Sixth Edition

Fundamentals of Investments
VALUATION AND MANAGEMENT

Bradford D. Jordan
University of Kentucky

Thomas W. Miller Jr.
Saint Louis University

Steven D. Dolvin, CFA
Butler University

FUNDAMENTALS OF INVESTMENTS: VALUATION AND MANAGEMENT

Published by McGraw-Hill/Irwin, a business unit of The McGraw-Hill Companies, Inc., 1221 Avenue of the Americas, New York, NY, 10020. Copyright © 2012, 2009, 2008, 2005, 2002, 2000 by The McGraw-Hill Companies, Inc. All rights reserved. No part of this publication may be reproduced or distributed in any form or by any means, or stored in a database or retrieval system, without the prior written consent of The McGraw-Hill Companies, Inc., including, but not limited to, in any network or other electronic storage or transmission, or broadcast for distance learning.

Some ancillaries, including electronic and print components, may not be available to customers outside the United States.

This book is printed on acid-free paper.
1 2 3 4 5 6 7 8 9 0 DOW/DOW 1 0 9 8 7 6 5 4 3 2 1

ISBN   978-0-07-131564-7
MHID   0-07-131564-0

www.mhhe.com

Fundamentals of Investments
VALUATION AND MANAGEMENT

The McGraw-Hill/Irwin Series in Finance, Insurance and Real Estate

Stephen A. Ross
Franco Modigliani Professor of Finance and Economics
Sloan School of Management
Massachusetts Institute of Technology
Consulting Editor

To my late father, S. Kelly Jordan Sr.,
a great stock picker.

BDJ

To my parents, Tom and Kathy Miller,
my wife Carolyn, and #21 —Thomas W. Miller III.

TWM Jr.

To my wife, Kourtney, and the "three L's"—my greatest
investment in this life.

SDD

About the Authors

Bradford D. Jordan
Gatton College of Business and Economics, University of Kentucky

Bradford D. Jordan is Professor of Finance and holder of the Richard W. and Janis H. Furst Endowed Chair in Finance at the University of Kentucky. He has a long-standing interest in both applied and theoretical issues in investments, and he has extensive experience teaching all levels of investments. Professor Jordan has published numerous research articles on issues such as valuation of fixed-income securities, tax effects in investments analysis, the behavior of security prices, IPO valuation, and pricing of exotic options. He is co-author of *Fundamentals of Corporate Finance* and *Essentials of Corporate Finance*, two of the most widely used finance textbooks in the world.

Thomas W. Miller Jr.
John Cook School of Business, Saint Louis University

Tom Miller is the Senior Fellow for Research and Faculty Development and Professor of Finance at the John Cook School of Business at Saint Louis University. Professor Miller has a long-standing interest in derivative securities and investments and has published numerous articles on various topics in these areas. Professor Miller has been honored with many research and teaching awards. Professor Miller is a co-author (with David Dubofsky) of *Derivatives: Valuation and Risk Management* (Oxford University Press). Professor Miller's interests include golf, skiing, American saddlebred horses, and playing tenor saxophone.

Steven D. Dolvin
College of Business, Butler University

Steven D. Dolvin, CFA, is an Associate Professor of Finance at Butler University. He teaches primarily in the area of investments, but he also oversees student-run portfolios in both public and private equity. He has received multiple teaching awards and has also published numerous articles in both academic and practitioner outlets. His principal areas of interest are IPOs, venture capital, financial education, retirement investing, and behavioral finance. His prior experience includes work in both corporate finance and investments, and he currently does investment consulting for both individuals and businesses. Professor Dolvin is also a CFA charterholder and is actively involved as a board member of his local society.

Preface

So why *did* we write this book?

As we toiled away, we asked ourselves this question many times, and the answer was always the same: *Our students made us.*

Traditionally, investments textbooks tend to fall into one of two camps. The first type has a greater focus on portfolio management and covers a significant amount of portfolio theory. The second type is more concerned with security analysis and generally contains fairly detailed coverage of fundamental analysis as a tool for equity valuation. Today, most texts try to cover all the bases by including some chapters drawn from one camp and some from another.

The result of trying to cover everything is either a very long book or one that forces the instructor to bounce back and forth between chapters. This frequently leads to a noticeable lack of consistency in treatment. Different chapters have completely different approaches: Some are computational, some are theoretical, and some are descriptive. Some do macroeconomic forecasting, some do mean-variance portfolio theory and beta estimation, and some do financial statements analysis. Options and futures are often essentially tacked on the back to round out this disconnected assortment.

The goal of these books is different from the goal of our students. Our students told us they come into an investments course wanting to learn how to make investment decisions. As time went by, we found ourselves supplying more and more supplemental materials to the texts we were using and constantly varying chapter sequences while chasing this elusive goal. We finally came to realize that the financial world had changed tremendously, and investments textbooks had fallen far behind in content and relevance.

What we really wanted, and what our students really needed, was a book that would do several key things:

- Focus on the students as investment managers by giving them information they can act on instead of concentrating on theories and research without the proper context.
- Offer strong, consistent pedagogy, including a balanced, unified treatment of the main types of financial investments as mirrored in the investment world.
- Organize topics in a way that would make them easy to apply—whether to a portfolio simulation or to real life—and support these topics with hands-on activities.

We made these three goals the guiding principles in writing this book. The next several sections explain our approach to each and why we think they are so important.

Who Is This Book For?

This book is aimed at introductory investments classes with students who have relatively little familiarity with investments. A typical student may have taken a principles of finance class and had some exposure to stocks and bonds, but not much beyond the basics. The introductory investments class is often a required course for finance majors, but students from other areas often take it as an elective. One fact of which we are acutely aware is that this may be the only investments class many students will ever take.

We intentionally wrote this book in a relaxed, informal style that engages the student and treats him or her as an active participant rather than a passive information absorber. We think the world of investments is exciting and fascinating, and we hope to share our considerable enthusiasm for investing with the student. We appeal to intuition and basic principles whenever possible because we have found that this approach effectively promotes understanding. We also make extensive use of examples throughout, drawing on material from the world around us and using familiar companies wherever appropriate.

By design, the text is not encyclopedic. As the table of contents indicates, we have a total of 20 chapters. Chapter length is about 30 to 40 pages, so the text is aimed at a single-term course; most of the book can be covered in a typical quarter or semester.

Aiming the book at a one-semester course necessarily means some picking and choosing, with regard to both topics and depth of coverage. Throughout, we strike a balance by introducing and covering the essentials while leaving some of the details to follow-up courses in security analysis, portfolio management, and options and futures.

How Does the Sixth Edition of This Book Expand upon the Goals Described Above?

Based on user feedback, we have made numerous improvements and refinements in the sixth edition of *Fundamentals of Investments: Valuation and Management*. We updated an appendix containing useful formulas. We updated every chapter to reflect current market practices and conditions, and we significantly expanded and improved the end-of-chapter material. Also, our chapters devoted to market efficiency and to behavioral finance continue to rate highly among readers.

To give some examples of our additional new content:

- Chapter 1 contains new sections on the crash of 2008, dollar-weighted average returns, and the equity risk premium.
- Chapter 2 contains a new section on the Investment Policy Statement (IPS) and new material on asset allocation, retirement accounts, and short sale constraints.
- Chapter 3 describes the new ticker symbols for exchange-traded options.
- Chapter 4 contains new material on target date funds and a greatly expanded section on exchange-traded funds, particularly leveraged ETFs. Considerable new material is introduced on hedge funds, particularly their fee structure and investment styles.
- Chapter 5 includes new material on the structure of private equity funds. In addition, the sections on the NYSE and NASDAQ contain much new material.
- Chapter 6 contains sections on how to analyze ROE, how to compute stock prices using the H-model, and how to compute stock prices using the free cash flow model.
- Chapter 7 contains new material on the market crash of 2008.
- Chapter 8 offers new material on heuristics, herding, and overcoming bias. Students have an opportunity to take an online quiz about overconfidence.
- Chapter 11 contains new material on the fallacy of time diversification.
- Chapter 12 includes new material on how to calculate beta using regression.
- Chapter 13 contains new material on calculating alpha using regression, calculating an information ratio, calculating a portfolio's R-squared, and Global Investment Performance Standards (GIPS).
- Chapter 15 contains a vastly improved section on option intrinsic value and option moneyness. The chapter also has new material on the "new" option symbols and credit default swaps (CDS).
- Chapter 17 updates the valuation of Starbucks Corporation.
- Chapter 18 contains some new material on bond ratings and alternatives to bond ratings.

In addition, we have updated learning objectives for each chapter. We have reworked our chapter summaries to reflect the chapter's learning objectives.

For the sixth edition, we significantly expanded and improved the end-of-chapter material. We added new problems throughout, and we have significantly increased the CFA™ content.

We updated the questions that test understanding of concepts with no calculations involved. In addition, our *What's on the Web?* questions give students assignments to perform based on information they retrieve from various Web sites. Finally, in selected chapters, we have included spreadsheet assignments, which ask students to create certain types of spreadsheets to solve problems.

We continue to emphasize the use of the Web in investments analysis, and we integrate Web-based content in several ways. First, wherever appropriate, we provide a commented link in the margin. These links send readers to selected, particularly relevant Web sites. Second, our *Work the Web* feature, expanded and completely updated for this edition, appears in most chapters. These boxed readings use screen shots to show students how to access, use, and interpret various types of key financial and market data. Finally, as previously noted, new end-of-chapter problems rely on data retrieved from the Web.

We continue to provide *Spreadsheet Analysis* exhibits, which we have enhanced for this edition. These exhibits illustrate directly how to use spreadsheets to do certain types of important problems, including such computationally intensive tasks as calculating Macaulay duration, finding Black-Scholes option prices, and determining optimal portfolios based on Sharpe ratios. We also continue to provide, where relevant, readings from *The Wall Street Journal*, which have been thoroughly updated for this edition.

CFA™ Mapping

Consider this description provided by the CFA Institute: "First awarded in 1963, the Chartered Financial Analyst (CFA) charter has become known as the gold standard of professional credentials within the global investment community. Investors recognize the CFA designation as the definitive standard for measuring competence and integrity in the fields of portfolio management and investment analysis." The importance and growing significance of the CFA charter are compelling reasons to integrate CFA curriculum material into our sixth edition.

Among the requirements to earn the CFA charter, candidates must pass three sequential levels of comprehensive exams. Each exam asks questions on a wide array of subject areas concerning the investment process. To help candidates study for the exams, the exams at each level are divided into so-called study sessions. Each of these study sessions has a core set of readings designed to help prepare the candidate for the exams. We carefully examined the content of each reading, as well as the stated learning outcomes, to determine which areas we covered in the fifth edition. Importantly, we also considered which areas might be added to the sixth edition.

As a result of this thorough process, in our sixth edition we expanded coverage on 10 readings and added completely new coverage of 15 readings. In total, our textbook contains material that touches over 70 percent of the readings from Level 1 of the CFA exam. Topics that we do not address from Level 1, such as basic statistics, accounting, and economics, are likely addressed in prerequisite courses taken before the investments course. In addition, we present some higher level material: We touch on about 35 percent of the readings from the Level 2 and 3 exams.

Of course, we make no claim that our textbook is a substitute for the CFA exam readings. Nonetheless, we believe that our sixth edition provides a terrific framework and introduction for students looking to pursue a career in investments—particularly for those interested in eventually holding the CFA charter. To provide a sense of studying for the CFA, the sixth edition includes an end-of-chapter case review. *Schweser,* a leading purveyor of CFA exam preparation packages, graciously provided extensive material from which we chose these case reviews.

We provide a mapping between the textbook and the CFA curriculum as follows. Each chapter opens with a CFA Exam box citing references to specific readings from the CFA curriculum that are covered within the chapter. The topic is identified and we indicate which level and study session the reading comes from. We label these topics CFA1, CFA2, CFA3, and so on, for easy reference. End-of-chapter problems in the book and in *Connect* are also labeled with these tags. Over 95 percent of our end-of-chapter material is related to the CFA exam. We believe that this integration has added tremendous value to the sixth edition.

Assurance-of-Learning Ready

Many educational institutions today are focused on the notion of assurance of learning, an important element of some accreditation standards. This edition is designed specifically to support your assurance-of-learning initiatives with a simple, yet powerful, solution. Listed below are the learning objectives for each chapter.

Each test bank question for this book maps to a specific chapter learning objective listed in the text. You can use the test bank software to easily query for learning outcomes and objectives that directly relate to the learning objectives for your course. You can then use the reporting features of the software to aggregate student results in similar fashion, making the collection and presentation of assurance-of-learning data simple and easy.

Chapter Learning Objectives

Chapter 1: A Brief History of Risk and Return
To become a wise investor (maybe even one with too much money), you need to know:

1. How to calculate the return on an investment using different methods.
2. The historical returns on various important types of investments.
3. The historical risks on various important types of investments.
4. The relationship between risk and return.

Chapter 2: The Investment Process
Don't sell yourself short. Instead, learn about these key investment subjects:

1. The importance of an investment policy statement.
2. The various types of securities brokers and brokerage accounts.
3. How to calculate initial and maintenance margin.
4. The workings of short sales.

Chapter 3: Overview of Security Types
Price quotes for all types of investments are easy to find, but what do they mean? Learn the answer for:

1. Various types of interest-bearing assets.
2. Equity securities.
3. Futures contracts.
4. Option contracts.

Chapter 4: Mutual Funds
You're probably going to be a mutual fund investor very soon, so you should definitely know the following:

1. The different types of mutual funds.
2. How mutual funds operate.
3. How to find information about how mutual funds have performed.
4. The workings of exchange-traded funds and hedge funds.

Chapter 5: The Stock Market
Take stock in yourself. Make sure you have a good understanding of:

1. The differences between private and public equity and between primary and secondary stock markets.
2. The workings of the New York Stock Exchange.
3. How NASDAQ operates.
4. How to calculate index returns.

Chapter 6: Common Stock Valuation

Separate yourself from the commoners by having a good understanding of these security valuation methods:

1. The basic dividend discount model.
2. The two-stage dividend growth model.
3. The residual income and free cash flow models.
4. Price ratio analysis.

Chapter 7: Stock Price Behavior and Market Efficiency

You should strive to have your investment knowledge fully reflect:

1. The foundations of market efficiency.
2. The implications of the forms of market efficiency.
3. Market efficiency and the performance of professional money managers.
4. What stock market anomalies, bubbles, and crashes mean for market efficiency.

Chapter 8: Behavioral Finance and the Psychology of Investing

Psych yourself up and get to know something about:

1. Prospect theory.
2. The implications of investor overconfidence and misperceptions of randomness.
3. Sentiment-based risk and limits to arbitrage.
4. The wide array of technical analysis methods used by investors.

Chapter 9: Interest Rates

It will be worth your time to increase your rate of interest in these topics:

1. Money market prices and rates.
2. Rates and yields on fixed-income securities.
3. Treasury STRIPS and the term structure of interest rates.
4. Nominal versus real interest rates.

Chapter 10: Bond Prices and Yields

Bonds can be an important part of portfolios. You will learn:

1. How to calculate bond prices and yields.
2. The importance of yield to maturity.
3. Interest rate risk and Malkiel's theorems.
4. How to measure the impact of interest rate changes on bond prices.

Chapter 11: Diversification and Risky Asset Allocation

To get the most out of this chapter, spread your study time across:

1. How to calculate expected returns and variances for a security.
2. How to calculate expected returns and variances for a portfolio.
3. The importance of portfolio diversification.
4. The efficient frontier and the importance of asset allocation.

Chapter 12: Return, Risk, and the Security Market Line

Studying some topics will yield an expected reward. For example, make sure you know:

1. The difference between expected and unexpected returns.
2. The difference between systematic risk and unsystematic risk.
3. The security market line and the capital asset pricing model.
4. The importance of beta.

Chapter 13: Performance Evaluation and Risk Management
To get a high evaluation of your performance, make sure you know:

1. How to calculate the best-known portfolio evaluation measures.
2. The strengths and weaknesses of three portfolio evaluation measures.
3. How to calculate a Sharpe-optimal portfolio.
4. How to calculate and interpret Value-at-Risk.

Chapter 14: Futures Contracts
You will derive many future benefits if you have a good understanding of:

1. The basics of futures markets and how to obtain price quotes for futures contracts.
2. The risks involved in futures market speculation.
3. How cash prices and futures prices are linked.
4. How futures contracts can be used to transfer price risk.

Chapter 15: Stock Options
Give yourself some in-the-money academic and professional options by understanding:

1. The basics of option contracts and how to obtain price quotes.
2. The difference between option payoffs and option profits.
3. The workings of some basic option trading strategies.
4. The logic behind the put-call parity condition.

Chapter 16: Option Valuation
Make sure the price is right by making sure that you have a good understanding of:

1. How to price options using the one-period and two-period binomial model.
2. How to price options using the Black-Scholes model.
3. How to hedge a stock portfolio using options.
4. The workings of employee stock options.

Chapter 17: Projecting Cash Flow and Earnings
Help yourself grow as a stock analyst by knowing:

1. How to obtain financial information about companies.
2. How to read basic financial statements.
3. How to use performance and price ratios.
4. How to use the percentage of sales method in financial forecasting.

Chapter 18: Corporate Bonds
Conform to your fixed-income knowledge covenants by learning:

1. The basic types of corporate bonds.
2. How callable bonds function.
3. The different types of corporate bonds.
4. The basics of bond ratings.

Chapter 19: Government Bonds
Before you loan money to Uncle Sam (and his relatives), you should know:

1. The basics of U.S. Treasury securities and how they are sold.
2. The workings of the STRIPS program and pricing Treasury bonds.
3. How federal agencies borrow money.
4. How municipalities borrow money.

Chapter 20 (*Web site only*): Mortgage-Backed Securities

Before you mortgage your future, you should know:

1. The workings of a fixed-rate mortgage.
2. Government's role in the secondary market for home mortgages.
3. The impact of mortgage prepayments.
4. How collateralized mortgage obligations are created and divided.

How Is This Book Relevant to the Student?

Fundamental changes in the investments universe drive our attention to relevance. The first major change is that individuals are being asked to make investment decisions for their own portfolios more often than ever before. There is, thankfully, a growing recognition that traditional "savings account" approaches to investing are decidedly inferior. At the same time, the use of employer-sponsored "investment accounts" has expanded enormously. The second major change is that the investments universe has exploded with an ever-increasing number of investment vehicles available to individual investors. As a result, investors must choose from an array of products, many of which are very complex, and they must strive to choose wisely.

Beyond this, students are more interested in subjects that affect them directly (as are we all). By taking the point of view of the student as an investor, we are better able to illustrate and emphasize the relevance and importance of the material.

Our approach is evident in the table of contents. Our first chapter is motivational; we have found that this material effectively "hooks" students and even motivates a semester-long discourse on risk and return. Our second chapter answers the student's next natural question: "How do I get started investing and how do I buy and sell securities?" The third chapter surveys the different types of investments available. After only three chapters, very early in the term, students have learned something about the risks and rewards from investing, how to get started investing, and what investment choices are available.

We close the first part of the text with a detailed examination of mutual funds. Without a doubt, mutual funds have become the most popular investment vehicles for individual investors. There are now more mutual funds than there are stocks on the NYSE! Given the size and enormous growth in the mutual fund industry, this material is important for investors. Even so, investments texts typically cover mutual funds in a cursory way, often banishing the material to a back chapter under the obscure (and obsolete) heading of "investment companies." Our early placement lets students quickly explore a topic they have heard a lot about and are typically interested in learning more about.

How Does This Book Allow Students to Apply the Investments Knowledge They Learn?

After studying this text, students will have the basic knowledge needed to move forward and actually act on what they have learned. We have developed two features to encourage students in making decisions as an investment manager. Learning to make good investment decisions comes with experience, while experience (regrettably) comes from making bad investment decisions. As much as possible, we press our students to get those bad decisions out of their systems before they start managing real money!

Not surprisingly, most students don't know how to get started in buying and selling securities. We have learned that providing some structure, especially with a portfolio simulation, greatly enhances the experience. Therefore, we have a series of *Get Real* boxes. These boxes (at the end of each chapter) usually describe actual trades for students to explore. The intention is to show students how to gain real experience with the principles and instruments covered in the chapter. The second feature is a series of *Stock-Trak* exercises that take students through specific trading situations using *Stock-Trak Portfolio Simulations,* which can be found in the book's Web site, www.mhhe.com/jmd6e.

Because we feel that portfolio simulations are so valuable, we have taken steps to assist instructors who, like us, plan to integrate portfolio simulations into their courses. Beyond the features mentioned above, we have organized the text so that the essential material needed before participating in a simulation is covered at the front of the book. Most notably, with every book, we have included a *free* subscription to *Stock-Trak Portfolio Simulations. Stock-Trak* is the leading provider of investment simulation services to the academic community; providing *Stock-Trak* free represents a significant cost savings to students. To our knowledge, ours is the first (and only) investments text to directly offer a full-featured online brokerage account simulation with the book at no incremental cost.

How Does This Book Maintain a Consistent, Unified Treatment?

In most investments texts, depth of treatment and presentation vary dramatically from instrument to instrument, which leaves the student without an overall framework for understanding the many types of investments. We stress early on that there are essentially only four basic types of financial investments—stocks, bonds, options, and futures. In parts 2 through 6, our simple goal is to take a closer look at each of these instruments. We take a unified approach to each by answering these basic questions:

1. What are the essential features of the instrument?
2. What are the possible rewards?
3. What are the risks?
4. What are the basic determinants of investment value?
5. For whom is the investment appropriate and under what circumstances?
6. How is the instrument bought and sold, and how does the market for the instrument operate?

By covering investment instruments in this way, we teach the students what questions to ask when looking at any potential investment.

Unlike other introductory investments texts, we devote several chapters beyond the basics to the different types of fixed-income investments. Students are often surprised to learn that the fixed-income markets are so much bigger than the equity markets and that money management opportunities are much more common in the fixed-income arena. Possibly the best way to see this is to look at recent CFA exams and materials and note the extensive coverage of fixed-income topics. We have placed these chapters toward the back of the text because we recognize not everyone will want to cover all this material. We have also separated the subject into several shorter chapters to make it more digestible for students and to allow instructors more control over what is covered.

Acknowledgments

We have received extensive feedback from reviewers at each step along the way, and we are very grateful to the following dedicated scholars and teachers for their time and expertise:

Aaron Phillips, California State University–Bakersfield

Allan O'Bryan, Rochester Community & Technical College

Allan Zebedee, San Diego State University

Ann Hackert, Idaho State University

Carl R. Chen, University of Dayton

Carla Rich, Pensacola Junior College

Caroline Fulmer, University of Alabama

Charles Appeadu, University of Wisconsin–Madison

Cheryl Frohlich, University of North Florida

Christos Giannikos, Bernard M. Baruch College

David Dubofsky, University of Louisville

David Louton, Bryant College

David Loy, Illinois State University

David Peterson, Florida State University

David Stewart, Winston-Salem State University

Deborah Murphy, University of Tennessee–Knoxville

Dina Layish, Binghamton University

Donald Wort, California State University–East Bay

Dwight Giles, Jefferson State Community College

Edward Miller, University of New Orleans

Felix Ayadi, Fayetteville State University

Gay B. Hatfield, University of Mississippi

George Jouganatos, California State University–Sacramento

Gioia Bales, Hofstra University

Haigang Zhou, Cleveland State University

Howard Van Auken, Iowa State University

Howard W. Bohnen, St. Cloud State University

Imad Elhaj, University of Louisville

It-Keong Chew, University of Kentucky

James Forjan, York College of Pennsylvania

Jeff Brookman, Idaho State University

Jeff Edwards, Portland Community College

Jeff Manzi, Ohio University

Jennifer Morton, Ivy Technical Community College of Indiana

Ji Chen, University of Colorado

Jim Tipton, Baylor University

Joan Anderssen, Arapahoe Community College

Joe Brocato, Tarleton State University

Joe Walker, University of Alabama–Birmingham

John Bockino, Suffolk County Community College

John Clinebell, University of Northern Colorado

John Finnigan, Marist College

John Ledgerwood, Bethune-Cookman College

John Paul Broussard, Rutgers, The State University of New Jersey

John Romps, St. Anselm College

John Stocker, University of Delaware

John Wingender, Creighton University

Johnny Chan, University of Dayton

Jorge Omar R. Brusa, University of Arkansas

Karen Bonding, University of Virginia

Kerri McMillan, Clemson University

Lalatendu Misra, University of Texas at San Antonio

Lawrence Blose, Grand Valley State University

Linda Martin, Arizona State University

Lisa Schwartz, Wingate University

M. J. Murray, Winona State University

Marc LeFebvre, Creighton University

Marie Kratochvil, Nassau Community College

Margo Kraft, Heidelberg College

Matthew Fung, Saint Peter's College

Michael C. Ehrhardt, University of Tennessee–Knoxville

Michael Gordinier, Washington University

Michael Nugent, SUNY–Stony Brook

Mukesh Chaudhry, Indiana University of Pennsylvania

Naresh Bansal, Saint Louis University

Nolan Lickey, Utah Valley State College

Nozar Hashemzadeh, Radford University

Patricia Clarke, Simmons College

Paul Bolster, Northeastern University

Percy S. Poon, University of Nevada, Las Vegas

Rahul Verma, University of Houston

Randall Wade, Rogue Community College

Richard Followill, University of Northern Iowa

Richard Lee Kitchen, Tallahassee Community College

Richard Proctor, Siena College

Richard W. Taylor, Arkansas State University

Robert Friederichs, Alexandria Technical College

Robert Kozub, University of Wisconsin–Milwaukee

Ronald Christner, Loyola University–New Orleans

Samira Hussein, Johnson County Community College

Sammie Root, Texas State University–San Marcos

Samuel H. Penkar, University of Houston

Scott Barnhart, Clemson University

Scott Beyer, University of Wisconsin–Oshkosh

Stephen Chambers, Johnson County Community College

Steven Lifland, High Point University

Stuart Michelson, University of Central Florida

Thomas M. Krueger, University of Wisconsin–La Crosse

Thomas Willey, Grand Valley State University

Tim Samolis, Pittsburgh Technical Institute

Vernon Stauble, San Bernardino Valley College

Ward Hooker, Orangeburg-Calhoun Technical College

William Compton, University of North Carolina–Wilmington

William Elliott, Oklahoma State University

William Lepley, University of Wisconsin–Green Bay

Yvette Harman, Miami University of Ohio

Zekeriah Eser, Eastern Kentucky University

We thank Lynn Kugele, University of Mississippi, for developing the Test Bank, and Spencer Jones, Carson-Newman College, for creating the Student Narrated PowerPoint slides. We thank R. Douglas Van Eaton, CFA for providing access to *Schweser's* preparation material for the CFA exam. We would especially like to acknowledge the careful reading and helpful suggestions made by professors Bidisha Chakrabarty and John Walker.

The following doctoral and MBA students did outstanding work on this text: Tim Riley, Paula Wimberley, and Matt Harlow; to them fell the unenviable task of technical proofreading and, in particular, careful checking of each calculation throughout the text and supplements.

We are deeply grateful to the select group of professionals who served as our development team on this edition: Michele Janicek, Executive Editor; Elizabeth Hughes, Development Editor; Melissa Caughlin, Senior Marketing Manager; Bruce Gin, Senior Project Manager; Cara Hawthorne, Designer; Debra Sylvester, Production Supervisor; and Brian Nacik, Media Project Manager.

Bradford D. Jordan

Thomas W. Miller Jr.

Steven D. Dolvin

Coverage

This book was designed and developed explicitly for a first course in investments taken by either finance majors or non–finance majors. In terms of background or prerequisites, the book is nearly self-contained, but some familiarity with basic algebra and accounting is assumed. The organization of the text has been designed to give instructors the flexibility they need to teach a quarter-long or semester-long course.

To present an idea of the breadth of coverage in the sixth edition of *Fundamentals of Investments*, the following grid is presented chapter by chapter. This grid contains some of the most significant new features and a few selected chapter highlights. Of course, for each chapter, features like opening vignettes, *Work the Web, Spreadsheet Analyses, Get Real, Investment Updates*, and end-of-chapter material have been thoroughly reviewed and updated.

Chapters and Learning Objectives	Selected Topics of Interest	Learning Outcome/Comment
PART ONE Introduction		
Chapter 1		
A Brief History of Risk and Return	Dollar returns and percentage returns. *New Material:* The crash of 2000.	Average returns differ by asset class.
	Return variability and calculating variance and standard deviation.	Return variability also differs by asset class.
	Arithmetic versus geometric returns. *New Material:* Dollar-weighted average returns.	Geometric average tells you what you actually earned per year, compounded annually. Arithmetic return tells you what you earned in a typical year. Dollar-weighted average return adjusts for investment inflows and outflows.
	The risk-return trade-off. *New Material:* The U.S. equity risk premium.	Historically, higher returns are associated with higher risk. Estimates of future equity risk premiums involve assumptions about the risk environment and investor risk aversion.
Chapter 2		
The Investment Process	*New Section:* The Investment Policy Statement. *New Material:* More on asset allocation.	By knowing their objectives and constraints, investors can capture risk and return trade-offs in an investment policy statement (IPS).
	Investor objectives, constraints, and strategies.	Presentation of issues like risk and return, resource constraints, market timing, and asset allocation.
	Investment professionals and types of brokerage accounts.	Discussion of the different types of financial advisors and brokerage accounts available to an individual investor.
	New Material: Retirement accounts.	Readers will know the workings of company-sponsored plans, such as a 401(k), and traditional individual retirement accounts (IRAs) and Roth IRAs.
	Short sales. *New Material:* Constraints on short sales.	Description of the process of short-selling stock and short-selling constraints imposed by regulations and market conditions.
	Forming an investment portfolio.	An investment portfolio must account for an investor's risk tolerance, objectives, constraints, and strategies.

Chapters and Learning Objectives	Selected Topics of Interest	Learning Outcome/Comment
Chapter 3		
Overview of Security Types	Classifying securities.	Interest-bearing, equity, and derivative securities.
	NASD's new TRACE system and transparency in the corporate bond market.	Up-to-date discussion of new developments in fixed income with respect to price, volume, and transactions reporting.
	Equity securities.	Obtaining price quotes for equity securities.
	Derivative securities: Obtaining futures contract and option contract price quotes using the Internet. *Updated Material:* New option ticker symbols.	Defining the types of derivative securities, interpreting their price quotes, and calculating gains and losses from these securities.
Chapter 4		
Mutual Funds	Advantages and drawbacks of investing in mutual funds.	Advantages include diversification, professional management, and minimum initial investment. Drawbacks include risk, costs, and taxes.
	Investment companies and types of funds.	Covers concepts like open-end versus closed-end funds and net asset value.
	Mutual fund organization, creation, costs, and fees.	Presents types of expenses and fees like front-end loads, 12b-1 fees, management fees, and turnover.
	Short-term funds, long-term funds, and fund performance. *New Material:* Target date funds.	Discussion of money market mutual funds versus the variety of available stock and bond funds and how to find their performance.
	Special funds like closed-end funds, exchange-traded funds (*expanded material*), and hedge funds (*greatly expanded material on hedge fund fees and hedge fund investment styles*). *New Material:* Leveraged ETFs.	The closed-end fund discount mystery and discussion of exchange-traded funds (ETFs), exchange-traded notes (ETNs), hedge fund investment styles, and the perils of leveraged ETFs.

PART TWO   Stock Markets

Chapter 5		
The Stock Market	The primary stock market. *New Material:* Types of private equity funds and the structure of private equity funds.	The workings of an initial public offering (IPO), a seasoned equity offering (SEO), the role of investment bankers, and the role of the Securities and Exchange Commission (SEC).
	The secondary stock market. *Updated Material:* The current structure of the NYSE and NASDAQ.	The role of dealers and brokers, the workings of the New York Stock Exchange (NYSE), and NASDAQ market operations.
	Stock Indexes, including the Dow Jones Industrial Average (DJIA) and the Standard & Poor's 500 Index (S&P 500).	The components of the DJIA and their dividend yields. The difference between price-weighted indexes and value-weighted indexes.
Chapter 6		
Common Stock Valuation	The basic dividend discount model (DDM) and several of its variants. *New Material:* Analyzing ROE using the DuPont formula.	Valuation using constant and nonconstant growth.
	The two-stage dividend growth model. *New Material:* The H-model.	Valuation of stocks with nonconstant growth rates.
	The residual income model. *New Section:* The Free Cash Flow Model.	Valuation of non-dividend-paying stocks. Valuation of stocks with negative earnings.
	Price ratio analysis.	Valuation using price-earnings, price–cash flow, and price-sales.
	New Material: Updated McGraw-Hill valuation detailed example.	Using *Value Line* information to value a stock using methods presented earlier in the chapter.

Chapters and Learning Objectives	Selected Topics of Interest	Learning Outcome/Comment
Chapter 7		
Stock Price Behavior and Market Efficiency	Forms of market efficiency.	The effects of information on stock prices with respect to market efficiency.
	Event studies using actual events surrounding Advanced Medical Optics.	Explains how new information gets into stock prices and how researchers measure it.
	Informed traders, insider trading, and illegal insider trading.	Example: Martha Stewart and ImClone.
	Updated Material: Market efficiency and the performance of professional money managers.	Discusses the performance of professional money managers versus static benchmarks.
	Updated Material: Anomalies.	Presentation of the day-of-the-week effect, the amazing January effect, the turn-of-the-year effect, and the turn-of-the-month effect.
	Bubbles and crashes. *New Material:* The crash of October 2008.	Shows the extent of famous events like the crash of 1929, the crash of October 1987, the Asian market crash, the "dot-com" bubble, and the crash of 2008.
Chapter 8		
Behavioral Finance and the Psychology of Investing	Introduction to behavioral finance.	The influence of reasoning errors on investor decisions.
	Prospect theory.	How investors tend to behave differently when faced with prospective gains and losses.
	Overconfidence, misperceiving randomness, and overreacting to chance events. *New Material:* Illusion of knowledge and the "snakebite effect."	Examines the consequences of these serious errors in judgment. *New Online Quiz:* Overconfidence.
	New Section: More on Behavioral Finance.	*New Material:* Heuristics, herding, and overcoming bias.
	Sentiment-based risk and limits to arbitrage.	3Com/Palm mispricing; the Royal Dutch/Shell price ratio.
	Technical analysis.	*Updated Material:* Advance/decline line indicators, market diary, relative strength charts, and technical analysis data for Microsoft Corp.

PART THREE   Interest Rates and Bond Valuation

Chapter 9		
Interest Rates	Interest rate history and a quick review of the time value of money.	A graphical presentation of the long-term history of interest rates.
	Money market rates and their prices.	Important money market concepts including pricing U.S. Treasury bills, bank discount yields versus bond equivalent yields, annual percentage rates, and effective annual returns.
	Rates and yields on fixed-income securities.	The Treasury yield curve, the term structure of interest rates, and Treasury STRIPS.
	Nominal versus real interest rates.	The Fisher hypothesis.
	Determinants of nominal interest rates.	Problems with traditional theories and modern term structure theory.
Chapter 10		
Bond Prices and Yields	Straight bond prices and yield to maturity (YTM).	Calculate straight bond prices, calculate yield to maturity.
	The concept of duration and bond risk measures based on duration.	Calculate and interpret a bond's duration. The dollar value of an "01," yield value of a 32nd.
	Dedicated portfolios and reinvestment risk.	Learn how to create a dedicated portfolio and show its exposure to reinvestment risk.
	Immunization.	Minimize the uncertainty concerning the value of a bond portfolio at its target date.

Chapters and Learning Objectives	Selected Topics of Interest	Learning Outcome/Comment
PART FOUR Portfolio Management		
Chapter 11		
Diversification and Risky Asset Allocation	Expected returns and variances.	Calculate expected returns and variances using equal and unequal probabilities.
	Portfolios and the effect of diversification on portfolio risk. *New Material:* The fallacy of time diversification.	Compute portfolio weights, expected returns, variances, and why diversification works.
	The importance of asset allocation.	The effect of correlation on the risk-return trade-off.
	The Markowitz efficient frontier and illustrating the importance of asset allocation using three securities.	Compute risk-return combinations using various portfolio weights for three assets.
Chapter 12		
Return, Risk, and the Security Market Line	Diversification, systematic and unsystematic risk.	Total risk is comprised of unsystematic and systematic risk and only unsystematic risk can be reduced through diversification.
	The security market line and the reward-to-risk ratio.	The security market line describes how the market rewards risk. All assets will have the same reward-to-risk ratio in a competitive financial market.
	Measuring systematic risk with beta (*updated and extended material on beta*). *New Material:* Calculating beta using regression.	The average beta is 1.00. Assets with a beta greater than 1.00 have more than average systematic risk.
	The capital asset pricing model (CAPM).	Expected return depends on the amount of and the reward for bearing systematic risk as well as the pure time value of money.
	Extending CAPM.	One of the most important extensions of the CAPM is the Fama-French three-factor model.
Chapter 13		
Performance Evaluation and Risk Management	Performance evaluation measures. *New Material:* Calculating alpha using regression; calculating an information ratio; calculating a portfolio's R-squared, and Global Investment Performance Standards (GIPS).	Calculate and interpret the Sharpe ratio, the Treynor ratio, and Jensen's alpha. Also, calculate alpha using regression, calculate an information ratio, and calculate a portfolio's R-squared.
	Sharpe-optimal portfolios.	The portfolio with the highest possible Sharpe ratio given the assets comprising the portfolio is Sharpe optimal.
	Value-at-Risk (VaR).	VaR is the evaluation of the probability of a significant loss.
	Example showing how to calculate a Sharpe-optimal portfolio.	Combines the concepts of a Sharpe ratio, a Sharpe-optimal portfolio, and VaR.
PART FIVE Futures and Options		
Chapter 14		
Futures Contracts	The basics of futures contracts and using them to hedge price risk. *Detailed Example:* Hedging an inventory using futures markets.	Futures quotes from the Internet and financial press, short and long hedging, futures accounts.
	Spot-futures parity.	Basis, cash markets, and cash-futures arbitrage.
	Stock index futures. *New Example:* Changing the beta of a stock portfolio to zero using stock index futures.	Index arbitrage, speculating with stock index futures, and hedging stock market risk with stock index futures.
	Hedging interest rate risk with futures.	Shows how to use portfolio duration when deciding how many futures contracts to use to hedge a bond portfolio.

Chapters and Learning Objectives	Selected Topics of Interest	Learning Outcome/Comment
Chapter 19		
Government Bonds	Government bonds basics emphasizing U.S. government debt.	Details of U.S. Treasury bills, notes, bonds, and STRIPS.
	U.S. savings bonds.	Covers important changes to these investment vehicles.
	Municipal bonds and their credit ratings.	Reviews important features of bonds issued by municipal governments.
Chapter 20 (*Web site only*)		
Mortgage-Backed Securities	Fixed-rate mortgages and prepayment.	Presents home mortgage principal and interest calculations.
	Secondary mortgage markets and reverse mortgages.	The function of GNMA and its clones, the PSA mortgage prepayment model.
	Collateralized mortgage obligations (CMOs).	Describes how cash flows from mortgage pools are carved up and distributed to investors.

Features

Pedagogical Features

From your feedback, we have included many pedagogical features in this text that will be valuable learning tools for your students. This walkthrough highlights some of the most important elements.

Chapter Openers

These one-paragraph introductions for each chapter present scenarios and common misconceptions that may surprise you. An explanation is more fully developed in the chapter.

Learning Objectives

Objectives next to the opener outline learning goals for the chapter.

CHAPTER 4
Mutual Funds

Learning Objectives

You're probably going to be a mutual fund investor very soon, so you should definitely know the following:

1. The different types of mutual funds.
2. How mutual funds operate.
3. How to find information about how mutual funds have performed.
4. The workings of Exchange-Traded Funds (ETFs) and hedge funds.

"Take calculated risks. That is quite different from being rash."

–George S. Patton

With only $2,000 to invest, you can easily own shares in Microsoft, GM, McDonald's, IBM, Coke, and many more stocks through a mutual fund. Or, you can invest in a portfolio of government bonds or other investments. Indeed, many thousands of different mutual funds are available to investors. In fact, there are about as many mutual funds as there are different stocks traded on the NASDAQ and the New York Stock Exchange combined. There are funds for aggressive investors, conservative investors, short-term investors, and long-term investors. There are bond funds, stock funds, international funds, and you-name-it funds. Is there a right fund for you? This chapter will help you find out. ■

As we discussed in an earlier chapter, if you do not wish to actively buy and sell individual securities on your own, you can invest in stocks, bonds, or other financial assets through a *mutual fund*. Mutual funds are simply a means of combining or pooling the funds of a large group of investors. The buy and sell decisions for the resulting pool are then made by a fund manager, who is compensated for the service provided.

Because mutual funds provide indirect access to financial markets for individual investors, they are a form of financial intermediary. In fact, mutual funds are now the largest type of intermediary in the United States, followed by commercial banks and life insurance companies.

CFA™ Exam Topics in This Chapter:

1 Discounted cash flow applications (L1, S2)
2 Alternative investments (L1, S18)
3 Soft dollar standards (L2, S1)
4 Alternative investments portfolio management (L3, S13)

Go to www.mhhe.com/jmd6e for a guide that aligns your textbook with CFA readings.

CFA™ Exam Map

This new feature maps topics within each chapter to readings from the CFA™ curriculum.

Check This

Every major section in each chapter ends with questions for review. This feature helps students test their understanding of the material before moving on to the next section.

CHECK THIS

4.4a What is the difference between a load fund and a no-load fund?

4.4b What are 12b-1 fees?

Key Terms

Key terms are indicated in bold and defined in the margin. The running glossary in the margin helps students quickly review the basic terminology for the chapter.

money market mutual fund
A mutual fund specializing in money market instruments.

MONEY MARKET MUTUAL FUNDS

As the name suggests, **money market mutual funds**, or MMMFs, specialize in money market instruments. As we describe elsewhere, these are short-term debt obligations issued by governments and corporations. Money market funds were introduced in the early 1970s and have grown tremendously. At the end of 2009, about 720 money market funds managed almost $3.4 trillion in assets. All money market funds are open-end funds.

Web Addresses

Web sites are called out in the margins, along with a notation of how they relate to the chapter material.

Visit
www.mfea.com
for info on thousands of
funds, including MMMFs.

MONEY MARKET FUND ACCOUNTING A unique feature of money market funds is that their net asset values are always $1 per share. This is purely an accounting gimmick, however. A money market fund simply sets the number of shares equal to the fund's assets. In other words, if the fund has $100 million in assets, then it has 100 million shares. As the fund earns interest on its investments, the fund owners are simply given more shares.

The reason money market mutual funds always maintain a $1 net asset value is to make them resemble bank accounts. As long as a money market fund invests in very safe, interest-

Investment Updates

These boxed readings, reprinted from various business press sources, provide additional real-world events and examples to illustrate the material in the chapter. Some articles from the past two years highlight very recent events, and others present events of more historical significance.

INVESTMENT UPDATES

GET A FRESH ANGLE ON YOUR FINANCES

Not sure whether you're saving enough or whether you have the right investment mix? To get a better handle on your portfolio, it sometimes helps to look at your finances from another angle.

1 How Much Do You Need in Conservative Investments to Feel Safe?

Investment advisors and Wall Street firms constantly exhort investors to consider their risk tolerance. For instance, we are often prodded to fill out those irritating questionnaires where we are asked whether our goal is "growth" or "capital preservation."

The answer, of course, is that we want both. Even retirees need growth from their portfolios. Even freshly

high-quality corporate bonds, municipals, money-market funds, and savings accounts. But don't stop there.

I would expand the list to include Social Security retirement benefits, pension income, mortgage debt, and any other loans you have. After all, you regularly receive income from Social Security and your pension, just as you would from a bond. Meanwhile, your debts involve making regular payments to other folks.

All these dealings affect your sense of financial security, and they should influence how you structure your portfolio. For instance, if you expect a traditional company pension when you retire, you effectively have a huge position in bonds and thus you might want to load up on stocks in your investment portfolio.

On the other hand, if you have a heap of debts, your

Work the Web

Various screenshots appear throughout the text. These exercises illustrate how to access specific features of selected Web sites in order to expand students' knowledge of current investment topics.

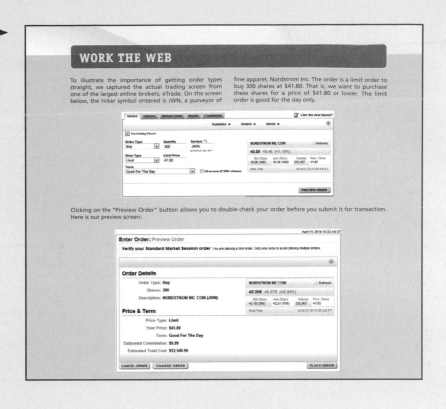

WORK THE WEB

To illustrate the importance of getting order types straight, we captured the actual trading screen from one of the largest online brokers, eTrade. On the screen below, the ticker symbol entered is JWN, a purveyor of fine apparel, Nordstrom Inc. The order is a limit order to buy 300 shares at $41.80. That is, we want to purchase these shares for a price of $41.80 or lower. The limit order is good for the day only.

Clicking on the "Preview Order" button allows you to double-check your order before you submit it for transaction. Here is our preview screen:

Numbered Examples

Example boxes are integrated throughout the chapters to reinforce the content and demonstrate to students how to apply what they've learned. Each example displays an intuitive or mathematical application in a step-by-step format. There is enough detail in the explanations so that the student doesn't have to look elsewhere for additional information.

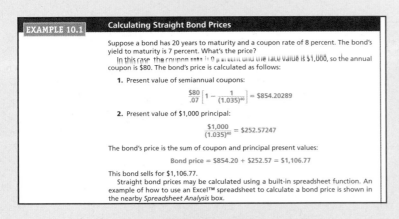

EXAMPLE 10.1

Calculating Straight Bond Prices

Suppose a bond has 20 years to maturity and a coupon rate of 8 percent. The bond's yield to maturity is 7 percent. What's the price?

In this case, the coupon rate is 8 percent and the face value is $1,000, so the annual coupon is $80. The bond's price is calculated as follows:

1. Present value of semiannual coupons:

$$\frac{\$80}{.07}\left[1 - \frac{1}{(1.035)^{40}}\right] = \$854.20289$$

2. Present value of $1,000 principal:

$$\frac{\$1,000}{(1.035)^{40}} = \$252.57247$$

The bond's price is the sum of coupon and principal present values:

$$\text{Bond price} = \$854.20 + \$252.57 = \$1,106.77$$

This bond sells for $1,106.77.

Straight bond prices may be calculated using a built-in spreadsheet function. An example of how to use an Excel™ spreadsheet to calculate a bond price is shown in the nearby *Spreadsheet Analysis* box.

Spreadsheet Analysis

Self-contained spreadsheet examples show students how to set up spreadsheets to solve problems—a vital part of every business student's education.

SPREADSHEET ANALYSIS

	A	B	C	D	E	F	G	H
1								
2		Calculating the Price of a Coupon Bond						
3								
4	A Treasury bond traded on March 30, 2010 matures in 20 years on March 30, 2030.							
5	Assuming an 8 percent coupon rate and a 7 percent yield to maturity, what is the							
6	price of this bond?							
7	Hint: Use the Excel function PRICE.							
8								
9		$110.6775	= PRICE("3/30/2010","3/30/2030",0.08,0.07,100,2,3)					
10								
11	For a bond with $1,000 face value, multiply the price by 10 to get $1,106.78.							
12								
13	This function uses the following arguments:							
14								
15		=PRICE("Now","Maturity", Coupon,Yield,100,2,3)						
16								
17	The 100 indicates redemption value as a percent of face value.							
18	The 2 indicates semi-annual coupons.							
19	The 3 specifies an actual day count with 365 days per year.							
20								
21								

Numbered Equations

Key equations are highlighted and numbered sequentially. For easy reference, an appendix at the end of the book lists these key equations by chapter.

arbitrage opportunities do not exist, and it therefore follows that a American call option price is never less than its intrinsic value (even when dividends are paid). That is:

$$\text{American call option price} \geq \text{MAX}[S - K, 0] \qquad (15.3)$$

AMERICAN PUTS A similar arbitrage argument applies to American put options. For example, suppose a current stock price is $S = \$40$, and a put option with a strike price of $K = \$50$ has a price of $P = \$5$. This \$5 put price is less than the option's intrinsic value of $K - S = \$10$. To exploit this profit opportunity, you first buy the put option at its price of $P = \$5$, and then buy the stock at its current price of $S = \$40$. At this point, you have acquired the stock for \$45, which is the sum of the put price plus the stock price.

Now you immediately exercise the put option, thereby selling the stock to the option writer at the strike price of $S = \$50$. Because you acquired the stock for \$45 and sold the stock for \$50, you have earned an arbitrage profit of \$5. Again, you would not realistically expect such an easy arbitrage opportunity to exist. Therefore, we conclude that the price of an American put option price is never less than its intrinsic value:

$$\text{American put option price} \geq \text{MAX}[K - S, 0] \qquad (15.4)$$

EUROPEAN CALLS Because European options cannot be exercised before expiration, we cannot use the arbitrage strategies that we used to set lower bounds for American options. We must use a different approach (which can be found in many textbooks that focus on options). It turns out that the lower bound for a European call option is greater than its intrinsic value.

$$\text{European call option price} \geq \text{MAX}[S - K/(1 + r)^T, 0] \qquad (15.5)$$

Figures and Tables

This text makes extensive use of real data and presents them in various figures and tables. Explanations in the narrative, examples, and end-of-chapter problems refer to many of these exhibits.

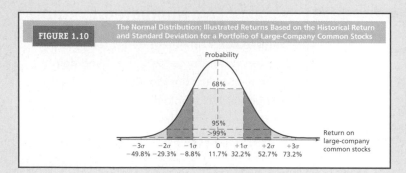

FIGURE 1.10 The Normal Distribution: Illustrated Returns Based on the Historical Return and Standard Deviation for a Portfolio of Large-Company Common Stocks

Summary and Conclusions

Each chapter ends with a summary that highlights the important points of the chapter. This material provides a handy checklist for students when they review the chapter.

5.7 Summary and Conclusions

This chapter introduces you to stock markets. We discussed who owns stocks, how the stock exchanges operate, and how stock market indexes are constructed and interpreted. This chapter covers many important aspects of stock markets, including the following items—grouped by the chapter's important concepts.

1. **The differences between private and public equity, and primary and secondary stock markets.**

A. Private equity funds are investment companies that invest in private companies. These investments range from early stage financing (i.e., venture capital) to large leveraged buyouts of public companies (i.e., going private).

B. The stock market is composed of a primary market, where stock shares are first sold, and a secondary market, where investors trade shares among themselves. In the primary market, companies raise money for investment projects. Investment bankers specialize in arranging financing for companies in the primary market. Investment bankers often act as underwriters, buying newly issued stock from the company and then reselling the stock to the public. The primary market is best known as the market for initial public offerings (IPOs).

C. In the secondary market, investors trade securities with other investors. Secondary market transactions are directed through three channels: directly with other investors, indirectly through a broker, or directly with a dealer. We saw that a broker matches buyers and sellers; a dealer buys and sells out of inventory.

Get Real

For instructors looking to give their students a taste of what it means to be an investment manager, this feature (at the end of each chapter) acts as a first step by explaining to students how to apply the material they just learned. The *Get Real* boxes encourage students—whether for practice in a trading simulation, or with real money—to make investment decisions, and they also give some helpful tips to keep in mind.

GET REAL

This chapter added to your understanding of put and call options by covering the rights, obligations, and potential gains and losses involved in trading options. How should you put this information to work? You need to buy and sell options to experience the gains and losses that options can provide. So, with a simulated brokerage account (such as Stock-Trak), you should first execute each of the basic option transactions: buy a call, sell a call, buy a put, and sell a put.

For help getting started, you can find an enormous amount of information about options on the Internet. A useful place to start is the Chicago Board Options Exchange (www.cboe.com). Excellent Web sites devoted to options education are the Options Industry Council (www.optionscentral.com) and the Options Clearing Corporation (www.optionsclearing.com). You might also look at the options section of Trading Markets (www.tradingmarkets.com) or Investor Links (www.investorlinks.com).

For information on option trading strategies, try entering the strategy name into an Internet search engine. For example, enter the search phrases "covered calls" or "protective puts" for online information about those strategies. For more general information, try the search phrase "options trading strategies" to find sites like Commodity World (www.commodityworld.com). For a sales pitch on writing covered calls, check out Write Call (www.writecall.com).

If you're having trouble understanding options ticker symbols, don't feel alone because almost everyone has trouble at first. For help on the net, try the search phrases "option symbols" or "options symbols" to find sites like www.optionscentral.com. Of course, the options exchanges listed above also provide complete information on the option ticker symbols they use.

Chapter Review Problems and Self-Test

1. **Call Option Payoffs (CFA3)**   You purchase 25 call option contracts on Blue Ox stock. The strike price is $22, and the premium is $1. If the stock is selling for $24 per share at expiration, what are your call options worth? What is your net profit? What if the stock were selling for $23? $22?

2. **Stock versus Options (CFA2)**   Stock in Bunyan Brewery is currently priced at $20 per share. A call option with a $20 strike price and 60 days to maturity is quoted at $2. Compare the percentage gains and losses from a $2,000 investment in the stock versus the option in 60 days for stock prices of $26, $20, and $18.

3. **Put-Call Parity (CFA1)**   A call option sells for $8. It has a strike price of $80 and six months until expiration. If the underlying stock sells for $60 per share, what is the price of a put option with an $80 strike price and six months until expiration? The risk-free interest rate is 6 percent per year.

Answers to Self-Test Problems

1. Blue Ox stock is selling for $24. You own 25 contracts, each of which gives you the right to buy 100 shares at $22. Your options are thus worth $2 per share on 2,500 shares, or $5,000. The option premium was $1, so you paid $100 per contract, or $2,500 total. Your net profit is $2,500. If the stock is selling for $23, your options are worth $2,500, so your net profit is exactly zero. If the stock is selling for $22, your options are worthless, and you lose the entire $2,500 you paid.

2. Bunyan stock costs $20 per share, so if you invest $2,000, you'll get 100 shares. The option premium is $2, so an option contract costs $200. If you invest $2,000, you'll get $2,000/$200 = 10 contracts. If the stock is selling for $26 in 60 days, your profit on the stock is $6 per share, or $600 total. The percentage gain is $600/$2,000 = 30%.

   In this case, your options are worth $6 per share, or $600 per contract. You have 10 contracts,

Chapter Review Problems and Self-Test

Students are provided with one to three practice problems per chapter with worked-out solutions to test their abilities in solving key problems related to the content of the chapter.

Test Your Investment Quotient

An average of 15 multiple-choice questions are included for each chapter, many of which are taken from past CFA exams. This text is unique in that it is the only text that presents CFA questions in multiple-choice format—which is how they appear on the actual exam. Answers to these questions appear in Appendix A.

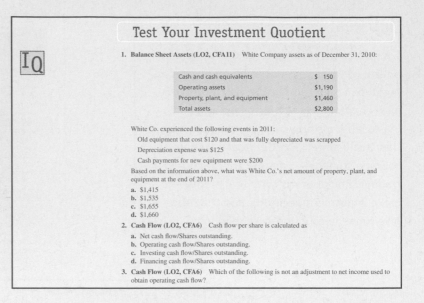

Test Your Investment Quotient

1. **Balance Sheet Assets (LO2, CFA11)** White Company assets as of December 31, 2010:

Cash and cash equivalents	$ 150
Operating assets	$1,190
Property, plant, and equipment	$1,460
Total assets	$2,800

White Co. experienced the following events in 2011:

Old equipment that cost $120 and that was fully depreciated was scrapped

Depreciation expense was $125

Cash payments for new equipment were $200

Based on the information above, what was White Co.'s net amount of property, plant, and equipment at the end of 2011?

  a. $1,415
  b. $1,535
  c. $1,655
  d. $1,660

2. **Cash Flow (LO2, CFA6)** Cash flow per share is calculated as

  a. Net cash flow/Shares outstanding.
  b. Operating cash flow/Shares outstanding.
  c. Investing cash flow/Shares outstanding.
  d. Financing cash flow/Shares outstanding.

3. **Cash Flow (LO2, CFA6)** Which of the following is not an adjustment to net income used to obtain operating cash flow?

Concept Questions

At the end of every chapter are 10 to 15 concept questions that further reinforce key concepts found throughout the chapter.

Concept Questions

1. **Money Market Instruments (LO1, CFA1)** What are the distinguishing features of a money market instrument?
2. **Preferred Stock (LO2)** Why is preferred stock "preferred"?
3. **WSJ Stock Quotes (LO2)** What is the PE ratio reported for stocks in *The Wall Street Journal*? In particular, how is it computed?
4. **Yields (LO1, CFA2)** The current yield on a bond is the coupon rate divided by the price. Thus, it is very similar to what number reported for common and preferred stocks?

Questions and Problems

A variety of problems (average of 20 per chapter) are included in each chapter to test students' understanding of the conceptual and mathematical elements. Each problem is labeled with the subject and the level—core or intermediate. Selected answers appear in Appendix B, and complete solutions are included in the Instructor Web site.

Questions and Problems

Core Questions

1. **Stock Quotations (LO2)** You found the following stock quote for DRK Enterprises, Inc., at your favorite Web site. You also find that the stock paid an annual dividend of $0.75, which resulted in a dividend yield of 1.30 percent. What was the closing price for this stock yesterday? How many round lots of stock were traded yesterday?

CFA Exam Review
by Schweser

Unique to this text! These reviews are excerpted from Schweser, a leader in CFA exam preparation. Each review addresses chapter content but in a way that is consistent with the format of the actual CFA exam.

What's on the Web?

← **What's on the Web?**

These end-of-chapter activities show students how to use and learn from the vast amount of financial resources available on the Internet.

1. **Ticker Symbols** Go to finance.yahoo.com and look up the ticker symbols for the following companies: 3M Company, International Business Machines, Dell Computer, Advanced Micro Devices, American Standard Company, and Bed, Bath & Beyond.
2. **Average Return and Standard Deviation** Go to finance.yahoo.com and enter the ticker symbol for your favorite stock. Now, look for the historical prices and find the monthly closing stock price for the last six years. Calculate the annual arithmetic average return, the standard deviation, and the geometric return for this period.

Stock-Trak Exercises

← **Stock-Trak Exercises**

Unique to this text! This text is the only book that incorporates Stock-Trak Portfolio Simulations® exercises. Stock-Trak is one of the most successful trading simulations with over 30,000 college students having trading accounts each semester (see Supplements for more information). Go to the next level in teaching your students about investments management by encouraging your students to use this product. Chapters with Stock-Trak Exercises will have the logo and the URL for the book's Web site. The actual exercise and questions related to the chapter will be presented in both the Student and Instructor portions of the Web site. Instructors and students must be registered for Stock-Trak in order to make trades (see the Supplement Section of the Preface or the insert card for more information).

To access the Stock-Trak Exercise for this chapter, please visit the book Web site at www.mhhe.com/jmd6e and choose the corresponding chapter.

Resources

Teaching and Learning Supplements

We have developed a number of supplements for both teaching and learning to accompany this text. Each product has been significantly revised for the sixth edition.

Digital Solutions

Online Learning Center (OLC):

Online Support at www.mhhe.com/jmd6e

The Online Learning Center (OLC) contains access to additional Web-based study and teaching aids created for this text, such as:

Student Support

Student-Narrated PowerPoints *created by Spencer Jones,* Carson-Newman College

Students all learn differently and these chapter PowerPoints were created with that rationale in mind. The interactive presentations provide detailed examples demonstrating how to solve key problems from the text. The slides are accompanied by an audio narration. They can be purchased as part of the premium content package available for $10 and then viewed online or uploaded onto an iPod.

Excel Templates

Corresponding to most end-of-chapter problems, each template allows the student to work through the problem using Excel, reinforcing each concept. Each end-of-chapter problem with a template is indicated by an Excel icon in the margin beside it.

Self-Study Chapter Quizzes

Quizzes consist of 10–15 multiple-choice questions on various chapter topics. They reveal a score instantly and provide feedback to help students study.

Other Features

Be sure to check out the other helpful features found on the OLC including key-term flashcards, helpful Web links, and more!

Instructor Support

The Instructor's Edition of the OLC contains the following assets:

PowerPoint Presentation, *prepared by Thomas W. Miller Jr.,* Saint Louis University

This product, created by one of the authors, contains over 300 slides with lecture outlines, examples, and images and tables from the text.

Instructor's Manual, *prepared by Steven D. Dolvin, CFA,* Butler University

Developed by one of the authors, the goals of this product are to outline chapter material clearly and provide extra teaching support. The first section of the Instructor's Manual includes an annotated outline of each chapter with suggested Web sites, references to PowerPoint slides, teaching tips, additional examples, and current events references.

Solutions Manual, *Prepared by Steven D. Dolvin, CFA,* Butler University

The Solutions Manual contains the complete worked-out solutions for the end-of-chapter questions and problems.

Test Bank, *prepared by Lynn Kugele,* University of Mississippi

With almost 1,500 questions, this Test Bank, in Microsoft Word, provides a variety of question formats (true-false, multiple choice, fill-in-the-blank, and problems) and levels of difficulty to meet any instructor's testing needs.

Computerized Test Bank (Windows)

This computerized version of the Test Bank utilizes McGraw-Hill's EZ Test testing software to quickly create customized exams. This user-friendly program allows instructors to sort questions by format; edit existing questions or add new ones; and scramble questions for multiple versions of the same test.

Videos ISBN 0-07-336379-0 (DVD format)

The McGraw-Hill/Irwin series of finance videos are 10-minute case studies on topics such as Financial Markets, Stocks, Bonds, Portfolio Management, Derivatives, and Going Public.

PageOut at www.pageout.net

Free to adopters, this Web page generation software is designed to help you create your own course Web site, without all of the hassle. In just a few minutes, even the most novice computer user can have a functioning course Web site.

Simply type your material into the template provided and PageOut instantly converts it to HTML. Next, choose your favorite of three easy-to-navigate designs and your class Web home page is created, complete with online syllabus, lecture notes, and bookmarks. You can even include a separate instructor page and an assignment page.

PageOut offers enhanced point-and-click features, including a Syllabus Page that applies a real-world link to original text material, an automatic grade book, and a discussion board where you and your students can exchange questions and post announcements. Ask your campus representative to show you a demo.

Additional Resources Packaged with Your New Text

Stock-Trak Portfolio Simulation

Give your students investment management experience! McGraw-Hill/Irwin has partnered with *Stock-Trak* and is providing a **free** subscription to the *Stock-Trak Portfolio Simulation* for one semester with the purchase of every new copy of *Fundamentals of Investments: Valuation and Management, Sixth Edition* by Jordan, Miller, and Dolvin. *Stock-Trak* gives students $1,000,000 and allows them to trade stocks, options, futures, bonds, mutual funds, and international stocks—no other simulation offers all these types of securities! More than 600 professors have used this service, and around 30,000 college students each semester participate. All trades are done on the Web at www.stocktrak.com. See this site for more information or use the Stock-Trak card bound into this text. Stock-Trak exercises are available on the book Web site, www.mhhe.com/jmd6e.

McGraw-Hill *Connect Finance*

Less Managing. More Teaching. Greater Learning.

McGraw-Hill *Connect Finance* is an online assignment and assessment solution that connects students with the tools and resources they'll need to achieve success. *Connect* helps prepare students for their future by enabling faster learning, more efficient studying, and higher retention of knowledge.

McGraw-Hill *Connect Finance* Features

Connect Finance offers a number of powerful tools and features to make managing assignments easier, so faculty can spend more time teaching. With *Connect Finance,* students can engage with their coursework anytime and anywhere, making the learning process more accessible and efficient. *Connect Finance* offers you the features described below.

Simple Assignment Management With *Connect Finance,* creating assignments is easier than ever, so you can spend more time teaching and less time managing. The assignment management function enables you to:

- Create and deliver assignments easily with selectable end-of-chapter questions and test bank items.
- Streamline lesson planning, student progress reporting, and assignment grading to make classroom management more efficient than ever.
- Go paperless with the eBook and online submission and grading of student assignments.

Smart Grading When it comes to studying, time is precious. *Connect Finance* helps students learn more efficiently by providing feedback and practice material when they need it, where they need it. When it comes to teaching, your time is also precious. The grading function enables you to:

- Have assignments scored automatically, giving students immediate feedback on their work and side-by-side comparisons with correct answers.
- Access and review each response; manually change grades or leave comments for students to review.
- Reinforce classroom concepts with practice tests and instant quizzes.

Instructor Library The *Connect Finance* Instructor Library is your repository for additional resources to improve student engagement in and out of class. You can select and use any asset that enhances your lecture.

Student Study Center The *Connect Finance* Student Study Center is the place for students to access additional resources. The Student Study Center:

- Offers students quick access to lectures, practice materials, eBooks, and more.
- Provides instant practice material and study questions, easily accessible on the go.
- Gives students access to the Self-Quiz and Study described below.

Self-Quiz and Study The Self-Quiz and Study (SQS) connects each student to the learning resources needed for success in the course. For each chapter, students:

- Take a practice test to initiate the SQS.
- Immediately upon completing the practice test, see how their performance compares to the chapter objectives to be achieved within each section of the chapter.
- Are pointed toward readings from the text, supplemental study material, and practice work that will improve their understanding and mastery of each learning objective.

Student Progress Tracking *Connect Finance* keeps instructors informed about how each student, section, and class is performing, allowing for more productive use of lecture and office hours. The progress-tracking function enables you to:

- View scored work immediately and track individual or group performance with assignment and grade reports.
- Access an instant view of student or class performance relative to learning objectives.

Lecture Capture through Tegrity Campus For an additional charge, Lecture Capture offers new ways for students to focus on the in-class discussion, knowing they can revisit important topics later. This can be delivered through *Connect* or separately. See below for more details.

McGraw-Hill *Connect Plus Finance*

McGraw-Hill reinvents the textbook learning experience for the modern student with *Connect Plus Finance*. A seamless integration of an eBook and *Connect Finance, Connect Plus Finance* provides all of the *Connect Finance* features plus the following:

- An integrated eBook, allowing for anytime, anywhere access to the textbook.
- Dynamic links between the problems or questions you assign to your students and the location in the eBook where that problem or question is covered.
- A powerful search function to pinpoint and connect key concepts in a snap.

In short, *Connect Finance* offers you and your students powerful tools and features that optimize your time and energies, enabling you to focus on course content, teaching, and student learning. *Connect Finance* also offers a wealth of content resources for both instructors and students. This state-of-the-art, thoroughly tested system supports you in preparing students for the world that awaits.

For more information about *Connect,* go to **www.mcgrawhillconnect.com**, or contact your local McGraw-Hill sales representative.

Tegrity Campus: Lectures 24/7

Tegrity Campus is a service that makes class time available 24/7 by automatically capturing every lecture in a searchable format for students to review when they study and complete assignments. With a simple one-click start-and-stop process, you capture all computer screens and corresponding audio. Students can replay any part of any class with easy-to-use browser-based viewing on a PC or Mac.

Educators know that the more students can see, hear, and experience class resources, the better they learn. In fact, studies prove it. With Tegrity Campus, students quickly recall key moments by using Tegrity Campus's unique search feature. This search helps students efficiently find what they need, when they need it, across an entire semester of class recordings. Help turn all your students' study time into learning moments immediately supported by your lecture.

To learn more about Tegrity watch a two-minute Flash demo at **http://tegritycampus .mhhe.com**.

McGraw-Hill Customer Care Contact Information

At McGraw-Hill, we understand that getting the most from new technology can be challenging. That's why our services don't stop after you purchase our products. You can e-mail our Product Specialists 24 hours a day to get product training online. Or you can search our knowledge bank of Frequently Asked Questions on our support Web site. For Customer Support, call **800-331-5094,** e-mail **hmsupport@mcgraw-hill.com**, or visit **www.mhhe.com/support**. One of our Technical Support Analysts will be able to assist you in a timely fashion.

Brief Contents

Contents

CHAPTER 1

A Brief History of Risk and Return

Learning Objectives

To become a wise investor (maybe even one with too much money), you need to know:

1. How to calculate the return on an investment using different methods.

2. The historical returns on various important types of investments.

3. The historical risks on various important types of investments.

4. The relationship between risk and return.

"All I ask is for the chance to prove that money can't make me happy."

–Spike Milligan

Who wants to be a millionaire? Actually, anyone can retire as a millionaire. How? Consider this: Suppose you, on your 25th birthday, invest $3,000. You have the discipline to invest $3,000 on each of your next 39 birthdays until you retire on your 65th birthday. How much will you have? The answer might surprise you. If you earn 10 percent per year, you will have about $1.46 million. Are these numbers realistic? Based on the history of financial markets, the answer appears to be yes. For example, over the last 84 or so years, the widely followed Standard & Poor's index of large-company common stocks has actually yielded about 12 percent per year. ■

The study of investments could begin in many places. After thinking it over, we decided that a brief history lesson is in order, so we start our discussion of risk and return by looking back at what has happened to investors in U.S. financial markets since 1925. In 1931, for example, the stock market lost 43 percent of its value. Just two years later, the market reversed itself and gained 54 percent. In more recent times, the stock market lost about 25 percent of its value on October 19, 1987, alone, and it gained almost 40 percent in 1995. From 2003 through 2007, the market gained about 80 percent. In 2008, the market fell almost 40 percent. In 2009, the market reversed course again, returning almost 20 percent.

CFA™ Exam Topics in This Chapter:

1 Discounted cash flow applications (L1, S2)
2 Statistical concepts and market returns (L1, S2)
3 Common probability distributions (L1, S3)
4 Sampling and estimation (L1, S3)
5 Dividend and dividend policy (L2, S8)
6 Evaluating portfolio performance (L3, S17)

Go to www.mhhe.com/jmd6e for a guide that aligns your textbook with CFA readings.

So what should you, as a stock market investor, expect when you invest your own money? In this chapter, we study more than eight decades of market history to find out.

In this chapter, we present the historical relation between risk and return. As you will see, this chapter has a lot of very practical information for anyone thinking of investing in financial assets such as stocks and bonds. For example, suppose you were to start investing in stocks today. Do you think your money would grow at an average rate of 5 percent per year? Or 10 percent? Or 20 percent? This chapter gives you an idea of what to expect (the answer may surprise you). The chapter also shows how risky certain investments can be, and it gives you the tools to think about risk in an objective way.

Our primary goal in this chapter is to see what financial market history can tell us about risk and return. Specifically, we want to give you a perspective on the numbers. What is a high return? What is a low return? More generally, what returns should we expect from financial assets such as stocks and bonds, and what are the risks from such investments? Beyond this, we hope that by studying what *did* happen in the past, we will at least gain some insight into what *can* happen in the future.

The history of risk and return is made day by day in global financial markets. The Internet is an excellent source of information on financial markets. Visit our Web site (at www.mhhe.com/jmd6e) for suggestions on where to find information on recent financial market events. We will suggest other sites later in the chapter.

Not everyone agrees on the value of studying history. On the one hand, there is philosopher George Santayana's famous comment, "Those who do not remember the past are condemned to repeat it." On the other hand, there is industrialist Henry Ford's equally famous comment, "History is more or less bunk." These extremes aside, perhaps everyone would agree with Mark Twain, who observed, with remarkable foresight (and poor grammar), that "October. This is one of the peculiarly dangerous months to speculate in stocks in. The others are July, January, September, April, November, May, March, June, December, August, and February."

Two key observations emerge from a study of financial market history. First, there is a reward for bearing risk, and, at least on average, that reward has been substantial. That's the good news. The bad news is that greater rewards are accompanied by greater risks. The fact that risk and return go together is probably the single most important fact to understand about investments, and it is a point to which we will return many times.

1.1   Returns

We wish to discuss historical returns on different types of financial assets. First, we need to know how to compute the return from an investment. We will consider buying shares of stock in this section, but the basic calculations are the same for any investment.

DOLLAR RETURNS

If you buy an asset of any type, your gain (or loss) from that investment is called the *return* on your investment. This return will usually have two components. First, you may receive some cash directly while you own the investment. Second, the value of the asset you purchase may change. In this case, you have a capital gain or capital loss on your investment.[1]

To illustrate, suppose you purchased 200 shares of stock in Harley-Davidson (ticker symbol: HOG) on January 1. At that time, Harley was selling for $25 per share, so your 200 shares cost you $5,000. At the end of the year, you want to see how you did with your investment.

---

[1] As a practical matter, what is and what is not a capital gain (or loss) is determined by the Internal Revenue Service. Even so, as is commonly done, we use these terms to refer to a change in value.

The first thing to consider is that over the year, a company may pay cash dividends to its shareholders. As a stockholder in Harley, you are a part owner of the company, and you are entitled to a portion of any money distributed. So if Harley chooses to pay a dividend, you will receive some cash for every share you own.

In addition to the dividend, the other part of your return is the capital gain or loss on the stock. This part arises from changes in the value of your investment. For example, consider these two cases:

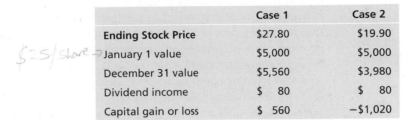

	Case 1	Case 2
Ending Stock Price	$27.80	$19.90
January 1 value	$5,000	$5,000
December 31 value	$5,560	$3,980
Dividend income	$ 80	$ 80
Capital gain or loss	$ 560	−$1,020

$25/share → (handwritten annotation pointing to January 1 value)

At the beginning of the year, on January 1, the stock was selling for $25 per share. As we calculated above, your total outlay for 200 shares is $5,000. Over the year, Harley paid dividends of $.40 per share. By the end of the year, then, you received dividend income of

$$\text{Dividend income} = \$.40 \times 200 = \$80$$

In Case 1, suppose that as of December 31, a HOG share was selling for $27.80, meaning that the value of your stock increased by $2.80 per share. Your 200 shares would be worth $5,560, so you have a capital gain of

$$\text{Capital gain} = (\$27.80 - \$25) \times 200 = \$560$$

On the other hand, if the price had dropped to, say, $19.90 (Case 2), you would have a capital loss of

$$\text{Capital loss} = (\$19.90 - \$25) \times 200 = -\$1,020$$

Notice that a capital loss is the same thing as a negative capital gain.

The **total dollar return** on your investment is the sum of the dividend income and the capital gain (or loss):

$$\text{Total dollar return} = \text{Dividend income} + \text{Capital gain (or loss)}$$

In case 1, the total dollar return is thus given by

$$\text{Total dollar return} = \$80 + \$560 = \$640$$

Overall, between the dividends you received and the increase in the price of the stock, the value of your investment increased from $5,000 to $5,000 + $640 = $5,640.

A common misconception often arises in this context. Suppose you hold on to your Harley-Davidson stock and don't sell it at the end of the year. Should you still consider the capital gain as part of your return? Isn't this only a "paper" gain and not really a cash gain if you don't sell it?

The answer to the first question is a strong yes, and the answer to the second is an equally strong no. The capital gain is every bit as much a part of your return as the dividend, and you should certainly count it as part of your return. The fact that you decide to keep the stock and don't sell (you don't "realize" the gain) is irrelevant because you could have converted it to cash if you had wanted to. Whether you choose to do so is up to you.

total dollar return

The return on an investment measured in dollars that accounts for all cash flows and capital gains or losses.

After all, if you insist on converting your gain to cash, you could always sell the stock and immediately reinvest by buying the stock back. There is no difference between doing this and just not selling (assuming, of course, that there are no transaction costs or tax consequences from selling the stock). Again, the point is that whether you actually cash out and buy pizzas (or whatever) or continue to hold the investment doesn't affect the return you actually earn.

PERCENTAGE RETURNS

It is usually more convenient to summarize information about returns in percentage terms than in dollar terms, because that way your return doesn't depend on how much you actually invested. With percentage returns the question we want to answer is: How much do we get *for each dollar* we invest?

To answer this question, let P_t be the price of the stock at the beginning of the year. Let D_{t+1} be the dividend paid on the stock during the year. The following cash flows are the same as those shown earlier, except that we have now expressed everything on a per-share basis:

	Case 1	Case 2
January 1 stock price, P_t	$25.00	$25.00
December 31 stock price, P_{t+1}	$27.80	$19.90
Dividend income, D_{t+1}	$ .40	$ .40
Capital gain or loss	$ 2.80	−$ 5.10

In our example, the price at the beginning of the year was $25 per share and the dividend paid during the year on each share was $.40. If we divide the dividend by the beginning stock price, the result is the **dividend yield**:

dividend yield
The annual stock dividend as a percentage of the initial stock price.

$$\text{Dividend yield} = D_{t+1} / P_t \qquad (1.1)$$
$$= \$.40 / \$25 = .0160 = 1.60\%$$

This calculation says that for each dollar we invested we received 1.60 cents in dividends.

capital gains yield
The change in stock price as a percentage of the initial stock price.

The second component of our percentage return is the **capital gains yield**. This yield is calculated as the change in the price during the year (the capital gain) divided by the beginning price. With the case 1 ending price, we get:

$$\text{Capital gains yield} = (P_{t+1} - P_t) / P_t \qquad (1.2)$$
$$= (\$27.80 - \$25.00) / \$25.00$$
$$= \$2.80 / \$25 = .1120 = 11.20\%$$

This 11.20 percent yield means that for each dollar invested we got about 11 cents in capital gains (HOG heaven).

Putting it all together, per dollar invested, we get 1.60 cents in dividends and 11.20 cents in capital gains for a total of 12.80 cents. Our **total percent return** is 12.80 cents on the dollar, or 12.80 percent. When a return is expressed on a percentage basis, we often refer to it as the *rate of return,* or just "return," on the investment. Notice that if we combine the formulas for the dividend yield and capital gains yield, we get a single formula for the total percentage return:

total percent return
The return on an investment measured as a percentage that accounts for all cash flows and capital gains or losses.

$$\text{Percentage return} = \text{Dividend yield} + \text{Capital gains yield} \qquad (1.3)$$
$$= D_{t+1} / P_t + (P_{t+1} - P_t) / P_t$$
$$= (D_{t+1} + P_{t+1} - P_t) / P_t$$

To check our calculations, notice that we invested $5,000 and ended up with $5,640. By what percentage did our $5,000 increase? As we saw, our gain was $5,640 − $5,000 = $640. This is an increase of $640 / $5,000, or 12.80 percent.

WORK THE WEB

To look up information on common stocks using the Web, you need to know the "ticker" symbol for the stocks in which you are interested. You can look up ticker symbols in many places, including one of our favorite sites, finance.yahoo.com. Here we have looked up (using the "Symbol Lookup" link) and entered ticker symbols for some well-known "tech" stocks: Dell, Cisco, Intel, and Microsoft.

YAHOO! FINANCE   Q Search

| dell csco intc msft | **GET QUOTES** | Finance Search | Mon, Feb 1, 2010, 10:15AM ET |

Once we hit "Get Quotes," this is what we got:

Views: Summary | Real-Time | **Basic edit** | DayWatch | Performance | ✚ New View

Symbol	Last Trade		Change		Volume	Intraday	Related Info
DELL	10:01AM ET	13.19	↑0.30	↑2.29%	2,738,649	[........]	Chart, Messages, Key Stats, more...
CSCO	10:01AM ET	22.88	↑0.41	↑1.82%	7,610,314	[........]	Chart, Messages, Key Stats, more...
INTC	10:01AM ET	19.69	↑0.29	↑1.50%	7,430,161	[........]	Chart, Messages, Key Stats, more...
MSFT	10:01AM ET	28.35	↑0.17	↑0.60%	12,228,301	[........]	Chart, Messages, Key Stats, more...

As you can see, we get the price for each stock, along with information about the change in price and volume (number of shares traded). You will find a lot of links to hit and learn more, so have at it!

EXAMPLE 1.1

Calculating Percentage Returns

Suppose you buy some stock in Concannon Plastics for $35 per share. After one year, the price is $49 per share. During the year, you received a $1.40 dividend per share. What is the dividend yield? The capital gains yield? The percentage return? If your total investment was $1,400, how much do you have at the end of the year?

Your $1.40 dividend per share works out to a dividend yield of

$$\text{Dividend yield} = D_{t+1} / P_t$$
$$= \$1.40 / \$35$$
$$= 4\%$$

The per-share capital gain is $14, so the capital gains yield is

$$\text{Capital gains yield} = (P_{t+1} - P_t) / P_t$$
$$= (\$49 - \$35) / \$35$$
$$= \$14 / \$35$$
$$= 40\%$$

The total percentage return is thus 4% + 40% = 44%.

If you had invested $1,400, you would have $2,016 at the end of the year. To check this, note that your $1,400 would have bought you $1,400 / $35 = 40 shares. Your 40 shares would then have paid you a total of 40 × $1.40 = $56 in cash dividends. Your $14 per share gain would give you a total capital gain of $14 × 40 = $560. Add these together and you get $616, which is a 44 percent total return on your $1,400 investment.

A NOTE ON ANNUALIZING RETURNS

So far, we have only considered annual returns. Of course, the actual length of time you own an investment will almost never be exactly a year. To compare investments, however, we will usually need to express returns on a per-year or "annualized" basis, so we need to do a little bit more work.

For example, suppose you bought 200 shares of Lowe's Companies, Inc. (LOW) at a price of $18 per share. In three months, you sell your stock for $19. You didn't receive any dividends. What is your return for the three months? What is your annualized return?

In this case, we say that your *holding period,* which is the length of time you own the stock, is three months. With a zero dividend, you know that the percentage return can be calculated as:

$$\text{Percentage return} = (P_{t+1} - P_t)/P_t = (\$19 - \$18)/\$18 = .0556 = 5.56\%$$

This 5.56 percent is your return for the three-month holding period, but what does this return amount to on a per-year basis? To find out, we need to convert this to an annualized return, meaning a return expressed on a per-year basis. Such a return is often called an **effective annual return**, or **EAR** for short. The general formula is this:

$$1 + EAR = (1 + \text{holding period percentage return})^m \qquad (1.4)$$

where *m* is the number of holding periods in a year.

In our example, the holding period percentage return is 5.56 percent, or .0556. The holding period is three months, so there are four (12 months/3 months) periods in a year. We calculate the annualized return, or *EAR*, as follows:

$$\begin{aligned}
1 + EAR &= (1 + \text{holding period percentage return})^m \\
&= (1 + .0556)^4 \\
&= 1.2416
\end{aligned}$$

So, your annualized return is 24.16 percent.

effective annual return (EAR)

The return on an investment expressed on a per-year, or "annualized," basis.

| EXAMPLE 1.2 | A "QWEST" for Returns |

Suppose you buy some stock in Qwest (no, that's not a typo, that's how the company spells it) at a price of $8 per share. Four months later, you sell for $8.40 per share. No dividend is paid. What is your annualized return on this investment?

For the four-month holding period, your return is:

$$\text{Percentage return} = (P_{t+1} - P_t) / P_t = (\$8.40 - \$8) / \$8 = .05 = 5\%$$

There are three four-month periods in a year, so the annualized return is:

$$1 + EAR = (1 + \text{holding period percentage return})^m = (1 + .05)^3 = 1.1576$$

Subtracting the one, we get an annualized return of .1576, or 15.76 percent.

| EXAMPLE 1.3 | More Annualized Returns |

Suppose you buy some stock in Johnson & Johnson (JNJ) at a price of $50 per share. Three *years* later, you sell it for $62.50. No dividends were paid. What is your annualized return on this investment?

The situation here is a bit different because your holding period is now longer than a year, but the calculation is basically the same. For the three-year holding period, your return is:

$$\text{Percentage return} = (P_{t+1} - P_t) / P_t = (\$62.50 - \$50) / \$50 = .25 = 25\%$$

(continued)

How many three-year holding periods are there in a single year? The answer is one-third, so *m* in this case is 1/3. The annualized return is:

$$1 + EAR = (1 + \text{holding period percentage return})^m$$
$$= (1 + .25)^{1/3}$$
$$= 1.0772$$

Subtracting the one, we get an annualized return of .0772, or 7.72 percent.

Now that you know how to calculate returns on a hypothetical stock, you should calculate returns for real stocks. The nearby *Work the Web* box using finance.yahoo.com describes how to begin. Meanwhile, in the next several sections, we will take a look at the returns that some common types of investments have earned over the last 84 years.

CHECK THIS

1.1a What are the two parts of total return?

1.1b What is the difference between a dollar return and a percentage return? Why are percentage returns usually more convenient?

1.1c What is an effective annual return (EAR)?

1.2 The Historical Record

We now examine year-to-year historical rates of return on five important categories of financial investments. These returns can be interpreted as what you would have earned if you had invested in portfolios of the following asset categories:

Annual historical financial market data can be downloaded (but not for free) at www.globalfinancialdata.com

1. Large-company stocks. The large-company stock portfolio is based on the Standard & Poor's (S&P's) 500 index, which contains 500 of the largest companies (in terms of total market value of outstanding stock) in the United States.

2. Small-company stocks. This is a portfolio composed of stock of smaller companies, where "small" corresponds to the smallest 20 percent of the companies listed on the New York Stock Exchange, again as measured by market value of outstanding stock.

3. Long-term corporate bonds. This is a portfolio of high-quality bonds with 20 years to maturity.

4. Long-term U.S. government bonds. This is a portfolio of U.S. government bonds with 20 years to maturity.

5. U.S. Treasury bills. This is a portfolio of Treasury bills (T-bills for short) with a three-month maturity.

If you are not entirely certain what these investments are, don't be overly concerned. We will have much more to say about each in later chapters. For now, just accept that these are some important investment categories. In addition to the year-to-year returns on these financial instruments, the year-to-year percentage changes in the Consumer Price Index (CPI) are also computed. The CPI is a standard measure of consumer goods price inflation.

Here is a bit of market jargon for you. A company's *total market capitalization* (or market "cap" for short) is equal to its stock price multiplied by the number of shares of stock. In other words, it's the total value of the company's stock. Large companies are often called "large-cap" stocks, and small companies are called "small-cap" stocks. We'll use these terms frequently.

FIGURE 1.1

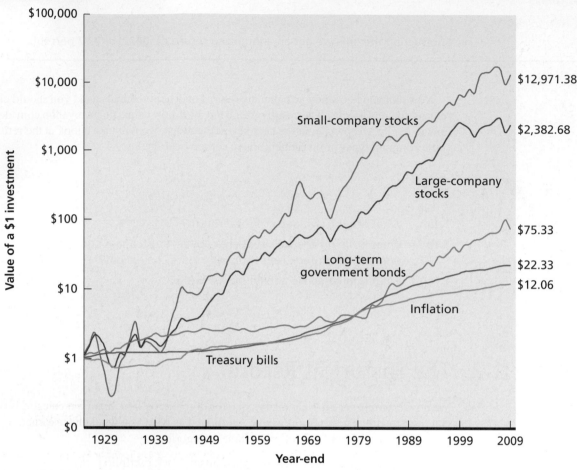

A $1 Investment in Different Types of Portfolios: 1926–2009 (Year-end 1925 = $1)

Source: *Global Financial Data* (www.globalfinancialdata.com) and Professor Kenneth R. French, Dartmouth College.

A FIRST LOOK

Before examining the different portfolio returns, we first take a look at the "big picture." Figure 1.1 shows what happened to $1 invested in these different portfolios at the beginning of 1926 and held over the 84-year period ending in 2009 (for clarity, the long-term corporate bonds are omitted). To fit all the information on a single graph, some modification in scaling is used. As is commonly done with financial time series, the vertical axis is scaled so that equal distances measure equal percentage (as opposed to dollar) changes in value. Thus, the distance between $10 and $100 is the same as that between $100 and $1,000, since both distances represent the same 900 percent increases.

Looking at Figure 1.1, we see that the small-company investment did the best overall. Every dollar invested grew to a remarkable $12,971.38 over the 84 years. The larger common stock portfolio did less well; a dollar invested in it grew to $2,382.68.

At the other end, the T-bill portfolio grew to only $22.33. This is even less impressive when we consider the inflation over this period. As illustrated, the increase in the price level was such that $12.06 is needed just to replace the original $1.

Given the historical record, why would anybody buy anything other than small-company stocks? If you look closely at Figure 1.1, you will probably see the answer—risk. The T-bill portfolio and the long-term government bond portfolio grew more slowly than did the stock portfolios, but they also grew much more steadily. The small stocks ended up on top, but, as you can see, they grew quite erratically at times. For example, the small stocks were the

FIGURE 1.2   Financial Market History

Total return indexes (1801–2009)

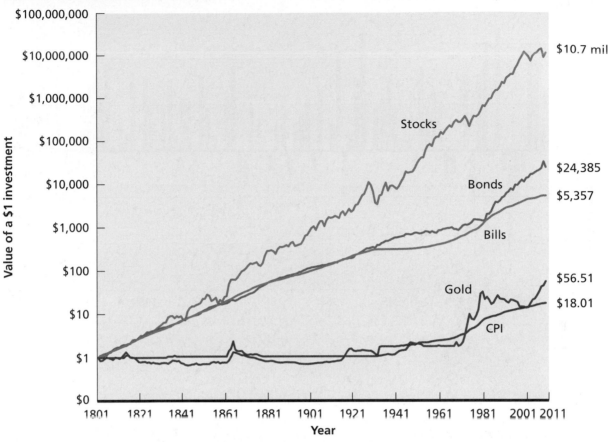

Source: Jeremy J. Siegel, *Stocks for the Long Run*, 3rd ed. (New York: McGraw-Hill, 2003). Update through 2009 provided by Jeremy J. Siegel. *Global Financial Data* (www.globalfinancialdata.com) and Professor Kenneth R. French, Dartmouth College.

worst performers for about the first 10 years and had a smaller return than long-term government bonds for almost 15 years.

A LONGER RANGE LOOK

The data available on the stock returns before 1925 are not comprehensive, but it is nonetheless possible to trace reasonably accurate returns in U.S. financial markets as far back as 1801. Figure 1.2 shows the values, in 2009, of $1 invested since 1801 in stocks, long-term bonds, short-term bills, and gold. The CPI is also included for reference.

Inspecting Figure 1.2, we see that $1 invested in stocks grew to an astounding $10.7 million over this 209-year period. During this time, the returns from investing in stocks dwarf those earned on other investments. Notice also in Figure 1.2 that, after two centuries, gold has managed to keep up with inflation, but that is about it.

What we see thus far is that there has been a powerful financial incentive for long-term investing. The real moral of the story is this: Get an early start!

A CLOSER LOOK

To illustrate the variability of the different investments and inflation, Figures 1.3 through 1.6 plot the year-to-year percentage returns in the form of vertical bars drawn from the horizontal axis. The height of a bar tells us the return for the particular year. For example, looking at the long-term government bonds (Figure 1.5), we see that the largest historical return (49.99 percent) occurred in 1982. This year was a good year for bonds. In comparing these charts, notice the differences in the vertical axis scales. With these differences in mind, you

Large-company stocks

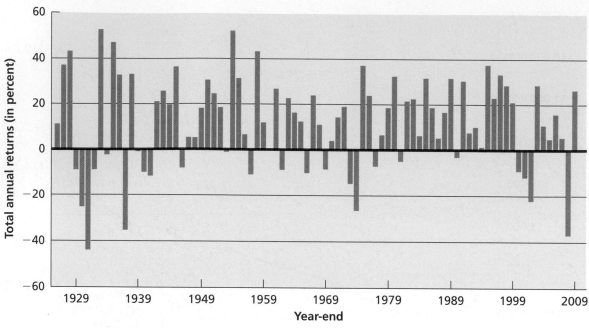

Source: Professor Kenneth R. French, Dartmouth College.

Small-company stocks

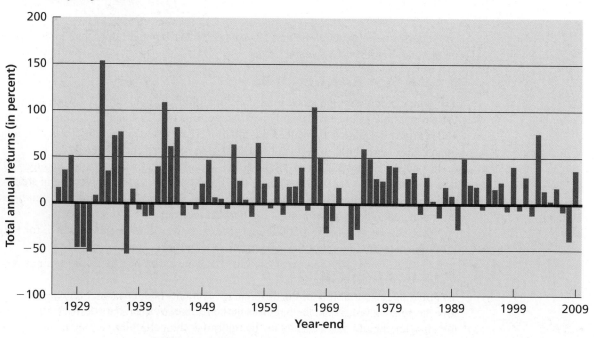

Source: Professor Kenneth R. French, Dartmouth College.

FIGURE 1.5 Year-to-Year Total Returns on Bonds and Bills: 1926–2009

Long-term U.S. government bonds

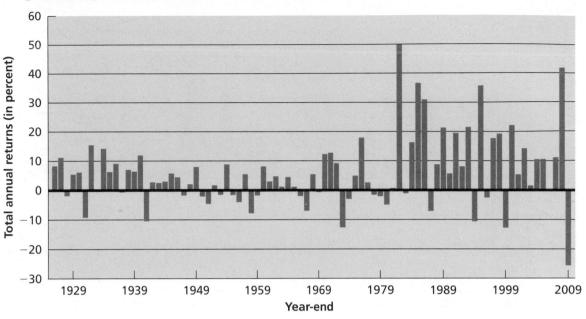

U.S. Treasury bills

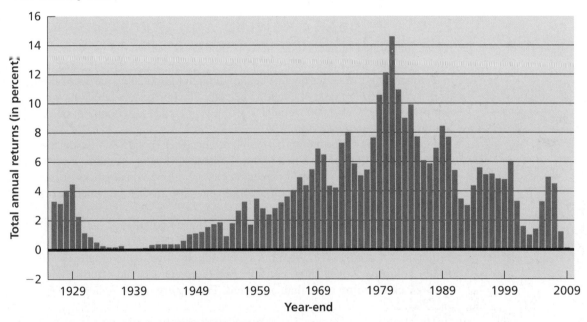

Source: *Global Financial Data* (www.globalfinancialdata.com).

can see how predictably the Treasury bills (bottom of Figure 1.5) behaved compared to the small-company stocks (Figure 1.4).

The returns shown in these bar graphs are sometimes very large. Looking at the graphs, we see, for example, that the largest single-year return was a remarkable 153 percent for the small-company stocks in 1933. In the same year, the large-company stocks returned "only" 53 percent. In contrast, the largest Treasury bill return was 14.6 percent, in 1981. For future reference, the actual year-to-year returns for the S&P 500, long-term U.S. government bonds, U.S. Treasury bills, and the CPI are shown in Table 1.1 on page 13.

FIGURE 1.6   Year-to-Year Inflation: 1926–2009

Inflation
Cumulative index and rates of change

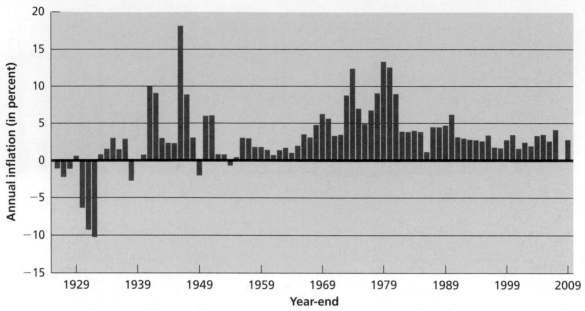

Source: *Global Financial Data* (www.globalfinancialdata.com).

2008: THE BEAR GROWLED AND INVESTORS HOWLED

As we mentioned in our chapter introduction, 2008 entered the record books as one of the worst years for stock market investors in U.S. history. Over the extended period beginning in October 2007 (when the decline began) through March 2009, the S&P 500 Index declined from 1,576 to 677, a drop of about 57 percent. Stock investors fared much better during the rest of 2009. The S&P 500 stood at 1,115 at year's end—a rebound of 65 percent from the March low.

Figure 1.7 shows the month-by-month performance of the S&P 500 during 2008. As indicated, returns were negative in 8 of the 12 months. Most of the damage occurred in the fall, with investors losing almost 17 percent in October alone. Small stocks fared no better. They fell 37 percent for the year (with a 21 percent drop in October), their worst performance since losing 58 percent in 1937.

As Figure 1.7 suggests, stock prices were highly volatile during 2008. Oddly, the S&P had 126 up days and 126 down days (remember the markets are closed weekends and holidays). Of course, the down days were much worse on average. To see how extraordinary volatility was in 2008, consider that there were 18 days during which the value of the S&P changed by more than 5 percent. There were only 17 such moves *between 1956 and 2007!*

The drop in stock prices in 2008 was a global phenomenon, and many of the world's major markets were off by much more than the S&P. China, India, and Russia, for example, all experienced declines of more than 50 percent. Tiny Iceland saw share prices drop by more than 90 percent for the year. Trading on the Icelandic exchange was temporarily suspended on October 9. In what has to be a modern record for a single day, stocks fell by 76 percent when trading resumed on October 14.

Did U.S. investors encounter any bright spots? The answer is yes: As stocks plummeted, bonds soared, particularly U.S. Treasury bonds. In fact, long-term Treasuries gained over 40 percent in 2008, while shorter term Treasury bonds were up 13 percent. Long-term corporate bonds did not fare as well, but still managed to finish in positive territory, up 9 percent.

TABLE 1.1 — Year-to-Year Total Returns: 1926–2009

Year	Large-Company Stocks	Long-Term U.S. Government Bonds	U.S. Treasury Bills	Consumer Price Index	Year	Large-Company Stocks	Long-Term U.S. Government Bonds	U.S. Treasury Bills	Consumer Price Index
1926	11.14%	7.90%	3.30%	-1.12%	1968	11.00%	5.33%	5.49%	4.72%
1927	37.13	10.36	3.15	-2.26	1969	-8.47	-7.45	6.90	6.20
1928	43.31	-1.37	4.05	-1.16	1970	3.94	12.24	6.50	5.57
1929	-8.91	5.23	4.47	0.58	1971	14.30	12.67	4.36	3.27
1930	-25.26	5.80	2.27	-6.40	1972	18.99	9.15	4.23	3.41
1931	-43.86	-8.04	1.15	-9.32	1973	-14.69	-12.66	7.29	8.71
1932	-8.85	14.11	0.88	-10.27	1974	-26.47	-3.28	7.99	12.34
1933	52.88	0.31	0.52	0.76	1975	37.23	4.67	5.87	6.94
1934	-2.34	12.98	0.27	1.52	1976	23.93	18.34	5.07	4.86
1935	47.22	5.88	0.17	2.99	1977	-7.16	2.31	5.45	6.70
1936	32.80	8.22	0.17	1.45	1978	6.57	-2.07	7.64	9.02
1937	-35.26	-0.13	0.27	2.86	1979	18.61	-2.76	10.56	13.29
1938	33.20	6.26	0.06	-2.78	1980	32.50	-5.91	12.10	12.52
1939	-0.91	5.71	0.04	0.00	1981	-4.92	-0.16	14.60	8.92
1940	-10.08	10.34	0.04	0.71	1982	21.55	49.99	10.94	3.83
1941	-11.77	-8.66	0.14	9.93	1983	22.56	-2.11	8.99	3.79
1942	21.07	2.67	0.34	9.03	1984	6.27	16.53	9.90	3.95
1943	25.76	2.50	0.38	2.96	1985	31.73	39.03	7.71	3.80
1944	19.69	2.88	0.38	2.30	1986	18.67	32.51	6.09	1.10
1945	36.46	5.17	0.38	2.25	1987	5.25	-8.09	5.88	4.43
1946	-8.18	4.07	0.38	18.13	1988	16.61	8.71	6.94	4.42
1947	5.24	-1.15	0.62	8.84	1989	31.69	22.15	8.44	4.65
1948	5.10	2.10	1.06	2.99	1990	-3.10	5.44	7.69	6.11
1949	18.06	7.02	1.12	-2.07	1991	30.46	20.04	5.43	3.06
1950	30.58	-1.44	1.22	5.93	1992	7.62	8.09	3.48	2.90
1951	24.55	-3.53	1.56	6.00	1993	10.08	22.32	3.03	2.75
1952	18.50	1.82	1.75	0.75	1994	1.32	-11.46	4.39	2.67
1953	-1.10	-0.88	1.87	0.75	1995	37.58	37.28	5.61	2.54
1954	52.40	7.89	0.93	-0.74	1996	22.96	-2.59	5.14	3.32
1955	31.43	-1.03	1.80	0.37	1997	33.36	17.70	5.19	1.70
1956	6.63	-3.14	2.66	2.99	1998	28.58	19.22	4.86	1.61
1957	-10.85	5.25	3.28	2.90	1999	21.04	-12.76	4.80	2.68
1958	43.34	-6.70	1.71	1.76	2000	-9.10	22.16	5.98	3.39
1959	11.90	-1.35	3.48	1.73	2001	-11.89	5.30	3.33	1.55
1960	0.48	7.74	2.81	1.36	2002	-22.10	14.08	1.61	2.38
1961	26.81	3.02	2.40	0.67	2003	28.68	1.62	1.03	1.88
1962	-8.78	4.63	2.82	1.33	2004	10.88	10.34	1.43	3.26
1963	22.69	1.37	3.23	1.64	2005	4.91	10.35	3.30	3.42
1964	16.36	4.43	3.62	0.97	2006	15.79	0.28	4.97	2.54
1965	12.36	1.40	4.06	1.92	2007	5.49	11.07	4.52	4.08
1966	-10.10	-1.61	4.94	3.46	2008	-37.00	41.78	1.24	0.09
1967	23.94	-6.38	4.39	3.04	2009	26.46	-25.61	0.15	2.72

Source: Author calculations based on data obtained from *Global Financial Data* (www.globalfinancialdata.com) and Professor Kenneth R. French, Dartmouth College.

FIGURE 1.7 S&P 500 Monthly Returns: 2008

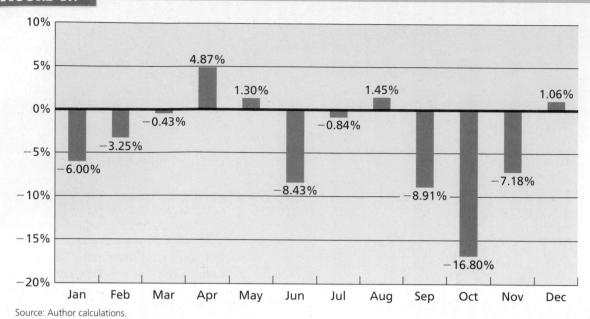

Source: Author calculations.

These returns were especially impressive considering that the rate of inflation, as measured by the CPI, was essentially zero.

What lessons should investors take away from this very recent bit of capital market history? First, and most obviously, stocks have significant risk! But note a second, equally important lesson: Depending on the mix, a diversified portfolio of stocks and bonds probably would have suffered in 2008, but the losses would have been much smaller than those experienced by an all-stock portfolio. In other words, diversification matters, a point we will examine in detail in our next chapter.

CHECK THIS

1.2a With 20-20 hindsight, which investment category performed best for the period 1926–35?

1.2b Why doesn't everyone just buy small-company stocks as investments?

1.2c What was the smallest return observed over the 84 years for each category of investments? Approximately when did it occur?

1.2d About how many times did large-company stocks (common stocks) return more than 30 percent? How many times did they return less than –20 percent?

1.2e What was the longest "winning streak" (years without a negative return) for large-company stocks? For long-term government bonds?

1.2f How often did the T-bill portfolio have a negative return?

1.3 Average Returns: The First Lesson

As you've probably begun to notice, the history of financial market returns in an undigested form is complicated. What we need are simple measures to accurately summarize and describe all these numbers. Accordingly, we discuss how to go about condensing detailed numerical data. We start by calculating average returns.

TABLE 1.2

Average Annual Returns: 1926–2009

Investment	Average Return
Large-company stocks	11.7%
Small-company stocks	17.7
Long-term corporate bonds	6.5
Long-term government bonds	5.9
U.S. Treasury bills	3.8
Inflation	3.1

Source: Author calculations using data from *Global Financial Data* (www.globalfinancialdata.com) and Professor Kenneth R. French, Dartmouth College.

CALCULATING AVERAGE RETURNS

The obvious way to calculate average returns on the different investments in Figures 1.3 to 1.5 is to simply add up the yearly returns and divide by 84. The result is the historical average of the individual values. For example, if you add the returns for large-company common stocks for the 84 years, you will get about 987 percent. The average annual return is thus 987/84 = 11.7%. You can interpret this 11.7 percent just like any other average. If you picked a year at random from the 84-year history and you had to guess the return in that year, the best guess is 11.7 percent.

AVERAGE RETURNS: THE HISTORICAL RECORD

Table 1.2 shows the average returns for the investments we have discussed. Because these averages do not reflect the impact of inflation, we include an average inflation rate. Notice that over this 84-year period the average inflation rate was 3.1 percent per year while the average return on U.S. Treasury bills was 3.8 percent per year. Thus, the average return on Treasury bills exceeded the average rate of inflation by only .7 percent per year. At the other extreme, the return on small-company common stocks exceeded the rate of inflation by about 17.7% − 3.1% = 14.6%. The real return of the large-company common stocks averaged 11.7% − 3.1% = 8.6% per year.

RISK PREMIUMS

Now that we have computed some average returns, it seems logical to see how they compare with each other. Based on our discussion above, one such comparison involves government-issued securities. These are free of much of the variability we see in, for example, the stock market.

The government borrows money by issuing debt, that is, bonds. These bonds come in different forms. The ones we focus on are Treasury bills. Treasury bills have the shortest time to maturity of the different types of government debt. Because the government can always raise taxes or print money to pay its expenses, Treasury bills are virtually free of any default risk. Thus, we will call the rate of return on such debt the **risk-free rate**, and we will use it as a kind of investing benchmark.

A particularly interesting comparison involves the virtually risk-free return on T-bills and the risky return on common stocks. The difference between these two returns can be interpreted as a measure of the *excess return* on the average risky asset (assuming that the stock of a large U.S. corporation has about average risk compared to all risky assets).

We call this the "excess" return because it is the additional return we earn by moving from a virtually risk-free investment to a risky one. Because this excess return can be interpreted as a reward for bearing risk, we will call it a **risk premium**.

THE U.S. EQUITY RISK PREMIUM: HISTORICAL AND INTERNATIONAL PERSPECTIVES. So far, in this chapter we have studied returns in U.S. stock and bond markets in the period 1926–2009. As we have discussed, the historical U.S. stock market risk premium has been substantial. Of course, whenever we use the past to predict the future,

risk-free rate
The rate of return on a riskless investment.

risk premium
The extra return on a risky asset over the risk-free rate; the reward for bearing risk.

TABLE 1.3

World Stock Market Capitalization 2008 and 2007

Region/Country	2008 Amount (in trillions)	Percent	2007 Amount (in trillions)	Percent
United States	$11.7	36.0%	$19.9	32.7%
Canada	1.0	3.1	2.2	3.6
Americas, excluding U.S. and Canada	1.1	3.4	2.2	3.6
Japan	3.1	9.5	4.3	7.1
Asia-Pacific, excluding Japan	6.1	18.8	13.6	22.3
United Kingdom	1.9	5.8	3.9	6.4
Germany	1.1	3.4	2.1	3.4
Europe, Africa, Middle East, excluding U.K. and Germany	6.5	20.0	12.7	20.9
Total	$32.5		$60.9	

Source: World Federation of Exchanges Database, www.world-exchanges.org/statistics/annual.

there is a danger that the past period isn't representative of what the future will hold. Perhaps U.S. investors got lucky over this period and earned particularly large returns. Data from earlier years is available, although it is not of the same quality. With that caveat in mind, researchers have tracked returns back to 1802. The U.S. equity risk premium in the pre-1926 era was smaller than it was in the post-1926 era. Using the U.S. return data from 1802 to 2006, the historical equity risk premium was 5.4 percent.

We have not looked at stock returns in other major countries. Actually, more than half of the value of tradable stock is not in the United States. From Table 1.3, we can see that while the total world stock market capitalization was $32.5 trillion in 2008, only about 36.0 percent was in the United States. Thanks to Professors Elroy Dimson, Paul Marsh, and Michael Staunton, data from earlier periods and other countries are now available to help us take a closer look at equity risk premiums. Table 1.4 shows the historical stock market risk premiums for 17 countries around the world in the period 1900 to 2005. Looking at the numbers, the U.S. historical equity risk premium is the eighth highest at 7.4 percent (which differs from our estimate below because of the different time periods examined). The overall world average risk premium is 7.1 percent. It seems clear that U.S. investors did well, but not exceptionally so relative to many other countries. The top performing countries according to the Sharpe ratio were the United States, Australia, and France; the worst performers were Denmark and Norway. Germany, Japan, and Italy might make an interesting case study because they have the highest stock returns over this period (despite World War I and II), but also the highest risk.

What is a good estimate of the U.S. equity risk premium going forward? Unfortunately, nobody can know for sure what investors expect in the future. If history is a guide, the expected U.S. equity risk premium could be 7.4 percent based upon estimates from 1900–2005. We should also be mindful that the average world equity risk premium was 7.1 percent over this same period. On the other hand, the relatively more recent period (1926–2009) suggests higher estimates of the U.S. equity risk premium and the earlier period (1802–1925) suggests lower estimates. Taking a slightly different approach, Professor Ivo Welch asked the opinions of 226 financial economists regarding the future U.S. equity risk premium. The median response was 7 percent.

We are comfortable with an estimate based on the historical U.S. equity risk premium of about 7 percent. Estimates of the future U.S. equity risk premium that are somewhat higher or lower could be reasonable, especially if we have good reason to believe the past is not representative of the future. The bottom line is that any estimate of the future equity risk premium will involve assumptions about the future risk environment as well as the amount of risk aversion of future investors. For example, in "The Worldwide Equity Premium: A

	TABLE 1.4	Annualized Equity Risk Premiums and Sharpe Ratios for 17 Countries: 1900–2005		

Country	(1) Historical Equity Risk Premiums (%)	(2) Standard Deviation (%)	(1)/(2) The Sharpe Ratio
Australia	8.49%	17.00%	0.50
Belgium	4.99	23.06	0.22
Canada	5.88	16.71	0.35
Denmark	4.51	19.85	0.23
France	9.27	24.19	0.38
Germany*	9.07	33.49	0.27
Ireland	5.98	20.33	0.29
Italy	10.46	32.09	0.33
Japan	9.84	27.82	0.35
Netherlands	6.61	22.36	0.30
Norway	5.70	25.90	0.22
South Africa	8.25	22.09	0.37
Spain	5.46	21.45	0.25
Sweden	7.98	22.09	0.36
Switzerland	5.29	18.79	0.28
U.K.	6.14	19.84	0.31
U.S.	7.41	19.64	0.38
Average	7.14%	22.75%	0.31

*1922–1923 omitted.

Source: Reprinted from *Handbook of the Equity Risk Premium*, Elroy Dimson, Paul Marsh, and Michael Staunton, "The Worldwide Equity Premium: A Smaller Puzzle," © 2007, with permission from Elsevier.

Smaller Puzzle," Dimson, Marsh, and Staunton argue that a good estimate of the world equity risk premium going forward is 5 percent. They attribute this lower estimate to nonrecurring factors that positively affected worldwide historical returns.

THE FIRST LESSON

From the data in Table 1.2, we can calculate risk premiums for the five different categories of investments. The results are shown in Table 1.5. Notice that the risk premium on T-bills is shown as zero in the table because they are our riskless benchmark. Looking at Table 1.5, we see that the average risk premium earned by the large-company common stock portfolio is $11.7\% - 3.8\% = 7.9\%$. This difference is a significant reward. The fact that it exists historically is an important observation, and it is the basis for our first lesson:

	TABLE 1.5	Average Annual Returns and Risk Premiums: 1926–2009	

Investment	Average Return	Risk Premium
Large-company stocks	11.7%	7.9%
Small-company stocks	17.7	13.9
Long-term corporate bonds	6.5	2.7
Long-term government bonds	5.9	2.1
U.S. Treasury bills	3.8	0.0

Source: Author calculations using data from *Global Financial Data* (www.globalfinancialdata.com) and Professor Kenneth R. French, Dartmouth College.

Risky assets, on average, earn a risk premium. Put another way, there is a reward, on average, for bearing risk.

Why is this so? Why, for example, is the risk premium for small stocks so much larger than the risk premium for large stocks? More generally, what determines the relative sizes of the risk premiums for the different assets? These questions are at the heart of the modern theory of investments. We will discuss the issues involved many times in the chapters ahead. For now, part of the answer can be found by looking at the historical variability of the returns of these different investments. So, to get started, we now turn our attention to measuring variability in returns.

CHECK THIS

1.3a   What do we mean by excess return and risk premium?

1.3b   What is the historical risk premium on small-company stocks? On U.S. Treasury bonds?

1.3c   What is the first lesson from financial market history?

1.4   Return Variability: The Second Lesson

We have already seen that the year-to-year returns on common stocks tend to be more volatile than returns on, say, long-term government bonds. We now discuss measuring this variability so we can begin examining the subject of risk.

FREQUENCY DISTRIBUTIONS AND VARIABILITY

To get started, we can draw a *frequency distribution* for large-company stock returns like the one in Figure 1.8. What we have done here is to count the number of times that an annual return on the large-company stock portfolio falls within each 10 percent range. For example,

FIGURE 1.8	Frequency Distribution of Returns on Large-Company Common Stocks: 1926–2009

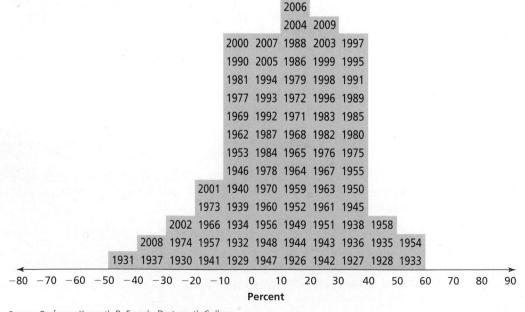

Source: Professor Kenneth R. French, Dartmouth College.

in Figure 1.8, the height of 15 for the bar within the interval 10 percent to 20 percent means that 15 of the 84 annual returns are in that range. Notice also that most of the returns are in the −10 to 40 percent range.

What we need to do now is to measure the spread in these returns. We know, for example, that the return on large-company stocks in a typical year was 11.7 percent. We now want to know by how much the actual return differs from this average in a typical year. In other words, we need a measure of the volatility of returns. The **variance** and its square root, the **standard deviation**, are the most commonly used measures of volatility. We describe how to calculate them next. If you've already studied basic statistics, you should notice that we are simply calculating an ordinary sample variance and standard deviation, just as you may have done many times before.

variance
A common measure of volatility.

standard deviation
The square root of the variance.

THE HISTORICAL VARIANCE AND STANDARD DEVIATION

The variance essentially measures the average squared difference between the actual returns and the average return. The bigger this number is, the more the actual returns tend to differ from the average return. Also, the larger the variance or standard deviation is, the more spread out the returns will be.

The way we calculate the variance and standard deviation depends on the specific situation. In this chapter, we are looking at historical returns. Therefore, the procedure we describe here is the correct one for calculating the *historical* variance and standard deviation. If we were examining projected future returns, then the procedure would be different. We describe this procedure in a later chapter.

To illustrate how we calculate the historical variance, suppose a particular investment had returns of 10 percent, 12 percent, 3 percent, and −9 percent over the last four years. The average return is (.10 + .12 + .03 − .09)/4 = .04, or 4 percent.

Notice that the return is never actually equal to 4 percent. Instead, the first return deviates from the average by .10 − .04 = .06, the second return deviates from the average by .12 − .04 = .08, and so on. To compute the variance, we square each of these deviations, add them up, and divide the result by the number of returns less 1, or 3 in this case. These calculations are summarized in the following table.

For an easy-to-read review of basic statistics, see www.robertniles.com/stats/

Year	(1) Actual Return	(2) Average Return	(3) Deviation (1) − (2)	(4) Squared Deviation
1	.10	.04	.06	.0036
2	.12	.04	.08	.0064
3	.03	.04	−.01	.0001
4	−.09	.04	−.13	.0169
Totals	.16		.00	.0270

In the first column, we write down the four actual returns. In the third column, we calculate the difference between the actual returns and the average by subtracting out 4 percent. Finally, in the fourth column, we square the numbers in Column 3 to get the squared deviations from the average.

The variance can now be calculated by dividing .0270, the sum of the squared deviations, by the number of returns less 1. Let Var(R) or σ^2 (read this as "sigma squared") stand for the variance of the return:

$$\text{Var}(R) = \sigma^2 = .027/(4 - 1) = .009$$

The standard deviation is the square root of the variance. So, if SD(R) or σ stands for the standard deviation of the return:

$$\text{SD}(R) = \sigma = \sqrt{.009} = .09487$$

INVESTORS HOPE THE '10S BEAT THE '00S

Since End of 1999, U.S. Stocks' Performance Has Been the All-Time Clunker; Even 1930s Beat It

The U.S. stock market is wrapping up what is likely to be its worst decade ever.*

In nearly 200 years of recorded stock-market history, no calendar decade has seen such a dismal performance as the 2000s.

Investors would have been better off investing in pretty much anything else, from bonds to gold or even just stuffing money under a mattress. Since the end of 1999, stocks traded on the New York Stock Exchange have lost an average of 0.5% a year thanks to the twin bear markets this decade.

Many investors were lured to the stock market by the bull market that began in the early 1980s and gained force through the 1990s. But coming out of the 1990s—when a 17.6% average annual gain made it the second-best decade in history behind the 1950s—stocks simply had gotten too expensive. Companies also pared dividends, cutting into investor returns. And in a time of financial panic like 2008, stocks were a terrible place to invest.

With two weeks to go in 2009, the declines since the end of 1999 make the last 10 years the worst calendar decade for stocks going back to the 1820s, when reliable stock market records begin, according to data compiled by Yale University finance professor William Goetzmann. He estimates it would take a 3.6% rise between now and year end for the decade to come in better than the 0.2% decline suffered by stocks during the Depression years of the 1930s.

The past decade also well underperformed other decades with major financial panics, such as in 1907 and 1893.

"The last 10 years have been a nightmare, really poor," for U.S. stocks, said Michele Gambera, chief economist at Ibbotson Associates.

While the overall market trend has been a steady march upward, the last decade is a reminder that stocks can decline over long periods of time, he said.

"It's not frequent, but it can happen," Mr. Gambera said.

To some degree these statistics are a quirk of the calendar, based on when the 10-year period starts and finishes. The 10-year periods ending in 1937 and 1938 were worse than the most recent calendar decade because they capture the full effect of stocks hitting their peak in 1929 and the October crash of that year.

From 2000 through November 2009, investors would have been far better off owning bonds, which posted gains ranging from 5.6% to more than 8% depending on the sector, according to Ibbotson. Gold was the best-performing asset, up 15% a year this decade after losing 3% each year during the 1990s.

This past decade looks even worse when the impact of inflation is considered.

Since the end of 1999, the Standard & Poor's 500-stock index has lost an average of 3.3% a year on an inflation-adjusted basis, compared with a 1.8% average annual gain during the 1930s when deflation afflicted the economy.

Even the 1970s, when a bear market was coupled with inflation, wasn't as bad as the most recent period. The S&P 500 lost 1.4% after inflation during that decade.

That is especially disappointing news for investors, considering that a key goal of investing in stocks is to increase money faster than inflation.

For investors counting on stocks for retirement plans, the most recent decade means many have fallen behind retirement goals. Many financial plans assume a 10% annual return for stocks over the long term, but over the last 20 years, the S&P 500 is registering 8.2% annual gains.

Should stocks average 10% a year for the next decade, that would lift the 30-year average return to only 8.8%. For those who started investing in 2000, a 10% return a year would get them up to only 4.4% a year.

There were ways to make money in U.S. stocks during the last decade. But the returns paled in comparison with those posted in the 1990s.

So what went wrong for the U.S. stock market? For starters, it turned out that the old rules of valuation matter.

The square root of the variance is used because the variance is measured in "squared" percentages and thus is hard to interpret. The standard deviation is an ordinary percentage, so the answer here could be written as 9.487 percent.

In the table on the previous page, notice that the sum of the deviations is equal to zero. This will always be the case, and it provides a good way to check your work. In general, if we have N historical returns, where N is some number, we can write the historical variance as:

$$\text{Var}(R) = \frac{1}{N-1} [(R_1 - \overline{R})^2 + \cdots + (R_N - \overline{R})^2]$$

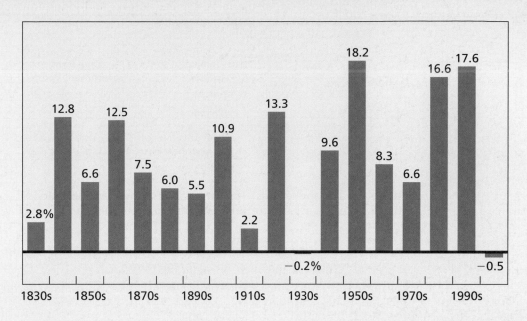

"We came into this decade horribly overpriced," said Jeremy Grantham, co-founder of money managers GMO LLC.

In late 1999, the stocks in the S&P 500 were trading at about an all-time high of 44 times earnings, based on Yale professor Robert Shiller's measure, which tracks prices compared with 10-year earnings and adjusts for inflation. That compares with a long-run average of about 16.

Buying at those kinds of values, "you'd better believe you're going to get dismal returns for a considerable chunk of time," said Mr. Grantham, whose firm predicted 10 years ago that the S&P 500 likely would lose nearly 2% a year in the 10 years through 2009.

Despite the woeful returns this decade, stocks today aren't a steal. The S&P is trading at a price-to-earnings ratio of about 20 on Mr. Shiller's measure.

Mr. Grantham thinks U.S. large-cap stocks are about 30% overpriced, which means returns should be about 30% less than their long-term average for the next seven years. That means returns of just 1.6% a year before adding in inflation.

Another hurdle for the stock market has been the decline in dividends that began in the late 1980s.

Over the long term, dividends have played an important role in helping stocks achieve a 9.5% average annual return since 1926. But since that year, the average yield on S&P 500 stocks was roughly 4%. This decade it has averaged about 1.8%.

This decline in dividends must be made up by price appreciation to maintain the long-run 9.5% average. If dividends do not rise to their long run average, perhaps total stock returns will only be about 7.5%.

*Correction and amplification: The 1950s represented the best decade for stock-market returns. A previous version of this article stated that the best decade was the 1990s.

Source: Tom Lauricella, *The Wall Street Journal*, December 20, 2009. Reprinted with permission of *The Wall Street Journal*. © 2009 Dow Jones & Company, Inc. All Rights Reserved Worldwide.

This formula tells us to do just what we did above: Take each of the N individual returns (R_1, R_2, ..., R_N) and subtract the average return, $\overline{R}$; square the results, and add up all these squares; and finally, divide this total by the number of returns less 1 (i.e., $N - 1$).[2] The standard deviation is the square root of Var(R). Standard deviations are a widely used measure of volatility.

[2] The reason for dividing by $N - 1$ rather than simply N is based on statistical sampling theory, which is beyond the scope of this book. Just remember that to calculate a variance about a sample average, you need to divide the sum of squared deviations from the average by $N - 1$.

EXAMPLE 1.4

Calculating the Variance and Standard Deviation

From Table 1.1, we see that the large-company stocks and long-term government bonds had these returns for the past four years:

Year	Large-Company Stocks	Long-Term Government Bonds
2006	0.1579	0.0028
2007	0.0549	0.1107
2008	−0.3700	0.4178
2009	0.2646	−0.2561

What are the average returns? The variances? The standard deviations?

To calculate the average returns, we add up the returns and divide by four. The results are:

$$\text{Large-company stocks, average return} = \overline{R} = .1074/4 = .02685$$
$$\text{Long-term government bonds, average return} = \overline{R} = .2752/4 = .0688$$

To calculate the variance for large-company stocks, we can summarize the relevant calculations (with rounding) as follows:

Year	(1) Actual Return	(2) Average Return	(3) Deviation (1) − (2)	(4) Squared Deviation
2006	0.1579	0.02685	0.1311	0.0172
2007	0.0549	0.02685	0.0281	0.0008
2008	−0.3700	0.02685	−0.3969	0.1575
2009	0.2646	0.02685	0.2378	0.0565
Totals	0.1075		0.0000	0.2320

Because there are four years of returns, we calculate the variance by dividing .2320 by (4 − 1) = 3:

	Large-Company Stocks	Long-Term Government Bonds
Variance (σ^2)	.2320/3 = .07733	.2335/3 = .07782
Standard deviation (σ)	$\sqrt{.07733}$ = .2781	$\sqrt{.07782}$ = .2790

For practice, verify that you get the same answers that we do for long-term government bonds. Notice that the standard deviation for long-term government bonds, 27.90 percent, is higher than the standard deviation for large-company stocks, 27.81 percent. Why is this relationship unusual?

THE HISTORICAL RECORD

Figure 1.9 summarizes much of our discussion of capital market history so far. It displays average returns, standard deviations, and frequency distributions of annual returns on a common scale. In Figure 1.9, notice, for example, that the standard deviation for the small-stock portfolio (37.1 percent per year) is more than 10 times larger than the T-bill

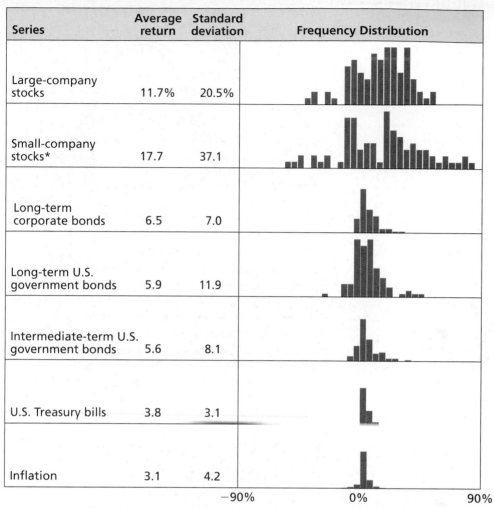

Series	Average return	Standard deviation	Frequency Distribution
Large-company stocks	11.7%	20.5%	
Small-company stocks*	17.7	37.1	
Long-term corporate bonds	6.5	7.0	
Long-term U.S. government bonds	5.9	11.9	
Intermediate-term U.S. government bonds	5.6	8.1	
U.S. Treasury bills	3.8	3.1	
Inflation	3.1	4.2	

-90%   0%   90%

*The 1933 small-company stocks total return was 153.2 percent.

Source: Author calculations using data from *Global Financial Data* (www.globalfinancialdata.com) and Professor Kenneth R. French, Dartmouth College.

portfolio's standard deviation (3.1 percent per year). We will return to discuss these facts momentarily.

NORMAL DISTRIBUTION

normal distribution

A symmetric, bell-shaped frequency distribution that is completely defined by its average and standard deviation.

For many different random events in nature, a particular frequency distribution, the **normal distribution** (or *bell curve*) is useful for describing the probability of ending up in a given range. For example, the idea behind "grading on a curve" comes from the fact that exam scores often resemble a bell curve.

Figure 1.10 illustrates a normal distribution and its distinctive bell shape. As you can see, this distribution has a much cleaner appearance than the actual return distributions illustrated in Figure 1.8. Even so, like the normal distribution, the actual distributions do appear to be at least roughly mound shaped and symmetric. When this shape is observed, the normal distribution is often a very good approximation.

Also, keep in mind that the distributions in Figure 1.9 are based on only 84 yearly observations, while Figure 1.10 is, in principle, based on an infinite number. So, if we had been able to observe returns for, say, 1,000 years, we might have filled in a lot of the irregularities

FIGURE 1.10

The Normal Distribution: Illustrated Returns Based on the Historical Return and Standard Deviation for a Portfolio of Large-Company Common Stocks

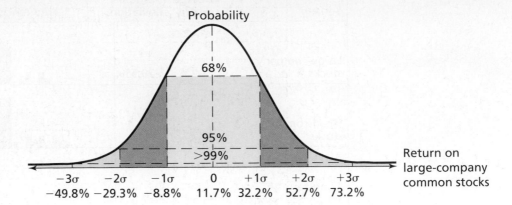

and ended up with a much smoother picture. For our purposes, it is enough to observe that the returns are at least roughly normally distributed.

The usefulness of the normal distribution stems from the fact that it is completely described by the average and the standard deviation. If you have these two numbers, then there is nothing else you need to know. For example, with a normal distribution, the probability that we end up within one standard deviation of the average is 68 percent, or about 2/3. The probability that we end up within two standard deviations is about 95 percent. Finally, the probability of being more than three standard deviations away from the average is less than 1 percent. These ranges and the probabilities are illustrated in Figure 1.10.

To see why this range is useful, recall from Figure 1.9 that the standard deviation of returns on the large-company common stocks is 20.5 percent. The average return is 11.7 percent. So, assuming that the frequency distribution is at least approximately normal, the probability that the return in a given year is in the range of −8.8 percent to 32.2 percent (11.7 percent plus or minus one standard deviation, 20.5 percent) is about 2/3. This range is illustrated in Figure 1.10. In other words, there is about one chance in three that the return will be *outside* this range. This literally tells you that, if you buy stocks in large companies, you should expect to be outside this range in one year out of every three. This reinforces our earlier observations about stock market volatility. However, there is only a 5 percent chance (approximately) that we would end up outside the range of −29.3 percent to 52.7 percent (11.7 percent plus or minus 2 × 20.5%). These points are also illustrated in Figure 1.10.

THE SECOND LESSON

Our observations concerning the year-to-year variability in returns are the basis for our second lesson from capital market history. On average, bearing risk is handsomely rewarded, but, in a given year, there is a significant chance of a dramatic change in value. Thus, our second lesson is this: The greater the potential reward, the greater is the risk.

Thus far in this chapter, we have emphasized the year-to-year variability in returns. We should note that even day-to-day movements can exhibit considerable volatility. For example, on September 29, 2008, the Dow Jones Industrial Average (DJIA) plummeted 777.68 points, or 6.98 percent. By historical standards, it was one of the worst days ever for the 30 stocks that comprise the DJIA (as well as for a majority of stocks in the market). Still, while the drop was the largest one-day decrease in the DJIA ever in terms of points, it was not in the top 10 largest one-day percentage decreases in history, as illustrated below:

Days with Greatest Net Loss				
Rank	Date	Close	Net Change	% Change
1	9/29/2008	10365.45	−777.68	−6.98
2	10/15/2008	8577.91	−733.08	−7.87
3	9/17/2001	8920.70	−684.81	−7.13
4	12/1/2008	8149.09	−679.95	−7.70
5	10/9/2008	8579.19	−678.91	−7.33
6	4/14/2000	10305.77	−617.78	−5.66
7	10/27/1997	7161.15	−554.26	−7.18
8	10/22/2008	8519.21	−526.00	−5.82
9	8/31/1998	7539.07	−512.61	−6.37
10	10/7/2008	9447.11	−508.39	−5.11

Days with Greatest Percentage Loss				
Rank	Date	Close	Net Change	% Change
1	10/19/1987	1738.74	−507.99	−22.61
2	10/28/1929	260.64	−40.58	−13.47
3	10/29/1929	230.07	−30.57	−11.73
4	10/5/1931	86.48	−10.40	−10.73
5	11/6/1929	232.13	−25.55	−9.92
6	8/12/1932	63.11	−5.79	−8.40
7	1/4/1932	71.59	−6.31	−8.10
8	10/26/1987	1793.93	−156.83	−8.04
9	10/15/2008	8577.91	−733.08	−7.87
10	6/16/1930	230.05	−19.64	−7.87

Source: Author calculations.

This discussion highlights the importance of looking at returns in terms of percentages rather than dollar amounts or index points. For example, before 2008, the biggest one-day loss in terms of points was on September 17, 2001, when the DJIA declined by about 685 points. The second worst was the 618-point drop of April 14, 2000. By contrast, the 5.79-point drop in the DJIA on August 12, 1932, marked the sixth worst percentage drop in the history of the index, but a 5.79-point loss in the DJIA in today's market would hardly be noticed. This is precisely why we relied on percentage returns when we examined market history in this chapter.[3]

Now that you know how to calculate and, more important, interpret average returns and standard deviations, the nearby *Spreadsheet Analysis* box shows how to do the calculations using Excel, which can really speed up things when we have a lot of data.

EXAMPLE 1.5   **Investing in Growth Stocks**

The term *growth stock* is frequently a euphemism for small-company stock. Are such investments suitable for "widows and orphans"? Before answering, you should consider the historical volatility. For example, from the historical record, what is the approximate probability that you will actually lose 16 percent or more of your money in a single year if you buy a portfolio of such companies?

(continued)

---

[3] By the way, as you may have noticed, what's kind of weird is that 6 of the 12 worst days in the history of the DJIA occurred in October, including the top 3. We have no clue as to why. Furthermore, looking back at the Mark Twain quote near the beginning of the chapter, how do you suppose he knew? Sounds like a case for *CSI: Wall Street*.

Looking back at Figure 1.9, we see that the average return on small stocks is 17.7 percent and the standard deviation is 37.1 percent. Assuming that the returns are approximately normal, there is about a 1/3 probability that you will experience a return outside the range of −19.4 percent to 54.8 percent (17.7% ± 37.1%).

Because the normal distribution is symmetric, the odds of being above or below this range are equal. There is thus a 1/6 chance (half of 1/3) that you will lose more than 19.4 percent. So, you should expect this to happen once in every six years, on average. Such investments can thus be *very* volatile, and they are not well suited for those who cannot afford the risk.

SPREADSHEET ANALYSIS

Using a Spreadsheet to Calculate Average Returns and Volatilities

Here is an Excel spreadsheet summarizing the formulas and analysis needed to calculate average returns and standard deviations using the 1990s as an example:

	A	B	C	D	E	F	G	H
1								
2		Using a spreadsheet to calculate average returns and standard deviations						
3								
4	Looking back in the chapter, the data suggest that the 1990s were one							
5	of the best decades for stock market investors. We will find out just how good by							
6	calculating the average returns and standard deviations for this period. Here are the							
7	year-by-year returns on the large-company stocks:							
8								
9		Year	Return(%)	Year	Return(%)			
10		1990	−3.10	1995	37.58			
11		1991	30.46	1996	22.96			
12		1992	7.62	1997	33.36			
13		1993	10.08	1998	28.58			
14		1994	1.32	1999	21.04			
15								
16		Average return (%):	18.99					
17		Standard deviation (%):	14.16					
18								
19	The formulas we used to do the calculations are just =AVERAGE(C10:C14;E10:E14)							
20	and =STDEV(C10:C14;E10:E14). Notice that the average return in the 1990s was 18.99							
21	percent per year, which is larger than the long-run average of 11.7 percent. At the same							
22	time, the standard deviation, 14.16 percent, was smaller than the 20.5 percent long-run value.							

CHECK THIS

1.4a In words, how do we calculate a variance? A standard deviation?

1.4b What is the second lesson from financial market history?

1.5 More on Average Returns

Thus far in this chapter, we have looked closely at simple average returns. But there is another way of computing an average return. The fact that average returns are calculated two different ways leads to some confusion, so our goal in this section is to explain the two approaches and also explain the circumstances under which each is appropriate. In addition, we include a measure of return that accounts for investor decisions to add funds to or remove funds from an investment.

ARITHMETIC VERSUS GEOMETRIC AVERAGES

Let's start with a simple example. Suppose you buy a particular stock for $100. Unfortunately, the first year you own it, it falls to $50. The second year you own the stock, its price increases to $100, leaving you where you started (no dividends were paid).

What was your average return on this investment? Common sense seems to say that your average return must be exactly zero since you started with $100 and ended with $100. But if we calculate the returns year-by-year, we see that you lost 50 percent the first year (you lost half of your money). The second year, you made 100 percent (you doubled your money). Your average return over the two years was thus $(-50\% + 100\%)/2 = 25\%$! So which is correct, 0 percent or 25 percent?

geometric average return

The average compound return earned per year over a multiyear period.

The answer is that both are correct; they just answer different questions. The 0 percent is called the **geometric average return**. The geometric average return answers the question *"What was your average compound return per year over a particular period?"*

The 25 percent is called the **arithmetic average return**. The arithmetic average return answers the question *"What was your return in an average year over a particular period?"*

arithmetic average return

The return earned in an average year over a multiyear period.

Notice that, in previous sections, the average returns we calculated were all arithmetic averages, so you already know how to calculate them. What we need to do now is (1) learn how to calculate geometric averages and (2) learn the circumstances under which one average is more meaningful than the other.

Finally, the order and size of losses and gains matters. For an example of this issue, see the nearby *Investment Updates* box.

TABLE 1.6

Geometric versus Arithmetic Average Returns: 1926–2009

Series	Geometric Mean	Arithmetic Mean	Standard Deviation
Large-company stocks	9.7%	11.7%	20.5%
Small-company stocks	11.9	17.7	37.1
Long-term corporate bonds	6.3	6.5	7.0
Long-term government bonds	5.3	5.9	11.9
Intermediate-term government bonds	5.3	5.6	8.1
U.S. Treasury bills	3.7	3.8	3.1
Inflation	3.0	3.1	4.2

CALCULATING GEOMETRIC AVERAGE RETURNS

If we have N years of returns, the geometric average return over these N years is calculated using this formula:

$$\text{Geometric average return} = [(1 + R_1) \times (1 + R_2) \times \cdots \times (1 + R_N)]^{1/N} - 1 \qquad (1.5)$$

This formula tells us that four steps are required:

1. Take each of the N annual returns $R_1, R_2, \ldots, R_N$ and add a 1 to each (after converting them to decimals!).
2. Multiply all the numbers from step 1 together.
3. Take the result from step 2 and raise it to the power of $1/N$.
4. Finally, subtract 1 from the result of step 3. The result is the geometric average return.

To illustrate how we calculate a geometric average return, suppose a particular investment had annual returns of 10 percent, 12 percent, 3 percent, and –9 percent over the last four years. The geometric average return over this four-year period is calculated as $(1.10 \times 1.12 \times 1.03 \times .91)^{1/4} - 1 = 3.66\%$. In contrast, the average arithmetic return is $(.10 + .12 + .03 - .09)/4 = 4.0\%$.

One thing you may have noticed in our examples thus far is that the geometric average returns seem to be smaller. It turns out that this will always be true (as long as the returns are not all identical, in which case the two "averages" would be the same). To illustrate, Table 1.6 shows the arithmetic averages and standard deviations from Figure 1.9, along with the geometric average returns.

As shown in Table 1.6, the geometric averages are all smaller, but the magnitude of the difference varies quite a bit. The reason is that the difference is greater for more volatile investments. In fact, there is a useful approximation. Assuming all the numbers are expressed in decimals (as opposed to percentages), the geometric average return is approximately equal to the arithmetic average return minus half the variance. For example, looking at the large-company stocks, the arithmetic average is .117 and the standard deviation is .205, implying that the variance is .042025. The approximate geometric average is thus $.117 - .042025/2 = .0960$, which is quite close to the actual value.

EXAMPLE 1.6

Calculating the Geometric Average Return

Calculate the geometric average return for the large-company stocks for the last four years in Table 1.1, 2006–2009.

First, convert percentages to decimal returns, add one, and then calculate their product.

(continued)

Year	Large-Company Stocks	Product
2006	15.79	1.1579
2007	5.49	× 1.0549
2008	−37.00	× 0.6300
2009	26.46	× 1.2646
		0.9731

Notice that the number 0.9731 is what our investment is worth after five years if we started with a one-dollar investment. The geometric average return is then calculated as

Geometric average return = $0.9731^{1/4} - 1 = -0.0068$, or −0.68%

Thus the geometric average return is about −0.68 percent in this example. In contrast, in Example 1.4, the average arithmetic return was calculated as 2.685 percent. Here is a tip: If you are using a financial calculator, you can put $1 in as the present value, $0.9731 as the future value, and 4 as the number of periods. Then, solve for the unknown rate. You should get the same answer we did.

EXAMPLE 1.7   **More Geometric Averages**

Take a look back at Figure 1.1. There, we showed the value of a $1 investment after 84 years. Use the value for the large-company stock investment to check the geometric average in Table 1.6.

In Figure 1.1, the large-company investment grew to $2,382.68 over 84 years. The geometric average return is thus

Geometric average return = $2,382.68^{1/84} - 1 = .0970$, or about 9.7%

This 9.7% is the value shown in Table 1.6. For practice, check some of the other numbers in Table 1.6 the same way.

ARITHMETIC AVERAGE RETURN OR GEOMETRIC AVERAGE RETURN?

When we look at historical returns, the difference between the geometric and arithmetic average returns isn't too hard to understand. To put it slightly differently, the geometric average tells you what you actually earned per year on average, compounded annually. The arithmetic average tells you what you earned in a typical year. You should use whichever one answers the question you want answered.

A somewhat trickier question concerns forecasting the future, and there is a lot of confusion about this point among analysts and financial planners. The problem is the following. If we have *estimates* of both the arithmetic and geometric average returns, then the arithmetic average is probably too high for longer periods and the geometric average is probably too low for shorter periods.

The good news is that there is a simple way of combining the two averages, which we will call *Blume's formula*.[4] Suppose we calculated geometric and arithmetic return averages from N years of data and we wish to use these averages to form a T-year average return forecast, $R(T)$, where T is less than N. Here's how we do it:

$$R(T) = \frac{T-1}{N-1} \times \textit{Geometric average} + \frac{N-T}{N-1} \times \textit{Arithmetic average}$$

For example, suppose that, from 25 years of annual returns data, we calculate an arithmetic average return of 12 percent and a geometric average return of 9 percent. From these

---

[4] This elegant result is due to Marshal Blume. ("Unbiased Estimates of Long-Run Expected Rates of Return," *Journal of the American Statistical Association,* September 1974, pp. 634–638.)

averages, we wish to make 1-year, 5-year, and 10-year average return forecasts. These three average return forecasts are calculated as follows:

$$R(1) = \frac{1-1}{24} \times 9\% + \frac{25-1}{24} \times 12\% = 12\%$$

$$R(5) = \frac{5-1}{24} \times 9\% + \frac{25-5}{24} \times 12\% = 11.5\%$$

$$R(10) = \frac{10-1}{24} \times 9\% + \frac{25-10}{24} \times 12\% = 10.875\%$$

Thus, we see that 1-year, 5-year, and 10-year forecasts are 12 percent, 11.5 percent, and 10.875 percent, respectively.

This concludes our discussion of geometric versus arithmetic averages. One last note: In the future, when we say "average return," we mean arithmetic average unless we explicitly say otherwise.

EXAMPLE 1.8

Forecasting Average Returns

Over the 84-year period 1926–2009, the geometric average return for large-company stocks was 9.7 percent and the arithmetic average return was 11.7 percent. Calculate average return forecasts for 1, 5, 10, and 25 years into the future.

In this case, we would use Blume's formula with values of $T = 1, 5, 10,$ and 25 and $N = 84$:

$$R(T) = \frac{T-1}{83} \times 9.7\% + \frac{84-T}{83} \times 11.7\%$$

T	$R(T)$
1	11.7%
5	11.6
10	11.5
25	11.1
84	9.7

Notice that short-term forecasts are closer to the arithmetic average return and long-term forecasts are closer to the geometric average return.

DOLLAR-WEIGHTED AVERAGE RETURNS

Suppose an investment had returns of 10 percent and −5 percent over the last two years. You know how to compute the arithmetic average (2.50 percent) and the geometric average (2.23 percent). You might not know that these average returns are accurate only if the investor made a single deposit at the start of the two-year period.

Many investors, however, make deposits or withdrawals through time. For example, some people add money to their investments over time as they save for retirement. Some people might be forced to withdraw funds to meet unexpected needs. Other investors attempt to "time the market" by adding funds because they believe their investments will soon increase in value. These "market timers" also sell part (or all) of their investments before an anticipated decline.

Whether investors can be successful at market timing is a topic of much debate, and one that we address in later chapters. Still, it is important to know how to calculate the return of an investment when an investor makes deposits and withdrawals. The relevant return measure in this case is called the **dollar-weighted average return**.

dollar-weighted average return

Average compound rate of return earned per year over a multiyear period accounting for investment inflows and outflows.

As an example, assume that you invest $1,000. After earning 10 percent the first year, you decide to invest another $4,000 (perhaps hoping the investment repeats its performance). Unfortunately for you, the return in year 2 was −5 percent. What was your net return?

To begin to answer this question, you need to know the ending value of your investment. At the end of the first year, your account had a value of $1,100, which is the initial investment plus the 10 percent return. You then deposited another $4,000, bringing the account value to $5,100 at the beginning of year 2. After losing 5 percent in year 2, your final value is $4,845.

Before we set out to calculate your exact return, you know that your return is negative. After all, you deposited $5,000 out of your own pocket but at the end of two years the investment is worth only $4,845. So, the arithmetic and geometric averages, which were both positive, do not account for this case.

To calculate the dollar-weighted average return, we need to find the average rate of return that equates our cash outflows to our cash inflows. In other words, what is the rate that makes the net present value of the investment equal zero? Here is a summary of your cash flows for this investment:

Time:	0	1	2
Cash flow:	−$1,000	−$4,000	+$4,845

In this summary, the negative cash flows are the deposits you made. The positive cash flow is the amount you have in the investment at the end of year 2.

In a corporate finance class, this calculation is known as the *internal rate of return,* or *IRR.* Finding the IRR requires trial and error, unless you use the help of a financial calculator or spreadsheet. To see how to do this in Excel, you can look at the nearby *Spreadsheet Analysis* box. The dollar-weighted rate of return for this investment is −2.6 percent. This makes sense because you had the greatest amount invested during the period when the return was the lowest, and you had the least amount invested when the return was the highest.

You know that the geometric average is always less than or equal to the arithmetic average. How about the relationship between the geometric average and the dollar-weighted average return? As you might guess, the relationship depends on when deposits and withdrawals were made. The geometric average return could be greater than, less than, or equal to the dollar-weighted average return. In fact, the geometric average is really just a special case of the dollar-weighted return, where the additional inflows and outflows happen to be zero.

SPREADSHEET ANALYSIS

	A	B	C	D	E	F	G	H
1								
2		Calculating dollar-weighted average returns						
3								
4	To find a rate of return that equates a series of uneven cash flows, we must identify							
5	when the cash flows were made and we must know their size. Then, we can use							
6	the built-in IRR function in Excel to calculate the dollar-weighted average return.							
7								
8		Time	Cash Flow					
9		0	−$1,000					
10		1	−$4,000					
11		2	$4,845					
12								
13			−2.6%	=IRR(C9:C11)				
14								
15	Note, Time 0 is the beginning of Year 1, while Time 1 is the end of Year 1.							
16								
17	Using the IRR function, we calculate a dollar-weighted average return of −2.6%.							
18								
19								

CHECK THIS

1.5a Over a five-year period, an investment in a broad market index yielded annual returns of 10, 16, −5, −8, and 7 percent. What were the arithmetic and geometric average annual returns for this index?

1.5b Over a 25-year period, an investment in a broad market index yielded an arithmetic average return of 4 percent and a geometric average return of 3.6 percent. Using Blume's formula, what would be the 5-year and 10-year average return forecasts?

1.5c Why is it important to control for the flow of funds into and out of an investment when calculating returns?

1.6 Risk and Return

In previous sections we explored financial market history to see what we could learn about risk and return. In this section we summarize our findings and then conclude our discussion by looking ahead at the subjects we will be examining in later chapters.

THE RISK-RETURN TRADE-OFF

Figure 1.11 shows our findings on risk and return from Figure 1.9. What Figure 1.11 shows is that there is a risk-return trade-off. At one extreme, if we are unwilling to bear any risk at all, but we are willing to forgo the use of our money for a while, then we can earn the risk-free rate. Because the risk-free rate represents compensation for just waiting, it is often called the *time value of money.*

If we are willing to bear risk, then we can expect to earn a risk premium, at least on average. Further, the more risk we are willing to bear, the greater is the risk premium. Investment advisors like to say that an investment has a "wait" component and a "worry" component. In our figure, the time value of money is the compensation for waiting, and the risk premium is the compensation for worrying.

There are two important caveats to this discussion. First, risky investments do not *always* pay more than risk-free investments. Indeed, that is precisely what makes them risky. In other words, there is a risk premium *on average,* but, over any particular time interval, there is no guarantee. Second, we have intentionally been a little imprecise about what we mean exactly by risk. As we will discuss in the chapters ahead, investors are not compensated for

FIGURE 1.11   Risk-Return Trade-Off

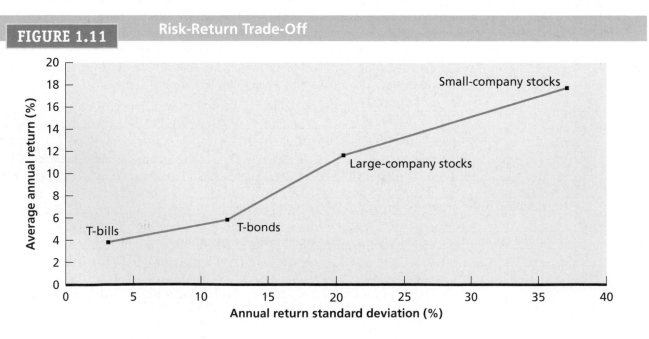

all risks. Some risks are cheaply and easily avoidable, and no reward is expected for bearing them. It is only those risks that cannot be easily avoided that are compensated (on average).

A LOOK AHEAD

In the remainder of this text, we focus exclusively on financial assets. An advantage of this approach is that it is limited to four major types: stocks, bonds, futures, and options, in the order that we cover them. This means that we won't be discussing collectibles such as classic automobiles, baseball cards, coins, fine art, or stamps. We also won't be discussing real estate or precious metals such as gold and platinum. It's not that these are unimportant; rather, they are very specialized. So, instead of treating them superficially, we leave a discussion of them for another day (and another book).

As we've indicated, to understand the potential reward from an investment, it is critical to first understand the risk involved. There is an old saying that goes like this: It's easy to make a small fortune investing in_____ (put your favorite investment here)—just start with a large fortune! The moral is that the key to successful investing is to make informed, intelligent decisions about risk. For this reason, we are going to pay particular attention to the factors that determine the value of the different assets we discuss and the nature of the associated risks.

One common characteristic that these assets have is that they are bought and sold around the clock and around the world in vast quantities. The way they are traded can be very different, however. We think it is important and interesting to understand exactly what happens when you buy or sell one of these assets, so we will be discussing the different trading mechanisms and the way the different markets function. We will also describe actual buying and selling at various points along the way to show you the steps involved and the results of placing buy and sell orders and having them executed.

1.7 Summary and Conclusions

This chapter presents some important concepts for investors, including the following items—grouped by the chapter's important concepts.

1. **How to calculate the return on an investment using different methods.**

A. We show how to calculate dollar returns and percentage returns over a time period. Returns have two parts: a capital gain (or loss) and dividend income. We also show how to convert returns over a period different from a year into annualized returns.

B. We demonstrate the two ways to calculate average returns over time: the arithmetic method and the geometric method. The arithmetic average return answers the question "What was your return in an average year over a particular period?" The geometric average return answers the question "What was your average compound return per year over a particular period?" Generally, when investors say "average return," they are referring to arithmetic average unless they explicitly say otherwise.

C. We also examine the effect of fund flows into and out of an investment. This case calls for calculating the dollar-weighted average return.

2. **The historical returns on various important types of investments.**

A. In order of their historical return from highest to lowest, we discuss returns on some important portfolios, including:

- *Small-company stocks.* This is a portfolio composed of the smallest (in terms of total market value of outstanding stock) of the companies listed on the New York Stock Exchange.

- *Large-company stocks.* This portfolio is based on the Standard & Poor's 500 index. This index contains 500 of the largest companies (in terms of total market value of outstanding stock) in the United States.

- *Long-term U.S. government bonds.* This is a portfolio of U.S. government bonds with 20 years to maturity.

- *U.S. Treasury bills.* This is a portfolio of Treasury bills (T-bills for short) with a three-month maturity.

B. One important historical return fact is that U.S. T-bill returns have barely outpaced inflation. Therefore, an investor must invest in stocks or bonds to earn a return higher than the inflation rate.

3. The historical risks on various important types of investments.

A. Historically, the risk (as measured by standard deviation of returns) of the portfolios described above is highest for small-company stocks. The next highest risk is for large-company stocks, followed by long-term government bonds and Treasury bills.

B. We draw two key lessons from historical risk:

- Risky assets, on average, earn a risk premium. That is, there is a reward for bearing risk. However, this expected reward is not realized each year.
- The greater the potential reward from a risky investment, the greater is the risk.

4. The relationship between risk and return.

A. When we put these two key lessons together, we concluded that there is a risk-return trade-off.

B. The only way to earn a higher return is to take on greater risk.

GET REAL

This chapter took you through some basic, but important, investment-related calculations. We then walked through the modern history of risk and return. How should you, as an investor or investment manager, put this information to work?

The answer is that you now have a rational, objective basis for thinking about what you stand to make from investing in some important broad asset classes. For the stock market as a whole, as measured by the performance of large-company stocks, you know that you might realistically expect to make 12 percent or so per year on average.

Equally important, you know that you won't make 12 percent in any one year; instead, you'll make more or less. You know that the standard deviation is about 20 percent per year, and you should know what that means in terms of risk. In particular, you need to understand that in one year out of every six, you should expect to lose more than 8 percent (12 percent minus one standard deviation), so this will be a relatively common event. The good news is that in one year out of six, you can realistically expect to earn more than 32 percent (12 percent plus one standard deviation).

The other important, practical thing to understand from this chapter is that a strategy of investing in very low-risk assets (such as T-bills) has historically barely kept up with inflation. This might be sufficient for some investors, but if your goal is to do better than that, then you will have to bear some amount of risk to achieve it.

Key Terms

1. **Calculating Returns (CFA1)** You bought 400 shares of Metallica Heavy Metal, Inc., at $30 per share. Over the year, you received $.75 per share in dividends. If the stock sold for $33 at the end of the year, what was your dollar return? Your percentage return?

2. **Calculating Returns and Variability (CFA2)** Using the following returns, calculate the arithmetic average returns, the variances, the standard deviations, and the geometric returns for the following stocks:

Year	Michele, Inc.	Janicek Co.
1	12%	5%
2	−4	−15
3	0	10
4	20	38
5	2	17

3. **Forecasting Returns** Over a 30-year period an asset had an arithmetic return of 12.8 percent and a geometric return of 10.7 percent. Using Blume's formula, what is your best estimate of the future annual returns over the next 5 years? 10 years? 20 years?

Answers to Self-Test Problems

1. Your dollar return is just your gain or loss in dollars. Here, we receive $.75 in dividends on each of our 400 shares, for a total of $300. In addition, each share rose from $30 to $33, so we make $3 × 400 shares = $1,200. Our total dollar return is thus $300 + $1,200 = $1,500.

   Our percentage return (or just "return" for short) is equal to the $1,500 we made divided by our initial outlay of $30 × 400 shares = $12,000; so $1,500/12,000 = .125 = 12.5%. Equivalently, we could have just noted that each share paid a $.75 dividend and each share gained $3, so the total dollar gain per share was $3.75. As a percentage of the cost of one share ($30), we get $3.75/30 = .125 = 12.5%.

2. First, calculate arithmetic averages as follows:

Michele, Inc.	Janicek Co.
12%	5%
−4	−15
0	10
20	38
2	17
30%	55%
Average return: 30/5 = 6%	55/5 = 11%

Using the arithmetic averages above, calculate the squared deviations from the arithmetic average returns and sum the squared deviations as follows:

Michele, Inc.		Janicek Co.	
$(12 − 6)^2 =$	36	$(5 − 11)^2 =$	36
$(−4 − 6)^2 =$	100	$(−15 − 11)^2 =$	676
$(0 − 6)^2 =$	36	$(10 − 11)^2 =$	1
$(20 − 6)^2 =$	196	$(38 − 11)^2 =$	729
$(2 − 6)^2 =$	16	$(17 − 11)^2 =$	36
	384		1,478

www.mhhe.com/jmd6e

Calculate return variances by dividing the sums of squared deviations by four, which is the number of returns less one.

Michele: $384/4 = 96$ Janicek: $1,478/4 = 369.5$

Standard deviations are then calculated as the square root of the variance.

Michele: $\sqrt{96} = 9.8\%$ Janicek: $\sqrt{369.5} = 19.22\%$

Geometric returns are then calculated as:

Michele: $[(1 + .12)(1 - .04)(1 + .00)(1 + .20)(1 + .02)]^{1/5} - 1 = 5.65\%$
Janicek: $[(1 + .05)(1 - .15)(1 + .10)(1 + .38)(1 + .17)]^{1/5} - 1 = 9.65\%$

3. To find the best forecast, we apply Blume's formula as follows:

$$R(5) = \frac{5 - 1}{29} \times 10.7\% + \frac{30 - 5}{29} \times 12.8\% = 12.51\%$$

$$R(10) = \frac{10 - 1}{29} \times 10.7\% + \frac{30 - 10}{29} \times 12.8\% = 12.15\%$$

$$R(20) = \frac{20 - 1}{29} \times 10.7\% + \frac{30 - 20}{29} \times 12.8\% = 11.42\%$$

Test Your Investment Quotient

1. **Prices and Returns (LO1, CFA1)**   You plan to buy a common stock and hold it for one year. You expect to receive both $1.50 from dividends and $26 from the sale of the stock at the end of the year. If you wanted to earn a 15 percent rate of return, what is the maximum price you would pay for the stock today?

   a. $22.61
   b. $23.91
   c. $24.50
   d. $27.50

2. **Returns (LO1, CFA1)**   A portfolio of non-dividend-paying stocks earned a geometric mean return of 5 percent between January 1, 1994, and December 31, 2000. The arithmetic mean return for the same period was 6 percent. If the market value of the portfolio at the beginning of 1994 was $100,000, the market value of the portfolio at the end of 2000 was *closest* to:

   a. $135,000
   b. $140,710
   c. $142,000
   d. $150,363

3. **Standard Deviation (LO4, CFA2)**   Which of the following statements about standard deviation is true? Standard deviation

   a. Is the square of the variance.
   b. Can be a positive or negative number.
   c. Is denominated in the same units as the original data.
   d. Is the arithmetic mean of the squared deviations from the mean.

4. **Normal Distribution (LO4, CFA3)**   An investment strategy has an expected return of 12 percent and a standard deviation of 10 percent. If the investment returns are normally distributed, the probability of earning a return less than 2 percent is closest to:

   a. 10 percent
   b. 16 percent
   c. 32 percent
   d. 34 percent

5. **Normal Distribution (LO4, CFA3)**   What are the mean and standard deviation of a standard normal distribution?

	Mean	Standard Deviation
a.	0	0
b.	0	1
c.	1	0
d.	1	1

6. **Normal Distribution (LO4, CFA3)** Given a data series that is normally distributed with a mean of 100 and a standard deviation of 10, about 95 percent of the numbers in the series will fall within which of the following ranges?

   a. 60 to 140
   b. 70 to 130
   c. 80 to 120
   d. 90 to 110

7. **Asset Types (LO3)** Stocks, bonds, options, and futures are the four major types of

   a. Debt
   b. Real assets
   c. Equity
   d. Financial assets

8. **Investment Returns (LO1, CFA1)** Suppose the value of an investment doubles in a one-year period. In this case, the rate of return on this investment over that one-year period is what amount?

   a. 100 percent even if the gain is not actually realized.
   b. 200 percent even if the gain is not actually realized.
   c. 100 percent only if the gain is actually realized.
   d. 200 percent only if the gain is actually realized.

9. **Historical Returns (LO2)** Which of the following asset categories has an annual returns history most closely linked to historical annual rates of inflation?

   a. U.S. Treasury bills
   b. Corporate bonds
   c. Large-company stocks
   d. Small-company stocks

10. **Historical Returns (LO2)** Based on the annual returns history since 1926, which asset category, on average, has yielded the highest risk premium?

    a. U.S. government bonds
    b. Corporate bonds
    c. Large-company stocks
    d. Small-company stocks

11. **Stat 101 (LO1, CFA1)** Over a four-year period, an investment in Outa'Synch common stock yields returns of –10, 40, 0, and 20. What is the arithmetic return over this period?

    a. 5 percent
    b. 7.5 percent
    c. 10 percent
    d. 12.5 percent

12. **Stat 101 (LO4, CFA3)** You calculate an average historical return of 20 percent and a standard deviation of return of 10 percent for an investment in Stonehenge Construction Co. You believe these values well represent the future distribution of returns. Assuming that returns are normally distributed, what is the probability that Stonehenge Construction will yield a negative return?

    a. 17 percent
    b. 33 percent
    c. 5 percent
    d. 2.5 percent

13. **Stat 101 (LO4, CFA3)** Which of the following statements about a normal distribution is incorrect?

    a. A normal distribution is symmetrically centered on its mean.
    b. The probability of being within one standard deviation from the mean is about 68 percent.
    c. The probability of being within two standard deviations from the mean is about 95 percent.
    d. The probability of a negative value is always one-half.

14. **Normal Distribution (LO4, CFA3)** Based on a normal distribution with a mean of 500 and a standard deviation of 150, the z-value for an observation of 200 is closest to:

    a. –2.00
    b. –1.75
    c. 1.75
    d. 2.00

15. **Normal Distribution (LO4, CFA2)**   A normal distribution would least likely be described as:
   a. Asymptotic.
   b. A discrete probability distribution.
   c. A symmetrical or bell-shaped distribution.
   d. A curve that theoretically extends from negative infinity to positive infinity.

Concept Questions

1. **Risk versus Return (LO3)**   Based on the historical record, rank the following investments in increasing order of risk. Rank the investments in increasing order of average returns. What do you conclude about the relationship between the risk of an investment and the return you expect to earn on it?
   a. Large stocks
   b. Treasury bills
   c. Long-term government bonds
   d. Small stocks

2. **Return Calculations (LO1, CFA1)**   A particular stock had a return last year of 4 percent. However, you look at the stock price and notice that it actually didn't change at all last year. How is this possible?

3. **Returns Distributions (LO4, CFA2)**   What is the probability that the return on small stocks will be less than -100 percent in a single year (think about it)? What are the implications for the distribution of returns?

4. **Arithmetic versus Geometric Returns (LO1, CFA1)**   What is the difference between arithmetic and geometric returns? Suppose you have invested in a stock for the last 10 years. Which number is more important to you, the arithmetic or geometric return?

5. **Blume's Formula (LO1)**   What is Blume's formula? When would you want to use it in practice?

6. **Inflation and Returns (LO1)**   Look at Table 1.1 and Figures 1.5 and 1.6. When were T-bill rates at their highest? Why do you think they were so high during this period?

7. **Inflation and Returns (LO1)**   The returns we have examined are not adjusted for inflation. What do you suppose would happen to our estimated risk premiums if we did account for inflation?

8. **Taxes and Returns (LO1)**   The returns we have examined are not adjusted for taxes. What do you suppose would happen to our estimated returns and risk premiums if we did account for taxes? What would happen to our volatility measures?

9. **Taxes and Treasury Bills (LO1)**   As a practical matter, most of the return you earn from investing in Treasury bills is taxed right away as ordinary income. Thus, if you are in a 40 percent tax bracket and you earn 5 percent on a Treasury bill, your aftertax return is only $.05 \times (1 - .40) = .03$, or 3 percent. In other words, 40 percent of your return goes to pay taxes, leaving you with just 3 percent. Once you consider inflation and taxes, how does the long-term return from Treasury bills look?

10. **The Long Run (LO4)**   Given your answer to the last question and the discussion in the chapter, why would any rational person do anything other than load up on 100 percent small stocks?

Questions and Problems

1. **Calculating Returns (LO1, CFA1)**   Suppose you bought 100 shares of stock at an initial price of $37 per share. The stock paid a dividend of $0.28 per share during the following year, and the share price at the end of the year was $41. Compute your total dollar return on this investment. Does your answer change if you keep the stock instead of selling it? Why or why not?

2. **Calculating Yields (LO1, CFA1)** In the previous problem, what is the capital gains yield? The dividend yield? What is the total rate of return on the investment?

3. **Calculating Returns (LO1, CFA1)** Rework Problems 1 and 2 assuming that you buy 750 shares of the stock and the ending share price is $32.

4. **Historical Returns (LO3)** What is the historical rate of return on each of the following investments? What is the historical risk premium on these investments?

   a. Long-term government bonds
   b. Treasury bills
   c. Large stocks
   d. Small stocks

5. **Calculating Average Returns (LO1, CFA1)** The rate of return on Cherry Jalopies, Inc., stock over the last five years was 17 percent, 11 percent, −2 percent, 3 percent, and 14 percent. Over the same period, the return on Straw Construction Company's stock was 16 percent, 18 percent, −6 percent, 1 percent, and 22 percent. What was the arithmetic average return on each stock over this period?

6. **Calculating Variability (LO4, CFA2)** Using the information from the previous problem, calculate the variances and the standard deviations for Cherry and Straw.

7. **Return Calculations (LO1, CFA1)** A particular stock has a dividend yield of 1.3 percent. Last year, the stock price fell from $56 to $49. What was the return for the year?

8. **Geometric Returns (LO1, CFA1)** Using the information from Problem 5, what is the geometric return for Cherry Jalopies, Inc.?

9. **Arithmetic and Geometric Returns (LO1, CFA1)** A stock has had returns of 21 percent, 12 percent, 7 percent, −13 percent, −4 percent, and 26 percent over the last six years. What are the arithmetic and geometric returns for the stock?

Intermediate Questions

10. **Returns and the Bell Curve (LO4, CFA3)** An investment has an expected return of 9 percent per year with a standard deviation of 21 percent. Assuming that the returns on this investment are at least roughly normally distributed, how frequently do you expect to earn between −12 percent and 30 percent? How often do you expect to earn less than −12 percent?

11. **Returns and the Bell Curve (LO4, CFA3)** An investment has an expected return of 8 percent per year with a standard deviation of 4 percent. Assuming that the returns on this investment are at least roughly normally distributed, how frequently do you expect to lose money?

12. **Using Returns Distributions (LO4, CFA2)** Based on the historical record, if you invest in long-term U.S. Treasury bonds, what is the approximate probability that your return will be less than −6.0 percent in a given year? What range of returns would you expect to see 95 percent of the time? 99 percent of the time?

13. **Using Returns Distributions (LO2, CFA2)** Based on the historical record, what is the approximate probability that an investment in small stocks will double in value in a single year? How about triple in a single year?

14. **Risk Premiums (LO2)** Refer to Table 1.1 for large-stock and T-bill returns for the period 1973–1977:

    a. Calculate the observed risk premium in each year for the common stocks.
    b. Calculate the average returns and the average risk premium over this period.
    c. Calculate the standard deviation of returns and the standard deviation of the risk premium.
    d. Is it possible that the observed risk premium can be negative? Explain how this can happen and what it means.

15. **Geometric Return (LO1, CFA1)** Your grandfather invested $1,000 in a stock 46 years ago. Currently the value of his account is $231,000. What is his geometric return over this period?

16. **Forecasting Returns (LO1)** You have found an asset with a 11.40 percent arithmetic average return and a 9.46 percent geometric return. Your observation period is 40 years. What is your best estimate of the return of the asset over the next 5 years? 10 years? 20 years?

17. **Geometric Averages (LO2)** Look back to Figure 1.1 and find the value of $1 invested in each asset class over this 84-year period. Calculate the geometric return for small-company stocks, large-company stocks, long-term government bonds, Treasury bills, and inflation.

18. **Arithmetic and Geometric Returns (LO1, CFA1)** A stock has returns of −12 percent, 15 percent, 11 percent, 19 percent, and −2 percent. What are the arithmetic and geometric returns?

19. **Arithmetic and Geometric Returns (LO1, CFA1)**   A stock has had the following year-end prices and dividends:

Year	Price	Dividend
0	$23.25	—
1	25.61	$0.15
2	26.72	0.18
3	25.18	0.20
4	27.12	0.24
5	30.43	0.28

What are the arithmetic and geometric returns for the stock?

20. **Arithmetic versus Geometric Returns (LO1, CFA1)**   You are given the returns for the following three stocks:

Year	Stock A	Stock B	Stock C
1	8%	3%	−24%
2	8	13	37
3	8	7	14
4	8	5	9
5	8	12	4

Calculate the arithmetic return, geometric return, and standard deviation for each stock. Do you notice anything about the relationship between an asset's arithmetic return, standard deviation, and geometric return? Do you think this relationship will always hold?

Spreadsheet Problems

21. **Return and Standard Deviation (LO4, CFA2)**   The 1980s was a good decade for investors in S&P 500 stocks. To find out how good, construct a spreadsheet that calculates the arithmetic average return, variance, and standard deviation for the S&P 500 returns during the 1980s using spreadsheet functions.

22. **Dollar-Weighted Average Return (LO3, CFA6)**   Suppose that an investor opens an account by investing $1,000. At the beginning of each of the next four years, he deposits an additional $1,000 each year, and he then liquidates the account at the end of the total five-year period. Suppose that the yearly returns in this account, beginning in year 1, are as follows: 12 percent, 5 percent, 8 percent, −7 percent, and −14 percent. Calculate the arithmetic and geometric average returns for this investment, and determine what the investor's actual dollar-weighted average return was for this five-year period. Why is the dollar-weighted average return higher or lower than the geometric average return?

CFA Exam Review by Schweser

[CFA1, CFA6]

Mega Marketing, an advertising firm specializing in the financial services industry, has just hired Kinara Yamisaka. Ms. Yamisaka was a finance major in college and is a candidate for the CFA program. She was hired to provide the firm with more depth in the area of investment performance analysis.

Mega is preparing advertising information for Vega Funds Limited. Vega has provided the following five-year annual return data, where year 5 is the most recent period:

Vega Funds Limited	
Year	Return
1	−10%
2	25
3	−5
4	30
5	5

To assess her understanding of returns, Ms. Yamisaka's supervisor asks her to calculate a number of different returns, including arithmetic, geometric, annualized, and money- (or dollar-) weighted returns. He also asks her to determine the impact of the following cash flow scenarios on Vega's returns:

Cash Flows	Scenario 1	Scenario 2	Scenario 3
Beginning market value	$100	$100	$100
End of year 2 deposit (withdrawal)	$0	$20	($10)
End of year 5 market value	?	?	?

1. What is Vega's geometric average return over the five-year period?
   a. 7.85 percent
   b. 9.00 percent
   c. 15.14 percent

2. What are Vega's money- (or dollar-) weighted average returns over the five-year period for Scenarios 2 and 3?

	Scenario 2	Scenario 3
a.	7.78%	7.96%
b.	7.96%	7.78%
c.	9.00%	7.85%

3. Ms. Yamisaka has determined that the average monthly return of another Mega client was 1.63 percent during the past year. What is the annualized rate of return?
   a. 5.13 percent
   b. 19.56 percent
   c. 21.41 percent

4. The return calculation method most appropriate for evaluating the performance of a portfolio manager is:
   a. Holding period
   b. Geometric
   c. Money-weighted (or dollar-weighted)

What's on the Web?

1. **Ticker Symbols**   Go to finance.yahoo.com and look up the ticker symbols for the following companies: 3M Company, International Business Machines, Dell Computer, Advanced Micro Devices, American Standard Company, and Bed, Bath & Beyond.

2. **Average Return and Standard Deviation**   Go to finance.yahoo.com and enter the ticker symbol for your favorite stock. Now, look for the historical prices and find the monthly closing stock price for the last six years. Calculate the annual arithmetic average return, the standard deviation, and the geometric return for this period.

Stock-Trak Exercises

To access the Stock-Trak Exercise for this chapter, please visit the book Web site at www.mhhe.com/jmd6e and choose the corresponding chapter.

www.mhhe.com/jmd6e

CHAPTER 2

The Investment Process

Learning Objectives

Don't sell yourself short. Instead, learn about these key investment subjects:

1. The importance of an investment policy statement.
2. The various types of securities brokers and brokerage accounts.
3. How to calculate initial and maintenance margin.
4. The workings of short sales.

"Don't gamble! Take all your savings and buy some good stock and hold it till it goes up. If it don't go up, don't buy it."

–Will Rogers

Are you planning to take a road trip on your upcoming fall or spring break? If so, you might do quite a few things to prepare for this adventure. Among them, you will probably consult an online road map to determine the best route to get you to your destination. You might also check for any expected construction delays. If you find any, you might look for ways to change your route. While road-trip planning might seem unrelated to investing, this process is similar to the approach that you should take with your investment portfolio. In this chapter, we discuss the general investment process. We begin with the investment policy statement, which serves as the investor's "road map."

We hope reading about the history of risk and return in our previous chapter generated some interest in investing on your own. To help you get started, this chapter covers the basics of the investing process. We begin by describing the investment policy statement. We then discuss how you go about buying and selling securities such as stocks and bonds. ■

CFA™ Exam Topics in This Chapter:

1 Discounted cash flow applications (L1, S2)
2 The asset allocation decision (L1, S12)
3 An introduction to portfolio management (L1, S12)
4 Organization and functioning of securities markets (L1, S13)
5 Security-market indexes (L1, S13)
6 Market efficiency and anomalies (L1, S13)
7 The portfolio management process and the investment policy statement (L2, S18)
8 Managing individual investor portfolios (L3, S4)
9 Taxes and private wealth management in a global context (L3, S4)
10 Asset allocation (L3, S8)
11 Execution of portfolio decisions (L3, S16)

Go to www.mhhe.com/jmd6e for a guide that aligns your textbook with CFA readings.

2.1 The Investment Policy Statement

Different investors will have very different investment objectives and strategies. For example, some will be very active, buying and selling frequently; others will be relatively inactive, buying and holding for long periods of time. Some will be willing to bear substantial risk in seeking out returns; for others, safety is a primary concern. In this section, we describe the investment policy statement, which is designed to reflect these issues.

The investment policy statement, or IPS, is typically divided into two sections: objectives and constraints. In thinking about investor objectives, the most fundamental question is: Why invest at all? For the most part, the only sensible answer is that we invest today to have more tomorrow. In other words, investment is simply deferred consumption; instead of spending today, we choose to wait because we wish to have (or need to have) more to spend later.

Given that we invest now to have more later, the particular objectives identified will depend on, among other things, the time horizon, liquidity needs, and taxes. We discuss these and other issues next.

OBJECTIVES: RISK AND RETURN

Probably the most fundamental decision that an investor must make concerns the amount of risk to take. Most investors are *risk-averse*, meaning that, all else equal, they dislike risk and want to expose themselves to the minimum risk level possible. However, as our previous chapter indicated, larger returns are generally associated with larger risks, so there is a trade-off. In formulating investment objectives, the individual must therefore balance return objectives with risk tolerance.

An individual's tolerance to risk is affected by their ability to take risk and their willingness to take risk. First, some investors are simply able to take on more risk, possibly due to a larger beginning portfolio or a longer time horizon. Second, although some investors are well-suited to take on risk, they simply are not willing to do so. Thus, risk tolerance is impacted by both an investor's ability and willingness to take on risk.

Attitudes toward risk are strictly personal preferences, and individuals with very similar economic circumstances can have very different degrees of risk aversion. For this reason, the first thing that must be assessed in evaluating the suitability of an investment strategy is risk tolerance. Unfortunately, this is not an easy thing to do. Most individuals have a difficult time articulating in any precise way their attitude toward risk (what's yours?). One reason is that risk is not a simple concept; it is not easily defined or measured. Nevertheless, the nearby *Investment Updates* box contains an article from *The Wall Street Journal* about risk tolerance that has a short quiz that might help you assess your attitude toward risk. When you take the quiz, remember there are no right or wrong answers. Afterwards, score your risk tolerance as shown at the end of the article.

INVESTOR CONSTRAINTS

In addition to attitude toward risk, an investor's investment strategy will be affected by various constraints. We discuss five of the most common and important constraints next.

RESOURCES Probably the most obvious constraint, and the one to which many students can most easily relate, is *resources*. Obviously, if you have no money, you cannot invest at all. Beyond that, certain types of investments and investment strategies generally have minimum requirements.

What is the minimum resource level needed? The answer to this question depends on the investment strategy, so there is no precise answer. Through mutual funds, initial investments in the stock market can be made for as little as $500, with subsequent investments as small as $100 or less. However, because minimum commission levels, account fees, and other costs are frequently associated with buying and selling securities, an investor interested in actively trading on her own would probably need an account in the $5,000 to $50,000 range.

HORIZON The investment *horizon* refers to the planned life of the investment. For example, individuals frequently save for retirement, where the investment horizon, depending on your age, can be very long. On the other hand, you might be saving to buy a house in the near future, implying a relatively short horizon.

How else can you build a portfolio?
Go to
moneycentral.msn.com
and search the site for
"Prepare to Invest"

Want to have a career in
financial advice? See
www.cfainstitute.org
and
www.cfp.net

Do-It-Yourself Crowd Has Quizzes to Rate Courage on Finances

Risk

There once was a time when risk assessment was the duty of stockbrokers or financial planners, who questioned clients to gauge their comfort level for volatility and potential losses. But with the explosion of online trading, investors have taken control of their own finances. In the process, they have cast aside the mental due diligence that ultimately determines whether they're sleepless in Cisco or bored by Boeing.

It's an age-old quest for balance. Investors who structure their portfolios so that they are comfortable with both the rewards and risks are the ones who sleep best when market downdrafts keep others awake at night. Moreover, they aren't the ones berating themselves for missing out on big gains when the market rebounds.

To help investors determine the level of risk they're most comfortable with, here's a statistically based risk-tolerance quiz constructed with the help of Investment Technologies Inc., a New York firm that provides investment tools and risk-assessment instruments to financial institutions such as banks and investment firms.

Financial companies increasingly rely on risk quizzes similar to this one, though often far more detailed, to better assess a client's true tolerance for market vicissitudes. As investors continue to take on increasing responsibility for their own money—through online trading or in self-managed 401(k) and IRA retirement accounts—"the issue of how individual investors make investment decisions is becoming a huge issue," says Brian Rom, president of Investment Technologies.

All manner of risk-assessment quizzes are available. Some are posted on financial Web sites, others are available from financial planners and investment companies. Some are relatively simple and are designed to match an investor with particular mutual funds or annuities.

The more sophisticated quizzes are based on statistical research that quantifies the psychological behavior of people and their money habits. Such "behavioral finance" studies have determined that many people typically aren't rational but are irrational when it comes to money and risk.

For example, research has shown that most people fear loss more than they value comparable gain. Offer someone a sure $50 or, on the flip of a coin, the possibility of winning $100 or winning nothing, and chances are they'll pocket the sure thing. Conversely, penalize them $50 to start, then offer a flip of a coin to lose $100 or lose nothing, and they'll invariably take the coin toss. Both scenarios are statistically equivalent, yet people tend to view "the possibility of recouping a loss as more important than the possibility of greater gain," even though the coin flip could mean an even greater loss, says James Corter, associate professor of statistics and education at New York's Columbia University.

The accompanying quiz is based on research done by Mr. Corter. At just eight questions, it is short, but it is backed by empirical studies and "has adequate reliability and validity," says Mr. Corter.

The quiz is designed to reveal where an individual falls along the risk spectrum. It is accompanied by a chart detailing where a variety of stock and bond investments, based on historical performance and volatility, fall along the risk spectrum, to give quiz takers an idea of the class of investments most likely to match an investor's temperament.

Certainly, no risk quiz can tell you everything about your financial courage, and your score here doesn't mean that if you fall into a more conservative category that you can't stomach a little exposure to volatile tech stocks. "But if you answer the questions candidly," says Ms. Bickel at TIAA-CREF, "and don't worry about whether you come out conservative or a swinger, you'll have an accurate portrayal of your risk level that you can use when building your portfolio."

Risk Tolerance

Do you know your risk tolerance? This short questionnaire can help you gain a better understanding of your tolerance for market vicissitudes. Answer the questions, tally the results, and match the score to the Suitable Investments.*

1. Choose the statement that best describes your interests in an investment program.

   A My primary aim is to achieve high long-term return in the value of my portfolio, even if that means accepting some significant short-term swings in values.

   B My primary interest is in stable growth in the value of my portfolio, even if that means somewhat lower returns over time.

   C I attach equal value to maximizing long-term returns and minimizing fluctuations in value.

2. How important are the following factors when you decide to purchase a stock or mutual fund?

   a) Short-term potential for the price to appreciate.

   b) Long-term potential for the price to appreciate.

   c) If a stock, the potential that the company will be bought or taken over.

   d) Gain or loss in the price over the past six months.

e) Gain or loss in the price over the past five years.

f) Stock was recommended by a friend or coworker.

g) Risk that the price could drop.

h) Potential that the investment will pay dividends.

Very Important	Somewhat Important	Not At All Important
A	B	C
A	B	C
A	B	C
A	B	C
A	B	C
A	B	C
A	B	C
A	B	C

3. a) Would you put $5,000 of your assets into an investment where you have a 70% chance of doubling your money (to $10,000) and a 30% chance of losing the entire $5,000?

   Yes   No

   b) How about an 80% chance of doubling to $10,000 and a 20% chance of losing the entire $5,000?

   Yes__ No__

   c) How about a 60% chance of doubling to $10,000 and a 40% chance of losing the entire $5,000?

   Yes__ No__

4. Suppose you have a choice between two mutual funds, both of which are broadly diversified into 6 asset classes (e.g., stocks, bonds, real estate, etc.). The charts below show the changes in value over the past 12 months for the assets in each portfolio. Which portfolio of assets do you prefer to invest in?

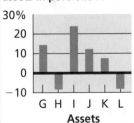

One-year returns for assets in portfolio A

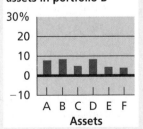

One-year returns for assets in portfolio B

5. Assume that you have made an investment that has dropped in value by $2,000 and you find yourself faced with the following choice (please circle only one option):

   A Sell and take the immediate $2,000 loss (a 100% chance of loss).

   B Hold on to it with a 50% chance of recouping the $2,000 and a 50% chance of losing an additional $2,000.

   C No preference.

6. Assume that you have recently invested $10,000 in a stock and that the value of this stock has dropped 15% in value in one week. You can discover no reason for this decline, and the broader market has not dipped accordingly. Which of the following actions would you be most likely to take? (Circle one answer only.)

   A Buy more.

   B Sell all your holdings in the fund immediately and put the money into a less volatile investment.

   C Sell half of your holdings in the fund immediately and put the money elsewhere.

   D Wait for the price to recover and then sell all your holdings in the fund.

   E Do nothing (occasional dips in price are to be expected).

7. The following charts show quarterly performance of two equity mutual funds over the past two years. Which do you prefer to invest in?

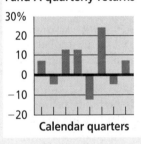

Fund A quarterly returns

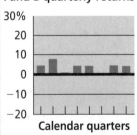

Fund B quarterly returns

8. As an investor in stock and bond markets, how would you rate your degree of experience relative to other individual investors? (Please circle one.)

   A Extremely experienced

   B More than average experience

   C Average experience

   D Less than average experience

   E Little or no experience

Source: Investment Technologies Inc.

Scoring

1 – A. 15; B. 0; C. 7

FOR EACH QUESTION:

2a) – A. 0; B. 1; C. 2

2b) through 2e)

    A. 2; B. 1; C. 0

FOR EACH QUESTION:

2f) through 2h)

    A. 0: B. 1; C. 2

FOR EACH QUESTION:

3a) through 3c)

    Yes. 5; No. 0

4 – A. 10; B. 0

5 – A. 0; B. 10; C. 10

6 – A. 15; B. 0; C. 5; D. 0; E. 10

7 – A. 10; B. 0

8 – A. 20; B. 15; C. 10; D. 5; E. 0

Score in Points	Suitable Investments*
0–11	Avoid risk! Open a money-market account—or buy a bigger mattress.
12–33	Gentlemen (and ladies) prefer bonds, and are most at home with high-grade corporate and government bonds of an intermediate duration.
34–55	You're still a bond buyer. But you're willing to live a bit closer to the edge with interest-only U.S. Treasury STRIPS.
56–77	Mix it up. Convertible bonds and stocks are to your liking. But safer utilities and large blue chips are as risky as you go. Real-estate investment trusts fit too.
78–99	Stock up on stocks. At the low end, you're comfortable with larger value stocks; at the high end, riskier midcap and growth stocks work.
100+	Viva Las Vegas, baby! Place your bets on 'Net stocks and new-tech issues. Risks are high, but so are the payoffs.

*Suitable investments are based upon an analysis of the volatility of 75 various bond and stock indexing, and apply to investment horizons of between 10 and 15 years.

Source: Jeff D. Opdyke, *The Wall Street Journal.* Reprinted with permission of *The Wall Street Journal.* © 2003 Dow Jones & Company Inc. All Rights Reserved Worldwide.

The reason that horizon is important is evident in our previous chapter. It is true that stocks outperformed the other investments in the long run, but there were short periods over which they did much worse. This fact means that, if you have to pay tuition in 30 days, stocks are probably not the best investment for that money. Thus, in thinking about the riskiness of an investment, one important consideration is when the money will be needed.

For more risk tolerance quizzes, visit
www.fool.com,
www.individual.ml.com,
and
moneycentral.msn.com

LIQUIDITY Some investors have to sell an asset quickly. In such cases, the asset's *liquidity* is particularly important. An asset with a high degree of liquidity is one that can be sold quickly without a significant price concession. Such an asset is said to be liquid.

Liquidity has two related parts. One part of liquidity is the ease with which an asset can be sold. The other part is how much you have to lower the price to sell the asset quickly. Liquidity is difficult to measure precisely, but some assets are clearly much more liquid than others. A good way to think about liquidity is to imagine buying an asset and then immediately reselling it. The less you would lose on this "round-trip" transaction, the more liquid is the asset.

TAXES Different types of investments are taxed very differently. When we talk about the return on an investment, what is really relevant is the *aftertax* return. As a result, taxes are a vital consideration. Higher tax bracket investors will naturally seek investment strategies with favorable tax treatments, while lower tax bracket (or tax-exempt) investors will focus more on pretax returns.

In addition, the way in which an investment is held can dramatically affect its tax status. The tax laws and other rules are in a constant state of flux, so we will stick to broad principles.

BUFFETT ON TAXES AND TRADING

Through my favorite comic strip, "Li'l Abner," I got a chance during my youth to see the benefits of delayed taxes, though I missed the lesson at the time. Making his readers feel superior, Li'l Abner bungled happily, but moronically, through life in Dogpatch. At one point he became infatuated with a New York temptress, Appassionatta Van Climax, but despaired of marrying her because he had only a single silver dollar and she was interested solely in millionaires. Dejected, Abner took his problem to Old Man Mose, the font of all knowledge in Dogpatch. Said the sage: Double your money 20 times and Appassionatta will be yours (1, 2, 4, 8, ... , 1,048,576).

My last memory of the strip is Abner entering a roadhouse, dropping his dollar into a slot machine, and hitting a jackpot that spilled money all over the floor. Meticulously following Mose's advice, Abner picked up two dollars and went off to find his next double. Whereupon I dumped Abner and began reading Ben Graham.

Mose clearly was overrated as a guru: Besides failing to anticipate Abner's slavish obedience to instructions, he also forgot about taxes. Had Abner been subject, say, to the 35% federal tax rate that Berkshire pays, and had he managed one double annually, he would after 20 years only have accumulated $22,370. Indeed, had he kept on both getting his annual doubles and paying a 35% tax on each, he would have needed 7½ years more to reach the $1 million required to win Appassionatta.

But what if Abner had instead put his dollar in a single investment and held it until it doubled the same 27½ times? In that case, he would have realized about $200 million pre-tax or, after paying a $70 million tax in the final year, about $130 million after-tax. For that, Appassionatta would have crawled to Dogpatch. Of course, with 27½ years having passed, how Appassionatta would have looked to a fellow sitting on $130 million is another question.

What this little tale tells us is that tax-paying investors will realize a far, far greater sum from a single investment that compounds internally at a given rate than from a succession of investments compounding at the same rate. But I suspect many Berkshire shareholders figured that out long ago.

Source: "Buffett on Taxes and Trading," *Change Alley: Global Finance and Intelligent Investing,* http://changealley.blogspot.com, accessed January 6, 2009.

The general idea is that certain types of accounts, particularly retirement savings accounts, receive preferential tax treatment. The tax break can be enormous, and, as a result, the amount you can invest each year in these accounts is strictly limited. There are also rules regarding when you can withdraw the money, and it is important to pay careful attention to them.

Taxes impact almost every step of the investment process, from the type of account you choose to the nature and length of the investments themselves. So we will discuss taxes throughout the remainder of the book, and throughout the rest of this chapter in particular. For now, though, consider the nearby *Investment Updates* box that provides some insight on the impact of taxes from one of the most famous and successful investors—Warren Buffett.

UNIQUE CIRCUMSTANCES Almost everyone will have some special or unique requirements or opportunities. For example, many companies will match certain types of investments made by employees on a dollar-for-dollar basis (typically up to some maximum per year). In other words, you double your money immediately with complete certainty. It is difficult to envision any other investment with such a favorable payoff. Therefore, investors should probably seize this opportunity even though there could be some undesirable liquidity, tax, or horizon considerations.

A list of possible special circumstances is essentially endless. To give a few examples, however, the number of dependents and their needs will vary from investor to investor. Therefore, the need to provide for dependents will be an important constraint for some investors. Some investors want to invest only in companies whose products and activities they consider to be socially or politically suitable. Some investors want to invest primarily in their own community or state. Other investors, such as corporate insiders, face regulatory and legal restrictions on their investing. Elected officials may have to avoid (or at least ethically *should* avoid) some types of investments out of conflict of interest concerns.

STRATEGIES AND POLICIES

Once the IPS is in place, the investor must determine the appropriate strategies to achieve the stated objectives. Investors need to address four key areas when they devise their investment strategy. These key areas are investment management, market timing, asset allocation, and security selection. We discuss each of these next.

INVESTMENT MANAGEMENT A basic decision that all investors make is who manages their investments. At one extreme, investors make all of the buy and sell decisions themselves. At the other extreme, investors make no buy and sell decisions. Instead, the investor hires someone to manage his or her investments.

Often investors make some investment decisions and hire professional managers to make other investment decisions. For example, suppose you divide your money among four different mutual funds. In this case, you have hired four different money managers. However, you decided what types of mutual funds to buy. Also, you chose the particular funds within each type. Finally, you decided how to divide your money among the funds.

At first blush, managing your money yourself might seem to be the cheapest way to go because you do not pay management fees. Upon reflection, this is not a cheap decision. First, you must consider the value of your time. For some investors, researching investments and making investment decisions is something of a hobby. For most investors, however, it is too time-consuming. The value of your time is a powerful incentive to hire professional money managers. Also, for some strategies, the costs of doing it yourself can exceed those of hiring someone even after considering fees. This higher cost is simply due to the higher level of commissions and other fees that individual investors generally have to pay. For example, it might not be a bad idea for some of your investment to be in real estate, but a small investor will find it very difficult to directly acquire a sound real estate investment at reasonable cost.

An interesting question regarding professional money managers concerns their performance. It certainly seems logical to argue that by hiring a professional investor to manage your money, you would earn more, at least on average. Surely the pros make better investment decisions than the amateurs! Surprisingly, this is not necessarily true. We will return to this subject in a later chapter. For now, we simply note that the possibility of a superior return might not be a compelling reason to prefer professional management.

MARKET TIMING A second basic investment decision you must make is whether you will try to buy and sell in anticipation of the future direction of the overall market. For example, you might move money into the stock market when you think stock prices will rise. Or you might move money out of the stock market when you think stock prices will fall. This trading activity is called **market timing**. Some investors actively move money around to try to time short-term market movements. Other investors are much less active, but they still try to time long-term market movements. At the extreme, a fully passive strategy is one in which you make no attempt to time the market.

Market timing certainly seems like a reasonable thing to do. After all, why leave money in an investment if you expect it to decrease in value? You might be surprised that a common recommendation is that investors *avoid* trying to time the market. Why? As we discuss in more detail in a later chapter, the simple reason is that successful market timing is, to put it mildly, extremely difficult. To outperform a completely passive strategy, you must be able to accurately predict the future. If you make even a small number of bad calls, you will likely never catch up.

ASSET ALLOCATION Another fundamental decision that you must make concerns the distribution of your investment across different types of assets. We saw in Chapter 1 that different asset types—small stocks, large stocks, bonds—have distinct risk and return characteristics. In formulating your investment strategy, you must decide what percentage of your money will be placed in each of these broad categories. This decision is called **asset allocation**.

An important asset allocation decision for many investors is how much to invest in common stocks and how much to invest in bonds. There are some basic rules of thumb for this decision, one of the simplest being to split the portfolio into 60 percent stocks and 40 percent bonds. A slightly more sophisticated rule of thumb is that your equity percentage should be

market timing
Buying and selling in anticipation of the overall direction of a market.

asset allocation
The distribution of investment funds among broad classes of assets.

equal to your age subtracted from 100 (or 120, depending on the source). Under this rule, a 22-year-old college student should have $100 - 22 = 78$ percent (or $120 - 22 = 98$ percent) of her portfolio in stocks. This approach gradually reduces your exposure to stocks as you get older. Most of the major investment firms and many Web sites maintain recommended asset allocation schemes, which can be custom-tailored for individuals depending on their risk tolerance, wealth, and retirement goals.

SECURITY SELECTION Finally, after deciding who will manage your investment, whether you will try to time the market, and the various asset classes you wish to hold, you must decide which specific securities to buy within each class. This is termed **security selection**.

security selection
Selection of specific securities within a particular class.

For example, you might decide that you want 30 percent of your money in small stocks. This is an asset allocation decision. Next, however, you must decide *which* small stocks to buy. Here again you must choose an active strategy or a passive strategy. With an active strategy, you would try to identify those small stocks that you think will perform best in the future. In other words, you are trying to pick "winners." Investigating particular securities within a broad class in an attempt to identify superior performers is often called *security analysis*.

With a passive security selection strategy, you might just acquire a diverse group of small stocks, perhaps by buying a mutual fund that holds shares in hundreds of small companies (such funds are discussed in detail in a later chapter).

A useful way to distinguish asset allocation from security selection is to note that asset allocation is a macro-level activity. That is, the focus is on whole markets or classes of assets. Security selection is a much more micro-level activity. The focus of security selection is on individual securities.

If we consider the active versus passive aspects of asset allocation and security selection simultaneously, four distinct investment strategies emerge. These strategies appear in the following two-by-two table:

	Security Selection	
Asset Allocation	Active	Passive
Active	I	II
Passive	III	IV

With strategy I, we actively move money between asset classes based on our beliefs and expectations about future performance. In addition, we try to pick the best performers in each class. This is a fully active strategy. At the other extreme, strategy IV is a fully passive strategy. In this strategy, we seldom change asset allocations or attempt to choose the likely best performers from a set of individual securities.

With strategy II, we actively vary our holdings by class, but we do not try to choose particular securities within each class. With this strategy, we might move back and forth between short-term government bonds and small stocks in an attempt to time the market. Finally, with strategy III, we do not vary our asset allocations, but we do select individual securities. A diehard stock picker would fall into this category. Such an investor holds 100 percent stocks and concentrates solely on buying and selling individual companies.

Between asset allocation and security selection, which one do you think is most important to the success of a portfolio? Because the news media tend to concentrate on the success and failure of individual stocks, you might be inclined to think security selection is the most important element of a successful investing strategy. Research shows, however, that asset allocation is the most important determinant of portfolio returns. In fact, many experts suggest that about 90 percent of the performance of a portfolio is determined by asset allocation, while only 10 percent is from security selection.

How is this possible? Well, consider the crash of 2008. If at the beginning of 2008 you had allocated all your money to bonds (as opposed to stocks), you would have done much better than an investor who had heavily allocated to stocks. This result could hold true even if the stock investor was excellent at selecting stocks. The idea is that equities tend to move together, so even good stocks can do poorly if all equities are doing poorly.

CHECK THIS

2.1a	What does the term "risk-averse" mean?
2.1b	What are some of the constraints investors face in making investment decisions?
2.1c	What is asset allocation?

2.2 Investment Professionals

Suppose you have created your IPS, detailing your objectives and constraints. So, what comes next? One way to get started is to open an account with a securities broker, such as Edward Jones or Merrill Lynch. Such accounts are often called *brokerage* or *trading accounts.* Opening a trading account is straightforward and really much like opening a bank account. You will be asked to supply some basic information about yourself and to sign an agreement (often simply called a customer's agreement) that spells out your rights and obligations and those of your broker. You then give your broker a check and instructions on how you want the money invested.

To illustrate, suppose that instead of going to Disneyland, you would rather own part of it. You therefore open an account with $10,000. You instruct your broker to purchase 100 shares of Walt Disney stock and to retain any remaining funds in your account. Your broker will locate a seller and purchase the stock on your behalf. Say shares of stock in Walt Disney Corporation are selling for about $33 per share, so your 100 shares will cost $3,300. In addition, for providing this service, your broker will generally charge you a commission. How much depends on a number of things, including the type of broker and the size of your order, but on this order, $50 wouldn't be an unusual commission charge. After paying for the stock and paying the commission, you would have $6,650 left in your account. Your broker will hold your stock for you or deliver the shares to you, whichever you wish. At a later date, you can sell your stock by instructing your broker to do so. You would receive the proceeds from the sale, less another commission charge. You can always add money to your account and purchase additional securities, and you can withdraw money from your account or even close it altogether.

In broad terms, this basic explanation is really all there is to it. As we begin to discuss in the next section, however, a range of services are available to you, and there are important considerations that you need to take into account before you actually begin investing.

CHOOSING A BROKER/ADVISOR

The first step in opening an account is choosing a broker. Brokers are traditionally divided into three groups: full-service brokers, discount brokers, and deep-discount brokers. What distinguishes the three groups is the level of service they provide and the resulting commissions they charge.

With a deep-discount broker, essentially the only services provided are account maintenance and order execution—that is, buying and selling. You generally deal with a deep-discount broker over the telephone or, increasingly, using a Web browser (see the next section on online brokers).

At the other extreme, a full-service broker will provide investment advice regarding the types of securities and investment strategies that might be appropriate for you to consider (or avoid). The larger brokerage firms do extensive research on individual companies and securities and maintain lists of recommended (and not recommended) securities. They maintain offices throughout the country, so, depending on where you live, you can actually stop in and speak to the person assigned to your account. A full-service broker will even manage your account for you if you wish.

Today, many full-service brokers are trying to specialize in wealth management. That is, these brokers manage many aspects of financial planning for high net worth investors. These high net worth accounts are exactly what you think they are—accounts with a lot of money in them. Particularly on the full-service side, many brokers have moved toward an advisory-based relationship with their clients. So, rather than charging commissions on every transaction, the investment advisor charges an annual fee, say 1–2 percent, based on the balance in the account. This fee covers all services associated with advice and trading. An advisory-based relationship brings potential benefits to the client and advisor. For example, without commissions, the advisor has little incentive to trade an account actively. As a result, the interests of the client and the advisor are more closely aligned.

Discount brokers fall somewhere between the two cases we have discussed so far, offering more investment counseling than the deep-discounters and lower commissions or fees than the full-service brokers. Which type of broker should you choose? It depends on how much advice and service you need or want. If you are the do-it-yourself type, then you may seek out the lower commissions. If you are not, then a full-service advisor might be more suitable. Often investors begin with a full-service broker, and then, as they gain experience and confidence, move on to a discount broker or a deep-discount broker.

We should note that the brokerage industry is very competitive, and differences between broker types seem to be blurring. Full-service brokers frequently discount commissions or fees to attract new customers (particularly those with large accounts), and you should not hesitate to ask about commission rates. Similarly, discount brokers have begun to offer securities research and extensive account management services. Basic brokerage services have become almost commoditylike, and, more and more, brokerage firms are competing by offering financial services such as retirement planning, credit cards, and check-writing privileges, to name a few.

ONLINE BROKERS

The most important recent change in the brokerage industry is the rapid growth of online brokers, also known as e-brokers or cyberbrokers. With an online broker, you place buy and sell orders over the Internet using a Web browser.

Before 1995, online accounts essentially did not exist. By 2010, many millions of investors were buying and selling securities online. Online investing has fundamentally changed the discount and deep-discount brokerage industry by slashing costs dramatically. In a typical online trade, no human intervention is needed by the broker as the entire process is handled electronically, so operating costs are held to a minimum. As costs have fallen, so have commissions. Even for relatively large trades, online brokers typically charge less than $20 per trade. For budget-minded investors and active stock traders, the attraction is clear.

Competition among online brokers is fierce. Some take a no-frills approach, offering only basic services and very low commission rates. Others, particularly the larger ones, charge a little more but offer a variety of services, including research and various banking services such as check-writing privileges, credit cards, debit cards, and even mortgages. As technology continues to improve and investors become more comfortable using it, online brokerages will almost surely become the dominant form because of their enormous convenience—and the low commission rates.

INVESTOR PROTECTION

THE FEDERAL DEPOSIT INSURANCE CORPORATION You probably know that a U.S. government agency called the Federal Deposit Insurance Corporation, or FDIC, protects money deposited into bank accounts. In fact, the FDIC currently insures deposits up to $250,000 per account in nearly every bank and thrift in the United States. However, savers have not always had deposit insurance.

In the 1920s and early 1930s, many banks failed. When these banks failed, the money held in bank accounts vanished. To help restore faith in the banking system, the U.S. Congress created the FDIC in 1933. So far, so good. Since the start of FDIC insurance on January 1, 1934, no depositor has lost a single cent of insured funds as a result of a bank failure.

However, the FDIC insures only bank deposits. That is, the FDIC does *not* insure stocks, bonds, mutual funds, or other investments offered by banks, thrift institutions, and brokerage firms—even those calling themselves investment banks.

INVESTMENT FRAUD Suppose someone swindles you by selling you shares in a fictitious company. Or suppose someone sells you shares in a real company, but does not transfer ownership to you. These two situations are examples of investment fraud.

Experts estimate that losses from investment fraud in the United States range from $10 billion to $40 billion a year. You should know that "insurance" for investment fraud does not exist in the United States, but state and federal securities agencies were established to help investors deal with cases of investment fraud. Of course, investors can help protect themselves against fraud simply by dealing with reputable brokerage firms.

THE SECURITIES INVESTOR PROTECTION CORPORATION Even reputable brokerage firms can go bankrupt or suffer financial difficulties. Fortunately for investors, all reputable brokerage firms belong to the **Securities Investor Protection Corporation**, or **SIPC**. In fact, almost all brokerage firms operating in the United States are required to be members of the SIPC. The SIPC insures your brokerage account for up to $500,000 in cash and securities, with a $250,000 cash maximum.

Congress chartered the SIPC in 1970, but SIPC is not a government agency; SIPC is a private insurance fund supported by the securities industry. SIPC has a narrow, but important, focus: restore funds to investors who have securities in the hands of bankrupt or financially troubled brokerage firms. When a brokerage firm is closed as a result of financial difficulties, sometimes customer assets are missing. In this case, the SIPC works to return customers' cash, bonds, stock, and other eligible securities. Without SIPC, investors at financially troubled brokerage firms might lose their securities or money forever.

Not every loss is protected by the SIPC. For example, the SIPC does not guarantee the value of securities held in an SIPC-covered brokerage account. In other words, you can still lose everything in an SIPC-covered account if the value of your securities falls to zero.

The SIPC gained the national spotlight with the Bernard "Bernie" Madoff scandal in 2009. Mr. Madoff ran a hedge fund that was really just a "Ponzi" scheme. In this system, Mr. Madoff would take deposits from investors. Rather than investing the money, however, he would simply create fictitious reports to detail investors' alleged holdings. If an investor wanted to withdraw funds, Mr. Madoff would use deposits by subsequent investors to fund the payout. Although the case is still being investigated, it is considered to be the largest investment fraud in Wall Street history, topping $65 billion. You can learn more about the relationship of the SIPC to this case in the nearby *Investment Updates* box that discusses how Bernie "Madoff with the money."

BROKER–CUSTOMER RELATIONS

There are several other important things to keep in mind when dealing with a broker or advisor. First, any advice you receive is *not* guaranteed. Far from it—buy and sell recommendations carry the explicit warning that you rely on them at your own risk. Your broker does have a duty to exercise reasonable care in formulating recommendations and not recommend anything grossly unsuitable, but that is essentially the extent of it.

Second, your broker or advisor works as your agent and has a legal duty to act in your best interest; however, brokerage firms are in the business of generating brokerage commissions. This fact will probably be spelled out in the account agreement that you sign. There is, therefore, the potential for a conflict of interest. On rare occasions, a broker is accused of "churning" an account, which refers to excessive trading for the sole purpose of generating commissions. In general, you are responsible for checking your account statements and notifying your broker in the event of any problems, and you should certainly do so. With an advisory relationship, churning is less likely.

Finally, in the unlikely event of a significant problem, your account agreement will probably specify very clearly that you must waive your right to sue and/or seek a jury trial. Instead, you agree that any disputes will be settled by arbitration and that arbitration is final and binding. Arbitration is not a legal proceeding, and the rules are much less formal. In essence, a panel is appointed by a self-regulatory body of the securities industry to review the case. The panel will be composed of a small number of individuals who are knowledgeable about the securities industry, but a majority of them will not be associated with the industry. The panel makes a finding, and, absent extraordinary circumstances, its findings cannot be appealed. The panel does not have to disclose factual findings or legal reasoning.

Securities Investor Protection Corporation (SIPC)

Insurance fund covering investors' brokerage accounts with member firms.

If you want to learn more about the SIPC, go to www.sipc.org and surf to the Answers to the Seven Most Asked Questions.

To learn more about dispute resolution, visit www.finra.org

SIPC SETS PAYOUTS IN MADOFF SCANDAL

The Securities Investor Protection Corp. said the amount it has committed to advance to Madoff victims has topped half a billion dollars, exceeding the total of all previous payouts since SIPC's inception in 1970.

Bernard Madoff, who is serving 150 years in federal prison, ran a multiyear Ponzi scheme involving billions of dollars.

In a briefing with reporters Wednesday, Irving Picard, the court-appointed trustee in charge of liquidating Bernard L. Madoff Investment Securities LLC, said he had identified $21.2 billion in cash investor losses, up from an estimate of $13 billion earlier this year.

Of those losses, SIPC has approved customer claims representing just $4.44 billion. And of that amount, SIPC has agreed to pay out $534 million. When a brokerage firm fails, SIPC can cover losses from theft and proven unauthorized trading of up to $500,000 per customer. Before the latest disbursements, SIPC had paid out $520 million since 1970.

The rest of customer losses will have to be covered out of whatever assets the trustee can gather in the liquidation process. Mr. Picard has recovered $1.4 billion in Madoff-related assets and expects that number soon will hit $1.5 billion.

Much of what the trustee is expected to recover will be from "clawback" suits against investors who pulled out money from the Madoff firm in recent years. Mr. Picard, who said there are pending lawsuits against investors seeking about $15 billion, is planning to bring other lawsuits.

Mr. Picard said he won't sue investors he determines to be hardship cases, such as those with medical problems.

The trustee and SIPC have received 15,974 customer claims. Some 11,000 claims were from investors who invested with Madoff indirectly through feeder funds. The SIPC hasn't paid any money to feeder-fund investors, and Mr. Picard said he still is trying to determine how to handle indirect claims.

"We'll have to see if people's names are on the accounts, whether they got an account statement from Madoff," Mr. Picard said. "There are a lot of other factors that will be looked at in making that determination."

The number of claims and estimated losses are likely to rise in the coming months. "We're finding we have additional claims we did not know about," Mr. Picard said.

Meanwhile, estimated losses could rise as he and his team get more details on customers' account histories. They have been able to reconstruct account records going back to 1983 and may be able to go back as far as the late 1970s, he said. The trustee uses a definition of "net equity" as the difference between what customers put in and what they took out.

Former Madoff investors are fighting the trustee's methodology, saying claims should be based on what was shown on November 2008 account statements, which reflected balances of nearly $65 billion, before the fraud collapsed in December.

CHECK THIS

2.2a   What are the differences between full-service and deep-discount brokers?

2.2b   What is the SIPC? How does SIPC coverage differ from FDIC coverage?

2.3 Types of Accounts

The account agreement that you sign has a number of important provisions and details specifying the types of trades that can be made and who can make them. Another important concern is whether the broker will extend credit and, if so, the terms under which credit will be extended. We discuss these, and other, issues next.

CASH ACCOUNTS

cash account
A brokerage account in which all transactions are made on a strictly cash basis.

A **cash account** is the simplest arrangement. Securities can be purchased to the extent that sufficient cash is available in the account. If additional purchases are desired, then the needed funds must be promptly supplied.

MARGIN ACCOUNTS

margin account
A brokerage account in which, subject to limits, securities can be bought and sold on credit.

call money rate
The interest rate brokers pay to borrow bank funds for lending to customer margin accounts.

margin
The portion of the value of an investment that is *not* borrowed.

With a **margin account**, you can, subject to limits, purchase securities on credit using money loaned to you by your broker. Such a purchase is called a *margin purchase*. The interest rate you pay on the money you borrow is based on the broker's **call money rate**, which is, loosely, the rate the broker pays to borrow the money. You pay some amount over the call money rate, called the *spread;* the exact spread depends on your broker and the size of the loan. Suppose the call money rate has been hovering around 7 percent. If a brokerage firm charges a 2.5 percent spread above this rate on loan amounts under $10,000, then you would pay a total of about 9.5 percent. However, this is usually reduced for larger loan amounts. For example, the spread may decline to .75 percent for amounts over $100,000.

Several important concepts and rules are involved in a margin purchase. For concreteness, we focus on stocks in our discussion. The specific margin rules for other investments can be quite different, but the principles and terminology are usually similar.

In general, when you purchase securities on credit, some of the money is yours and the rest is borrowed. The amount that is yours is called the **margin**. Margin is usually expressed as a percentage. For example, if you take $7,000 of your own money and borrow an additional $3,000 from your broker, your total investment will be $10,000. Of this $10,000, $7,000 is yours, so the margin is $7,000/$10,000 = .70, or 70 percent.

It is useful to create an account balance sheet when thinking about margin purchases (and some other issues we'll get to in just a moment). To illustrate, suppose you open a margin account with $5,000. You tell your broker to buy 100 shares of 3M Company (MMM). Shares in 3M Company are selling for $80 per share, so the total cost will be $8,000. Because you have only $5,000 in the account, you borrow the remaining $3,000. Immediately following the purchase, your account balance sheet would look like this:

Assets		Liabilities and Account Equity	
100 shares of 3M	$8,000	Margin loan	$3,000
		Account equity	5,000
Total	$8,000	Total	$8,000

On the left-hand side of this balance sheet, we list the account assets, which, in this case, consist of the $8,000 in 3M stock you purchased. On the right-hand side, we first list the $3,000 loan you took out to help you pay for the stock. This amount is a liability because, at some point, the loan must be repaid. The difference between the value of the assets held in the account and the loan amount is $5,000. This amount is your *account equity,* that is, the net value of your investment. Notice that your margin is equal to the account equity divided by the value of the stock owned and held in the account: $5,000/$8,000 = .625, or 62.5 percent.

EXAMPLE 2.1

The Account Balance Sheet

You want to buy 1,000 shares of Pfizer (PFE) at a price of $24 per share. You put up $18,000 and borrow the rest. What does your account balance sheet look like? What is your margin?

The 1,000 shares of Pfizer cost $24,000. You supply $18,000, so you must borrow $6,000. The account balance sheet looks like this:

Assets		Liabilities and Account Equity	
1,000 shares of Pfizer	$24,000	Margin loan	$ 6,000
		Account equity	18,000
Total	$24,000	Total	$24,000

Your margin is the account equity divided by the value of the stock owned:

$$\text{Margin} = \$18,000/\$24,000$$
$$= .75, \text{ or } 75 \text{ percent}$$

---

initial margin

The minimum margin that must be
supplied on a securities purchase.

INITIAL MARGIN When you first purchase securities on credit, there is a minimum margin that you must supply. This percentage is called the **initial margin**. The minimum percentage (for stock purchases) is set by the Federal Reserve (the "Fed"). However, the exchanges and individual brokerage firms may require higher initial margin amounts.

The Fed's power to set initial margin requirements was established in the Securities Exchange Act of 1934. In subsequent years, initial margin requirements ranged from a low of 45 percent to a high of 100 percent. Since 1974, the minimum has been 50 percent (for stock purchases). In other words, if you have $10,000 of your own cash, you can borrow up to an additional $10,000, but no more.

We emphasize that these initial margin requirements apply to stocks. In contrast, for the most part, there is little initial margin requirement for government bonds. On the other hand, margin is not allowed at all on certain other types of securities.

EXAMPLE 2.2	Calculating Initial Margin

Suppose you have $3,000 in cash in a trading account with a 50 percent initial margin requirement. What is the largest order you can place (ignoring commissions)? If the initial margin were 60 percent, how would your answer change?

When the initial margin is 50 percent, you must supply half of the total (and you borrow the other half). So, $6,000 is the largest order you could place. When the initial margin is 60 percent, your $3,000 must equal 60 percent of the total. In other words, it must be the case that

$$\$3,000 = 0.60 \times \text{Total order}$$
$$\text{Total order} = \$3,000/.60$$
$$= \$5,000$$

As this example illustrates, the higher the initial margin required, the less you can borrow. When the margin is 50 percent, you can borrow $3,000. When the margin is 60 percent, you can borrow only $2,000.

maintenance margin

The minimum margin that must
be present at all times in a margin
account.

MAINTENANCE MARGIN In addition to the initial margin requirement set by the Fed, brokerage firms and exchanges generally have a **maintenance margin** requirement. For example, the New York Stock Exchange (NYSE) requires a minimum of 25 percent maintenance margin. This amount is the minimum margin required at all times after the purchase.

The maintenance margin set by your broker is sometimes called the "house" margin requirement. The level is established by your broker, who may vary it depending on what you are buying. For low-priced and very volatile stocks, the house margin can be as high as 100 percent, meaning no margin at all.

margin call

A demand for more funds that
occurs when the margin in
an account drops below the
maintenance margin.

A typical maintenance margin would be 30 percent. If your margin falls below 30 percent, then you may be subject to a **margin call**, which is a demand by your broker to add to your account, pay off part of the loan, or sell enough securities to bring your margin back up to an acceptable level. In some cases, you will be asked to restore your account to the initial margin level. In other cases, you will be asked to restore your account to the maintenance margin level. If you do not or cannot comply, your securities may be sold. The loan will be repaid out of the proceeds, and any remaining amounts will be credited to your account.

To illustrate, suppose your account has a 50 percent initial margin requirement and a 30 percent maintenance margin. Suppose stock in Vandelay Industries is selling for $50 per share. You have $20,000, and you want to buy as much of this stock as you possibly can. With a 50 percent initial margin, you can buy up to $40,000 worth, or 800 shares. The account balance sheet looks like this:

Assets		Liabilities and Account Equity	
800 shares @$50/share	$40,000	Margin loan	$20,000
		Account equity	20,000
Total	$40,000	Total	$40,000

Unfortunately, right after your purchase, Vandelay Industries reveals that it has been artificially inflating earnings for the last three years (this is not good). Share prices plummet to $35 per share. What does the account balance sheet look like when this happens? Are you subject to a margin call?

To create the new account balance sheet, we recalculate the total value of the stock. The margin loan stays the same, so the account equity is adjusted as needed:

Assets		Liabilities and Account Equity	
800 shares @$35/share	$28,000	Margin loan	$20,000
		Account equity	8,000
Total	$28,000	Total	$28,000

As shown, the total value of your "position" (i.e., the stock you hold) falls to $28,000, a $12,000 loss. You still owe $20,000 to your broker, so your account equity is $28,000 − $20,000 = $8,000. Your margin is therefore $8,000/$28,000 = .286, or 28.6 percent. You are below the 30 percent minimum, so you are subject to a margin call.

THE EFFECTS OF MARGIN Margin is a form of *financial leverage*. Any time you borrow money to make an investment, the impact is to magnify both your gains and losses, hence the use of the term "leverage." The easiest way to see this is through an example. Imagine that you have $30,000 in an account with a 60 percent initial margin. You now know that you can borrow up to an additional $20,000 and buy $50,000 worth of stock (why?). The call money rate is 5.50 percent; you must pay this rate plus a .50 percent spread. Suppose you buy 1,000 shares of Coca-Cola Co. (KO) at $50 per share. One year later, shares in Coca-Cola Co. are selling for $60 per share. Assuming the call money rate does not change and ignoring dividends, what is your return on this investment?

At the end of the year, your 1,000 shares are worth $60,000. You owe 6 percent interest on the $20,000 you borrowed, or $1,200. If you pay off the loan with interest, you will have $60,000 − $21,200 = $38,800. You started with $30,000 and ended with $38,800, so your net gain is $8,800. In percentage terms, your return was $8,800/$30,000 = .2933, or 29.33 percent.

How would you have done without the financial leverage created from the margin purchase? In this case, you would have invested just $30,000. At $50 per share, you would have purchased 600 shares. At the end of the year, your 600 shares would be worth $60 apiece, or $36,000 total. Your dollar profit is $6,000, so your percentage return would be $6,000/$30,000 = .20, or 20 percent. If we compare this to the 29.33 percent that you made above, it's clear that you did substantially better by leveraging.

The downside is that you would do much worse if Coca-Cola's stock price fell (or didn't rise very much). For example, if Coca-Cola shares had fallen to $40 a share, you would have lost (check these calculations for practice) $11,200, or 37.33 percent on your margin investment, compared to $6,000, or 20 percent on the unmargined investment. This example illustrates how leveraging an investment through a margin account can cut both ways.

EXAMPLE 2.3   **A Marginal Investment?**

A year ago, you bought 300 shares of Pepsico, Inc. (PEP) at $55 per share. You put up the 60 percent initial margin. The call money rate plus the spread you paid was 8 percent. What is your return if the price today is $50? Compare this to the return you would have earned if you had not invested on margin.

Your total investment was 300 shares at $55 per share, or $16,500. You supplied 60 percent, or $9,900, and you borrowed the remaining $6,600. At the end of the year, you owe $6,600 plus 8 percent interest, or $7,128. If the stock sells for $50, then your position is worth 300 × $50 = $15,000. Deducting the $7,128 leaves $7,872 for you. Since you originally invested $9,900, your dollar loss is $9,900 − $7,872 = $2,028. Your percentage return is −$2,028/$9,900 = −20.48 percent.

(continued)

If you had not leveraged your investment, you would have purchased $9,900/$55 = 180 shares. These would have been worth $180 \times \$50 = \$9,000$. You therefore would have lost $900; your percentage return would have been $-\$900/\$9,900 = -9.09$ percent, compared to the -20.48 percent that you lost on your leveraged position.

EXAMPLE 2.4

How Low Can It Go?

In our previous example (Example 2.3), suppose the maintenance margin was 40 percent. At what price per share would you have been subject to a margin call?

To answer, let $P*$ be the critical price. You own 300 shares, so, at that price, your stock is worth $300 \times P*$. You borrowed $6,600, so your account equity is equal to the value of your stock less the $6,600 you owe, or $300 \times P* - \$6,600$. We can summarize this information as follows:

$$\text{Amount borrowed} = \$6,600$$
$$\text{Value of stock} = 300 \times P*$$
$$\text{Account equity} = 300 \times P* - \$6,600$$

From our preceding discussion, your percentage margin is your dollar margin (or account equity) divided by the value of the stock:

$$\text{Margin} = \frac{\text{Account equity}}{\text{Value of stock}}$$
$$= \frac{300 \times P* - \$6,600}{300 \times P*}$$

To find the critical price, we will set this margin equal to the maintenance margin and solve for $P*$:

$$\text{Maintenance margin} = \frac{\text{Number of shares} \times P* - \text{Amount borrowed}}{\text{Number of shares} \times P*}$$

Solving for $P*$ yields

$$P* = \frac{\text{Amount borrowed/Number of shares}}{1 - \text{Maintenance margin}}$$

Finally, setting the maintenance margin equal to 40 percent, we obtain this critical price, $P*$:

$$P* = \frac{\$6,600/300}{1 - .40}$$
$$= \frac{\$6,600}{180} = \$36.67$$

At any price below $36.67, your margin will be less than 40 percent, and you will be subject to a margin call. So, $36.67 is the lowest possible price that could be reached before you are subject to a margin call.

As Example 2.4 shows, you can calculate the critical price (the lowest price before you get a margin call) as follows:

$$P* = \frac{\text{Amount borrowed/Number of shares}}{1 - \text{Maintenance margin}} \tag{2.1}$$

For example, suppose you had a margin loan of $40,000, which you used to purchase, in part, 1,000 shares. The maintenance margin is 37.5 percent. What's the critical stock price, and how do you interpret it?

See if you don't agree that the critical stock price, P^*, is $40/.625 = $64. The interpretation is straightforward: If the stock price falls below $64, you are subject to a margin call.

ANNUALIZING RETURNS ON A MARGIN PURCHASE

Things get a little more complicated when we consider holding periods different from a year on a margin purchase. For example, suppose the call money rate is 9 percent, and you pay a spread of 2 percent over that. You buy 1,000 shares of Costco (COST) at $60 per share, but you put up only half the money. In three months, Costco is selling for $63 per share, and you sell your Costco shares. What is your annualized return assuming no dividends are paid?

In this case, you invested $60,000, half of which, $30,000, is borrowed. How much do you have to repay in three months? Here we have to adjust for the fact that the interest rate is 11 percent per year, but you only borrowed the money for three months. In this case, the amount you repay is equal to:

$$\text{Amount repaid} = \text{Amount borrowed} \times (1 + \text{interest rate year})^t$$

where t is the fraction of a year. In our case, t would be 3 months/12 months, or .25. So, plugging in our numbers, we get:

$$
\begin{aligned}
\text{Amount repaid} &= \text{Amount borrowed} \times (1 + \text{interest rate per year})^t \\
&= \$30,000 \times (1 + .11)^{.25} \\
&= \$30,000 \times 1.02643 \\
&= \$30,792.90
\end{aligned}
$$

So, when you sell your stock, you get $63,000, of which $30,792.90 is used to pay off the loan, leaving you with $32,207.10. You invested $30,000, so your dollar gain is $2,207.10, and your percentage return for your three-month holding period is $2,207.10/$30,000 = .0736, or 7.36 percent.

Finally, we have to convert this 7.36 percent to an annualized return. There are four three-month periods in a year, so:

$$
\begin{aligned}
1 + EAR &= (1 + \text{holding period percentage return})^m \\
&= (1 + .0736)^4 \\
&= 1.3285
\end{aligned}
$$

So, your annualized return is 32.85 percent.

HYPOTHECATION AND STREET NAME REGISTRATION

As part of your margin account agreement, you must agree to various conditions. We discuss two of the most important next.

HYPOTHECATION Any securities you purchase in your margin account will be held by your broker as collateral against the loan made to you. This practice protects the broker because the securities can be sold by the broker if the customer is unwilling or unable to meet a margin call. Putting securities up as collateral against a loan is called **hypothecation**. In fact, a margin agreement is sometimes called a hypothecation agreement. In addition, to borrow the money that it loans to you, your broker will often *re*-hypothecate your securities, meaning that your broker will pledge them as collateral with its lender, normally a bank.

hypothecation
Pledging securities as collateral against a loan.

STREET NAME REGISTRATION Securities in a margin account are normally held in **street name**. This means that the brokerage firm is actually the registered owner. If this were not the case, the brokerage firm could not legally sell the securities should a customer refuse to meet a margin call or otherwise fail to live up to the terms of the margin agreement. With this arrangement, the brokerage firm is the "owner of record," but the account holder is the "beneficial owner."

street name
An arrangement under which a broker is the registered owner of a security.

When a security is held in street name, anything mailed to the security owner, such as an annual report or a dividend check, goes to the brokerage firm. The brokerage firm then passes these on to the account holder. Street name ownership is actually a great convenience to the owner. In fact, because it is usually a free service, even customers with cash accounts generally choose street name ownership. Some of the benefits are:

1. Since the broker holds the security, there is no danger of theft or other loss of the security. This is important because a stolen or lost security cannot be easily or cheaply replaced.

2. Any dividends or interest payments are automatically credited, and they are often credited more quickly (and conveniently) than they would be if the owner received the check in the mail.

3. The broker provides regular account statements showing the value of securities held in the account and any payments received. Also, for tax purposes, the broker will provide all the needed information on a single form at the end of the year, greatly reducing the owner's record-keeping requirements.

RETIREMENT ACCOUNTS

COMPANY-SPONSORED PLANS If you are employed by a company, particularly a medium to large company, you will probably have access to a company-sponsored retirement plan such as a 401(k). In a typical plan, you (as the employee) can decide how much money you contribute to the plan by making deductions from your paychecks. In many cases, your employer also makes contributions to the plan. For example, your company could make dollar-for-dollar matching contributions up to a certain percentage of your salary. Even after your contributions hit the maximum amount your employer will match, you can still contribute additional funds. The amount of your total contribution is limited by the Internal Revenue Service (IRS). As of 2010, the contribution limit is $16,500—but this limit is adjusted for inflation annually.

You decide how your 401(k) contributions are invested. Although some companies have retirement plans that allow employees to choose almost any security, most plans use a "menu" format. That is, the company provides a set, or a menu, of investment choices for their employees. Most likely, these choices are mutual funds.

The general investing approach described earlier in this chapter applies to your retirement plan. You decide your percentage allocations to asset classes (like stocks, bonds, and T-bills) and then choose particular assets (e.g., mutual funds) in each asset class. For example, you might decide that you want 75 percent of your retirement funds invested in stocks. Then, you have to make the decision whether you want to invest in U.S. stocks, stocks in other regions of the world, stocks in specific countries, large-company stocks, small-company stocks, or a combination of these categories.

The primary benefit of company-sponsored plans is that they are considered "qualified" accounts for tax purposes. In a qualified account, any money that you deposit into the account is deducted from your taxable income. As a result, your yearly tax bill will be lower, and your net out-of-pocket cost of your deposit is lower. For example, if you are in the 25 percent tax bracket and decide to deposit $12,000 next year, your net out-of-pocket cost is only $9,000. Why? You will pay $3,000 (.25 × $12,000) less in taxes than you would if you had not made this deposit. Of course, nothing is free. You must pay taxes on the withdrawals you make during retirement.

INDIVIDUAL RETIREMENT ACCOUNTS (IRAs) People who do not have access to a company-sponsored plan, or those who simply want another retirement account, can use individual retirement accounts (IRAs). Because an IRA is set up directly with a broker or a bank, these accounts can contain a wide range of assets. In 2010, the maximum contribution to an IRA was $5,000. Annoyingly, the amount you can contribute falls as your income rises. As a result, IRA accounts are not available for every investor.

In terms of tax treatment, there are basically two types of IRAs. With the first type, you pay taxes today on money you earn. If you then invest these aftertax dollars in a retirement savings account, you pay no taxes at all when you take the money out later. This means that dividends, interest, and capital gains are not taxed, which is a big break. Currently, this type of account is called a Roth individual retirement account (Roth IRA).

With the second type of account, you do not pay taxes on the money you earn today if you invest it. Such accounts are "tax-deferred" and are the way most employer-sponsored retirement accounts (such as 401(k) plans) are set up. Later, when you retire, you owe income taxes on whatever you take out of the account.

The two types of accounts really come down to this: You either pay taxes today and do not pay taxes later, or vice versa. It would be great if you could invest pretax dollars and never pay taxes. Alas, this is tax avoidance—which is illegal. Therefore, investors must decide whether to pay taxes now or pay taxes later.

Some circumstances make a Roth IRA preferable to a more traditional tax-deferred IRA. For example, younger investors who are currently in a low tax bracket might be well-suited for a Roth IRA. The reason is that the benefit of tax-free investment growth outweighs the cost of making contributions with income left after taxes. From a behavioral standpoint, a Roth might also be preferred. When determining the amount to contribute, an investor is prone to pick a dollar amount, say, the maximum $5,000. With the Roth IRA, however, investors are actually "investing" more because they are also paying the tax on that portion up front. In any case, whether you choose a Roth or a traditional IRA will depend on personal characteristics like your age and your tax bracket.

OTHER ACCOUNT ISSUES

In an earlier section, we discussed the evolution of the financial services industry from a broker-based system to an advisor-based platform. As a result, different account types have become popular, particularly for investors who desire a more "hands-off" approach to managing their portfolio. For example, if you do not wish to manage your account yourself, you can set up an *advisory account*. In this case, you pay someone else to make buy and sell decisions on your behalf. You are responsible for paying any commissions or other costs, as well as a management fee.

In a relatively recent innovation, brokerage firms have begun to offer *wrap accounts*. In such an account, you choose a money manager or a set of money managers from a group offered by the brokerage firm. All of the costs, commissions, and expenses associated with your account are "wrapped" into a single fee that you pay, hence the name. If you simply authorize your broker to trade for you, then there is no management fee, but you are still responsible for any commissions. This arrangement is termed a *discretionary account*.

Most of the large brokerage firms offer accounts that provide for complete money management, including check-writing privileges, credit cards, and margin loans, especially for larger investors. Such accounts are generally called *asset management accounts*. The terms of these accounts differ from broker to broker, and the services provided frequently change in response to competition.

Finally, if you want to buy and sell a broad variety of individual securities, then a brokerage account is almost a requirement. It is true that some companies and other entities (such as the U.S. government) do sell directly to the public, at least at certain times and possibly with restrictions. So, you can buy securities directly in some cases. In fact, you could buy and sell through the want ads in your local paper if you were so inclined, but given the modest commissions charged by deep-discount brokers, this hardly seems worth the trouble.

You should be aware that if you do not wish to buy and sell securities actively, but you do want to own stocks, bonds, or other financial assets, there is an alternative to a brokerage account: a *mutual fund*. Mutual funds are a means of combining or pooling the funds of a large group of investors. The buy and sell decisions for the resulting pool are then made by a fund manager, who is compensated for the service. Mutual funds have become so important that we devote an entire chapter to them (Chapter 4).

CHECK THIS

2.3a	What is the difference between a cash and margin account?	
2.3b	What is the effect of a margin purchase on gains and losses?	
2.3c	What is a margin call?	

2.4 Types of Positions

Once you have created your investment policy statement and decided which type of investment professional you will employ, your next step is to determine the types of positions you will hold in your account. The two basic positions are long and short.

An investor who buys and owns shares of stock is said to be *long* in the stock or to have a *long position*. An investor with a long position will make money if the price of the stock increases and lose money if it goes down. In other words, a long investor hopes that the price will increase.

Now consider a different situation. Suppose you thought, for some reason, that the stock in a particular company was likely to *decrease* in value. You obviously wouldn't want to buy any of it. If you already owned some, you might choose to sell it.

Beyond this, you might decide to engage in a **short sale**. In a short sale, you actually sell a security that you do not own. This is referred to as *shorting* the stock. After the short sale, the investor is said to have a *short position* in the security.

Financial assets of all kinds are sold short, not just shares of stock, and the terms "long" and "short" are universal. However, the mechanics of a short sale differ quite a bit across security types. Even so, regardless of how the short sale is executed, the essence is the same. An investor with a long position benefits from price increases, and, as we will see, an investor with a short position benefits from price decreases. For the sake of illustration, we focus here on shorting shares of stock. Procedures for shorting other types of securities are discussed in later chapters.

BASICS OF A SHORT SALE

How can you sell stock you don't own? It is easier than you might think: You borrow the shares of stock from your broker and then you sell them. At some future date, you will buy the same number of shares that you originally borrowed and return them, thereby eliminating the short position. Eliminating the short position is often called *covering the position* or, less commonly, *curing the short*.

You might wonder where your broker will get the stock to loan you. Normally, it will simply come from other margin accounts. Often, when you open a margin account, you are asked to sign a loan-consent agreement, which gives your broker the right to loan shares held in the account. If shares you own are loaned out, you still receive any dividends or other distributions and you can sell the stock if you wish. In other words, the fact that some of your stock may have been loaned out is of little or no consequence as far as you are concerned.

An investor with a short position will profit if the security declines in value. For example, assume that you short 2,000 shares of Xerox Corp. (XRX) at a price of $10 per share. You receive $20,000 from the sale (more on this in a moment). A month later, the stock is selling for $8 per share. You buy 2,000 shares for $16,000 and return the stock to your broker, thereby covering your short position. Because you received $20,000 from the sale and it cost you only $16,000 to cover, you made $4,000.

Conventional Wall Street wisdom states that the way to make money is to "buy low, sell high." With a short sale, we hope to do exactly that, just in opposite order—"sell high, buy low." If a short sale strikes you as a little confusing, it might help to think about the everyday use of the terms. Whenever we say that we are "running short" on something, we mean we

short sale

A sale in which the seller does not actually own the security that is sold.

don't have enough of it. Similarly, when someone says "don't sell me short," they mean don't bet on them not to succeed.

The Long and Short of It

Suppose you short 2,000 shares of Alcoa, Inc. (AA), at $15 per share. Six months later you cover your short. If Alcoa is selling for $10 per share at that time, did you make money or lose money? How much? What if you covered at $20?

If you shorted at $15 per share and covered at $10, you originally sold 2,000 shares at $15 and later bought them back at $10, so you made $5 per share, or $10,000. If you covered at $20, you lost $10,000.

SHORT SALES: SOME DETAILS

When you short a stock, you must borrow it from your broker, so you must fulfill various requirements. First, there is an initial margin and a maintenance margin. Second, after you sell the borrowed stock, the proceeds from the sale are credited to your account, but you cannot use them. They are, in effect, frozen until you return the stock. Finally, if any dividends are paid on the stock while you have a short position, you must pay them.

To illustrate, we will again create an account balance sheet. Suppose you want to short 100 shares of Verizon Communications, Inc. (VZ), when the price is $30 per share. This short sale means you will borrow shares of stock worth a total of $30 × 100 = $3,000. Your broker has a 50 percent initial margin and a 40 percent maintenance margin on short sales.

An important thing to keep in mind with a margin purchase of securities is that margin is calculated as the value of your account equity relative to the value of the securities purchased. With a short sale, margin is calculated as the value of your account equity relative to the value of the securities sold short. Thus, in both cases, margin is equal to equity value divided by security value.

In our Verizon Communications example, the initial value of the securities sold short is $3,000 and the initial margin is 50 percent, so you must deposit at least half of $3,000, or $1,500, in your account. With this in mind, after the short sale, your account balance sheet is as follows:

Assets		Liabilities and Account Equity	
Proceeds from sale	$3,000	Short position	$3,000
Initial margin deposit	1,500	Account equity	1,500
Total	$4,500	Total	$4,500

There are many sites devoted to the fine art of short selling. Try www.bearmarketcentral.com

As shown, four items appear on the account balance sheet:

1. *Proceeds from sale.* This is the $3,000 you received when you sold the stock. This amount will remain in your account until you cover your position. Note that you will not earn interest on this amount—it will just sit there as far as you are concerned.

2. *Margin deposit.* This is the 50 percent margin that you had to post. This amount will not change unless there is a margin call. Depending on the circumstances and your particular account agreement, you may earn interest on the initial margin deposit.

3. *Short position.* Because you must eventually buy back the stock and return it, you have a liability. The current cost of eliminating that liability is $3,000.

4. *Account equity.* As always, the account equity is the difference between the total account value ($4,500) and the total liabilities ($3,000).

We now examine two scenarios: (1) the stock price falls to $20 per share, and (2) the stock price rises to $40 per share.

If the stock price falls to $20 per share, then you are still liable for 100 shares, but the cost of those shares is now just $2,000. Your account balance sheet becomes:

Assets		Liabilities and Account Equity	
Proceeds from sale	$3,000	Short position	$2,000
Initial margin deposit	1,500	Account equity	2,500
Total	$4,500	Total	$4,500

Notice that the left-hand side doesn't change. The same $3,000 you originally received is still held, and the $1,500 margin you deposited is still there also. On the right-hand side, the short position is now a $2,000 liability, down from $3,000. Finally, the good news is that the account equity rises by $1,000, so this is your gain. Your margin is equal to account equity divided by the security value (the value of the short position), $2,500/$2,000 = 1.25, or 125 percent.

However, if the stock price rises to $40, things are not so rosy. Now, the 100 shares for which you are liable are worth $4,000:

Assets		Liabilities and Account Equity	
Proceeds from sale	$3,000	Short position	$4,000
Initial margin deposit	1,500	Account equity	500
Total	$4,500	Total	$4,500

Again, the left-hand side doesn't change. The short liability rises by $1,000, and, unfortunately for you, the account equity declines by $1,000, the amount of your loss.

To make matters worse, when the stock price rises to $40, you are severely undermargined. The account equity is $500, but the value of the stock sold short is $4,000. Your margin is $500/$4,000 = 12.5 percent. Since this is well below the 40 percent maintenance margin, you are subject to a margin call. You have two options: (1) buy back some or all of the stock and return it, or (2) add funds to your account.

EXAMPLE 2.6 **A Case of The Shorts**

You shorted 5,000 shares of Collerado Industries at a price of $30 per share. The initial margin is 50 percent, and the maintenance margin is 40 percent. What does your account balance sheet look like following the short?

Following the short, your account becomes:

Assets		Liabilities and Account Equity	
Proceeds from sale	$150,000	Short position	$150,000
Initial margin deposit	75,000	Account equity	75,000
Total	$225,000	Total	$225,000

Notice that you shorted $150,000 worth of stock, so, with a 50 percent margin requirement, you deposited $75,000.

EXAMPLE 2.7

Margin Calls

In our previous example (Example 2.6), at what price per share would you be subject to a margin call?

To answer this one, let $P*$ be the critical price. The short liability then is 5,000 shares at a price of $P*$, or $5,000 \times P*$. The total account value is $225,000, so the account equity is $225,000 - 5,000 \times P*$. We can summarize this information as follows:

$$\text{Short position} = 5,000 \times P*$$

$$\text{Account equity} = \$225,000 - 5,000 \times P*$$

Notice that the total account value, $225,000, is the sum of your initial margin deposit plus the proceeds from the sale, and this amount does not change. Your margin is the account equity relative to the short liability:

$$\text{Margin} = \frac{\text{Account equity}}{\text{Value of stock}}$$

$$= \frac{\text{Initial margin deposit} + \text{Short proceeds} - \text{Number of shares} \times P*}{\text{Number of shares} \times P*}$$

$$= \frac{\$150,000 + 75,000 - 5,000 \times P*}{5,000 \times P*}$$

To find the critical price, we will set this margin equal to the maintenance margin and solve for $P*$:

Maintenance margin

$$= \frac{\text{Initial margin deposit} + \text{Short proceeds} - \text{Number of shares} \times P*}{\text{Number of shares} \times P*}$$

Solving for $P*$ yields:

$$P* = \frac{(\text{Initial margin deposit} + \text{Short proceeds})/\text{Number of shares}}{1 + \text{Maintenance margin}}$$

Finally, setting the maintenance margin equal to 40 percent, we obtain this critical price, $P*$:

$$P* = \frac{\$225,000/5,000}{1.40} = \$32.14$$

At any price *above* $32.14, your margin will be less than 40 percent, so you will be subject to a margin call. So $32.14 is the highest possible price that could be reached before you are subject to a margin call.

As Example 2.7 shows, you can calculate the critical price on a short sale (the highest price before you get a margin call) as follows:

$$P* = \frac{(\text{Initial margin deposit} + \text{Short proceeds})/\text{Number of shares}}{1 + \text{Maintenance margin}}$$

For example, suppose you shorted 1,000 shares at $50. The initial margin is 50 percent, and the maintenance margin is 40 percent. What's the critical stock price, and how do you interpret it?

Noting that the initial margin deposit is $25,000 (50 percent of the short proceeds), see if you don't agree that the critical stock price, $P*$, is $75/1.40 = $53.57. So, if the stock price rises above $53.57, you're subject to a margin call.

You can find the short interest for the current month in many financial publications. But what if you want a longer history of the shares sold short for a particular company? At www.nasdaq.com, you can find the short interest for companies listed on the NASDAQ for the previous 11 months. We went to the site and looked up Yahoo!, and here is what we found:

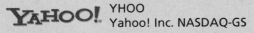

YHOO
Yahoo! Inc. NASDAQ-GS

Settlement Date	Short Interest	Avg Daily Share Volume	Days To Cover
10/30/2009	29,898,547	25,969,381	1.151300
10/15/2009	29,962,155	22,767,581	1.316001
9/30/2009	32,514,374	40,403,980	1.000000
9/15/2009	33,821,416	28,360,885	1.192537
8/31/2009	32,806,719	22,224,522	1.476150
8/14/2009	38,708,292	33,262,975	1.163705
7/31/2009	38,928,957	48,031,220	1.000000
7/15/2009	47,037,295	16,579,959	2.836997
6/30/2009	48,568,110	19,766,704	2.457067

As you can see, the short interest in Yahoo! fell from about 48 million shares in June 2009 to about 30 million shares in October 2009. Why would you want a history of short sales? Some investors use short sales as a technical indicator, which we discuss in a later chapter. Here's a question for you: What do you think "Days to Cover" means?

At this point, you might wonder whether short selling is a common practice among investors. Actually, it is quite common and a substantial volume of stock sales are initiated by short sellers. In fact, the amount of stock held short for some companies can be several tens of millions of shares, and the total number of shares held short across all companies can be several billion shares. To measure the extent of short selling in a particular stock, many investors refer to **short interest**, which is simply the amount of common stock held in short positions. A nearby *Work the Web* box shows how to find short interest for a particular company.

short interest
The amount of common stock held in short positions.

SHORT-SALE CONSTRAINTS

Although short selling stock is relatively easy, you do need to be aware of some constraints related to this type of position. For example, sell orders marked as short sales used to be subject to the **NYSE uptick rule**. According to the NYSE uptick rule, a short sale can be executed only if the last price change was an uptick. For example, suppose the last two trades were executed at 55.50 and then 55.63. The last price change was an uptick of .13, and a short sale can be executed at a price of 55.63 or higher. Alternatively, suppose the last two trades were executed at 55.50 and 55.25, where the last price change was a downtick of .25. In this case, a short sale can be executed only at a price higher than 55.25.

NYSE uptick rule
Rule for short sales requiring that before a short sale can be executed, the last price change must be an uptick.

The NYSE originally enacted the uptick rule to make it more difficult for speculators to drive down a stock's price by repeated short sales. Interestingly, the uptick rule was a NYSE rule only and did not necessarily apply to short-sale transactions executed elsewhere. The uptick rule was repealed in June 2007. However, as you can read in our nearby *Investment Updates* box, the U.S. federal government is seriously considering reinstating the rule.

INVESTMENT UPDATES

SEC MAY RECONSIDER "UPTICK RULE"

The Securities and Exchange Commission will consider as soon as next month restoring a rule that puts the brakes on short-selling in falling markets.

The SEC is expected to propose bringing back the "uptick" rule, which prevented traders from initiating a short sale unless the price of a stock in its most recent trade was higher than the previous price. In a short sale, investors borrow shares and sell them, hoping for the price to fall.

The uptick rule was initially created following the stock market crash of 1929 to prevent bearish investors from ganging up on shares. After years of economic studies that showed the rule wasn't having an impact on market volatility, the SEC abolished it in 2007, around the time financial turmoil was getting under way.

Many traders and others blame the SEC's decision as a factor behind the precipitous declines of some shares over the past two years. Some say that the rule's absence hurt investor psychology, even if it didn't cause market volatility. Reinstating the uptick rule could give the market "a huge shot of confidence," says Brian Bartsch, a trader with Cohen Capital Group.

The SEC is expected to put out for public comment a proposal that would modernize the old uptick rule, a person familiar with the matter said. It is also expected to ask questions about methods of doing so, a person familiar with the matter said.

Under one suggestion, a short sale could take place if someone made a higher bid on a share, even if no trade was completed. The SEC also intends to ask about a potential "circuit-breaker" that could be triggered if a stock fell by a certain amount, the person said. This concept would allow short-selling generally but ban it or limit it via the uptick rule or some other means if the circuit were tripped.

Source: Kara Scannell, *The Wall Street Journal*, March 10, 2009.
Reprinted with permission of *The Wall Street Journal*. © 2009 Dow Jones & Company, Inc. All Rights Reserved Worldwide.

There are other constraints related to government oversight. For example, during the crash of 2008, the Securities and Exchange Commission (SEC) instituted a ban on short selling in an original set of 799 financial companies. The SEC's goal was to limit the downward slide in the market, which the SEC perceived to be strongly related to excessive short selling. Even after the ban, however, financial stocks continued to slide. Combined with other negative effects, many insiders question how effective this ban actually was. Check out our nearby *Investment Updates* box for some additional insight on the short-selling ban.

Besides government intervention, short-sellers face other constraints. For example, not enough shares might be available to short, whether from your particular broker or simply across the entire market. Without shares available to borrow, the short sale cannot take place. This constraint can create effects similar to those of the outright ban instituted by the SEC: reduced liquidity, increased volatility, and inefficient pricing.

We conclude our discussion of short sales with a *very* important observation. With a long position, the most you can ever lose is your total investment. In other words, if you buy $10,000 worth of stock, $10,000 is the most you can lose because the worst that can happen is the stock price drops to zero. However, if you short $10,000 in stock, you can lose *much more* than $10,000 because the stock price can keep rising without any particular limit. In fact, as our previous chapter showed, stock prices do tend to rise, at least on average. With this in mind, potential short sellers should remember the following classic bit of Wall Street wisdom: "He that sells what isn't his'n, must buy it back or go to prison!"[1]

CHECK THIS

2.4a   What is a short sale?

2.4b   Why might an investor choose to short a stock?

2.4c   What is the maximum possible loss on a short sale? Explain.

---

[1] Of course, the same is true for "she that sells what isn't hers'n"; it just doesn't rhyme as well.

2.5 Forming an Investment Portfolio

Let's review the investment process so far. We began by crafting our investment policy statement, detailing our objectives and constraints. Next, we discussed the type of investment professional that might best fit our situation. Then, once the account was opened, we considered whether we wanted a traditional cash account or if we were interested in increasing financial leverage (i.e., risk) using margin. Last, we had to decide whether we wanted to include long or short positions (or both) in our portfolio. With this basic structure in place, we can now consider actual examples of how we would put this process into practice.

Do you remember the risk tolerance quiz that you took earlier in the chapter? What was your score? In this section, we will give you an example of how to take this score, and other investor characteristics, and form an actual portfolio. Of course, many approaches are possible, and we can touch on only a few.

SOME RISK TOLERANCE SCORES

To start, we gave the risk tolerance quiz to 10 students, staff, and faculty at a well-known private university in St. Louis. Their scores and some other information appear in Table 2.1 (their names are changed, but no one is innocent).

As you can see, the scores have a wide range: from 27 to 85. If you look closely, you will see that the average score for the males and females in this very small set of quiz takers is about the same. However, the average score for those investors with little or no investment experience is 47. Those with at least some investment experience have an average score of 61. What do these scores mean?

| TABLE 2.1 | Risk Tolerance Test Results |

Name	Age	Sex	Investment Experience	Score
Lynn	23	F	Little or none	27
Lucy	50	F	Little or none	38
Isabel	28	F	Little or none	73
Brigit	38	F	Little or none	67
Lauren	22	F	Little or none	37
Patrick	29	M	Little or none	41
Imelda	59	F	Less than average	30
Homer	54	M	Average	52
Bart	25	M	Average	77
Marie	21	F	More than average	85

RISK AND RETURN

Risk tolerance is the first thing to assess in evaluating the suitability of an investment strategy. Let's look at the test results for Marie and Imelda.

Marie and Imelda have a sufficient cash reserve. That is, both Marie and Imelda have at least six months' living expenses readily available in a money market account. Of course, these amounts are not the same, largely because of housing and transportation cost differences. Having a sufficient cash reserve means that Marie and Imelda can proceed with building an investment portfolio.

MARIE Marie is a 21-year-old accounting student with more than average investment experience. According to the *Investment Updates* quiz, her score of 85 means Marie should: "Stock up on stocks. On the low end, you're comfortable with larger value stocks; at the high end, riskier midcap and growth stocks work." Okay, but how much of her portfolio should she devote to stock?

To help determine Marie's percentage stock allocation, we will use the rule of thumb from the previous section. That is, an investor's percentage allocation to stock should be equal to his or her age subtracted from 100. For Marie, this is $100 - 21 = 79$ percent (let's call it 80 percent).

Marie has 30+ years to retirement, so she does not have to worry about short-term market volatility. In addition, she is studying diligently so that she can begin her auditing career and earn a steady and relatively high income. Therefore, for now, having 80 percent of her investments devoted to stock seems appropriate.

IMELDA Imelda is about 59 years old. She is a college professor with many advanced degrees. Imelda's score of 30 means that: "Gentlemen (and ladies) prefer bonds, and are most at home with high-grade corporate and government bonds of an intermediate duration."

For Imelda, the rule of thumb shows that she should consider having a portfolio with $100 - 59 = 41$ percent in stocks (let's call it 40 percent). Imelda has 5+ years to retirement, but many years left to enjoy life. Therefore, Imelda has to worry about market volatility in the short term. Her worry stems from the fact that her lofty income will not be available to her when she retires. As a result, Imelda will really have to think long and hard about whether 40 is the appropriate percentage to have invested in stock. Further, using margin would be inappropriate, because the added risk would not be consistent with her risk tolerance.

INVESTOR CONSTRAINTS

In our example, both Marie and Imelda have sufficient *resources*[2] to set up the brokerage accounts that they will use for their investment portfolio, but they have different investment

---

[2] All investor constraints, strategies, and policies appear in *italics*.

horizons. For simplicity, we will assume that both investors prefer highly *liquid* investments. With respect to *taxes*, Marie is currently in a low tax bracket. Therefore, she is likely to elect to pay taxes now and invest in a Roth IRA. Imelda will most likely defer taxes because she is currently in a high tax bracket. So Imelda will most likely try to invest as many pretax dollars as she can. Marie and Imelda will both have to factor in *special circumstances*. For example, Marie might very well have some dependents to support beginning in the next five years or so. Imelda has adult children, but her grandchildren will certainly appreciate her financial support in the years ahead.

STRATEGIES AND POLICIES

With respect to *investment management*, both Marie and Imelda want to avoid the time-consuming activities associated with managing her own investment portfolio. However, each will monitor her portfolio on a monthly basis. Marie and Imelda are convinced that attempts at *market timing* will result in investment underperformance. In addition, both think that *security selection* is a dangerous trap for the unwary. As a result, they both decide to invest in mutual funds (but they have not told us which ones).

Both investors have yet to decide on their *asset allocation*. The asset allocation strategy should provide the highest rate of return given the acceptable level of risk and after accounting for portfolio constraints. Based on their financial resources, financial goals, time horizon, tax status, and risk tolerance, our investors have selected the initial asset allocations seen in Table 2.2.

In addition, you can see that our investors have set holding limits on each asset class. That is, they want to make sure that they do not overinvest in any particular asset class. This can happen if an asset class performs well in relation to the rest.

MORE ON ASSET ALLOCATION

ALLOCATION ACROSS ACCOUNTS Earlier in this chapter, you learned that asset allocation is more important than security selection. Many factors affect asset allocation decisions. Consider the asset allocation given for Imelda in Table 2.2. This allocation plan should reflect her entire portfolio of assets.

For example, suppose Imelda has three different investment accounts: a 401(k), a Roth IRA, and a traditional brokerage account. The asset allocation she has selected does not need to be the same in every account. Can you identify why she might want to choose a different allocation in the 401(k) as opposed to the traditional account?

TABLE 2.2	**Sample Asset Allocations**				
		Marie, 21		**Imelda, 59**	
Asset Class		**Initial Allocation**	**Holding Limit**	**Initial Allocation**	**Holding Limit**
Small-cap stock fund		40%	20–50%	10%	10–20%
Midcap stock fund		20	10–30	5	0–10
Large-cap stock fund		15	5–20	20	10–30
International stock fund		5	0–10	5	0–10
REIT fund		5	0–10	20	15–30
High-yield bond fund		5	0–15	0	0–5
High-quality bond fund		5	0–10	40	25–50
International bond fund		5	0–10	0	0–5

Among the possible reasons, an important one is taxes. Historically, investors pay a lower tax rate on capital gains than they do on cash income. Long-term investments in stocks usually generate considerable capital gains (and some stocks pay a steady stream of dividends). Long-term fixed-income investments usually provide cash income in the form of coupons. The tax-savvy investor would hold non-dividend-paying stocks in taxable brokerage accounts and would hold fixed-income assets in qualified (i.e., tax-deferred) plans. In the case of stocks that pay dividends, the tax-savvy investor would have to judge whether the future dividends will outweigh capital gains and plan accordingly.

Another reason is that with the company-sponsored plan, Imelda would be able to choose from only the menu of funds offered. What happens if a particular asset category is not on the menu? Or, suppose a particular asset category is on the menu, but, in Imelda's opinion, the fund offered just isn't that good? In this case, Imelda could choose the best fund(s) available, regardless of its asset category. Then, she would use her other accounts to complete her overall asset allocation plan.

STRATEGIC VERSUS TACTICAL ALLOCATION As objectives or constraints change, investors will modify their asset allocation. Generally, these changes are infrequent. In other words, a properly selected asset allocation will be relatively stable. This targeted allocation is referred to as the *strategic allocation*. Over time, because asset classes have relatively higher or lower returns, the portfolio will be rebalanced to the targeted strategic allocation.

What if you were actively following the financial markets and you thought that stocks were overvalued relative to bonds? Or, suppose you thought that international stocks will perform better than U.S. stocks? In cases like these, you might use a *tactical asset allocation*. With a tactical asset allocation, you attempt to make smaller, short-term changes to your strategic allocation. The purpose? You are trying to capture added return.

After a period of time, you would shift your allocation back to the longer term strategic allocation. Note well, however, that this tactical asset allocation approach is similar to market timing. You should be aware that considerable debate exists on whether tactical allocation is truly beneficial.

REITS

REIT

A company that owns income-producing real estate.

To learn more about REITS, go to www.investinreits.com

Some quiz results in the *Investment Updates* box earlier in the chapter suggested that investors consider REITs. REITs is an acronym for real estate investment trust(s). You might be unfamiliar with REITs. Briefly, a **REIT** is a company that owns income-producing real estate such as apartments, shopping centers, offices, hotels, and warehouses. The shares of many REITs trade on major stock exchanges. Therefore, REITs provide for a way to make a diversified investment in professionally managed income-producing real estate without having to deal directly with tenants. REITs are risky assets because cash flows from the properties are not guaranteed. However, the portfolio of properties varies from REIT to REIT. Therefore, not all REITs have the same risk.

✓ **CHECK THIS**

2.5a   Besides risk tolerance, what are some other constraints, strategies, and policies that investors use in forming an investment portfolio?

2.5b   Why could two investors of the same age wind up with different investment portfolios?

2.5c   What is the difference between strategic and tactical asset allocation?

2.6 Summary and Conclusions

In this chapter, we cover many aspects of the investing process—which we summarize by the chapter's important concepts.

1. **The importance of an investment policy statement.**

    A. The investment policy statement (IPS) identifies the objectives (risk and return) of an investor, as well as the constraints the investor faces in achieving these objectives.
    B. The IPS provides an investing "road map" and will influence the strategies, type of account, and holdings an investor chooses.

2. **The various types of securities brokers and brokerage accounts.**

    A. Opening a brokerage account is straightforward and really much like opening a bank account. You supply information and sign agreements with your broker. Then you write a check and provide instructions on how you want your money invested.
    B. Brokers are traditionally divided into three groups: full-service brokers, discount brokers, and deep-discount brokers. What distinguishes the three groups is the level of service they provide and the resulting commissions they charge. In recent years, the boundaries among the groups have blurred.
    C. Your broker does not have a duty to provide you with guaranteed purchase and sale recommendations. However, your broker does have a duty to exercise reasonable care in formulating recommendations. Your broker has a legal duty to act in your best interest. However, your broker relies on commissions generated from your account. Therefore, on rare occasions, a broker is accused of "churning" an account (i.e., promoting excessive trading). When you open your brokerage account, you generally agree that disputes will be resolved by binding arbitration.

3. **How to calculate initial and maintenance margin.**

    A. If you have a "cash account," you can purchase securities only to the extent that you can pay for them in full. If you want to buy more stock, you must deposit more cash into your account.
    B. If you have a "margin account," you can purchase securities on credit using money loaned to you by your broker. Generally, you can borrow only half the amount needed to buy the securities.
    C. When you first purchase securities on credit, you must supply a specified minimum amount of money. This minimum amount of money is called initial margin.
    D. After you have purchased securities on margin, the securities can decline in value. If they do, you must follow established rules concerning the amount of money you must keep in your account. This minimum is called maintenance margin. If your account balance falls below the maintenance margin level, you will receive a margin call. In this chapter, we show you how to calculate initial and maintenance margin levels and their effects on your returns.

4. **The workings of short sales.**

    A. An investor who buys and owns shares of stock is said to be long in the stock, or to have a long position. An investor with a long position makes money only if the price of the stock increases.
    B. If you think, for whatever reason, that shares of stock in a particular company are likely to decline in value, you can engage in a short sale. In a short sale, you actually sell a security that you do not own. This is referred to as shorting the stock. After the short sale, the investor is said to have a short position in the security. An investor with a short position makes money only if the shares decrease in value.
    C. In this chapter we describe in detail the short-sale process for shares of stock. We also stress the potentially unlimited losses that can arise from a short position.

This chapter covered the basics of policy statements, brokerage accounts, some important trade types, and, finally, some big-picture issues regarding investment strategies. How should you, as an investor or investment manager, put this information to work?

The answer is that you need to open a brokerage account! Investing is like many activities; the best way to learn is by making mistakes. Unfortunately, making mistakes with real money is an expensive way to learn, so we don't recommend trying things like short sales with real money, at least not at first.

Instead, to learn about how to trade and gain some experience with making (and losing) money, you should open a Stock-Trak account (or a similar simulated brokerage account). Take it seriously. Try various trade types and strategies and see how they turn out. The important thing to do is to follow your trades and try to understand why you made or lost money and also why you made or lost the amount you did.

In a similar vein, you should carefully review your account statements to make sure you understand exactly what each item means and how your account equity is calculated.

After you have gained some experience trading "on paper," you should open a real account as soon as you can pull together enough money. Try visiting some online brokers such as TDAmeritrade to find out the minimum amount you need to open an account. The amount has been declining. In 2010, you could open a cash account for as little as $500, but to open a margin account, you need in the area of $2,000. Or, you can visit www.sharebuilder.com and www.buyandhold.com to open accounts with no money at all!

Looking back at Chapter 1, you know that it's important to get started early. Once you have a real account, however, it's still a good idea to keep a separate "play money" account to test trading ideas to make sure you really understand them before committing your precious real money.

Key Terms

asset allocation 48
call money rate 54
cash account 53
hypothecation 58
initial margin 55
maintenance margin 55
margin 54
margin account 54
margin call 55

market timing 48
NYSE uptick rule 65
REIT 70
Securities Investor Protection
   Corporation (SIPC) 52
security selection 49
short interest 65
short sale 61
street name 58

Chapter Review Problems and Self-Test

1. **The Account Balance Sheet (CFA4)** Suppose you want to buy 10,000 shares of Intel Corporation at a price of $30 per share. You put up $200,000 and borrow the rest. What does your account balance sheet look like? What is your margin?

2. **Short Sales (CFA5)** Suppose that in the previous problem you shorted 10,000 shares instead of buying. The initial margin is 60 percent. What does the account balance sheet look like following the short?

3. **Margin Calls (CFA4)** You purchased 500 shares of stock at a price of $56 per share on 50 percent margin. If the maintenance margin is 30 percent, what is the critical stock price?

Answers to Self-Test Problems

1. The 10,000 shares of Intel cost $300,000. You supply $200,000, so you must borrow $100,000. The account balance sheet looks like this:

Assets		Liabilities and Account Equity	
10,000 shares of Intel	$300,000	Margin loan	$100,000
		Account equity	200,000
Total	$300,000	Total	$300,000

Your margin is the account equity divided by the value of the stock owned:

$$\text{Margin} = \$200,000/\$300,000$$
$$= .666 \ldots$$
$$= 67\%$$

2. Following the short, your account is as follows:

Assets		Liabilities and Account Equity	
Proceeds from sale	$300,000	Short position	$300,000
Initial margin deposit	180,000	Account equity	180,000
Total	$480,000	Total	$480,000

Notice that you shorted $300,000 worth of stock, so, with a 60 percent margin requirement, you deposited $180,000.

3. The lowest price the stock can drop before you receive a margin call is:

$$P^* = \frac{\text{Amount borrowed/Number of shares}}{1 - \text{Maintenance margin}}$$

You borrowed $500 \times \$56 \times .50 = \$14,000$. Therefore:

$$P^* = \frac{14,000/500}{1 - .30} = \$40.00$$

You will receive a margin call if the stock drops below $40.00.

Test Your Investment Quotient

1. **Investment Objectives (LO1, CFA8)** An individual investor's investment objectives should be expressed in terms of:
   a. Risk and return.
   b. Capital market expectations.
   c. Liquidity needs and time horizon.
   d. Tax factors and legal and regulatory constraints.

2. **Asset Allocation (LO1, CFA2)** Which of the following best reflects the importance of the asset allocation decision to the investment process? The asset allocation decision:
   a. Helps the investor decide on realistic investment goals.
   b. Identifies the specific securities to include in a portfolio.
   c. Determines most of the portfolio's returns and volatility over time.
   d. Creates a standard by which to establish an appropriate investment horizon.

3. **Leverage (LO3, CFA4)** You deposit $100,000 cash in a brokerage account and purchase $200,000 of stocks on margin by borrowing $100,000 from your broker. Later, the value of your stock holdings falls to $150,000, whereupon you get nervous and close your account. What is the percentage return on your investment (ignore interest paid)?

   a. 0 percent
   b. −25 percent
   c. −50 percent
   d. −75 percent

4. **Leverage (LO4, CFA5)** You deposit $100,000 cash in a brokerage account and short sell $200,000 of stocks. Later, the value of the stocks held short rises to $250,000, whereupon you get nervous and close your account. What is the percentage return on your investment?

   a. 0 percent
   b. −25 percent
   c. −50 percent
   d. −75 percent

5. **Account Margin (LO3, CFA4)** You deposit $100,000 cash in a brokerage account and purchase $200,000 of stocks on margin by borrowing $100,000 from your broker. Later, the value of your stock holdings falls to $175,000. What is your account margin in dollars?

   a. $50,000
   b. $75,000
   c. $100,000
   d. $150,000

6. **Account Margin (LO3, CFA4)** You deposit $100,000 cash in a brokerage account and purchase $200,000 of stocks on margin by borrowing $100,000 from your broker. Later, the value of your stock holdings falls to $150,000. What is your account margin in percent?

   a. 25 percent
   b. 33 percent
   c. 50 percent
   d. 75 percent

7. **Account Margin (LO4, CFA5)** You deposit $100,000 cash in a brokerage account and short sell $200,000 of stocks on margin. Later, the value of the stocks held short rises to $225,000. What is your account margin in dollars?

   a. $50,000
   b. $75,000
   c. $100,000
   d. $150,000

8. **Account Margin (LO4, CFA5)** You deposit $100,000 cash in a brokerage account and short sell $200,000 of stocks on margin. Later, the value of the stocks held short rises to $250,000. What is your account margin in percent?

   a. 20 percent
   b. 25 percent
   c. 33 percent
   d. 50 percent

9. **Margin Calls (LO3, CFA4)** You deposit $100,000 cash in a brokerage account and purchase $200,000 of stocks on margin by borrowing $100,000 from your broker, who requires a maintenance margin of 30 percent. Which of the following is the largest value for your stock holdings for which you will still receive a margin call?

   a. $200,000
   b. $160,000
   c. $140,000
   d. $120,000

10. **Margin Calls (LO4, CFA5)** You deposit $100,000 cash in a brokerage account and short sell $200,000 of stocks. Your broker requires a maintenance margin of 30 percent. Which of the following is the lowest value for the stocks you are holding short for which you will still receive a margin call?

   a. $260,000
   b. $240,000

    c. $220,000

    d. $200,000

11. **Investment Decisions (LO1, CFA7)** Which of the following investment factors, strategies, or tactics is the least relevant to a passive investment policy?

    a. Market timing

    b. Asset allocation

    c. Political environment

    d. Tax status

12. **Investment Decisions (LO1, CFA2)** Which of the following investment factors, strategies, or tactics is most associated with an active investment policy?

    a. Market timing

    b. Asset allocation

    c. Security selection

    d. Tax status

13. **Investment Decisions (LO1, CFA8)** Which of the following investment strategies or tactics will likely consume the greatest amount of resources, time, effort, and so on, when implementing an active investment policy?

    a. Market timing

    b. Asset allocation

    c. Security selection

    d. Tax strategy

14. **Investment Decisions (LO1, CFA2)** Which of the following investment strategies or tactics is likely the most relevant in the decision to short sell a particular stock?

    a. Market timing

    b. Asset allocation

    c. Security selection

    d. Tax strategy

15. **Investment Constraints (LO1, CFA5)** Which of the following investment constraints is expected to have the most fundamental impact on the investment decision process for a typical investor?

    a. Investor's tax status

    b. Investor's time horizon

    c. Investor's need for liquidity

    d. Investor's attitude toward risk

Concept Questions

1. **Margin (LO3, CFA4)** What does it mean to purchase a security on margin? Why might you do it?

2. **Short Sales (LO4, CFA5)** What does it mean to sell a security short? Why might you do it?

3. **Margin Requirements (LO3, CFA4)** What is the reason margin requirements exist?

4. **Allocation versus Selection (LO1, CFA2)** What is the difference between asset allocation and security selection?

5. **Allocation versus Timing (LO1, CFA10)** Are market timing and tactical asset allocation similar? Why or why not?

6. **Brokers versus Advisors (LO2, CFA11)** To an investor, what is the difference between using an advisor and using a broker?

7. **Broker–Customer Relations (LO2, CFA11)** Suppose your broker tips you on a hot stock. You invest heavily, but, to your considerable dismay, the stock plummets in value. What recourse do you have against your broker?

8. **Long Profits (LO4, CFA5)** An important difference between a long position in stock and a short position concerns the potential gains and losses. Suppose a stock sells for $18 per share, and you buy 500 shares. What are your potential gains and losses?

9. **Liquidity (LO4, CFA5)** The liquidity of an asset directly affects the risk of buying or selling that asset during adverse market conditions. Describe the liquidity risk you face with a short stock position during a market rally, and a long stock position during a market decline.

10. **Taxes (LO4, CFA9)** How will personal tax rates impact the choice of a traditional versus a Roth IRA?

Questions and Problems

Core Questions

1. **Calculating Margin (LO3, CFA4)** Carson Corporation stock sells for $17 per share, and you've decided to purchase as many shares as you possibly can. You have $31,000 available to invest. What is the maximum number of shares you can buy if the initial margin is 60 percent?

2. **Margin (LO3, CFA4)** You purchase 750 shares of 2nd Chance Co. stock on margin at a price of $35. Your broker requires you to deposit $14,000. What is your margin loan amount? What is the initial margin requirement?

3. **Margin Return (LO3, CFA4)** In the previous problem, suppose you sell the stock at a price of $42. What is your return? What would your return have been had you purchased the stock without margin? What if the stock price is $34 when you sell the stock?

4. **Margin (LO3, CFA4)** Repeat the previous two problems assuming the initial margin requirement is 30 percent. Does this suggest a relationship between the initial margin and returns?

5. **Margin Purchases (LO3, CFA4)** You have $22,000 and decide to invest on margin. If the initial margin requirement is 55 percent, what is the maximum dollar purchase you can make?

6. **Margin Calls (LO3, CFA4)** You buy 400 shares of stock at a price of $55 and an initial margin of 60 percent. If the maintenance margin is 30 percent, at what price will you receive a margin call?

7. **Margin Calls (LO3, CFA5)** You decide to buy 1,200 shares of stock at a price of $34 and an initial margin of 55 percent. What is the maximum percentage decline in the stock before you will receive a margin call if the maintenance margin is 35 percent?

8. **Margin Calls on Short Sales (LO4, CFA5)** The stock of Flop Industries is trading at $17. You feel the stock price will decline, so you short 900 shares at an initial margin of 60 percent. If the maintenance margin is 30 percent, at what share price will you receive a margin call?

9. **Margin Calls on Short Sales (LO4, CFA5)** You short sold 1,000 shares of stock at a price of $36 and an initial margin of 55 percent. If the maintenance margin is 35 percent, at what share price will you receive a margin call? What is your account equity at this stock price?

10. **Taxes and Returns (LO1, CFA9)** You purchased a stock at the end of the prior year at a price of $81. At the end of this year the stock pays a dividend of $1.80 and you sell the stock for $97. What is your return for the year? Now suppose that dividends are taxed at 15 percent and long-term capital gains (over 11 months) are taxed at 30 percent. What is your aftertax return for the year?

Intermediate Questions

11. **Calculating Margin (LO3, CFA4)** Using the information in Problem 1, construct your equity account balance sheet at the time of your purchase. What does your balance sheet look like if the share price rises to $24? What if it falls to $14 per share? What is your margin in both cases? Round the number of shares down to the nearest number of whole shares.

12. **Calculating Margin (LO3, CFA4)** You've just opened a margin account with $11,000 at your local brokerage firm. You instruct your broker to purchase 600 shares of Landon Golf stock, which currently sells for $46 per share. What is your initial margin? Construct the equity account balance sheet for this position.

13. **Margin Call (LO3, CFA4)** Suppose you purchase 500 shares of stock at $48 per share with an initial cash investment of $8,000. If your broker requires a 30 percent maintenance margin, at what share price will you be subject to a margin call? If you want to keep your position open despite the stock price plunge, what alternatives do you have?

14. **Margin and Leverage (LO3, CFA4)** In the previous problem, suppose the call money rate is 5 percent and you are charged a 1.5 percent premium over this rate. Calculate your return on investment for each of the following share prices one year later. Ignore dividends.
    a. $56
    b. $48
    c. $32

76 Part 1 ■ Introduction

Suppose instead you had simply purchased $8,000 of stock with no margin. What would your rate of return have been now?

15. **Margin and Leverage (LO3, CFA4)**   Suppose the call money rate is 6.8 percent, and you pay a spread of 1.9 percent over that. You buy 1,000 shares at $51 per share with an initial margin of 40 percent. One year later, the stock is selling for $57 per share, and you close out your position. What is your return assuming no dividends are paid?

16. **Margin and Leverage (LO3, CFA4)**   Suppose the call money rate is 4.5 percent, and you pay a spread of 2.5 percent over that. You buy 800 shares of stock at $34 per share. You put up $15,000. One year later, the stock is selling for $48 per share, and you close out your position. What is your return assuming a dividend of $.64 per share is paid?

17. **Margin Interest (LO3, CFA4)**   Suppose you take out a margin loan for $50,000. The rate you pay is an 8.4 percent effective rate. If you repay the loan in six months, how much interest will you pay?

18. **Margin Interest (LO3, CFA4)**   Suppose you take out a margin loan for $39,000. You pay a 5.8 percent effective rate. If you repay the loan in two months, how much interest will you pay?

19. **Annualized Returns (CFA1)**   Suppose you hold a particular investment for seven months. You calculate that your holding-period return is 6 percent. What is your annualized return?

20. **Annualized Returns (CFA1)**   In the previous question, suppose your holding period was five months instead of seven. What is your annualized return? What do you conclude in general about the length of your holding period and your annualized return?

21. **Annualized Returns (CFA1)**   Suppose you buy stock at a price of $57 per share. Five months later, you sell it for $61. You also received a dividend of $.60 per share. What is your annualized return on this investment?

22. **Calculating Returns (CFA1)**   Looking back at Problem 12, suppose the call money rate is 6 percent and your broker charges you a spread of 1.25 percent over this rate. You hold the stock for six months and sell at a price of $53 per share. The company paid a dividend of $.25 per share the day before you sold your stock. What is your total dollar return from this investment? What is your effective annual rate of return?

23. **Short Sales (LO4, CFA5)**   You believe that Rose, Inc., stock is going to fall and you've decided to sell 800 shares short. If the current share price is $47, construct the equity account balance sheet for this trade. Assume the initial margin is 100 percent.

24. **Short Sales (LO4, CFA5)**   Repeat the previous problem assuming you short the 800 shares on 75 percent margin.

25. **Calculating Short Sale Returns (LO4, CFA5)**   You just sold short 750 shares of Wetscope, Inc., a fledgling software firm, at $96 per share. You cover your short when the price hits $86.50 per share one year later. If the company paid $.75 per share in dividends over this period, what is your rate of return on the investment? Assume an initial margin of 60 percent.

26. **Short Sales (LO4, CFA5)**   You believe the stock in Freeze Frame Co. is going to fall, so you short 600 shares at a price of $72. The initial margin is 50 percent. Construct the equity balance sheet for the original trade. Now construct an equity balance sheet for a stock price of $63 and a stock price of $77. What is your margin at each of these stock prices? What is your effective annual return if you cover your short position at each of these prices in five months?

CFA Exam Review by Schweser

[CFA1, CFA7, CFA10, CFA11]

Barbara Analee, a registered nurse and businesswoman, recently retired at age 50 to pursue a life as a blues singer. She had been running a successful cosmetics and aesthetics business. She is married to Tom, a retired scientist (age 55). They have saved $3 million in their portfolio and now they want to travel the world. Their three children are all grown and out of college and have begun their own families. Barbara now has two grandchildren. Barbara and Tom feel that they have achieved a comfortable portfolio level to support their family's needs for the foreseeable future.

To meet their basic living expenses, Tom and Barbara feel they need $75,000 per year in today's dollars (before taxes) to live comfortably. As a trained professional, Barbara likes to be actively involved in intensively researching investment opportunities. Barbara and Tom want to be able to provide $10,000 per year (pretax) indexed for inflation to each of their grandchildren over the next 10 years for their college education. They also want to set aside $15,000 each year (pretax) indexed for inflation for traveling for her musical performances around the United States. They have no debt. Most of their portfolio is currently in large-cap U.S. stocks and Treasury notes.

They have approached Pamela Jaycoo, CFA, for guidance on how to best achieve their financial goals. Inflation is expected to increase at an annual rate of 3 percent into the foreseeable future.

1. What is the Analee's return objective?

   a. 6.67 percent
   b. 6.17 percent
   c. 3.83 percent

2. What is their tolerance for risk?

   a. Average
   b. Below average
   c. Above average

3. What is Barbara's willingness and ability to assume risk?

Willingness	Ability
a. Above average	Average
b. Below average	Average
c. Above average	Above average

4. Based on the information in the case, which one of the following portfolios should the Analees choose?

	Expected Return	Allocation		
		Portfolio A	Portfolio B	Portfolio C
U.S. large stocks	9%	20%	5%	10%
U.S. small stocks	10	20	15	10
Foreign stocks	12	15	15	10
Corp. bonds	5	15	0	35
Gov. bonds	3	10	0	25
Venture capital	11	5	30	0
REITs	15	10	30	0
Cash	1	5	5	10
Pretax return		8.8%	11.6%	5.7%
Aftertax return		5.6%	7.4%	3.6%
Aftertax yield		1.9%	1.9%	2.8%

   a. Portfolio A
   b. Portfolio B
   c. Portfolio C

What's on the Web?

1. **Risk Tolerance** As we discussed in the chapter, risk tolerance is based on an individual's personality and investment goals. There are numerous risk tolerance questionnaires on the Web. One, provided by Merrill Lynch, is located at individual.ml.com. Go to the Web site, locate the questionnaire, and take the quiz. How conservative or aggressive are you?

2. **Short Interest** You can find the number of short sales on a particular stock at finance.yahoo.com. Go to the site and find the number of shares short sold for ExxonMobil (XOM) under the "Key Statistics" link. How many shares are sold short in the current month? What about the previous month? What do the "Percent of Float" and "Short Ratio" mean?

3. **Broker Call Money Rate** What is the current broker call money rate? To find out, go to www.money-rates.com and look up the call money rate.

4. **Margin Purchases**   Suppose you have a margin account with TDAmeritrade. You purchase 1,000 shares of IBM stock on 50 percent margin at today's price. Go to finance.yahoo.com to find your purchase price. Ignoring transaction costs, how much will you borrow? Next, go to www.money-rates.com to find the current broker call money rate. Finally, go to www.TDAmeritrade.com to find out how much above the current broker call money rate you will pay. If you keep your investment for one year, how much will you pay in interest assuming the margin rate stays the same? What does the stock price have to be in one year for you to break even on your investment?

Stock-Trak Exercises

To access the Stock-Trak Exercise for this chapter, please visit the book Web site at www.mhhe.com/jmd6e and choose the corresponding chapter.

CHAPTER 3

Overview of Security Types

Learning Objectives

Price quotes for all types of investments are easy to find, but what do they mean? Learn the answers for:

1. Various types of interest-bearing assets.
2. Equity securities.
3. Futures contracts.
4. Option contracts.

"An investment operation is one which upon thorough analysis promises safety of principal and an adequate return. Operations not meeting these requirements are speculative."

–Benjamin Graham

You invest $5,000 in Yahoo! common stock and just months later sell the shares for $7,500, realizing a 50 percent return. Not bad! At the same time, your neighbor invests $5,000 in Yahoo! stock options, which are worth $25,000 at expiration—a 400 percent return. Yahoo! Alternatively, your Yahoo! shares fall in value to $2,500, and you realize a 50 percent loss. Too bad! But at the same time your neighbor's Yahoo! stock options are now worthless. Clearly, there is a big difference between stock shares and stock options. Security type matters. ∎

Our goal in this chapter is to introduce you to some of the different types of securities that are routinely bought and sold in financial markets around the world. As we mentioned in Chapter 1, we will be focusing on financial assets such as bonds, stocks, futures, and options in this book, so these are the securities we briefly describe here. The securities we discuss are covered in much greater detail in the chapters ahead, so we touch on only some of their most essential features in this chapter.

For each of the securities we examine, we ask three questions. First, what is its basic nature and what are its distinguishing characteristics? Second, what are the potential gains and losses from owning it? Third, how are its prices quoted in the financial press?

CFA™ Exam Topics in This Chapter:

1 Discounted cash flow applications (L1, S2)
2 Features of debt securities (L1, S15)
3 Forward markets and contracts (L1, S17)
4 Option markets and contracts (L1, S17)

Go to www.mhhe.com/jmd6e for a guide that aligns your textbook with CFA readings.

3.1 Classifying Securities

To begin our overview of security types, we first develop a classification scheme for the different securities. As shown in Table 3.1, financial assets can be grouped into three broad categories, and each of these categories can be further subdivided into a few major subtypes. This classification is not exhaustive, but it covers the major types of financial assets. In the sections that follow, we describe these assets in the order they appear in Table 3.1.

When we examine some of these security types in more detail, we will see that the distinctions can become a little blurred, particularly with some recently created financial instruments; as a result, some financial assets are hard to classify. The primary reason is that some instruments are hybrids, meaning that they are combinations of the basic types.

As you may have noticed in our discussion, financial assets, such as bonds and stocks, are often called securities. They are often called financial "instruments" as well. In certain contexts, there are distinctions between these terms, but they are used more or less interchangeably in everyday discussion, so we will stick with common usage.

TABLE 3.1	Classification of Financial Assets	
	Basic Types	**Major Subtypes**
	Interest-bearing	Money market instruments
		Fixed-income securities
	Equities	Common stock
		Preferred stock
	Derivatives	Futures
		Options

CHECK THIS

3.1a   What are the three basic types of financial assets?

3.1b   Why are some financial assets hard to classify?

3.2 Interest-Bearing Assets

Broadly speaking, interest-bearing assets (as the name suggests) pay interest. Some pay interest implicitly and some pay it explicitly, but the common denominator is that the value of these assets depends, at least for the most part, on interest rates. The reason that these assets pay interest is that they all begin life as a loan of some sort, so they are all debt obligations of some issuer.

There are many types of interest-bearing assets. They range from the relatively simple to the astoundingly complex. We discuss some basic types and their features next. The more complex types are discussed in later chapters.

MONEY MARKET INSTRUMENTS

money market instruments

Debt obligations of large corporations and governments with an original maturity of one year or less.

For the most part, **money market instruments** are the simplest form of interest-bearing asset. Money market instruments generally have the following two properties:

1. They are essentially IOUs sold by large corporations or governments to borrow money.
2. They mature in less than one year from the time they are sold, meaning that the loan must be repaid within one year.

Most money market instruments trade in very large denominations, and most, but not all, are quite liquid.

The most familiar example of a money market instrument is a Treasury bill, or T-bill for short. Every week, the U.S. Treasury borrows billions of dollars by selling T-bills to the public. Like many (but not all) money market instruments, T-bills are sold on a *discount basis*. This simply means that T-bills are sold at a price that is less than their stated face value. In other words, an investor buys a T-bill at one price and later, when the bill matures, receives the full face value. The difference is the interest earned.

U.S. Treasury bills are the most liquid type of money market instrument—that is, the type with the largest and most active market. Other types of money market instruments traded in active markets include bank certificates of deposit (or CDs) and corporate and municipal money market instruments.

The potential gain from buying a money market instrument is fixed because the owner is promised a fixed future payment. The most important risk is the risk of default, which is the possibility that the borrower will not repay the loan as promised. With a T-bill, there is no possibility of default, so, as we saw in Chapter 1, T-bills are essentially risk-free. In fact, most money market instruments have relatively low risk, but there are exceptions, and a few spectacular defaults have occurred in the past.

Prices for different money market instruments are quoted in the financial press in different ways. In fact, usually interest rates are quoted, not prices, so some calculation is necessary to convert rates to prices. The procedures are not complicated, but they involve a fair amount of detail, so we save them for another chapter.

FIXED-INCOME SECURITIES

fixed-income securities

Longer-term debt obligations, often of corporations and governments, that promise to make fixed payments according to a preset schedule.

Fixed-income securities are exactly what the name suggests: securities that promise to make fixed payments according to some preset schedule. The other key characteristic of a fixed-income security is that, like a money market instrument, it begins life as a loan of some sort. Fixed-income securities are therefore debt obligations. They are typically issued by corporations and governments. Unlike money market instruments, fixed-income securities have lives that exceed 12 months at the time they are issued.

The words "note" and "bond" are generic terms for fixed-income securities, but "fixed income" is more accurate. This term is being used more frequently as securities are increasingly being created that don't fit within traditional note or bond frameworks but are nonetheless fixed-income securities.

EXAMPLES OF FIXED-INCOME SECURITIES To give one particularly simple example of a fixed-income security, near the end of every month, the U.S. Treasury sells between $25 billion and $35 billion of two-year notes to the public. If you buy a two-year note when it is issued, you will receive a check every six months for two years for a fixed amount, called the bond's *coupon*, and in two years you will receive the face amount on the note.

Suppose you buy $1 million in face amount of a 4 percent, two-year note. The 4 percent is called the *coupon rate*, and it tells you that you will receive 4 percent of the $1 million face value each year, or $40,000, in two $20,000 semiannual "coupon" payments. In two years, in addition to your final $20,000 coupon payment, you will receive the $1 million face value. The price you would pay for this note depends on market conditions. U.S. government security prices are discussed in detail in a later chapter.

current yield

Annual coupon divided by the current bond price.

You must be careful not to confuse the *coupon rate* with **current yield**. The current yield is the annual coupon divided by the current bond price. For most bonds, the coupon rate never changes. But the current yield fluctuates with the price of the bond.

EXAMPLE 3.1	A "Note-Worthy" Investment?

Suppose you buy $100,000 in face amount of a just-issued five-year U.S. Treasury note. If the coupon rate is 5 percent, what will you receive over the next five years if you hold on to your investment?

You will receive 5 percent of $100,000, or $5,000, per year, paid in two semiannual coupons of $2,500. In five years, in addition to the final $2,500 coupon payment, you will receive the $100,000 face amount.

WORK THE WEB

Corporate bond quotes have become more available with the rise of the Internet. One site where you can find current corporate bond prices is www.nasdbondinfo.com. We went there and looked for bonds issued by 3M Co. (MMM), long known as Minnesota Mining and Manufacturing Company. Here is a look at some of these bonds:

Bond Symbol	Issuer Name	Coupon	Maturity	Callable	Ratings			Last Sale	
					Moody's	S&P	Fitch	Price	Yield
MMM.GS	3M COMPANY	4.50	11/01/2011	No	Aa2	AA-	NR	106.571	0.945
MMM.GQ	3M COMPANY	4.65	12/15/2012	No	Aa2	AA-	NR	109.181	1.500
MMM.GR	3M COMPANY	4.38	08/15/2013	No	Aa2	AA-	NR	107.810	2.143
MMM.GD	3M COMPANY	0.04	09/30/2027	No	Aa2	AA-	NR	97.500	-
MMM.GB	3M COMPANY	6.38	02/15/2028	Yes	Aa2	AA-	NR	114.332	5.150

December 15, 2009

We will focus on the last bond in the list. The bond has a coupon rate of 6.38 percent and matures on February 15, 2028. The last sale price of this bond was 114.332, which gives a yield to maturity of 5.15 percent. Then, by clicking on the link for this bond, we obtained this more detailed information for the bond:

Item Description

Bond Type:	US Corporate Debentures	Industry:	Industrial
Last Price:	$114.332	Industry Sub-Sector	Manufacturing
Yield:	5.15000%	Tax Status:	-
Callable:	Yes	Insurance	-
Moody's Rating (Assignment Date):	Aa2 (05/01/2009)	Redemption Type:	-
S&P Rating (Assignment Date):	AA- (03/18/2009)	Pre-refund:	No
Fitch Rating (Assignment Date):	NR (10/27/2000)		
Pay Frequency:	Semi-Annual		
First Coupon Date:	08/15/1998		

Not only does the site provide the most recent price and yield information, but we also find out that the fixed coupon rate is paid semiannually, and the bond is callable. The credit rating for this bond is Aa2 from Moody's and AA- from Standard & Poor's.

WWW

Check out bond basics
www.investing
inbonds.com

WWW

To learn more about
TRACE, visit
www.finra.org

To give a slightly different example, suppose you take out a 48-month car loan. Under the terms of the loan, you promise to make 48 payments of $400 per month. It may not look like it to you, but in taking out this loan, you have issued a fixed-income security to your bank. In fact, your bank may turn around and sell your car loan (perhaps bundled with a large number of other loans) to an investor. Actually, car loans are not sold all that often, but there is a very active market in student loans, which are routinely bought and sold in huge quantities.

FIXED-INCOME PRICE QUOTES Corporate bond dealers now report trade information through what is known as the Trade Reporting and Compliance Engine (TRACE). As this is written, daily transaction prices are reported on thousands of bonds. A nearby *Work the Web* box shows you how to get data from TRACE through one handy Web site.

FIGURE 3.1 Corporate Bond Trading

Print this page
Last updated: 12/14/2009 at 6:45 PM ET

Market Breadth

	All Issues	Investment Grade	High Yield	Convertibles
Total Issues Traded	5,779	4,079	1,475	225
Advances	2,833	1,915	770	148
Declines	2,414	1,834	516	64
Unchanged	216	108	100	64
52 Week High	625	345	249	31
52 Week Low	46	32	14	31
Dollar Volume *	17,674	11,956	4,595	1,123

About This Information:
End of Day data. Activity as reported to FINRA TRACE (Trade Reporting and Compliance Engine). The Market breadth information represents activity in all TRACE eligible publicly traded securities. The most active information represent the most active fixed-coupon bonds (ranked by par value traded). Inclusion in Investment Grade or High Yield tables based on TRACE dissemination criteria. "C" indicates yield is unavailable because of issue's call criteria.

* Par value in millions.

Most Active Investment Grade Bonds

Issuer Name	Symbol	Coupon	Maturity	Rating Moody's/S&P/Fitch	High	Low	Last	Change	Yield %
CITIGROUP	C.GOR	6.375%	Aug 2014	A3/A/A+	107.481	105.333	106.967	-0.099	4.689
CITIBANK NA	C.HSO	2.250%	Dec 2012	Aaa/AAA/AAA	101.922	100.000	101.879	-0.111	1.602
JPMORGAN CHASE & CO	JPM.LUA	1.650%	Feb 2011	Aaa/AAA/AAA	101.523	101.162	101.523	0.391	0.356
JPMORGAN CHASE & CO	JPM.LUC	2.200%	Jun 2012	Aaa/AAA/AAA	102.306	95.596	102.164	0.082	1.317
CITIBANK NA	C.HSP	1.625%	Mar 2011	Aaa/AAA/AAA	101.355	101.355	101.355	0.046	0.570
MORGAN STANLEY	MS.HDO	2.900%	Dec 2010	Aaa/AAA/AAA	102.450	102.292	102.321	-0.036	0.470
PETROBRAS INTL FINANCE CO	PBR.GO	7.875%	Mar 2019	Baa1/BBB-/BBB	116.300	115.250	116.125	0.275	5.613
TIME WARNER CABLE	TWCA.GM	8.250%	Apr 2019	Baa2/BBB/BBB	121.080	120.721	121.064	0.550	5.342
ANADARKO PETROLEUM CORP	APC.HE	5.950%	Sep 2016	Baa3/BBB-/BBB-	110.302	106.000	110.215	1.581	4.194
CENTENNIAL COMM CORP	CYCL.GK	10.000%	Jan 2013	—/A/A	105.250	105.100	105.250	0.000	4.077

Source: www.wsj.com, December 15, 2009. Reprinted with permission of *The Wall Street Journal*. © 2009 Dow Jones & Company, Inc. All Rights Reserved Worldwide.

As shown in Figure 3.1, *The Wall Street Journal* provides an online daily snapshot of the data from TRACE by reporting information on the most active investment-grade bonds. Information for the most active high-yield bonds and convertible bonds is available, too. Most of the information is self-explanatory.

EXAMPLE 3.2 **Corporate Bond Quotes**

In Figure 3.1, which bond has the longest maturity? Assuming a face value of $1,000 each, how much would you have to pay for 100 of these bonds?

The bond with the longest maturity is the Time Warner Cable bond with an 8.25 percent coupon. It matures in April 2019. Based on the reported last price, the price you would pay is $121.064 percent of face value per bond. Assuming a $1,000 face value, this amount is $1,210.64 per bond, or $121,064 for 100 bonds.

The potential gains from owning a fixed-income security come in two forms. First, there are the fixed payments promised and the final payment at maturity. In addition, the prices of most fixed-income securities rise when interest rates fall, so there is the possibility of a gain from a favorable movement in rates. An unfavorable change in interest rates will produce a loss.

Another significant risk for many fixed-income securities is the possibility that the issuer will not make the promised payments. This risk depends on the issuer. It doesn't exist for U.S. government bonds, but for many other issuers the possibility is very real. Finally, unlike most money market instruments, fixed-income securities are often quite illiquid, again depending on the issuer and the specific type.

CHECK THIS

3.2a	What are the two basic types of interest-bearing assets?
3.2b	What are the two basic features of a fixed-income security?

3.3 Equities

Equities are probably the most familiar type of security. They come in two forms: common stock and preferred stock. Of these, common stock is much more important, so we discuss it first.

COMMON STOCK

WWW

Are you a Foolish
investor? Go to
www.fool.com
and find the 13 steps.

Common stock represents ownership in a corporation. If you own 1,000 shares of IBM, for example, then you own about .0000763 percent of IBM (IBM has roughly 1.31 billion shares outstanding). It's really that simple. As a part owner, you are entitled to your pro rata share of anything paid out by IBM, and you have the right to vote on important matters regarding IBM. If IBM were to be sold or liquidated, you would receive your share of whatever was left over after all of IBM's debts and other obligations (such as wages) were paid.

The potential benefits from owning common stock come primarily in two forms. First, many companies (but not all) pay cash dividends to their shareholders. However, neither the timing nor the amount of any dividend is guaranteed. At any time, it can be increased, decreased, or omitted altogether. Dividends are paid strictly at the discretion of a company's board of directors, which is elected by the shareholders.

The second potential benefit from owning stock is that the value of your stock may rise because share values overall increase or because the future prospects for your particular company improve (or both). The downside is just the reverse: your shares may lose value if either the economy or your particular company falters. As we saw back in Chapter 1, both the potential rewards and the risks from owning common stock have been substantial, particularly shares of stock in smaller companies.

PREFERRED STOCK

The other type of equity security, preferred stock, differs from common stock in several important ways. First, the dividend on a preferred share is usually fixed at some amount and never changed. Further, in the event of liquidation, preferred shares have a particular face value. The reason that preferred stock (or preference stock, as it is sometimes termed) is called "preferred" is that a company must pay the fixed dividend on its preferred stock before any dividends can be paid to common shareholders. In other words, preferred shareholders must be paid first.

The dividend on a preferred stock can be omitted at the discretion of the board of directors, so, unlike a debt obligation, there is no legal requirement that the dividend be paid (as long as the common dividend is also skipped). However, some preferred stock is *cumulative,* meaning that any and all skipped dividends must be paid in full (although without interest) before common shareholders can receive a dividend.

Potential gains from owning preferred stock consist of the promised dividend plus any gains from price increases. The potential losses are just the reverse: the dividend may be skipped, and the value of your preferred shares may decline from either marketwide decreases in value or diminished prospects for your particular company's future business (or both).

Preferred stock issues are not rare, but they are much less frequently encountered than common stock issues. Most preferred stock is issued by large companies, particularly banks and public utilities.

In many ways, preferred stock resembles a fixed-income security; in fact, it is sometimes classified that way. In particular, preferred stocks usually have a fixed payment and a fixed liquidation value (but no fixed maturity date). The main difference is that preferred stock is not a debt obligation. Also, for accounting and tax purposes, preferred stock is treated as equity.

FIGURE 3.2   Closing Prices: Most Widely Held

Most Widely Held: Closing Table

Friday, January 02, 2009

NOTICE TO READERS: This table will no longer update because we lost our source. We apologize for the inconvenience.

Alphabetical listing of stocks with the largest institutional ownership based on the most recent Form 13-F SEC filings.

Stocks' trends based on a comparison of three moving averages (20-day, 50-day and 100-day), as supplied by www.investorsintelligence.com, based on the Dow Jones Wilshire 5000 universe. **Bullish** (▲) Shorter-term moving averages hold above longer-term (20-day>50-day>100-day). **Bearish** (▼) Shorter-term moving averages have crossed below longer-term (20-day<50-day<100-day). **No trend** (◄►) No trend symbol means the company is not in the DJ Wilshire 5000 universe.

Trend	Company	Symbol	Volume	DAILY Close	DAILY Chg	DAILY % Chg	YTD % chg	52 WEEK High	52 WEEK Low	52 WEEK % Chg
▼	AES Corp	AES	4,482,481	$8.64	0.40	4.85	4.9	$22.48	$5.80	-59.1
◄►	AT & T Inc	T	17,910,823	29.42	0.92	3.23	3.2	41.94	20.90	-28.1
▼	Abbott Labs	ABT	6,141,264	53.56	0.19	0.36	0.4	61.09	45.75	-4.0
▼	Alcoa Inc	AA	30,346,605	12.11	0.85	7.55	7.5	44.77	6.80	-65.3
▼	Altria Group Inc	MO	17,150,923	15.20	0.14	0.93	0.9	24.55	14.34	-34.2
▼	American Express	AXP	9,944,782	19.33	0.78	4.20	4.2	52.63	16.55	-60.7
▼	Amer Int'l Group	AIG	30,704,752	1.69	0.12	7.64	7.6	59.42	1.25	-96.9
▲	Amgen Inc	AMGN	5,671,545	58.99	1.24	2.15	2.1	66.51	39.16	31.7
▼	Apple Inc	AAPL	25,645,808	90.75	5.40	6.33	6.3	192.24	79.14	-49.6
▼	Applied Materials	AMAT	8,460,726	10.67	0.54	5.33	5.3	21.75	7.80	-36.4
▼	Bank of America	BAC	81,080,655	14.33	0.25	1.78	1.8	45.08	10.01	-64.0
▼	Bank of NY Mellon	BK	5,660,821	28.52	0.19	0.67	0.7	49.38	20.49	-40.8
▼	Boston Scientific	BSX	9,445,638	7.88	0.14	1.81	1.8	14.22	5.41	-30.3
▲	Bristol-Myers	BMY	8,857,354	23.88	0.63	2.71	2.7	27.37	16.00	-7.3
▼	CVS Caremark	CVS	5,704,577	29.38	0.64	2.23	2.2	44.29	23.19	-21.2
▼	Chevron Corp	CVX	11,735,919	76.52	2.55	3.45	3.4	104.63	55.50	-18.0
▼	Cisco Systems	CSCO	37,078,688	16.96	0.66	4.05	4.0	27.72	14.20	-35.1

Source: www.wsj.com, January 3, 2009. Reprinted with permission of *The Wall Street Journal*. © 2009 Dow Jones & Company Inc. All Rights Reserved Worldwide.

Preferred stock is a good example of why it is sometimes difficult to neatly and precisely classify every security type. To further complicate matters, some preferred stock issues have dividends that are not fixed. So it seems clear that these securities are not fixed-income securities. However, some bond issues make no fixed payments and allow the issuer to skip payments under certain circumstances. As we mentioned earlier, these are examples of hybrid securities.

To give a more difficult example, consider a *convertible bond*. Such a bond is an ordinary bond in every way except that it can be exchanged for a fixed number of shares of stock anytime at the bondholder's discretion. Whether this is really a debt or equity instrument is difficult (or even impossible) to say.

COMMON STOCK PRICE QUOTES

Unlike fixed-income securities, the price quotes on common and preferred stock are fairly uniform. Part of the common stock page found at www.wsj.com can be seen in Figure 3.2. Locate the entry for Apple (AAPL).

In the first column, you see a red arrow pointed downward. This arrow is a trend indicator that says the average price for Apple stock over the past 20 days is lower than the average price for Apple stock over the past 50 days. In addition, the average price for Apple stock over the past 50 days is less than the average price for Apple stock over the past 100 days. We have much more to say about technical indicators, including trend indicators, in a later chapter.

The second and third columns contain the company name and its ticker symbol. The next piece of information, Volume, is the actual number of shares traded for the day: 25,645,808. Because investors usually trade stock in multiples of 100 shares, called "round lots," sometimes you will see volume figures reported in multiples of hundreds.

WORK THE WEB

Throughout this chapter, we have looked at information available online at www.wsj.com. One problem is that prices reported are sometimes from the previous day. Before you trade, you'll want more up-to-date prices, particularly in fast-moving markets. Using an Internet server, such as Yahoo!, let's get some intraday prices. Here, we entered a ticker symbol ("JWN" for Nordstrom, Inc.).

Most of the information here is self-explanatory. The abbreviation "Market Cap" is short for "market capitalization," which is the total value of all outstanding shares. Notice, on this particular day, JWN was up 1.26 percent, compared to the $40.42 ("Prev Close") that you would see in the print version of *The Wall Street Journal*. We'll discuss other unfamiliar terms, such as "Bid" and "Ask," a little later in the book. For now, a good exercise is to select a detailed quote yourself and find out what information is in the links below the stock quote.

As noted, the free quotes available at finance.yahoo.com during the day are generally delayed by 20 minutes or so. These days, you can also see "real-time" quotes. These are even provided at the top of the quote.

For example, if you wanted to report Apple's volume in round lots, you would report volume as 256,458.

The next three columns contain Apple's share price at the close of trading, the share price change ("Chg") measured in dollars, and the percent change from the previous day's closing price ("% Chg"). You can see that Apple shares closed at $90.75, which is $5.40 higher than the previous day. In percent change terms, you can verify that the closing price is 6.33 percent higher than the previous closing price. The closing price is the last price at which a trade occurred before regular trading hours ended at 4:00 P.M. EST.

The last three numbers (labeled "52 WEEK High," "Low," and "% Chg") are the highest and lowest price per share that the stock has sold for over the past 52 weeks. Thus, Apple's stock sold for as high as $192.24 per share and as low as $79.14 per share. Based on its share price 52 weeks ago, Apple shares have declined by 49.6 percent.

You can also get preferred stock quotes at www.wsj.com. They appear in a separate section with a relatively simple format. Of course, the information contained in *The Wall Street Journal* and at www.wsj.com can be obtained online in many other places, too. The above *Work the Web* box describes one way.

INVESTMENT UPDATES

THE TALE OF THE TAPE

The on-air "ticker tape" is a familiar sight on television, particularly on financially oriented shows and networks. The most widely watched such channel is CNBC. All day long, at the bottom of the screen, two rolls of information scroll by.

On CNBC, the upper band shows trading on the New York Stock Exchange, and the lower band shows trading on the NASDAQ Stock Market. A lot of other information (too much, in fact, for us to cover here) will also scroll by.

To learn more, go to nasdaq.com and install "The NASDAQ Stock Ticker" toolbar (or desktop). Follow the installation instructions, and you will be able to create your own ticker that you can display on your computer screen. A personalized ticker allows you to track just the stocks that interest you the most. We created our own ticker:

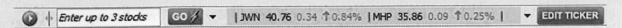

If you click on "custom," you can add your own list of stock symbols. You can make this ticker run forward or backward, and you can even pause it. If you see an interesting news headline flash by, you can click on it and read the pop-up window. Many other free stock tickers are available online. (We Googled "free stock ticker" and got about 22,000 results.)

The display is called a "ticker" because, at one time, it was printed on a thin strip of "ticker tape" (paper) by a "ticker" machine (so named because of the sound it made while printing). In fact, the reason for ticker symbols in the first place was to make information quicker and easier to print. Perhaps you have seen old film footage of a "ticker tape parade" in New York. The paper that rains down on the celebrities and dignitaries is ticker tape.

Ticker machines date to an era before television (if you can imagine such a time). The first one was introduced in 1867 and was later improved upon by none other than Thomas Edison. To learn more, visit the Web site www.stocktickercompany.com.

FIGURE 3.3 Top Yielding Stocks, Basic Resources Sector

Stock Scan: Dividend Stocks

TOP-YIELDING STOCKS

GO TO: WAYS TO INVEST FOR DIVIDENDS: Stocks With Fastest Dividend Growth | High-Yielding Mutual Funds | ETFs

Monday, December 14, 2009   Find Historical Data | WHAT'S THIS?

Stocks with the highest dividend yields in the day's best performing U.S. sectors, ranked by dividend yield.

| Div amt | Div % yld | Index/Core stock | Symbol | Mkt cap† | DAILY | | | YTD % chg | 52-WEEK RANGE | | | | P/E ratio |
					Close	Chg	% Chg		Low	Close (●)	High	% Chg	
...	2.17	Basic Resources	...	...	2281.87	46.50	2.08	69.0	1021.16		2343.49	73.0	...
$1.52	10.31	Penn Virginia GP Hldgs	PVG	$576	$14.75	-0.13	-0.87	48.5	$8.08		$17.42	22.9	17
1.88	9.16	Penn Virginia Res	PVR	1,063	20.52	0.21	1.03	80.5	9.10		20.81	73.3	32
2.16	8.99	Natural Res Prtnrs	NRP	1,668	24.02	-0.13	-0.54	37.7	15.86		25.47	32.0	18
3.04	7.26	Alliance Rsrc Prtn	ARLP	1,520	41.90	2.11	5.30	55.9	23.87		42.41	60.5	13
1.76	7.04	AllianceHldgGP LP	AHGP	1,496	24.99	0.56	2.29	68.9	12.29		25.00	58.9	14
1.06	6.84	Brookfield Infrastr Ptrns	BIP	348	15.49	0.05	0.32	38.3	7.15		18.64	40.2	8
1.44	3.36	Nucor Corp	NUE	13,430	42.83	0.58	1.37	-7.3	29.84		51.08	-0.5	-*
0.40	3.27	Worthington Indus	WOR	969	12.22	0.23	1.92	10.9	6.99		16.42	-5.3	-*
0.36	2.91	Glatfelter	GLT	562	12.35	0.12	0.98	32.8	4.57		12.43	39.5	6
0.40	2.80	Neenah Paper	NP	209	14.31	-0.24	-1.65	61.9	3.26		15.50	67.6	-*

"REBALANCING" YOUR PORTFOLIO CAN BE A TOUGH RIDE

Another market truism—regular rebalancing of your portfolio guarantees higher return and lower risk—has bit the dust. Rebalancing ensures that you buy low and sell high. It can work. But that doesn't mean it always works.

History suggests that resetting back to a target mix of stocks and bonds should add about half a percentage point per year to your average rate of return—over the course of several decades. In the short run, however, if stocks keep dropping for years on end, then rebalancing mightn't add anything; in fact, it can subtract.

Much like the choice of whether to invest in stocks at all, rebalancing is a bet about the future. Buying low and selling high is a great idea over time, but not all the time. As many investors have learned painfully over the past 16 months or so, if what you bought keeps going lower and what you sold keeps going higher, then rebalancing will backfire.

Consider two simplified examples. First, with the help of Morningstar Inc., we will look at the worst bear market on record, the Great Depression; then let's study the past 15 years, with two huge bull markets and two nasty bears.

From its peak in August and September 1929, what is now the Standard & Poor's 500 index went on to lose more than 83%, hitting bottom in June 1932. Over the same period, intermediate Treasury bonds went up 12.4%. Even with dividends reinvested, an all-stock portfolio didn't recover its 1929 high until January 1945. At that point, bonds were up 00.3%.

If you had gone 50/50 in stocks and bonds at the start and let it ride, you would have lost 35.5% by June 1932. Had you rebalanced every 12 months, selling enough bonds and buying enough stocks to get you back to your half-and-half split, you would have lost 48.2%. Rebalancing more often than annually would have made your losses even worse.

In short, you would have been better off crawling into a cave for three years than rebalancing.

On the upswing, rebalancing earned its keep. By the beginning of 1945, a portfolio that was 50/50 in 1929 and never readjusted would have gained 40.5% cumulatively, while rebalancing your portfolio at least annually would have yielded a cumulative gain of at least 53.7%. Once both stocks and bonds went up, especially since they went up at different rates, rebalancing could work its cure.

What about the past 15 years?

If you'd invested $10,000 in a 50/50 mix of stocks and bonds in December 1993, you'd have had $24,419 by December 1999. Then it was almost straight downhill; by September 2002, you would have had $19,240 left. Rebalancing would have yielded almost the same result. That's because bonds went up almost every single month over that period, while stocks kept crashing.

After 2002 came another long upswing and then the recent brutal drop. How would this have affected your original $10,000 invested in 1993? If you rebalanced annually, by this February [2009] you still would have had $24,967 left. That is $4,000 more than if you had been 100% in stocks all along and $2,400 more than if you had invested your money 50/50 and never touched it after that.

What's the lesson from all this?

For younger investors with horizons of several decades, rebalancing is probably a chance worth taking. But you shouldn't feel compelled to rebalance constantly; once a year is plenty. Pick a date that will never vary and that you will always remember, like your birthday. If you are retired, rebalancing into stocks could hurt more than it may help; catching a butcher-block full of falling knives is a risk you mightn't be able to afford to take. I will still rebalance on my next birthday, because I am nowhere near retirement and I know I don't know what the future holds.

The bottom line: Whether rebalancing will heal or hurt your portfolio depends not only on what the markets do but also how they do it. Even techniques that are supposed to reduce risk carry risks of their own.

To interpret this information, you will need to know the company's ticker symbol. The ticker symbol is a unique combination of letters assigned to each company. Nordstrom's ticker symbol, for example, is JWN.

Stock price information is also available all day long on television and on the Web. Our *Investment Updates* box on page 88 explains how to interpret a very common sight on television, the on-air ticker. As explained there, once you understand the display, you can actually create your own ticker to track the investments that interest you the most.

Some investors want a list of companies that pay dividends. A sample of such a list from www.wsj.com appears in Figure 3.3. Notice that much of the information is similar to the information in Figure 3.2. However, you can find some additional information on dividends, dividend yields, and price-earnings ratios.

You can see that this list is for a group of stocks in the "Basic Resources Sector." Locate the entry for Nucor Corp. (NUE). Nucor is classified in the Basic Resources Sector because Nucor manufactures steel.

The first two columns in Figure 3.3 are the dividend amount and dividend yield, $1.44 and 3.36 percent, respectively, for Nucor. Like most dividend-paying companies, Nucor pays dividends on a quarterly basis. The dividend number reported here, $1.44, is actually four times the most recent quarterly dividend. The dividend yield is this annualized dividend divided by the closing price.

The last column contains the price-earnings ratio, or "P/E ratio." This ratio, as the name suggests, is equal to the price per share divided by earnings per share. Earnings per share is calculated as the sum of earnings per share over the last four quarters. We will discuss dividends, dividend yields, and price-earnings ratios in detail in a later chapter.

CHECK THIS

3.3a   What are the two types of equity securities?

3.3b   Why is preferred stock sometimes classified as a fixed-income security?

3.4 Derivatives

There is a clear distinction between real assets, which are essentially tangible items, and financial assets, which are pieces of paper describing legal claims. Financial assets can be further subdivided into primary and derivative assets. A **primary asset** (sometimes called a *primitive asset*) is a security that was originally sold by a business or government to raise money, and a primary asset represents a claim on the assets of the issuer. Thus, stocks and bonds are primary financial assets.

In contrast, as the name suggests, a **derivative asset** is a financial asset that is derived from an existing primary asset rather than issued by a business or government to raise capital. As we will see, derivative assets usually represent claims either on other financial assets, such as shares of stock or even other derivative assets, or on the future price of a real asset such as gold. Beyond this, it is difficult to give a general definition of the term "derivative asset" because there are so many different types, and new ones are created almost every day. On the most basic level, however, any financial asset that is not a primary asset is a derivative asset.

To give a simple example of a derivative asset, imagine that you and a friend buy 1,000 shares of a dividend-paying stock, perhaps the Nucor stock we discussed. You each put up half the money, and you agree to sell your stock in one year. Furthermore, the two of you agree that you will get all the dividends paid while your friend gets all the gains or absorbs all the losses on the 1,000 shares.

This simple arrangement takes a primary asset, shares of Nucor stock, and creates two derivative assets, the dividend-only shares that you hold and the no-dividend shares held by your friend. Derivative assets such as these actually exist, and there are many variations on this basic theme.

Two types of derivative assets, futures and options, are particularly important. Many other types exist, but they can usually be built up from these two basic types, possibly by combining them with other primary assets. Futures are the simpler of the two, so we discuss them first.

FUTURES CONTRACTS

In many ways, a futures contract is the simplest of all financial assets. A **futures contract** is just an agreement made today regarding the terms of a trade that will take place later. For example, suppose you know that you will want to buy 100 ounces of gold in six months.

primary asset
Security originally sold by a business or government to raise money.

derivative asset
A financial asset that is derived from an existing traded asset rather than issued by a business or government to raise capital. More generally, any financial asset that is not a primary asset.

futures contract
An agreement made today regarding the terms of a trade that will take place later.

One thing you could do is to strike a deal today with a seller in which you promise to pay, say, $1,000 per ounce in six months for the 100 ounces of gold. In other words, you and the seller agree that six months from now, you will exchange $100,000 for 100 ounces of gold. The agreement that you have created is a futures contract.

With your futures contract, you have locked in the price of gold six months from now. Suppose that gold is actually selling for $1,050 per ounce in six months. You benefit from having entered into the futures contract because you have to pay only $1,000 per ounce. However, if gold is selling for $950, you lose because you are forced to pay $1,000 per ounce. Thus, a futures contract is risky because the future price of gold can differ from the futures contract price today. Notice that with your futures contract, no money changes hands today.

After entering into the futures contract, what happens if you change your mind in, say, four months, and you want out of the contract? The answer is that you can sell your contract to someone else. You would generally have a gain or a loss when you sell. The contract still has two months to run. If market participants generally believe that gold will be worth more than $1,000 when the contract matures in two months, then your contract is valuable, and you would have a gain if you sold it. If, on the other hand, market participants think gold will not be worth $1,000, then you would have a loss on the contract if you sold it because you would have to pay someone else to take it off your hands.

Futures contracts are traded all over the world on many types of assets, and futures contracts can be traced back to ancient civilizations. As we discuss in detail in a later chapter, there are two broad categories of futures contracts: *financial futures* and *commodity futures*. The difference is that, with financial futures, the underlying asset is intangible, usually stocks, bonds, currencies, or money market instruments. With commodity futures, the underlying asset is a real asset, typically either an agricultural product (such as cattle or wheat) or a natural resource product (such as gold or oil).

FUTURES PRICE QUOTES

An important feature of traded futures contracts is that they are *standardized*, meaning that one contract calls for the purchase of a specific quantity of the underlying asset. Further, the contract specifies in detail what the underlying asset is and where it is to be delivered. For example, with a wheat contract, one contract specifies that 5,000 bushels of a particular type of wheat will be delivered at one of a few approved locations on a particular date in exchange for the agreed-upon futures price.

In Figure 3.4, futures price quotations for U.S. Treasury bonds (or "T-bonds" for short) are seen as they appear online at www.wsj.com. A nearby *Work the Web* contains links for

---

FIGURE 3.4   Futures Trading

Interest Rate Futures | Index | Agricultural | Currency | Metals & Petroleum

Monday, December 14, 2009   Find Historical Data | WHAT'S THIS?

KEY TO EXCHANGES: CBT: Chicago Board of Trade; CME: Chicago Mercantile Exchange; CMX: Comex; DME: Dubai Mercantile Exchange; ENXT: Euronext.liffe; EUREX: EUREX; ICE-EU: ICE Futures Europe; ICE-US: ICE Futures U.S.; KC: Kansas City Board of Trade; ME: Montreal Exchange; MPLS: Minneapolis Grain Exchange; NYM: New York Mercantile Exchange, or Nymex; SGX-DT: Singapore Exchange Derivatives Trading Ltd

Treasury Bonds (CBT)-$100,000; pts 32nds of 100%

	Open	High	Low	Settle	Chg	LIFETIME High	(▲▼)	Low	Open Int
Dec 09	119-030	119-090	118-220	119-030	+6.0	136-300		110-000	23,707
Mar 10	117-210	118-070	117-170	118-010	+6.0	123-030		112-120	677,820
Jun 10	116-120	116-150	116-120	116-180	+6.0	121-040		112-090	83

Est vol 147,350; vol Fri 281,506; open int, 701,611, −6,425.

Futures price quotes have also become more available with the rise of the Internet. The primary site for finding futures price quotes is www.cmegroup.com.

At the CME Group, futures contracts for grains (e.g., corn, wheat, soybeans), interest rates (U.S. Treasury notes and bonds, German bonds), and Dow Jones Index Futures are listed. A complete list of all the contracts traded can be found on the Web site. Each futures contract has some unique aspects. For example, here is a sample soybean futures screen from the CME Group's Web site.

Soybeans Futures

Quotes | Contract Specifications | Performance Bonds / Margins | Product Calendar | Learn More

| Quotes | Time & Sales | Volume | Settlements | | | | | | Trade Date: 12/15/2009 |

Globex Futures | Open Outcry Futures — Market Data is delayed at least 10 minutes

View Spread Quotes ▸ — Turn Auto-refresh OFF | ℹ About this Report

Month	Charts	Last	Change	Prior Settle	Open	High	Low	Volume	Hi / Lo Limit	Updated
Jan 2010 OPT	⬚ ⬚	1054'6	-0'2	1055'0	1054'6	1068'4	1049'4	79885	1125'0 985'0	1:55:53 PM CST 12/15/2009
Mar 2010 OPT	⬚ ⬚	1061'6	0'0	1061'6	1061'0	1074'6	1056'0	46756	1131'6 991'6	1:55:53 PM CST 12/15/2009
May 2010 OPT	⬚ ⬚	1066'2	0'0	1066'2	1066'0	1077'6	1060'0	13125	1136'2 996'2	1:55:53 PM CST 12/15/2009
Jul 2010 OPT	⬚ ⬚	1070'6	+1'2	1069'4	1069'2	1081'2	1063'4	15705	1139'4 999'4	1:55:53 PM CST 12/15/2009
Aug 2010 OPT	⬚ ⬚	1066'4 a	+2'4	1064'0	1065'0	1074'4	1060'0	665	1134'0 994'0	1:40:23 PM CST 12/15/2009
Sep 2010 OPT	⬚ ⬚	1044'6 a	+0'6	1044'0	1041'4	1050'4 b	1036'6	416	1114'0 974'0	1:40:23 PM CST 12/15/2009

Locate the line that starts with May 2010. This is a very active futures contract that calls for May delivery of 5,000 bushels of soybeans. Note that these quotes are obtained at the end of the day's trading. By convention, soybean prices are still quoted in cents and eighths of a cent even though the minimum price change is one-fourth cent, or two-eighths of a cent. Under the "Last" column, you can see an entry of 1066'2, which is 1,066 and 2/8 cents, or $10.66⅛. The daily low was 1060'0, which is 1060 and 0/8 cents, or $10.60.

The volume of 13,125 says that there have been 13,125 futures contracts traded. This volume represents 13,125 × 5,000 = 65,625,000 bushels.

Understanding futures markets, their use, and their quoting conventions takes a great deal of study. Your school might even offer a course where you can study futures markets in depth.

futures price quotes. Looking at Figure 3.4, we see these are quotes for delivery of T-bonds with a total par, or face, value of $100,000. The letters CBT indicate to us where this contract is traded; in this case, it is the Chicago Board of Trade (part of the CME Group).

The first column in Figure 3.4 tells us the delivery date for the bond specified by the contract. For example, the "Dec 09" indicates that the first contract listed is for T-bond delivery in December 2009. The second is for delivery in March 2010. Following the delivery month, we have a series of prices. In order, we have the open price, the high price, the low price, and the settle price. The open price is the price at the start of the trading day, the high and low are highest and lowest prices for the day, and the settle is a price reflecting the trades at the end of the day. The "Chg" is the change in the settle price from the previous trading day.

The columns labeled "LIFETIME High" and "LIFETIME Low" refer to the highest and lowest prices over the life of this contract. Finally, the "Open Int" tells us how many contracts are currently outstanding.

To get a better idea of how T-bond futures contracts work, suppose you buy one December contract at the settle price. What you have done is agree to buy T-bonds with a total par value of $100,000 in September at a price of 119-03 per $100 of par value, where the "03" represents 3/32. Thus, 119-03 can also be written as 119 3/32, which represents a price of $119,093.75 per $100,000 face value. No money changes hands today. However, if you take no further action, when December rolls around your T-bonds will be delivered, and you must pay for them at that time.

Actually, most futures contracts don't result in delivery. Most buyers and sellers close out their contracts before the delivery date. To close out a contract, you take the opposite side. For example, suppose that with your one T-bond contract, you later decide you no longer wish to be in it. To get out, you simply sell one contract, thereby canceling your position.

GAINS AND LOSSES ON FUTURES CONTRACTS

Futures contracts have the potential for enormous gains and losses. To see why, let's consider again buying T-bond contracts based on the settle prices in Figure 3.4. To make matters somewhat more interesting, suppose you buy 15 March contracts at the settle price of 118-01 per $100 of par value.

One month later, perhaps because of falling inflation, the futures price of T-bonds for March delivery rises five dollars to 123-01. This may not seem like a huge increase, but it generates a substantial profit for you. You have locked in a price of 118-01 per $100 par value. The price has risen to 123-01, so you make a profit of $5 per $100 of par value, or $5,000 per $100,000 face value. With 15 contracts, each of which calls for delivery of $100,000 in face value of T-bonds, you make a tidy profit of 15 × $5,000 = $75,000. Of course, if the price had decreased by five dollars, you would have lost $75,000 on your 15-contract position.

EXAMPLE 3.3   **Future Shock**

It is July. Suppose you purchase five September T-bond contracts at a settle price of 115-22. How much will you pay today? Suppose in one month you close your position and the September futures price at that time is 110-21. Did you make or lose money? How much?

When you purchase the five contracts, you pay nothing today because the transaction is for September. However, you have agreed to pay 115-22 per $100 par value. If, when you close your position in a month, the futures price is 110-21, you have a loss of 115-22 − 110-21 = 5 1/32 per $100 par value, or 5 1/32 × 1,000 = $5,031.25 per contract. Your total loss is thus $5,031.25 × 5 contracts, or $25,156.25 in all (ouch!).

CHECK THIS

3.4a   What is a futures contract?

3.4b   What are the general types of futures contracts?

3.4c   Explain how you make or lose money on a futures contract.

3.5 Option Contracts

option contract
An agreement that gives the owner the right, but not the obligation, to buy or sell a specific asset at a specified price for a set period of time.

An **option contract** is an agreement that gives the owner the right, but not the obligation, to buy or sell (depending on the type of option) a specific asset at a specific price for a specific period of time. The most familiar options are stock options. These are options to buy or sell shares of stock, and they are the focus of our discussion here. Options are a very flexible investment tool, and a great deal is known about them. We present some of the most important concepts here; our detailed coverage begins in a later chapter.

OPTION TERMINOLOGY

Options come in two flavors, calls and puts. The owner of a **call option** has the right, but not the obligation, to *buy* an underlying asset at a fixed price for a specified time. The owner of a **put option** has the right, but not the obligation, to *sell* an underlying asset at a fixed price for a specified time.

Options occur frequently in everyday life. Suppose, for example, that you are interested in buying a used car. You and the seller agree that the price will be $3,000. You give the seller $100 to hold the car for one week, meaning that you have one week to come up with the $3,000 purchase price, or else you lose your $100.

This agreement is a call option. You paid the seller $100 for the right, but not the obligation, to buy the car for $3,000. If you change your mind because, for example, you find a better deal elsewhere, you can just walk away. You'll lose your $100, but that is the price you paid for the right, but not the obligation, to buy. The price you pay to purchase an option, the $100 in this example, is called the **option premium**.

A few other definitions will be useful. First, the specified price at which the underlying asset can be bought or sold with an option contract is called the **strike price**, the *striking price,* or the *exercise price.* Using an option to buy or sell an asset is called *exercising* the option.

The *last trading day* for all listed stock options in the United States is the third Friday of the option's expiration month (except when Friday falls on a holiday, in which case the last trading day is the third Thursday). The *expiration day* for stock options is the Saturday immediately following the last trading day. The expiration day is the last day (in the case of *American-style* options) or the only day (in the case of *European-style* options) on which an option may be *exercised.*

OPTIONS VERSUS FUTURES

Our discussion thus far illustrates the two crucial differences between an option contract and a futures contract. The first is that the purchaser of a futures contract is *obligated* to buy the underlying asset at the specified price (and the seller of a futures contract is obligated to sell). The owner of a call option has the right, but not the obligation, to buy.

The second important difference is that when you buy a futures contract you pay no money at the time of purchase (and you receive none if you sell). However, if you buy an option contract, you pay the premium at the time of the purchase; if you sell an option contract, you receive the premium at the time of the sale.

OPTION PRICE QUOTES

Like futures contracts, most option contracts are standardized. One call option contract, for example, gives the owner the right to buy 100 shares (one round lot) of stock. Similarly, one put option contract gives the owner the right to sell 100 shares.

Figure 3.5 presents intraday 20-minute delay quotes for call and put options on Nike common stock. The data is from finance.yahoo.com. To obtain these option quotes, enter a ticker symbol (here: NKE), then find and click the option link. At the time these quotes were obtained, Nike stock was trading at $74.68.

The first column in Figure 3.5 lists strike prices for options with September expiration. More precisely, these options expire at the close of trading on September 17, 2010. Option data for other expiration months can be obtained by clicking on other views.

The second column is the unique symbol for each option. Until early 2010, option ticker symbols had five letters. For example, the Nike September 75 call option would have been designated NKEIO. The "NKE" stands for Nike; the "I" represents September (for calls, expiration months corresponded to the letters A through L, so, for calls, the ninth month was assigned the ninth letter of the alphabet, I); and the "O" would refer to the strike price. Note that the symbol for the Nike September 75 put option would have been NKEUO. For

FIGURE 3.5   Options Trading

| View By Expiration: **Sep 10** | Oct 10 | Jan 11 | Apr 11 | Jan 12 | Jan 13 | | | | | | |

Call Options — Expire At Close Friday, September 17, 2010

Strike	Symbol	Last	Chg	Bid	Ask	Vol	Open Int
65.00	NKE100918C00065000	**7.07**	0.00	9.55	9.70	1	1
67.50	NKE100918C00067500	**4.55**	0.00	7.10	7.30	62	119
70.00	NKE100918C00070000	**4.83**	↑ 0.31	4.60	4.75	6	817
72.50	NKE100918C00072500	**2.43**	↑ 0.71	2.25	2.33	7	1,512
75.00	NKE100918C00075000	**0.64**	↑ 0.32	0.51	0.54	139	2,256
80.00	NKE100918C00080000	**0.04**	0.00	N/A	0.04	1	258

Put Options — Expire At Close Friday, September 17, 2010

Strike	Symbol	Last	Chg	Bid	Ask	Vol	Open Int
65.00	NKE100918P00065000	**0.02**	0.00	N/A	0.04	25	1,204
67.50	NKE100918P00067500	**0.04**	↓ 0.02	0.02	0.04	2	1,725
70.00	NKE100918P00070000	**0.11**	0.00	0.04	0.07	45	1,606
72.50	NKE100918P00072500	**0.34**	0.00	0.15	0.17	11	1,493
75.00	NKE100918P00075000	**0.89**	↓ 0.64	0.86	0.91	418	1,100
80.00	NKE100918P00080000	**6.35**	0.00	5.30	5.45	3	197

☐ Highlighted options are in-the-money.

Source: finance.yahoo.com, September 13, 2010.

puts, expiration months corresponded to the letters M through X. So, for puts, the ninth month would have received the twenty-first letter of the alphabet, U.

The method of decoding option symbols described above had been the industry standard for years. Beginning in early 2010, however, the exchanges incorporated a new system for option symbols. The idea is to expand the symbol from 5 basic letters to a larger combination of letters and numbers. The goal is to reduce confusion by explicitly stating the underlying stock symbol, option expiration date, whether the option is a call or a put, the dollar part of the strike price, and the decimal part of the strike price. Figure 3.5 provides the "new" option symbols for Nike. Whether quadrupling the size of the ticker will reduce confusion, we do not know. We discuss this change in more detail in a later chapter.

Returning to Figure 3.5, columns three and four list last sale prices and the change from the previous close. Current bid and ask prices appear in the next two columns. The bid price is the price *you* will receive if you want to sell an option at the prevailing market price; the ask price is the price *you* will pay if you want to buy an option at the prevailing market price. Volume and open interest numbers appear in the last two columns. Volume is the number of contracts traded that day. Open interest is the number of contracts outstanding.

Referring to the Nike 75 call options, we see that 139 call option contracts have been traded so far in this trading day, and the last transaction price for this option was $0.64 per share. Because each listed option contract actually involves 100 shares, the price per contract was $0.64 × 100 = $64.00.

The bid and ask prices reflect current market conditions, not the market conditions that prevailed at the time of the last transaction price. Based on the bid and ask prices, what price would you pay now for one of these call options? Remember, the ask price is the price *you* pay, so you would pay $0.54 per share, or $54 for the contract. If you were selling, you would sell at the bid price of $0.51 per share, or $51 for the contract.

Suppose you wanted the right to buy 500 shares of Nike for $70 sometime before September 17, 2010. What would you buy? Based on the information in Figure 3.5, how much would you have to pay?

You want the right to buy, so you want to purchase call options. Because each contract is for 100 shares, and you want the right to buy 500 shares, you need five contracts. The contract you want would be described as the Nike September 70 call option. From Figure 3.5, the quoted option premium to buy the contract with a $70 strike and a September expiration is $4.75, so one contract would cost $4.75 × 100 = $475. The cost for five contracts would therefore be 5 × $475 = $2,375.

EXAMPLE 3.4

Put Options

Suppose you want the right to sell 200 shares of Nike sometime before September 17, 2010 at a price of $70. In light of the information in Figure 3.5, what contract should you buy? How much will it cost you?

You want the right to sell stock at a fixed price, so you want to buy put options. Specifically, you want to buy two September 70 put contracts. In Figure 3.5, the ask premium for this contract is given as $0.07. Recalling that this is the premium per share, one contract will cost you $7, so two contracts would cost $14. Because each option contract is for 100 shares, we must multiply the quoted option price by 100.

GAINS AND LOSSES ON OPTION CONTRACTS

As with futures contracts, option contracts have the potential for large gains and losses. Let's consider our previous example in which you paid $2,375 for five Nike September 70 call contracts. Suppose you hold on to your contracts until September rolls around, and they are just about to expire. What are your gains (or losses) if Nike is selling for $90 per share? $50 per share?

If Nike is selling for $90 per share, you will profit handsomely. You have the right to buy 500 shares at a price of $70 per share. Because the stock is worth $90, your options are worth $20 per share, or $10,000 in all. So you invested $2,375 and ended up with more than 4 times that. Not bad.

If the stock ends up at $50 per share, however, the result is not so pretty. You have the right to buy the stock for $70 when it is selling for $50, so your call options expire worthless. You lose the entire $2,375 you originally invested. In fact, if the stock price is anything less than $70, you lose $2,375.

EXAMPLE 3.5

More on Puts

In Example 3.4, you bought two Nike September 70 put contracts for $14. Suppose that September arrives, and Nike is selling for $55 per share. How did you do? What's the break-even stock price, that is, the stock price at which you just make enough to cover your $14 cost?

Your put contracts give you the right to sell 200 shares of Nike at a price of $70 per share. If the stock is worth only $55 per share, your put options are worth $15 per share, or $3,000 in all. To determine the break-even stock price, notice that you paid $0.07 per share for the option. The break-even stock price is thus $70 − $0.07 = $69.93.

INVESTING IN STOCKS VERSUS OPTIONS

To get a better idea of the potential gains and losses from investing in stocks compared to investing in options, let's suppose you have $10,000 to invest. You're looking at Macron Technology, which is currently selling for $50 per share. You also notice that a call option with a $50 strike price and three months to maturity is available. The premium is $4. Macron pays no dividends.

You're considering investing all $10,000 either in the stock or in the call options. What is your return from these two investments, if, in three months, Macron is selling for $55 per share? What about $45 per share?

First, if you buy the stock, your $10,000 will purchase two round lots, meaning 200 shares. A call contract costs $400 (why?), so you can buy 25 of them. Notice that your 25 contracts give you the right to buy 2,500 shares at $50 per share.

If, in three months, Macron is selling for $55, your stock will be worth 200 shares × $55 = $11,000. Your dollar gain will be $11,000 less the $10,000 you invested, or $1,000. Because you invested $10,000, your return for the three-month period is $1,000/$10,000 = 10%. If Macron is selling for $45 per share, then you lose $1,000, and your return is −10 percent.

If Macron is selling for $55, your call options are worth $55 − $50 = $5 each, but now you control 2,500 shares, so your options are worth 2,500 shares × $5 = $12,500 total. You invested $10,000, so your dollar return is $12,500 − $10,000 = $2,500, and your percentage return is $2,500/$10,000 = 25%, compared to 10 percent on the stock investment. However, if Macron is selling for $45 when your options mature, then you lose everything, and your return is −100 percent.

EXAMPLE 3.6

Put Returns

In our example for Macron Technology, suppose a put option is also available with a premium of $2.50. Calculate your percentage return for the three-month holding period if the stock price declines to $47 per share. What is your annualized return?

One put contract costs $250, so you can buy 40 of them. Notice that your 40 contracts give you the right to sell 4,000 shares at $50 per share.

If, in three months, Macron is selling for $47, your put options are worth $50 − $47 = $3 each. You control 4,000 shares, so your options are worth 4,000 shares × $3 = $12,000 total. You invested $10,000, so your dollar return is $12,000 − $10,000 = $2,000, and your percentage return is $2,000/$10,000 = 20%.

To annualize your return, we need to compute the effective annual return, recognizing that there are 4 three-month periods in a year:

$$1 + EAR = 1.20^4$$
$$1 + EAR = 2.0736$$
$$EAR = 1.0736 = 107.36\%$$

Your annualized return is thus about 107 percent.

CHECK THIS

3.5a What is a call option? A put option?

3.5b If you buy a call option, what do you hope will happen to the underlying stock? What if you buy a put option?

3.5c What are the two key differences between a futures contract and an option contract?

3.6 Summary and Conclusions

In this chapter we examine the basic types of financial assets. We discuss three broad classes: interest-bearing assets, equity securities, and derivative assets—futures and options. For each of the broad classes, we ask three questions. First, what is its basic nature and what are its distinguishing characteristics? Second, what are the potential gains and losses from owning it? Third, how are its prices quoted online and in the financial press? We cover many aspects of these investments. We provide a brief description of these investments broken down by the chapter's important concepts.

1. **Various types of interest-bearing assets.**

   A. Each of these major groups can be further subdivided. Interest-bearing assets include money market instruments and fixed-income securities.

   B. Money market instruments generally have the following two properties: (1) they are essentially IOUs sold by large corporations or governments to borrow money; and (2) they mature in less than one year from the time they are sold, meaning that the loan must be repaid within one year.

   C. Fixed-income securities are securities that promise to make fixed payments according to some preset schedule. Another key characteristic of a fixed-income security is that it begins life as a loan of some sort. That is, fixed-income securities are debt obligations. Corporations and governments issue fixed-income securities. Unlike money market instruments, fixed-income securities have lives that exceed 12 months at the time they are issued.

2. **Equity securities.**

   A. The two major equity types are common stock and preferred stock. Common stock represents ownership in a corporation. If you own 1,000 shares of General Electric, then you own a very small percentage of GE's outstanding shares. Nonetheless, you are a part-owner of GE. As a part-owner, you are entitled to your pro rata share of anything paid out by GE, and you have the right to vote on important matters regarding the company.

   B. Preferred stock differs from common stock in several important ways. First, the dividend on a preferred share is usually fixed at some amount and never changed. Second, if the company liquidates, preferred shares have a particular face value. The reason preferred stock is called "preferred" is that a company must pay the fixed dividend on its preferred stock before any dividends can be paid to common shareholders. In other words, preferred shareholders must be paid first.

3. **Futures contracts.**

   A. In many ways, a futures contract is the simplest of all financial assets. A futures contract is just an agreement made today regarding the terms of a trade that will take place later.

   B. As an example of a futures contract, suppose you know that you will want to buy 100 ounces of gold in six months. One thing you could do is to strike a deal today with a seller in which you promise to pay, say, $1,100 per ounce in six months for the 100 ounces of gold. In other words, you and the seller agree that six months from now, you will exchange $110,000 for 100 ounces of gold. The agreement that you have created is a futures contract.

4. **Option contracts.**

   A. An option contract is an agreement that gives the owner the right, but not the obligation, to buy or sell (depending on the type of option) a specific asset at a specific price for a specific period of time.

   B. The most familiar options are stock options. These are options to buy or sell shares of stock, and they are the focus of our discussion here. Options are a very flexible investment tool, and a great deal is known about them. We present some of the most important option concepts in this chapter.

GET REAL

This chapter covered the basics of the four main types of financial assets: stocks, bonds, futures, and options. In addition to discussing basic features, we alerted you to some of the risks associated with these instruments. We particularly stressed the large potential gains and losses possible with derivative assets. How should you, as an investor or investment manager, put this information to work?

Following up on our previous chapter, you need to execute each of the possible transaction types suggested by this chapter in a simulated brokerage account. Your goal is to experience some of the large gains (and losses) to understand them on a personal level. Try to do at least the following:

1. Buy a corporate or government bond.

2. Buy agriculture, natural resource, and financial futures contracts.

3. Sell agriculture, natural resource, and financial futures contracts.

4. Buy put and call option contracts.

5. Sell put and call option contracts

In each case, once you have created the position, be sure to monitor it regularly by checking prices, trading activity, and relevant news using *The Wall Street Journal* or an online information service to understand why it changes in value.

One thing you will discover if you execute these trades is that some of these investments carry relatively low risk and some carry relatively high risk. Which are which? Under what circumstances is each of these investments appropriate? We will have more to say about these investments later, but you'll get a lot more out of our discussion (and have some fun stories to tell) if you already have some personal experience. As always, it's better to become educated about these things with play money before you commit real money.

Key Terms

call option 94
current yield 82
derivative asset 90
fixed-income securities 82
futures contract 90
money market instruments 81

option contract 93
option premium 94
primary asset 90
put option 94
strike price 94

Chapter Review Problems and Self-Test

1. **Corporate Bond Quotes (CFA2)** In Figure 3.1, locate the Citigroup bond that matures in the year 2014. What is the coupon rate on this issue? Suppose you purchase $100,000 in face value. How much will this cost? Assuming semiannual payments, what will you receive in coupon payments?

2. **Call Options (CFA4)** In Figure 3.5, locate the Nike September 65 call option. If you buy 10 contracts, how much will you pay? Suppose that just as the option is about to expire, Nike is selling for $75.50 per share. What are your options worth? What is your profit/loss?

1. Based on Figure 3.1, the Citigroup bond that matures in 2014 has a 6.375 percent coupon rate. The last price, as a percentage of face value, is 106.967, or 106.967 percent. If you buy $100,000 in face value, you would thus pay $106,967. You will receive 6.375 percent of $100,000, or $6,375, in coupon payments every year, paid in two $3,187.50 semiannual installments.

2. From Figure 3.5, the September 65 call ask premium is 9.70, or $9.70. Because one contract involves 100 shares, the cost of a contract is $970, and 10 contracts would cost $9,700. In September, if Nike is selling for $75.50, then you have the right to buy 10 contracts × 100 shares = 1,000 shares at $65. Your contracts are thus worth $75.50 − $65.00 = $10.50 per share, or $10,500 total. Because they cost you $9,700, your gain is $800.

Test Your Investment Quotient

1. **Money Market Securities (LO1, CFA1)**   Which of the following is not a common characteristic of money market securities?

    a. Sold on a discount basis.
    b. Mature in less than one year.
    c. Most important risk is default risk.
    d. All of the above are characteristics.

2. **Money Market Securities (LO1, CFA1)**   Which of the following money market securities is the most liquid?

    a. U.S. Treasury bills.
    b. Bank certificates of deposit.
    c. Corporate money market debt.
    d. Municipality money market debt.

3. **Options (LO4, CFA4)**   A European option can be exercised

    a. Only after American options.
    b. Anytime up to and including the expiration date.
    c. Only on the day before the expiration date.
    d. Only on a European exchange.

4. **Fixed-Income Securities (LO1, CFA2)**   Your friend told you she just received her semiannual coupon payment on a U.S. Treasury note with a $100,000 face value that pays a 6 percent annual coupon. How much money did she receive from this coupon payment?

    a. $3,000
    b. $6,000
    c. $30,000
    d. $60,000

5. **Common Stock (LO2, CFA1)**   A corporation with common stock issued to the public pays dividends

    a. At the discretion of management, who are elected by the shareholders.
    b. At the discretion of shareholders, since they own the corporation.
    c. At the discretion of the company's board of directors, who are elected by shareholders.
    d. At the discretion of the company's board of directors, who are appointed by management.

6. **Futures Contracts (LO3, CFA3)**   You buy (go long) five copper futures contracts at 100 cents per pound, where the contract size is 25,000 pounds. At contract maturity, copper is selling for 102 cents per pound. What is your profit (+) or loss (−) on the transaction?

    a. −$2,500
    b. +$2,500
    c. −$25,000
    d. +$25,000

7. **Futures Contracts (LO3, CFA3)**   You sell (go short) 10 gold futures contracts at $400 per ounce, where the contract size is 100 ounces. At contract maturity, gold is selling for $410 per ounce. What is your profit (+) or loss (−) on the transaction?

    a. −$1,000
    b. +$1,000

c. −$10,000

   d. +$10,000

8. **Option Contracts (LO4, CFA4)**   You buy 100 CJC call option contracts with a strike price of 95 at a quoted price of $1. At option expiration, CJC sells for $97. What is your net profit on the transaction?

   a. $2,000

   b. $5,000

   c. $10,000

   d. $20,000

9. **Option Contracts (LO4, CFA4)**   You buy 100 CJC put option contracts with a strike price of 92 at a quoted price of $8. At option expiration, CJC sells for $83.80. What is your net profit on the transaction?

   a. $200

   b. $1,000

   c. $2,000

   d. $10,000

10. **Short Sales (LO4)**   Which of the following statements about short selling is true?

   a. A short position may be hedged by writing call options.

   b. A short position may be hedged by purchasing put options.

   c. Short sellers may be subject to margin calls if the stock price increases.

   d. Stocks that pay large dividends should be sold short before the ex-dividend date and bought afterward to take advantage of the large price declines in a short time period.

Concept Questions

1. **Money Market Instruments (LO1, CFA1)**   What are the distinguishing features of a money market instrument?

2. **Preferred Stock (LO2)**   Why is preferred stock "preferred"?

3. **WSJ Stock Quotes (LO2)**   What is the PE ratio reported for stocks in *The Wall Street Journal*? In particular, how is it computed?

4. **Yields (LO1, CFA2)**   The current yield on a bond is the coupon rate divided by the price. Thus, it is very similar to what number reported for common and preferred stocks?

5. **Volume Quotations (LO1, LO2, LO3, LO4)**   Explain how volume is quoted for stocks, corporate bonds, futures, and options.

6. **Futures Contracts (LO3, CFA3)**   Changes in what price lead to gains and/or losses in futures contracts?

7. **Futures Contracts (LO3, CFA3)**   What is the open interest on a futures contract? What do you think will usually happen to open interest as maturity approaches?

8. **Futures versus Options (LO3, CFA4)**   What is the difference between a futures contract and an option contract? Do the buyer of a futures contract and the buyer of an option contract have the same rights? What about the seller?

9. **Asset Types (LO1, LO2, LO3, LO4)**   What is the distinction between a real asset and a financial asset? What are the two basic types of financial assets, and what does each represent?

10. **Puts versus Calls (LO4, CFA4)**   Suppose a share of stock is selling for $100. A put and a call are offered, both with $100 strike prices and nine months to maturity. Intuitively, which do you think is more valuable?

Questions and Problems

Core Questions

1. **Stock Quotations (LO2)**   You found the following stock quote for DRK Enterprises, Inc., at your favorite Web site. You also found that the stock paid an annual dividend of $0.75, which resulted in a dividend yield of 1.30 percent. What was the closing price for this stock yesterday? How many round lots of stock were traded yesterday?

Company	Symbol	DAILY				YTD	52 WEEK		
		Vol	Close	Chg	%Chg	%Chg	High	Low	%Chg
DRK Enterprises	DRK	18,649,130	??	0.26	−0.39%	8.73%	78.19	51.74	27.4%

2. **Stock Quotations (LO2)** In the previous problem, assume the company has 95 million shares of stock outstanding and a PE ratio of 16. What was net income for the most recent four quarters?

3. **Dividend Yields (LO2, CFA1)** You find a stock selling for $69.80 that has a dividend yield of 2.8 percent. What was the last quarterly dividend paid?

4. **Earnings per Share (LO2)** In the previous problem, if the company has a PE ratio of 21.5, what is the earnings per share (EPS) for the company?

5. **Bonds (LO1, CFA2)** You purchase 3,000 bonds with a par value of $1,000 for $980 each. The bonds have a coupon rate of 7.2 percent paid semiannually, and mature in 10 years. How much will you receive on the next coupon date? How much will you receive when the bonds mature?

6. **Futures Profits (LO3, CFA3)** The contract size for platinum futures is 50 troy ounces. Suppose you need 500 troy ounces of platinum and the current futures price is $1,530 per ounce. How many contracts do you need to purchase? How much will you pay for your platinum? What is your dollar profit if platinum sells for $1,565 a troy ounce when the futures contract expires? What if the price is $1,475 at expiration?

7. **Option Profits (LO4, CFA4)** You purchase 7 call option contracts with a strike price of $75 and a premium of $3.85. If the stock price at expiration is $83.61, what is your dollar profit? What if the stock price is $69.56?

8. **Stock Quotations (LO2)** You found the following stock quote for Gigantus Corporation in today's newspaper. What was the stock selling for on January 1?

Company	Symbol	DAILY				YTD	52 WEEK		
		Vol	Close	Chg	%Chg	%Chg	High	Low	%Chg
Gigantus	GIG	12,805,325	48.92	0.72	1.47%	−1.20%	62.81	45.93	6.5%

Use the following bond quote for the next two questions:

Company	Symbol	Coupon	Maturity	Rating Moody's/ S&P/Fitch	High	Low	Last	Change	Yield%
Int'l Systems	ISU.GO	6.850%	May, 2032	Baa2/BBB/BB−	102.817	91.865	93.231	1.650	7.482%

9. **Bond Quotations (LO1, CFA2)** What is the yield to maturity of the bond? What is the current yield of the bond?

10. **Bond Quotations (LO1, CFA2)** If you currently own 25 of the bonds, how much will you receive on the next coupon date?

Intermediate Questions

Use the following corn futures quotes for the next three problems:

Corn 5,000 bushels						
	Open	High	Low	Settle	Chg	Open Int
Mar	455'1	457'0	451'6	452'0	−2'6	597,913
May	467'0	468'0	463'0	463'2	−2'6	137,547
July	477'0	477'0	472'4	473'0	−2'0	153,164
Sep	475'0	475'0	471'6	472'2	−2'0	29,258

11. **Futures Quotations (LO3, CFA3)** How many of the March contracts are currently open? How many of these contracts should you sell if you wish to deliver 225,000 bushels of corn in March? If you actually make delivery, how much will you receive? Assume you locked in the settle price.

12. **Futures Quotations (LO3, CFA3)** Suppose you sell 25 of the May corn futures at the high price of the day. You close your position later when the price is 465'3. Ignoring commission, what is your dollar profit on this transaction?

13. **Using Futures Quotations (LO3, CFA3)** Suppose you buy 15 of the September corn futures contracts at the last price of the day. One month from now, the futures price of this contract is 462'1, and you close out your position. Calculate your dollar profit on this investment.

Use the following quotes for JC Penney stock options for the next three problems:

View By Expiration: Dec 09 | Jan 10 | Feb 10 | **May 10** | Jan 11 | Jan 12

CALL OPTIONS				Expire at close Fri, May 21, 2010		
Strike	Last	Chg	Bid	Ask	Vol	Open Int
22.50	6.24	0.00	6.20	6.40	1	11
25.00	5.20	0.00	4.50	4.70	152	187
26.00	5.70	0.00	3.90	4.10	2	8
27.00	4.50	0.00	3.30	3.50	11	36
28.00	2.90	0.00	2.90	3.00	3	173
29.00	2.50	0.00	2.40	2.55	16	335
30.00	2.08	0.00	2.05	2.15	25	368
31.00	2.20	0.00	1.65	1.80	26	403
32.00	1.45	0.00	1.40	1.50	51	388

PUT OPTIONS				Expire at close Fri, May 21, 2010		
Strike	Last	Chg	Bid	Ask	Vol	Open Int
15.00	0.25	0.00	0.15	0.25	26	114
17.50	0.40	0.00	0.35	0.45	52	156
20.00	0.90	0.00	0.65	0.75	35	622
22.50	1.30	0.00	1.20	1.30	2	2,214
25.00	1.95	0.00	2.00	2.10	2	470
26.00	2.55	0.00	2.40	2.50	8	12
27.00	2.86	0.00	2.85	2.95	10	21
28.00	3.50	0.00	3.30	3.50	75	390
29.00	4.30	0.00	3.90	4.00	27	621
30.00	4.70	0.00	4.50	4.70	79	1,000
31.00	4.80	0.00	5.10	5.40	4	258

14. **Options Quotations (LO4, CFA4)** If you wanted to purchase the right to sell 2,000 shares of JC Penney stock in May 2010 at a strike price of $27 per share, how much would this cost you?

15. **Options Quotations (LO4, CFA4)** Which put contract sells for the lowest price? Which one sells for the highest price? Explain why these respective options trade at such extreme prices.

16. **Using Options Quotations (LO4 , CFA4)** In Problem 14, suppose JC Penney stock sells for $22.91 per share immediately before your options' expiration. What is the rate of return on your investment? What is your rate of return if the stock sells for $32.54 per share (think about it)? Assume your holding period for this investment is exactly three months.

17. **Options (LO4, CFA4)** You've located the following option quote for Eric-Cartman, Inc. (ECI):

ECI			Call		Put	
Option/Strike		Exp.	Vol.	Last	Vol.	Last
20.25	10	Sep	29	5.50	...	...
20.25	15	Sep	333	7	69	1
20.25	25	Dec	5	2	...	...
20.25	30	Sep	76	2	188	8.75
20.25	35	Oct	89	0.50	...	...

Two of the premiums shown can't possibly be correct. Which two? Why?

18. **Annualized Returns (LO2, CFA1)** Suppose you have $28,000 to invest. You're considering Miller-Moore Equine Enterprises (MMEE), which is currently selling for $40 per share. You also notice that a call option with a $40 strike price and six months to maturity is available. The premium is $4.00. MMEE pays no dividends. What is your annualized return from these two investments if, in six months, MMEE is selling for $48 per share? What about $36 per share?

19. **Annualized Returns (LO2, CFA1)** In the previous question, suppose a dividend of $.80 per share is paid. Comment on how the returns would be affected.

20. **Option Returns (LO4, CFA4)** In Problem 18, suppose a put option with a $40 strike is also available with a premium of $2.80. Calculate your percentage return for the six-month holding period if the stock price declines to $36 per share.

What's on the Web?

1. **Option Prices** You want to find the option prices for ConAgra Foods (CAG). Go to finance.yahoo.com, get a stock quote, and follow the "Options" link. What is the option premium and strike price for the highest and lowest strike price options that are nearest to expiring? What are the option premium and strike price for the highest and lowest strike price options expiring next month?

2. **Futures Quotes** Go to www.cmegroup.com and find the contract specifications for corn futures. What is the size of the corn futures contract? On the Web site, find the settle price for the corn futures contract that will expire the soonest. If you go long 10 contracts, how much will the corn cost at the current price?

3. **LEAPS** Go to www.cboe.com, highlight the "Products" tab, then follow the "LEAPS" link. What are LEAPS? What are the two types of LEAPS? What are the benefits of equity LEAPS? What are the benefits of index LEAPS?

4. **FLEX Options** Go to www.cboe.com, highlight the "Institutional" tab, then follow the "FLEX Options" link. What is a FLEX option? When do FLEX options expire? What is the minimum size of a FLEX option?

Stock-Trak Exercises

To access the Stock-Trak Exercise for this chapter, please visit the book Web site at www.mhhe.com/jmd6e and choose the corresponding chapter.

CHAPTER 4

Mutual Funds

Learning Objectives

You're probably going to be a mutual fund investor very soon, so you should definitely know the following:

1. The different types of mutual funds.

2. How mutual funds operate.

3. How to find information about how mutual funds have performed.

4. The workings of Exchange-Traded Funds (ETFs) and hedge funds.

"Take calculated risks. That is quite different from being rash."

–George S. Patton

With only $2,000 to invest, you can easily own shares in Microsoft, GM, McDonald's, IBM, Coke, and many more stocks through a mutual fund. Or, you can invest in a portfolio of government bonds or other investments. Indeed, many thousands of different mutual funds are available to investors. In fact, there are about as many mutual funds as there are different stocks traded on the NASDAQ and the New York Stock Exchange combined. There are funds for aggressive investors, conservative investors, short-term investors, and long-term investors. There are bond funds, stock funds, international funds, and you-name-it funds. Is there a right fund for you? This chapter will help you find out. ■

As we discussed in an earlier chapter, if you do not wish to actively buy and sell individual securities on your own, you can invest in stocks, bonds, or other financial assets through a *mutual fund*. Mutual funds are simply a means of combining or pooling the funds of a large group of investors. The buy and sell decisions for the resulting pool are then made by a fund manager, who is compensated for the service provided.

Because mutual funds provide indirect access to financial markets for individual investors, they are a form of financial intermediary. In fact, mutual funds are now the largest type of intermediary in the United States, followed by commercial banks and life insurance companies.

CFA™ Exam Topics in This Chapter:

1 Discounted cash flow applications (L1, S2)

2 Alternative investments (L1, S18)

3 Soft dollar standards (L2, S1)

4 Alternative investments portfolio management (L3, S13)

Go to www.mhhe.com/jmd6e for a guide that aligns your textbook with CFA readings.

Mutual funds have become so important that we devote this entire chapter to them. The number of funds and the different fund types available have grown tremendously in recent years. As of the beginning of 2010, an estimated 88.5 million Americans in 51.2 million households owned mutual funds, up from just 5 million households in 1980. Investors contributed $390 billion to mutual funds in 2009, and, by the end of the year, mutual fund assets totaled $11.1 *trillion*.

One of the reasons for the proliferation of mutual funds and fund types is that mutual funds have become, on a very basic level, consumer products. They are created and marketed to the public in ways that are intended to promote buyer appeal. As every business student knows, product differentiation is a basic marketing tactic, and in recent years mutual funds have become increasingly adept at practicing this common marketing technique.

In fact, if you are not already a mutual fund investor, you very likely will be in the near future. The reason has to do with a fundamental change in the way businesses of all types provide retirement benefits for employees. It used to be that most large employers offered so-called defined benefit pensions. With such a plan, when you retire, your employer pays you a pension typically based on years of service and salary. The key is that the pension benefit you receive is based on a predefined formula, hence the name.

Defined benefit plans are rapidly being replaced by "defined contribution" plans. Defined contribution plans are essentially the same as 401(k) plans discussed elsewhere. With a defined contribution plan, your employer will contribute money each pay period to a retirement account on your behalf, but you have to select where the funds go. With this arrangement, the benefit you ultimately receive depends entirely on how your investments do; your employer only makes contributions. Most commonly, you must choose from a group of mutual funds for your investments, so it is very important that you understand the different types of mutual funds, as well as their risk and return characteristics.

4.1 Advantages and Drawbacks of Mutual Fund Investing

ADVANTAGES

Investing in mutual funds offers many advantages. Three of these are diversification, professional management, and the size of the initial investment.

DIVERSIFICATION When you invest in a mutual fund, you are investing in a portfolio, or basket, of securities. As you will learn in detail in later chapters, holding a diversified portfolio helps you reduce risk. How? A mutual fund might invest in hundreds (or thousands) of securities. If the value of one of them falls to zero, this decline will have a small impact on the mutual fund value. Diversification helps you reduce risk, but diversification does not eliminate risk. It is still possible for you to lose money when you invest in a mutual fund. Also note that not all mutual funds are diversified. For example, some intentionally specialize in specific industries or countries.

PROFESSIONAL MANAGEMENT Professional money managers make investment decisions for mutual funds. That is, the mutual fund manager makes the decision of when to add or remove particular securities from the mutual fund. This means that you, as the investor holding the mutual fund, do not have to make these crucial decisions.

MINIMUM INITIAL INVESTMENT Most mutual funds have a minimum initial purchase of $2,500, but some are as low as $1,000. After your initial purchase, subsequent purchases are sometimes as low as $50. Of course, these amounts vary from fund to fund.

DRAWBACKS

As with any type of investment, some drawbacks are associated with mutual funds. In particular, three of them are risk, costs, and taxes.

RISK Let us start with a point that should be obvious. The value of your mutual fund investment, unlike a bank deposit, could fall and be worth less than your initial investment. You should also realize that no government or private agency guarantees the value of a mutual fund.

A not so obvious point is that some investors think that there is a cost to diversification. Diversification greatly reduces the risk of loss from holding one (or a few) securities. However, by spreading your investments over many securities, you limit your chances for large returns if one of these securities increases dramatically in value. We happen to think that this is a cost worth bearing.

COSTS Investing in mutual funds entails fees and expenses that do not usually accrue when purchasing individual securities directly. We detail most of these costs later in the chapter.

TAXES When you invest in a mutual fund, you will pay federal income tax (and state and local taxes, if applicable) on:

- Distributions (dividends and capital gains) made by the mutual fund.
- Profits you make when you sell mutual fund shares.

There are some exceptions. A notable one is the receipt of distributions in tax-deferred retirement accounts such as individual retirement accounts (IRAs).

CHECK THIS

| 4.1a | What are some advantages of investing in mutual funds? |
| 4.1b | What are some drawbacks of investing in mutual funds? |

4.2 Investment Companies and Fund Types

investment company
A business that specializes in pooling funds from individual investors and investing them.

At the most basic level, a company that pools funds obtained from individual investors and invests them is called an **investment company**. In other words, an investment company is a business that specializes in managing financial assets for individual investors. All mutual funds are, in fact, investment companies. As we will see, however, not all investment companies are mutual funds.

In the sections that follow, we will be discussing various aspects of mutual funds and related entities. Figure 4.1 is a big-picture overview of some of the different types of funds and how they are classified. It will serve as a guide for the next several sections. We will define the various terms that appear as we go along.

OPEN-END VERSUS CLOSED-END FUNDS

As Figure 4.1 shows, there are two fundamental types of investment companies, *open-end funds* and *closed-end funds*. The difference is very important. Whenever you invest in a mutual fund, you do so by buying shares in the fund. However, how shares are bought and sold depends on which type of fund you are considering.

open-end fund
An investment company that stands ready to buy and sell shares at any time.

With an **open-end fund**, the fund itself will sell new shares to anyone wishing to buy and will redeem (i.e., buy back) shares from anyone wishing to sell. When an investor wishes to buy open-end fund shares, the fund simply issues them and then invests the money received. When someone wishes to sell open-end fund shares, the fund sells some of its assets and

FIGURE 4.1 Fund Types

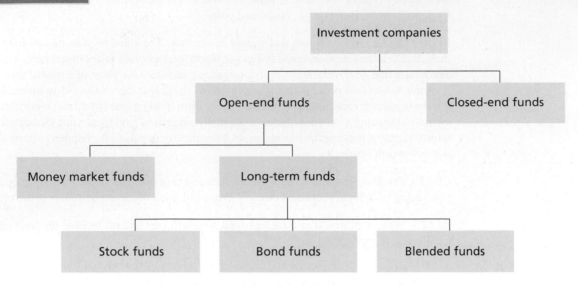

uses the cash to redeem the shares. As a result, with an open-end fund, the number of shares outstanding fluctuates through time.

closed-end fund
An investment company with a fixed number of shares that are bought and sold only in the open stock market.

With a **closed-end fund**, the number of shares is fixed and never changes. If you want to buy shares, you must buy them from another investor. Similarly, if you wish to sell shares that you own, you must sell them to another investor.

Thus, the key difference between an open-end fund and a closed-end fund is that, with a closed-end fund, the fund itself does not buy or sell shares. In fact, as we discuss below, shares in closed-end funds are listed on stock exchanges just like ordinary shares of stock, where their shares are bought and sold in the same way. Open-end funds are more popular among individual investors than closed-end funds.

The distinction between open-end funds and closed-end funds is not always as clear cut as one would think. For example, some open-end funds "close their doors" to new investors. The typical reason for this decision is fund size. If the fund gets too large, exercising effective control over the fund's investments will be difficult for the fund managers. When an open-end fund no longer accepts new investors, existing investors generally can continue to add money to the fund. Of course, existing investors can withdraw money from the fund.

Strictly speaking, the term "mutual fund" actually refers only to an open-end investment company. Thus, the phrase "closed-end fund" is a bit of an oxymoron, kind of like jumbo shrimp, and the phrase "open-end mutual fund" is a redundancy, an unnecessary repetition, or restatement. Nonetheless, particularly in recent years, the term "investment company" has all but disappeared from common use, and investment companies are now generically called mutual funds. We will stick with this common terminology to avoid any confusion.

NET ASSET VALUE

net asset value
The value of assets less liabilities held by a mutual fund, divided by the number of shares outstanding. Abbreviated NAV.

A mutual fund's **net asset value** is an important consideration. Net asset value is calculated by taking the total value of the assets held by the fund less any liabilities and then dividing by the number of outstanding shares. For example, suppose a mutual fund has $105 million in assets and $5 million in liabilities based on current market values and a total of 5 million shares outstanding. Based on the value of net assets held by the fund, $100 million, each share has a value of $100 million/5 million = $20. This $20 is the fund's net asset value, often abbreviated as NAV.

With one important exception, the net asset value of a mutual fund will change essentially every day simply because the value of the assets held by the fund fluctuates. The one exception concerns money market mutual funds, which we discuss in a later section.

Net Asset Value

As of late 2009, the Pimco Total Return fund had about $192.6 billion in invested assets, making it the largest fund in the world. If the fund had 17.56 billion shares outstanding, what is its net asset value?

The net asset value is simply the asset value per share, or $192.6 billion/17.56 billion = $10.97.

As we noted, an open-end fund will generally redeem or buy back shares at any time. The price you will receive for shares you sell is the net asset value. Thus, in our example above, you could sell your shares back to the fund and receive $20 each. Because the fund stands ready to redeem shares at any time, shares in an open-end fund are always worth their net asset value.

In contrast, because the shares of closed-end funds are bought and sold in the stock markets, their share prices at any point in time may or may not be equal to their net asset values. We examine this issue in more detail in a later section.

CHECK THIS

4.2a   What is an investment company?

4.2b   What is the difference between an open-end fund and a closed-end fund?

4.3 Mutual Fund Operations

In this section, we discuss some essentials of mutual fund operations. We focus on how mutual funds are created, marketed, regulated, and taxed. Our discussion here deals primarily with open-end funds, but much of it applies to closed-end funds as well. Further details on closed-end funds are provided in a later section.

MUTUAL FUND ORGANIZATION AND CREATION

A mutual fund is simply a corporation. Like a corporation, a mutual fund is owned by its shareholders. The shareholders elect a board of directors; the board of directors is responsible for hiring a manager to oversee the fund's operations. Although mutual funds often belong to a larger "family" of funds, every fund is a separate company owned by its shareholders.

Most mutual funds are created by investment advisory firms, which are businesses that specialize in managing mutual funds. Investment advisory firms are also called mutual fund companies. Increasingly, such firms have additional operations such as discount brokerages and other financial services.

There are hundreds of investment advisory firms in the United States. The largest, and probably best known, is Fidelity Investments, with more than 300 mutual funds, about $1.4 trillion in assets under management, and more than 20 million customers. Dreyfus, Franklin, and Vanguard are some other well-known examples. Many brokerage firms, such as Merrill Lynch and Charles Schwab, also have large investment advisory operations.

Investment advisory firms create mutual funds simply because they wish to manage them to earn fees. A typical management fee might be .75 percent of the total assets in the fund per year. A fund with $200 million in assets would not be especially large, but could nonetheless generate management fees of about $1.5 million per year. Thus, there is a significant economic incentive to create funds and attract investors to them.

For example, a company like Fidelity might one day decide that there is a demand for a fund that buys stock in companies that grow and process citrus fruits. Fidelity could form a mutual fund that specializes in such companies and call it something like the Fidelity Lemon Fund.[1] A fund manager would be appointed, and shares in the fund would be offered to the public. As shares were sold, the money received would be invested. If the fund were a success, a large amount of money would be attracted and Fidelity would benefit from the fees it earns. If the fund was not a success, the board could vote to liquidate it and return shareholders' money or merge it with another fund.

As our hypothetical example illustrates, an investment advisory firm such as Fidelity can (and often will) create new funds from time to time. Through time, this process leads to a family of funds all managed by the same advisory firm. Each fund in the family will have its own fund manager, but the advisory firm will generally handle the record keeping, marketing, and much of the research that underlies the fund's investment decisions.

In principle, the directors of a mutual fund in a particular family, acting on behalf of the fund shareholders, could vote to fire the investment advisory firm and hire a different one. As a practical matter, this rarely, if ever, occurs. At least part of the reason is that the directors are originally appointed by the fund's founder, and they are routinely reelected. Unhappy shareholders generally "vote with their feet"—that is, sell their shares and invest elsewhere.

TAXATION OF INVESTMENT COMPANIES

As long as an investment company meets certain rules set by the Internal Revenue Service, it is treated as a "regulated investment company" for tax purposes. This is important because a regulated investment company does not pay taxes on its investment income. Instead, the fund passes through all realized investment income to fund shareholders, who then pay taxes on these distributions as though they owned the securities directly. Essentially, the fund simply acts as a conduit, funneling gains and losses to fund owners.

To qualify as a regulated investment company, the fund must follow three basic rules. The first rule is that it must in fact be an investment company holding almost all of its assets as investments in stocks, bonds, and other securities. The second rule limits the fund to using no more than 5 percent of its assets when acquiring a particular security. This is a diversification rule. The third rule is that the fund must pass through all realized investment income to fund shareholders.

THE FUND PROSPECTUS AND ANNUAL REPORT

Mutual funds are required by law to produce a document known as a *prospectus*. The prospectus must be supplied to any investor wishing to purchase shares. Mutual funds must also provide an annual report to their shareholders. The annual report and the prospectus, which are sometimes combined, contain financial statements along with specific information concerning the fund's expenses, gains and losses, holdings, objectives, and management. We discuss many of these items in the next few sections.

CHECK THIS

4.3a   How do mutual funds usually get started?

4.3b   How are mutual funds taxed?

4.4 Mutual Fund Costs and Fees

All mutual funds have various expenses that are paid by the fund's shareholders. These expenses can vary considerably from fund to fund, however, and one of the most important considerations in evaluating a fund is its expense structure. All else the same, lower expenses are preferred, of course, but, as we discuss, matters are not quite that cut-and-dried.

---

[1] Fidelity would probably come up with a better name.

TYPES OF EXPENSES AND FEES

Basically, there are four types of expenses or fees associated with buying and owning mutual fund shares:

1. Sales charges or "loads."
2. 12b-1 fees.
3. Management fees.
4. Trading costs.

We discuss each of these in turn.

SALES CHARGES Many mutual funds charge a fee whenever shares are purchased. These fees are generally called **front-end loads**. Funds that charge loads are called *load funds*. Funds that have no such charges are called *no-load funds*.

front-end load
A sales charge levied on purchases of shares in some mutual funds.

When you purchase shares in a load fund, you pay a price in excess of the net asset value, called the *offering price*. The difference between the offering price and the net asset value is the *load*. Shares in no-load funds are sold at net asset value.

Front-end loads can range as high as 8.5 percent, but 5 percent or so would be more typical. Some funds, with front-end loads in the 2 percent to 3 percent range, are described as *low-load funds*.

Front-end loads are expressed as a percentage of the offering price, not the net asset value. For example, suppose a load fund has an offering price of $100 and a net asset value of $98. The front-end load is $2, which, as a percentage of the $100 offering price, is $2/$100 = 2 percent. The way front-end loads are calculated understates the load slightly. In our example here, you are paying $100 for something worth only $98, so the load is really $2/$98 = 2.04 percent.

EXAMPLE 4.2 | **Front-End Loads**

On a particular day, according to *The Wall Street Journal*, the Common Sense Growth fund had a net asset value of $13.91. The offering price was $15.20. Is this a load fund? What is the front-end load?

Because the offering price, which is the price you must pay to purchase shares, exceeds the net asset value, this is definitely a load fund. The load can be calculated by taking the difference between the offering price and the net asset value, $1.29, and dividing by the $15.20 offering price. The result is a hefty front-end load of 8.5 percent.

CDSC
A sales charge levied when investors redeem shares (also called a "back-end" load).

Some funds have "back-end" loads, which are charges levied on redemptions. These loads are often called *contingent deferred sales charges* and abbreviated **CDSC**. The CDSC usually declines through time. It might start out at 6 percent for shares held less than one year, then drop to 3 percent for shares held for two years, and disappear altogether on shares held for three or more years. Some funds offer "level" loads. That is, investors pay an added fee, typically 1 percent, every year they are in the fund.

Different loads are typically designated with letters. For example, front-end loads are often known as A-shares. Back-end loads are designated B-shares, and level loads are called C-shares. You might think that B-shares would be preferred to A-shares, because the back-end load would decline over time. You must look at all the fees involved, however. With the back-end and level loads, the fund companies often increase other fees associated with the fund (such as the 12b-1 fee discussed next). So, two factors that influence your preference for share type are their relative expense structures and your anticipated holding period.

12b-1 fees
Named for SEC Rule 12b-1, which allows funds to spend up to 1 percent of fund assets annually to cover distribution and marketing costs.

12B-1 FEES So-called **12b-1 fees** are named after the Securities and Exchange Commission (SEC) rule that permits them. Mutual funds are allowed to use a portion of the fund's assets to cover distribution and marketing costs. Funds that market directly to the public may use 12b-1 fees to pay for advertising and direct mailing costs. Funds that rely on brokers and other sales force personnel often use 12b-1 fees to provide compensation for their services. The total amount of these fees could be .25 percent to 1.0 percent of the fund's assets per year, although .25 percent is common.

Frequently, 12b-1 fees are used in conjunction with a CDSC. Such funds will often have no front-end load, but they effectively make it up through these other costs. Such funds may look like no-load funds, but they are really disguised load funds. Mutual funds with no front-end or back-end loads and no or minimal 12b-1 fees are often called "pure" no-load funds to distinguish them from the "not-so-pure" funds that may have no loads but still charge hefty 12b-1 fees.

MANAGEMENT FEES We briefly discussed management fees in an earlier section. Fees are usually based first on the size of the fund. Often, an incentive provision increases the fee if the fund outperforms some benchmark, like the S&P 500 Index. Management fees generally range from .25 percent to 1.5 percent of total fund assets every year.

TRADING COSTS Mutual funds have brokerage expenses from trading just like individuals do. As a result, mutual funds that do a lot of trading will have relatively high trading costs.

Trading costs can be difficult to get a handle on because they are not reported directly. However, in the prospectus, funds are required to report something known as **turnover**. A fund's turnover is a measure of how much trading a fund does. It is calculated as the lesser of a fund's total purchases or sales during a year, divided by average daily assets.[2]

turnover
A measure of how much trading a fund does, calculated as the lesser of total purchases or sales during a year divided by average daily assets.

EXAMPLE 4.3

Turnover

Suppose a fund had average daily assets of $50 million during a particular year. It bought $80 million worth of stock and sold $70 million during the year. What is its turnover?

The lesser of purchases or sales is $70 million, and average daily assets are $50 million. Turnover is thus $70/$50 = 1.4 times.

A fund with a turnover of 1.0 has, in effect, sold off its entire portfolio and replaced it once during the year. Similarly, a turnover of .50 indicates that, loosely speaking, the fund replaced half of its holdings during the year. All else the same, a higher turnover indicates more frequent trading and higher trading costs.

While increased trading obviously adds to the amount of commissions paid, it also has some related costs. For example, increased trading will result in gains (and potentially losses) being recognized in the fund. As these gains occur, capital gains will be passed through to the underlying investors. Potentially, these capital gains will increase taxes for the investors.

Another aspect of increased trading relates to the commissions themselves. Typically, an investment manager will have either an in-house or third-party broker who fulfills the trades. This relationship, however, is not always determined by who is the lowest cost provider. In fact, some fund managers purposefully choose higher cost providers. Why? The higher cost might provide added research or other materials that the fund manager considers beneficial in managing the fund. This added commission is referred to as *soft dollars*.

EXPENSE REPORTING

Mutual funds are required to report expenses in a fairly standardized way in the prospectus. The exact format varies, but the information reported is generally the same. There are three parts to an expense statement. Figure 4.2 shows this information as it was reported for the Fidelity Low-Priced Stock Fund.

The first part of the statement shows shareholder transaction expenses, which are generally loads and deferred sales charges. As indicated, for this fund, there is no front-end load

---

[2] Purchases and sales for a fund are usually different because of purchases and redemptions of fund shares by shareholders. For example, if a fund is growing, purchases will exceed sales.

| FIGURE 4.2 | Mutual Fund Expenses |

Fidelity®

Low-Priced Stock Fund

(fund number 316, trading symbol FLPSX)

Prospectus

October 9, 2009

Fee Table

The following table describes the fees and expenses that are incurred when you buy, hold, or sell shares of the fund.

The annual fund operating expenses provided below for the fund do not reflect the effect of any reduction of certain expenses during the period.

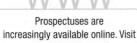

Prospectuses are increasingly available online. Visit www.fidelity.com to see some examples.

Shareholder fees (paid by the investor directly)

Sales charge (load) on purchases and reinvested distributions [A]	None
Deferred sales charge (load) on redemptions	None
Redemption fee on shares held less than 90 days (as a % of amount redeemed) [B]	1.50%

[A] The fund may impose a 3.00% sales charge on purchases upon 60 days notice to shareholders.

[B] A redemption fee may be charged when you sell your shares or if your shares are redeemed because your fund balance falls below the balance minimum for any reason, including solely due to declines in net asset value per share.

Annual operating expenses (paid from fund assets)

Management fee	0.72%
Distribution and/or Service (12b-1) fees	None
Other expenses	0.27%
Total annual fund operating expenses	0.99%

This **example** helps you compare the cost of investing in the fund with the cost of investing in other mutual funds.

Let's say, hypothetically, that the fund's annual return is 5% and that your shareholder fees and the fund's annual operating expenses are exactly as described in the fee table. This example illustrates the effect of fees and expenses, but is not meant to suggest actual or expected fees and expenses or returns, all of which may vary. For every $10,000 you invested, here's how much you would pay in total expenses if you sell all of your shares at the end of each time period indicated:

1 year	$	101
3 years	$	315
5 years	$	547
10 years	$	1,213

on shares purchased or on dividends received that are reinvested in the fund (mutual fund shareholders frequently reinvest any dividends received from the fund). The next item shows that there is no CDSC. The third item, labeled "redemption fee," refers to a back-end load that is applied under certain circumstances.

The second part of the statement, "Annual operating expenses," includes the management and 12b-1 fees. This fund's management fee was .72 percent of assets. There was no 12b-1 fee. The other expenses include things like legal, accounting, and reporting costs along with director fees. At .27 percent of assets, these costs are not trivial. The sum of these three items is the fund's total operating expense expressed as a percentage of assets, .99 percent in this case. To put the fees in perspective, this fund has about $28.9 billion in assets, so operating costs were about $286 million, of which about $208 million was paid to the fund manager.

The third part of the expense report gives a hypothetical example showing the total expense you would incur over time per $10,000 invested. The example is strictly hypothetical, however, and is only a rough guide. As shown in Figure 4.2, your costs would amount to $1,213 after 10 years per $10,000 invested, assuming a return of 5 percent per year. This third part of the expense statement is not all that useful, really. What matters for this fund is that expenses appear to run about .99 percent per year, so that is what you pay (in addition to loads, if applicable).

One thing to watch out for is that funds may have 12b-1 fees but may choose not to incur any distribution or marketing costs. Similarly, the fund manager can choose to rebate some of the management fee in a particular year (especially if the fund has done poorly). These actions create a low expense figure for a given year, but this does not mean that expenses won't be higher in the future.

WHY PAY LOADS AND FEES?

Because pure no-load funds exist, you might wonder why anyone would buy load funds or funds with substantial CDSC or 12b-1 fees. Finding a good answer to this question is becoming increasingly difficult. At one time, there simply weren't many no-load funds, and those that existed weren't widely known. Today, there are many good no-load funds, and competition among funds is forcing many funds to lower or do away with loads and other fees.

Having said this, there are basically two reasons that you might want to consider a load fund or a fund with above-average fees. First, you may simply want a fund run by a particular manager. A good example of this is the Fidelity Magellan Fund we mentioned earlier. For many years, it was run by Peter Lynch, who is widely regarded as one of the most successful managers in the history of the business. The Magellan Fund was a load fund, leaving you no choice but to pay the load to obtain Lynch's expertise. As we discuss in a later chapter, however, the historical performance of managers might not be a good reason to select a fund.

The other reason to consider paying a load is that you want a specialized type of fund. For example, you might be interested in investing in a fund that invests only in a particular foreign country, such as Brazil. We'll discuss such specialty funds in a later section, but for now we note that there is less competition among specialty funds, and, as a result, loads and fees tend to be higher.

CHECK THIS

4.4a   What is the difference between a load fund and a no-load fund?

4.4b   What are 12b-1 fees?

4.5 Short-Term Funds

Mutual funds are usually divided into two major groups, short-term funds and long-term funds. Short-term funds are collectively known as *money market mutual funds*. Long-term funds essentially include everything that is not a money market fund. We discuss long-term funds in our next section; here we focus on money market funds.

THERE'S NO SUCH THING AS A "SAFE" INVESTMENT

For conservative investors burned by supposedly "safe" investments, the credit crisis and slow-motion market crash hammered home one point: Everything carries some measure of risk, and even the stodgiest-seeming products require scrutiny.

Some of the first cracks appeared among ultrashort bond funds, which many investors regarded as almost as safe as cash. Starting in late 2007, many of these funds hit the skids, thanks to mortgage-related securities and other complex holdings that dropped during the credit crunch. Schwab YieldPlus Fund, for example, lost a startling 35% in 2008, while Fidelity Ultra-Short Bond lost 8%.

The market for auction-rate securities froze up early last year, stranding investors who thought they were holding a cash-like vehicle. A big money-market fund "broke the buck" last September, sparking panic among investors who generally expect these funds to maintain a $1 share price.

And target-date funds—even those designed for investors on the brink of retirement—dealt investors a blow as all their supposedly diversified holdings seemed to go down at once.

Many of these products have caught the attention of regulators, who have proposed tighter rules for money-market funds and examined target-date funds' strategies.

Such moves may make products marginally safer, but the burden remains on investors to know what they own, and to understand the risks.

But it's getting easier for investors to do their homework as financial advisors and analysts take a harder look at "safe" investments. Morningstar recently rolled out new ratings for target-date funds, analyzing the funds' holdings, fees, managers and other factors.

And with some people now asking about such issues as diversifying cash among multiple institutions, advisors say, investors are rethinking even their lowest-risk holdings.

Source: Eleanor Laise, *The Wall Street Journal*, September 11, 2009. Reprinted with permission of *The Wall Street Journal*. © 2009 Dow Jones & Company, Inc. All Rights Reserved Worldwide.

MONEY MARKET MUTUAL FUNDS

money market mutual fund

A mutual fund specializing in money market instruments.

As the name suggests, **money market mutual funds**, or MMMFs, specialize in money market instruments. As we describe elsewhere, these are short-term debt obligations issued by governments and corporations. Money market funds were introduced in the early 1970s and have grown tremendously. At the end of 2009, about 720 money market funds managed almost $3.4 trillion in assets. All money market funds are open-end funds.

Most money market funds invest in high-quality, low-risk instruments with maturities of less than 90 days. As a result, they have relatively little risk. However, some buy riskier assets or have longer maturities than others, so they do not all carry equally low risk, as the nearby *Investment Updates* box illustrates. For example, some buy only very short-term U.S. government securities and are therefore essentially risk-free. Others buy mostly securities issued by corporations, which entail some risk. We discuss the different types of money market instruments and their relative risks elsewhere in the book.

MONEY MARKET FUND ACCOUNTING A unique feature of money market funds is that their net asset values are always $1 per share. This is purely an accounting gimmick, however. A money market fund simply sets the number of shares equal to the fund's assets. In other words, if the fund has $100 million in assets, then it has 100 million shares. As the fund earns interest on its investments, the fund owners are simply given more shares.

The reason money market mutual funds always maintain a $1 net asset value is to make them resemble bank accounts. As long as a money market fund invests in very safe, interest-bearing, short-maturity assets, its net asset value will not drop below $1 per share. There is no guarantee, however, that the NAV will stay above $1, as the *Investment Updates* box suggests. The term "breaking the buck" is used to describe a drop below $1 in net asset value. Breaking the buck is a very rare occurrence. Following the crash of 2008, a few money

WWW

Visit
www.mfea.com
for info on thousands of funds, including MMMFs.

market funds, beginning with the Reserve Primary Fund, experienced substantial losses in their underlying holdings, causing them to break the buck. Further, some funds were unable to maintain the $1 mark, because returns on short-term securities fell to the point where they were insufficient to cover fund costs. Rather than breaking the buck, many of these money market funds simply shut down.

TAXES AND MONEY MARKET FUNDS Money market funds are either taxable or tax-exempt. Taxable funds are more common; of the $3.4 trillion in total money market fund assets at the end of 2009, taxable funds accounted for about 87.8 percent. As the name suggests, the difference in the two fund types lies in their tax treatment. As a general rule, interest earned on state and local government (or "municipal") securities is exempt from federal income tax. Nontaxable money market funds therefore buy only these types of tax-exempt securities.

Some tax-exempt funds go even further. Interest paid by one state is often subject to state taxes in another. Some tax-exempt funds therefore buy only securities issued by a single state. For residents of that state, the interest earned is free of both federal and state taxes. For beleaguered New York City residents, there are even "triple-tax-free" funds that invest only in New York City obligations, thereby allowing residents to escape federal, state, and local income taxes on the interest received.

Because of their favorable tax treatment, tax-exempt money market instruments have much lower interest rates, or *yields*.[3] For example, in late 2009, taxable money market funds offered about .43 percent interest, whereas tax-exempt funds offered only .27 percent interest. Which is better depends on your individual tax bracket. If you're in a 40 percent bracket, then the taxable fund is paying only $.0043 \times (1 - .40) = .0026$, or .26 percent, on an aftertax basis, so you are slightly better off with the tax-exempt fund.

EXAMPLE 4.4   **Taxes and Money Market Fund Yields**

In our discussion just above, suppose you were in a 20 percent tax bracket. Which type of fund is more attractive?

On an aftertax basis, the taxable fund is offering $.0043 \times (1 - .20) = .0034$, or .34 percent, so the taxable fund is more attractive.

MONEY MARKET DEPOSIT ACCOUNTS

Most banks offer what are called "money market" deposit accounts, or MMDAs, which are much like money market mutual funds. For example, both money market funds and money market deposit accounts generally have limited check-writing privileges.

There is a very important distinction between such a bank-offered money market account and a money market fund, however. A bank money market account is a bank deposit and offers FDIC protection, whereas a money market fund does not. A money market fund will generally offer SIPC protection, but this is not a perfect substitute. Confusingly, some banks offer both money market accounts and, through a separate, affiliated entity, money market funds.

CHECK THIS

4.5a   What is a money market mutual fund? What are the two types?

4.5b   How do money market mutual funds maintain a constant net asset value?

---

[3] We discuss how yields on money market instruments are calculated in another chapter.

4.6 Long-Term Funds

WWW

One of the best mutual
fund sites is
www.morningstar.com

There are many different types of long-term funds. Historically, mutual funds were classified as stock, bond, or balanced funds. As a part of the rapid growth in mutual funds, however, placing all funds into these three categories is becoming increasingly difficult. Also, providers of mutual fund information do not use the same classification schemes.

Mutual funds have different goals, and a fund's objective is the major determinant of the fund type. All mutual funds must state the fund's objective in the prospectus. For example, the Fidelity Independence Fund states:

> The fund's objective is capital appreciation. Normally, the fund's strategy is to invest primarily in common stocks of domestic and foreign issuers. The fund strategy may result in the realization of capital gains without considering the tax consequences to shareholders. Fidelity Management & Research Company (FMR) is not constrained by any particular investment style and may invest in "growth" stocks, "value" stocks, or both, at any given time.

Thus, this fund invests in different types of stocks with the goal of capital appreciation. This fund is clearly a stock fund, and it might further be classified as a "capital appreciation" fund or "aggressive growth" fund, depending on whose classification scheme is used.

Mutual fund objectives are an important consideration; unfortunately, the truth is they frequently are too vague to provide useful information. For example, a very common objective reads like this: "The Big Bucks Fund seeks capital appreciation, income, and capital preservation." Translation: The fund seeks to (1) increase the value of its shares, (2) generate income for its shareholders, and (3) not lose money. Well, don't we all! More to the point, funds with very similar-sounding objectives can have very different portfolios and, consequently, very different risks. As a result, it is a mistake to look only at a fund's stated objective: Actual portfolio holdings speak louder than prospectus promises.

STOCK FUNDS

Stock funds exist in great variety. We consider nine separate general types and some subtypes. We also consider some new varieties that don't fit in any category.

CAPITAL APPRECIATION VERSUS INCOME The first four types of stock funds trade off capital appreciation and dividend income.

1. *Capital appreciation.* As in our example just above, these funds seek maximum capital appreciation. They generally invest in companies that have, in the opinion of the fund manager, the best prospects for share price appreciation without regard to dividends, company size, or, for some funds, country. Often this means investing in unproven companies or companies perceived to be out-of-favor.

2. *Growth.* These funds also seek capital appreciation, but they tend to invest in larger, more established companies. Such funds may be somewhat less volatile as a result. Dividends are not an important consideration.

3. *Growth and income.* Capital appreciation is still the main goal, but at least part of the focus is on dividend-paying companies.

4. *Equity income.* These funds focus almost exclusively on stocks with relatively high dividend yields, thereby maximizing the current income of the portfolio.

Among these four fund types, the greater the emphasis on growth, the greater the risk, at least as a general matter. Again, however, these are only rough classifications. Equity income funds, for example, frequently invest heavily in public utility stocks; such stocks had heavy losses in the first part of the 1990s.

COMPANY SIZE–BASED FUNDS These next three fund types focus on companies in a particular size range.

1. *Small company.* As the name suggests, these funds focus on stocks in small companies, where "small" refers to the total market value of the stock. Such funds are often called "small-cap" funds, where "cap" is short for total market value or capitalization. In Chapter 1, we saw that small stocks have traditionally performed very well, at least over the long run, hence the demand for funds that specialize in such stocks. With small-company mutual funds, what constitutes small is variable, ranging from perhaps $10 million up to $1 billion or so in total market value, and some funds specialize in smaller companies than others. Since most small companies don't pay dividends, these funds necessarily emphasize capital appreciation.

2. *Midcap.* These funds usually specialize in stocks that are too small to be in the S&P 500 Index but too large to be considered small-cap stocks.

3. *Large company.* Large-capitalization, or "large-cap," funds invest in companies with large market values. Most large-cap firms have a market value in excess of $5 billion.

INTERNATIONAL FUNDS Research has shown that diversifying internationally can significantly improve the risk-return trade-off for investors. The number of international funds grew rapidly during the 1980s and early 1990s. However, that growth slowed sharply in the late 1990s. Their number shrank in the early 2000s, but their numbers have increased since 2005. The two fund groups that invest outside the U.S. are:

1. *Global.* These funds have substantial international holdings but also maintain significant investments in U.S. stocks.

2. *International.* These funds are like global funds, except they focus on non-U.S. equities.

Among international funds, some specialize in specific regions of the world, such as Europe, the Pacific Rim, or South America. Others specialize in individual countries. Today, there is at least one mutual fund specializing in essentially every country in the world that has a stock market, however small.

International funds that specialize in countries with small or recently established stock markets are often called *emerging markets funds.* Almost all single-country funds, and especially emerging markets funds, are not well-diversified and have historically been extremely volatile.

Many funds that are not classified as international funds may actually have substantial overseas investments, so this is one thing to watch out for. It is not unusual for a fund to call itself a "growth" fund and actually invest heavily outside the United States.

SECTOR FUNDS Sector funds specialize in specific sectors of the economy and often focus on particular industries or particular commodities. There are far too many different types to list here. There are funds that only buy software companies, and funds that only buy hardware companies. There are funds that specialize in natural gas producers, oil producers, and precious metals producers. In fact, essentially every major industry in the U.S. economy is covered by at least one fund.

One thing to notice about sector funds is that, like single-country funds, they are obviously not well-diversified. Every year, many of the best performing mutual funds (in terms of total return) are sector funds simply because whatever sector of the economy is hottest will generally have the largest stock price increases. Funds specializing in that sector will do well. In the same vein, and for the same reason, the worst performing funds are also almost always some type of sector fund. When it comes to mutual funds, past performance is almost always an unreliable guide to future performance; nowhere is this more true than with sector funds.

OTHER FUND TYPES AND ISSUES Three other types of stock funds that don't fit easily into one of the above categories bear discussing: *index funds,* so-called *social conscience funds,* and *tax-managed funds.*

1. *Index funds.* Index funds simply hold the stocks that make up a particular index in the same relative proportions as the index. The most important index funds are

S&P 500 funds, which are intended to track the performance of the S&P 500, the large stock index we discussed in Chapter 1. By their nature, index funds are passively managed, meaning that the fund manager trades only as necessary to match the index. Such funds are appealing in part because they are generally characterized by low turnover and low operating expenses. Another reason index funds have grown rapidly is that there is considerable debate over whether mutual fund managers can consistently beat the averages. If they can't, the argument runs, why pay loads and management fees when it's cheaper just to buy the averages by indexing? To put the importance of index funds into perspective, as of late 2009, the largest stock index mutual fund in the United States was the Vanguard 500 Index Fund, with $87.3 billion in assets. This fund, as the name suggests, is an S&P 500 Index fund.

To learn more about "social conscience" funds, visit www.socialinvest.org and www.domini.com

Is vice nice? Visit www.usamutuals.com/vicefund to find out.

2. *Social conscience funds.* These funds are a relatively new creation. They invest only in companies whose products, policies, or politics are viewed as socially desirable. The specific social objectives range from environmental issues to personnel policies. The Parnassus Fund is a well-known example, avoiding the alcoholic beverage, tobacco, gambling, weapons, and nuclear power industries. Of course, consensus on what is socially desirable or responsible is hard to find. In fact, there are so-called sin funds (and sector funds) that specialize in these very industries! See the nearby *Investment Updates* box for some information on other unique funds.

3. *Tax-managed funds.* Taxable mutual funds are generally managed without regard for the tax liabilities of fund owners. Fund managers focus on (and are frequently rewarded based on) total pretax returns. However, recent research has shown that some fairly simple strategies can greatly improve the aftertax returns to shareholders and that focusing just on pretax returns is not a good idea for taxable investors. Tax-managed funds try to hold down turnover to minimize realized capital gains, and they try to match realized gains with realized losses. Such strategies work particularly well for index funds. For example, the Schwab 1000 Fund is a fund that tracks the Russell 1000 Index, a widely followed 1,000-stock index. However, the fund will deviate from strictly following the index to a certain extent to avoid realizing taxable gains, and, as a result, the fund holds turnover to a minimum. Fund shareholders have largely escaped taxes as a result. We predict that funds promoting such strategies will become increasingly common as investors become more aware of the tax consequences of fund ownership.

TAXABLE AND MUNICIPAL BOND FUNDS

Most bond funds invest in domestic corporate and government securities, although some invest in foreign government and non-U.S. corporate bonds as well. As we will see, there are a relatively small number of bond fund types. Basically, five characteristics distinguish bond funds:

1. *Maturity range.* Different funds hold bonds of different maturities, ranging from quite short (2 years) to quite long (25–30 years).

2. *Credit quality.* Some bonds are much safer than others in terms of the possibility of default. United States government bonds have no default risk, while so-called junk bonds have significant default risk.

3. *Taxability.* Municipal bond funds buy only bonds that are free from federal income tax. Taxable funds buy only taxable issues.

4. *Type of bond.* Some funds specialize in particular types of fixed-income instruments such as mortgages.

5. *Country.* Most bond funds buy only domestic issues, but some buy foreign company and government issues.

THE 10 STRANGEST MUTUAL FUNDS

When mutual funds step off the beaten path, there's no telling what will happen. In the past, for example, oddball funds have fought the war on terror (the Ancora Homeland Security Fund), tried to prop up the sky (the Chicken Little Growth Fund), and fantasized about swinging a presidential election (the Blue Fund). And although those three particular funds failed, others have stepped in to carry the torch and preserve a long and proud tradition of eccentric investing styles. Here are the 10 quirkiest funds we could find:

The Congressional Effect Fund (CEFFX) This fund exists to answer the question posed in enormous letters at the top of its website: "How much investment wealth does Congress destroy?" As the question suggests, the fund has a rather cynical view of the country's political leaders. In fact, its manager sees politicians' disruptive influences as so far-reaching that when Congress is in session, he pulls completely out of the stock market and moves the entire portfolio into treasuries, cash, and money market funds.

The StockCar Stocks Index Fund (SCARX) At first glance, this fund, which tracks an index of companies that support NASCAR's Sprint Cup Series, is a dream come true for racing fans. But a more careful look reveals a different story—most of its holdings are only tangentially related to NASCAR. Investors might be surprised to see that aside from car-related names, the fund's top holdings include Disney, Target, Coca-Cola, and Sony.

The Blue Chip Winery Fund Jokingly called the best "liquid" investments on the market, wine funds once enjoyed some popularity. But unlike a good glass of wine—or investment, for that matter—these funds have usually not gotten better with age, and most of the ones that were around several years ago have since crashed and burned. Instead of buying actual bottles of wine, it will invest exclusively in real estate holdings like wineries and storage facilities.

The Herzfeld Caribbean Basin Fund (NASDAQCM: CUBA) While most managers talk about investing with long time horizons, few are willing to stake large chunks of their fortunes on an event that may never happen in the lifetime of their funds. But for the past 15 years, fund manager Thomas Herzfeld has been doing just that as he patiently waits for the Cuba embargo to come crashing down.

The Marketocracy Masters 100 Fund (MOFQX) If you're a mutual fund investor, chances are there has been a time when you've loudly ranted about how you can do a better job than your fund manager. With this fund, you get the opportunity to be your own manager—at least kind of, and only if you beat out thousands of other investors. On Marketocracy.com, investors create hypothetical online portfolios; currently, there are roughly 30,000 active users. Of the portfolios they produce, Marketocracy takes its favorites—up to 100 at a time—and uses them to select the Masters 100's actual holdings.

The Vice Fund (VICEX) As its name suggests, this fund invests in "sin stocks," and its list of top holdings is littered with companies that conscientious investors love to hate: Lorillard, British American Tobacco, and Altria. Mixed in with these big names in tobacco are defense and weapons giants like Lockheed Martin and Raytheon, beer companies such as Carlsberg A/S and Molson Coors, and some gambling picks.

The Monetta Young Investor Fund (MYIFX) Ever wonder what would happen if you put your third-grade child in charge of a mutual fund? Chances are it would include plenty of Disney and McDonald's shares. It's no coincidence that those companies are among this fund's top holdings. And while Monetta doesn't literally have an army of elementary school students serving as its stock pickers, one of its stated purposes is to act as if it did.

The Timothy Plan Aggressive Growth Fund (TAAGX) Have you ever wanted a complimentary moral audit? On this fund's website, that's only one of several services offered to potential clients who are interested in investing in accordance with Christian values. There's also a "Hall of Shame," which lists companies the fund avoids, and a section to help parents identify potentially offensive video games. Like the other Timothy Plan funds, the Aggressive Growth Fund stays away from companies that are connected to alcohol, tobacco, gambling, and pornography.

The Adaptive Allocation Fund (AAXCX) Since the fund's advisor is a company called Critical Math, it unsurprisingly takes a rather formulaic approach to investing. In fact, the fund, which launched in 2006, uses upwards of 80 "fundamental" models—in addition to a number of "technical" models—to decide where to invest. With these models, the fund's managers take the jack-of-all-trades approach to a new level, giving themselves the ability to invest any portion of the portfolio in essentially any type of security for as long of a time period as they see fit.

The Women's Leadership Fund. Swiss company Naissance Capital will launch this fund next year with the goal of promoting gender-conscious investing. When the fund opens its doors, it will focus on companies that have significant female representation in their leadership teams.

Source: Rob Silverblatt, *U.S. News & World Report*, December 2, 2009.

SHORT-TERM AND INTERMEDIATE-TERM FUNDS As the names suggest, these two fund types focus on bonds in a specific maturity range. Short-term maturities are generally considered to be less than five years. Intermediate-term would be less than 10 years. There are both taxable and municipal bond funds with these maturity targets.

One thing to be careful of with these types of funds is that the credit quality of the issues can vary from fund to fund. One fund could hold very risky intermediate-term bonds, while another might hold only U.S. government issues with similar maturities.

GENERAL FUNDS For both taxable and municipal bonds, this fund category is kind of a catch-all. Funds in this category simply don't specialize in any particular way. Our warning just above concerning varied credit quality applies here. Maturities can differ substantially as well.

HIGH-YIELD FUNDS High-yield municipal and taxable funds specialize in low-credit quality issues. Such issues have higher yields because of their greater risks. As a result, high-yield bond funds can be quite volatile.

MORTGAGE FUNDS A number of funds specialize in so-called mortgage-backed securities such as GNMA (Government National Mortgage Association, referred to as "Ginnie Mae") issues. We discuss this important type of security in detail in a later chapter. There are no municipal mortgage-backed securities (yet), so these are all taxable bond funds.

WORLD FUNDS A relatively limited number of taxable funds invest worldwide. Some specialize in only government issues; others buy a variety of non-U.S. issues. These are all taxable funds.

INSURED FUNDS This is a type of municipal bond fund. Municipal bond issuers frequently purchase insurance that guarantees the bond's payments will be made. Such bonds have very little possibility of default, so some funds specialize in them.

SINGLE-STATE MUNICIPAL FUNDS Earlier we discussed how some money market funds specialize in issues from a single state. The same is true for some bond funds. Such funds are especially important in large states such as California and other high-tax states. Confusingly, this classification refers only to long-term funds. Short and intermediate single-state funds are classified with other maturity-based municipal funds.

STOCK AND BOND FUNDS

This last major fund group includes a variety of funds. The only common feature is that these funds don't invest exclusively in either stocks or bonds. For this reason, they are often called "blended" or "hybrid" funds. We discuss a few of the main types.

BALANCED FUNDS Balanced funds maintain a relatively fixed split between stocks and bonds. They emphasize relatively safe, high-quality investments. Such funds provide a kind of "one-stop" shopping for fund investors, particularly smaller investors, because they diversify into both stocks and bonds.

ASSET ALLOCATION FUNDS Two types of funds carry this label. The first is an extended version of a balanced fund. Such a fund holds relatively fixed proportional investments in stocks, bonds, money market instruments, and perhaps real estate or some other investment class. The target proportions may be updated or modified periodically.

The other type of asset allocation fund is often called a *flexible portfolio fund*. Here, the fund manager may hold up to 100 percent in stocks, bonds, or money market instruments, depending on her views about the likely performance of these investments. These funds essentially try to time the market, guessing which general type of investment will do well (or least poorly) over the months ahead.

CONVERTIBLE FUNDS Some bonds are convertible, meaning they can be swapped for a fixed number of shares of stock at the option of the bondholder. Some mutual funds specialize in these bonds.

INCOME FUNDS An income fund emphasizes generating dividend and coupon income on its investments, so it would hold a variety of dividend-paying common stocks, as well as preferred stocks and bonds of various maturities.

TARGET DATE FUNDS Also known as life-cycle funds, the asset allocation chosen by target date funds is based on the anticipated retirement date of the investors holding the fund. For example, if a fund company offers a Target Date 2040 fund, the fund is for people planning to retire in or around the year 2040. Because of its long-term investment horizon, this fund will probably hold a portfolio that is heavily allocated to stocks—both domestic and international. As the years pass, the fund manager will increase the asset allocation to fixed income and decrease the equity holdings of the portfolio. This approach is like the equity allocation guideline we discuss elsewhere. Using this guideline, your percentage equity allocation should be 100 (or 120) minus your age. Target date funds appeal to investors who want a "hands-off" approach to investing. A potential downside to target date funds is that they sometimes add a layer of management fees—but these extra fees have become less common in recent years.

MUTUAL FUND OBJECTIVES: RECENT DEVELOPMENTS

As we mentioned earlier, a mutual fund's stated objective may not be all that informative. In recent years, there has been a trend toward classifying a mutual fund's objective based on its actual holdings. For example, Figure 4.3 illustrates the classifications used by *The Wall Street Journal*.

A key thing to notice in Figure 4.3 is that most general-purpose funds (as opposed to specialized types such as sector funds) are classified based on the market "cap" of the stocks they hold (small, midsize, or large) and also on whether the fund tends to invest in either "growth" or "value" stocks (or both). We will discuss growth versus value stocks in a later chapter; for now, it is enough to know that "growth" stocks are those considered more likely to grow rapidly. "Value" stocks are those that look to be relatively undervalued and thus may be attractive for that reason. Notice that, in this scheme, *all* stocks are "growth," "value," or a blend of the two, a classic example of the Lake Wobegon effect.[4]

The mutual fund "style" box is an increasingly common sight. A style box is a way of visually representing a fund's investment focus by placing the fund into one of nine boxes like this:

As shown, this particular fund focuses on large-cap, value stocks.

These newer mutual fund objectives are also useful for screening mutual funds. As our nearby *Work the Web* box shows, many Web sites have mutual fund selectors that allow you to find funds with particular characteristics.

---

[4] Lake Wobegon is a mystical place in Minnesota made famous by Garrison Keillor where "the men are strong, the women are beautiful, and all the children are above average." See www.phc.mpr.org for more.

FIGURE 4.3 Mutual Fund Objectives

MUTUAL-FUND OBJECTIVES

Categories compiled by The Wall Street Journal, based on classifications by Lipper Inc.

STOCK FUNDS

Emerging Markets (EM): Funds investing in emerging-market equity securities, where the "emerging market" is defined by a country's GNP per capita and other economic measures.

Equity Income (EI): Funds seeking high current income and growth of income by investing in equities.

European Region (EU): Funds investing in markets or operations concentrated in the European region.

Global Stock (GL): Funds investing in securities traded outside of the U.S. and may own U.S. securities as well.

Gold Oriented (AU): Funds investing in gold mines, gold-mining finance houses, gold coins or bullion.

Health/Biotech (HB): Funds investing in companies related to health care, medicine and biotechnology.

International Stock (IL) (non-U.S.): Canadian; International; International Small Cap.

Latin American (LT): Funds investing in markets or operations concentrated in Latin American region.

Large-Cap Growth (LG): Funds investing in large companies with long-term earnings that are ex-pected to grow significantly faster than the earnings of stocks in major indexes. Funds normally have above-average price-to-earnings ratios, price-to-book ratios and three-year earnings growth.

Large-Cap Core (LC): Funds investing in large companies, with wide latitude in the type of shares they buy. On average, the price-to-earnings ratios, price-to-book ratios, and three-year earnings growth are in line with those of the U.S. diversified large-cap funds' universe average.

Large-Cap Value (LV): Funds investing in large companies that are considered undervalued relative to major stock indexes based on price-to-earnings ratios, price-to-book ratios or other factors.

Midcap Growth (MG): Funds investing in midsize companies with long-term earnings that are ex-pected to grow significantly faster than the earnings of stocks in major indexes. Funds normally have above-average price-to-earnings ratios, price-to-book ratios and three-year earnings growth.

Midcap Core (MC): Funds investing in midsize companies, with wide latitude in the type of shares they buy. On average, the price-to-earnings ratios, price-to-book ratios, and three-year earnings growth are in line with those of the U.S. diversified midcap funds' universe average.

Midcap Value (MV): Funds investing in midsize companies that are considered undervalued relative to major stock indexes based on price-to-earnings ratios, price-to-book ratios or other factors.

Multicap Growth (XG): Funds investing in companies of various sizes, with long-term earnings ex-pected to grow significantly faster than the earnings of stocks in major indexes. Funds normally have above-average price-to-earnings ratios, price-to-book ratios, and three-year earnings growth.

Multicap Core (XC): Funds investing in companies of various sizes with average price-to-earnings ratios, price-to-book ratios and earnings growth.

Multicap Value (XV): Funds investing in companies of various size, normally those that are consid-ered undervalued relative to major stock indexes based on price-to-earnings ratios, price-to-book ratios or other factors.

Natural Resources (NR): Funds investing in natural-resource stocks.

Pacific Region (PR): Funds that invest in China Region; Japan; Pacific Ex-Japan; Pacific Region.

Science & Technology (TK): Funds investing in science and technology stocks. Includes telecommunication funds.

Sector (SE): Funds investing in financial services; real estate; specialty & miscellaneous.

S&P 500 Index (SP): Funds that are passively managed and are designed to replicate the performance of the Standard & Poor's 500-stock Index on a reinvested basis.

Small-Cap Growth (SG): Funds investing in small companies with long-term earnings that are expected to grow significantly faster than the earnings of stocks in major indexes. Funds normally have above-average price-to-earnings ratios, price-to-book ratios, and three-year earnings growth.

Small-Cap Core (SC): Funds investing in small companies, with wide latitude in the type of shares they buy. On average, the price-to-earnings ratios, price-to-book ratios, and three-year earnings growth are in line with those of the U.S. diversified small-cap funds' universe average.

Small-Cap Value (SV): Funds investing in small companies that are considered undervalued relative to major stock indexes based on price-to-earnings ratios, price-to-book ratios or other factors.

Specialty Equity (SQ): Funds investing in all market-capitalization ranges, with no restrictions for any one range. May have strategies that are distinctly different from other diversified stock funds.

Utility (UT): Funds investing in utility stocks.

TAXABLE-BOND FUNDS

Short-Term Bond (SB): Ultra-short Obligation; Short Investment Grade Debt; Short-Intermediate Investment Grade Debt.

Short-Term U.S. (SU): Short U.S. Treasury; Short U.S. Government; Short-Intermediate U.S. Government debt.

Intermediate Bond (IB): Funds investing in investment-grade debt issues (rated in the top four grades) with dollar-weighted average maturities of five to 10 years.

Intermediate U.S. (IG): Intermediate U.S. Government; Intermediate U.S. Treasury.

Long-Term Bond (AB): Funds investing in corporate- and government-debt issues in the top grades.

Long-Term U.S. (LU): General U.S. Government; General U.S. Treasury; Target Maturity.

General U.S. Taxable (GT): Funds investing in general bonds.

High-Yield Taxable (HC): Funds aiming for high current yields from fixed-income securities and tend to invest in lower-grade debt.

Mortgage (MT): Adjustable Rate Mortgage; GNMA; U.S. Mortgage.

World Bond (WB): Emerging Markets Debt; Global Income; International Income; Short World MultiMarket Income.

MUNICIPAL-DEBT FUNDS

Short-Term Muni (SM): California Short-Intermediate Muni Debt; Other States Short-Intermediate Muni Debt; Short-Intermediate Muni Debt; Short Muni Debt.

Intermediate Muni (IM): Intermediate-term Muni Debt including single states.

General Muni (GM): Funds investing in muni-debt issues in the top-four credit ratings.

Single-State Municipal (SS): Funds investing in debt of individual states.

High-Yield Municipal (HM): Funds investing in lower-rated muni debt.

Insured Muni (NM): California Insured Muni Debt; Florida Insured Muni Debt; Insured Muni Debt; New York Insured Muni Debt.

STOCK & BOND FUNDS

Balanced (BL): Primary objective is to conserve principal, by maintaining a balanced portfolio of both stocks and bonds.

Stock/Bond Blend (MP): Multipurpose funds such as Balanced Target Maturity; Convertible Securities; Flexible Income; Flexible Portfolio; Global Flexible and Income funds, that invest in both stocks and bonds.

Source: Reprinted with permission of *The Wall Street Journal.* © 2008 Dow Jones & Company, Inc. All Rights Reserved Worldwide.

CHECK THIS

4.6a What are the three major types of long-term funds? Give several examples of each and describe their investment policies.

4.6b What do single-state municipal funds, single-country stock funds, and sector stock funds have in common?

4.6c What are the distinguishing characteristics of a bond fund?

WORK THE WEB

As we have discussed in this chapter, there are many thousands of mutual funds. So how do you pick one? One answer is to visit one of the many mutual fund sites on the Web and use a fund selector. Here is an example of how they are used. We went to www.morningstar.com and clicked on the "Fund Screener." Note that you might have to register to have access to this feature. There are many other fund selectors on the Web. For example, www.wsj.com offers one for subscribers to *The Wall Street Journal*.

Using the Morningstar fund screener, we indicated that we were interested in a domestic stock fund that invests in small-cap growth stocks with relatively low expenses, no loads, and several other features. Out of a database of more than 15,000 funds, here is what was returned:

| Change Criteria | Results of Search | New Search | 💡 Analyst Insights | Instructions |

View: Snapshot ⌄ Results: 1-25 of 30 Previous 25 | Next 25

Check boxes to: Test in a Portfolio | Add to my Portfolio   **Score These Results**

▲ Fund Name	Morningstar Category	Morningstar Rating	YTD Return (%)	Expense Ratio (%)	Total Assets ($ mil)
Baron Growth	Small Growth	★★★★★	29.60	1.32	5,187
Baron Small Cap	Small Growth	★★★★	27.75	1.32	2,732
Eagle Small Cap Growth A	Small Growth	★★★★	25.40	1.25	323
Eagle Small Cap Growth R5	Small Growth	★★★★	25.92	0.90	323
Evergreen Growth A Load W	Small Growth	★★★★	32.10	1.25	288
ING Baron Small Cap Growt	Small Growth	★★★★	30.97	1.08	668
ING Baron Small Cap Growt	Small Growth	★★★★	30.69	1.31	668
Ivy Small Cap Growth A Lo	Small Growth	★★★★	37.07	1.56	369
Ivy Small Cap Growth Y	Small Growth	★★★★	37.44	1.34	369
JPMorgan Small Cap Growth	Small Growth	★★★★	30.73	1.25	400
MassMutual Select Small C	Small Growth	★★★★	31.71	1.51	467
MassMutual Select Small C	Small Growth	★★★★	32.09	1.27	467
MassMutual Select Small C	Small Growth	★★★★	32.35	0.98	467
MassMutual Select Small C	Small Growth	★★★★	32.24	1.12	467
MFS New Discovery I	Small Growth	★★★★	53.09	1.25	637
MFS New Discovery R3	Small Growth	★★★★	52.79	1.55	637
MFS New Discovery R4	Small Growth	★★★★	53.06	1.30	637
Nicholas Limited Edition	Small Growth	★★★★★	21.41	1.12	137
Pioneer Oak Ridge Small C	Small Growth	★★★★★	20.47	1.40	451
Royce 100 Svc	Small Growth	★★★★★	32.81	1.49	202
Royce Value Plus Svc	Small Growth	★★★★	32.70	1.43	2,977
Van Kampen Small Cap Grow	Small Growth	★★★★★	10.91	1.38	941
Van Kampen Small Cap Grow	Small Growth	★★★★	10.94	1.15	941
Waddell & Reed Small Cap	Small Growth	★★★★	37.31	1.55	672
Waddell & Reed Small Cap	Small Growth	★★★★	38.13	1.06	672
Small Growth Avg			27.99	1.61	434
S&P 500			21.06		

Check boxes to: Test in a Portfolio | Add to my Portfolio   **Score These Results**

View: Snapshot ⌄ Results: 1-25 of 30 Previous 25 | Next 25

This search narrowed things down in a hurry! Now we have a list of 30 funds, the first 25 of which are shown here in alphabetical order. Clicking on the name of the fund takes you to the Morningstar Web site on the fund, where you can learn more about the fund.

4.7 Mutual Fund Performance

We close our discussion of open-end mutual funds by looking at some of the performance information reported in the financial press. We then discuss the usefulness of such information for selecting mutual funds.

MUTUAL FUND PERFORMANCE INFORMATION

Mutual fund performance is very closely tracked by a number of organizations. Financial publications of all types periodically provide mutual fund data, and many provide lists of recommended funds. We examine *Wall Street Journal* information in this section, but by no means is this the only source or the most comprehensive.[5] However, *The Wall Street Journal* (and its online version) is a particularly timely source because it reports mutual fund year-to-date returns on a daily basis, and it provides a summary of average investment performance by fund category on a regular basis. The information we consider here applies only to open-end funds.

Figure 4.4 reproduces "Mutual-Fund Yardsticks," a feature appearing online at www.wsj.com. This table compares the recent investment performance of the major fund categories, ranked by performance. Figure 4.4 includes yardsticks for many categories of equity funds, bond funds, and balanced stock and bond funds.

Figure 4.5 is a small section of the mutual fund price quotations regularly reported by *The Wall Street Journal* online. All of the funds listed in Figure 4.5 belong to the large family of funds managed by Fidelity Investments. We highlighted the Blue Chip Growth Fund (abbreviated BluCh). As its name suggests, the Blue Chip Fund has a large-cap focus.[6]

The first piece of information given is the fund's symbol, FBGRX. Following the symbol is the latest net asset value, NAV, for the fund. Following the NAV are three performance measures. The first number is the daily change in the fund's NAV. In this case, the NAV of the Blue Chip Growth Fund rose $0.07 from the previous day's level. Next we have the year-to-date (YTD) return, 5.5 percent. The last column is the three-year annualized return for this fund, 1.4 percent. An "NS" in this column just means that the fund did not exist at the start of the period.

If you click on "BluCh," a screen appears with detailed performance measures. Figure 4.6 shows part of this screen. You can see in Figure 4.6 that this fund falls into the category of "Large-Cap Growth." Below the fund category, you can see a series of performance measures. The first number is the year-to-date return, 5.53 percent (which was rounded to 5.5 percent in Figure 4.5). Next we have annualized returns for the previous 1, 3, 5, and 10 years. Thus, the Blue Chip Fund averaged −2.44 percent per year over the previous 10 years. This return slightly exceeds the large-cap growth category but falls quite a bit short of the S&P 500 Index. Note, however, that both benchmarks lost money over the last 10 years.

At the bottom of Figure 4.6, you see a letter grade assigned to each of the 1-, 3-, 5-, and 10-year returns. A grade of "A" means that the fund's return is in the top 20 percent of all funds in the same category. A grade of "B" means the next 20 percent, and so on. Notice that the grades are strictly relative, so mutual funds, in effect, are graded on the curve!

HOW USEFUL ARE FUND PERFORMANCE RATINGS?

If you look at the performance ratings reported in Figure 4.6, you might wonder why anyone would buy a fund in a category other than those with the highest returns. Well, the lessons learned in Chapter 1 suggest the answer is these historical returns do not consider the riskiness of the various fund categories. For example, if the market has done well, the best ranked funds may simply be the riskiest funds, since the riskiest funds normally perform the best in a rising market. In a market downturn, however, these best ranked funds are most likely to become the worst ranked funds, since the riskiest funds normally perform the worst in a falling market.

---

[5] For more detailed information, publications from companies such as Morningstar, Weisenberger, and Value Line are often available in the library or online. Of course, a mutual fund's prospectus and annual report contain a great deal of information as well.

[6] A blue chip stock is a well-established, profitable, very well regarded company. A good example might be IBM. The term "blue chip" refers to the game of poker, in which chips are used for betting. Traditionally, the blue chips are the most valuable.

FIGURE 4.4   Mutual Fund Yardsticks

Mutual Fund Yardsticks

Friday, March 26, 2010

Mutual-fund categories and their benchmarks ranked by one-year total return. Yardsticks are based on categories compiled by The Wall Street Journal, based on Lipper, Inc. fund investment objectives. Performance for Yardsticks is based on an arithmetic average of all the mutual funds in the category.

| | DAILY | | TOTAL RETURN (%) | | | Annualized | |
Investment Objective	Chg	% Chg	4-wk	YTD	1-yr	3-yr	5-yr
Vanguard Small Co. index	-0.02	-0.07	7.94	9.51	63.51	-2.62	4.46
Small-Cap Value Funds	0.01	0.02	7.27	9.34	63.45	-4.30	3.11
Mid-Cap Value Funds	0.03	0.11	6.04	7.63	56.17	-4.44	3.41
Small-Cap Core Funds	unch.	-0.01	6.89	7.79	54.78	-4.38	2.97
Mid-Cap Core Funds	0.01	0.02	5.90	7.25	54.02	-3.84	3.30
Small-Cap Growth Funds	-0.02	-0.10	7.66	7.08	52.26	-4.04	2.68
Science & Technology	-0.03	-0.05	6.90	2.73	50.56	-1.00	4.64
European Region	0.18	0.81	5.76	-0.95	49.89	-8.54	3.55
Mid-Cap Growth Funds	unch.	unch.	6.26	6.53	48.94	-2.98	3.68
International	0.14	0.81	5.55	0.77	48.13	-6.98	3.94
Multi-Cap Value Funds	0.02	0.07	5.56	5.97	48.00	-6.88	1.09
Global Funds	0.08	0.42	5.31	2.49	46.73	-4.81	3.52
Multi-Cap Growth Funds	0.01	0.05	5.88	4.39	45.61	-2.57	3.66
Multi-Cap Core Funds	0.04	0.11	5.37	4.89	45.37	-4.44	2.30
High Yield Taxable Bond	0.01	0.12	2.58	3.95	45.23	3.26	5.19
S & P 500 Daily Reinv	1.43	0.07	5.74	5.10	43.12	-4.61	2.03
Large-Cap Value Funds	0.02	0.07	5.42	5.31	42.65	-6.76	0.99
Large-Cap Core Funds	0.01	0.04	5.33	4.53	41.72	-4.51	1.86
Dow Jones Ind Dly Reinv	16.18	0.08	5.22	4.72	40.95	-1.81	3.44
Large-Cap Growth Funds	0.01	0.04	5.53	3.73	40.27	-2.32	2.68
Equity Income	0.02	0.08	4.85	4.23	40.02	-4.59	2.37
Stock & Bond Funds	0.02	0.20	3.89	3.09	37.30	-2.28	3.61
Health & Biotechnology	-0.11	-0.43	4.38	5.99	34.92	1.87	5.49
Balanced	0.04	0.16	3.18	3.05	31.27	-0.86	3.18
General Taxable Bond	0.02	0.12	1.08	2.80	26.52	4.63	5.21
Utility	0.04	0.20	2.25	-2.69	23.74	-6.09	4.66
Long Term Investment Grade Corporate Bond	0.03	0.19	0.40	2.58	23.38	4.40	4.44
Intmdt Investment Grade Corporate Bond	0.02	0.17	0.11	2.23	15.97	4.73	4.53
Single State Municipal Debt	-0.01	-0.05	unch.	1.37	13.35	2.52	3.43
General Municipal Debt	-0.01	-0.05	-0.06	1.35	13.32	2.42	3.17
Short Term Investment Grade Corp Bond	0.01	0.09	0.04	1.39	10.31	3.36	3.56
Mortgage	0.02	0.12	0.23	2.07	8.57	5.52	4.97
Intermediate Term Municipal Debt	-0.01	-0.10	-0.53	0.96	8.06	3.80	3.64
Intermediate Term US Treasury/Govt Bond	0.02	0.18	-0.37	0.52	5.30	4.64	4.20
Lipper L-T Govt Bond Index	0.40	0.08	-0.65	1.18	4.12	5.03	4.67
Long Term US Treasury/Govt Bond	0.02	0.17	-0.81	1.01	1.43	4.50	4.16

Source: Lipper

These problems with performance measures deal with the evaluation of historical performance. However, there is an even more fundamental criterion. Ultimately, we don't care about historical performance; we care about *future* performance. Whether historical performance is useful in predicting future performance is the subject of ongoing debate. However, one thing we can say is that some of the poorest-performing funds are those with very high costs. These costs act as a constant drag on performance, and such funds tend to have persistently poorer returns than otherwise similar funds.

FIGURE 4.5   Mutual Funds: Closing Quotes

Mutual Funds: Closing Quotes

F

GO TO: A | B | C | D | E | G | H | I | J | K | L | M | N | O | P | Q | R | S | T | U | V | W | X | Y | Z

Friday, November 13, 2009

Alphabetical listing by fund family.

Family/ Fund	Symbol	NAV	Chg	YTD % return	3-yr % chg
Fidelity Invest					
100Index	FOHIX	8.29	...	4.5	NS
13030LarCap	FOTTX	6.89	...	4.4	NS
AdvStrRRA	FSRAX	8.57	0.01	1.1	0.0
AggrInt	FIVFX	11.70	0.08	3.2	-7.5
AilSectEq	FSAEX	11.95	0.01	4.5	NS
AMgr20%	FASIX	12.20	0.01	2.1	2.5
AMgr50%	FASMX	14.27	0.03	3.0	0.3
AMgr70%	FASGX	14.84	0.04	3.6	-1.7
AMgr85%	FAMRX	12.09	0.04	3.8	-2.7
AstMgr30R	FTANX	9.37	0.02	0.6	NO
AZMun	FSAZX	11.30	-0.01	1.0	3.8
Balanc	FBALX	16.97	0.02	3.7	-1.5
BluCh	FBGRX	40.05	0.07	5.5	1.4
BlueChipVal	FBCVX	10.50	0.02	5.4	-9.2
CAMun	FCTFX	11.85	-0.01	1.8	3.0
CAShITxFr t	FCSTX	10.58	-0.01	0.6	4.7
Canad r	FICDX	50.80	-0.09	4.8	2.8
CapAp	FDCAX	23.28	0.03	8.6	-3.0
CapDevA p	FDTTX	9.23	0.04	5.6	-4.6
CapDevO	FDETX	9.45	0.04	5.7	-4.2
ChinaReg	FHKCX	27.60	0.24	-1.0	9.9
CpInc r	FAGIX	8.90	0.03	4.7	7.2
CngS	CNGRX	422.77	0.16	1.3	-0.3
Contra	FCNTX	59.98	0.09	3.1	-0.7

Source: www.wsj.com, March 27, 2010. Reprinted with permission of *The Wall Street Journal*.
© 2010 Dow Jones & Company, Inc. All Rights Reserved Worldwide.

FIGURE 4.6 Detailed Performance Measures

FIDELITY SECURITIES FUND: FIDELITY BLUE CHIP GROWTH FUND FBGRX

As of 3/26/10	1-Day Net Change	1-Day Return	YTD Total Return	Category
NAV: 40.05	▲ 0.07	▲ 0.18%	▲ 5.53%	Large-Cap Growth

LIPPER LEADER SCORECARD

⑤ ⑤ ④ ① ⑤

Total Return Consistent Return Preservation Tax Efficiency Expense

LIPPER Higher ⑤ ④ ③ ② ① Lower

More on Lipper Leaders

TOTAL RETURNS (%) 3, 5 and 10 year returns are annualized.

	YTD	1Yr	3Yr	5Yr	10Yr
Fund	5.53	53.51	1.44	3.85	-2.44
Category	3.75	40.32	-2.32	2.67	-3.54
Index (S&P 500)	5.10	43.10	-4.60	2.00	-0.90
% Rank in Category	9	4	7	24	31
Quintile Rank	A	A	A	B	B

Source: www.wsj.com, March 27, 2010. Reprinted with permission of *The Wall Street Journal*. © 2010 Dow Jones & Company, Inc. All Rights Reserved Worldwide.

CHECK THIS

4.7a Which mutual fund in Figure 4.5 had the best year-to-date return? The worst?

4.7b What are some of the problems with comparing historical performance numbers?

4.8 Closed-End Funds, Exchange-Traded Funds, and Hedge Funds

It is probably fitting that we close our mutual fund chapter with a discussion of closed-end funds, exchange-traded funds, and hedge funds. As we will see, such funds have some unusual aspects.

CLOSED-END FUNDS PERFORMANCE INFORMATION

As we described earlier, the major difference between a closed-end fund and an open-end fund is that closed-end funds don't buy and sell shares. Instead, there is a fixed number of shares in the fund, and these shares are bought and sold on the open market. More than 600 closed-end funds have their shares traded on U.S. stock exchanges, which is far fewer than the roughly 8,000 long-term, open-end mutual funds available to investors.

Figure 4.7 shows some quotes for a particular type of closed-end fund, "World Income" funds. As the name suggests, these funds generally invest outside the United States, and they are a relatively common type (single-state municipal funds are the most common). The entry for the Templeton Global Income Fund is highlighted.

Examining the entry for the Templeton Global Income Fund, the first entry after the name is the ticker symbol. Next, we have the NAV, the market price per share, and the fund's premium or discount. The final column is the one-year return based on the fund's NAV.

An important thing to notice is that the fund's NAV as of March 26, 2010, $9.70, does not equal its market price, $10.05. The percentage difference is ($10.05 − $9.70)/$9.70 = .0361, or 3.61 percent, which is the number shown in the second to last column. We will say more about this premium in a moment, but notice that (1) essentially all the closed-end funds have either premiums or discounts, (2) the premiums and discounts can be relatively large, and (3) the premiums and discounts fluctuate.

FIGURE 4.7   Closed-End Funds

CLOSED-END FUNDS: World Income	Return to Major Categories	Return to Expanded Categories	About Closed End Funds			

Friday, March 26, 2010

Fund	Weekly Statistics (as of 3/26/2010)			52 Week Market Return %
	NAV	Mkt Price	Prem/Disc %	
Aberdeen Asia-Pac Inc (FAX)	6.68	6.53	-2.25	42.23
Aberdeen Global Income (FCO)	11.85	11.90	+0.42	46.40
AllianceBernstein Gl Hi (AWF)	14.41	14.20	-1.46	90.42
DWS Glbl High Income (LBF)	8.27	7.42	-10.28	36.29
Eaton Vance Sht Dur Dl (EVG) [a]	18.20	16.95	-6.87	42.90
Evergreen Intl Bal Inc (EBI)	16.18	13.95	-13.78	38.20
First Tr/Abrdn Gl Op Inc (FAM)	17.08	16.34	-4.33	71.52
Global High Income (GHI) [a]	13.34	14.19	+6.37	83.56
Global Income (GIFD)	4.62	3.76	-18.61	57.99
Morg Stan Em Mkt Dom Dbt (EDD)	17.10	15.16	-11.35	72.71
Morg Stan Emrg Mkts Debt (MSD)	11.65	10.62	-8.84	56.18
Nuveen Glbl Gvt Enh Inc (JGG)	16.70	16.52	-1.08	16.39
Nuveen Mlti-Curr ShTrmGl (JGT)	16.26	14.90	-8.36	29.13
PIMCO Inc Oppty (PKO)	23.61	24.12	+2.16	84.18
PIMCO Str Glbl Govt (RCS)	9.32	10.89	+16.85	69.86
Strategic Global Income (SGL) [a]	11.85	10.99	-7.26	51.95
Templeton Emrg Mkts Inc (TEI)	15.69	14.66	-6.56	67.31
Templeton Global Income (GIM)	9.70	10.05	+3.61	40.51
Western Asset EM Debt (ESD)	19.77	18.08	-8.55	66.99
Western Asset EM Income (EMD)	14.02	12.74	-9.13	67.00
Western Asset Gl Cr D Op (GDO)	19.34	18.63	-3.67	NS
Western Asset Gl Hi Inc (EHI)	12.54	11.66	-7.02	83.66
Western Asset Gl Prt Inc (GDF)	11.41	12.51	+9.64	106.27
Western Asset Wrldwd Inc (SBW)	14.30	13.20	-7.69	70.03

Source: Lipper Inc.

Source: www.wsj.com, March 27, 2010. Reprinted with permission of *The Wall Street Journal*.

THE CLOSED-END FUND DISCOUNT MYSTERY

Wall Street has many unsolved puzzles, and one of the most famous and enduring has to do with prices of shares in closed-end funds. As we noted earlier, shares in closed-end funds trade in the marketplace. Furthermore, as the Templeton Global Income Fund shows, share prices can differ from net asset values. In fact, many closed-end funds sell at a discount or premium relative to their net asset values, and this difference is sometimes substantial.

For example, suppose a closed-end fund owns $100 million worth of stock. It has 10 million shares outstanding, so the NAV is clearly $10. It would not be at all unusual, however, for the share price to be only $9, indicating a 10 percent discount. What is puzzling about this discount is that you can apparently buy $10 worth of stock for only $9!

To make matters even more perplexing, as we have noted, the typical discount fluctuates over time. Sometimes, the discount is very wide; at other times, it almost disappears. Despite a great deal of research, the closed-end fund discount phenomenon remains largely unexplained.

Because of the discount available on closed-end funds, it is often argued that funds with the largest discounts are attractive investments. The problem with this argument is that it assumes that the discount will narrow or disappear. Unfortunately, this may or may not happen; the discount might get even wider.

Sometimes, certain closed-end funds sell at a premium, implying that investors are willing to pay more than the NAV for shares. This case is not quite as perplexing; after all, investors in load funds do the same thing. The reasons we discussed for paying loads might apply to these cases.

We close our discussion with a cautionary note. When a closed-end fund is first created, its shares are offered for sale to the public. For example, a closed-end fund might raise $50 million by selling 5 million shares to the public at $10 per share (the original offer price is almost always $10), which is the fund's NAV. Fine. But, here's the rub.

MUTUAL FUNDS vs. ETFs

Across a crowded room, index funds and exchange traded funds (ETFs) are pretty good lookers. Both have low costs, diversification, and approval from Mom and Dad. But it's what's on the inside that counts.

So let's take a deeper look at these two worthy contenders for our investment dollars.

How They Work

Mutual Funds

Traditional, actively managed mutual funds usually begin with a load of cash and a fund management team. Investors send their C-notes to the fund, are issued shares, and the Porsche piloting team of investment managers figures out what to buy. Some of these stock pickers are very good at this. The other 80% of them, not so much.

Index mutual funds work similarly to traditional ones except that the managers ride the bus and eat sack lunches. (Actually, there are rarely human managers. Most index funds are computer-driven.) More importantly, index mutual funds put money into stocks that as a whole track a chosen benchmark. Because there's less "research" to pay for—like trips to California to visit that refinery's headquarters (and a little wine tasting . . . I mean, we're in the neighborhood . . .)—index mutual funds generally have lower expenses.

If the fund is popular or its salesmen make it so (yes, funds often have a sales force), it attracts gobs of money. The more money that comes in, the more shares must be created, and the more stocks investment managers (or Hal, the index robot) must go out and buy for the fund.

ETFs

ETFs work almost in reverse. They begin with an idea—tracking an index—and are born of stocks instead of money.

What does that mean? Major investing institutions like Fidelity Investments or the Vanguard Group already control billions of shares. To create an ETF, they simply peel a few million shares off the top of the pile, putting together a basket of stocks to represent the appropriate index, say, the NASDAQ composite or the TBOPP index we made up. They deposit the shares with a holder and receive a number of creation units in return. (In effect they're trading stocks for creation units, or buying their way into the fund using equities instead of money.)

A creation unit is a large block, perhaps 50,000 shares, of the ETF. These creation units are then split up by the recipients into the individual shares that are traded on the market. More creation units (and more market shares) can be made if institutional investors deposit more shares into the underlying hopper. Similarly, the pool of outstanding ETF shares can be dried up if one of the fat cats swaps back creation units for underlying shares in the basket.

The variation in the fund structures mean subtle but important differences at the end of the chain for individual investors.

The Business of Buying

That's the birds and the bees of ETFs and mutual funds. Now let's take 'em for a spin and see how they handle our money.

Timing Trades

With traditional mutual funds, you order your shares and buy them for the NAV (net asset value) at the end of the day. Period. (Unless you're a favored client engaged in illegal, after-hours trading, but that's another story . . . .)

If you pay $10, then you are likely to discover two unpleasant facts quite soon. First, the fund promoter will be paid, say, 7 percent of the proceeds right off the top, or about $3.5 million (this will be disclosed in the prospectus). This fee will come out of the fund, leaving a total value of $46.5 million and a NAV of $9.30. Further, as we have seen, the shares could trade at a discount relative to NAV in the market, so you would lose another piece of your investment almost immediately. In short, newly offered closed-end funds are generally very poor investments.

EXCHANGE-TRADED FUNDS

Exchange-traded funds, or ETFs, are a relatively recent innovation. Although they have been around since 1993, they really began to grow in the late 1990s. As of 2010, more than 700 ETFs were being traded. Over 400 ETFs have been created since 2007, and more are in the works. An ETF is basically an index fund that seeks to achieve the same return as a

For more on ETFs, visit
www.morningstar.com

Since ETFs trade like stocks, you can buy and sell them all day long. Though doing that, like any day trading, will likely land you in the gutter searching for loose change, it does have some advantage for the Foolish investor. Limit orders are one. You can tell your broker (or the computerized lackey) to purchase your ETF shares only at a certain price. If the market jumps 3% with excitement over some major world event—like a peace pact between Britney and Christina—you can use a limit order to make sure you don't pick up your shares at the top of the soon-to-be-crashing wave of misguided enthusiasm.

Shorting is another possibility. Yes, you black-turtleneck-wearing, world-weary pessimists out there can bet against the index with ETFs, and profit if and when it falls in value.

Making the Minimum

If you've ever visited our table of no-load index funds, you might have sprinted away from the computer shrieking. Under the column titled "account minimum," you see numbers as high as $50,000. That's the price of entry for some index mutual funds. Got less than that? Take your money elsewhere. Or rifle the couch cushions for loose change. Or open an IRA, where minimums are generally much lower.

ETFs, on the other hand, have no minimums. You can purchase as few shares as you like. Want one lonely little share? You can get it. Just make sure that you *choose your broker wisely* so that you don't shell out too much in commissions for your purchases.

Averaging, Joe?

A few years back, it might not have made sense to dollar cost-average into ETFs. If you were trying to buy a few hundred dollars' worth of a fund once a month, the brokerage fees would have taken a big bite of your nest egg and made a no-load index mutual fund a much better bet because mutual funds do not generally charge transaction fees.

But with the advent of ultra low-cost, or even no-cost brokerages, it's now cost-efficient to make small, frequent purchases of ETF shares. Of course, you'll have to put in the buy orders yourself, as you would to purchase a regular stock.

Options for Experts

Though we don't recommend them for beginning Fools, ETFs offer advanced trading possibilities. Options are one. These complex little investments give you the right to "call" or "put" (buy or sell) shares of the ETF at some point in the future for some specific price. There's no calling and putting when it comes to mutual funds.

Dividend Differences

Most mutual fund investors take advantage of their fund's automatic dividend reinvestment feature. That saves them the hassle of deciding what to do with the cash that comes their way periodically. If and when the mutual fund pays out a cash dividend, your cut of the dough is automatically reinvested in shares, or partial shares of the fund.

With dividend-paying ETFs, that moolah winds up in your brokerage account instead, just like the dividend on a regular stock. If you want to reinvest that cash, you have to make another purchase—and you'll get smacked with your usual trading fee unless your broker allows you to reinvest dividends for no extra cost. Many do.

Source: *The Motley Fool*, September 14, 2009. © 2009 *The Motley Fool*. All Rights Reserved.

particular market index. Therefore, when you buy an ETF, it is as if you are buying the basket of stocks that make up the index.

The most popular ETFs represent well-known indexes like the S&P 500, the NASDAQ 100, and the Dow Jones Industrial Average. The best known ETF is a "Standard & Poor's Depositary Receipt," or SPDR (pronounced "spider"). This ETF (ticker symbol SPY) is simply the S&P 500 Index. The other two ETFs have catchy nicknames, too. The "Cubes" (QQQQ—former ticker, QQQ) is the NASDAQ 100 Index. "Diamonds" (DIA) is the ETF that tracks the Dow Jones Industrial Average.

If you decide to invest in these three ETFs, you will have plenty of trading partners. In late 2009, average daily trading volume for Diamonds was about 12 million shares. For the Cubes, traders exchange more than 100 million shares on a daily basis. However, daily trading volume in Spiders routinely tops 200 million shares (that's a lot of spiders).

Investigate other ETFs at
www.nasdaq.com
or
www.nyse.com

More specialized ETFs also exist. For example, suppose, for some reason, you hold mostly large-cap stocks. You can get a small piece of many small-cap stocks with the Vanguard Small Cap ETF (VB). Maven of the Medici? If so, the Italy Index (EWI) might be for you. Have you played enough Monopoly to convince yourself that "The Donald" better duck? Then perhaps you will land on the Vanguard REIT ETF (VNQ). You just cannot decide whether to invest in Europe, Australasia, or the Far East? Why decide when you can have a portfolio of 21 country indexes by purchasing shares of the EAFE Index (EFA)? Many other ETFs are available.

CREATING AN ETF How are ETFs created? The process begins when a potential ETF sponsor files a plan with the Securities and Exchange Commission (SEC) to create an ETF. Normally, the sponsors are investment companies, like Fidelity Investments or the Vanguard Group, that control billions of shares in a wide variety of securities. To get the shares necessary to create an ETF, the sponsor arranges to set aside the shares representing the basket of securities that forms the ETF index. These few million (or so) shares are placed into a trust.

To complete the process, "creation units" are formed. Creation units are simply claims (like a claim check) on the bundles of shares held in the trust. Because these creation units are legal claims backed by the shares in the trust, traders will gladly trade these creation units. Creation units are generally for 50,000 shares of the ETF. Therefore, the creation units are split up into the individual ETF shares that are traded on the market. The ability of investors to redeem these units keeps the ETF from trading at a significant premium or discount to NAV.

ETFs AND INDEX FUNDS Earlier, we said that an ETF was basically an index fund. But an ETF is not exactly like an index fund. What makes an ETF different from an index fund is that, as the name suggests, an ETF actually trades like a closed-end fund. ETFs can be bought and sold during the day, they can be sold short, and you can buy options on them. ETFs generally have very low expenses, lower even than index funds, but you must pay a commission when you buy and sell shares. The nearby *Investment Updates* box details these differences.

Figure 4.8 reproduces an end-of-trading-day listing of ETFs by gainers, decliners, and most actives. You can see that an ETF called Spiders tops the list of active ETFs (its ticker symbol is SPY). When you surf over to this list, you can click on any ETF and get a detailed description. If you do so for SPY, you will see that the SPY has a low expense ratio, .09, or just under one-tenth of 1 percent. You will also see that the purpose of the SPY is to track the total return on the S&P 500 Index.

By surfing around the ETF section at online.wsj.com, you will see that the SPY is not the only ETF on the S&P 500 Index. Its trading volume, however, dwarfs its main competitor—an ETF called the iShares S&P 500 (ticker symbol IVV). You might think that perhaps the IVV and other iShares are somehow associated with Apple Computer. They are not. The IVV and other iShares are affiliated with Barclays Global Investors. The SPY is affiliated with State Street Global Markets (ticker symbol STT).

LEVERAGED ETFs The recent growth in the number of types of ETFs has been explosive. A particularly interesting, but potentially dangerous, ETF growth area is in leveraged ETFs. The fund managers of a leveraged ETF create a portfolio designed to provide a return that tracks the underlying index. But by also using derivative contracts, the managers can magnify, or leverage, the return on the underlying index.

Rydex Investments, for example, offers two of these leveraged funds: the Rydex 2X S&P 500 (symbol RSU) and the Rydex Inverse 2X S&P 500 (symbol RSW). The first fund (RSU) is designed to provide twice the return of the S&P 500. In other words, if the S&P 500 return on a given day is 1 percent, the RSU should provide a return of 2 percent. Terrific! What's the danger? Well, leverage works both ways. Losses are magnified by 2, too. The second fund (RSW) is designed to move in twice the direction *opposite* the return of the S&P 500 index. If the S&P 500 gains 1 percent, then RSW should lose 2 percent. You can see that the RSW provides a way for investors to go (twice) short on the S&P 500.

These leveraged ETFs seem to track their underlying indexes on a short-term basis, that is, day by day. Over longer periods of time, however, their performance is probably not what you would expect. The Rydex funds, for example, began trading on November 7, 2007. Over the next two

FIGURE 4.8   Exchange-Traded Funds

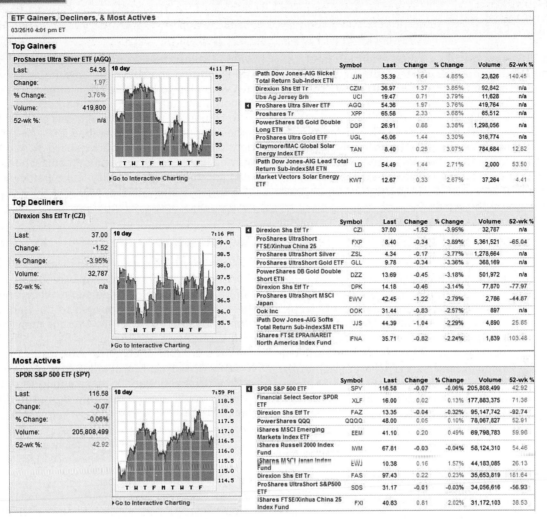

years, the S&P 500 lost 22.4 percent. Given its objective, the RSU fund should have lost 44.8 percent, which is twice the return of the S&P 500. The inverse fund, the RSW, should have gained twice the return of the S&P 500, or 44.8 percent. Over this two-year period, however, the long fund (RSU) lost 56.5 percent, and the inverse fund (RSW) *lost* 7.3 percent. How is this possible?

The answer does not lie with Rydex Investments. Instead, the answer depends on arithmetic versus geometric averages that we discuss elsewhere. Recall that geometric (or compounded) returns are lower than arithmetic returns, with volatility fueling the difference. In the Rydex example, both leveraged funds add extra volatility to the series of S&P 500 Index returns. As a result, returns from any leveraged funds will be less than expected.

As an example, consider a week during which the S&P 500 earns the following daily returns: 1, −2, 2, 1, and 3 percent, respectively. You can check that the arithmetic average is 1 percent, while the geometric average is just slightly less, .986 percent. This difference seems trivial. Consider the returns for a twice-leveraged fund. The arithmetic average is exactly double, 2 percent. The geometric average, however, is only $[(1.02)(.96)(1.04)(1.02)(1.06)]^{(1/5)} - 1 = .0194$, or 1.94 percent.

What is the lesson? The longer we hold these investments and/or the more volatile the underlying index, the less accurate a leveraged fund will be in tracking their stated objective. Should you use leveraged ETFs? This question is difficult to answer, but the nearby *Investment Updates* box provides some insight.

LEVERAGED ETFs: BUYER BEWARE!

Leveraged ETFs have gotten a lot of attention lately. Although the fund companies that produced them have thrived from their popularity, that party may soon be over.

Unfortunately, many investors don't fully understand how these vehicles work. Leveraged ETFs are designed to deliver some multiple of the daily performance of whatever underlying index the ETF tracks. But over time, daily movements in the underlying index can create losses for those who hold shares over longer periods of time—even if the index rises on the whole.

For instance, say you pay $1,000 for a leveraged ETF when the underlying index is at 1,000. The index drops 10 points every day for 10 days, and then rises 10 points every day for the next 10. With a standard index ETF, you'd be back to break-even. But with a leveraged 2x ETF, you would actually have a small loss. And even more strangely, an inverse leveraged 2x ETF would have exactly the same loss. So far in 2009, that effect has pushed many pairs of leveraged funds, such as the Direxion Daily Financial Bull 3x ETF (NYSE: FAS) and the Direxion Daily Financial Bear 3x ETF (NYSE: FAZ), down in tandem.

Even Wall Street Is Taking a Step Back

Regulators recently voiced concern over the sustainability of these investment vehicles as long-term investments. The independent regulatory organization FINRA warned about the risks of inverse and leveraged ETFs this spring, stating that they are "unsuitable for retail investors who plan to hold them for longer than one trading session, particularly in volatile markets."

In response, many of the big cats on Wall Street have either stopped selling leveraged ETFs, or placed restrictions on sales. Fidelity and Schwab (NASDAQ: SCHW) have warned investors about using them, while UBS (NYSE: UBS) and the Morgan Stanley Smith Barney joint venture of Morgan Stanley (NYSE: MS) and Citigroup (NYSE: C) have simply stopped selling them for the moment.

Are They Bad?

I believe there are cases in which leveraged ETFs can give short-term investors a powerful way to seek profits. They can be effective if you understand them, and if you use them the way they're supposed to be used. But they're simply not structured for the average individual investor with a long-term horizon.

Whether leveraged ETFs will survive depends on whether there's a real market for risky short-term investments. If you want to make a long-term investment, though, you'll almost certainly do better just steering clear of them.

Source: Jennifer Schonberger, *The Motley Fool*, September 14, 2009.
© 2009 *The Motley Fool*. All Rights Reserved.

EXCHANGE-TRADED NOTES In mid-2006, Barclays Bank introduced exchange-traded notes (ETNs). To investors, exchange-traded notes (ETNs) look very similar to exchange-traded funds. Like most ETFs, ETNs are designed to allow investors to achieve the same return as a particular index. Also like ETFs, investors can go long or short an ETN.

Originally, ETNs were created to provide investors with exposure to the risks and returns of commodities, a traditionally volatile arena. However, ETNs now exist for currencies and for at least one emerging market—India.

As of late 2009, the largest ETN is the iPath Dow Jones-AIG Commodity Total Return Index (DJP), a Barclays Bank product. This ETN tracks the returns of a portfolio of 19 futures contracts. However, in this index, by rule, any commodity group, including energy, can comprise only 33 percent of the index. By contrast, the iPath GSCI Total Return Index (GSP) tracks the returns of a portfolio of 24 futures contracts, but 75 percent of this index is energy-related. Want more exposure? The iPath GSCI Crude Oil Total Return Index (OIL) provides investors with 100 percent exposure to returns on crude oil futures contracts.

The iPath ETNs are actually debt securities issued by Barclays Bank. Essentially, these ETNs promise to pay investors the return on a commodity index, less Barclays's .75 percent annual fee. However, ETNs are not limited to one bank. For example, Deutsche Bank and Goldman Sachs also have ETNs. Other banks will surely follow.

There is an important difference between ETFs and ETNs. Essentially, the holder of an ETF holds a fractional ownership of the shares placed in trust to create the ETF. With ETNs, however, this is not the case. ETNs are unsecured debt securities. Holders of ETNs are relying on the solvency of the issuing bank when they hold ETNs. Therefore, ETN holders face the risk that the issuing bank might default on the promised payments of the ETN. In addition, ETNs are taxed differently, which complicates matters.

HEDGE FUNDS

Hedge funds are a special type of investment company. They are like mutual funds in that a fund manager invests a pool of money obtained from investors. Hedge funds are generally free to pursue almost any investment style they wish. In contrast, as we have discussed, mutual funds are relatively limited in their permitted investment strategies. For example, mutual funds are usually not allowed to do things like sell short or use large degrees of leverage.

When you hear the words "hedge fund," you might think that these funds are low-risk investments (as in saying "hedging your bets"). Some hedge funds do try to exploit arbitrage opportunities on a low-risk basis. Most hedge funds, however, undertake aggressive, risk-enhancing strategies. We discuss hedge fund investment styles below. First, we compare hedge funds and mutual funds.

Hedge funds are generally not subject to the same disclosure requirements as mutual funds. Further, hedge funds are not required to maintain any particular degree of diversification or liquidity. Unlike mutual funds, for example, hedge funds do not redeem shares on demand. Instead, hedge funds typically designate particular liquidation dates, possibly only once every quarter. Even then, investors need to provide advance notice that they plan to withdraw funds. One reason for such a policy is that the fund might have investments in illiquid assets. As a result, quick redemptions by some investors could damage the investment value for the other investors.

Obviously, investing in hedge funds is not suitable for all investors. To prevent unsophisticated investors from getting involved, hedge funds accept only "qualified" (or accredited) investors. To be considered a qualified investor, you must be an institution or an individual investor with a net worth of about $1 million or a recurring annual income of more than $200,000 (i.e., you need to be "rich").

Accepting only qualified investors is one factor that allows hedge funds to avoid many of the restrictions and regulations placed on mutual funds. Two other factors are: (1) hedge funds do not offer their securities for sale to the public, and (2) hedge funds generally limit the number of investors in any particular fund to no more than 50–100 institutions or individuals.

HEDGE FUND REGULATION Traditionally, hedge funds were only lightly regulated. Despite protests from the hedge fund industry, the Securities and Exchange Commission (SEC) recently initiated some regulations.

As of February 2006, the SEC requires hedge funds to register as investment advisors. However, many hedge fund managers registered with the SEC before this new requirement. Hedge fund managers do not have to register each of their hedge funds. Instead, they must provide some basic information to the SEC and must have a person on staff whose duties include helping the hedge fund comply with SEC rules. Registered hedge fund managers can be inspected at random by the SEC.

As with many rules, there are exceptions. For example, hedge funds that manage less than $30 million do not have to register. Also, hedge funds that "lock up" their investors' money for two or more years do not have to register (by "lock up" we mean that investors cannot withdraw their money).

HEDGE FUND FEES Hedge funds typically have a special fee structure, where, in addition to a general management fee of 1 to 2 percent of fund assets, the manager is paid a special performance fee. This special performance fee is often in the range of 20 to 40 percent of profits realized by the fund's investment strategy. The most common fee structure is 2/20, which is a short way to say that the manager charges an annual 2 percent management fee and also retains 20 percent of the profit earned in the fund. More structures are possible and some are quite elaborate.

One positive aspect of the performance fee is that the hedge fund manager has an incentive to earn as much profit as possible. There are, however, some potentially negative consequences, too. Suppose, for example, the performance bonus is awarded each year. What might the hedge fund manager do if the fund appeared to be certain to lose money this year? One possible strategy is for the manager to have the fund absorb as much loss as possible this year. As a result, the manager would be in a better position to make a large percentage profit for the fund next year (and a healthy performance fee for the manager).

Hedge fund investors are savvy. To prevent the fund from being manipulated by its managers, many fee structures also include constraints (or hurdles) for the manager to meet. A common example is called a "high-water mark." When a hedge fund fee structure includes a high-water mark, the manager will receive performance fees only when the fund value is higher than its previous highest value. Suppose a manager makes the fund absorb large losses this year. Under this fee structure, the annual 2 percent management fee is still paid. To receive performance fees, however, the manager must bring the hedge fund value to a level above the previous high-water mark. Then, the manager receives a 20 percent bonus of these "new" profits.

Why do hedge fund investors willingly pay high fees? The obvious answer is that the returns earned are high enough to be considered reasonable. Significant debate exists about the issue of hedge fund fees. Many experts opine that when fees are subtracted from hedge fund returns, hedge fund investors are not much better off than investors holding a portfolio that represents the overall stock market.

If these experts are correct, why would anyone invest in a hedge fund instead of a market index fund? The answer relates to the principle of diversification. As you will read elsewhere in this book, investments that appear to have a high level of risk, or those that offer only a nominal return, might turn out to be good additions to a portfolio. In other words, these investments might bring significant diversification benefits to an investment portfolio.

HEDGE FUND STYLES Worldwide there are thousands of hedge funds, and the number keeps growing. Big hedge funds may require a minimum investment of $1 million or more. Small hedge funds may require a minimum investment of only $50,000 or less. Whether large or small, each fund develops its own investment style or niche. For example, a hedge fund may focus on a particular sector, like technology, or a particular global region, like Asia or eastern Europe.

Alternatively, a hedge fund may pursue a particular investment strategy. We highlight some common investment styles just below. At the end of each investment style description, we identify its level of expected return volatility.

Information about starting your own hedge fund is available at Turn Key Hedge Funds
www.turnkeyhedgefunds.com

1. *Market neutral:* The goal of this strategy is to offset risk by holding opposite positions in pairs of securities. These hedge funds are also called *long-short funds.* The managers of these funds take long positions in a set of securities that the managers believe are underpriced. Then, the manager matches these investments with corresponding short positions in overpriced, or even fairly priced, securities. Properly constructed, the resulting portfolio makes money regardless of how the overall market performs. Hence the name "market neutral." Be aware that some funds offset all long positions, whereas other funds match only a portion. *Expected volatility: Low.*

2. *Arbitrage:* The goal of the managers of these funds is to identify a mispricing in relationships between securities which theoretically should not exist. Arbitrage fund managers look at pricing relationships for securities offered by the same company, or for investments across time or countries. For example, a hedge fund manager might buy convertible bonds of a company and short-sell the common stock of the same company. *Expected volatility: Low.*

3. *Distressed securities:* The managers of these hedge funds concentrate their investments in securities that are being offered at deep discounts resulting from company-specific or sectorwide distress. For example, a manager of a distressed securities fund might buy securities of firms facing bankruptcy. *Expected volatility: Low to moderate.*

4. *Macro:* These hedge fund managers attempt to profit from changes in global economies brought about by governmental policies that affect interest rates, currencies, or commodity prices. Macro fund managers often use leverage and derivative securities to increase the impact of market moves. *Expected volatility: High.*

5. *Short selling:* In contrast to a long-short fund, a manager of a pure short hedge fund only short sells. In addition, these managers use leverage through the use of margin. *Expected volatility: High.*

6. *Market timing:* Managers of these hedge funds attempt to identify trends in particular sectors or overall global markets. These managers often take concentrated positions and generally use leverage to increase the fund's exposure to predicted movements. *Expected volatility: High.*

As you can see from this list, many approaches are possible, and each has its own risk level. What is the lesson? Even after you make your millions and become a qualified investor, you still have your work cut out trying to identify the best hedge fund for your portfolio. Suppose you just cannot decide? Well, you might want to use a "fund of funds," which we discuss in the next section.

FUNDS OF FUNDS A significant portion of the money invested in hedge funds is funneled through "funds of funds." A fund of funds is just what the name suggests: An investment company that invests in hedge funds. For an investor, a fund of funds has the advantage that the fund manager may have expertise in selecting hedge funds; moreover, having multiple hedge funds offers a diversification benefit. However, a fund of funds charges fees of its own, on top of the already hefty hedge fund fees, so these advantages come with a cost.

STARTING YOUR OWN HEDGE FUND Ever dream about becoming an investment portfolio manager? You can by starting your own hedge fund. It may be easier than you think. A hedge fund is typically structured as a limited partnership in which the manager is a general partner and the investors are limited partners. Rather than stumble through the legal details, we simply advise that you will need the services of a lawyer familiar with investment companies, but the bottom line is that it's not difficult to do. Actually, the hardest part about setting up your own hedge fund is finding willing investors. Essentially, you need to find well-to-do individuals who have faith in your investment ideas. Bear in mind that you will have to register your hedge fund if you have more than 15 investors. Make sure you know all the regulatory requirements that might be imposed on your hedge fund.

CHECK THIS

4.8a   What is a closed-end fund and how does it differ from a mutual fund?

4.8b   What is meant by the net asset value (NAV) of a closed-end fund?

4.8c   What is a hedge fund? What are the important differences between a hedge fund and a mutual fund?

4.8d   What is a market-neutral investment strategy? Why is this strategy available to hedge funds but not to mutual funds?

4.9 Summary and Conclusions

We covered many aspects of mutual fund investing in this chapter. We saw that there are thousands of mutual funds and dozens of types. We summarize a few of the more important distinctions grouped by the chapter's important concepts.

1. **The different types of mutual funds.**

   A. At the most basic level, a company that pools funds obtained from individual investors and invests them is called an investment company. In other words, an investment company is a business that specializes in managing financial assets for individual investors. All mutual funds are, in fact, investment companies.

B. There are two fundamental types of investment companies, open-end funds and closed-end funds. When an investor wishes to buy open-end fund shares, the fund simply issues them and then invests the money received. In a closed-end fund, the number of shares is fixed and never changes. If you want to buy shares, you must buy them from another investor.

C. Mutual funds have different investment horizons. Money market mutual funds are an example of funds with a short-term investment horizon. Examples of funds with longer term investment horizons include:

- Stock funds that may specialize in capital appreciation, income, company size, international stocks, sector-specific stocks, or indexes.

- Bond funds that may specialize in short-term bonds, intermediate-term bonds, high-yield bonds, mortgages, or international bonds.

- Stock and bond funds that may keep a fixed balance among stocks, bonds, and cash or try to outguess the market by moving portfolio weights among stocks, bonds, and cash balances.

2. How mutual funds operate.

A. Mutual funds are corporations. Like other corporations, a mutual fund is owned by its shareholders. The shareholders elect a board of directors; the board of directors is responsible for hiring a manager to oversee the fund's operations.

B. Although mutual funds often belong to a larger "family" of funds, every fund is a separate company owned by its shareholders. Most mutual funds are created by investment advisory firms, which are businesses that specialize in managing mutual funds. Investment advisory firms are also called mutual fund companies. Increasingly, such firms have additional operations such as discount brokerages and other financial services.

C. There are hundreds of investment advisory firms in the United States. The largest, and probably best known, is Fidelity Investments, with more than 300 mutual funds, about $1.4 trillion in assets under management, and more than 20 million customers. Dreyfus, Franklin, and Vanguard are some other well-known examples. Many brokerage firms, such as Merrill Lynch and Charles Schwab, also have large investment advisory operations.

D. Investment advisory firms create mutual funds simply because they wish to manage them to earn fees. A typical management fee might be .75 percent of the total assets in the fund per year. A fund with $200 million in assets would not be especially large but could nonetheless generate management fees of about $1.5 million per year.

3. How to find information about mutual fund performance.

A. Funds have very different objectives and, as a result, very different risk and return potentials. Furthermore, funds with similar-sounding objectives can, in fact, be quite different. It is important to consider a fund's actual holdings and investment policies, not just read its stated objective.

B. Mutual fund information is widely available, but performance information should be used with caution. The best performing funds are often those with the greatest risks or those that just happened to be in the right investment at the right time.

4. The workings of exchange-traded funds and hedge funds.

A. An exchange-traded fund (ETF) is basically an index fund that seeks to achieve the same return as a particular market index. Therefore, when you buy an ETF, it is as if you are buying the basket of stocks that make up the index.

B. The most popular ETFs represent well-known indexes like the S&P 500, the NASDAQ 100, or the Dow Jones Industrial Average.

C. Many more specialized ETFs exist. For example, with an ETF, you can get a small piece of many small-cap stocks or midcap stocks, or you can invest in country-specific funds or in real estate.

D. Hedge funds are also investment companies, but they face fewer regulations than a typical mutual fund because they take only a limited number of qualified investors.

E. Hedge fund strategies vary from low risk (e.g., market neutral, arbitrage) to high risk (e.g., short selling, market timing). No matter the approach, though, the fee structure tends to be similar, with about a 2 percent management fee and a 20 percent share of profits.

GET REAL

This chapter covered the essentials of mutual funds. How should you, as an investor or investment manager, put this information to work?

The first thing to do is to start looking at mutual fund prospectuses. These are written to be accessible to novice investors (or, at least, they are *supposed* to be written that way). The best way to begin exploring is to visit Web sites. Almost any large mutual fund company will have extensive online information available. Links to some of the better known families are available at our Web page. It is important to look at different funds within a given family and also to look across families. Compare growth funds to growth funds, for example. This adventure will give you some of the real-life background you need to select the types of funds most suitable for you or someone else.

Once you have examined prospectuses on different funds, it's time to invest. Beginning with your simulated account, pick a few funds, invest, and observe the outcomes. Open-end mutual funds are probably the place most of you will begin investing real dollars. An initial purchase can be made with a relatively small amount, perhaps $500, and subsequent purchases can be made in amounts of as little as $100 or less.

Most important of all, the majority of employers now provide employees with retirement plans. The way these work is that, typically, your employer will make a contribution to a mutual fund you select (often from a fairly limited set). Your employer may even match, or more than match, a contribution you make. Such plans may be the only retirement benefit offered, but they can be an extraordinary opportunity for those who take full advantage of them by getting the largest possible match and then investing in a suitable fund. It's an important choice, so the more knowledge you have regarding mutual funds, the better your outcome is likely to be.

Key Terms

12b-1 fees 111
CDSC 111
closed-end fund 108
front-end load 111
hedge fund 135

investment company 107
money market mutual fund 115
net asset value 108
open-end fund 107
turnover 112

Chapter Review Problems and Self-Test

1. **Front-End Loads (CFA2)** The Madura HiGro Fund has a net asset value of $50 per share. It charges a 3 percent load. How much will you pay for 100 shares?

2. **Turnover (CFA2)** The Starks Income Fund's average daily total assets were $100 million for the year just completed. Its stock purchases for the year were $20 million, while its sales were $12.5 million. What was its turnover?

1. You will pay 100 times the offering price. Since the load is computed as a percentage of the offering price, we can compute the offering price as follows:

$$\text{Net asset value} = (1 - \text{Front-end load}) \times \text{Offering price}$$

   In other words, the NAV is 97 percent of the offering price. Since the NAV is $50, the offering price is $50/.97 = $51.55. You will pay $5,155 in all, of which $155 is a load.

2. Turnover is the lesser of purchases or sales divided by average daily assets. In this case, sales are smaller at $12.5, so turnover is $12.5/$100 = .125 times.

Test Your Investment Quotient

1. **Investment Companies (LO2, CFA2)**   Which of the following statements typically does not characterize the structure of an investment company?

   a. An investment company adopts a corporate form of organization.
   b. An investment company invests a pool of funds belonging to many investors in a portfolio of individual investments.
   c. An investment company receives an annual management fee ranging from 3 to 5 percent of the total value of the fund.
   d. The board of directors of an investment company hires a separate investment management company to manage the portfolio of securities and handle other administrative duties.

2. **Expense Statement (LO3)**   Which of the following is *not* part of the expense statement?

   a. Shareholder transactions expenses
   b. Shareholder demographic profile
   c. Annual operating expenses
   d. A hypothetical example of expenses

3. **Mutual Fund Investing (LO2, CFA2)**   Which of the following is the least likely advantage of mutual fund investing?

   a. Diversification
   b. Professional management
   c. Convenience
   d. Mutual fund returns are normally higher than market average returns

4. **Open-End Funds (LO2, CFA2)**   An open-end mutual fund is owned by which of the following?

   a. An investment company
   b. An investment advisory firm
   c. A "family of funds" mutual fund company
   d. Its shareholders

5. **Closed-End Funds (LO2, CFA2)**   Which of the following is most true of a closed-end investment company?

   a. The fund's share price is usually greater than net asset value.
   b. The fund's share price is set equal to net asset value.
   c. Fund shares outstanding vary with purchases and redemptions by shareholders.
   d. Fund shares outstanding are fixed at the issue date.

6. **Closed-End Funds (LO2, CFA2)**   A closed-end fund is owned by which of the following?

   a. An investment company
   b. An investment advisory firm
   c. A "family of funds" mutual fund company
   d. Its shareholders

7. **Exchange-Traded Funds (LO4, CFA2)**   Which of the following statements regarding exchange-traded funds (ETFs) is false?

   a. ETFs are funds that can be traded on a stock market.
   b. ETF investors own shares of the underlying fund sponsor.
   c. ETF shares can be sold short.
   d. ETF shares can be bought on margin.

8. **Closed-End Funds (LO1, CFA2)** Closed-end funds and exchange-traded funds (ETFs) have which of the following characteristics in common?

   a. Shares of both closed-end funds and ETFs trade in the secondary market.
   b. Both closed-end funds and ETFs stand ready to redeem shares.
   c. The structures of closed-end funds and ETFs prevent shares from trading at a significant premium or discount to NAV.
   d. Neither ETF nor closed-end fund managers receive a management fee.

9. **Mutual Fund Investing (LO1, CFA2)** Growth, value, large-cap, and small-cap investing are all examples of:

   a. Style investment strategies
   b. Sector investment strategies
   c. Index investment strategies
   d. Lifestyle investment strategies

10. **Mutual Fund Investing (LO1, CFA4)** One of the main advantages to investing in a fund of funds (FOF) is that FOFs provide:

   a. Improved diversification of assets
   b. Higher expected returns
   c. Lower management fees
   d. Higher volatility of returns

11. **Fund Types (LO1, CFA2)** Which mutual fund type will most likely incur the smallest tax liability for its investors?

   a. Index fund
   b. Municipal bond fund
   c. Income fund
   d. Growth fund

12. **Fund Types (LO1)** Which mutual fund type will most likely incur the greatest overall risk levels for its investors?

   a. Large-cap index fund
   b. Insured municipal bond fund
   c. Money market mutual fund
   d. Small-cap growth fund

13. **Mutual Fund Fees (LO2, CFA2)** Which of the following mutual fund fees is assessed on an annual basis?

   a. 12b-1 fees
   b. Front-end load
   c. Back-end load
   d. Contingent deferred sales charge (CDSC)

14. **Mutual Fund Fees (LO2, CFA2)** Which of the following mutual fund fees will most likely be the biggest expense for a long-term fund investor?

   a. 12b-1 fees
   b. Front-end load
   c. Back-end load
   d. Contingent deferred sales charge (CDSC)

15. **Mutual Fund Fees (LO2, CFA3)** Which of the following mutual fund fees and expenses is the most difficult for investors to assess?

   a. Sales charges or "loads"
   b. 12b-1 fees
   c. Management fees
   d. Trading costs

Concept Questions

1. **Fund Ownership (LO2)** Who actually owns a mutual fund? Who runs it?

2. **Loads (LO2)** Given that no-load funds are widely available, why would a rational investor pay a front-end load? More generally, why don't fund investors always seek out funds with the lowest loads, management fees, and other fees?

3. **Money Market Funds (LO2, CFA1)**   Is it true that the NAV of a money market mutual fund never changes? How is this possible?

4. **Money Market Deposit Accounts (LO2, CFA1)**   What is the difference between a money market deposit account and a money market mutual fund? Which is riskier?

5. **ETFs versus Index Mutual Funds (LO4, CFA2)**   ETFs and index mutual funds hold similar underlying assets. Why might an investor prefer one over the other?

6. **Open-End versus Closed-End Funds (LO2, CFA2)**   An open-end mutual fund typically keeps a percentage, often around 5 percent, of its assets in cash or liquid money market assets. How does this affect the fund's return in a year in which the market increases in value? How about during a bad year? Closed-end funds do not typically hold cash. What is it about the structure of open-end and closed-end funds that would influence this difference?

7. **12b-1 Fees (LO2, CFA2)**   What are 12b-1 fees? What expenses are 12b-1 fees intended to cover? Many closed-end mutual funds charge a 12b-1 fee. Does this make sense to you? Why or why not?

8. **Open-End versus Closed-End Funds (LO2, CFA2)**   If you were concerned about the liquidity of mutual funds shares that you held, would you rather hold shares in a closed-end fund or an open-end fund? Why?

9. **Mutual Fund Performance (LO3)**   Refer to Figure 4.5. Look at the 3-year performance for the funds listed. Why do you suppose there are so few poor performers? Hint: Think about the hit TV show *Survivor*.

10. **Hedge Fund Fees (LO4, CFA4)**   How does a high-water mark constrain hedge fund managers from earning excess performance management fees?

Questions and Problems

Core Questions

1. **Net Asset Value (LO2, CFA2)**   The World Income Appreciation Fund has current assets with a market value of $8.5 billion and has 410 million shares outstanding. What is the net asset value (NAV) for this mutual fund?

2. **Front-End Loads (LO2)**   Suppose the mutual fund in the previous problem has a current market price quotation of $22.18. Is this a load fund? If so, calculate the front-end load.

3. **Calculating NAV (LO2, CFA2)**   The Emerging Growth and Equity Fund is a "low-load" fund. The current offer price quotation for this mutual fund is $17.86, and the front-end load is 1.5 percent. What is the NAV? If there are 19.2 million shares outstanding, what is the current market value of assets owned by the fund?

4. **Money Market Funds (LO2, CFA1)**   The Aqua Liquid Assets Money Market Mutual Fund has a NAV of $1 per share. During the year, the assets held by this fund appreciated by 2.5 percent. If you had invested $50,000 in this fund at the start of the year, how many shares would you own at the end of the year? What will the NAV of this fund be at the end of the year? Why?

5. **NAV (LO2, CFA2)**   An open-end mutual fund has the following stocks:

Stock	Shares	Stock Price
A	6,000	$98
B	33,000	19
C	4,600	89
D	82,500	12

If there are 50,000 shares of the mutual fund, what is the NAV?

6. **NAV (LO2, CFA2)**   Suppose the fund in the previous problem has liabilities of $110,000. What is the NAV of the fund now?

7. **Front-End Load (LO2)**   In the previous problem, assume the fund is sold with a 5 percent front-end load. What is the offering price of the fund?

8. **Turnover (LO2, CFA3)** A mutual fund sold $36 million of assets during the year and purchased $42 million in assets. If the average daily assets of the fund was $110 million, what was the fund turnover?

9. **Closed-End Funds (LO2, CFA2)** A closed-end fund has total assets of $240 million and liabilities of $110,000. Currently, 11 million shares are outstanding. What is the NAV of the fund? If the shares currently sell for $19.25, what is the premium or discount on the fund?

10. **Mutual Fund Returns (LO2, CFA1)** You invested $10,000 in a mutual fund at the beginning of the year when the NAV was $34.87. At the end of the year the fund paid $.42 in short-term distributions and $.61 in long-term distributions. If the NAV of the fund at the end of the year was $38.21, what was your return for the year?

Intermediate Questions

11. **Calculating Turnover (LO2, CFA3)** A sector fund specializing in commercial bank stocks had average daily assets of $3.4 billion during the year. This fund sold $1.25 billion worth of stock during the year, and its turnover ratio was .42. How much stock did this mutual fund purchase during the year? What other costs are associated with higher turnover?

12. **Calculating Fees (LO2)** In the previous problem, suppose the annual operating expense ratio for the mutual fund is .75 percent, and the management fee is .45 percent. How much money did the fund's management earn during the year? If the fund doesn't charge any 12b-1 fees, how much were miscellaneous and administrative expenses during the year?

13. **Calculating Fees (LO2, CFA1)** You purchased 2,000 shares in the New Pacific Growth Fund on January 2, 2010, at an offering price of $47.10 per share. The front-end load for this fund is 5 percent, and the back-end load for redemptions within one year is 2 percent. The underlying assets in this mutual fund appreciate (including reinvested dividends) by 8 percent during 2010, and you sell back your shares at the end of the year. If the operating expense ratio for the New Pacific Growth Fund is 1.95 percent, what is your total return from this investment? What do you conclude about the impact of fees in evaluating mutual fund performance?

14. **Hedge Funds (LO4, CFA4)** You invested $750,000 with a market-neutral hedge fund manager. The fee structure is 2/20, and the fund has a high-water-mark provision. Suppose the first year the fund manager loses 10 percent, and the second year she gains 20 percent. What are the management and performance fees paid each year? Assume management fees are paid at the beginning of each year and performance fees are taken at the end of each year.

15. **ETFs versus Mutual Funds (LO4, CFA2)** Suppose you just inherited $25,000 from your Aunt Louise. You have decided to invest in an S&P Index fund, but you haven't decided yet whether to use an ETF or a mutual fund. Suppose the ETF has an annual expense ratio of .12 percent, while the mutual fund charges .23 percent. The mutual fund has no load, but the ETF purchase would carry a $25 commission. Assuming this is a long-term holding and you are not concerned about being able to margin or short-sell, which is the better approach?

16. **Expenses and Returns (LO2, CFA1)** The Bruin Stock Fund sells Class A shares that have a front-end load of 5.75 percent, a 12b-1 fee of .23 percent, and other fees of .73 percent. There are also Class B shares with a 5 percent CDSC that declines 1 percent per year, a 12b-1 fee of 1.00 percent, and other fees of .73 percent. If the portfolio return is 10 percent per year and you plan to sell after the third year, should you invest in Class A or Class B shares? What if your investment horizon is 20 years?

17. **Expenses and Returns (LO2, CFA1)** You are going to invest in a stock mutual fund with a 6 percent front-end load and a 1.75 percent expense ratio. You also can invest in a money market mutual fund with a 3.30 percent return and an expense ratio of .10 percent. If you plan to keep your investment for two years, what annual return must the stock mutual fund earn to exceed an investment in the money market fund? What if your investment horizon is 10 years?

18. **Taxes and MMMFs (LO2, CFA1)** Suppose you're evaluating three alternative MMMF investments. The first fund buys a diversified portfolio of municipal securities from across the country and yields 3.5 percent. The second fund buys only taxable, short-term commercial paper and yields 5.4 percent. The third fund specializes in the municipal debt from the state of New Jersey and yields 3.4 percent. If you are a New Jersey resident, your federal tax bracket is 35 percent, and your state tax bracket is 8 percent, which of these three MMMFs offers you the highest aftertax yield?

19. **Taxes and MMMFs (LO2, CFA1)** In the previous problem, which MMMF offers you the highest yield if you are a resident of Texas, which has no state income tax?

20. **Closed-End Funds (LO2, CFA2)** The Argentina Fund has $560 million in assets and sells at a 7.8 percent discount to NAV. If the quoted share price for this closed-end fund is $15.42, how many shares are outstanding? If you purchase 1,000 shares of this fund, what will the total shares outstanding be now?

21. **Closed-End Fund Discounts (LO2, CFA2)** Suppose you purchase 5,000 shares of a closed-end mutual fund at its initial public offering; the offer price is $10 per share. The offering prospectus discloses that the fund promoter gets an 8 percent fee from the offering. If this fund sells at a 7 percent discount to NAV the day after the initial public offering, what is the value of your investment?

CFA Exam Review by Schweser

[CFA2, CFA4]

Suzanne Harlan has a large, well-diversified stock and bond portfolio. She wants to try some alternative investments, such as hedge funds, and has contacted Lawrence Phillips, CFA, to help assemble a new portfolio.

Before agreeing to make recommendations for Ms. Harlan, Mr. Phillips wants to determine if she is a good candidate for alternative investments. He gives her a standard questionnaire. Here are some of her comments:

- I'm interested in high returns. I'm not afraid of risk, and I'm investing money for the benefit of my heirs.
- I pay a lot of attention to expense and return data from my investments and track their performance closely.
- Investors have told me that assessing the quality of hedge funds is difficult, so I'm interested in purchasing a fund of funds where I can diversify my risk while potentially sharing in some outsized returns.
- I pay several million dollars in taxes every year, and I want any additional investments to be tax-friendly.
- My neighbors founded Kelly Tool and Die 20 years ago. They are declaring bankruptcy, and I am interested in obtaining a partial interest in the business.

Ms. Harlan then tells Mr. Phillips that it is imperative that the returns of any investments he recommends must be in some way comparable to a benchmark.

Mr. Phillips is not excited about the business idea or the fund of funds. However, he does know of several managers of individual hedge funds. He talks her out of fund of funds and suggests she put her money in the Stillman Fund, which concentrates on spinoffs, generally buying the spun-off company and shorting the parent company.

1. In an attempt to talk Ms. Harlan out of investing in a fund of funds, Mr. Phillips addressed the advantages of investing in individual funds. Which of the following would be his most compelling argument?
   a. The lower expenses of individual funds
   b. The likelihood of style drift in a fund of funds
   c. The lack of benchmark for a fund of funds

2. What is Ms. Harlan's tolerance for risk?
   a. Distressed security
   b. Arbitrage
   c. Market neutral

3. Which of Ms. Harlan's responses is most likely to make Mr. Phillips consider her a bad candidate for investing in hedge funds?
   a. I pay a lot of attention to expense and return data from my investments and track their performance closely.
   b. I pay several million dollars in taxes every year, and I want any additional investments to be tax-friendly.
   c. I'm interested in high returns. I'm not afraid of risk, and I'm investing money for the benefit of my heirs.

4. If Ms. Harlan is truly concerned about benchmarks, she should avoid which of her suggested investments?

   a. None of them
   b. Kelly Tool and Die
   c. Hedge funds

What's on the Web?

1. **Bond Funds**   One of the best Internet sites for information on mutual funds is www.morningstar.com. Go to the Web site and find the ticker symbol for the Harbor Bond Fund. Find all of the following information on the Web site for this fund: loads, expense ratio, top five holdings, bond quality ratings, the fund's rank in its category for the last seven years, and the Morningstar rating. Next, find out how the Morningstar star ranking system works.

2. **Stock Funds**   Go to www.morningstar.com and find the ticker symbol for a domestic stock fund. Enter the ticker symbol and find the following information for the fund: manager and manager start date, year-to-date return, three-year return, five-year return, front-end or back-end loads, actual and maximum 12b-1 fees, management fees, expense ratio, the top 25 holdings, and the fund address and phone number.

3. **Morningstar Fund Selector**   Find the mutual fund screener on the Morningstar Web site. How many funds fit the following criteria: domestic stock fund, minimum initial purchase equal to or less than $500, expense ratio less than or equal to category average, and turnover less than 75 percent?

Stock-Trak Exercises

To access the Stock-Trak Exercise for this chapter, please visit the book Web site at www.mhhe.com/jmd6e and choose the corresponding chapter.

www.mhhe.com/jmd6e

PART 2

CHAPTER 5

The Stock Market

Learning Objectives

Take stock in yourself. Make sure you have a good understanding of:

1. The differences between private and public equity, and primary and secondary stock markets.

2. The workings of the New York Stock Exchange.

3. How NASDAQ operates.

4. How to calculate index returns.

"One of the funny things about the stock market is that every time one man buys, another sells, and both think they are astute."

–William Feather

"If you don't know who you are, the stock market is an expensive place to find out."

–Adam Smith (pseud. for George J. W. Goodman)

On May 17, 1792, a group of commodity brokers met and signed the now famous Buttonwood Tree Agreement, thereby establishing the forerunner of what soon became the New York Stock Exchange. On April 4, 2007, the NYSE and Euronext completed their merger. The new company, known as NYSE Euronext, operates large and liquid stock exchanges in Amsterdam, Brussels, Paris, New York, and other world cities. The NYSE is the world's best known stock exchange. It's big, too. In the first quarter of 2010, daily trading volume at the NYSE averaged 1.7 billion shares. Established in 1971, and now famous as an arena for "tech" stock investing, daily trading volume at the NASDAQ averaged about 2.3 billion shares in the first quarter of 2010. Together, the NYSE and NASDAQ account for the vast majority of stock trading in the United States. ■

CFA™ Exam Topics in This Chapter:

1 Organization and functioning of securities markets (L1, S13)

2 Security-market indexes (L1, S13)

3 Alternative investments (L1, S18)

4 Private company valuation (L2, S12)

5 Alternate investments portfolio management (L3, S13)

6 Execution of portfolio decisions (L3, S16)

Go to www.mhhe.com/jmd6e for a guide that aligns your textbook with CFA readings.

With this chapter, we begin in earnest our study of stock markets. This chapter presents a "big picture" overview of how a stock market works and how to read and understand stock market information reported in the financial press.

5.1 Private Equity versus Selling Securities to the Public

PRIVATE EQUITY

The broad term *private equity* is often used to label the financing for nonpublic companies. For example, one day, you and a friend have a great idea for a new computer software product that helps users communicate using the next generation Meganet. Filled with entrepreneurial zeal, you christen the product MegaComm and set about bringing it to market.

Working nights and weekends, you are able to create a prototype of your product. It doesn't actually work, but at least you can show it around to illustrate your idea. To develop a working product, you need to hire programmers, buy computers, rent office space, and so on. Unfortunately, because you are both college students, your combined assets are not sufficient to fund a pizza party, much less a start-up company. You need what is often referred to as OPM—other people's money.

Your first thought might be to approach a bank for a loan. You would probably discover, however, that banks are generally not interested in making loans to start-up companies with no assets (other than an idea) run by fledgling entrepreneurs with no track record. Instead, your search for capital would very likely lead you to the **venture capital (VC)** market, an important part of the private equity market.

Firms other than start-ups might need financing. Thus, in addition to venture capital, other areas of private equity include middle-market firms and large leveraged buyouts. We discuss each of these below, but before we do, we provide a general overview of a typical private equity fund. A private equity fund raises money from investors and invests in private companies.

THE STRUCTURE OF PRIVATE EQUITY FUNDS

Although they have differences, private equity funds and hedge funds share some characteristics. For example, both private equity funds and hedge funds are investment companies set up as limited partnerships that pool money from investors and then invest the money on behalf of these investors.

Of course, investors pay private equity funds a management fee to make investment decisions and, in most cases, the investors also pay a performance fee. Similar to hedge funds, private equity funds typically use a 2/20 fee structure (i.e., a 2 percent annual management fee and 20 percent of profits).

Similar to the hedge funds, private equity funds also have built-in constraints to prevent the fund managers from taking excessive compensation. Specifically, private equity funds generally have a high-water-mark provision and typically have a "clawback" provision. The aim of a clawback provision is to make sure that the manager receives only the agreed-upon performance fee.

Here is how a clawback works. Suppose the private equity fund is set up to have a two-year life. In its first year of operation, the private equity fund earns a 25 percent return. For every $1,000 in the fund, the managers of this private equity fund "receive" a hefty performance fee of $50 (20 percent of the $250 profit). In its second year, the private equity fund investors suffer a 10 percent loss. Under the terms of a typical clawback provision, the managers have to "give back" the first year's performance fee when the fund is liquidated at the end of year 2. At liquidation, the managers earn a fee of $25 for every $1,000 in the fund (20 percent of the accumulated two-year profit of $125). Because the fund managers generally do not take any performance fees until the fund is liquidated, the performance fee for private equity firms is known as "carried interest."

Like hedge funds, the fees paid to the private equity managers significantly reduce the net return of the fund. The benefit of such investments is frequently debated. Right now, the general thinking is that the average net return to investors in private equity funds is about equal to the return of small-cap stocks. So, is there any benefit to adding this type of investment to a portfolio? The answer depends on whether private equity funds provide significant diversification benefits to investors.

Even if private equity funds do provide diversification benefits, they might not be a reasonable choice for most investors. First, an investor in private equity funds must be a qualified investor—that is, "rich." Second, the funds are really illiquid, possibly even more illiquid than hedge funds. A typical private equity fund is started by raising money from investors. After the money is raised, the managers invest in private companies, with the intention of improving them and subsequently exiting, preferably through an initial public offering (IPO). This process obviously can take some time. This process means that a typical fund will have a stated life of 7–10 years—which makes for an illiquid investment.

TYPES OF PRIVATE EQUITY FUNDS

For a list of well-known VC firms, see www.vfinance.com

VENTURE CAPITAL The term *venture capital* does not have a precise meaning, but it generally refers to financing for new, often high-risk ventures. For example, before it went public, Internet auctioneer eBay was venture capital financed. Individual venture capitalists invest their own money, whereas venture capital firms specialize in pooling funds from various sources and investing them.

Venture capitalists and venture capital firms recognize that many or even most new ventures will not fly, but the occasional one will. The potential profits are enormous in such cases. To limit their risk, venture capitalists generally provide financing in stages. At each stage, enough money is invested to reach the next milestone or planning stage. For example, the *first-stage* (or first "round") *financing* might be enough to get a prototype built and a manufacturing plan completed. Based on the results, the *second-stage financing* might be a major investment needed to actually begin manufacturing, marketing, and distribution. There might be many such stages, each of which represents a key step in the process of growing the company.

The Internet is a tremendous source of venture capital information, both for suppliers and demanders of capital. For example, see www.nvca.org

Venture capital firms often specialize in different stages. Some specialize in very early "seed money," or ground floor, financing. In contrast, financing in the later stages might come from venture capitalists specializing in so-called mezzanine-level financing, where *mezzanine level* refers to the level just above the ground floor. This mezzanine-level financing could come in the form of either debt or equity. In either case, it will likely be structured to limit downside risk and retain upside profit potential. Examples of such securities include preferred stock that is convertible into common stock, or a bond that has some attached call options.

The fact that financing is available in stages and is contingent on specified goals being met is a powerful motivating force for the firm's founders. Often, the founders receive relatively little in the way of salary and have substantial portions of their personal assets tied up in the business. At each stage of financing, the value of the founder's stake grows and the probability of success rises. If goals are not met, the venture capitalist will withhold further financing, thereby limiting future losses.

In addition to providing financing, venture capitalists generally will actively participate in running the firm, providing the benefit of experience with previous start-ups as well as general business expertise. This is especially true when the firm's founders have little or no hands-on experience in running a company.

If a start-up succeeds, the big payoff frequently comes when the company is sold to another company or goes public. Either way, investment bankers are often involved in the process.

MIDDLE MARKET When you hear the term "venture capital," you probably are thinking about investment into start-up companies. There are, however, many examples of private equity investments other than start-up companies. For example, many small, regional private equity funds concentrate their investments in "middle market" companies. These companies are ongoing concerns (i.e., not start-ups) with a known performance history. Typically, these companies are small, and many are family owned and operated.

LEHMAN AND PE A YEAR LATER: BY THE NUMBERS

Lehman Brothers Holdings Inc.'s bankruptcy one year ago had an undeniably huge impact on private equity. Over the past year, the bankruptcy and the economic downturn that followed rendered raising debt nearly impossible, brought deal-making to a halt, sent fund-raising into a tailspin and has pushed many portfolio companies into bankruptcy or to the edge of it.

Here, a look at some of the numbers. Our sources are our own publications (LBO Wire and Private Equity Analyst), as well as industry data tracker Dealogic.

Nine months: Amount of time it took for financial sponsor-backed loan volume to exceed $50 billion in 2009

Seven weeks: Amount of time it took in 2008

$55.4 billion: Financial sponsor-backed loan volume this year as of Sept. 14

$213.9 billion: Financial sponsor-backed loan volume as of the same date in 2008

$19.6 billion: Dollar volume of U.S. buyout transactions between Sept. 15, 2008, and Aug. 17, 2009

Roughly $61 billion: The full-year 2008 figure

Roughly $375 billion: The full-year 2007 figure

At least 75: Number of private equity-backed U.S. portfolio company bankruptcies since Sept. 15, 2008

$2.75 billion: Valuation of the largest U.S. buyout so far in 2009—of Skype by a Silver Lake–led group

$4.1 billion: Valuation of the largest U.S. buyout in 2008—of ConvaTec Ltd. by Avista Capital Partners and Nordic Capital

$45 billion: Valuation of the largest buyout ever—of TXU Corp., now Energy Future Holdings Corp., by Kohlberg Kravis Roberts & Co. and TPG Capital in 2007

$1.7 billion: Financial sponsor fees paid to banks this year through Sept. 14, 2009

106: The number of banks that have failed between Sept. 15, 2008, and Sept. 15, 2009, according to the Federal Deposit Insurance Corp.'s Web site

At least 10: Number of U.S. banks that have received or are planning to receive capital from private equity firms or individuals who head PE firms since Sept. 15, 2008 (Indymac, BankUnited, First Bank & Trust Co., First National Bank of Cainesville, Flagstar Bancorp, Guaranty Bancorp, Webster Financial Corp., FirstCity Bank of Commerce, First Bankshares Inc., First Southern Bank)

$71 billion: Amount raised by U.S.-based private equity, venture capital, mezzanine and secondary firms in 2009 through Sept. 9

Roughly $175 billion: Amount raised by mid-September of last year

Source: Laura Kreutzer, *The Wall Street Journal*. Reprinted by permission of *The Wall Street Journal*. © 2009 Dow Jones & Company, Inc. All Rights Reserved Worldwide.

Why would an established, middle market company even be in the market for more capital? Many times, these companies need capital if they wish to expand beyond their existing region. Other times, the founders of the firm want to retire from the business. In the latter case, the private equity fund might be interested in purchasing a portion or all of the business so that others can take over running the company.

LEVERAGED BUYOUTS You might be familiar with the term "going public," a process (which we discuss below) where a privately owned company sells ownership shares to the public market. What if, however, the opposite happens? What if the company (or someone else) purchases all the shares held by the public at large? This process is called taking the company private. Because most publicly traded companies have a large market capitalization, the cost of going private is high. So a manager or investor who wants to take a company private probably needs to borrow a significant amount of money. Taking a company private using borrowed money is called a leveraged buyout (LBO).

With its need for borrowed money, the activity level in the LBO market depends on credit markets. For example, in the middle of the first decade of the 2000s, the LBO market was quite active. The LBO market came to a standstill, however, for some time after the crash of 2008. While the LBO market has regained some activity, it is still trying to recover. To read more about the impact of the crash of 2008, check out the nearby *Investment Updates* box.

How big is the "typical" LBO? Unfortunately, there is no "typical" LBO. We can give you an idea, however, of the potential size of such deals. For example, during the height of the LBO boom just mentioned, the private equity firm Cerberus bought Chrysler for $25 billion; Apollo and TPG funds bought Harrah's Entertainment for $31 billion; and a group led by Goldman Sachs bought the energy firm TXU for $45 billion.

No matter the situation—venture capital, middle market, or LBO—the process and securities used will generally follow the structure we identified in the previous sections. The main difference among the types of private equity funds is really just the types of firms in which the funds are investing.

SELLING SECURITIES TO THE PUBLIC

The goal of the private equity funds we just discussed is to invest in a private company, improve its performance, and then exit the business with a profit. Exiting the firm could be accomplished by selling to another investor. Typically, however, the preferred route is to sell the firm to the general public.

What about private companies that do not have private equity investors? Well, the managers of these companies might decide to raise additional capital by selling shares directly to the general investing public. In either case, shares of stock in the firm would then be listed on a stock exchange.

primary market
The market in which new securities are originally sold to investors.

secondary market
The market in which previously issued securities trade among investors.

When we talk about the *stock market*, we are talking about securities that have been sold to the public. The stock market consists of a **primary market** and a **secondary market**. In the primary, or new-issue market, shares of stock are first brought to the market and sold to investors. In the secondary market, existing shares are traded among investors.

In the primary market, companies issue new securities to raise money. In the secondary market, investors are constantly appraising the values of companies by buying and selling shares previously issued by these companies. We next discuss the operation of the primary market for common stocks, and then we turn our attention to the secondary market for stocks.

THE PRIMARY MARKET FOR COMMON STOCK

The primary market for common stock is how new securities are first brought to market. It is best known as the market for **initial public offerings (IPOs)**. An IPO occurs when a company offers stock for sale to the public for the first time. Typically, the company is small and growing, and it needs to raise capital for further expansion.

initial public offering (IPO)
An initial public offering occurs when a company offers stock for sale to the public for the first time.

seasoned equity offering (SEO)
The sale of additional shares of stock by a company whose shares are already publicly traded.

An IPO is sometimes called an *unseasoned equity offering* because shares are not available to the public before the IPO. If a company already has shares owned by the public, it can raise equity with a **seasoned equity offering (SEO)**. The terms *secondary* and *follow-on offering* also refer to an SEO. A seasoned equity offering of common stock can be made using a general cash offer or a rights offer. In a **general cash offer**, securities are offered to the general public on a "first-come, first served" basis. With a **rights offer**, securities are initially offered only to existing owners. Rights offerings are rare in the United States but common in other countries.

general cash offer
An issue of securities offered for sale to the general public on a cash basis.

rights offer
A public issue of securities in which securities are first offered to existing shareholders (also called a rights offering).

Obviously, all initial public offerings are cash offers. To illustrate how an IPO occurs, let's look in on the software company that you started several years ago. Suppose your company was initially set up as a privately held corporation with 100,000 shares of stock, all sold for one dollar per share. The reason your company is privately held is that shares were not offered for sale to the general public. Instead, you bought 50,000 shares for yourself and sold the remaining 50,000 shares to a few supportive friends and relatives (who were taking the role of venture capitalists).

Fortunately, your company has prospered beyond all expectations. However, company growth is now hampered by a lack of capital. At an informal stockholders' meeting, it is agreed to take the company public. Not really knowing how to do this, you consult your accountant, who recommends an **investment banking firm**. An investment banking firm, among other things, specializes in arranging financing for companies by finding investors to buy newly issued securities.

investment banking firm
A firm specializing in arranging financing for companies.

After lengthy negotiations, including an examination of your company's current financial condition and plans for future growth, your investment banker suggests an issue of 4 million shares of common stock. Two million shares will be distributed to the original stockholders (you and your original investors) in exchange for their old shares. These 2 million shares distributed to the original stockholders ensure that effective control of the corporation will remain in their hands.

After much haggling, your investment banker agrees to **underwrite** the stock issue by purchasing the other 2 million shares from your company for $10 per share. The net effect of this transaction is that you have sold half the company to the underwriter for $20 million. The proceeds from the sale will allow your company to construct its own headquarters building and to double its staff of programmers and sales consultants.

Your investment banker will not keep the 2 million shares but instead will resell them in the primary market. She thinks the stock can probably be sold for $11 per share in an IPO. The difference between the $11 the underwriter sells the stock for and the $10 per share you received is called the **underwriter spread**, or discount. It is the basic compensation received by the underwriter. Sometimes the underwriter will get noncash compensation in the form of warrants and stock in addition to the spread.

Underwriters combine to form an underwriting group called a **syndicate** to share the risk and to help sell the issue. In a syndicate, one or more managers arrange the offering. This manager is designated as the lead manager, or principal manager. The lead manager typically has the responsibility of pricing the securities. The other underwriters in the syndicate serve primarily to distribute the issue.

Two basic types of underwriting are involved in a cash offer: firm commitment and best efforts. A third type of underwriting is Dutch auction underwriting.

FIRM COMMITMENT UNDERWRITING In **firm commitment underwriting**, the issuer sells the entire issue to the underwriters, who then attempt to resell it. This is the most prevalent type of underwriting in the United States. This is really just a purchase-resale arrangement, and the underwriter's fee is the spread. For a new issue of seasoned equity, the underwriters can look at the market price to determine what the issue should sell for, and 95 percent of all such new issues are firm commitments.

If the underwriter cannot sell all of the issue at the agreed-upon offering price, it may have to lower the price on the unsold shares. Nonetheless, with firm commitment underwriting, the issuer receives the agreed-upon amount, and all the risk associated with selling the issue is transferred to the underwriter.

Because the offering price usually isn't set until the underwriters have investigated how receptive the market is to the issue, this risk is usually minimal. Also, because the offering price usually is not set until just before selling commences, the issuer doesn't know precisely what its net proceeds will be until that time.

BEST EFFORTS UNDERWRITING In **best efforts underwriting**, the underwriter is legally bound to use "best efforts" to sell the securities at the agreed-upon offering price. Beyond this, the underwriter does not guarantee any particular amount of money to the issuer. This form of underwriting has become very uncommon in recent years; firm commitments are now the dominant form.

DUTCH AUCTION UNDERWRITING With **Dutch auction underwriting**, the underwriter does not set a fixed price for the shares to be sold. Instead, the underwriter conducts an auction in which investors bid for shares. The offer price is determined based on the submitted bids. A Dutch auction is also known by the more descriptive name *uniform price auction*. This approach to selling securities to the public is relatively new in the IPO market and has not been widely used there, but it is very common in the bond markets. For example, it is the sole procedure used by the U.S. Treasury to sell enormous quantities of notes, bonds, and bills to the public.

Dutch auction underwriting was much in the news in 2004 because Web search company Google elected to use this approach. The best way to understand a Dutch or uniform

---

underwrite
To assume the risk of buying newly issued securities from a company and reselling them to investors.

underwriter spread
Compensation to the underwriter, determined by the difference between the underwriter's buying price and offering price.

syndicate
A group of underwriters formed to share the risk and to help sell an issue.

firm commitment underwriting
The type of underwriting in which the underwriter buys the entire issue, assuming full financial responsibility for any unsold shares.

best efforts underwriting
The type of underwriting in which the underwriter sells as much of the issue as possible, but can return any unsold shares to the issuer without financial responsibility.

Dutch auction underwriting
The type of underwriting in which the offer price is set based on competitive bidding by investors. Also known as a *uniform price auction.*

price auction is to consider a simple example. Suppose The Roserita Company wants to sell 400 shares to the public. The company receives five bids as follows:

Bidder	Quantity	Price
A	100 shares	$16
B	100 shares	14
C	200 shares	12
D	100 shares	12
E	200 shares	10

Thus, bidder A is willing to buy 100 shares at $16 each, bidder B is willing to buy 100 shares at $14, and so on. The Roserita Company examines the bids to determine the highest price that will result in all 400 shares being sold. So, for example, at $14, A and B would buy only 200 shares, so that price is too high. Working our way down, all 400 shares won't be sold until we hit a price of $12, so $12 will be the offer price in the IPO. Bidders A through D will receive shares; bidder E will not.

There are two additional important points to observe in our example: First, all the winning bidders will pay $12, even bidders A and B, who actually bid a higher price. The fact that all successful bidders pay the same price is the reason for the name "uniform price auction." The idea in such an auction is to encourage bidders to bid aggressively by providing some protection against bidding a price that is too high.

Second, notice that at the $12 offer price, there are actually bids for 500 shares, which exceeds the 400 shares Roserita wants to sell. Thus, there has to be some sort of allocation. How this is done varies a bit, but, in the IPO market, the approach has been to simply compute the ratio of shares offered to shares bid at the offer price or better, which, in our example, is 400/500 = .8, and allocate bidders that percentage of their bids. In other words, bidders A through D would each receive 80 percent of the shares they bid at a price of $12 per share.

As is common with an IPO, some restrictions are imposed on you as part of the underwriting contract. Most important, you and the other original stockholders agree not to sell any of your personal stockholdings for six months after the underwriting (this is called the "lockup" period). This ties most of your wealth to the company's success and makes selling the stock to investors a more credible undertaking by the underwriter. Essentially, investors are assured that you will be working hard to expand the company and increase its earnings.

After the underwriting terms are decided, much of your time will be devoted to the mechanics of the offering. In particular, before shares can be sold to the public, the issue must obtain an approved registration with the **Securities and Exchange Commission (SEC)**. The SEC is the federal regulatory agency charged with regulating U.S. securities markets.

SEC regulations governing IPOs are especially strict. To gain SEC approval, you must prepare a **prospectus**, normally with the help of outside accounting, auditing, and legal experts. The prospectus contains a detailed account of your company's financial position, its operations, and its investment plans for the future. Once the prospectus is prepared, it is submitted to the SEC for approval. The SEC makes no judgment about the quality of your company or the value of your stock. Instead, it only checks to make sure that various rules regarding full disclosure and other issues have been satisfied.

While awaiting SEC approval, your investment banker will circulate a preliminary prospectus among investors to generate interest in the stock offering. This document is commonly called a **red herring** because the cover page is stamped in red ink, indicating that final approval for the stock issue has not yet been obtained. The preliminary prospectus is essentially complete except for the final offering price and a few other pieces of information. These are not set because market conditions might change while SEC approval is being sought. Upon obtaining SEC approval, the prospectus will be

For more on IPOs, check out IPO Central at www.hoovers.com

Securities and Exchange Commission (SEC)
Federal regulatory agency charged with enforcing U.S. securities laws and regulations.

prospectus
Document prepared as part of a security offering detailing a company's financial position, its operations, and investment plans for the future.

red herring
A preliminary prospectus not yet approved by the SEC.

updated and completed, and your underwriter can begin selling your company's shares to investors.

To publicize an offering, the underwriter will usually place announcements in newspapers and other outlets. Because of their appearance, these announcements are known as *tombstones*, and they are a familiar sight in the financial press. A sample tombstone as it appeared in *The Wall Street Journal* is shown in Figure 5.1.

As Figure 5.1 shows, a typical tombstone states the name of the company, some information about the stock issue being sold, and the underwriters for the issue. All but very small issues generally involve more than one underwriter, and the names of the participating underwriters are usually listed at the bottom of the tombstone. Those listed first are the "lead" underwriters, who are primarily responsible for managing the issue process.

Initial public stock offerings vary in size a great deal. The 2 million share issue for your hypothetical software company discussed above is a fairly small issue. One of the largest public offerings in the United States was AT&T Wireless, a subsidiary of AT&T. The new shares were offered at $29.50 per share to create a $70 billion public offering.

THE SECONDARY MARKET FOR COMMON STOCK

In the secondary market for common stock, investors buy and sell shares with other investors. If you think of the primary market as the new-car showroom at an automotive dealer, where cars are first sold to the public, then the secondary market is just the used-car lot.

Secondary market stock trading among investors is directed through three channels. An investor may trade:

1. Directly with other investors.
2. Indirectly through a broker who arranges transactions for others.
3. Directly with a dealer who buys and sells securities from inventory.

As we discussed in Chapter 2, for individual investors, almost all common stock transactions are made through a broker. However, large institutional investors, such as pension funds and mutual funds, trade through both brokers and dealers, and also trade directly with other institutional investors.

DEALERS AND BROKERS

dealer
A trader who buys and sells securities from inventory.

broker
An intermediary who arranges security transactions among investors.

bid price
The price a dealer is willing to pay.

ask price
The price at which a dealer is willing to sell. Also called the *offer* or *offering* price.

spread
The difference between the bid and ask prices.

Because most securities transactions involve dealers and brokers, it is important that you understand exactly what these terms mean. A **dealer** maintains an inventory and stands ready to buy and sell at any time. By contrast, a **broker** brings buyers and sellers together but does not maintain an inventory. Thus, when we speak of used-car dealers and real estate brokers, we recognize that the used-car dealer maintains an inventory, whereas the real estate broker normally does not.

In the securities markets, a dealer stands ready to buy securities from investors wishing to sell them and to sell securities to investors wishing to buy them. An important part of the dealer function involves maintaining an inventory to accommodate temporary buy and sell order imbalances. The price a dealer is willing to pay is called the **bid price**. The price at which a dealer will sell is called the **ask price** (sometimes called the offer or offering price). The difference between the bid and ask prices is called the **spread**.

A dealer attempts to profit by selling securities at a price higher than the average price paid for them. Of course, this is a goal for all investors, but the distinguishing characteristic of securities dealers is that they hold securities in inventory only until the first opportunity to resell them. Essentially, trading from inventory is their business.

Dealers exist in all areas of the economy, of course, not just in the stock markets. For example, your local university bookstore is both a primary and secondary market textbook dealer. If you buy a new book, then this is a primary market transaction. If you buy a used book, this is a secondary market transaction, and you pay the store's ask price. If you sell the

FIGURE 5.1   IPO Tombstone

This announcement is neither an offer to sell nor a solicitation of an offer to buy any of these securities.
The offering is made only by the Prospectus.

New Issue

11,500,000 Shares

World Wrestling Federation Entertainment, Inc.

Class A Common Stock

Price $17.00 Per Share

Copies of the Prospectus may be obtained in any State in which this announcement
is circulated from only such of the Underwriters, including the undersigned,
as may lawfully offer these securities in such State.

U.S. Offering

9,200,000 Shares

This portion of the underwriting is being offered in the United States and Canada.

Bear, Stearns & Co. Inc.

       Credit Suisse First Boston

              Merrill Lynch & Co.

                  Wit Capital Corporation

Allen & Company Incorporated	Banc of America Securities LLC	Deutsche Banc Alex. Brown
Donaldson, Lufkin & Jenrette	A.G. Edwards & Sons, Inc.	Hambrecht & Quist ING Barings
Prudential Securities SG Cowen	Wasserstein Perella Securities, Inc.	Advest, Inc.
Axiom Capital Management, Inc.	Blackford Securities Corp.	J.C. Bradford & Co.
Joseph Charles & Assoc., Inc.	Chatsworth Securities LLC	Gabelli & Company, Inc.
Gaines, Berland Inc. Jefferies & Company, Inc.	Josephthal & Co. Inc.	Neuberger Berman, LLC
Raymond James & Associates, Inc.	Sanders Morris Mundy	
Tucker Anthony Cleary Gull		Wachovia Securities, Inc.

International Offering

2,300,000 Shares

This portion of the underwriting is being offered outside of the United States and Canada.

Bear, Stearns International Limited

       Credit Suisse First Boston

              Merrill Lynch International

book back, you receive the store's bid price, often half the ask price. The bookstore's spread is the difference between the bid and the ask price.

In contrast, a securities broker arranges transactions between investors, matching investors wishing to buy securities with investors wishing to sell securities. Brokers may match investors with other investors, investors with dealers, and sometimes even dealers with dealers. The distinctive characteristic of securities brokers is that they do not buy or sell securities for their own account. Facilitating trades by others is their business.

Most common stock trading is directed through an organized stock exchange or a trading network. Whether on a stock exchange or through a trading network, the goal is to match investors wishing to buy stocks with investors wishing to sell stocks. The largest, most active organized stock exchange in the United States is the New York Stock Exchange (NYSE). Other well-known stock exchanges include the Chicago Stock Exchange (CHX), the Boston Stock Exchange (BSE), the National Stock Exchange (NSX), and the Philadelphia Stock Exchange (PHLX). The major competitor to the organized stock exchanges is the vast trading network known as NASDAQ. We next discuss the workings of the NYSE, and then we turn to a discussion of NASDAQ.

CHECK THIS

5.1a	Is an IPO a primary or a secondary market transaction?
5.1b	Which is bigger, the bid price or the ask price? Why?
5.1c	What is the difference between a securities broker and a securities dealer?

5.2 The New York Stock Exchange

The New York Stock Exchange (NYSE, pronounced "ny-see"), popularly known as the Big Board, celebrated its bicentennial in 1992. It has occupied its current building on Wall Street since the turn of the twentieth century. For more than 200 years, the NYSE operated as a not-for-profit corporation. However, on March 8, 2006, the NYSE went public (ticker NYX) and is now a publicly traded for-profit corporation. On April 4, 2007, NYSE Holdings merged with Euronext N.V. and launched NYSE Euronext. NYSE Euronext is currently the world's largest exchange.

Our subsequent discussion in this chapter concerning the NYSE reflects the structure of the exchange as it exists at the time of this writing. How this structure will evolve over time will depend on the numerous changes that are being initiated in the U.S. financial markets. NYSE's decision to become publicly owned will be affected by regulatory changes and technological innovations that are changing the landscape for financial markets all across the globe.

NYSE MEMBERSHIP HISTORY

NYSE exchange member
Before 2006, the NYSE exchange members were the owners of the exchange.

Historically, the NYSE had 1,366 **exchange members**. Before 2006, the exchange members were said to own "seats" on the exchange, and, collectively, the members of the exchange were also the owners. For this and other reasons, seats were valuable and were bought and sold fairly regularly. Seat prices reached a record $4 million in 2005.

In 2006, all of this changed when the NYSE became a publicly owned corporation called NYSE Group, Inc. Naturally, its stock is listed on the NYSE. Now, instead of purchasing seats, exchange members must purchase trading licenses, the number of which is limited to 1,500. In 2010, a license would set you back a cool $40,000—per year. Being a **license holder** entitles you to buy and sell securities on the floor of the exchange. Different members play different roles in this regard.

NYSE license holder
Having a license entitles the holder to buy and sell securities on the floor of the exchange.

For up-to-date
info on the NYSE,
surf to
www.nyse.com

specialists
Formerly, sole dealers in a small number of securities on the floor of the NYSE; often called a market makers.

display book
A chronological record of all limit, stop, and short-sale orders that had been placed with a specialist; also contains an inventory of the specialist's holdings.

designated market maker (DMM)
A new class of market maker at the NYSE; replaced the role of specialists on the exchange floor.

supplemental liquidity provider (SLP)
A new class of market maker at the NYSE; located off the floor of the exchange.

commission brokers
Firms that execute customer orders to buy and sell stock transmitted to the exchange floor.

floor brokers
NYSE members who execute orders for commission brokers on a fee basis; sometimes called two-dollar brokers.

Super Display Book system (SDBK)
The new server-based electronic trading system at the NYSE.

SuperDOT system
The NYSE's well-known, now defunct, electronic trading system.

Arca
All-electronic securities exchange listing stocks, options, and ETFs.

Before the NYSE went public, NYSE members collectively owned the exchange. Today, the shareholders own the exchange. At the end of February 2010, the NYSE had about 260 million shares outstanding.

DESIGNATED MARKET MAKERS

During much of the history of the NYSE, nearly all securities listed for trading were divided among **specialists**. A specialist acted as the exclusive dealer, or intermediary, for a set of securities. Specialists posted bid prices and ask prices for each security assigned to them. Specialists were obligated to make and maintain a fair, orderly market for the securities assigned to them. Specialists make a market by standing ready to buy at bid prices and sell at ask prices when a temporary disparity arises between the flow of buy orders and the flow of sell orders for a security. In this capacity, they act as dealers for their own accounts. The specialists had an exclusive, advance look at incoming orders that flowed to the **display book**. Because of this advance look, specialists had an information advantage when they were making quotes and matching orders. Under this system, specialists, however, could "work" orders, that is, try to improve trading prices for customers.

Because of competition from other exchanges and other trading technologies, the market share of the NYSE has eroded. As one of several strategies aimed at staying competitive, in 2009 the NYSE replaced the role of specialists with two classes of market makers, called **designated market maker (DMM)** and **supplemental liquidity provider (SLP)**.

What were specialists are now the DMMs. The DMMs are assigned a set of securities by the exchange and are obligated to maintain a fair and orderly market in these stocks, as specialists had been. There are some differences, however, between the two roles. The DMMs do not face the restrictions on trading that specialists had and are given some other rights. For example, they can now compete against other exchange members for trades, rather than stand at the back of the line for trades. Specialists had to step back from a trade if a floor broker order (or SuperDOT order when it was active) had the same price. A DMM, however, has equal standing among traders and does not have to step back from orders. Unlike the specialist system, however, DMMs do not receive an advance look at incoming orders.

Under the multidealer structure, however, DMMs do not have an exclusive right to make markets in their assigned securities. A newly created class of market maker is called the supplemental liquidity provider (SLP). SLPs can trade the same stocks as the DMMs. SLPs can trade only from offices outside the exchange. DMMs are located on the floor of the exchange. DMMs must quote bid prices *and* ask prices for at least 5 percent of the trading day. SLPs, however, are required to quote bid prices *or* ask prices for at least 5 percent of the day.

As an incentive to provide liquidity to the market, the exchange pays DMMs 30 cents per 100 shares when they make a trade. Because they face lower quoting requirements, the SLPs get 15 cents per 100 shares traded. Floor brokers have no quoting requirements, but the exchange encourages their trading activity by paying them 4 cents per 100 shares traded.

OTHER NYSE PARTICIPANTS

The business of a **commission broker** is to execute customer orders to buy and sell stocks. A commission broker's primary responsibility to customers is to get the best possible prices for their orders. The exact number varies, but about 500 commission brokers are affiliated with the NYSE. NYSE commission brokers typically are employees of brokerage companies such as Merrill Lynch (now owned by Bank of America).

Floor brokers are used by commission brokers who are too busy to handle certain orders themselves. Such commission brokers will delegate some orders to floor brokers for execution. Floor brokers are sometimes called two-dollar brokers, a name earned at a time when the standard fee for their service was only $2. In recent years, floor brokers have become less important on the exchange floor.

A substitute for floor brokers is the efficient NYSE **Super Display Book system (SDBK)**, which recently replaced the well-known **SuperDOT system** (the *DOT* stands for designated order turnaround). Based on the NYSE's electronic trading engine, **Arca**, the NYSE SDBK is a server-based system. The NYSE Arca is a fully electronic exchange for growth-oriented companies. This all-electronic exchange lists stocks, options, and exchange-traded funds (ETFs).

Trading via the SDBK is remarkably fast. NYSE customers can have their trades executed within 5 milliseconds (down from a relatively sluggish 350 milliseconds in 2007). How fast is this trading? For comparison, when Danica Patrick is running her Number 7 Go Daddy Chevrolet at 200 miles per hour, she races only about 1.5 feet in 5 milliseconds.

floor traders
NYSE license holders who trade securities for their own accounts.

A small number of NYSE members are **floor traders** who independently trade for their own accounts. Floor traders try to anticipate temporary price fluctuations and profit from them by buying low and selling high. In recent decades, the number of floor traders has declined substantially, suggesting that profiting from short-term trading on the exchange floor has become increasingly difficult.

THE NYSE HYBRID MARKET

To keep pace with technology advances and innovations in global financial markets, the NYSE has been increasingly building an automated trading platform structure. The NYSE rolled out a faster automated execution system called the Hybrid platform beginning in late 2006. The NYSE continues to make improvements in the Hybrid platform.

Hybrid trading combines the exchange's automated technology with the advantages of an auction market. In the Hybrid market, DMMs and floor brokers interact with the market electronically as well as in person. This design allows the Hybrid market to offer more choice in how investor orders are executed on the exchange.

The Hybrid trading system has evolved because human judgment provided by living market makers is valuable (1) in less liquid stocks, (2) during the opening and closing of trading sessions, and (3) during times of market duress. In normal times for the average stock, however, the automated platform is an efficient option.

NYSE-LISTED STOCKS

A company is said to be "listed" on the NYSE Euronext if its stock is traded there. At the end of December 2008, the approximately 8,500 companies listed on the NYSE Euronext represented a total global market value of approximately $16.7 trillion (€12.3 trillion). This total includes many large companies so well known that we easily recognize them by their initials—for example, IBM, MMM, and CAT. This total also includes many companies that are not so readily recognized. For example, relatively few investors would instantly recognize AEP as American Electric Power, but many would recognize AXP as American Express.

U.S. companies that wish to have their stock listed for trading on the "Big Board" must apply for the privilege. If the application is approved, the company must pay an initial listing fee. In 2009, this fee was $50,000, plus a per-share listing fee of $.0032, or $3,200 per million shares.

Once listed, if a firm lists additional shares of a class of previously listed securities, it pays the following listing fees. For the first 75 million shares, the fee is $4,800 per million shares. For the next 225 million shares, it is $3,750 per million shares. For each million shares above 300 million, the fee is $1,900. The minimum initial listing fee is $125,000 and the maximum listing fee is $250,000.

In addition to an initial listing fee, the NYSE assesses an annual listing fee. In 2009, the annual listing fee was $930 per million shares (subject to a $38,000 minimum fee).

The NYSE has minimum requirements for companies wishing to apply for listing. Although the requirements might change from time to time, examples of minimum requirements in effect in 2010 for U.S. domestic stocks included:

1. The company must have at least 2,200 shareholders, and average monthly trading volume for the most recent six months must be at least 100,000 shares.

2. At least 1.1 million stock shares must be held in public hands.

3. Publicly held shares must have at least $100 million in market value ($40 million for IPOs).

4. The company must have aggregate earnings of $10 million before taxes in the previous three years and $2 million pretax earnings in each of the preceding two years.

In practice, most companies with stock listed on the NYSE easily exceed these minimum listing requirements. You can read copious details and minutia about listing at the NYSE if you surf over to http://nysemanual.nyse.com.

CHECK THIS

5.2a	What are the types of license holders at the New York Stock Exchange?
5.2b	What are the two types of market makers at the NYSE? What do they do?
5.2c	What is the SDBK?

5.3 Operation of the New York Stock Exchange

Now that we have a basic idea of how the NYSE is organized and who the major players are, we turn to the question of how trading actually takes place. Fundamentally, the business of the NYSE is to attract and process *order flow*—the flow of customer orders to buy and sell stocks. Customers of the NYSE are the millions of individual investors and tens of thousands of institutional investors who place their orders to buy and sell NYSE-listed stock shares with member-firm brokers.

Historically, the NYSE has been quite successful in attracting order flow. For example, in 2007, the average stock trading volume on the NYSE was well over 2 billion shares per day. In recent years, however, volume at the NYSE has decreased in proportion to the volume at the NASDAQ and Electronic Communication Networks (ECNs).

About one-third of all NYSE stock trading volume is attributable to individual investors, and almost half is derived from institutional investors. The remainder represents NYSE member trading, which is largely attributed to specialists acting as market makers.

NYSE FLOOR ACTIVITY

Quite likely you have seen film footage of the NYSE trading floor on television, or you may have visited the NYSE and viewed exchange floor activity from the gallery (when it was open). Either way, you saw a big room, about the size of a small basketball gym. This big room is aptly called "the big room." There are several other, smaller rooms that you normally do not see. Another is called "the garage" because that is what it was before it was taken over for securities trading. Two others were called the "blue room" because, well, the room is painted blue, and the "extended blue room." In November 2007, the NYSE closed the blue room and the extended blue room.

On the floor of the exchange are a number of stations, each with a roughly figure-eight shape. These stations have multiple counters with numerous computer terminal screens above and on the sides. People operate behind and in front of the counters in relatively stationary positions.

Other people move around on the exchange floor, frequently returning to the many telephone booths positioned along the exchange walls. In all, you may have been reminded of worker ants moving around an ant colony. It is natural to wonder: What are all those people doing down there (and why are so many wearing funny-looking coats)?

As an overview of exchange floor activity, here is a quick look at what goes on. Each of the counters at the figure-eight shaped stations is a **DMM's post**. DMMs normally operate in front of their posts to monitor and manage trading in the stocks assigned to them. Clerical employees working for the DMMs operate behind the counters. Moving from the many telephone booths out to the exchange floor and back again are swarms of floor brokers, receiving relayed customer orders, walking out to the posts where the orders can be executed, and returning to confirm order executions and receive new customer orders.

To better understand activity on the NYSE trading floor, imagine yourself as a floor broker. Your phone clerk has just handed you an order to sell 3,000 shares of KO (the ticker symbol for Coca-Cola common stock) for a customer of the brokerage company that

DMM's post
Fixed place on the exchange floor where the DMM operates.

market order

A customer order to buy or sell securities marked for immediate execution at the current market price.

employs you. The order is a **market order**, meaning that the customer wants to sell the stock at the best possible price as soon as possible. You immediately walk (running violates exchange rules) to the post where KO stock is traded.

Upon approaching the post where KO is traded, you check the terminal screen for information on the current market price for KO stock. The screen reveals that the last executed trade for KO was at 70.63 and that the current bid is 70.50 per share. You could immediately sell at 70.50, but that would be too easy.

Instead, as the customer's representative, you are obligated to get the best possible price. It is your job to "work" the order, and your job depends on providing satisfactory order execution service. So you look around for another broker who represents a customer who wants to buy KO stock. Luckily, you quickly find another broker at the post with a market order to buy 3,000 shares of KO. Noticing that the posted asking price is 70.76 per share, you both agree to execute your orders with each other at a price of 70.63. This price, halfway between the posted bid and ask prices, saves each of your customers approximately $.13 \times 3,000 = $390 compared to the posted prices.

In a trade of this type, in which one floor broker buys from another, the DMM acts only as a broker assisting in matching buy orders and sell orders. On an actively traded stock, many floor brokers can be buying and selling. In such cases, trading is said to occur "in the crowd." Thus, the DMM functions as a broker as long as buyers and sellers are available. The DMM steps in as a dealer only when necessary to fill an order that would otherwise go unfilled.

In reality, not all orders are executed so easily. For example, suppose you are unable to find another broker quickly with an order to buy 3,000 shares of KO. Because you have a market order, you may have no choice but to sell at the posted bid price of 70.50. In this case, the need to execute an order quickly takes priority, and the DMM provides the necessary liquidity to allow immediate order execution.

Note an important caveat concerning this discussion of NYSE floor operations. If you think about it, there's no way that the NYSE could trade more than a billion shares a day just using humans. It's just not physically possible. What actually happens is that over 99 percent of orders are processed electronically. Based on volume of orders submitted, however, that number drops to about 75 percent. The implication is that larger orders are handled by floor brokers, but smaller orders are not. In fact, much of the trading in liquid stocks during normal times happens completely electronically.

SPECIAL ORDER TYPES

limit order

Customer order to buy or sell securities with a specified "limit" price. The order can be executed only at the limit price or better.

stop order

Customer order to buy or sell securities when a preset "stop" price is reached.

Many orders are transmitted to the NYSE floor as **limit orders**. A limit order is an order to buy or sell stock, where the customer specifies a maximum price he is willing to pay in the case of a buy order, or a minimum price he will accept in the case of a sell order. For example, suppose that as a NYSE floor broker, you receive a limit order to sell 3,000 shares of KO stock at 70.75. This means that the customer is not willing to accept any price below 70.75 per share, even if it means missing the trade.

A **stop order** may appear similar to a limit order, but there is an important difference. With a stop order, the customer specifies a "stop" price. This stop price serves as a trigger point. No trade can occur until the stock price reaches this stop price. When the stock price reaches the stop price, the stop order is immediately converted into a market order. Because the order is now a market order, the customer may get a price that is better or worse than the stop price. Thus, the stop price only serves as a trigger point for conversion into a market order. Unlike a limit price, the stop price places no limit on the price at which a trade can occur. Once converted to a market order, the trade is executed just like any other market order.

The most common type of stop order is a *stop-sell* order, which is an order to sell shares if the stock price falls to a specified stop price below the current stock price. This type of order is generally called a *stop-loss* because it is usually intended to limit losses on a long position. The other type is a *stop-buy* order, which is an order to buy shares if the price rises to a specified stop price above the current stock price. Stop-buy orders are often placed in conjunction with short sales, again as a means of limiting losses.

Placing stop-loss orders is frequently touted as a smart trading strategy, but there are a couple of issues we should mention. For concreteness, suppose you buy 1,000 shares of

TABLE 5.1 — Stock Market Order Types

Order Type	Buy	Sell
Market order	Buy at best price available for immediate execution.	Sell at best price available for immediate execution.
Limit order	Buy at best price available, but not more than the preset limit price. Forgo purchase if limit is not met.	Sell at best price available, but not less than the preset limit price. Forgo sale if limit is not met.
Stop order	Convert to a market order to buy when the stock price crosses the stop price from below.	Convert to a market order to sell when the stock price crosses the stop price from above. Also known as a "stop-loss."
Stop-limit order	Convert to a limit order to buy when the stock price crosses the stop price from below.	Convert to a limit order to sell when the stock price crosses the stop price from above.

GoGo Corp. at $20. You simultaneously place a stop-sell order at $15. Thus you seem to have limited your potential loss to $5 per share.

Unfortunately, after the market closes, a rumor circulates that GoGo has uncovered a significant accounting fraud. The next morning, the stock opens at $8, meaning the first trade occurs at $8 per share. Because this price is below your $15 stop price, a market order to sell your stock will be placed and executed, and you'll lose much more than $5 per share. What you discover is that your stop-loss guarantees only that a market order to sell will be placed as soon as the stock trades at $15 *or below*.

Adding insult to injury, after your stock is sold, a creditable announcement is made indicating that the rumor is false. GoGo shares promptly bounce back to $20, but you were sold out at a big loss. Thus, a second danger in blindly using stop-loss orders is that volatile conditions can lead to an unfavorable stop sale. Table 5.1 summarizes the characteristics of limit and stop orders.

A limit price can be attached to a stop order to create a *stop-limit order*. This is different from a simple stop order in that once the stock price reaches the preset stop price the order is converted into a limit order. By contrast, a simple stop order is converted into a market order. At this point, the limit order is just like any other limit order. Notice that with a stop-limit order you must specify two prices, the stop and the limit. The two prices can be the same, or they can be different. In our GoGo Corp. example, you could place a stop-limit sell order at $15 stop, $12 limit. This order converts to a limit order to sell at $12 or better if the price ever hits $15 or below. Thus you will never sell below $12. Of course, you may never sell at all unless your limit price is reached! Our nearby *Work the Web* box shows how these orders are entered in an actual online brokerage account.

Another type of order that requires special attention is the *short-sale order*. As explained elsewhere, a short sale involves borrowing stock shares and then selling the borrowed shares in the hope of buying them back later at a lower price. Short-sale loans are normally arranged through the customer's broker. New York Stock Exchange rules require that when shares are sold as part of a short-sale transaction, the order must be marked as a short-sale transaction when it is transmitted to the NYSE floor.

Finally, colored coats are worn by many of the people on the floor of the exchange. The color of the coat indicates the person's job or position. Clerks, runners, visitors, exchange officials, and so on, wear particular colors to identify themselves. Also, since things can get a little hectic on a busy day with the result that good clothing may not last long, the cheap coats offer some protection. Nevertheless, many specialists and floor brokers wear a good business suit every day simply out of habit and pride.

CHECK THIS

5.3a What are the four main types of orders to buy and sell common stocks?

5.3b What do DMMs do?

5.3c What is a limit order? How do limit and stop orders differ?

To illustrate the importance of getting order types straight, we captured the actual trading screen from one of the largest online brokers, eTrade. On the screen below, the ticker symbol entered is JWN, a purveyor of fine apparel, Nordstrom Inc. The order is a limit order to buy 300 shares at $41.80. That is, we want to purchase these shares for a price of $41.80 or lower. The limit order is good for the day only.

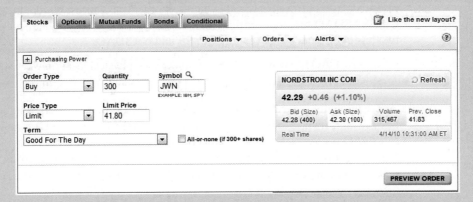

Clicking on the "Preview Order" button allows you to double-check your order before you submit it for transaction. Here is our preview screen:

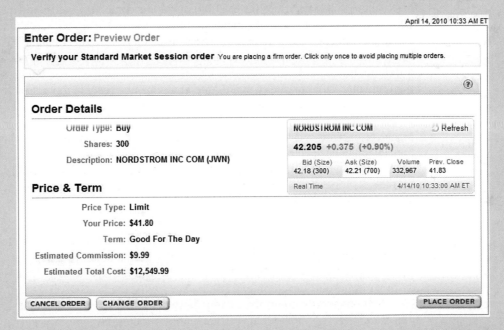

After checking to make sure we have entered everything correctly, we just hit the "Place Order" button to submit our order.

5.4 NASDAQ

In terms of total dollar volume of trading, the second largest stock market in the United States is NASDAQ (say "Naz-dak"). In fact, in terms of companies listed and, on most days recently, number of shares traded, NASDAQ is bigger than the NYSE. The somewhat odd name is derived from the acronym NASDAQ, which stands for National Association of Securities Dealers Automated Quotations system. But NASDAQ is now a proper name in its own right.

NASDAQ OPERATIONS

Introduced in 1971, the NASDAQ market is a computer network of securities dealers who disseminate timely security price quotes to NASDAQ subscribers. These dealers act as market makers for securities listed on NASDAQ. As market makers, NASDAQ dealers post bid and ask prices at which they accept sell and buy orders, respectively. With each price quote, they also post the number of stock shares that they obligate themselves to trade at their quoted prices.

Like NYSE DMMs, NASDAQ market makers trade on an inventory basis, using their inventory as a buffer to absorb buy and sell order imbalances. Unlike the NYSE DMM system, NASDAQ features multiple market makers for actively traded stocks. Thus, there are two basic differences between the NYSE and NASDAQ:

1. NASDAQ is a computer network and has no physical location where trading takes place.
2. NASDAQ has a multiple market maker system rather than the DMM/SLP system.

over-the-counter (OTC) market

Securities market in which trading is almost exclusively done through dealers who buy and sell for their own inventories.

Traditionally, a securities market largely characterized by dealers who buy and sell securities for their own inventories is called an **over-the-counter (OTC) market**. Consequently, NASDAQ is often referred to as an OTC market. In their efforts to promote a distinct image, NASDAQ officials prefer that the term OTC not be used when referring to the NASDAQ market. Nevertheless, old habits die hard, and many people still refer to NASDAQ as an OTC market.

The NASDAQ is actually made up of three separate markets: the NASDAQ Global Select Market, the NASDAQ Global Market, and the NASDAQ Capital Market. As the market for NASDAQ's larger and more actively traded securities, the NASDAQ Global Select Market listed about 1,200 securities (as of 2009), including some very well-known companies. The Global Market companies are somewhat smaller in size. NASDAQ lists about 1,450 of these companies. Finally, the smallest companies listed on NASDAQ are in the NASDAQ Capital Market. About 550 companies are listed in this market. As you might guess, an important difference among the markets is that the Global Select Market has the most stringent listing requirements. Of course, as Capital Market companies become more established, they may move up to the Global Market or the Global Select Market.

The success of the NASDAQ Global Select Market as a competitor to NYSE and other organized exchanges can be judged by its ability to attract stock listings by companies that traditionally might have chosen to be listed on the NYSE. Some of the best-known companies in the world such as Microsoft, Apple Computer, Intel, Dell, Yahoo!, Starbucks, and, of course, Google list their securities on NASDAQ.

NASDAQ PARTICIPANTS

As we mentioned previously, the NASDAQ has historically been a dealer market, characterized by competing market makers. In early 2010, about 3,000 companies were listed on the NASDAQ system. More than 500 NASDAQ member firms act as market makers.

electronic communications network (ECN)

A Web site that allows investors to trade directly with each other.

In an important development, in the late 1990s, the NASDAQ system was opened to so-called **electronic communications networks (ECNs)**. ECNs are basically Web sites that allow investors to trade directly with one another. Investor buy and sell orders placed on ECNs are transmitted to the NASDAQ and displayed along with market maker bid and ask prices. As a result, the ECNs open up the NASDAQ by essentially allowing individual investors to enter orders through their brokers, not just market makers. As a result, the ECNs act to increase liquidity and competition.

inside quotes

Highest bid quotes and the lowest ask quotes offered by dealers for a security.

If you check prices on the Web for both NASDAQ- and NYSE-listed stocks, you'll notice an interesting difference. For NASDAQ stocks, you can actually see the bid and ask prices as well as recent transactions information. The bid and ask prices for the NASDAQ listings you see represent **inside quotes**, that is, the highest bid and the lowest ask prices. For a relatively small fee (or possibly even free from your broker), you can even have access to "Level II" quotes, which show all of the posted bid and ask prices and, frequently, the identity of the market maker. Of course, NYSE DMMs post bid and ask prices as well; they are just not disclosed to the general public. These quotes are known as "Level III" and they are available by subscription at a cost substantially higher than that for Level II NASDAQ quotes.

DIRECT EDGE APPLIES FOR EXCHANGE STATUS

Direct Edge Holdings, an electronic-trading firm, took another step forward in its plans to become a full-fledged stock exchange this week by filing an application with the Securities and Exchange Commission.

The Jersey City, N.J., company, which currently operates the third-largest U.S. stock trading venue, expects to receive SEC approval by year end, said Chief Executive William O'Brien.

Attaining exchange status will help Direct Edge compete more directly with NYSE Euronext's New York Stock Exchange and NASDAQ OMX Group Inc.'s NASDAQ Stock Market.

The two incumbent stock exchanges have seen their market share in trading U.S. stocks fall sharply over the past year as electronic rivals gain ground.

Last fall, BATS Trading, another electronic trading network, converted into an exchange called BATS Exchange after receiving SEC approval.

"We're confident we will get through the regulatory process and join the other exchanges at the table," said Mr. O'Brien, who worked at NASDAQ before joining Direct Edge in mid-2007.

"Being an exchange also will give us the freedom to explore entries into other areas, such as listings, and it will make us a sustainable competitor for a long period of time," he said.

In April, about 12.5% of U.S. stock trades were "matched" on Direct Edge's platforms, versus 4% a year ago, the company said.

Direct Edge has benefited from the consolidation of broker-dealers over the past year, said Diego Perfumo, an exchange analyst with Equity Research Desk.

Following the collapse of Lehman Brothers Holdings Inc. and Bear Stearns Cos., investors have concentrated orders among fewer dealers, including Direct Edge shareholders Knight Capital Group Inc., Citadel Derivatives Group and Goldman Sachs Group Inc., Mr. Perfumo said.

Closely held Direct Edge has 75 employees and operates two high-speed electronic networks that have used competitive pricing and services to lure trades.

Source: Serena Ng, *The Wall Street Journal,* May 8, 2009. Reprinted with permission of *The Wall Street Journal.* © 2009 Dow Jones & Company, Inc. All Rights Reserved Worldwide.

CHECK THIS

| 5.4a | How does NASDAQ differ from the NYSE? |
| 5.4b | What are the different levels of access to the NASDAQ network? |

5.5 NYSE and NASDAQ Competitors

third market

Off-exchange market for securities listed on an organized exchange.

fourth market

Market for exchange-listed securities in which investors trade directly with other investors, usually through a computer network.

The NYSE and NASDAQ face strong competition in the market for order execution services from securities trading firms operating in the **third market**. The phrase "third market" refers to trading in exchange-listed securities that occurs off the exchange on which the security is listed. For example, a substantial volume of NYSE-listed stock trading is executed through independent securities trading firms.

NASDAQ and NYSE also face substantial competition from the **fourth market**. The term "fourth market" refers to direct trading of exchange-listed securities among investors. A good example of a company engaged in fourth-market trading activity is Direct Edge, an ECN that has applied to the SEC to become an exchange (see the nearby *Investment Updates* box). As we discussed in our previous section, however, these fourth-market ECNs are increasingly becoming integrated into the NASDAQ system.

The third and fourth markets are not the only NYSE and NASDAQ competitors. Regional exchanges also attract substantial trading volume away from NYSE and NASDAQ. For example, thousands of stocks are dually listed on NYSE and either on NASDAQ or on at least one regional exchange.

Where do companies go when they can't (or don't want to) meet the listing requirements of the larger stock markets? Two options are the Over-the-Counter Bulletin Board (OTCBB) and the Pink Sheets. These two electronic markets are part of the Wild, Wild West of stock trading. The somewhat odd names have simple explanations. The OTCBB began as an electronic bulletin board that was created to facilitate OTC trading in nonlisted stocks. The name "Pink Sheets" just reflects the fact that prices for such stocks once were quoted on pink sheets of paper.

The well-known markets such as the NASDAQ and the NYSE have relatively strict listing requirements. If a company fails to meet these requirements, it can be delisted.

The OTCBB and the Pink Sheets, on the other hand, have no listing requirements. The OTCBB does require that companies file financial statements with the SEC (or other relevant agency), but the Pink Sheets does not.

Stocks traded on these markets often have very low prices and are frequently referred to as "penny stocks," "microcaps," or even "nanocaps." Relatively few brokers do any research on these companies, so information is often spread through word of mouth or the Internet, probably not the most reliable of sources. In fact, for many stocks, these markets often look like big electronic rumor mills and gossip factories. To get a feel for what trading looks like, we captured two typical screens from www.otcmarkets.com.

Market Statistics

Data delayed 15-20 minutes

OTCBB ▾ | Vol Actives ▾ | GO

Name	Symbol	Last	Tick	Chg	% Chg	Open	High	Low	Volume
iVoice Inc.	IVOI	0.0006	▲	0.0001	20.00%	0.0005	0.0006	0.0005	201.64 m
Trey Resources Inc.	TYRIA	0.0003	▬	0.00	0.00%	0.0003	0.0004	0.0002	154.61 m
China Crescent Enterprises Inc.	CCTR	0.0219	▼	-0.0004	-1.79%	0.0239	0.024	0.0202	70.08 m
Cyberlux Corp.	CYBL	0.0002	▬	0.00	0.00%	0.0002	0.0002	0.0001	68.46 m
Fresh Harvest Products Inc.	FRHV	0.1014	▼	-0.0336	-24.89%	0.1405	0.1535	0.096	39.08 m
Zevotek Inc.	ZVTK	0.0055	▬	0.00	0.00%	0.0059	0.0059	0.0054	29.88 m
Cord Blood America Inc.	CBAI	0.0091	▼	-0.0003	-3.19%	0.0092	0.0093	0.009	23.72 m
Camelot Entertainment Group Inc. NEW	CMGR	0.0001	▬	0.00	0.00%	0.0001	0.0001	0.0001	22.16 m
Artfest International Inc.	ARTS	0.0091	▼	-0.0009	-9.00%	0.01	0.011	0.0085	17.65 m
Wellstar International Inc.	WLSI	0.0008	▬	0.00	0.00%	0.0008	0.0008	0.0007	15.42 m

First, let's look at the returns. iVoice, Inc., had a return to this point in the day of 20 percent! That's not something you see very often. The current stock price was essentially zero. The shares are selling for $.0006, an increase of $.0001 per share.

To be listed on the Pink Sheets, a company just has to find a market maker willing to trade in the company's stock. Companies list on the Pink Sheets for various reasons. Small companies that do not wish to meet listing requirements are one type. Foreign companies often list on the Pink Sheets because they do not prepare their

financial statements according to Generally Accepted Accounting Principles (GAAP), a requirement for listing on U.S. stock exchanges. Many are companies that had formerly been listed on bigger stock markets and were either delisted involuntarily or chose to "go dark" for various reasons.

Total trading volume for the stocks at the OTCBB and Pink Sheets is usually quite brisk. As you can see, the trading volume at the Pink Sheets had already surpassed 2.6 billion at 9:44 a.m. (meaning there was about six hours left in the trading day). However, total dollar volume at

Some companies do not meet the listing requirements of the NYSE or NASDAQ. Even if they do meet these requirements, the company's management might decide to list shares elsewhere. A nearby *Work the Web* box describes two choices.

CHECK THIS

5.5a   What is the third market for securities?

5.5b   What is the fourth market for securities?

Current OTC Market Activity
Wed, Apr 14, 2010 09:44:19 AM

Market Makers | **Most Active** | **Advancers** | **Decliners**

$ Volume | Share Volume | # Trades | More >>

Market Maker	$ Volume	Share Volume	# Trades
Knight Equity Markets, LP	13,022,841	673,047,481	4,401
Archipelago Trading Services Inc.	9,561,020	15,799,460	1,511
UBS Securities, LLC	6,797,823	118,289,189	2,246
Jane Street Markets, LLC	5,715,755	343,028	374
Automated Trading Desk Fincl Svcs	5,107,453	130,030,567	2,361
E*Trade Capital Markets, LLC	4,257,697	354,786,838	2,117
Intl Trading, Inc.	3,465,233	474,482	226
Pershing Trading Company	2,743,021	20,460,557	888
Hudson Securities, Inc	2,657,049	55,354,433	1,006
E*Trade Capital Markets, LLC IMM	2,653,191	391,935	163

'Market Maker data only includes Pink Link transactions.

Total Share Volume: 2,640,736,500

Total $ Volume: 162,852,466

both exchanges is not as impressive. For example, notice that as of 9:44 a.m., total dollar volume at the Pink Sheets was only $162 million. At the end of a "typical" day in 2010, total dollar trading volume at the Pink Sheets surpasses $300 million. By contrast, average daily volume for Microsoft Corp. (MSFT) is about 57 million shares at the NASDAQ. With a stock price of about $29 per share, this means that total dollar trading volume for Microsoft is about $1.7 billion, or about 6 times more than the entire Pink Sheets for just this one NASDAQ stock.

All in all, the OTCBB and Pink Sheets can be pretty wild places to trade. Low stock prices allow huge percentage returns on small stock price movements. Be advised, however, that attempts at manipulation and fraud are commonplace. Also, many stocks on these markets are often very thinly traded, meaning there is little volume. It is not unusual for a stock listed on either market to have zero trades on a given day. Even two or three days in a row without a trade in a particular stock is not uncommon.

5.6 Stock Market Information

Many newspapers publish current price information for a selection of stocks. In the United States, the newspaper best known for reporting stock price information is *The Wall Street Journal* and its online version, www.wsj.com. Investors interested in an overview of stock market activity refer to daily summaries. Among other things, these summaries contain information regarding several stock market indexes. Immediately below, we describe the most important stock market indexes.

FIGURE 5.2   Dow Jones Industrial Average

Source: Reprinted by permission of *The Wall Street Journal.* © 2009 Dow Jones & Company, Inc. All Rights Reserved Worldwide.

THE DOW JONES INDUSTRIAL AVERAGE

The most widely followed barometer of day-to-day stock market activity is the Dow Jones Industrial Average (DJIA), often called the "Dow" for short. The DJIA is an index of the stock prices of 30 large companies representative of American industry. There are two more specialized Dow Jones averages, a utilities average and a transportation average. We will focus on the industrial average. Figure 5.2 reproduces a chart of the DJIA from www.wsj.com.

Figure 5.2 shows daily high, low, and closing prices for the DJIA from December 2008 through most of November 2009. The vertical bars in the chart indicate the range of index high and low values on each trading day. The tick mark on the right side of each day's bar marks the closing value of the index on that day. We therefore see that, based on closing prices, the Dow reached a high of about 10,500 during this period compared to a low of about 6,500. Figure 5.3 contains a list of the 30 well-known companies in the DJIA and their dividend yields.

Although the Dow is the most familiar stock market index, a number of other indexes are widely followed. In fact, as we begin to discuss next, the Dow is not the most representative index by any means, and the way it is computed presents various problems that can make it difficult to interpret.

STOCK MARKET INDEXES

The Dow Jones Industrial Average Web page is informative, but market watchers might be interested in more detail regarding recent stock market activity. A more comprehensive view of stock market trading is contained in Figure 5.4, which is also published daily at www.wsj.com.

The Web page we examine here, "Major Stock Indexes," reports information about a variety of stock market indexes in addition to the Dow Jones averages. Of the non–Dow Jones indexes shown, by far the best known and most widely followed is the Standard & Poor's Index of 500 stocks, commonly abbreviated as the S&P 500, or often just the S&P.

For more on the Dow, visit www.djaverages.com

What are the Russell indexes? Visit www.russell.com to find out.

Yields On Dow Stocks

Wednesday, March 31, 2010

Components of the Dow Jones Averages, ranked by dividend yield based on recent price and annualized dividend amount. This page is updated twice a month. (See charts of the Dow Jones Averages.)

DOW JONES INDUSTRIALS

Company	Indicated Yield	Indicated Annual Div	Price 3/31/2010	Change From 12/31/2009
AT&T Corp.	6.50	1.68	25.84	-2.19
Verizon	6.13	1.90	31.02	-2.11
DuPont	4.40	1.64	37.24	+3.57
Pfizer	4.20	0.72	17.15	-1.04
Merck	4.07	1.52	37.35	+0.81
Kraft Foods	3.84	1.16	30.24	+3.06
Chevron Corp	3.59	2.72	75.83	-1.16
McDonald's	3.30	2.20	66.72	+4.28
Coca-Cola	3.20	1.76	55.00	-2.00
Johnson & Johnson	3.01	1.96	65.20	+0.79
Home Depot	2.94	0.95	32.35	+3.42
Intel	2.83	0.63	22.26	+1.86
Procter & Gamble	2.78	1.76	63.27	+2.64
Caterpillar	2.67	1.68	62.85	+5.86
3M	2.51	2.10	83.57	+0.90
Exxon-Mobil	2.51	1.68	66.98	-1.21
Travelers Cos.	2.45	1.32	53.94	+4.08
Boeing	2.31	1.68	72.61	+18.48
United Tech	2.31	1.70	73.61	+4.20
General Electric	2.20	0.40	18.20	+3.07
Wal-Mart Stores	2.18	1.21	55.60	+2.15
Microsoft	1.78	0.52	29.27	-1.22
American Express	1.75	0.72	41.26	+0.74
IBM	1.72	2.20	128.25	-2.65
Walt Disney	1.00	0.35	34.91	+2.66
Alcoa	0.84	0.12	14.24	-1.88
Hewlett-Packard	0.60	0.32	53.15	+1.64
J.P. Morgan Chase	0.45	0.20	44.75	+3.08
Bank of America Corp	0.22	0.04	17.85	+2.79
Cisco Systems	-	-	26.03	+2.09

Source: Reprinted by permission of *The Wall Street Journal.* © 2010 Dow Jones & Company, Inc. All Rights Reserved Worldwide.

FIGURE 5.4 Stock Market Major Indexes

Stock Indexes: Closing Data Bank

Friday, April 09, 2010

Find Historical Data | WHAT'S THIS?

Index	DAILY					YTD % chg	52 WEEK			3-yr % chg*
	High	Low	Close	Chg	% Chg		High	Low	% Chg	
Dow Jones										
Industrial Average	11000.98	10926.92	10997.35	70.28	0.64	5.5	10997.35	7841.73	36.0	-4.4
Transportation Average	4508.54	4454.30	4507.65	50.95	1.14	10.0	4507.65	2924.86	50.8	-3.5
Utility Average	385.04	380.06	384.92	2.27	0.59	-3.3	406.72	326.11	14.3	-9.2
65 Composite	3748.19	3717.32	3747.43	29.06	0.78	5.1	3747.43	2689.77	35.6	-5.0
Total Stock Market	12450.82	12364.24	12447.93	83.69	0.68	8.3	12447.93	8496.08	42.4	-5.3
Broad Stock Market	2928.32	2907.66	2927.62	19.96	0.69	8.1	2927.62	2005.04	41.8	-5.4
Large-Cap Growth TSM	2817.61	2797.53	2816.80	18.00	0.64	7.1	2816.80	1910.94	43.7	-1.4
Large-Cap Value TSM	2592.08	2572.73	2591.28	18.55	0.72	7.8	2591.28	1844.67	36.0	-10.0
Mid-Cap Growth TSM	4125.25	4081.06	4125.24	37.97	0.93	11.0	4125.24	2513.81	60.1	1.4
Mid-Cap Value TSM	4117.83	4076.48	4117.83	31.73	0.78	12.1	4121.89	2563.73	54.7	-3.5
Small-Cap Growth TSM	3599.26	3562.35	3599.26	21.15	0.59	12.5	3599.26	2165.53	62.5	-0.9
Small-Cap Value TSM	5315.01	5253.90	5315.01	43.55	0.83	14.6	5315.01	3187.98	60.1	-4.1
Micro-Cap TSM	6521.73	6501.64	6520.67	16.06	0.25	16.3	6520.67	3746.11	71.8	-6.8
Select REIT	163.52	160.53	163.49	2.88	1.79	13.5	164.60	86.37	73.8	-11.1
Internet	119.51	118.25	119.51	0.71	0.60	9.0	119.51	72.63	63.2	5.5
Barron's 400	284.96	282.68	284.96	1.26	0.44	8.2	285.17	184.77	51.4	-3.6
Nasdaq Stock Market										
Composite	2454.12	2432.93	2454.05	17.24	0.71	8.1	2454.05	1608.21	48.5	-0.2
Nasdaq 100	1994.48	1978.04	1994.43	13.70	0.69	7.2	1994.43	1309.37	48.8	3.3
Q-50	141.83	140.05	141.83	1.61	1.15	13.8	141.83	88.75	57.0	2.5
Biotech	950.93	944.57	950.93	0.73	0.08	12.7	963.38	653.15	39.8	5.4
Computer	1229.22	1215.49	1228.55	12.10	0.99	5.2	1228.55	760.75	57.7	4.8
Industrials	1939.27	1922.08	1939.27	13.42	0.70	11.0	1939.27	1210.88	56.5	-3.8
Insurance	3824.60	3795.75	3809.35	-7.13	-0.19	5.2	3829.47	2895.28	21.1	-2.2
Banks	1948.81	1936.43	1943.47	0.07	unch.	17.7	1943.47	1497.78	17.4	-15.6
Telecommunications	229.91	227.74	229.80	1.47	0.64	6.0	229.97	164.83	35.4	-1.9
Standard & Poor's										
500 Index	1194.66	1187.15	1194.37	7.93	0.67	7.1	1194.37	832.39	39.4	-6.1
100 Index	545.65	542.62	545.46	3.44	0.63	6.1	545.46	389.82	35.7	-6.2
MidCap 400	814.48	804.54	814.48	7.03	0.87	12.1	814.48	520.35	51.8	-1.9
SmallCap 600	372.41	368.45	372.41	1.80	0.49	12.0	372.41	240.42	50.1	-3.8
SuperComp 1500	274.39	272.54	274.34	1.84	0.68	7.7	274.34	189.36	40.8	-5.7
New York Stock Exchange										
Composite	7630.52	7565.42	7629.05	63.72	0.84	6.2	7629.05	5220.12	41.9	-6.8
Financial	5210.08	5160.94	5210.08	49.12	0.95	10.4	5210.08	3192.36	54.1	-18.2
Health Care	6471.89	6423.52	6466.67	41.78	0.65	0.6	6732.71	4663.28	35.7	-3.4
Energy	11742.83	11601.95	11733.05	131.94	1.14	2.8	12007.48	8490.84	31.5	-1.2

Source: Reprinted by permission of *The Wall Street Journal*. © 2010 Dow Jones & Company, Inc. All Rights Reserved Worldwide.

We have seen this index before. In Chapter 1, we used it as a benchmark to track the performance of large-company common stocks for the last eight decades.

If you were to scrutinize the various indexes in Figure 5.4, you would quickly find essentially four differences between them: (1) the market covered; (2) the types of stocks included; (3) how many stocks are included; and (4) how the index is calculated.

The first three of these differences are straightforward. Some indexes listed in Figure 5.4, such as the Dow Jones Utilities, focus on specific industries. Others, such as the NASDAQ Composite, focus on particular markets. Some have a small number of stocks, like the Dow Jones Industrial Average. Others, like the New York Stock Exchange Composite, have a large number.

How stock market indexes are computed is not quite so straightforward, but it is important to understand. There are two major types of stock market index: price-weighted and value-weighted. With a **price-weighted index**, stocks are held in the index in proportion to their share prices. With a **value-weighted index**, stocks are held in proportion to the aggregate market value of the companies in the index.

The best way to understand the difference between price and value weighting is to consider an example. To keep things relatively simple, we suppose that there are only two companies in the entire market. We have the following information about their shares outstanding, share prices, and total market values:

price-weighted index
Stock market index in which stocks are held in proportion to their share price.

value-weighted index
Stock market index in which stocks are held in proportion to the aggregate market value of the companies in the index.

	Shares Outstanding	Price per Share		Total Market Value	
		Beginning of Year	End of Year	Beginning of Year	End of Year
Company A	50 million	$10	$14	$500 million	$700 million
Company B	1 million	$50	$40	$ 50 million	$ 40 million

As shown, Company A has a lower share price but many more shares outstanding. Ignoring dividends, notice that Company A's stock price rose by 40 percent ($10 to $14) while Company B's stock price fell by 20 percent ($50 to $40).

The question we want to answer here is simply. How did the market do for the year? There are several ways we could answer this question. We could first focus on what happened to the average share price. The average share price was ($10 + $50)/2 = $30 at the beginning of the year, and ($14 + $40)/2 = $27 at the end, so the average share price fell. If we take the average share price as our index, then our index fell from 30 to 27, for a change of −3 points. Because the index began at 30, this is a −3/30 = −.10, or a 10% decrease. In this case, investors say that the market was "off" by 10 percent.

This is an example of a price-weighted index. Because Company B's stock price is five times bigger than Company A's, it carries five times as much weight in the index. This explains why the index was down even though Company A's stock gained 40 percent whereas Company B's stock only lost 20 percent. The Dow Jones indexes are price weighted.

Alternatively, instead of focusing on the price of a typical share, we could look at what happened to the total value of a typical company. Here we notice that the average total value, in millions, rose from ($500 + $50)/2 = $275 to ($700 + $40)/2 = $370. If we take average total company value as our index, then our index rose from 275 to 370, a 35 percent *increase*.

This is an example of a value-weighted index. The influence a company has in this case depends on its overall change in total market value, not just its stock price change. Because Company A has a much larger total value, it carries a much larger weight in the index. With the exception of the Dow Jones indexes, most of the other indexes in Figure 5.4, including the Standard & Poor's, are value weighted.

Now we have a problem. One index tells us the market was down by 10 percent, while the other tells us it was up by 35 percent. Which one is correct? The answer seems fairly obvious. The total value of the market as a whole grew from $550 million to $740 million, so the market as a whole increased in value. Put differently, investors as a whole owned stock worth $550 million at the beginning of the year and $740 million at the end of the year. So, on the whole, stock market investors earned 35 percent, even though the average share price went down.

www

Take a look at the "value" and "growth" indexes at www.mscibarra.com

This example shows that a price-weighted index can be misleading as an indicator of total market value. The basic flaw in a price-weighted index is that the effect a company has on the index depends on the price of a single share. However, the price of a single share is only part of the story. Unless the number of shares is also considered, the true impact on the overall market isn't known, and a distorted picture can emerge.

EXAMPLE 5.1

Caution: Indexes Under Construction

Suppose there are only two stocks in the market and the following information is given:

	Shares Outstanding	Price per Share	
		Beginning of Year	End of Year
Betty Co.	10 million	$10	$11
Gray Bull, Inc.	20 million	$20	$25

Construct price- and value-weighted indexes and calculate the percentage changes in each.

The average share price rose from $15 to $18, or $3, so the price-weighted index would be up by 3/15 = 20 percent. Average total market value, in millions, rose from $250 to $305, so the value-weighted index rose by 55/250 = 22 percent.

MORE ON PRICE-WEIGHTED INDEXES

Earlier we indicated that the Dow Jones averages are price weighted. Given this, you may wonder why the Dow Jones Industrial Average has such a high value when the stock prices used to calculate the average are much smaller. To answer this question, we must explain one last detail about price-weighted indexes.

The extra detail concerns the effects of stock splits on price-weighted indexes. For example, in a 2-for-1 stock split, all current shareholders receive two new shares in exchange for each old share that they own. However, the total value of the company does not change because it is still the same company after the stock split. There are just twice as many shares, each worth half as much.

A stock split has no effect on a value-weighted index since the total value of the company does not change. But it can have a dramatic effect on a price-weighted index. To see this, consider what happens to the price-weighted and value-weighted indexes we created above when Company B enacts a 2-for-1 stock split. Based on beginning prices, with a 2-for-1 split, Company B's shares fall to $25. The price-weighted index falls to (10 + 25)/2 = 17.50 from 30, even though nothing really happened.

For a price-weighted index, the problem of stock splits can be addressed by adjusting the divisor each time a split occurs. Once again, an example is the best way to illustrate. In the case stated just above, suppose we wanted the index value to stay at 30 even though B's price per share fell to $25 as a result of the split. The only way to accomplish this is to add together the new stock prices and divide by something less than 2.

This new number is called the *index divisor*, and it is adjusted as needed to remove the effect of stock splits. To find the new divisor in our case, the stock prices are $25 and $10, and we want the index to equal 30. We solve for the new divisor, d, as follows:

$$\text{Index level} = \frac{\text{Sum of stock prices}}{\text{Divisor}}$$

$$30 = \frac{25 + 10}{d}$$

$$d = \frac{35}{30} = 1.16666\ldots$$

The new divisor is thus approximately 1.17.

Adjusting the divisor takes care of the problem in one sense, but it creates another problem. Because we are no longer dividing the sum of the share prices by the number of companies in the index, we can no longer interpret the change in the index as the change in price of an average share.

EXAMPLE 5.2

Adjusting the Divisor

Take a look back at Example 5.1. Suppose that Gray Bull splits 5-for-1. Based on beginning information, what is the new divisor?

Following a 5-for-1 split, Gray Bull's share price will fall from $20 to $4. With no adjustment to the divisor, the price-weighted index would drop from 15 to (10 + 4)/2 = 7. To keep the index at its old level of 15, we need to solve for a new divisor such that (10 + 4)/d = 15. In this case, the new divisor would be 14/15 = .93333. This example shows how the divisor can drop below 1.0.

THE DOW JONES DIVISORS

The method we described of adjusting the divisor on a price-weighted index for stock splits is the method used to adjust the Dow Jones averages. Through time, with repeated adjustments for stock splits, the divisor becomes smaller and smaller. At the start of trading on June 8, 2009, two once-dominant business icons, Citigroup, Inc. (C), and General Motors Corp. (GM) were removed from the DJIA. Travelers Cos. (TRV) and Cisco Systems, Inc. (CSCO), took their places. As of April 12, 2010, the DJIA divisor was a nice, round .132319125. Because there are 30 stocks in the index, the divisor on the DJIA would be 30 if it were never adjusted, so it has declined substantially. Divisors for the other Dow Jones averages have similarly odd values.

Given its shortcomings, you might wonder why the financial press continues to report the Dow Jones averages. The reason is tradition. The Dow Jones averages have been around for more than 100 years, and each new generation of investors becomes accustomed to its quirks.

MORE ON INDEX FORMATION: BASE-YEAR VALUES

We next discuss one or two more details about indexes. First, to ease interpretation, the starting value of an index is usually set equal to some simple base number, like 100 or 1,000. For example, if you were to create a value-weighted index for the NYSE, the actual value of the index would be very large and cumbersome, so adjusting it makes sense.

To illustrate, suppose we have a value-weighted index with a starting value of 1.4 million. If we want the starting value to be 100, we just divide the starting value, and every subsequent value, by 1.4 million and then multiply by 100. So, if the next value of the index is 1.6 million, the "reindexed" value would be 1.6 million/1.4 million × 100 = 114.29, which is easily interpreted as a 14.29 percent increase over a base of 100.

EXAMPLE 5.3

Reindexing

You've calculated values for an index over a four-year period as follows:

Year 1:	1,687 million
Year 2:	1,789 million
Year 3:	1,800 million
Year 4:	1,700 million

Suppose you wanted the index to start at 1,000. What would the reindexed values be?

To reindex these numbers, we need to (1) divide each of them by the starting value, 1,687 million, and then (2) multiply each by 1,000. Thus, we have:

Year 1:	1,687 million/1,687 million × 1,000 = 1,000.00
Year 2:	1,789 million/1,687 million × 1,000 = 1,060.46
Year 3:	1,800 million/1,687 million × 1,000 = 1,066.98
Year 4:	1,700 million/1,687 million × 1,000 = 1,007.71

Finally, an important consideration in looking at indexes is whether dividends are included. Most indexes don't include them. As a result, the change in an index measures only the capital gain (or loss) component of your return. When you're trying to evaluate how a particular type of stock market investment has done over time, dividends have to be included to get an accurate picture.

So which index is the best? The most popular alternative to the DJIA is the value-weighted S&P 500. You might further wonder, however, why this popular index limits itself to 500 stocks. The answer is timeliness and accuracy. Almost all stocks in the S&P 500 index trade every day, and therefore accurate daily updates of market prices are available each day. Stocks that do not trade every day can cause **index staleness**. Index staleness occurs when an index does not reflect all current price information because some of the stocks in the index have not traded recently. Also, as a practical matter, the largest 500 companies account for a large portion of the value of the overall stock market.

index staleness
Condition that occurs when an index does not reflect all current price information because some of the stocks in the index have not traded recently.

CHECK THIS

5.6a   What is the difference between price- and value-weighting in the construction of stock market indexes? Give an example of a well-known index of each type.

5.6b   Which is better, price or value weighting? Why?

5.6c   Which stock market index is likely to contain the greater degree of index staleness, the DJIA or the NYSE Composite index? Why?

5.7   Summary and Conclusions

This chapter introduces you to stock markets. We discussed who owns stocks, how the stock exchanges operate, and how stock market indexes are constructed and interpreted. This chapter covers many important aspects of stock markets, including the following items—grouped by the chapter's important concepts.

1. **The differences between private and public equity, and primary and secondary stock markets.**

   A.   Private equity funds are investment companies that invest in private companies. These investments range from early stage financing (i.e., venture capital) to large leveraged buyouts of public companies (i.e., going private).

   B.   The stock market is composed of a primary market, where stock shares are first sold, and a secondary market, where investors trade shares among themselves. In the primary market, companies raise money for investment projects. Investment bankers specialize in arranging financing for companies in the primary market. Investment bankers often act as underwriters, buying newly issued stock from the company and then reselling the stock to the public. The primary market is best known as the market for initial public offerings (IPOs).

   C.   In the secondary market, investors trade securities with other investors. Secondary market transactions are directed through three channels: directly with other investors, indirectly through a broker, or directly with a dealer. We saw that a broker matches buyers and sellers; a dealer buys and sells out of inventory.

2. **The workings of the New York Stock Exchange (NYSE).**

   A.   Most common stock trading is directed through an organized stock exchange or through a trading network. The largest organized stock exchange in the United States is the New York Stock Exchange (NYSE). Popularly known as the Big Board, NYSE was once owned by its members. Today, however, the NYSE itself is a publicly traded company—so, it is owned by its shareholders.

   B.   The three major types of NYSE license holders are commission brokers, DMMs, and floor traders. We discussed the role of each in the functioning of the exchange.

3. How NASDAQ operates.

A. The NASDAQ market is a computer network of securities dealers who post timely security price quotes to NASDAQ subscribers. These dealers act as market makers for securities listed on the NASDAQ.

B. Unlike the NYSE, the NASDAQ relies on multiple market makers instead of using a specialist system. Because it is a computer network, the NASDAQ has no physical location.

C. The NASDAQ network operates with three levels of information access:

- Level I provides timely and accurate price quotes which are freely available on the Internet.

- Level II allows users to view price quotes from all NASDAQ market makers. This level allows access to inside quotes. Inside quotes are the highest bid and lowest asked quotes for a NASDAQ-listed security.

- Level III is for use by NASDAQ market makers only. With this access, market makers can change their quotes.

4. How to calculate index returns.

A. Investors interested in an overview of stock market activity refer to the returns on several stock market indexes.

B. The most widely followed barometer of day-to-day stock market activity is the Dow Jones Industrial Average (DJIA), often called the "Dow" for short. The DJIA is an index of the stock prices of 30 large companies representative of American industry. The DJIA is a price-weighted index.

C. Another widely followed index is the Standard & Poor's Index of 500 stocks, commonly abbreviated as the S&P 500, or often just the S&P. The S&P 500 Index is a value-weighted index.

D. Many newspapers and Web sites publish current price information for indexes as well as stocks. In the United States, the newspaper best known for reporting stock price information is *The Wall Street Journal*—with its companion Web site, www.wsj.com.

GET REAL

This chapter covered the operations and organization of the major stock markets. It also covered some of the most important order types and the construction of stock market indexes. How should you, as an investor or investment manager, put this information to work?

First, as in some previous chapters, you need to submit as many as possible of the different order types suggested by this chapter in a simulated brokerage account—like Stock-Trak (note that not all simulated brokerage accounts allow all trade types). Your goal is to gain experience with the different order types and what they mean and accomplish for you as an investor or investment manager.

In each case, once you have placed the order, be sure to monitor the price of the stock in question to see if any of your orders should be executed. When an order is executed, compare the result to the stop or limit price to see how you did.

The second thing to do is to start observing the different indexes and learning how they are computed, what's in them, and what they are intended to cover. For example, the NASDAQ 100 is made up of the largest NASDAQ stocks. Is this index broadly representative of big stocks in general? Of NASDAQ stocks in general? Learn about other indexes, like the Russell 2000, at www.russell.com.

Key Terms

Arca 156
ask price 153
best efforts underwriting 151
bid price 153
broker 153
commission brokers 156
dealer 153
designated market maker (DMM) 156
display book 156
DMM's post 158
Dutch auction underwriting 151
electronic communications
   network (ECN) 162
firm commitment underwriting 151
floor brokers 156
floor traders 157
fourth market 163
general cash offer 150
index staleness 172
initial public offering (IPO) 150
inside quotes 162
investment banking firm 150
limit order 159
market order 159
NYSE exchange member 155

NYSE license holder 155
over-the-counter (OTC)
   market 162
price-weighted index 169
primary market 150
prospectus 152
red herring 152
rights offer 150
seasoned equity offering (SEO) 150
secondary market 150
Securities and Exchange
   Commission (SEC) 152
specialists 156
spread 153
stop order 159
Super Display Book system (SDBK) 156
SuperDOT system 156
supplemental liquidity provider (SLP) 156
syndicate 151
third market 163
underwrite 151
underwriter spread 151
venture capital (VC) 147
value-weighted index 169

Chapter Review Problems and Self-Test

1. **Index Construction (CFA2)**   Suppose there are only two stocks in the market and the following information is given:

	Shares Outstanding	Price per Share	
		Beginning of Year	End of Year
Ally Co.	100 million	$ 60	$ 66
McBeal, Inc.	400 million	$120	$100

   Construct price- and value-weighted indexes and calculate the percentage changes in each.

2. **Stock Splits (CFA2)**   In the previous problem, suppose that McBeal splits 3-for-1. Based on beginning information, what is the new divisor?

Answers to Self-Test Problems

1. The average share price at the beginning of the year is ($60 + 120)/2 = $90. At the end of the year, the average price is $83. Thus, the average price declined by $7 from $90, a percentage drop of −$7/$90 = −7.78%. Total market cap at the beginning of the year is $60 × 100 + $120 × 400 = $54 billion. It falls to $46.6 billion, a decline of $7.4 billion. The percentage decline is −$7.4 billion/$54 billion = −13.7%, or almost twice as much as the price-weighted index.

2. Following a 3-for-1 split, McBeal's share price falls from $120 to $40. To keep the price-weighted index at its old level of 90, we need a new divisor such that (60 + 40)/d = 90. In this case, the new divisor would be 100/90 = 1.1111.

Test Your Investment Quotient

1. **New York Stock Exchange (LO2, CFA1)**   Which of the following is false?

   a. DMMs can trade for their own accounts.

   b. DMMs earn income from providing liquidity.

   c. On the NYSE, all buy and sell orders are negotiated through a commission broker.

   d. DMMs stand ready to trade at quoted bid and ask prices.

2. **Private Equity (LO1, CFA5)**   Private equity funds that concentrate in early stage financing would likely be what type of fund?

   a. Venture capital

   b. Middle market

   c. Leveraged buyouts

   d. Distressed assets

3. **Private Equity (LO1, CFA4)**   The compensation constraint that requires private equity fund managers to "give back" performance fees when subsequent losses occur is a _____ provision.

   a. High-water-mark

   b. Clawback

   c. Zenith

   d. Index

4. **Value-Weighted Index (LO4, CFA2)**   An analyst gathered the following data about stocks J, K, and L, which together form a value-weighted index:

	December 31, Year 1		December 31, Year 2	
Stock	Price	Shares Outstanding	Price	Shares Outstanding
J	$40	10,000	$50	10,000
K	$30	6,000	$20	12,000*
L	$50	9,000	$40	9,000

*2-for-1 stock split.

The ending value-weighted index (base index = 100) is closest to:

   a. 92.31

   b. 93.64

   c. 106.80

   d. 108.33

5. **Dow Jones Index (LO4, CFA2)**   The divisor for the Dow Jones Industrial Average (DJIA) is most likely to decrease when a stock in the DJIA

   a. Has a stock split.

   b. Has a reverse split.

   c. Pays a cash dividend.

   d. Is removed and replaced.

6. **New York Stock Exchange (LO2, CFA1)**   Which of the following activities are *not* conducted by DMMs on the NYSE?

   a. Acting as dealers for their own accounts.

   b. Monitoring compliance with margin requirements.

   c. Providing liquidity to the market.

   d. Posting bid and ask prices.

7. **Stock Markets (LO1, CFA1)**   What is a securities market characterized by dealers who buy and sell securities for their own inventories called?

   a. A primary market.

   b. A secondary market.

   c. An over-the-counter market.

   d. An institutional market.

8. **Stock Markets (LO1, CFA1)**   What is the over-the-counter market for exchange-listed securities called?

   a. Third market
   b. Fourth market
   c. After-market
   d. Block market

9. **Stock Indexes (LO4, CFA2)**   If the market price of each of the 30 stocks in the Dow Jones Industrial Average changes by the same percentage amount during a given day, which stock will have the greatest impact on the DJIA?

   a. The one whose stock trades at the highest dollar price per share.
   b. The one whose total equity has the highest market value.
   c. The one having the greatest amount of equity in its capital structure.
   d. The one having the lowest volatility.

10. **Stock Indexes (LO4, CFA2)**   In calculating the Standard & Poor's stock price indexes, how are adjustments for stock splits made?

    a. By adjusting the divisor.
    b. Automatically, due to the manner in which the index is calculated.
    c. By adjusting the numerator.
    d. Quarterly, on the last trading day of each quarter.

11. **Stock Indexes (LO4, CFA2)**   Which of the following indexes includes the largest number of actively traded stocks?

    a. The NASDAQ Composite Index.
    b. The NYSE Composite Index.
    c. The Wilshire 5000 Index.
    d. The Value Line Composite Index.

12. **Private Equity (LO1, CFA5)**   Private equity funds that concentrate in smaller, family-owned companies with established cash flows are typically referred to as

    a. Venture capital
    b. Middle market
    c. Leveraged buyouts
    d. Distressed assets

13. **Private Equity (LO1, CFA4)**   The compensation constraint that requires private equity fund managers to meet a particular return target before performance fees can be taken is a _____ provision.

    a. High-water-mark
    b. Clawback
    c. Zenith
    d. Index

14. **Private Equity (LO1, CFA4)**   Private equity funds will often use convertible preferred stock or bonds with attached call options. These types of securities are used because they

    a. Increase the risk of the transaction.
    b. Shorten the life of the investment.
    c. Allow upside potential associated with a successful venture.
    d. Meet SEC regulations for such investments.

15. **Stock Indexes (LO4, CFA2)**   Which one of the following statements regarding the Dow Jones Industrial Average is false?

    a. The DJIA contains 30 well-known large-company stocks.
    b. The DJIA is affected equally by dollar changes in low- and high-priced stocks.
    c. The DJIA is affected equally by percentage changes in low- and high-priced stocks.
    d. The DJIA divisor must be adjusted for stock splits.

Concept Questions

1. **Primary and Secondary Markets (LO1, CFA5)**   If you were to visit your local Chevrolet retailer, there is both a primary and a secondary market in action. Explain. Is the Chevy retailer a dealer or a broker?

2. **Brokers (LO1, CFA1)**   Why would commission brokers be willing to pay more than $40,000 per year just for the right to trade on the NYSE?

3. **Market and Limit Orders (LO1, CFA6)**   What is the difference between a market order and a limit order? What is the potential downside to each type of order?

4. **Stop That! (CFA6)**   What is a stop-loss order? Why might it be used? Is it sure to stop a loss?

5. **Order Types (CFA6)**   Suppose Microsoft is currently trading at $100. You want to buy it if it reaches $120. What type of order should you submit?

6. **Order Types (CFA6)**   Suppose Dell is currently trading at $65. You think that if it reaches $70, it will continue to climb, so you want to buy it if and when it gets there. Should you submit a limit order to buy at $70?

7. **NASDAQ Quotes (LO3, CFA1)**   With regard to the NASDAQ, what are inside quotes?

8. **Index Composition (CFA2)**   There are basically four factors that differentiate stock market indexes. What are they? Comment on each.

9. **Index Composition (CFA2)**   Is it necessarily true that, all else the same, an index with more stocks is better? What is the issue here?

10. **Private Equity (LO1, CFA5)**   Why would venture capitalists provide financing in stages?

Questions and Problems

Core Questions

1. **Price-Weighted Divisor (LO4, CFA2)**   Able, Baker, and Charlie are the only three stocks in an index. The stocks sell for $93, $312, and $78, respectively. If Baker undergoes a 2-for-1 stock split, what is the new divisor for the price-weighted index?

2. **Price-Weighted Divisor (LO4, CFA2)**   In the previous problem, assume that Baker undergoes a 3-for-1 stock split. What is the new divisor now?

3. **Order Books (LO2, CFA1)**   You find the following order book on a particular stock. The last trade on the stock was at $70.54.

Buy Orders		Sell Orders	
Shares	Price	Shares	Price
250	$70.53	100	$70.56
100	70.52	400	70.57
900	70.51	1,000	70.59
75	70.49	700	70.60
		900	70.61

   a. If you place a market buy order for 100 shares, at what price will it be filled?
   b. If you place a market sell order for 100 shares, at what price will it be filled?
   c. Suppose you place a market order to buy 400 shares. At what price will it be filled?

4. **Price-Weighted Index (LO4, CFA2)**   You are given the following information concerning two stocks that make up an index. What is the price-weighted return for the index?

	Shares Outstanding	Price per Share	
		Beginning of Year	End of Year
Kirk, Inc.	35,000	$37	$41
Picard Co.	26,000	84	93

5. **Value-Weighted Index (LO4, CFA2)**   Calculate the index return for the information in the previous problem using a value-weighted index.

6. **Reindexing (LO4, CFA2)** In Problem 5, assume that you want to reindex with the index value at the beginning of the year equal to 100. What is the index level at the end of the year?

7. **Index Level (LO4, CFA2)** In Problem 5, assume the value-weighted index level was 408.16 at the beginning of the year. What is the index level at the end of the year?

8. **Reindexing (LO4, CFA2)** Suppose you calculated the total market value of the stocks in an index over a five-year period:

Year 1: 4,387 million
Year 2: 4,671 million
Year 3: 5,032 million
Year 4: 4,820 million
Year 5: 5,369 million

Suppose you wanted the index to start at 1,000. What would the reindexed values be?

Intermediate Questions

9. **Price-Weighted Divisor (LO4, CFA2)** Look back at Problem 1. Assume that Able undergoes a 1-for-3 reverse stock split. What is the new divisor?

10. **DJIA (LO4, CFA2)** On November 20, 2009, the DJIA opened at 10,327.91. The divisor at that time was .132319125. Suppose on this day the prices for 29 of the stocks remained unchanged and one stock increased $5.00. What would the DJIA level be at the end of the day?

11. **DJIA (LO4, CFA2)** In November 2009, IBM was the highest priced stock in the DJIA and Alcoa was the lowest. The closing price for IBM on November 19, 2009, was $127.54 and the closing price for Alcoa was $13.22. Suppose the next day the other 29 stock prices remained unchanged and IBM increased 5 percent. What would the new DJIA level be? Now assume only Alcoa increased by 5 percent. Find the new DJIA level.

12. **DJIA (LO4, CFA2)** Looking back at the previous two problems, what would the new index level be if all stocks on the DJIA increased by $1.00 per share on the next day?

13. **Price-Weighted Divisor (LO4, CFA2)** You construct a price-weighted index of 40 stocks. At the beginning of the day the index is 8,465.52. During the day, 39 stock prices remain the same, and one stock price increases $5.00. At the end of the day, your index value is 8,503.21. What is the divisor on your index?

14. **Price-Weighted Indexes (LO4, CFA2)** Suppose the following three defense stocks are to be combined into a stock index in January 2010 (perhaps a portfolio manager believes these stocks are an appropriate benchmark for his or her performance):

	Shares (millions)	Price		
		1/1/10	1/1/11	1/1/12
Douglas McDonnell	340	$103	$106	$118
Dynamics General	450	45	39	53
International Rockwell	410	74	63	79

a. Calculate the initial value of the index if a price-weighting scheme is used.
b. What is the rate of return on this index for the year ending December 31, 2010? For the year ending December 31, 2011?

15. **Price-Weighted Indexes (LO4, CFA2)** In the previous problem, suppose that Douglas McDonnell shareholders approve a 3-for-1 stock split on January 1, 2011. What is the new divisor for the index? Calculate the rate of return on the index for the year ending December 31, 2011, if Douglas McDonnell's share price on January 1, 2012, is $39.33 per share.

16. **Value-Weighted Indexes (LO4, CFA2)** Repeat Problem 14 if a value-weighted index is used. Assume the index is scaled by a factor of 10 million; that is, if the average firm's market value is $5 billion, the index would be quoted as 500.

17. **Value-Weighted Indexes (LO4, CFA2)** In the previous problem, will your answers change if Douglas McDonnell stock splits? Why or why not?

18. **Equally Weighted Indexes (LO4, CFA2)** In addition to price-weighted and value-weighted indexes, an equally weighted index is one in which the index value is computed from the

average rate of return of the stocks comprising the index. Equally weighted indexes are frequently used by financial researchers to measure portfolio performance.

    a. Using the information in Problem 14, compute the rate of return on an equally weighted index of the three defense stocks for the year ending December 31, 2010.

    b. If the index value is set to 100 on January 1, 2010, what will the index value be on January 1, 2011? What is the rate of return on the index for 2011?

19. Equally Weighted versus Value-Weighted Indexes (LO4, CFA2) Historically there have been periods where a value-weighted index has a higher return than an equally weighted index and other periods where the opposite has occurred. Why do you suppose this would happen? Hint: Look back to Chapter 1.

20. Geometric Indexes (LO4) Another type of index is the geometric index. The calculation of a geometric index is similar to the calculation of a geometric return:

$$1 + R_G = [(1 + R_1)(1 + R_2) \dots (1 + R_N)]^{1/N}$$

The difference in the geometric index construction is the returns used are the returns for the different stocks in the index for a particular period, such as a day or year. Construct the geometric index returns for Problem 14 over each of the two years. Assume the beginning index level is 100.

21. Interpreting Index Values (CFA2) Suppose you want to replicate the performance of several stock indexes, some of which are price-weighted, others value-weighted, and still others equally weighted. Describe the investment strategy you need for each of the index types. Are any of the three strategies passive, in that no portfolio rebalancing need be performed to perfectly replicate the index (assuming no stock splits or cash distributions)? Which of the three strategies do you think is most often followed by small investors? Which strategy is the most difficult to implement?

CFA Exam Review by Schweser

[CFA6]

George White, CFA, and Elizabeth Plain, CFA, manage an account for Briggs and Meyers Securities. In managing the account, White and Plain use a variety of strategies, and they trade in different markets. They use both market and limit orders to execute their trades, which are often based on algorithmic methods. Their supervisor has asked them to compose a summary of their trading records to see how various strategies have worked.

Their supervisor also asks them to assess the costs and risks of the various types of trades. The supervisor specifically asks Mr. White and Ms. Plain to explain the difference in risks associated with market and limit orders. After Mr. White and Ms. Plain explain how limit orders can give a better price, the supervisor asks why they wouldn't always use limit orders.

As part of the discussion, Ms. Plain explains the issue of spread. She uses a recent example where the quoted bid and ask prices of GHT stock were $25.40 and $25.44, respectively.

1. Which of the following statements regarding market orders is *most* accurate? Market orders:

    a. Have price uncertainty, and limit orders have execution uncertainty.

    b. Have execution uncertainty, and limit orders have price uncertainty.

    c. And limit orders both have execution uncertainty and no price uncertainty.

2. In the example given by Ms. Plain, what was the spread for the GHT stock just prior to execution?

    a. $.06

    b. $.02

    c. $.04

3. Assume that when Mr. White and Ms. Plain entered their buy order for GHT, the price of the stock increased to $25.45. This is the price at which the trade was executed. Given this impact, the effective spread was _____ that in question 2 above.

    a. Lower than

    b. Higher than

    c. The same as

What's on the Web?

1. **DJIA** As you have seen, in a price-weighted index, a stock with a higher price has a higher weight in the index return. To find out the weight of the stocks in the DJIA, go to www.djindexes.com. Which stock in the DJIA has the highest weight? The lowest weight?

2. **DJIA** You want to find the current divisor for the DJIA. Go to www.djindexes.com and look up the current divisor.

3. **S&P 500** To find out the most recent changes in the S&P 500, go to www.standardandpoors.com. Once at the Web site, find the 10 most recent additions and deletions to the stocks in the index.

4. **Nikkei 225** The Nikkei 225 Index is a highly followed index that measures the performance of the Japanese stock market. Go to e.nikkei.com and find out if the Nikkei 225 is a price-weighted or value-weighted index. What is the divisor for this index? When was the latest reconstitution of the index? Which stocks were added? Which stocks were deleted? Hint: Look in the "Help" section.

Stock-Trak Exercises

To access the Stock-Trak Exercise for this chapter, please visit the book Web site at www.mhhe.com/jmd6e and choose the corresponding chapter.

CHAPTER 6

Common Stock Valuation

Learning Objectives

Separate yourself from the commoners by having a good understanding of these security valuation methods:

1. The basic dividend discount model.
2. The two-stage dividend growth model.
3. The residual income and free cash flow models.
4. Price ratio analysis.

"If a business is worth a dollar and I can buy it for 40 cents, something good may happen to me."

–Warren Buffett

"Prediction is difficult, especially about the future."

–Niels Bohr[1]

Common stock valuation is one of the most challenging tasks in financial analysis. A fundamental assertion of finance holds that the value of an asset is based on the present value of its future cash flows. Accordingly, common stock valuation attempts the difficult task of predicting the future. Consider that the dividend yield for a typical large-company stock might be about 2 percent. This implies that the present value of dividends to be paid over the next 10 years constitutes only a portion of the current stock price. Thus, much of the value of a typical stock is derived from dividends to be paid more than 10 years away! ∎

---

[1] This quote has also been attributed to Yogi Berra, Samuel Goldwyn, and Mark Twain.

CFA™ Exam Topics in This Chapter:

1 Financial reporting quality: Red flags and accounting warning signs (L1, S10)

2 Cost of capital (L1, S11)

3 An introduction to security valuation (L1, S14)

4 Company analysis and stock valuation (L1, S14)

5 Introduction to price multiples (L1, S14)

6 Equity valuation: Applications and processes (L2, S10)

7 Discounted dividend valuation (L2, S11)

8 Free cash flow valuation (L2, S12)

9 Market-based valuation (L2, S12)

10 Residual income valuation (L2, S12)

Go to www.mhhe.com/jmd6e for a guide that aligns your textbook with CFA readings.

In this chapter, we examine several methods commonly used by financial analysts to assess the economic value of common stocks. These methods are grouped into two categories: discount models and price ratio models. After studying these models, we provide an analysis of a real company to illustrate the use of the methods discussed in this chapter.

6.1 Security Analysis: Be Careful Out There

It may seem odd that we start our discussion with an admonition to be careful, but in this case, we think it is a good idea. The methods we discuss in this chapter are examples of those used by many investors and security analysts to assist in making buy and sell decisions for individual stocks. The basic idea is to identify both "undervalued" or "cheap" stocks to buy and "overvalued" or "rich" stocks to sell. In practice, however, many stocks that look cheap may in fact be correctly priced for reasons not immediately apparent to the analyst. Indeed, the hallmark of a good analyst is a cautious attitude and a willingness to probe further and deeper before committing to a final investment recommendation.

The type of security analysis we describe in this chapter falls under the heading of **fundamental analysis**. Numbers such as a company's earnings per share, cash flow, book equity value, and sales are often called *fundamentals* because they describe, on a basic level, a specific firm's operations and profits (or lack of profits).

Fundamental analysis represents the examination of these and other accounting statement-based company data used to assess the value of a company's stock. Information regarding such things as management quality, products, and product markets is often examined as well.

We urge you to be cautious when you apply these techniques. Further, the simpler the technique, the more cautious you should be. As our later chapter on market efficiency explains, there is good reason to believe that too-simple techniques that rely on widely available information are not likely to yield systematically superior investment results. In fact, they could lead to unnecessarily risky investment decisions. This is especially true for ordinary investors (like most of us) who do not have timely access to the information that a professional security analyst working for a major securities firm would possess.

As a result, our goal here is not to teach you how to "pick" stocks with a promise that you will become rich. Certainly, one chapter in an investments text is not likely to be sufficient to acquire that level of investment savvy. Still, an appreciation of the techniques in this chapter is important simply because buy and sell recommendations made by securities firms are frequently couched in the terms we introduce here. Much of the discussion of individual companies in the financial press relies on these concepts as well, so some background is necessary just to interpret commonly presented investment information. In essence, you must learn both the jargon and the concepts of security analysis.

fundamental analysis
Examination of a firm's accounting statements and other financial and economic information to assess the economic value of a company's stock.

Visit the New York Society of Security Analysts Web site at www.nyssa.org

✔ **CHECK THIS**

6.1a	What is fundamental analysis?
6.1b	What is a "rich" stock? What is a "cheap" stock?
6.1c	Why does valuing a stock necessarily involve predicting the future?

6.2 The Dividend Discount Model

A fundamental principle of finance says that the value of a security equals the sum of its future cash flows, where the cash flows are adjusted for risk and the time value of money. A popular model used to value common stock is the **dividend discount model**, or **DDM**. The dividend discount model values a share of stock as the sum of all expected future dividend payments, where the dividends are adjusted for risk and the time value of money.

dividend discount model (DDM)
Method of estimating the value of a share of stock as the present value of all expected future dividend payments.

For example, suppose a company pays a dividend at the end of each year. Let D_t denote a dividend to be paid t years from now, and let P_0 represent the present value of the future dividend stream. Also, let k denote the appropriate risk-adjusted discount rate. Using the dividend discount model, the present value of a share of this company's stock is measured as this sum of discounted future dividends:

$$P_0 = \frac{D_1}{(1+k)} + \frac{D_2}{(1+k)^2} + \frac{D_3}{(1+k)^3} + \cdots + \frac{D_T}{(1+k)^T} \qquad (6.1)$$

In equation (6.1), we assume that the last dividend is paid T years from now. The value of T depends on the time of the *terminal*, or last, dividend. Thus, if $T = 3$ years and $D_1 = D_2 = D_3 = \$100$, the present value, P_0, is stated as:

$$P_0 = \frac{\$100}{(1+k)} + \frac{\$100}{(1+k)^2} + \frac{\$100}{(1+k)^3}$$

If the discount rate is $k = 10$ percent, then a quick calculation yields $P_0 = \$248.69$. Thus, the stock price should be about $250 per share.

EXAMPLE 6.1	**Using the Dividend Discount Model**

Suppose again that a stock pays three annual dividends of $100 per year and the discount rate is $k = 15$ percent. In this case, what is the price of the stock today?

With a 15 percent discount rate, we have:

$$P_0 = \frac{\$100}{(1.15)} + \frac{\$100}{(1.15)^2} + \frac{\$100}{(1.15)^3}$$

Check that the answer is $P_0 = \$228.32$.

EXAMPLE 6.2	**Using the Dividend Discount Model Again**

Suppose instead that the stock pays three annual dividends of $10, $20, and $30 in years 1, 2, and 3, respectively, and the discount rate is $k = 10$ percent. What is the price of the stock today?

In this case, we have:

$$P_0 = \frac{\$10}{(1.10)} + \frac{\$20}{(1.10)^2} + \frac{\$30}{(1.10)^3}$$

Check that the answer is $P_0 = \$48.16$.

CONSTANT PERPETUAL GROWTH

constant perpetual growth model

A version of the dividend discount model in which dividends grow forever at a constant rate, and the growth rate is strictly less than the discount rate.

A particularly simple and useful form of the dividend discount model is called the **constant perpetual growth model**. In this case, we assume the firm will pay dividends that grow at the constant rate g forever. In the constant perpetual growth model, stock prices are calculated using this formula:

$$P_0 = \frac{D_0(1+g)}{k-g} \qquad (g < k) \qquad (6.2)$$

Because $D_0(1 + g) = D_1$, we can also write the constant perpetual growth model as:

$$P_0 = \frac{D_1}{k-g} \qquad (g < k) \qquad (6.3)$$

Either way, we have a very simple, and very widely used, formula for the price of a share of stock based on its future dividend payments.

Notice that the constant perpetual growth model requires that the growth rate be strictly less than the discount rate, that is, $g < k$. It looks as if the share value would be negative if this were not true. Actually, the formula is simply not valid in this case. The reason is that a perpetual dividend growth rate greater than the discount rate implies an *infinite* value because the present value of the dividends keeps getting bigger and bigger. Because no security can have infinite value, the requirement that $g < k$ simply makes good economic sense.

To illustrate the constant perpetual growth model, suppose that the growth rate is $g = 4$ percent, the discount rate is $k = 9$ percent, and the current dividend is $D_0 = \$10$. In this case, a simple calculation yields:

$$P_0 = \frac{\$10(1.04)}{.09 - .04} = \$208$$

EXAMPLE 6.3

Using the Constant Perpetual Growth Model

Suppose dividends for a particular company are projected to grow at 5 percent forever. If the discount rate is 15 percent and the current dividend is $10, what is the value of the stock?

$$P_0 = \frac{\$10(1.05)}{.15 - .05} = \$105$$

With these inputs, the stock should sell for $105.

HOW DO WE GET THE FORMULA FOR CONSTANT PERPETUAL GROWTH? Good question. Many people wonder how such a simple-looking formula, equation (6.3), emerges when we add up an infinite number of dividends. Recall that perpetual dividend growth means that dividends will grow forever. This means today's stock price, P_0, equals

$$P_0 = \frac{D_1}{(1+k)} + \frac{D_1(1+g)}{(1+k)^2} + \frac{D_1(1+g)^2}{(1+k)^3} + \frac{D_1(1+g)^3}{(1+k)^4} \cdots \qquad (6.4)$$

Equation (6.4) says that the stock price today is equal to the sum of the discounted amounts of all future dividends. To get the formula for today's stock price when assuming constant perpetual growth, we begin by multiplying both sides of equation (6.4) by the amount $[(1+g)/(1+k)]$. Equation (6.4) then becomes

$$P_0 \left[\frac{(1+g)}{(1+k)} \right] = \frac{D_1}{(1+k)} \left[\frac{(1+g)}{(1+k)} \right] + \frac{D_1(1+g)}{(1+k)^2} \left[\frac{(1+g)}{(1+k)} \right] \qquad (6.5)$$

$$+ \frac{D_1(1+g)^2}{(1+k)^3} \left[\frac{(1+g)}{(1+k)} \right] + \cdots$$

$$= \frac{D_1(1+g)}{(1+k)^2} + \frac{D_1(1+g)^2}{(1+k)^3} + \frac{D_1(1+g)^3}{(1+k)^4} + \cdots$$

Then we simply subtract equation (6.5) from equation (6.4). If you look closely, you can see that when we do this, we can cancel a lot of terms. In fact, we can cancel *all* the terms on the right side of equation (6.5) and all but the first term on the right side of equation (6.4). Using a little bit of algebra, we show what happens when we subtract equation (6.5) from equation (6.4):

$$P_0 - P_0 \frac{(1+g)}{(1+k)} = \frac{D_1}{(1+k)} + \frac{D_1(1+g)}{(1+k)^2} - \frac{D_1(1+g)}{(1+k)^2} \qquad (6.6)$$

$$+ \frac{D_1(1+g)^2}{(1+k)^3} - \frac{D_1(1+g)^2}{(1+k)^3} + \cdots$$

$$P_0 \left[1 - \frac{(1+g)}{(1+k)} \right] = \frac{D_1}{(1+k)}$$

$$P_0 \left[\frac{(1+k)}{(1+k)} - \frac{(1+g)}{(1+k)} \right] = \frac{D_1}{(1+k)}$$

$$P_0 \left[\frac{(k-g)}{(1+k)} \right] = \frac{D_1}{(1+k)}$$

$$P_0 = \frac{D_1}{(1+k)} \cdot \frac{(1+k)}{(k-g)}$$

$$P_0 = \frac{D_1}{k-g}$$

There. Now you know how we get a formula for the price of a share of stock when we assume that dividends grow at a constant rate forever. We apply this formula in the following section.

APPLICATIONS OF THE CONSTANT PERPETUAL GROWTH MODEL In practice, the constant perpetual growth model is the most popular dividend discount model because it is so simple to use. Certainly, the model satisfies Einstein's famous dictum: "Simplify as much as possible, but no more." However, experienced financial analysts are keenly aware that the constant perpetual growth model can be usefully applied only to companies with a history of relatively stable earnings and if dividend growth is expected to continue into the distant future.

A standard example of an industry for which the constant perpetual growth model can often be usefully applied is the electric utility industry. Consider American Electric Power, which is traded on the New York Stock Exchange under the ticker symbol AEP. In late 2009, AEP was paying an annual dividend of $1.64; thus we set $D_0 = \$1.64$.

To use the constant perpetual growth model, we also need a discount rate and a growth rate. An old quick and dirty rule of thumb for a risk-adjusted discount rate for electric utility companies is the yield to maturity on 20-year maturity U.S. Treasury bonds, plus 2 percent. At the time this example was written, the yield on 20-year maturity T-bonds was about 3.75 percent. Adding 2 percent, we get a discount rate of $k = 5.75$ percent.

In 2008, AEP increased its dividend by 3.8 percent, and AEP did not change its dividend in 2009. The average of these dividend growth rates is about 2 percent. This growth rate is consistent with the projected earnings growth rate for the overall electric utilities industry. A growth rate of 2 percent appears to be a sensible estimate of future growth for AEP.

Putting it all together, we have $k = 5.75$ percent, $g = 2$ percent, and $D_0 = \$1.64$. Using these numbers, we obtain this estimate for the value of a share of AEP stock:

$$P_0 = \frac{\$1.64(1.02)}{.0575 - .02} = \$44.61$$

This estimate is somewhat above the late 2009 AEP stock price of $31.83, possibly suggesting that AEP stock was undervalued.

We emphasize the word "possibly" here because we made several assumptions in the process of coming up with this estimate. A change in any of these assumptions could easily lead us to a different conclusion. In particular, we made assumptions about the discount rate, the growth rate, and the steady nature of dividend growth. What happens when we change these assumptions? We will return to this point several times in future discussions.

EXAMPLE 6.4	**Valuing DTE Energy Co. (formerly Detroit ED)**

In 2009, the utility company DTE Energy (DTE) paid a $2.12 dividend. Using $D_0 = \$2.12$, $k = 5.75$ percent, and an industry average growth rate of $g = 2$ percent, calculate a present value estimate for DTE. Compare this with the late 2009 DTE stock price of $40.29.

Plugging in the relevant numbers, we immediately have:

$$P_0 = \frac{\$2.12(1.02)}{.0575 - .02} = \$57.66$$

This estimate is somewhat above the late 2009 DTE stock price of $40.29, possibly suggesting that DTE stock was undervalued.

---

geometric average dividend growth rate

A dividend growth rate based on a geometric average of historical dividends.

arithmetic average dividend growth rate

A dividend growth rate based on an arithmetic average of historical dividends.

HISTORICAL GROWTH RATES

In the constant growth model, a company's historical average dividend growth rate is frequently taken as an estimate of future dividend growth. Sometimes historical growth rates are provided in published information about the company. Other times it is necessary to calculate a historical growth rate yourself. There are two ways to do this: (1) using a **geometric average dividend growth rate** or (2) using an **arithmetic average dividend growth rate**. Both methods are relatively easy to implement, as we will now illustrate.

To illustrate the difference between a geometric average and an arithmetic average of historical dividend growth, suppose that The Broadway Joe Company paid the following dividends at the end of each of the years indicated immediately below.

2010:	$2.20	2007:	$1.75
2009:	2.00	2006:	1.70
2008:	1.80	2005:	1.50

We begin with a geometric average growth rate because it is the easiest to calculate. Notice that five years elapsed between the $1.50 dividend paid at the end of 2005 and the $2.20 dividend paid at the end of 2010. A geometric average growth rate is equivalent to a constant rate of growth over the five-year period that would grow the dividend from $1.50 to $2.20. That is, it is the growth rate that solves this growth equation:

$$\$2.20 = \$1.50(1 + g)^5$$

$$g = \left(\frac{\$2.20}{\$1.50}\right)^{1/5} - 1 = .08$$

Thus, in this case, the five-year geometric average dividend growth rate is 8 percent. Notice that this calculation is similar to our calculation of the geometric average return in Chapter 1.

In general, if D_0 is the earliest dividend used and D_N is the latest dividend used to calculate a geometric average dividend growth rate over N years, the general equation used is:

$$g = \left[\frac{D_N}{D_0}\right]^{1/N} - 1 \tag{6.7}$$

In the above example, $D_0 = \$1.50$, $D_N = \$2.20$, and $N = 5$, which yields $g = 8\%$.

An arithmetic average growth rate takes a little more effort to calculate, because it requires that we first calculate each year's dividend growth rate separately and then calculate an arithmetic average of these annual growth rates. For our Broadway Joe example, the arithmetic average of five years of dividend growth is calculated as follows:

Year	Dividend	Yearly Growth Rates
2010	$2.20	10.00% = (2.20 − 2.00)/2.00
2009	2.00	11.11% = (2.00 − 1.80)/1.80
2008	1.80	2.86% = (1.80 − 1.75)/1.75
2007	1.75	2.94% = (1.75 − 1.70)/1.70
2006	1.70	13.33% = (1.70 − 1.50)/1.50
2005	1.50	
		SUM/N = 40.24%/5 = 8.05%

The sum of the five yearly growth rates is 40.24%. Dividing by five yields an arithmetic average growth rate of 40.24%/5 = 8.05%. Notice that this arithmetic average growth rate is close to the geometric average growth rate of 8.0 percent. This is usually the case for dividend growth rates, but not always. A large difference between the two means that the dividend grew erratically, which calls into question the use of the constant growth formula.

EXAMPLE 6.5

Erratic Dividend Growth

To illustrate how the geometric average and the arithmetic average of historical dividend growth can differ, consider the following dividends paid by the Joltin' Joe Company:

2010:	$2.20	2007:	$2.00
2009:	2.00	2006:	1.50
2008:	1.80	2005:	1.50

(continued)

For Joltin' Joe, the arithmetic average of five years of dividend growth is calculated as follows:

Year	Dividend	Yearly Growth Rates
2010	$2.20	10.00% = (2.20 − 2.00)/2.00
2009	2.00	11.11% = (2.00 − 1.80)/1.80
2008	1.80	−10.00% = (1.80 − 2.00)/2.00
2007	2.00	33.33% = (2.00 − 1.50)/1.50
2006	1.50	0.00% = (1.50 − 1.50)/1.50
2005	1.50	
		44.44%/5 = 8.89%

In this case, the sum of the five yearly growth rates is 44.44 percent. Dividing by five yields an arithmetic average growth rate of 44.44%/5 = 8.89%. Notice that this arithmetic average growth rate is somewhat larger than the geometric average growth rate of 8.0 percent, which you can verify using equation (6.7).

As the Joltin' Joe example shows, sometimes the arithmetic and geometric growth rate averages can yield rather different results. In practice, most analysts prefer to use a geometric average when calculating an average historical dividend growth rate. In any case, a historical average growth rate may or may not be a reasonable estimate of future dividend growth. Many analysts adjust their estimates to reflect other information available to them, for example, whether the growth rate appears to be sustainable.

THE SUSTAINABLE GROWTH RATE

As we have seen, when using the constant perpetual growth model, it is necessary to come up with an estimate of g, the growth rate of dividends. In our previous discussions, we described two ways to do this: (1) using the company's historical average growth rate or (2) using an industry median or average growth rate. We now describe a third way, known as the **sustainable growth rate**, which involves using a company's earnings to estimate g.

As we have discussed, a limitation of the constant perpetual growth model is that it should be applied only to companies with stable dividend and earnings growth. Essentially, a company's earnings can be paid out as dividends to its stockholders or kept as **retained earnings** within the firm to finance future growth. The proportion of earnings paid to stockholders as dividends is called the **payout ratio**. The proportion of earnings retained for reinvestment is called the **retention ratio**.

If we let D stand for dividends and EPS stand for earnings per share, then the payout ratio is simply D/EPS. Because anything not paid out is retained, the retention ratio is just 1 minus the payout ratio. For example, if a company's current dividend is $4 per share, and its earnings per share are currently $10, then the payout ratio is $4/$10 = .40, or 40 percent, and the retention ratio is 1 − .40 = .60, or 60 percent.

A firm's sustainable growth rate is equal to its return on equity (ROE) times its retention ratio.[2]

$$\text{Sustainable growth rate} = \text{ROE} \times \text{Retention ratio}$$
$$= \text{ROE} \times (1 - \text{Payout ratio}) \qquad (6.8)$$

Return on equity is commonly computed using an accounting-based performance measure and is calculated as a firm's net income divided by shareholders' equity:

$$\text{Return on equity (ROE)} = \text{Net Income / Equity} \qquad (6.9)$$

sustainable growth rate
A dividend growth rate that can be sustained by a company's earnings.

retained earnings
Earnings retained within the firm to finance growth.

payout ratio
Proportion of earnings paid out as dividends.

retention ratio
Proportion of earnings retained for reinvestment.

[2] Strictly speaking, this formula is correct only if ROE is calculated using beginning-of-period shareholders' equity. If ending figures are used, then the precise formula is ROE × Retention ratio / [1 − (ROE × Retention ratio)]. However, the error from not using the precise formula is usually small, so most analysts might not bother with it.

Calculating Sustainable Growth

In 2009, American Electric Power (AEP) had a return on equity (ROE) of 10 percent, earnings per share (EPS) of $2.90, and paid dividends of $D_0 = 1.64. What was AEP's retention rate? Its sustainable growth rate?

AEP's dividend payout was $1.64/$2.90 = .566, or about 56.6 percent. Its retention ratio was thus 1 − .566 = .434, or 43.4 percent. Finally, AEP's sustainable growth rate was .10 × .434 = .0434, or 4.34 percent.

Valuing American Electric Power (AEP)

Using AEP's sustainable growth rate of 4.34 percent (see Example 6.6) as an estimate of perpetual dividend growth and its current dividend of $1.64, what is the value of AEP's stock assuming a discount rate of 5.75 percent?

If we plug the various numbers into the perpetual growth model, we obtain a value of $P_0 = $1.64(1.0434)/(.0575 − .0434) = 121.36.

In late 2009, share prices for AEP were $31.83. In this case, using the sustainable growth rate to value the stock gives a poor estimate.

Valuing DTE Energy Co. (DTE)

In 2009, DTE had a return on equity (ROE) of 8 percent, earnings per share (EPS) of $3.00, and a per-share dividend of $D_0 = 2.12. Assuming a 5.75 percent discount rate, what is the value of DTE's stock?

DTE's payout ratio was $2.12/$3.00 = .7067, or about 70.7 percent. Thus, DTE's retention ratio was 1 − .707 = .293, or 29.3 percent. DTE's sustainable growth rate is thus 8% × .293 = 2.34%. Finally, using the constant growth model, we obtain a value of $2.12(1.0234)/(.0575 − .0234) = $63.62. Clearly, something is wrong because the actual price was $40.29. Can you explain the causes of this difference?

A common problem with sustainable growth rates is that they are sensitive to year-to-year fluctuations in earnings. As a result, security analysts routinely adjust sustainable growth rate estimates to smooth out the effects of earnings variations. Unfortunately, there is no universally standard method to adjust a sustainable growth rate, and analysts depend a great deal on personal experience and their own subjective judgment. Our nearby *Work the Web* box contains more information on analyst-estimated growth rates.

ANALYZING ROE

Two factors are needed to estimate a sustainable growth rate: the dividend payout ratio and ROE. For most firms, dividend policy is relatively stable. Thus, any major changes in the firm's sustainable growth rate likely stem from changes in ROE. Therefore, an understanding of ROE is critical when you are analyzing a stock price.

You might recall from other finance classes that ROE, net income divided by equity, can be broken down into three components. This "decomposition" is so important that it has a name: *the DuPont formula*. The DuPont formula is:

$$\text{ROE} = \frac{\text{Net income}}{\text{Sales}} \times \frac{\text{Sales}}{\text{Assets}} \times \frac{\text{Assets}}{\text{Equity}} \tag{6.10}$$

The DuPont formula shows that ROE has three parts. The first part is the firm's *net profit margin*, which measures the amount of net income for each dollar of sales. The second part measures asset efficiency, and it is referred to as *asset turnover*. Asset efficiency measures how much sales a firm gets from its assets. The third part is called the *equity multiplier*. The equity multiplier captures the amount of leverage (or debt) used by the firm. If the equity multiplier equals one, then the firm has no debt.

WORK THE WEB

We discussed use of the sustainable growth formula to estimate a company's growth rate; however, the formula is not foolproof. Changes in the variables of the model can have a dramatic effect on growth rates. One of the most important tasks of an equity analyst is estimating future growth rates. These estimates require a detailed analysis of the company. One place to find earnings and sales growth rates on the Web is Yahoo! Finance at finance.yahoo .com. Here, we pulled up a quote for Coca-Cola (KO) and followed the "Analysts Estimates" link. Below you will see an abbreviated look at the results.

Earnings Est	Current Qtr Dec-09	Next Qtr Mar-10	Current Year Dec-09	Next Year Dec-10
Avg. Estimate	0.67	0.75	3.07	3.42
No. of Analysts	10	6	13	14
Low Estimate	0.63	0.73	3.03	3.35
High Estimate	0.72	0.78	3.10	3.60
Year Ago EPS	0.64	0.65	3.15	3.07

Revenue Est	Current Qtr Dec-09	Next Qtr Mar-10	Current Year Dec-09	Next Year Dec-10
Avg. Estimate	7.22B	7.79B	30.80B	32.81B
No. of Analysts	7	5	9	8
Low Estimate	6.72B	7.60B	30.20B	31.00B
High Estimate	7.59B	8.02B	31.31B	33.80B
Year Ago Sales	7.13B	7.17B	31.94B	30.80B
Sales Growth (year/est)	1.3%	8.7%	-3.6%	6.5%

As shown, analysts expect revenue (sales) of $30.80 billion in 2009, growing to $32.81 billion in 2010, an increase of 6.5 percent. We also have the following table comparing Coca-Cola to some benchmarks:

Growth Est	KO	Industry	Sector	S&P 500
Current Qtr.	4.7%	9.5%	71.2%	-34.1%
Next Qtr.	15.4%	13.4%	71.6%	18.0%
This Year	-2.5%	2.2%	12.7%	0.7%
Next Year	11.4%	11.0%	24.9%	24.8%
Past 5 Years (per annum)	11.425%	N/A	N/A	N/A
Next 5 Years (per annum)	6.5%	8.05%	9.63%	N/A
Price/Earnings (avg. for comparison categories)	18.72	16.84	18.65	17.59
PEG Ratio (avg. for comparison categories)	2.88	2.09	1.94	N/A

As you can see, estimated earnings growth this year for KO is below the estimates for the industry and the S&P 500. What about next year? Here is an assignment for you: What is the PEG ratio? Locate a financial glossary on the Web (there are lots of them) to find out.

You can now see the ways that managers of a firm can increase the firm's sustainable growth rate. They can pay out a smaller percentage of the earnings. A lower payout ratio will increase the growth rate. If managers find ways to increase profitability or increase asset efficiency, ROE increases. Finally, the managers can increase debt. The resulting increase in the equity multiplier means that ROE increases. Looking at the sustainable growth rate formula, you can see that if ROE increases, so does the sustainable growth rate.

After you graduate from college, suppose you get hired as a financial analyst. If you know how to analyze ROE, you can judge how strategies being used by management will impact the future growth rate of the firm. Then, you just might be able to estimate a potential stock price for this firm.

CHECK THIS

6.2a Compare the dividend discount model, the constant growth model, and the constant perpetual growth model. How are they alike? How do they differ?

6.2b What is a geometric average growth rate? How is it calculated?

6.2c What is a sustainable growth rate? How is it calculated?

6.2d What are the components of ROE?

6.3 The Two-Stage Dividend Growth Model

In the previous section, the dividend discount model used one growth rate. You might have already thought that a single growth rate is often unrealistic. You might be thinking that companies experience temporary periods of unusually high or low growth, with growth eventually converging to an industry average or an economywide average. In these cases, financial analysts frequently use a **two-stage dividend growth model**.

two-stage dividend growth model
A dividend discount model that assumes a firm will temporarily grow at a rate different from its long-term growth rate.

A two-stage dividend growth model assumes that a firm will initially grow at a rate g_1 during a first stage of growth lasting T years and thereafter grow at a rate g_2 during a perpetual second stage of growth. The formula for the two-stage dividend growth model is stated as follows:

$$P_0 = \frac{D_0(1 + g_1)}{k - g_1}\left[1 - \left(\frac{1 + g_1}{1 + k}\right)^T\right] + \left(\frac{1 + g_1}{1 + k}\right)^T\left[\frac{D_0(1 + g_2)}{k - g_2}\right] \qquad (6.11)$$

At first glance, you might think that this expression looks a little complicated. Well, you are right. Let's make it easier by looking at each part of the formula. We'll start with the part of the formula to the left of the + sign in equation (6.11). To show how we get this part of the formula, we pretend that dividends grow at the constant rate g_1 forever. We do this because we want to know the value today of all the dividends beginning one date from now to date T—the date where the dividend growth rate changes from g_1 to g_2. To begin, look at Figure 6.1.

You already know the formula for the value of the sum of all dividends that will be received beginning one date from now and growing at a constant rate g_1 in perpetuity. In Figure 6.1, (A_0) represents the value today of this set of cash flows. That is,

$$A_0 = \frac{D_0(1 + g_1)}{k - g_1} \qquad (6.12)$$

Now for something just a little bit different. Let us focus our attention on date T. Starting at date T, the value of the sum of all dividends that we will receive beginning one date from T (i.e., at date $T + 1$) and growing at a constant rate g_1 in perpetuity is

$$B_T = \frac{D_0(1 + g_1)^{T+1}}{k - g_1} \qquad (6.13)$$

What is the value of these dividends today? To answer this, we discount this amount by $1/(1 + k)^T$:

$$B_0 = \frac{1}{(1 + k)^T}\left[\frac{D_0(1 + g_1)^{T+1}}{k - g_1}\right] \qquad (6.14)$$

FIGURE 6.1   A Handy Dividend Timeline

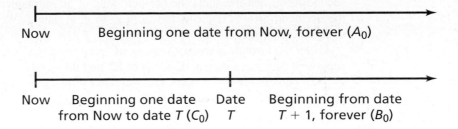

What happens if we subtract B_0 from A_0? Looking at the timeline in Figure 6.1, you can see that we are left with the value of all dividends beginning one date from now and ending at date T. That is,

$$C_0 = \frac{D_0(1 + g_1)}{k - g_1} - \frac{1}{(1 + k)^T}\left[\frac{D_0(1 + g_1)^{T+1}}{k - g_1}\right] \tag{6.15}$$

To help make equation (6.15) easier to calculate, we can rewrite $D_0(1 + g_1)^{T+1}$ as $D_0(1 + g_1)(1 + g_1)^T$. Therefore, equation (6.15) becomes

$$C_0 = \frac{D_0(1 + g_1)}{k - g_1} - \frac{1}{(1 + k)^T}\left[\frac{D_0(1 + g_1)(1 + g_1)^T}{k - g_1}\right]$$

or, with some rearranging,

$$C_0 = \frac{D_0(1 + g_1)}{k - g_1} - \frac{D_0(1 + g_1)}{k - g_1}\left[\frac{(1 + g_1)^T}{(1 + k)^T}\right]$$

which is the term to the left of the plus sign in equation (6.11):

$$C_0 = \frac{D_0(1 + g_1)}{k - g_1}\left[1 - \left(\frac{1 + g_1}{1 + k}\right)^T\right]$$

Now we have all the parts needed to write the term to the right of the plus sign in equation (6.11). All we have to do is ask, what is the value now of all dividends received beginning at date $T + 1$ if dividends grow in perpetuity at the rate g_2 after date T? To answer this question, we have to know what the dividend is at date $T + 1$. We know the current dividend D_0 increases each date by $(1 + g_1)$ until date T. Beginning at date T, the growth rate becomes g_2. Therefore, the dividend at date $T + 1$ is the amount $D_0(1 + g_1)^T(1 + g_2)$. We add an asterisk (*) to B_0 to alert us to the fact that the dividend growth rate has changed. So,

$$B_0^* = \frac{1}{(1 + k)^T}\left[\frac{D_0(1 + g_1)^T(1 + g_2)}{k - g_2}\right] \tag{6.16}$$

We see that equations (6.14) and (6.16) are quite similar. The difference is the value of the dividend at date $T + 1$. In equation (6.14), this dividend value is $D_0(1 + g_1)^{T+1}$, or $D_0(1 + g_1)(1 + g_1)^T$. In equation (6.16), this value is $D_0(1 + g_1)^T(1 + g_2)$.

With some rearranging, equation (6.16) becomes the term to the right of the plus sign in equation (6.11). That is,

$$B_0^* = \frac{1}{(1 + k)^T}\left[\frac{D_0(1 + g_1)^T(1 + g_2)}{k - g_2}\right]$$

or

$$B_0^* = \left(\frac{1 + g_1}{1 + k}\right)^T\left[\frac{D_0(1 + g_2)}{k - g_2}\right]$$

To recap, equation (6.11) has two parts. The first term on the right-hand side measures the present value of the first T dividends, which is the value A_0 in equation (6.12). The second term then measures the present value of all subsequent dividends, assuming that the dividend growth rate changes from g_1 to g_2 at date T. We show that this value is B_0^* in equation (6.16).

Using the formula is mostly a matter of "plug and chug" with a calculator. For example, suppose a firm has a current dividend of $2, and dividends are expected to grow at the rate $g_1 = 20$ percent for $T = 5$ years, and thereafter grow at the rate $g_2 = 5$ percent. With a discount rate of $k = 12$ percent, the stock price today, P_0, is calculated as:

$$P_0 = \frac{\$2(1.20)}{.12 - .20}\left[1 - \left(\frac{1.20}{1.12}\right)^5\right] + \left(\frac{1.20}{1.12}\right)^5\left[\frac{\$2(1.05)}{.12 - .05}\right]$$

$$= \$12.36 + \$42.36$$

$$= \$54.72$$

In this calculation, the total present value of $54.72 is the sum of a $12.36 present value for the first five dividends plus a $42.36 present value for all subsequent dividends.

EXAMPLE 6.9

Using the Two-Stage Model

Suppose a firm has a current dividend of $D_0 = \$5$, which is expected to "shrink" at the rate $g_1 = -10$ percent for $T = 5$ years and thereafter grow at the rate $g_2 = 4$ percent. With a discount rate of $k = 10$ percent, what is the value of the stock?

Using the two-stage model, the stock price today, P_0, is calculated as:

$$P_0 = \frac{\$5(.90)}{.10 - (-.10)}\left[1 - \left(\frac{.90}{1.10}\right)^5\right] + \left(\frac{.90}{1.10}\right)^5\left[\frac{\$5(1.04)}{.10 - .04}\right]$$

$$= \$14.25 + \$31.78$$

$$= \$46.03$$

The total present value of $46.03 is the sum of a $14.25 present value of the first five dividends plus a $31.78 present value of all subsequent dividends.

The two-stage growth formula requires that the second-stage growth rate be strictly less than the discount rate, that is, $g_2 < k$. However, the first-stage growth rate g_1 can be greater than, less than, or equal to the discount rate.

EXAMPLE 6.10

Valuing American Express (AXP)

American Express trades on the New York Stock Exchange under the ticker symbol AXP. In 2009, AXP was paying a dividend of $.72 and analysts forecasted five-year growth rates of 11.00 percent for AXP and 11.25 percent for the financial services industry. Assume the growth rate for the financial services industry will remain constant. Then, assuming AXP's growth rate will revert to the industry average after five years, what value would we place on AXP, if we use a discount rate of 14 percent?

$$P_0 = \frac{\$.72\,(1.1100)}{.14 - .1100}\left[1 - \left(\frac{1.1100}{1.14}\right)^5\right] + \left(\frac{1.1100}{1.14}\right)^5\left[\frac{\$.72\,(1.1125)}{.14 - .1125}\right]$$

$$= \$26.64 \times .1248 + .8752 \times \$29.13$$

$$= \$3.32 + \$25.49$$

$$= \$28.81$$

This present value estimate is less than AXP's late 2009 share price of $41.68. Is AXP overvalued? What other factors could explain the difference?

EXAMPLE 6.11   **Pepsi! Pepsi! Pepsi! (PEP)**

Pepsi shares trade on the New York Stock Exchange under the ticker symbol PEP. In 2009, Pepsi was paying a dividend of $1.75 and analysts forecasted a five-year growth rate of 10.50 percent for Pepsi and an 8.05 percent growth rate for the soft-drink industry. Suppose Pepsi grows at 10.5 percent for five years and then at 8.05 percent thereafter. Assuming a 12 percent discount rate, what value would we place on PEP?

Plugging this information into the two-stage dividend growth model, we get:

$$P_0 = \frac{\$1.75 \times (1.105)}{.12 - .105}\left[1 - \left(\frac{1.105}{1.12}\right)^5\right] + \left(\frac{1.105}{1.12}\right)^5 \frac{\$1.75 \times (1.0805)}{.12 - .0805}$$

$$P_0 = (\$128.92 \times .0652) + (.9348 \times \$47.87)$$

$$P_0 = \$8.41 + \$44.75$$

$$P_0 = \$53.16$$

This estimate is about 15 percent below PEP's late 2009 share price of $62.94. Suppose we try a second-stage growth rate of 9 percent. In this case we get:

$$P_0 = \frac{\$1.75 \times (1.105)}{.12 - .105}\left[1 - \left(\frac{1.105}{1.12}\right)^5\right] + \left(\frac{1.105}{1.12}\right)^5 \frac{\$1.75 \times (1.09)}{.12 - .09}$$

$$P_0 = (\$128.92 \times .0652) + (.9348 \times \$63.58)$$

$$P_0 = \$8.41 + \$59.43$$

$$P_0 = \$67.84$$

This new estimate is closer to the actual price of PEP. This example illustrates how sensitive stock price estimates using dividend growth models can be to small changes in estimated growth rates.

NONCONSTANT GROWTH IN THE FIRST STAGE

Visit AXP and PEP Web sites at
www.americanexpress.com
and
www.pepsico.com

The last case we consider is nonconstant growth in the first stage. As a simple example of nonconstant growth, consider the case of a company that is currently not paying dividends. You predict that, in five years, the company will pay a dividend for the first time. The dividend will be $.50 per share. You expect that this dividend will then grow at a rate of 10 percent per year indefinitely. The required return on companies such as this one is 20 percent. What is the price of the stock today?

To see what the stock is worth today, we first find out what it will be worth once dividends are paid. We can then calculate the present value of that future price to get today's price. The first dividend will be paid in five years, and the dividend will grow steadily from then on. Using the dividend growth model, we can say that the price in four years will be:

$$P_4 = D_4 \times (1 + g)/(k - g)$$
$$= D_5/(k - g)$$
$$= \$.50/(.20 - .10)$$
$$= \$5$$

If the stock will be worth $5 in four years, then we can get the current value by discounting this price back four years at 20 percent:

$$P_0 = \$5/1.20^4 = \$5/2.0736 = \$2.41$$

The stock is therefore worth $2.41 today.

FIGURE 6.2   Time Line

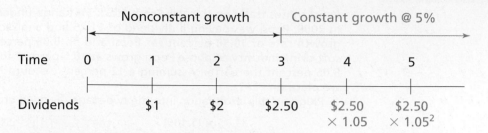

The problem of nonconstant growth is only slightly more complicated if the dividends are not zero for the first several years. For example, suppose that you have come up with the following dividend forecasts for the next three years:

Year	Expected Dividend
1	$1.00
2	2.00
3	2.50

After the third year, the dividend will grow at a constant rate of 5 percent per year. The required return is 10 percent. What is the value of the stock today?

In dealing with nonconstant growth, a time line can be very helpful. Figure 6.2 illustrates one for this problem. The important thing to notice is when constant growth starts. As we've shown, for this problem, constant growth starts at time 3. This means that we can use our constant growth model to determine the stock price at time 3, P_3. By far the most common mistake in this situation is to incorrectly identify the start of the constant growth phase and, as a result, calculate the future stock price at the wrong time.

The value of the stock is the present value of all future dividends. To calculate this present value, we first have to compute the present value of the stock price three years down the road, just as we did before. We then have to add in the present value of the dividends that will be paid between now and then. So, the price in three years is:

$$P_3 = D_3 \times (1 + g)/(k - g)$$
$$= \$2.50 \times 1.05/(.10 - .05)$$
$$= \$52.50$$

We can now calculate the total value of the stock as the present value of the first three dividends plus the present value of the price at time 3, P_3.

$$P_0 = \frac{D_1}{(1 + k)^1} + \frac{D_2}{(1 + k)^2} + \frac{D_3}{(1 + k)^3} + \frac{P_3}{(1 + k)^3}$$
$$= \frac{\$1}{1.10} + \frac{2}{1.10^2} + \frac{2.50}{1.10^3} + \frac{52.50}{1.10^3}$$
$$= \$.91 + 1.65 + 1.88 + 39.44$$
$$= \$43.88$$

The value of the stock today is thus $43.88.

EXAMPLE 6.12   **"Supernormal" Growth**

Chain Reaction, Inc., has been growing at a phenomenal rate of 30 percent per year because of its rapid expansion and explosive sales. You believe that this growth rate will last for three more years and that the rate will then drop to 10 percent per year. If the growth rate then remains at 10 percent indefinitely, what is the total value

(continued)

of the stock? Total dividends just paid were $5 million, and the required return is 20 percent.

Chain Reaction's situation is an example of supernormal growth. It is unlikely that a 30 percent growth rate can be sustained for any extended length of time. To value the equity in this company, we first need to calculate the total dividends over the supernormal growth period:

Year	Total Dividends (in millions)
1	$5.00 × 1.3 = $ 6.500
2	6.50 × 1.3 = 8.450
3	8.45 × 1.3 = 10.985

The price at time 3 can be calculated as:

$$P_3 = D_3 \times (1 + g)/(k - g)$$

where g is the long-run growth rate. So we have:

$$P_3 = \$10.985 \times 1.10/(.20 - .10) = \$120.835 \text{ million}$$

To determine the value today, we need the present value of this amount plus the present value of the total dividends:

$$P_0 = \frac{D_1}{(1 + k)^1} + \frac{D_2}{(1 + k)^2} + \frac{D_3}{(1 + k)^3} + \frac{P_3}{(1 + k)^3}$$

$$= \frac{\$6.50}{1.20} + \frac{8.45}{1.20^2} + \frac{10.985}{1.20^3} + \frac{120.835}{1.20^3}$$

$$= \$5.42 + 5.87 + 6.36 + 69.93$$

$$= \$87.58$$

The total value of the stock today is thus $87.58 million. If there were, for example, 20 million shares, then the stock would be worth $87.58/20 = $4.38 per share.

THE H-MODEL

In Example 6.12, we assumed a supernormal growth rate of 30 percent per year for three years, and then growth at a perpetual 10 percent. For most firms, however, growth does not follow this disjointed path. The growth rate is more likely to start at a high level and then fall over time until reaching its perpetual level.

There are many possibilities for how we assume the growth rate declines over time. One popular approach is the H-model, which assumes a linear decline in growth. Let's revisit our example. Suppose the growth rate begins at 30 percent and reaches 10 percent in year 4 and beyond. Using the H-model, we would assume that the company's growth rate would decline by 20 percent from the end of year 1 to the beginning of year 4.

If we assume a linear decline, then the growth rate would fall by 6.67 percent per year (20 percent/3 years). Using the H-model, our growth estimates would be 30, 23.33, 16.66, and 10 percent over years 1 through 4, respectively. With these growth estimates, you can repeat Example 6.12. You should find that the firm value is $75.93 million, with a per-share value of $3.80. As we would expect, this value is lower than our initial estimate because we are assuming lower growth rates in years 2 and 3 compared to the original example.

DISCOUNT RATES FOR DIVIDEND DISCOUNT MODELS

You may wonder where the discount rates used in the preceding examples come from. The answer is that they come from the *capital asset pricing model* (CAPM). Although a detailed discussion of the CAPM is deferred to a later chapter, we can point out here that, based on the CAPM, the discount rate for a stock can be estimated using this formula:

Discount rate = U.S. T-bill rate + (Stock beta × Stock market risk premium)   (6.17)

The components of this formula, as we use it here, are defined as follows:

U.S. T-bill rate:	Return on 90-day U.S. T-bills
Stock beta:	Risk relative to an average stock
Stock market risk premium:	Risk premium for an average stock

The basic intuition for this approach appears in Chapter 1. There we saw that the return we expect to earn on a risky asset had two parts, a "wait" component and a "worry" component. We labeled the wait component as the *time value of money,* and we noted that it can be measured as the return we earn from an essentially riskless investment. Here we use the return on a 90-day Treasury bill as the riskless return.

We called the worry component the *risk premium,* and we noted that the greater the risk, the greater the risk premium. Depending on the exact period studied, the risk premium for the U.S. market as a whole over the past 80 or so years has averaged about 8.5 percent. This 8.5 percent can be interpreted as the risk premium for bearing an average amount of stock market risk. Remember, though, the risk premium has been neither constant through time nor consistent across countries. Based on recent history and global metrics, we proposed that a risk premium around 7 percent might be more applicable over the coming years.

Finally, when we look at a particular stock, we recognize that it may be more or less risky than an average stock. A stock's **beta** is a measure of a single stock's risk relative to an average stock, and we discuss beta at length in a later chapter. For now, it suffices to know that the market average beta is 1.0. A beta of 1.5 indicates that a stock has 50 percent more risk than the average stock, so its risk premium is 50 percent higher. A beta of .50 indicates that a stock is 50 percent less risky than average and has a smaller risk premium.

beta
Measure of a stock's risk relative to the stock market average.

Over time, T-bill rates have averaged about 4 percent. Taking the concept of stock beta as given for now, a stock beta of .8 yields an estimated discount rate of $4.0\% + (.8 \times 7\%) = 9.6\%$. Similarly, a stock beta of 1.2 yields the discount rate of $4.0\% + (1.2 \times 7\%) = 12.4\%$. For the remainder of this chapter, we will use discount rates calculated according to this CAPM formula.

OBSERVATIONS ON DIVIDEND DISCOUNT MODELS

We have examined three dividend discount models: the constant perpetual growth model, the two-stage dividend growth model, and the nonconstant growth model. Each model has advantages and disadvantages. Certainly, the main advantage of the constant perpetual growth model is that it is simple to compute. However, it has several disadvantages: (1) it is not usable for firms not paying dividends, (2) it is not usable when the growth rate is greater than the discount rate, (3) it is sensitive to the choice of growth rate and discount rate, (4) discount rates and growth rates may be difficult to estimate accurately, and (5) constant perpetual growth is often an unrealistic assumption.

The two-stage dividend growth model offers several improvements: (1) it is more realistic, since it accounts for low, high, or zero growth in the first stage, followed by constant long-term growth in the second stage, and (2) it is usable when the first-stage growth rate is greater than the discount rate. However, the two-stage model is also sensitive to the choice of discount rate and growth rates, and it is not useful for companies that don't pay dividends. The nonconstant growth model is more flexible in this regard, but it still remains sensitive to the discount and growth rates assumed.

Financial analysts readily acknowledge the limitations of dividend discount models. Consequently, they also turn to other valuation methods to expand their analyses. In the next few sections, we discuss some popular stock valuation methods based on residual income, free cash flow, and price ratios.

CHECK THIS

6.3a   What are the three parts of a CAPM-determined discount rate?

6.3b   Under what circumstances is a two-stage dividend discount model appropriate?

6.4 The Residual Income Model

To this point, we have been valuing only firms that pay dividends. What about the many companies that don't pay dividends? As it turns out, there is an elegant and simple model that we can use.

RESIDUAL INCOME

At the beginning of any period, we can think of the book, or the accounting, equity in a firm as representing the total amount of money that stockholders have tied up in the company. Let B_{t-1} stand for the book equity per share at the beginning of a period that ends at time t. Over the period, the stockholders have a required return on that investment of k. Thus, the required return in dollars, or required earnings per share ($REPS$), during the period that ends at time t is:

$$REPS_t = B_{t-1} \times k$$

The difference between actual earnings, EPS_t, and required earnings, $REPS_t$, during a period is called the *residual income, RI*, and is given by:

$$RI_t = EPS_t - REPS_t = EPS_t - B_{t-1} \times k$$

Economic Value Added (EVA)
A financial performance measure based on the difference between a firm's actual earnings and required earnings.

Residual income is sometimes called **Economic Value Added**, or **EVA** for short. It is also called "abnormal" earnings. Whatever it is called, it is the excess of actual earnings over required earnings. We can also think of it as the value created by a firm in period t.

Next, we can write the value of a share of stock as the sum of two parts. The first part is the current book value of the firm (i.e., what is currently invested). The second part is the present value of all future residual earnings. That is,

$$P_0 = B_0 + \frac{EPS_1 - B_0 \times k}{(1+k)^1} + \frac{EPS_2 - B_1 \times k}{(1+k)^2} + \frac{EPS_3 - B_2 \times k}{(1+k)^3} + \cdots \qquad (6.18)$$

When we developed the constant perpetual growth model for dividend-paying stocks, we made the simplifying assumption that *dividends* grow at a constant rate of g. Here we make the similar assumption that *earnings* grow at a constant rate of g. With this assumption, we can simplify equation (6.18) to:

$$P_0 = B_0 + \frac{EPS_0(1+g) - B_0 \times k}{k-g} \qquad (6.19)$$

residual income model (RIM)
A method for valuing stock in a company that does not pay dividends.

Equation (6.19) is known as the **residual income model**, or **RIM**. If we write both terms in equation (6.19) with a common denominator, we get another way to write the residual income model:

$$P_0 = \frac{EPS_1 - B_0 \times g}{k-g} \qquad (6.20)$$

THE RIM VERSUS THE CONSTANT GROWTH DDM

The RIM is closely related to the constant perpetual growth dividend model. To see the connection, assume that the change in book value per share on a stock is equal to earnings per share minus dividends. This is known as the **clean surplus relationship (CSR)**, written as:

clean surplus relationship (CSR)
An accounting relationship in which earnings minus dividends equals the change in book value per share.

$$EPS_1 - D_1 = B_1 - B_0 \qquad \text{or} \qquad D_1 = EPS_1 + B_0 - B_1$$

Note that in practice the CSR does not exactly hold because various "dirty" surplus changes to book equity are allowed. But it is usually a good approximation, particularly over the long run.

Assuming that earnings and dividends per share grow at rate g, the CSR shows that book value per share must also grow at rate g, so we can write:

$$D_1 = EPS_1 + B_0 - B_1 = EPS_1 + B_0 - B_0(1+g) = EPS_1 - B_0 \times g \qquad (6.21)$$

Plugging the expression for D_1 from equation (6.21) into equation (6.20), we see right away that the residual income model is mathematically the same as the constant perpetual growth model:

$$P_0 = \frac{EPS_1 - B_0 \times g}{k - g} = \frac{D_1}{k - g}$$

So these two approaches are really the same, but the RIM is more flexible because we can apply it to any stock, not just dividend payers.

Although we do not present them, there are other forms of the RIM. For example, a two-stage residual income model incorporates two different periods of growth. Also, the case of nonconstant growth for a number of years followed by constant growth can be handled by another form of the residual income model.

EXAMPLE 6.13

Just Ducky

Shares of Duckwall–ALCO Stores, Inc., trade on the NASDAQ with the ticker symbol DUCK. This company operates as a regional broadline retailer in the central U.S. Currently, DUCK pays no dividends, so we cannot use a dividend discount model. Suppose it is July 1, 2010, and DUCK shares are trading at $10.94. We have the following data:

Share Information	July 1, 2010 (Time 0)
EPS_0	$1.20
Dividends	$0
Book value per share, B_0	$5.886

Assume $g = 9$ percent and $k = 13$ percent. Using the residual income model,

$$P_0 = B_0 + \frac{EPS_0(1 + g) - B_0 \times k}{k - g}$$

$$= \$5.886 + \frac{\$1.20(1.09) - \$5.886 \times .13}{.13 - .09}$$

$$= \$5.886 + \frac{\$1.308 - \$.7652}{.04}$$

$$= \$19.46$$

Verify this price using equation (6.20). Be careful to use g, not $(1 + g)$. Is the market price for DUCK shares too low? If you say yes, what are you assuming about the values for g and k?

EXAMPLE 6.14

The Growth of DUCK

Using the relevant data in Example 6.13 and the residual income model, what growth rate g results in a price of $10.94?

$$P_0 = B_0 + \frac{EPS_0(1 + g) - B_0 \times k}{k - g}$$

$$\$10.94 = 5.886 + \frac{1.20(1 + g) - 5.886 \times .13}{.13 - g}$$

$$\$5.054 \times (.13 - g) = 1.20 + 1.20g - .7652$$

$$\$.6570 - 5.054g = 1.20g + .4348$$

$$.2222 = 6.254g$$

$$g = .0355, \text{ or } 3.55\%$$

6.4a What does the residual income model do that the perpetual constant growth model cannot do?

6.4b What is the critical assumption that makes the residual income model mathematically equal to the perpetual constant growth model?

6.5 The Free Cash Flow Model

The residual income model allows us to value companies that do not pay dividends. But when we used the residual income model, we assumed that the company had positive earnings. Some companies do not pay dividends and have negative earnings. How do we value them? You might think that such companies have little value. Remember that we calculate earnings based on accounting rules that use tax codes. Even though a company has negative earnings, it may have positive cash flows—and a positive value.

The key to understanding how a company can have negative earnings and positive cash flows is how we handle *depreciation*—the writing down of assets. Depreciation reduces earnings, but it impacts cash flow positively because depreciation is counted as an expense. Higher expenses mean lower taxes paid, all else equal. To value companies when we account for depreciation, we turn to a model that examines "free cash flow."

FREE CASH FLOW

Free cash flow (FCF) converts reported earnings into cash flow by adjusting for items that impact earnings and cash flows differently. Formal models can be used to calculate free cash flow (you probably saw some of them in your corporate finance class). Most stock analysts, however, use a relatively simple formula to calculate FCF. Specifically, we define FCF as:

$$\text{FCF} = \text{Net income} + \text{Depreciation} - \text{Capital spending} \quad (6.22)$$

From this equation, you can see how it is possible for a company to have negative earnings (i.e., net income) but have a positive (free) cash flow. Of course, if the company undertakes a large capital expenditure, it can have positive earnings and a negative cash flow.

Most analysts agree that in examining a company's financial performance, cash flow can be more informative than net income. To see why, consider the hypothetical example of two identical companies: Twiddle-Dee Co. and Twiddle-Dum Co. Suppose that both companies have the same constant revenues and expenses in each year over a three-year period. These constant revenues and cash expenses (excluding depreciation) yield the same constant annual cash flows, and they are stated as follows:

	Twiddle-Dee	Twiddle-Dum
Revenues	$5,000	$5,000
Cash expenses	−3,000	−3,000
Cash flow	$2,000	$2,000

Thus, both companies have the same $2,000 cash flow in each of the three years of this hypothetical example.

Next, suppose that both companies incur total depreciation of $3,000 spread out over the three-year period. Standard accounting practices sometimes allow a manager to choose among several depreciation schedules. Twiddle-Dee Co. chooses straight-line depreciation, and Twiddle-Dum Co. chooses accelerated depreciation. These two depreciation schedules are tabulated below:

	Twiddle-Dee	Twiddle-Dum
Year 1	$1,000	$1,500
Year 2	1,000	1,000
Year 3	1,000	500
Total	$3,000	$3,000

Note that total depreciation over the three-year period is the same for both companies. However, Twiddle-Dee Co. has the same $1,000 depreciation in each year, while Twiddle-Dum Co. has accelerated depreciation of $1,500 in the first year, $1,000 in the second year, and $500 depreciation in the third year.

Now, let's look at the resulting annual cash flows and net income figures for the two companies, recalling that in each year, Cash flow = Net income + Depreciation (when capital expenditures = 0):

	Twiddle-Dee		Twiddle-Dum	
	Cash Flow	Net Income	Cash Flow	Net Income
Year 1	$2,000	$1,000	$2,000	$ 500
Year 2	2,000	1,000	2,000	1,000
Year 3	2,000	1,000	2,000	1,500
Total	$6,000	$3,000	$6,000	$3,000

Note that Twiddle-Dum Co.'s net income is lower in the first year and higher in the third year than Twiddle-Dee Co.'s net income. This is purely a result of Twiddle-Dum Co.'s accelerated depreciation schedule, and has nothing to do with Twiddle-Dum Co.'s actual profitability. However, an inexperienced analyst observing Twiddle-Dum Co.'s rapidly rising annual earnings figures might incorrectly label Twiddle-Dum as a growth company. An experienced analyst would observe that there was no cash flow growth to support this naive conclusion.

THE FCF MODEL VERSUS THE CONSTANT GROWTH DDM

A basic finance principle is that the price of an asset should equal the present value of its expected future cash flows. The dividend discount model (DDM) assumed that dividends were the relevant cash flow for equity investors, which is the proper approach. What differs when we look at FCF? Well, as opposed to dividends, which are paid directly to stockholders, FCF could be used to pay off debt holders and stockholders. Thus, when we use the FCF approach, we are valuing the entire company, not just its equity.

You should remember the basic accounting identity: Assets = Liabilities + Equity. With the DDM, we can value equity directly. With FCF, we are actually valuing the overall market value of the company's assets. We can, however, use the FCF approach to value equity, too. The approach has two steps. First we find the value of the company and then we subtract the value of the company's debt. We are left with our estimate of the equity value.

There is another issue to consider. Specifically, when we estimate the required return for the DDM using the CAPM, we use the company's equity beta. If we are valuing the entire company, however, we need to use the "asset" beta.

A beta measures risk. In a later chapter we discuss betas at length, but for now all you need to know about betas is that they measure risk. Asset betas measure the risk of the industry to which the company belongs. Two firms in the same industry should have approximately the same asset betas. Their equity betas, however, could be quite different. Why? Investors can increase portfolio risk by using margin (i.e., borrowing money to buy stock). A business can do the same by using debt in its capital structure. So, when we value the company, we must "convert" reported equity betas into asset betas by adjusting for the amount of leverage being used. The following formula is one way to accomplish this conversion:

$$B_{Equity} = B_{Asset} \times [1 + \frac{Debt}{Equity}(1 - t)] \tag{6.23}$$

Note that when a company has no debt, its equity beta equals its asset beta. Also notice that a higher amount of debt increases the equity beta. This makes sense because stockholders face more risk when the company takes on more debt. All else equal, the cash flows to stockholders are more risky when the company has more debt.

Note that we account for the tax rate, t. We do so because the interest cost on the debt is tax deductible. Because the company can deduct interest as an expense, the government effectively subsidizes part of the cost of debt. This subsidy creates a more stable cash flow associated with debt, thereby reducing risk for the equity holders, all else equal. In an extreme example, the government might return money to a company that has a negative taxable income.

Once we have an estimate of FCF, the growth rate of FCF, and the proper discount rate, we can value the company using, for example, a "DDM" formula. We have "DDM" in quotes because we are using FCF, not dividends, in the formula. Example 6.15 shows you how to value a company using FCF.

EXAMPLE 6.15 | **Free Cash Flow Valuation**

Landon Air is a new airline that flies only a circular route from Indianapolis to Lexington to St. Louis to Indianapolis. Landon Air has a net income of $25 million, depreciation expense of $10 million, and capital expenditures of $3 million. Landon Air has an expected constant growth rate in FCF of 3 percent, and an average tax rate of 35 percent. Assume that Landon Air has a debt-to-equity ratio of .4 (with $100 million of debt); the current equity beta is 1.2; the risk-free rate is 4 percent; and the market risk premium is 7 percent. Landon Air pays no dividends. What is Landon Air's current equity value?

The first step is to calculate Landon Air's asset beta. Using equation (6.23):

$$1.2 = B_{Asset} \times [1 + .4 \times (1 - .35)]$$
$$1.2 = B_{Asset} \times 1.26$$
$$B_{Asset} = .95$$

The next step is to use this beta to calculate Landon Air's required return, which we can still do using the CAPM:[3]

$$k = 4.00 + 7(.95) = 10.65\%$$

Next, we need to know Landon Air's free cash flow, which we can calculate using equation (6.22):

$$FCF = \$25 + 10 - 3 = \$32 \text{ million}$$

Now that we have these values, we can use the constant growth model to find the current value for Landon Air:

$$\text{Firm value} = \frac{\$32 \times (1 + .03)}{.1065 - .03} = \$430.85 \text{ million}$$

If Landon Air has $100 million in debt outstanding, then Landon Air's equity value is $330.85 million. To get the per share equity value, we would then divide this total equity value by the total number of shares outstanding.

---

[3] The required return we get from the CAPM using the asset beta is equivalent to weighted average cost of capital, or WACC.

CHECK THIS

6.5a   How is it possible for a company to have negative earnings but still have positive free cash flow?

6.5b   Why is a firm's equity beta different from its asset beta? When would these two measures of risk be the same?

6.6 Price Ratio Analysis

Price ratios are widely used by financial analysts, more so even than dividend discount models. Of course, all valuation methods try to accomplish the same thing, which is to appraise the economic value of a company's stock. However, analysts readily agree that no single method can adequately handle this task on all occasions. In this section, we therefore examine several of the most popular price ratio methods and provide examples of their use in financial analysis.

PRICE-EARNINGS RATIOS

price-earnings (P/E) ratio
Current stock price divided by annual earnings per share (EPS).

earnings yield (E/P)
Inverse of the P/E ratio: earnings per share divided by price per share.

The most popular price ratio used to assess the value of common stock is a company's **price-earnings ratio**, abbreviated as **P/E ratio**. In fact, as we saw in Chapter 3, P/E ratios are reported in the financial press every day. As we discussed, a price-earnings ratio is calculated as the ratio of a firm's current stock price divided by its annual earnings per share (EPS).

The inverse of a P/E ratio is called an **earnings yield**, and it is measured as earnings per share divided by the current stock price (**E/P**). Clearly, an earnings yield and a price-earnings ratio are simply two ways to measure the same thing. In practice, earnings yields are less commonly stated and used than P/E ratios.

Because most companies report earnings each quarter, annual earnings per share can be calculated either as the most recent quarterly earnings per share times four or as the sum of the last four quarterly earnings per share figures. Most analysts prefer the first method of multiplying the latest quarterly earnings per share value times four. However, some published data sources, including *The Wall Street Journal,* report annual earnings per share as the sum of the last four quarters' figures. The difference is usually small, but it can sometimes be a source of confusion.

growth stocks
A term often used to describe high-P/E stocks.

Financial analysts often refer to high-P/E stocks as **growth stocks**. To see why, notice that a P/E ratio is measured as the *current* stock price over *current* earnings per share. Now, consider two companies with the same current earnings per share, where one company is a high-growth company and the other is a low-growth company. Which company do you think should have a higher stock price, the high-growth company or the low-growth company?

This question is a no-brainer. All else equal, we would be surprised if the high-growth company did not have a higher stock price, and therefore a higher P/E ratio. In general, companies with higher expected earnings growth will have higher P/E ratios, which is why high-P/E stocks are often referred to as growth stocks.

WWW

Visit the Starbucks and GM Web sites at
www.starbucks.com
and
www.gm.com

To give an example, Starbucks Corporation is a specialty coffee retailer with a history of aggressive sales growth. Its stock trades on NASDAQ under the ticker symbol SBUX. In late 2009, SBUX stock traded at $21.78 with earnings per share (EPS) of $.52, and so had a P/E ratio of $21.78/$.52 = 41.88. This P/E ratio is well above the average P/E ratio of about 16.8 for the S&P 500 (of which SBUX is a member). SBUX has never paid a dividend. Instead, Starbucks reinvests all earnings. So far this strategy has been successful, as the firm has grown rapidly.

value stocks
A term often used to describe low-P/E stocks.

The reason high-P/E stocks are called growth stocks seems obvious enough; however, in a seeming defiance of logic, low-P/E stocks are often referred to as **value stocks**. The reason is that low-P/E stocks are often viewed as "cheap" relative to *current* earnings. (Notice again the emphasis on "current.") This suggests that these stocks may represent good investment values, and hence the term value stocks.

In mid-2007, shares of the well-known S&P 500 auto company General Motors (GM) were trading at a price of $31.08. With earnings per share of EPS = $3.75, the P/E ratio was $31.08/$3.75 = 8.29. This was well below the S&P 500 average, and so General Motors might have been considered a value stock. Given its recent bankruptcy, it might not have been such a value after all.

Having said all this, we want to emphasize that the terms "growth stock" and "value stock" are mostly just commonly used labels. Of course, only time will tell whether a high-P/E stock actually turns out to be a high-growth stock, or whether a low-P/E stock is really a good value, as the GM example illustrates.

Although P/E ratios seem quite "easy" to evaluate, you need to be aware that P/E ratios are not that stable. To illustrate, consider a company that has a one-time write-off that significantly reduces earnings. If the write-off is truly a one-time event, then the share price should not be impacted too severely. In this case, the price remains stable but earnings are much lower—resulting in a faux increase in the P/E ratio. An unwary investor might even think that this company is a growth stock. The facts about the write-off, however, do not support this conclusion. What would happen if there was a one-time positive impact on earnings? The lesson: A high or low P/E ratio is not necessarily bad or good.

Because it is difficult to compare companies that have different P/E ratios, investment managers often calculate the PEG ratio. The PEG ratio is calculated by dividing the P/E ratio by the expected earnings growth rate. Although not perfect, the PEG ratio provides investors with a better method to compare companies.

PRICE-CASH FLOW RATIOS

price-cash flow (P/CF) ratio

Current stock price divided by current cash flow per share.

cash flow

In the context of the price-cash flow ratio, usually taken to be net income plus depreciation.

Instead of price-earnings (P/E) ratios, many analysts prefer to look at price-cash flow (P/CF) ratios. A **price-cash flow (P/CF) ratio** is measured as a company's current stock price divided by its current annual **cash flow** per share. Like earnings, cash flow is normally reported quarterly and most analysts multiply the last quarterly cash flow figure by four to obtain annual cash flow. Again, like earnings, many published data sources report annual cash flow as a sum of the latest four quarterly cash flows.

Financial analysts typically use both price-earnings ratios and price-cash flow ratios. They point out that when a company's earnings per share is not significantly larger than its cash flow per share (CFPS), this is a signal, at least potentially, of good-quality earnings. The term "quality" means that the accounting earnings mostly reflect actual cash flow, not just accounting numbers. When earnings are bigger than cash flow, this may be a signal of poor quality earnings.

Going back to some of our earlier examples, Starbucks Corporation had cash flow per share of CFPS = $1.87, yielding a P/CF ratio of $21.78/$1.87 = 11.65. Notice that cash flow per share was roughly triple earnings per share of $.52, suggesting high-quality earnings.

PRICE-SALES RATIOS

price-sales (P/S) ratio

Current stock price divided by annual sales per share.

An alternative view of a company's performance is provided by its **price-sales (P/S) ratio**. A price-sales ratio is calculated as the current price of a company's stock divided by its current annual sales revenue per share. A price-sales ratio focuses on a company's ability to generate sales growth. Essentially, a high P/S ratio would suggest high sales growth, while a low P/S ratio might indicate sluggish sales growth.

For example, Starbucks Corporation had sales per share of $13.15 to yield a price-sales ratio of P/S = $21.78/$13.15 = 1.66. We should note that there can be a large variation in price-sales ratios for two companies, particularly if they are in very different kinds of businesses. Security analysts recognize that price-sales ratios cannot be compared in isolation from other important information.

PRICE-BOOK RATIOS

price-book (P/B) ratio

Market value of a company's common stock divided by its book (or accounting) value of equity.

A very basic price ratio for a company is its **price-book (P/B) ratio**, sometimes called the market-book ratio. A price-book ratio is measured as the market value of a company's outstanding common stock divided by its book value of equity.

TABLE 6.1	Price Ratio Analysis for Intel Corporation (INTC) Late 2009 Stock Price: $19.40		
	Earnings	**Cash Flow**	**Sales**
Five-year average price ratio	20.96 (P/E)	10.85 (P/CF)	3.14 (P/S)
Current value per share	$ .92 (EPS)	$ 1.74 (CFPS)	$ 6.76 (SPS)
Growth rate	8.5%	7.5%	7.0%
Expected stock price	$20.92	$20.29	$22.71

Price-book ratios are appealing because book values represent, in principle, historical cost. The stock price is an indicator of current value, so a price-book ratio simply measures what the equity is worth today relative to what it cost. A ratio bigger than 1.0 indicates that the firm has been successful in creating value for its stockholders. A ratio smaller than 1.0 indicates that the company is actually worth less than it cost.

This interpretation of the price-book ratio seems simple enough, but the truth is that because of varied and changing accounting standards, book values are difficult to interpret. For this and other reasons, price-book ratios may not have as much information value as they once did.

APPLICATIONS OF PRICE RATIO ANALYSIS

Check out the Intel Web site at
www.intel.com

Price-earnings ratios, price-cash flow ratios, and price-sales ratios are commonly used to calculate estimates of expected future stock prices. This is done by multiplying a historical average price ratio by an expected future value for the price-ratio denominator variable. For example, Table 6.1 summarizes such a price ratio analysis for Intel Corporation (INTC) based on late 2009 information.

In Table 6.1, the five-year average ratio row contains five-year average P/E, P/CF, and P/S ratios. The current value row contains values for earnings per share, cash flow per share, and sales per share; and the growth rate row contains five-year projected growth rates for EPS, CFPS, and SPS.

The expected price row contains expected stock prices one year hence. The basic idea is this. Because Intel had an average P/E ratio of 20.96, we will assume that Intel's stock price will be 20.96 times its earnings per share one year from now. To estimate Intel's earnings one year from now, we note that Intel's earnings are projected to grow at a rate of 8.5 percent per year. If earnings continue to grow at this rate, next year's earnings will be equal to this year's earnings times 1.085. Putting it all together, we have

$$\begin{aligned}
\text{Expected price} &= \text{Historical P/E ratio} \times \text{Projected EPS} \\
&= \text{Historical P/E ratio} \times \text{Current EPS} \\
&\quad \times (1 + \text{Projected EPS growth rate}) \\
&= 20.96 \times \$.92 \times 1.085 \\
&= \$20.92
\end{aligned}$$

The same procedure is used to calculate an expected price based on cash flow per share:

$$\begin{aligned}
\text{Expected price} &= \text{Historical P/CF ratio} \times \text{Projected CFPS} \\
&= \text{Historical P/CF ratio} \times \text{Current CFPS} \\
&\quad \times (1 + \text{Projected CFPS growth rate}) \\
&= 10.85 \times \$1.74 \times 1.075 \\
&= \$20.29
\end{aligned}$$

Finally, an expected price based on sales per share is calculated as

$$\begin{aligned}
\text{Expected price} &= \text{Historical P/S ratio} \times \text{Projected SPS} \\
&= \text{Historical P/S ratio} \times \text{Current SPS} \\
&\quad \times (1 + \text{Projected SPS growth rate}) \\
&= 3.14 \times \$6.76 \times 1.07 \\
&= \$22.71
\end{aligned}$$

	Earnings	Cash Flow	Sales
Five-year average price ratio	19.5 (P/E)	10.42 (P/CF)	1.47 (P/S)
Current value per share	$ 2.26 (EPS)	$ 2.39 (CFPS)	$20.76 (SPS)
Growth rate	12.0%	10.5%	8.0%
Expected stock price	$49.36	$27.52	$32.96

See Mickey's Web site at
www.disney.go.com

Notice that in the case of Intel, the price ratio methods yield prices ranging from about $20 to about $23. However, when this analysis was made in late 2009 Intel's stock price was around $19.40. This difference may be explained by the fact that price ratios for Intel have fallen sharply in recent years. For example, Intel's P/E ratio fell from a high of 45.8 in 2002 to just 26.3 in 2009. With such a large price-ratio decline, a historical average price ratio may be inaccurate.

EXAMPLE 6.16

Going to Disneyland

Table 6.2 contains information about Walt Disney Corporation. Calculate expected share prices using each of the three price ratio approaches we have discussed.

For example, using the P/E approach, we come up with the following estimates of the price of Walt Disney stock in one year:

$$\text{Expected price} = \text{Historical P/E ratio} \times \text{Current EPS} \times (1 + \text{Projected EPS growth})$$

$$= 19.5 \times \$2.26 \times 1.120$$

$$= \$49.36$$

CHECK THIS

6.6a   Why are high-P/E stocks sometimes called growth stocks?

6.6b   Why might an analyst prefer a price-cash flow ratio to a price-earnings ratio?

6.7 An Analysis of the McGraw-Hill Company

Stock market investors have available to them many sources of information about the financial performance of companies with publicly traded stock shares. Indeed, the sheer volume of information available can often be overwhelming. For this reason, several sources publish reference summaries for individual companies.

One well-known example is the *Value Line Investment Survey*, a published reference with frequent updates. *Value Line* provides what many serious investors consider to be the best one-page company summaries available. Current updates to the *Value Line Investment Survey* are available at most stock brokerage offices and many public libraries. In addition, these updates are available (to subscribers) as PDF files on *Value Line*'s Web site. Figure 6.3 presents a one-page summary for the McGraw-Hill Company published by *Value Line* in November 2009. We will make frequent reference to information found in the *Value Line* summary in the discussion of McGraw-Hill.

As shown in the title bar of Figure 6.3, McGraw-Hill stock trades on the New York Stock Exchange (NYSE) under the ticker symbol MHP. When this survey went to press in November 2009, McGraw-Hill's stock price was $28.73, with a P/E ratio of 12.2. *Value Line* calculates a P/E ratio as the most recent stock price divided by the latest six months' earnings

Visit the McGraw-Hill Web site at
www.mcgraw-hill.com

FIGURE 6.3 *Value Line* Analysis Chart

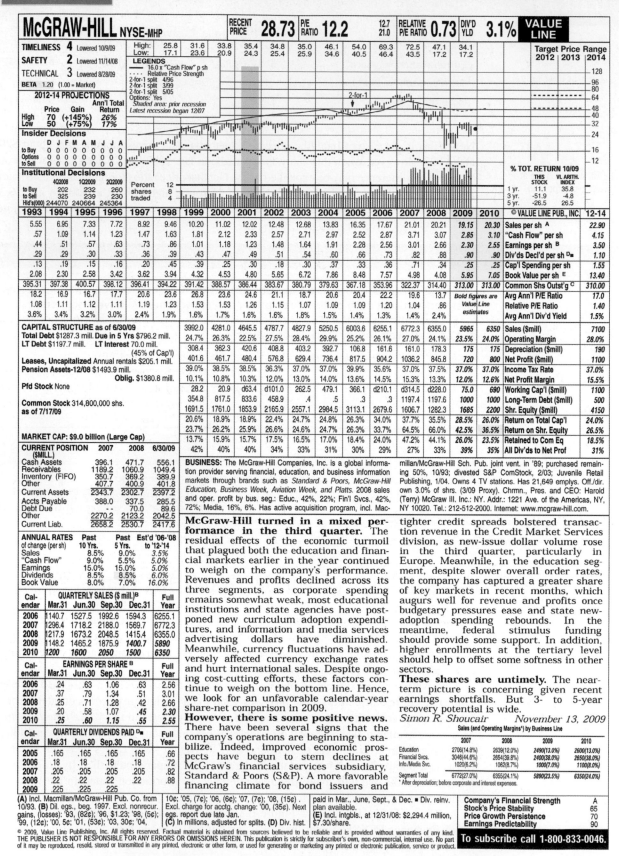

per share plus earnings per share estimated for the next six months. McGraw-Hill's relative P/E ratio of .73 is obtained by dividing its current P/E by the median P/E ratio of all stocks under review by *Value Line*. The dividend yield of 3.1 percent is calculated by dividing estimated dividends for the coming year by the current stock price.

At this point, as you look over *Value Line*'s summary in Figure 6.3, you will realize that *Value Line* has packed a considerable amount of information onto a single page. Because there is so much information on the one-page *Value Line* survey, we can cover only some of the items on the page. Most items are well-explained in Figure 6.4, which contains a complete sample explanation page. However, some items in Figure 6.3 may differ from those in Figure 6.4 reflecting changes made by *Value Line*. In the following discussion, we refer only to information needed to illustrate the analytic methods discussed previously in this chapter.

Check out Value Line's
Web site at
www.valueline.com

USING THE DIVIDEND DISCOUNT MODEL

Our first task is to estimate a discount rate for McGraw-Hill. The *Value Line Investment Survey* reports a beta of 1.20 for McGraw-Hill stock. Using a Treasury bill rate of 4.0 percent and a historical stock market risk premium of 7 percent, we obtain a CAPM discount rate estimate for McGraw-Hill of $4.0\% + 1.20 \times 7\% = 12.4\%$.

Our next task is to calculate a sustainable growth rate. *Value Line* reports projected 2010 earnings per share of $2.55 and projected 2010 dividends per share of $.90, implying a retention ratio of $1 - \$.90/\$2.55 = .65$. *Value Line* also reports a projected 2010 return on equity of ROE = 36.5 percent (reported as "Return on Shr. Equity"). Putting these together yields a sustainable growth rate of $.65 \times 36.5\% = 23.73\%$, which may be somewhat high for a mature company like McGraw-Hill.

Finally, with a discount rate and sustainable growth rate we can calculate a share price for McGraw-Hill. Using a constant dividend growth rate model with the 2009 dividend of $D_0 = \$.90$, a discount rate of $k = 12.4$ percent, and a growth rate of 23.73 percent, we get:

$$P_0 = \frac{\$.90 \times 1.2373}{.124 - .2373}$$

$$= \$-9.83$$

which cannot be. The negative price is due to a growth rate greater than the discount rate, indicating we cannot use the constant dividend growth rate model. As a good analyst would, we'll try something else.

USING THE RESIDUAL INCOME MODEL

In reality, a sustainable growth rate of over 23 percent is not feasible. *Value Line* reports that the actual dividend growth rate over the previous five years was 8.5 percent (from the box labeled "Annual Rates"). You can audit this number by calculating a simple or geometric average dividend growth rate using dividends per share from 2004 through 2009.

Let's assume that "today" is January 1, 2010. Also, let's keep the 8.5 percent growth rate and 12.4 percent discount rate. From the *Value Line Investment Survey* (VL), we can fill in columns two and three of the table below:

		Forecast	
	End-of-Year 2009 (time 0)	2010 (VL)	2010 (CSR)
Beginning BV per share	NA	$5.95	$5.95
EPS	$2.30	$2.55	$2.4955*
DIV	$ .90	$ .90	$1.9897**
Ending BV per share	$5.95	$7.05	$6.4558*

* 2.30 × 1.085; 5.95 × 1.085.
** 2.4955 − (6.4558 − 5.95).

FIGURE 6.4 *Value Line* Analysis Chart

The Legends box contains the "cash flow" multiple, the amounts and dates of recent stock splits and an indication if options on the stock are traded.

Monthly price ranges of the stock— plotted on a ratio (logarithmic) grid to show percentage changes in true proportion. For example, a ratio chart equalizes the move of a $10 stock that rises to $11 with that of a $100 stock that rises to $110. Both have advanced 10% and over the same space on a ratio grid.

The "cash flow" line— reported earnings plus depreciation ("cash flow") multiplied by a number selected to correlate the stock's 3- to 5-year projected target price, with "cash flow" projected out to 2004.

Recent price— see page 2 of the *Summary & Index* for the date, just under "Index to Stocks."

P/E ratio— the recent price divided by the latest six months' earnings per share plus earnings estimated for the next six months.

Trailing and median P/E— the first is the recent price divided by the sum of reported earnings for the past 4 quarters; the second is an average of the price/earnings ratios over the past 10 years.

Value Line's Ranks— the rank for Timeliness; the rank for Safety; the Technical rank. Beta, the stock's sensitivity to fluctuations of the market as a whole, is included in this box but is not a rank. (*See Glossary for Industry rank.*)

Relative P/E ratio— the stock's current P/E divided by the median P/E for all stocks under Value Line review.

The projected stock price in 2006-08. Also, the total expected % gain/loss before dividends and the Annual Total Return (% including dividends).

Dividend yield— cash dividends estimated to be declared in the next 12 months divided by the recent price.

The record of insider decisions— the number of times officers and directors bought or sold stock or exercised options during the past nine months.

The stock's highest and lowest price of the year.

Target Price Range— the range in which a stock price is likely to trade in the years 2006-08. Also shown in the "Projections" box on the left.

Stock purchases/sales by institutions— the number of times institutions with more than $100 million of assets under management bought or sold stock during the past three quarters and the total number of shares held by those institutions at the end of each quarter.

Relative Price Strength describes the stock's past price performance relative to the Value Line Arithmetic Composite Average of approximately 1,700 stocks. (A rising line indicates the stock price has been rising more than the Value Line universe.)

Statistical Array— historical financial data appears in regular type.

The % Total Return shows the price appreciation and dividends of a stock and the Value Line Arithmetic Composite Index for the past 1, 3, and 5 years.

The capital structure as of the indicated recent date showing, among other things, the $ amount and % of capital in long-term debt and preferred stock. We also show the number of times that interest charges were earned.

Statistical Array— Value Line estimates appearing in the area on the right side are in *bold italics*.

Current position— total current assets and total current liabilities, and their detail.

The percent of shares traded monthly— the number of shares traded each month as a % of the total outstanding.

Annual rates of change (on a compound per-share basis). Actual for each of the past 5 and 10 years, estimated for the next 3 to 5 years.

Business Data— a brief description of the company's business and major products along, with other important data.

Quarterly sales are shown on a gross basis. Quarterly earnings on a per-share basis (estimates in bold type).

Analyst's Commentary— an approximately 350-word report on recent developments and prospects—issued every three months on a preset schedule.

Quarterly dividends paid are actual payments. The total of dividends paid in four quarters may not equal the figure shown in the annual series on dividends declared in the Statistical Array. (Sometimes a dividend declared at the end of the year will be paid in the first quarter of the following year.)

Footnotes explain a number of things, such as the way earnings are reported, whether basic or diluted.

Value Line's Indexes of Financial Strength, Stock's Price Stability, Price Growth Persistence, and Earnings Predictability. (*See Glossary for definitions.*)

The expected date of receipt by subscribers. *The Survey* is mailed on a schedule that aims for delivery to every subscriber on Friday afternoon.

Source: *Value Line,* "How to Invest in Common Stocks: A Guide to Using the Value Line Investment Survey," 2007.

The fourth column comes from using the clean surplus relationship (CSR). Here, we grow EPS and book value per share using a growth rate of 8.5 percent. Then we calculate the dividend "plug" that makes the change in book value equal to EPS minus dividends.

Now we can estimate two prices for McGraw-Hill shares using the RIM—one from data provided by *Value Line* and one from data using the clean surplus relationship. In addition, we can compare these values using a constant dividend growth rate model that uses a dividend growth rate of 8.5 percent. Using the RIM, we get:

$$P_0 = 5.95 + \frac{2.4955 - 5.95 \times .124}{.124 - .085} = \$51.02 \quad \text{(CSR)}$$

$$P_0 = 5.95 + \frac{2.55 - (7.05 - 5.95)}{.124 - .085} = \$43.13 \quad \text{(VL)}$$

Using the DDM, we get:

$$P_0 = \frac{1.9897}{.124 - .085} = \$51.02 \quad \text{(CSR)}$$

$$P_0 = \frac{.90}{.124 - .085} = \$23.08 \quad \text{(VL)}$$

The $.90 used is *Value Line*'s estimate of next year's dividend, D_1, because *Value Line* forecasts no dividend growth between 2009 and 2010. As you would expect, both the RIM and the DDM indicate a price of $51.02 for McGraw-Hill when we use the CSR. This share value is much higher than McGraw-Hill's recently reported stock price of $28.73. RIM and DDM prices using data from *Value Line* differ, however, because of "dirty surplus."

USING PRICE RATIO ANALYSIS

Value Line reports annual growth rates for sales, cash flow, earnings, dividends, and book values in the box labeled "Annual Rates." These include historical five-year and ten-year growth rates, along with expected growth rates for the next three to five years. We will estimate expected future stock prices using five-year average price ratios that we will calculate along with expected growth rates supplied by *Value Line*.

The *Value Line* survey reports annual average price-earnings ratios, but it does not report average price to cash flow per share ratios, P/CF, or average price to sales per share ratios, P/S. In this case, because all these numbers are on a per-share basis, a quick way to calculate an average P/CF ratio is to multiply an average P/E ratio by the ratio of earnings per share to cash flow per share. That is, P/CFPS = P/E × EPS/CFPS (recall that the "E" in P/E stands for EPS, so they cancel).

For example, McGraw-Hill's 2008 average P/E was 13.70, EPS was $2.66, CFPS was $3.07, and SPS was $20.21. Thus, a quick calculation of McGraw-Hill's 2008 average P/CF ratio is 13.70 × 2.66/3.07 = 11.87. Similarly, the average P/S ratio, (P/EPS) × (EPS/SPS), is 13.70 × $2.66/$20.21 = 1.80. In Table 6.3, we provide average price ratio calculations for P/CF and P/S ratios for the years 2004 through 2008, along with five-year averages for each price ratio.

We use the five-year average price ratios calculated in Table 6.3 in the price ratio analysis presented in Table 6.4. We use the expected growth rates for earnings, cash flow, and

TABLE 6.3	Price Ratio Calculations for McGraw-Hill Co. (MHP)					
	2004	**2005**	**2006**	**2007**	**2008**	**Average**
P/E	20.60	20.40	22.20	19.60	13.70	19.30
EPS	1.91	2.28	2.56	3.01	2.66	2.48
CFPS	2.97	2.52	2.87	3.71	3.07	3.03
SPS	13.83	16.35	17.67	20.01	20.21	17.61
P/CF	13.25	18.46	19.80	15.90	11.87	15.86
P/S	2.84	2.84	3.22	2.95	1.80	2.73

TABLE 6.4

Price Ratio Analysis for McGraw-Hill Co. (MHP) November 2009 Stock Price: $28.73

	Earnings	Cash Flow	Sales
Five-year average price ratio	19.30 (P/E)	15.86 (P/CF)	2.73 (P/S)
Current value per share, 2008	$ 2.66 (EPS)	$ 3.07 (CFPS)	$20.21 (SPS)
Growth rate	5.00%	5.00%	3.50%
Expected share price	$53.90	$51.12	$57.10

sales provided by *Value Line* (from the "Annual Rates" box) to calculate expected share prices for McGraw-Hill *one year from now*. For ease, we restate the three formulas used to calculate expected prices below. As an exercise, you should verify the expected share prices in Table 6.4.

$$\text{Expected share price} = \text{P/E ratio} \times \text{EPS} \times (1 + \text{EPS growth rate})$$

$$\text{Expected share price} = \text{P/CF ratio} \times \text{CFPS} \times (1 + \text{CFPS growth rate})$$

$$\text{Expected share price} = \text{P/S ratio} \times \text{SPS} \times (1 + \text{SPS growth rate})$$

We can now summarize our analysis by listing the stock prices obtained by the different ways we have described in this chapter, along with the model used to derive them.

DDM, with calculated sustainable growth rate:	Not defined
DDM, historical growth rate, *Value Line* input:	$23.08
DDM, historical growth rate, CSR:	$51.02
RIM, historical growth rate, *Value Line* input:	$43.13
RIM, historical growth rate, CSR:	$51.02
Price-earnings model:	$53.90
Price-cash flow model:	$51.12
Price-sales model:	$57.10

Notice the wide range of share values we obtained by our various ways. This is not uncommon in security analysis, and it suggests how daunting a task security analysis sometimes can be. In this case, the DDM (*Value Line* historical growth) yields the closest value to the observed stock price of $28.73. The goal is not to find a model that yields a value closest to the current price. Rather, the goal is to find a model about which we are confident. For example, suppose you believe the DDM is the most appropriate model and that the inputs from *Value Line* are the most accurate. If so, then you might conclude that McGraw-Hill shares are somewhat overpriced. If you look across other valuation methods, however, you would come to the opposite conclusion. What is the lesson? A fair amount of subjectivity is entailed in the valuation process, even though we can look at financial data objectively.

CHECK THIS

6.7a Locate *Value Line*'s projected growth rate in dividends. How does it compare to the sustainable growth rate we estimated? The historical growth rates? Revalue the stock using the constant perpetual dividend model and this growth rate.

6.7b Assume that the sustainable growth rate we calculated is the growth rate for the next five years only and that dividends will grow thereafter at the rate projected by *Value Line* analysts. Using these growth rates, revalue the stock using the two-stage dividend growth model.

6.8 Summary and Conclusions

In this chapter, we examined several methods of fundamental analysis used by financial analysts to value common stocks. The methods we examined are the learning objectives for the chapter. We illustrated many of these methods with a detailed analysis of the McGraw-Hill Company.

1. **The Basic Dividend Discount Model.**

   A. Dividend discount models value common stock as the sum of all expected future dividend payments, where the dividends are adjusted for risk and the time value of money.
   B. The dividend discount model is often simplified by assuming that dividends will grow at a constant growth rate. A particularly simple form of the dividend discount model is the case in which dividends grow at a constant perpetual growth rate. The simplicity of the constant perpetual growth model makes it the most popular dividend discount model. However, it should be applied only to companies with stable earnings and dividend growth.
   C. Dividend models require an estimate of future growth. We described the sustainable growth rate, which is measured as a firm's return on equity times its retention ratio, and illustrated its use.

2. **The Two-Stage Dividend Growth Model.**

   A. Companies often experience temporary periods of unusually high or low growth, where growth eventually converges to an industry average. In such cases, analysts frequently use a two-stage dividend growth model.
   B. The two-stage growth model can be used with two separate growth rates for two distinct time periods, or with growth rates that linearly converge toward the constant growth rate. This latter case is referred to as the H-model.
   C. The two-stage growth model can be used where there is a period with nonconstant dividend growth and a period of constant dividend growth.

3. **The Residual Income and Free Cash Flow Models.**

   A. The difference between actual and required earnings in any period is called residual income. Residual income is sometimes called Economic Value Added.
   B. The residual income model is a method that can be used to value a share of stock in a company that does not pay dividends. To derive the residual income model, a series of constant growth assumptions are made for EPS, assets, liabilities, and equity. Together, these growth assumptions result in a sustainable growth rate.
   C. The clean surplus relationship is an accounting relationship that says earnings minus dividends equals the change in book value per share. The clean surplus relationship might not hold in actual practice. But if the clean surplus relationship is true, then the residual income model is mathematically equivalent to the constant perpetual growth model.
   D. The free cash flow (FCF) model values the entire firm by concentrating on FCF, which is defined as net income plus depreciation minus capital spending.
   E. Because the FCF model values the whole firm, we must use an asset beta, rather than an equity beta.

4. **Price Ratio Analysis.**

   A. Price ratios are widely used by financial analysts. The most popular price ratio is a company's price-earnings ratio. A P/E ratio is calculated as the ratio of a firm's stock price divided by its earnings per share (EPS).
   B. Financial analysts often refer to high-P/E stocks as growth stocks and low-P/E stocks as value stocks. In general, companies with high expected earnings growth will have high P/E ratios, which is why high-P/E stocks are referred to as growth stocks. Low-P/E stocks are referred to as value stocks because they are viewed as cheap relative to current earnings.

C. Instead of price-earnings ratios, many analysts prefer to look at price-cash flow (P/CF) ratios. A price-cash flow ratio is measured as a company's stock price divided by its cash flow per share. Most analysts agree that cash flow can provide more information than net income about a company's financial performance.

D. An alternative view of a company's performance is provided by its price-sales (P/S) ratio. A price-sales ratio is calculated as the price of a company's stock divided by its annual sales revenue per share. A price-sales ratio focuses on a company's ability to generate sales growth. A high P/S ratio suggests high sales growth, while a low P/S ratio suggests low sales growth.

E. A basic price ratio for a company is its price-book (P/B) ratio. A price-book ratio is measured as the market value of a company's outstanding common stock divided by its book value of equity. A high P/B ratio suggests that a company is potentially expensive, while a low P/B value suggests that a company may be cheap.

F. A common procedure using price-earnings ratios, price-cash flow ratios, and price-sales ratios is to calculate estimates of expected future stock prices. However, each price ratio method yields a different expected future stock price. Because each method uses different information, each makes a different prediction.

GET REAL

This chapter introduced you to some of the basics of common stock valuation and fundamental analysis. It focused on three important tools used by stock analysts in the real world to assess whether a particular stock is "rich" or "cheap": dividend discount models, residual income models, free cash flow models, and price ratio analysis. How should you, as an investor or investment manager, put this information to use?

The answer is that you need to pick some stocks and get to work! As we discussed in the chapter, experience and judgment are needed to use these models, and the only way to obtain these is through practice. Try to identify a few stocks that look cheap and buy them in a simulated brokerage account such as Stock-Trak. At the same time, find a few that look rich and short them. Start studying P/E ratios. Scan *The Wall Street Journal* (or a similar source of market information) and look at the range of P/Es. What's a low P/E? What's a high one? Do they really correspond to what you would call growth and value stocks?

The Internet is a copious source for information on valuing companies. Try, for example, Stock Sheet (www.stocksheet.com), Market Watch (www.marketwatch .com), Hoovers Online (www.hoovers.com), and Zacks (www.zacks.com). Don't forget to check out the Motley Fool (www.fool.com).

Several trade associations have informative Web sites that can be helpful. For individual investors there is the American Association of Individual Investors (www.aaii .com) and for professional security analysts there is the New York Society of Security Analysts (www.nyssa.org). The CFA Institute (www.cfainstitute.org) provides a financial analyst's certification that is highly respected among security analysts.

Key Terms

arithmetic average dividend growth rate 185
beta 196
cash flow 203
clean surplus relationship (CSR) 197

constant perpetual growth model 183
dividend discount model (DDM) 182
earnings yield (E/P) 202
Economic Value Added (EVA) 197

Chapter Review Problems and Self-Test

1. **The Perpetual Growth Model (CFA1)**   Suppose dividends for Layton's Pizza Company are projected to grow at 6 percent forever. If the discount rate is 16 percent and the current dividend is $2, what is the value of the stock?

2. **The Two-Stage Growth Model (CFA3)**   Suppose the Titanic Ice Cube Co.'s dividend grows at a 20 percent rate for the next three years. Thereafter, it grows at a 12 percent rate. What value would we place on Titanic assuming a 15 percent discount rate? Titanic's most recent dividend was $3.

3. **Residual Income Model (CFA10)**   Suppose Al's Infrared Sandwich Company has a current book value of $10.85 per share. The most recent earnings per share were $2.96, and earnings are expected to grow at 6 percent forever. The appropriate discount rate is 8.2 percent. Assume the clean surplus relationship is true. Assuming the company maintains a constant retention ratio, what is the value of the company according to the residual income model if there are no dividends?

4. **Price Ratio Analysis (CFA3)**   The table below contains some information about the Jordan Air Co. Provide expected share prices using each of the three price ratio approaches we have discussed.

Price Ratio Analysis For Jordan Air (Current Stock Price: $40)

	Earnings	Cash Flow	Sales
Five-year average price ratio	25 (P/E)	7 (P/CF)	1.5 (P/S)
Current value per share	$2.00 (EPS)	$6.00 (CFPS)	$30.00 (SPS)
Growth rate	10%	16%	14%

Answers to Self-Test Problems

1. Plugging the relevant numbers into the constant perpetual growth formula results in:

$$P_0 = \frac{\$2(1.06)}{.16 - .06} = \$21.20$$

As shown, the stock should sell for $21.20.

2. Plugging all the relevant numbers into the two-stage formula gets us:

$$P_0 = \frac{\$3(1.20)}{.15 - .20}\left[1 - \left(\frac{1.20}{1.15}\right)^3\right] + \left(\frac{1.20}{1.15}\right)^3 \frac{\$3(1.12)}{.15 - .12}$$

$$= \$9.81 + \$127.25$$

$$= \$137.06$$

Thus, the stock should sell for about $137.

3. Recall the formula for the residual income model when the clean surplus relationship is true:

$$P_0 = B_0 + \frac{EPS_0(1 + g) - B_0 \times k}{k - g}$$

www.mhhe.com/jmd6e

Next, make a table of all the information that you need to put into the formula:

Al's Infrared Sandwich Company	Time 0, i.e., Now
Beginning book value, B_0	$10.85
Earnings per share, EPS_0	$ 2.96
Growth rate, g	6%
Discount rate, k	8.2%

We can now solve the problem.

$$P_0 = \$10.85 + \frac{\$2.96(1 + .06) - \$10.85 \times .082}{.082 - .06}$$

$$P_0 = \$113.03$$

4. Using the P/E approach, we come up with the following estimate of the price of Jordan Air in one year:

$$\text{Estimated price} = \text{Average P/E} \times \text{Current EPS} \times (1 + \text{Growth rate})$$

$$= 25 \times \$2 \times 1.10$$

$$= \$55$$

Using the P/CF approach, we get:

$$\text{Estimated price} = \text{Average P/CF} \times \text{Current CFPS} \times (1 + \text{Growth rate})$$

$$= 7 \times \$6 \times 1.16$$

$$= \$48.72$$

Finally, using the P/S approach, we get:

$$\text{Estimated price} = \text{Average P/S} \times \text{Current SPS} \times (1 + \text{Growth rate})$$

$$= 1.5 \times \$30 \times 1.14$$

$$= \$51.30$$

Test Your Investment Quotient

1. **Sustainable Growth (LO1, CFA7)**   A company has a return on equity of ROE = 20 percent, and from earnings per share of EPS = $5, it pays a $2 dividend. What is the company's sustainable growth rate?

   a. 8 percent
   b. 10 percent
   c. 12 percent
   d. 20 percent

2. **Sustainable Growth (LO1, CFA7)**   If the return on equity for a firm is 15 percent and the retention ratio is 40 percent, the sustainable growth rate of earnings and dividends is which of the following?

   a. 6 percent
   b. 9 percent
   c. 15 percent
   d. 40 percent

3. **Dividend Discount Model (LO1, CFA3)**   A common stock pays an annual dividend per share of $2.10. The risk-free rate is 7 percent and the risk premium for this stock is 4 percent. If the annual dividend is expected to remain at $2.10, the value of the stock is closest to:

   a. $19.09
   b. $30.00
   c. $52.50
   d. $70.00

4. **Dividend Discount Model (LO1, CFA3)** The constant growth dividend discount model will not produce a finite value if the dividend growth rate is which of the following?

   a. Above its historical average.
   b. Above the required rate of return.
   c. Below its historical average.
   d. Below the required rate of return.

5. **Dividend Discount Model (LO1, CFA3)** In applying the constant growth dividend discount model, a stock's intrinsic value will do which of the following when the required rate of return is lowered?

   a. Decrease.
   b. Increase.
   c. Remain unchanged.
   d. Decrease or increase, depending on other factors.

6. **Dividend Discount Model (LO1, CFA3)** The constant growth dividend discount model would typically be most appropriate for valuing the stock of which of the following?

   a. New venture expected to retain all earnings for several years.
   b. Rapidly growing company.
   c. Moderate growth, mature company.
   d. Company with valuable assets not yet generating profits.

7. **Dividend Discount Model (LO1, CFA7)** A stock has a required return of 15 percent, a constant growth rate of 10 percent, and a dividend payout ratio of 50 percent. What should the stock's P/E ratio be?

   a. 3.0
   b. 4.5
   c. 9.0
   d. 11.0

8. **Dividend Discount Model (LO1, CFA7)** Which of the following assumptions does the constant growth dividend discount model require?

   I. Dividends grow at a constant rate.
   II. The dividend growth rate continues indefinitely.
   III. The required rate of return is less than the dividend growth rate.

   a. I only
   b. III only
   c. I and II only
   d. I, II, and III

9. **Dividend Discount Model (LO2, CFA3)** A stock will not pay dividends until three years from now. The dividend then will be $2.00 per share, the dividend payout ratio will be 40 percent, and return on equity will be 15 percent. If the required rate of return is 12 percent, which of the following is closest to the value of the stock?

   a. $27
   b. $33
   c. $53
   d. $67

10. **Dividend Discount Model (LO1, CFA3)** Assume that at the end of the next year, Company A will pay a $2.00 dividend per share, an increase from the current dividend of $1.50 per share. After that, the dividend is expected to increase at a constant rate of 5 percent. If you require a 12 percent return on the stock, what is the value of the stock?

    a. $28.57
    b. $28.79
    c. $30.00
    d. $31.78

11. **Dividend Discount Model (LO1, CFA7)** A share of stock will pay a dividend of $1.00 one year from now, with dividend growth of 5 percent thereafter. In the context of a dividend discount model, the stock is correctly priced at $10 today. According to the constant dividend growth model, if the required return is 15 percent, what should the value of the stock be two years from now?

    a. $11.03
    b. $12.10

    c. $13.23

    d. $14.40

12. **Free Cash Flow (LO3, CFA7)** A firm has net income of $230 million. Included in this net income is a depreciation expense of $52 million. In addition, the firm had $42 million of capital expenditures. The firm's FCF is closest (in millions) to:

    a. $282

    b. $188

    c. $218

    d. $240

13. **Free Cash Flow (LO3, CFA7)** A firm had a free cash flow (FCF) in the prior year of $125 million. The FCF is expected to grow at 3 percent per year into perpetuity. The appropriate discount rate is 12 percent. What is the firm's current value (in millions) based on the FCF model?

    a. $1,042

    b. $1,389

    c. $1,555

    d. $1,431

14. **Price Ratios (LO4, CFA5)** Two similar companies acquire substantial new production facilities, which they both will depreciate over a 10-year period. However, Company A uses accelerated depreciation while Company B uses straight-line depreciation. In the first year that the assets are depreciated, which of the following is most likely to occur?

    a. A's P/CF ratio will be higher than B's.

    b. A's P/CF ratio will be lower than B's.

    c. A's P/E ratio will be higher than B's.

    d. A's P/E ratio will be lower than B's.

15. **Price Ratios (LO4, CFA3)** An analyst estimates the earnings per share and price-to-earnings ratio for a stock market series to be $43.50 and 26 times, respectively. The dividend payout ratio for the series is 65 percent. The value of the stock market series is closest to

    a. 396

    b. 735

    c. 1,131

    d. 1,866

16. **P/E Ratio (LO4, CFA5)** An analyst gathered the following information about a stock market index:

Required rate of return:	16%
Expected dividend payout ratio:	30%
Expected return on equity investment:	20%

    The expected price-earnings (P/E) ratio of the index is closest to

    a. 3.5

    b. 7.0

    c. 15.0

    d. 35.00

17. **P/E Ratio (LO3, CFA5)** A company's return on equity is greater than its required return on equity. The earnings multiplier (P/E) for that company's stock is most likely to be positively related to the

    a. Risk-free rate.

    b. Market risk premium.

    c. Earnings retention ratio.

    d. Stock's capital asset pricing model beta.

18. **Residual Income Model (LO4, CFA10)** The residual income model separates the value of the firm into two basic components. What are these two components?

    a. The current book value and the present value of future earnings.

    b. The value of earnings per share and the value of cash flow per share.

    c. The current value of the firm's shares and the future value of its shares.

    d. The time value of money and the value of bearing risk.

19. **Residual Income (LO4, CFA10)** Residual income is
   a. The actual earnings less expected earnings.
   b. Any increase in the value of the firm.
   c. The value of profitable investment projects.
   d. The value added by economical use of assets.

20. **Clean Surplus Relation (LO4, CFA10)** The clean surplus relation says that
   a. Assets minus liabilities minus shareholder's equity equals the change in current assets plus debt payments.
   b. The difference between earnings and dividends equals the change in book value.
   c. Dividends minus earnings equals one minus the payout ratio.
   d. The difference between earnings and dividends equals the change in surplus inventory.

Concept Questions

1. **Dividend Discount Model (LO1, CFA3)** What is the basic principle behind dividend discount models?

2. **P/E Ratios (LO4, CFA5)** Why do growth stocks tend to have higher P/E ratios than value stocks?

3. **Residual Income Model (LO3, CFA10)** What happens in the residual income model when EPS is negative?

4. **FCF Valuation (LO3, CFA2)** Why do we need to convert the typical equity beta to value a firm using FCF?

5. **Stock Valuation (LO1, CFA3)** Why does the value of a share of stock depend on dividends?

6. **Stock Valuation (LO3, CFA6)** A substantial percentage of the companies listed on the NYSE and the NASDAQ don't pay dividends, but investors are nonetheless willing to buy shares in them. How is this possible given your answer to the previous question?

7. **Dividends (LO3, CFA6)** Referring to the previous two questions, under what circumstances might a company choose not to pay dividends?

8. **Constant Perpetual Growth Model (LO1, CFA7)** Under what two assumptions can we use the constant perpetual growth model presented in the chapter to determine the value of a share of stock? How reasonable are these assumptions?

9. **Dividend Growth Models (LO1, CFA3)** Based on the dividend growth models presented in the chapter, what are the two components of the total return of a share of stock? Which do you think is typically larger?

10. **Stock Valuation (LO3, CFA4)** If a firm has no dividends and has negative earnings, which valuation models are appropriate?

Questions and Problems

Core Questions

1. **Dividend Valuation (LO1, CFA3)** JJ Industries will pay a regular dividend of $2.40 per share for each of the next four years. At the end of the four years, the company will also pay out a $40 per share liquidating dividend, and the company will cease operations. If the discount rate is 10 percent, what is the current value of the company's stock?

2. **Dividend Valuation (LO1, CFA3)** In the previous problem, suppose the current share price is $50. If all other information remains the same, what must the liquidating dividend be?

3. **Free Cash Flow Model (LO3, CFA8)** You are going to value Lauryn's Doll Co. using the FCF model. After consulting various sources, you find that Lauryn has a reported equity beta of 1.4, a debt-to-equity ratio of .3, and a tax rate of 30 percent. Based on this information, what is Lauryn's asset beta?

4. **Free Cash Flow Model (LO3, CFA8)** Using your answer to the previous question, calculate the appropriate discount rate assuming a risk-free rate of 4 percent and a market risk premium of 7 percent.

5. **Free Cash Flow Model (LO3, CFA2)** Lauryn's Doll Co. had net income last year of $30 million. Included in net income was a depreciation expense of $4 million. In addition, Lauryn paid out $5 million in capital expenditures. What is Lauryn's FCF for the year?

6. **Free Cash Flow Model (LO3, CFA2)** Using your answers from questions 3 through 5, value Lauryn's Doll Co. assuming her FCF is expected to grow at a rate of 2 percent into perpetuity. Is this value the value of the equity?

7. **Perpetual Dividend Growth (LO1, CFA7)** Atlantis Seafood Company stock currently sells for $50 per share. The company is expected to pay a dividend of $3.26 per share next year, and analysts project that dividends should increase at 3.0 percent per year for the indefinite future. What must the relevant discount rate be for Atlantis stock?

8. **Perpetual Dividend Growth (LO1, CFA7)** Xytex Products just paid a dividend of $1.40 per share, and the stock currently sells for $42. If the discount rate is 11 percent, what is the dividend growth rate?

9. **Perpetual Dividend Growth (LO1, CFA7)** Star Light & Power increases its dividend 3.8 percent per year every year. This utility is valued using a discount rate of 9 percent, and the stock currently sells for $38 per share. If you buy a share of stock today and hold on to it for at least three years, what do you expect the value of your dividend check to be three years from today?

10. **Sustainable Growth (LO1, CFA7)** Johnson Products earned $3.10 per share last year and paid a $1.25 per share dividend. If ROE was 16 percent, what is the sustainable growth rate?

11. **Sustainable Growth (LO4, CFA7)** Joker stock has a sustainable growth rate of 8 percent, ROE of 14 percent, and dividends per share of $1.65. If the P/E ratio is 19, what is the value of a share of stock?

12. **Capital Asset Pricing Model (LO1, CFA2)** A certain stock has a beta of 1.2. If the risk-free rate of return is 4.1 percent and the market risk premium is 7.5 percent, what is the expected return of the stock? What is the expected return of a stock with a beta of .85?

13. **Residual Income Model (LO3, CFA10)** Bill's Bakery expects earnings per share of $2.56 next year. Current book value is $4.70 per share. The appropriate discount rate for Bill's Bakery is 11 percent. Calculate the share price for Bill's Bakery if earnings grow at 3 percent forever.

14. **Residual Income Model (LO3, CFA10)** For Bill's Bakery described in the previous question, suppose instead that current earnings per share are $2.56. Calculate the share price for Bill's Bakery now.

Intermediate Questions

15. **Two-Stage Dividend Growth Model (LO2, CFA3)** Could I Industries just paid a dividend of $1.10 per share. The dividends are expected to grow at a 25 percent rate for the next six years and then level off to a 4 percent growth rate indefinitely. If the required return is 12 percent, what is the value of the stock today?

16. **H-Model (LO2, CFA7)** The dividend for Should I, Inc., is currently $1.25 per share. It is expected to grow at 20 percent next year and then decline linearly to a 5 percent perpetual rate beginning in four years. If you require a 15 percent return on the stock, what is the most you would pay per share?

17. **Multiple Growth Rates (LO2, CFA7)** Netscrape Communications does not currently pay a dividend. You expect the company to begin paying a $4 per share dividend in 15 years, and you expect dividends to grow perpetually at 5.5 percent per year thereafter. If the discount rate is 15 percent, how much is the stock currently worth?

18. **Multiple Growth Rates (LO2, CFA7)** PerfectlySoft Corp. is experiencing rapid growth. Dividends are expected to grow at 25 percent per year during the next three years, 20 percent over the following year, and then 5 percent per year thereafter indefinitely. The required return on this stock is 14 percent, and the stock currently sells for $56.20 per share. What is the projected dividend for the coming year?

19. **Multiple Growth Rates (LO1, CFA7)** Leisure Lodge Corporation is expected to pay the following dividends over the next four years: $15.00, $10.00, $5.00, $2.20. Afterwards, the company pledges to maintain a constant 4 percent growth rate in dividends forever. If the required return on the stock is 12 percent, what is the current share price?

20. **Multiple Required Returns (LO1, CFA7)** Sea Side, Inc., just paid a dividend of $1.68 per share on its stock. The growth rate in dividends is expected to be a constant 5.5 percent per year

indefinitely. Investors require an 18 percent return on the stock for the first three years, then a 13 percent return for the next three years, and then an 11 percent return thereafter. What is the current share price?

21. **Price Ratio Analysis (LO4, CFA3)**   Given the information below for Seger Corporation, compute the expected share price at the end of 2011 using price ratio analysis.

Year	2005	2006	2007	2008	2009	2010
Price	$94.50	$100.40	$99.10	$97.90	$121.50	$136.80
EPS	4.34	5.05	5.22	6.06	7.00	8.00
CFPS	7.27	8.24	8.71	10.12	11.80	13.10
SPS	52.60	58.52	57.90	60.69	71.60	78.70

22. **Dividend Growth Analysis (LO1, CFA3)**   In the previous problem, suppose the dividends per share over the same period were $1.00, $1.08, $1.17, $1.25, $1.35, and $1.40, respectively. Compute the expected share price at the end of 2010 using the perpetual growth method. Assume the market risk premium is 7.5 percent, Treasury bills yield 4 percent, and the projected beta of the firm is .90.

23. **Price Ratio Analysis for Internet Companies (LO4, CFA9)**   Given the information below for HooYah! Corporation, compute the expected share price at the end of 2011 using price ratio analysis.

Year	2005	2006	2007	2008	2009	2010
Price	$ 8.00	$ 44.50	$116.00	$193.00	$83.00	$13.50
EPS	−4.00	−3.30	−1.80	−0.55	0.04	0.06
CFPS	−9.00	−6.50	−2.80	−0.25	0.03	0.08
SPS	5.00	13.50	18.10	20.30	23.80	21.95

24. **Price Ratio Analysis for Internet Companies (LO4, CFA9)**   Given the information below for StartUp.Com, compute the expected share price at the end of 2011 using price ratio analysis.

Year	2007	2008	2009	2010
Price	N/A	$ 68.12	$ 95.32	$104.18
EPS	N/A	−7.55	−4.30	−3.68
CFPS	N/A	−11.05	−8.20	−5.18
SPS	N/A	4.10	6.80	8.13

25. **Price Ratio Analysis (LO4, CFA3)**   The current price of Parador Industries stock is $74 per share. Current earnings per share are $3.40, the earnings growth rate is 6 percent, and Parador does not pay a dividend. The expected return on Parador stock is 13 percent. What one-year ahead P/E ratio is consistent with Parador's expected return and earnings growth rate?

26. **Price Ratio Analysis (LO4, CFA3)**   The current price of Parador Industries stock is $74 per share. Current sales per share are $18.75, the sales growth rate is 8 percent, and Parador does not pay a dividend. The expected return on Parador stock is 13 percent. What one-year ahead P/S ratio is consistent with Parador's expected return and sales growth rate?

Use the following information to answer Problems 27–31.
Abbott Laboratories (ABT) engages in the discovery, development, manufacture, and sale of a line of health care and pharmaceutical products. Below you will find selected information from *Value Line*. Use the *Value Line* estimated 2009 figures as the actual year-end figures for the company. The beta reported was .60 and the risk-free rate was 3.13 percent. Assume a market risk premium of 7 percent.

2005	2006	2007	2008	2009	2010	©VALUE LINE PUB., INC.
14.51	14.62	16.72	19.40	19.70	21.45	Sales per sh
3.42	3.51	4.05	4.32	4.95	5.50	"Cash Flow" per sh
2.50	2.52	2.84	3.03	3.65	4.15	Earnings per sh A
1.10	1.18	1.30	1.44	1.60	1.76	Div'ds Decl'd per sh B■
.78	.87	1.07	.85	1.10	1.15	Cap'l Spending per sh
9.37	9.14	11.47	11.48	12.95	14.90	Book Value per sh C
1539.2	1537.2	1549.9	1522.4	1545.0	1540.0	Common Shs Outst'g D
18.1	17.9	19.2	18.3	Bold figures are		Avg Ann'l P/E Ratio
.96	.97	1.02	1.12	Value Line		Relative P/E Ratio
2.4%	2.6%	2.4%	2.6%	estimates		Avg Ann'l Div'd Yield
22338	22476	25914	29528	30450	33000	Sales ($mill)
27.6%	28.2%	26.2%	25.5%	29.2%	29.3%	Operating Margin
1358.9	1558.8	1854.9	1838.8	2000	2075	Depreciation ($mill)
3908.5	3841.8	4429.3	4734.2	5640	6400	Net Profit ($mill)
24.3%	23.5%	19.3%	19.2%	20.0%	20.0%	Income Tax Rate
17.5%	17.1%	17.1%	16.0%	18.5%	19.4%	Net Profit Margin
3970.5	d669.3	4939.4	5450.7	6500	6515	Working Cap'l ($mill)
4571.5	7009.7	9487.8	8713.3	10000	8000	Long-Term Debt ($mill)
14415	14054	17779	17480	20000	22950	Shr. Equity ($mill)
21.0%	18.8%	17.0%	18.8%	19.0%	21.0%	Return on Total Cap'l
27.1%	27.3%	24.9%	27.1%	28.0%	28.0%	Return on Shr. Equity
15.4%	14.7%	13.9%	14.6%	16.0%	16.0%	Retained to Com Eq
43%	46%	44%	46%	44%	43%	All Div'ds to Net Prof

The high and low share price each year were:

	2005	2006	2007	2008	2009
High	$50.00	$49.90	$59.50	$61.10	$57.40
Low	37.50	39.20	48.80	45.80	41.30

27. **Constant Perpetual Growth Model (LO1, CFA7)** What is the sustainable growth rate and required return for Abbott Laboratories? Using these values, calculate the 2010 share price of Abbott Laboratories Industries stock according to the constant dividend growth model.

28. **Price Ratios (LO4, CFA5)** Using the P/E, P/CF, and P/S ratios, estimate the 2010 share price for Abbott Laboratories. Use the average stock price each year to calculate the price ratios.

29. **Residual Income Model (LO3, CFA10)** Assume the sustainable growth rate and required return you calculated in Problem 27 are valid. Use the clean surplus relationship to calculate the share price for Abbott Laboratories with the residual income model.

30. **Clean Surplus Dividend (LO3, CFA10)** Use the information from the previous problem and calculate the stock price with the clean surplus dividend. Do you get the same stock price as in the previous problem? Why or why not?

31. **Stock Valuation (LO1, LO3, LO4)** Given your answers in the previous questions, do you feel Abbott Laboratories is overvalued or undervalued at its current price of around $50? At what price do you feel the stock should sell?

32. **Residual Income Model and Nonconstant Growth (LO3, CFA10)** When a stock is going through a period of nonconstant growth for T periods, followed by constant growth forever, the residual income model can be modified as follows:

$$P_0 = \sum_{t=1}^{T} \frac{EPS_t + B_{t-1} - B_t}{(1+k)^t} + \frac{P_T}{(1+k)^T}$$

where

$$P_T = B_T + \frac{EPS_T (1 + g) - B_T \times k}{k - g}$$

Al's Infrared Sandwich Company had a book value of $12.95 at the beginning of the year, and the earnings per share for the past year were $3.41. Molly Miller, a research analyst at Miller, Moore & Associates, estimates that the book value and earnings per share will grow at 12.5 and 11 percent per year for the next four years, respectively. After four years, the growth rate is expected to be 6 percent. Molly believes the required return for the company is 8.2 percent. What is the value per share for Al's Infrared Sandwich Company?

CFA Exam Review by Schweser

[CFA2, CFA7, CFA8]

Beachwood Builders merged with Country Point Homes on December 31, 1992. Both companies were builders of midscale and luxury homes in their respective markets. In 2010, because of tax considerations and the need to segment the business, Beachwood decided to spin off Country Point, its luxury subsidiary, to its shareholders. Beachwood retained Bernheim Securities to value the spin-off of Country Point as of December 31, 2010.

When the books closed on 2010, Beachwood had $140 million in debt outstanding due in 2019 at a coupon rate of 8 percent, which is a spread of 2 percent above the current risk-free rate. Beachwood also had 5 million common shares outstanding. It pays no dividends, has no preferred shareholders, and faces a tax rate of 30 percent. Bernheim is assuming a market risk premium of 11 percent.

The common equity allocated to Country Point for the spin-off was $55.6 million as of December 31, 2010. There was no long-term debt allocated from Beachwood.

The managing directors in charge of Bernheim's construction group, Denzel Johnson and Cara Nguyen, are prepping for the valuation presentation. Ms. Nguyen tells Mr. Johnson that Bernheim estimated Country Point's net income at $10 million in 2010, growing $5 million per year through 2014. Based on Ms. Nguyen's calculations, Country Point will be worth $223.7 million in 2014. Ms. Nguyen decided to use a cost of equity for Country Point in the valuation equal to its return on equity at the end of 2010 (rounded to the nearest percentage). Ms. Nguyen also gives Mr. Johnson the table she obtained from Beachwood projecting depreciation and capital expenditures ($ in millions):

	2010	2011	2012	2013	2014
Depreciation	$5	$6	$5	$ 6	$ 5
Capital expenditures	7	8	9	10	12

1. What is the estimate of Country Point's free cash flow to the firm (FCFF) in 2012?

   a. 25
   b. 16
   c. 11

2. What is the cost of capital that Ms. Nguyen used for her valuation of Country Point?

   a. 18 percent
   b. 17 percent
   c. 15 percent

3. Given Ms. Nguyen's estimate of Country Point's terminal value in 2014, what is the growth assumption she must have used for free cash flow after 2014?

   a. 7 percent
   b. 9 percent
   c. 3 percent

4. The value of beta for Country Point is:

   a. 1.09
   b. 1.27
   c. 1.00

5. What is the estimated value of Country Point in a proposed spin-off?

   a. $144.5 million
   b. $162.6 million
   c. $178.3 million

What's on the Web?

1. **Sustainable Growth Rate**   You can find the home page for Caterpillar, Inc., at www.cat.com. Go to this page and find the most recent annual report for Caterpillar. Calculate the sustainable growth rate for each of the past two years. Are these values the same? Why or why not?

2. **Sustainable Growth Rate**   Go to finance.yahoo.com and find the analysts' estimates for DuPont's (DD) growth rate over the next five years. How does this compare to the industry, sector, and S&P 500 growth rates? Now find the EPS and dividends per share for DuPont and calculate the sustainable growth rate. How does your number compare to analysts' estimates for the company? Why might these estimates differ?

3. **Perpetual Dividend Growth Model**   Go to finance.yahoo.com and find the following information: the beta, the most recent annual dividend, and analysts' estimated growth rate for Johnson & Johnson (JNJ). Next, find the three-month Treasury bill yield on finance.yahoo.com. Assuming the market risk premium is 9 percent, what is the required return for JNJ? What is the value of JNJ stock using the perpetual dividend growth model? Does JNJ appear overpriced, underpriced, or correctly priced? Why might this analysis be inappropriate, or at least misleading?

Stock-Trak Exercises

To access the Stock-Trak Exercise for this chapter, please visit the book Web site at www.mhhe.com/jmd6e and choose the corresponding chapter.

CHAPTER 7

Stock Price Behavior and Market Efficiency

Learning Objectives

You should strive to have your investment knowledge fully reflect:

1. The foundations of market efficiency.

2. The implications of the forms of market efficiency.

3. Market efficiency and the performance of professional money managers.

4. What stock market anomalies, bubbles, and crashes mean for market efficiency.

"A market is the combined behavior of thousands of people responding to information, misinformation, and whim."

–Kenneth Chang

"If you want to know what's happening in the market, ask the market."

–Japanese Proverb

Controversial, intriguing, and baffling issues are at the heart of this chapter. We begin by investigating a very basic question: Can you, as an investor, consistently "beat the market"? You may be surprised to learn that evidence strongly suggests that the answer to this question is probably not. We show that even professional money managers have trouble beating the market. At the end of the chapter, we describe some market phenomena that sound more like carnival side shows, such as the "amazing January effect." ■

CFA™ Exam Topics in This Chapter:

1 Efficient capital markets (L1, S13)

2 Equity portfolio management (L3, S11)

Go to www.mhhe.com/jmd6e for a guide that aligns your textbook with CFA readings.

7.1 Introduction to Market Efficiency

Market efficiency is probably the most controversial and intriguing issue in investments. The debate that has raged around market efficiency for decades shows few signs of abating. The central issue in the market efficiency debate is: Can you (or anyone else) consistently "beat the market"?

If the answer to this question is no, then the market is said to be efficient. The **efficient markets hypothesis (EMH)** asserts that, as a practical matter, organized financial markets like the New York Stock Exchange are efficient. The controversy surrounding the EMH centers on this assertion.

In the sections that follow, we discuss many issues surrounding the EMH. You will notice that we focus our discussion on stock markets. The reason is that the debate on the EMH and the associated research have largely centered on these markets. However, the same principles and arguments would also apply to any organized financial market, such as the markets for government bonds, corporate bonds, commodity futures, and options.

CHECK THIS

7.1a What is the central issue in the market efficiency debate?

7.1b How would you state the efficient markets hypothesis?

7.2 What Does "Beat the Market" Mean?

Good question. As we discussed in Chapter 1 and elsewhere, there is a risk-return trade-off. On average at least, we expect riskier investments to have larger returns than less risky assets. So the fact that an investment appears to have a high or low return doesn't tell us much. We need to know if the return was high or low relative to the risk involved.

Instead, to determine if an investment is superior to another, we need to compare **excess returns**. The excess return on an investment is the difference between what that investment earned and what other investments with the same risk earned. A positive excess return means that an investment has outperformed other investments of the same risk. Thus, *consistently earning a positive excess return* is what we mean by "beating the market."

CHECK THIS

7.2a What is an excess return?

7.2b What does it mean to "beat the market"?

7.3 Foundations of Market Efficiency

Three economic forces can lead to market efficiency: (1) investor rationality, (2) independent deviations from rationality, and (3) arbitrage. These conditions are so powerful that any one of them can result in market efficiency. We discuss aspects of these conditions in detail throughout this chapter. Given their importance, however, we briefly introduce each of them here. In our discussions, we use the term "rational" to mean only that investors do not systematically overvalue or undervalue financial assets in light of the information that they possess.

If every investor always made perfectly rational investment decisions, earning an excess return would be difficult, if not impossible. The reason is simple: If everyone is fully rational, equivalent risk assets would all have the same expected returns. Put differently, no bargains would be there to be had, because relative prices would all be correct.

However, even if the investor rationality condition does not hold, the market could still be efficient. Suppose that many investors are irrational, and a company makes a relevant announcement about a new product. Some investors will be overly optimistic, some will be overly pessimistic, but the net effect might be that these investors cancel each other out. In a sense, the irrationality is just noise that is diversified away. As a result, the market could still be efficient (or nearly efficient). What is important here is that irrational investors don't all (or mostly all) have similar beliefs. However, even under this condition, called "independent deviations from rationality," the market still may be efficient.

Let us now think of a market with many irrational traders and further suppose that their collective irrationality does not balance out. In this case, observed market prices can be too high or too low relative to their risk. Now suppose there are some well-capitalized, intelligent, and rational investors. This group of traders would see these high or low market prices as a profit opportunity and engage in arbitrage—buying relatively inexpensive stocks and selling relatively expensive stocks.

If these rational arbitrage traders dominate irrational traders, the market will still be efficient. We sometimes hear the expression "Market efficiency doesn't require that *everybody* be rational, just that *somebody* is." In our next section, we look more closely at market efficiency and discuss several different forms.

CHECK THIS

7.3a What three economic conditions cause market efficiency?

7.3b How would well-capitalized, intelligent, and rational investors profit from market inefficiency?

7.4 Forms of Market Efficiency

Now that we have a little more precise notion of what beating the market means, we can be a little more precise about market efficiency. A market is efficient *with respect to some particular information* if that information is not useful in earning a positive excess return. Notice the emphasis we place on "with respect to some particular information."

For example, it seems unlikely that knowledge of Shaquille O'Neal's free-throw shooting percentage (low) would be of any use in beating the market. If so, we would say that the market is efficient with respect to the information in Shaq's free-throw percentage. On the other hand, if you have prior knowledge concerning impending takeover offers, you could most definitely use that information to earn a positive excess return. Thus, the market is not efficient with regard to this information. We hasten to add that such information is probably "insider" information, and insider trading is generally, though not always, illegal (in the United States, at least). As we discuss later in the chapter, using insider information illegally might well earn you a stay in a jail cell and a stiff financial penalty.

Thus, the question of whether a market is efficient is meaningful only relative to some type of information. Put differently, if you are asked whether a particular market is efficient, you should always reply, "With respect to what information?" Three general types of information are particularly interesting in this context, and it is traditional to define three forms of market efficiency: weak, semistrong, and strong.

The particular sets of information used in the three forms of market efficiency are *nested*. That is, the information set in the strong form includes the information set in the semistrong form, which in turn includes the information set in the weak form. Figure 7.1 shows the relationships among the information sets.

FIGURE 7.1   Information Sets for Market Efficiency

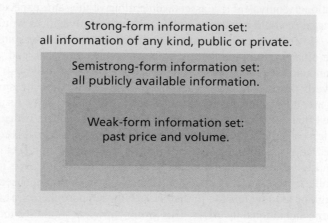

A weak-form efficient market is one in which the information reflected in past prices and volume figures is of no value in beating the market. As we discuss in our next chapter, one form of stock market analysis, called "technical analysis," is based on using past prices and volume to predict future prices. If a market is weak-form efficient, however, then technical analysis is of no use whatsoever. You might as well read tea leaves as stock price charts if the market is weak-form efficient.

In a semistrong-form efficient market, publicly available information of any and all kinds is of no use in beating the market. If a market is semistrong-form efficient, then the fundamental analysis techniques we described in a previous chapter are useless. Also, notice that past prices and volume data are publicly available information, so if a market is semistrong-form efficient, it is also weak-form efficient.

The implications of semistrong-form efficiency are, at a minimum, semistaggering. What it literally means is that nothing in the library, for example, is of any value in earning a positive excess return. How about a firm's financial statement? Useless. How about information in the financial press? Worthless. This book? Sad to say, if the market is semistrong-form efficient, nothing in this book will be of any use in beating the market. You can imagine that this form of market efficiency is hotly disputed.

Finally, in a strong-form efficient market no information of any kind, public or private, is useful in beating the market. Notice that if a market is strong-form efficient, it is necessarily weak- and semistrong-form efficient as well. Ignoring the issue of legality, possession of nonpublic inside information of many types clearly would enable you to earn essentially unlimited returns, so this case is not particularly interesting. Instead, the market efficiency debate focuses on the first two forms.

CHECK THIS

7.4a   What role does information play in determining whether markets are efficient?

7.4b   What are the forms of market efficiency?

7.5   Why Would a Market Be Efficient?

The driving force toward market efficiency is simply competition and the profit motive. Investors constantly try to identify superior-performing investments. Using the most advanced information processing tools available, investors and security analysts constantly appraise stock values, buying those stocks that look even slightly undervalued and selling those that look even slightly overvalued. This constant appraisal and subsequent trading activity (as well as all the research behind these activities) act to ensure that prices never differ much from their efficient market price.

To give you an idea of how strong the incentive is to identify superior investments, consider a large mutual fund such as the Fidelity Magellan Fund. As we mentioned in Chapter 4, this is one of the largest equity funds in the United States, with about $23 billion under management (as of late 2009). Suppose Fidelity was able through its research to improve the performance of this fund by 20 basis points for one year only (recall that a basis point is 1 percent of 1 percent, i.e., 0.0001). How much would this one-time 20-basis point improvement be worth?

The answer is 0.0020 times $23 billion, or $46 million. Thus, Fidelity would be willing to spend up to $46 million to boost the performance of this one fund by as little as one-fifth of one percent for a single year only. As this example shows, even relatively small performance enhancements are worth tremendous amounts of money and thereby create the incentive to unearth relevant information and use it.

Because of this incentive, the fundamental characteristic of an efficient market is that prices are correct in the sense that they fully reflect relevant information. If and when new information comes to light, prices may change, and they may change by a lot. It just depends on the nature of the new information. However, in an efficient market, right here, right now, price is a consensus opinion of value, where that consensus is based on the information and intellect of hundreds of thousands, or even millions, of investors around the world.

CHECK THIS

7.5a   What is the driving force behind market efficiency?

7.5b   Why does this driving force work?

7.6 Some Implications of Market Efficiency

DOES OLD INFORMATION HELP PREDICT FUTURE STOCK PRICES?

In its weakest form, the efficient markets hypothesis is the simple statement that stock prices fully reflect all past information. If this is true, this means that studying past price movements in the hopes of predicting future stock price movements is really a waste of time.

In addition, a very subtle prediction is at work here. That is, no matter how often a particular stock price path has related to subsequent stock price changes in the past, there is no assurance that this relationship will occur again in the future.

Researchers have used sophisticated statistical techniques to test whether past stock price movements are of any value in predicting future stock price movements. This turns out to be a surprisingly difficult question to answer clearly and without qualification.

In short, although some researchers have been able to show that future returns are partly predictable by past returns, the predicted returns are not *economically* important, which means that predictability is not sufficient to earn an excess return. In addition, trading costs generally swamp attempts to build a profitable trading system on the basis of past returns. Researchers have been unable to provide evidence of a superior trading strategy that uses only past returns. That is, trading costs matter, and buy-and-hold strategies involving broad market indexes are extremely difficult to outperform. (If you know how to outperform a broad market index after accounting for trading costs, please share it with us.)

RANDOM WALKS AND STOCK PRICES

If you were to ask people you know whether stock market prices are predictable, many of them would say yes. To their surprise, and perhaps yours, it is very difficult to predict stock market prices. In fact, considerable research has shown that stock prices change through time as if they are random. That is, stock price increases are about as likely as stock price decreases.

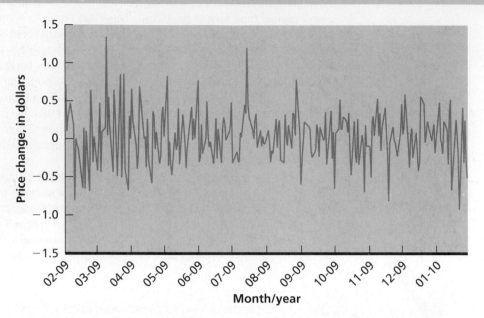

When the path that a stock price follows shows no discernible pattern, then the stock's price behavior is largely consistent with the notion of a **random walk**. A random walk is related to the weak-form version of the efficient markets hypothesis because past knowledge of the stock price is not useful in predicting future stock prices.

random walk
No discernible pattern to the path that a stock price follows through time.

Figure 7.2 illustrates daily price changes for Intel stock from February 2, 2009, through January 29, 2010. To qualify as a true random walk, Intel stock price changes would have to be truly independent from day to day. In addition, the distribution of possible stock prices each day must be the same. Even so, the graph of daily price changes for Intel stock is essentially what a random walk looks like. It is certainly hard to see any pattern in the daily price changes of Intel.

HOW DOES NEW INFORMATION GET INTO STOCK PRICES?

In its semistrong form, the efficient markets hypothesis is the simple statement that stock prices fully reflect publicly available information. Stock prices change when traders buy and sell shares based on their view of the future prospects for the stock. The future prospects for the stock are influenced by unexpected news announcements. Examples of unexpected news announcements might include an increase or decrease in the dividend paid by a stock, an increase or decrease in the forecast for future earnings, lawsuits over company practices, or changes in the leadership team. As shown in Figure 7.3, prices could adjust to a positive news announcement in three basic ways.

- *Efficient market reaction:* The price instantaneously adjusts to, and fully reflects, new information. There is no tendency for subsequent increases or decreases to occur.

- *Delayed reaction:* The price partially adjusts to the new information, but days elapse before the price completely reflects new information.

- *Overreaction and correction:* The price overadjusts to the new information; it overshoots the appropriate new price but eventually falls to the new price.

EVENT STUDIES

On Friday, May 25, 2007, executives of Advanced Medical Optics, Inc. (EYE), recalled a contact lens solution called Complete MoisturePlus Multi Purpose Solution. Advanced Medical Optics took this voluntary action after the Centers for Disease Control and Prevention (CDC) found a link between the solution and a rare cornea infection. The medical name for this infection is acanthamoeba keratitis, or AK for short.

FIGURE 7.3   Possible Market Price Reactions to a News Announcement

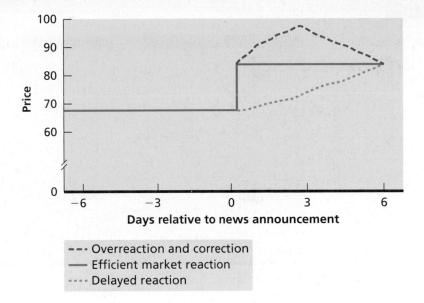

--- Overreaction and correction
— Efficient market reaction
···· Delayed reaction

About two out of every million contact lens users in the United States each year are afflicted with AK. Although instances of AK are rare, AK is serious—this infection can lead to vision loss, and sometimes it can lead to the need for a cornea transplant. The CDC determined that the risk of developing AK is about seven times greater for consumers using the Complete Moisture-Plus contact lens solution than for those consumers using other contact lens solutions.

Executives at Advanced Medical Optics chose to recall their product even though they did not find evidence their manufacturing process introduced the parasite that can lead to AK. Further, company officials believed that the occurrences of AK were most likely the result of end users who failed to follow safe procedures when installing contact lenses.

Nevertheless, the recall was announced following the market close on Friday, May 25, 2007. Following the long weekend, EYE shares opened on Tuesday, May 29, 2007, at $34.37, down $5.83 from the Friday close of $40.20. Figure 7.4 is a plot of the price per share of Advanced Medical Optics (EYE) in the days surrounding this news announcement.

event study
A research method designed to help study the effects of news on stock prices.

Researchers use a technique known as an **event study** to test the effects of news announcements on stock prices. When researchers look for effects of news on stock prices, however, they must make sure that overall market news is accounted for in their analysis. The reason is simple. Suppose the whole market had fallen drastically on May 29, 2007. How would researchers be able to separate the overall market decline from the isolated news concerning Advanced Medical Optics?

abnormal returns
The remaining return on a stock after overall market returns have been removed.

To answer this question, researchers calculate **abnormal returns**. The equation to calculate an abnormal return is simply:

$$\text{Abnormal return} = \text{Observed return} - \text{Expected return} \qquad (7.1)$$

The expected return can be calculated using a market index (like the NASDAQ 100 Index or the S&P 500 Index) or by using a long-term average return on the stock. Researchers then align the abnormal return on a stock to the days relative to the news announcement. Usually, researchers assign the value of zero to the day a news announcement is made. One day after the news announcement is assigned a value of $+1$, two days after the news announcement is assigned a value of $+2$, and so on. Similarly, one day before the news announcement is assigned the value of -1.

According to the efficient markets hypothesis, the abnormal return today should relate only to information released on that day. Any previously released information should have no effect on abnormal returns because this information has been available to all traders. Also, the return today cannot be influenced by information that traders do not yet know.

FIGURE 7.4

The Price of Shares for Advanced Medical Optics, May 14, 2007, through June 15, 2007

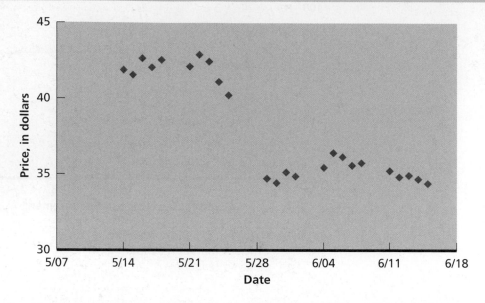

FIGURE 7.5

Cumulative Abnormal Returns for Advanced Medical Optics, March 30, 2007, through July 25, 2007

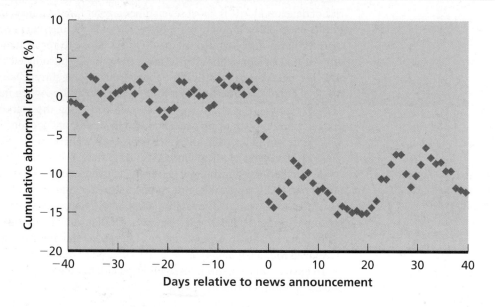

To evaluate abnormal returns, researchers usually accumulate them over some period. Figure 7.5 is a plot of the cumulative abnormal returns for Advanced Medical Optics beginning 40 days before the announcement. The first cumulative abnormal return, or CAR, is just equal to the abnormal return on day −40. The CAR on day −39 is the sum of the first two abnormal returns, the CAR on day −38 is the sum of the first three, and so on. By examining CARs, we can see if there was an over- or underreaction to an announcement.

As you can see in Figure 7.5, Advanced Medical's cumulative abnormal return hovered around zero before the announcement. After the news was released, there was a large, sharp downward movement in the CAR. The stock price gyrated as additional news was released, but the overall pattern of cumulative abnormal returns is essentially what the efficient markets hypothesis would predict. That is, there is a band of cumulative abnormal returns, a sharp break in cumulative abnormal returns, and another band of cumulative abnormal returns.

CHECK THIS

7.6a How is a random walk affiliated with the efficient markets hypothesis?

7.6b What are the possible market price reactions to a news announcement?

7.6c How do researchers use event studies to examine the effects of news announcements on stock prices?

7.7 Informed Traders and Insider Trading

Recall that if a market is strong-form efficient, no information of any kind, public or private, is useful in beating the market. However, inside information of many types clearly would enable you to earn essentially unlimited returns. This fact generates an interesting question: Should any of us be able to earn returns based on information that is not known to the public?

In the United States (and in many other countries, though not all), making profits on nonpublic information is illegal. This ban is said to be necessary if investors are to have trust in U.S. stock markets. The United States Securities and Exchange Commission (SEC) is charged with enforcing laws concerning illegal trading activities. As a result, it is important for you to be able to distinguish between informed trading, insider trading, and legal insider trading.

INFORMED TRADING

informed trader
An investor who makes a buy or sell decision based on public information and analysis.

When an investor makes a decision to buy or sell a stock based on publicly available information and analysis, this investor is said to be an **informed trader**. The information that an informed trader possesses might come from reading *The Wall Street Journal,* reading quarterly reports issued by a company, gathering financial information from the Internet, talking to other traders, or a host of other sources.

INSIDER TRADING

Some informed traders are also insider traders. When you hear the term *insider trading,* you most likely think that such activity is illegal. However, as you will see at the end of this section, not all insider trading is illegal.

material nonpublic information
Private knowledge that can substantially influence the share price of a stock.

WHO IS AN INSIDER? For the purposes of defining illegal insider trading, an insider is someone who has **material nonpublic information**. Such information is both not known to the public and, if it were known, would impact the stock price. A person can be charged with insider trading when he or she acts on such information in an attempt to make a profit.

Frequently, when an illegal insider trade occurs, there is a *tipper* and a *tippee*. The tipper is the person who has, on purpose, divulged material nonpublic information. The tippee is the person who has knowingly used such information in an attempt to make a profit. For example, a tipper could be a CEO who spills some inside information to a friend who does not work for the company. If the friend then knowingly uses this inside information to make a trade, this tippee is guilty of insider trading.

Proving that a trader is a tippee is difficult for the SEC, because keeping track of insider information flows and subsequent trades is difficult. For example, suppose a person makes a trade based on the advice of a stockbroker. Even if the broker based this advice on material nonpublic information, the trader might not have been aware of the broker's knowledge. The SEC must prove that the trader was, in fact, aware that the broker's information was based on material nonpublic information.

Sometimes, people accused of insider trading claim that they just "overheard" someone talking. Suppose, for example, you are at a restaurant and overhear a conversation between Bill Gates and his CFO concerning some potentially explosive news regarding Microsoft, Inc. If you then go out and make a trade in an attempt to profit from what you overheard, you would be violating the law (even though the information was "innocently obtained").

When you take possession of material nonpublic information, you become an insider and are bound to obey insider trading laws. Note that in this case, Bill Gates and his CFO, although careless, are not necessarily in violation of insider trading laws.

LEGAL INSIDER TRADING A company's corporate insiders can make perfectly legal trades in the stock of their company. To do so, they must comply with the reporting rules made by the U.S. Securities and Exchange Commission. When they make a trade and report it to the SEC, these trades are reported to the public. In addition, corporate insiders must declare that trades that they made were based on public information about the company, rather than "inside" information. Most public companies also have guidelines that must be followed. For example, companies commonly allow insiders to trade only during certain windows throughout the year, often sometime after earnings have been announced.

IT'S NOT A GOOD THING: WHAT DID MARTHA DO? Martha Stewart became one of America's most successful entrepreneurs by telling people how to entertain, cook, and decorate their homes. She built her superhomemaker personality into a far-flung international enterprise. When her company went public in 1999, the initial public offering raised $873 million. Today, Martha Stewart Living Omnimedia, Inc. (MSO), has a market capitalization of around $266 million and employs about 750 people (plus interns).

Ms. Stewart was in the legal news because the U.S. Securities and Exchange Commission believed that Martha Stewart was told by her friend Sam Waksal, who founded a company called ImClone, that a cancer drug being developed by ImClone had been rejected by the Food and Drug Administration. This development was bad news for ImClone. Martha Stewart sold her 3,928 shares in ImClone on December 27, 2001. On that day, ImClone traded below $60 per share, a level that Ms. Stewart claimed triggered an existing stop-loss order. However, the SEC believed that Ms. Stewart illegally sold her shares because she had information concerning FDA rejection before it became public.

The FDA rejection was announced after the market closed on Friday, December 28, 2001. This news was a huge blow to ImClone shares, which closed at about $46 per share on the following Monday (the first trading day after the information became public). Shares in ImClone subsequently fell to under $10 per share about six months later, in mid-2002. Ironically, shares of ImClone rallied to sell for more than $80 per share in mid-2004.

In June 2003, Martha Stewart and her stockbroker, Peter Bacanovic, were indicted on nine federal counts. They both pleaded not guilty. Ms. Stewart's trial began in January 2004. Just days before the jury began to deliberate, however, Judge Miriam Cedarbaum dismissed the most serious charge—securities fraud. Ms. Stewart, however, was convicted on all four counts of obstructing justice and lying to investigators.

Judge Cedarbaum fined Martha Stewart $30,000 and sentenced her to five months in prison, two years of probation, and five months of home confinement after her release. The fine was the maximum allowed under federal rules; the sentence was the minimum the judge could impose. Peter Bacanovic, Martha Stewart's broker at the time, was fined $4,000 and was sentenced to five months in prison and two years of probation.

So, to summarize, Martha Stewart was accused, but not convicted, of insider trading. She was accused, and convicted, of obstructing justice and misleading investigators. Although her conviction bars her from taking on the duties of an executive officer, MSO still paid Martha about $5.5 million in 2009 (base pay plus perks).

CHECK THIS

7.7a	What makes a stock trader an informed trader?
7.7b	What traders are considered to be insiders?
7.7c	What is the difference between legal insider trading and illegal insider trading?

7.8 How Efficient Are Markets?

ARE FINANCIAL MARKETS EFFICIENT?

Financial markets are one of the most extensively documented human endeavors. Colossal amounts of financial market data are collected and reported every day. These data, particularly stock market data, have been exhaustively analyzed to test market efficiency.

You would think that with all this analysis going on, we would know whether markets are efficient, but really we don't. Instead, what we seem to have, at least in the minds of many researchers, is a growing realization that beyond a point, we just can't tell.

For example, it is not difficult to program a computer to test trading strategies that are based solely on historic prices and volume figures. Many such strategies have been tested, and the bulk of the evidence indicates that such strategies are not useful.

More generally, market efficiency is difficult to test for four basic reasons:

1. The risk-adjustment problem.
2. The relevant information problem.
3. The dumb luck problem.
4. The data snooping problem.

We briefly discuss each in turn.

The first issue, the risk-adjustment problem, is the easiest to understand. Earlier, we noted that beating the market means consistently earning a positive excess return. To determine whether an investment has a positive excess return, we have to adjust for its risk. As we discuss elsewhere in this book, the truth is that we are not even certain exactly what we mean by risk, much less how to measure it precisely and then adjust for it. Thus, what appears to be a positive excess return may just be the result of a faulty risk-adjustment procedure.

The second issue, the relevant information problem, is even more troublesome. Remember that the concept of market efficiency is meaningful only relative to some particular information. As we look back in time and try to assess whether some particular market behavior was inefficient, we have to recognize that we cannot possibly know all the information that may have been underlying that market behavior.

For example, suppose we see that 10 years ago the price of a stock shot up by 100 percent over a short period of time, and then subsequently collapsed. We dig through all the historical information we can find, but we can find no reason for this behavior. What can we conclude? Nothing, really. For all we know, an undocumented rumor existed of a takeover that never materialized, and relative to this information, the price behavior was perfectly efficient.

In general, there is no way to tell whether we have all the relevant information. Without *all* the relevant information, we cannot tell if some observed price behavior is inefficient. Put differently, any price behavior, no matter how bizarre, might be efficient, and therefore explainable, with respect to *some* information.

The third problem has to do with evaluating investors and money managers. One type of evidence frequently cited to prove that markets can be beaten is the enviable track record of certain legendary investors. For example, *The Wall Street Journal* article reproduced in the nearby *Investment Updates* box gives some information on the track record of superstar investor Warren Buffett.

A hidden argument in the *Investment Updates* box is that because some investors seem to be able to beat the market, it must be the case that there are market inefficiencies. Is this correct? Maybe yes, maybe no. You may be familiar with the following expression: "If you put an immortal monkey in front of a typewriter, this monkey will eventually produce *Hamlet*." In a similar manner, suppose we have thousands of monkeys who are tasked with picking stocks for a portfolio. We would find that some of these monkeys would appear to be amazingly talented and rack up extraordinary gains. As you surely recognize, however, this is just caused by random chance.

Similarly, if we track the performance of thousands of money managers over some period of time, some managers will accumulate remarkable track records and a lot of publicity. Are

WARREN BUFFETT, UNPLUGGED

Warren Buffett, the billionaire investor and insurance executive, was in his office here this summer when he received a faxed letter about a company he'd never heard of.

The letter was from an advisor to Forest River Inc., an Elkhart, Ind., recreational vehicle maker. He proposed that Mr. Buffett buy the company for $800 million.

Mr. Buffett liked what he saw: The company had a big market share and little debt.

The next day, Mr. Buffett offered to buy Forest River and to let its founder, Peter Liegl, continue running it. He sealed the deal, at an undisclosed price, in a 20-minute meeting one week later. As the meeting wrapped up, Mr. Buffett told Mr. Liegl not to expect to hear from him more than once a year. Says Mr. Liegl: "It was easier to sell my business than to renew my driver's license."

Mr. Buffett says he knows an attractive acquisition candidate when he sees it. "If I don't know it in five to 10 minutes," Mr. Buffett says, "then I'm not going to know it in 10 weeks."

Mr. Buffett, an Omaha native, learned about investing under the tutelage of the classic "value" investor Benjamin Graham, who preached buying beaten-down stocks with good underlying value. He became a broker in 1951 at Buffett-Falk & Co., his father's stock-brokerage firm in Omaha, before going to work for Mr. Graham in New York three years later. In 1965, Mr. Buffett bought control of Berkshire, a foundering New Bedford, Mass., fabric mill. He soon purchased National Indemnity Cos., an Omaha insurer, which gave Berkshire $20 million of assets.

Mr. Buffett calculates that since 1951, he has generated an average annual return of about 31%. The average return for the Standard & Poor's 500 over that period is 11% a year. A $1,000 investment in Berkshire in 1965 would be worth about $5.5 million today. Over the past decade, Berkshire shares have tripled in price, returning twice as much, in percentage terms, as the S&P 500.

Mr. Buffett, with a personal net worth of $43 billion, is the nation's second-richest man, after Bill Gates. His nearly 55-year record has brought him recognition as one of the best investors ever, earned him fierce loyalty from Berkshire shareholders, and inspired legions of investors who attempt to ape his moves.

Though his empire has grown, Mr. Buffett says his routine has changed little over the years. He says he spends the better part of most workdays thinking and reading. He fields a handful of phone calls, and on most days, he confers with the chiefs of a few Berkshire subsidiaries. He seldom holds meetings. "There isn't much going on here," he says of his office on a typical day.

Around midday, a call came in from David Sokol, chief executive of Berkshire's MidAmerican Energy subsidiary.

Mr. Buffett put his hands behind his head and cradled the phone against his shoulder, nodding when Mr. Sokol told him that MidAmerican had received a government approval for its pending acquisition of PacifiCorp (a utility) for $5.1 billion in cash, plus $4.3 billion of assumed debt. Mr. Buffett, sipping a Coke from a Styrofoam cup, soon ended the conversation.

Mr. Buffett tends to stick to investments for the long haul, even when the going gets bumpy. Mr. Sokol recalls bracing for an August 2004 meeting at which he planned to break the news to Mr. Buffett that the Iowa utility needed to write off about $360 million for a soured zinc project. Mr. Sokol says he was stunned by Mr. Buffett's response: "David, we all make mistakes." Their meeting lasted only 10 minutes.

"I would have fired me if I was him," Mr. Sokol says.

"If you don't make mistakes, you can't make decisions," Mr. Buffett says. "You can't dwell on them."

Mr. Buffett has relied on gut instinct for decades to run Berkshire Hathaway Inc. Watch him at work inside his $136 billion investment behemoth, and what you see resembles no other modern financial titan. He spends most of his day alone in an office with no computer, no stock-quote machine or stock-data terminal. He keeps a muted television set tuned to CNBC, the financial-news network. Although he occasionally carries a cell phone on the road, he does not use one in Omaha. He keeps no calculator on his desk, preferring to do most calculations in his head. "I deplore false precision in math," he says, explaining that he does not need exact numbers for most investment decisions. On the cabinet behind his desk are two black phones with direct lines to his brokers on Wall Street.

On a recent Wednesday morning, Mr. Buffett had barely settled into his seat when one of them rang. It was John Freund, his longtime broker from Citigroup Inc.'s investment-banking unit. Mr. Freund briefed Mr. Buffett on a stock position he had been building for Berkshire. "If we bought a couple million, that would be fine," Mr. Buffett said, giving Mr. Freund a parameter for how many shares he wanted to buy that day. (Mr. Buffett declines to identify the stock.)

By the end of the day, Mr. Buffett had bought $140 million of the stock for Berkshire's investment portfolio—equal to the entire asset value of many mutual funds.

Even with such heavy trading, Mr. Buffett's desk isn't littered with stock research. "I don't use analysts or fortune tellers," he says. "If I had to pick one, I don't know which it would be."

Source: Susan Pulliam and Karen Richardson, *The Wall Street Journal*, November 12, 2005. Reprinted with permission of *The Wall Street Journal*. © 2005 Dow Jones & Company, Inc. All Rights Reserved Worldwide.

they good or are they lucky? If we could track them for many decades, we might be able to tell, but for the most part, money managers are not around long enough for us to accumulate sufficient data. We discuss the performance of money managers as a group later in the chapter.

Our final problem has to do with what is known as "data snooping." Instead of monkeys at typewriters, think of what can happen if thousands of finance researchers with thousands of computers are all studying the same data and are looking for inefficiencies. Apparent patterns, or anomalies, will surely be found.

In fact, researchers *have* discovered extremely simple patterns that, at least historically, have been both highly successful and very hard to explain. We discuss some of these later in the chapter. These discoveries raise another problem: ghosts in the data. If we look long enough and hard enough at any data, we are bound to find some apparent patterns by sheer chance. But are these patterns real? Only time will tell.

Notwithstanding the four problems we have discussed, based on the last 20 to 30 years of scientific research, three generalities about market efficiency seem in order. First, short-term stock price and market movements appear to be very difficult, or even impossible, to predict with any accuracy (at least with any objective method of which we are aware). Second, the market reacts quickly and sharply to new (i.e., unanticipated) information, and the vast majority of studies of the impact of new information find little or no evidence that the market underreacts or overreacts to new information in a way that can be profitably exploited. Third, *if* the stock market can be beaten, the way to do it is at least not *obvious,* so the implication is that the market is not grossly inefficient.

SOME IMPLICATIONS OF MARKET EFFICIENCY

To the extent that you think a market is efficient, there are some important investment implications. Going back to Chapter 2, we saw that the investment process can be viewed as having two parts: asset allocation and security selection. Even if all markets are efficient, asset allocation is still important because the way you divide your money among the various types of investments will strongly influence your overall risk-return relation.

However, if markets are efficient, then security selection is less important, and you do not have to worry too much about overpaying or underpaying for any particular security. In fact, if markets are efficient, you would probably be better off just buying a large basket of stocks and following a passive investment strategy. Your main goal would be to hold your costs to a minimum while maintaining a broadly diversified portfolio. We discussed index funds, which exist for just this purpose, in Chapter 4.

In broader terms, if markets are efficient, then little role exists for professional money managers. You should not pay load fees to buy mutual fund shares, and you should shop for low management fees. You should not work with full-service brokers, and so on.

If markets are efficient, there is one other thing that you should not do: You should not try to time the market. Recall that market timing amounts to moving money in and out of the market based on your expectations of future market direction. By trying to time the market, all you will accomplish is to guarantee that you will, on average, underperform the market.

In fact, market efficiency aside, market timing is hard to recommend. Historically, most of the gains earned in the stock market have tended to occur over relatively short periods of time. If you miss even a single one of these short market runups, you will likely never catch up. Put differently, successful market timing requires phenomenal accuracy to be of any benefit, and anything less than that will, based on the historical record, result in underperforming the market.

CHECK THIS

7.8a   What are the four basic reasons market efficiency is difficult to test?

7.8b   What are the implications to investors if markets are efficient?

7.9 Market Efficiency and the Performance of Professional Money Managers

Let's have a stock market investment contest in which you are going to take on professional money managers. Of course, the professional money managers have at their disposal their skill, banks of computers, and scores of analysts to help pick their stocks. Does this sound like an unfair match? Well, it is—you have a terrific advantage.

It's true. You can become an expert investor by using the following investment strategy: Hold a broad-based market index. One such index that you can easily buy is a mutual fund called the Vanguard 500 Index Fund (there are other market index mutual funds, too). This low-fee mutual find is designed to produce investment results that correspond to the price and yield performance of the S&P 500 Index. The fund tracks the performance of the S&P 500 Index by investing its assets in the stocks that make up the S&P 500 Index. By the way, this fund is popular—as of February 2010, the Vanguard 500 Index Fund was one of the largest stock mutual funds in the United States, with over $46 billion in assets.

As discussed in a previous chapter, a general equity mutual fund (GEF) is simply a pool of money invested in stocks that is overseen by a professional money manager. The number of GEFs has grown substantially during the past 20 years. Figure 7.6 shows the growth in the number of GEFs from 1986 through 2009. The solid blue line shows the total number of funds that have existed for at least one year, while the solid red line shows the number of funds that have existed for at least 10 years. From Figure 7.6, you can see that it is difficult for professional money managers to keep their funds in existence for 10 years (if it were easy, there would not be much difference between the solid blue line and the solid red line).

Figure 7.6 also shows the number of these funds that beat the performance of the Vanguard 500 Index Fund. You can see that there is much more variation in the dashed blue line than in the dashed red line. What this means is that in any given year, it is hard to predict how many professional money managers will beat the Vanguard 500 Index Fund. But the

| FIGURE 7.6 | The Growth of Actively Managed Equity Funds, 1986–2009 |

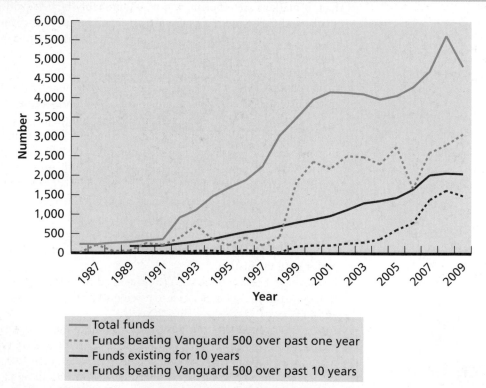

Source: Author calculations.

FIGURE 7.7

Percentage of Managed Equity Funds Beating the Vanguard 500 Index Fund, One-Year Returns

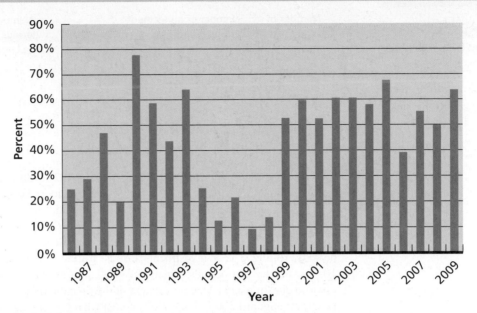

Source: Author calculations.

FIGURE 7.8

Percentage of Managed Equity Funds Beating the Vanguard 500 Index Fund, 10-Year Returns

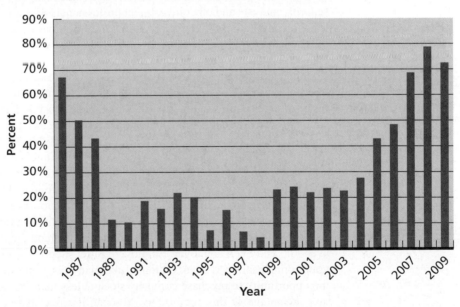

Source: Author calculations.

low level and low variation of the dashed red line means that the percentage of professional money managers who can beat the Vanguard 500 Index Fund over a 10-year investment period is low and stable.

Figures 7.7 and 7.8 are bar charts that show the percentage of managed equity funds that beat the Vanguard 500 Index Fund. Figure 7.7 uses return data for the previous year only, while Figure 7.8 uses return data for the previous 10 years. As you can see from Figure 7.7, in only 12 of the 24 years spanning 1986 through 2009 did more than half the professional money managers beat the Vanguard 500 Index Fund. The performance is worse

TABLE 7.1

The Performance of Professional Money Managers versus the Vanguard 500 Index Fund

Length of Each Investment Period (Years)	Span	Number of Investment Periods	Number of Investment Periods Half the Funds Beat Vanguard	Percent	Number of Investment Periods Three-Fourths of the Funds Beat Vanguard	Percent
1	1980–2009	30	14	46.7%	2	6.7%
3	1982–2009	28	11	39.3	0	0.0
5	1984–2009	26	9	34.6	0	0.0
10	1989–2009	21	3	14.3	1	4.8

Source: Author calculations.

when it comes to 10-year investment periods (1977–1986 through 2000–2009). As shown in Figure 7.8, in only 5 of these 24 investment periods did more than half the professional money managers beat the Vanguard 500 Index Fund.

Table 7.1 presents more evidence concerning the performance of professional money managers. Using data from 1980 through 2009, we divide this time period into 1-year investment periods, rolling 3-year investment periods, rolling 5-year investment periods, and rolling 10-year investment periods. Then, after we calculate the number of investment periods, we ask two questions: (1) what percentage of the time did half the professionally managed funds beat the Vanguard 500 Index Fund? and (2) what percentage of the time did three-fourths of the professionally managed funds beat the Vanguard 500 Index Fund?

As you see in Table 7.1, the performance of professional money managers is generally quite poor relative to the Vanguard 500 Index Fund. In addition, the performance of professional money managers declines the longer the investment period.

The figures and table in this section raise some difficult and uncomfortable questions for security analysts and other investment professionals. If markets are inefficient, and tools like fundamental analysis are valuable, why don't mutual fund managers do better? Why can't mutual fund managers even beat a broad market index?

The performance of professional money managers is especially troublesome when we consider the enormous resources at their disposal and the substantial survivorship bias that exists. The survivorship bias comes into being because managers and funds that do especially poorly disappear. If beating the market was possible, then this Darwinian process of elimination should lead to a situation in which the survivors, as a group, are capable of doing so. The fact that professional money managers seem to lack the ability to outperform a broad market index is consistent with the notion that, overall, the equity market is efficient.

So if the market is this efficient, what is the role for portfolio managers? The role of a portfolio manager in an efficient market is to build a portfolio to meet the specific needs of individual investors. You have learned that a basic principle of investing is to hold a well-diversified portfolio. However, exactly which diversified portfolio is optimal varies by investor.

Some factors that influence portfolio choice include the investor's age, tax bracket, risk aversion, and even employer. Employer? Sure, suppose you work for Starbucks and part of your compensation is stock options. Like many companies, Starbucks offers its employees the opportunity to purchase company stock at less than market value. Of course, you would take advantage of this opportunity. You can imagine that you could wind up with a lot of Starbucks stock in your portfolio, which means you are not holding a diversified portfolio. The role of your portfolio manager would be to help you add other assets to your portfolio so that it is once again well diversified.

CHECK THIS

7.9a How well do professional money managers perform, on average, against a broad market index?

7.9b What are the implications of this performance to investors?

7.10 Anomalies

In this section, we discuss some aspects of stock price behavior that are both baffling and potentially hard to reconcile with market efficiency. Researchers call these *market anomalies*. Keep three facts in mind as you read about market anomalies. First, anomalies are generally "small," in that they do not involve many dollars relative to the overall size of the stock market. Second, many anomalies are fleeting and tend to disappear when discovered. Finally, anomalies are not easily used as the basis for a trading strategy, because transaction costs render many of them unprofitable.

THE DAY-OF-THE-WEEK EFFECT

In the stock market, which day of the week has, on average, the biggest return? The question might strike you as silly; after all, what would make one day different from any other on average? On further reflection, though, you might realize that one day is different: Monday.

When we calculate a daily return for the stock market, we take the percentage change in closing prices from one trading day to the next. For every day except Monday this is a 24-hour period. However, because the markets are closed on the weekends, the average return on Monday is based on the percentage change from Friday's close to Monday's close, a 72-hour period. Thus, the average Monday return would be computed over a three-day period, not just a one-day period. Therefore, because of this longer time period, we would predict that Monday should have the highest return; in fact Monday's average return should be three times as large.

Given this reasoning, it may come as a surprise to you to learn that Monday has the lowest average return. In fact, Monday is the only day with a *negative* average return. This is the **day-of-the-week effect**. Table 7.2 shows the average return by day of the week for the S&P 500 for the period January 1950 through December 2009.

In the 60 years spanning 1950 to 2009, the negative return on Monday is significant, both in a statistical sense and in an economic sense. This day-of-the-week effect does not appear to be a fluke; it exists in other markets, such as the bond market, and it exists in stock markets outside the United States. It has defied explanation since it was first documented in the early 1980s. As you can see in Table 7.2, the effect is strong in the 1950–1979 time period. The effect is not apparent in the 1980–2009 time period.

Still, critics of the efficient markets hypothesis point to this strange return behavior as evidence of market inefficiency. While this return behavior is odd, exploiting it presents a problem. That is, how this return behavior can be used to earn a positive excess return is not clear. This murkiness is especially true in the 1980–2009 time period (i.e., in the period following the time when the effect was first documented). So whether this strange return behavior points to inefficiency is hard to say.

THE AMAZING JANUARY EFFECT

We saw in Chapter 1 that returns from small-cap common stocks have significantly outdistanced the returns from large-cap common stocks. Beginning in the early 1980s, researchers reported that the difference was too large even to be explained by differences in risk. In other words, small stocks appeared to earn positive excess returns.

day-of-the-week effect
The tendency for Monday to have a negative average return.

TABLE 7.2	Average Daily S&P 500 Returns, by Day of the Week (Dividends Included)				
			Weekday		
Time Period	Monday	Tuesday	Wednesday	Thursday	Friday
1950–2009	−0.068%	0.040%	0.084%	0.041%	0.076%
1950–1979	−0.137	0.001	0.094	0.061	0.115
1980–2009	0.003	0.080	0.075	0.022	0.037

Source: Author calculations.

Further research found that, in fact, a substantial percentage of the return on small stocks has historically occurred early in the month of January, particularly in the few days surrounding the turn of the year. Even closer research documents that this peculiar phenomenon is more pronounced for stocks that have experienced significant declines in value, or "losers."

Thus, we have the famous "small-stock-in-January-especially-around-the-turn-of-the-year-for-losers effect," or SSIJEATTOTYFLE for short. For obvious reasons, this phenomenon is usually just dubbed the **January effect**. To give you an idea of how big this effect is, we first plotted average returns by month going back to 1926 for large stocks in Figure 7.9A. As shown, the average return per month has been just under 1 percent.

In Figure 7.9A, there is nothing remarkable about January; the largest average monthly return for large stocks occurred in December (followed closely by July); the lowest in September. From a statistical standpoint, there is nothing too exceptional about these large stock returns. After all, some month has to be the highest, and some month has to be the lowest.

Figure 7.9B, however, shows average returns by month for small stocks (notice the difference in vertical axis scaling between Figures 7.9A and 7.9B). The month of January definitely jumps out. Over the 84 years covered, small stocks gained, on average, about 6.5 percent in the month of January alone! Comparing Figures 7.9A and 7.9B, we see, outside the month of January, small stocks have not done especially well relative to large stocks. To a lesser extent, we see that small stocks have done better than large stocks in February, but large stocks have done better than small stocks by about the same amount in October.

The January effect appears to exist in many major markets around the world, so it's not unique to the United States (it's actually more pronounced in some other markets). It also exists in some markets other than stock markets. Critics of market efficiency point to enormous gains to be had from simply investing in January and ask: How can an efficient market have such unusual behavior? Why don't investors take advantage of this opportunity and thereby drive it out of existence?

In Table 7.3, you can see that, on average, small stock returns were 5.34 percent higher than large stock returns in the 1926–2009 time period. The next best month in this period (February) is essentially canceled out by the worst month (October). When we break the 1926–2009 time period into smaller time intervals, you can see that the January effect has diminished over time. In fact, in the 1982–2009 time period, the *best* monthly difference of 2.42 percent (January) is essentially canceled out by the worst monthly difference of −2.40 percent (October).

FIGURE 7.9A   Large Stocks' Average Monthly Returns, 1926–2009, Dividends Included

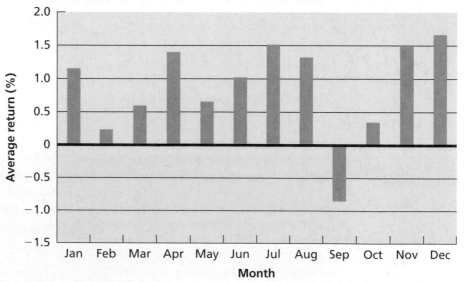

Source: Author calculations.

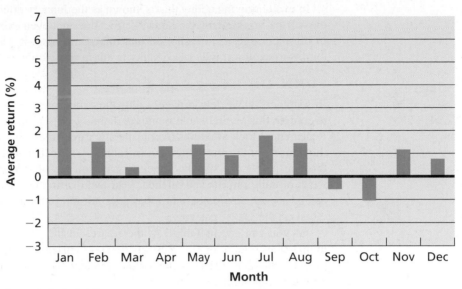

Source: Author calculations.

TABLE 7.3 — **Monthly Returns of Small Stocks Minus Monthly Returns of Large Stocks, by Various Time Periods, 1926–2009**

| Time Period | Best Difference | | Next Best Difference | | Worst Difference | |
	Percent	Month	Percent	Month	Percent	Month
1926–2009	5.34%	January	1.30%	February	−1.37%	October
1926–1953	7.35	January	1.85	May	−3.01	December
1954–1981	6.26	January	0.84	February	1.73	October
1982–2009	2.42	January	1.38	February	−2.40	October

Source: Author calculations.

Unlike the day-of-the-week effect, the January effect is at least partially understood. Two factors are thought to be important. The first is tax-loss selling. Investors have a strong tax incentive to sell stocks that have gone down in value to realize the loss for tax purposes. This trading leads to a pattern of selling in these stocks near the end of the year and buying after the turn of the year. In large stocks, this activity wouldn't have much effect, but in the smaller stocks, it could.

The tax-loss selling argument is plausible because researchers have looked to see whether the January effect existed in the United States before there was an income tax—and they found no January effect. However, the January effect has been found in other countries that didn't (or don't) have calendar tax years or didn't (or don't) have capital gains taxes. However, foreign investors in those markets (such as U.S. investors) did (or do). So, debate continues about the tax-loss selling explanation.

The second factor has to do with institutional investors. The argument here has several pieces, but the gist of it is that these large investors compensate portfolio managers based on their performance over the calendar year. Portfolio managers therefore pile into small stocks at the beginning of the year because of their growth potential, bidding up prices. Over the course of the year, they shed the stocks that do poorly because they don't want to be seen as having a bunch of "losers" in their portfolio (this is called "window dressing"). Also, because performance is typically measured relative to the S&P 500, portfolio managers who begin to lag because of losses in small stocks have an incentive to sell them and buy S&P 500 stocks to make sure they don't end up too far behind the S&P 500. Managers who are well ahead late in the year also have an incentive to move into S&P 500 stocks to preserve their leads (this is called "bonus lock-in").

In evaluating the oddity that is known as the January effect, keep in mind that, unlike the day-of-the-week effect, the January effect does not even exist for the market as a whole, so, in big-picture terms, it is not all that important. Also, it doesn't happen every year, so attempts to exploit it will occasionally result in substantial losses.

TURN-OF-THE-YEAR EFFECT

Researchers have delved deeply into the January effect to see whether the effect is due to returns during the whole month of January or to returns bracketing the end of the year. Researchers look at returns over a specific three-week period and compare these returns to the returns for the rest of the year. In Table 7.4, we calculated daily market returns from 1962 through 2009. The specific three-week period we call "Turn-of-the-Year Days" is the last week of daily returns in a calendar year and the first two weeks of daily returns in the next calendar year. Any daily return that does not fall into this three-week period is put into the "Rest-of-the-Days" category.

As you can see in Table 7.4, the returns in the "Turn-of-the-Year Days" category are higher than returns in the "Rest-of-the-Days" category. Further, the difference is apparent in the 1986–2009 period. The difference, however, was more than twice as large in the 1962–1985 period.

TURN-OF-THE-MONTH EFFECT

Financial market researchers have also investigated whether a turn-of-the-month effect exists. In Table 7.5, we took daily stock market returns and separated them into two categories. If the daily return is from the last day of any month or the following three days of the following month, it is put into the "Turn-of-the-Month Days" category. All other daily returns are put into the "Rest-of-the-Days" category.

As you can see in Table 7.5, the returns in the "Turn-of-the-Month Days" category are higher than the returns in the "Rest-of-the-Days" category. As with the turn-of-the-year anomaly, the turn-of-the-month effect is apparent in each of the three time periods we report. Interestingly, the effect appears to be almost as strong in the 1986–2009 period as in the 1962–1985 period. Again, the fact that this effect exists is puzzling to proponents of the EMH.

The day-of-the-week, turn-of-the-month, turn-of-the-year, and the January effect are examples of calendar anomalies. There are noncalendar anomalies as well. Two well-known noncalendar anomalies have to do with earnings announcements and price-earnings ratios.

TABLE 7.4 — **The Turn-of-the-Year Effect**

| | Market Return on the: | | |
Time Period	Turn-of-the-Year Days (%)	Rest-of-the-Days (%)	Difference (%)
1962–2009	0.128%	0.034%	0.094%
1962–1985	0.167	0.029	0.138
1986–2009	0.089	0.039	0.050

Source: Author calculations.

TABLE 7.5 — **The Turn-of-the-Month Effect**

| | Market Return on the: | | |
Time Period	Turn-of-the-Month Days (%)	Rest-of-the-Days (%)	Difference (%)
1962–2009	0.127%	0.019%	0.108%
1962–1985	0.129	0.016	0.114
1986–2009	0.125	0.023	0.102

Source: Author calculations.

THE EARNINGS ANNOUNCEMENT PUZZLE

As you saw earlier in this chapter, unexpected news releases can have a dramatic impact on the price of a stock. One news item that is particularly important to investors is an earnings announcement. These announcements contain information about past earnings and future earnings potential.

Researchers have shown that substantial price adjustments do occur in anticipation of the actual earnings. According to the EMH, stock prices should then respond very quickly to unanticipated news, or the earnings "surprise." However, researchers have found that it takes days (or even longer) for the market price to adjust fully. In addition, some researchers have found that buying stocks after positive earnings surprises is a profitable investment strategy.

THE PRICE-EARNINGS (P/E) PUZZLE

As we have discussed elsewhere, the P/E ratio is widely followed by investors and is used in stock valuation. Researchers have found that, on average, stocks with relatively low P/E ratios outperform stocks with relatively high P/E ratios, even after adjusting for other factors, like risk. Because a P/E ratio is publicly available information, according to the EMH, it should already be reflected in stock prices. However, purchasing stocks with relatively low P/E ratios appears to be a potentially profitable investment strategy.

There are many other noncalendar anomalies. For example, the market appears to do worse on cloudy days than sunny days. But rather than continuing with a laundry list of anomalies—however much fun they might provide—we will instead turn to some spectacular events in market history.

CHECK THIS

7.10a   What is the day-of-the-week effect?

7.10b   What is the amazing January effect?

7.10c   What is the turn-of-the-year effect?

7.11 Bubbles and Crashes

As a famous songwriter penned, "History shows again and again, how nature points up the folly of men."[1] Nowhere is this statement seemingly more appropriate in finance than in a discussion of bubbles and crashes.

bubble
A situation where observed prices soar far higher than fundamentals and rational analysis would suggest.

A **bubble** occurs when market prices soar far in excess of what normal and rational analysis would suggest. Investment bubbles eventually pop because they are not based on fundamental values. When a bubble does pop, investors find themselves holding assets with plummeting values. You can read the nearby *Investment Updates* box for a more lighthearted side of bubbles.

crash
A situation where market prices collapse significantly and suddenly.

A **crash** is a significant and sudden drop in marketwide values. Crashes are generally associated with a bubble. Typically, a bubble lasts much longer than a crash. A bubble can form over weeks, months, or even years. Crashes, on the other hand, are sudden, generally lasting less than a week. However, the disastrous financial aftermath of a crash can last for years.

THE CRASH OF 1929

During the Roaring Twenties, the stock market was supposed to be the place where everyone could get rich. The market was widely believed to be a no-risk situation. Many people invested their life savings without learning about the potential pitfalls of investing. At the time, investors could purchase stocks by putting up 10 percent of the purchase price and borrowing the remainder from a broker. This level of leverage was one factor that led to the sudden market downdraft in October 1929.

---

[1] Lyrics from "Godzilla," by Donald "Buck Dharma" Roeser (as performed by Blue Oyster Cult).

A FEAR OF BUBBLES

The list of irrational fears enobled as "phobias"—by whatever bodies decide such things—is astonishing. Children, clowns and flowers all appear, apparently scaring enough people witless to warrant official, faux-Greek monikers of their own. So it seems quite odd that there's no official term for "fear of bubbles." Plenty of people in and around the world's financial markets have one, and rather badly, so it might be nice to give their trepidation an official name.*

Those of more bearish persuasion have been disposed to see bubbles forming in risk assets, like equities, all year, and have been wringing their hands about it. These folk argue stock rises have gone far beyond anything economic fundamentals would dictate. The indexes' strength is a product of enormous emergency liquidity provision, rather than genuine improvement "on the ground." With returns on safe, government-backed assets laughably low, investors are piling thoughtlessly into more risky things, headlong and heedless of the economics.

The soothing defense, mounted most recently by analysts at Deutsche Bank, talking about Asian markets, is that, far from boiling over, equity markets have simply made good on losses they incurred when everyone thought the world was going to end. Now we're sure it isn't, well sure-ish, stocks have just returned to levels we were seeing before credit crunched.

This is a long way from a watertight argument, of course. There's nothing special about pre-crunch market levels, nor anything intrinsically heartwarming or "right" about revisiting them. And, last time we were up here, the markets weren't on the state life support they now get.

But the soothers then go on to list various indicators of equity value, price/earnings ratios, long-term profit levels, that sort of thing, all of which supposedly prove things aren't getting too bubbly so far.

And in any case, the fact is that those who have bet on rising markets, so far, have been vindicated. While those who said it's all just a growing bubble and stayed away have missed out terribly.

Investors can perhaps be forgiven for not worrying much why a market is rising, as long as it keeps doing so.

And, even if central-bank liquidity is doing most of the heavy lifting here, there's no sign it will be withdrawn in the near future. The latest comments from the Fed attest to interest rates staying low for an extended period, even if such action could lead to "excessive risk-taking in financial markets." Negative inflation, negligible interest rates, plentiful liquidity and improving profit margins are likely to drive increasing equity valuations into the New Year, even if the economics continue to underwhelm. If all that makes a bubble it's one that will probably get bigger and scarier for a while yet.

*Fouskalaphobia is as close as we can get.

Source: David Cottle, *The Wall Street Journal,* November 25, 2009. Reprinted with permission of *The Wall Street Journal.* © 2009 Dow Jones & Company, Inc. All Rights Reserved Worldwide.

As you can see in Figure 7.10, on Friday, October 25, the Dow Jones Industrial Average closed up about a point, at 301.22. On Monday, October 28, it closed at 260.64, down 13.5 percent. On Tuesday, October 29, the Dow closed at 230.07, with an interday low of 212.33, which is about 30 percent lower than the closing level on the previous Friday. On this day, known as "Black Tuesday," NYSE volume of 16.4 million shares was more than four times normal levels.

Although the Crash of 1929 was a large decline, it pales with respect to the ensuing bear market. As shown in Figure 7.11, the DJIA rebounded about 20 percent following the October 1929 crash. However, the DJIA then began a protracted fall, reaching the bottom at 40.56 on July 8, 1932. This level represents about a 90 percent decline from the record high level of 386.10 on September 3, 1929. By the way, the DJIA did not surpass its previous high level until November 24, 1954, more than 25 years later.

THE CRASH OF OCTOBER 1987

Once, when we spoke of *The* Crash, we meant October 29, 1929. That was until October 1987. The Crash of 1987 began on Friday, October 16. On huge volume (at the time) of about 338 million shares, the DJIA fell 108 points to close at 2,246.73. It was the first time in history that the DJIA fell by more than 100 points in one day.

FIGURE 7.10

Dow Jones Industrial Average, October 21, 1929, to October 31, 1929

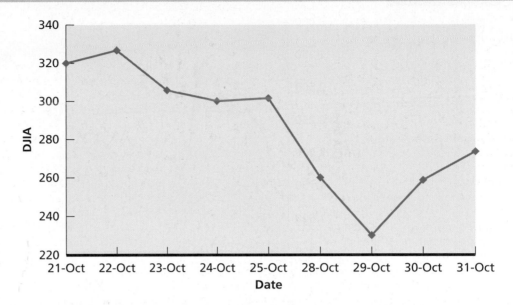

FIGURE 7.11

Dow Jones Industrial Average, October 1928 to October 1932

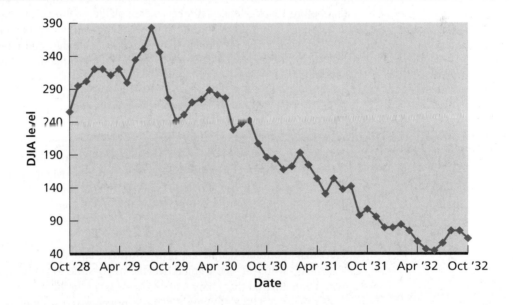

October 19, 1987, now wears the mantle of "Black Monday." This day was indeed a dark and stormy one on Wall Street; the market lost about 22.6 percent of its value on a new record volume of about 600 million shares traded. The DJIA plummeted 508.32 points to close at 1,738.74.

During the day on Tuesday, October 20, the DJIA continued to plunge in value, reaching an intraday low of 1,616.21. But the market rallied and closed at 1,841.01, up 102 points. From the then market high on August 25, 1987, of 2,746.65 to the intraday low on October 20, 1987, the market had fallen over 40 percent.

After the Crash of 1987, however, there was no protracted depression. In fact, as you can see in Figure 7.12, the DJIA took only two years to surpass its previous market high made in August 1987.

What happened? It's not exactly ancient history, but, here again, debate rages. One faction says that irrational investors had bid up stock prices to ridiculous levels until Black Monday, when

FIGURE 7.12 | Dow Jones Industrial Average, October 1986 to October 1990

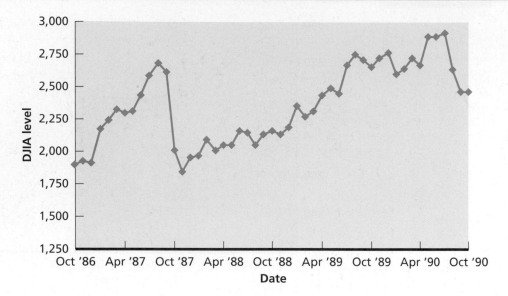

the bubble burst, leading to panic selling as investors dumped their stocks. The other faction says that before Black Monday, markets were volatile, volume was heavy, and some ominous signs about the economy were filtering in. From the close on October 13 to the close on October 16, 1987, for example, the market fell by over 10 percent, the largest three-day drop since May 1940 (when German troops broke through French lines near the start of World War II). To top it all off, market values had risen sharply because of a dramatic increase in takeover activity, but Congress was in session and was actively considering antitakeover legislation.

Another factor is that beginning a few years before the Crash of 1987, large investors had developed techniques known as *program trading* designed for very rapid selling of enormous quantities of shares of stock following a market decline. These techniques were still largely untested because the market had been strong for years. However, following the huge sell-off on October 16, 1987, sell orders came pouring in on Monday at a pace never before seen. In fact, these program trades were (and are) blamed by some for much of what happened.

One of the few things we know for certain about the Crash of 1987 is that the stock exchanges suffered a meltdown. The NYSE simply could not handle the volume. Posting of prices was delayed by hours, so investors had no idea what their positions were worth. The specialists couldn't handle the flow of orders, and some specialists actually began selling. NASDAQ went off-line when it became impossible to get through to market makers. It has even been alleged that many stopped answering the phone.

On the two days following the crash, prices *rose* by about 14 percent, one of the biggest short-term gains ever. Prices remained volatile for some time, but as antitakeover talk in Congress died down, the market recovered.

The Crash of 1987 led to some significant market changes. Upgrades have made it possible to handle much heavier trading volume, for example. One of the most interesting changes was the introduction of **NYSE circuit breakers**. Different circuit breakers are triggered if the DJIA drops by 10, 20, or 30 percent. These 10, 20, and 30 percent decline levels in the DJIA, respectively, will result in the following actions:

Level 1 Halt. A 10 percent drop in the DJIA will halt trading for one hour if the decline occurs before 2 P.M.; for one half hour if the decline occurs between 2 and 2:30 P.M.; and it will have no effect if the decline occurs between 2:30 and 4:00 P.M.

Level 2 Halt. A 20 percent drop in the DJIA will halt trading for two hours if the decline occurs before 1 P.M.; for one hour if the decline occurs between 1 and 2 P.M.; and for the remainder of the day if it occurs between 2 and 4 P.M.

NYSE circuit breakers

Rules that kick in to slow or stop trading when the DJIA declines by more than a preset amount in a trading session.

Level 3 Halt. A 30 percent drop will halt trading for the remainder of the day regardless of when the decline occurs.

These specific circuit breaker trigger limits were implemented in 1998. Point drops that trigger the circuit breakers are calculated quarterly. For the second quarter of 2010, Level 1, 2, and 3 halts will occur at DJIA drops of 1,050, 2,150, and 3,200 points, respectively. Because circuit breakers are designed to slow a market decline, they are often called "speed bumps." Naturally, how well they work is a matter of debate.

One of the most remarkable things about the crash is how little impact it seems to have had. If you look back at the data in Chapter 1, you will see that the market was actually up slightly in 1987. The postcrash period was one of the better times to be in the market, and the Crash of 1987 increasingly looks like a blip in one of the most spectacular market increases that U.S. investors have ever seen. One thing is clearly true: October is the cruelest month for market investors. Indeed two years after the Crash of 1987, a minicrash occurred on October 13, 1989, as the DJIA fell 190 points in the afternoon (following the collapse of a proposed buyout of United Airlines).

THE ASIAN CRASH

The crash of the Nikkei Index, which began in 1990, lengthened into a particularly long bear market. It is quite like the Crash of 1929 in that respect.

The Asian crash started with a booming bull market in the 1980s. Japan and emerging Asian economies seemed to be forming a powerful economic force. The "Asian economy" became an investor outlet for those wary of the U.S. market after the Crash of 1987.

To give you some idea of the bubble that was forming in Japan between 1955 and 1989, real estate prices in Japan increased by 70 times, and stock prices increased 100 times over. In 1989, price-earnings ratios of Japanese stocks climbed to unheard of levels as the Nikkei Index soared past 39,000. In retrospect, there were numerous warning signals about the Japanese market. At the time, however, optimism about the continued growth in the Japanese market remained high. Crashes never seem to occur when the outlook is poor, so, as with other crashes, many people did not see the impending Nikkei crash.

As you can see in Figure 7.13, in three years from December 1986 to the peak in December 1989, the Nikkei 225 Index rose from about 15,000 to about 39,000. Over the next three years, the index fell to about the 15,000 level. In April 2003, the Nikkei Index stood at a level that was 80 percent off its peak in December 1989.

| FIGURE 7.13 | Nikkei 225 Index, January 1984 to January 2010 |

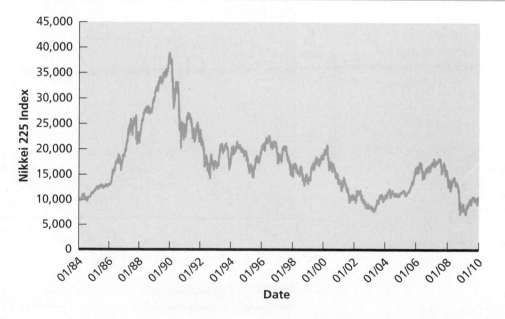

THE "DOT-COM" BUBBLE AND CRASH

WWW

The growth of the World Wide Web is documented at www.zakon.org/robert/internet/timeline

How many Web sites do you think existed at the end of 1994? Would you believe only about 10,000? By the end of 1999, the number of active Web sites stood at about 9,500,000 and at the end of 2009, there were over 200 million active Web sites.

By the mid-1990s, the rise in Internet use and its international growth potential fueled widespread excitement over the "new economy." Investors did not seem to care about solid business plans—only big ideas. Investor euphoria led to a surge in Internet IPOs, which were commonly referred to as "dot-coms" because so many of their names ended in ".com." Of course, the lack of solid business models doomed many of the newly formed companies. Many of them suffered huge losses and some folded relatively shortly after their IPOs.

The extent of the dot-com bubble and subsequent crash is presented in Table 7.6 and Figure 7.14, which compare the Amex Internet Index and the S&P 500 Index. As shown in Table 7.6, the Amex Internet Index soared from a level of 114.68 on October 1, 1998, to its peak of 688.52 in late March 2000, an increase of 500 percent. The Amex Internet Index then fell to a level of 58.59 in early October 2002, a drop of 91 percent. By contrast, the S&P 500 Index rallied about 31 percent in the same 1998–2000 time period and fell 40 percent during the 2000–2002 time period.

TABLE 7.6			Values of the Amex Internet Index and the S&P 500 Index			
Date	Amex Internet Index Value	Gain to Peak from Oct. 1, 1998 (%)	Loss from Peak to Trough (%)	S&P 500 Index Value	Gain to Peak from Oct. 1, 1998 (%)	Loss from Peak to Trough (%)
October 1, 1998	114.68			986.39		
Late March 2000 (peak)	688.52	500%		1,293.72	31%	
Early October 2002 (trough)	58.59		−91%	776.76		−40%

Source: Author calculations.

FIGURE 7.14	Values of the Amex Internet Index and the S&P 500 Index, October 1995 through December 2009

— Amex Internet Index
— S&P 500 Index

THE CRASH OF OCTOBER 2008

Elsewhere, we detail the stock market crash of 2008, where many market indexes fell more than 40 percent. Given the recent nature of these events, debate as to the fundamental cause is ongoing. Much of the preceding bubble (and crash), however, appears to have been a function of "easy money." Unqualified borrowers frequently received large, so-called subprime home loans at low "teaser" rates, which, after a certain amount of time, were reset at more reasonable levels, meaning that required monthly payments increased. If real estate prices were still rising, owners could easily refinance. When prices began to level off and fall, however, the number of bankruptcies increased significantly. These bankruptcies set off a downward spiral effect in securities related to real estate, which we discuss in more detail in another chapter.

To get a clearer picture of the progression of 2008, take a close look at Figure 7.15. This figure details the monthly closing price of the Dow Jones Industrial Average (DJIA). You can see that it declined steeply over almost the entire year. The months of October and November were particularly severe. Recall that this was the time during which investment banks such as Lehman Brothers and Bear Stearns (which had taken highly leveraged positions in real estate) went under or were acquired. Figure 7.16 shows the daily values for the DJIA from October 3 through October 17, 2008.

FIGURE 7.15

Dow Jones Industrial Average, January 2008 through April 2010

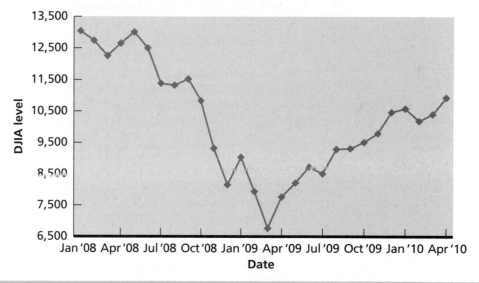

FIGURE 7.16

Dow Jones Industrial Average, October 3, 2008, to October 17, 2008

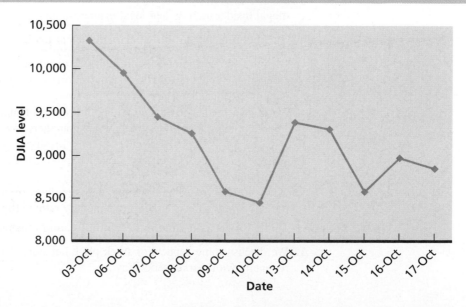

CHECK THIS

7.11a What is a stock market bubble? A stock market crash?

7.11b What are NYSE circuit breakers? What are they intended to do?

7.11c What is a major difference between the Crash of October 1929 and the Crash of October 1987?

7.11d Do you think the Crash of October 2008 resembles the Crash of October 1929 or the Crash of October 1987? Why?

7.12 Summary and Conclusions

In this chapter, we examined market price behavior and market efficiency. Market efficiency is probably the most controversial and intriguing issue in investments. We cover many aspects of market efficiency in this chapter—which we summarize by the chapter's important concepts.

1. **The foundations of market efficiency.**

   A. The efficient markets hypothesis (EMH) asserts that, as a practical matter, organized financial markets like the New York Stock Exchange are efficient.

   B. Researchers who study efficient markets often ask whether it is possible to "beat the market." We say that you beat the market if you can consistently earn returns in excess of those earned by other investments having the same risk.

   C. If a market is efficient, earning these excess returns is not possible, except by luck. The controversy surrounding the EMH centers on this assertion.

2. **The implications of the forms of market efficiency.**

   A. The EMH states that the market is efficient with respect to some particular information if that information is not useful in earning a positive excess return.

   B. The forms of market efficiency and their information sets are:

   - *Weak form:* Past price and volume information.
   - *Semistrong form:* All publicly available information.
   - *Strong form:* All information of any kind, public or private.

   C. We discuss how information affects market prices by influencing traders to act on the arrival of information. We show you how to distinguish among informed trading, illegal insider trading, and legal insider trading.

3. **Market efficiency and the performance of professional money managers.**

   A. Testing market efficiency is difficult. We discussed four reasons for this: (1) the risk-adjustment problem, (2) the relevant information problem, (3) the dumb luck problem, and (4) the data snooping problem.

   B. We then presented evidence concerning tests of market efficiency. One lesson we demonstrate is that professional money managers have been unable to beat the market consistently—despite their tremendous resources, experience, opportunities, and incentives. Also, this fact is true despite patterns and other oddities that have occurred historically in the stock market.

   C. The fact that professional money managers have been unable to beat the market supports the notion that markets are generally rather efficient.

4. **What stock market anomalies, bubbles, and crashes mean for market efficiency.**

   A. We discuss some aspects of stock price behavior that are both baffling and hard to reconcile with market efficiency.

B. We discuss the day-of-the-week effect, the amazing January effect, the turn-of-the-year effect, the turn-of-the-month effect, the earnings announcement puzzle, and the price-earnings (P/E) puzzle.

C. We present some market history concerning some famous bubbles and crashes, including the Crash of October 1929, the Crash of October 1987, the Asian crisis, the dot-com bubble and crash, and the Crash of 2008.

GET REAL

This chapter covered market efficiency. In it, we raised a significant question: Can you, or indeed anyone, consistently beat the market? In other words, is the market efficient? This is a question that every investor needs to think about because it has direct, practical implications for investing and portfolio management.

If you think the market is relatively efficient, then your investment strategy should focus on minimizing costs and taxes. Asset allocation is your primary concern, and you will still need to establish the risk level you are comfortable with. But beyond this, you should be a buy-and-hold investor, transacting only when absolutely necessary. Investments such as low-cost, low-turnover mutual funds make a lot of sense. Tools for analyzing the market are irrelevant at best. Thus, in some ways, the appropriate investment strategy is kind of boring, but it's the one that will pay off over the long haul in an efficient market.

In contrast, if you think the market is not particularly efficient, then you've got to be a security picker. You also have to decide what market analyzing tools will be the ones you use. This is also true if you are in the money management business; you have to decide which specific stocks or bonds to hold.

In the end, the only way to find out if you've got what it takes to beat the market is to try, and the best way to try is with a simulated brokerage account such as Stock-Trak. Be honest with yourself: You think you can beat the market; most novice investors do. Some change their minds and some don't. As to which tools to use, you will just have to find out which ones work (or don't work) for you.

Key Terms

Chapter Review Problems and Self-Test

1. **Market Research (CFA1)** Smolira Investment Trust (SIT) runs a retirement account for college professors, with a current market value of $2 billion. Alchemy, Inc., offers to conduct market research in an attempt to sift through the market data to find a way to increase the return to SIT's portfolio by 30 basis points this year. Alchemy is offering to conduct the research for the sum of $9 million. Is this price too high or too low?

2. **Picking a Money Manager (CFA1)**   You are helping your very rich aunt Molly decide where to invest her portfolio. She is planning to take a 10-year world tour after she invests the bulk of her portfolio. She thinks that picking a money manager is unimportant because she believes any professional money manager must be able to beat the market. She's just planning to pick a professional money manager at random. What do you tell her?

Answers to Self-Test Problems

1. Assuming that Alchemy, Inc., actually can conduct research that allows Smolira Investment Trust (SIT) to increase its portfolio return by 30 basis points this year, SIT would be willing to pay up to $2,000,000,000 times 0.0030 = $6,000,000 for this research. So the price of $9 million is too high.

2. You could show her Figure 7.8. In this figure, it is clear that picking a professional manager at random gives her about a 25 to 30 percent chance of beating a market fund like the Vanguard 500 Index Fund. If she invests her sizable portfolio in the Vanguard 500 Index Fund, she has about a 70 to 75 percent chance of beating a professional money manager picked at random.

Test Your Investment Quotient

1. **Efficient Markets Hypothesis (LO4, CFA1)**   A market anomaly refers to
   a. An exogenous shock to the market that is sharp but not persistent.
   b. A price or volume event that is inconsistent with historical price or volume trends.
   c. A trading or pricing structure that interferes with efficient buying or selling of securities.
   d. Price behavior that differs from the behavior predicted by the efficient markets hypothesis.

2. **Efficient Markets Hypothesis (LO1, CFA1)**   Which of the following assumptions does not imply an informationally efficient market?
   a. Security prices adjust rapidly to reflect new information.
   b. The timing of one news announcement is independent of other news announcements.
   c. The risk-free rate exists, and investors can borrow and lend unlimited amounts at the risk-free rate.
   d. Many profit-maximizing participants, each acting independently of the others, analyze and value securities.

3. **Efficient Markets Hypothesis (LO2, CFA1)**   After lengthy trial and error, you discover a trading system that would have doubled the value of your investment every six months if applied over the last three years. Which of the following problems makes it difficult to conclude that this is an example of market inefficiency?
   a. Risk-adjustment problem
   b. Relevant information problem
   c. Dumb luck problem
   d. Data snooping problem

4. **Efficient Markets Hypothesis (LO2, CFA1)**   In discussions of financial market efficiency, which of the following is not one of the stylized forms of market efficiency?
   a. Strong form
   b. Semistrong form
   c. Weak form
   d. Economic form

5. **Beating the Market (LO3, CFA2)**   Which of the following is not considered a problem when evaluating the ability of a trading system to "beat the market"?
   a. Risk-adjustment problem
   b. Relevant information problem
   c. Data measurement problem
   d. Data snooping problem

6. **Calendar Anomalies (LO4, CFA2)**   Which month of the year, on average, has had the highest stock market returns as measured by a small-stock portfolio?
   a. January
   b. March
   c. June
   d. December

7. **NYSE Circuit Breakers** Which of the following intraday changes in the Dow Jones Industrial Average (DJIA) will trigger a circuit breaker halting NYSE trading for one hour?

    a. 10 percent drop before 2 P.M.
    b. 10 percent drop after 2 P.M.
    c. 10 percent rise before 2 P.M.
    d. 10 percent rise after 2 P.M.

8. **Efficient Markets Hypothesis (LO2, CFA1)** The SEC has regulations that prohibit trading on inside information. If the market is _____ -form efficient, such regulation is not needed.

    a. Weak
    b. Semistrong
    c. Technical
    d. Strong

9. **The January Effect (LO4, CFA2)** Which of the following is a possible explanation of the January effect?

    I. Institutional window dressing
    II. Bonus demand
    III. Tax-loss selling

    a. I only
    b. I and II only
    c. I and III only
    d. I, II, and III

10. **NYSE Circuit Breakers** Circuit breakers implemented by the NYSE were designed to

    a. Reduce the January effect.
    b. Reduce the effect of technical trading.
    c. Eliminate program trading.
    d. Slow a market decline.

11. **Market Efficiency Implications (LO2, CFA2)** Assume the market is semistrong-form efficient. The best investment strategy is to

    a. Examine the past prices of a stock to determine the trend.
    b. Invest in an actively managed mutual fund whose manager searches for underpriced stocks.
    c. Invest in an index fund.
    d. Examine the financial statements for a company to find stocks that are not selling at intrinsic value.

12. **Market Efficiency Implications (LO2, CFA2)** Assume the market is weak-form efficient. If this is true, technical analysts _____ earn excess returns and fundamental analysts _____ earn excess returns.

    a. Could; could
    b. Could; could not
    c. Could not; could not
    d. Could not; could

13. **Efficient Markets Hypothesis (LO1, CFA1)** Which of the following is *not* true concerning the efficient markets hypothesis?

    a. Markets that are less organized are not as likely to be efficient.
    b. Markets with wide fluctuations in prices cannot be efficient.
    c. The efficient markets hypothesis deals only with the stock market.
    d. Prices in an efficient market are fair on average.

14. **Efficient Markets Hypothesis (LO2, CFA1)** You purchase a stock that you expect to increase in value over the next year. One year later, after the discovery that the CEO embezzled funds and the company is close to bankruptcy, the stock has fallen in price. Which of the following statements is true?

    a. This is a violation of weak-form efficiency.
    b. This is a violation of semistrong-form efficiency
    c. This is a violation of all forms of market efficiency.
    d. This is not a violation of market efficiency.

15. **Efficient Markets Hypothesis (LO2, CFA1)** Which of the following statements concerning market efficiency is true?

   a. If the market is weak-form efficient, it is also semistrong-form efficient.
   b. If the market is semistrong-form efficient, it is also strong-form efficient.
   c. If the market is weak-form efficient, it is also strong-form efficient.
   d. If the market is semistrong-form efficient, it is also weak-form efficient.

Concept Questions

1. **Efficient Markets (LO2, CFA1)** A stock market analyst is able to identify mispriced stocks by comparing the average price for the last 10 days to the average price for the last 60 days. If this is true, what do you know about the market?

2. **Efficient Markets (LO2, CFA1)** Critically evaluate the following statement: "Playing the stock market is like gambling. Such speculative investing has no social value, other than the pleasure people get from this form of gambling."

3. **Misconceptions about Efficient Markets (LO3, CFA2)** Several celebrated investors and stock pickers have recorded huge returns on their investments over the past two decades. Is the success of these particular investors an invalidation of an efficient stock market? Explain.

4. **Interpreting Efficient Markets (LO2, CFA2)** For each of the following scenarios, discuss whether profit opportunities exist from trading in the stock of the firm under the conditions that (1) the market is not weak-form efficient, (2) the market is weak-form but not semistrong-form efficient, (3) the market is semistrong-form but not strong-form efficient, and (4) the market is strong-form efficient.

   a. The stock price has risen steadily each day for the past 30 days.
   b. The financial statements for a company were released three days ago, and you believe you've uncovered some anomalies in the company's inventory and cost control reporting techniques that are understating the firm's true liquidity strength.
   c. You observe that the senior management of a company has been buying a lot of the company's stock on the open market over the past week.
   d. Your next-door neighbor, who happens to be a computer analyst at the local steel plant, casually mentions that a German steel conglomerate hinted yesterday that it might try to acquire the local firm in a hostile takeover.

5. **Performance of the Pros (LO3)** In the mid- to late-1990s, the performance of the pros was unusually poor—on the order of 90 percent of all equity mutual funds underperformed a passively managed index fund. How does this bear on the issue of market efficiency?

6. **Efficient Markets (LO1, CFA1)** A hundred years ago or so, companies did not compile annual reports. Even if you owned stock in a particular company, you were unlikely to be allowed to see the balance sheet and income statement for the company. Assuming the market is semistrong-form efficient, what does this say about market efficiency then compared to now?

7. **Efficient Markets Hypothesis (LO2, CFA1)** You invest $10,000 in the market at the beginning of the year, and by the end of the year your account is worth $15,000. During the year the market return was 10 percent. Does this mean that the market is inefficient?

8. **Efficient Markets Hypothesis (LO1, CFA1)** Which of the following statements are true about the efficient markets hypothesis?

   a. It implies perfect forecasting ability.
   b. It implies that prices reflect all available information.
   c. It implies an irrational market.
   d. It implies that prices do not fluctuate.
   e. It results from keen competition among investors.

9. **Semistrong Efficiency (LO2, CFA2)** If a market is semistrong-form efficient, is it also weak-form efficient? Explain.

10. **Efficient Markets Hypothesis (LO2, CFA1)** What are the implications of the efficient markets hypothesis for investors who buy and sell stocks in an attempt to "beat the market"?

11. **Efficient Markets Hypothesis (LO2, CFA1)** Aerotech, an aerospace technology research firm, announced this morning that it hired the world's most knowledgeable and

prolific space researchers. Before today, Aerotech's stock had been selling for $100. Assume that no other information is received over the next week and the stock market as a whole does not move.

    a. What do you expect will happen to Aerotech's stock?

    b. Consider the following scenarios:

        i. The stock price jumps to $118 on the day of the announcement. In subsequent days it floats up to $123, then falls back to $116.

        ii. The stock price jumps to $116 and remains at that level.

        iii. The stock price gradually climbs to $116 over the next week.

    Which scenario(s) indicate market efficiency? Which do not? Why?

12. Efficient Markets Hypothesis (LO2, CFA1)   When the 56-year-old founder of Gulf & Western, Inc., died of a heart attack, the stock price immediately jumped from $18.00 a share to $20.25, a 12.5 percent increase. This is evidence of market inefficiency, because an efficient stock market would have anticipated his death and adjusted the price beforehand. Assume that no other information is received and the stock market as a whole does not move. Is this statement about market efficiency true or false? Explain.

13. Efficient Markets Hypothesis (LO2, CFA1)   Today, the following announcement was made: "Early today the Justice Department reached a decision in the Universal Product Care (UPC) case. UPC has been found guilty of discriminatory practices in hiring. For the next five years, UPC must pay $2 million each year to a fund representing victims of UPC's policies." Assuming the market is efficient, should investors not buy UPC stock after the announcement because the litigation will cause an abnormally low rate of return? Explain.

14. Efficient Markets Hypothesis (LO2, CFA1)   Newtech Corp. is going to adopt a new chip-testing device that can greatly improve its production efficiency. Do you think the lead engineer can profit from purchasing the firm's stock before the news release on the device? After reading the announcement in *The Wall Street Journal,* should you be able to earn an abnormal return from purchasing the stock if the market is efficient?

15. Efficient Markets Hypothesis (LO2, CFA1)   TransTrust Corp. has changed how it accounts for inventory. Taxes are unaffected, although the resulting earnings report released this quarter is 20 percent higher than what it would have been under the old accounting system. There is no other surprise in the earnings report and the change in the accounting treatment was publicly announced. If the market is efficient, will the stock price be higher when the market learns that the reported earnings are higher?

16. Efficient Markets Hypothesis (LO3, CFA1)   The Durkin Investing Agency has been the best stock picker in the country for the past two years. Before this rise to fame occurred, the Durkin newsletter had 200 subscribers. Those subscribers beat the market consistently, earning substantially higher returns after adjustment for risk and transaction costs. Subscriptions have skyrocketed to 10,000. Now, when the Durkin Investing Agency recommends a stock, the price instantly rises several points. The subscribers currently earn only a normal return when they buy recommended stock because the price rises before anybody can act on the information. Briefly explain this phenomenon. Is Durkin's ability to pick stocks consistent with market efficiency?

17. Efficient Markets Hypothesis (LO2, CFA1)   Your broker commented that well-managed firms are better investments than poorly managed firms. As evidence, your broker cited a recent study examining 100 small manufacturing firms that eight years earlier had been listed in an industry magazine as the best-managed small manufacturers in the country. In the ensuing eight years, the 100 firms listed have not earned more than the normal market return. Your broker continued to say that if the firms were well managed, they should have produced better-than-average returns. If the market is efficient, do you agree with your broker?

18. Efficient Markets Hypothesis (LO2, CFA1)   A famous economist just announced in *The Wall Street Journal* his findings that the recession is over and the economy is again entering an expansion. Assume market efficiency. Can you profit from investing in the stock market after you read this announcement?

19. Efficient Markets Hypothesis (LO2, CFA1)   Suppose the market is semistrong-form efficient. Can you expect to earn excess returns if you make trades based on

    a. Your broker's information about record earnings for a stock?

    b. Rumors about a merger of a firm?

    c. Yesterday's announcement of a successful new product test?

20. **Efficient Markets Hypothesis (LO2, CFA1)**   The efficient markets hypothesis implies that all mutual funds should obtain the same expected risk-adjusted returns. Therefore, we can simply pick mutual funds at random. Is this statement true or false? Explain.

21. **Efficient Markets Hypothesis (LO2, CFA1)**   Assume that markets are efficient. During a trading day, American Golf, Inc., announces that it has lost a contract for a large golfing project, which, prior to the news, it was widely believed to have secured. If the market is efficient, how should the stock price react to this information if no additional information is released?

22. **Efficient Markets Hypothesis (LO2, CFA2)**   Prospectors, Inc., is a publicly traded gold prospecting company in Alaska. Although the firm's searches for gold usually fail, the prospectors occasionally find a rich vein of ore. What pattern would you expect to observe for Prospectors' cumulative abnormal returns if the market is efficient?

Questions and Problems

Core Questions

1. **Cumulative Abnormal Returns (LO2, CFA2)**   On November 14, Thorogood Enterprises announced that the public and acrimonious battle with its current CEO had been resolved. Under the terms of the deal, the CEO would step down from his position immediately. In exchange, he was given a generous severance package. Given the information below, calculate the cumulative abnormal return (CAR) around this announcement. Assume the company has an expected return equal to the market return. Graph and interpret your results. Do your results support market efficiency?

Date	Market Return (%)	Company Return (%)
11/7	0.5	0.4
11/8	0.3	0.4
11/9	−0.2	−0.3
11/10	−0.6	−0.5
11/11	1.3	1.1
11/14	−0.1	1.8
11/15	0.1	0.1
11/16	0.9	0.7
11/17	0.2	0.3
11/18	−0.2	0.0
11/19	0.3	0.2

2. **Cumulative Abnormal Returns (LO2, CFA2)**   The following diagram shows the cumulative abnormal returns (CAR) for oil exploration companies announcing oil discoveries over a 30-year period. Month 0 in the diagram is the announcement month. Assume that no other information is received and the stock market as a whole does not move. Is the diagram consistent with market efficiency? Why or why not?

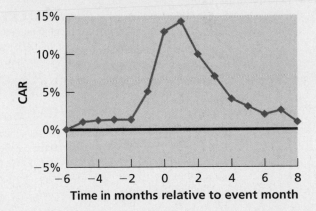

Time in months relative to event month

3. **Cumulative Abnormal Returns (LO2, CFA2)** The following figures present the results of four cumulative abnormal returns (CAR) studies. Indicate whether the results of each study support, reject, or are inconclusive about the semistrong form of the efficient markets hypothesis. In each figure, time 0 is the date of an event.

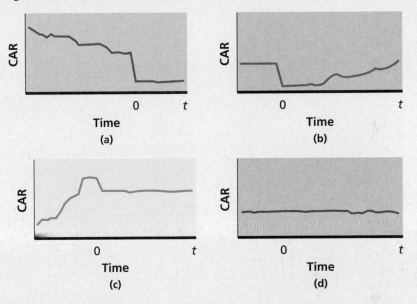

4. **Cumulative Abnormal Returns (LO2, CFA2)** A study analyzed the behavior of the stock prices of firms that had lost antitrust cases. Included in the diagram are all firms that lost the initial court decision, even if the decision was later overturned on appeal. The event at time 0 is the initial, pre-appeal court decision. Assume no other information was released, aside from that disclosed in the initial trial. The stock prices all have a beta of 1. Is the diagram consistent with market efficiency? Why or why not?

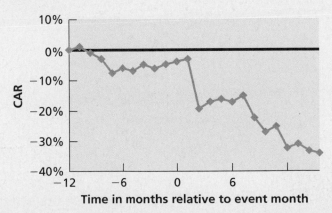

Time in months relative to event month

5. **Cumulative Abnormal Returns (LO2, CFA2)** Ross Co., Westerfield, Inc., and Jordan Company announced a new agreement to market their respective products in China on July 18 (7/18), February 12 (2/12), and October 7 (10/7), respectively. Given the information below, calculate the cumulative abnormal return (CAR) for these stocks as a group. Assume all companies have an expected return equal to the market return. Graph and interpret your results. Do your results support market efficiency?

	Ross Co.			Westerfield, Inc.			Jordan Company	
Date	Market Return	Company Return	Date	Market Return	Company Return	Date	Market Return	Company Return
7/12	−0.2	−0.4	2/8	−0.7	−0.9	10/1	0.3	0.5
7/13	0.1	0.3	2/9	−0.8	−0.9	10/2	0.2	0.8
7/16	0.6	0.8	2/10	0.6	0.4	10/3	0.9	1.3
7/17	−0.4	−0.2	2/11	0.8	1.0	10/6	−0.1	−0.5
7/18	−1.9	1.3	2/12	−0.1	0.1	10/7	−2.4	−0.5
7/19	−0.8	−0.6	2/15	1.3	1.4	10/8	0.3	0.3
7/20	−0.9	−1.0	2/16	0.7	0.7	10/9	−0.5	−0.4
7/23	0.6	0.4	2/17	−0.1	0.0	10/10	0.1	−0.1
7/24	0.1	0.0	2/18	0.5	0.4	10/13	−0.2	−0.6

CHAPTER 8

Behavioral Finance and the Psychology of Investing

Learning Objectives

Psych yourself up and get a good understanding of:

1. Prospect theory.
2. The implications of investor overconfidence and misperceptions of randomness.
3. Sentiment-based risk and limits to arbitrage.
4. The wide array of technical analysis methods used by investors.

"The investor's chief problem, and even his worst enemy, is likely to be himself."

–Benjamin Graham

"There are three factors that influence the market: Fear, Greed, and Greed."

–Market folklore

Be honest: Do you think of yourself as a better than average driver? If you do, you are not alone. About 80 percent of the people who are asked this question will say yes. Evidently, we tend to overestimate our abilities behind the wheel. Is the same thing true when it comes to making investment decisions? ■

You will probably not be surprised when we say that human beings sometimes make errors in judgment. How these errors, and other aspects of human behavior, affect investors and asset prices falls under the general heading of "behavioral finance." In the first part of this chapter, our goal is to acquaint you with some common types of mistakes investors make and their financial implications. As you will see, researchers have identified a wide variety of potentially damaging behaviors. In the second part of the chapter, we describe a trading strategy known as "technical analysis." Some investors use technical analysis as a tool to try

CFA™ Exam Topics in This Chapter:

1 Technical analysis (L1, S3)
2 Efficient capital markets (L1, S54)
3 Heuristic-driven bias (L3, S3)
4 Frame dependence (L3, S3)
5 Inefficient markets (L3, S3)
6 Portfolios, pyramids, emotions, and biases (L3, S3)
7 Investment decision making in defined contribution pension plans (L3, S3)
8 Managing individual investor portfolios (L3, S4)

Go to www.mhhe.com/jmd6e for a guide that aligns your textbook with CFA readings.

to exploit patterns in prices. These patterns are thought to exist (by advocates of technical analysis) because of predictable behavior by investors.

8.1 Introduction to Behavioral Finance

Sooner or later, you are going to make an investment decision that winds up costing you a lot of money. Why is this going to happen? You already know the answer. Sometimes you make sound decisions, but you just get unlucky when something happens that you could not have reasonably anticipated. At other times (and painful to admit) you just make a bad decision, one that could have (and should have) been avoided. The beginning of investment wisdom is to recognize the circumstances that lead to poor decisions and thereby cut down on the damage done by investment blunders.

behavioral finance
The area of finance dealing with the implications of investor reasoning errors on investment decisions and market prices.

As we previously noted, the area of research known as **behavioral finance** attempts to understand and explain how reasoning errors influence investor decisions and market prices. Much of the research done in the area of behavioral finance stems from work in the area of cognitive psychology, which is the study of how people, including investors, think, reason, and make decisions. Errors in reasoning are often called *cognitive errors*.

Some proponents of behavioral finance believe that cognitive errors by investors will cause market inefficiencies. Recall that in a previous chapter, we identified three economic conditions that lead to market efficiency: (1) investor rationality, (2) independent deviations from rationality, and (3) arbitrage. For a market to be inefficient, all three of these conditions must be absent. That is, it must be the case that a substantial portion of investors make irrational investment decisions, and the collective irrationality of these investors then must lead to an overly optimistic or pessimistic market situation that cannot be corrected via arbitrage by rational, well-capitalized investors. Whether this actually occurs in financial markets is the subject of a raging debate, and we are not going to take sides. Instead, our goal is to introduce you to the ideas and issues.

CHECK THIS

8.1a   What is behavioral finance?
8.1b   What three conditions must be absent for a market to be inefficient?

8.2 Prospect Theory

prospect theory
An alternative theory to classical, rational economic decision making, which emphasizes, among other things, that investors tend to behave differently when they face prospective gains and losses.

Prospect theory, developed in the late 1970s, is a collection of ideas that provides an alternative to classical, rational economic decision making. The foundation of prospect theory rests on the idea that investors are much more distressed by prospective losses than they are happy about prospective gains. Researchers have found that a typical investor considers the pain of a $1 loss to be about twice as great as the pleasure received from the gain of $1. Also, researchers have found that investors respond in different ways to identical situations. The difference depends on whether the situation is presented in terms of losses or in terms of gains.

Investors seem to be willing to take more risk to avoid the loss of a dollar than they are to make a dollar profit. Also, if an investor has the choice between a sure gain and a gamble that could increase or decrease the sure gain, the investor is likely to choose the sure gain. Choosing a sure gain over a gamble is called *risk-averse behavior*. If the same investor is faced with a sure loss and a gamble that could increase or decrease the sure loss, the investor is likely to take the gamble. Choosing the gamble over the sure loss is called *risk-taking behavior*.

This focus on gains and losses and the tendency of investors to be risk-averse with regard to gains, but risk-taking when it comes to losses, is the essence of prospect theory. In contrast, a fully rational investor (in an economic sense) is presumed to care only about his or her overall wealth, not the gains and losses associated with individual pieces of that wealth.

To give a simple example, suppose you own just two stocks (which is, of course, a bad idea from a diversification standpoint). On a particular day, one stock goes up sharply, but the other goes down so that your total wealth is unchanged. On another day, neither stock changes price at all. In both cases, your total wealth was unaffected, but in the first case you would probably be upset that your big gain was canceled out. If you are, you are focusing on the individual pieces, not the big picture. As we will see in the next few subsections, this kind of thinking can lead to potentially damaging errors in judgment.

FRAME DEPENDENCE

Another important aspect of prospect theory is the notion that people focus on *changes* in wealth versus *levels* of wealth. **Frame dependence** is a result of this phenomenon.

frame dependence

The theory that simply how a problem is described—that is, framed—matters to people.

If an investment problem is presented in two different (but really equivalent) ways, investors often make inconsistent choices. That is, how a problem is described, or framed, seems to matter to people. Some people believe that frames are transparent; that is, investors should be able to see through the way the question is asked. Do they? Do you? Try this: Jot down your answers in the following two scenarios.

Scenario One. Suppose we give you $1,000. You have the following choice:
  A. You can receive another $500 for sure.
  B. You can flip a fair coin. If the coin-flip comes up heads, you get another $1,000, but if it comes up tails, you get nothing.

Scenario Two. Suppose we give you $2,000. You have the following choice:
  A. You can lose $500 for sure.
  B. You can flip a fair coin. If the coin-flip comes up heads, you lose $1,000, but if it comes up tails, you lose nothing.

What were your answers? Did you choose option A in the first scenario and option B in the second? If that's what you did, you are guilty of just focusing on gains and losses, and not paying attention to what really matters, namely, the impact on your wealth. However, you are not alone. About 85 percent of the people who are presented with the first scenario choose option A, and about 70 percent of the people who are presented with the second scenario choose option B.

If you look closely at the two scenarios, you will see that they are actually identical. You end up with $1,500 for sure if you pick option A, or else you end up with a 50-50 chance of either $1,000 or $2,000 if you pick option B. So you should pick the same option in both scenarios. Which option you prefer is up to you, but the point is that you should never pick option A in one scenario and option B in the other. But people do so because the phrasing, or framing, of the question leads people to answer the questions differently. This scenario is an example of frame dependence.

Similar behavior has been documented among participants of company-sponsored retirement plans, such as 401(k) plans. Historically, participants were required to "opt into" the plans—meaning they were required to sign up to participate. Under this approach, less than half of all eligible employees chose to enroll. More recently, however, companies have been allowed to enroll employees automatically, while offering them the option to "opt out" of the plan. Although the choices are identical, the outcomes have been much different. Specifically, after the change the percentage of workers who participated in the plans significantly increased. So, simply by framing the decision differently (opting *in* versus opting *out*), the behavior of participants was influenced.

Our frame dependence examples offer several important investment lessons. First, an investor can always frame a decision problem in broad terms (like wealth) or in narrow terms (like gains and losses). Second, broad and narrow frames often lead the investor to make different choices. Although using a narrow frame (like gains and losses) is human nature, doing so can lead to irrational decisions. Therefore, using broad frames, like overall wealth, results in better investment decisions.

LOSS AVERSION

When you add a new stock to your portfolio, it is human nature for you to associate the stock with its purchase price. As the price of the stock changes through time, you will have unrealized gains or losses when you compare the current price to the purchase price. Through time, you will mentally account for these gains and losses, and how you feel about the investment depends on whether you are ahead or behind.

When you add stocks to your portfolio, you unknowingly create a personal relationship with each of your stocks. As a result, selling one of them becomes more difficult. It is as if you have to "break up" with this stock, or "fire" it from your portfolio. As with personal relationships, these "stock relationships" can be complicated and, believe it or not, make selling stocks difficult at times. This is often referred to as the *status quo bias*, or the *endowment effect*.

In fact, you may have particular difficulty selling a stock at a price lower than your purchase price. If you sell a stock at a loss, you may have a hard time thinking that purchasing the stock in the first place was correct. You may feel this way even if the decision to buy was actually a very good decision. A further complication is that you will also think that if you can just somehow "get even," you will be able to sell the stock without any hard feelings. This phenomenon is known as **loss aversion**, which is the reluctance to sell investments, such as shares of stock, after they have fallen in value. Loss aversion, often a function of **anchoring**, is also called the "break-even" or "disposition effect." Those suffering from it are sometimes said to have "get-evenitis." Legendary investor Warren Buffett offers the following advice: "The stock doesn't know you own it. You have feelings about it, but it has no feelings about you. The stock doesn't know what you paid. People shouldn't get emotionally involved with their stocks."

To see if you are likely to suffer from loss aversion, consider the following two investments:

> **Investment One**. A year ago, you bought shares in Fama Enterprises for $40 per share. Today, these shares are worth $20 each.

> **Investment Two**. A year ago, you bought shares in French Company for $5 per share. Today, these shares are worth $20 each.

What will you do? Will you (1) sell one of these stocks and hold the other; (2) sell both of these stocks; or (3) hold both of these stocks?

Because you are reading about loss aversion, you will undoubtedly recognize that if you choose to keep the shares in Fama Enterprises, you might be suffering from loss aversion. Why do we say might? Well, consider this. Suppose you are considering a new investment in Fama Enterprises. Does your rational analysis say that it is reasonable to purchase shares at $20? If the rational answer is no, then you should sell. If the rational answer is yes, then you do not suffer from loss aversion. However, if you argued to yourself that if shares in Fama Enterprises were a good buy at $40, then they must be a steal at $20, you probably have a raging case of loss aversion. So, to summarize, there are two important lessons from this example:

- **Lesson One**: The market says that shares in Fama Enterprises are worth $20. The market does not care that you paid $40 a year ago.

- **Lesson Two**: You should not care about your purchase price of Fama Enterprises either. You must evaluate your shares at their current price.

How about the shares in French Company? Do you sell them and take the profit? Once again, the lessons are the same. The market says that shares in French Company are worth

effect are all consistent with
ent errors have been docu-

us on avoiding short-
mple, you might fail
fear of loss in the

ng a decision because
an optimal. Regret

money after bad."
of unfavorable

ing that you own
the endowment
than they would

eal buying
cts of

The fact that you paid $5 a year ago is not relevant. Note that selling
ᵗᵃx consequences. Your careful analysis should acknowledge the
fees, and their impact on the net proceeds available to you

? Perhaps the most famous case of loss aversion, or
when 28-year-old Nicholas Leeson caused the collapse
Barings Bank. At the end of 1992, Leeson had lost about
ecret account. By the end of 1993, his losses were about
med to £208 million at the end of 1994 (at the time, this was
tting to these losses, Leeson gambled more of the bank's money
and catch-up." On February 23, 1995, Leeson's losses were
llion) and his trading irregularities were uncovered. Although he
osecution, he was caught, arrested, tried, convicted, and impris-
orced him.

ou will suffer from a case of loss aversion as severe as Nicholas
ersion does affect everyday investors. For example, we know that
sell "winners" more frequently than they sell "losers." If a typical
had 100 stocks with unrealized gains, the investor might sell 15 of
. If the same investor had 100 stocks with unrealized losses, the investor
ll 10 of them and keep 90. That is, individual investors are typically about
likely to sell a stock that has gone up in price than they are to sell a stock
in price.

t is worse when investors hold mutual funds. With mutual funds, when inves-
to sell, they are more than 2.5 times as likely to sell a winning fund than a losing
about professional money managers who manage the mutual funds? They also
om loss aversion.

are all
abil-
e will
)? In
our
e of

ex-
ny

NTAL ACCOUNTING AND HOUSE MONEY

hen people engage in **mental accounting**, they tend to segment their money into mental
buckets." Spending regular income differently from bonuses and investing prudently in
one's retirement account while taking wild risks with a separate stock account are two examples of mental accounting.

Casinos in Las Vegas (and elsewhere) know all about a concept called "playing with
house money." The casinos have found that gamblers are far more likely to take big risks
with money that they have won from the casino (i.e., the "house money"). Also, casinos have
found that gamblers are not as upset about losing house money as they are about losing the
money they brought with them to gamble. As you can see, the house money effect is a result
of mental accounting.

It may seem natural for you to feel that some money is precious because you earned it
through hard work, sweat, and sacrifice, whereas other money is less precious because it
came to you as a windfall. But these feelings are plainly irrational because any dollar you
have buys the same amount of goods and services no matter how you obtained that dollar.
The lessons are:

- **Lesson One**. There are no "paper profits." Your profits are yours.
- **Lesson Two**. All your money is your money. That is, you should not separate your
  money into bundles labeled "house money" and "my money."

Let us return to the shares of Fama Enterprises and French Company. Suppose both were
to decline to $15. You might feel very differently about the decline depending on which
stock you looked at. With Fama Enterprises, the decline makes a bad situation even worse.
Now you are down $25 per share on your investment. On the other hand, with French Com-
pany, you only "give back" some of your "paper profit." You are still way ahead. This kind
of thinking is playing with house money. Whether you lose from your original investment or
from your investment gains is irrelevant.

Frame dependence, mental accounting, and the house money [effect are] the predictions of prospect theory. Many other types of judgm[ent are docu]mented. Here are a few examples:

- **Myopic loss aversion**: This behavior is the tendency to fo[cus on short]term losses, even at the expense of long-term gains. For exa[mple, you fear] to invest "retirement" money into stocks because you have a [fear of loss in the] near term.

- **Regret aversion**: This aversion is the tendency to avoid mak[ing a decision because] you fear that, in hindsight, the decision would have been less t[han optimal. Regret] aversion relates to myopic loss aversion.

- **Sunk cost fallacy**: This mistake is the tendency to "throw good [money after bad."] An example is to keep buying a stock or mutual fund in the face [of adverse] developments.

- **Endowment effect**: This effect is the tendency to consider somet[hing you own] to be worth more than it would be if you did not own it. Because o[f the endowment] effect, people sometimes demand more money to give up somethin[g than they would] be willing to pay to acquire it.

- **Money illusion**: This illusion means that you are confused between [real buying] power and nominal buying power (i.e., you do not account for the eff[ects of] inflation).

CHECK THIS

8.2a What is the basic prediction of prospect theory?

8.2b What is frame dependence?

8.2c How does loss aversion affect investment decisions?

8.3 Overconfidence

A serious error in judgment you can make as an investor is to be overconfident. We [are] overconfident about our abilities in many areas (recall our question about your drivin[g abil]ity at the beginning of the chapter). Here is another example. Ask yourself: What grad[e will] I receive in this course (in spite of the arbitrary and capricious nature of the professo[r)? In] our experience, almost everyone will either say A or, at worst, B. Sadly, when we ask [our] students this question, we always feel confident (but not overconfident) that at least som[e of] our students are going to be disappointed.

Concerning investment behavior, overconfidence appears in several ways. The classic [ex]ample is diversification, or the lack of it. Investors tend to invest too heavily in the compa[ny] for which they work. When you think about it, this loyalty can be very bad financially. This [is] because both your earning power (your income) and your retirement nest egg depend on o[ne] company.

Other examples of the lack of diversification include investing too heavily in the sto[ck] of local companies. You might also do this because you read about them in the local new[s or] you know someone who works there. That is, you might be unduly confident that you h[av]e a high degree of knowledge about local companies versus distant companies.

OVERCONFIDENCE AND TRADING FREQUENCY

If you are overconfident about your investment skill, you are likely to trade too much. You [ ] should know that researchers have found that investors who make relatively more trades [ ] have lower returns than investors who trade less frequently. Based on brokerage accoun[t] activity over a particular period, researchers found that the average household earned a[ ] annual return of 16.4 percent. However, those households that traded the most earned an annual return of only 11.4 percent. The moral is clear: Excessive trading is hazardous to your wealth.

OVERTRADING AND GENDER: "IT'S (BASICALLY) A GUY THING"

In a study published in 2001, Professors Brad Barber and Terrance Odean further examined the effects of overconfidence. As identified above, two possible effects of overconfidence are that it leads to more trading and more trading leads to lower returns. If investors could be divided into groups that differed in overconfidence, then these effects could be examined in greater detail.

Barber and Odean use the fact that psychologists have found that men are more overconfident than women in the area of finance. So, do men trade more than women? Do portfolios of men underperform the portfolios of women? Barber and Odean show that the answer to both questions is yes.

Barber and Odean examined the trading accounts of men and women and found that men trade about 50 percent more than women. They found that both men and women reduce their portfolio returns through excessive trading. However, men did so by 94 basis points more per year than women. The difference is even bigger between single men and single women. Single men traded 67 percent more than single women, and single men reduced their return by 144 basis points compared to single women.

Using four risk measures, and accounting for the effects of marital status, age, and income, Professors Barber and Odean also found that men invested in riskier positions than women. Young and single people held portfolios that displayed more return volatility and contained a higher percentage of stocks in small companies. Investors with higher incomes also accepted more market risk. These results are comforting because it seems to make sense that the relatively young and the relatively wealthy should be willing to take more investment risk, particularly if they do not have dependents.

WHAT IS A DIVERSIFIED PORTFOLIO TO THE EVERYDAY INVESTOR?

It is clear to researchers that most investors have a poor understanding of what constitutes a well-diversified portfolio. Researchers have discovered that the average number of stocks in a household portfolio is about four, and the median is about three.

Ask yourself: What percentage of these households beat the market? If you are like most people, your answer is too low. Researchers have found, however, that even when accounting for trading costs, about 43 percent of the households outperformed the market. Surprised? The lack of diversification is the source of your surprise.

Think about it like this. Suppose all investors held just one stock in their account. If there are many stocks, about half the individual stock returns outperform the market average. Therefore, about half the investors will beat the market. Quickly: Did you think that you would certainly be in that half that would beat the market? If you did, this should show you that you might be prone to overconfidence. To measure your level of overconfidence, see the nearby *Work the Web* box.

ILLUSION OF KNOWLEDGE

Overconfident investors tend to underestimate the risk of individual stocks and their overall portfolios. This aspect of overconfidence typically stems from a belief that information you hold is superior to information held by other investors. You believe, therefore, that you are able to make better judgments. This belief is referred to as the *illusion of knowledge*.

A possible example of this behavior was observed in 2009 following the bankruptcy of General Motors. As part of the reorganization process, GM's management announced that existing shares were worthless (i.e., had a value of $0 per share). Nonetheless, these existing shares continued to trade, albeit at low, but positive, value. If management stated the shares

As we noted, overconfidence is a common behavioral characteristic. When we compare ourselves to others, we tend to consider ourselves better, whether it be as a driver, an investor, or a leader. While some people are more overconfident than others, it is safe to say that we have probably all exhibited this at some point. To see how overconfident you are, consider the following survey that comes from www.tim-richardson.net/misc/estimation_quiz.html:

Self-Test of Overconfidence

For each of the following 10 items, provide a low and high guess such that you are 90 percent sure the correct answer falls between the two.

Your challenge is to be neither too narrow (i.e., overconfident) nor too wide (i.e., underconfident).

If you successfully meet this challenge, your result should be at least 8 correct (94% likelihood).

You can be 99.9% sure of getting at least 6 correct.

Question	Low	High	Units
1. Martin Luther King's age at death			
2. Length of the Nile River			KM ○ MILES ⊙
3. Number of countries that are members of OPEC			
4. Number of books in the Old Testament			
5. Diameter of the moon			KM ○ MILES ⊙
6. Weight of an empty Boeing 747			KG ○ POUNDS ⊙
7. Year in which Wolfgang Amadeus Mozart was born			
8. Gestation period (in days) of an Asian elephant			
9. Air distance from London to Tokyo			KM ○ MILES ⊙
10. Deepest (known) point in the oceans			METRES ○ FEET ⊙

Submit   Reset

Once you have completed the quiz, go to the Web site to see how you score. Are you average or above average when it comes to being overconfident?

Source: From *Decision Traps* by J. Edward Russo and Paul J. H. Schoemaker. © 1989 by J. Edward Russo and Paul J. H. Schoemaker. Used by permission of Doubleday, a division of Random House, Inc.

were worthless, why would anyone continue to buy them? No one knows for sure. A possible explanation, however, is that this "noise trading" was driven by investors with an illusion of knowledge. These investors thought that they knew more about the prospects of GM's common stock than did the managers of GM.

SNAKEBITE EFFECT

Are you an avid skateboarder? If not, maybe you never tried it, or maybe it simply has never appealed to you. Or, you might have tried skateboarding but gave it up because of a bad experience (say, a broken leg, arm, both, or worse). If this category is yours, you could well have experienced the snakebite effect.

As it relates to investing, the snakebite effect refers to the unwillingness of investors to take a risk following a loss. This effect is sometimes considered to have the opposite influence of overconfidence. The snakebite effect makes people less confident in the investment process following a loss. This particular phenomenon has been well documented in fund flows to mutual funds. More money tends to be liquidated from mutual funds following some significant market declines. In other market declines, less money than "normal" tends to flow toward mutual funds. Unfortunately, this action is the opposite of what rational investors do—that is, "buy low, sell high."

CHECK THIS

8.3a	How does overconfidence appear in investment behavior?
8.3b	What are the effects of trading frequency on portfolio performance?
8.3c	How does the snakebite effect impact investors?

8.4 Misperceiving Randomness and Overreacting to Chance Events

representativeness heuristic

Concluding that causal factors are at work behind random sequences.

Cognitive psychologists have discovered that the human mind is a pattern-seeking device. As a result, we can conclude that causal factors or patterns are at work behind sequences of events even when the events are truly random. In behavioral finance, this is known as the **representativeness heuristic**, which says that if something is random, it should look random. But what does random look like?

Suppose we flip a coin 20 times and write down whether we get a head or a tail. Then we do it again. The results of our two sets of 20 flips are:

First 20:   T T T H T T T H T T H H H T H H T H H H

Second 20:   T H T H H T T H T H T H T H T T H T H T H H

Do these sequences of heads and tails both look random to you? Most people would say that the first 20 and the second 20 somehow look "different," even though both are random sequences and both have 10 heads and 10 tails.

Let's look at this a bit differently by graphing the results. We'll start at zero. If a head occurs, we will subtract one; if a tail occurs, we will add one. Table 8.1 lists the results. Suppose we graph the two sets of 20 flips in Figure 8.1. Do the two series look different to you? Do you think the line labeled First 20 has a pattern to it, but the line labeled Second 20 appears to be random? If you do, your mind saw a pattern in a random sequence of coin flips, even though both patterns are the result of random coin flips with 10 heads and 10 tails.

The representativeness heuristic assumes that people tend to ignore base rates. In a well-known research study by Professors Daniel Kahneman and Amos Tversky, subjects were shown personality descriptions and asked to estimate the probability that the person described was a lawyer. One group was told that the description was drawn from a sample of 30 lawyers and 70 engineers. The second group was told that the description was drawn from a sample of 70 lawyers and 30 engineers. Both groups, however, produced a similar probability that the personality sketch was that of a lawyer. You might conclude that people often find what they are looking for in the data.

Although making fun of lawyers is, for some, a happy pastime, representativeness has a major impact on investors. As an example, consider what you would do if someone asked you to choose between investing in Microsoft or Retalix. You might attempt to do some detailed research and choose the "better" company. Most investors, however, are prone to choose Microsoft simply because it is well-known. This example shows the common error of confusing a good company with a good investment.

THE "HOT-HAND" FALLACY

Basketball fans generally believe that success breeds success. Suppose we look at the recent performance of two basketball players named LeBron and Shaquille. Both of these players make half of their shots. But LeBron just made two shots in a row, while Shaquille just missed two shots in a row. Researchers have found that if they ask

TABLE 8.1

The Results of Two Sets of 20 Coin Flips

Flip Number	First 20 Flips			Second 20 Flips		
	Result	+1/−1	Accumulated Sum	Result	+1/−1	Accumulated Sum
			0			0
1	T	1	1	T	1	1
2	T	1	2	H	−1	0
3	T	1	3	T	1	1
4	H	−1	2	H	−1	0
5	T	1	3	H	−1	−1
6	T	1	4	T	1	0
7	T	1	5	T	1	1
8	H	−1	4	H	−1	0
9	T	1	5	T	1	1
10	T	1	6	H	−1	0
11	H	−1	5	T	1	1
12	H	−1	4	H	−1	0
13	H	−1	3	T	1	1
14	T	1	4	T	1	2
15	H	−1	3	H	−1	1
16	H	−1	2	T	1	2
17	T	1	3	H	−1	1
18	H	−1	2	T	1	2
19	H	−1	1	H	−1	1
20	H	−1	0	H	−1	0
Number of heads	10			10		
Number of tails	10			10		

FIGURE 8.1

The Pattern of Two Different Sets of 20 Coin Flips

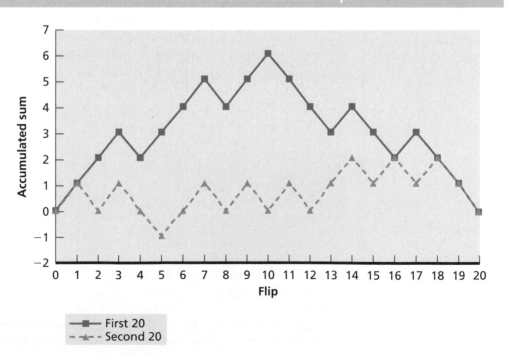

TABLE 8.2	Shooting Percentages and the History of Previous Attempts	
Shooting Percentage on Next Shot	**History of Previous Attempts**	
46%	Made 3 in a row	
50	Made 2 in a row	
51	Made 1	
52	First shot of the game	
54	Missed 1	
53	Missed 2 in a row	
56	Missed 3 in a row	

100 basketball fans which player has the better chance of making the next shot, 91 of them will say LeBron, because he has a "hot hand." Further, 84 of these fans believe that it is important for teammates to pass the ball to LeBron after he has made two or three shots in a row.

But—and the sports fans among you will have a hard time with this—researchers have found that the hot hand is an illusion. That is, players really do not deviate much from their long-run shooting averages, although fans, players, announcers, and coaches think they do. Cognitive psychologists actually studied the shooting percentage of one professional basketball team for a season. The findings are presented in Table 8.2. Detailed analysis of shooting data failed to show that players make or miss shots more or less frequently than what would be expected by chance. That is, statistically speaking, all the shooting percentages in Table 8.2 are the "same."

The shooting percentages in Table 8.2 may suggest that teams tried harder to defend a shooter who has made the last two or three shots. To take this possibility into account, researchers have also studied percentages for undefended shots—free throws. Researchers told fans that a certain player was a 70 percent free throw shooter and was about to shoot two foul shots. They asked fans to predict what would happen on the second shot if the player

1. Made the first free throw.

2. Missed the first free throw.

Fans thought that this 70 percent free throw shooter would make 74 percent of the second free throws after making the first free throw, but would only make 66 percent of the second free throws after missing the first free throw. Researchers studied free throw data from a professional basketball team over two seasons. They found that the result of the first free throw does not matter when it comes to making or missing the second free throw. On average, the shooting percentage on the second free throw was 75 percent when the player made the first free throw. On average, the shooting percentage on the second free throw was also 75 percent when the player missed the first free throw.

It is true that basketball players shoot in streaks. But these steaks are within the bounds of long-run shooting percentages. So it is an illusion that players are either "hot" or "cold." If you are a believer in the "hot hand," however, you are likely to reject these facts because you "know better" from watching your favorite teams over the years. You are being fooled by randomness, because randomness often appears in clusters.

clustering illusion
Human belief that random events that occur in clusters are not really random.

The **clustering illusion** is our human belief that random events that occur in clusters are not really random. For example, it strikes most people as very unusual if heads comes up four times in a row during a series of coin flips. However, if a fair coin is flipped 20 times, there is about a 50 percent chance of getting four heads in a row. Ask yourself, if you flip four heads in a row, do you think you have a "hot hand" at coin flipping?

Mutual fund investing is one area where investors seem to fall prey to the clustering illusion. Every year, funds that have had exceptionally good performance receive large inflows of investor money. Despite the universal disclaimer that "past performance is no guarantee of future results," investors nonetheless clearly chase past returns.

THE GAMBLER'S FALLACY

People commit the gambler's fallacy when they assume that a departure from what occurs on average, or in the long run, will be corrected in the short run. Another way to think about the gambler's fallacy is that because an event has not happened recently, it has become "overdue" and is more likely to occur. People sometimes refer (wrongly) to the "law of averages" in such cases.

Roulette is a random gambling game where gamblers can make various bets on the spin of the wheel. There are 38 numbers on an American roulette table, 2 green ones, 18 red ones, and 18 black ones. One possible bet is to bet whether the spin will result in a red number or in a black number. Suppose a red number has appeared five times in a row. Gamblers will often become confident that the next spin will be black, when the true chance remains at about 50 percent (of course, it is exactly 18 in 38).

The misconception arises from the human intuition that the overall odds of the wheel must be reflected in a small number of spins. That is, gamblers often become convinced that the wheel is "due" to hit a black number after a series of red numbers. Gamblers do know that the odds of a black number appearing are always unchanged: 18 in 38. But gamblers cannot help but feel that after a long series of red numbers, a black one must appear to restore the "balance" between red and black numbers over time. Thousands of betting systems exist that claim to be able to generate money by betting opposite to recent outcomes. One simple example in roulette is to wait until four red numbers in a row appear—then bet on black. Internet hucksters sell "guaranteed" betting systems that are basically based on the gambler's fallacy. None of them work. Think about it. If these betting systems actually worked, why would they be for sale?

The hot-hand fallacy and the gambler's fallacy can be thought of as forecasting errors. Professors Kahneman and Tversky discovered that people place too much weight on recent experiences. Overweighting what recently happened can help explain both of these fallacies. The difference between them lies in the belief that future events will resemble past events (hot-hand fallacy) or that a turnaround is due (gambler's fallacy).

Of course, there are many other related investor errors and biases. Here is a partial list:

- **Law of small numbers**: If you believe in the law of small numbers, you believe that a small sample of outcomes always resembles the long-run distribution of outcomes. If your investment guru has been right five out of seven times recently, you might believe that his long-run average of being correct is also five out of seven. The law of small numbers is related to recency bias and to the gambler's fallacy.

- **Recency bias**: Humans tend to give recent events more importance than less recent events. For example, during the great bull market that occurred from 1995 to 1999, many investors thought the market would continue its big gains for a long time—forgetting that bear markets also occur (which happened from 2000 to 2002). Recency bias is related to the law of small numbers.

- **Self-attribution bias**: This bias occurs when you attribute good outcomes to your own skill, but blame bad outcomes on luck.

- **Wishful thinking bias**: You suffer from wishful thinking bias when you believe what you want to believe. Wishful thinking bias relates to self-attribution bias.

- **False consensus**: This is the tendency to think that other people are thinking the same thing about a stock you own (or are going to buy). False consensus relates to overconfidence.

- **Availability bias**: You suffer from availability bias when you put too much weight on information that is easily available and place too little weight on information that is hard to obtain. Your financial decisions will suffer if you consider only information that is easy to obtain.

Visit
www.behaviouralfinance.net
for many other terms and concepts
of behavioral finance.

8.5 More on Behavioral Finance

HEURISTICS

You have probably had to evaluate some stocks, and maybe even pick the ones you think are best. In doing so, you surely found that a large amount of information is available—stock reports, analyst estimates, financial statements, and the list goes on. How can you, or any investor, possibly evaluate all this information correctly? Sadly, the answer is, one cannot do so. So, how do most investors make decisions? Most likely, investment decisions are made by using rules of thumb, or heuristics (fancy name).

A heuristic simplifies the decision-making process by identifying a defined set of criteria to evaluate. Unfortunately, investors often choose inappropriate criteria. For example, investors might choose criteria that identify good companies, but not necessarily good investments.

Another example involves 401(k) plans. Researchers have found that most investors simply allocate among their investment choices equally. This choice presents some serious implications. For retirement plans that offer more bond funds than stock funds, participants will choose a conservative portfolio (i.e., more bonds than stocks). For retirement plans that offer more stock funds than bond funds, participants will choose a more aggressive portfolio (i.e., more stocks than bonds). This behavior is referred to as the "$1/n$ phenomenon," as investors simply allocate $1/n$ percent to each of the n funds available. This heuristic-based allocation simplifies the decision process, but it is definitely not optimal for many investors.

HERDING

Have you ever watched a nature documentary that shows schools of fish? If you have, recall how the fish move if a danger is detected. Do the fish scatter? No. They tend to move together in a quick and pronounced manner. This behavior is known as *herding*.

While we are well aware of such behavior among animals, this behavior is also common among investors. For example, many academic studies conclude that stock analysts tend to exhibit herding behavior in their earnings forecasts and stock ratings. Where one analyst goes, others follow—presumably from the fear of being left behind. This behavior might be a preservation behavior similar to the fish. For example, if an analyst rates a stock a strong buy, while everyone else is saying sell or hold, the lone analyst faces risk. If he is right, he will be considered a genius. If he is incorrect, however, he will probably lose his job. Does avoiding this "survival of the fittest" outcome motivate analysts to herd? Analysts would probably say no, but the evidence seems to point to herding.

This behavior is also common among individual investors. Among many triggers, one prominent one seems to be media interaction. After a stock is highlighted in an investment periodical or on a television show, volume tends to increase, as does stock price. Many of you are probably familiar with Jim Cramer, the host of the TV show *Mad Money*. When Mr. Cramer recommends a stock, it shows a significant uptick on the following day. Why is this? Maybe Mr. Cramer has added new information to the market, or maybe investors are simply herding by following his recommendation.

HOW DO WE OVERCOME BIAS?

Proponents of behavioral finance generally contend that most biases are coded in our DNA, meaning we are born with them. While this contention is debatable, we can generally agree on things we can do to help overcome, or at least reduce, the negative impact of these behaviors on our investment decisions.

WALL STREET'S MATH WIZARDS FORGOT A FEW VARIABLES

In the aftermath of the great meltdown of 2008, Wall Street's quants have been cast as the financial engineers of profit-driven innovation run amok. They, after all, invented the exotic securities that proved so troublesome.

But the real failure, according to finance experts and economists, was in the quants' mathematical models of risk that suggested the arcane stuff was safe.

The risk models proved myopic, they say, because they were too simple-minded. They focused mainly on figures like the expected returns and the default risk of financial instruments. What they didn't sufficiently take into account was human behavior, specifically the potential for widespread panic. When lots of investors got too scared to buy or sell, markets seized up and the models failed.

That failure suggests new frontiers for financial engineering and risk management, including trying to model the mechanics of panic and the patterns of human behavior.

"What wasn't recognized was the importance of a different species of risk—liquidity risk," said Stephen Figlewski, a professor of finance at the Leonard N. Stern School of Business at New York University. "When trust in counterparties is lost, and markets freeze up so there are no prices," he said, it "really showed how different the real world was from our models."

In the future, experts say, models need to be opened up to accommodate more variables and more dimensions of uncertainty.

The drive to measure, model and perhaps even predict waves of group behavior is an emerging field of research that can be applied in fields well beyond finance.

Much of the early work has been done tracking online behavior. The Web provides researchers with vast data sets for tracking the spread of all manner of things—news stories, ideas, videos, music, slang and popular fads—through social networks. That research has potential applications in politics, public health, online advertising and Internet commerce. And it is being done by academics and researchers at Google, Microsoft, Yahoo!, and Facebook.

Financial markets, like online communities, are social networks. Researchers are looking at whether the mechanisms and models being developed to explore collective behavior on the Web can be applied to financial markets. A team of six economists, finance experts and computer scientists at Cornell was recently awarded a grant from the National Science Foundation to pursue that goal.

"The hope is to take this understanding of contagion and use it as a perspective on how rapid changes of behavior can spread through complex networks at work in financial markets," explained Jon M. Kleinberg, a computer scientist and social network researcher at Cornell.

At the Massachusetts Institute of Technology, Andrew W. Lo, director of the Laboratory for Financial Engineering, is taking a different approach to incorporating human behavior into finance. His research focuses on applying insights from disciplines, including evolutionary biology and cognitive neuroscience, to create a new perspective on how financial markets work, which Mr. Lo calls "the adaptive-markets

---

The most important thing is to know all potential biases. So, by reading this chapter, you are better prepared than most investors. Simply by understanding what errors you could make, you are less likely to make them (you are, aren't you?). The importance of this knowledge is illustrated in the nearby *Investment Updates* box.

Other actions you can take to reduce bias include diversifying your portfolio, avoiding situations (or media) that you know will unduly influence you, and creating objective investment criteria. Although these actions are not guaranteed to completely eliminate biases, they should at least give you an advantage over other investors who have not taken such precautions.

CHECK THIS

8.5a   What is the "1/*n* phenomenon"?

8.5b   Explain herding behavior by investors.

8.5c   What potential bias might affect how you invest?

8.6 Sentiment-Based Risk and Limits to Arbitrage

It is important to realize that the efficient markets hypothesis does not require every investor to be rational. As we have noted, all that is required for a market to be efficient is that at least some investors are smart and well-financed. These investors are prepared to buy and sell to

hypothesis." It is a departure from the "efficient-market" theory, which asserts that financial markets get asset prices right given the available information and that a sufficient number of well-capitalized people behave rationally.

Efficient-market theory, of course, has dominated finance and econometric modeling for decades, though it is being sharply questioned in the wake of the financial crisis. "It is not that efficient market theory is wrong, but it's a very incomplete model," Mr. Lo said.

Mr. Lo is confident that his adaptive-markets approach can help model and quantify liquidity crises in a way traditional models, with their narrow focus on expected returns and volatility, cannot. "We're going to see three-dimensional financial modeling and eventually N-dimensional modeling," he said.

J. Doyne Farmer, a former physicist at Los Alamos National Laboratory and a founder of a quantitative trading firm, finds the behavioral research intriguing but awfully ambitious, especially to build into usable models. Instead, Mr. Farmer, a professor at the interdisciplinary Sante Fe Institute, is doing research on models of markets, institutions and their complex interactions, applying a hybrid discipline called econophysics.

To explain, Mr. Farmer points to the huge buildup of the credit-default-swap market, to a peak of $60 trillion. And in 2006, the average leverage on mortgage securities increased to 16 to 1 (it is now 1.5 to 1). Put the two together, he said, and you have a serious problem.

"You don't need a model of human psychology to see that there was a danger of impending disaster," Mr. Farmer observed. "But economists have failed to make models that accurately model such phenomena and adequately address their couplings."

When a bridge over a river collapses, the engineers who built the bridge have to take responsibility. But typically, critics call for improvement and smarter, better-trained engineers—not fewer of them. The same pattern seems to apply to financial engineers. At M.I.T., the Sloan School of Management is starting a one-year master's in finance this fall because the field has become too complex to be adequately covered as part of a traditional M.B.A. program, and because of student demand. The new finance program, Mr. Lo noted, had 179 applicants for 25 places.

In the aftermath of the economic crisis, financial engineers, experts say, will probably shift more to risk management and econometric analysis and concentrate less on devising exotic new instruments. Still, the recent efforts by investment banks to create a trading market for "life settlements," life insurance policies that the ill or elderly sell for cash, suggest that inventive sales people are browsing for new asset classes to securitize, bundle and trade.

"Good or bad, moral or immoral, people are going to make markets and trade via computers, and this is a natural area for financial engineers," says Emanuel Derman, a professor at Columbia University and a former Wall Street quant.

Source: Steve Lohr. From *The New York Times*, September 13, 2009.

take advantage of any mispricing in the marketplace. This activity is what keeps markets efficient. Sometimes, however, a problem arises in this context.

LIMITS TO ARBITRAGE

limits to arbitrage
The notion that the price of an asset may not equal its correct value because of barriers to arbitrage.

The term **limits to arbitrage** refers to the notion that under certain circumstances, rational, well-capitalized traders may be unable to correct a mispricing, at least not quickly. The reason is that strategies designed to eliminate mispricings are often risky, costly, or somehow restricted. Three important impediments are:

- *Firm-specific risk:* This issue is the most obvious risk facing a would-be arbitrageur. Suppose that you believe that the observed price on Ford stock is too low, so you purchase many, many shares. Then, some unanticipated negative news drives the price of Ford stock even lower. Of course, you could try to hedge some firm-specific risk by shorting shares in another stock, say, Honda. But there is no guarantee that the price of Honda will fall if some firm-specific event triggers a decline in the price of Ford. It might even rise, leaving you even worse off. Furthermore, in many, if not most, cases there might not even be a stock that could be considered a close substitute.

noise trader
A trader whose trades are not based on information or meaningful financial analysis.

- *Noise trader risk:* A **noise trader** is someone whose trades are not based on information or financially meaningful analysis. Noise traders could, in principle, act together to worsen a mispricing in the short run. Noise trader risk is important because the worsening of a mispricing could force the arbitrageur to liquidate early and sustain steep losses. As the economist John Maynard Keynes once famously observed, "Markets can remain irrational longer than you can remain solvent."[1]

Noise trader risk is also called **sentiment-based risk**, meaning the risk that an asset's price is being influenced by sentiment (or irrational belief such as illusion of knowledge) rather than fact-based financial analysis. If sentiment-based risk exists, then it is another source of risk beyond the systematic and unsystematic risks we discussed in an earlier chapter.

- *Implementation costs:* These costs include transaction costs such as bid-ask spreads, brokerage commissions, and margin interest. In addition, there might be some short-sale constraints. One short-sale constraint arises when there are not enough shares of the security to borrow so that the arbitrageur can take a large short position. Another short-sale constraint stems from legal restrictions. Many money managers, especially pension fund and mutual fund managers, are not allowed to sell short.

When these or other risks and costs are present, a mispricing may persist because arbitrage is too risky or too costly. Collectively, these risks and costs create barriers or limits to arbitrage. How important these limits are is difficult to say, but we do know that mispricings occur, at least on occasion. To illustrate, we next consider two well-known examples.

THE 3COM/PALM MISPRICING

On March 2, 2000, a profitable provider of computer networking products and services, 3Com, sold 5 percent of one of its subsidiaries to the public via an initial public offering (IPO). At the time, the subsidiary was known as Palm (now owned by Hewlett-Packard).

3Com planned to distribute the remaining Palm shares to 3Com shareholders at a later date. Under the plan, if you owned 1 share of 3Com, you would receive 1.5 shares of Palm. So, after 3Com sold part of Palm via the IPO, investors could buy Palm shares directly, or they could buy them indirectly by purchasing shares of 3Com.

What makes this case interesting is what happened in the days that followed the Palm IPO. If you owned one 3Com share, you would be entitled, eventually, to 1.5 shares of Palm. Therefore, each 3Com share should be worth *at least* 1.5 times the value of each Palm share. We say "at least" because the other parts of 3Com were profitable. As a result, each 3Com share should have been worth much more than 1.5 times the value of one Palm share. But, as you might guess, things did not work out this way.

The day before the Palm IPO, shares in 3Com sold for $104.13. After the first day of trading, Palm closed at $95.06 per share. Multiplying $95.06 by 1.5 results in $142.59, which is the minimum value one would expect to pay for 3Com. But the day Palm closed at $95.06, 3Com shares closed at $81.81, more than $60 lower than the price implied by Palm. It gets stranger.

A 3Com price of $81.81 when Palm is selling for $95.06 implies that the market values the rest of 3Com's businesses (per share) at $81.81 − $142.59 = −$60.78. Given the number of 3Com shares outstanding at the time, this means the market placed a *negative* value of about −$22 billion for the rest of 3Com's businesses. Of course, a stock price cannot be negative. This means, then, that the price of Palm relative to 3Com was much too high.

To profit from this mispricing, investors would purchase shares of 3Com and short shares of Palm. In a well-functioning market, this action would force the prices into alignment quite quickly. What happened?

As you can see in Figure 8.2, the market valued 3Com and Palm shares in such a way that the non-Palm part of 3Com had a negative value for about two months, from March 2, 2000, until May 8, 2000. Even then, it took approval by the IRS for 3Com to proceed with the planned distribution of Palm shares before the non-Palm part of 3Com once again had a positive value.

---

[1] This remark is generally attributed to Keynes, but whether he actually said it is not known.

FIGURE 8.2

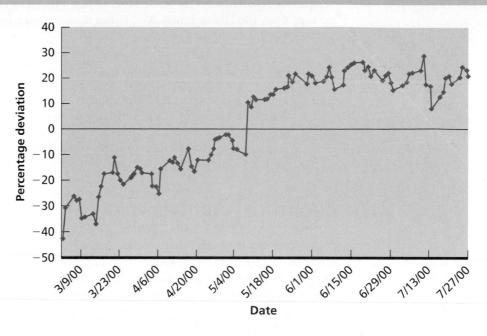

FIGURE 8.3

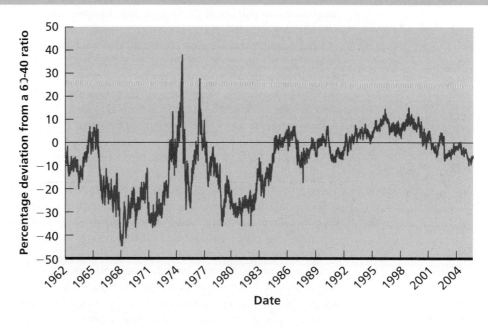

THE ROYAL DUTCH/SHELL PRICE RATIO

Another fairly well-known example of a mispricing involves two large oil companies. In 1907, Royal Dutch of the Netherlands and Shell of the United Kingdom agreed to merge their business enterprises and split profits on a 60-40 basis. So, whenever the stock prices of Royal Dutch and Shell are not in a 60-40 ratio, there is a potential opportunity to make an arbitrage profit. If, for example, the ratio were 50-50, you would buy Royal Dutch, and short sell Shell.

Figure 8.3 plots the daily deviations from the 60-40 ratio of the Royal Dutch price to the Shell price. If the prices of Royal Dutch and Shell are in a 60-40 ratio, there is a zero percentage deviation. If the price of Royal Dutch is too high compared to the Shell price, there is a positive deviation. If the price of Royal Dutch is too low compared to the price of Shell, there is a negative deviation. As you can see in Figure 8.3, there have been large and persistent deviations from the 60-40 ratio. In fact, the ratio was seldom at 60-40 for most of the time from 1962 through mid-2005 (when the companies merged).

CHECK THIS

8.6a What does the term "limits to arbitrage" mean?

8.6b If there were no limits to arbitrage, what would have been the relationship between 1 share of 3Com and 1.5 shares of Palm?

8.6c If there were no limits to arbitrage, what would have been the relationship between the prices of Royal Dutch and Shell?

8.7 Technical Analysis

technical analysis
Using past price data and other nonfinancial data to identify future trading opportunities.

Many investors try to predict future stock price movements based on investor sentiment, errors in judgment, and/or historical price movements. These investors are using **technical analysis**. Unlike fundamental analysis, technical analysis does not rely on traditional valuation techniques like those presented in our earlier chapters.

WHY DOES TECHNICAL ANALYSIS CONTINUE TO THRIVE?

Proponents of the efficient markets hypothesis do not believe that technical analysis can assist investors in predicting future stock price movements. If that is the case, why is technical analysis still used? In fact, in this Internet and computer age, technical analysis is actually thriving. Why?

One possible reason that technical analysis still exists is that an investor can derive thousands of successful technical analysis systems by using historical security prices. Past movements of security prices are easy to fit into a wide variety of technical analysis systems. As a result, proponents of technical analysis can continuously tinker with their systems and find methods that fit historical prices. This process is known as "backtesting." Alas, successful investment is all about future prices.

Another possible reason that technical analysis still exists is simply that it sometimes works. Again, given a large number of possible technical analysis systems, it is possible that many of them will work (or appear to work) in the short run.

To give an example of a technical analysis tool, or a technical "indicator," consider trying to analyze market sentiment. The term "market sentiment" refers to the prevailing mood among investors about the future outlook of an individual security or the market. Market sentiment is generally classified as optimistic (bullish), neutral (undecided), or pessimistic (bearish).

Market sentiment usually takes time to change. That is, it takes time for, say, 80 percent of the investors to become bullish if only 50 percent of the investors are currently bullish. Investors who rely on market sentiment often believe that once 80 percent of the investors are bullish or bearish, a consensus has been reached. Further, once a consensus is reached, investors take this as a sign of an impending turn in the direction of the market. One way to measure market sentiment is to ask investors whether they think the market is going up or down. Suppose you ask 50 investors whether they are "bullish" or "bearish" on the market over the next month. Twenty say that they are bearish. The market sentiment index (MSI) can then be calculated as:

$$MSI = \frac{\text{Number of bearish investors}}{\text{Number of bullish investors} + \text{Number of bearish investors}}$$

$$MSI = \frac{20}{30 + 20} = 0.40$$

The MSI has a maximum value of 1.00, which occurs when every investor you ask is bearish on the market. The MSI has a minimum value of 0.00, which occurs when every investor you ask is bullish on the market. Note that if you are constructing a sentiment index, you will have to decide how many investors to ask, the identity of these investors, and their investment time frame, that is, daily, weekly, monthly, quarterly, or longer. You can construct a sentiment index for any financial asset for any investment time interval you choose.

People who calculate and use sentiment indexes often view them as "contrarian indicators." This means that if most other investors are bearish, perhaps the market is "oversold" and prices are due to rebound. Or if most other investors are bullish, perhaps the market is "overbought" and prices will be heading down.

The following saying is useful when you are trying to remember how to interpret the MSI: "When the MSI is high, it is time to buy; when the MSI is low, it is time to go." Note that there is no theory to guide investors as to what level of the MSI is "high" and what level is "low." This lack of precise guidance is a common problem with a technical indicator like the MSI.

Technical analysis techniques are centuries old, and their number is enormous. Many, many books on the subject have been written. For this reason, we only touch on the subject and introduce some of its key ideas in the next few sections. Although we focus on the use of technical analysis in the stock market, you should be aware that it is very widely used in commodity markets, and most comments herein apply to those markets as well.

Recall that investors with a positive outlook on the market are often called "bulls," and their outlook is characterized as "bullish." A rising market is called a "bull market." In contrast, pessimistic investors are called "bears," and their dismal outlook is characterized as "bearish." A falling market is called a "bear market." Technical analysts essentially search for bullish or bearish signals, meaning positive or negative indicators about stock prices or market direction.

DOW THEORY

Dow theory
A method for predicting market direction that relies on the Dow Industrial and the Dow Transportation averages.

Dow theory is a method of analyzing and interpreting stock market movements that dates back to the turn of the twentieth century. The theory is named after Charles Dow, a cofounder of the Dow Jones Company and an editor of the Dow Jones–owned newspaper, *The Wall Street Journal.*

The essence of Dow theory is that there are, at all times, three forces at work in the stock market: (1) a primary direction or trend, (2) a secondary reaction or trend, and (3) daily fluctuations. According to the theory, the primary direction is either bullish (up) or bearish (down), and it reflects the long-run direction of the market.

WWW

Learn more about Dow theory at
www.dowtheory.com
and
www.thedowtheory.com

However, the market can, for limited periods of time, depart from its primary direction. These departures are called secondary reactions or trends and may last for several weeks or months. These are eliminated by *corrections*, which are reversions to the primary direction. Daily fluctuations are essentially noise and are of no real importance.

The basic purpose of the Dow theory is to signal changes in the primary direction. To do this, two stock market averages, the Dow Jones Industrial Average (DJIA) and the Dow Jones Transportation Average (DJTA), are monitored. If one of these departs from the primary trend, the movement is viewed as secondary. However, if a departure in one is followed by a departure in the other, then this is viewed as a *confirmation* that the primary trend has changed. The Dow theory was, at one time, very well known and widely followed. It is less popular today, but its basic principles underlie more contemporary approaches to technical analysis.

ELLIOTT WAVES

Elliott wave theory
A method for predicting market direction that relies on a series of past market price swings (i.e., waves).

In the early 1930s, an accountant named Ralph Nelson Elliott developed the **Elliott wave theory**. While recuperating from life-threatening anemia (as well as his disastrous losses in the Crash of October 1929), Elliott read a book on Dow theory and began to study patterns of market price movements. Elliott discovered what he believed to be a persistent and recurring pattern that operated between market tops and bottoms. His theory was that these patterns, which he called "waves," collectively expressed investor sentiment. Through use of sophisticated measurements that he called "wave counting," a wave theorist could forecast market turns with a high degree of accuracy.

In 1935, Elliott published his theory in his book called *The Wave Principle.* His main theory was that there was a repeating eight-wave sequence. The first five waves, which he called "impulsive," were followed by a three-wave "corrective" sequence. Figure 8.4 shows

FIGURE 8.4   Basic Elliott Wave Pattern

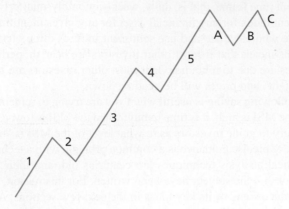

support level

Price or level below which a
stock or the market as a whole
is unlikely to fall.

resistance level

Price or level above which a
stock or the market as a whole
is unlikely to rise.

the basic Elliott wave pattern. The impulse waves are labeled numerically, 1 through 5, while the corrective waves are labeled A, B, and C.

The basic Elliott wave theory gets very complicated because, under the theory, each wave can subdivide into finer wave patterns that are classified into a multitude of structures. Notwithstanding the complex nature of the Elliott wave theory, it is still a widely followed indicator.

SUPPORT AND RESISTANCE LEVELS

A key concept in technical analysis is the identification of support and resistance levels. A **support level** is a price or level below which a stock or the market as a whole is unlikely to fall. A **resistance level** is a price or level above which a stock or the market as a whole is unlikely to rise.

The idea behind these levels is straightforward. As a stock's price (or the market as a whole) falls, it reaches a point where investors increasingly believe that it can fall no further—the point at which it "bottoms out." Essentially, purchases by bargain-hungry investors ("bottom feeders") pick up at that point, thereby "supporting" the price. A resistance level is formed by reverse logic. As a stock's price (or the market as a whole) rises, it reaches a point where investors increasingly believe that it can go no higher—the point at which it "tops out." Once it does, sales by profit-hungry investors ("profit takers") pick up, thereby "resisting" further advances.

Resistance and support areas are usually viewed as psychological barriers. As the DJIA approaches levels with three zeros, such as 11,000, increased talk of "psychologically important" prices appears in the financial press. A "breakout" occurs when a stock (or the market as a whole) closes below a support level or above a resistance level. A breakout is usually interpreted to mean that the price move will continue in that direction.

As this discussion illustrates, much colorful language is used under the heading of technical analysis. We will see many more examples just ahead.

TECHNICAL INDICATORS

Technical analysts rely on a variety of technical indicators to forecast the direction of the market. Every day, *The Wall Street Journal* publishes a variety of such indicators. An excerpt of the "Diaries" section (from www.wsj.com) appears in Figure 8.5.

Much, but not all, of the information presented is self-explanatory. The first item listed in Figure 8.5 is the number of issues, i.e., stocks, traded. This number fluctuates because, on any given day, there may be zero trading volume in some stocks listed on the NYSE. In the rows that follow, we see the number of price advances, the number of price declines, and the number of unchanged prices. The number of stock prices reaching new highs and new lows as of that day is also listed.

One popular technical indicator is called the *advance/decline line*. This indicator shows, for some given period, the cumulative difference between advancing stocks and

FIGURE 8.5   Market Diaries

Markets Diary: Closing Snapshot

DIARIES
GO TO:

Volume by Market | Breakdown of Volume | Crossing Session | Weekly Totals

Monday, November 30, 2009   Find Historical Data [ ] | WHAT'S THIS?

NYSE	Latest close	% Chg from 65-day avg	Previous close	Week ago
Issues traded	3,156	0.1	3,086	3,156
Advances	1,739	9.4	450	2,365
Declines	1,233	-14.9	2,547	664
Unchanged	184	59.1	89	127
New highs	55	-68.2	36	190
New lows	15	272.1	12	1
Adv. volume*	775,229,960	23.7	22,198,690	796,137,850
Decl. volume*	564,259,270	-8.7	631,394,730	170,657,940
Total volume*	1,348,282,850	6.5	654,832,520	980,047,020
Closing tick	+353	...	-844	+296
Closing Arms (TRIN)†	1.03	...	5.03	0.76
Block trades*	n.a.	n.a.	3,580	4,689

Nasdaq	Latest close	% Chg from 65-day avg	Previous close	Week ago
Issues traded	2,855	1.2	2,733	2,853
Advances	1,336	4.6	446	1,898
Declines	1,238	-9.0	2,122	742
Unchanged	281	53.4	165	213
New highs	40	-50.8	26	129
New lows	33	141.8	30	12
Adv. volume*	1,123,351,896	0.5	105,269,781	1,337,438,650
Decl. volume*	816,139,733	-22.9	859,393,340	455,642,794
Total volume*	1,986,058,768	-10.2	971,998,305	1,840,174,611
Closing tick	+113	...	-946	-5
Closing Arms (TRIN)†	0.78	...	1.72	0.87
Block trades*	n.a.	n.a.	3,573	7,026

NYSE Amex	Latest close	% Chg from 65-day avg	Previous close	Week ago
Issues traded	559	-0.9	527	547
Advances	254	1.9	122	273
Declines	217	-11.3	329	220
Unchanged	88	25.5	76	54
New highs	6	-73.5	4	13
New lows	5	75.7	2	7
Adv. volume*	12,312,124	14.1	4,150,900	6,727,751
Decl. volume*	12,328,800	33.7	8,209,834	5,125,110
Total volume*	25,864,804	18.2	12,858,134	13,539,961
Closing tick	+31	...	-13	+11
Closing Arms (TRIN)†	1.17	...	0.73	0.95
Block trades*	n.a.	n.a.	n.a.	n.a.

*Primary market NYSE & NYSE Amex only. †Compares the ratio of advancing to declining issues with the ratio of volume of shares rising and falling. Arms Index or TRIN = (advancing issues / declining issues) / (volume of advancing issues / volume of declining issues.) Generally, an Arms of less than 1.00 indicates buying demand; above 1.00 indicates selling pressure.

Source: Reprinted with permission of *The Wall Street Journal*. © 2009 Dow Jones & Company, Inc. All Rights Reserved Worldwide.

TABLE 8.3

Advance/Decline Line Calculation

Weekday	Stocks Advancing	Stocks Declining	Difference	Cumulative Difference
Monday	2,486	566	1,920	1,920
Tuesday	1,374	1,660	−286	1,634
Wednesday	1,395	1,653	−258	1,376
Thursday	574	2,498	−1,924	−548
Friday	1,283	1,741	−458	−1,006

declining stocks. For example, Table 8.3 contains advance and decline information for the November 16, 2009, to November 20, 2009, trading week.

In Table 8.3, notice how we take the difference between the number of stocks advancing and declining on each day and then cumulate the difference through time. For example, on Monday, 1,920 more stocks advanced than declined. On Tuesday, 286 fewer stocks advanced than declined. Over the two days, the cumulative advance/decline is thus $1,920 - 286 = 1,634$.

This cumulative advance/decline number, once plotted, is the advance/decline line. A downward-sloping advance/decline line would be considered a bearish signal, whereas an upward-sloping advance/decline line is a bullish signal. The advance/decline line is often used to measure market "breadth." If the market is going up, for example, then technical analysts view it as a good sign if there is market breadth. That is, the signal is more bullish if the advance is accompanied by a steeply upwardly sloping advance/decline line.

The next few rows in Figure 8.5 deal with trading volume. These rows represent trading volume for advancing stocks, declining stocks, and unchanged stocks (which is calculated by subtracting advancing volume and declining volume from volume traded). For a technical analyst, heavy advancing volume is generally viewed as a bullish signal of buyer interest. This is particularly true if more stocks are up than down and if a lot of new highs appear as well.

The last three numbers in Figure 8.5 are also of interest to technicians. The first, labeled "Closing tick," is the difference between the number of stocks that closed on an uptick and those that closed on a downtick. From our discussion of the NYSE short sale rule in a previous chapter, you know that an uptick occurs when the last price change was positive; a downtick is just the reverse. The tick gives an indication of where the market was heading as it closed.

The entry labeled "Closing Arms (TRIN)" is the ratio of average trading volume in declining stocks to average trading volume in advancing stocks. It is calculated as follows:

$$\text{Arms} = \frac{\text{Declining Volume/Declining Stocks}}{\text{Advancing Volume/Advancing Stocks}} \tag{8.1}$$

The ratio is named after its inventor, Richard Arms; it is often called the "TRIN," which is an acronym for "TR(ading) IN(dex)." Notice that the numerator in this ratio is just the average volume for stocks that declined on that day. The denominator is the average volume for advancing stocks. Values greater than 1.00 are considered bearish because the indication is that declining shares had heavier volume. Using the number from Figure 8.5 for Monday, we can calculate the Arms value as follows:[2]

$$\text{Arms} = \frac{564,259,270/1,233}{775,229,960/1,739} = \frac{457,631}{445,791} = 1.03$$

which rounds to the value shown in Figure 8.5. A caveat: Some sources reverse the numerator and the denominator when they calculate this ratio.

The final piece of information in Figure 8.5, "Block trades," refers to trades in excess of 10,000 shares. At one time, these trades were taken to be indicators of buying or selling by large institutional investors. Today these trades are routine, and it is difficult to see how this information is particularly useful.

---

[2] The footnote in Figure 8.5 contains a mathematically equivalent way to calculate Arms.

RELATIVE STRENGTH CHARTS

relative strength
A measure of the performance of one investment relative to another.

Relative strength charts illustrate the performance of one company, industry, or market relative to another. If you look back at the *Value Line* exhibit in Chapter 6, you will see a plot labeled "relative strength." Very commonly, such plots are created to analyze how a stock has done relative to its industry or the market as a whole.

To illustrate how such plots are constructed, suppose that on some particular day, we invest equal amounts, say $100, in both Coke and Pepsi (the amount does not matter; what matters is that the original investment is the same for both). On every subsequent day, we take the ratio of the value of our Coke investment to the value of our Pepsi investment, and we plot it. A ratio bigger than 1.0 indicates that, on a relative basis, Coke has outperformed Pepsi, and vice versa. Thus, a value of 1.20 indicates that Coke has done 20 percent better than Pepsi over the period studied. Notice that if both stocks are down, a ratio bigger than 1.0 indicates that Coke is down by less than Pepsi.

EXAMPLE 8.1

Relative Strength

Consider the following series of monthly stock prices for two hypothetical companies:

Month	Susan, Inc.	Carolyn Co.
1	$25	$50
2	24	48
3	22	45
4	22	40
5	20	39
6	19	38

On a relative basis, how has Susan, Inc., done compared to Carolyn Co.?

To answer, suppose we had purchased four shares of Susan, Inc., and two shares of Carolyn Co. for an investment of $100 in each. We can calculate the value of our investment in each month and then take the ratio of Susan, Inc., to Carolyn Co. as follows:

	Investment Value		
Month	Susan, Inc. (4 shares)	Carolyn Co. (2 shares)	Relative Strength
1	$100	$100	1.00
2	96	96	1.00
3	88	90	0.98
4	88	80	1.10
5	80	78	1.03
6	76	76	1.00

What we see is that over the first four months both stocks were down, but Susan, Inc., outperformed Carolyn Co. by 10 percent. However, after six months the two had done equally well (or equally poorly).

Learn more about charting at www.stockcharts.com Select "Chart School."

CHARTING

Technical analysts rely heavily on charts showing recent market activity in terms of either prices or, less frequently, volume. In fact, technical analysis is sometimes called "charting," and technical analysts are often called "chartists." There are many types of charts, but the basic idea is that by studying charts of past market prices (or other information), the chartist

FIGURE 8.6 Open-High-Low-Close Bar Chart for Sun Microsystems

Sun Microsystems, Inc. (SUNW) Nasdaq Nat. Mkt. © StockCharts.com
14-Mar-2000 4:00pm Open 46.12 High 47.38 Low 43.38 Last 43.69 Volume 33.8M Chg -1.75 ▼

identifies particular patterns that signal the direction of a stock or the market as a whole. We briefly describe some charting techniques next.

OPEN-HIGH-LOW-CLOSE CHARTS (OHLC) Perhaps the most popular charting method is the bar chart. The most basic bar chart uses the stock's opening, high, low, and closing prices for the period covered by each bar. If the technician is constructing a daily bar chart, the technician will use the daily opening, high, low, and closing prices of the stock. The high and low prices are represented by the top and bottom of the vertical bar and the opening and closing prices are shown by short horizontal lines crossing the vertical bar. The example of a bar chart in Figure 8.6 for Sun Microsystems is from www.stockcharts.com.

PRICE CHANNEL A price channel is a chart pattern using OHLC data that can slope upward, downward, or sideways. Price channels belong to the group of price patterns known as *continuation patterns*. A continuation pattern is a pattern where the price of the stock is expected to continue along its main direction. A price channel has two boundaries, an upper trendline and a lower trendline. The upper trendline marks resistance and the lower trendline marks support. If the overall price movement of the stock is downward, the upper trendline is called the main trendline, and the lower trendline is called the channel line. The example of a price channel for ChevronTexaco in Figure 8.7 is from the Web site www.stockcharts.com.

HEAD AND SHOULDERS A head and shoulders chart pattern belongs to a group of price charts known as *reversal patterns*. Reversal pattern charts also use OHLC data. These chart patterns signal that a reversal from the main trendline is possibly going to occur. Because it belongs to the reversal pattern group, a head and shoulders pattern is identified as either a *head and shoulders top* or a *head and shoulders bottom*. The example of a head and shoulders top for CNET Networks in Figure 8.8 is also from the Web site www.stockcharts.com.

As you can see, the head and shoulders top formation has three components: the *left shoulder*, the *head*, and the *right shoulder*. To qualify as a head and shoulders top pattern, the shoulders must be lower than the head. Then, a *neckline support* is drawn between the valleys formed by the left and right shoulders. The reversal signal is generated when the neckline is *pierced*. In the case of CNET, once the stock price fell below $45, the stock plunged to $25. Of course, there are *false piercings*, which do not result in a sudden downdraft of the stock.

MOVING AVERAGES Moving averages are used to generate price reversal signals. As the name implies, a moving average is simply the average closing price of a stock over a fixed

FIGURE 8.7

Price Channel Chart for ChevronTexaco

FIGURE 8.8

Head and Shoulders Chart for CNET Networks, Inc.

length of time, say 20 days. Each day, the new closing price is added to the calculation, and the oldest closing price is dropped from the calculation.

Moving averages are either simple or exponential. In a *simple moving average,* all days are given equal weighting. In an *exponential moving average,* more weight is given to the most recently observed price. Market technicians, like many investors, often believe that the latest price observed for a stock is the most important piece of information about the stock. In Example 8.2, we present data for a three-day simple moving average and data for a three-day exponential moving average, where two-thirds of the average weight is placed on the most recent price.

EXAMPLE 8.2

Three-Day Simple Moving Average and Three-Day Exponential Moving Average

Day	Closing Price	Three-Day Simple Moving Average	Three-Day Exponential Moving Average
1	$89.00	—	—
2	88.44	—	$88.72
3	87.60	$88.35	87.97
4	86.20	87.41	86.79
5	85.75	86.52	86.10
6	84.57	85.51	85.08
7	83.64	84.65	84.12
8	76.70	81.64	79.17
9	76.65	79.00	77.49
10	75.48	76.28	76.15

To calculate the first three-day simple moving average, we need three closing prices. The first simple moving average entry is simply:

$$(\$89.00 + \$88.44 + \$87.60)/3 = \$88.35$$

The second simple moving average entry is:

$$(\$88.44 + \$87.60 + \$86.20)/3 = \$87.41$$

To calculate a three-day exponential moving average, we begin by averaging the first two days:

$$(\$89.00 + \$88.44)/2 = \$88.72$$

This number appears first in the exponential moving average column. To obtain the next one, you must decide how much weight is placed on the latest price. As noted above, we selected a 2/3, or 0.667, weight. To calculate the next exponential moving average entry, we multiply the latest closing price by 0.667 and the average of the first two days by 0.333:

$$(0.667)(\$87.60) + (0.333)(\$88.72) = \$87.97$$

The next exponential moving average entry is:

$$(0.667)(\$86.20) + (0.333)(\$87.97) = \$86.79$$

You can see that the simple moving average and the exponential moving average generate different numbers. The exponential moving average responds more quickly to the latest price information than does the simple moving average.

For a description of many technical indicators, including other moving average indicators, see www.crediblecharts.com.

In practice, 50-day moving averages are frequently compared to 200-day moving averages. The 200-day moving average might be thought of as indicative of the long-run trend, while the 50-day average might be thought of as a short-run trend. If the 200-day average was rising while the 50-day average was falling, the indication might be that price declines are expected in the short term, but the long-term outlook is favorable. Alternatively, the indication might be that there is a danger of a change in the long-term trend. Our nearby *Work the Web* box gives an example.

PUTTING IT ALL TOGETHER Quite often, a market technician will be using multiple chart indicators to help in making trading decisions. Let's examine the collection of technical information available from the Web site www.bigcharts.com. We set the Web site controls starting with "Advanced Chart" to give us three months of daily data for Microsoft (MSFT). In

Charts are easy to draw online. Two of the best sites are www.stockcharts.com and www.bigcharts.com. Another really good site is finance.yahoo.com. We provide an example using its basic technical analysis, but the menu presents many technical analysis options.

As illustrated, we have drawn a moving average chart for Starbucks. The jagged line tracks Starbucks's daily stock price over the past year. The two smoother lines are the 50-day and 200-day moving averages. Notice the 50-day average crosses the 200-day average in early May from below. Such a crossing is sometimes interpreted as a signal to buy. In this case, the signal has been true so far. Notice that the stock price rose from about $14 to about $22 in about six months.

addition, we asked the Web site to provide us with 9-day and 18-day exponential moving averages, Bollinger bands, volume, *MACD,* and *money flow*. The results appear in Figure 8.9.

BOLLINGER BANDS John Bollinger created Bollinger bands in the early 1980s. The purpose of Bollinger bands is to provide *relative* levels of high and low prices. Bollinger bands represent a 2-standard deviation bound calculated from the moving average (this is why Bollinger bands do not remain constant). In Figure 8.9, the Bollinger bands surround a 20-day moving average. The Bollinger bands are the maroon bands that appear in the top chart. Bollinger bands have been interpreted in many ways by their users. For example, when the stock price is relatively quiet, the Bollinger bands are tight, which indicates a possible pent-up tension that must be released by a subsequent price movement.

MACD MACD stands for moving average convergence divergence. The MACD indicator shows the relationship between two moving averages of prices. The MACD is derived by dividing one moving average by another and then comparing this ratio to a third moving average, the signal line. In the MSFT example, the MACD uses a 12-day and a 26-day moving average and a 9-day signal line. The convergence/divergence of these three averages is represented by the solid black bars in the third chart of Figure 8.9. The basic MACD trading rule is to sell when the MACD falls below its signal line and to buy when the MACD rises above its signal line.

MONEY FLOW The idea behind money flow is to identify whether buyers are more eager to buy the stock than sellers are to sell it. In its purest form, money flow looks at each trade. To calculate the money flow indicator, the technician multiplies price and volume for the trades that occur at a price higher than the previous trade price. The technician then sums this money flow. From this sum, the technician subtracts another money flow: the accumulated total of

FIGURE 8.9

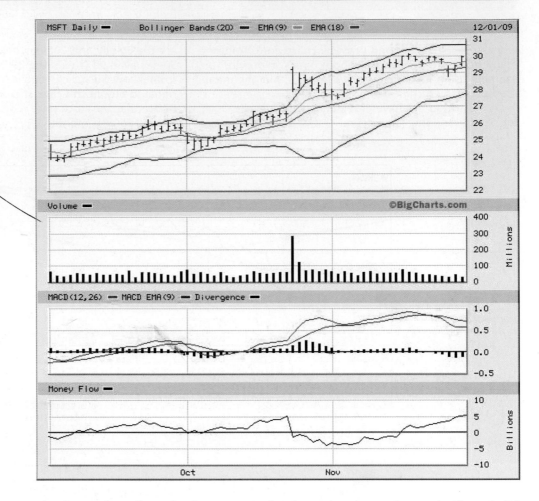

price times volume for trades that occur at prices lower than the previous trade. Example 8.3 shows how to calculate money flow using hypothetical data.

Traders using money flow look for a divergence between money flow and price. If price remains stable but money flow becomes highly positive, this is taken as an indicator that the stock price will soon increase. Similarly, if the stock price remains stable but the money flow becomes quite negative, this is taken as an indicator that the stock price will soon decrease. In Figure 8.9, the positive accumulation of money flow for Microsoft signals to followers of money flow that further price gains for Microsoft are in order.

EXAMPLE 8.3

Calculating Money Flow

Price	Up (+); Down (−); Unchanged (0)	Volume	Price × Volume	Money Flow (+)	Money Flow (−)	Net Money Flow
10						
11	+	1,000	11,000	11,000		
12	+	100	1,200	12,200		
12	0	500	6,000			
11	−	500	5,500		5,500	
10	−	50	500		6,000	
At the end of the day:						6,200

FIBONACCI NUMBERS

Traders using technical analysis are interested in timing their purchase or sale of a stock. As you know by now, these traders look for support or resistance stock price levels. As strange as it may seem, one source that traders use is known as the *golden mean*. The golden mean is sometimes abbreviated by the Greek letter phi (ϕ). The golden mean, ϕ, is approximately equal to 1.618 (it is precisely equal to $(\sqrt{5} + 1)/2$). The golden mean is mathematically interesting, because, among other things, $\phi^2 = \phi + 1$.

The golden mean also results from a series of numbers known as *Fibonacci numbers*. The infinite Fibonacci series grows as follows:

$$1,1,2,3,5,8,13,21,34,55,89,144,233,377,610,987 \ldots$$

Note that the series begins with 1,1 and grows by adding the two previous numbers together (for example, $21 + 34 = 55$). Let's look at the ratio of some number to their predecessor in the series:

$$21/13 = 1.6154$$
$$34/21 = 1.6190$$
$$55/34 = 1.6176$$
$$89/55 = 1.6182$$

The ratio converges to 1.618, or ϕ. Market technicians are interested in ϕ because:

$$(\phi - 1)/\phi = 0.618/1.618 = 0.382$$
$$1/\phi = 1.000/1.618 = 0.618 = \phi - 1$$

For an excellent source on Fibonacci numbers and the golden mean, visit www.maths.surrey.ac.uk/ hosted-sites/r.knott/Fibonacci

Market technicians use these numbers to predict support and resistance levels. For example, as a stock increases in value over time, it will occasionally pull back in value. Suppose a stock has increased from $40 to $60, and has recently begun to fall a bit in value. Using the $(\phi - 1)/\phi$ ratio, market technicians would predict the primary support area would occur at $52.36 ($60 − $40 = $20; $20 × 0.382 = $7.64; $60 − $7.64 = $52.36). A similar calculation that uses the $1/\phi$ ratio of 0.618 instead of 0.382 results in the secondary support area of $47.64. If the stock were to pierce this secondary support level and close below it, the rally would be declared over. Market technicians would then begin to look for opportunities to sell the stock short if it subsequently rallied.

Nature provides many instances involving Fibonacci numbers. The number of petals on a flower is often a Fibonacci number. For example, black-eyed susans have 13 petals and ordinary daisies have 34. Also, pinecones and pineapples have spirals containing 8 or 13 scales. There are so many other examples that some observers classify Fibonacci numbers as a "law of nature." Because of this, some market technicians believe that the Fibonacci numbers should also apply to market prices.

OTHER TECHNICAL INDICATORS

We close our discussion of technical analysis by describing a few additional technical indicators. The "odd-lot" indicator looks at whether odd-lot purchases (purchases of fewer than 100 shares) are up or down. One argument is that odd-lot purchases represent the activities of smaller, unsophisticated investors, so when they start buying, it's time to sell. This is a good example of a "contrarian" indicator. In contrast, some argue that because short selling is a fairly sophisticated tactic, increases in short selling are a negative signal.

Some indicators can seem a little silly. For example, there is the "hemline" indicator, which is also known as the "bull markets and bare knees" indicator. Through much of the nineteenth century, long skirts dominated women's fashion and the stock market experienced many bear markets. In the 1920s, flappers revealed their knees and the stock market boomed. Even the stock market crash of October 1987 was predicted by hemlines. During the 1980s, miniskirts flourished, but by October 1987, a fashion shift had women wearing longer skirts.

One of the more famous (or fatuous, depending on how you look at it) indicators is the Super Bowl indicator, which forecasts the direction of the market based on whether the

THE SUPER GUIDE TO INVESTING

Every January, about 90 million people in the United States watch television for a prediction of how well the stock market is going to do in the upcoming year. So you missed it this year? Maybe not. The stock market predictor we are talking about is the Super Bowl!

The Super Bowl indicator has become one of the more famous (or infamous) technical indicators of stock market performance. Here's how it works. In the 1960s, the original National Football League (NFL) and the upstart American Football League (AFL) were fighting for dominance. The Super Bowl indicator says that if a team from the original AFL wins the Super Bowl, the market posts a negative return for the year, and if a team from the original NFL wins, the market will post a gain for the year.

So how has the Super Bowl predictor performed? Take a look at the chart we obtained from www.cnn.com.

For the first 31 Super Bowls, the indicator was correct 28 out of 31 times! The Miami Dolphins are perhaps the best market predictor. When Miami won the Super Bowl in 1973, the market proceeded to drop by 14.7 percent. The next year was an even better indicator. The next year, the Dolphins beat the Minnesota Vikings and the S&P 500 lost 26.5 percent, the worst one-year performance in its history. When the Dolphins lost the Super Bowl in 1972, 1983, and 1985, the S&P 500 posted double-digit gains in each of those years.

So are you ready to bet the ranch on the Super Bowl indicator? It's probably not a good thing. Beginning with the 1998 game through the one in 2009, the Super Bowl indicator has an unimpressive record of 4-5-3. Let's look at the winning years: 2002, 2005, 2006, and 2009. The New England Patriots, an AFL team, won the Super Bowl in 2002 and 2005 and the S&P 500 dropped 30 percent in 2002 (but only .6 percent in 2005). The Pittsburgh Steelers, an original NFL team, won in 2006 and 2009, and the S&P 500 was up for the year about 14 percent and 21 percent, respectively.

Let's look at some other years. The performance in 2001 is not as clear. The Baltimore Ravens won the Super Bowl that year and the market lost 7.6 percent. The Ravens are the descendants of the original Cleveland Browns, a member of the original NFL. In this case, the Super Bowl indicator was incorrect. However, purists (especially in Cleveland) argue that since the Browns have been revived, the

Ravens cannot be considered a member of the original NFL. But the Ravens did beat the New York Giants, an old NFL team. In 2003, the expansion Tampa Bay Buccaneers beat an original AFL team, the Oakland Raiders, and the market went up about 28 percent.

In 2007, the Indianapolis Colts won (easily), but it didn't matter. Both the Colts and their opponent, the Chicago Bears, are original NFL teams, so 2007 has to be an up year according to the indicator. For 2007, the market was up about 3 percent. In 2010, the New Orleans Saints, an original NFL team, beat the Indianapolis Colts, also an original NFL team. So, will 2010 be an up year like 2007? In the first quarter of 2010, the market was up about 4 percent. Stay tuned. Or, better yet, just watch the Super Bowl commercials.

The Predictor (32-8-4)

Bullish years (24)
49ers - '82, '85, '89, '95
Bears- '86
Colts - '71
Cowboys - '72, '93, '94, '96
Giants - '87, '91
Packers, '67, '68, '97
Redskins - '83, '88, '92
Steelers - '75, '76, '79, '80, '06, '09

Bearish years (8)
Dolphins - '73, '74
Jets, '69
Patriots, '02, '05
Raiders - '77, '81, '84

Indicator missed (8)
Broncos - '98, '99
Chiefs - '70
49ers - '90
Cowboys - '78
Rams -'00
Patriots - '04
Giants - '08

Inconclusive (4)
Ravens - '01*
Buccaneers - '03**
Colts - '07***
Saints - '10****

*Created when the old NFL Cleveland Browns moved to Baltimore, the NFL says the Ravens started life as an AFC team in 1996, which would mean the predictor was accurate.
**Expansion team
***A former NFL team beat an original NFL team.
****An original NFL team beat a former NFL team.

National Football Conference or the American Football Conference wins. A Super Bowl win by a National Football Conference team or an American Football Conference team that used to be in the old National Football League (i.e., Pittsburgh Steelers, Baltimore Colts) is bullish. This probably strikes you as absurd, so you might be surprised to learn that for the period 1967–1988, the Super Bowl indicator forecast the direction of the stock market with more than 90 percent accuracy. The nearby *Investment Updates* box contains more details about this indicator.

If you want a more recent indicator of stock market performance from the world of sports, consider the Daytona 500 indicator. Winning this race (the "Super Bowl of NAS-CAR") is an accomplishment for the driver, yet it doesn't seem to carry over to the stock of the winning driver's sponsor. For example, in 2005, Jeff Gordon won the Daytona 500 and stock in his sponsor company, Du Pont, was down 13 percent for the year. Things were even worse for Du Pont stock when Gordon won in 1997; the stock lost 36 percent on the year.

Overall, in the last 15 years before 2005, stock in the sponsor of the winning driver trailed the market by about 20 percent per year. The trend continued in 2006 after Jimmie Johnson won the Daytona 500. The stock of his sponsor, Lowe's, dropped about 6.5 percent during the year, but the S&P 500 increased about 14 percent. In 2007, however, the indicator did not do so well. Kevin Harvick won the race and shares of one of his main sponsors, Shell, outpaced the S&P 500 by about 13 percent.

In a recent three-year period, the indicator has had some "hard bad" racin' luck—running smack dab into privately held companies and wholly owned subsidiaries. For example, Ryan Newman won the 2008 race with Alltel as his sponsor. Alltel was held by Goldman Sachs Private Equity and TPC Group during 2008. Verizon bought Alltel in early 2009. Matt Kenseth won the 2009 race with DeWalt Tools as his primary sponsor. DeWalt is a subsidiary of Stanley Black & Decker. Bass Pro Shops was Jamie McMurray's primary sponsor for the 2010 race winner. The privately held purveyor of outdoor sports equipment, however, subsequently dropped its sponsorship. What a bad streak of luck for this spurious indicator.

There are lots of other technical trading rules. How seriously should you take them? That's up to you, but our advice is to keep in mind that life is full of odd coincidences. Just because a bizarre stock market predictor seems to have worked well in the past doesn't mean that it's going to work in the future.

CHECK THIS

8.7a	What is technical analysis?
8.7b	What is the purpose of charting a stock's past price?
8.7c	What is the purpose of using technical indicators?

8.8 Summary and Conclusions

The topic of this chapter is behavioral finance and technical analysis. In this chapter, we cover many aspects of this evolving area in finance. We summarize these aspects of the chapter's important concepts.

1. Prospect theory.

   A. Prospect theory is a collection of ideas that provides an alternative to classical, rational economic decision making. The foundation of prospect theory rests on the idea that investors are much more distressed by prospective losses than they are happy about prospective gains.

   B. Researchers have found that a typical investor considers the pain of a $1 loss to be about twice as great as the pleasure received from the gain of $1. Also, researchers have found that investors respond in different ways to identical situations. The difference depends on whether the situation is presented in terms of losses or in terms of gains.

C. Researchers have identified other befuddling examples of investor behavior. Three of them are:

- *Frame dependence:* If an investment problem is presented in two seemingly different (but actually equivalent) ways, investors often make inconsistent choices. That is, how a problem is described, or framed, seems to matter to people.

- *Mental accounting:* Through time, you will mentally account for gains and losses in your investments. How you feel about the investment depends on whether you are ahead or behind. This behavior is known as mental accounting.

- *House money:* Casinos in Las Vegas (and elsewhere) know all about a concept called "playing with house money." The casinos have found that gamblers are far more likely to take big risks with money won from the casino (i.e., the "house money") than with their "hard-earned cash." Casinos also know that gamblers are not as upset about losing house money as they are about losing the money they brought with them to gamble. This is puzzling because all your money is your money.

2. The implications of investor overconfidence and misperceptions of randomness.

A. One key to becoming a wise investor is to avoid certain types of behavior. By studying behavioral finance, you can see the potential damage to your (or your client's) portfolio from overconfidence and psychologically induced errors.

B. The evidence is relatively clear on one point: Investors probably make mistakes. A much more difficult question, and one where the evidence is not at all clear, is whether risks stemming from errors in judgment by investors can influence market prices and lead to market inefficiencies. An important point is that market efficiency does not require that all investors behave in a rational fashion. It just requires that some do.

3. Sentiment-based risk and limits to arbitrage.

A. "Limits to arbitrage" is a term that refers to the notion that under certain circumstances, rational, well-capitalized traders may be unable to correct a mispricing, at least not quickly. The reason is that strategies designed to eliminate mispricings are often risky, costly, or somehow restricted. Three important such problems are firm-specific risk, noise trader risk, and implementation costs.

B. When these or other risks and costs are present, a mispricing may persist because arbitrage is too risky or too costly. Collectively, these risks and costs create barriers or limits to arbitrage. How important these limits are is difficult to say, but we do know that mispricings occur, at least on occasion. Two well-known examples are 3Com/Palm and Royal Dutch/Shell.

4. The wide array of technical analysis methods used by investors.

A. Many investors try to predict future stock price movements based on investor sentiment, errors in judgment, or historical price movements. Such investors rely on the tools of technical analysis, and we present numerous specific methods used by technical analysts.

B. Whether these tools or methods work is much debated. We close this chapter by noting the possibility that market prices are influenced by factors like errors in judgment by investors, sentiment, emotion, and irrationality. If they are, however, we are unaware of any scientifically proven method investors such as you can use to profit from these influences.

GET REAL

This chapter deals with various aspects of behavioral finance. How do you go about incorporating these concepts into the management of your portfolio? First, recall that one of the major lessons from this chapter is that, at times, you may be your own worst enemy when you are investing.

But suppose that you are able to harness your own psychological flaws that unduly influence your investment decisions. To profit from insights from behavioral finance, you might try to shift your portfolio to take advantage of situations where you perceive other market participants have incorrectly valued certain stocks, bonds, derivatives, market sectors, or even countries. Shifting portfolio weights to take advantage of these opportunities is called a "dynamic" trading strategy.

Here is one example of using a dynamic trading strategy. Consider a typical value/growth portfolio weight-shifting scheme. When there is a great deal of market overreaction, perhaps signaled by high market volatility, you would increase, or tilt, your relative portfolio weight toward value stocks. When there is a great deal of market underreaction, perhaps signaled by low market volatility, you would increase your relative weighting in growth stocks. The problem, of course, is knowing when and how to tilt your portfolio to take advantage of what you perceive to be market overreactions and underreactions. At times, you can do very well when you tilt your portfolio. Other times, to use an old commodity market saying, "you get your head handed to you."

A great amount of information is available on the Internet about behavioral finance and building portfolios. One interesting place to start is the research section at www.psychonomics.com. Make sure that the money that you are using to test any trading scheme is only a small portion of your investment portfolio.

Key Terms

anchoring 262
behavioral finance 260
clustering illusion 269
Dow theory 277
Elliott wave theory 277
frame dependence 261
limits to arbitrage 273
loss aversion 262
mental accounting 263

noise trader 273
prospect theory 260
relative strength 281
representativeness heuristic 267
resistance level 278
sentiment-based risk 274
support level 278
technical analysis 276

Chapter Review Problems and Self-Test

1. **It's All Relative (CFA1)**   Consider the following series of monthly stock prices for two companies:

Week	Phat Co.	GRRL Power
1	$10	$80
2	12	82
3	16	80
4	15	84
5	14	85
6	12	88

On a relative basis, how has Phat done compared to GRRL Power?

2. Simple Moving Averages (CFA1) Using the prices from the previous problem, calculate the three-month simple moving average prices for both companies.

Answers to Self-Test Problems

1. Suppose we had purchased eight shares of Phat and one share of GRRL Power. We can calculate the value of our investment in each month and then take the ratio of Phat to GRRL Power as follows:

	Investment Value		
Week	Phat Co. (8 shares)	GRRL Power (1 share)	Relative Strength
1	$80	$80	1.00
2	96	82	1.17
3	128	80	1.60
4	120	84	1.43
5	112	85	1.32
6	96	88	1.09

Phat Co. has significantly outperformed GRRL Power over much of this period; however, after six weeks, the margin has fallen to about 9 percent from as high as 60 percent.

2. The moving averages must be calculated relative to the share price; also note that results cannot be computed for the first two weeks because of insufficient data.

Week	Phat Co.	Phat Co. Moving Average	GRRL Power	GRRL Power Moving Average
1	$10	—	$80	—
2	12	—	82	—
3	16	$12.67	80	$80.67
4	15	14.33	84	82.00
5	14	15.00	85	83.00
6	12	13.67	88	85.67

Test Your Investment Quotient

1. **Technical Analysis (LO4, CFA1)** Which of the following is a basic assumption of technical analysis in contrast to fundamental analysis?

   a. Financial statements provide information crucial in valuing a stock.
   b. A stock's market price will approach its intrinsic value over time.
   c. Aggregate supply and demand for goods and services are key determinants of stock value.
   d. Security prices move in patterns, which repeat over long periods.

2. **Technical Analysis (LO4, CFA1)** Which of the following is least likely to be of interest to a technical analyst?

   a. A 15-day moving average of trading volume.
   b. A relative strength analysis of stock price momentum.
   c. Company earnings and cash flow growth.
   d. A daily history of the ratio of advancing stocks over declining stocks.

3. **Dow Theory (LO4, CFA1)** Dow theory asserts that three forces are at work in the stock market at any time. Which of the following is *not* one of these Dow theory forces?

   a. Daily price fluctuations
   b. A secondary reaction or trend
   c. A primary direction or trend
   d. Reversals or overreactions

www.mhhe.com/jmd6e

4. **Technical Indicators (LO4, CFA1)** The advance/decline line is typically used to

   a. Measure psychological barriers.
   b. Measure market breadth.
   c. Assess bull market sentiment.
   d. Assess bear market sentiment.

5. **Technical Indicators (LO4, CFA1)** The closing Arms (TRIN) ratio is the ratio of

   a. Average trading volume in declining stocks to advancing stocks.
   b. Average trading volume in NYSE stocks to NASDAQ stocks.
   c. The number of advancing stocks to the number of declining stocks.
   d. The number of declining stocks to the number of advancing stocks.

6. **Technical Indicators (LO4, CFA1)** Resistance and support areas for a stock market index are viewed as technical indicators of

   a. Economic barriers
   b. Psychological barriers
   c. Circuit breakers
   d. Holding patterns

7. **Behavioral Finance Concepts (LO1, CFA4)** When companies changed the structure of 401(k) plans to allow employees to opt out rather than in, the participation rates significantly increased. This is an example of:

   a. Representativeness
   b. The house money effect
   c. Frame dependence
   d. A heuristic

8. **Behavioral Finance Concepts (LO1, CFA3)** When someone who wins money is more willing to lose the gains, this is referred to as:

   a. Representativeness
   b. The house money effect
   c. Frame dependence
   d. A heuristic

9. **Behavioral Finance Concepts (LO2, CFA2)** Investors are generally more likely to choose a well-known company when faced with a choice between two firms. This is an example of:

   a. Representativeness
   b. The house money effect
   c. Frame dependence
   d. A heuristic

10. **Behavioral Finance Concepts (LO2, CFA3)** Many investors try to simplify the investment process by using rules of thumb to make decisions. This is an example of:

    a. Representativeness
    b. The house money effect
    c. Frame dependence
    d. A heuristic

11. **Behavioral Finance Concepts (LO2, CFA8)** All of the following are ways to help reduce behavioral biases except:

    a. Learning about the biases.
    b. Diversifying your portfolio.
    c. Watching more financial news programs.
    d. Creating objective investment criteria.

12. **Behavioral Finance Concepts (LO1, CFA2)** Which of the following topics related to behavioral finance deals with the idea that investors experience more pain from a loss than pleasure from a comparable gain?

    a. Frame dependence
    b. Prospect theory
    c. Loss aversion
    d. Mental accounting

13. **Limits to Arbitrage (LO3)** Which of the following is not a reason that rational, well-capitalized investors can correct a mispricing, at least not immediately?

   a. Firm-specific risk
   b. Implementation costs
   c. Aversion risk
   d. Noise trader risk

14. **Technical Indicators (LO4, CFA1)** Which of the following techniques deals with the breadth of the market?

   a. Price channels
   b. Advance/decline lines
   c. Bollinger bands
   d. Support and resistance lines

15. **Technical Indicators (LO4, CFA1)** Which of the following techniques does not assume there are psychologically important barriers in stock prices?

   a. Price channels
   b. Advance/decline lines
   c. Bollinger bands
   d. Support and resistance lines

Concept Questions

1. **Dow Theory (LO4, CFA1)** In the context of Dow theory, what are the three forces at work at all times? Which is the most important?

2. **Technical Analysis (LO4, CFA1)** To a technical analyst, what are support and resistance areas?

3. **Mental Accounting (LO1, CFA4)** Briefly explain mental accounting and identify the potential negative effect of this bias.

4. **Heuristics (LO2, CFA2)** Why do 401(k) plans with more bond choices tend to have participants with portfolios more heavily allocated to fixed income?

5. **Overconfidence (LO2, CFA5)** In the context of behavioral finance, why do men tend to underperform women with regard to the returns in their portfolios?

6. **Overconfidence (LO2, CFA6)** What is the "illusion of knowledge" and how does it impact investment performance?

7. **Dow Theory (LO4, CFA1)** Why do you think the industrial and transportation averages are the two that underlie Dow theory?

8. **Limits to Arbitrage (LO3)** In the chapter, we discussed the 3Com/Palm and Royal Dutch/Shell mispricings. Which of the limits to arbitrage would least likely be the main reason for these mispricings? Explain.

9. **Contrarian Investing (LO4, CFA1)** What does it mean to be a contrarian investor? How would a contrarian investor use technical analysis?

10. **Technical Analysis (LO4, CFA1)** A frequent argument against the usefulness of technical analysis is that trading on a pattern has the effect of destroying the pattern. Explain what this means.

11. **Gaps (LO4, CFA1)** Gaps are another technical analysis tool used in conjunction with open-high-low-close charts. A gap occurs when either the low price for a particular day is higher than the high price from the previous day, or the high price for a day is lower than the low price from the previous day. Do you think gaps are a bullish or bearish signal? Why?

12. **Probabilities (LO2, CFA3)** Suppose you are flipping a fair coin in a coin-flipping contest and have flipped eight heads in a row. What is the probability of flipping a head on your next coin flip? Suppose you flipped a head on your ninth toss. What is the probability of flipping a head on your tenth toss?

13. **Prospect Theory (LO1, CFA2)** How do prospect theory and the concept of a rational investor differ?

14. **Frame Dependence (LO1, CFA4)** How can frame dependence lead to irrational investment decisions?

15. **Noise Trader Risk (LO3, CFA3)** What is noise trader risk? How can noise trader risk lead to market inefficiencies?

Questions and Problems

1. **Advance/Decline Lines (LO4, CFA1)**   Use the data below to construct the advance/decline line for the stock market. Volume figures are in thousands of shares and are from November 2–6, 2009.

	Stocks Advancing	Advancing Volume	Stocks Declining	Declining Volume
Monday	1,634	825,503	1,402	684,997
Tuesday	1,876	928,360	1,171	440,665
Wednesday	1,640	623,369	1,410	719,592
Thursday	2,495	1,101,332	537	173,003
Friday	1,532	508,790	1,459	498,585

2. **Calculating Arms Ratio (LO4, CFA1)**   Using the data in the previous problem, construct the Arms ratio on each of the five trading days.

3. **Simple Moving Averages (LO4, CFA1)**   The table below shows the closing monthly stock prices for Amazon.com and Google during 2009. Calculate the simple three-month moving average for each month for both companies.

AMZN	GOOG
$51.28	$307.65
58.82	338.53
64.79	337.99
73.44	348.06
80.52	395.97
77.99	417.23
83.66	421.59
85.76	443.05
81.19	461.67
93.36	495.85
118.81	536.12
135.91	583.00

4. **Exponential Moving Averages (LO4, CFA1)**   Using the stock prices in Problem 3, calculate the exponential three-month moving average for both stocks where two-thirds of the average weight is placed on the most recent price.

5. **Exponential Moving Averages (LO4, CFA1)**   Using the stock prices in Problem 3, calculate the exponential three-month moving average for Amazon.com and Google. Place 50 percent of the average weight on the most recent price. How does this exponential moving average compare to your result from the previous problem?

6. **Market Sentiment Index (LO4, CFA1)**   A group of investors was polled each week for the last five weeks about whether they were bullish or bearish concerning the market. Construct the market sentiment index for each week based on these polls. Assuming the market sentiment index is being used as a contrarian indicator, which direction would you say the market is headed?

Week	Bulls	Bears
1	58	63
2	53	68
3	47	74
4	50	71
5	43	78

www.mhhe.com/jmd6e

7. **Money Flow (LO4, CFA1)** You are given the following information concerning the trades made on a particular stock. Calculate the money flow for the stock based on these trades. Is the money flow a positive or negative signal in this case?

Price	Volume
$70.12	
70.14	1,900
70.13	1,400
70.09	1,800
70.05	2,100
70.07	2,700
70.03	3,000

8. **Moving Averages (LO4, CFA1)** Suppose you are given the following information on the S&P 500:

Date	Close
11/2/2009	1,042.88
11/3/2009	1,045.51
11/4/2009	1,046.50
11/5/2009	1,066.63
11/6/2009	1,069.30
11/9/2009	1,093.08
11/10/2009	1,093.01
11/11/2009	1,098.51
11/12/2009	1,087.24
11/13/2009	1,093.48

Calculate the simple three-day moving average for the S&P 500 and the exponential three-day moving average where two-thirds of the weight is placed on the most recent close. Why would you want to know the moving average for an index? If the close on November 13, 2009, was above the three-day moving average, would it be a buy or sell signal?

9. **Support and Resistance Levels (LO4, CFA1)** Below you will see a stock price chart for Cisco Systems from finance.yahoo.com. Do you see any resistance or support levels? What do support and resistance levels mean for the stock price?

10. **Advance/Decline Lines and Arms Ratio (LO4, CFA1)** Use the data below to construct the advance/decline line and Arms ratio for the market. Volume is in thousands of shares.

	Stocks Advancing	Advancing Volume	Stocks Declining	Declining Volume
Monday	2,530	995,111	519	111,203
Tuesday	2,429	934,531	639	205,567
Wednesday	1,579	517,007	1,407	498,094
Thursday	2,198	925,424	823	313,095
Friday	1,829	592,335	1,188	384,078

11. **Money Flow (LO4, CFA1)** A stock had the following trades during a particular period. What was the money flow for the stock? Is the money flow a positive or negative signal in this case?

Price	Volume
$61.85	
61.81	1,000
61.82	1,400
61.85	1,300
61.84	800
61.87	1,100
61.88	1,400
61.92	600
61.91	1,200
61.93	1,600

Intermediate Questions

12. **Fibonacci Numbers (LO4, CFA1)** A stock recently increased in price from $26 to $42. Using φ, what are the primary and secondary support areas for the stock?

13. **Simple Moving Averages (LO4, CFA1)** Below you will find the closing stock prices for eBay over a three-week period. Calculate the simple three-day and five-day moving averages for the stock and graph your results. Are there any technical indications of the future direction of the stock price?

Date	Close
10/26/2009	$23.33
10/27/2009	23.15
10/28/2009	22.75
10/29/2009	23.01
10/30/2009	22.27
11/2/2009	22.44
11/3/2009	22.51
11/4/2009	22.55
11/5/2009	23.24
11/6/2009	23.34
11/9/2009	23.27
11/10/2009	23.43
11/11/2009	23.76
11/12/2009	23.91
11/13/2009	23.74

14. **Exponential Moving Averages (LO4, CFA1)** Use the information from the previous problem to calculate the three-day and five-day exponential moving averages for eBay and graph your results. Place two-thirds of the average weight on the most recent stock price. Are there any technical indications of the future direction of the stock price?

15. **Put/Call Ratio (LO4, CFA1)** Another technical indicator is the put/call ratio. The put/call ratio is the number of put options traded divided by the number of call options traded. The put/call ratio can be constructed on the market or an individual stock. Below you will find the number of puts and calls traded over a four-week period for all stocks:

Week	Puts	Calls
1	1,874,986	1,631,846
2	1,991,650	1,772,815
3	2,187,450	1,976,277
4	2,392,751	2,182,270

How would you interpret the put/call ratio? Calculate the put/call ratio for each week. From this analysis, does it appear the market is expected to be upward trending or downward trending?

CFA Exam Review by Schweser

[CFA2, CFA3, CFA4, CFA5, CFA6]

Terry Shriver and Mary Trickett are portfolio managers for High End Investment Managers. As part of their annual review of their client portfolios, they consider the appropriateness of their client portfolios given their clients' investment policy. Their boss, Jill Castillo, is concerned that Shriver and Trickett allow the clients' behavioral biases to enter into the asset allocation decision, so she has asked them to review their notes from meetings with clients. The information below is excerpted from their notes regarding the clients named.

Tom Higgins: "In the past five years, I have consistently outperformed the market averages in my stock portfolio. It really does not take a genius to beat a market average, but I am proud to say that I have beaten the market averages by at least 2 percent each year and have not once lost money. I would continue managing my portfolio myself, but with a new baby and a promotion, I just don't have time."

Joanne McHale: "The last three quarters were bad for my portfolio. I have lost about a third of my value, primarily because I invested heavily in two aggressive growth mutual funds that had bad quarters. I need to get back one-third of my portfolio's value because I am only 15 years away from retirement and I don't have a defined-benefit pension plan. Because of this, I am directing Mary Trickett to invest my savings in technology mutual funds. Their potential return is much higher, and I believe I can recover my losses with them."

Jack Sims: "I enjoy birdwatching and hiking. I am an avid environmental advocate and will only invest in firms that share my concern for the environment. My latest investment was in Washington Materials, which was recently featured in an environmental magazine for its outstanding dedication to environmental protection."

1. Which of the following best describes Tom Higgins's behavioral characteristic in investment decisions?

   a. Tom is overconfident.
   b. Tom uses frame dependence.
   c. Tom uses anchoring.

2. Which of the following best describes the potential problem with Mr. Higgins's investment strategy?

   a. He will underestimate the risk of his portfolio and underestimate the impact of an event on stocks.
   b. He will overestimate the risk of his portfolio and overestimate the impact of an event on stocks.
   c. He will underestimate the risk of his portfolio and overestimate the impact of an event on stocks.

3. Which of the following best describes Joanne McHale's behavioral characteristic in investment decisions?

   a. Joanne is loss averse.
   b. Joanne uses the *ceteris paribus* heuristic.
   c. Joanne is experiencing the snakebite effect.

4. Which of the following best describes Jack Sims's behavioral characteristic in investment decisions?

   a. Jack is overconfident.
   b. Jack uses frame dependence.
   c. Jack uses representativeness.

5. Which of the following would Mr. Higgins, Ms. McHale, and Mr. Sims be least likely to use when making investment decisions?

   a. Heuristics
   b. Their personal experiences
   c. Fundamental analysis

What's on the Web?

1. **Bollinger Bands**   You can learn more about Bollinger bands at www.chartsmart.com. What does the site say about using Bollinger bands in technical analysis? Now go to finance.yahoo.com, and enter your favorite stock. Find the technical analysis section and view the Bollinger bands for your stock. What does the chart tell you about this stock?

2. **Relative Strength**   Relative strength measures the performance of a stock against a "bogey," which is either another stock or suitable index. Pick your favorite stock and go to the technical analysis area of finance.yahoo.com. Compare the relative strength of your stock against a close competitor and the S&P 500 Index. How is this stock performing relative to these bogeys?

3. **Triangles**   Go to english.borsanaliz.com. How many different types of triangles are listed on the site? What does each type of triangle mean to a technical analyst?

4. **Market Volume**   An important tool for most technical traders is market volume. Go to www.marketvolume.com. Look on the site to find the reasons market volume is considered important.

Stock-Trak Exercises

To access the Stock-Trak Exercise for this chapter, please visit the book Web site at www.mhhe.com/jmd6e and choose the corresponding chapter.

PART 3

CHAPTER 9

Interest Rates

Learning Objectives

It will be worth your time to increase your rate of interest in these topics:

1. Money market prices and rates.

2. Rates and yields on fixed-income securities.

3. Treasury STRIPS and the term structure of interest rates.

4. Nominal versus real interest rates.

"We reckon hours and minutes to be dollars and cents."

–Thomas Chandler Haliburton

(from *The Clockmaker*)

Benjamin Franklin stated a fundamental truth of commerce when he sagely advised young tradesmen to "remember that time is money." In finance, we call this the time value of money. But how much time corresponds to how much money? Interest constitutes a rental payment for money, and an interest rate tells us how much money for how much time. But there are many interest rates, each corresponding to a particular money market. Interest rates state money prices in each of these markets. ■

This chapter is the first dealing specifically with interest-bearing assets. As we discussed in a previous chapter, there are two basic types of interest-bearing assets: money market instruments and fixed-income securities. For both types of asset, interest rates are a key determinant of asset values. Furthermore, because trillions of dollars in interest-bearing assets are outstanding, interest rates play a pivotal role in financial markets and the economy.

Because interest rates are one of the most closely watched financial market indicators, we devote this entire chapter to them. We first discuss the many different interest rates that are commonly reported in the financial press, along with some of the different ways interest rates are calculated and quoted. We then go on to describe the basic determinants and separable components of interest rates.

CFA™ Exam Topics in This Chapter:

1 The time value of money (L1, S2)

2 Discounted cash flow applications (L1, S2)

3 Money, the price level, and inflation (L1, S6)

4 U.S. inflation, unemployment, and business cycles (L1, S6)

5 Risks associated with investing in bonds (L1, S15)

6 Understanding yield spreads (L1, S15)

7 Introduction to the valuation of debt securities (L1, S16)

8 Yield measures, spot rates, and forward rates (L1, S16)

9 Term structure and volatility of interest rates (L2, S14)

Go to www.mhhe.com/jmd6e for a guide that aligns your textbook with CFA readings.

9.1 Interest Rate History and Money Market Rates

Recall from Chapter 3 that money market instruments are debt obligations that have a maturity of less than one year at the time they are originally issued. Each business day, *The Wall Street Journal* publishes a list of current interest rates for several categories of money market securities in its "Money Rates" report. We will discuss each of these interest rates and the securities they represent following a quick look at the history of interest rates.

INTEREST RATE HISTORY

In Chapter 1, we saw how looking back at the history of returns on various types of investments gave us a useful perspective on rates of return. Similar insights are available from interest rate history. For example, in November 2009, short-term interest rates were about 0.35 percent and long-term rates were about 4.1 percent. We might ask, "Are these rates unusually high or low?" To find out, we examine Figure 9.1, which graphically illustrates 209 years of interest rates in the United States.

Two interest rates are plotted in Figure 9.1, one for bills and one for bonds. Both rates are based on U.S. Treasury securities, or close substitutes. We discuss bills and bonds in detail in this chapter and the next chapter. For now, it is enough to know that bills are short term and bonds are long term, so what is plotted in Figure 9.1 are short- and long-term  interest rates.

Probably the most striking feature in Figure 9.1 is the fact that the highest interest rates in U.S. history occurred in the not-too-distant past. Rates began rising sharply in the 1970s and then peaked at extraordinary levels in the early 1980s. They have generally declined since then. The other striking aspect of U.S. interest rate history is the very low short-term interest rates that prevailed from the 1930s to the 1960s as well as in the

---

FIGURE 9.1 Interest Rate History (U.S. Interest Rates, 1800–2009)

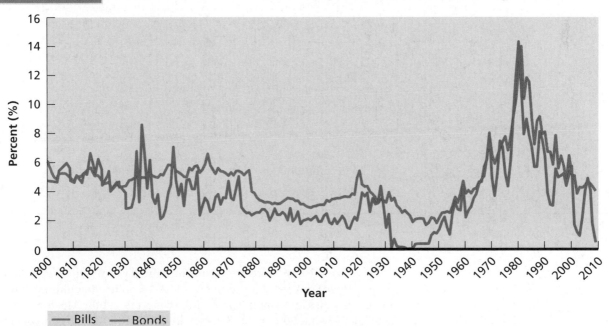

Source: Adapted from Jeremy J. Siegel, *Stocks for the Long Run,* 3rd ed., © McGraw-Hill, 2002; Global Financial Data, and the Federal Reserve Bank of St. Louis.

EXAMPLE 9.1

A Quick Review of the Time Value of Money

Undoubtedly, your instincts tell you that $1,000 received in three years is not the same as $1,000 received today. But if you are going to receive $1,000 today, what is an equivalent amount of money received in three years?

Fortunately, an equation tells us exactly what this is:

$$\text{Future value} = \text{Present value} \times (1 + r)^N \tag{9.1}$$

In this equation, the r represents a periodic interest rate (expressed as a decimal), and the N represents the number of periods (expressed as an integer). Although the periods could be weeks, months, or years, the important thing to remember is that the interest rate must be expressed as an interest rate *per period*.

Suppose you have $1,000 to invest and you can invest at an annual rate of 3.5 percent per year. In equation (9.1) the per-period interest rate enters as 0.035. If you invest for three years ($N = 3$), the amount you will have in three years is:

$$\$1,108.718 = \$1,000 \times (1 + 0.035)^3 \tag{9.2}$$

which would be rounded to $1,108.72.

You can also use equation (9.1) to tell you how much a future amount is worth today. If we divide both sides of equation (9.1) by $(1 + r)^N$ and rearrange terms, we get:

$$\text{Present value} = \frac{\text{Future value}}{(1 + r)^N} \tag{9.3}$$

which, by the rules of exponents, can be written as:

$$\text{Present value} = \text{Future value} \times (1 + r)^{-N} \tag{9.4}$$

That is, $(1 + r)^{-N}$ is just another way to write $1/(1 + r)^N$.

If you remember the relationship between equations (9.1) and (9.4), you will soon become very comfortable with *compounding*, which is equation (9.1), and *discounting*, which is equation (9.4).

To continue with our numerical example, first note that $(1 + 0.035)^3 = 1.108718$. Therefore, using equation (9.3),

$$\text{Present value} = \frac{\text{Future value}}{(1 + r)^N}$$

$$\$1,000 = \frac{\$1,081.718}{1.081718}$$

Suppose you invest $500 for 4 percent for six years. How much money will you have at the end of six years?

$$\text{Future value} = \text{Present value} \times (1 + r)^N$$

$$\$632.66 = \$500 \times (1.04)^6$$

Now suppose you will be getting $800 in four years. What is an equivalent amount today if you discount at 3.7 percent?

$$\text{Present value} = \text{Future value} \times (1 + r)^{-N}$$

$$\$691.79 = \$800 \times (1 + 0.037)^{-4}$$

past few years. These rate levels were the result, in large part, of deliberate actions by the Federal Reserve Board to keep short-term rates low—a policy that ultimately proved unsustainable and even disastrous in the years following the 1960s. Much was learned by the experience, however, and now the Federal Reserve is generally more concerned with controlling inflation. As we discuss just below, however, these actions may be forced upon the Federal Reserve by the condition of the market.

SOME TREASURY YIELDS TURN NEGATIVE

Some Treasury bills maturing at the start of next year traded at negative rates Thursday, a sign of investors' strong demand for the safest securities at a time when T-bills are in scarce supply.

When market participants buy Treasury bills at negative rates, they are essentially paying the government to keep their money safe.

Rates on issues maturing in early January and February slid as low as −0.03%, traders said. Some issues maturing in the first two weeks of December also slipped, trading at flat to a bit negative Thursday.

The rate on the three-month T-bill fell as low as 0.007% and was at 0.013% late Thursday.

Bill yields last fell below zero in late 2008 amid the financial market panic that was triggered by the bankruptcy of Lehman Brothers Holdings Inc. The decline this time, though, isn't driven by the same sorts of fears—it is more about a scarce supply of T-bills amid strong demand for safe assets, given the hazy economic outlook.

The amount of T-bills in the market has shrunk with the government letting the bills in its Supplementary Financing Program—which financed the ballooning deficit through the issuance of bills—mature rather than sell new bills to roll over the debt. At the same time, money-market investors face fewer options to park their cash.

Treasury bond prices also powered forward as investors continued to position for a long period of low interest rates. In late afternoon trade, the 10-year note was up 5/32 point, or $1.56 per $1,000 face value, at 100 7/32. Its yield fell to 3.349% from 3.368% Wednesday, as yields move inversely to prices. The two-year was up 2/32 point to 100 18/32 to yield 0.717%, and the 30-year bond was up 7/32 to 101 16/32 to yield 4.287%.

Source: Deborah Lynn Blumberg, *The Wall Street Journal,* November 19, 2009. Reprinted with permission of *The Wall Street Journal.* © 2009 Dow Jones & Company, Inc. All Rights Reserved Worldwide.

With long-term rates around 4 percent as this chapter was written, many market observers have commented that these interest rate levels are extraordinarily low. Based on the history of interest rates illustrated in Figure 9.1, however, 4 percent may be low relative to the last 30 years, but it is not at all low compared to rates during the 170-year period from 1800 to 1970. Indeed, long-term rates would have to fall well below 4 percent to be considered low by historical standards. Example 9.1 shows how investors use interest rates.

Why have interest rates been at such low levels over the last few years? We noted that the low rates can be attributable to the actions of the Federal Reserve, but other factors are at play as well. With the Crash of 2008, many investors undertook a "flight to quality," implying selling risky assets and moving into safe ones. See our nearby *Investment Updates* box for more on this issue.

This flight to quality increases the demand for Treasury securities, particularly short-term bills. Based on the formulas in Example 9.1, you will see that as prices rise due to increased demand, the interest rates will fall. So, the reduction in rates could really be primarily a result of the crash. After the crash, market participants increased their purchases of extremely safe assets like U.S. Treasury bills.

prime rate
The basic interest rate on short-term loans that the largest commercial banks charge to their most creditworthy corporate customers.

bellwether rate
Interest rate that serves as a leader or as a leading indicator of future trends, e.g., interest rates as a bellwether of inflation.

MONEY MARKET RATES

Figure 9.2 reproduces a *Wall Street Journal* "Money Rates" report of interest rates for the most important money market instruments. A commonly quoted interest rate is the **prime rate**. The prime rate is a key short-term interest rate since it is the basis for interest rates that large commercial banks charge on short-term loans (rates are quoted as prime plus or minus a spread). The prime rate is well known as a **bellwether rate** of bank lending to business. Besides a prime rate for the United States, the "Money Rates" report also lists foreign prime rates for Canada, the European Central Bank, Japan, Switzerland, Great Britain, Australia, and Hong Kong.

FIGURE 9.2   Money Market Interest Rates

Money Rates

Friday, April 23, 2010   Find Historical Data | WHAT'S THIS?

INFLATION

GO TO:

International Rates | U.S Government rates | Secondary Market | Other short-term rates | Weekly Survey

U.S. consumer price index

	March index level	% CHG FROM Feb. '10	% CHG FROM March '09
All items	217.631	0.4	2.3
Core	221.059	0.2	1.1

INTERNATIONAL RATES

GO TO:

Inflation | U.S Government rates | Secondary Market | Other short-term rates | Weekly Survey

Prime rates [U.S. Effective Date: 12/16/2008]

	Latest	Wk ago	52-WEEK High	52-WEEK Low
U.S.	3.25	3.25	3.25	3.25
Canada	2.25	2.25	2.25	2.25
Euro zone	1.00	1.00	1.25	1.00
Japan	1.475	1.475	1.475	1.475
Switzerland	0.53	0.52	0.55	0.51
Britain	0.50	0.50	0.50	0.50
Australia	4.25	4.25	4.25	3.00
Hong Kong	5.25	5.25	5.25	5.00

Overnight repurchase

	Latest	Wk ago	52-WEEK High	52-WEEK Low
U.S.	0.18	0.23	0.31	0.03
U.K. (BBA)	0.500	0.507	0.543	0.407
Euro zone	0.28	0.28	1.40	0.28

U.S. GOVERNMENT RATES

GO TO:

Inflation | International Rates | Secondary Market | Other short-term rates | Weekly Survey

Discount [Effective Date: 2/19/2010]

Latest	Wk ago	52-WEEK High	52-WEEK Low
0.75	0.75	0.75	0.50

Federal funds [Effective Date: 12/16/2008]

	Latest	Wk ago	52-WEEK High	52-WEEK Low
Effective rate	0.20	0.21	0.26	0.09
Target rate	0-0.25	0-0.25	0-0.25	0-0.25
High	0.3800	0.3800	0.5000	0.2500
Low	0.1400	0.0500	0.3200	0.0000
Bid	0.2000	0.1800	0.2500	0.0000
Offer	0.2800	0.2200	0.8333	0.0200

Treasury bill auction [Auction Date: 4/23/2010]

	Latest	Wk ago	52-WEEK High	52-WEEK Low
4 weeks	0.140	0.145	0.160	0.000
13 weeks	0.145	0.155	0.195	0.040
26 weeks	0.220	0.240	0.350	0.130

SECONDARY MARKET

GO TO:

Inflation | International Rates | U.S Government rates | Other short-term rates | Weekly Survey

Freddie Mac

30-year mortgage yields

	Latest	Wk ago	52-WEEK High	52-WEEK Low
30 days	4.84	4.76	5.95	4.26
60 days	4.91	4.84	5.55	4.33
One-year RNY	2.500	2.500	3.375	2.500

Fannie Mae

30-year mortgage yields

	Latest	Wk ago	52-WEEK High	52-WEEK Low
30 days	4.866	4.802	5.502	4.263
60 days	4.931	4.871	5.591	4.364

Bankers acceptance

	Latest	Wk ago	52-WEEK High	52-WEEK Low
30 days	0.22	0.22	0.55	0.21
60 days	0.25	0.25	1.00	0.23
90 days	0.26	0.26	1.20	0.25
120 days	0.28	0.28	1.35	0.26
150 days	0.33	0.33	1.45	0.31
180 days	0.36	0.36	1.60	0.35

OTHER SHORT-TERM RATES

GO TO:

Inflation | International Rates | U.S Government rates | Secondary Market | Weekly Survey

Call money [Effective Date: 12/16/2008]

Latest	Wk ago	52-WEEK High	52-WEEK Low
2.00	2.00	2.00	2.00

Commercial paper

	Latest	Wk ago	52-WEEK High	52-WEEK Low
30 to 39 days	0.21	...	...	...
40 to 59 days	0.22	...	...	...
60 to 89 days	0.23	...	...	...
90 to 119 days	0.28	...	...	...
120 to 149 days	0.31	...	...	...
150 to 179 days	0.35	...	...	...
180 to 209 days	0.41	...	...	...
210 to 239 days	0.47	...	...	...
240 to 270 days	0.49	...	...	...

Dealer commercial paper

	Latest	Wk ago	52-WEEK High	52-WEEK Low
30 days	0.23	0.21	0.45	0.20
60 days	0.27	0.25	0.85	0.20
90 days	0.32	0.28	1.00	0.21

Euro commercial paper

	Latest	Wk ago	52-WEEK High	52-WEEK Low
30 day	n.a.	n.a.	0.73	0.10
Two month	n.a.	n.a.	0.96	0.18
Three month	0.42	0.42	1.15	0.35
Four month	0.50	0.50	1.27	0.40
Five month	0.57	0.57	1.31	0.50
Six month	0.68	0.68	1.40	0.61

London interbank offered rate, or Libor

	Latest	Wk ago	52-WEEK High	52-WEEK Low
One month	0.26438	0.25563	0.43500	0.22813
Three month	0.32063	0.30531	1.07250	0.24875
Six month	0.49281	0.46438	1.62125	0.38250
One year	0.97875	0.94438	1.93063	0.83406

Euro interbank offered rate

	Latest	Wk ago	52-WEEK High	52-WEEK Low
One month	0.405	0.405	0.990	0.397
Three month	0.645	0.644	1.400	0.634
Six month	0.957	0.954	1.593	0.944
One year	1.226	1.224	1.764	1.211

Hibor

	Latest	Wk ago	52-WEEK High	52-WEEK Low
One month	0.090	0.080	0.231	0.050
Three month	0.139	0.130	0.849	0.099
Six month	0.249	0.248	1.119	0.210
One year	0.557	0.548	1.499	0.500

Asian dollars

	Latest	Wk ago	52-WEEK High	52-WEEK Low
One month	0.274	0.261	0.441	0.235
Three month	0.317	0.305	1.084	0.255
Six month	0.479	0.455	1.638	0.384
One year	0.957	0.922	1.938	0.839

Certificates of Deposit

	Latest	Wk ago	52-WEEK High	52-WEEK Low
One month	0.230	0.210	0.450	0.200
Three month	0.320	0.280	1.000	0.210
Six Month	0.450	0.400	1.550	0.250

Merrill Lynch Ready Assets Trust

	Latest	Wk ago	52-WEEK High	52-WEEK Low
	0.000	0.000	0.330	0.000

Eurodollars (mid rates)

	LATEST Offer	LATEST Bid	Wk ago	52-WEEK High	52-WEEK Low
One month	0.20	0.40	0.30	0.65	0.30
Two month	0.30	0.50	0.40	1.00	0.35
Three month	0.40	0.60	0.50	1.25	0.40
Four month	0.35	0.55	0.45	1.35	0.40
Five month	0.35	0.55	0.45	1.45	0.40
Six month	0.45	0.65	0.55	1.65	0.50

Notes on data:
U.S. prime rate and discount rate are effective December 16, 2008. U.S. prime rate is the base rate on corporate loans posted by at least 70% of the 10 largest U.S. banks; Other prime rates aren't directly comparable; lending practices vary widely by location; Discount rate is the charge on loans to depository institutions by the New York Federal Reserve Banks; Federal-funds rate is on reserves traded among commercial banks for overnight use in amounts of $1 million or more; Call money rate is the charge on loans to brokers on stock-exchange collateral; Dealer commercial paper rates are for high-grade unsecured notes sold through dealers by major corporations; Freddie Mac RNY is the required net yield for the one-year 2% rate-capped ARM. Libor is the British Bankers' Association average of interbank offered rates for dollar deposits in the London market; Libor Swaps quoted are mid-market, semi-annual swap rates and pay the floating 3-month Libor rate..

Sources: Merrill Lynch; Bureau of Labor Statistics; Thomson Reuters; General Electric Capital Corp.; ICAP plc; Tullett Prebon Information, Ltd.

Federal funds rate

Interest rate that banks charge each other for overnight loans of $1 million or more.

The **Federal funds rate** (or just "Fed funds") is a fundamental interest rate for commercial bank activity. The Fed funds rate is the interest rate that banks charge each other for overnight loans of $1 million or more. This interbank rate is set by continuous bidding among banks, where banks wishing to lend funds quote "offer rates" (rates at which they are willing to lend), and banks wishing to borrow funds quote "bid rates" (rates they are willing to pay). Notice that four different rates are stated. Two rates are from the day's trading session: *high* is the day's highest rate offered and *low* is the day's lowest bid rate. The other two rates are a snapshot at the end of the day: *bid* represents the rate to borrow and *offered* represents the rate to lend.

The Federal Reserve's **discount rate** is another pivotal interest rate for commercial banks. The discount rate is the interest rate that the Fed offers to commercial banks for overnight reserve loans. You might recall from your Money and Banking class that banks are required to maintain reserves equal to some fraction of their deposit liabilities. When a bank cannot supply sufficient reserves from internal sources, it must borrow reserves from other banks through the Federal funds market. Therefore, the Fed discount rate and the Fed funds rate are usually closely linked.

The Federal Reserve Bank is the central bank of the United States. The "Fed" has the responsibility to manage interest rates and the money supply to control inflation and promote stable economic growth. The discount rate is a basic tool of monetary policy for the Federal Reserve Bank. An announced change in the discount rate is often interpreted as a signal of the Federal Reserve's intentions regarding future monetary policy. For example, by increasing the discount rate, the Federal Reserve may be signaling that it intends to pursue a tight-money policy, most likely to control budding inflationary pressures. Similarly, by decreasing the discount rate, the Federal Reserve may be signaling an intent to pursue a loose-money policy to stimulate economic activity. Of course, many times a discount rate change is simply a case of the Federal Reserve catching up to financial market conditions rather than leading them. Indeed, the Federal Reserve often acts like the lead goose, who, upon looking back and seeing the flock heading in another direction, quickly flies over to resume its position as "leader" of the flock.

Another important interest rate reported is the **call money rate**, or simply the call rate. "Call money" refers to loans from banks to security brokerage firms, and the call rate is the interest rate that brokerage firms pay on call money loans. As we discussed in Chapter 2, brokers use funds raised through call money loans to make margin loans to customers to finance leveraged stock and bond purchases. The call money rate is the basic rate that brokers use to set interest rates on customer call money loans. Brokers typically charge their customers the call money rate plus a premium, where the broker and the customer may negotiate the premium. For example, a broker may charge a customer the basic call money rate plus 1 percent for a margin loan to purchase common stock.

Commercial paper is short-term, unsecured debt issued by large corporations. The commercial paper market is dominated by financial corporations, such as banks and insurance companies, or financial subsidiaries of large corporations. A leading commercial paper rate is the rate that General Electric Capital Corporation (the finance arm of General Electric) pays on short-term debt issues. This commercial paper rate is a benchmark for this market because General Electric Capital is one of the largest single issuers of commercial paper. Most other corporations issuing commercial paper will pay a slightly higher interest rate than this benchmark rate. Commercial paper is a popular investment vehicle for portfolio managers and corporate treasurers with excess funds on hand that they wish to invest on a short-term basis. Euro commercial paper refers to commercial paper denominated in euros rather than dollars.

One important interest rate reported in Figure 9.2 is the rate on **certificates of deposit**, or **CDs**. Certificates of deposit represent large-denomination deposits of $100,000 or more at commercial banks for a specified term. The interest rate paid on CDs usually varies according to the term of the deposit. For example, a six-month CD may pay a higher interest rate than a three-month CD, which in turn may pay a higher interest rate than a one-month CD.

Large-denomination certificates of deposit are generally negotiable instruments, meaning that they can be bought and sold among investors. Consequently, they are often called negotiable certificates of deposit, or negotiable CDs. Negotiable CDs can be bought and sold through a broker. The large-denomination CDs described here should not be confused with the small-denomination CDs that banks offer retail customers. These small-denomination

---

discount rate
The interest rate that the Fed offers to commercial banks for overnight reserve loans.

For the latest on money market rates visit www.money-rates.com

call money rate
The interest rate brokerage firms pay for call money loans, which are bank loans to brokerage firms. This rate is used as the basis for customer rates on margin loans.

Visit General Electric Capital at www.gecapsol.com

commercial paper
Short-term, unsecured debt issued by large corporations.

certificate of deposit (CD)
Large-denomination deposits of $100,000 or more at commercial banks for a specified term.

CDs are simply bank time deposits. They normally pay a lower interest rate than large-denomination CDs and are not negotiable instruments.

A **banker's acceptance** is essentially a postdated check upon which a commercial bank has guaranteed payment. Banker's acceptances are normally used to finance international trade transactions. For example, as an importer, you wish to purchase computer components from a company in Singapore and pay for the goods three months after delivery, so you write a postdated check. You and the exporter agree, however, that once the goods are shipped, your bank will guarantee payment on the date specified on the check.

After your goods are shipped, the exporter presents the relevant documentation, and, if all is in order, your bank stamps the word *ACCEPTED* on your check. At this point your bank has created an acceptance, which means it has promised to pay the acceptance's face value (the amount of the check) at maturity (the date on the check). The exporter can then hold on to the acceptance or sell it in the money market. The banker's acceptance rate published in "Money Rates" is the interest rate for acceptances issued by the largest commercial banks.

Eurodollars are U.S. dollar denominated deposits at foreign banks or foreign branches of U.S. banks. Eurodollar rates are interest rates paid for large-denomination Eurodollar certificates of deposit. Eurodollar CDs are negotiable and are traded in a large, very active Eurodollar money market. The "Money Rates" report lists Eurodollar rates for various maturities obtained from transactions occurring late in the day.

The **London Interbank Offered Rate (LIBOR)** is the interest rate offered by London commercial banks for dollar deposits from other banks. The LIBOR rate is perhaps the most frequently cited rate used to represent the London money market. Bank lending rates are often stated as LIBOR plus a premium, where the premium is negotiated between the bank and its customer. For example, a corporation may be quoted a loan rate from a London bank at LIBOR plus 2 percent. Euro LIBOR refers to deposits denominated in euros—the common currency of 16 European Union countries. Like LIBOR, the Euro LIBOR rate is calculated by the British Bankers Association (BBA) from quotes provided by London banks. The EURIBOR is an interest rate that also refers to deposits denominated in euros. However, the EURIBOR is based largely on interest rates from banks in the European Union interbank market. HIBOR is an interest rate based on Hong Kong dollars. HIBOR is the interest rate between banks in the Hong Kong interbank market.

U.S. Treasury bills, or just **T-bills**, represent short-term U.S. government debt issued through the U.S. Treasury. The Treasury bill market is the world's largest market for new debt securities with one year or less to maturity. As such, the Treasury bill market leads all other credit markets in determining the general level of short-term interest rates. "Money Rates" reports Treasury bill interest rates set during the most recent weekly Treasury bill auction. Interest rates determined at each Treasury bill auction are closely watched by professional money managers throughout the world. The overnight repurchase, or "repo," rate is essentially the rate charged on overnight loans that are collateralized by U.S. Treasury securities.

The Federal Home Loan Mortgage Corporation (FHLMC), commonly called "Freddie Mac," and the Federal National Mortgage Association (FNMA), commonly called "Fannie Mae," are government-sponsored agencies that purchase large blocks of home mortgages and combine them into mortgage pools, where each pool may represent several tens of millions of dollars of home mortgages. The interest rates reported in "Money Rates" are an indicator of rates on newly created home mortgages. Because home mortgages are long-term obligations, these are not actually money market rates. However, with several trillion dollars of mortgages outstanding, the mortgage market has a considerable influence on money market activity.

banker's acceptance
A postdated check on which a bank has guaranteed payment; commonly used to finance international trade transactions.

Eurodollars
U.S. dollar denominated deposits at foreign banks or foreign branches of U.S. banks.

London Interbank Offered Rate (LIBOR)
Interest rate that international banks charge one another for overnight Eurodollar loans.

WWW

For more on LIBOR, visit
www.bba.org.uk

U.S. Treasury bill (T-bill)
A short-term U.S. government debt instrument issued by the U.S. Treasury.

CHECK THIS

9.1a   Which money market interest rates are most important to commercial banks?

9.1b   Which money market interest rates are most important to nonbank corporations?

9.2 Money Market Prices and Rates

pure discount security
An interest-bearing asset that makes a single payment of face value at maturity with no payments before maturity.

Money market securities typically make a single payment of face value at maturity and make no payments before maturity. Such securities are called **pure discount securities** because they sell at a discount relative to their face value. In this section, we discuss the relationship between the price of a money market instrument and the interest rate quoted on it.

One of the things you will notice in this section is that market participants quote interest rates in several different ways. This inconsistent treatment presents a problem when we wish to compare rates on different investments. Therefore, we must put rates on a common footing before we can compare them.

After going through the various interest rate conventions and conversions needed to compare them, you might wonder why everybody doesn't just agree to compute interest rates and prices in some uniform way. Well perhaps they should, but they definitely do not. As a result, we must review some of the various procedures actually used in money markets. We hope you come to recognize that the calculations are neither mysterious nor even especially difficult, although they are rooted in centuries-old procedures and may sometimes be tedious. However, given the billions of dollars of securities traded every day based on these numbers, it is important to understand them.

One other thing to notice is that the word "yield" appears frequently. For now, you can take it as given that the yield on an interest-bearing asset is simply a measure of the interest rate being offered by the asset. We will discuss the topic of yields in greater detail in the next chapter.

basis point
With regard to interest rates or bond yields, one basis point is 1 percent of 1 percent.

Bond yields and many interest rates are quoted as a percentage with two decimal places, such as 5.82 percent. With this quote, the smallest possible change would be .01 percent, or .0001. This amount, which is 1 percent of 1 percent, is called a **basis point**. So, if an interest rate of 5.82 percent rose to 5.94 percent, we would say this rate rose by $94 - 82 = 12$ basis points. The quantity to the left of the decimal point (i.e., the "5") is called the "handle." Traders frequently omit the handle when quoting or discussing rates since, presumably, anyone actively trading would know it.

BANK DISCOUNT RATE QUOTES

bank discount basis
A method for quoting interest rates on money market instruments.

Interest rates for some key money market securities, including Treasury bills and banker's acceptances, are quoted on a **bank discount basis**, or simply discount basis. An interest rate quoted on a discount basis is often called a discount yield. If we are given an interest rate quoted on a bank discount basis for a particular money market instrument, then we calculate the price of that instrument as follows:

$$\text{Current price} = \text{Face value} \times \left(1 - \frac{\text{Days to maturity}}{360} \times \text{Discount yield}\right) \quad \text{(9.5)}$$

The term "discount yield" here simply refers to the quoted interest rate. It should not be confused with the Federal Reserve's discount rate discussed earlier.

To give an example, suppose a banker's acceptance has a face value of $1 million that will be paid in 90 days. If the interest rate, quoted on a discount basis, is 5 percent, what is the current price of the acceptance?

As the following calculation shows, a discount yield of 5 percent and maturity of 90 days gives a current price of $987,500.

$$\$987,500 = \$1,000,000 \times \left(1 - \frac{90}{360} \times .05\right)$$

The difference between the face value of $1 million and the price of $987,500 is $12,500 and is called the "discount." This discount is the interest earned over the 90-day period until the acceptance matures.

Notice that the formula used to calculate the acceptance price assumes a 360-day business year. This practice dates back to a time when calculations were performed manually. Assuming a 360-day business year, with exactly four 90-day quarters rather than a true 365-day calendar year, made manual discount calculations simpler and less subject to error.

Consequently, if $1 million is discounted over a full calendar year of 365 days using a bank discount yield of 5 percent and an assumed 360-day business year, the resulting price of $949,305.56 is calculated as follows:

$$\$949,305.56 = \$1,000,000 \times \left(1 - \frac{365}{360} \times .05\right)$$

EXAMPLE 9.2

Money Market Prices

The rate on a particular money market instrument, quoted on a discount basis, is 4 percent. The instrument has a face value of $100,000 and will mature in 71 days. What is its price? What if it had 51 days to maturity?

Using the bank discount basis formula, we have:

$$\text{Current price} = \text{Face value} \times \left(1 - \frac{\text{Days to maturity}}{360} \times \text{Discount yield}\right)$$

$$\$99,211.11 = \$100,000 \times \left(1 - \frac{71}{360} \times .04\right)$$

Check for yourself that the price in the second case of a 51-day maturity is $99,433.33.

TREASURY BILL QUOTES

For price and yield data on U.S. Treasury securities visit money.cnn.com and surf to "Bonds and Interest Rates" under the "Markets" tab.

In its online version, *The Wall Street Journal* reports current interest rates on U.S. Treasury bills each business day. Figure 9.3 reproduces a "Treasury bills" interest rate report. The maturity of each bill issue is stated in year-month-day format. The two columns following the maturity give the bid and ask discounts for each bill issue. The bid discount is used by Treasury bill dealers to state what they are willing to pay for a Treasury bill, and the ask discount is used to state what price a dealer will accept to sell a Treasury bill. The next column shows the change in the ask discount from the previous day.

For example, consider the bill that matures on February 11, 2010, with a bid discount rate of .028 percent and an ask discount rate of .020 percent. This bill matures in 79 days. For a $1 million face value Treasury bill, the corresponding bid and ask prices can be calculated by using the discounts shown, along with our bank discount basis pricing formula. For example, the bid price would be:

$$\text{Bid price} = \$999,938.56 = \$1,000,000 \times \left(1 - \frac{79}{360} \times .00028\right)$$

Check that the ask price would be $999,956.11.

EXAMPLE 9.3

T-Bill Prices

Suppose you wanted to buy a T-bill with 85 days to maturity and a face value of $5,000,000. How much would you have to pay if the ask discount is 3.41 percent?

Because you are buying, you must pay the ask price. To calculate the ask price, we use the ask discount in the bank discount basis formula:

$$\text{Ask price} = \$4,959,743.06 = \$5,000,000 \times \left(1 - \frac{85}{360} \times .0341\right)$$

Calculate a bid price for this T-bill assuming a bid discount of 3.42 percent. Notice that the ask price is higher than the bid price even though the ask discount is lower than the bid discount. The reason is that a bigger discount produces a lower price.

Treasury bill prices may be calculated using a built-in spreadsheet function. An example of how to use an Excel™ spreadsheet to calculate a Treasury bill price is shown in the nearby *Spreadsheet Analysis* box.

FIGURE 9.3 U.S. Treasury Bills

TREASURY BILLS

GO TO: Notes and Bonds

Tuesday, November 24, 2009

Treasury bill bid and ask data are representative over-the-counter quotations as of 3pm Eastern time quoted as a discount to face value. Treasury bill yields are to maturity and based on the asked quote.

Maturity	Bid	Ask	Chg	Ask yield
2009 Nov 27	0.035	0.030	+0.025	0.031
2009 Dec 03	0.035	0.030	-0.002	0.030
2009 Dec 10	0.048	0.040	+0.003	0.041
2009 Dec 17	0.048	0.040	unch.	0.041
2009 Dec 24	0.058	0.050	+0.003	0.051
2009 Dec 31	0.050	0.045	-0.002	0.046
2010 Jan 07	0.010	0.005	unch.	0.005
2010 Jan 14	0.010	0.005	-0.003	0.005
2010 Jan 21	0.010	0.003	unch.	0.003
2010 Jan 28	0.010	0.003	unch.	0.003
2010 Feb 04	0.018	0.010	-0.002	0.010
2010 Feb 11	0.028	0.020	-0.002	0.020
2010 Feb 18	0.028	0.020	unch.	0.020
2010 Feb 25	0.045	0.035	unch.	0.036
2010 Mar 04	0.048	0.038	unch.	0.038
2010 Mar 11	0.053	0.043	-0.005	0.043
2010 Mar 18	0.058	0.048	-0.002	0.048
2010 Mar 25	0.050	0.040	-0.002	0.041
2010 Apr 01	0.060	0.050	-0.003	0.051
2010 Apr 08	0.083	0.073	+0.003	0.074
2010 Apr 15	0.090	0.085	-0.005	0.086
2010 Apr 22	0.095	0.088	unch.	0.089
2010 Apr 29	0.088	0.080	-0.003	0.081
2010 May 06	0.115	0.108	-0.005	0.109
2010 May 13	0.125	0.118	-0.005	0.119

Source: Reprinted with permission of *The Wall Street Journal*, © 2009 Dow Jones & Company, Inc. All Rights Reserved Worldwide.

The last column in Figure 9.3 lists the ask yield for each Treasury bill issue. It is important to realize that the ask yield is *not* quoted on a discount basis. Instead, it is a "bond equivalent yield." Unlike a discount rate, a bond equivalent yield assumes a 365-day calendar year. Bond equivalent yields are principally used to compare yields on Treasury bills with yields on other money market instruments as well as Treasury bonds and other bonds (we discuss these long-term yields in the next chapter).

BANK DISCOUNT YIELDS VERSUS BOND EQUIVALENT YIELDS

A bank discount yield is converted to a bond equivalent yield using the following formula:

$$\text{Bond equivalent yield} = \frac{365 \times \text{Discount yield}}{360 - \text{Days to maturity} \times \text{Discount yield}} \quad (9.6)$$

This conversion formula is correct for maturities of six months or less. Calculation of bond equivalent yields for maturities greater than six months is a little more complicated, and we will not discuss it here, particularly because T-bills with maturities greater than six months are less common.

For example, suppose the ask discount rate on a T-bill with 170 days to maturity is 3.22 percent. What is the bond equivalent yield? Plugging into the conversion formula, a 3.22 percent discount is converted into a bond equivalent yield as follows:

$$.03315 = \frac{365 \times .0322}{360 - 170 \times .0322}$$

The bond equivalent yield is thus 3.315 percent.

EXAMPLE 9.4 **Bond Equivalent Yields**

Suppose a T-bill has 45 days to maturity and an ask discount of 5 percent. What is the bond equivalent yield?

Using the bond equivalent yield conversion formulas, we have:

$$.05101 = \frac{365 \times .05}{360 - 45 \times .05}$$

The bond equivalent yield is thus 5.101 percent.

Bond equivalent yields may be calculated using a built-in spreadsheet function. An example of how to use an Excel™ spreadsheet to calculate a bond equivalent yield is shown in the nearby *Spreadsheet Analysis* box.

SPREADSHEET ANALYSIS

	A	B	C	D	E	F	G	H
1								
2			Treasury Bill Price and Yield Calculations					
3								
4	A Treasury bill traded on February 23, 2010 pays $100 on May 15, 2010. Assuming							
5	a discount rate of 1.05 percent, what are its price and bond equivalent yield?							
6	Hint: Use the Excel functions TBILLPRICE and TBILLEQ.							
7								
8		$99.7638	=TBILLPRICE("2/23/2010","5/15/2010",0.0105)					
9								
10		1.067%	=TBILLEQ("2/23/2010","5/15/2010",0.0105)					
11								
12								
13	A credit card charges a nominal annual interest rate of 15 percent. With interest							
14	charged monthly, what is the effective annual rate (EAR) on this credit card?							
15	Hint: Use the Excel function EFFECT.							
16								
17		16.075%	=EFFECT(0.15,12)					

One common cause of confusion about bond equivalent yield calculations is the way that leap years are handled. The rule is that we must use 366 days if February 29 occurs within the next 12 months. For example, 2016 will be a leap year. So, beginning on March 1, 2015, we must use 366 days in the numerator of equation (9.6). Then, beginning on March 1, 2016, we must revert to using 365 days.

| EXAMPLE 9.5 | Back to the Future: Leap Year Bond Equivalent Yields |

Calculate the ask yield (bond equivalent yield) for a T-bill price quoted in December 2011 with 119 days to maturity and an ask discount of 5.41 percent.

Because the 12-month period following the date of the price quote includes February 29, we must use 366 days. Plugging this into the conversion formula, we get:

$$.0560 = \frac{366 \times .0541}{360 - 119 \times .0541}$$

Therefore, 5.60 percent is the ask yield stated as a bond equivalent yield.

We can calculate a Treasury bill ask price using the ask yield, which is a bond equivalent yield, as follows:

$$\text{Bill price} = \frac{\text{Face value}}{1 + \text{Bond equivalent yield} \times \text{Days to maturity}/365} \tag{9.7}$$

For example, we have calculated the 3.315 percent bond equivalent yield on a T-bill with 170 days to maturity and a 3.22 percent ask discount rate. If we calculate its price using this bond equivalent yield, we get:

$$\$984,795 = \frac{\$1,000,000}{1 + .03315 \times 170/365}$$

Check that, ignoring a small rounding error, you get the same price using the bank discount formula.

BOND EQUIVALENT YIELDS, APRs, AND EARs

Money market rates not quoted on a discount basis are generally quoted on a "simple" interest basis. Simple interest rates are calculated just like the annual percentage rate (APR) on a consumer loan. So, for the most part, money market rates are either bank discount rates or APRs. For example, CD rates are APRs.

In fact, the bond equivalent yield on a T-bill with less than six months to maturity is also an APR. As a result, like any APR, it understates the true interest rate, which is usually called the *effective annual rate,* or EAR. In the context of the money market, EARs are sometimes referred to as effective annual yields, effective yields, or annualized yields. Whatever it is called, to find out what a T-bill, or any other money market instrument, is *really* going to pay you, yet another conversion is needed. We will get to the needed conversion in a moment.

First, however, recall that an APR is equal to the interest rate per period multiplied by the number of periods in a year. For example, if the rate on a car loan is 1 percent per month, then the APR is $1\% \times 12 = 12\%$. In general, if we let m be the number of periods in a year, an APR is converted to an EAR as follows:

$$1 + EAR = \left(1 + \frac{APR}{m}\right)^m \tag{9.8}$$

For example, on our 12 percent APR car loan, the EAR can be determined by:

$$1 + EAR = \left(1 + \frac{.12}{12}\right)^{12}$$

$$= 1.01^{12}$$

$$= 1.126825$$

$$EAR = 12.6825\%$$

Thus, the rate on the car loan is really 12.6825 percent per year.

EXAMPLE 9.6

APRs and EARs

A typical credit card may quote an APR of 18 percent. On closer inspection, you will find that the rate is actually 1.5 percent per month. What annual interest rate are you *really* paying on such a credit card?

With 12 periods in a year, an APR of 18 percent is converted to an EAR as follows:

$$1 + EAR = \left(1 + \frac{.18}{12}\right)^{12}$$

$$= 1.015^{12}$$

$$= 1.1956$$

$$EAR = 19.56\%$$

Thus, the rate on this credit card is really 19.56 percent per year.

Effective annual rates may be calculated using a built-in spreadsheet function. An example of how to use an Excel™ spreadsheet to calculate an effective annual rate is shown in the *Spreadsheet Analysis* box on page 310.

Now, to see that the bond equivalent yield on a T-bill is just an APR, we can first calculate the price on the bill we considered earlier (3.22 percent ask discount, 170 days to maturity). Using the bank discount formula, the ask price, for $1 million in face value, is:

$$\text{Ask price} = \$984,794 = \$1,000,000 \times \left(1 - \frac{170}{360} \times .0322\right)$$

The discount is $15,206. Thus, on this 170-day investment, you earn $15,206 in interest on an investment of $984,794. On a percentage basis, you earned:

$$1.544\% = \frac{\$15,206}{\$984,794}$$

In a 365-day year, there are 365/170 = 2.147 periods of 170-day length. So if we multiply what you earned over the 170-day period by the number of 170-day periods in a year, we get:

$$3.315\% = 2.147 \times 1.544\%$$

This is the bond equivalent yield we calculated earlier.

Finally, for this T-bill we can calculate the EAR using this 3.315 percent:

$$1 + EAR = \left(1 + \frac{.03315}{2.147}\right)^{2.147}$$

$$= 1.03344$$

$$EAR = 3.344\%$$

In the end, we have three different rates for this simple T-bill. The last one, the EAR, finally tells us what we really want to know: What rate are we actually going to earn?

EXAMPLE 9.7 | **Discounts, APRs, and EARs**

A money market instrument with 60 days to maturity has a quoted ask price of 99, meaning $99 per $100 face value. What are the banker's discount yield, the bond equivalent yield, and the effective annual return?

First, to get the discount yield, we have to use the bank discount formula and solve for the discount yield:

$$\$99 = \$100 \times \left(1 - \frac{60}{360} \times \text{Discount yield}\right)$$

With a little algebra, we see that the discount yield is 6 percent.

We convert this to a bond equivalent yield as follows:

$$6.145\% = \frac{365 \times .06}{360 - 60 \times .06}$$

The bond equivalent yield is thus 6.145 percent.

Finally, to get the EAR, note that there are 365/60 = 6.0833 sixty-day periods in a year, so:

$$1 + EAR = \left(1 + \frac{.06145}{6.0833}\right)^{6.0833}$$
$$= 1.06305$$
$$EAR = 6.305\%$$

This example illustrates the general result that the discount rate is lower than the bond equivalent yield, which in turn is less than the EAR.

CHECK THIS

9.2a What are the three different types of interest rate quotes that are important for money market instruments?

9.2b How are T-bill rates quoted? How are CD rates quoted?

9.2c Of the three different types of interest rate quotes, which is the largest? Which is the smallest? Which is the most relevant?

9.3 Rates and Yields on Fixed-Income Securities

Thus far, we have focused on short-term interest rates, where "short-term" means one year or less. Of course, these are not the only interest rates we are interested in, so we now begin to discuss longer-term rates by looking at fixed-income securities. To keep this discussion to a manageable length, we defer the details of how some longer-term rates are computed to another chapter.

Fixed-income securities include long-term debt contracts from a wide variety of issuers. The largest single category of fixed-income securities is debt issued by the U.S. government. The second largest category of fixed-income securities is mortgage debt issued to finance real estate purchases. The two other large categories of fixed-income securities are debt issued by corporations and debt issued by municipal governments. Each of these categories represents several trillion dollars of outstanding debt. Corporate bonds and municipal government bonds are covered in later chapters.

Because of its sheer size, the leading world market for debt securities is the market for U.S. Treasury securities. Interest rates for U.S. Treasury debt are closely watched throughout the world, and daily reports can be found in most major newspapers. *The Wall Street Journal* provides a daily summary of activity in the U.S. Treasury market in its "Credit Markets" column, as seen in the nearby *Investment Updates* box.

WWW

For more information on fixed-income securities visit www.sifma.org

WWW

For the latest U.S. Treasury rates, check www.bloomberg.com

CREDIT MARKETS

For Treasurys, Jobs Call the Tune

Progress on Labor Could Weaken Market Early in 2010

Dubai's unraveling credit is likely to continue to capture attention worldwide, but the most compelling news for investors in U.S. Treasurys this week will be much closer to home.

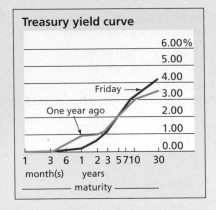

Treasury yield curve

The last payrolls report published in 2009, due Friday, could be pivotal for the fortunes of the Treasury market in the new year.

Although government bonds look well supported to the end of the year, any substantial signs of turnaround in the U.S.'s troubled labor market could put Treasurys on the back foot from the outset of the new year—at a time when the U.S. government still needs to raise trillions in debt to finance its hefty deficit.

The suspension of payments on Dubai World's $60 billion of debt last week drove anxious trading that could well bring more buyers to the safety of government bonds once business picks up as trading resumes after the Thanksgiving-holiday week.

Larry Milstead, head of U.S. government and agency trading at R.W. Pressprich & Co., said he doesn't expect Dubai's problems to spread, though "it's worth watching closely," given the continued fragility of credit markets on both sides of the Atlantic.

Payrolls should easily eclipse such distractions by the end of the week. These figures are the biggest threat to a month-long government bond rally powered chiefly by the conviction that the economic recovery can't take hold, nor can the Fed raise interest rates, while unemployment keeps rising.

Jobs are the major ingredient missing in the economic recovery: October's payrolls figure put the rate at a 26-year high of 10.2%, and there's no consensus that the peak has been reached. The balance of forecasts among economists surveyed by Dow Jones Newswires on Friday was for that level to hold in November.

Demand for the safety of government bonds is at its strongest when economic times look bleak, so it's no surprise that the persistently weak labor market has supported Treasurys. The last set of unemployment figures helped unleash a month of declines in yields, which move inversely to prices.

Late Friday, the benchmark 10-year note Treasury yielded 3.202%, down 0.16 percentage point on the week, as the yield falls as the price rises. RBS Securities strategist Aaron Kohli sees potential for the 10-year yield to drop to 3.17% this week.

Treasurys look set for a continued rally to year end, thanks in part to increased demand among investors for the highest-quality assets to make their year-end accounts look their best.

But the new year brings a host of returning anxieties for the government-bond market that could have a far swifter impact if combined with a resurgent labor force.

Although this week brings a rare hiatus in the Treasury Department's hefty schedule of note auctions, debt sales in record-breaking volumes are in the cards for the foreseeable future. Dealers are forecasting debt sales in the current fiscal year (ending September 30th) of $1.2 trillion to $1.75 trillion.

The Treasury plans $478 billion in sales for the first quarter of 2010.

That supply could weigh more heavily on prices in the new year, particularly as corporate credit markets reopen, providing higher-yielding alternatives to government paper.

THE TREASURY YIELD CURVE

Treasury yield curve

A graph of Treasury yields plotted against maturities.

Every day in its online version, *The Wall Street Journal* contains a graphical display of the current **Treasury yield curve**, which is a plot of Treasury yields against maturities. The *Investment Updates* box above contains an example. Yields are measured along the vertical axis, and maturities are measured along the horizontal axis. The line marked "Friday" represents the most recent yield curve, while the other line represents the yield curve from one year ago. Thus, the "Treasury yield curve" box illustrates both where Treasury interest rates are now and where they were recently.

What does the current Treasury yield curve look like? You can find the answer on the Web in many different places. We went to www.bloomberg.com, and here is what we found on November 25, 2009. As you can see, Bloomberg shows you the yield curve for today and yesterday. For this day, the yield curve shifted slightly upward, as can be seen from the increase in the yield (or decrease in price) for each maturity. This yield curve would be considered a normal, upward-sloping yield curve. The short-term rates are about 0.04 percent, and the six-month rate is about 0.13 percent. Here's a question for you: What is the yield premium for the 10-year over the 5-year? The 30-year over the 10-year?

U.S. Treasuries

	COUPON	MATURITY DATE	CURRENT PRICE/YIELD	PRICE/YIELD CHANGE	TIME
3-MONTH	0.000	02/25/2010	0.04 / .04	0.006 / .006	11:00
6-MONTH	0.000	05/27/2010	0.13 / .13	-0.002 / -.002	11:16
12-MONTH	0.000	11/18/2010	0.24 / .24	-0.018 / -.018	11:15
2-YEAR	0.750	11/30/2011	100-00½ / .74	-0-01 / .016	11:21
3-YEAR	1.375	11/15/2012	100-14+ / 1.22	-0-01½ / .016	11:20
5-YEAR	2.125	11/30/2014	99-29½ / 2.14	-0-02+ / .017	11:23
7-YEAR	3.125	10/31/2016	101-28 / 2.82	-0-04+ / .022	11:23
10-YEAR	3.375	11/15/2019	100-12 / 3.33	-0-07 / .026	11:23
30-YEAR	4.375	11/15/2039	101-13½ / 4.29	-0-23 / .042	11:23

YIELD CURVE   ☐ CURRENT ☐ PREVIOUS CLOSE

© Bloomberg L.P.

The Treasury yield curve is fundamental to bond market analysis because it represents the interest rates that financial markets are charging to the world's largest debtor with the world's highest credit rating—the U.S. government. In essence, the Treasury yield curve represents interest rates for default-free lending across the maturity spectrum. As such, almost all other domestic interest rates are determined with respect to U.S. Treasury interest rates. A *Work the Web* box in this section shows how to get yield curves online.

RATES ON OTHER FIXED-INCOME INVESTMENTS

Figure 9.4 displays interest rates based on bond market indexes that are constructed by two securities firms, Barclays Capital and Merrill Lynch. Current interest rates and the highest and lowest interest rates over the previous 52-week period are reported for a number of bond indexes. These bond market "tracking benchmark" indexes provide yield information on many different types of bonds. Because we will be discussing these in much more detail in several subsequent chapters, we touch on them only briefly here.

Two important indexes represent U.S. Treasury securities with 1- to 10-year maturities ("Intermediate") and 10- to 30-year maturities ("Long-Term"). Another index represents U.S. government agency debt with 10- to 20-year maturities and debt with more than 20 years to

FIGURE 9.4 Tracking Bond Benchmarks

Tracking Bond Benchmarks

Friday, April 23, 2010

Closing index values, return on investment and yields paid to investors compared with 52-week highs and lows for different types of bonds. Preliminary data and data shown as "n.a." will update around 12p.m. the following business day.

Index	Close	% Chg	YTD total return	52-wk % Chg	YIELD (%), 52-WEEK RANGE			SPREAD, 52-WEEK RANGE (●) Latest		
					Latest	Low	High	Latest	Low	High
Broad Market Barclays Capital										
U.S. Government/Credit	1674.40	-0.20	1.98	7.74	3.070	2.810	4.070	n.a.	50.00	172.00
Barclays Aggregate	1473.88	-0.15	2.18	7.65	3.490	3.150	4.580	n.a.	46.00	158.00
Hourly Treasury Indexes Barclays Capital										
Composite (Price Return)	1369.62	-0.20	0.23	-3.26	2.490	1.920	2.740	-5.00	-6.00	-5.00
Composite (Total Return)	11260.16	-0.20	1.22	0.01	2.490	1.920	2.740	-5.00	-6.00	6.00
Intermediate (Price Return)	1242.17	-0.18	0.26	-2.41	2.190	1.590	2.370	-6.00	-7.00	-5.00
Intermediate (Total Return)	9708.51	-0.17	1.16	0.59	2.190	1.590	2.370	-6.00	-7.00	-5.00
Long-Term (Price Return)	1752.87	-0.35	0.05	-7.70	4.420	3.720	4.640	-4.00	-5.00	-4.00
Long-Term (Total Return)	16801.16	-0.33	1.61	-3.03	4.420	3.720	4.640	-4.00	-5.00	4.00
U.S. Corporate Indexes Barclays Capital										
U.S. Corporate	1850.39	-0.24	3.25	22.03	4.400	4.320	7.270	n.a.	139.00	473.00
Intermediate	1877.96	-0.20	3.14	19.67	3.840	3.740	7.090	n.a.	132.00	496.00
Long-term	2131.32	-0.36	3.57	29.71	6.090	6.000	7.860	n.a.	159.00	402.00
Double-A-rated (AA)	395.62	-0.29	2.45	14.70	3.550	3.440	5.540	n.a.	86.60	328.00
Triple-B-rated (Baa)	432.91	-0.22	4.15	28.71	4.870	4.810	8.750	n.a.	173.00	610.00
High Yield Bonds Merrill Lynch										
High Yield Constrained*	n.a.	n.a.	n.a.	n.a.	n.a.	8.030	16.726	n.a.	551.00	1490.00
Triple-C-rated (CCC)	n.a.	n.a.	n.a.	n.a.	n.a.	11.010	32.045	n.a.	874.00	3066.00
High Yield 100	n.a.	n.a.	n.a.	n.a.	n.a.	6.779	10.395	n.a.	461.00	858.00
Europe High Yield Constrained	n.a.	n.a.	n.a.	n.a.	n.a.	7.981	23.326	n.a.	592.00	1887.00
Global High Yield Constrained	n.a.	n.a.	n.a.	n.a.	n.a.	8.080	17.696	n.a.	561.00	1552.00
U.S. Agency Indexes Barclays Capital										
U.S. Agency	1375.10	-0.10	1.26	2.81	2.140	1.780	2.730	n.a.	14.00	62.00
10-20 years	1271.46	-0.10	1.19	2.89	1.950	1.800	2.530	n.a.	12.00	60.00
20-plus years	2008.66	-0.22	2.34	1.77	4.960	4.500	5.700	n.a.	43.00	90.00
Mortgage-Backed Barclays Capital										
Mortgage-Backed	1570.86	-0.06	1.81	5.03	4.070	3.450	4.850	n.a.	3.00	64.00
Ginnie Mae (GNMA)	1538.29	-0.06	2.25	5.25	4.110	3.680	4.900	n.a.	15.00	95.00
Freddie Mae (FHLMC)	1415.63	-0.07	1.75	5.05	4.080	3.430	4.880	n.a.	1.00	65.00
Fannie Mae (FNMA)	912.03	-0.06	1.69	4.94	4.050	3.400	4.810	n.a.	-1.00	55.00
Mortgage-Backed Merrill Lynch										
Ginnie Mae (GNMA)	570.48	-0.14	2.33	2.98	4.290	3.178	4.921	n.a.	-15.00	33.00
Fannie Mae (FNMA)	542.95	-0.14	1.80	0.43	4.410	3.480	4.870	n.a.	-21.00	31.00
Freddie Mae (FHLMC)	335.06	-0.14	1.91	0.42	4.420	3.567	4.930	n.a.	-17.00	37.00
U.S. Corporate Debt Merrill Lynch										
1-10 Year Maturities	1387.06	-0.19	3.53	20.70	3.950	3.862	7.389	n.a.	146.00	543.00
10+ Year Maturities	1642.73	-0.34	4.18	31.27	6.100	6.042	7.926	n.a.	168.00	428.00
Corporate Master	1954.46	-0.23	3.69	23.13	4.470	4.388	7.518	n.a.	151.00	516.00
High Yield	1045.22	0.06	6.85	47.16	7.900	7.900	16.590	n.a.	539.00	1467.00
Yankee Bonds	1446.68	-0.17	3.24	17.16	3.820	3.751	6.129	n.a.	119.00	396.00
Tax-Exempt Merrill Lynch										
Muni Master	n.a.	n.a.	n.a.	n.a.	n.a.	2.875	3.761	n.a.	35.00	66.00
7-12 years	265.65	-0.03	2.65	6.16	3.260	2.893	3.988	n.a.	49.00	79.00
12-22 years	279.79	0.03	2.93	7.73	4.230	3.878	5.015	n.a.	32.00	68.00
22-plus years	258.57	0.00	3.09	14.58	5.050	4.722	5.820	n.a.	57.00	127.00
Bond Buyer 6% Muni	115.16	0.05	2.67	7.65	5.140	4.930	5.620	...	...	...
Yankee Barclays	1804.08	-0.18	2.55	13.77	3.610	3.460	5.260	n.a.	94.00	300.00

Source: Reprinted with permission of *The Wall Street Journal.* © 2010 Dow Jones & Company Inc. All Rights Reserved Worldwide.

maturity. A variety of government agencies borrow money in financial markets. The Tennessee Valley Authority (TVA) is an example of such an agency.

In recent years, U.S. government agencies have issued debt with maturities as long as 50 years. U.S. government agency debt does not carry the same credit guarantee as U.S. Treasury debt, and therefore interest rates on agency debt reflect a premium over interest rates on Treasury debt. Also, agency securities are often subject to state taxes, whereas Treasury securities are not.

In the "U.S. Corporate Indexes" section, you can see rates on debt issued by domestic corporations according to their maturity. Notice that corporate debt with a low credit quality ("High Yield") pays a higher interest rate than U.S. government agency debt. As you can see in Figure 9.4, medium credit quality corporate debt ("Triple-B-rated") pays a higher interest rate than high credit quality corporate debt ("Double-A-rated"). "High Yield Bonds" refers to corporate bonds with above-average default risk. These bonds are usually avoided by conservative investors, but they may be attractive to investors who understand and are willing to accept the risks involved. Because of their much higher credit risk, the interest rates for these bonds are significantly higher than those for even medium-quality corporate bonds.

"Yankee bonds" are issued by foreign corporations for sale in the United States. These bonds are denominated in U.S. dollars so investors do not have to worry that changing foreign exchange rates will affect debt values.

As we noted previously, the Federal Home Loan Mortgage Corporation (FHLMC), or Freddie Mac, and the Federal National Mortgage Association (FNMA), or Fannie Mae, are government-sponsored agencies that repackage home mortgages into mortgage pools, where each pool represents several tens of millions of dollars of home mortgages. A third agency, the Government National Mortgage Association (GNMA), better known as "Ginnie Mae," is also an active mortgage repackager. The interest rates reported for these agencies correspond to indexes constructed from many mortgage pools.

"Tax-exempts" are bonds issued by municipal governments. Coupon interest payments on most municipal bonds are exempt from federal income taxes, and they are often exempt from state income taxes as well. The interest rates reported in the "Tax Exempt" table are based on indexes for high-quality municipal bonds corresponding to maturities of 7–12 years and 12–22 years for general obligation bonds (GOs) and 22-plus years for revenue bonds.

General obligation bonds are secured by the general taxing power of the issuing municipality. Revenue bonds are secured by revenues generated from specific projects, such as toll roads, airports, or user fees for services. Because of their tax-exempt status, interest rates on high-quality municipal bonds are generally lower than interest rates on comparable U.S. Treasury securities.

CHECK THIS

9.3a	What is the yield curve? Why is it important?
9.3b	Why are corporate bond yields higher than Treasury bond yields?
9.3c	Why are municipal bond yields lower than Treasury bond yields?
9.3d	What are Yankee bonds?

9.4 The Term Structure of Interest Rates

term structure of interest rates
Relationship between time to maturity and interest rates for default-free, pure discount instruments.

The yield curve tells us the relationship between Treasury bond yields and time to maturity. The **term structure of interest rates** (or just "term structure") is a similar, but not identical, relationship. Recall that a pure discount instrument has a single payment of face value at maturity with no other payments until then. Treasury bonds are *not* pure discount instruments because they pay coupons every six months. Pure discount instruments with more than a year to maturity are often called "zero coupon bonds," or just "zeroes," because they are, in effect, bonds with a zero coupon rate.

The term structure of interest rates is the relationship between time to maturity and interest rates for default-free, pure discount instruments. So, the difference between the yield curve and the term structure is that the yield curve is based on coupon bonds, whereas the term structure is based on pure discount instruments. The term structure is sometimes called the "zero coupon yield curve" to distinguish it from the Treasury yield curve.

TREASURY STRIPS

Until about 1987, the term structure of interest rates was not directly observable simply because default-free, pure discount instruments with maturities greater than one year did not exist or reliable data on them were not available. Today, however, the term structure of interest rates can be easily seen by examining yields on **U.S. Treasury STRIPS**.

STRIPS are pure discount instruments created by "stripping" the coupons and principal payments of U.S. Treasury notes and bonds into separate parts and then selling the parts separately. The term STRIPS stands for Separate Trading of Registered Interest and Principal of Securities. For example, a Treasury note with 10 years to maturity will make 20 semiannual coupon payments during its life and will also make a principal payment at maturity. This note can therefore be separated, or stripped, into 21 separate parts, and each part can be bought and sold separately. The Treasury originally allowed notes and bonds with 10 years or more to maturity (at the time they are issued) to be stripped. Today, any note or bond is strippable.

Figure 9.5 is a sample U.S. Treasury STRIPS daily report of individual STRIPS prices and yields from *The Wall Street Journal*'s Web site, www.wsj.com. STRIPS can be created from a coupon payment, a Treasury bond principal payment, or a Treasury note principal payment. Figure 9.5 shows some STRIPS from each of these possible sources. Of course, Figure 9.5 contains only a partial list of all available STRIPS.

The first column of Figure 9.5 gives the maturity of each STRIPS listed. The next two columns contain bid and ask prices for each STRIPS. As always, the bid price is a quote of what dealers were willing to pay to buy the STRIPS, and the ask price is a quote of what dealers were willing to accept to sell the STRIPS. The next-to-the-last column in Figure 9.5 reports the change in the ask price quote from the previous day.

The last column in Figure 9.5 lists ask yields, which are yields on the STRIPS based on their ask price quotes. Notice that each maturity has a different ask yield, or interest rate. This shows us that interest rates determined in financial markets generally differ according to the maturity of a security.

STRIPS prices are stated as a price per $100 of face value. In the very recent past, STRIPS prices were quoted in dollars and thirty-seconds of a dollar. That is, a quote of, say, 84:08 stood for 84 and 8/32 of a dollar, or $84.25. Today, however, STRIPS prices are quoted to three decimal points. For example, suppose a coupon interest STRIPS has an ask price quote of 93.668. This means that the price per $100 face value is $93.668. Thus, the skill of being able to divide by 32 is no longer highly valued, at least in STRIPS trading.

YIELDS FOR U.S. TREASURY STRIPS

An ask yield for a U.S. Treasury STRIPS is an APR (APRs were discussed earlier in this chapter). It is calculated as two times the true semiannual rate. Calculation of the yield on a STRIPS is a standard time value of money calculation. The price today of the STRIPS is the *present value*; the face value received at maturity is the *future value*. As shown in Example 9.1, the relationship between present value and future value is:

$$\text{Present value} = \frac{\text{Future value}}{(1 + r)^N}$$

FIGURE 9.5 Treasury STRIPS (November 2009)

Treasury Bond, Stripped Principal

2010 Feb 15	99.989	99.999	unch.	0.00
2010 Aug 15	99.856	99.866	0.014	0.19
2010 Nov 15	99.732	99.742	0.022	0.27
2015 Feb 15	88.601	88.611	0.311	2.33
2015 Aug 15	86.583	86.593	0.332	2.53
2015 Nov 15	85.586	85.595	0.356	2.62
2016 Feb 15	84.547	84.557	0.339	2.71
2016 May 15	83.229	83.239	0.372	2.86
2016 Aug 15	82.859	82.869	0.384	2.82
2016 Nov 15	80.965	80.975	0.278	3.05

Stripped Coupon Interest

2010 Feb 15	99.998	100.000	unch.	0.00
2010 May 15	99.995	100.000	unch.	0.00
2010 Aug 15	99.896	99.906	0.009	0.13
2010 Nov 15	99.763	99.773	0.017	0.23
2011 Feb 15	99.634	99.644	0.058	0.29
2011 May 15	99.720	99.730	0.077	0.18
2011 Aug 15	99.173	99.183	0.090	0.48
2011 Nov 15	99.176	99.186	0.103	0.41

Treasury Note, Stripped Principal

2010 Feb 15	99.984	99.994	-0.002	0.03
2010 Feb 15	99.984	99.994	-0.002	0.03
2010 May 15	99.938	99.948	0.004	0.11
2010 May 15	99.937	99.947	0.004	0.11
2010 Aug 15	99.853	99.863	0.015	0.19
2011 Feb 15	99.585	99.595	0.070	0.33
2011 Aug 15	99.113	99.123	0.090	0.51
2012 Feb 15	98.132	98.142	0.110	0.85
2012 Aug 15	97.261	97.271	0.133	1.02
2012 Nov 15	96.585	96.594	0.138	1.17

Source: Reprinted with permission of *The Wall Street Journal.*

In this equation, r is the rate per period and N is the number of periods. Notice that a period is not necessarily one year long.[1] For Treasury STRIPS, the number of periods is two times the number of years to maturity, here denoted by $2M$, and the interest rate is the "yield to maturity" (YTM) divided by 2:

$$\text{STRIPS price} = \frac{\text{Face value}}{(1 + YTM/2)^{2M}} \qquad (9.9)$$

Consider a STRIPS with an ask price of 55.568, a reported yield of 4.40, and 13.5 years to maturity. The actual semiannual rate is $4.40\%/2 = 2.20\%$. Also, 13.5 years to maturity converts to $2 \times 13.5 = 27$ semiannual periods. To check that the reported price is correct given the reported yield, we plug in future value, rate per period, and number of periods:

$$\text{STRIPS price} = \frac{\$100}{(1 + .022)^{27}}$$
$$= 55.568$$

If we need to go the other way and calculate the ask yield on a STRIPS given its price, we can rearrange the basic present value equation to solve it for r:

$$r = \left(\frac{\text{Future value}}{\text{Present value}}\right)^{1/N} - 1$$

For STRIPS, $N = 2M$ is the number of semiannual periods, and $r = YTM/2$ is the semiannual interest rate, so the formula is:

$$YTM = 2 \times \left[\left(\frac{\text{Face value}}{\text{STRIPS price}}\right)^{1/2M} - 1\right] \qquad (9.10)$$

Consider a STRIPS maturing in six years with an ask price of 73.031. Its yield to maturity of 5.3072 percent as calculated immediately below would be reported as 5.31 percent.

$$.053072 = 2 \times \left[\left(\frac{100}{73.031}\right)^{1/12} - 1\right]$$

As another example, consider a STRIPS maturing in 20 years with an ask price of 26.188. As calculated immediately below, its yield to maturity of 6.8129 percent would be reported as 6.81 percent.

$$.068129 = 2 \times \left[\left(\frac{100}{26.188}\right)^{1/40} - 1\right]$$

CHECK THIS

9.4a What is the yield to maturity (YTM) on a STRIPS maturing in five years if its ask price quote is 77.75?

9.4b What is the YTM of a STRIPS maturing in 15 years if its ask price quote is 36.813?

9.4c What is the YTM of a STRIPS maturing in 25 years if its ask price quote is 18.656?

9.5 Nominal versus Real Interest Rates

nominal interest rates
Interest rates as they are normally observed and quoted, with no adjustment for inflation.

There is a fundamental distinction between *nominal* and *real* interest rates. **Nominal interest rates** are interest rates as we ordinarily observe them, for example, as they are reported in *The Wall Street Journal*. Thus, all the money market rates we discussed earlier in this chapter and the STRIPS yields we discussed just above are nominal rates.

---

[1] Any financial calculator can perform these calculations, but we will work them the hard way so that you can learn how to do them with any calculator.

FIGURE 9.6   Real T-Bill Rates, 1950 through 2009

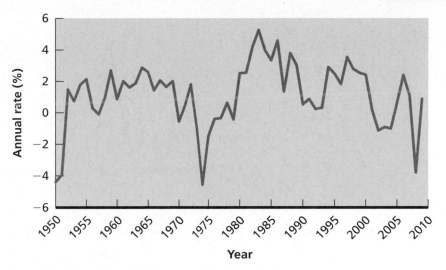

Year

Source: Federal Reserve Board of Governors and Global Financial Data.

REAL INTEREST RATES

real interest rates
Interest rates adjusted for the effect of inflation, calculated as the nominal rate less the rate of inflation.

Real interest rates are nominal rates adjusted for the effects of price inflation. To obtain a real interest rate, simply subtract an inflation rate from a nominal interest rate:

$$\text{Real interest rate} = \text{Nominal interest rate} - \text{Inflation rate} \qquad (9.11)$$

The real interest rate is so-called because it measures the real change in the purchasing power of an investment. For example, if the nominal interest rate for a one-year certificate of deposit is 7 percent, then a one-year deposit of $100,000 will grow to $107,000. But if the inflation rate over the same year is 4 percent, you would need $104,000 after one year passes to buy what cost $100,000 today. Thus, the real increase in purchasing power for your investment is only $3,000, and, therefore, the real interest rate is only 3 percent.

Figure 9.6 displays real interest rates based on annual rates of return on U.S. Treasury bills and inflation rates over the 59-year period 1950 through 2009. As shown in Figure 9.6, following a negative spike at the beginning of the Korean War in 1950, real interest rates for Treasury bills were generally positive until the Organization of Petroleum-Exporting Countries' (OPEC) oil embargo in 1973. After this, real rates were generally negative until the Federal Reserve Board initiated a tight-money policy to fight an inflationary spiral in the late 1970s. The tight-money policy caused the 1980s to begin with historically high real interest rates. Throughout the 1980s, real Treasury bill rates were falling as inflation subsided. During this 50-year period the average real Treasury bill interest rate was slightly less than 1 percent.

THE FISHER HYPOTHESIS

Fisher hypothesis
Assertion that the general level of nominal interest rates follows the general level of inflation.

The relationship between nominal interest rates and the rate of inflation is often couched in terms of the *Fisher hypothesis*, which is named for the famous economist Irving Fisher, who formally proposed it in 1930. The **Fisher hypothesis** simply asserts that the general level of nominal interest rates follows the general level of inflation.

According to the Fisher hypothesis, interest rates are on average higher than the rate of inflation. Therefore, it logically follows that short-term interest rates reflect current inflation, while long-term interest rates reflect investor expectations of future inflation. Figure 9.7 graphs nominal interest rates and inflation rates used to create Figure 9.6. Notice that when inflation rates were high, Treasury bill returns tended to be high also, as predicted by the Fisher hypothesis.

FIGURE 9.7 Inflation Rates and T-Bill Rates, 1950 through 2009

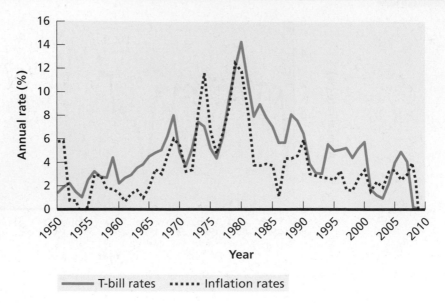

Source: Federal Reserve Board of Governors and Global Financial Data.

INFLATION-INDEXED TREASURY SECURITIES

In recent years, the U.S. Treasury has issued securities that guarantee a fixed rate of return in excess of realized inflation rates. These inflation-indexed Treasury securities pay a fixed coupon rate on their current principal and adjust their principal semiannually according to the most recent inflation rate. For investors wanting long-term protection against inflation along with the safety of U.S. Treasury bonds, inflation-indexed Treasury securities are perhaps the perfect investment.

For example, suppose an inflation-indexed note is issued with a coupon rate of 3.5 percent and an initial principal of $1,000. Six months later, the note will pay a coupon of $1,000 \times 3.5\%/2 = $17.50. Assuming 2 percent inflation over the six months since issuance, the note's principal is then increased to $1,000 \times 102\% = $1,020. Six months later, the note pays $1,020 \times 3.5\%/2 = $17.85, and its principal is again adjusted to compensate for recent inflation.

Price and yield information for inflation-indexed Treasury securities is reported online at www.wsj.com in the same section with other Treasury securities, as shown in Figure 9.8. Locating the listing for inflation-indexed Treasury securities in Figure 9.8, we see that the first and second columns report the maturity and the fixed coupon rate, respectively. The third, fourth, and fifth columns report current bid prices and ask prices and the price change from the previous trading day. Prices for inflation-indexed securities are reported as a percentage of current accrued principal. The sixth and seventh columns list an inflation-adjusted yield to maturity and current accrued principal reflecting all cumulative inflation adjustments.

CHECK THIS

9.5a What is the difference between a nominal interest rate and a real interest rate?

9.5b What does the Fisher hypothesis assert?

9.5c What is the distinguishing feature of inflation-indexed Treasury securities?

FIGURE 9.8 Inflation-Indexed Treasury Securities

Treasury Inflation-Protected Securities

Friday, April 23, 2010   Find Historical Data 🔲 | WHAT'S THIS?

Treasury Inflation-Protected Securities, or TIPS, are securities whose principal is tied to the Consumer Price Index (CPI). The principal increases with inflation and decreases with deflation. When the security matures, the U.S. Treasury pays the original or adjusted principal, whichever is greater. TIPS pay interest every six months. Figures after periods in bid and ask quotes represent 32nds; 101.26 means 101 26/32, or 101.8125% of 100% face value; 99.01 means 99 1/32, or 99.03125% of face value.

Maturity	Coupon	Bid	Ask	Chg	Yield*	Accrued principal
2011 Jan 15	3.500	103.08	103.08	unch.	-0.969	1245
2011 Apr 15	2.375	102.31	102.31	- 1	-0.678	1091
2012 Jan 15	3.375	107.02	107.03	+ 1	-0.705	1220
2012 Apr 15	2.000	104.30	104.30	+ 1	-0.491	1068
2012 Jul 15	3.000	108.01	108.02	+ 1	-0.594	1205
2013 Apr 15	0.625	102.05	102.06	unch.	-0.110	1025
2013 Jul 15	1.875	106.01	106.02	+ 1	-0.002	1180
2014 Jan 15	2.000	106.13	106.14	- 1	0.265	1172
2014 Apr 15	1.250	103.20	103.21	- 1	0.326	1024
2014 Jul 15	2.000	106.24	106.25	unch.	0.383	1149
2015 Jan 15	1.625	104.24	104.25	- 1	0.596	1135
2015 Jul 15	1.875	106.06	106.07	- 2	0.664	1114
2016 Jan 15	2.000	106.24	106.25	- 1	0.788	1091
2016 Jul 15	2.500	110.00	110.01	- 1	0.841	1073
2017 Jan 15	2.375	108.26	108.27	- 1	1.011	1074
2017 Jul 15	2.625	110.28	110.29	unch.	1.055	1045
2018 Jan 15	1.625	103.09	103.10	- 1	1.175	1034
2018 Jul 15	1.375	101.07	101.08	- 1	1.217	1005
2019 Jan 15	2.125	106.18	106.19	- 1	1.322	1009
2019 Jul 15	1.875	104.07	104.08	- 2	1.384	1015
2020 Jan 15	1.375	99.09	99.10	- 2	1.453	1002
2025 Jan 15	2.375	106.20	106.21	+ 2	1.857	1149
2026 Jan 15	2.000	101.17	101.18	+ 2	1.885	1091
2027 Jan 15	2.375	106.13	106.14	+ 3	1.924	1074
2028 Jan 15	1.750	96.29	96.30	+ 2	1.955	1034
2028 Apr 15	3.625	124.14	124.15	+ 3	1.999	1340
2029 Jan 15	2.500	108.06	108.07	+ 2	1.973	1009
2029 Apr 15	3.875	129.18	129.19	+ 3	1.994	1318
2032 Apr 15	3.375	124.10	124.11	+ 3	2.000	1221
2040 Feb 15	2.125	102.19	102.20	+ 5	2.008	1002

*-Yld. to maturity on accrued principal.

Source: Thomson Reuters

9.6 Traditional Theories of the Term Structure

Yield curves have been studied by financial economists for well over a century. During this period a number of different theories have been proposed to explain why yield curves may be upward sloping at one point in time and then downward sloping or flat at another point in time. We discuss three of the most popular traditional theories of the term structure in this section. We then present a modern perspective on the term structure in the following section.

EXPECTATIONS THEORY

expectations theory
The term structure of interest rates is a reflection of financial market beliefs regarding future interest rates.

According to the **expectations theory** of the term structure of interest rates, the shape of a yield curve expresses financial market expectations regarding future interest rates. Essentially, an upward-sloping yield curve predicts an increase in interest rates, and a downward-sloping yield curve predicts a decrease in interest rates. A flat yield curve expresses the sentiment that interest rates are not expected to change in the near future.

EXPECTATIONS AND FORWARD RATES The basic principles of the expectations theory can be explained with a two-period example. Let r_1 stand for the current market interest rate on a one-year investment, and let r_2 be the current market interest rate on a two-year investment. Also, let $r_{1,1}$ be the market interest rate on a one-year investment that will be available in one year. Of course, this rate is not known today.

For a two-year investment, you have two strategies available. First, you can invest for two years at the rate r_2. In this case, \$1 invested today will become \$$(1 + r_2)^2$ in two years. For example, if $r_2 = 10$ percent, you would have \$1 $\times (1.10)^2 = \$1.21$ in two years for every dollar you invest.

Alternatively, you can invest for one year at the rate r_1, and, at the end of one year, you can reinvest the proceeds at the rate $r_{1,1}$. In this case, \$1 invested today will become \$$(1 + r_1)(1 + r_{1,1})$ in two years. For example, suppose $r_1 = 10$ percent and, after a year passes, it turns out that $r_{1,1} = 8$ percent. Then you would end up with \$1 $\times 1.10 \times 1.08 = \$1.19$. Alternatively, suppose that after a year passes it turns out that $r_{1,1} = 12$ percent; then you would have \$1 $\times 1.10 \times 1.12 = \$1.23$. Notice that this second strategy entails some uncertainty since the next year's interest rate, $r_{1,1}$, is not known when you originally select your investment strategy.

forward rate
An expected future interest rate implied by current interest rates.

The expectations theory of the term structure of interest rates asserts that, on average, the two-year investment proceeds, \$$(1 + r_2)^2$ and \$$(1 + r_1)(1 + r_{1,1})$, will be equal. In fact, we can obtain what is known as the implied **forward rate**, $f_{1,1}$, by setting the two total proceeds equal to each other:

$$(1 + r_2)^2 = (1 + r_1)(1 + f_{1,1})$$

Solving for the forward rate, $f_{1,1}$, we see that:

$$f_{1,1} = \frac{(1 + r_2)^2}{1 + r_1} - 1$$

Notice that this forward interest rate is simply a future interest rate implied by current interest rates.

According to expectations theory, the forward rate $f_{1,1}$ is an accurate predictor of the rate $r_{1,1}$ to be realized one year in the future. Thus, if $r_2 = 10$ percent and $r_1 = 8$ percent, then $f_{1,1} = 12$ percent, approximately. This forward rate predicts that the one-year interest rate one year from now will increase from 10 percent to 12 percent (recall r_2 is the rate per year for two years). Alternatively, if $r_2 = 10$ percent and $r_1 = 12$ percent, then $f_{1,1} = 8$ percent, approximately. This forward rate predicts that the one-year interest rate one year from now will decrease from 10 percent to 8 percent.

In general, if $r_2 > r_1$, such that the term structure is upward sloping, then expectations theory predicts an interest rate increase. Similarly, if $r_2 < r_1$, indicating a downward-sloping term structure, then expectations theory predicts an interest rate decrease. Thus, the slope of the term structure points in the predicted direction of future interest rate changes.

EXAMPLE 9.8   **Looking Forward**

Suppose the yield on a two-year STRIPS is 7 percent and the yield on a one-year STRIPS is 6 percent. Based on the expectations theory, what will the yield on a one-year STRIPS be one year from now?

According to the expectations theory, the implied forward rate is an accurate predictor of what the interest rate will be. Thus, solving for the forward rate, we have:

$$(1 + r_2)^2 = (1 + r_1)(1 + f_{1,1})$$

$$(1 + .07)^2 = (1 + .06)(1 + f_{1,1})$$

and the forward rate is:

$$f_{1,1} = \frac{1.07^2}{1.06} - 1 = 8.00943\%$$

Based on the expectations theory, the rate next year will be about 8 percent. Notice that this is higher than the current rate, as we would predict since the term structure is upward sloping.

EXPECTATIONS THEORY AND THE FISHER HYPOTHESIS The expectations theory is closely related to the Fisher hypothesis we discussed earlier. The relationship between the expectations theory of interest rates and the Fisher hypothesis is stated as follows. If expected future inflation is higher than current inflation, then we are likely to see an upward-sloping term structure where long-term interest rates are higher than short-term interest rates. Similarly, if future inflation is expected to be lower than its current level, we would then be likely to see a downward-sloping term structure where long-term interest rates are lower than short-term interest rates.

In other words, taken together, the expectations theory and the Fisher hypothesis assert that an upward-sloping term structure tells us that the market expects that nominal interest rates and inflation are likely to be higher in the future.

MATURITY PREFERENCE THEORY

Another traditional theory of the term structure asserts that lenders prefer to lend short-term to avoid tying up funds for long periods of time. In other words, they have a preference for shorter maturities. At the same time, borrowers prefer to borrow long-term to lock in secure financing for long periods of time.

maturity preference theory

Long-term interest rates contain a maturity premium necessary to induce lenders into making longer-term loans.

According to the **maturity preference theory**, then, borrowers have to pay a higher rate to borrow long-term rather than short-term to essentially bribe lenders into loaning funds for longer maturities. The extra interest is called a *maturity premium*.[2]

The Fisher hypothesis, maturity preference theory, and expectations theory can coexist without problem. For example, suppose the shape of a yield curve is basically determined by expected future interest rates according to expectations theory. But where do expected future interest rates come from? According to the Fisher hypothesis, expectations regarding future interest rates are based on expected future rates of inflation. Thus, expectations theory and the Fisher hypothesis mesh quite nicely.

Furthermore, a basic yield curve determined by inflationary expectations could also accommodate maturity preference theory. All we need to do is add a maturity premium to longer term interest rates. In this view, long-term, default-free interest rates have three components: a real rate, an anticipated future inflation rate, and a maturity premium.

---

[2] Traditionally, maturity preference theory has been known as "liquidity" preference theory and the maturity premium was termed a "liquidity" premium. However, as we discussed in a previous chapter, the term "liquidity" is universally used to indicate the relative ease with which an asset can be sold. Also, the term "liquidity premium" now has a different meaning. To avoid confusion and to make this theory more consistent with modern views of liquidity, interest rates, and the term structure, we have adopted the more descriptive name of maturity premium.

MARKET SEGMENTATION THEORY

An alternative theory of the term structure of interest rates is the **market segmentation theory**, which asserts that debt markets are segmented according to the various maturities of debt instruments available for investment. By this theory, each maturity represents a separate, distinct market. For example, one group of lenders and borrowers may prefer to lend and borrow using securities with a maturity of 10 years, while another group may prefer to lend and borrow using securities with a maturity of 5 years. Segmentation theory simply states that interest rates corresponding to each maturity are determined separately by supply and demand conditions in each market segment.

Another theory of the term structure, known as the *preferred habitat theory,* is essentially a compromise between market segmentation and maturity preference. In the preferred habitat theory, as in the market segmentation theory, different investors have different preferred maturities. The difference is that they can be induced to move to less preferred maturities by a higher interest rate. In the maturity preference theory, the preferred habitat is always toward shorter maturities rather than longer maturities.

CHECK THIS

9.6a According to the expectations theory, what does an upward-sloping term structure indicate?

9.6b What basic assertion does maturity preference theory make about investor preferences? If this assertion is correct, how does it affect the term structure of interest rates?

9.6c What is a maturity premium?

9.7 Determinants of Nominal Interest Rates: A Modern Perspective

Our understanding of the term structure of interest rates has increased significantly in the last few decades. Also, the evolution of fixed-income markets has shown us that, at least to some extent, traditional theories discussed in our previous section may be inadequate to explain the term structure. We discuss some problems with these theories next and then move on to a modern perspective.

PROBLEMS WITH TRADITIONAL THEORIES

To illustrate some problems with traditional theories, we could examine the behavior of the term structure in the last two decades. What we would find is that the term structure is almost always upward sloping. But contrary to the expectations hypothesis, interest rates have not always risen. Furthermore, as we saw with STRIPS term structure, it is often the case that the term structure turns down at very long maturities. According to the expectations hypothesis, market participants apparently expect rates to rise for 20 or so years and then decline. This seems to be stretching things a bit.

In terms of maturity preference, the world's biggest borrower, the U.S. government, borrows much more heavily short term than long term. Furthermore, many of the biggest buyers of fixed-income securities, such as pension funds, have a strong preference for *long* maturities. It is hard to square these facts with the behavioral assumptions underlying the maturity preference theory.

Finally, in terms of market segmentation, the U.S. government borrows at all maturities. Many institutional investors, such as mutual funds, are more than willing to move among maturities to obtain more favorable rates. At the same time, some bond trading operations do nothing other than buy and sell various maturity issues to exploit even very small perceived premiums. In short, in the modern fixed-income market, market segmentation does not seem to be a powerful force.

MODERN TERM STRUCTURE THEORY

Going back to Chapter 1, we saw that long-term government bonds had higher returns, on average, than short-term T-bills. They had substantially more risk as well. In other words, there appears to be a risk-return trade-off for default-free bonds as well, and long-term bonds appear to have a risk premium.

Notice that this risk premium doesn't result from the possibility of default since it exists on default-free U.S. government debt. Instead, it exists because longer-term bond prices are more volatile than shorter-term prices. As we discuss in detail in the next chapter, the reason is that, for a given change in interest rates, long-term bond prices change more than short-term bonds. Put differently, long-term bond prices are much more sensitive to interest rate changes than short-term bonds. This is called *interest rate risk*, and the risk premium on longer-term bonds is called the *interest rate risk premium*.

The interest rate risk premium carried by long-term bonds leads us to a modern reinterpretation of the maturity preference hypothesis. All else equal, investors do prefer short-term bonds to long-term bonds. The reason is simply that short-term bonds are less risky. As a result, long-term bonds have to offer higher yields to compensate investors for the extra interest rate risk.

Putting it together, the modern view of the term structure suggests that nominal interest rates on default-free securities can be stated as follows:

$$NI = RI + IP + RP \tag{9.12}$$

where: NI = Nominal interest rate
RI = Real interest rate
IP = Inflation premium
RP = Interest rate risk premium

In equation (9.12), the real rate of interest is assumed to be the same for all securities, and, on average, the real interest rate (RI) is positive, as predicted by the Fisher hypothesis.

As we discussed above, the inflation premium (IP) reflects investor expectations of future price inflation. The inflation premium may be different for securities with different maturities because expected inflation may be different over different future horizons. For example the expected average rate of inflation over the next two years may be different from the expected average rate of inflation over the next five years.

In addition to the real rate and the inflation premium, nominal rates reflect an interest rate risk premium (RP) which increases with the maturity of the security being considered. As a result, if interest rates are expected to remain constant through time, the term structure would have a positive slope. This is consistent with maturity preference theory. Indeed, for zero coupon bonds the interest rate risk premium and the maturity premium are the same thing.

The separate effects of the inflation premium and the interest rate risk premium are difficult to distinguish. For example, the yields for U.S. Treasury STRIPS in Figure 9.5 reveal a substantial yield premium for long-maturity STRIPS over short-term STRIPS. This yield premium for long-maturity STRIPS reflects the combined effects of the inflation premium and the risk premium. However, it is unclear how much of the total premium is caused by an inflation premium and how much is caused by a risk premium. Figure 9.9 shows how nominal interest rates can be separated into the real interest rate, the inflation premium, and the interest rate risk premium.

LIQUIDITY AND DEFAULT RISK

Thus far we have examined the components of interest rates on default-free, highly liquid securities such as Treasury STRIPS. We now expand our coverage to securities that are less liquid, not default-free, or both, to present a more detailed decomposition of nominal interest rates. When we are finished, what we will see is that nominal interest rates for individual securities can be decomposed into five basic components as follows:

$$NI = RI + IP + RP + LP + DP \tag{9.13}$$

FIGURE 9.9 The Term Structure of Interest Rates

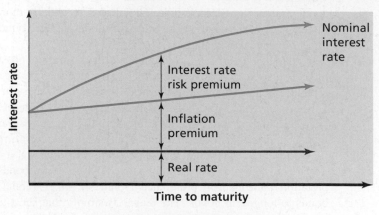

(a) Upward-sloping term structure

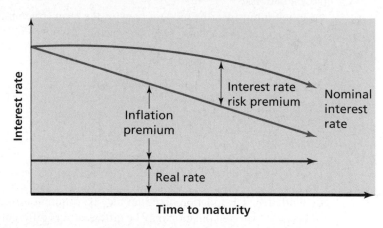

(b) Downward-sloping term structure

where: NI = Nominal interest rate
RI = Real interest rate
IP = Inflation premium
RP = Interest rate risk premium
LP = Liquidity premium
DP = Default premium

We have already discussed the first three components of the nominal interest rate. We now consider the two new ones on our list, the default and liquidity premiums.

The *liquidity premium* (LP) is a reflection of the fact that two otherwise identical securities may have very different degrees of liquidity. All else the same, the one with less liquidity would have to offer a higher yield as compensation. For Treasury securities, "on-the-run issues" are the most actively traded (i.e., liquid) bonds. The on-the-run issue is the most recently issued Treasury note or bond of a given maturity.

The fifth, and final, component of a nominal interest rate is a *default premium* (DP). Investors demand a default premium to assume the risk of holding a security that might default on its promised payments. Naturally, the greater the risk of default for a particular bond issue, the larger the default premium required by investors. The topic of default risk is discussed in detail for corporate bonds and municipal bonds in later chapters.

In addition to the five basic components we have discussed, another important determinant of nominal interest rates is tax status. As we briefly discussed in an earlier chapter, municipal bonds are not taxed at the federal level, but all other bonds are (including Treasury bonds). All else the same, taxable bonds must pay higher rates than nontaxable bonds. As a result, the rate on a high-quality municipal issue will normally be less than the rate on a Treasury issue, even though the Treasury is more liquid and has no default risk.

9.8 Summary and Conclusions

The time value of money is arguably the most important principle of finance. Interest rates are a convenient way to measure and state the time value of money. Furthermore, understanding interest rates is essential for understanding money market and fixed-income securities. This chapter covers many topics relating to interest rates. They are grouped here by the learning objectives of the chapter.

1. **Money market prices and rates.**

   A. Money market is the name of the financial market for short-term borrowing and lending. In the money market, the borrowing and lending period is generally less than a year.
   B. Important short-term money market rates include the prime rate, the Federal funds rate, and the Federal Reserve's discount rate. The prime rate is a bellwether of bank lending to business, while the Federal funds rate and the Federal Reserve's discount rate are indicators of the availability of money and credit within the banking system.

2. **Rates and yields on fixed-income securities.**

   A. Fixed-income securities promise a regular payment during the life of the security. In addition, most fixed-income securities also promise a lump sum payment at the end of the life of the security. Generally, when they are issued, fixed-income securities have a life ranging from 2 to 30 years.
   B. The Treasury yield curve plots the relationship between yields on U.S. Treasury securities and their maturities. The Treasury yield curve is fundamental to bond market analysis because it represents the interest rates that financial markets are charging to the world's largest debtor with the world's highest credit rating—the U.S. government.

3. **Treasury STRIPS and the term structure of interest rates.**

   A. The term structure of interest rates is the fundamental relationship between time to maturity and interest rates for default-free, pure discount instruments such as U.S. Treasury STRIPS.
   B. A number of different theories—including the expectations theory, the maturity preference theory, and the market segmentation theory—have been proposed to explain why the term structure of interest rates and yield curves may be upward sloping at one point in time and then downward sloping or flat at another time. In a modern view of the term structure, yields on default-free, pure discount bonds are determined by the real rate of interest, expectations of future inflation, and an interest rate risk premium.

4. **Nominal versus real interest rates.**

   A. Nominal interest rates are interest rates that we ordinarily observe. Nominal interest rates have five basic components: the real rate, an inflation premium, an interest rate risk premium, a liquidity premium, and a default premium. The real interest rate is the nominal interest rate adjusted for the effects of inflation.
   B. U.S. Treasury securities are free of default risk and are generally free from liquidity risk. For other debt issues, however, these two nominal interest rate components are very important.
   C. When nominal interest rates change, long-term bond prices change more than short-term bonds. Put differently, long-term bond prices are much more sensitive to interest rate changes than are short-term bonds. This difference in price changes is called interest rate risk.

D. The liquidity premium reflects the fact that two otherwise identical securities could have starkly different degrees of liquidity. All else the same, the one with less liquidity would have to offer a higher yield as compensation. The fifth component of a nominal interest rate, the default premium, reflects the extra yield that investors demand to assume the risk of holding a security that might default on its promised payments.

GET REAL

This chapter covered the essentials of interest rates. How should you, as an investor or investment manager, put this information to work?

The best thing to do is to buy, perhaps in a simulated brokerage account, a variety of instruments discussed in this chapter. STRIPS, in particular, are an important investment vehicle for both institutional and individual investors. To gain some practical experience with the risks and rewards from STRIPS investing, you should invest equal dollar amounts in several different STRIPS with different maturities. Pick short-term (a few years), intermediate-term (10 or so years), and long-term (25 years or longer), for example. Once you make these investments, monitor their yields and prices.

A good place to start with a study of interest rates is to visit some federal government Web sites. Try the U.S. Treasury (www.ustreas.gov), the Bureau of Public Debt (www.publicdebt.treas.gov), the Federal Reserve Board of Governors (www.federalreserve.gov), and the New York (www.newyorkfed.org) and St. Louis (www.stlouisfed.org) Federal Reserve banks. For the latest money market rates see Money Rates (www.money-rates.com), and, for bank lending rates, check out Banx (www.banx.com) or Bankrate (www.bankrate.com). Price and yield data for U.S. Treasury securities can be found at CNN (money.cnn.com).

Key Terms

bank discount basis 307
banker's acceptance 306
basis point 307
bellwether rate 303
call money rate 305
certificate of deposit (CD) 305
commercial paper 305
discount rate 305
Eurodollars 306
expectations theory 324
Federal funds rate 304
Fisher hypothesis 321

forward rate 324
London Interbank Offered Rate (LIBOR) 306
market segmentation theory 326
maturity preference theory 325
nominal interest rates 320
prime rate 303
pure discount security 307
real interest rates 321
term structure of interest rates 317
Treasury yield curve 314
U.S. Treasury bill (T-bill) 306
U.S. Treasury STRIPS 318

Chapter Review Problems and Self-Test

1. **Money Market Prices (LO1, CFA2)** The rate on a particular money market instrument, quoted on a discount basis, is 5 percent. The instrument has a face value of $100,000 and will mature in 40 days. What is its price?

2. **Bond Equivalent Yields (LO1, CFA1)** Suppose a T-bill has 75 days to maturity and an ask discount of 4 percent. What is the bond equivalent yield?

Answers to Self-Test Problems

1. Using the bank discount basis formula, we have:

$$\text{Current price} = \text{Face value} \times \left(1 - \frac{\text{Days to maturity}}{360} \times \text{Discount yield}\right)$$

$$\$99{,}444.44 = \$100{,}000 \times \left(1 - \frac{40}{360} \times .05\right)$$

You would pay $99,444.44.

2. Using the bond equivalent yield conversion formula, we have:

$$4.09\% = \frac{365 \times .04}{360 - 75 \times .04}$$

The bond equivalent yield is thus 4.09 percent.

Test Your Investment Quotient

1. **Interest Rates (LO2, CFA2)**   Which of the following interest rates is a bellwether (leading indicator) rate of bank lending to business?

   a. Unsecured business loan rate.
   b. Prime rate.
   c. Commercial paper rate.
   d. Banker's acceptance rate.

2. **Interest Rates (LO2, CFA2)**   Among the following interest rates, which is normally the highest rate?

   a. Commercial paper rate.
   b. U.S. Treasury bill rate.
   c. Federal funds rate.
   d. Federal Reserve discount rate.

3. **T-Bill Yields (LO1, CFA2)**   A U.S. Treasury bill with 180 days to maturity has a discount yield of 5 percent and a face value of $100,000. What is its current price?

   a. $97,500
   b. $95,000
   c. $92,500
   d. $90,000

4. **T-Bill Yields (LO1, CFA2)**   A U.S. Treasury bill with 90 days to maturity has a price of $95,000. What is its discount yield?

   a. 5 percent
   b. 10 percent
   c. 15 percent
   d. 20 percent

5. **T-Bill Yields (LO1, CFA2)**   A 30-day U.S. Treasury bill is selling at a 12 percent yield on a discount basis. Which of the following is the approximate bond equivalent yield?

   a. 6.0 percent
   b. 11.7 percent
   c. 12.0 percent
   d. 12.3 percent

6. **Effective Annual Rates (LO2, CFA1)**   A credit card company states an annual percentage rate (APR) of 12 percent, which is actually a rate of 1 percent per month. What is the EAR?

   a. 12 percent
   b. 12.68 percent
   c. 13.08 percent
   d. 13.76 percent

7. **STRIPS Yields (LO3, CFA6)**   A U.S. Treasury STRIPS maturing in 10 years has a current price of $502.57 for $1,000 of face value. What is the yield to maturity of this STRIPS?

   a. 7.0 percent
   b. 7.12 percent

    c. 8.0 percent

    d. 8.12 percent

8. **STRIPS Yields (LO3, CFA6)** A U.S. Treasury STRIPS with $1,000 face value maturing in five years has a yield to maturity of 7 percent. What is the current price of this STRIPS?

    a. $930

    b. $712.99

    c. $708.92

    d. $650

9. **Bond Yields (LO2, CFA1)** An analyst finds that the semiannual interest rate that equates the present value of the bond's cash flow to its current market price is 3.85 percent. Consider the following possible alternatives:

    I.   The bond equivalent yield on this security is 7.70 percent.

    II. The effective annual yield on the bond is 7.85 percent.

    III. The bond's yield-to-maturity is 7.70 percent.

    IV. The bond's horizon return is 8.35 percent.

    Which of these alternatives are true?

    a. I and II only

    b. II, III, and IV only

    c. I, II, and III only

    d. III only

10. **Forward Rates (LO3, CFA8)** An analyst gathered the following spot rates:

Time (years)	Annual Spot Rate
1	15.0%
2	12.5
3	10.0
4	7.5

    The one-year forward rate two years from now is closest to

    a. −4.91 percent

    b. 5.17 percent

    c. 10.05 percent

    d. 7.5 percent

11. **Zeroes (LO2)** If an investor's required return is 12 percent, the value of a 10-year maturity zero coupon bond with a maturity value of $1,000 is closest to:

    a. $312

    b. $688

    c. $1,000

    d. $1,312

12. **Fisher Hypothesis (LO4, CFA4)** The Fisher hypothesis essentially asserts which of the following?

    a. Nominal interest rates follow inflation.

    b. Real interest rates follow inflation.

    c. Inflation follows real interest rates.

    d. Inflation follows nominal interest rates.

13. **Term Structure Theory (LO3, CFA9)** Which one of the following statements about the term structure of interest rates is true?

    a. The expectations hypothesis indicates a flat yield curve if anticipated future short-term rates exceed current short-term rates.

    b. The expectations hypothesis contends that the long-term rate is equal to the anticipated short-term rate.

    c. The liquidity premium theory indicates that, all else being equal, longer maturities will have lower yields.

    d. The market segmentation theory contends that borrowers and lenders prefer particular segments of the yield curve.

14. **Term Structure Theory (LO3, CFA9)** Which one of the following is *not* an explanation of the relationship between a bond's interest rate and its term to maturity?

    a. Default (credit) risk hypothesis
    b. Expectations hypothesis
    c. Liquidity preference hypothesis
    d. Segmentation hypothesis

15. **Term Structure Theory (LO3, CFA3)** Which theory explains the shape of the yield curve by considering the relative demands for various maturities?

    a. Relative strength theory
    b. Segmentation theory
    c. Unbiased expectations theory
    d. Liquidity premium theory

16. **Term Structure Theory (LO3, CFA3)** The concepts of spot and forward rates are most closely associated with which one of the following explanations of the term structure of interest rates?

    a. Expectations hypothesis
    b. Liquidity premium theory
    c. Preferred habitat hypothesis
    d. Segmented market theory

17. **Forward Rates (LO3, CFA8)** The current one-year interest rate is 6 percent and the current two-year interest rate is 7 percent. What is the implied forward rate for next year's one-year rate?

    a. 9 percent
    b. 8 percent
    c. 7 percent
    d. 6 percent

18. **Forward Rates (LO3, CFA8)** The current one-year interest rate is 7 percent and the current two-year interest rate is 6 percent. What is the implied forward rate for next year's one-year rate?

    a. 7 percent
    b. 6 percent
    c. 5 percent
    d. 4 percent

19. **Forward Rates (LO3, CFA8)** The 6-month Treasury bill spot rate is 4 percent, and the 1-year Treasury bill spot rate is 5 percent. The implied 6-month forward rate 6 months from now is which of the following?

    a. 3.0 percent
    b. 4.5 percent
    c. 5.5 percent
    d. 5.9 percent

20. **Forward Rates (LO3, CFA8)** An analyst gathers the following information:

Years to Maturity	Spot Rate
1	5.00%
2	6.00
3	6.50

Based on the data above, the one-year implied forward rate two years from now is *closest* to:

    a. 6.25 percent
    b. 7.01 percent
    c. 7.26 percent
    d. 7.51 percent

Concept Questions

1. **Interest Rate History (LO2, CFA6)** Based on the history of interest rates, what is the range of short-term rates that has occurred in the United States? The range of long-term rates? What is a typical value for each?

2. **Discount Securities (LO1, CFA2)** What are pure discount securities? Give two examples.

3. **Fed Funds versus the Discount Rate (LO1, CFA5)** Compare and contrast the Fed funds rate and the discount rate. Which do you think is more volatile? Which market do you think is more active? Why?

4. **Commercial Paper (LO1, CFA2)** Compare and contrast commercial paper and Treasury bills. Which would typically offer a higher interest rate? Why?

5. **LIBOR (LO1, CFA6)** What is LIBOR? Why is it important?

6. **Bank Discount Rates (LO1, CFA2)** Why do you suppose rates on some money market instruments are quoted on a bank discount basis? (*Hint:* Why use a 360-day year?)

7. **STRIPS (LO3)** What are the three different types of Treasury STRIPS that are publicly traded?

8. **Nominal and Real Rates (LO4, CFA4)** When we observe interest rates in the financial press, do we see nominal or real rates? Which are more relevant to investors?

9. **Munis versus Treasuries (LO2, CFA5)** Which would have a higher yield, a municipal bond or a Treasury bond of the same maturity?

10. **Term Structure (LO4, CFA5)** Discuss how each of the following theories for the term structure of interest rates could account for a downward-sloping term structure of interest rates:

    a. Pure expectations
    b. Liquidity preference
    c. Market segmentation

Questions and Problems

1. **STRIPS (LO3, CFA7)** What is the price of a Treasury STRIPS with a face value of $100 that matures in 10 years and has a yield to maturity of 3.5 percent?

2. **STRIPS (LO3, CFA7)** A Treasury STRIPS matures in 8.5 years and has a yield to maturity of 5.4 percent. If the par value is $100,000, what is the price of the STRIPS? What is the quoted price?

3. **STRIPS (LO3, CFA7)** A Treasury STRIPS is quoted at 81.265 and has 8 years until maturity. What is the yield to maturity?

4. **STRIPS (LO3, CFA2)** What is the yield to maturity on a Treasury STRIPS with 7 years to maturity and a quoted price of 65.492?

5. **Fisher Effect (LO4, CFA4)** A stock had a return of 8.9 percent last year. If the inflation rate was 2.1 percent, what was the approximate real return?

6. **Fisher Effect (LO4, CFA4)** Your investments increased in value by 11.6 percent last year but your purchasing power increased by only 9.1 percent. What was the approximate inflation rate?

7. **Treasury Bill Prices (LO1, CFA2)** What is the price of a U.S. Treasury bill with 43 days to maturity quoted at a discount yield of 1.85 percent? Assume a $1 million face value.

8. **Treasury Bill Prices (LO1, CFA1)** In the previous problem, what is the bond equivalent yield?

9. **Treasury Bill Prices (LO1, CFA2)** How much would you pay for a U.S. Treasury bill with 112 days to maturity quoted at a discount yield of 3.82 percent? Assume a $1 million face value.

10. **Treasury Bill Prices (LO1, CFA1)** In the previous problem, what is the bond equivalent yield?

11. **Treasury Bills (LO1, CFA2)** A Treasury bill with 82 days to maturity is quoted at 98.921. What is the bank discount yield, the bond equivalent yield, and the effective annual return?

12. **Treasury Bills (LO1, CFA2)** A Treasury bill purchased in December 2011 has 55 days until maturity and a bank discount yield of 3.74 percent. What is the price of the bill as a percentage of face value? What is the bond equivalent yield?

13. **Money Market Prices (LO1, CFA2)** The treasurer of a large corporation wants to invest $20 million in excess short-term cash in a particular money market investment. The prospectus quotes the instrument at a true yield of 5.93 percent; that is, the EAR for this investment is 5.93 percent. However, the treasurer wants to know the money market yield on this instrument

334 Part 3 ■ Interest Rates and Bond Valuation

to make it comparable to the T-bills and CDs she has already bought. If the term of the instrument is 90 days, what are the bond-equivalent and discount yields on this investment?

Use the following information to answer the next six questions:

U.S. Treasury STRIPS, close of business February 15, 2010:

Maturity	Price	Maturity	Price
Feb 11	96.203	Feb 14	84.195
Feb 12	92.125	Feb 15	79.642
Feb 13	87.987	Feb 16	72.681

14. **Treasury STRIPS (LO3, CFA1)**   Calculate the quoted yield for each of the STRIPS given in the table above. Does the market expect interest rates to go up or down in the future?

15. **Treasury STRIPS (LO3, CFA1)**   What is the yield of the two-year STRIPS expressed as an EAR?

16. **Forward Interest Rates (LO3, CFA3)**   According to the pure expectations theory of interest rates, how much do you expect to pay for a one-year STRIPS on February 15, 2011? What is the corresponding implied forward rate? How does your answer compare to the current yield on a one-year STRIPS? What does this tell you about the relationship between implied forward rates, the shape of the zero coupon yield curve, and market expectations about future spot interest rates?

17. **Forward Interest Rates (LO3, CFA8)**   According to the pure expectations theory of interest rates, how much do you expect to pay for a five-year STRIPS on February 15, 2011? How much do you expect to pay for a two-year STRIPS on February 15, 2013?

18. **Forward Interest Rates (LO3, CFA8)**   This problem is a little harder. Suppose the term structure is set according to pure expectations and the maturity preference theory. To be specific, investors require no compensation for holding investments with a maturity of one year, but they demand a premium of .30 percent for holding investments with a maturity of two years. Given this information, how much would you pay for a one-year STRIPS on February 15, 2011? What is the corresponding implied forward rate? Compare your answer to the solutions you found in Problem 16. What does this tell you about the effect of a maturity premium on implied forward rates?

19. **Bond Price Changes (LO3, CFA7)**   Suppose the (quoted) yield on each of the six STRIPS increases by .25 percent. Calculate the percentage change in price for the one-year, three-year, and six-year STRIPS. Which one has the largest price change? Now suppose that the quoted price on each STRIPS decreases by .500. Calculate the percentage change in (quoted) yield for the one-year, three-year, and six-year STRIPS. Which one has the largest yield change? What do your answers tell you about the relationship between prices, yields, and maturity for discount bonds?

20. **Inflation and Returns (LO3, CFA1)**   You observe that the current interest rate on short-term U.S. Treasury bills is 2.64 percent. You also read in the newspaper that the GDP deflator, which is a common macroeconomic indicator used by market analysts to gauge the inflation rate, currently implies that inflation is 1.3 percent. Given this information, what is the approximate real rate of interest on short-term Treasury bills? Is it likely that your answer would change if you used some alternative measure for the inflation rate, such as the CPI? What does this tell you about the observability and accuracy of real interest rates compared to nominal interest rates?

21. **Forward Interest Rates (LO3, CFA8)**   Consider the following spot interest rates for maturities of one, two, three, and four years.

$$r_1 = 4.3\% \qquad r_2 = 4.9\% \qquad r_3 = 5.6\% \qquad r_4 = 6.4\%$$

What are the following forward rates, where $f_{1,k}$ refers to a forward rate for the period beginning in one year and extending for k years?

$$f_{1,1} = \qquad ;\ f_{1,2} = \qquad ;\ f_{1,3} =$$

Hint: Use the equation $(1 + r_1)(1 + f_{1,k})^k = (1 + r_{k+1})^{k+1}$ to solve for $f_{1,k}$.

22. **Forward Interest Rates (LO3, CFA9)** Based on the spot interest rates in the previous question, what are the following forward rates, where $f_{k,1}$ refers to a forward rate beginning in k years and extending for 1 year?

$$f_{2,1} = \qquad ; \quad f_{3,1} =$$

Hint: Use the equation $(1 + r_k)^k(1 + f_{k,1}) = (1 + r_{k+1})^{k+1}$ to solve for $f_{k,1}$.

23. **Expected Inflation Rates (LO4, CFA4)** Based on the spot rates in Question 21, and assuming a constant real interest rate of 2 percent, what are the expected inflation rates for the next four years?

Hint: Use the Fisher hypothesis and the unbiased expectations theory.

Spreadsheet Problems

24. **Treasury Bills (LO1, CFA2)** A Treasury bill that settles on July 17, 2010, pays $100,000 on August 21, 2010. Assuming a discount rate of 2.48 percent, what is the price and bond equivalent yield?

25. **Effective Annual Rate (LO2, CFA1)** You have a car loan with a nominal rate of 7.29 percent. With interest charged monthly, what is the effective annual rate (EAR) on this loan?

CFA Exam Review by Schweser

[CFA3, CFA8, CFA9]

James Wallace, CFA, is a fixed-income fund manager at a large investment firm. Each year the firm recruits a group of new college graduates. Recently, Mr. Wallace was asked to teach the fixed-income portion of the firm's training program. Mr. Wallace wants to start by teaching the various theories of the term structure of interest rates, and the implications of each theory for the shape of the Treasury yield curve. To evaluate the trainees' understanding of the subject, he creates a series of questions.

The following interest rate scenario is used to derive examples on the different theories used to explain the shape of the term structure and for all computational problems in Mr. Wallace's lecture. He assumes a rounded day count of .5 year for each semiannual period.

Period (months)	LIBOR Forward Rates	Implied Spot Rates
0 × 6	5.00%	5.00%
6 × 12	5.50	5.25
12 × 18	6.00	5.50
18 × 24	6.50	5.75
24 × 30	6.75	5.95
30 × 36	7.00	6.12

1. Mr. Wallace asks the trainees which of the following explains an upward-sloping yield curve according to the pure expectations theory.

   a. The market expects short-term rates to rise through the relevant future.
   b. There is greater demand for short-term securities than for long-term securities.
   c. There is a risk premium associated with more distant maturities.

2. Mr. Wallace asks the trainees which of the following explains an upward-sloping yield curve according to the market segmentation theory.

   a. The market expects short-term rates to rise through the relevant future.
   b. There is greater demand for short-term securities than for long-term securities.
   c. There is a risk premium associated with more distant maturities.

3. According to the expectations theory, which of the following is *closest* to the one-year implied forward rate one year from now?

   a. 6.58 percent
   b. 5.75 percent
   c. 6.25 percent

4. Mr. Wallace is particularly interested in the effects of a steepening yield curve. Which of the following is most accurate for a steepening curve?

   a. The price of short-term Treasuries increases relative to long-term treasuries.
   b. The price of long-term Treasuries increases relative to short-term treasuries.
   c. The price of short-term Treasury securities increases.

What's on the Web?

1. **Yield Curve** What is the shape of the Treasury yield curve today? Go to www.bloomberg.com and find out. Is the yield curve upward sloping or downward sloping? According to the expectations theory, are interest rates in the future expected to be higher or lower than they are today?

2. **STRIPS** Go to www.treasurydirect.gov and search the site for STRIPS to find information on Treasury STRIPS. Answer the following questions: Which Treasury securities are eligible to be stripped? What are minimum par amounts for stripping? How do I buy STRIPS? Why do investors hold STRIPS?

3. **STRIPS** Go to www.bondsonline.com and find the quotes for STRIPS that are offered for sale on the site. How many STRIPS are offered for sale? What is the lowest and highest yield to maturity? Are there STRIPS with the same maturity that have different prices? How could this happen?

CHAPTER 10

Bond Prices and Yields

Learning Objectives

Bonds can be an important part of portfolios. You will learn:

1. How to calculate bond prices and yields.

2. The importance of yield to maturity.

3. Interest rate risk and Malkiel's theorems.

4. How to measure the impact of interest rate changes on bond prices.

"More money has been lost reaching for yield than at the point of a gun."

–Raymond Devoe

Interest rates go up and bond prices go down. But which bonds go down the most and which go down the least? Interest rates go down and bond prices go up. But which bonds go up the most and which go up the least? For bond portfolio managers, these are important questions about interest rate risk. For anyone managing a bond portfolio, an understanding of interest rate risk rests on an understanding of the relationship between bond prices and yields. ■

In the preceding chapter on interest rates, we introduced the subject of bond yields. As we promised there, we now return to this subject and discuss bond prices and yields in some detail. We first describe how bond yields are determined and how they are interpreted. We then go on to examine what happens to bond prices as yields change. Finally, once we have a good understanding of the relation between bond prices and yields, we examine some of the fundamental tools of bond risk analysis used by fixed-income portfolio managers.

CFA™ Exam Topics in This Chapter:

1 Long-term liabilities and leases (L1, S9)

2 Features of debt securities (L1, S15)

3 Risks associated with investing in bonds (L1, S15)

4 Overview of bond sectors and instruments (L1, S15)

5 Introduction to the valuation of debt securities (L1, S16)

6 Introduction to the measurement of interest rate risk (L1, S16)

7 Fixed-income portfolio management (L3, S9)

Go to www.mhhe.com/jmd6e for a guide that aligns your textbook with CFA readings.

10.1 Bond Basics

A bond essentially is a security that offers the investor a series of fixed interest payments during its life, along with a fixed payment of principal when it matures. So long as the bond issuer does not default, the schedule of payments does not change. When originally issued, bonds normally have maturities ranging from 2 years to 30 years, but bonds with maturities of 50 or 100 years also exist. Bonds issued with maturities of less than 10 years are usually called notes. A very small number of bond issues have no stated maturity, and these are referred to as perpetuities or consols.

STRAIGHT BONDS

The most common type of bond is the so-called straight bond. By definition, a straight bond is an IOU that obligates the issuer to pay the bondholder a fixed sum of money at the bond's maturity along with constant, periodic interest payments during the life of the bond. The fixed sum paid at maturity is referred to as bond principal, par value, stated value, or face value. The periodic interest payments are called coupons. Perhaps the best example of straight bonds are U.S. Treasury bonds issued by the federal government to finance the national debt. However, corporations and municipal governments also routinely issue debt in the form of straight bonds.

In addition to a straight bond component, many bonds have special features. These features are sometimes designed to enhance a bond's appeal to investors. For example, convertible bonds have a conversion feature that grants bondholders the right to convert their bonds into shares of common stock of the issuing corporation. As another example, "putable" bonds have a put feature that grants bondholders the right to sell their bonds back to the issuer at a prespecified price.

These and other special features are attached to many bond issues, but we defer discussion of special bond features until later chapters. For now, it is only important to know that when a bond is issued with one or more special features, strictly speaking, it is no longer a straight bond. However, bonds with attached special features will normally have a straight bond component, namely, the periodic coupon payments and fixed principal payment at maturity. For this reason, straight bonds are important as the basic unit of bond analysis.

The prototypical example of a straight bond pays a series of constant semiannual coupons, along with a face value of $1,000 payable at maturity. This example is used in this chapter because it is common and realistic. For example, most corporate bonds are sold with a face value of $1,000 per bond, and most bonds (in the United States at least) pay constant semiannual coupons.

COUPON RATE AND CURRENT YIELD

A familiarity with bond yield measures is important for understanding the financial characteristics of bonds. As we briefly discussed in Chapter 3, two basic yield measures for a bond are its coupon rate and current yield.

A bond's **coupon rate** is defined as its annual coupon amount divided by its par value, or, in other words, its annual coupon expressed as a percentage of face value:

$$\text{Coupon rate} = \frac{\text{Annual coupon}}{\text{Par value}} \qquad (10.1)$$

For example, suppose a $1,000 par value bond pays semiannual coupons of $40. The annual coupon is then $80, and, stated as a percentage of par value, the bond's coupon rate is $80/$1,000 = 8%. A coupon rate is often referred to as the *coupon yield* or the *nominal yield*. Notice that the word "nominal" here has nothing to do with inflation.

A bond's **current yield** is its annual coupon payment divided by its current market price:

$$\text{Current yield} = \frac{\text{Annual coupon}}{\text{Bond price}} \qquad (10.2)$$

For example, suppose a $1,000 par value bond paying an $80 annual coupon has a price of $1,032.25. The current yield is $80/$1,032.25 = 7.75%. Similarly, a price of $969.75

coupon rate

A bond's annual coupon divided by its par value. Also called *coupon yield* or *nominal yield*.

current yield

A bond's annual coupon divided by its market price.

implies a current yield of $80/$969.75 = 8.25\%$. Notice that whenever there is a change in the bond's price, the coupon rate remains constant. However, a bond's current yield is inversely related to its price, and it changes whenever the bond's price changes.

CHECK THIS

10.1a   What is a straight bond?

10.1b   What is a bond's coupon rate? Its current yield?

10.2 Straight Bond Prices and Yield to Maturity

yield to maturity (YTM)
The discount rate that equates a bond's price with the present value of its future cash flows. Also called *promised yield* or just *yield*.

The single most important yield measure for a bond is its **yield to maturity**, commonly abbreviated as **YTM**. By definition, a bond's yield to maturity is the discount rate that equates the bond's price with the computed present value of its future cash flows. A bond's yield to maturity is sometimes called its *promised yield*, but, more commonly, the yield to maturity of a bond is simply referred to as its *yield*. In general, if the term "yield" is being used with no qualification, it means yield to maturity.

STRAIGHT BOND PRICES

For straight bonds, the following standard formula is used to calculate a bond's price given its yield:

$$\text{Bond price} = \frac{C/2}{YTM/2}\left[1 - \frac{1}{(1 + YTM/2)^{2M}}\right] + \frac{FV}{(1 + YTM/2)^{2M}}$$

This formula can be simplified just a bit as follows:

$$\text{Bond price} = \frac{C}{YTM}\left[1 - \frac{1}{(1 + YTM/2)^{2M}}\right] + \frac{FV}{(1 + YTM/2)^{2M}} \qquad (10.3)$$

where: C = Annual coupon, the sum of two semiannual coupons
FV = Face value
M = Maturity in years
YTM = Yield to maturity

In this formula, the coupon used is the annual coupon, which is the sum of the two semiannual coupons. As discussed in our previous chapter for U.S. Treasury STRIPS, the yield on a bond is an annual percentage rate (APR), calculated as twice the true semiannual yield. As a result, the yield on a bond somewhat understates its effective annual rate (EAR).

The straight bond pricing formula has two separate components. The first component is the present value of all the coupon payments. Since the coupons are fixed and paid on a regular basis, you may recognize that they form an ordinary annuity, and the first piece of the bond pricing formula is a standard calculation for the present value of an annuity. The other component represents the present value of the principal payment at maturity, and it is a standard calculation for the present value of a single lump sum.

Calculating bond prices is mostly "plug and chug" with a calculator. In fact, a good financial calculator or spreadsheet should have this formula built into it. In any case, we will work through a few examples the long way just to illustrate the calculations.

Suppose a bond has a $1,000 face value, 20 years to maturity, an 8 percent coupon rate, and a yield of 9 percent. What's the price? Using the straight bond pricing formula, the price of this bond is calculated as follows:

1. Present value of semiannual coupons:

$$\frac{\$80}{.09}\left[1 - \frac{1}{(1.045)^{40}}\right] = \$736.06338$$

2. Present value of $1,000 principal:

$$\frac{\$1{,}000}{(1.045)^{40}} = \$171.92870$$

The price of the bond is the sum of the present values of coupons and principal:

$$\text{Bond price} = \$736.06 + \$171.93 = \$907.99$$

So, this bond sells for $907.99.

EXAMPLE 10.1

Calculating Straight Bond Prices

Suppose a bond has 20 years to maturity and a coupon rate of 8 percent. The bond's yield to maturity is 7 percent. What's the price?

In this case, the coupon rate is 8 percent and the face value is $1,000, so the annual coupon is $80. The bond's price is calculated as follows:

1. Present value of semiannual coupons:

$$\frac{\$80}{.07}\left[1 - \frac{1}{(1.035)^{40}}\right] = \$854.20289$$

2. Present value of $1,000 principal:

$$\frac{\$1{,}000}{(1.035)^{40}} = \$252.57247$$

The bond's price is the sum of coupon and principal present values:

$$\text{Bond price} = \$854.20 + \$252.57 = \$1{,}106.77$$

This bond sells for $1,106.77.

Straight bond prices may be calculated using a built-in spreadsheet function. An example of how to use an Excel™ spreadsheet to calculate a bond price is shown in the *Spreadsheet Analysis* box below.

SPREADSHEET ANALYSIS

	A	B	C	D	E	F	G	H
1								
2		Calculating the Price of a Coupon Bond						
3								
4	A Treasury bond traded on March 30, 2010, matures in 20 years on March 30, 2030.							
5	Assuming an 8 percent coupon rate and a 7 percent yield to maturity, what is the							
6	price of this bond?							
7	Hint: Use the Excel function PRICE.							
8								
9		$110.6775	= PRICE("3/30/2010","3/30/2030",0.08,0.07,100,2,3)					
10								
11	For a bond with $1,000 face value, multiply the price by 10 to get $1,106.78.							
12								
13	This function uses the following arguments:							
14								
15		=PRICE("Now","Maturity", Coupon,Yield,100,2,3)						
16								
17	The 100 indicates redemption value as a percent of face value.							
18	The 2 indicates semi-annual coupons.							
19	The 3 specifies an actual day count with 365 days per year.							
20								
21								

PREMIUM AND DISCOUNT BONDS

Bonds are commonly distinguished according to whether they are selling at par value or at a discount or premium relative to par value. These three relative price descriptions—premium, discount, and par bonds—are defined as follows:

1. **Premium bonds:** Bonds with a price greater than par value are said to be selling at a premium. The yield to maturity of a premium bond is less than its coupon rate.

2. **Discount bonds:** Bonds with a price less than par value are said to be selling at a discount. The yield to maturity of a discount bond is greater than its coupon rate.

3. **Par bonds:** Bonds with a price equal to par value are said to be selling at par. The yield to maturity of a par bond is equal to its coupon rate.

The important thing to notice is that whether a bond sells at a premium or discount depends on the relation between its coupon rate and its yield. If the coupon rate exceeds the yield, the bond will sell at a premium. If the coupon is less than the yield, the bond will sell at a discount.

EXAMPLE 10.2

Premium and Discount Bonds

Consider two bonds, both with eight years to maturity and a 7 percent coupon. One bond has a yield to maturity of 5 percent while the other has a yield to maturity of 9 percent. Which of these bonds is selling at a premium and which is selling at a discount? Verify your answer by calculating each bond's price.

For the bond with a 9 percent yield to maturity, the coupon rate of 7 percent is less than the yield, indicating a discount bond. The bond's price is calculated as follows:

$$\frac{\$70}{.09}\left[1 - \frac{1}{(1.045)^{16}}\right] + \frac{\$1,000}{(1.045)^{16}} = \$887.66$$

For the bond with a 5 percent yield to maturity, the coupon rate of 7 percent is greater than the yield, indicating a premium bond. The bond's price is calculated as follows:

$$\frac{\$70}{.05}\left[1 - \frac{1}{(1.025)^{16}}\right] + \frac{\$1,000}{(1.025)^{16}} = \$1,130.55$$

The relationship between bond prices and bond maturities for premium and discount bonds is graphically illustrated in Figure 10.1 for bonds with an 8 percent coupon rate. The vertical axis measures bond prices, and the horizontal axis measures bond maturities.

Figure 10.1 also describes the paths of premium and discount bond prices as their maturities shorten with the passage of time, assuming no changes in yield to maturity. As shown,

FIGURE 10.1   Premium, Par, and Discount Bond Prices

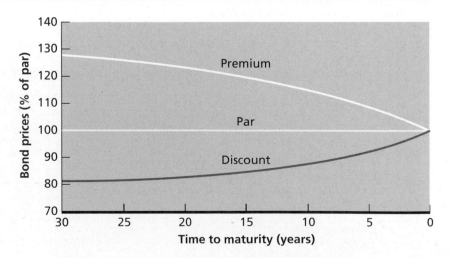

the time paths of premium and discount bond prices follow smooth curves. Over time, the price of a premium bond declines and the price of a discount bond rises. At maturity, the price of each bond converges to its par value.

Figure 10.1 illustrates the general result that, for discount bonds, holding the coupon rate and yield to maturity constant, the longer the term to maturity of the bond the greater is the discount from par value. For premium bonds, holding the coupon rate and yield to maturity constant, the longer the term to maturity of the bond the greater is the premium over par value.

Even though bond prices change (almost constantly) with interest rates, most bonds are actually issued at par. When a company issues a bond at par, the company is picking a coupon rate that matches the required return on the bond when the bond is issued. You know that the company could simply change the number of bonds it issues to generate a desired level of proceeds. Therefore, why would it matter whether bonds are issued at par? The answer relates to accounting rules that require companies to amortize premiums and discounts to par over the life of the bonds. So, pricing at par allows companies to avoid the unnecessary burden associated with accounting for these rules.

EXAMPLE 10.3 | **Premium Bonds**

Consider two bonds, both with a 9 percent coupon rate and the same yield to maturity of 7 percent, but with different maturities of 5 and 10 years. Which has the higher price? Verify your answer by calculating the prices.

First, because both bonds have a 9 percent coupon and a 7 percent yield, both bonds sell at a premium. Based on what we know, the one with the longer maturity will have a higher price. We can check these conclusions by calculating the prices as follows:

5-year maturity premium bond price:

$$\frac{\$90}{.07}\left[1 - \frac{1}{(1.035)^{10}}\right] + \frac{\$1,000}{(1.035)^{10}} = \$1,083.17$$

10-year maturity premium bond price:

$$\frac{\$90}{.07}\left[1 - \frac{1}{(1.035)^{20}}\right] + \frac{\$1,000}{(1.035)^{20}} = \$1,142.12$$

Notice that the longer maturity premium bond has a higher price, as we predicted.

EXAMPLE 10.4 | **Discount Bonds**

Now consider two bonds, both with a 9 percent coupon rate and the same yield to maturity of 11 percent, but with different maturities of 5 and 10 years. Which has the higher price? Verify your answer by calculating the prices.

These are both discount bonds. (Why?) The one with the shorter maturity will have a higher price. To check, the prices can be calculated as follows:

5-year maturity discount bond price:

$$\frac{\$90}{.11}\left[1 - \frac{1}{(1.055)^{10}}\right] + \frac{\$1,000}{(1.055)^{10}} = \$924.62$$

10-year maturity discount bond price:

$$\frac{\$90}{.11}\left[1 - \frac{1}{(1.055)^{20}}\right] + \frac{\$1,000}{(1.055)^{20}} = \$880.50$$

In this case, the shorter maturity discount bond has the higher price.

Current information on Treasury bond prices and yields is available, among other places, at www.zionsdirect.com. As a guest on the site, you can search for bonds. From the home page, select "Bonds Store" and then "Search Bonds." At this area of the site, you can search for municipal bonds, investment-grade corporate bonds, high-yield corporate bonds, agency bonds, U.S. Treasury bonds, and other bonds. We wanted to look at some U.S. Treasury bonds that mature between 2013 and 2019 with a yield more than 3 percent. If you want to buy any of these bonds, you must be a client of the bank.

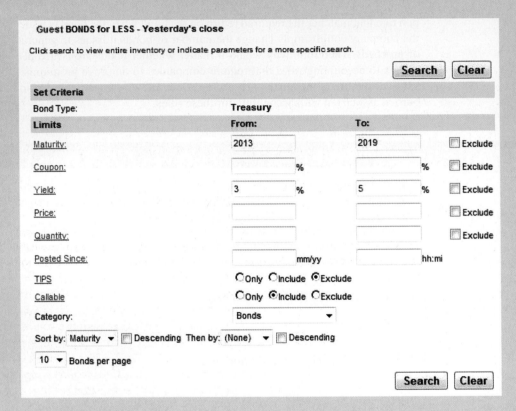

RELATIONSHIPS AMONG YIELD MEASURES

We have discussed three different bond rates or yields in this chapter—the coupon rate, the current yield, and the yield to maturity. We've seen the relationship between coupon rates and yields for discount and premium bonds. We can extend this to include current yields by simply noting that the current yield is always between the coupon rate and the yield to maturity (unless the bond is selling at par, in which case all three are equal).

Putting together our observations about yield measures, we have the following:

Premium bonds:	Coupon rate > Current yield > Yield to maturity
Discount bonds:	Coupon rate < Current yield < Yield to maturity
Par value bonds:	Coupon rate = Current yield = Yield to maturity

Thus, when a premium bond and a discount bond both have the same yield to maturity, the premium bond has a higher current yield than the discount bond. However, as shown in Figure 10.1, the advantage of a high current yield for a premium bond is offset by the fact that the price of a premium bond must ultimately fall to its face value when the bond matures. Similarly, the disadvantage of a low current yield for a discount bond is offset by the fact that the price of a discount bond must ultimately rise to its face value at maturity. For these reasons, current yield is not a reliable guide to what an actual yield will be.

If you wish to get current price and yield information for Treasury note and bond issues, try the Internet. The nearby *Work the Web* box displays a typical search query and the search results from a popular Web site.

A NOTE ON BOND PRICE QUOTES

If you buy a bond between coupon payment dates, the price you pay will usually be more than the price you are quoted. The reason is that standard convention in the bond market is to quote prices net of "accrued interest," meaning that accrued interest is deducted to arrive at the quoted price. This quoted price is called the **clean price**. The price you actually pay, however, includes the accrued interest. This price is the **dirty price**, also known as the *full* or *invoice price*.

An example is the easiest way to understand these issues. Suppose you buy a bond with a 12 percent annual coupon, payable semiannually. You actually pay $1,080 for this bond, so $1,080 is the dirty, or invoice, price. Further, on the day you buy it, the next coupon is due in four months, so you are between coupon dates. Notice that the next coupon will be $60.

The accrued interest on a bond is calculated by taking the fraction of the coupon period that has passed, in this case two months out of six, and multiplying this fraction by the next coupon, $60. So, the accrued interest in this example is $2/6 \times \$60 = \$20$. The bond's quoted price (i.e., its clean price) would be $\$1,080 - \$20 = \$1,060$.[1]

Keep in mind that clean prices and accrued interest are purely a quoting convention. The price that matters to you is the invoice price, because that is what you will actually pay for the bond. The only thing that's important about accrued interest on a bond is that it may impact the taxes you owe on the first coupon you receive.

clean price
The price of a bond net of accrued interest; this is the price that is typically quoted.

dirty price
The price of a bond including accrued interest, also known as the *full* or *invoice price*. This is the price the buyer actually pays.

CHECK THIS

10.2a A straight bond's price has two components. What are they?

10.2b What do you call a bond that sells for more than its face value?

10.2c What is the relationship between a bond's price and its term to maturity when the bond's coupon rate is equal to its yield to maturity?

10.2d Does current yield more strongly overstate yield to maturity for long-maturity or short-maturity premium bonds?

---

[1] The way accrued interest is calculated actually depends on the type of bond being quoted, for example, Treasury or corporate. The difference has to do with exactly how the fractional coupon period is calculated. In our example just above, we implicitly treated the months as having exactly the same length (i.e., 30 days each, 360 days in a year), which is consistent with the way corporate bonds are quoted. In contrast, for Treasury bonds, actual day counts are used. If you look back at our *Spreadsheet Analysis* exhibit, you'll see that we had to specify this treatment to value our Treasury bond.

10.3 More on Yields

In the previous section, we focused on finding a straight bond's price given its yield. In this section, we reverse direction to find a bond's yield given its price. We then discuss the relationship among the various yield measures we have seen. We finish the section with some additional yield calculations.

Before we begin the process of calculating yields, you should be aware of an important assumption made when yield is calculated. This assumption is that an investor will be able to reinvest the coupon interest payments at a rate equal to the yield to maturity of the bond. Therefore, an investor will earn the bond's yield to maturity only if the investor holds the bond to maturity and if all the coupon interest payments received are reinvested at a rate equal to the bond's yield to maturity. The actual rate earned on the bond can be lower or higher than the yield to maturity—it depends on how long the investor holds the bond and the rate at which the coupon payments are reinvested.

CALCULATING YIELDS

To calculate a bond's yield given its price, we use the same straight bond formula used previously. The only way to find the yield is by trial and error. Financial calculators and spreadsheets do it this way at very high speed.

To illustrate, suppose we have a 6 percent bond with 10 years to maturity. Its price is 90, meaning 90 percent of face value. Assuming a $1,000 face value, the price is $900 and the coupon is $60 per year. What's the yield?

To find out, all we can do is try different yields until we come across the one that produces a price of $900. However, we can speed things up quite a bit by making an educated guess using what we know about bond prices and yields. We know the yield on this bond is greater than its 6 percent coupon rate because it is a discount bond. So let's first try 8 percent in the straight bond pricing formula:

$$\frac{\$60}{.08}\left[1 - \frac{1}{(1.04)^{20}}\right] + \frac{\$1,000}{(1.04)^{20}} = \$864.10$$

SPREADSHEET ANALYSIS

	A	B	C	D	E	F	G	H
1								
2		Calculating the Yield to Maturity of a Coupon Bond						
3								
4	A Treasury bond traded on March 30, 2010, matures in 8 years on March 30, 2018.							
5	Assuming an 8 percent coupon rate and a price of 110, what is this bond's yield							
6	to maturity?							
7	Hint: Use the Excel function YIELD.							
8								
9		6.3843%		= YIELD("3/30/2010","3/30/2018",0.08,110,100,2,3)				
10								
11	This function uses the following arguments:							
12								
13		= YIELD("Now","Maturity",Coupon,Price,100,2,3)						
14								
15	Price is entered as a percent of face value.							
16	The 100 indicates redemption value as a percent of face value.							
17	The 2 indicates semi-annual coupons.							
18	The 3 specifies an actual day count with 365 days per year.							
19								
20								

The price with an 8 percent yield is $864.10, which is somewhat less than the $900 price, but not too far off.

To finish, we need to ask whether the 8 percent we used was too high or too low. We know that the higher the yield, the lower is the price, thus 8 percent is a little too high. So let's try 7.5 percent:

$$\frac{\$60}{.075}\left[1 - \frac{1}{(1.0375)^{20}}\right] + \frac{\$1,000}{(1.0375)^{20}} = \$895.78$$

Now we're very close. We're still a little too high on the yield (since the price is a little low). If you try 7.4 percent, you'll see that the resulting price is $902.29, so the yield is between 7.4 and 7.5 percent (it's actually 7.435 percent).

EXAMPLE 10.5

Calculating YTM

Suppose a bond has eight years to maturity, a price of 110, and a coupon rate of 8 percent. What is its yield?

This is a premium bond, so its yield is less than the 8 percent coupon. If we try 6 percent, we get (check this) $1,125.61. The yield is therefore a little bigger than 6 percent. If we try 6.5 percent, we get (check this) $1,092.43, so the answer is slightly less than 6.5 percent. Check that 6.4 percent is almost exact (the exact yield is 6.3843 percent).

Yields to maturity may be calculated using a built-in spreadsheet function. An example of how to use an Excel™ spreadsheet to calculate a yield to maturity of a coupon bond is shown in the nearby *Spreadsheet Analysis* box.

YIELD TO CALL

callable bond

A bond is callable if the issuer can buy it back before it matures.

call price

The price the issuer of a callable bond must pay to buy it back.

make-whole call price

The present value of the bond's remaining cash flows.

The discussion in this chapter so far has assumed that a bond will have an actual maturity equal to its originally stated maturity. However, this is not always so because most bonds are **callable bonds**. When a bond issue is callable, the issuer can buy back outstanding bonds before the bonds mature. In exchange, bondholders receive a special **call price**, which is often equal to face value, although it may be slightly higher. When a call price is equal to face value, the bond is said to be *callable at par*.

When a bond is called, the bondholder does not receive any more coupon payments. Therefore, some callable bonds are issued with a provision known as a **make-whole call price**. The make-whole call price is calculated as the present value of the bond's remaining cash flows. The discount rate used to calculate the present value is often the yield of a comparable maturity Treasury bond plus a prespecified premium. The first bonds issued to the investment public with a make-whole call provision were the Quaker State Corporation bonds issued in 1995. Since then, callable bond issues with make-whole call provisions have become common.

Bonds are called at the convenience of the issuer, and a call usually occurs after a fall in market interest rates allows issuers to refinance outstanding debt with new bonds paying lower coupons. However, an issuer's call privilege is often restricted so that outstanding bonds cannot be called until the end of a specified **call protection period**, also termed a *call deferment period*. As a typical example, a bond issued with a 20-year maturity may be sold to investors subject to the restriction that it is callable anytime after an initial five-year call protection period.

call protection period

The period during which a callable bond cannot be called. Also called a *call deferment period*.

yield to call (YTC)

Measure of return that assumes a bond will be redeemed at the earliest call date.

If a bond is callable, its yield to maturity may no longer be a useful number. Instead, the **yield to call**, commonly abbreviated **YTC**, may be more meaningful. Yield to call is a yield measure that assumes a bond issue will be called at its earliest possible call date.

We calculate a bond's yield to call using the straight bond pricing formula we have been using with two changes. First, instead of time to maturity, we use time to the first possible call date. Second, instead of face value, we use the call price. The resulting formula is thus:

$$\text{Callable bond price} = \frac{C}{YTC}\left[1 - \frac{1}{(1 + YTC/2)^{2T}}\right] + \frac{CP}{(1 + YTC/2)^{2T}} \qquad (10.4)$$

where: C = Constant annual coupon
  CP = Call price of the bond
  T = Time in years until earliest possible call date
  YTC = Yield to call assuming semiannual coupons

Calculating a yield to call requires the same trial-and-error procedure as calculating a yield to maturity. Most financial calculators either will handle the calculation directly or can be tricked into it by just changing the face value to the call price and the time to maturity to time to call.

To give a trial-and-error example, suppose a 20-year bond has a coupon of 8 percent, a price of 98, and is callable in 10 years. The call price is 105. What are its yield to maturity and yield to call?

Based on our earlier discussion, we know the yield to maturity is slightly bigger than the coupon rate. (Why?) After some calculation, we find it to be 8.2 percent.

To find the bond's yield to call, we pretend it has a face value of 105 instead of 100 ($1,050 versus $1,000) and will mature in 10 years. With these two changes, the procedure is exactly the same. We can try 8.5 percent, for example:

$$\frac{\$80}{.085}\left[1 - \frac{1}{(1.0425)^{20}}\right] + \frac{\$1,050}{(1.0425)^{20}} = \$988.51$$

Because $988.51 is a little too high, the yield to call is slightly bigger than 8.5 percent. If we try 8.6, we find that the price is $981.83, so the yield to call is about 8.6 percent (it's 8.6276 percent).

A natural question comes up in this context. Which is bigger, the yield to maturity or the yield to call? The answer depends on the call price. However, if the bond is callable at par (as many are), then, for a premium bond, the yield to maturity is greater. For a discount bond, the reverse is true.

Many financial data sources will provide both the yield to maturity and the yield to call. What if, however, the data source gives you only a single yield value? Which one does it give you? Well, the answer is: It depends. Generally speaking, the lower of the two yields is reported. If so, this fact implies that the yield to maturity is typically reported for discount bonds, while the yield to call is given for premium bonds.

SPREADSHEET ANALYSIS

	A	B	C	D	E	F	G	H
1								
2				Calculating Yield to Call				
3								
4	A bond traded on March 30, 2010, matures in 15 years on March 30, 2025, and may							
5	be called anytime after March 30, 2015, at a call price of 105. The bond pays an							
6	8.5 percent coupon and currently trades at par. What are the yield to maturity							
7	and yield to call for this bond?							
8								
9	Yield to maturity is based on the 2025 maturity and the current price of 100.							
10								
11		8.5000%		= YIELD("3/30/2010","3/30/2025",0.085,100,100,2,3)				
12								
13	Yield to call is based on the 2015 call date and the call price of 105.							
14								
15		9.3080%		= YIELD("3/30/2010","3/30/2015",0.085,100,105,2,3)				
16								
17								

EXAMPLE 10.6	Yield to Call

An 8.5 percent coupon bond maturing in 15 years is callable at 105 in 5 years. If the price is 100, which is bigger, the yield to call or the yield to maturity?

Since this is a par bond callable at a premium, the yield to call is bigger. We can verify this by calculating both yields. Check that the yield to maturity is 8.50 percent, whereas the yield to call is 9.308 percent.

Yields to call may be calculated using a built-in spreadsheet function. An example of how to use an Excel™ spreadsheet to calculate a yield to call is shown in the nearby *Spreadsheet Analysis* box.

CHECK THIS

10.3a   What does it mean for a bond to be callable?

10.3b   What is the difference between yield to maturity and yield to call?

10.3c   Yield to call is calculated just like yield to maturity except for two changes. What are the changes?

10.4 Interest Rate Risk and Malkiel's Theorems

interest rate risk
The possibility that changes in interest rates will result in losses in a bond's value.

Bond yields are essentially interest rates, and, like interest rates, they fluctuate through time. When interest rates change, bond prices change. This is called **interest rate risk**. The term "interest rate risk" refers to the possibility of losses on a bond from changes in interest rates.

PROMISED YIELD AND REALIZED YIELD

realized yield
The yield actually earned or "realized" on a bond.

The terms *yield to maturity* and *promised yield* both seem to imply that the yield originally stated when a bond is purchased is what you will actually earn if you hold the bond until it matures. Actually, this is not generally correct. The return or yield you actually earn on a bond is called the **realized yield**, and an originally stated yield to maturity is almost never exactly equal to the realized yield.

The reason a realized yield will almost always differ from a promised yield is that interest rates fluctuate, causing bond prices to rise or fall. One consequence is that if a bond is sold before maturity, its price may be higher or lower than originally anticipated, and, as a result, the actually realized yield will be different from the promised yield.

Another important reason why realized yields generally differ from promised yields relates to the bond's coupons. We will get to this in the next section. For now, you should know that, for the most part, a bond's realized yield will equal its promised yield only if its yield doesn't change at all over the life of the bond, an unlikely event.

INTEREST RATE RISK AND MATURITY

While changing interest rates systematically affect all bond prices, it is important to realize that the impact of changing interest rates is not the same for all bonds. Some bonds are more sensitive to interest rate changes than others. To illustrate, Figure 10.2 shows how two bonds with different maturities can have different price sensitivities to changes in bond yields.

In Figure 10.2, bond prices are measured on the vertical axis, and bond yields are measured on the horizontal axis. Both bonds have the same 8 percent coupon rate, but one bond has a 5-year maturity while the other bond has a 20-year maturity. Both bonds display the inverse relationship between bond prices and bond yields. Since both bonds have the same 8 percent coupon rate, and both sell for par, their yields are 8 percent.

FIGURE 10.2 Bond Prices and Yields

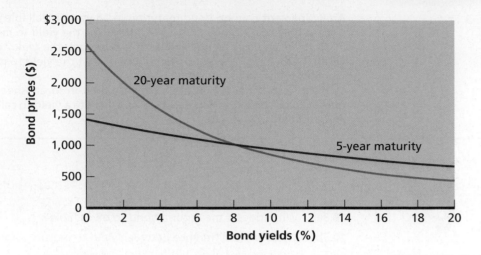

However, when bond yields are greater than 8 percent, the 20-year maturity bond has a lower price than the 5-year maturity bond. In contrast, when bond yields are less than 8 percent, the 20-year maturity bond has a higher price than the 5-year maturity bond. Essentially, falling yields cause both bond prices to rise, but the longer maturity bond experiences a larger price increase than the shorter maturity bond. Similarly, rising yields cause both bond prices to fall, but the price of the longer maturity bond falls by more than the price of the shorter maturity bond.

MALKIEL'S THEOREMS

The effect illustrated in Figure 10.2, along with some other important relationships among bond prices, maturities, coupon rates, and yields, is succinctly described by Burton Malkiel's five bond price theorems.[2] These five theorems are:

1. Bond prices and bond yields move in opposite directions. As a bond's yield increases, its price decreases. Conversely, as a bond's yield decreases, its price increases.

2. For a given change in a bond's yield to maturity, the longer the term to maturity of the bond, the greater will be the magnitude of the change in the bond's price.

3. For a given change in a bond's yield to maturity, the size of the change in the bond's price increases at a diminishing rate as the bond's term to maturity lengthens.

4. For a given change in a bond's yield to maturity, the resulting percentage change in the bond's price is inversely related to the bond's coupon rate.

5. For a given absolute change in a bond's yield to maturity, the magnitude of the price increase caused by a decrease in yield is greater than the price decrease caused by an increase in yield.

The first, second, and fourth of these theorems are the simplest and most important. The first one says that bond prices and yields move in opposite directions. The second one says that longer term bonds are more sensitive to changes in yields than shorter term bonds. The fourth one says that lower coupon bonds are more sensitive to changes in yields than higher coupon bonds.

---

[2] Burton C. Malkiel, "Expectations, Bond Prices, and the Term Structure of Interest Rates," *Quarterly Journal of Economics*, May 1962, pp. 197–218.

TABLE 10.1	Bond Prices and Yields		
		Time to Maturity	
Yields	**5 Years**	**10 Years**	**20 Years**
7%	$1,041.58	$1,071.06	$1,106.78
9%	960.44	934.96	907.99
Price difference	$ 81.14	$ 136.10	$ 198.79

TABLE 10.2	Twenty-Year Bond Prices and Yields		
		Coupon Rates	
Yields	**6 Percent**	**8 Percent**	**10 Percent**
6%	$1,000.00	$1,231.15	$1,462.30
8%	802.07	1,000.00	1,197.93
10%	656.82	828.41	1,000.00

The third theorem says that a bond's sensitivity to interest rate changes increases as its maturity grows, but at a diminishing rate. In other words, a 10-year bond is much more sensitive to changes in yield than a 1-year bond. However, a 30-year bond is only slightly more sensitive than a 20-year bond. Finally, the fifth theorem says essentially that the loss you would suffer from, say, a 1 percent increase in yields is less than the gain you would enjoy from a 1 percent decrease in yields.

Table 10.1 illustrates the first three of these theorems by providing prices for 8 percent coupon bonds with maturities of 5, 10, and 20 years and yields to maturity of 7 percent and 9 percent. Be sure to check these for practice. As the first theorem says, bond prices are lower when yields are higher (9 percent versus 7 percent). As the second theorem indicates, the differences in bond prices between yields of 7 percent and 9 percent are greater for bonds with a longer term to maturity. However, as the third theorem states, the effect increases at a diminishing rate as the maturity lengthens. To see this, notice that $136.10 is 67.7 percent larger than $81.14, while $198.79 is only 46.1 percent larger than $136.10.

To illustrate the last two theorems, we present prices for 20-year maturity bonds with coupon rates and yields to maturity of 6 percent, 8 percent, and 10 percent (again, calculate these for practice) in Table 10.2. To illustrate the fourth theorem, compare the loss on the 6 percent and the 8 percent bonds as yields move from 8 percent to 10 percent. The 6 percent bond loses ($656.82 − $802.07)/$802.07 = −18.1%. The 8 percent bond loses ($828.41 − $1,000)/$1,000 = −17.2%, showing that the bond with the lower coupon is more sensitive to a change in yields. You can (and should) verify that the same is true for a yield increase.

Finally, to illustrate the fifth theorem, take a look at the 8 percent coupon bond in Table 10.2. As yields decrease by 2 percent from 8 percent to 6 percent, its price climbs by $231.15. As yields rise by 2 percent, the bond's price falls by $171.59.

As we have discussed, bond maturity is an important factor determining the sensitivity of a bond's price to changes in interest rates. However, bond maturity is an incomplete measure of bond price sensitivity to yield changes. For example, we have seen that a bond's coupon rate is also important. An improved measure of interest rate risk for bonds that accounts for both differences in maturity and differences in coupon rates is our next subject. A nearby *Investment Updates* box discusses the importance of bonds in an investment portfolio.

GET A FRESH ANGLE ON YOUR FINANCES

Not sure whether you're saving enough or whether you have the right investment mix? To get a better handle on your portfolio, it sometimes helps to look at your finances from another angle.

1 How Much Do You Need in Conservative Investments to Feel Safe?

Investment advisors and Wall Street firms constantly exhort investors to consider their risk tolerance. For instance, we are often prodded to fill out those irritating questionnaires where we are asked whether our goal is "growth" or "capital preservation."

The answer, of course, is that we want both. Even retirees need growth from their portfolios. Even freshly minted college graduates hanker after some stability.

My advice: Forget risk tolerance. Instead, divide your portfolio into two parts. Designate one portion for "getting rich" and the other for "making sure I'm not poor."

How should you split your savings between the two? That brings us to our first question. Think about how much you need in conservative investments, like high-quality bonds, certificates of deposit, and savings accounts, to cover expected costs, pay for financial emergencies, and have a general sense of financial security.

If you are retired, this stash of safe money might be equal to your living expenses for the next three or five years. If you are still hauling in a paycheck, your conservative investments could amount to just three months' living expenses.

Once you have enough in conservative investments to soothe your fears, that will free you up to be more aggressive with the rest of your portfolio. You might invest your "getting rich" money in a mix of U.S. shares, foreign stocks, real-estate investment trusts, high-yield "junk" bonds and foreign bonds.

What if these investments hit a rough patch? With any luck, you won't be too unnerved, thanks to the financial cushion provided by your safe money.

2 How Much Do You Really Have in Bonds?

When you tote up your holdings of conservative investments, you probably count CDs, Treasury bonds, high-quality corporate bonds, municipals, money-market funds, and savings accounts. But don't stop there.

I would expand the list to include Social Security retirement benefits, pension income, mortgage debt, and any other loans you have. After all, you regularly receive income from Social Security and your pension, just as you would from a bond. Meanwhile, your debts involve making regular payments to other folks.

All these dealings affect your sense of financial security, and they should influence how you structure your portfolio. For instance, if you expect a traditional company pension when you retire, you effectively have a huge position in bonds and thus you might want to load up on stocks in your investment portfolio.

On the other hand, if you have a heap of debts, your financial position is much more precarious and you may want to take less risk with your investments. On that score, consider your mortgage, which probably is your biggest debt. Let's say you have a $300,000 home and a $200,000 mortgage. The temptation is to deduct your mortgage from your home's value and declare that your total real-estate investment is $100,000.

But in truth, your real-estate exposure is equal to your home's full $300,000 value. Think about it: Whether you are mortgaged to the hilt or you are debt-free, you still benefit from every dollar of home-price appreciation and suffer every dollar of loss.

Meanwhile, I would view your $200,000 mortgage as a "negative bond" because, instead of earning interest, you are paying it. Suppose you also have $75,000 in government bonds, which means you have lent money to Uncle Sam. Overall, you owe a lot more money than you are owed—to the tune of $125,000.

In fact, your financial position may be more perilous than a couple whose portfolio is 100% in stocks but who own their home free and clear. The implication: You may want to tamp down risk, either by buying more bonds or by making extra principal payments on your mortgage.

Source: Jonathan Clements, *The Wall Street Journal*, October 16, 2005. Reprinted with permission of *The Wall Street Journal*. © 2005 Dow Jones & Company, Inc. All Rights Reserved Worldwide.

CHECK THIS

10.4a True or false: A bond price's sensitivity to interest rate changes increases at an increasing rate as maturity lengthens.

10.4b Which is more sensitive to an interest rate shift: a low-coupon bond or a high-coupon bond?

10.5 Duration

duration

A widely used measure of a bond's sensitivity to changes in bond yields.

To account for differences in interest rate risk across bonds with different coupon rates and maturities, the concept of **duration** is widely applied. As we will explore in some detail, duration measures a bond's sensitivity to interest rate changes. The idea behind duration was first presented by Frederick Macaulay in an early study of U.S. financial markets.[3] Today, duration is a very widely used measure of a bond's price sensitivity to changes in bond yields.

MACAULAY DURATION

There are several duration measures. The original version is called *Macaulay duration*. The usefulness of Macaulay duration stems from the fact that it satisfies the following approximate relationship between percentage changes in bond prices and changes in bond yields:

$$\text{Percentage change in bond price} \approx -\text{Duration} \times \frac{\text{Change in } YTM}{(1 + YTM/2)} \tag{10.5}$$

As a consequence, two bonds with the same duration, but not necessarily the same maturity, have approximately the same price sensitivity to a change in bond yields. This approximation is quite accurate for relatively small changes in yields, but it becomes less accurate when large changes are considered.

To see how we use this result, suppose a bond has a Macaulay duration of six years, and its yield decreases from 10 percent to 9.5 percent. The resulting percentage change in the price of the bond is calculated as follows:

$$-6 \times \frac{.095 - .10}{1.05} = 2.86\%$$

Thus, the bond's price rises by 2.86 percent in response to a yield decrease of 50 basis points.

EXAMPLE 10.7

Macaulay Duration

A bond has a Macaulay duration of 11 years, and its yield increases from 8 percent to 8.5 percent. What will happen to the price of the bond?

The resulting percentage change in the price of the bond can be calculated as follows:

$$-11 \times \frac{.085 - .08}{1.04} = -5.29\%$$

The bond's price declines by approximately 5.29 percent in response to a 50 basis point increase in yield.

MODIFIED DURATION

Some analysts prefer to use a variation of Macaulay duration called *modified duration*. The relationship between Macaulay duration and modified duration for bonds paying semiannual coupons is simply:

$$\text{Modified duration} = \frac{\text{Macaulay duration}}{(1 + YTM/2)} \tag{10.6}$$

As a result, based on modified duration, the approximate relationship between percentage changes in bond prices and changes in bond yields is just:

$$\text{Percentage change in bond price} \approx -\text{Modified duration} \times \text{Change in } YTM \tag{10.7}$$

---

[3] Frederick Macaulay, *Some Theoretical Problems Suggested by the Movements of Interest Rates, Bond Yields, and Stock Prices in the United States since 1856* (New York: National Bureau of Economic Research, 1938).

In other words, to calculate the percentage change in the bond's price, we just multiply the modified duration by the change in yields.

EXAMPLE 10.8

Modified Duration

A bond has a Macaulay duration of 8.5 years and a yield to maturity of 9 percent. What is its modified duration?

The bond's modified duration is calculated as follows:

$$\frac{8.5}{1.045} = 8.134$$

Notice that we divided the yield by 2 to get the semiannual yield.

EXAMPLE 10.9

Modified Duration

A bond has a modified duration of seven years. Suppose its yield increases from 8 percent to 8.5 percent. What happens to its price?

We can very easily determine the resulting percentage change in the price of the bond using its modified duration:

$$-7 \times (.085 - .08) = -3.5\%$$

The bond's price declines by about 3.5 percent.

CALCULATING MACAULAY DURATION

Macaulay duration is often described as a bond's *effective maturity*. For this reason, duration values are conventionally stated in years. The first fundamental principle for calculating the duration of a bond concerns the duration of a zero coupon bond. Specifically, the duration of a zero coupon bond is equal to its maturity. Thus, on a pure discount instrument, such as the U.S. Treasury STRIPS, no calculation is necessary to come up with Macaulay duration.

The second fundamental principle for calculating duration concerns the duration of a coupon bond with multiple cash flows. The duration of a coupon bond is a weighted average of individual maturities of all the bond's separate cash flows. The weights attached to the maturity of each cash flow are proportionate to the present values of each cash flow.

A sample duration calculation for a bond with three years until maturity is illustrated in Table 10.3. The bond sells at par value. It has an 8 percent coupon rate and an 8 percent yield to maturity.

TABLE 10.3

Calculating Bond Duration

Years	Cash Flow	Discount Factor	Present Value	Years × Present Value ÷ Bond Price
0.5	$ 40	.96154	$ 38.4615	.0192 years
1	40	.92456	36.9822	.0370
1.5	40	.88900	35.5599	.0533
2	40	.85480	34.1922	.0684
2.5	40	.82193	32.8771	.0822
3	1,040	.79031	821.9271	2.4658
			$1,000.00	2.7259 years
			Bond Price	Bond Duration

As shown in Table 10.3, calculating a bond's duration can be laborious—especially if the bond has a large number of separate cash flows. Fortunately, relatively simple formulas are available for many of the important cases. For example, if a bond is selling for par value, its duration can be calculated easily using the following formula:

$$\text{Par value bond duration} = \frac{(1 + YTM/2)}{YTM}\left[1 - \frac{1}{(1 + YTM/2)^{2M}}\right] \tag{10.8}$$

where: M = Bond maturity in years
         YTM = Yield to maturity assuming semiannual coupons

For example, using YTM = 8% and M = 3 years we obtain the same duration value (2.7259 years) computed in Table 10.3.

EXAMPLE 10.10

Duration for a Par Value Bond

Suppose a par value bond has a 6 percent coupon and 10 years to maturity. What is its duration?
   Since the bond sells for par, its yield is equal to its coupon rate, 6 percent. Plugging this into the par value bond duration formula, we have:

$$\text{Par value bond duration} = \frac{(1 + .06/2)}{.06}\left[1 - \frac{1}{(1 + .06/2)^{20}}\right]$$

After a little work on a calculator, we find that the duration is 7.66 years.

The par value bond duration formula (equation 10.8) is useful for calculating the duration of a bond that is actually selling at par value. Unfortunately, the general formula for bonds not necessarily selling at par value is somewhat more complicated. The general duration formula for a bond paying constant semiannual coupons is:

$$\text{Duration} = \frac{1 + YTM/2}{YTM} - \frac{(1 + YTM/2) + M(CPR - YTM)}{YTM + CPR[(1 + YTM/2)^{2M} - 1]} \tag{10.9}$$

where: CPR = Constant annual coupon rate
         M = Bond maturity in years
         YTM = Yield to maturity assuming semiannual coupons

Although somewhat tedious for manual calculations, this formula is used in many computer programs that calculate bond durations. Some popular personal computer spreadsheet packages and financial calculators have built-in functions to help you perform this calculation.

EXAMPLE 10.11

Duration for a Discount Bond

A bond has a yield to maturity of 7 percent. It matures in 12 years. Its coupon rate is 6 percent. What is its modified duration?
   We first must calculate the Macaulay duration using the unpleasant-looking formula just above. We finish by converting the Macaulay duration to modified duration. Plugging into the duration formula, we have:

$$\text{Duration} = \frac{1 + .07/2}{.07} - \frac{(1 + .07/2) + 12(.06 - .07)}{.07 + .06[(1 + .07/2)^{24} - 1]}$$

$$= \frac{1.035}{.07} - \frac{1.035 + 12(-.01)}{.07 + .06(1.035^{24} - 1)}$$

After a little button pushing, we find that the duration is 8.56 years. Finally, converting to modified duration, we find that the modified duration is equal to 8.56/1.035 = 8.27 years.

(continued)

Bond durations may be calculated using a built-in spreadsheet function. An example of how to use an Excel™ spreadsheet to calculate a Macaulay duration and modified duration is shown in the *Spreadsheet Analysis* box below.

SPREADSHEET ANALYSIS

	A	B	C	D	E	F	G	H
1								
2			**Calculating Macaulay and Modified Durations**					
3								
4	A Treasury bond traded on March 30, 2010, matures in 12 years on March 30, 2022.							
5	Assuming a 6 percent coupon rate and a 7 percent yield to maturity, what are the							
6	Macaulay and modified durations of this bond?							
7	Hint: Use the Excel functions DURATION and MDURATION.							
8								
9		8.561	= DURATION("3/30/2010","3/30/2022",0.06,0.07,2,3)					
10								
11		8.272	= MDURATION("3/30/2010","3/30/2022",0.06,0.07,2,3)					
12								
13	These DURATION AND MDURATION functions use the following arguments:							
14								
15		= DURATION("Now","Maturity",Coupon,Yield,2,3)						
16								
17	The 2 indicates semi-annual coupons.							
18	The 3 specifies an actual day count with 365 days per year.							
19								
20								

PROPERTIES OF DURATION

Macaulay duration has a number of important properties. For straight bonds, the basic properties of Macaulay duration can be summarized as follows:

1. All else the same, the longer a bond's maturity, the longer is its duration.
2. All else the same, a bond's duration increases at a decreasing rate as maturity lengthens.
3. All else the same, the higher a bond's coupon, the shorter is its duration.
4. All else the same, a higher yield to maturity implies a shorter duration, and a lower yield to maturity implies a longer duration.

As we saw earlier, a zero coupon bond has a duration equal to its maturity. The duration on a bond with coupons is always less than its maturity. Because of the second principle, durations much longer than 10 or 15 years are rarely seen. An exception to some of these principles involves very long maturity bonds selling at a very steep discount. This exception rarely occurs in practice, so these principles are generally correct.

A graphical illustration of the relationship between duration and maturity is presented in Figure 10.3, where duration is measured on the vertical axis and maturity is measured on the horizontal axis. In Figure 10.3, the yield to maturity for all bonds is 10 percent. Bonds with coupon rates of 0 percent, 5 percent, 10 percent, and 15 percent are presented. As the figure shows, the duration of a zero coupon bond rises step for step with maturity. For the coupon bonds, however, the duration initially moves closely with maturity, as our first duration principle suggests, but, consistent with the second principle, the lines begin to flatten out after four or five years. Also, consistent with our third principle, the lower coupon bonds have higher durations.

FIGURE 10.3   Bond Duration and Maturity

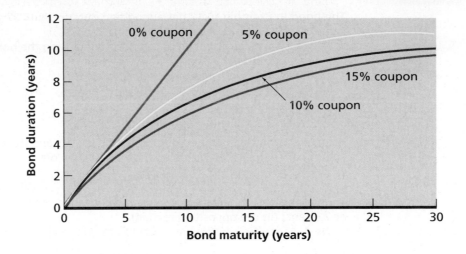

CHECK THIS

10.5a	What does duration measure?
10.5b	What is the duration of a zero coupon bond?
10.5c	What happens to a bond's duration as its maturity grows?

10.6 Bond Risk Measures Based on Duration

In this section, we examine some risk measures that are either based on duration or closely related to it. These measures are commonly used by bond traders and other fixed-income professionals.

DOLLAR VALUE OF AN 01

dollar value of an 01
Change in bond price resulting from a change in yield to maturity of one basis point.

A popular measure of interest rate risk among bond professionals is the **dollar value of an 01** (say "dollar value of an oh-one"), which measures the change in bond price resulting from a one basis point change in yield to maturity, where one basis point is 1 percent of 1 percent, that is, .01 percent, or .0001. The dollar value of an 01 is also known as the *value of a basis point*. The dollar value of an 01 can be stated through the modified duration of a bond as follows:

$$\text{Dollar value of an 01} \approx \text{Modified duration} \times \text{Bond price} \times 0.0001 \qquad (10.10)$$

YIELD VALUE OF A 32nd

yield value of a 32nd
Change in yield to maturity that would lead to a 1/32 change in bond price.

When bond prices are quoted in 1/32's of a point, as they are, for example, with U.S. Treasury notes and bonds, the **yield value of a 32nd** is often used by bond professionals as an additional or alternative measure of interest rate risk. The yield value of a 32nd is the change in yield to maturity that would lead to a 1/32 change in bond price. A simple way to obtain the yield value of a 32nd is to multiply the dollar value of an 01 by 32 and then invert the result:

$$\text{Yield value of a 32nd} \approx \frac{1}{32 \times \text{Dollar value of an 01}} \qquad (10.11)$$

EXAMPLE 10.12 | **Bond Risk Measures Based on Duration**

The bond in Example 10.11 has a modified duration of 8.27 years. What is its dollar value of an 01? What is its yield value of a 32nd?

We must first calculate the price of this bond using the bond pricing formula provided earlier in this chapter:

$$\text{Bond price} = \frac{6}{.07}\left[1 - \frac{1}{(1 + .035)^{24}}\right] + \frac{100}{(1 + .035)^{24}}$$

$$= \$91.971$$

Then, plugging the modified duration of 8.27 years and the bond price as a percentage of par value, 91.971, into equation (10.10), we obtain the dollar value of an 01:

$$\text{Dollar value of an 01} \approx 8.27 \times 91.971 \times .0001 = .07606$$

Thus, a one basis point change in yield will change the bond price by about $0.076, or 7.6 cents (in the opposite direction).

Next we multiply by 32 and invert to obtain the yield value of a 32nd:

$$\text{Yield value of a 32nd} \approx \frac{1}{32 \times .07606} = .41086$$

Now we see that a change in yield of .41 basis point, or .0041 percent, would lead to a change in bond price of about 1/32. As a check, we calculate a bond price obtained by changing the yield from 7 percent to 7.0041 percent:

$$\text{Bond price} = \frac{6}{.070041}\left[1 - \frac{1}{(1 + .03500205)^{24}}\right] + \frac{100}{(1 + .03500205)^{24}}$$

$$= \$91.94$$

The resulting price change is $0.0314 \approx \$91.97 - \$91.94$. Because 1/32 of a point corresponds to $0.03125, we see that our computed yield value of a 32nd is quite accurate.

CHECK THIS

10.6a What is the relationship between modified duration and the dollar value of an 01?

10.6b What is the relationship between the dollar value of an 01 and the yield value of a 32nd?

10.7 Dedicated Portfolios and Reinvestment Risk

Duration has another property that makes it a vital tool in bond portfolio management. To explore this subject, we first need to introduce two important concepts, dedicated portfolios and reinvestment risk.

DEDICATED PORTFOLIOS

dedicated portfolio
A bond portfolio created to prepare for a future cash outlay.

A firm can invest in coupon bonds when it is preparing to meet a future liability or other cash outlay. A bond portfolio formed for such a specific purpose is called a **dedicated portfolio**. When the future liability payment of a dedicated portfolio is due on a known date, this date is commonly called the portfolio's *target date*.

Pension funds provide a good example of dedicated portfolio management. A pension fund normally knows years in advance the amount of benefit payments it must make to its beneficiaries. The fund can then purchase coupon bonds today to prepare for these future payments.

Let's work through an example. Suppose the Safety First pension fund estimates that it must pay benefits of about $100 million in five years. Safety First then decides to buy coupon bonds yielding 8 percent. These coupon bonds pay semiannual coupons, mature in five years, and are currently selling at par. If interest rates *do not change over the next five years,* how much money does Safety First need to invest today in these coupon bonds to have $100 million in five years?

Fortunately, we can use equation (10.3)—and some ingenuity—to answer this question. Recall that equation (10.3) says that today's bond price, P, is the present value of the coupons plus the present value of the promised face value. However, in the case of Safety First, we want to solve for a future value. So let's make equation (10.3) into an equation for future value by multiplying by the amount $(1 + YTM/2)^{2M}$:

$$P = \frac{C}{YTM}\left[1 - \frac{1}{(1 + YTM/2)^{2M}}\right] + \frac{\text{Face value}}{(1 + YTM/2)^{2M}}$$

$$P(1 + YTM/2)^{2M} = \frac{C}{YTM}[(1 + YTM/2)^{2M} - 1] + \text{Face value} \qquad (10.12)$$

Equation (10.12) shows us that the future value of all the payments made on a bond over its life is just the current value, P, multiplied by $(1 + YTM/2)^{2M}$. In the case of Safety First, we know the future value is $100,000,000, so we have:

$$\text{Future value} = \$100,000,000 = P(1 + YTM/2)^{2M} \qquad (10.13)$$

We can rearrange equation (10.13) to solve for the present value:

$$\text{Present value} = P = \$100,000,000/(1 + YTM/2)^{2M}$$

The bonds being considered by Safety First have a yield to maturity of 8 percent and mature in five years, so:

$$\text{Present value} = P = \$100,000,000/(1 + .08/2)^{2\times 5}$$
$$= \$100,000,000/(1 + .04)^{10}$$
$$= \$67,556,417$$

Thus, Safety First needs to invest about $67.5 million today. Because the bonds in question sell for par, this $67.5 million is also the total face value of the bonds.

With this face value, the coupon payment every six months is thus $67,556,417 \times .08/2 = $2,702,257. When Safety First invests each of these coupons at 8 percent (i.e., the YTM), the total future value of the coupons is $32,443,583. Safety First will also receive the face value of the coupon bonds in five years, or $67,556,417. In five years, Safety First will have $32,443,583 + $67,556,417 = $100,000,000.

Therefore, Safety First needs about $67.5 million to construct a dedicated bond portfolio to fund a future liability of $100 million. However, consider another important fact: We calculated this amount assuming that Safety First can invest each coupon amount at 8 percent over the next five years. If the assumption is true (i.e., interest rates do not change over the next five years), Safety First's bond fund will grow to the amount needed.

REINVESTMENT RISK

As we have seen, the bond investment strategy of the Safety First pension fund will be successful if all coupons received during the life of the investment *can be reinvested at a constant 8 percent YTM.* However, in reality, yields at which coupons can be reinvested are uncertain, and a target date surplus or shortfall is therefore likely to occur.

The uncertainty about the future or target date portfolio value that results from the need to reinvest bond coupons at yields that cannot be predicted in advance is called

reinvestment rate risk. Thus, the uncertain portfolio value on the target date represents reinvestment risk. In general, more distant target dates entail greater uncertainty and reinvestment risk.

To examine the impact of reinvestment risk, we continue with the example of the Safety First pension fund's dedicated bond portfolio. We will add one small wrinkle. We assume that Safety First buys 8 percent coupon bonds that are selling at par. However, we will not assume that interest rates stay constant at 8 percent.

Instead, consider two cases, one in which all bond coupons are reinvested at a 7 percent YTM, and one in which all coupons are reinvested at a 9 percent YTM. The value of the portfolio on the target date will be the payment of the fixed $67.5 million principal plus the future value of the 10 semiannual coupons compounded at either 7 percent or 9 percent. Note that the coupon rate is 8 percent in both cases.

As shown in Table 10.4, a value of $99.258 million is realized by a 7 percent reinvestment YTM, and a target date portfolio value of $100.762 million is realized through a 9 percent reinvestment YTM. The difference between these two amounts, about $1.5 million, represents reinvestment risk.

As this example illustrates, a maturity matching strategy for a dedicated bond portfolio has reinvestment risk. Further, we changed interest rates by only 1 percent. Reinvestment risk can be much greater than what we have shown. Our example also understates a pension fund's total reinvestment risk because it considers only a single target date. In reality, pension funds have a series of target dates, and a shortfall at one target date typically coincides with shortfalls at other target dates too.

A simple solution for reinvestment risk is to purchase zero coupon bonds that pay a fixed principal at a maturity chosen to match a dedicated portfolio's target date. Because there are no coupons to reinvest, there is no reinvestment risk. However, a zero coupon bond strategy has its drawbacks, too. As a practical matter, U.S. Treasury STRIPS are the only zero coupon bonds issued in sufficient quantity to even begin to satisfy the dedicated portfolio needs of pension funds, insurance companies, and other institutional investors.

However, U.S. Treasury securities have lower yields than even the highest quality corporate bonds. A yield difference of only .25 percent between Treasury securities and corporate bonds can make a substantial difference in the initial cost of a dedicated bond portfolio.

TABLE 10.4　　**Reinvestment Rate Risk**

Year	Six-Month Period	Payment	Reinvestment YTM: 7.00% Coupon Rate: 8.00% Payment Value, End of Year 5	Reinvestment YTM: 8.00% Coupon Rate: 8.00% Payment Value, End of Year 5	Reinvestment YTM: 9.00% Coupon Rate: 8.00% Payment Value, End of Year 5
1	1	$2,702,257	$ 3,682,898	$ 3,846,154	$ 4,015,811
	2	2,702,257	3,558,356	3,698,225	3,842,881
2	3	2,702,257	3,438,025	3,555,985	3,677,398
	4	2,702,257	3,321,763	3,419,217	3,519,041
3	5	2,702,257	3,209,433	3,287,708	3,367,503
	6	2,702,257	3,100,902	3,161,258	3,222,491
4	7	2,702,257	2,996,040	3,039,671	3,083,724
	8	2,702,257	2,894,725	2,922,761	2,950,932
5	9	2,702,257	2,796,836	2,810,347	2,823,858
	10	2,702,257	2,702,257	2,702,257	2,702,257
Future value of coupons			$31,701,236	$ 32,443,583	$ 33,205,896
Face value received (at End of Year 5)			$67,556,417	$ 67,556,417	$ 67,556,417
Target date portfolio value			$99,257,653	$100,000,000	$100,762,313

For example, suppose that Treasury STRIPS have a yield of 7.75 percent. Using semiannual compounding, the present value of these zero coupon bonds providing a principal payment of $100 million at a five-year maturity is calculated as follows:

$$\text{STRIPS price} = \frac{\$100,000,000}{(1 + 0.0775/2)^{2 \times 5}}$$

$$= \frac{\$100,000,000}{(1 + 0.03875)^{10}}$$

$$= \$68,373,787$$

This cost of $68.374 million based on a 7.75 percent yield is significantly higher than the previously stated cost of $67.556 million based on an 8 percent yield. From the perspective of the Safety First pension fund, this represents a hefty premium to pay to eliminate reinvestment risk. Fortunately, as we discuss in the next section, other methods are available at lower cost.

CHECK THIS

10.7a What is a dedicated portfolio?

10.7b What is reinvestment rate risk?

10.8 Immunization

immunization
Constructing a portfolio to minimize the uncertainty surrounding its target date value.

Constructing a dedicated portfolio to minimize the uncertainty in its target date value is called **immunization**. In this section, we show how duration can be used to immunize a bond portfolio against reinvestment risk.

PRICE RISK VERSUS REINVESTMENT RATE RISK

To understand how immunization is accomplished, suppose you own a bond with eight years to maturity. However, your target date is actually just six years from now. If interest rates rise, are you happy or unhappy?

Your initial reaction is probably "unhappy" because you know that as interest rates rise, bond values fall. However, things are not so simple. Clearly, if interest rates rise, then, in six years, your bond will be worth less than it would have been at a lower rate. This is called **price risk**. However, it is also true that you will be able to reinvest the coupons you receive at a higher interest rate. As a result, your reinvested coupons will be worth more. In fact, the net effect of an interest rate increase might be to make you *better* off.

price risk
The risk that bond prices will decrease, which arises in dedicated portfolios when the target date value of a bond or bond portfolio is not known with certainty.

As our simple example illustrates, for a dedicated portfolio, interest rate changes have two effects. Interest rate increases act to decrease bond prices (price risk) but increase the future value of reinvested coupons (reinvestment rate risk). In the other direction, interest rate decreases act to increase bond values but decrease the future value of reinvested coupons. The key observation is that these two effects—price risk and reinvestment rate risk—tend to offset each other.

You might wonder if it is possible to engineer a portfolio in which these two effects offset each other more or less precisely. As we illustrate next, the answer is most definitely yes.

IMMUNIZATION BY DURATION MATCHING

The key to immunizing a dedicated portfolio is to match its duration to its target date. If this is done, then the impacts of price and reinvestment rate risk will almost exactly offset, and interest rate changes will have a minimal impact on the target date value of the portfolio. In fact, immunization is often simply referred to as duration matching.

To see how a duration matching strategy can be applied to reduce target date uncertainty, suppose the Safety First pension fund initially purchases $67.5 million of par value bonds paying 8 percent coupons with a maturity of 6.2 years instead of 5 years. Why 6.2 years?

FIGURE 10.4 ■ Bond Price and Reinvestment Rate Risk

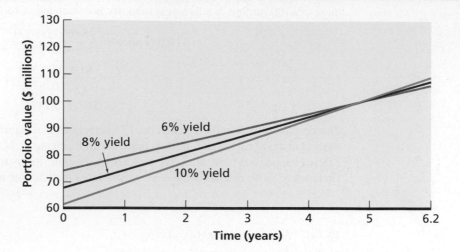

From the par value duration formula, equation (10.8), a maturity of 6.2 years corresponds to a duration of 5 years. Thus, the duration of Safety First's dedicated bond portfolio is now matched to its five-year portfolio target date.

Suppose that immediately after the bonds are purchased, a one-time shock causes bond yields to either jump up to 10 percent or jump down to 6 percent. As a result, all coupons are reinvested at either a 10 percent yield or a 6 percent yield, depending on which way rates jump.

This example is illustrated in Figure 10.4, where the left vertical axis measures initial bond portfolio values, and the right vertical axis measures bond portfolio values realized by holding the portfolio until the bonds mature in 6.2 years. The horizontal axis measures the passage of time from initial investment to bond maturity. The positively sloped lines plot bond portfolio values through time for bond yields that have jumped to either 10 percent or 6 percent immediately after the initial investment of $67.5 million in par value 8 percent coupon bonds. This example assumes that after their initial jump, bond yields remain unchanged.

As shown in Figure 10.4, the initial jump in yields causes the value of Safety First's bond portfolio to jump in the opposite direction. If yields increase, bond prices fall, but coupons are reinvested at a higher interest rate, thereby leading to a higher portfolio value at maturity. In contrast, if yields decrease, bond prices rise, but a lower reinvestment rate reduces the value of the portfolio at maturity.

However, what is remarkable is that regardless of whether yields rise or fall, there is almost no difference in Safety First's portfolio value at the duration-matched five-year target date. Thus, the immunization strategy of matching the duration of Safety First's dedicated portfolio to its portfolio target date has almost entirely eliminated reinvestment risk.

DYNAMIC IMMUNIZATION

The example of the Safety First pension fund immunizing a dedicated bond portfolio by a duration matching strategy assumed that the bond portfolio was subject to a single yield shock. In reality, bond yields change constantly. Therefore, successful immunization requires that a dedicated portfolio be rebalanced frequently to maintain a portfolio duration equal to the portfolio's target date.

For example, by purchasing bonds with a maturity of 6.2 years, the Safety First pension fund had matched the duration of the dedicated portfolio to the fund's 5-year target date. One year later, however, the target date is four years away, and bonds with a duration of four years are required to maintain a duration matching strategy. Assuming interest rates haven't changed, the par value duration formula shows that a maturity of 4.7 years corresponds to a duration of 4 years. Thus, to maintain a duration-matched target date, the Safety First fund must sell its originally purchased bonds now with a maturity of 5.2 years and replace them with bonds having a maturity of 4.7 years.

dynamic immunization
Periodic rebalancing of a dedicated bond portfolio to maintain a duration that matches the target maturity date.

The strategy of periodically rebalancing a dedicated bond portfolio to maintain a portfolio duration matched to a specific target date is called **dynamic immunization**. The advantage of dynamic immunization is that reinvestment risk caused by continually changing bond yields is greatly reduced. The drawback of dynamic immunization is that each portfolio rebalancing incurs management and transaction costs. Therefore, portfolios should not be rebalanced too frequently. In practice, rebalancing on an intermittent basis, say, each quarter, is a reasonable compromise between the costs of rebalancing and the benefits of dynamic immunization.

CHECK THIS

10.8a What are the two effects on the target date value of a dedicated portfolio of a shift in yields? Explain why they tend to offset.

10.8b How can a dedicated portfolio be immunized against shifts in yields?

10.8c Why is rebalancing necessary to maintain immunization?

10.9 Summary and Conclusions

This chapter covers the basics of bonds, bond yields, duration, and immunization. Among other items, we covered the following topics—grouped by the chapter's important concepts.

1. **How to calculate bond prices and yields.**

   A. The straight bond pricing formula has two separate components. The first component is the present value of all the coupon payments. Because the coupons are fixed and paid on a regular basis, you may recognize that they form an ordinary annuity, and the first piece of the bond pricing formula is a standard calculation for the present value of an annuity. The other component represents the present value of the principal payment at maturity, and it is a standard calculation for the present value of a single lump sum.

   B. Calculating bond prices is mostly "plug and chug" with a calculator. In fact, a good financial calculator or spreadsheet should have this formula built into it. However, it is important to be able to work bond calculations the "long way" so that you know how the formulas work.

   C. Bonds are generally distinguished according to whether they are selling at par value or at a discount or premium relative to par value. Bonds with a price greater than par value are said to be selling at a premium; bonds with a price less than par value are said to be selling at a discount.

2. **The importance of yield to maturity.**

   A. There are three different yield measures: coupon yield or rate, current yield, and yield to maturity. Each is calculated using a specific equation, and which is the biggest or smallest depends on whether the bond is selling at a discount or a premium.

   B. Important relationships among bond prices, maturities, coupon rates, and yields are described by Malkiel's five bond price theorems.

   C. A stated yield to maturity is almost never equal to an actually realized yield because yields are subject to bond price risk and coupon reinvestment rate risk.

3. **Interest rate risk and Malkiel's theorems.**

   A. Bond prices and bond yields move in opposite directions. As a bond's yield increases, its price decreases. Conversely, as a bond's yield decreases, its price increases.

   B. For a given change in a bond's yield to maturity, the longer the term to maturity of the bond, the greater will be the magnitude of the change in the bond's price.

   C. For a given change in a bond's yield to maturity, the size of the change in the bond's price increases at a diminishing rate as the bond's term to maturity lengthens.

   D. For a given change in a bond's yield to maturity, the absolute magnitude of the resulting change in the bond's price is inversely related to the bond's coupon rate.

E. For a given absolute change in a bond's yield to maturity, the magnitude of the price increase caused by a decrease in yield is greater than the price decrease caused by an increase in yield.

4. How to measure the impact of interest rate changes on bond prices.

A. Bond price risk is the risk that a bond sold before maturity must be sold at a price different from the price predicted by an originally stated yield to maturity. Coupon reinvestment risk is the risk that bond coupons must be reinvested at yields different from an originally stated yield to maturity.

B. To account for differences in interest rate risk across bonds with different coupon rates and maturities, the concept of duration is widely applied. Duration is a direct measure of a bond's price sensitivity to changes in bond yields.

C. Bond portfolios are often created for the purpose of preparing for a future liability payment. Portfolios formed for such a specific purpose are called dedicated portfolios. When the future liability payment of a dedicated portfolio is due on a known date, that date is called the portfolio's target date.

D. Minimizing the uncertainty of the value of a dedicated portfolio's future target date value is called immunization. A strategy of matching a bond portfolio's duration to the target maturity date accomplishes this goal.

GET REAL

This chapter covered bond basics. How should you, as an investor or investment manager, put this information to work?

Now that you've been exposed to basic facts about bonds, their prices, and their yields, you might try applying the various principles we have discussed. Do this by buying some bonds, perhaps in a simulated brokerage account, and then observing the behavior of their prices and yields. Buying Treasury bonds is the best place to start.

With a simulated brokerage account (such as Stock-Trak), buy two Treasury bonds with the same maturity but different coupons. This will let you see the impact of coupon rates on price volatility. Similarly, buy two bonds with very different maturities but similar coupon rates. You'll see firsthand how maturity determines the risk of a bond.

While you're at it, calculate the durations of the bonds you buy. As their yields fluctuate, check that the percentage change in price is very close to what your calculated duration suggests it should be.

To learn more about bond prices and yields, visit some interesting Web sites such as Bonds Online (www.bondsonline.com), Investing in Bonds (www.investinginbonds.com), and James Baker & Assoc. (www.jamesbaker.com).

Key Terms

callable bond 347
call price 347
call protection period 347
clean price 345
coupon rate 339
current yield 339
dedicated portfolio 358
dirty price 345
dollar value of an 01 357
duration 353

dynamic immunization 363
immunization 361
interest rate risk 349
make-whole call price 347
price risk 361
realized yield 349
reinvestment rate risk 360
yield to call (YTC) 347
yield to maturity (YTM) 340
yield value of a 32nd 357

Chapter Review Problems and Self-Test

1. **Straight Bond Prices (LO1, CFA5)**   Suppose a bond has 10 years to maturity and a coupon rate of 6 percent. The bond's yield to maturity is 8 percent. What's the price?

2. **Premium Bonds (LO1, CFA3)**   Suppose we have two bonds, both with a 6 percent coupon rate and the same yield to maturity of 4 percent, but with different maturities of 5 and 15 years. Which has the higher price? Verify your answer by calculating the prices.

3. **Macaulay Duration (LO4, CFA6)**   A bond has a Macaulay duration of nine years, and its yield increases from 6 percent to 6.25 percent. What will happen to the price of the bond?

Answers to Self-Test Problems

1. Here, the coupon rate is 6 percent and the face value is $1,000, so the annual coupon is $60. The bond's price is calculated as follows:

   Present value of semiannual coupons:

   $$\frac{\$60}{.08}\left[1 - \frac{1}{(1.04)^{20}}\right] = \$407.70979$$

   Present value of $1,000 principal:

   $$\frac{\$1,000}{(1.04)^{20}} = \$456.38695$$

   The bond's price is the sum of coupon and principal present values:

   $$\text{Bond price} = \$407.71 + \$456.39 = \$864.10$$

2. Because both bonds have a 6 percent coupon and a 4 percent yield, both bonds sell at a premium, and the one with the longer maturity will have a higher price. We can verify these conclusions by calculating the prices as follows:

   5-year maturity premium bond price:

   $$\frac{\$60}{.04}\left[1 - \frac{1}{(1.02)^{10}}\right] + \frac{\$1,000}{(1.02)^{10}} = \$1,089.83$$

   15-year maturity premium bond price:

   $$\frac{\$60}{.04}\left[1 - \frac{1}{(1.02)^{30}}\right] + \frac{\$1,000}{(1.02)^{30}} = \$1,223.96$$

   Notice that the longer maturity premium bond has a higher price, just as we thought.

3. The resulting percentage change in the price of the bond can be calculated as follows:

   $$-9 \times \frac{.0625 - .06}{1.03} = -2.18\%$$

   The bond's price declines by approximately 2.18 percent in response to a 25 basis point increase in yields.

Test Your Investment Quotient

1. **Yield to Maturity (LO2, CFA3)**   The yield to maturity on a bond is
   a. Below the coupon rate when the bond sells at a discount and above the coupon rate when the bond sells at a premium.
   b. The interest rate that makes the present value of the payments equal to the bond price.
   c. Based on the assumption that all future payments received are reinvested at the coupon rate.
   d. Based on the assumption that all future payments received are reinvested at future market rates.

2. **Bond Yields (LO1, CFA5)** In which one of the following cases is the bond selling at a discount?

    a. Coupon rate is greater than current yield, which is greater than yield to maturity.
    b. Coupon rate, current yield, and yield to maturity are all the same.
    c. Coupon rate is less than current yield, which is less than yield to maturity.
    d. Coupon rate is less than current yield, which is greater than yield to maturity.

3. **Bond Yields (LO1, CFA3)** When are yield to maturity and current yield on a bond equal?

    a. When market interest rates begin to level off.
    b. If the bond sells at a price in excess of its par value.
    c. When the expected holding period is greater than one year.
    d. If the coupon and market interest rate are equal.

4. **Bond Yields (LO1, CFA5)** Which of the following states the correct relationship among yield measures for discount bonds?

    a. Coupon rate < Current yield < Yield to maturity
    b. Current yield < Coupon rate < Yield to maturity
    c. Coupon rate < Yield to maturity < Current yield
    d. Yield to maturity < Coupon rate < Current yield

5. **Bond Yields (LO1, CFA5)** Which of the following states the correct relationship among yield measures for premium bonds?

    a. Coupon rate > Current yield > Yield to maturity
    b. Current yield > Coupon rate > Yield to maturity
    c. Coupon rate > Yield to maturity > Current yield
    d. Yield to maturity > Coupon rate > Current yield

6. **Bond Prices (LO1, CFA3)** Consider a five-year bond with a 10 percent coupon that is presently trading at a yield to maturity of 8 percent. If market interest rates do not change, one year from now the price of this bond

    a. Will be higher
    b. Will be lower
    c. Will be the same
    d. Cannot be determined

7. **Bond Prices (LO1, CFA2)** Using semiannual compounding, what would the price of a 15-year, zero coupon bond that has a par value of $1,000 and a required return of 8 percent be?

    a. $308
    b. $315
    c. $464
    d. $555

8. **Bond Prices (LO1, CFA2)** If an investor's required return is 12 percent, the value of a 10-year maturity zero coupon bond with a maturity value of $1,000 is *closest* to

    a. $312
    b. $688
    c. $1,000
    d. $1,312

9. **Duration (LO4, CFA3)** Another term for bond duration is

    a. Actual maturity
    b. Effective maturity
    c. Calculated maturity
    d. Near-term maturity

10. **Duration (LO4, CFA6)** Which of the following is not a property of duration?

    a. A longer maturity generally yields a longer duration.
    b. Duration generally increases at a decreasing rate as maturity lengthens.
    c. A bigger coupon generally yields a longer duration.
    d. A higher yield to maturity generally yields a shorter duration.

11. **Duration (LO4, CFA4)** Which statement is true for the Macaulay duration of a zero coupon bond?

    a. It is equal to the bond's maturity in years.
    b. It is equal to one-half the bond's maturity in years.

c. It is equal to the bond's maturity in years divided by its yield to maturity.

d. It cannot be calculated because of the lack of coupons.

12. **Duration (LO4, CFA6)**   Which of the following states the correct relationship between Macaulay duration and modified duration?

a. Modified duration = Macaulay duration/$(1 + YTM/2)$

b. Modified duration = Macaulay duration $\times (1 + YTM/2)$

c. Modified duration = Macaulay duration/YTM

d. Modified duration = Macaulay duration $\times YTM$

13. **Duration (LO4, CFA6)**   Which one of the following bonds has the shortest duration?

a. Zero coupon, 10-year maturity

b. Zero coupon, 13-year maturity

c. 8 percent coupon, 10-year maturity

d. 8 percent coupon, 13-year maturity

14. **Duration (LO4, CFA6)**   Identify the bond that has the longest duration (no calculations necessary).

a. 20-year maturity with an 8 percent coupon

b. 20-year maturity with a 12 percent coupon

c. 15-year maturity with a 0 percent coupon

d. 10-year maturity with a 15 percent coupon

15. **Duration (LO4, CFA3)**   Which bond has the longest duration?

a. 8-year maturity, 6 percent coupon

b. 8-year maturity, 11 percent coupon

c. 15-year maturity, 6 percent coupon

d. 15-year maturity, 11 percent coupon

16. **Duration (LO4, CFA3)**   The duration of a bond normally increases with an increase in

a. Term to maturity

b. Yield to maturity

c. Coupon rate

d. All of the above

17. **Duration (LO4, CFA6)**   When interest rates decline, what happens to the duration of a 30-year bond selling at a premium?

a. It increases

b. It decreases

c. It remains the same

d. It increases at first, then declines

18. **Duration (LO4, CFA6)**   An 8 percent, 20-year corporate bond is priced to yield 9 percent. The Macaulay duration for this bond is 8.85 years. Given this information, how many years is the bond's modified duration?

a. 8.12

b. 8.47

c. 8.51

d. 9.25

19. **Using Duration (LO4, CFA2)**   A 9-year bond has a yield to maturity of 10 percent and a modified duration of 6.54 years. If the market yield changes by 50 basis points, what is the change in the bond's price?

a. 3.27 percent

b. 3.66 percent

c. 6.54 percent

d. 7.21 percent

20. **Using Duration (LO4, CFA3)**   A 6 percent coupon bond paying interest semiannually has a modified duration of 10 years, sells for $800, and is priced at a yield to maturity (YTM) of 8 percent. If the YTM increases to 9 percent, the predicted change in price, using the duration concept, is which of the following amounts?

a. $76.56

b. $76.92

c. $77.67

d. $80.00

21. **Immunization (LO4, CFA7)** Which of the following strategies is most likely to yield the best interest rate risk immunization results for a bond portfolio?

   a. Maturity matching
   b. Duration matching
   c. Buy and hold
   d. Investing in interest rate–sensitive stocks

22. **Immunization (LO4, CFA7)** Consider two dedicated bond portfolios both with the same 10-year target dates. One is managed using a buy-and-hold strategy with reinvested coupons. The other is managed using a dynamic immunization strategy. The buy-and-hold portfolio is most likely to outperform the immunized portfolio under what kind of interest rate environment?

   a. Steadily rising interest rates.
   b. Steadily falling interest rates.
   c. Constant interest rates.
   d. Performance will be the same under any environment.

23. **Bond Yields (LO1, CFA5)** A zero coupon bond paying $100 at maturity 10 years from now has a current price of $50. Its yield to maturity is *closest* to which of the following?

   a. 5 percent
   b. 6 percent
   c. 7 percent
   d. 8 percent

24. **Bond Price (LO1, CFA5)** A newly issued 10-year option-free bond is valued at par on June 1, 2010. The bond has an annual coupon of 8.0 percent. On June 1, 2013, the bond has a yield to maturity of 7.1 percent. The first coupon is reinvested at 8.0 percent and the second coupon is reinvested at 7.0 percent. The price of the bond on June 1, 2013, is closest to

   a. 100.0 percent of par
   b. 102.5 percent of par
   c. 104.8 percent of par
   d. 105.4 percent of par

25. **Interest Rate Risk (LO3, CFA6)** The interest rate risk of a noncallable bond is most likely to be positively related to the

   a. Risk-free rate
   b. Bond's coupon rate
   c. Bond's time to maturity
   d. Bond's yield to maturity

Concept Questions

1. **Bond Prices (LO1, CFA3)** What are premium, discount, and par bonds?

2. **Bond Features (LO1, CFA2)** In the United States, what is the normal face value for corporate and U.S. government bonds? How are coupons calculated? How often are coupons paid?

3. **Coupon Rates and Current Yields (LO1, CFA3)** What are the coupon rate and current yield on a bond? What happens to these if a bond's price rises?

4. **Interest Rate Risk (LO3, CFA4)** What is interest rate risk? What are the roles of a bond's coupon and maturity in determining its level of interest rate risk?

5. **Bond Yields (LO1, CFA2)** For a premium bond, which is greater, the coupon rate or the yield to maturity? Why? For a discount bond? Why?

6. **Bond Yields (LO2, CFA4)** What is the difference between a bond's promised yield and its realized yield? Which is more relevant? When we calculate a bond's yield to maturity, which of these are we calculating?

7. **Interpreting Bond Yields (LO2, CFA3)** Is the yield to maturity (YTM) on a bond the same thing as the required return? Is YTM the same thing as the coupon rate? Suppose that today a 10 percent coupon bond sells at par. Two years from now, the required return on the same bond is 8 percent. What is the coupon rate on the bond now? The YTM?

8. **Interpreting Bond Yields (LO2, CFA3)** Suppose you buy a 9 percent coupon, 15-year bond today when it's first issued. If interest rates suddenly rise to 15 percent, what happens to the value of your bond? Why?

9. **Bond Prices versus Yields (LO1, CFA3)** (a) What is the relationship between the price of a bond and its YTM? (b) Explain why some bonds sell at a premium to par value, and other bonds sell at a discount. What do you know about the relationship between the coupon rate and the YTM for premium bonds? What about discount bonds? For bonds selling at par value? (c) What is the relationship between the current yield and YTM for premium bonds? For discount bonds? For bonds selling at par value?

10. **Yield to Call (LO1, CFA5)** For callable bonds, the financial press generally reports either the yield to maturity or the yield to call. Often yield to call is reported for premium bonds, and yield to maturity is reported for discount bonds. What is the reasoning behind this convention?

Questions and Problems

Core Questions

1. **Bond Prices (LO1, CFA5)** Aloha Inc. has 7 percent coupon bonds on the market that have 12 years left to maturity. If the YTM on these bonds is 9.1 percent, what is the current bond price?

2. **Bond Yields (LO1, CFA2)** Rolling Company bonds have a coupon rate of 6.0 percent, 14 years to maturity, and a current price of $1,086. What is the YTM? The current yield?

3. **Bond Prices (LO1, CFA3)** A bond has a coupon rate of 8.2 percent and 13 years until maturity. If the yield to maturity is 7.4 percent, what is the price of the bond?

4. **Bond Prices (LO1, CFA3)** A bond with 25 years until maturity has a coupon rate of 7.2 percent and a yield to maturity of 8 percent. What is the price of the bond?

5. **Yield to Maturity (LO1, CFA5)** A bond sells for $902.30 and has a coupon rate of 6 percent. If the bond has 12 years until maturity, what is the yield to maturity of the bond?

6. **Yield to Maturity (LO1, CFA5)** A bond with a maturity of 14.5 years sells for $1,047. If the coupon rate is 8.2 percent, what is the yield to maturity of the bond?

7. **Yield to Maturity (LO1, CFA5)** May Industries has a bond outstanding that sells for $928. The bond has a coupon rate of 7.5 percent and nine years until maturity. What is the yield to maturity of the bond?

8. **Yield to Maturity (LO1, CFA5)** Atlantis Fisheries issues zero coupon bonds on the market at a price of $289 per bond. Each bond has a face value of $1,000 payable at maturity in 20 years. What is the yield to maturity for these bonds?

9. **Yield to Call (LO1, CFA5)** Atlantis Fisheries zero coupon bonds referred to above are callable in 10 years at a call price of $500. Using semiannual compounding, what is the yield to call for these bonds?

10. **Yield to Call (LO1, CFA5)** If instead the Atlantis Fisheries zero coupon bonds referred to above are callable in 10 years at a call price of $475, what is their yield to call?

Intermediate Questions

11. **Coupon Rates (LO1, CFA2)** Ghost Rider Corporation has bonds on the market with 10 years to maturity, a YTM of 7.5 percent, and a current price of $938. What must the coupon rate be on the company's bonds?

12. **Bond Prices (LO1, CFA5)** Great Wall Pizzeria issued 10-year bonds one year ago at a coupon rate of 8.40 percent. If the YTM on these bonds is 9.2 percent, what is the current bond price?

13. **Bond Yields (LO1, CFA3)** Soprano's Spaghetti Factory issued 25-year bonds two years ago at a coupon rate of 7.5 percent. If these bonds currently sell for 92 percent of par value, what is the YTM?

14. **Bond Price Movements (LO1, CFA3)** A zero coupon bond with a 6 percent YTM has 20 years to maturity. Two years later, the price of the bond remains the same. What's going on here?

15. **Realized Yield (LO2)** For the bond referred to in the previous question, what would be the realized yield if it were held to maturity?

16. **Bond Price Movements (LO1, CFA5)** Bond P is a premium bond with an 8 percent coupon, a YTM of 6 percent, and 15 years to maturity. Bond D is a discount bond with an 8 percent coupon, a YTM of 10 percent, and also 15 years to maturity. If interest rates remain unchanged, what do you expect the price of these bonds to be 1 year from now? In 5 years? In 10 years? In 14 years? In 15 years? What's going on here?

17. **Interest Rate Risk (LO3, CFA4)** Both bond A and bond B have 6 percent coupons and are priced at par value. Bond A has 5 years to maturity, while bond B has 15 years to maturity. If interest rates suddenly rise by 2 percent, what is the percentage change in price of bond A? Of bond B? If rates were to suddenly fall by 2 percent instead, what would the percentage change in price of bond A be now? Of bond B? Illustrate your answers by graphing bond prices versus YTM. What does this problem tell you about the interest rate risk of longer term bonds?

18. **Interest Rate Risk (LO3, CFA4)** Bond J is a 4 percent coupon bond. Bond K is a 8 percent coupon bond. Both bonds have 10 years to maturity and have a YTM of 7 percent. If interest rates suddenly rise by 2 percent, what is the percentage price change of these bonds? What if rates suddenly fall by 2 percent instead? What does this problem tell you about the interest rate risk of lower coupon bonds?

19. **Finding the Bond Maturity (LO1, CFA2)** LKD Co. has 10 percent coupon bonds with a YTM of 8.6 percent. The current yield on these bonds is 9.2 percent. How many years do these bonds have left until they mature?

20. **Finding the Bond Maturity (LO1, CFA2)** You've just found a 10 percent coupon bond on the market that sells for par value. What is the maturity on this bond?

21. **Realized Yields (LO2)** Suppose you buy a 6 percent coupon bond today for $1,080. The bond has 10 years to maturity. What rate of return do you expect to earn on your investment? Two years from now, the YTM on your bond has increased by 2 percent, and you decide to sell. What price will your bond sell for? What is the realized yield on your investment? Compare this yield to the YTM when you first bought the bond. Why are they different? Assume interest payments are reinvested at the original YTM.

22. **Yield to Call (LO1, CFA3)** Fooling Company has a 10 percent callable bond outstanding on the market with 25 years to maturity, call protection for the next 5 years, and a call premium of $100. What is the yield to call (YTC) for this bond if the current price is 108 percent of par value?

23. **Calculating Duration (LO4, CFA6)** What is the Macaulay duration of a 7 percent coupon bond with six years to maturity and a current price of $935.50? What is the modified duration?

24. **Using Duration (LO4, CFA6)** In the previous problem, suppose the yield on the bond suddenly increases by 2 percent. Use duration to estimate the new price of the bond. Compare your answer to the new bond price calculated from the usual bond pricing formula. What do your results tell you about the accuracy of duration?

25. **Dollar Value of an 01 (LO4, CFA2)** What is the dollar value of an 01 for the bond in Problem 23?

26. **Yield Value of a 32nd (LO4, CFA2)** A Treasury bond with 8 years to maturity is currently quoted at 106:16. The bond has a coupon rate of 7.5 percent. What is the yield value of a 32nd for this bond?

27. **Calculating Duration (LO4, CFA6)** A bond with a coupon rate of 8 percent sells at a yield to maturity of 9 percent. If the bond matures in 11 years, what is the Macaulay duration of the bond? What is the modified duration?

28. **Calculating Duration (LO4, CFA6)** Assume the bond in the previous problem has a yield to maturity of 7 percent. What is the Macaulay duration now? What does this tell you about the relationship between duration and yield to maturity?

29. **Calculating Duration (LO4, CFA6)** You find a bond with 19 years until maturity that has a coupon rate of 8 percent and a yield to maturity of 7 percent. What is the Macaulay duration? The modified duration?

30. **Using Duration (LO4, CFA3)** Suppose the yield to maturity on the bond in the previous problem increases by .25 percent. What is the new price of the bond using duration? What is the new price of the bond using the bond pricing formula? What if the yield to maturity increases by 1 percent? By 2 percent? By 5 percent? What does this tell you about using duration to estimate bond price changes for large interest rate changes?

31. **Bootstrapping (LO1)** One method used to obtain an estimate of the term structure of interest rates is called bootstrapping. Suppose you have a one-year zero coupon bond with a rate of r_1 and a two-year bond with an annual coupon payment of C. To bootstrap the two-year rate, you can set up the following equation for the price (P) of the coupon bond:

$$P = \frac{C_1}{1 + r_1} + \frac{C_2 + \text{Par value}}{(1 + r_2)^2}$$

Because you can observe all of the variables except r_2, the spot rate for two years, you can solve for this interest rate. Suppose there is a zero coupon bond with one year to maturity that sells for $949 and a two-year bond with a 7.5 percent coupon paid annually that sells for $1,020. What is the interest rate for two years? Suppose a bond with three years until maturity and an 8.5 percent annual coupon sells for $1,029. What is the interest rate for three years?

32. **Bootstrapping (LO1)** You find that the one-, two-, three-, and four-year interest rates are 4.2 percent, 4.5 percent, 4.9 percent, and 5.1 percent. What is the yield to maturity of a four-year bond with an annual coupon rate of 6.5 percent? *Hint:* Use the bootstrapping technique in the previous problem to find the price of the bond.

Spreadsheet Problems

33. **Yield to Maturity (LO1, CFA3)** A Treasury bond that settles on August 10, 2010, matures on April 15, 2015. The coupon rate is 6.5 percent and the quoted price is 106:17. What is the bond's yield to maturity? Use an actual day count with 365 days per year.

34. **Bond Yields (LO1, CFA3)** A bond that settles on June 7, 2010, matures on July 1, 2030, and may be called at any time after July 1, 2015, at a price of 108. The coupon rate on the bond is 8 percent and the price is 111.50. What is the yield to maturity and yield to call on this bond? Use the NASD 30/360-day count basis.

35. **Duration (LO4, CFA6)** A Treasury bond that settles on October 18, 2010, matures on March 30, 2029. The coupon rate is 7.8 percent and the bond has a 6.85 yield to maturity. What are the Macaulay duration and modified duration?

CFA Exam Review by Schweser

[CFA3, CFA6, CFA7]

Frank Myers, CFA, is a fixed-income portfolio manager for a large pension fund. A member of the Investment Committee, Fred Spice, is very interested in learning about the management of fixed-income portfolios. Mr. Spice has approached Mr. Myers with several questions.

Mr. Myers has decided to illustrate fixed-income trading strategies using a fixed-rate bond and note. Both bonds have semiannual coupons. Unless otherwise stated, all interest rate changes are parallel. The characteristics of these securities are shown in the table below.

	Fixed-Rate Bond	Fixed-Rate Note
Price	107.18	100.00
Yield to maturity	5.00%	5.00%
Periods to maturity	18	8
Modified duration	6.9848	3.5851

1. Mr. Spice asks Mr. Myers how a fixed-income manager would position his portfolio to capitalize on his expectations of increasing interest rates. Which of the following would be the most appropriate strategy?

   a. Lengthen the portfolio duration.
   b. Buy fixed-rate bonds.
   c. Shorten the portfolio duration.

2. Mr. Spice asks Mr. Myers to quantify the value changes from changes in interest rates. To illustrate, Mr. Myers computes the value change for the fixed-rate note. He assumes an increase in interest rates of 100 basis points. Which of the following is the best estimate of the change in value for the fixed-rate note?

   a. −$7.17
   b. −$3.59
   c. $3.59

3. For an increase of 100 basis points in the yield to maturity, by what amount would the fixed-rate bond's price change?

   a. −$7.49
   b. −$5.73
   c. −$4.63

4. Mr. Spice wonders how a fixed-income manager could position his portfolio to capitalize on the expectation of an upward-shifting and twisting term structure. For the twist, interest rates on long-term bonds increase by more than those on shorter-term notes.

   a. Sell bonds and buy notes.
   b. Buy bonds and sell notes.
   c. Buy both bonds and notes.

What's on the Web?

1. **Bond Markets**   Go to www.bondsonline.com. What is the outlook for the bond market today? What are the major news items today that are expected to influence the bond market?

2. **Government Bonds**   Go to www.bloomberg.com and look up the yields for U.S. government bonds under "Market Data." You should also find a listing for foreign government bonds. Are the yields on all government bonds the same? Why or why not?

PART 4

CHAPTER 11

Diversification and Risky Asset Allocation

Learning Objectives

To get the most out of this chapter, spread your study time across:

1. How to calculate expected returns and variances for a security.

2. How to calculate expected returns and variances for a portfolio.

3. The importance of portfolio diversification.

4. The efficient frontier and the importance of asset allocation.

"It is the part of a wise man not to venture all his eggs in one basket."

–Miguel de Cervantes

Intuitively, we all know that diversification is important for managing investment risk. But how exactly does diversification work, and how can we be sure we have an efficiently diversified portfolio? Insightful answers can be gleaned from the modern theory of diversification and asset allocation. ∎

In this chapter, we examine the role of diversification and asset allocation in investing. Most of us have a strong sense that diversification is important. After all, Don Cervantes's advice against "putting all your eggs in one basket" has become a bit of folk wisdom that seems to have stood the test of time quite well. Even so, the importance of diversification has not always been well understood. Diversification is important because portfolios with many investments usually produce a more consistent and stable total return than portfolios with just one investment. When you own many stocks, even if some of them decline in price, others are likely to increase in price (or stay at the same price).

You might be thinking that a portfolio with only one investment could do very well if you pick the right solitary investment. Indeed, had you decided to hold only Dell stock during the 1990s or shares of Medifast (MED) in the 2000s, your portfolio would have been very profitable. However, which single investment do you make today that will be very profitable in the future? That's the problem. If you pick the wrong one, you could get wiped out. Knowing which

CFA™ Exam Topics in This Chapter:

1 Discounted cash flow applications (L1, S2)
2 Statistical concepts and market returns (L1, S2)
3 Probability concepts (L1, S2)
4 The asset allocation decision (L1, S12)
5 An introduction to portfolio management (L1, S12)
6 Portfolio concepts (L2, S18)
7 Asset allocation (L3, S8)

Go to www.mhhe.com/jmd6e for a guide that aligns your textbook with CFA readings.

investment will perform the best in the future is impossible. Obviously, if we knew, then there would be no risk. Therefore, investment risk plays an important role in portfolio diversification.

The role and impact of diversification on portfolio risk and return were first formally explained in the early 1950s by financial pioneer Harry Markowitz. These aspects of portfolio diversification were an important discovery—Professor Markowitz shared the 1986 Nobel Prize in Economics for his insights on the value of diversification.

Surprisingly, Professor Markowitz's insights are not related to how investors care about risk or return. In fact, we can talk about the benefits of diversification without having to know how investors feel about risk. Realistically, however, it is investors who care about the benefits of diversification. Therefore, to help you understand Professor Markowitz's insights, we make two assumptions. First, we assume that investors prefer more return to less return, and second, we assume that investors prefer less risk to more risk. In this chapter, variance and standard deviation are measures of risk.

11.1 Expected Returns and Variances

In Chapter 1, we discussed how to calculate average returns and variances using historical data. We begin this chapter with a discussion of how to analyze returns and variances when the information we have concerns future returns and their probabilities. We start here because the notion of diversification involves future returns and variances of future returns.

EXPECTED RETURNS

See how traders attempt to profit from expected returns at www.411stocks.com

We start with a straightforward case. Consider a period of time such as a year. We have two stocks, say, Starcents and Jpod. Starcents is expected to have a return of 25 percent in the coming year; Jpod is expected to have a return of 20 percent during the same period.

In a situation such as this, if all investors agreed on these expected return values, why would anyone want to hold Jpod? After all, why invest in one stock when the expectation is that another will do better? Clearly, the answer must depend on the different risks of the two investments. The return on Starcents, although *expected* to be 25 percent, could turn out to be significantly higher or lower. Similarly, Jpod's *realized* return could be significantly higher or lower than expected.

For example, suppose the economy booms. In this case, we think Starcents will have a 70 percent return. But if the economy tanks and enters a recession, we think the return will be –20 percent. In this case, we say that there are *two states of the economy,* which means that there are two possible outcomes. This scenario is oversimplified, of course, but it allows us to illustrate some key ideas without a lot of computational complexity.

Suppose we think boom and recession are equally likely to happen, that is, a 50–50 chance of each outcome. Table 11.1 illustrates the basic information we have described and some additional information about Jpod. Notice that Jpod earns 30 percent if there is a recession and 10 percent if there is a boom.

Obviously, if you buy one of these stocks, say, Jpod, what you earn in any particular year depends on what the economy does during that year. Suppose these probabilities stay the same through time. If you hold Jpod for a number of years, you'll earn 30 percent about half the time and 10 percent the other half. In this case, we say your **expected return** on Jpod, $E(R_J)$, is 20 percent:

expected return
Average return on a risky asset expected in the future.

$$E(R_J) = .50 \times 30\% + .50 \times 10\% = 20\%$$

In other words, you should expect to earn 20 percent from this stock, on average.

For Starcents, the probabilities are the same, but the possible returns are different. Here we lose 20 percent half the time, and we gain 70 percent the other half. The expected return on Starcents, $E(R_S)$, is thus 25 percent:

$$E(R_S) = .50 \times -20\% + .50 \times 70\% = 25\%$$

Table 11.2 illustrates these calculations.

In Chapter 1, we defined a risk premium as the difference between the returns on a risky investment and a risk-free investment, and we calculated the historical risk premiums on

TABLE 11.1

States of the Economy and Stock Returns

State of Economy	Probability of State of Economy	Security Returns If State Occurs	
		Starcents	Jpod
Recession	.50	−20%	30%
Boom	.50	70	10
	1.00		

TABLE 11.2

Calculating Expected Returns

		Starcents		Jpod	
(1) State of Economy	(2) Probability of State of Economy	(3) Return If State Occurs	(4) Product (2) × (3)	(5) Return If State Occurs	(6) Product (2) × (5)
Recession	.50	× −20% =	−10%	30%	15%
Boom	.50	70	35	10	05
	1.00		$E(R_S) = 25\%$		$E(R_J) = 20\%$

some different investments. Using our projected returns, we can calculate the *projected* or *expected risk premium* as the difference between the expected return on a risky investment and the certain return on a risk-free investment.

For example, suppose risk-free investments are currently offering an 8 percent return. We will say that the risk-free rate, which we label R_f, is 8 percent. Given this, what is the projected risk premium on Jpod? On Starcents? Because the expected return on Jpod, $E(R_J)$, is 20 percent, the projected risk premium is:

$$\text{Risk premium} = \text{Expected return} - \text{Risk-free rate} \qquad (11.1)$$
$$= E(R_J) - R_f$$
$$= 20\% - 8\%$$
$$= 12\%$$

Similarly, the risk premium on Starcents is $25\% - 8\% = 17\%$.

In general, the expected return on a security or other asset is simply equal to the sum of the possible returns multiplied by their probabilities. So, if we have 100 possible returns, we would multiply each one by its probability and then add up the results. The sum would be the expected return. The risk premium would then be the difference between this expected return and the risk-free rate.

EXAMPLE 11.1

Unequal Probabilities

Look again at Tables 11.1 and 11.2. Suppose you thought a boom would occur 20 percent of the time instead of 50 percent. What are the expected returns on Starcents and Jpod in this case? If the risk-free rate is 10 percent, what are the risk premiums?

The first thing to notice is that a recession must occur 80 percent of the time $(1 - .20 = .80)$ because there are only two possibilities. With this in mind, Jpod has a 30 percent return in 80 percent of the years and a 10 percent return in 20 percent of the years. To calculate the expected return, we just multiply the possibilities by the probabilities and add up the results:

$$E(R_J) = .80 \times 30\% + .20 \times 10\% = 26\%$$

If the returns are written as decimals:

$$E(R_J) = .80 \times .30 + .20 \times .10 = .26$$

(*continued*)

Table 11.3 summarizes the calculations for both stocks. Notice that the expected return on Starcents is −2 percent.

The risk premium for Jpod is 26% − 10% = 16% in this case. The risk premium for Starcents is negative: −2% − 10% = −12%. This is a little unusual, but, as we will see, it's not impossible.

TABLE 11.3

Calculating Expected Returns

		Starcents		Jpod	
(1)	**(2)**	**(3)**	**(4)**	**(5)**	**(6)**
State of Economy	**Probability of State of Economy**	**Return If State Occurs**	**Product (2) × (3)**	**Return If State Occurs**	**Product (2) × (5)**
Recession	.80	−20%	−16%	30%	24%
Boom	.20	70	14	10	2
	1.00		$E(R_S) = -2\%$		$E(R_J) = 26\%$

CALCULATING THE VARIANCE OF EXPECTED RETURNS

To calculate the variances of the expected returns on our two stocks, we first determine the squared deviations from the expected return. We then multiply each possible squared deviation by its probability. Next we add these up, and the result is the variance.

To illustrate, one of our stocks in Table 11.2, Jpod, has an expected return of 20 percent. In a given year, the return will actually be either 30 percent or 10 percent. The possible deviations are thus 30% − 20% = 10% or 10% − 20% = −10%. In this case, the variance is:

$$\text{Variance} = \sigma^2 = .50 \times (10\%)^2 + .50 \times (-10\%)^2$$
$$= .50 \times (.10)^2 + .50 \times (-.10)^2 = .01$$

WWW

There's more on risk measures at www.investopedia.com and www.teachmefinance.com

Notice that we used decimals to calculate the variance. The standard deviation is the square root of the variance:

$$\text{Standard deviation} = \sigma = \sqrt{.01} = .10 = 10\%$$

Table 11.4 contains the expected return and variance for both stocks. Notice that Starcents has a much larger variance. Starcents has the higher expected return, but Jpod has less risk. You could get a 70 percent return on your investment in Starcents, but you could also lose 20 percent. However, an investment in Jpod will always pay at least 10 percent.

Which of these stocks should you buy? We can't really say; it depends on your personal preferences regarding risk and return. We can be reasonably sure, however, that some investors would prefer one and some would prefer the other.

You've probably noticed that the way we calculated expected returns and variances of expected returns here is somewhat different from the way we calculated returns and variances in Chapter 1 (and, probably, different from the way you learned it in your statistics course). The reason is that we were examining historical returns in Chapter 1, so we estimated the average return and the variance based on some actual events. Here, we have projected *future* returns and their associated probabilities. Therefore, we must calculate expected returns and variances of expected returns.

TABLE 11.4

Expected Returns and Variances

	Starcents	Jpod
Expected return, $E(R)$	.25, or 25%	.20, or 20%
Variance of expected return, σ^2	.2025	.0100
Standard deviation of expected return, σ	.45, or 45%	.10, or 10%

EXAMPLE 11.2

More Unequal Probabilities

Going back to Table 11.3 in Example 11.1, what are the variances on our two stocks once we have unequal probabilities? What are the standard deviations?

Converting all returns to decimals, we can summarize the needed calculations as follows:

(1) State of Economy	(2) Probability of State of Economy	(3) Return Deviation from Expected Return	(4) Squared Return Deviation	(5) Product (2) × (4)
Starcents				
Recession	.80	$-.20 - (-.02) = -.18$	.0324	.02592
Boom	.20	$.70 - (-.02) = .72$	.5184	.10368
				$\sigma_S^2 = .12960$
Jpod				
Recession	.80	$.30 - .26 = .04$	.0016	.00128
Boom	.20	$.10 - .26 = -.16$	.0256	.00512
				$\sigma_J^2 = .00640$

Based on these calculations, the standard deviation for Starcents is $\sigma_S = \sqrt{.1296} = 36\%$. The standard deviation for Jpod is much smaller, $\sigma_J = \sqrt{.0064}$, or 8%.

CHECK THIS

11.1a   How do we calculate the expected return on a security?

11.1b   In words, how do we calculate the variance of an expected return?

11.2 Portfolios

portfolio

Group of assets such as stocks and bonds held by an investor.

Thus far in this chapter, we have concentrated on individual assets considered separately. However, most investors actually hold a **portfolio** of assets. All we mean by this is that investors tend to own more than just a single stock, bond, or other asset. Given that this is so, portfolio return and portfolio risk are of obvious relevance. Accordingly, we now discuss portfolio expected returns and variances.

PORTFOLIO WEIGHTS

There are many equivalent ways of describing a portfolio. The most convenient approach is to list the percentages of the total portfolio's value that are invested in each portfolio asset. We call these percentages the **portfolio weights**.

portfolio weight

Percentage of a portfolio's total value invested in a particular asset.

For example, if we have $50 in one asset and $150 in another, then our total portfolio is worth $200. The percentage of our portfolio in the first asset is $50/$200 = .25, or 25%. The percentage of our portfolio in the second asset is $150/$200 = .75, or 75%. Notice that the weights sum up to 1.00 (100%) because all of our money is invested somewhere.[1]

PORTFOLIO EXPECTED RETURNS

Let's go back to Starcents and Jpod. You put half your money in each. The portfolio weights are obviously .50 and .50. What is the pattern of returns on this portfolio? The expected return?

---

[1] Some of it could be in cash, of course, but we would then just consider cash to be another of the portfolio assets.

TABLE 11.5

Expected Portfolio Return

(1) State of Economy	(2) Probability of State of Economy	(3) Portfolio Return If State Occurs	(4) Product (2) × (3)
Recession	.50	.50 × −20% + .50 × 30% = 5%	2.5
Boom	.50	.50 × 70% + .50 × 10% = 40%	20.0
			$E(R_p) = 22.5\%$

To answer these questions, suppose the economy actually enters a recession. In this case, half your money (the half in Starcents) loses 20 percent. The other half (the half in Jpod) gains 30 percent. Your portfolio return, R_p, in a recession will thus be:

$$R_p = .50 \times -20\% + .50 \times 30\% = 5\%$$

Table 11.5 summarizes the remaining calculations. Notice that when a boom occurs, your portfolio would return 40 percent:

$$R_p = .50 \times 70\% + .50 \times 10\% = 40\%$$

As indicated in Table 11.5, the expected return on your portfolio, $E(R_p)$, is 22.5 percent.

We can save ourselves some work by calculating the expected return more directly. Given these portfolio weights, we could have reasoned that we expect half of our money to earn 25 percent (the half in Starcents) and half of our money to earn 20 percent (the half in Jpod). Our portfolio expected return is thus:

$$E(R_p) = .50 \times E(R_S) + .50 \times E(R_J)$$
$$= .50 \times 25\% + .50 \times 20\%$$
$$= 22.5\%$$

This is the same portfolio return that we calculated in Table 11.5.

This method to calculate the expected return on a portfolio works no matter how many assets are in the portfolio. Suppose we had n assets in our portfolio, where n is any number at all. If we let x_i stand for the percentage of our money in Asset i, then the expected return is:

$$E(R_p) = x_1 \times E(R_1) + x_2 \times E(R_2) + \cdots + x_n \times E(R_n) \tag{11.2}$$

Equation (11.2) says that the expected return on a portfolio is a straightforward combination of the expected returns on the assets in that portfolio. This result seems somewhat obvious, but, as we will examine next, the obvious approach is not always the right one.

EXAMPLE 11.3

More Unequal Probabilities

Suppose we had the following projections on three stocks:

State of Economy	Probability of State of Economy	Returns Stock A	Returns Stock B	Returns Stock C
Boom	.50	10%	15%	20%
Bust	.50	8%	4%	0%

We want to calculate portfolio expected returns in two cases. First, what would be the expected return on a portfolio with equal amounts invested in each of the three stocks? Second, what would be the expected return if half of the portfolio were in A, with the remainder equally divided between B and C?

(continued)

From our earlier discussion, the expected returns on the individual stocks are:

$$E(R_A) = 9.0\% \quad E(R_B) = 9.5\% \quad E(R_C) = 10.0\%$$

(Check these for practice.) If a portfolio has equal investments in each asset, the portfolio weights are all the same. Such a portfolio is said to be *equally weighted.* Since there are three stocks in this case, the weights are all equal to 1/3. The portfolio expected return is thus:

$$E(R_P) = 1/3 \times 9.0\% + 1/3 \times 9.5\% + 1/3 \times 10.0\% = 9.5\%$$

In the second case, check that the portfolio expected return is 9.375%.

PORTFOLIO VARIANCE OF EXPECTED RETURNS

From the preceding discussion, the expected return on a portfolio that contains equal investments in Starcents and Jpod is 22.5 percent. What is the standard deviation of return on this portfolio? Simple intuition might suggest that half of our money has a standard deviation of 45 percent, and the other half has a standard deviation of 10 percent. So the portfolio's standard deviation might be calculated as follows:

$$\sigma_P = .50 \times 45\% + .50 \times 10\% = 27.5\%$$

Unfortunately, this approach is *completely incorrect!*

Let's see what the standard deviation really is. Table 11.6 summarizes the relevant calculations. As we see, the portfolio's standard deviation is much less than 27.5 percent—it's only 17.5 percent. What is illustrated here is that the variance on a portfolio is *not* generally a simple combination of the variances of the assets in the portfolio.

We can illustrate this point a little more dramatically by considering a slightly different set of portfolio weights. Suppose we put 2/11 (about 18 percent) in Starcents and the other 9/11 (about 82 percent) in Jpod. If a recession occurs, this portfolio will have a return of:

$$R_P = 2/11 \times -20\% + 9/11 \times 30\% = 20.91\%$$

If a boom occurs, this portfolio will have a return of:

$$R_P = 2/11 \times 70\% + 9/11 \times 10\% = 20.91\%$$

Notice that the return is the same no matter what happens. No further calculation is needed: This portfolio has a *zero* variance and no risk!

This portfolio is a nice bit of financial alchemy. We take two quite risky assets and, by mixing them just right, we create a riskless portfolio. It seems very clear that combining assets into portfolios can substantially alter the risks faced by an investor. This observation is crucial. We will begin to explore its implications in the next section.[2]

---

[2] Earlier, we had a risk-free rate of 8 percent. Now we have, in effect, a 20.91 percent risk-free rate. If this situation actually existed, there would be a very profitable opportunity! In reality, we expect that all riskless investments would have the same return.

| TABLE 11.6 | Calculating Portfolio Variance and Standard Deviation |

(1) State of Economy	(2) Probability of State of Economy	(3) Portfolio Returns If State Occurs	(4) Squared Deviation from Expected Return*	(5) Product (2) × (4)
Recession	.50	5%	$(5 - 22.5)^2 = 306.25$	153.125
Boom	.50	40	$(40 - 22.5)^2 = 306.25$	153.125
			Variance, $\sigma_P^2 = 306.25$	
			Standard deviation, $\sigma_P = \sqrt{306.25} = 17.5\%$	

* Notice that we used percents for all returns. Verify that if we wrote returns as decimals, we would get a variance of .030625 and a standard deviation of .175, or 17.5%.

EXAMPLE 11.4

Portfolio Variance and Standard Deviations

In Example 11.3, what are the standard deviations of the two portfolios?

To answer, we first have to calculate the portfolio returns in the two states. We will work with the second portfolio, which has 50 percent in Stock A and 25 percent in each of stocks B and C. The relevant calculations are summarized as follows:

State of Economy	Probability of State of Economy	Returns			
		Stock A	Stock B	Stock C	Portfolio
Boom	.50	10%	15%	20%	13.75%
Bust	.50	8	4	0	5.00

The portfolio return when the economy booms is calculated as:

$$R_p = .50 \times 10\% + .25 \times 15\% + .25 \times 20\% = 13.75\%$$

The return when the economy goes bust is calculated the same way. Check that it's 5 percent and also check that the expected return on the portfolio is 9.375 percent. Expressing returns in decimals, the variance is thus:

$$\sigma_p^2 = .50 \times (.1375 - .09375)^2 + .50 \times (.05 - .09375)^2 = .0019141$$

The standard deviation is:

$$\sigma_p = \sqrt{.0019141} = .04375, \text{ or } 4.375\%$$

Check: Using equal weights, verify that the portfolio standard deviation is 5.5 percent.

Note: If the standard deviation is 4.375 percent, the variance should be somewhere between 16 and 25 (the squares of 4 and 5, respectively). If we square 4.375, we get 19.141. To express a variance in percentage, we must move the decimal *four* places to the right. That is, we must multiply .0019141 by 10,000—which is the square of 100.

CHECK THIS

11.2a What is a portfolio weight?

11.2b How do we calculate the variance of an expected return?

11.3 Diversification and Portfolio Risk

Our discussion to this point has focused on some hypothetical securities. We've seen that portfolio risks can, in principle, be quite different from the risks of the assets that make up the portfolio. We now look more closely at the risk of an individual asset versus the risk of a portfolio of many different assets. As we did in Chapter 1, we will examine some stock market history to get an idea of what happens with actual investments in U.S. capital markets.

THE EFFECT OF DIVERSIFICATION: ANOTHER LESSON FROM MARKET HISTORY

In Chapter 1, we saw that the standard deviation of the annual return on a portfolio of large-company common stocks was about 20 percent per year. Does this mean that the standard deviation of the annual return on a typical stock in that group is about 20 percent? As you might suspect by now, the answer is no. This observation is extremely important.

To examine the relationship between portfolio size and portfolio risk, Table 11.7 illustrates typical average annual standard deviations for equally weighted portfolios that contain different numbers of randomly selected NYSE securities.

TABLE 11.7

Portfolio Standard Deviations

(1) Number of Stocks in Portfolio	(2) Average Standard Deviation of Annual Portfolio Returns	(3) Ratio of Portfolio Standard Deviation to Standard Deviation of a Single Stock
1	49.24%	1.00
2	37.36	.76
4	29.69	.60
6	26.64	.54
8	24.98	.51
10	23.93	.49
20	21.68	.44
30	20.87	.42
40	20.46	.42
50	20.20	.41
100	19.69	.40
200	19.42	.39
300	19.34	.39
400	19.29	.39
500	19.27	.39
1,000	19.21	.39

Source: These figures are from Table 1 in Meir Statman, "How Many Stocks Make a Diversified Portfolio?" *Journal of Financial and Quantitative Analysis* 22 (September 1987), pp. 353–64. They were derived from E. J. Elton and M. J. Gruber, "Risk Reduction and Portfolio Size: An Analytic Solution," *Journal of Business* 50 (October 1977), pp. 415–37.

In column 2 of Table 11.7, we see that the standard deviation for a "portfolio" of one security is just under 50 percent per year at 49.24 percent. What this means is that if you randomly select a single NYSE stock and put all your money into it, your standard deviation of return would typically have been about 50 percent per year. Obviously, such a strategy has significant risk! If you were to randomly select two NYSE securities and put half your money in each, your average annual standard deviation would have been about 37 percent.

The important thing to notice in Table 11.7 is that the standard deviation declines as the number of securities is increased. By the time we have 100 randomly chosen stocks (and 1 percent invested in each), the portfolio's volatility has declined by 60 percent, from 50 percent per year to 20 percent per year. With 500 securities, the standard deviation is 19.27 percent per year, similar to the 20 percent per year we saw in Chapter 1 for large-company common stocks. The small difference exists because the portfolio securities, portfolio weights, and the time periods covered are not identical.

An important foundation of the diversification effect is the random selection of stocks. When stocks are chosen at random, the resulting portfolio represents different sectors, market caps, and other features. Consider what would happen, however, if you formed a portfolio of 30 stocks, but all were technology companies. In this case, you might think you have a diversified portfolio. But because all these stocks have similar characteristics, you are actually close to "having all your eggs in one basket."

Similarly, during times of extreme market stress, such as the Crash of 2008, many seemingly unrelated asset categories tend to move together—down. Thus, diversification, although generally a good thing, doesn't always work as we might hope. We discuss other elements of diversification in more detail in a later section. For now, read the nearby *Investment Updates* box for another perspective on this fundamental investment issue.

BACK TO THE DRAWING BOARD

The recent financial crisis has all but torn up the investment rule book—received wisdoms have been found wanting if not plain wrong.

Investors are being forced to decide whether the theoretical foundations upon which their portfolios are constructed need to be repaired or abandoned. Some are questioning the wisdom of investing in public markets at all.

Many professional investors have traditionally used a technique known as modern portfolio theory to help decide which assets they should put money in. This approach examines the past returns and volatility of various asset classes and also looks at their correlation—how they perform in relation to each other. From these numbers wealth managers calculate the optimum percentage of a portfolio that should be invested in each asset class to achieve an expected rate of return for a given level of risk.

It is a relatively neat construct. But it has its problems. One is that past figures for risk, return and correlation are not always a good guide to the future. In fact, they may be downright misleading. "These aren't natural sciences we're dealing with," says Kevin Gardiner, head of investment strategy for Europe, the Middle East and Africa at Barclays Wealth in London. "It's very difficult to establish underlying models and correlations. And even if you can establish those, it's extremely difficult to treat them with any confidence on a forward-looking basis."

Modern portfolio theory assumes that diversification always reduces risk—and because of this, diversification is often described as the only free lunch in finance. But Lionel Martellini, professor of finance at Edhec Business School in Nice, believes that this isn't always true. "Modern portfolio theory focuses on diversifying your risk away," he says. "But the crisis has shown the limits of the approach. The concept of risk diversification is okay in normal times, but not during times of extreme market moves."

Wealth investors are beginning to question the usefulness of an approach that doesn't always work, especially if they can't tell when it is going to give up the ghost. So what are the alternatives? On what new foundations should investors be looking to construct their portfolios?

There are two schools of thought and, unhelpfully, they are diametrically opposed. On the one hand, there are those that suggest investors need to accept the limits of mathematical models and should adopt a more intuitive, less scientific approach. On the other hand, there are those who say that there is nothing wrong with mathematical models per se. It is just that they need to be refined and improved.

Mr. Gardiner is in the former camp. "It's not that there's a new model or set of theories to be discovered," he says. "There is no underlying model or structure that defines the way financial markets and economics works. There is no stability out there. All you can hope to do is establish one or two rules of thumb that perhaps work most of the time."

He argues that investment models can not only lead investors to make mistakes, they can lead lots of investors to make the same mistakes at the same time, which exacerbates the underlying problems.

Prof. Martellini, however, believes more complex models can offer investors a sound basis for portfolio construction. Last September, he and fellow Edhec academics published a paper describing a new portfolio construction system, which Prof. Martellini contends will be a great improvement on modern portfolio theory. It relies on combining three investment principles already in use by large institutional investors and applying them to private client portfolios. Crucially, this approach has a different outcome for each individual investor, and therefore does not result in a plethora of virtually identical portfolios. Prof. Martellini says: "These three principles go beyond modern portfolio theory, and if they are implemented would make private investment portfolios behave much better."

The first principle is known as liability-driven investment. With this approach, investors make asset allocations that give the best chance of meeting their own unique future financial commitments, rather than simply trying to maximize risk-adjusted returns.

Modern portfolio theory is founded on the premise that cash is a risk-free asset. But if the investor knows, say, that he or she wants to buy a property in five years' time, then an asset would have to be correlated with real-estate prices to reduce risk for them.

The second principle is called life-cycle investing. This takes account of the investor's specific time horizons, something which modern portfolio theory doesn't cater for. The final part of the puzzle involves controlling the overall risk of the client's investments to make sure it is in line with their risk appetite—this is called risk-controlled investing.

There is also a third option to choosing a more discretionary approach to investment or looking to improve investment models: to shun the markets altogether. Edward Bonham Carter, chief executive of Jupiter Investment Management Group, believes that, rather than a bull or bear market, we are currently experiencing a "hippo" market.

Hippos spend long periods almost motionless in rivers and lakes. But when disturbed, they can lash out, maiming anything in reach. Nervous of this beast, wealthy investors are starting to back away from publicly quoted instruments whose prices are thrashing around wildly. David Scott, founder of Vestra Wealth, says: "I would say half my wealthier clients are more interested in building their businesses than playing the market."

Source: John Ferry and Mike Foster, *The Wall Street Journal*, November 17, 2009. Reprinted with permission of *The Wall Street Journal*. © 2009 Dow Jones & Company, Inc. All Rights Reserved Worldwide.

FIGURE 11.1   Portfolio Diversification

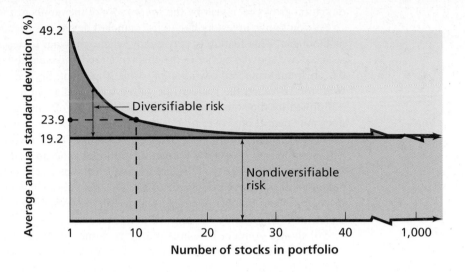

THE PRINCIPLE OF DIVERSIFICATION

Figure 11.1 illustrates the point we've been discussing. What we have plotted is the standard deviation of the return versus the number of stocks in the portfolio. Notice in Figure 11.1 that the benefit in terms of risk reduction from adding securities drops off as we add more and more. By the time we have 10 securities, most of the diversification effect is already realized, and by the time we get to 30 or so, there is very little remaining benefit.

The diversification benefit does depend on the time period over which returns and variances are calculated. For example, the data in Table 11.7 precede 1987. Scholars recently revisited diversification benefits by looking at stock returns and variances from 1986 to 1997 and found that 50 stocks were needed to build a highly diversified portfolio in this time period. The point is that investors should be thinking in terms of 30 to 50 individual stocks when they are building a diversified portfolio.

Figure 11.1 illustrates two key points. First, some of the riskiness associated with individual assets can be eliminated by forming portfolios. The process of spreading an investment across assets (and thereby forming a portfolio) is called *diversification*. The **principle of diversification** tells us that spreading an investment across many assets will eliminate some of the risk. Not surprisingly, risks that can be eliminated by diversification are called "diversifiable" risks.

The second point is equally important. There is a minimum level of risk that cannot be eliminated by simply diversifying. This minimum level is labeled "nondiversifiable risk" in Figure 11.1. Taken together, these two points are another important lesson from financial market history: Diversification reduces risk, but only up to a point. Put another way, some risk is diversifiable and some is not.

principle of diversification

Spreading an investment across a number of assets will eliminate some, but not all, of the risk.

THE FALLACY OF TIME DIVERSIFICATION

Has anyone ever told you, "You're young, so you should have a large amount of equity (or other risky assets) in your portfolio"? While this advice could be true, the argument frequently used to support this strategy is generally incorrect. In particular, the common argument goes something like this: Although stocks are more volatile in any given year, over time this volatility cancels itself out. Although this argument sounds logical, it is incorrect. Investment professionals refer to this flawed logic as the *time diversification fallacy*.

How can such logical-sounding advice be so faulty? Consider the following line of reasoning. You might (or might not) remember from your statistics class that we can add variances together. This fact means that an annual variance grows each year by multiplying the annual variance by the number of years. Standard deviations cannot be added together. Because the standard deviation is the square root of the variance, however, an annual standard deviation grows each year by the *square root* of the number of years.

As you know, investors like to use standard deviations because they have the same units as the mean. This feature is very handy when you want to describe investment returns and risks. As we showed earlier in the chapter, a randomly selected portfolio of large-cap stocks has an annual standard deviation of about 20 percent. So, for example, if we held this portfolio for 16 years, the standard deviation would be about 80 percent, which is 20 percent multiplied by the square root of 16. Bottom line: Volatility increases over time—volatility does not "cancel out" over time.

Take a look at Figure 11.2. The figure examines the growth in a $1,000 investment over a 40-year period. It assumes that returns follow a random walk, but that the overall average will be consistent with the return of the S&P 500. The figure suggests that while investing in equity gives you a greater chance of having a portfolio with an extremely large value, it also increases the probability of ending with a really low value. By definition, this is volatility—a wider range of possible outcomes, that is, more risk.

So, should younger investors put more money in equity? The answer is probably still yes—but for logically sound reasons that differ from the reasoning underlying the fallacy of time diversification. If you are young and your portfolio suffers a steep decline in a particular year, what could you do? You could make up for this loss by changing your work habits (e.g., your type of job, hours, second job). People approaching retirement

| FIGURE 11.2 | S&P 500 Random Walk Model—Risk and Return |

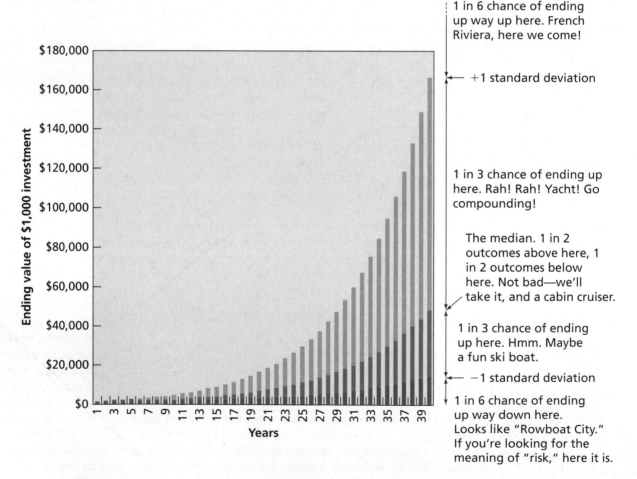

Source: http://homepage.mac.com/j.norstad. Used with permission.

have little future earning power, so a major loss in their portfolio will have a much greater impact on their wealth. Thus, the portfolios of young people should contain relatively more equity (i.e., risk).

CHECK THIS

11.3a What happens to the standard deviation of return for a portfolio if we increase the number of securities in the portfolio?

11.3b What is the principle of diversification?

11.3c What is the time diversification fallacy?

11.4 Correlation and Diversification

We've seen that diversification is important. What we haven't discussed is how to get the most out of diversification. For example, in our previous section, we investigated what happens if we simply spread our money evenly across randomly chosen stocks. We saw that significant risk reduction resulted from this strategy, but you might wonder whether even larger gains could be achieved by a more sophisticated approach. As we begin to examine that question here, the answer is yes.

WHY DIVERSIFICATION WORKS

correlation

The tendency of the returns on two assets to move together.

Why diversification reduces portfolio risk as measured by the portfolio's standard deviation is important and worth exploring in some detail. The key concept is **correlation**, which is the extent to which the returns on two assets move together. If the returns on two assets tend to move up and down together, we say they are *positively* correlated. If they tend to move in opposite directions, we say they are *negatively* correlated. If there is no particular relationship between the two assets, we say they are *uncorrelated*.

Measure portfolio diversification using Instant X-ray at www.morningstar.com (use the search feature)

The *correlation coefficient*, which we use to measure correlation, ranges from -1 to $+1$, and we will denote the correlation between the returns on two assets, say A and B, as $\text{Corr}(R_A, R_B)$. The Greek letter ρ (rho) is often used to designate correlation as well. A correlation of $+1$ indicates that the two assets have a *perfect* positive correlation. For example, suppose that whatever return Asset A realizes, either up or down, Asset B does the same thing by exactly twice as much. In this case, they are perfectly correlated because the movement on one is completely predictable from the movement on the other. Notice, however, that perfect correlation does not necessarily mean they move by the same amount.

A zero correlation means that the two assets are uncorrelated. If we know that one asset is up, then we have no idea what the other one is likely to do; there simply is no relation between them. Perfect negative correlation [$\text{Corr}(R_A, R_B) = -1$] indicates that they always move in opposite directions. Figure 11.3 illustrates the three benchmark cases of perfect positive, perfect negative, and zero correlation.

Diversification works because security returns are generally not perfectly correlated. We will be more precise about the impact of correlation on portfolio risk in just a moment. For now, it is useful to simply think about combining two assets into a portfolio. If the two assets are highly positively correlated (the correlation is near $+1$), then they have a strong tendency to move up and down together. As a result, they offer limited diversification benefit. For example, two stocks from the same industry, say, General Motors and Ford, will tend to be relatively highly correlated because the companies are in essentially the same business, and a portfolio of two such stocks is not likely to be very diversified.

In contrast, if the two assets are negatively correlated, then they tend to move in opposite directions; whenever one zigs, the other tends to zag. In such a case, the diversification benefit will be substantial because variation in the return on one asset tends to be offset by variation in the opposite direction from the other. In fact, if two assets have a perfect

FIGURE 11.3   Correlations

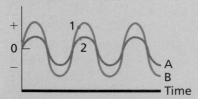

Perfect positive correlation
Corr $(R_A, R_B) = +1$

Both the return on Security A and the return on Security B are higher than average at the same time. Both the return on Security A and the return on Security B are lower than average at the same time.

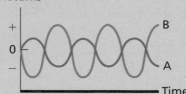

Perfect negative correlation
Corr $(R_A, R_B) = -1$

Security A has a higher-than-average return when Security B has a lower-than-average return, and vice versa.

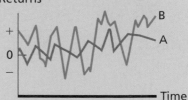

Zero correlation
Corr $(R_A, R_B) = 0$

The return on Security A is completely unrelated to the return on Security B.

negative correlation [Corr(R_A, R_B) = −1], then it is possible to combine them such that all risk is eliminated. Looking back at our example involving Jpod and Starcents in which we were able to eliminate all of the risk, what we now see is that they must be perfectly negatively correlated.

To illustrate the impact of diversification on portfolio risk further, suppose we observed the actual annual returns on two stocks, A and B, for the years 2006–2010. We summarize these returns in Table 11.8. In addition to actual returns on stocks A and B, we also calculated the returns on an equally weighted portfolio of A and B in Table 11.8. We label this portfolio as AB. In 2006, for example, Stock A returned 10 percent and Stock B returned 15 percent. Because Portfolio AB is half invested in each, its return for the year was:

$$1/2 \times 10\% + 1/2 \times 15\% = 12.5\%$$

The returns for the other years are calculated similarly.

At the bottom of Table 11.8, we calculated the average returns and standard deviations on the two stocks and the equally weighted portfolio. These averages and standard deviations are calculated just as they were in Chapter 1 (check a couple just to refresh your memory). The impact of diversification is apparent. The two stocks have standard deviations in the 13 percent to 14 percent per year range, but the portfolio's volatility is only 2.2 percent. In fact, if we compare the portfolio to Stock A, it has a higher return (11 percent vs. 9 percent) and much less risk.

Figure 11.4 illustrates in more detail what is occurring with our example. Here we have three bar graphs showing the year-by-year returns on Stocks A and B and Portfolio AB.

TABLE 11.8   Annual Returns on Stocks A and B

Year	Stock A	Stock B	Portfolio AB
2006	10%	15%	12.5%
2007	30	−10	10.0
2008	−10	25	7.5
2009	5	20	12.5
2010	10	15	12.5
Average returns	9	13	11.0
Standard deviations	14.3	13.5	2.2

FIGURE 11.4 Imapact of Diversification

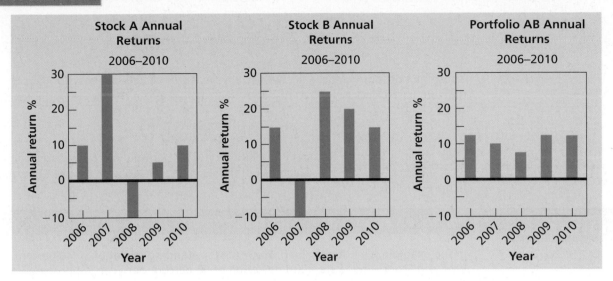

Examining the graphs, we see that in 2007, for example, Stock A earned 30 percent while Stock B lost 10 percent. The following year, Stock B earned 25 percent, while A lost 10 percent. These ups and downs tend to cancel out in our portfolio, however, with the result that there is much less variation in return from year to year. In other words, the correlation between the returns on stocks A and B is relatively low.

Calculating the correlation between stocks A and B is not difficult, but it would require us to digress a bit. Instead, we will explain the needed calculation in the next chapter, where we build on the principles developed here.

CALCULATING PORTFOLIO RISK

We've seen that correlation is an important determinant of portfolio risk. To further pursue this issue, we need to know how to calculate portfolio variances directly. For a portfolio of two assets, A and B, the variance of the return on the portfolio, σ_P^2, is given by equation (11.3):

$$\sigma_P^2 = x_A^2 \sigma_A^2 + x_B^2 \sigma_B^2 + 2x_A x_B \sigma_A \sigma_B \text{Corr}(R_A, R_B) \tag{11.3}$$

In this equation, x_A and x_B are the percentages invested in assets A and B. Notice that $x_A + x_B = 1$. (Why?)

For a portfolio of three assets, the variance of the return on the portfolio, σ_P^2, is given by equation (11.4):

$$\sigma_P^2 = x_A^2 \sigma_A^2 + x_B^2 \sigma_B^2 + x_C^2 \sigma_C^2 + 2x_A x_B \sigma_A \sigma_B \text{Corr}(R_A, R_B) \\ + 2x_A x_C \sigma_A \sigma_C \text{Corr}(R_A, R_C) + 2x_B x_C \sigma_B \sigma_C \text{Corr}(R_B, R_C) \tag{11.4}$$

Note that six terms appear in equation (11.4). There is a term involving the squared weight and the variance of the return for each of the three assets (A, B, and C) as well as a *cross-term* for each pair of assets. The cross-term involves pairs of weights, pairs of standard deviations of returns for each asset, and the correlation between the returns of the asset pair. If you had a portfolio of six assets, you would have an equation with 21 terms. (Can you write this equation?) If you had a portfolio of 50 assets, the equation for the variance of this portfolio would have 1,275 terms! Let's return to equation (11.3).

Equation (11.3) looks a little involved, but its use is straightforward. For example, suppose Stock A has a standard deviation of 40 percent per year and Stock B has a standard deviation of 60 percent per year. The correlation between them is .15. If you put half your money in each, what is your portfolio standard deviation?

To answer, we just plug the numbers into equation (11.3). Note that x_A and x_B are each equal to .50, while σ_A and σ_B are .40 and .60, respectively. Taking $\text{Corr}(R_A, R_B) = .15$, we have:

$$\sigma_P^2 = .50^2 \times .40^2 + .50^2 \times .60^2 + 2 \times .50 \times .50 \times .40 \times .60 \times .15$$
$$= .25 \times .16 + .25 \times .36 + .018$$
$$= .148$$

Thus, the portfolio variance is .148. As always, variances are not easy to interpret since they are based on squared returns, so we calculate the standard deviation by taking the square root:

$$\sigma_P = \sqrt{.148} = .3847 = 38.47\%$$

Once again, we see the impact of diversification. This portfolio has a standard deviation of 38.47 percent, which is less than either of the standard deviations on the two assets that are in the portfolio.

EXAMPLE 11.5 — Portfolio Variance and Standard Deviation

In the example we just examined, Stock A has a standard deviation of 40 percent per year and Stock B has a standard deviation of 60 percent per year. Suppose now that the correlation between them is .35. Also suppose you put one-fourth of your money in Stock A. What is your portfolio standard deviation?

If you put 1/4 (or .25) in Stock A, you must have 3/4 (or .75) in Stock B, so $x_A = .25$ and $x_B = .75$. Making use of our portfolio variance equation (11.3), we have:

$$\sigma_P^2 = .25^2 \times .40^2 + .75^2 \times .60^2 + 2 \times .25 \times .75 \times .40 \times .60 \times .35$$
$$= .0625 \times .16 + .5625 \times .36 + .0315$$
$$= .244$$

Thus the portfolio variance is .244. Taking the square root, we get:

$$\sigma_P = \sqrt{.244} = .49396 \approx 49\%$$

This portfolio has a standard deviation of 49 percent, which is between the individual standard deviations. This shows that a portfolio's standard deviation isn't necessarily less than the individual standard deviations.

The impact of correlation in determining the overall risk of a portfolio has significant implications. For example, consider an investment in international equity. Historically, this sector has had slightly lower returns than large-cap U.S. equity, but the international equity volatility has been much higher.

If investors prefer more return to less return, and less risk to more risk, why would anyone allocate funds to international equity? The answer lies in the fact that the correlation of international equity to U.S. equity is not close to $+1$. Although international equity is quite risky by itself, adding international equity to an existing portfolio of U.S. investments can reduce risk. In fact, as we discuss in the next section, adding the international equity could actually make our portfolio have a better return-to-risk (or more efficient) profile.

Another important point about international equity and correlations is that correlations are not constant over time. Investors expect to receive significant diversification benefits from international equity, but if correlations increase, much of the benefit will be lost. When does this happen? Well, in the Crash of 2008, correlations across markets increased significantly, as all asset classes (with the exception of short-term government debt) declined in value. As investors, we must be mindful of the differences between expected and actual outcomes—particularly during crashes and bear markets.

THE IMPORTANCE OF ASSET ALLOCATION, PART 1

asset allocation
How an investor spreads portfolio dollars among assets.

Why are correlation and **asset allocation** important, practical, real-world considerations? Well, suppose that as a very conservative, risk-averse investor, you decide to invest all of your money in a bond mutual fund. Based on your analysis, you think this fund has an

TABLE 11.9

Risk and Return with Stocks and Bonds

Portfolio Weights		Expected Return	Standard Deviation (Risk)
Stocks	Bonds		
1.00	.00	12.00%	15.00%
.95	.05	11.70	14.31
.90	.10	11.40	13.64
.85	.15	11.10	12.99
.80	.20	10.80	12.36
.75	.25	10.50	11.77
.70	.30	10.20	11.20
.65	.35	9.90	10.68
.60	.40	9.60	10.21
.55	.45	9.30	9.78
.50	.50	9.00	9.42
.45	.55	8.70	9.12
.40	.60	8.40	8.90
.35	.65	8.10	8.75
.30	.70	7.80	8.69
.25	.75	7.50	8.71
.20	.80	7.20	8.82
.15	.85	6.90	9.01
.10	.90	6.60	9.27
.05	.95	6.30	9.60
.00	1.00	6.00	10.00

expected return of 6 percent with a standard deviation of 10 percent per year. A stock fund is available, however, with an expected return of 12 percent, but the standard deviation of 15 percent is too high for your taste. Also, the correlation between the returns on the two funds is about .10.

Is the decision to invest 100 percent in the bond fund a wise one, even for a very risk-averse investor? The answer is no; in fact, it is a bad decision for any investor. To see why, Table 11.9 shows expected returns and standard deviations available from different combinations of the two mutual funds. In constructing the table, we begin with 100 percent in the stock fund and work our way down to 100 percent in the bond fund by reducing the percentage in the stock fund in increments of .05. These calculations are all done just like our examples just above; you should check some (or all) of them for practice.

Beginning on the first row in Table 11.9, we have 100 percent in the stock fund, so our expected return is 12 percent, and our standard deviation is 15 percent. As we begin to move out of the stock fund and into the bond fund, we are not surprised to see both the expected return and the standard deviation decline. However, what might be surprising to you is the fact that the standard deviation falls only so far and then begins to rise again. In other words, beyond a point, adding more of the lower risk bond fund actually *increases* your risk!

The best way to see what is going on is to plot the various combinations of expected returns and standard deviations calculated in Table 11.9 as we do in Figure 11.5. We simply placed the standard deviations from Table 11.9 on the horizontal axis and the corresponding expected returns on the vertical axis.

Examining the plot in Figure 11.5, we see that the various combinations of risk and return available all fall on a smooth curve (in fact, for the geometrically inclined, it's a hyperbola). This curve is called an **investment opportunity set** because it shows the possible combinations of risk and return available from portfolios of these two assets. One important thing to

investment opportunity set

Collection of possible risk–return combinations available from portfolios of individual assets.

FIGURE 11.5 | Risk and Return with Stocks and Bonds

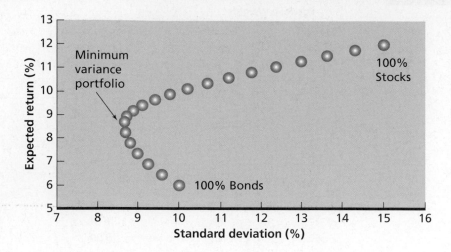

notice is that, as we have shown, there is a portfolio that has the smallest standard deviation (or variance—same thing) of all. It is labeled "minimum variance portfolio" in Figure 11.5. What are (approximately) its expected return and standard deviation?

Review modern portfolio theory at www.moneychimp.com

Now we see clearly why a 100 percent bonds strategy is a poor one. With a 10 percent standard deviation, the bond fund offers an expected return of 6 percent. However, Table 11.9 shows us that a combination of about 60 percent stocks and 40 percent bonds has almost the same standard deviation, but a return of about 9.6 percent. Comparing 9.6 percent to 6 percent, we see that this portfolio has a return that is fully 60 percent greater ($6\% \times 1.6 = 9.6\%$) with the same risk. Our conclusion? Asset allocation matters.

Going back to Figure 11.5, notice that any portfolio that plots below the minimum variance portfolio is a poor choice because, no matter which one you pick, there is another portfolio with the same risk and a much better return. In the jargon of finance, we say that these undesirable portfolios are *dominated* and/or *inefficient*. Either way, we mean that given their level of risk, the expected return is inadequate compared to some other portfolio of equivalent risk. A portfolio that offers the highest return for its level of risk is said to be an **efficient portfolio**. In Figure 11.5, the minimum variance portfolio and all portfolios that plot above it are therefore efficient.

efficient portfolio
A portfolio that offers the highest return for its level of risk.

EXAMPLE 11.6 | More Portfolio Variance and Standard Deviation

Looking at Table 11.9, suppose you put 57.627 percent in the stock fund. What is your expected return? Your standard deviation? How does this compare with the bond fund?

If you put 57.627 percent in stocks, you must have 42.373 percent in bonds, so $x_A = .57627$ and $x_B = .42373$. From Table 11.9, you can see that the standard deviation for stocks and bonds is 15 percent and 10 percent, respectively. Also, the correlation between stocks and bonds is .10. Making use of our portfolio variance equation (11.3), we have:

$$\sigma_P^2 = .57627^2 \times .15^2 + .42373^2 \times .10^2 + 2 \times .57627 \times .42373 \times .15 \times .10 \times .10$$

$$= .332 \times .0225 + .180 \times .01 + .0007325$$

$$= .01$$

Thus, the portfolio variance is .01, so the standard deviation is .1, or 10 percent. Check that the expected return is 9.46 percent. Compared to the bond fund, the standard deviation is now identical, but the expected return is almost 350 basis points higher.

MORE ON CORRELATION AND THE RISK-RETURN TRADE-OFF

Given the expected returns and standard deviations on the two assets, the shape of the investment opportunity set in Figure 11.5 depends on the correlation. The lower the correlation, the more bowed to the left the investment opportunity set will be. To illustrate, Figure 11.6 shows the investment opportunity for correlations of −1, 0, and +1 for two stocks, A and B. Notice that Stock A has an expected return of 12 percent and a standard deviation of 15 percent, while Stock B has an expected return of 6 percent and a standard deviation of 10 percent. These are the same expected returns and standard deviations we used to build Figure 11.5, and the calculations are all done the same way; just the correlations are different. Notice also that we use the symbol ρ to stand for the correlation coefficient.

In Figure 11.6, when the correlation is +1, the investment opportunity set is a straight line connecting the two stocks, so, as expected, there is little or no diversification benefit. As the correlation declines to zero, the bend to the left becomes pronounced. For correlations between +1 and zero, there would simply be a less pronounced bend.

Finally, as the correlation becomes negative, the bend becomes quite pronounced, and the investment opportunity set actually becomes two straight-line segments when the correlation hits −1. Notice that the minimum variance portfolio has a *zero* variance in this case.

FIGURE 11.6	Risk and Return with Two Assets

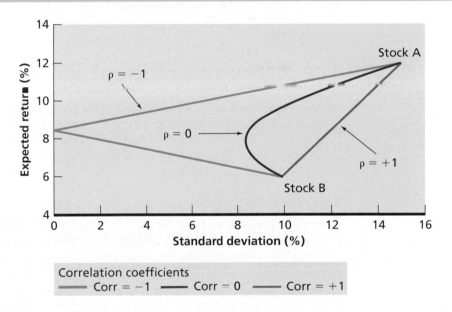

It is sometimes desirable to be able to calculate the percentage investments needed to create the minimum variance portfolio. For a two-asset portfolio, equation (11.5) shows the weight in asset A, x_A^*, that achieves the minimum variance.

$$x_A^* = \frac{\sigma_B^2 - \sigma_A \sigma_B \text{Corr}(R_A, R_B)}{\sigma_A^2 + \sigma_B^2 - 2\sigma_A \sigma_B \text{Corr}(R_A, R_B)} \qquad (11.5)$$

A question at the end of the chapter asks you to prove that equation (11.5) is correct.

Looking back at Table 11.9, what combination of the stock fund and the bond fund has the lowest possible standard deviation? What is the minimum possible standard deviation?

Recalling that the standard deviations for the stock fund and bond fund were .15 and .10, respectively, and noting that the correlation was .1, we have:

$$x_A^* = \frac{.10^2 - .15 \times .10 \times .10}{.15^2 + .10^2 - 2 \times .15 \times .10 \times .10}$$

$$= .288136$$

$$\approx 28.8\%$$

Thus, the minimum variance portfolio has 28.8 percent in stocks and the balance, 71.2 percent, in bonds. Plugging these into our formula for portfolio variance, we have:

$$\sigma_P^2 = .288^2 \times .15^2 + .712^2 \times .10^2 + 2 \times .288 \times .712 \times .15 \times .10 \times .10$$

$$= .007551$$

The standard deviation is the square root of .007551, about 8.7 percent. Notice that this is where the minimum occurs in Figure 11.5.

CHECK THIS

11.4a   Fundamentally, why does diversification work?

11.4b   If two stocks have positive correlation, what does this mean?

11.4c   What is an efficient portfolio?

11.5 The Markowitz Efficient Frontier

In the previous section, we looked closely at the risk-return possibilities available when we consider combining two risky assets. Now we are left with an obvious question: What happens when we consider combining three or more risky assets? As we will see, at least on a conceptual level, the answer turns out to be a straightforward extension of our previous examples that use two risky assets.

THE IMPORTANCE OF ASSET ALLOCATION, PART 2

As you saw in equation (11.4), the formula to compute a portfolio variance with three assets is a bit cumbersome. Indeed, the amount of calculation increases greatly as the number of assets in the portfolio grows. The calculations are not difficult, but using a computer is highly recommended for portfolios consisting of more than three assets!

We can, however, illustrate the importance of asset allocation using only three assets. How? Well, a mutual fund that holds a broadly diversified portfolio of securities counts as only one asset. So, with three mutual funds that hold diversified portfolios, we can construct a diversified portfolio with these three assets. Suppose we invest in three index funds—one that represents U.S. stocks, one that represents U.S. bonds, and one that represents foreign stocks. Then we can see how the allocation among these three diversified portfolios matters. (Our *Get Real* box at the end of the chapter presents a more detailed discussion of mutual funds and diversification.)

Figure 11.7 shows the result of calculating the expected returns and portfolio standard deviations when there are three assets. To illustrate the importance of asset allocation, we calculated expected returns and standard deviations from portfolios composed of three key investment types: U.S. stocks, foreign (non-U.S.) stocks, and U.S. bonds. These asset classes *are not* highly correlated in general; therefore, we assume a zero correlation in all cases.

FIGURE 11.7 Markowitz Efficient Portfolio

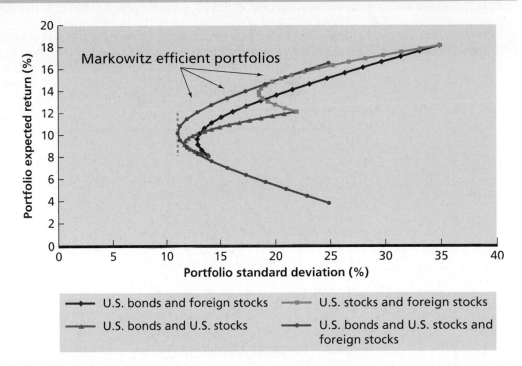

When we assume that all correlations are zero, the return to this portfolio is still:

$$R_P = x_F R_F + x_S R_S + x_B R_B \qquad (11.6)$$

But when all correlations are zero, the variance of the portfolio becomes:

$$\sigma_P^2 = x_F^2 \sigma_F^2 + x_S^2 \sigma_S^2 + x_B^2 \sigma_B^2 \qquad (11.7)$$

Suppose the expected returns and standard deviations are as follows:

	Expected Returns	Standard Deviations
Foreign stocks, *F*	18%	35%
U.S. stocks, *S*	12	22
U.S. bonds, *B*	8	14

We can now compute risk-return combinations as we did in our two-asset case. We create tables similar to Table 11.9, and then we can plot the risk-return combinations.

In Figure 11.7, each point plotted is a possible risk-return combination. Comparing the result with our two-asset case in Figure 11.5, we see that now not only do some assets plot below the minimum variance portfolio on a smooth curve, but we have portfolios plotting inside as well. Only combinations that plot on the upper left-hand boundary are efficient; all the rest are inefficient. This upper left-hand boundary is called the **Markowitz efficient frontier**, and it represents the set of risky portfolios with the maximum return for a given standard deviation.

Figure 11.7 makes it clear that asset allocation matters. For example, a portfolio of 100 percent U.S. stocks is highly inefficient. For the same standard deviation, there is a portfolio with an expected return almost 400 basis points, or 4 percent, higher. Or, for the same expected return, there is a portfolio with about half as much risk! Our nearby *Work the Web* box shows you how an efficient frontier can be created online.

The analysis in this section can be extended to any number of assets or asset classes. In principle, it is possible to compute efficient frontiers using thousands of assets. As a practical matter, however, this analysis is most widely used with a relatively small number of asset classes. For example, most investment banks maintain so-called model portfolios. These are simply recommended asset allocation strategies typically involving three to six asset categories.

Markowitz efficient frontier

The set of portfolios with the maximum return for a given standard deviation.

Check out the online journal at
www.efficientfrontier.com

Several Web sites allow you to perform a Markowitz-type analysis. One free site that provides this, and other, information is www75.wolframalpha.com. Once there, click on the "Examples" link, then select Money and Finance.

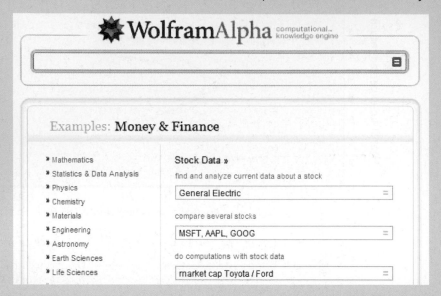

The page above will appear. Click on the box that says "compare several stocks." You will be able to enter the stocks or funds you want to evaluate. Once you have entered the data, the Web site provides some useful information. We are interested in the efficient frontier, which you will find at the bottom of the page labeled "Mean-variance optimal portfolio." The output suggests the optimal portfolio allocation for the stocks we have selected, as well as for the S&P 500, bonds, and T-bills.

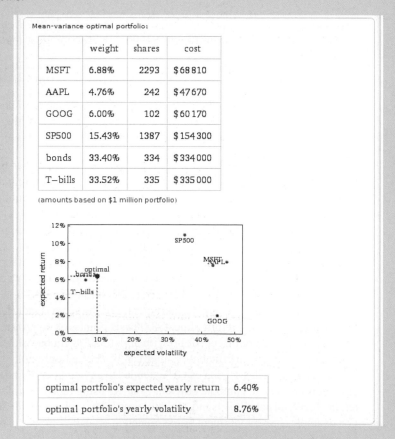

A primary reason that the Markowitz analysis is not usually extended to large collections of individual assets has to do with data requirements. The inputs into the analysis are (1) expected returns on all assets; (2) standard deviations on all assets; and (3) correlations between every pair of assets. Moreover, these inputs have to be measured with some precision, or we just end up with a garbage-in, garbage-out (GIGO) system.

Suppose we just look at 2,000 NYSE stocks. We need 2,000 expected returns and standard deviations. We already have a problem because returns on individual stocks cannot be predicted with precision at all. To make matters worse, however, we need to know the correlation between every *pair* of stocks. With 2,000 stocks, there are $2,000 \times 1,999/2 = 1,999,000$, or almost 2 million unique pairs![3] Also, as with expected returns, correlations between individual stocks are very difficult to predict accurately. We will return to this issue in our next chapter, where we show that there may be an extremely elegant way around the problem.

CHECK THIS

11.5a What is the Markowitz efficient frontier?

11.5b Why is Markowitz portfolio analysis most commonly used to make asset allocation decisions?

11.6 Summary and Conclusions

In this chapter, we covered the basics of diversification and portfolio risk and return. The most important thing to carry away from this chapter is an understanding of diversification and why it works. Once you understand this concept, then the importance of asset allocation becomes clear.

Our diversification story is not complete, however, because we have not considered one important asset class: riskless assets. This will be the first task in our next chapter. However, in this chapter, we covered many aspects of diversification and risky assets. We recap some of these aspects, grouped below by the learning objectives of the chapter.

1. **How to calculate expected returns and variances for a security.**

   A. In Chapter 1, we discussed how to calculate average returns and variances using historical data. When we calculate expected returns and expected variances, we have to use calculations that account for the probabilities of future possible returns.

   B. In general, the expected return on a security is equal to the sum of the possible returns multiplied by their probabilities. So, if we have 100 possible returns, we would multiply each one by its probability and then add up the results. The sum is the expected return.

   C. To calculate the variances, we first determine the squared deviations from the expected return. We then multiply each possible squared deviation by its probability. Next we add these up, and the result is the variance. The standard deviation is the square root of the variance.

2. **How to calculate expected returns and variances for a portfolio.**

   A. A portfolio's expected return is a simple weighted combination of the expected returns on the assets in the portfolio. This method of calculating the expected return on a portfolio works no matter how many assets are in the portfolio.

   B. The variance of a portfolio is generally *not* a simple combination of the variances of the assets in the portfolio. Review Equations (11.3) and (11.4) to verify this fact.

---

[3] With 2,000 stocks, there are $2,000^2 = 4,000,000$ possible pairs. Of these, 2,000 involve pairing a stock with itself. Further, we recognize that the correlation between A and B is the same as the correlation between B and A, so we only need to actually calculate half of the remaining 3,998,000 correlations.

3. **The importance of portfolio diversification.**

A. Diversification is a very important consideration. The principle of diversification tells us that spreading an investment across many assets can reduce some, but not all, of the risk. Based on U.S. stock market history, for example, about 60 percent of the risk associated with owning individual stocks can be eliminated by naïve diversification.

B. Diversification works because asset returns are not perfectly correlated. All else the same, the lower the correlation, the greater is the gain from diversification.

C. It is even possible to combine some risky assets in such a way that the resulting portfolio has zero risk. This is a nice bit of financial alchemy.

4. **The efficient frontier and the importance of asset allocation.**

A. When we consider the possible combinations of risk and return available from portfolios of assets, we find that some are inefficient (or dominated portfolios). An inefficient portfolio is one that offers too little return for its risk.

B. For any group of assets, there is a set that is efficient. That set is known as the Markowitz efficient frontier. The Markowitz efficient frontier simultaneously represents (1) the set of risky portfolios with the maximum return for a given standard deviation, and (2) the set of risky portfolios with the minimum standard deviation for a given return.

GET REAL

This chapter explained diversification, a very important consideration for real-world investors and money managers. The chapter also explored the famous Markowitz efficient portfolio concept, which shows how (and why) asset allocation affects portfolio risk and return.

Building a diversified portfolio is not a trivial task. Of course, as we discussed many chapters ago, mutual funds provide one way for investors to build diversified portfolios, but there are some significant caveats concerning mutual funds as a diversification tool. First of all, investors sometimes assume a fund is diversified simply because it holds a relatively large number of stocks. However, with the exception of some index funds, most mutual funds will reflect a particular style of investing, either explicitly, as stated in the fund's objective, or implicitly, as favored by the fund manager. For example, in the mid- to late-1990s, stocks as a whole did very well, but mutual funds that concentrated on smaller stocks generally did not do well at all.

It is tempting to buy a number of mutual funds to ensure broad diversification, but even this may not work. Within a given fund family, the same manager may actually be responsible for multiple funds. In addition, managers within a large fund family frequently have similar views about the market and individual companies.

Thinking just about stocks for the moment, what does an investor need to consider to build a well-diversified portfolio? At a minimum, such a portfolio probably needs to be diversified across industries, with no undue concentrations in particular sectors of the economy; it needs to be diversified by company size (small, midcap, and large), and it needs to be diversified across "growth" (i.e., high-P/E) and "value" (low-P/E) stocks. Perhaps the most controversial diversification issue concerns international diversification. The correlation between international stock exchanges is surprisingly low, suggesting large benefits from diversifying globally.

Perhaps the most disconcerting fact about diversification is that it leads to the following paradox: A well-diversified portfolio will always be invested in something that does not do well! Put differently, such a portfolio will almost always have both winners and losers. In many ways, that's the whole idea. Even so, it requires a lot of financial discipline to stay diversified when some portion of your portfolio seems to be doing poorly. The payoff is that, over the long run, a well-diversified portfolio should provide much steadier returns and be much less prone to abrupt changes in value.

Key Terms

asset allocation 388
correlation 385
efficient portfolio 390
expected return 374
investment opportunity set 389

Markowitz efficient frontier 393
portfolio 377
portfolio weight 377
principle of diversification 383

Chapter Review Problems and Self-Test

Use the following table of states of the economy and stock returns to answer the review problems:

State of Economy	Probability of State of Economy	Security Returns If State Occurs	
		Roten	Bradley
Bust	.40	−10%	30%
Boom	.60	40	10
	1.00		

1. **Expected Returns (CFA1)**   Calculate the expected returns for Roten and Bradley.
2. **Standard Deviations (CFA2)**   Calculate the standard deviations for Roten and Bradley.
3. **Portfolio Expected Returns (CFA3)**   Calculate the expected return on a portfolio of 50 percent Roten and 50 percent Bradley.
4. **Portfolio Volatility (CFA5)**   Calculate the volatility of a portfolio of 50 percent Roten and 50 percent Bradley.

Answers to Self-Test Problems

1. We calculate the expected return as follows:

		Roten		Bradley	
(1) State of Economy	(2) Probability of State of Economy	(3) Return If State Occurs	(4) Product (2) × (3)	(5) Return If State Occurs	(6) Product (2) × (5)
Bust	.40	−10%	−.04	30%	.12
Boom	.60	40	.24	10	.06
			$E(R) = 20\%$		$E(R) = 18\%$

2. We calculate the standard deviation as follows:

(1) State of Economy	(2) Probability of State of Economy	(3) Return Deviation from Expected Return	(4) Squared Return Deviation	(5) Product (2) × (4)
Roten				
Bust	.40	−.30	.09	.036
Boom	.60	.20	.04	.024
				$\sigma^2 = .06$
Bradley				
Bust	.40	.12	.0144	.00576
Boom	.60	−.08	.0064	.00384
				$\sigma^2 = .0096$

Taking square roots, the standard deviations are 24.495 percent for Roten and 9.798 percent for Bradley.

3. We calculate the expected return on a portfolio of 50 percent Roten and 50 percent Bradley as follows:

(1) State of Economy	(2) Probability of State of Economy	(3) Portfolio Return If State Occurs	(4) Product (2) × (3)
Bust	.40	10%	.04
Boom	.60	25	.15
			$E(R_p) = 19\%$

4. We calculate the volatility of a portfolio of 50 percent Roten and 50 percent Bradley as follows:

(1) State of Economy	(2) Probability of State of Economy	(3) Portfolio Return If State Occurs	(4) Squared Deviation from Expected Return	(5) Product (2) × (4)
Bust	.40	.10	.0081	.00324
Boom	.60	.25	.0036	.00216
				$\sigma_P^2 = .00540$
				$\sigma_P = 7.3485\%$

Test Your Investment Quotient

www.mhhe.com/jmd6e

IQ

1. **Diversification (LO3, CFA6)**   Starcents has an expected return of 25 percent and Jpod has an expected return of 20 percent. What is the likely investment decision for a risk-averse investor?

   a. Invest all funds in Starcents.
   b. Invest all funds in Jpod.
   c. Do not invest any funds in Starcents and Jpod.
   d. Invest funds partly in Starcents and partly in Jpod.

2. **Return Standard Deviation (LO1, CFA2)**   Starcents experiences returns of 5 percent or 45 percent, each with an equal probability. What is the return standard deviation for Starcents?

   a. 30 percent
   b. 25 percent
   c. 20 percent
   d. 10 percent

3. **Return Standard Deviation (LO1, CFA2)**   Jpod experiences returns of 0 percent, 25 percent, or 50 percent, each with a one-third probability. What is the approximate return standard deviation for Jpod?

   a. 30 percent
   b. 25 percent
   c. 20 percent
   d. 10 percent

4. **Expected Return (LO1, CFA1)**   An analyst estimates that a stock has the following return probabilities and returns depending on the state of the economy:

State of Economy	Probability	Return
Good	.1	15%
Normal	.6	13
Poor	.3	7

What is the expected return of the stock?

   a. 7.8 percent
   b. 11.4 percent
   c. 11.7 percent
   d. 13.0 percent

5. **Risk Aversion (LO3, CFA4)** Which of the following statements best reflects the importance of the asset allocation decision to the investment process? The asset allocation decision

   a. Helps the investor decide on realistic investment goals.
   b. Identifies the specific securities to include in a portfolio.
   c. Determines most of the portfolio's returns and volatility over time.
   d. Creates a standard by which to establish the appropriate investment time horizon.

6. **Efficient Frontier (LO4, CFA5)** The Markowitz efficient frontier is best described as the set of portfolios that has

   a. The minimum risk for every level of return.
   b. Proportionally equal units of risk and return.
   c. The maximum excess rate of return for every given level of risk.
   d. The highest return for each level of beta used on the capital asset pricing model.

7. **Diversification (LO3, CFA3)** An investor is considering adding another investment to a portfolio. To achieve the maximum diversification benefits, the investor should add an investment that has a correlation coefficient with the existing portfolio closest to

   a. −1.0
   b. −.5
   c. .0
   d. +1.0

8. **Risk Premium (LO2, CFA1)** Starcents has an expected return of 25 percent, Jpod has an expected return of 20 percent, and the risk-free rate is 5 percent. You invest half your funds in Starcents and the other half in Jpod. What is the risk premium for your portfolio?

   a. 20 percent
   b. 17.5 percent
   c. 15 percent
   d. 12.5 percent

9. **Return Standard Deviation (LO2, CFA5)** Both Starcents and Jpod have the same return standard deviation of 20 percent, and Starcents and Jpod returns have zero correlation. You invest half your funds in Starcents and the other half in Jpod. What is the return standard deviation for your portfolio?

   a. 20 percent
   b. 14.14 percent
   c. 10 percent
   d. 0 percent

10. **Return Standard Deviation (LO2, CFA5)** Both Starcents and Jpod have the same return standard deviation of 20 percent, and Starcents and Jpod returns have a correlation of +1. You invest half your funds in Starcents and the other half in Jpod. What is the return standard deviation for your portfolio?

    a. 20 percent
    b. 14.14 percent
    c. 10 percent
    d. 0 percent

11. **Return Standard Deviation (LO2, CFA5)** Both Starcents and Jpod have the same return standard deviation of 20 percent, and Starcents and Jpod returns have a correlation of −1. You invest half your funds in Starcents and the other half in Jpod. What is the return standard deviation for your portfolio?

    a. 20 percent
    b. 14.14 percent
    c. 10 percent
    d. 0 percent

12. **Minimum Variance Portfolio (LO2, CFA4)** Both Starcents and Jpod have the same return standard deviation of 20 percent, and Starcents and Jpod returns have zero correlation. What is the minimum attainable standard deviation for a portfolio of Starcents and Jpod?

    a. 20 percent
    b. 14.14 percent
    c. 10 percent
    d. 0 percent

13. **Minimum Variance Portfolio (LO2, CFA4)**   Both Starcents and Jpod have the same return standard deviation of 20 percent, and Starcents and Jpod returns have a correlation of −1. What is the minimum attainable return variance for a portfolio of Starcents and Jpod?

   a. 20 percent
   b. 14.14 percent
   c. 10 percent
   d. 0 percent

14. **Minimum Variance Portfolio (LO2, CFA4)**   Stocks A, B, and C each have the same expected return and standard deviation. The following shows the correlations between returns on these stocks:

	Stock A	Stock B	Stock C
Stock A	+1.0		
Stock B	+0.9	+1.0	
Stock C	+0.1	−0.4	+1.0

Given these correlations, which of the following portfolios constructed from these stocks would have the lowest risk?

   a. One equally invested in stocks A and B.
   b. One equally invested in stocks A and C.
   c. One equally invested in stocks B and C.
   d. One totally invested in stock C.

15. **Markowitz Efficient Frontier (LO4, CFA5)**   Which of the following portfolios cannot lie on the efficient frontier as described by Markowitz?

	Portfolio	Expected Return	Standard Deviation
a.	W	9%	21%
b.	X	5	7
c.	Y	15	36
d.	Z	12	15

Concept Questions

1. **Diversification and Market History (LO3, CFA6)**   Based on market history, what is the average annual standard deviation of return for a single, randomly chosen stock? What is the average annual standard deviation for an equally weighted portfolio of many stocks?

2. **Interpreting Correlations (LO2, CFA3)**   If the returns on two stocks are highly correlated, what does this mean? If they have no correlation? If they are negatively correlated?

3. **Efficient Portfolios (LO4, CFA5)**   What is an efficient portfolio?

4. **Expected Returns (LO2, CFA3)**   True or false: If two stocks have the same expected return of 12 percent, then any portfolio of the two stocks will also have an expected return of 12 percent.

5. **Portfolio Volatility (LO2, CFA5)**   True or false: If two stocks have the same standard deviation of 45 percent, then any portfolio of the two stocks will also have a standard deviation of 45 percent.

6. **Time Diversification (LO3, CFA6)**   Why should younger investors be willing to hold a larger amount of equity in their portfolios?

7. **Asset Allocation (LO4, CFA7)**   Assume you are a very risk-averse investor. Why might you still be willing to add an investment with high volatility to your portfolio?

8. **Minimum Variance Portfolio (LO2, CFA4)**   Why is the minimum variance portfolio important in regard to the Markowitz efficient frontier?

9. **Markowitz Efficient Frontier (LO4, CFA5)** True or false: It is impossible for a single asset to lie on the Markowitz efficient frontier.

10. **Portfolio Variance (LO2, CFA5)** Suppose two assets have zero correlation and the same standard deviation. What is true about the minimum variance portfolio?

Questions and Problems

1. **Expected Returns (LO1, CFA1)** Use the following information on states of the economy and stock returns to calculate the expected return for Dingaling Telephone:

State of Economy	Probability of State of Economy	Security Return If State Occurs
Recession	.30	−8%
Normal	.40	13
Boom	.30	23

2. **Standard Deviations (LO1, CFA2)** Using the information in the previous question, calculate the standard deviation of returns.

3. **Expected Returns and Deviations (LO1, CFA2)** Repeat Questions 1 and 2 assuming that all three states are equally likely.

Use the following information on states of the economy and stock returns to answer Questions 4–7:

State of Economy	Probability of State of Economy	Security Returns If State Occurs Roll	Ross
Bust	.40	−10%	21%
Boom	.60	28	8

4. **Expected Returns (LO1, CFA1)** Calculate the expected returns for Roll and Ross by filling in the following table (verify your answer by expressing returns as percentages as well as decimals):

		Roll		Ross	
(1) State of Economy	(2) Probability of State of Economy	(3) Return If State Occurs	(4) Product (2) × (3)	(5) Return if State Occurs	(6) Product (2) × (5)
Bust					
Boom					

5. **Standard Deviations (LO1, CFA2)** Calculate the standard deviations for Roll and Ross by filling in the following table (verify your answer using returns expressed in percentages as well as decimals):

(1) State of Economy	(2) Probability of State of Economy	(3) Return Deviation from Expected Return	(4) Squared Return Deviation	(5) Product (2) × (4)
Roll				
Bust				
Boom				
Ross				
Bust				
Boom				

6. **Portfolio Expected Returns (LO2, CFA3)** Calculate the expected return on a portfolio of 55 percent Roll and 45 percent Ross by filling in the following table:

(1) State of Economy	(2) Probability of State of Economy	(3) Portfolio Return If State Occurs	(4) Product (2) × (3)
Bust			
Boom			

7. **Portfolio Volatility (LO2, CFA5)** Calculate the volatility of a portfolio of 35 percent Roll and 65 percent Ross by filling in the following table:

(1) State of Economy	(2) Probability of State of Economy	(3) Portfolio Return If State Occurs	(4) Squared Deviation from Expected Return	(5) Product (2) × (4)
Bust				
Boom				
$\sigma_p^2 =$				
$\sigma_p =$				

8. **Calculating Returns and Standard Deviations (LO1, CFA2)** Based on the following information, calculate the expected return and standard deviation for the two stocks.

State of Economy	Probability of State of Economy	Rate of Return If State Occurs	
		Stock A	Stock B
Recession	.25	.04	−.20
Normal	.55	.09	.13
Boom	.20	.12	.33

9. **Returns and Standard Deviations (LO2, CFA5)** Consider the following information:

State of Economy	Probability of State of Economy	Rate of Return If State Occurs		
		Stock A	Stock B	Stock C
Boom	.10	.18	.48	.33
Good	.30	.11	.18	.15
Poor	.40	.05	−.09	−.05
Bust	.20	−.03	−.32	−.09

   a. Your portfolio is invested 25 percent each in A and C, and 50 percent in B. What is the expected return of the portfolio?
   b. What is the variance of this portfolio? The standard deviation?

10. **Portfolio Returns and Volatilities (LO2, CFA5)** Fill in the missing information in the following table. Assume that Portfolio AB is 40 percent invested in Stock A.

Year	Stock A	Stock B	Portfolio AB
2006	11%	21%	
2007	37	−38	
2008	−21	48	
2009	26	16	
2010	13	24	
Average return			
Standard deviation			

Intermediate Questions

11. **Portfolio Returns and Volatilities (LO2, CFA5)** Given the following information, calculate the expected return and standard deviation for a portfolio that has 35 percent invested in Stock A, 45 percent in Stock B, and the balance in Stock C.

State of Economy	Probability of State of Economy	Returns		
		Stock A	Stock B	Stock C
Boom	.60	15%	18%	20%
Bust	.40	10	0	−10

12. **Portfolio Variance (LO2, CFA5)** Use the following information to calculate the expected return and standard deviation of a portfolio that is 50 percent invested in 3 Doors, Inc., and 50 percent invested in Down Co.:

	3 Doors, Inc.	Down Co.
Expected return, $E(R)$	14%	10%
Standard deviation, σ	42	31
Correlation	.30	

13. **More Portfolio Variance (LO4, CFA3)** In the previous question, what is the standard deviation if the correlation is +1? 0? −1? As the correlation declines from +1 to −1 here, what do you see happening to portfolio volatility? Why?

14. **Minimum Variance Portfolio (LO4, CFA4)** In Problem 12, what are the expected return and standard deviation on the minimum variance portfolio?

15. **Asset Allocation (LO4, CFA4)** Fill in the missing information assuming a correlation of .30.

Portfolio Weights		Expected Return	Standard Deviation
Stocks	Bonds		
1.00		12%	21%
.80			
.60			
.40			
.20			
.00		7%	12%

16. **Minimum Variance Portfolio (LO4, CFA4)** Consider two stocks, Stock D, with an expected return of 13 percent and a standard deviation of 31 percent, and Stock I, an international company, with an expected return of 16 percent and a standard deviation of 42 percent. The correlation between the two stocks is −.10. What is the weight of each stock in the minimum variance portfolio?

17. **Minimum Variance Portfolio (LO2, CFA4)** What are the expected return and standard deviation of the minimum variance portfolio in the previous problem?

18. **Minimum Variance Portfolio (LO4, CFA4)** Asset K has an expected return of 11 percent and a standard deviation of 32 percent. Asset L has an expected return of 6 percent and a standard deviation of 12 percent. The correlation between the assets is .25. What are the expected return and standard deviation of the minimum variance portfolio?

19. **Minimum Variance Portfolio (LO4, CFA4)** The stock of Bruin, Inc., has an expected return of 14 percent and a standard deviation of 42 percent. The stock of Wildcat Co. has an expected return of 12 percent and a standard deviation of 57 percent. The correlation between the two stocks is .25. Is it possible for there to be a minimum variance portfolio since the highest-return stock has the lowest standard deviation? If so, calculate the expected return and standard deviation of the minimum variance portfolio.

20. **Portfolio Variance (LO2, CFA3)** You have a three-stock portfolio. Stock A has an expected return of 12 percent and a standard deviation of 41 percent, Stock B has an expected return of 16 percent and a standard deviation of 58 percent, and Stock C has an expected return of 13 percent and a standard deviation of 48 percent. The correlation between Stocks A and B is .30, between Stocks A

and C is .20, and between Stocks B and C is .05. Your portfolio consists of 45 percent Stock A, 25 percent Stock B, and 30 percent Stock C. Calculate the expected return and standard deviation of your portfolio. The formula for calculating the variance of a three-stock portfolio is:

$$\sigma_P^2 = x_A^2\sigma_A^2 + x_B^2\sigma_B^2 + x_C^2\sigma_C^2 + 2x_Ax_B\sigma_A\sigma_B\text{Corr}(R_A, R_B) \\ + 2x_Ax_C\sigma_A\sigma_C\text{Corr}(R_A, R_C) + 2x_Bx_C\sigma_B\sigma_C\text{Corr}(R_B, R_C)$$

21. **Minimum Variance Portfolio (LO4, CFA4)**   You are going to invest in Asset J and Asset S. Asset J has an expected return of 13 percent and a standard deviation of 54 percent. Asset S has an expected return of 10 percent and a standard deviation of 19 percent. The correlation between the two assets is .50. What are the standard deviation and expected return of the minimum variance portfolio? What is going on here?

22. **Portfolio Variance (LO2, CFA3)**   Suppose two assets have perfect positive correlation. Show that the standard deviation on a portfolio of the two assets is simply:

$$\sigma_P = x_A \times \sigma_A + x_B \times \sigma_B$$

(*Hint*: Look at the expression for the variance of a two-asset portfolio. If the correlation is +1, the expression is a perfect square.)

23. **Portfolio Variance (LO2, CFA5)**   Suppose two assets have perfect negative correlation. Show that the standard deviation on a portfolio of the two assets is simply:

$$\sigma_P = \pm(x_A \times \sigma_A - x_B \times \sigma_B)$$

(*Hint*: See previous problem.)

24. **Portfolio Variance (LO2, CFA5)**   Using the result in Problem 23, show that whenever two assets have perfect negative correlation it is possible to find a portfolio with a zero standard deviation. What are the portfolio weights? (*Hint*: Let x be the percentage in the first asset and $(1 - x)$ be the percentage in the second. Set the standard deviation to zero and solve for x.)

25. **Portfolio Variance (LO2, CFA4)**   Derive our expression in the chapter for the portfolio weight in the minimum variance portfolio. (Danger! Calculus required!) (*Hint*: Let x be the percentage in the first asset and $(1 - x)$ the percentage in the second. Take the derivative with respect to x, and set it to zero. Solve for x.)

CFA Exam Review by Schweser

[CFA3, CFA5, CFA6]

Andy Green, CFA, and Sue Hutchinson, CFA, are considering adding alternative investments to the portfolio they manage for a private client. After much discussion, they have decided to add a hedge fund to the portfolio. In their research, Mr. Green focuses on hedge funds that have the highest returns, while Ms. Hutchinson focuses on finding hedge funds that can reduce portfolio risk while maintaining the same level of return.

After completing their research, Mr. Green proposes two funds: the New Horizon Emerging Market Fund (NH), which takes long-term positions in emerging markets, and the Hi Rise Real Estate Fund (HR), which holds a highly leveraged real estate portfolio. Ms. Hutchinson proposes two hedge funds: the Quality Commodity Fund (QC), which takes conservative positions in commodities, and the Beta Naught Fund (BN), which manages an equity long/short portfolio that targets a market risk of zero. The table below details the statistics for the existing portfolio, as well as for the four potential funds. The standard deviation of the market's return is 18 percent.

	Existing	NH	HR	QC	BN
Average return	10%	20%	10%	6%	4%
Standard deviation	16%	50%	16%	16%	25%
Beta	0.8	0.9	0.4	−0.2	0
Correlation with existing portfolio		0.32	0.45	−0.23	0.00

Mr. Green and Ms. Hutchinson have agreed to select the fund that will provide a portfolio with the highest return-to-risk ratio (i.e., average return relative to standard deviation). They have decided to invest 10 percent of the portfolio in the selected fund.

As an alternative to one fund, Mr. Green and Ms. Hutchinson have discussed investing 5 percent in the Beta Naught Fund (BN) and 5 percent in one of the other three funds. This new 50/50 hedge fund would then serve as the 10 percent allocation in the portfolio.

1. Mr. Green and Ms. Hutchinson divided up their research into return enhancement and diversification benefits. Based upon the stated goals of their research, which of the two approaches is more likely to lead to an appropriate choice?

    a. Green's research.
    b. Hutchinson's research.
    c. Neither is appropriate.

2. Which of the following is closest to the expected return of the client's portfolio if 10 percent of the portfolio is invested in the New Horizon (NH) Emerging Market Fund?

    a. 11 percent
    b. 10.2 percent
    c. 11.8 percent

3. Which of the following is closest to the expected standard deviation of the client's portfolio if 10 percent of the portfolio is invested in the Quality Commodity (QC) Fund?

    a. 9.6 percent
    b. 14.1 percent
    c. 16.0 percent

4. Which of the following is closest to the expected return of a portfolio that consists of 90 percent of the original portfolio, 5 percent of the Hi Rise (HR) Real Estate Fund, and 5 percent of the Beta Naught (BN) Fund?

    a. 9.0 percent
    b. 10.4 percent
    c. 9.7 percent

5. When combined with Beta Naught in a 50/50 portfolio, which of the other three funds will produce a portfolio that has the lowest standard deviation?

    a. New Horizon only.
    b. Quality Commodity only.
    c. Either Hi Rise or Quality Commodity.

CHAPTER 12

Return, Risk, and the Security Market Line

Learning Objectives

Studying some topics will yield an expected reward. For example, make sure you know:

1. The difference between expected and unexpected returns.

2. The difference between systematic risk and unsystematic risk.

3. The security market line and the capital asset pricing model.

4. The importance of beta.

"To win, you have to risk loss."

–Franz Klammer

An important insight of modern financial theory is that some investment risks yield an expected reward, while other risks do not. Essentially, risks that can be eliminated by diversification do not yield an expected reward, and risks that cannot be eliminated by diversification do yield an expected reward. Thus, financial markets are somewhat fussy regarding what risks are rewarded and what risks are not. ■

Chapter 1 presented some important lessons from capital market history. The most noteworthy, perhaps, is that there is a reward, on average, for bearing risk. We called this reward a *risk premium.* The second lesson is that this risk premium is positively correlated with an investment's risk.

In this chapter, we return to an examination of the reward for bearing risk. Specifically, we have two tasks to accomplish. First, we have to define risk more precisely and then discuss how to measure it. Second, once we have a better understanding of just what we mean by "risk," we will go on to quantify the relation between risk and return in financial markets.

When we examine the risks associated with individual assets, we find two types of risk: systematic and unsystematic. This distinction is crucial because, as we will see, systematic risk affects almost all assets in the economy, at least to some degree, whereas unsystematic risk affects at most only a small number of assets. This observation allows us to say a great deal about the risks and returns on individual assets. In particular, it is the basis

CFA™ Exam Topics in This Chapter:

1 Cost of capital (L1, S11)

2 Introduction to asset pricing models (L1, S12)

3 Return concepts (L2, S10)

Go to www.mhhe.com/jmd6e for a guide that aligns your textbook with CFA readings.

for a famous relationship between risk and return called the *security market line,* or SML. To develop the SML, we introduce the equally famous beta coefficient, one of the center-pieces of modern finance. Beta and the SML are key concepts because they supply us with at least part of the answer to the question of how to go about determining the expected return on a risky investment.

12.1 Announcements, Surprises, and Expected Returns

In our previous chapter, we discussed how to construct portfolios and evaluate their returns. We now begin to describe more carefully the risks and returns associated with individual securities. Thus far, we have measured volatility by looking at the difference between the actual return on an asset or portfolio, R, and the expected return, $E(R)$. We now look at why those deviations exist.

EXPECTED AND UNEXPECTED RETURNS

To begin, consider the return on the stock of a hypothetical company called Flyers. What will determine this stock's return in, say, the coming year?

The return on any stock traded in a financial market is composed of two parts. First, the normal, or expected, return from the stock is the part of the return that investors predict or expect. This return depends on the information investors have about the stock, and it is based on the market's understanding today of the important factors that will influence the stock in the coming year.

The second part of the return on the stock is the uncertain, or risky, part. This is the portion that comes from unexpected information revealed during the year. A list of all possible sources of such information would be endless, but here are a few basic examples:

News about Flyers's product research.

Government figures released on gross domestic product.

The latest news about exchange rates.

The news that Flyers's sales figures are higher than expected.

A sudden, unexpected drop in interest rates.

Based on this discussion, one way to express the return on Flyers stock in the coming year would be:

based on known info

$$\text{Total return} - \text{Expected return} = \text{Unexpected return} \qquad (12.1)$$

or

$$R - E(R) = U$$

where R stands for the actual total return in the year, $E(R)$ stands for the expected part of the return, and U stands for the unexpected part of the return. What this says is that the actual return, R, differs from the expected return, $E(R)$, because of surprises that occur during the year. In any given year, the unexpected return will be positive or negative, but, through time, the average value of U will be zero. This simply means that, on average, the actual return equals the expected return.

ANNOUNCEMENTS AND NEWS

We need to be careful when we talk about the effect of news items on stock returns. For example, suppose Flyers's business is such that the company prospers when gross domestic product (GDP) grows at a relatively high rate and suffers when GDP is relatively stagnant. In this case, in deciding what return to expect this year from owning stock in Flyers, investors either implicitly or explicitly must think about what GDP is likely to be for the coming year.

When the government actually announces GDP figures for the year, what will happen to the value of Flyers stock? Obviously, the answer depends on what figure is released. More to the point, however, the impact depends on how much of that figure actually represents new information.

At the beginning of the year, market participants will have some idea or forecast of what the yearly GDP figure will be. To the extent that shareholders have predicted GDP, that prediction will already be factored into the expected part of the return on the stock, $E(R)$. On the other hand, if the announced GDP is a surprise, then the effect will be part of U, the unanticipated portion of the return.

As an example, suppose shareholders in the market had forecast that the GDP increase this year would be .5 percent. If the actual announcement this year is exactly .5 percent, the same as the forecast, then the shareholders don't really learn anything, and the announcement isn't news. There should be no impact on the stock price as a result. This is like receiving redundant confirmation about something that you suspected all along; it reveals nothing new.

To give a more concrete example, Nabisco once announced it was taking a massive $300 million charge against earnings for the second quarter in a sweeping restructuring plan. The company also announced plans to cut its workforce sharply by 7.8 percent, eliminate some package sizes and small brands, and relocate some of its operations. This all seems like bad news, but the stock price didn't even budge. Why? Because it was already fully expected that Nabisco would take such actions, and the stock price already reflected the bad news.

A common way of saying that an announcement isn't news is to say that the market has already discounted the announcement. The use of the word "discount" here is different from the use of the term in computing present values, but the spirit is the same. When we discount a dollar to be received in the future, we say it is worth less to us today because of the time value of money. When an announcement or a news item is discounted into a stock price, we say that its impact is already a part of the stock price because the market already knew about it.

Going back to Flyers, suppose the government announces that the actual GDP increase during the year has been 1.5 percent. Now shareholders have learned something, namely, that the increase is 1 percentage point higher than they had forecast. This difference between the actual result and the forecast, 1 percentage point in this example, is sometimes called the *innovation* or the *surprise*.

This distinction explains why what seems to be bad news can actually be good news. For example, Gymboree, a retailer of children's apparel, had a 3 percent decline in same-store sales for a particular month, yet its stock price shot up 13 percent on the news. In the retail business, same-store sales, which are sales by existing stores in operation at least a year, are a crucial barometer, so why was this decline good news? The reason was that analysts had been expecting significantly sharper declines, so the situation was not as bad as previously thought.

A key fact to keep in mind about news and price changes is that news about the future is what matters. For example, America Online (AOL) once announced third-quarter earnings that exceeded Wall Street's expectations. That seems like good news, but America Online's stock price promptly dropped 10 percent. The reason was that America Online also announced a new discount subscriber plan, which analysts took as an indication that future revenues would be growing more slowly. Similarly, shortly thereafter, Microsoft reported a 50 percent jump in profits, exceeding projections. That seems like *really* good news, but Microsoft's stock price proceeded to decline sharply. Why? Because Microsoft warned that its phenomenal growth could not be sustained indefinitely, so its 50 percent increase in current earnings was not such a good predictor of future earnings growth.

To summarize, an announcement can be broken into two parts, the anticipated, or expected, part plus the surprise, or innovation:

$$\text{Announcement} = \text{Expected part} + \text{Surprise} \qquad (12.2)$$

The expected part of any announcement is the part of the information that the market uses to form the expectation, $E(R)$, of the return on the stock. The surprise is the news that influences the unanticipated return on the stock, U.

WWW

Visit the earnings calendar in the free services section at www.earningswhispers.com

WWW

See recent earnings surprises at earnings.nasdaq.com
or
biz.yahoo.com/z/extreme.html

Our discussion of market efficiency in a previous chapter bears on this discussion. We are assuming that relevant information known today is already reflected in the expected return. This assumption is identical to saying that the current price reflects relevant publicly available information. We are thus implicitly assuming that markets are at least reasonably efficient in the semistrong-form sense. Henceforth, when we speak of news, we will mean the surprise part of an announcement and not the portion that the market had expected and therefore already discounted.

EXAMPLE 12.1   **In the News**

Suppose Intel were to announce that earnings for the quarter just ending were up by 40 percent relative to a year ago. Do you expect that the stock price would rise or fall on the announcement?

The answer is that you can't really tell. Suppose the market was expecting a 60 percent increase. In this case, the 40 percent increase would be a negative surprise, and we would expect the stock price to fall. On the other hand, if the market was expecting only a 20 percent increase, there would be a positive surprise, and we would expect the stock to rise on the news.

CHECK THIS

12.1a What are the two basic parts of a return on common stock?

12.1b Under what conditions will an announcement have no effect on common stock prices?

12.2 Risk: Systematic and Unsystematic

It is important to distinguish between expected and unexpected returns because the unanticipated part of the return, that portion resulting from surprises, is the significant risk of any investment. After all, if we always receive exactly what we expect, then the investment is perfectly predictable and, by definition, risk-free. In other words, the risk of owning an asset comes from surprises—unanticipated events.

There are important differences, though, among various sources of risk. Look back at our previous list of news stories. Some of these stories are directed specifically at Flyers, and some are more general. Which of the news items are of specific importance to Flyers?

Announcements about interest rates or GDP are clearly important for nearly all companies, whereas the news about Flyers's product research or its sales is of specific interest to Flyers investors only. We distinguish between these two types of events, because, as we will see, they have very different implications.

SYSTEMATIC AND UNSYSTEMATIC RISK

systematic risk
Risk that influences a large number of assets. Also called *market risk.*

The first type of surprise, the one that affects most assets, we label **systematic risk**. A systematic risk is one that influences a large number of assets, each to a greater or lesser extent. Because systematic risks have marketwide effects, they are sometimes called *market risks.*

unsystematic risk
Risk that influences a single company or a small group of companies. Also called *unique* or *asset-specific risk.*

The second type of surprise we call **unsystematic risk**. An unsystematic risk is one that affects a single asset, or possibly a small group of assets. Because these risks are unique to individual companies or assets, they are sometimes called *unique* or *asset-specific risks.* We use these terms interchangeably.

As we have seen, uncertainties about general economic conditions, such as GDP, interest rates, or inflation, are examples of systematic risks. These conditions affect nearly all companies to some degree. An unanticipated increase, or surprise, in inflation, for example, affects wages and the costs of supplies that companies buy. This surprise affects the value of the assets that companies own, and it affects the prices at which companies sell their products. Forces such as uncertainties about general economic conditions are the essence of systematic risk, because all companies are susceptible to these forces.

In contrast, the announcement of an oil strike by a particular company will primarily affect that company and, perhaps, a few others (such as primary competitors and suppliers). It is unlikely to have much of an effect on the world oil market, however, or on the affairs of companies not in the oil business, so this is an unsystematic event.

SYSTEMATIC AND UNSYSTEMATIC COMPONENTS OF RETURN

WWW

Analyze risk at
www.portfolioscience.com

The distinction between a systematic risk and an unsystematic risk is never really as exact as we would like it to be. Even the most narrow and peculiar bit of news about a company ripples through the economy. This ripple effect happens because every enterprise, no matter how tiny, is a part of the economy. It's like the proverb about a kingdom that was lost because one horse lost a horseshoe nail. However, not all ripple effects are equal—some risks have a much broader effect than others.

The distinction between the two types of risk allows us to break down the surprise portion, U, of the return on the Flyers stock into two parts. Earlier, we had the actual return broken down into its expected and surprise components: $R - E(R) = U$. We now recognize that the total surprise component for Flyers, U, has a systematic and an unsystematic component, so:

$$R - E(R) = U = \text{Systematic portion} + \text{Unsystematic portion} \qquad (12.3)$$

Because it is traditional, we will use the Greek letter epsilon ϵ to stand for the unsystematic portion. Because systematic risks are often called "market" risks, we use the letter m to stand for the systematic part of the surprise. With these symbols, we can rewrite the formula for the total return:

$$R - E(R) = U = m + \epsilon \qquad (12.4)$$

The important thing about the way we have broken down the total surprise, U, is that the unsystematic portion, ϵ, is unique to Flyers. For this reason, it is unrelated to the unsystematic portion of return on most other assets. To see why this is important, we need to return to the subject of portfolio risk.

EXAMPLE 12.2 | **Systematic versus Unsystematic Events**

Suppose Intel were to unexpectedly announce that its latest computer chip contains a significant flaw in its floating point unit that left it unable to handle numbers bigger than a couple of gigatrillion (meaning that, among other things, the chip cannot calculate Intel's quarterly profits). Is this a systematic or unsystematic event?

Obviously, this event is for the most part unsystematic. However, it would also benefit Intel's competitors to some degree and, at least potentially, harm some users of Intel products such as personal computer makers. Thus, as with most unsystematic events, there is some spillover, but the effect is mostly confined to a relatively small number of companies.

12.2a What are the two basic types of risk?

12.2b What is the distinction between the two types of risk?

CHECK THIS

12.3 Diversification, Systematic Risk, and Unsystematic Risk

In the previous chapter, we introduced the principle of diversification. What we saw was that some of the risk associated with individual assets can be diversified away and some cannot. We are left with an obvious question: Why is this so? It turns out that the answer hinges on the distinction between systematic and unsystematic risk.

DIVERSIFICATION AND UNSYSTEMATIC RISK

By definition, an unsystematic risk is one that is particular to a single asset or, at most, a small group of assets. For example, if the asset under consideration is stock in a single company, such things as successful new products and innovative cost savings will tend to increase the value of the stock. Unanticipated lawsuits, industrial accidents, strikes, and similar events will tend to decrease future cash flows and thereby reduce share value.

Here is the important observation: If we hold only a single stock, then the value of our investment will fluctuate because of company-specific events. If we hold a large portfolio, on the other hand, some of the stocks in the portfolio will go up in value because of positive company-specific events, and some will go down in value because of negative events. The net effect on the overall value of the portfolio will be relatively small, however, because these effects will tend to cancel each other out.

Now we see why some of the variability associated with individual assets is eliminated by diversification. When we combine assets into portfolios, the unique, or unsystematic, events—both positive and negative—tend to "wash out" once we have more than just a few assets. This is an important point that bears repeating:

> Unsystematic risk is essentially eliminated by diversification, so a portfolio with many assets has almost no unsystematic risk.

In fact, the terms *diversifiable risk* and *unsystematic risk* are often used interchangeably.

DIVERSIFICATION AND SYSTEMATIC RISK

We've seen that unsystematic risk can be eliminated by diversification. What about systematic risk? Can it also be eliminated by diversification? The answer is no because, by definition, a systematic risk affects almost all assets. As a result, no matter how many assets we put into a portfolio, systematic risk doesn't go away. Thus, for obvious reasons, the terms *systematic risk* and *nondiversifiable risk* are used interchangeably.

Because we have introduced so many different terms, it is useful to summarize our discussion before moving on. What we have seen is that the total risk of an investment can be written as:

$$\text{Total risk} = \text{Systematic risk} + \text{Unsystematic risk} \qquad (12.5)$$

Systematic risk is also called *nondiversifiable risk* or *market risk*. Unsystematic risk is also called *diversifiable risk, unique risk,* or *asset-specific risk*. Most important, for a well-diversified portfolio, unsystematic risk is negligible. For such a portfolio, essentially all risk is systematic.

CHECK THIS

12.3a Why is some risk diversifiable? Why is some risk not diversifiable?

12.3b Why can't systematic risk be diversified away?

12.4 Systematic Risk and Beta

We now begin to address another question: What determines the size of the risk premium on a risky asset? Put another way, why do some assets have a larger risk premium than other assets? The answer, as we discuss next, is also based on the distinction between systematic and unsystematic risk.

THE SYSTEMATIC RISK PRINCIPLE

Thus far, we've seen that the total risk associated with an asset can be decomposed into two components: systematic and unsystematic risk. We have also seen that unsystematic risk can be essentially eliminated by diversification. The systematic risk present in an asset, on the other hand, cannot be eliminated by diversification.

Based on our study of capital market history in Chapter 1, we know that there is a reward, on average, for bearing risk. However, we now need to be more precise about what we mean by risk. The **systematic risk principle** states that the reward for bearing risk depends only on the systematic risk of an investment.

The underlying rationale for this principle is straightforward: Because unsystematic risk can be eliminated at virtually no cost (by diversifying), there is no reward for bearing it. In other words, the market does not reward risks that are borne unnecessarily.

The systematic risk principle has a remarkable and very important implication:

The expected return on an asset depends only on its systematic risk.

This principle has an obvious corollary: No matter how much total risk an asset has, only the systematic portion is relevant in determining the expected return (and the risk premium) on that asset. This observation is consistent with our previous discussion on portfolio diversification. For example, recall that we noted that purchasing a security with high volatility could actually reduce total portfolio risk. How is this possible? Well, in the current context, if this high volatility is primarily a result of unsystematic risk, then much of the volatility is diversified away. In other words, this stock, although highly volatile, had low systematic, or market, risk.

MEASURING SYSTEMATIC RISK

Because systematic risk is the crucial determinant of an asset's expected return, we need some way of measuring the level of systematic risk for different investments. The specific measure we will use is called the **beta coefficient**, designated by the Greek letter β. A beta coefficient, or just beta for short, tells us how much systematic risk a particular asset has relative to an average asset. By definition, an average asset has a beta of 1.0 relative to itself. An asset with a beta of .50, therefore, has half as much systematic risk as an average asset. Likewise, an asset with a beta of 2.0 has twice as much systematic risk.

Table 12.1 presents the estimated beta coefficients for the stocks of some well-known companies. (Note that *Value Line* rounds betas to the nearest .05.) The range of betas in Table 12.1 is typical for stocks of large U.S. corporations. You should realize, however, that betas outside this range occur.

The important thing to remember is that the expected return, and thus the risk premium, on an asset depends only on its systematic risk. Because assets with larger betas have greater systematic risks, they will have greater expected returns. Thus, from Table 12.1, an investor who buys stock in ExxonMobil, with a beta of .75, should expect to earn less and lose less, on average, than an investor who buys stock in Harley-Davidson, with a beta of about 1.50.

One cautionary note is in order: Not all betas are created equal. For example, in Table 12.1, *Value Line*, a widely used source of betas, reports a beta for IBM of .90. At the same time, however, another widely used source, *S&P Stock Reports*, puts IBM's beta at .73, substantially lower. The difference results from the different procedures used to calculate beta coefficients. We will have more to say on this subject when we explain how betas are calculated in a later section. Our nearby *Work the Web* box shows one way to find betas online.

---

systematic risk principle
The reward for bearing risk depends only on the systematic risk of an investment.

beta coefficient (β)
Measure of the relative systematic risk of an asset. Assets with betas larger (smaller) than 1 have more (less) systematic risk than average.

Find betas at
finance.yahoo.com
and
www.smartmoney.com

Suppose you want to find the beta for a company like Continental Airlines, Inc. One way is to go to the Web. We went to finance.yahoo.com, looked up Continental Airlines (CAL), and followed the "Key Statistics" link. This is part of what we found:

FINANCIAL HIGHLIGHTS			TRADING INFORMATION	
Fiscal Year			**Stock Price History**	
Fiscal Year Ends:	31-Dec		Beta:	1.10
Most Recent Quarter (mrq):	30-Sep-09		52-Week Change[3]:	2.84%
Profitability			S&P500 52-Week Change[3]:	30.13%
Profit Margin (ttm):	-4.91%		52-Week High (08-Jan-09)[3]:	21.83
Operating Margin (ttm):	-0.50%		52-Week Low (09-Mar-09)[3]:	6.37
Management Effectiveness			50-Day Moving Average[3]:	13.50
Return on Assets (ttm):	-0.31%		200-Day Moving Average[3]:	12.35
Return on Equity (ttm):	-82.68%		**Share Statistics**	
Income Statement			Average Volume (3 month)[3]:	7,184,440
Revenue (ttm):	12.93B		Average Volume (10 day)[3]:	5,867,890
Revenue Per Share (ttm):	104.901		Shares Outstanding[5]:	138.45M
Qtrly Revenue Growth (yoy):	-20.20%		Float:	138.35M
Gross Profit (ttm):	2.46B		% Held by Insiders[1]:	0.07%
EBITDA (ttm):	373.00M		% Held by Institutions[1]:	92.70%
Net Income Avl to Common (ttm):	-635.00M		Shares Short (as of 13-Nov-09)[3]:	17.68M
Diluted EPS (ttm):	-5.15		Short Ratio (as of 13-Nov-09)[3]:	2.1
Qtrly Earnings Growth (yoy):	N/A		Short % of Float (as of 13-Nov-09)[3]:	16.20%
			Shares Short (prior month)[3]:	14.75M

The reported beta for Continental Airlines is 1.10, which means that Continental Airlines has about 1.10 times the systematic risk of a typical stock.

TABLE 12.1 Beta Coefficients

	Beta, β	
Company	Value Line	Standard & Poor's
ExxonMobil	0.75	0.35
IBM	0.90	0.73
Starbucks	1.15	1.36
Walmart	0.60	0.26
Microsoft	0.80	0.96
Harley-Davidson	1.50	2.32
eBay	1.15	1.74
Nordstrom	1.45	1.72
Southwest Airlines	0.95	1.10
Yahoo!	0.95	0.80

Source: *Value Line* Investment Survey and *S&P Stock Reports.*

Total Risk versus Beta

Consider the following information on two securities. Which has greater total risk? Which has greater systematic risk? Greater unsystematic risk? Which asset will have a higher risk premium?

	Standard Deviation	Beta
Security A	40%	.50
Security B	20	1.50

From our discussion in this section, Security A has greater total risk, but it has substantially less systematic risk. Because total risk is the sum of systematic and unsystematic risk, Security A must have greater unsystematic risk. Finally, from the systematic risk principle, Security B will have a higher risk premium and a greater expected return, despite the fact that it has less total risk.

PORTFOLIO BETAS

Earlier, we saw that the riskiness of a portfolio has no simple relation to the risks of the assets in the portfolio. By contrast, a portfolio beta can be calculated just like a portfolio expected return. For example, looking again at Table 12.1, suppose you put half of your money in Starbucks and half in Yahoo!. Using *Value Line* betas, what would the beta of this combination be? Because Starbucks has a beta of 1.15 and Yahoo! has a beta of 0.95, the portfolio's beta, β_p would be:

$$\beta_p = .50 \times \beta_{\text{Starbucks}} + .50 \times \beta_{\text{Yahoo!}}$$
$$= .50 \times 1.15 + .50 \times .95$$
$$= 1.05$$

In general, if we had a large number of assets in a portfolio, we would multiply each asset's beta by its portfolio weight and then add the results to get the portfolio's beta.

Portfolio Betas

Suppose we have the following information

Security	Amount Invested	Expected Return	Beta
Stock A	$1,000	8%	.80
Stock B	2,000	12	.95
Stock C	3,000	15	1.10
Stock D	4,000	18	1.40

What is the expected return on this portfolio? What is the beta of this portfolio? Does this portfolio have more or less systematic risk than an average asset?

To answer, we first have to calculate the portfolio weights. Notice that the total amount invested is $10,000. Of this, $1,000/$10,000 = 10% is invested in Stock A. Similarly, 20 percent is invested in Stock B, 30 percent is invested in Stock C, and 40 percent is invested in Stock D. The expected return, $E(R_p)$, is thus:

$$E(R_p) = .10 \times E(R_A) + .20 \times E(R_B) + .30 \times E(R_C) + .40 \times E(R_D)$$
$$= .10 \times 8\% + .20 \times 12\% + .30 \times 15\% + .40 \times 18\%$$
$$= 14.9\%$$

Similarly, the portfolio beta, β_p, is:

$$\beta_p = .10 \times \beta_A + .20 \times \beta_B + .30 \times \beta_C + .40 \times \beta_D$$
$$= .10 \times .80 + .20 \times .95 + .30 \times 1.10 + .40 \times 1.40$$
$$= 1.16$$

This portfolio thus has an expected return of 14.9 percent and a beta of 1.16. Because the beta is larger than 1, this portfolio has greater systematic risk than an average asset.

CHECK THIS

12.4a   What is the systematic risk principle?

12.4b   What does a beta coefficient measure?

12.4c   How do you calculate a portfolio beta?

12.4d   True or false: The expected return on a risky asset depends on that asset's total risk. Explain.

12.5 The Security Market Line

We're now in a position to see how risk is rewarded in the marketplace. To begin, suppose that Asset A has an expected return of $E(R_A) = 16\%$ and a beta of $\beta_A = 1.6$. Further suppose that the risk-free rate is $R_f = 4\%$. Notice that a risk-free asset, by definition, has no systematic risk (or unsystematic risk), so a risk-free asset has a beta of zero.

BETA AND THE RISK PREMIUM

Consider a portfolio made up of Asset A and a risk-free asset. We can calculate some different possible portfolio expected returns and betas by varying the percentages invested in these two assets. For example, if 25 percent of the portfolio is invested in Asset A, then the expected return is:

$$E(R_p) = .25 \times E(R_A) + (1 - .25) \times R_f$$
$$= .25 \times 16\% + .75 \times 4\%$$
$$= 7\%$$

Similarly, the beta on the portfolio, β_p, would be:

$$\beta_p = .25 \times \beta_A + (1 - .25) \times 0$$
$$= .25 \times 1.6$$
$$= .40$$

WWW

For more information on
risk management visit
www.fenews.co.uk

Notice that, because the weights have to add up to 1, the percentage invested in the risk-free asset is equal to 1 minus the percentage invested in Asset A.

One thing that you might wonder about is whether the percentage invested in Asset A can exceed 100 percent. The answer is yes. This can happen if the investor borrows at the risk-free rate and invests the proceeds in stocks. For example, suppose an investor has $100 and borrows an additional $50 at 4 percent, the risk-free rate. The total investment in Asset A would be $150, or 150 percent of the investor's wealth. This process would be similar to buying on margin, discussed in an earlier chapter. The expected return in this case would be:

$$E(R_p) = 1.50 \times E(R_A) + (1 - 1.50) \times R_f$$
$$= 1.50 \times 16\% - .50 \times 4\%$$
$$= 22\%$$

The beta on the portfolio would be:

$$\beta_p = 1.50 \times \beta_A + (1 - 1.50) \times 0$$
$$= 1.50 \times 1.6$$
$$= 2.4$$

We can calculate some other possibilities, as follows:

Percentage of Portfolio in Asset A	Portfolio Expected Return	Portfolio Beta
0%	4%	.0
25	7	.4
50	10	.8
75	13	1.2
100	16	1.6
125	19	2.0
150	22	2.4

In Figure 12.1A, we plot these portfolio expected returns against portfolio betas. Notice that all the combinations fall on a straight line.

THE REWARD-TO-RISK RATIO

What is the slope of the straight line in Figure 12.1A? As always, the slope of a straight line is equal to the rise over the run. In this case, as we move out of the risk-free asset into Asset A, the expected return goes from 4 percent to 16 percent, a rise of 12 percent. At the same time, the beta increases from zero to 1.6, a run of 1.6. The slope of the line is thus 12%/1.6 = 7.5%.

Notice that the slope of our line is just the risk premium on Asset A, $E(R_A) - R_f$, divided by Asset A's beta, β_A:

$$\text{Slope} = \frac{E(R_A) - R_f}{\beta_A}$$
$$= \frac{16\% - 4\%}{1.6}$$
$$= 7.50\%$$

 What this tells us is that Asset A offers a *reward-to-risk* ratio of 7.5 percent.[1] In other words, Asset A has a risk premium of 7.50 percent per "unit" of systematic risk.

THE BASIC ARGUMENT

Now suppose we consider a second asset, Asset B. This asset has a beta of 1.2 and an expected return of 12 percent. Which investment is better, Asset A or Asset B? You might think that we really cannot say—some investors might prefer A; some investors might prefer B. Actually, however, we can say: A is better because, as we will demonstrate, B offers inadequate compensation for its level of systematic risk, at least relative to A.

To begin, we calculate different combinations of expected returns and betas for portfolios of Asset B and a risk-free asset, just as we did for Asset A. For example, if we put 25 percent in Asset B and the remaining 75 percent in the risk-free asset, the portfolio's expected return will be:

$$E(R_p) = .25 \times E(R_B) + (1 - .25) \times R_f$$
$$= .25 \times 12\% + .75 \times 4\%$$
$$= 6\%$$

---

[1] This ratio is sometimes called the *Treynor index*, after one of its originators.

FIGURE 12.1 | Betas and Portfolio Returns

A. Portfolio expected returns and betas for Asset A

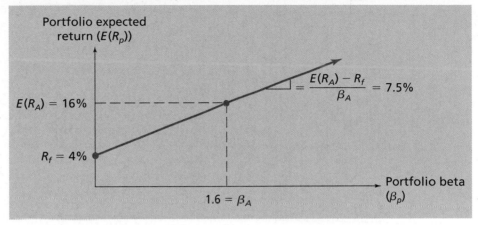

B. Portfolio expected returns and betas for Asset B

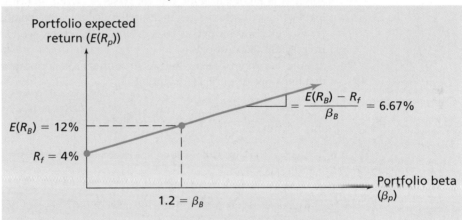

C. Portfolio expected returns and betas for both assets

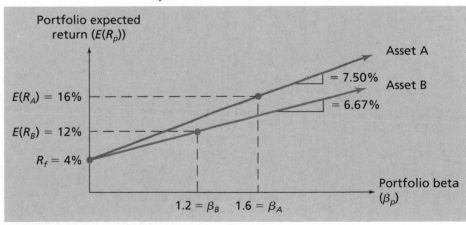

Similarly, the beta on the portfolio, β_p, would be:

$$\beta_p = .25 \times \beta_B + (1 - .25) \times 0$$
$$= .25 \times 1.2$$
$$= .30$$

Some other possibilities are as follows:

Percentage of Portfolio in Asset B	Portfolio Expected Return	Portfolio Beta
0%	4%	.0
25	6	.3
50	8	.6
75	10	.9
100	12	1.2
125	14	1.5
150	16	1.8

When we plot these combinations of portfolio expected returns and portfolio betas in Figure 12.1B, we get a straight line, just as we did for Asset A.

The key thing to notice is that when we compare the results for Assets A and B, as in Figure 12.1C, the line describing the combinations of expected returns and betas for Asset A is higher than the one for Asset B. What this result tells us is that for any given level of systematic risk (as measured by beta), some combination of Asset A and the risk-free asset always offers a larger return. Therefore, we can state that Asset A is a better investment than Asset B.

Another way of seeing that Asset A offers a superior return for its level of risk is to note that the slope of our line for Asset B is:

$$\text{Slope} = \frac{E(R_B) - R_f}{\beta_B}$$

$$= \frac{12\% - 4\%}{1.2}$$

$$= 6.67\%$$

Thus, Asset B has a reward-to-risk ratio of 6.67 percent, which is less than the 7.5 percent offered by Asset A.

THE FUNDAMENTAL RESULT

The situation we described for Assets A and B could not persist in a well-organized, active market because investors would be attracted to Asset A and away from Asset B. As a result, Asset A's price would rise and Asset B's price would fall. Because prices and expected returns move in opposite directions, A's expected return would decline and B's would rise.

This buying and selling would continue until the two assets plot on exactly the same line, which means they would offer the same reward for bearing risk. In other words, in an active, competitive market, we must have the situation that:

$$\frac{E(R_A) - R_f}{\beta_A} = \frac{E(R_B) - R_f}{\beta_B} \tag{12.6}$$

This is the fundamental relation between risk and return.

Our basic argument can be extended to more than just two assets. In fact, no matter how many assets we had, we would always reach the same conclusion:

The reward-to-risk ratio must be the same for all assets in a competitive financial market.

This result is really not too surprising. What it says is that, for example, if one asset has twice as much systematic risk as another asset, its risk premium will simply be twice as large.

EXAMPLE 12.5

Using Reward-to-Risk Ratios

Suppose we see that the reward-to-risk ratio for all assets equals 7.2. If the risk-free rate is 4 percent, what is the required return for an arbitrary asset i, with (1) beta equal 1? (2) beta equal 0?

To answer question (1), write down the reward-to-risk equation, and set it equal to 7.2. Because we know the risk-free rate and the beta of the asset, we can easily solve for the expected return of the asset:

$$\frac{E(R_i) - R_f}{\beta_i} = 7.2$$

$$\frac{E(R_i) - 4.0}{1} = 7.2$$

Therefore, $E(R_i) = 11.2$ percent.

Question (2) is a bit trickier. We cannot use the approach of (1) directly, because we would have to divide by zero. But let's think. Beta is the measure of risk in the reward-to-risk equation. If the portfolio has zero risk, its expected return should not reflect a premium for carrying risk. Therefore, the answer is 4 percent, the rate of return on the risk-free asset.

Because all assets in the market must have the same reward-to-risk ratio, they all must plot on the same line. This argument is illustrated in Figure 12.2, where the subscript i on the return R_i and beta β_i indexes Assets A, B, C, and D. As shown, Assets A and B plot directly on the line and thus have the same reward-to-risk ratio.

If an asset is plotted above the line, such as C in Figure 12.2, its reward-to-risk ratio is too high because its expected return is too high. An expected return has two inputs: the expected price and the price today. The expected return is calculated as $E(R) = [E(P) - P_{today}]/P_{today}$, or $[E(P)/P_{today}] - 1$. To *lower* the expected return for Asset C, its price today must *increase* until the reward-to-risk ratio for Asset C plots exactly on the line. Similarly, if an asset is plotted below the line, such as D in Figure 12.2, its reward-to-risk ratio is too low because its expected return is too low. To *increase* the expected return for Asset D, its price today must *fall* until the reward-to-risk ratio for Asset D also plots exactly on the line.

The arguments we have presented apply to active, competitive, well-functioning markets. Active financial markets, such as the NYSE, best meet these criteria. Other markets, such as real asset markets, may or may not. For this reason, these concepts are most useful in examining active financial markets.

FIGURE 12.2

Expected Returns and Systematic Risk

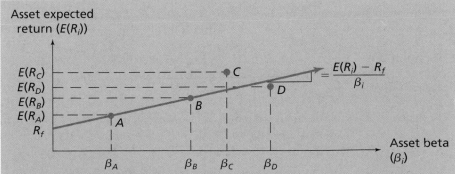

The fundamental relationship between beta and expected return is that all assets must have the same reward-to-risk ratio, $[E(R_i) - R_f]/\beta_i$. This means that they would all plot on the same straight line. Assets A and B are examples of this behavior. Asset C's expected return is too high; Asset D's is too low.

EXAMPLE 12.6

Buy Low, Sell High

A security is said to be *overvalued* relative to another security if its price today is too high given its expected return and risk. Suppose you observe the following:

Security	Beta	Expected Return
Melan Co.	1.3	14 %
Choly Co.	.8	10
Baby Co.	1.0	11.5

The risk-free rate is currently 6 percent. Is one of the securities overvalued relative to the others?

To answer, we compute the reward-to-risk ratios. For Melan, this ratio is (14% − 6%)/1.3 = 6.15%; for Choly, this ratio is 5 percent; and for Baby, it is 5.5 percent. What we conclude is that Choly offers an insufficient expected return for its level of risk, at least relative to Melan and Baby. Because its expected return is too low, its price is too high. In other words, Choly is overvalued relative to Melan and Baby, and we would expect to see its price fall relative to Melan and Baby. Notice that we could also say Melan and Baby are *undervalued* relative to Choly. What can you say about the relative pricing of Melan and Baby?

THE SECURITY MARKET LINE

The line that results when we plot expected returns and beta coefficients is obviously of some importance, so it's time we gave it a name. This line, which we use to describe the relationship between systematic risk and expected return in financial markets, is usually called the **security market line (SML)**, and it is one of the most important concepts in modern finance.

security market line (SML)
Graphical representation of the linear relationship between systematic risk and expected return in financial markets.

MARKET PORTFOLIOS We will find it very useful to know the equation of the SML. Although there are many different ways we could write it, we will discuss the most frequently seen version. Suppose we consider a portfolio made up of all of the assets in the market. Such a portfolio is called a *market portfolio*, and we will express the expected return on this market portfolio as $E(R_M)$.

Because all the assets in the market must plot on the SML, so must a market portfolio made up of those assets. To determine where it plots on the SML, we need to know the beta of the market portfolio, β_M. Because this portfolio is representative of all of the assets in the market, it must have average systematic risk. In other words, it has a beta of 1. We could therefore express the slope of the SML as:

$$\text{SML slope} = \frac{E(R_M) - R_f}{\beta_M} = \frac{E(R_M) - R_f}{1} = E(R_M) - R_f$$

market risk premium
The risk premium on a market portfolio, i.e., a portfolio made of all assets in the market.

The term $E(R_M) - R_f$ is often called the **market risk premium** because it is the risk premium on a market portfolio.

THE CAPITAL ASSET PRICING MODEL To finish up, if we let $E(R_i)$ and β_i stand for the expected return and beta, respectively, on any asset in the market, then we know that the asset must plot on the SML. As a result, we know that its reward-to-risk ratio is the same as that of the overall market:

$$\frac{E(R_i) - R_f}{\beta_i} = E(R_M) - R_f$$

If we rearrange this, then we can write the equation for the SML as:

$$E(R_i) = R_f + [E(R_M) - R_f] \times \beta_i \tag{12.7}$$

FIGURE 12.3   Security Market Line (SML)

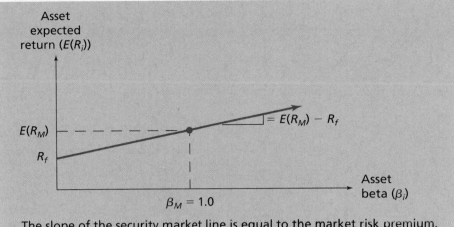

The slope of the security market line is equal to the market risk premium, i.e., the reward for bearing an average amount of systematic risk. The equation describing the SML can be written as:

$$E(R_i) = R_f + [E(R_M) - R_f] \times \beta_i$$

which is the capital asset pricing model (CAPM).

EXAMPLE 12.7   **Risk and Return**

Suppose the risk-free rate is 4 percent, the market risk premium is 8.6 percent, and a particular stock has a beta of 1.3. Based on the CAPM, what is the expected return on this stock? What would the expected return be if the beta were to double?

With a beta of 1.3, the risk premium for the stock is 1.3 × 8.6%, or 11.18 percent. The risk-free rate is 4 percent, so the expected return is 15.18 percent. If the beta were to double to 2.6, the risk premium would double to 22.36 percent, so the expected return would be 26.36 percent.

---

capital asset pricing model (CAPM)

A theory of risk and return for securities in a competitive capital market.

Equation (12.7) is the famous **capital asset pricing model (CAPM)**.[2] What the CAPM shows is that the expected return for an asset depends on three things:

1. *The pure time value of money.* As measured by the risk-free rate, R_f, this is the reward for merely waiting for your money, without taking any risk.

2. *The reward for bearing systematic risk.* As measured by the market risk premium, $E(R_M) - R_f$, this component is the reward the market offers for bearing an average amount of systematic risk.

3. *The amount of systematic risk.* As measured by β_i, this is the amount of systematic risk present in a particular asset relative to that in an average asset.

By the way, the CAPM works for portfolios of assets just as it does for individual assets. In an earlier section, we saw how to calculate a portfolio's beta in the CAPM equation.

Figure 12.3 summarizes our discussion of the SML and the CAPM. As before, we plot expected return against beta. Now we recognize that, based on the CAPM, the slope of the SML is equal to the market risk premium, $E(R_M) - R_f$.

There's a CAPM calculator (if you really need it!) at www.moneychimp.com

---

[2] Our discussion of the CAPM is actually closely related to the more recent development, arbitrage pricing theory (APT). The theory underlying the CAPM is more complex than we have indicated here, and it has implications beyond the scope of this discussion. As we present it here, the CAPM has essentially identical implications to those of the APT, so we don't distinguish between them.

TABLE 12.2 **Risk and Return Summary**

1. **Total risk.** The *total risk* of an investment is measured by the variance or, more commonly, the standard deviation of its return.

2. **Total return.** The *total return* on an investment has two components: the expected return and the unexpected return. The unexpected return comes about because of unanticipated events. The risk from investing stems from the possibility of an unanticipated event.

3. **Systematic and unsystematic risks.** *Systematic risks* (also called *market risks*) are unanticipated events that affect almost all assets to some degree because the effects are economywide. *Unsystematic risks* are unanticipated events that affect single assets or small groups of assets. Unsystematic risks are also called *unique* or *asset-specific risks.*

4. **The effect of diversification.** Some, but not all, of the risk associated with a risky investment can be eliminated by *diversification*. The reason is that unsystematic risks, which are unique to individual assets, tend to wash out in a large portfolio, but systematic risks, which affect all of the assets in a portfolio to some extent, do not.

5. **The systematic risk principle and beta.** Because unsystematic risk can be freely eliminated by diversification, the *systematic risk principle* states that the reward for bearing risk depends only on the level of systematic risk. The level of systematic risk in a particular asset, relative to the average, is given by the *beta* of that asset.

6. **The reward-to-risk ratio and the security market line.** The *reward-to-risk ratio* for Asset i is the ratio of its risk premium, $E(R_i) - R_f$, to its beta, β_i:

$$\frac{E(R_i) - R_f}{\beta_i}$$

   In a well-functioning market, this ratio is the same for every asset. As a result, when asset expected returns are plotted against asset betas, all assets plot on the same straight line, called the *security market line* (SML).

7. **The capital asset pricing model.** From the SML, the expected return on Asset i can be written:

$$E(R_i) = R_f + [E(R_M) - R_f] \times \beta_i$$

   This is the *capital asset pricing model* (CAPM). The expected return on a risky asset thus has three components. The first is the pure time value of money (R_f); the second is the market risk premium, $E(R_M) - R_f$; and the third is the beta for the asset (β_i).

This concludes our presentation of concepts related to the risk-return trade-off. Table 12.2 summarizes the various concepts in the order in which we discussed them.

CHECK THIS

12.5a What is the fundamental relationship between risk and return in active markets?

12.5b What is the security market line (SML)? Why must all assets plot directly on it in a well-functioning market?

12.5c What is the capital asset pricing model (CAPM)? What does it tell us about the required return on a risky investment?

12.6 More on Beta

In our last several sections, we discussed the basic economic principles of risk and return. We found that the expected return on a security depends on its systematic risk, which is measured using the security's beta coefficient, β. In this final section, we examine beta in more detail. We first illustrate more closely what it is that beta measures. We then show how betas can be estimated for individual securities, and we discuss why different sources report different betas for the same security.

A CLOSER LOOK AT BETA

Going back to the beginning of the chapter, we discussed how the actual return on a security, R, could be written as follows:

$$R - E(R) = m + \epsilon \tag{12.8}$$

Recall that in equation (12.8), m stands for the systematic or marketwide portion of the unexpected return. Based on our discussion of the CAPM, we can now be a little more precise about this component.

Specifically, the systematic portion of an unexpected return depends on two things. First, it depends on the size of the systematic effect. We will measure this as $R_M - E(R_M)$, which is simply the difference between the actual return on the overall market and the expected return. Second, as we have discussed, some securities have greater systematic risk than others, and we measure this risk using beta. Putting it together, we have:

$$m = [R_M - E(R_M)] \times \beta \tag{12.9}$$

In other words, the marketwide, or systematic, portion of the return on a security depends on both the size of the marketwide surprise, $R_M - E(R_M)$, and the sensitivity of the security to such surprises, β.

Now, if we combine equations (12.8) and (12.9), we have:

$$R - E(R) = m + \epsilon \tag{12.10}$$
$$= [R_M - E(R_M)] \times \beta + \epsilon$$

Equation (12.10) gives us some additional insight into beta by telling us why some securities have higher betas than others. A high-beta security is simply one that is relatively sensitive to overall market movements, whereas a low-beta security is one that is relatively insensitive. In other words, the systematic risk of a security is just a reflection of its sensitivity to overall market movements.

A hypothetical example is useful for illustrating the main point of equation (12.10). Suppose a particular security has a beta of 1.2, the risk-free rate is 5 percent, and the expected return on the market is 12 percent. From the CAPM, we know that the expected return on the security is:

$$E(R) = R_f + [E(R_M) - R_f] \times \beta$$
$$= .05 + (.12 - .05) \times 1.2$$
$$= .134$$

Thus, the expected return on this security is 13.4 percent. However, we know that in any year the actual return on this security will be more or less than 13.4 percent because of unanticipated systematic and unsystematic events.

Columns 1 and 2 of Table 12.3 list the actual returns on our security, R, for a five-year period along with the actual returns for the market as a whole, R_M, for the same period. Given these actual returns and the expected returns on the security (13.4 percent) and the market as a whole (12 percent), we can calculate the unexpected returns on the security, $R - E(R)$,

TABLE 12.3			\multicolumn{1}{c}{Decomposing Total Returns}			
	Actual Returns		Unexpected Returns		Systematic Portion	Unsystematic Portion (ϵ)
Year	R	R_M	$R - E(R)$	$R_M - E(R_M)$	$[R_M - E(R_M)] \times \beta$	$[R - E(R)] - [R_M - E(R_M)] \times \beta$
1	20 %	15%	6.6%	3%	3.6%	3%
2	−24.6	−3	−38	−15	−18	−20
3	23	10	9.6	−2	−2.4	12
4	36.8	24	23.4	12	14.4	9
5	3.4	7	−10	−5	−6	−4

FIGURE 12.4   Unexpected Returns and Beta

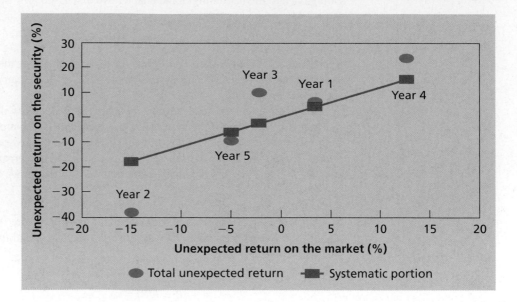

along with the unexpected return on the market as a whole, $R_M - E(R_M)$. The results are shown in columns 3 and 4 of Table 12.3.

Next we decompose the unexpected returns on the security—that is, we break them down into their systematic and unsystematic components in columns 5 and 6. From equation (12.9), we calculate the systematic portion of the unexpected return by taking the security's beta, 1.2, and multiplying it by the market's unexpected return:

$$\text{Systematic portion} = m = [R_M - E(R_M)] \times \beta$$

Finally, we calculate the unsystematic portion by subtracting the systematic portion from the total unexpected return:

$$\text{Unsystematic portion} = \epsilon = [R - E(R)] - [R_M - E(R_M)] \times \beta$$

Notice that the unsystematic portion is essentially whatever is left over after we account for the systematic portion. For this reason, it is sometimes called the "residual" portion of the unexpected return.

Figure 12.4 illustrates the main points of this discussion by plotting the unexpected returns on the security in Table 12.3 against the unexpected return on the market as a whole. These are the individual points in the graph, each labeled with its year. We also plot the systematic portions of the unexpected returns in Table 12.3 and connect them with a straight line. Notice that the slope of the straight line is equal to 1.2, the beta of the security. As indicated, the distance from the straight line to an individual point is the unsystematic portion of the return, ϵ, for a particular year.

WHERE DO BETAS COME FROM?

As our discussion to this point shows, beta is a useful concept. It allows us to estimate the expected return on a security, it tells how sensitive a security's return is to unexpected market events, and it lets us separate out the systematic and unsystematic portions of a security's return. In our example just above, we were given that the beta was 1.2, so the required calculations were all pretty straightforward. Suppose, however, that we didn't have the beta ahead of time. In this case, we would have to estimate it.

A security's beta is a measure of how sensitive the security's return is to overall market movements. That sensitivity depends on two things: (1) how closely correlated the security's return is with the overall market's return and (2) how volatile the security is relative to the market. Specifically, going back to our previous chapter, let $\text{Corr}(R_i, R_M)$ stand for the

TABLE 12.4   Calculating Beta

Year	Returns Security (1)	Returns Market (2)	Return Deviations Security (3)	Return Deviations Market (4)	Squared Deviations Security (5)	Squared Deviations Market (6)	Product of Deviations (7)
1	.10	.08	.00	−.04	.0000	.0016	.0000
2	−.08	−.12	−.18	−.24	.0324	.0576	.0432
3	−.04	.16	−.14	.04	.0196	.0016	−.0056
4	.40	.26	.30	.14	.0900	.0196	.0420
5	.12	.22	.02	.10	.0004	.0100	.0020
Totals	.50	.60	0	0	.1424	.0904	.0816

	Average Returns	Variances	Standard Deviations
Security	.50/5 = .10 = 10%	.1424/4 = .0356	$\sqrt{.0356}$ = .1887 = 18.87%
Market	.60/5 = .12 = 12%	.0904/4 = .0226	$\sqrt{.0226}$ = .1503 = 15.03%

Covariance = $\text{Cov}(R_i, R_M)$ = .0816/4 = .0204

Correlation = $\text{Corr}(R_i, R_M)$ = .0204/(.1887 × .1503) = .72

Beta = β = .72 × (.1887/.1503) = .9039 ≈ .9

correlation between the return on a particular security i and the overall market. As before, let σ_i and σ_M be the standard deviations on the security and the market, respectively. Given these numbers, the beta for the security, β_i, is simply:

$$\beta_i = \text{Corr}(R_i, R_M) \times \sigma_i/\sigma_M \qquad (12.11)$$

In other words, the beta is equal to the correlation multiplied by the ratio of the standard deviations.

From previous chapters, we know how to calculate the standard deviations in equation (12.11). However, we have not yet discussed how to calculate correlations. A simple and straightforward way to proceed is to construct a worksheet like Table 12.4.

The first six columns of Table 12.4 are familiar from Chapter 1. The first two contain five years of returns on a particular security and the overall market. We add these up and divide by 5 to get the average returns of 10 percent and 12 percent for the security and the market, respectively, as shown in the table. In the third and fourth columns we calculate the return deviations by taking each individual return and subtracting out the average return. In columns 5 and 6 we square these return deviations. To calculate the variances, we total these squared deviations and divide by $5 - 1 = 4$. We calculate the standard deviations by taking the square root of the variances, and we find that the standard deviations for the security and the market are 18.87 percent and 15.03 percent, respectively.

Now we come to the part that's new. In the last column of Table 12.4, we have calculated the *product* of the return deviations by simply multiplying columns 3 and 4. When we total these products and divide by $5 - 1 = 4$, the result is called the **covariance**.

Covariance, as the name suggests, is a measure of the tendency of two things to vary together. If the covariance is positive, then the tendency is to move in the same direction, and vice versa for a negative covariance. A zero covariance means there is no particular relation. For our security in Table 12.4, the covariance is +.0204, so the security tends to move in the same direction as the market.

A problem with covariances is that, like variances, the actual numbers are hard to interpret (the sign, of course, is not). For example, our covariance is .0204, but, just from this number, we can't really say if the security has a strong tendency to move with the market or only a weak one. To fix this problem, we divide the covariance by the product of the two standard deviations. The result is the correlation coefficient, introduced in the previous chapter.

covariance

A measure of the tendency of two things to move or vary together.

SPREADSHEET ANALYSIS

	A	B	C	D	E	F	G	H
1								
2			Using a Spreadsheet to Calculate Beta					
3								
4	To illustrate how to calculate betas, correlations, and covariances using a spreadsheet,							
5	we have entered the information from Table 12.4 into the spreadsheet below. Here, we							
6	use Excel functions to do all the calculations.							
7								
8				Returns				
9			Year	Security	Market			
10			1	10%	8%	Note: The Excel Format is		
11			2	−8%	−12%	set to percent, but the		
12			3	−4%	16%	numbers are entered as		
13			4	40%	26%	decimals.		
14			5	12%	22%			
15								
16			Average:	10%	12%	(Using the =AVERAGE function)		
17			Std. Dev.:	18.87%	15.03%	(Using the =STDEV function)		
18			Correlation:	0.72		=CORREL(D10:D14,E10:E14)		
19								
20			Beta:	0.90				
21								
22	Excel also has a covariance function, =COVAR, but we do not use it because it divides							
23	by n instead of n-1. Verify that you get a Beta of about 0.72 if you use the COVAR							
24	function divided by the variance of the Market Returns (Use the Excel function, =VAR).							
25								
26	Question 1: How would you correct the covariance calculation?							
27	Question 2: What happens when you use =SLOPE, an Excel function?							
28								

From Table 12.4, the correlation between our security and the overall market is .72. Recalling that correlations range from -1 to $+1$, this .72 tells us that the security has a fairly strong tendency to move with the overall market, but that tendency is not perfect.

Now, we have reached our goal of calculating the beta coefficient. As shown in the last row of Table 12.4, from equation (12.11), we have:

$$\beta_i = \text{Corr}(R_i, R_M) \times \sigma_i / \sigma_M$$
$$= .72 \times (.1887/.1503)$$
$$= .90$$

We find that this security has a beta of .9, so it has slightly less than average systematic risk. As our nearby *Spreadsheet Analysis* box shows, these calculations can be done easily with a spreadsheet.

ANOTHER WAY TO CALCULATE BETA

At the bottom of the previous *Spreadsheet Analysis* you will notice Question 2, which suggests using the built-in slope function in Excel. If you use this function, be sure to select the market returns as the "*x* data" and the security returns as the "*y* data." When you do, you will find that the result is the security's beta of .90.

To understand why the slope function gives us the beta, consider Figure 12.5A, which is a simple scatter plot of the market and security returns. Notice that we plotted the market returns on the *x* axis and the security returns on the *y* axis. Looking at the plot, we see that the security has a positive relationship with the market.

To capture the nature of this relationship, consider Figure 12.5B, which adds a simple trend line to the data. We refer to this as the *characteristic line*. Notice that the line almost crosses at the origin.

Recall that beta measures relative movement. For example, a security with a beta of 1 is expected to move, on average, with the market. In this case, what would the characteristic

FIGURE 12.5   Graphical Representation of Calculating Beta

A. Scatter plot

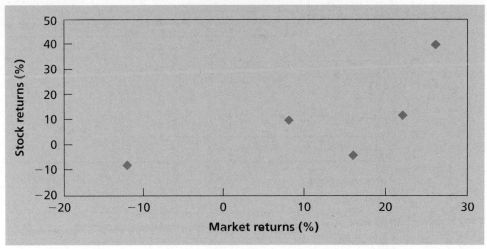

B. Characteristic line

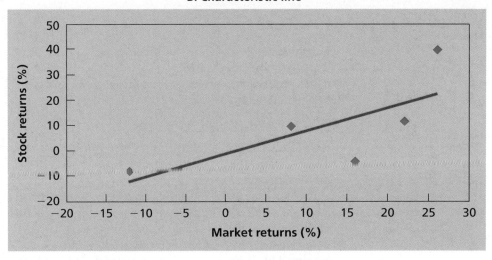

line look like? It would be a line with a 45 degree angle, or a slope of 1. This slope indicates that as the market goes up 1 percent, we would expect the stock to do the same. In mathematics terms, the measure of rise over run is slope. So, if we define the market as the *x* data and the stock as the *y* data, the slope is effectively the beta of the security.

Applying this method to Figure 12.5B, what do you think the beta is? Notice that when the market has a return of 10 percent, the security is expected to have a return slightly less than 10 percent. The characteristic line thus suggests that the beta for this security is less than 1 because the stock return is less than a corresponding market return. Because comovements in returns seem to be rather close, however, our answer of .90 seems appropriate.

You might recall from your statistics class an alternative method for estimating a "line of best fit." Hopefully you remember this as a simple linear regression. In this case, we are going to "regress" the returns of the security (*y* data) on the returns of the market (*x* data). Fortunately, Excel also has a built-in regression function. If you look at the next *Spreadsheet Analysis,* you can see a portion of the output from this process.

You will notice that the output provides an estimate of the intercept, as well as a coefficient (or slope) on the *x* data (i.e., the market returns). You should see that the estimated value is .90, which is consistent with our earlier calculations.

You might wonder why this approach is necessary if we can simply go to the Internet and look up the data. Well, the ability to calculate your own beta is important for several reasons.

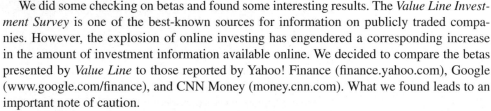

	A	B	C	D	E	F
1						
2		Using a Regression in Excel to Calculate Beta				
3						
4						
5	*Regression Statistics*					
6	Multiple R	0.7192				
7	R Square	0.5173				
8	Adjusted R Square	0.3563				
9	Standard Error	15.1375				
10	Observations	5				
11						
12	ANOVA					
13		*df*	*SS*	*MS*	*F*	*Significance F*
14	Regression	1	736.5663	736.5664	3.214418126	1.1709
15	Residual	3	687.4336	229.1445428		
16	Total	4	1424			
17						
18		*Coefficients*	*Standard Error*	*t Stat*	*P-value*	
19	Intercept	−0.8319	9.0736	−0.0917	0.9327	
20	Market Returns	0.9027	0.5035	1.7929	0.1709	

For example, as we discuss just below, many Internet sites will report different betas for a stock, so being able to understand which estimate is the best can be helpful. In addition, what if you are trying to evaluate a fund manager or an investment that is not publicly traded? Well, in this case you will have to "build a beta" yourself.

WHY DO BETAS DIFFER?

Based on what we've studied so far, you can see that beta is a pretty important topic. You might wonder, then, are all published betas created equal? Read on for a partial answer to this question.

We did some checking on betas and found some interesting results. The *Value Line Investment Survey* is one of the best-known sources for information on publicly traded companies. However, the explosion of online investing has engendered a corresponding increase in the amount of investment information available online. We decided to compare the betas presented by *Value Line* to those reported by Yahoo! Finance (finance.yahoo.com), Google (www.google.com/finance), and CNN Money (money.cnn.com). What we found leads to an important note of caution.

Consider Amazon.com, the big online retailer. The beta reported for it on the Internet was about 3.05. This estimate was much larger than *Value Line*'s beta for Amazon of 1.20. Amazon .com wasn't the only stock that showed a divergence in betas. In fact, for most of the technology companies we looked at, *Value Line* reported betas that were significantly lower than their online cousins. For example, the online beta for eBay was approximately 2.95, while *Value Line* reported a beta of 1.15. Similarly, the online beta for 1-800-Flowers.com was about 2.85 versus a *Value Line* beta of 1.20. Interested in something less high-tech? The online beta for Martha Stewart Living was around 3.50, compared to *Value Line*'s beta of 1.45.

We also found some unusual, and even hard to believe, estimates for beta. Campbell Soup Co. had a very low online beta of .04 (*Value Line* reported .75). The online beta for PepsiCo was .05, compared to *Value Line*'s .70. Perhaps the most outrageous numbers were the ones reported for the International Fight League and Catcher Holdings, Inc.; the estimated betas for those companies were 60.88 and −87 (notice the minus sign!), respectively. *Value Line* did not report a beta for these companies. How do you suppose we should interpret a beta of −87?

There are a few lessons to be learned from these examples. The important thing to remember is that betas are estimated from actual data. Different sources estimate differently, possibly using different data. We discuss some of the key differences next.

First, there are two issues concerning data. Betas can be calculated using daily, weekly, monthly, quarterly, or annual returns. In principle, it does not matter which is chosen, but with real data, different estimates will result. Second, betas can be estimated over relatively short periods such as a few weeks or over long periods of 5 to 10 years (or even more).

The trade-off here is not hard to understand. Betas obtained from high-frequency returns, such as daily returns, are less reliable than those obtained from less frequent returns, such as monthly returns. This argues for using monthly or longer returns. On the other hand, any time we estimate something, we would like to have a large number of recent observations. This argues for using weekly or daily returns. There is no ideal balance; the most common choices are three to five years of monthly data or a single year of weekly data. The betas we get from a year of weekly data are more current in the sense that they reflect only the previous year, but they tend to be less stable than those obtained from longer periods.

Another issue has to do with choice of a market index. All along, we have discussed the return on the "overall market," but we have not been very precise about how to measure this. By far the most common choice is to use the S&P 500 stock market index to measure the overall market, but this is not the only alternative. Different sources use different indexes to capture the overall market, and different indexes will lead to different beta estimates.

You might wonder whether some index is the "correct" one. The answer is yes, but a problem comes up. In principle, in the CAPM, when we speak of the overall market, what we really mean is the market for *every* risky asset of every type. In other words, what we would need is an index that included all the stocks, bonds, real estate, precious metals, and everything else in the entire world (not just the United States). Obviously, no such index exists, so instead we must choose some smaller index to proxy for this much larger one.

A few sources (including *Value Line,* one source for Table 12.1) calculate betas the way we described in Table 12.4, but then they go on to adjust them for statistical reasons. The nature of the adjustment goes beyond our discussion, but such adjustments are another reason why betas differ across sources.

The bottom-line lesson is that we are interested in knowing what the beta of the stock will be in the future, but betas have to be estimated using historical data. Anytime we use the past to predict the future, there is the danger of a poor estimate. In our case, it is very unlikely that International Fight League has a beta anything like 60.88 or that Catcher Holdings has a beta of −87. Instead, we can conclude that these beta estimates are almost certainly poor. The moral of the story is that, as with any financial tool, beta is not a black box that should be taken without question.

12.7 Extending CAPM

The previous two sections introduced you to the famous capital asset pricing model, or CAPM for short. For investors, the CAPM has a stunning implication: What you earn, through time, on your portfolio depends only on the level of systematic risk you bear. The corollary is equally striking: As a diversified investor, you do not need to be concerned with the total risk or volatility of any individual asset in your portfolio—it is simply irrelevant.

Of course, we should note that the CAPM is a theory, and, as with any theory, whether it is correct is a question for the data. So does the CAPM work or not? Put more directly, does expected return depend on beta, and beta alone, or do other factors come into play? There is no more hotly debated question in all of finance.

In this section, we first present a short history of attempts to test the CAPM. Then we discuss one of the most important extensions of the CAPM, the so-called Fama-French three-factor model.

A (VERY) BRIEF HISTORY OF TESTING CAPM

The CAPM was introduced in the mid-1960s (but, perhaps surprisingly, tests of this model began to appear only in the early 1970s). When researchers test the CAPM, they essentially look to see whether average returns are linearly related to beta. That is, they want to know if asset returns and beta line up as shown in Figure 12.3. The earliest tests of the CAPM suggested that return

SONIC SOLUTIONS, NABI AND BRISTOW ADVANCE

Small-capitalization stocks rose, outperforming their larger-cap peers as traders swarmed to this riskier corner of the market.

The energy and technology sectors helped lead the sector higher. Also helping small caps, Federal Reserve Chairman Ben Bernanke reiterated that interest rates will remain low, which tends to further jolt bank lending and aid smaller firms.

Investors had been shunning these more volatile securities for stable large-cap stocks in recent weeks as skepticism about the market's rally since March had increased. In the last four weeks of trading, the Russell 2000 index of small-cap stocks has fallen 2% while the Dow Jones Industrial Average is up 4%.

As long as investors remain confident in the Fed's commitment to keeping borrowing costs cheap, the market will likely keep rising, said Carl Gardiner, portfolio manager of the Cullen Small Cap Value Fund. "Outside of that mini-correction we had a few weeks back, it looks like people are off to the races pushing the market higher," he said.

Monday's action was the second-consecutive session that small caps gained, marking the first time they moved in the same direction for consecutive days in more than two weeks.

The Russell 2000 index of small-cap stocks rose 16.59 points, or 2.83%, to 602.87, its highest close since Oct. 22. The index gained 3.89% over the last two trading days, marking the largest two-day percentage gain since July 23. The Standard & Poor's Small Cap 600 index gained 8.76, or 2.82%, to 319.22.

For the purposes of this column, small-caps are considered those companies with a market capitalization of less than $2 billion.

The S&P 600's energy sector was its best performer, closing up 3.1%. Bristow Group (NYSE) rose $2.23, or 6.5%, to $36.41, while Tetra Technologies (NYSE) increased 66 cents, or 6.4% to 10.95.

Sonic Solutions rose 85 cents, or 9.4%, to 9.90, as Brigantine Advisors raised its investment rating on the broadband video and home connectivity company to "buy" from "hold."

Nabi Biopharmaceuticals soared 94 cents, or 26%, to 4.50. The Boca Raton, Fla., company reached a worldwide licensing pact with large-cap GlaxoSmithKline for NicVAX, an investigational vaccine for the treatment of nicotine addiction and the prevention of smoking relapse.

Source: Steven Russolillo, *The Wall Street Journal*, November 17, 2009. Reprinted with permission of *The Wall Street Journal*. © 2009 Dow Jones & Company, Inc. All Rights Reserved Worldwide.

and risk (as measured by beta) showed a reasonable relationship. However, the relationship was not so strong that financial researchers were content to move on and test other theories.

To summarize years of testing, the relationship between returns and beta appeared to vary depending on the time period that was studied. Over some periods, the relationship was strong. In others, it was apparent but not strong. In others, it was seemingly nonexistent. Over the years, researchers refined their techniques to measure betas. In addition, the question was raised whether researchers could calculate betas at all. The basic argument was that betas could not be calculated relative to the overall market portfolio because we cannot observe the true market portfolio. Nonetheless, despite this insightful critique, researchers continue to test CAPM and debate the findings of CAPM research to this day.

Despite the debate between CAPM critics and CAPM champions, some important ideas have emerged. Few researchers question these general principles:

- Investing has two dimensions: risk and return.
- It is inappropriate to look at the risk of an individual security. What is appropriate is how the individual security contributes to the risk of a diversified portfolio.
- Risk can be decomposed into systematic risk and nonsystematic risk.
- Investors will be compensated only for taking systematic risk.

THE FAMA-FRENCH THREE-FACTOR MODEL

To illustrate some aspects of the debate surrounding CAPM, we now briefly explore the Fama-French three-factor model, which gets its name from its creators, Professors Eugene Fama and Kenneth French. Table 12.5 illustrates an important finding from years of research into stock market returns. As shown, two groups of stocks have tended to do noticeably

TABLE 12.5	Average Annual Percentage Returns from 25 Portfolios Formed on Size (Cap) and Book to Market, 1927–2009				
	(Lowest B/M) 1	2	3	4	(Highest B/M) 5
1 (smallest cap)	11.46	19.22	20.77	23.86	30.22
2	11.52	16.82	18.90	18.85	19.85
3	12.08	15.53	16.80	17.34	19.28
4	12.21	13.33	15.09	16.36	17.93
5 (largest cap)	10.80	12.38	13.15	13.78	15.01

Source: Author calculations using data from the Web site of Ken French.

better than the market as a whole: (1) stocks with a small-market capitalization (small-cap stocks) and (2) stocks that have a higher than average ratio of book (or accounting) value to market value of equity (so-called value stocks).

Table 12.5 is formed as follows. First, for each year of historical data, a large set of stocks are ranked on the basis of their market cap, or size. The smallest 20 percent of the stocks are placed into the market cap quintile number 1, the next smallest 20 percent are placed into market cap quintile number 2, and so on. Then, the same set of stocks are ranked on the basis of their book/market (B/M) ratio. The smallest 20 percent are placed into B/M quintile number 1, the next smallest 20 percent are placed into B/M quintile number 2, and so on.

Let's look at the cell with an average annual return of 11.46 percent. This number is calculated as follows. After the sorting described above, we put stocks into portfolios according to both of their quintile scores, for a total of 25 (= 5 × 5) portfolios. So, for example, the stocks with both the smallest cap and the lowest B/M end up in the quintile 1–1 portfolio. As shown in Table 12.5, over the time period 1927 to 2009, the average annual return for stocks in the quintile 1–1 portfolio is 11.46 percent.

Three things should jump out at you in Table 12.5. Notice that the cell 1–5, which contains stocks with the smallest cap and highest B/M, has had the highest returns. Looking down each column, you can see that in four columns the highest return belongs to the smallest cap quintile (we see this pattern in columns 2, 3, 4, and 5). Looking across each row, you can see that in every row, the highest return belongs to the highest B/M quintile.

You can download lots of data behind the Fama-French model at http://mba.tuck.dartmouth.edu/ pages/faculty/ken.french/

Based on further analysis of these data, Professors Fama and French concluded that differences in beta were not sufficient to explain the differences in returns in Table 12.5. Consequently, they argue that two additional factors beyond beta must be considered to understand differences in expected returns on stocks, namely, market cap and B/M. Thus, their model of stock returns has a total of three factors. There is an ongoing academic debate about whether these extra factors are truly sources of systematic risk. As shown in the *Investments Updates* nearby, some investors, however, do believe in a relationship between market-capitalization and risk.

12.8 Summary and Conclusions

This chapter covers the essentials of risk and return. Along the way, we introduced a number of definitions and concepts. The most important of these is the security market line, or SML. The SML is important because it tells us the reward offered in financial markets for bearing risk. Because we covered quite a bit of ground, it's useful to summarize the basic economic logic underlying the SML as follows.

1. **The difference between expected and unexpected returns.**

A. The return on any stock traded in a financial market is composed of two parts. The expected return from the stock is the part of the return that investors predict or expect. This return depends on the information investors have about the stock, and it is based on the market's understanding today of the important factors that will influence the stock in the coming year.

B. The second part of the return on the stock is the uncertain, or risky, part. This is the portion that comes from unexpected information revealed during the year.

2. The difference between systematic risk and unsystematic risk.

A. Based on capital market history, there is a reward for bearing risk. This reward is the risk premium on an asset.

B. The total risk associated with an asset has two parts: systematic risk and unsystematic risk. Unsystematic risk can be freely eliminated by diversification (this is the principle of diversification), so only systematic risk is rewarded. As a result, the risk premium on an asset is determined by its systematic risk. This is the systematic risk principle.

3. The security market line and the capital asset pricing model.

A. An asset's systematic risk, relative to the average, can be measured by its beta coefficient, β_i. The risk premium on an asset is then given by the market risk premium multiplied by the asset's beta coefficient, $[E(R_M) - R_f] \times \beta_i$.

B. The expected return on an asset, $E(R_i)$, is equal to the risk-free rate, R_f, plus the asset's risk premium: $E(R_i) = R_f + [E(R_M) - R_f] \times \beta_i$. This is the equation of the SML, and it is often called the capital asset pricing model (CAPM).

4. The importance of beta.

A. Systematic risk is the crucial determinant of an asset's expected return. Therefore, we need some way of measuring the level of systematic risk for different investments.

B. The specific measure we use is called the beta coefficient, designated by the Greek letter β. A beta coefficient, or just beta for short, tells us how much systematic risk a particular asset has relative to an average asset.

C. By definition, an average asset has a beta of 1.0 relative to itself. An asset with a beta of .50, therefore, has half as much systematic risk as an average asset.

D. Toward the end of the chapter, we showed how betas are calculated and we discussed some of the main reasons different sources report different beta coefficients. We closed the chapter by presenting a discussion of the Fama-French three-factor model, an important extension to the basic CAPM.

GET REAL

An immediate implication of the CAPM is that you, as an investor, need to be aware of the level of systematic risk you are carrying. Look up the betas of the stocks you hold in your simulated brokerage account and compute your portfolio's systematic risk. Is it bigger or smaller than 1.0? More important, is the portfolio's beta consistent with your desired level of portfolio risk?

Betas are particularly useful for understanding mutual fund risk and return. Since most mutual funds are at least somewhat diversified (the exceptions being sector funds and other specialized funds), they have relatively little unsystematic risk, and their betas can be measured with some precision. Look at the funds you own and learn their betas (www.morningstar.com is a good source). Are the risk levels what you intended? As you study mutual fund risk, you will find some other measures exist, most of which are closely related to the measures discussed in this chapter. Take a few minutes to understand these as well.

Does expected return depend on beta, and beta alone, or do other factors come into play? There is no more hotly debated question in all of finance, and the research that exists to date is inconclusive. (Some researchers would dispute this!) At a minimum, beta appears to be a useful measure of market-related volatility, that is, risk. Whether beta is a useful measure of expected return (much less a comprehensive one) awaits more research. Lots more research.

Key Terms

beta coefficient (β) 412
capital asset pricing model (CAPM) 421
covariance 425
market risk premium 420

security market line (SML) 420
systematic risk 409
systematic risk principle 412
unsystematic risk 409

Chapter Review Problems and Self-Test

1. Risk and Return (CFA2) Suppose you observe the following situation:

Security	Beta	Expected Return
Sanders	1.8	22.00%
Janicek	1.6	20.44

If the risk-free rate is 7 percent, are these two stocks correctly priced relative to each other? What must the risk-free rate be if they are correctly priced?

2. CAPM (CFA1) Suppose the risk-free rate is 8 percent. The expected return on the market is 16 percent. If a particular stock has a beta of .7, what is its expected return based on the CAPM? If another stock has an expected return of 24 percent, what must its beta be?

Answers to Self-Test Problems

1. If we compute the reward-to-risk ratios, we get (22% − 7%)/1.8 = 8.33% for Sanders versus 8.4% for Janicek. Relative to Sanders, Janicek's expected return is too high, so its price is too low.

  If they are correctly priced, then they must offer the same reward-to-risk ratio. The risk-free rate would have to be such that:

$$\frac{22\% - R_f}{1.8} = \frac{20.44\% - R_f}{1.6}$$

With a little algebra, we find that the risk-free rate must be 8 percent:

$$22\% - R_f = (20.44\% - R_f)(1.8/1.6)$$
$$22\% - 20.44\% \times 1.125 = R_f - R_f \times 1.125$$
$$R_f = 8\%$$

2. Because the expected return on the market is 16 percent, the market risk premium is 16% − 8% = 8% (the risk-free rate is also 8 percent). The first stock has a beta of .7, so its expected return is 8% + 8% × .7 = 13.6%.

  For the second stock, notice that the risk premium is 24% − 8% = 16%. Because this is twice as large as the market risk premium, the beta must be exactly equal to 2. We can verify this using the CAPM:

$$E(R_i) = R_f + [E(R_M) - R_f] \times \beta_i$$
$$24\% = 8\% + (16\% - 8\%) \times \beta_i$$
$$\beta_i = 16\%/8\% = 2.0$$

Test Your Investment Quotient

1. Portfolio Return (LO3, CFA1) According to the CAPM, what is the rate of return of a portfolio with a beta of 1?

a. Between R_M and R_f
b. The risk-free rate, R_f
c. Beta × ($R_M - R_f$)
d. The return on the market, R_M

2. **Stock Return (LO1, CFA3)** The return on a stock is said to have which two of the following basic parts?

   a. An expected return and an unexpected return.
   b. A measurable return and an unmeasurable return.
   c. A predicted return and a forecast return.
   d. A total return and a partial return.

3. **News Components (LO1, CFA3)** A news announcement about a stock is said to have which two of the following parts?

   a. An expected part and a surprise.
   b. Public information and private information.
   c. Financial information and product information.
   d. A good part and a bad part.

4. **News Effects (LO1, CFA3)** A company announces that its earnings have increased 50 percent over the previous year, which matches analysts' expectations. What is the likely effect on the stock price?

   a. The stock price will increase.
   b. The stock price will decrease.
   c. The stock price will rise and then fall after an overreaction.
   d. The stock price will not be affected.

5. **News Effects (LO1, CFA3)** A company announces that its earnings have decreased 25 percent from the previous year, but analysts expected a small increase. What is the likely effect on the stock price?

   a. The stock price will increase.
   b. The stock price will decrease.
   c. The stock price will rise and then fall after an overreaction.
   d. The stock price will not be affected.

6. **News Effects (LO1, CFA3)** A company announces that its earnings have increased 25 percent from the previous year, but analysts actually expected a 50 percent increase. What is the likely effect on the stock price?

   a. The stock price will increase.
   b. The stock price will decrease.
   c. The stock price will rise and then fall after an overreaction.
   d. The stock price will not be affected.

7. **News Effects (LO1, CFA3)** A company announces that its earnings have decreased 50 percent from the previous year, but analysts only expected a 25 percent decrease. What is the likely effect on the stock price?

   a. The stock price will increase.
   b. The stock price will decrease.
   c. The stock price will rise and then fall after an overreaction.
   d. The stock price will not be affected.

8. **Security Risk (LO2, CFA2)** The systematic risk of a security is also called its

   a. Perceived risk
   b. Unique or asset-specific risk
   c. Market risk
   d. Fundamental risk

9. **Security Risk (LO2, CFA2)** Which type of risk is essentially eliminated by diversification?

   a. Perceived risk
   b. Market risk
   c. Systematic risk
   d. Unsystematic risk

10. **Security Risk (LO2, CFA2)** The systematic risk principle states that

    a. Systematic risk doesn't matter to investors.
    b. Systematic risk can be essentially eliminated by diversification.
    c. The reward for bearing risk is independent of the systematic risk of an investment.
    d. The reward for bearing risk depends only on the systematic risk of an investment.

11. **Security Risk (LO2, CFA2)** The systematic risk principle has an important implication, which is

    a. Systematic risk is preferred to unsystematic risk.
    b. Systematic risk is the only risk that can be reduced by diversification.
    c. The expected return on an asset is independent of its systematic risk.
    d. The expected return on an asset depends only on its systematic risk.

12. **CAPM (LO3, CFA1)** A financial market's security market line (SML) describes

    a. The relationship between systematic risk and expected returns.
    b. The relationship between unsystematic risk and expected returns.
    c. The relationship between systematic risk and unexpected returns.
    d. The relationship between unsystematic risk and unexpected returns.

13. **Risk Aversion (LO3, CFA2)** Which of the following is *not* an implication of risk aversion for the investment process?

    a. The security market line is upward sloping.
    b. The promised yield on AAA-rated bonds is higher than on A-rated bonds.
    c. Investors expect a positive relationship between expected return and risk.
    d. Investors prefer portfolios that lie on the efficient frontier to other portfolios with equal rates of return.

14. **Unsystematic Risk (LO2, CFA2)** In the context of capital market theory, unsystematic risk

    a. Is described as unique risk.
    b. Refers to nondiversifiable risk.
    c. Remains in the market portfolio.
    d. Refers to the variability in all risk assets caused by macroeconomic factors and other aggregate market-related variables.

15. **Security Market Line (LO3, CFA1)** Which of the following statements about the security market line (SML) is false?

    a. Properly valued assets plot exactly on the SML.
    b. The SML leads all investors to invest in the same portfolio of risky assets.
    c. The SML provides a benchmark for evaluating expected investment performance.
    d. The SML is a graphic representation of the relationship between expected return and beta.

Concept Questions

1. **Diversifiable Risk (LO2, CFA2)** In broad terms, why is some risk diversifiable? Why are some risks nondiversifiable? Does it follow that an investor can control the level of unsystematic risk in a portfolio, but not the level of systematic risk?

2. **Announcements and Prices (LO1, CFA3)** Suppose the government announces that, based on a just-completed survey, the growth rate in the economy is likely to be 2 percent in the coming year, compared to 5 percent for the year just completed. Will security prices increase, decrease, or stay the same following this announcement? Does it make any difference whether the 2 percent figure was anticipated by the market? Explain.

3. **Announcements and Risk (LO2, CFA3)** Classify the following events as mostly systematic or mostly unsystematic. Is the distinction clear in every case?

    a. Short-term interest rates increase unexpectedly.
    b. The interest rate a company pays on its short-term debt borrowing is increased by its bank.
    c. Oil prices unexpectedly decline.
    d. An oil tanker ruptures, creating a large oil spill.
    e. A manufacturer loses a multi-million-dollar product liability suit.
    f. A Supreme Court decision substantially broadens producer liability for injuries suffered by product users.

4. **Announcements and Risk (LO2, CFA3)**   Indicate whether the following events might cause stocks in general to change price, and whether they might cause Big Widget Corp.'s stock to change price.

   a. The government announces that inflation unexpectedly jumped by 2 percent last month.
   b. Big Widget's quarterly earnings report, just issued, generally fell in line with analysts' expectations.
   c. The government reports that economic growth last year was at 3 percent, which generally agreed with most economists' forecasts.
   d. The directors of Big Widget die in a plane crash.
   e. Congress approves changes to the tax code that will increase the top marginal corporate tax rate. The legislation had been debated for the previous six months.

5. **Diversification and Risk (LO2)**   True or false: The most important characteristic in determining the expected return of a well-diversified portfolio is the variances of the individual assets in the portfolio. Explain.

6. **Announcements (LO1, CFA3)**   As indicated by examples in this chapter, earnings announcements by companies are closely followed by, and frequently result in, share price revisions. Two issues should come to mind. First, earnings announcements concern past periods. If the market values stocks based on expectations of the future, why are numbers summarizing past performance relevant? Second, these announcements concern accounting earnings. Such earnings may have little to do with cash flow, so, again, why are they relevant?

7. **Beta (LO4, CFA2)**   Is it possible that a risky asset could have a beta of zero? Explain. Based on the CAPM, what is the expected return on such an asset? Is it possible that a risky asset could have a negative beta? What does the CAPM predict about the expected return on such an asset? Can you give an explanation for your answer?

8. **Relative Valuation (LO3, CFA2)**   Suppose you identify a situation in which one security is overvalued relative to another. How would you go about exploiting this opportunity? Does it matter if the two securities are both overvalued relative to some third security? Are your profits certain in this case?

9. **Reward-to-Risk Ratio (LO3, CFA2)**   Explain what it means for all assets to have the same reward-to-risk ratio. How can you increase your return if this holds true? Why would we expect that all assets have the same reward-to-risk ratio in liquid, well-functioning markets?

10. **Systematic versus Firm-Specific Risk (LO2, CFA2)**   Dudley Trudy, CFA, recently met with one of his clients. Trudy typically invests in a master list of 30 securities drawn from several industries. After the meeting concluded, the client made the following statement: "I trust your stock-picking ability and believe that you should invest my funds in your five best ideas. Why invest in 30 companies when you obviously have stronger opinions on a few of them?" Trudy plans to respond to his client within the context of Modern Portfolio Theory.

    a. Contrast the concept of systematic and firm-specific risk and give one example of each.
    b. Critique the client's suggestion. Discuss the impact of the systematic risk and firm-specific risk on portfolio risk as the number of securities in a portfolio is increased.

Questions and Problems

Core Questions

1. **Stock Betas (LO3, CFA2)**   A stock has an expected return of 13.2 percent, the risk-free rate is 3.5 percent, and the market risk premium is 7.5 percent. What must the beta of this stock be?

2. **Market Returns (LO3, CFA1)**   A stock has an expected return of 10.5 percent, its beta is .60, and the risk-free rate is 3 percent. What must the expected return on the market be?

3. **Risk-Free Rates (LO3, CFA1)**   A stock has an expected return of 14 percent, a beta of 1.70, and the expected return on the market is 10 percent. What must the risk-free rate be?

4. **Market Risk Premium (LO3, CFA1)**   A stock has a beta of .8 and an expected return of 13 percent. If the risk-free rate is 4.5 percent, what is the market risk premium?

5. **Portfolio Betas (LO4, CFA2)**   You own a stock portfolio invested 10 percent in Stock Q, 25 percent in Stock R, 50 percent in Stock S, and 15 percent in Stock T. The betas for these four stocks are 1.4, .6, 1.5, and .9, respectively. What is the portfolio beta?

6. **Portfolio Betas (LO4, CFA1)** You own 400 shares of Stock A at a price of $60 per share, 500 shares of Stock B at $85 per share, and 900 shares of Stock C at $25 per share. The betas for the stocks are .8, 1.4, and .5, respectively. What is the beta of your portfolio?

7. **Stock Betas (LO4, CFA1)** You own a portfolio equally invested in a risk-free asset and two stocks. If one of the stocks has a beta of 1.50, and the total portfolio is exactly as risky as the market, what must the beta be for the other stock in your portfolio?

8. **Expected Returns (LO3, CFA2)** A stock has a beta of .85, the expected return on the market is 11 percent, and the risk-free rate is 4.1 percent. What must the expected return on this stock be?

9. **CAPM and Stock Price (LO3, CFA3)** A share of stock sells for $35 today. The beta of the stock is 1.2, and the expected return on the market is 12 percent. The stock is expected to pay a dividend of $.80 in one year. If the risk-free rate is 5.5 percent, what should the share price be in one year?

10. **Portfolio Weights (LO4, CFA2)** A stock has a beta of .9 and an expected return of 9 percent. A risk-free asset currently earns 4 percent.

    a. What is the expected return on a portfolio that is equally invested in the two assets?
    b. If a portfolio of the two assets has a beta of .5, what are the portfolio weights?
    c. If a portfolio of the two assets has an expected return of 8 percent, what is its beta?
    d. If a portfolio of the two assets has a beta of 1.80, what are the portfolio weights? How do you interpret the weights for the two assets in this case? Explain.

Intermediate Questions

11. **Portfolio Risk and Return (LO3, CFA1)** Asset W has an expected return of 12.0 percent and a beta of 1.1. If the risk-free rate is 4 percent, complete the following table for portfolios of Asset W and a risk-free asset. Illustrate the relationship between portfolio expected return and portfolio beta by plotting the expected returns against the betas. What is the slope of the line that results?

Percentage of Portfolio in Asset W	Portfolio Expected Return	Portfolio Beta
0%		
25		
50		
75		
100		
125		
150		

12. **Relative Valuation (LO3, CFA2)** Stock Y has a beta of 1.15 and an expected return of 14 percent. Stock Z has a beta of .70 and an expected return of 9 percent. If the risk-free rate is 5 percent and the market risk premium is 7 percent, are these stocks correctly priced?

13. **Relative Valuation (LO3, CFA2)** In the previous problem, what would the risk-free rate have to be for the two stocks to be correctly priced relative to each other?

14. **CAPM (LO3, CFA1)** Using the CAPM, show that the ratio of the risk premiums on two assets is equal to the ratio of their betas.

15. **Relative Valuation (LO3, CFA2)** Suppose you observe the following situation:

Security	Beta	Expected Return
Peat Co.	1.05	12.3
Re-Peat Co.	.90	11.8

Assume these securities are correctly priced. Based on the CAPM, what is the expected return on the market? What is the risk-free rate?

16. **Calculating Beta (LO3, CFA2)** Show that another way to calculate beta is to take the covariance between the security and the market and divide by the variance of the market's return.

17. **Calculating Beta (LO4, CFA2)** Fill in the following table, supplying all the missing information. Use this information to calculate the security's beta.

	Returns		Return Deviations		Squared Deviations		Product of
Year	Security	Market	Security	Market	Security	Market	Deviations
2007	8	5					
2008	−18	−14					
2009	21	15					
2010	38	21					
2011	16	7					

18. **Analyzing a Portfolio (LO4, CFA2)** You have $100,000 to invest in a portfolio containing Stock X, Stock Y, and a risk-free asset. You must invest all of your money. Your goal is to create a portfolio that has an expected return of 13 percent and that has only 70 percent of the risk of the overall market. If X has an expected return of 31 percent and a beta of 1.8, Y has an expected return of 20 percent and a beta of 1.3, and the risk-free rate is 7 percent, how much money will you invest in Stock Y? How do you interpret your answer?

19. **Systematic versus Unsystematic Risk (LO2, CFA3)** Consider the following information on Stocks I and II:

State of Economy	Probability of State of Economy	Rate of Return If State Occurs	
		Stock I	Stock II
Recession	.30	.05	−.18
Normal	.40	.19	.14
Irrational exuberance	.30	.13	.29

The market risk premium is 8 percent, and the risk-free rate is 5 percent. Which stock has the most systematic risk? Which one has the most unsystematic risk? Which stock is "riskier"? Explain.

20. **Systematic and Unsystematic Risk (LO2, CFA3)** The beta for a certain stock is 1.15, the risk-free rate is 5 percent, and the expected return on the market is 13 percent. Complete the following table to decompose the stock's return into the systematic return and the unsystematic return.

	Actual Returns		Unexpected Returns		Systematic Portion	Unsystematic Portion (ϵ)
Year	R	R_M	$R - E(R)$	$R_M - E(R_M)$	$[R_M - E(R_M)] \times \beta$	$[R - E(R)] - [R_M - E(R_M)] \times \beta$
2006	10	12				
2007	11	8				
2008	−8	−11				
2009	−6	14				
2010	28	7				

21. **CAPM (LO3, CFA2)** Landon Stevens is evaluating the expected performance of two common stocks, Furhman Labs, Inc., and Garten Testing, Inc. The risk-free rate is 4 percent, the expected return on the market is 11.5 percent, and the betas of the two stocks are 1.4 and .9, respectively. Stevens's own forecasts of the returns on the two stocks are 12.75 percent for Furhman Labs and 11.50 percent for Garten. Calculate the required return for each stock. Is each stock undervalued, fairly valued, or overvalued?

22. Calculating Beta (CFA1) You are given the following information concerning a stock and the market:

| | Returns | |
Year	Market	Stock
2005	18%	34%
2006	11	27
2007	12	3
2008	−14	−21
2009	37	16
2010	15	22

Calculate the average return and standard deviation for the market and the stock. Next, calculate the correlation between the stock and the market, as well as the stock's beta. Use a spreadsheet to calculate your answers.

CFA Exam Review by Schweser

[CFA1, CFA2]

Janet Bellows, a portfolio manager, is attempting to explain asset valuation to a junior colleague, Bill Clay. Ms. Bellows's explanation focuses on the capital asset pricing model (CAPM). Of particular interest is her discussion of the security market line (SML) and its use in security selection. After a short review of the CAPM and SML, Ms. Bellows decides to test Mr. Clay's knowledge of valuation using the CAPM. Ms. Bellows provides the following information for Mr. Clay:

- The risk-free rate is 7 percent.
- The market risk premium during the previous year was 5.5 percent.
- The standard deviation of market returns is 35 percent.
- This year, the market risk premium is estimated to be 7 percent.
- Stock A has a beta of 1.30 and is expected to generate a 15.5 percent return.
- The correlation of Stock B with the market is .88.
- The standard deviation of Stock B's returns is 58 percent.

Then Ms. Bellows provides Mr. Clay with the following information about Ohio Manufacturing, Texas Energy, and Montana Mining:

	Ohio	Texas	Montana
Beta	0.50		1.50
Required return	10.5%	11.0%	
Expected return	12.0%	10.0%	15.0%
S&P 500 expected return		14.0%	

1. Based on the stock and market data provided above, which of the following data regarding Stock A is most accurate?

	Required Return	Recommendation
a.	16.1%	Sell
b.	16.1%	Buy
c.	14.15%	Sell

2. The beta of Stock B is closest to:

   a. .51
   b. 1.07
   c. 1.46

3. Which of the following represents the best investment advice?

   a. Avoid Texas because its expected return is lower than its required return.
   b. Buy Montana and Texas because their required returns are lower than their expected returns.
   c. Buy Montana because it is expected to return more than Texas, Ohio, and the market.

4. If the market risk premium decreases by 1 percent while the risk-free rate remains the same, the security market line:

   a. Becomes steeper.
   b. Becomes flatter.
   c. Parallel shifts downward.

What's on the Web?

1. **Expected Return**   You want to find the expected return for Home Depot using CAPM. First you need the risk-free rate. Go to www.bloomberg.com and find the current interest rate for three-month Treasury bills. Use the average large-company stock risk premium from Chapter 1 as the market risk premium. Next, go to finance.yahoo.com, enter the ticker symbol HD for Home Depot, and find the beta for Home Depot. What is the expected return for Home Depot using CAPM? What assumptions have you made to arrive at this number?

2. **Portfolio Beta**   You have decided to invest in an equally weighted portfolio consisting of American Express, Procter & Gamble, Johnson & Johnson, and United Technologies and need to find the beta of your portfolio. Go to finance.yahoo.com and find the beta for each of the companies. What is the beta for your portfolio?

3. **Beta**   Which stock has the highest and lowest beta? Go to finance.yahoo.com and find the stock screener. Enter 0 as the maximum beta and enter search. How many stocks currently have a beta less than 0? Which stock has the lowest beta? Go back to the stock screener and enter 3 as the minimum value. How many stocks have a beta greater than 3? What about 4? Which stock has the highest beta?

4. **Security Market Line**   Go to finance.yahoo.com and enter the ticker symbol GE for General Electric. Find the beta for this company and the target stock price in one year. Using the current share price and the target stock price, compute the expected return for this stock. Don't forget to include the expected dividend payments over the next year. Now go to www.bloomberg.com and find the current interest rate for three-month Treasury bills. Using this information, calculate the expected return of the market using the reward-to-risk ratio. Does this number make sense? Why or why not?

CHAPTER 13

Performance Evaluation and Risk Management

Learning Objectives

To get a high evaluation of your investments' performance, make sure you know:

1. How to calculate the best-known portfolio evaluation measures.

2. The strengths and weaknesses of these portfolio evaluation measures.

3. How to calculate a Sharpe-optimal portfolio.

4. How to calculate and interpret Value-at-Risk.

"It is not the return on my investment that I am concerned about; it is the return of my investment!"

–Will Rogers

"The stock market will fluctuate!"

–J. P. Morgan

Humorist Will Rogers expressed concern about "the return *of* [his] investment." Famed financier J. P. Morgan, when asked by a reporter what he thought the stock market would do, replied with his well-known quote. Both Will Rogers and J. P. Morgan understood a basic fact of investing—investors holding risky assets ask worrisome questions like: How well are my investments doing? How much money am I making (or losing)? and What are my chances of incurring a significant loss? ■

This chapter examines methods to deal with two related problems faced by investors in risky assets. These are (1) evaluating risk-adjusted investment performance and (2) assessing and managing the risks involved with specific investment strategies. Both subjects have come up previously in our text, but we have deferred a detailed discussion of them until now.

CFA™ Exam Topics in This Chapter:

1 Introduction to the Global Investment Performance Standards (L1, S1)
2 Global Investment Performance Standards I (L1, S1)
3 Statistical concepts and market returns (L1, S2)
4 Correlation and regression (L2, S3)
5 Risk management (L2, S14)
6 Evaluating portfolio performance (L3, S17)
7 Global Investment Performance Standards II (L3, S18)

Go to www.mhhe.com/jmd6e for a guide that aligns your textbook with CFA readings.

We first consider the problem of performance evaluation. Specifically, suppose we have investment returns data for several portfolios covering a recent period, and we wish to evaluate how well these portfolios have performed relative to other portfolios or some investment benchmark. The need for this form of scrutiny arises in a number of situations, including:

- An investor planning to choose a mutual fund wants to first compare the investment performance of several dozen candidate funds.

- A pension fund administrator wants to select a money manager and thus needs to compare the investment performance of a group of money managers.

- An employer wants to compare the performance of several investment companies before selecting one for inclusion in her company-sponsored 401(k) retirement plan.

In the first section of this chapter, we examine several useful evaluation measures of portfolio performance and discuss how they might be applied to these and similar situations.

In the second part of the chapter, we discuss the important problem of risk management from the perspective of an investor or money manager concerned with the possibility of a large loss. Specifically, we examine methods to assess the probabilities and magnitudes of losses we might expect to experience during a set future time period. These risk assessment techniques are commonly employed in a number of situations, including:

- A New York Stock Exchange specialist wants to know how much of a loss is possible with a 5 percent probability during the coming day's trading from the specialist firm's inventory.

- The foreign currency manager of a commercial bank wants to know how much of a loss is possible with a 2 percent probability on the bank's foreign currency portfolio during the coming week.

- A futures exchange clearinghouse wants to know how much margin funds should be deposited by exchange members to cover extreme losses that might occur with a "once in a century" probability.

Methods used to assess risk in these and similar scenarios fall into the category commonly referred to as "Value-at-Risk." Value-at-Risk techniques are widely applied by commercial banks, securities firms, and other financial institutions to assess and understand the risk exposure of portfolios under their management.

13.1 Performance Evaluation

Investors have a natural (and very rational) interest in how well particular investments have done. This is true whether the investor manages his or her own portfolio or has money managed by a professional. Concern with investment performance motivates the topic of **performance evaluation**. In general terms, performance evaluation focuses on assessing how well a money manager achieves high returns balanced with acceptable risks.

Going back to our discussion of efficient markets in an earlier chapter, we raised the question of risk-adjusted performance and whether anyone can consistently earn an "excess" return, thereby "beating the market." The standard example is an evaluation of investment performance achieved by the manager of a mutual fund. Such a performance evaluation is more than an academic exercise, because its purpose is to help investors decide whether they would entrust investment funds with the fund manager. Our goal here is to introduce you to the primary tools used to make this assessment.

performance evaluation
The assessment of how well a money manager achieves a balance between high returns and acceptable risks.

PERFORMANCE EVALUATION MEASURES

A variety of measures are used to evaluate investment performance. Here, we examine some of the best-known and most popular measures: the Sharpe ratio, the Treynor ratio, Jensen's alpha, the information ratio, and R-squared. But before we do so, let us first briefly discuss a naive measure of performance evaluation—the **raw return** on a portfolio.

raw return
States the total percentage return on an investment with no adjustment for risk or comparison to any benchmark.

The raw return on an investment portfolio, here denoted by R_p, is simply the total percentage return on the portfolio with no adjustment for risk or comparison to any benchmark. Calculating percentage returns was discussed in Chapter 1. The fact that a raw portfolio return does not reflect any consideration of risk suggests that its usefulness is limited when making investment decisions. After all, risk is important to almost every investor.

THE SHARPE RATIO

Sharpe ratio
Measures investment performance as the ratio of portfolio risk premium over portfolio return standard deviation.

A basic measure of investment performance that includes an adjustment for risk is the Sharpe ratio, originally proposed by Nobel laureate William F. Sharpe. The **Sharpe ratio** is computed as a portfolio's risk premium divided by the standard deviation of the portfolio's return:

$$\text{Sharpe ratio} = \frac{R_p - R_f}{\sigma_p} \qquad (13.1)$$

In this case, the portfolio risk premium is the raw portfolio return less a risk-free return, that is, $R_p - R_f$, which we know is the basic reward for bearing risk. The return standard deviation, σ_p, is a measure of risk, which we have discussed in previous chapters.

More precisely, return standard deviation is a measure of the *total* risk (as opposed to systematic risk) for a security or a portfolio. Thus, the Sharpe ratio is a reward-to-risk ratio that focuses on total risk. Because total risk is used to make the adjustment, the Sharpe ratio is probably most appropriate for evaluating relatively diversified portfolios.

Visit Professor Sharpe at
www.stanford.edu/~wfsharpe

EXAMPLE 13.1

Look Sharpe

Over a recent three-year period, the average annual return on a portfolio was 20 percent, and the annual return standard deviation for the portfolio was 25 percent. During the same period, the average return on 90-day Treasury bills was 5 percent. What is the Sharpe ratio for this portfolio during this three-year period?

Referring to the equation above, we calculate:

$$\text{Sharpe ratio} = \frac{.20 - .05}{.25} = .6$$

This indicates that the Sharpe ratio of portfolio excess return to total risk is .6.

THE TREYNOR RATIO

Treynor ratio
Measures investment performance as the ratio of portfolio risk premium over portfolio beta.

Another standard measure of investment performance that includes an adjustment for systematic risk is the Treynor ratio (or index), originally suggested by Jack L. Treynor. The **Treynor ratio** is computed as a portfolio's risk premium divided by the portfolio's beta coefficient:

$$\text{Treynor ratio} = \frac{R_p - R_f}{\beta_p} \qquad (13.2)$$

As with the Sharpe ratio, the Treynor ratio is a reward-to-risk ratio. The key difference is that the Treynor ratio looks at systematic risk only, not total risk.

EXAMPLE 13.2

The Treynor Ratio

Over a three-year period, the average return on a portfolio was 20 percent, and the beta for the portfolio was 1.25. During the same period, the average return on 90-day Treasury bills was 5 percent. What is the Treynor ratio for this portfolio during this period?

Referring to the Treynor ratio equation above, we calculate:

$$\text{Treynor ratio} = \frac{.20 - .05}{1.25} = .12$$

This reveals that the Treynor ratio of portfolio excess return to portfolio beta is .12.

FIGURE 13.1 Jensen's Alpha

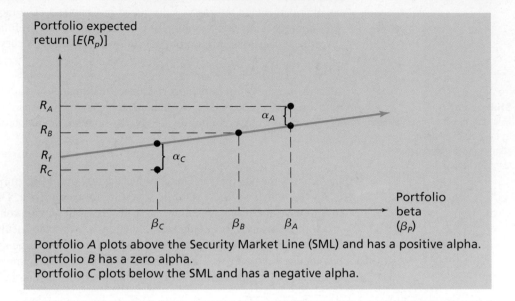

Portfolio *A* plots above the Security Market Line (SML) and has a positive alpha.
Portfolio *B* has a zero alpha.
Portfolio *C* plots below the SML and has a negative alpha.

You may recall that we saw the Treynor ratio in a previous chapter. There we said that in an active, competitive market, a strong argument can be made that all assets (and portfolios of those assets) should have the same Treynor ratio, that is, the same reward-to-risk ratio, where "risk" refers to systematic risk. To the extent that they don't, then there is evidence that at least some portfolios have earned excess returns.

Both the Sharpe and Treynor ratios are relative measures. A relative measure means that no absolute number represents a "good" or "bad" performance. Rather, to evaluate the performance, the ratios must be compared to those of other managers—or to a benchmark index. So, it is possible for a manager to have negative Sharpe and Treynor ratios and still be considered "good." This odd result occurs if the benchmark also experiences a negative return for the period under review. In relative terms, the negative ratios of the manager still outperform the benchmark.

JENSEN'S ALPHA

Another common measure of investment performance that draws on capital asset pricing theory for its formulation is Jensen's alpha, proposed by Professor Michael C. Jensen. **Jensen's alpha** is computed as the raw portfolio return less the expected portfolio return predicted by the capital asset pricing model (CAPM).

Recall from a previous chapter that, according to the CAPM, a portfolio expected return, $E(R_p)$, can be written as:

$$E(R_p) = R_f + [E(R_M) - R_f] \times \beta_p \tag{13.3}$$

To compute Jensen's alpha, we compare the actual return, R_p, to the predicted return. The difference is the alpha, denoted α_p:

$$\text{Jensen's alpha} = \alpha_p = R_p - E(R_p) \tag{13.4}$$
$$= R_p - \{R_f + [E(R_M) - R_f] \times \beta_p\}$$

Jensen's alpha is easy to understand. It is simply the excess return above or below the security market line, and, in this sense, it can be interpreted as a measure of by how much the portfolio "beat the market." This interpretation is illustrated in Figure 13.1, which shows a portfolio with a positive (*A*), zero (*B*), and negative (*C*) alpha, respectively. As shown, a positive alpha is a good thing because the portfolio has a relatively high return given its level of systematic risk.

Jensen's alpha

Measures investment performance as the raw portfolio return less the return predicted by the capital asset pricing model.

Jensen's Alpha

Over a three-year period, the average annual return on a portfolio was 20 percent, and the beta for the portfolio was 1.25. During the same period, the average annual return on 90-day Treasury bills was 5 percent, and the average return on the market portfolio was 15 percent. What is Jensen's alpha for this portfolio during this period? Referring to the Jensen-alpha equation above, we calculate:

$$.20 - [.05 + (.15 - .05)1.25] = .025$$

This shows that the portfolio had an alpha measure of portfolio excess return of 2.5 percent.

ANOTHER METHOD TO CALCULATE ALPHA

Previously, we discussed the characteristic line, which graphs the relationship between the return of an investment (on the y axis) and the return of the market or benchmark (on the x axis). Recall that the slope of this line represents the investment's beta. Beta gives us the predicted movement in the return of the stock for a given movement in the market or benchmark. With only a slight modification, we can extend this approach to calculate an investment's alpha.

Consider the following equation, which simply rearranges equation (13.3):

$$E(R_p) - R_f = [E(R_m) - R_f] \times \beta_p \tag{13.5}$$

If you compare this equation to the equation for the characteristic line, the only difference is that a risk-free rate appears. In fact, we could define the returns of the portfolio and the market as excess returns—meaning we subtract the risk-free rate from the returns of the portfolio. Doing so provides the following equation, which is similar to that of the characteristic line:

$$E(R_{p,RP}) = E(R_{m,RP}) \times \beta_p \tag{13.6}$$

As an example, consider the outcome when we evaluate an S&P 500 Index fund. We expect that the returns on the fund (excluding any expenses) will match the returns of the market. In this case, the resulting graph of the returns of the fund versus the market would look something like Figure 13.2. The slope of this line is 1. This slope makes sense because the fund is exactly tracking the market (i.e., beta = 1). Further, the alpha would be zero because the fund is earning no positive (or negative) excess return. Instead, it is simply returning exactly what the market does (and at the same level of risk).

FIGURE 13.2 **Index Fund Excess Returns versus Market Excess Returns**

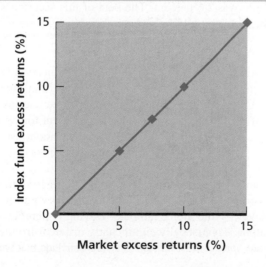

FIGURE 13.3 Security Returns versus Market Returns

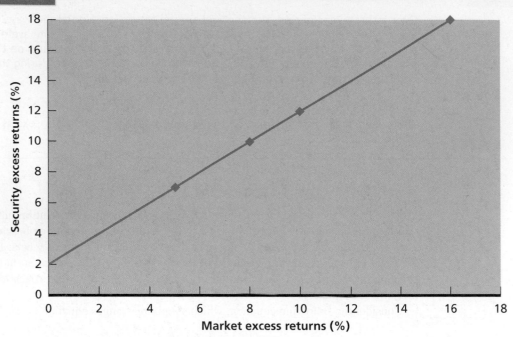

What would happen, though, if an actively managed fund took on the same amount of risk as the market (i.e., a beta of 1), but the fund earned exactly 2 percent more than the market every period? Well, if we graphed this hypothetical situation, it would look something like Figure 13.3. Notice that the slope (i.e., beta) is still 1, but the *x* intercept is now 2. This is actually the fund's alpha, which we could verify using equation (13.4).

Suppose that we have a fund whose returns are not consistently higher (or lower) than the market by a fixed amount. How could we estimate this fund's alpha? Well, similar to our previous beta calculation, we can apply a simple linear regression. In this case, we would regress the excess return of the investment on the excess return of the market. The intercept of this estimated equation is the fund's alpha. As an example of this approach, consider the nearby *Spreadsheet Analysis*.

In the spreadsheet example, the intercept estimate is −.0167. This estimate is given in the same units as the original data. So, the alpha is estimated to be −1.67 percent per year. We can verify this number using equation (13.4). The average return of the security over the five-year period is 10 percent, while the average market return was 12 percent and the average risk-free rate was 2.6 percent. The beta of this security is .96, which is the coefficient estimate on the *x* variable. With these numbers:

$$\text{Alpha} = 10\% - [2.6\% + (12.0\% - 2.6\%) \times .96] = -1.62\%$$

You will notice that the regression method and equation (13.4) produce similar, but not exact, alphas and betas. Part of the difference stems from using an average risk-free rate (as in equation [13.4]) versus using each year's risk-free rate (as in the regression technique). For example, if you use a risk-free rate of 2.6 percent for each year and run a new regression, the beta is .90. Inserting this beta into the equation just above, however, results in an alpha of −1.06 percent, which is about equal to the alpha estimate from this new regression, −1.08 percent.

Although equation (13.4) is easy to use, the regression approach has some potential advantages over equation (13.4). For example, the output of the regression will include a significance level for the alpha estimate. Having a significance level allows us to decide whether the alpha is statistically significantly different from zero. Using the *t*-statistic and *p*-value from our *Spreadsheet Analysis* box, we conclude that we are only 15 percent confident

SPREADSHEET ANALYSIS

	A	B	C	D	E	F
1						
2			Using a Spreadsheet to Calculate Alpha			
3						
4	To illustrate how to calculate alpha, we have replicated the returns of a security and the market					
5	over a five year period. In addition, we have listed the risk-free rate. From these, we have					
6	calculated the excess return for the security and the market, which is simply the return over					
7	and above the risk-free rate.					
8						
9			Returns			Excess Returns	
10	Year	Security	Market	Risk-free	Security	Market
11	1	10%	8%	3%	7%	5%
12	2	−8%	−12%	2%	−10%	−14%
13	3	−4%	16%	4%	−8%	12%
14	4	40%	26%	1%	39%	25%
15	5	12%	22%	3%	9%	19%
16						
17	We then choose the regression function under the data analysis tab. We enter cells E11:E15 as					
18	the y-data and cells F11:F15 as the x-data. The resulting output is:					
19						
20	SUMMARY OUTPUT					
21						
22	*Regression Statistics*					
23	Multiple R	0.741036				
24	R Square	0.549135				
25	Adjusted R Square	0.398846				
26	Standard Error	0.152192				
27	Observations	5				
28						
29		*Coefficients*	*Standard Error*	*t Stat*	*p-value*	
30	Intercept	−0.016692	0.08296698	−0.20118	0.853423	
31	X Variable 1	0.964804	0.504734054	1.91151	0.1519	

(1 minus the *p*-value) that this estimated alpha value is different from zero. The information ratio we discuss just below provides a similar analysis.

Another advantage of the regression approach is that you can pick the most relevant benchmark for the comparison. Data providers such as *Morningstar* and *Value Line* will report an alpha for most mutual funds, but they decide which index to use for comparison. For example, consider evaluating a value-oriented mutual fund. Most sources will quote alphas relative to the S&P 500 Index. To be more specific, however, you most likely should evaluate the fund versus a subset of the S&P 500, such as the S&P 500 Value Index.

INFORMATION RATIO

Consider a mutual fund that reports a positive alpha. How do we know whether this alpha is statistically significantly different from zero or simply represents a result of random chance? We have discussed evaluating the significance level of the alpha estimate that comes from the regression. An alternative is to calculate the fund's **information ratio**.

The information ratio is calculated as a fund's alpha divided by its tracking error. The **tracking error** measures the volatility of the fund's returns relative to its benchmark. As an example, consider the fund we evaluated in the *Spreadsheet Analysis* in the previous section. In the first year, the fund earned an excess return (above the risk-free rate) of 7 percent and the market had an excess return of 5 percent. The difference between these two values is 2 percent. Over the five years, the differences between the two excess returns are 2 percent, 4 percent, −20 percent, 14 percent, and −10 percent, respectively. The tracking error is the standard deviation of these return differences, which in this case is 13.2 percent (check this number for practice).

information ratio
Alpha divided by tracking error.

tracking error
A measure of how volatile a portfolio is relative to its benchmark.

So, this fund's information ratio is −1.67 percent divided by 13.2 percent, which is −.13. Because standard deviation is always positive, the information ratio will always have the same sign as the alpha. The information ratio allows us to compare investments that have the same alpha, or compare investments with different alphas and tracking errors. For example, if two funds both have alphas of 1.5 percent, we most likely prefer the one with the higher information ratio because less risk (or volatility) is associated with this fund.

EXAMPLE 13.4

Information Ratio

A fund has an alpha of .8 percent and a tracking error of 5.9 percent. What is the fund's information ratio?

$$\text{Information ratio} = .8/5.9 = .14$$

R-SQUARED

Elsewhere, we discussed the importance of an investment's correlation to other securities. Recall that correlation measures how returns for a particular security move relative to returns for another security. Correlation also plays a key role in performance measurement.

Suppose a particular fund has had a large alpha over the past three years. All else equal, we might say that this fund is a good choice. However, what if the fund is a sector-based fund that invests only in gold? Well, it is possible that the large alpha is simply due to a run-up in gold prices over the period and is not reflective of good management or future potential.

R-squared
A portfolio or security's squared correlation to the market or benchmark.

To evaluate this type of risk we can calculate **R-squared,** which is simply the squared correlation of the fund to the market. For example, if this fund's correlation with the market was .6, then the R-squared value is $.6^2 = .36$. R-squared represents the percentage of the fund's movement that can be explained by movements in the market.

Because correlation ranges only from −1 to +1, R-squared values will range from 0 to 100 percent. An R-squared of 100 indicates that all movements in the security are driven by the market, indicating a correlation of −1 or +1. A high R-squared value (say greater than .80) might suggest that the performance measures (such as alpha) are more representative of potential longer term performance. The same is true for interpreting a security's beta.

EXAMPLE 13.5

R-Squared

A portfolio has a correlation to the market of .9. What is the R-squared? What percentage of the portfolio's return is driven by the market? What percentage comes from asset-specific risk?

$$R\text{-squared} = .9^2 = .81$$

This value implies that 81 percent of the portfolio's return is driven by the market. Thus, 19 percent (i.e., 100 − 81 percent) is driven by risk specific to the portfolio's holdings.

CHECK THIS

13.1a	What is the Sharpe ratio of portfolio performance?
13.1b	What is the Treynor ratio of portfolio performance?
13.1c	What is Jensen's alpha?
13.1d	Why can Jensen's alpha be interpreted as measuring by how much an investment portfolio beat the market?
13.1e	What is the information ratio?
13.1f	What is R-squared?

13.2 Comparing Performance Measures

Table 13.1 presents investment performance data for three risky portfolios, *A*, *B*, and *C*, along with return data for the market portfolio and a risk-free portfolio, denoted by *M* and *F*, respectively. Based on the performance data in Table 13.1, Table 13.2 provides computed performance measures for portfolios *A*, *B*, *C*, and a market portfolio, *M*. The market portfolio is a benchmark of investment performance. Often the familiar S&P 500 Index is the adopted proxy for the market portfolio.

As shown in Table 13.2, the Sharpe ratio ranks the three risky portfolios in the ascending order of performance *A*, *B*, and *C*. By contrast, the Treynor ratio ranks these three risky portfolios in the reversed order of performance *C*, *B*, and *A*. Jensen's alpha yields another portfolio ranking altogether, with the ascending order of performance *C*, *A*, and *B*.

The example above illustrates that the three performance measures can yield substantially different performance rankings. The fact that each of the three performance measures can produce such different results leaves us with the burning question: "Which performance measure should we use to evaluate portfolio performance?"

Well, the simple answer is: "It depends." If you wish to select a performance measure to evaluate an entire portfolio held by an investor, then the Sharpe ratio is appropriate. But if you wish to choose a performance measure to individually evaluate securities or portfolios for possible inclusion in a broader (or "master") portfolio, then either the Treynor ratio or Jensen's alpha is appropriate.

In broader terms, all three measures have strengths and weaknesses. Jensen's alpha is, as we have seen, easy to interpret. Comparing Jensen's alpha and the Treynor ratio, we see that they are really very similar. The only difference is that the Treynor ratio standardizes everything, including any excess return, relative to beta. If you were to take Jensen's alpha and divide it by beta, then you would have a Jensen-Treynor alpha, which measures excess return relative to beta, which is similar to the information ratio.

A common weakness of the Jensen and Treynor measures is that both require a beta estimate. As we discussed in our last chapter, betas from different sources can differ substantially, and, as a result, what appears to be a positive alpha might just be due to a mismeasured beta.

The Sharpe ratio has the advantage that no beta is necessary, and standard deviations can be calculated unambiguously. The drawback is that total risk is frequently not what really matters. However, for a relatively well-diversified portfolio, most of the risk is systematic, so there's not much difference between total risk and systematic risk. For this reason, for doing things like evaluating mutual funds, the Sharpe ratio is probably the most frequently used. Furthermore, if a mutual fund is not very diversified, then its standard deviation would

TABLE 13.1	Investment Performance Data		
Portfolio	R_p	σ_p	β_p
A	12%	40%	.5
B	15	30	.75
C	20	22	1.4
M	15	15	1
F	5	0	0

TABLE 13.2	Portfolio Performance Measurement		
Portfolio	Sharpe Ratio	Treynor Ratio	Jensen's Alpha
A	.175	.14	2 %
B	.333	.133	2.5
C	.682	.107	1
M	.667	.10	0

The various performance measures we have discussed are frequently used to evaluate mutual funds, or, more accurately, mutual fund managers. For example, the information below concerns the Fidelity Low-Priced Stock Fund, which is a small-cap value fund. We obtained the numbers from www.morningstar.com by entering the fund's ticker symbol (FLPSX) and following the "Ratings and Risk" link. By the way, you will see the abbreviation "MPT" in this context quite a bit. MPT is an acronym for "modern portfolio theory," which is the general label for things related to Markowitz-type portfolio analysis and the CAPM.

For this fund, the beta is 1.10, so the degree of market risk is above average. The fund's alpha is 3.51 per-cent, which could indicate superior past performance. The fund's standard deviation is 22.90 percent. The mean reported, −1.08 percent, is the geometric return of the fund over the past three years. The Sharpe ratio for the fund is −.14. Of course, we cannot judge this value in isolation. The fund's R-squared is 91, which means that 91 percent of its returns are driven by the market's return. Note that the index is compared to the S&P 500 and a "Best-Fit" Index. Although the fund being measured is a small-cap value fund, Morningstar selected its Mid Core index, a mid-cap index, as the best-fit index. This example illustrates the importance of being able to understand how to compute all these measures.

Volatility Measurements	Trailing 3-Yr through 11-30-09 | *Trailing 5-Yr through 11-30-09		
Standard Deviation	22.90	Sharpe Ratio	-0.14
Mean	-1.08	Bear Market Decile Rank*	7

Modern Portfolio Theory Statistics			Trailing 3-Yr through 11-30-09
	Standard Index S&P 500 TR	**Best Fit Index** Morningstar Mid Core TR USD	
R-Squared	91	97	
Beta	1.10	0.92	
Alpha	3.51	2.03	

S&P 500 index data: S&P 500 Copyright © 2009

be larger, resulting in a smaller Sharpe ratio. Thus, the Sharpe ratio, in effect, penalizes a portfolio for being undiversified.

To see how these performance measures are used in practice, have a look at our nearby *Work the Web* box, which shows some actual numbers for a mutual fund.

EXAMPLE 13.6

Picking Portfolios

Suppose you are restricted to investing all of your money in only a single portfolio from among the choices A, B, and C presented in Table 13.1. Which portfolio should you choose?

Because you can select only a single portfolio, the Sharpe-ratio measure of portfolio performance should be used. Referring to Table 13.2, we see that portfolio C has the highest Sharpe ratio of excess return per unit of total risk. Therefore, portfolio C should be chosen.

EXAMPLE 13.7

Picking Portfolios Again

Suppose you are considering whether portfolios A, B, and C presented in Table 13.1 should be included in a master portfolio. Should you select one, two, or all three portfolios for inclusion in your master portfolio?

Since you are selecting portfolios for inclusion in a master portfolio, either the Treynor ratio or Jensen's alpha should be used. Suppose you decide to consider any portfolio that outperforms the market portfolio M, based on either the Treynor ratio or Jensen's alpha. Referring to Table 13.2, we see that all three portfolios have Treynor ratios and Jensen's alphas greater than the market portfolio. Therefore, you should decide to include all three portfolios in your master portfolio.

GLOBAL INVESTMENT PERFORMANCE STANDARDS

As the previous example illustrates, comparing investments is sometimes difficult, because the various performance metrics can provide different rankings. In the previous example, this difference was caused purely by the nature of the returns. However, even if the various metrics provided a similar ranking, we could still make an incorrect choice in selecting an investment manager.

How is this possible? Well, remember the adage "garbage in, garbage out." Sadly, this principle applies to the performance measurement process. In particular, our metrics are often based on returns (and other inputs) that are self-reported by the firms we are evaluating. This is particularly true for managers who do not offer a publicly traded portfolio.

To provide a measure of consistency in reported performance, the CFA Institute developed the Global Investment Performance Standards (GIPS). These standards provide investment firms with guidance for calculating and reporting their performance results to prospective (and current) clients. By standardizing the process, GIPS provide investors with the ability to make comparisons across managers.

Firms are not required by law to comply with GIPS. Rather, compliance with these standards is voluntary. Firms that do comply, however, are recognized by the CFA Institute, which might give these firms more credibility among potential investors.

WWW

For some specifics on the actual standards, check out www.gipsstandards.org

CHECK THIS

13.2a Explain the difference between systematic risk measured by beta and total risk measured by standard deviation. When are they essentially the same?

13.2b Alter the returns data in Table 13.1 so that portfolios *A*, *B*, and *C* all have a raw return of 15 percent. Which among these three portfolios then have a Treynor ratio or Jensen's alpha greater than that of the market portfolio *M*?

13.2c What is the purpose of the CFA Institute's Global Investment Performance Standards (GIPS)?

SHARPE-OPTIMAL PORTFOLIOS

In this section, we show how to obtain a funds allocation with the highest possible Sharpe ratio. Such a portfolio is said to be "Sharpe optimal." The method is closely related to the procedure of obtaining a Markowitz efficient frontier discussed in a previous chapter. This fact is no surprise because both methods are used to achieve an optimal balance of risk and return for investment portfolios.

To illustrate the connection, have a look at Figure 13.4. This figure shows the investment opportunity set of risk-return possibilities for a portfolio of two assets, a stock fund and a bond fund. Now the question is: "Of all of these possible portfolios, which one is Sharpe optimal?" To find out, consider the portfolio labeled *A* in the figure. Notice that we have drawn a straight line from the risk-free rate running through this point.

What is the slope of this straight line? As always, the slope of a straight line is the "rise over the run." In this case, the return rises from the risk-free rate, R_f, to the expected return on portfolio *A*, so the rise is $E(R_A) - R_f$. At the same time, risk moves from zero for a risk-free asset up to the standard deviation on portfolio *A*, so the run is $\sigma_A - 0 = \sigma_A$. Thus, the slope is $[E(R_A) - R_f]/\sigma_A$, which is just the Sharpe ratio for portfolio *A*.

So, the slope of a straight line drawn from the risk-free rate to a portfolio in Figure 13.4 tells us the Sharpe ratio for that portfolio. This is always the case, even if there are many assets, not just two. The problem of finding the Sharpe-optimal portfolio thus boils down to finding the line with the steepest slope. Looking again at Figure 13.4, we quickly figure out that the line with the steepest slope is always going to be the one that just touches (i.e., is tangent to) the investment opportunity set. We have labeled this portfolio *T* (for tangent).

FIGURE 13.4 The Sharpe-Optimal Portfolio

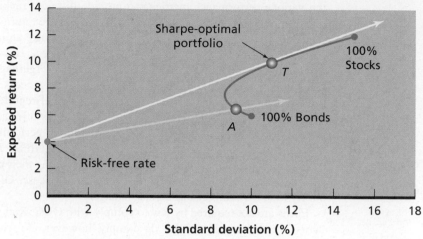

Portfolio *T* has the highest Sharpe ratio of any possible combination of these two assets, so it is Sharpe optimal.

We now have an interesting and important result. The Markowitz efficient frontier tells us which portfolios are efficient, but it does not tell us which of the efficient portfolios is the best. What Figure 13.4 shows is that, of those efficient portfolios, one is the very best, at least in the sense of being Sharpe optimal.

To illustrate how to find the Sharpe optimal portfolio, recall from Chapter 11 that the returns of the stock and bond funds are 12 percent and 6 percent. The standard deviations are 15 percent and 10 percent, respectively, and the correlation is .10. From our discussion in Chapter 11, we know that the expected return on a portfolio of two assets is given by:

$$E(R_p) = x_S E(R_S) + x_B E(R_B)$$

where x_S and x_B are the percentages invested in the stock and bond fund, respectively. Also from Chapter 11, the variance on a portfolio of these two assets is:

$$\sigma_P^2 = x_S^2 \sigma_S^2 + x_B^2 \sigma_B^2 + 2x_S x_B \sigma_S \sigma_B \text{Corr}(R_S, R_B)$$

Putting it all together, the Sharpe ratio for our two-asset portfolio looks like this:

$$\frac{E(R_p) - R_f}{\sigma_p} = \frac{x_S E(R_S) + x_B E(R_B) - R_f}{\sqrt{x_S^2 \sigma_S^2 + x_B^2 \sigma_B^2 + 2x_S x_B \sigma_S \sigma_B \text{Corr}(R_S, R_B)}} \tag{13.7}$$

Our task is to find the values of x_S and x_B that make this ratio as large as possible. This looks like a tough job, but, as our nearby *Spreadsheet Analysis* box shows, it can be done relatively easily. As shown there, assuming a risk-free interest rate of 4 percent, the highest possible Sharpe ratio is .553 based on a 70–30 mix between stocks and bonds.

You can use the Solver tool to solve for the weights that maximize the Sharpe ratio. In the nearby *Spreadsheet Analysis,* we did just that. Once the formulas are entered for the portfolio return, standard deviation, and Sharpe ratio, we can solve for the portfolio weights that give us the highest possible Sharpe ratio. We do not have to worry about the weight in bonds because the weight in bonds is simply equal to 1 minus the weight in stocks.

You can see in the *Spreadsheet Analysis* that we ask Solver to change the portfolio weight in stocks so that the maximum Sharpe ratio is obtained. Note that we also required that the weights in stocks and bonds both be equal to or greater than zero. If any of the returns, standard deviations, or correlations are changed, the Solver tool must be rerun. Build this spreadsheet yourself and see if you get the same answer we did. Then, change the correlation between stocks and bonds to .20. Does the Sharpe ratio increase or decrease? What happens to the weights?

	A	B	C	D	E	F	G	H
1								
2		Optimal Sharpe Ratio with Two Risky Assets, Stocks and Bonds						
3								
4		Expected Returns:						
5		Stocks =	0.12					
6		Bonds =	0.06			Portfolio Return, E(Rp) =		0.102
7								
8		Risk-Free Rate =	0.04			Portfolio Standard Deviation, SD(Rp) =		0.112
9								
10		Standard Deviations:				Sharpe Ratio =		0.553
11		Stocks =	0.15					
12		Bonds =	0.10					
13					Portfolio Weights to Maximize Sharpe Ratio:			
14		Correlation between					Stocks =	0.7000
15		Stocks and Bonds =	0.10				Bonds =	0.3000
16							(= 1 − H14)	
17								
18	Formulas for Portfolio Return, Portfolio Standard Deviation, and Sharpe Ratio:							
19								
20		E(Rp) = H14*C5+H15*C6						
21								
22		SD(Rp) = SQRT(H14*H14*C11*C11+H15*H15*C12*C12+2*H14*H15*C15*C11*C12)						
23								
24	Sharpe Ratio = (E(Rp) - RF) / SD(Rp) = (H6-C8)/H8							
25								
26	Using SOLVER® to compute portfolio weights that maximize the Sharpe Ratio:							
27								

Solver Parameters ? X

Set Target Cell: H10

Equal To: ⊙ Max ○ Min ○ Value of: 0

By Changing Cells:
H14

Subject to the Constraints:
H14 >= 0
H15 >= 0

[Solve] [Close] [Guess] [Options] [Add] [Change] [Delete] [Reset All] [Help]

EXAMPLE 13.8

Sharpe-Optimal Portfolio Calculations

Suppose you have the following expected return and risk information for stocks and bonds that will be used to form a Sharpe-optimal portfolio.

$$E(R_S) = .12 \quad \sigma_S = .15 \quad E(R_B) = .06 \quad \sigma_B = .10 \quad Corr(R_S, R_B) = .10 \quad R_F = .04$$

In the case of just two risky assets, stocks and bonds, the formulas for the portfolio weights for the optimal Sharpe portfolio are:

$$x_S = \frac{\sigma_B^2 \times [E(R_S) - R_F] - Corr(R_S, R_B) \times \sigma_S \times \sigma_B \times [E(R_B) - R_F]}{\sigma_B^2 \times [E(R_S) - R_F] + \sigma_S^2 \times [E(R_B) - R_F] - [E(R_S) + E(R_B) - 2 \times R_F] \times Corr(R_S, R_B) \times \sigma_S \times \sigma_B}$$

(continued)

and

$$x_B = 1 - x_S$$

Calculate the Sharpe-optimal portfolio weights and the expected return and standard deviation for the Sharpe-optimal portfolio.

Inserting the expected return and risk information into these formulas yields these optimal Sharpe portfolio weights for stocks and bonds:

$$x_S = \frac{.10^2 \times [.12 - .04] - .10 \times .15 \times .10 \times [.06 - .04]}{.10^2 \times [.12 - .04] + .15^2 \times [.06 - .04] - [.12 + .06 - 2 \times .04] \times .10 \times .15 \times .10}$$
$$= .70$$

and

$$x_B = 1 - x_S = 1 - .70 = .30$$

With these results, we now have all the information needed to calculate the expected return and standard deviation for the Sharpe-optimal portfolio:

$$E(R_P) = x_S E(R_S) + x_B E(R_B)$$
$$= .70 \times .12 + .30 \times .06$$
$$= .102, \text{ or } 10.2\%$$

$$\sigma_P = \sqrt{x_S^2 \sigma_S^2 + x_B^2 \sigma_B^2 + 2 x_S x_B \sigma_S \sigma_B \text{Corr}(R_S, R_B)}$$
$$= \sqrt{.70^2 \times .15^2 + .30^2 \times .10^2 + 2 \times .70 \times .30 \times .15 \times .10 \times .10}$$
$$= .112, \text{ or } 11.2\%$$

CHECK THIS

13.2d What is a Sharpe-optimal portfolio?

13.2e Among the many Markowitz efficient portfolios, which one is Sharpe optimal?

13.3 Investment Risk Management

investment risk management
Concerns a money manager's control over investment risks, usually with respect to potential short-run losses.

In the first part of this chapter, we discussed performance evaluation within a framework of optimizing the trade-off between risk and return for an investment portfolio. In the remainder of this chapter, we examine **investment risk management** within the framework of a money manager's concern over potential losses for an investment portfolio within a specific time horizon. We focus on what is known as the Value-at-Risk approach. However, risk can be viewed in many different ways, and, for some alternative viewpoints, we suggest reading the nearby *Investment Updates* boxes.

VALUE-AT-RISK

Value-at-Risk (VaR)
Assesses risk by stating the probability of a loss a portfolio might experience within a fixed time horizon with a specified probability.

An important goal of this chapter is to learn how to assess portfolio risk using **Value-at-Risk**. In essence, the Value-at-Risk (usually abbreviated VaR) method involves evaluating the probability of a significant loss. The basic approach we describe here is widely used by many different financial institutions.

normal distribution
A statistical model for assessing probabilities related to many phenomena, including security returns.

The VaR measure of investment risk is closely related to something we discussed way back in Chapter 1. There we said that if the returns on an investment follow a **normal distribution**, then we can state the probability that a portfolio's return will be within a certain range. Since a normal distribution is completely specified by its mean and standard deviation, these are all that we need to state this probability.

SHARPE POINT: RISK GAUGE IS MISUSED

gauge- calculate the amount or extent

William F. Sharpe was probably the biggest expert in the room when economists from around the world gathered in Sonoma, Calif., to hash out a pressing problem in July: How to gauge hedge-fund risk.

About 40 years ago, Dr. Sharpe, now a retired professor from Stanford University, created a simple calculation for measuring the return that investors should expect for the level of volatility they are accepting. The so-called Sharpe Ratio became a cornerstone of modern finance, as investors used it to help select money managers and mutual funds. But at the Sonoma meeting, the use of the ratio was criticized by many prominent academics—including Dr. Sharpe himself.

The ratio is commonly used—"misused," Dr. Sharpe says—for promotional purposes by hedge funds. "That is very disturbing," says the 71-year-old Dr. Sharpe. Hedge funds often use complex strategies that are vulnerable to surprise events and elude any simple formula for measuring risk. "Past average experience may be a terrible predictor of future performance," Dr. Sharpe says.

"This is becoming more of a problem because there is a movement to offer retail versions of hedge funds," says Andrew Lo, a Massachusetts Institute of Technology finance professor and a partner in the AlphaSimplex Group, a hedge fund that manages $350 million. "The typical retail investor might very well be misled by amazing looking Sharpe Ratios."

"Hedge funds can manipulate the ratio to misrepresent their performance," adds Dr. Sharpe, a founder of Financial Engines, a Palo Alto, Calif., investment advisor and manager. In a recent study, Dr. Lo found that the annual Sharpe Ratio for hedge funds can be overstated by as much as 65%. "You can legitimately generate very attractive Sharpe Ratios and still, in time, lose money," he says. "People should not take the Sharpe Ratio at face value."

Even if it isn't manipulated, Dr. Sharpe says, it doesn't foreshadow hedge-fund woes because "no number can." The formula can't predict such troubles as the inability to sell off investments quickly if they start to head south, nor can it account for extreme unexpected events. Long-Term Capital Management, a huge hedge fund in Connecticut, had a glowing Sharpe Ratio before it abruptly collapsed in 1998 when Russia devalued its currency and defaulted on debt.

In Hong Kong, the government bars hedge funds from opening unless they can prove they aren't going to fail—and yet there is no adequate measure, says Sally Wong, executive director of the Hong Kong Investment Funds Association. Her problem with the Sharpe Ratio is that it assumes that a fund's returns will remain even over time. "Many hedge-fund strategies have greater downside events," Ms. Wong says. She favors another measure, the Sortino Ratio. That is similar to the Sharpe Ratio, but instead of using the standard deviation as the denominator, it uses downside deviation—the amount a portfolio strays from its average downturns—to distinguish between "good" and "bad" volatility.

But even the namesake of that ratio is troubled by its use for evaluating hedge funds. "I think it's used too much because it makes hedge funds look good," says Frank Sortino, who developed the ratio 20 years ago and is director of the Pension Research Institute in San Francisco. "It's misleading to say the least," he adds. "I hate that they're using my name."

Dr. Sharpe feels similarly. "I never named it the Sharpe Ratio," he says of his formula. "I called it the Reward-to-Variability ratio."

Source: Ianthe Jeanne Dugan, *The Wall Street Journal*, August 31, 2005. Reprinted with permission of *The Wall Street Journal*. © 2005 Dow Jones & Company, Inc. All Rights Reserved Worldwide.

For example, suppose you own an S&P 500 Index fund. What is the probability of a return of −7 percent or worse in a particular year? As we saw in Chapter 1, since 1925, the return on the S&P 500 Index has averaged 13 percent per year with a standard deviation of about 20 percent per year. A return of −7 percent is exactly one standard deviation below the average (.13 − .20 = −.07). We know from Chapter 1 (and basic statistics) that the odds of being within one standard deviation are about 2/3, or .67. Being *within* one standard deviation of the mean of .13 means being *between* .13 plus .20 and .13 minus .20, i.e., between −.07 and +.33.

If the odds of being within this range are 2/3, then the odds of being *outside* this range are about 1/3. Finally, if we are outside this range, then half of the time we'll be above this range and half of the time we'll be below. Half of 1/3 is 1/6, so we'll experience a return of −.07 or worse 1/6, or about 17 percent, of the time.

Putting it together, if you own an S&P 500 Index fund, this risk assessment can be stated:

$$\text{Prob}(R_p \leq -.07) = 17\%$$

WWW

Learn all about VaR at
www.gloriamundi.org

HOW TO PLAY THE GAME OF RISK WHEN INVESTING YOUR MONEY

If we want our portfolios to go up, we need to spend a little time looking down. Take too much risk with our investments, and we could end up selling in a panic at the worst possible time. Take too little risk, and we will likely clock unnecessarily low returns. So how do we settle on the right amount of risk? Here are some thoughts on this messy notion:

Looking for Danger

High risk is meant to lead to high returns. But what do we mean by "high risk"? If we bet all our money on a couple of hot stocks, we are undoubtedly taking a ton of risk. But there is every chance we will lose our shirts. Instead, when academics talk about risk getting rewarded, they are referring to market risk. When investing in stocks, we can eliminate the risk of owning any one stock by spreading our money across a fistful of different companies. But even if we do that, we will still take a hit if the broad market declines. This market risk, which we can't diversify away, is the risk we get rewarded for taking.

What does this mean for our portfolios? If we want higher long-run returns, we need to take more market risk, by keeping less in conservative investments and more in stocks. But to be confident of getting our reward, we need to ensure that our stock portfolios are well diversified. This diversification has the added advantage of bolstering our tenacity. Have shares just tumbled 20%? If all we own are a couple of stocks, we will no doubt fret over whether our shares will ever bounce back. But if we own a broadly diversified portfolio, we will have greater confidence that our stocks should eventually generate decent gains.

Looking Up

To gauge risk, investment experts have traditionally looked at an investment's volatility, as reflected in statistical measures such as standard deviation and beta. Standard deviation is a gauge of how far an investment's results have strayed from its average performance, while beta measures an investment's price gyrations relative to a broad market index.

But investors often dismiss such statistical measures, complaining that they aren't bothered when volatility works to their advantage and generates big gains. Instead, what they care about is losses, and it is these losses that risk measures should seek to capture. But in fact, upside volatility is a great measure of downside risk. Consider technology stocks. Their dismal performance in the recent bear market was foretold by their equally astonishing rise during the late 1990s bull market.

Looking Out

When measuring risk, some experts don't just look at volatility. They also consider longer-run performance. For instance, if we hold stocks for 20 years, we are unlikely to

lose money and we will almost certainly outpace bonds. That has led some commentators to argue that stocks are less risky than bonds. But this is nonsense. If we look out far enough, the highest-returning investments will always appear to be the least risky. Indeed, I fear such foolishness could lead folks to bet far too much on stocks.

"Over a long enough period, risk and return become the same thing," says William Bernstein, author of "The Intelligent Asset Allocator" and an investment advisor in North Bend, Ore. "The reason stocks have seemed so low risk is because the returns have been so high. But the high returns may not be true going forward." Moreover, not everybody has a 20-year time horizon, and not many investors can ignore short-term market turmoil. "People feel risk in their gut in the short term and in their brain in the long term," Mr. Bernstein says. "Unfortunately, they react to their gut."

Looking Pale

How much risk can each of us stomach? Mutual-fund companies and investment advisors have questionnaires that try to help folks figure out whether they are aggressive or conservative investors. But often, people later discover that their risk tolerance is far higher or lower. What to do? Eleanor Blayney, a financial planner in McLean, Va., says investors should spend time studying their own investment history. "The best indicator of risk tolerance is past behavior," she argues. In particular, Ms. Blayney likes to ask clients what they believe their best and worst investment decisions were. She says aggressive investors tend to fret about missing out on gains, while conservative investors tend to dwell on their losses.

Looking for Safety

Even if we set out to take a lot of risk, we often gravitate toward investments we perceive to be safe. For instance, we may choose to invest a hefty amount in the stock market. But when it comes to picking individual stocks, we often select companies we view as safe. Indeed, if we didn't think a stock was a pretty safe bet, we probably wouldn't have the courage to buy.

Result? We tend to invest in widely admired corporations or those shares that have lately performed well. Meanwhile, we shy away from companies that have had financial problems or have suffered steep share-price declines, even though studies suggest that these tarnished companies often generate market-beating gains. "People will accept that risk gets rewarded if they are forced to listen to the finance-professor spiel," says Hersh Shefrin, a finance professor at Santa Clara University in California. "They will accept the notion intellectually. But emotionally, they associate good stocks with safe stocks."

Source: Jonathan Clements, *The Wall Street Journal*, February 2, 2002. Reprinted with permission of *The Wall Street Journal*. © 2002 Dow Jones & Company, Inc. All Rights Reserved Worldwide.

Your VaR statistic is thus a return of −.07 or worse with a probability of 17 percent. By the way, here is an important note: When we say a loss of −.07 or worse, we mean that, *one year from now*, your portfolio value is down by 7 percent or more.

EXAMPLE 13.9

VaR Risk Statistic

You agree with J. P. Morgan that the stock market will fluctuate and have become concerned with how these fluctuations might affect your stock portfolio. Having read about the VaR method for measuring investment risk, you decide to apply it to your portfolio.

Suppose you believe that there is a 5 percent chance of a return of −18 percent or worse in the coming week. Mathematically, this risk assessment can be stated as:

$$\text{Prob } (R_p \leq -18\%) = 5\%$$

Taken together, this −18 percent or worse expected loss and 5 percent probability form a VaR "statistic" for your stock portfolio.

CHECK THIS

13.3a What is the probability of realizing a portfolio return one or more standard deviations below the expected mean return?

13.3b What is the probability of realizing a portfolio return two or more standard deviations below the expected mean return?

13.3c Your portfolio has a mean return of 15 percent and a return standard deviation of 25 percent. What portfolio return is two standard deviations below the mean?

13.4 More on Computing Value-at-Risk

In this section we extend our discussion of computing VaR. Our goal is mainly to examine how to evaluate horizons that are shorter or longer than one year. The easiest way to do this is to take our earlier example concerning the S&P 500 and extend it a bit.

Once again, suppose you own an S&P 500 Index fund. What is the probability of a loss of 30 percent or more over the next *two* years? To answer, we need to know the average two-year return and the average two-year return standard deviation. Getting the average two-year return is easy enough; we just have to double the one-year average. So, the two-year average return is $2 \times .13 = .26$, or 26 percent.

The two-year standard deviation is a little trickier. The two-year *variance* is just double the one-year variance. In our case, the one-year variance is $.20^2 = .04$, and the two-year variance is thus .08. As always, to get the two-year standard deviation, we take the square root of this, which is .28, or 28 percent. The main thing to notice is that the two-year standard deviation is not just double the one-year number. In fact, if you look at it, the two-year number is equal to the one-year number multiplied by the square root of 2, or 1.414.

Now we can answer our question. A two-year loss of 30 percent is equal to the two-year average return of 26 percent less two standard deviations: $.26 - 2 \times .28 = -.30$. From Chapter 1, we know that the odds of being within two standard deviations are 95 percent, so the odds of being outside this range are 5 percent. The odds of being on the bad side (the loss side) are half that, namely, 2.5 percent.

Learn about the risk management profession at www.garp.com

In general, if we let T stand for the number of years, then the expected return on a portfolio over T years, $E(R_{p,T})$ can be written as:

$$E(R_{p,T}) = E(R_p) \times T \tag{13.8}$$

Similarly, the standard deviation can be written as:

$$\sigma_{p,T} = \sigma_p \times \sqrt{T} \tag{13.9}$$

If the time period is less than a year, the T is just a fraction of a year.

WWW

Check out risk grades at
www.riskmetrics.com

When you do a VaR analysis, you have to pick the time horizon and loss level probability. You can pick any probability you want, of course, but the most common are 1, 2.5, and 5 percent. We know that 2.5 percent, which is half of 5 percent, corresponds to two standard deviations (actually 1.96 to be more precise) below the expected return. To get the 1 percent and 5 percent numbers, you would need to find an ordinary "z" table to tell you the number of standard deviations. We'll save you the trouble. The 1 percent level is 2.326 standard deviations below the average, and the 5 percent level is 1.645 "sigmas" below.

Wrapping up our discussion, the VaR statistics for these three levels can be summarized as follows:

$$\text{Prob}[R_{p,T} \le E(R_p) \times T - 2.326 \times \sigma_p\sqrt{T}] = 1\% \tag{13.10}$$

$$\text{Prob}[R_{p,T} \le E(R_p) \times T - 1.96 \times \sigma_p\sqrt{T}] = 2.5\%$$

$$\text{Prob}[R_{p,T} \le E(R_p) \times T - 1.645 \times \sigma_p\sqrt{T}] = 5\%$$

Notice that if T, the number of years, is equal to 1, the 1 percent level corresponds to once in a century. Similarly, 5 percent is once every 20 years, and 2.5 percent is once every 40 years. Examples 13.10 through 13.13 show you how to use VaR statistics.

EXAMPLE 13.10 **VaR Risk Statistic**

The Ned Kelley Hedge Fund focuses on investing in bank and transportation companies in Australia with above-average risk. The average annual return is 15 percent with an annual return standard deviation of 50 percent. What loss level can we expect over a two-year investment horizon with a probability of .17?

We assume a two-year expected return of 30 percent. The one-year variance is $.50^2 = .25$, so the two-year variance is .50. Taking the square root, we get a two-year standard deviation of .7071, or 70.71 percent. A loss probability of .17 corresponds to one standard deviation below the mean, so the answer to our question is $.30 - .7071 = -.4071$, a substantial loss. We can write this succinctly as:

$$\text{Prob}(R_p \le -40.71\%) = 17\%$$

Notice that there is a 17 percent chance of a 40.71 percent loss or worse over the next two years.

EXAMPLE 13.11 **VaR Risk Statistic**

Going back to the Ned Kelley Hedge Fund in our previous example, what loss level might we expect over six months with a probability of .17?

The six-month expected return is half of 15 percent, or 7.5 percent. The six-month standard deviation is $.5 \times \sqrt{1/2} = .3536$. So the answer to our question is $.075 - .3536 = -.2786$. Again, we can write this succinctly as:

$$\text{Prob}(R_p \le -27.86\%) = 17\%$$

Thus there is a 17 percent chance of a 27.86 percent loss or worse over the next six months.

EXAMPLE 13.12

A One-in-Twenty Loss

For the Ned Kelley Hedge Fund specified in our previous examples, what is the expected loss for the coming year with a probability of 5 percent?

In this case, with an annual return mean of 15 percent and an annual return standard deviation of 50 percent, set $T = 1$ for a one year time horizon and calculate this VaR statistic:

$$\text{Prob}[R_{p,1} \le E(R_p) \times 1 - 1.645\sigma_p \times \sqrt{1}] = \text{Prob}(R_{p,1} \le 15\% - 1.645 \times 50\%)$$
$$= \text{Prob}(R_{p,1} \le -67.25\%) = 5\%$$

Thus we can expect a loss of 67.25 percent or worse over the next year with a 5 percent probability.

EXAMPLE 13.13

A One-in-a-Hundred Loss

For the Ned Kelley Hedge Fund specified in our previous examples, what is the expected loss for the coming month with a 1 percent probability?

Setting $T = 1/12$ for a one-month time horizon, we calculate this VaR statistic:

$$\text{Prob}[R_{p,T} \le E(R_p) \times 1/12 - 2.326\sigma_p \times \sqrt{1/12}]$$
$$= \text{Prob}(R_{p,T} \le 1.25\% - 2.326 \times 50\% \times .2887)$$
$$= \text{Prob}(R_{p,T} \le -32.32\%) = 1\%$$

Thus we can expect a loss of 32.32 percent or more with a 1 percent probability over the next month.

As an application of Value-at-Risk, consider the problem of determining VaR statistics for a Sharpe-optimal stock and bond portfolio. As with any VaR problem for a portfolio, remember that the key to the problem is to first determine the expected return and standard deviation for the portfolio. From our discussion in Chapter 11 and earlier in this chapter, we know that the expected return and standard deviation of a stock and bond portfolio are specified by these two equations:

$$E(R_P) = x_S E(R_S) + x_B E(R_B)$$

$$\sigma_P = \sqrt{x_S^2 \sigma_S^2 + x_B^2 \sigma_B^2 + 2x_S x_B \sigma_S \sigma_B \text{Corr}(R_S, R_B)}$$

Thus, the problem of calculating VaR statistics for a Sharpe-optimal portfolio is the same for any portfolio once the appropriate portfolio weights are determined.

CHECK THIS

13.4a Your portfolio allocates 40 percent of funds to ABC stock and 60 percent to XYZ stock. ABC has a return mean and standard deviation of 15 percent and 20 percent, respectively. XYZ stock has a return mean and standard deviation of 25 percent and 30 percent, respectively. What is the portfolio return standard deviation if the return correlation between ABC and XYZ stocks is zero?

13.4b Based on your answer to the previous question, what is the smallest expected loss for your portfolio in the coming year with a probability of 1 percent? What is the smallest expected loss for your portfolio in the coming month with a probability of 5 percent?

13.5 Summary and Conclusions

In this chapter, we covered the related topics of performance measurement and risk management.

1. **How to calculate the best-known portfolio evaluation measures.**

   A. Our goal with performance measurement is essentially to rank investments based on their risk-adjusted returns. We introduced and discussed the most frequently used tools to do this: the Sharpe ratio, the Treynor ratio, Jensen's alpha, the information ratio, and R-squared.

   B. As we saw, each has a somewhat different interpretation. Also, which one is the most suitable depends on the specific question to be answered.

2. **The strengths and weaknesses of these portfolio evaluation measures.**

   A. Sharpe ratio. *Strength:* No beta estimate is necessary, and standard deviations can be calculated unambiguously. *Weakness:* Total risk is frequently not what really matters. However, for a relatively well-diversified portfolio, most of the risk is systematic, so there's not much difference between total risk and systematic risk.

   B. Treynor ratio. *Strength:* The Treynor ratio standardizes everything, including any excess return, relative to beta. *Weakness:* The Treynor measure requires a beta estimate.

   C. Jensen's alpha. *Strength:* Jensen's alpha is easy to interpret. *Weakness:* The Jensen measure requires a beta estimate. Betas from different sources can differ substantially, and, as a result, what appears to be a positive alpha might just be due to a mismeasured beta.

   D. The information ratio and R-squared help to determine the accuracy of the other metrics.

3. **How to calculate a Sharpe-optimal portfolio.**

   A. The slope of a straight line drawn from the risk-free rate to a portfolio on a return–standard deviation graph tells us the Sharpe ratio for that portfolio. This is always the case, even with many assets, not just two. The portfolio with the highest slope is called Sharpe-optimal.

   B. The problem of finding the Sharpe-optimal portfolio boils down to finding the portfolio with the steepest slope. The line with the steepest slope is always going to be the one that just touches (i.e., is tangent to) the investment opportunity set. That portfolio is sometimes labeled portfolio T (for tangent).

   C. The Markowitz efficient frontier tells us which portfolios are efficient. The Markowitz efficient frontier does not tell us which one of the efficient portfolios is the best. Given a risk-free rate, the Sharpe-optimal portfolio is the best portfolio, at least as measured by the Sharpe ratio.

4. **How to calculate and interpret Value-at-Risk.**

   A. We introduce the popular and widely used method to assess portfolio risk called "Value-at-Risk," or VaR. Here the goal is usually to assess the probability of a large loss within a fixed time frame.

   B. Investors use this tool both to better understand the risks of their existing portfolios and to assess the risks of potential investments. The VaR measure is closely related to something we discussed way back in Chapter 1.

   C. If the returns on an investment follow a normal distribution, then we can state the probability that a portfolio's return will be within a certain range. Because a normal distribution is completely specified by its mean and standard deviation, these two statistics are all that we need to state the probability of a loss of a certain size.

This chapter covered the essentials of performance evaluation and investment risk management. With thousands of mutual funds and investment companies competing for performance while trying to control risk, these topics are especially important. If you wish to learn more about these subjects, a good place to start is the Internet.

Some useful and informative Web sites on investment performance analysis are Performance Analysis (www.andreassteiner.net/performanceanalysis), an informative Web site on investment performance analysis; Professor William F. Sharpe (www. stanford.edu/~wfsharpe), Web site of the Nobel laureate who created the Sharpe ratio; and FinPlan (www.finplan.com), a financial planning Web site with a useful section on investment performance analysis. You can also consult www.garp .com, which is the Web site of the Global Association of Risk Professionals (GARP), an independent organization of financial risk management practitioners and researchers.

Because financial institutions generally prefer that their risk profiles be kept private, a large part of the world of financial risk management is hidden from public view. Nevertheless, the field of risk management is large and growing. If you want to know more about this fascinating subject, some interesting Web sites that provide a wealth of information are Gloria Mundi (www.gloriamundi.org), a site that tells you all about Value-at-Risk; Risk Metrics (www.riskmetrics.com), a leading risk management consultancy group; and Margrabe (www.margrabe.com), the Web site of a professional risk management consultant.

Key Terms

information ratio 447	*R*-squared 448
investment risk management 454	Sharpe ratio 443
Jensen's alpha 444	tracking error 447
normal distribution 454	Treynor ratio 443
performance evaluation 442	Value-at-Risk (VaR) 454
raw return 442	

Chapter Review Problems and Self-Test

1. **Performance Measures (CFA6)**   Compute Sharpe ratios, Treynor ratios, and Jensen's alphas for portfolios *A*, *B*, and *C* based on the following returns data, where *M* and *F* stand for the market portfolio and risk-free rate, respectively:

Portfolio	R_p	σ_p	β_p
A	10%	30%	0.75
B	15	25	1.00
C	20	40	1.50
M	15	15	1.00
F	5	0	0.00

2. **Value-at-Risk (VaR) (CFA5)** A portfolio manager believes her $100 million stock portfolio will have a 10 percent return standard deviation during the coming week and that her portfolio's returns are normally distributed. What is the probability of her losing $10 million or more? What is the dollar loss expected with a 5 percent probability? What is the dollar loss expected with a 1 percent probability?

Answers to Self-Test Problems

1. Using equations (13.1), (13.2), and (13.4) yields these performance measurement values:

Portfolio	Sharpe Ratio	Treynor Ratio	Jensen's Alpha
A	.167	.0667	−2.5%
B	.400	.10	0
C	.375	.10	0
M	.667	.10	0

2. Because a mean is not given but the time horizon is only one week, we can simply assume a mean of zero. Thus the probability of a $10 million or greater loss is the probability of a loss of one or more return standard deviations. For a normal distribution, a realization 1.645 or more standard deviations below the mean occurs with about a 5 percent probability, yielding a potential loss of at least $1.645 \times \$10$ million = $16.45 million. For a normal distribution, a realization 2.326 or more standard deviations below the mean occurs with about a 1 percent probability, yielding a potential loss of at least $2.326 \times \$10$ million = $23.26 million.

Test Your Investment Quotient

1. **Beta and Standard Deviation (LO2, CFA3)** Beta and standard deviation differ as risk measures in that beta measures

   a. Only unsystematic risk, whereas standard deviation measures total risk.
   b. Only systematic risk, whereas standard deviation measures total risk.
   c. Both systematic and unsystematic risk, whereas standard deviation measures only unsystematic risk.
   d. Both systematic and unsystematic risk, whereas standard deviation measures only systematic risk.

   Answer Questions 2 through 8 based on the following information.

	Risk and Return Data		
Portfolio	Average Return	Standard Deviation	Beta
P	17%	20%	1.1
Q	24	18	2.1
R	11	10	0.5
S	16	14	1.5
S&P 500	14	12	1.0

   A pension fund administrator wants to evaluate the performance of four portfolio managers. Each manager invests only in U.S. common stocks. During the most recent five-year period, the average annual total return on the S&P 500 was 14 percent, and the average annual rate on Treasury bills was 8 percent. The table above shows risk and return measures for each portfolio.

2. **Treynor Ratio (LO1, CFA6)** The Treynor portfolio performance measure for Portfolio P is

   a. 8.18
   b. 7.62
   c. 6.00
   d. 5.33

3. **Sharpe Ratio (LO1, CFA6)**   The Sharpe portfolio performance measure for Portfolio Q is
   a. .45
   b. .89
   c. .30
   d. .57

4. **Jensen's Alpha (LO1, CFA6)**   The Jensen's alpha portfolio performance measure for Portfolio R is
   a. 2.4 percent
   b. 3.4 percent
   c. 0 percent
   d. −1 percent

5. **Treynor Ratio (LO1, CFA6)**   Which portfolio has the highest Treynor ratio?
   a. P
   b. Q
   c. R
   d. S

6. **Sharpe Ratio (LO1, CFA6)**   Which portfolio has the highest Sharpe ratio?
   a. P
   b. Q
   c. R
   d. S

7. **Jensen's Alpha (LO1, CFA6)**   Which portfolio has the highest Jensen's alpha?
   a. P
   b. Q
   c. R
   d. S

8. **Sharpe Ratio (LO1, CFA6)**   Assuming uncorrelated returns, the Sharpe ratio for a master portfolio with equal allocations to Portfolio S and Portfolio Q is
   a. .71
   b. 1.4
   c. .95
   d. 1.05

9. **Normal Distribution (LO4)**   Given a data series that is normally distributed with a mean of 100 and a standard deviation of 10, about 95 percent of the numbers in the series will fall within
   a. 60 to 140
   b. 70 to 130
   c. 80 to 120
   d. 90 to 110

10. **Normal Distribution (LO4)**   Given a data series that is normally distributed with a mean of 100 and a standard deviation of 10, about 99 percent of the numbers in the series will fall within
    a. 60 to 140
    b. 80 to 120
    c. 70 to 130
    d. 90 to 110

11. **Normal Distribution (LO4)**   A normal distribution is completely specified by its
    a. Mean and correlation
    b. Variance and correlation
    c. Variance and standard deviation
    d. Mean and standard deviation

12. **Standard Normal Distribution (LO4, CFA5)**   A normal random variable is transformed into a standard normal random variable by
    a. Subtracting its mean and dividing by its standard deviation.
    b. Adding its mean and dividing by its standard deviation.
    c. Subtracting its mean and dividing by its variance.
    d. Adding its mean and multiplying by its standard deviation.

13. **Standard Normal Distribution (LO4, CFA5)** The probability that a standard normal random variable is either less than −1 or greater than +1 is

   a. 2 percent
   b. 5 percent
   c. 10 percent
   d. 31.74 percent

14. **Standard Normal Distribution (LO4, CFA5)** The probability that a standard normal random variable is either less than −1.96 or greater than +1.96 is approximately

   a. 2 percent
   b. 5 percent
   c. 10 percent
   d. 31.74 percent

15. **Value-at-Risk (VaR) (LO4, CFA5)** The Value-at-Risk statistic for an investment portfolio states

   a. The probability of an investment loss.
   b. The value of the risky portion of an investment portfolio.
   c. The smallest investment loss expected with a specified probability.
   d. The largest investment loss expected with a specified probability.

Concept Questions

1. **Performance Evaluation Ratios (LO2, CFA6)** Explain the difference between the Sharpe ratio and the Treynor ratio.

2. **Performance Evaluation Measures (LO2, CFA6)** What is a common weakness of Jensen's alpha and the Treynor ratio?

3. **Jensen's Alpha (LO2, CFA6)** Explain the relationship between Jensen's alpha and the security market line (SML) of the capital asset pricing model (CAPM).

4. **Sharpe Ratio (LO2, CFA6)** What is one advantage and one disadvantage of the Sharpe ratio?

5. **Comparing Alphas (LO2, CFA6)** Suppose that two investments have the same alpha. What things might you consider to help you determine which investment to choose?

6. **Optimal Sharpe Ratio (LO3, CFA6)** What is meant by a Sharpe-optimal portfolio?

7. **Optimal Sharpe Ratio (LO3)** What is the relationship between the Markowitz efficient frontier and the optimal Sharpe ratio?

8. **Value-at-Risk (VaR) Statistic (LO4, CFA5)** Explain the meaning of a Value-at-Risk statistic in terms of a smallest expected loss and the probability of such a loss.

9. **Value-at-Risk (VaR) Statistic (LO4, CFA5)** The largest expected loss for a portfolio is −20 percent with a probability of 95 percent. Relate this statement to the Value-at-Risk statistic.

10. **Performance Measures (LO2, CFA6)** Most sources report alphas and other metrics relative to a standard benchmark, such as the S&P 500. When might this method be an inappropriate comparison?

Questions and Problems

Core Questions

1. **Standard Deviation (LO4, CFA5)** You find a particular stock has an annual standard deviation of 54 percent. What is the standard deviation for a two-month period?

2. **Standard Deviation (LO4, CFA5)** You find the monthly standard deviation of a stock is 9.20 percent. What is the annual standard deviation of the stock?

3. **Performance Evaluation (LO1, CFA6)**   You are given the following information concerning three portfolios, the market portfolio, and the risk-free asset:

Portfolio	R_p	σ_p	β_p
X	12%	29%	1.25
Y	11	24	1.10
Z	8	14	.75
Market	10	19	1.00
Risk-free	4	0	0

What is the Sharpe ratio, Treynor ratio, and Jensen's alpha for each portfolio?

4. **Information Ratio (LO1, CFA6)**   Assume that the tracking error of Portfolio X in the previous problem is 11.4 percent. What is the information ratio for Portfolio X?

5. **R-Squared (LO1, CFA6)**   In Problem 3, assume that the correlation of returns on Portfolio Y to returns on the market is .75. What is the percentage of Portfolio Y's return that is driven by the market?

6. **Information Ratio (LO1, CFA6)**   The Layton Growth Fund has an alpha of 1.4 percent. You have determined that Layton's information ratio is .2. What must Layton's tracking error be relative to its benchmark?

7. **Value-at-Risk (VaR) Statistic (LO4, CFA5)**   DW Co. stock has an annual return mean and standard deviation of 10 percent and 28 percent, respectively. What is the smallest expected loss in the coming year with a probability of 5 percent?

8. **Value-at-Risk (VaR) Statistic (LO4, CFA5)**   Woodpecker, Inc., stock has an annual return mean and standard deviation of 18 percent and 44 percent, respectively. What is the smallest expected loss in the coming month with a probability of 2.5 percent?

9. **Value-at-Risk (VaR) Statistic (LO4, CFA5)**   Your portfolio allocates equal funds to the DW Co. and Woodpecker, Inc., stocks referred to in the previous two questions. The return correlation between DW Co. and Woodpecker, Inc., is zero. What is the smallest expected loss for your portfolio in the coming month with a probability of 2.5 percent?

10. **Sharpe Ratio (LO1, CFA6)**   What is the formula for the Sharpe ratio for a stock and bond portfolio with a zero correlation between stock and bond returns?

Intermediate Questions

11. **Sharpe Ratio (LO1, CFA6)**   What is the formula for the Sharpe ratio for an equally weighted portfolio of stocks and bonds?

12. **Sharpe Ratio (LO1, CFA6)**   What is the formula for the Sharpe ratio for a portfolio of stocks and bonds with equal expected returns, i.e., $E(R_S) = E(R_B)$, and a zero return correlation?

13. **Value-at-Risk (VaR) Statistic (LO4, CFA5)**   A stock has an annual return of 11 percent and a standard deviation of 54 percent. What is the smallest expected loss over the next year with a probability of 1 percent? Does this number make sense?

14. **Value-at-Risk (VaR) Statistic (LO4, CFA5)**   For the stock in the previous problem, what is the smallest expected gain over the next year with a probability of 1 percent? Does this number make sense? What does this tell you about stock return distributions?

15. **Value-at-Risk (VaR) Statistic (LO4, CFA5)**   Tyler Trucks stock has an annual return mean and standard deviation of 10 percent and 26 percent, respectively. Michael Moped Manufacturing stock has an annual return mean and standard deviation of 18 percent and 62 percent, respectively. Your portfolio allocates equal funds to Tyler Trucks stock and Michael Moped Manufacturing stock. The return correlation between Tyler Trucks and Michael Moped Manufacturing is .5. What is the smallest expected loss for your portfolio in the coming month with a probability of 5 percent?

16. **Value-at-Risk (VaR) Statistic (LO4, CFA5)**   Using the same return means and standard deviations as in the previous question for Tyler Trucks and Michael Moped Manufacturing stocks, but assuming a return correlation of $-.5$, what is the smallest expected loss for your portfolio in the coming month with a probability of 5 percent?

17. **Value-at-Risk (VaR) Statistic (LO4, CFA5)**   Your portfolio allocates equal amounts to three stocks. All three stocks have the same mean annual return of 14 percent. Annual return standard deviations for these three stocks are 30 percent, 40 percent, and 50 percent. The return correlations among all three stocks are zero. What is the smallest expected loss for your portfolio in the coming year with a probability of 1 percent?

18. **Optimal Sharpe Portfolio Value-at-Risk (LO3, CFA5)** You are constructing a portfolio of two assets, Asset A and Asset B. The expected returns of the assets are 12 percent and 15 percent, respectively. The standard deviations of the assets are 29 percent and 48 percent, respectively. The correlation between the two assets is .25 and the risk-free rate is 5 percent. What is the optimal Sharpe ratio in a portfolio of the two assets? What is the smallest expected loss for this portfolio over the coming year with a probability of 2.5 percent?

Answer Problems 19 and 20 based on the following information.

You have been given the following return information for a mutual fund, the market index, and the risk-free rate. You also know that the return correlation between the fund and the market is .97.

Year	Fund	Market	Risk-Free
2008	−15.2%	−24.5%	1%
2009	25.1	19.5	3
2010	12.4	9.4	2
2011	6.2	7.6	4
2012	−1.2	−2.2	2

19. **Performance Metrics (LO1, CFA6)** What are the Sharpe and Treynor ratios for the fund?

20. **Jensen's Alpha (LO1, CFA6)** Calculate Jensen's alpha for the fund, as well as its information ratio.

Spreadsheet Problem

21. **Optimal Sharpe Ratio (LO3)** You are constructing a portfolio of two assets. Asset A has an expected return of 10 percent and a standard deviation of 21 percent. Asset B has an expected return of 15 percent and a standard deviation of 62 percent. The correlation between the two assets is .30 and the risk-free rate is 4 percent. What is the weight of each asset in the portfolio of the two assets that has the largest possible Sharpe ratio?

22. **Performance Metrics (LO1, CFA4)** You have been given the following return information for two mutual funds (Papa and Mama), the market index, and the risk-free rate.

Year	Papa Fund	Mama Fund	Market	Risk-Free
2008	−12.6%	−22.6%	−24.5%	1%
2009	25.4	18.5	19.5	3
2010	8.5	9.2	9.4	2
2011	15.5	8.5	7.6	4
2012	2.6	−1.2	−2.2	2

Calculate the Sharpe ratio, Treynor ratio, Jensen's alpha, information ratio, and *R*-squared for both funds and determine which is the best choice for your portfolio.

CFA Exam Review by Schweser

[CFA3, CFA6]

Kelli Blakely is a portfolio manager for the Miranda Fund, a core large-cap equity fund. The market proxy and benchmark for performance measurement is the S&P 500. Although the Miranda portfolio generally mirrors the S&P sector weightings, Ms. Blakely is allowed a significant amount of flexibility.

Ms. Blakely was able to produce exceptional returns last year (as outlined in the table below). Much of this performance is attributable to her pessimistic outlook, which caused her to change her asset class exposure to 50 percent stocks and 50 percent cash. The S&P's allocation was 97 percent stocks and 3 percent cash. The risk-free rate of cash returns was 2 percent.

	Miranda	S&P 500
Return	10.2%	−22.5%
Standard deviation	37%	44%
Beta	1.10	

1. What are the Sharpe ratios for the Miranda Fund and the S&P 500?

	Miranda	S&P 500
a.	0.2216	−0.5568
b.	0.3515	−0.2227
c	0.0745	−0.2450

2. What is the Treynor measure for the Miranda Fund and the S&P 500?

	Miranda	S&P 500
a.	0.2216	−0.5568
b.	0.3515	−0.2227
c	0.0745	−0.2450

3. What is the Jensen measure for the Miranda Fund?

   a. 0.2216
   b. 0.3515
   c. 0.0745

What's on the Web?

1. **Morningstar Ratings**   Go to www.morningstar.com and find out how to interpret the "Bear Market Decile Rank." While you are at the Web site, also learn more about the best-fit index numbers. What do the best-fit index numbers mean?

2. **Morningstar Risk**   Go to www.morningstar.com and find out how Morningstar calculates the "Morningstar Rating" category. What percentage of funds are rated as Below Average by Morningstar? What percentage are rated Average?

3. **Modified VaR**   Go to www.alternativesoft.com and learn about modified VaR proposed at the Web site. Why would you want to use a modified VaR?

4. **VaR Data**   You can calculate your own VaR statistics by downloading recent security price data off the Web. Go to finance.yahoo.com and enter the ticker symbol ^ GSPC (don't forget the caret when entering ticker symbols for stock indexes). Now click on the link for "Historical Prices." There you will see that you can get daily, weekly, or monthly price data for any period desired by setting the beginning and ending dates as indicated under "Historical Prices." You can also download the price data into a spreadsheet. Go to the bottom of the page and click on the link "Download to Spreadsheet." With the downloaded price data, you will need to calculate returns and then return averages and standard deviations. Using these, calculate the VaR statistics for your data as discussed and illustrated in this chapter.

CHAPTER 14

Futures Contracts

"There are two times in a man's life when he should not speculate: when he can't afford it and when he can."

–Mark Twain

"When you bet on a sure thing—hedge!"

–Robert Half

Futures contracts can be used for speculation or for risk management. For would-be speculators, Mark Twain's advice is well worth considering. In addition to their risk dimension, trading in futures contracts adds a time dimension to commodity markets. A futures contract separates the date of the agreement—when a delivery price is specified—from the date when delivery and payment actually occur. Both buyers and sellers can manage risk effectively when these dates are separated. This fundamental feature of futures contracts is one of the reasons that futures contracts have withstood the test of time. ∎

This chapter covers modern-day futures contracts. The first sections discuss the basics of futures contracts and how their prices are quoted in the financial press. From there, we move into a general discussion of how futures contracts are used for speculation and risk management. We also present the theoretical relationship between current cash prices and futures prices.

CFA™ Exam Topics in This Chapter:

1 Derivative markets and instruments (L1, S17)
2 Forward markets and contracts (L1, S17)
3 Futures markets and contracts (L1, S17)
4 Investing in commodities (L1, S18)

5 Futures markets and contracts (L2, S16)
6 Risk management applications of forward and futures strategies (L3, S15)

Go to www.mhhe.com/jmd6e for a guide that aligns your textbook with CFA readings.

14.1 Futures Contracts Basics

forward contract
Agreement between a buyer and a seller, who both commit to a transaction at a future date at a price set by negotiation today.

futures contract
Contract between a seller and a buyer specifying a commodity or financial instrument to be delivered and price paid at contract maturity. Futures contracts are managed through an organized futures exchange.

futures price
Price negotiated by buyer and seller at which the underlying commodity or financial instrument will be delivered and paid for to fulfill the obligations of a futures contract.

By definition, a **forward contract** is a formal agreement between a buyer and a seller who both commit to a commodity transaction at a future date at a price set by negotiation today. The genius of forward contracting is that it allows a producer to sell a product to a willing buyer before it is actually produced. By setting a price today, both buyer and seller remove price uncertainty as a source of risk. With less risk, buyers and sellers mutually benefit and commerce is stimulated. This principle has been understood and practiced for centuries.

Futures contracts represent a step beyond forward contracts. Futures contracts and forward contracts accomplish the same economic task, which is to specify a price today for future delivery. This specified price is called the **futures price**. However, while a forward contract can be struck between any two parties, futures contracts are managed through an organized futures exchange. Sponsorship through a futures exchange is a major distinction between a futures contract and a forward contract.

As we discuss later, because futures contracts are listed on exchanges, they come with many standardized features, such as the size of the contract and the delivery date. This standardization comes with trade-offs relative to forward contracts. For example, on the negative side, the fixed size of the futures contract means that buyers and sellers might not be able to match a particular position exactly.

On the positive side, the standardization of futures contracts facilitates the trading of contracts after they are created—thereby increasing liquidity. Further, because futures contracts are managed by the exchange, they have less counterparty risk, because the exchange ensures that both sides of the trade can cover any potential losses they might incur. For most investors, the advantages of futures contracts well outweigh the disadvantages.

MODERN HISTORY OF FUTURES TRADING

The Chicago Board of Trade (CBOT) was the first organized futures exchange in the United States. The CBOT was established in 1848 and grew with the westward expansion of American ranching and agriculture. The CBOT became the largest, most active futures exchange in the world. Other early American futures exchanges include the MidAmerica Commodity Exchange (founded in 1868), New York Cotton Exchange (1870), New York Mercantile Exchange (1872), Chicago Mercantile Exchange (1874), Minneapolis Grain Exchange (1881), New York Coffee Exchange (1882), and the Kansas City Board of Trade (1882).

For more than 100 years, American futures exchanges devoted their activities exclusively to commodity futures. However, a revolution began in the 1970s with the introduction of financial futures. Unlike commodity futures, which call for delivery of a physical commodity, financial futures require delivery of a financial instrument. The first financial futures were foreign currency contracts introduced in 1972 at the International Monetary Market (IMM), a division of the Chicago Mercantile Exchange (CME).

Next came interest rate futures, introduced at the Chicago Board of Trade in 1975. An interest rate futures contract specifies delivery of a fixed-income security. For example, an interest rate futures contract might specify a U.S. Treasury bill, note, or bond as the underlying instrument. Two of the most actively traded futures contracts at the CME Group are interest rate futures contracts: Eurodollars (formerly at the CME) and Treasury notes (formerly at the CBOT).

Stock index futures were introduced in 1982 at the Kansas City Board of Trade (KBT), the Chicago Mercantile Exchange, and the New York Futures Exchange (NYFE). A stock index futures contract specifies a particular stock market index as its underlying instrument.

Financial futures have been so successful that they now constitute the bulk of all futures trading. This success is largely attributed to the fact that financial futures have become an indispensable tool for financial risk management by corporations and portfolio managers. As we will see, futures contracts can be used to reduce risk through hedging strategies or to increase risk through speculative strategies. In this chapter, we discuss futures contracts generally, but, since this text deals with financial markets, we will ultimately focus on financial futures.

During 2007, several important commodity exchanges merged. For example, in January 2007, the IntercontinentalExchange (ICE), which listed mainly energy contracts, purchased the New York Board of Trade (NYBOT) for about $1 billion. The NYBOT listed "soft" commodities, such as coffee, sugar, cocoa, and cotton. The NYBOT was once the New York Cotton Exchange (NYCE). Through previous mergers the NYBOT had acquired the Coffee, Sugar, and Cocoa Exchange (CSCE) as well as the New York Futures Exchange (NYFE). We are fairly confident that you are able to name three commodities that formerly were traded at the CSCE and one commodity that traded at the NYCE. But we'd be surprised if you knew that orange juice futures contracts were traded at the NYCE.

On July 9, 2007, the Chicago Mercantile Exchange finalized its merger with its long-time rival, the Chicago Board of Trade. In this whopper of a deal, the CME bought the CBOT for about $8 billion. The book value of the new company, The CME Group, Inc., was about $26 billion.

FUTURES CONTRACT FEATURES

Futures contracts are a type of derivative security because the value of the contract is derived from the value of an underlying instrument. For example, the value of a futures contract to buy or sell gold is derived from the market price of gold. However, because a futures contract represents a zero-sum game between a buyer and a seller, the net value of a futures contract is always zero. That is, any gain realized by the buyer is exactly equal to a loss realized by the seller, and vice versa.

Futures are contracts and, in practice, exchange-traded futures contracts are standardized to facilitate convenience in trading and price reporting. Standardized futures contracts have a set contract size specified according to the particular underlying instrument. For example, a standard gold futures contract specifies a contract size of 100 troy ounces. This means that a single gold futures contract obligates the seller to deliver 100 troy ounces of gold to the buyer at contract maturity. In turn, the contract also obligates the buyer to accept the gold delivery and pay the negotiated futures price for the delivered gold.

To properly understand a futures contract, we must know the specific terms of the contract. In general, futures contracts must stipulate at least the following five contract terms:

1. The identity of the underlying commodity or financial instrument.

2. The futures contract size.

3. The futures maturity date, also called the expiration date.

4. The delivery or settlement procedure.

5. The futures price.

First, a futures contract requires that the underlying commodity or financial instrument be clearly identified. This is stating the obvious, but it is important that the obvious is clearly understood in financial transactions.

Second, the size of the contract must be specified. As stated earlier, the standard contract size for gold futures is 100 troy ounces. For U.S. Treasury note and bond futures, the standard contract size is $100,000 in par value notes or bonds, respectively.

The third contract term that must be stated is the maturity date. Contract maturity is the date on which the seller is obligated to make delivery and the buyer is obligated to make payment.

Fourth, the delivery process must be specified. For commodity futures, delivery normally entails sending a warehouse receipt for the appropriate quantity of the underlying commodity. After delivery, the buyer pays warehouse storage costs until the commodity is sold or otherwise disposed.

Finally, the futures price must be mutually agreed on by the buyer and seller. The futures price (or contract settlement price) is quite important, because it is the price that the buyer will pay and the seller will receive for delivery at expiration of the contract.

For financial futures, delivery is often accomplished by a transfer of registered ownership. For example, ownership of U.S. Treasury bills, notes, and bonds is registered at the Federal Reserve in computerized book-entry form. Futures delivery is accomplished by a notification to the Fed to make a change of registered ownership.

WORK THE WEB

One problem with futures quotes from newspapers is that the prices are from the previous trading day. If you need quotes from today, one of the best places to find intraday quotes is the Web site of the futures exchange.

We wanted to find current prices for the Standard & Poor's (S&P) futures, so we went to www.cmegroup.com, surfed around a bit, and found:

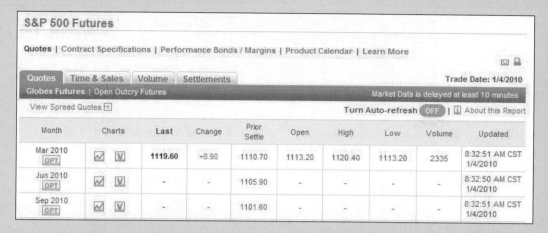

The Web site reports information on many different futures contracts on the S&P 500. You can see that of the contracts that expire in different months of 2010, only one had traded at the time we went to the Web site.

You will notice that you can get quoted prices from two sources, Globex and Open Outcry (look under the tabs above). Open Outcry means that these futures contracts are physically traded in the "trading pit," located in Chicago. The Globex platform is a global electronic trading system. That is, traders have the choice of submitting orders through the traditional pit-trading system or through a computer-driven electronic trading system.

Other financial futures feature cash settlement, which means that the buyer and seller simply settle up in cash with no actual delivery. We discuss cash settlement in more detail when we discuss stock index futures. The important thing to remember for now is that delivery procedures are selected for convenience and low cost. Specific delivery procedures are set by the futures exchange and may change slightly from time to time.

FUTURES PRICES

For futures markets information for many more contracts, visit www.wsj.com

The largest volume of futures trading in the United States takes place in Chicago. However, futures trading is also quite active at futures exchanges in New York, Kansas City, and Minneapolis. Current futures prices for contracts traded at the major futures exchanges are reported each day in *The Wall Street Journal.* Our nearby *Work the Web* box shows how to get prices online, and Figure 14.1 reproduces a portion of the daily "Futures Prices" report of *The Wall Street Journal.*

In this section of the *Journal,* the information is divided into sections according to categories of the underlying commodities or financial instruments. For example, the section "Agriculture Futures" lists futures price information for wheat, oats, soybeans, live cattle, (live) lean hogs, coffee, sugar, and cocoa, among others. The section "Metal & Petroleum Futures" reports price information for copper, gold, and petroleum products. Separate sections report financial futures, which include "Interest Rate," "Currency," and "Index" categories.

Each section states the contract name, futures exchange, and contract size, along with price information for various contract maturities. For example, under "Metal & Petroleum Futures" we find the Copper contract traded at the Commodities Exchange (CMX), i.e., the COMEX (which is a division of the New York Mercantile Exchange). The standard contract size for copper is 25,000 pounds per contract. The futures price is quoted in cents per pound.

FIGURE 14.1 Futures Prices

From Platinum to Orange Juice: Futures Contracts

Commodity futures prices, including open interest, or the number of contracts outstanding. Nearby-month contracts are listed first. Most-active contracts are also listed, plus other notable months.

KEY TO EXCHANGES: CBT: Chicago Board of Trade; **CME:** Chicago Mercantile Exchange; **CMX:** Comex; **KC:** Kansas City Board of Trade; **MPLS:** Minneapolis Grain Exchange; **NYBOT:** New York Board of Trade; **NYM:** New York Mercantile Exchange, or Nymex

Metal & Petroleum Futures

	Open	High hi lo	Low	Settle	Chg	Open interest
Copper-High (CMX)-25,000 lbs.; cents per lb.						
Jan	328.30	333.60 ▲	328.30	332.55	2.95	2,145
March	330.20	336.20	329.35	334.50	3.15	114,914
Gold (CMX)-100 troy oz.; $ per troy oz.						
Jan	1096.50	1097.10	1086.00	1091.50	-5.50	2,519
Feb	1098.50	1098.70	1086.60	1092.50	-5.60	318,077
April	1098.70	1098.70	1087.90	1093.80	-5.70	47,106
June	1098.40	1099.50	1089.40	1095.00	-5.70	33,153
Aug	1096.10	1100.50	1091.60	1096.20	-5.80	16,023
Dec	1100.00	1104.00	1094.50	1100.10	-5.90	22,812
Platinum (NYM)-50 troy oz.; $ per troy oz.						
Jan	1462.10	1470.60	1441.70	1452.30	-14.80	1,793
April	1471.10	1482.90	1455.00	1463.30	-12.70	30,040
Silver (CMX)-5,000 troy oz.; cnts per troy oz.						
Jan	1699.0	1699.0	1676.0	1677.9	-31.2	294
March	1710.5	1717.5	1676.5	1680.2	-30.8	78,677
Crude Oil, Light Sweet (NYM)-1,000 bbls.; $ per bbl.						
Feb	78.80	79.80	78.46	79.28	0.41	279,550
March	79.50	80.49	79.21	80.03	0.44	165,753
June	81.26	82.10	81.10	81.79	0.37	108,332
Dec	84.09	84.79	83.81	84.47	0.28	148,067
Dec'11	87.19	87.70	87.08	87.45	0.21	52,140
Dec'12	88.70	88.90	88.70	88.98	0.30	62,625
Heating Oil No. 2 (NYM)-42,000 gal.; $ per gal.						
Jan	2.1094	2.1250	2.1025	2.1093	.0065	14,360
Feb	2.1212	2.1364	2.1135	2.1202	.0036	91,082
Gasoline-NY RBOB (NYM)-42,000 gal.; $ per gal.						
Jan	2.0140	2.0440	2.0125	2.0406	.0300	11,200
Feb	2.0320	2.0612	2.0284	2.0566	.0276	82,084
Natural Gas (NYM)-10,000 MMBtu.; $ per MMBtu.						
Feb	5.840	5.929	5.672	5.709	-.131	120,795
March	5.805	5.891	5.655	5.685	-.129	130,623
April	5.768	5.840	5.617	5.649	-.129	74,422
May	5.781	5.858	5.665	5.678	-.120	39,165
Aug	5.969	6.050	5.878	5.884	-.111	28,396
Oct	6.100	6.180	6.005	6.014	-.109	43,921

Agriculture Futures

	Open	High hi lo	Low	Settle	Chg	Open interest
Corn (CBT)-5,000 bu.; cents per bu.						
March	416.00	416.75	400.50	413.75	-3.25	489,587
Dec	443.50	444.50	428.50	442.00	-3.25	199,077
Ethanol (CBT)-29,000 gal.; $ per gal.						
Jan	1.905	1.939	1.905	1.939	.016	466
April	1.878	1.907	1.878	1.900	.009	989
Oats (CBT)-5,000 bu.; cents per bu.						
March	268.00	276.75	267.25	276.25	7.25	9,453
May	276.50	284.50	275.25	284.25	6.50	900
Soybeans (CBT)-5,000 bu.; cents per bu.						
Jan	1033.00	1043.75	1026.75	1036.25	-1.75	27,176
March	1042.00	1052.25	1035.25	1044.50	-2.50	210,019
Soybean Meal (CBT)-100 tons; $ per ton.						
Jan	315.00	321.30	313.00	316.20	1.30	11,702
March	307.00	312.40	305.00	308.20	.60	70,506
Soybean Oil (CBT)-60,000 lbs.; cents per lb.						
Jan	39.43	39.51	39.11	39.49	.06	28,357
March	39.81	39.95	39.54	39.92	.07	112,332
Rough Rice (CBT)-2,000 cwt.; cents per cwt.						
Jan	1450.50	1453.00	1429.50	1440.00	-17.00	1,102
March	1488.00	1488.00	1462.50	1471.50	-16.50	12,681
Wheat (CBT)-5,000 bu.; cents per bu.						
March	540.00	550.00	540.00	544.75	3.75	183,421
July	565.75	574.00	565.25	569.75	3.50	64,554
Wheat (KC)-5,000 bu.; cents per bu.						
March	536.25	545.00	536.25	540.50	2.50	61,997
Dec	594.75	600.00	591.25	594.75	1.75	35,680
Wheat (MPLS)-5,000 bu.; cents per bu.						
March	549.00	555.00	548.75	551.25	2.25	20,484
July	574.50	578.25	573.00	575.50	2.25	8,946
Cattle-Feeder (CME)-50,000 lbs.; cents per lb.						
Jan	94.900	95.400	94.850	95.125	.150	5,119
March	94.550	95.150	94.475	94.875	.150	15,667
Cattle-Live (CME)-40,000 lbs.; cents per lb.						
Dec	84.250	84.700	84.125	84.600	.375	722
Feb'10	85.000	85.500	84.675	85.050	-.075	133,501
Hogs-Lean (CME)-40,000 lbs.; cents per lb.						
Feb	65.450	65.950	65.025	65.625	.200	72,955
April	69.975	70.550	69.675	70.500	.475	50,220
Pork Bellies (CME)-40,000 lbs.; cents per lb.						
Feb	86.250	87.900	85.250	86.300	.800	307
Lumber (CME)-110,000 bd. ft.; $ per 1,000 bd. ft.						
Jan	205.80	206.80	202.20	203.50	-1.30	1,829
March	234.10	235.00	231.60	234.80	1.30	5,223
Milk (CME)-200,000 lbs.; cents per lb.						
Dec	14.93	14.94	14.92	14.92	.01	4,762
Jan'10	14.32	14.32	14.22	14.25	-.08	3,990
Cocoa (ICE-US)-10 metric tons; $ per ton.						
March	3,231	3,269	3,231	3,247	10	70,865
May	3,261	3,284	3,261	3,267	9	24,597
Coffee (ICE-US)-37,500 lbs.; cents per lb.						
March	136.50	138.15	136.00	136.65	.30	77,722
May	138.05	139.95	137.90	138.45	.30	25,435

	Open	High hi lo	Low	Settle	Chg	Open interest
Sugar-World (ICE-US)-112,000 lbs.; cents per lb.						
March	26.77	27.40	26.55	26.96	.19	335,849
May	24.99	25.40	24.80	25.06	.08	143,256
Sugar-Domestic (ICE-US)-112,000 lbs.; cents per lb.						
March	34.95	35.00 ▲	34.00	34.66	-.34	2,815
July	31.00	31.02 ▲	31.00	31.00	.60	2,642
Cotton (ICE-US)-50,000 lbs.; cents per lb.						
March	75.07	75.59	74.78	75.43	.36	127,741
July	76.95	77.13	76.32	77.10	.34	21,988
Orange Juice (ICE-US)-15,000 lbs.; cents per lb.						
Jan	137.60	138.50 ▲	132.65	132.80	-4.65	1,065
March	141.85	141.85	136.00	136.90	-3.75	26,417

Interest Rate Futures

	Open	High hi lo	Low	Settle	Chg	Open interest
Treasury Bonds (CBT)-$100,000; pts 32nds of 100%						
March	115-150	115-290	115-100	115-280	15.0	662,891
June	114-050	114-140	114-020	114-140	15.0	132
Treasury Notes (CBT)-$100,000; pts 32nds of 100%						
March	115-205	115-275	115-180	115-270	6.0	1,155,807
June	114-065	114-130	114-065	114-140	6.0	88
5 Yr. Treasury Notes (CBT)-$100,000; pts 32nds of 100%						
Dec	116-007	116-012	115-295	116-017	2.0	12,433
March'10	114-205	114-242	114-167	114-215	1.0	745,589
2 Yr. Treasury Notes (CBT)-$200,000; pts 32nds of 100%						
Dec	108-255	108-262	108-242	108-257	1.2	8,299
March'10	108-070	108-090	108-062	108-072	.2	837,504
30 Day Federal Funds (CBT)-$5,000,000; 100 - daily avg.						
Dec	99.880	99.880	99.878	99.878	...	74,355
Feb'10	99.835	99.840	99.830	99.835	.005	93,596
1 Month Libor (CME)-$3,000,000; pts of 100%						
Jan	99.7625	99.7625	99.7525	99.7550	.0075	14,027
Feb	99.7400	99.7525	99.7375	99.7425	.0050	13,846
Eurodollar (CME)-$1,000,000; pts of 100%						
Jan	99.7275	99.7400 ▲	99.7275	99.7400	.0075	126,678
March	99.6300	99.6550	99.6250	99.6450	.0200	1,143,617
June	99.3200	99.3450	99.3150	99.3350	.0250	846,275
Dec	98.5100	98.5500	98.5050	98.5350	.0400	735,521

Currency Futures

	Open	High hi lo	Low	Settle	Chg	Open interest
Japanese Yen (CME)-¥12,500,000; $ per 100¥						
March	1.0874	1.0884	1.0782	1.0818	-.0062	94,744
June	1.0860	1.0889	1.0794	1.0827	-.0061	371
Canadian Dollar (CME)-CAD 100,000; $ per CAD						
March	.9586	.9586	.9452	.9475	-.0111	98,772
June	.9527	.9553	.9453	.9474	-.0111	1,244
British Pound (CME)-£62,500; $ per £						
March	1.5897	1.6088	1.5825	1.6061	.0164	84,300
June	1.5895	1.6078	1.5816	1.6053	.0164	418
Swiss Franc (CME)-CHF 125,000; $ per CHF						
March	.9651	.9664	.9599	.9648	-.0001	37,974
June	.9653	.9671	.9610	.9656	-.0001	55
Australian Dollar (CME)-AUD 100,000; $ per AUD						
March	.8876	.8893	.8835	.8872	-.0005	98,206
June	.8788	.8799	.8746	.8781	-.0004	241
Mexican Peso (CME)-MXN 500,000; $ per 10MXN						
Jan				.76300	-.00325	0
March	.76125	.76275	.75675	.75775	-.00325	95,283
Euro (CME)-€125,000; $ per €						
March	1.4346	1.4360	1.4271	1.4333	-.0017	142,271
June	1.4345	1.4354	1.4269	1.4329	-.0017	1,213

Index Futures

	Open	High hi lo	Low	Settle	Chg	Open interest
DJ Industrial Average (CBT)-$10 x index						
March	10485	10495	10426	10490	3	10,711
Mini DJ Industrial Average (CBT)-$5 x index						
March	10485	10494	10424	10490	3	63,818
S&P 500 Index (CME)-$250 x index						
March	1121.60	1122.50	1113.00	1122.10	0.40	321,736
June	1116.20	1118.00	1111.00	1117.40	0.40	2,278
Mini S&P 500 (CME)-$50 x index						
March	1121.25	1122.50	1113.00	1122.00	0.25	2,397,986
June	1115.50	1117.75	1106.25	1117.50	0.50	2,132
Nasdaq 100 (CME)-$100 x index						
March	1872.00	1880.00	1863.00	1876.75	4.25	10,380
Mini Nasdaq 100 (CME)-$20 x index						
March	1871.0	1880.3	1862.3	1876.8	4.3	294,073
June	1870.0	1877.5	1861.0	1874.8	4.0	662
Mini Russell 2000 (ICE-US)-$100 x index						
March	629.90	633.30	624.90	630.70	.20	339,063
June	626.10	630.00	624.10	628.40	...	448
Mini Russell 1000 (ICE-US)-$100 x index						
March	613.30	615.95	613.30	615.95	.30	21,486
U.S. Dollar Index (ICE-US)-$1,000 x index						
March	78.30	78.55	78.15	78.28	.09	58,266
June	78.70	78.92	78.55	78.64	.11	4,917

Source: Thomson Reuters

EXAMPLE 14.1

Futures Quotes

In Figure 14.1, locate the gold and wheat contracts. Where are they traded? What are the contract sizes for the gold and wheat contracts and how are their futures prices specified?

The gold contract trades on the CMX, the COMEX Division of the New York Mercantile Exchange. One gold contract calls for delivery of 100 troy ounces. The gold futures price is quoted in dollars per troy ounce.

Wheat contracts are traded on the Chicago Board of Trade (CBT), the Kansas City Board of Trade (KC), and the Minneapolis Grain Exchange (MPLS). One wheat contract calls for delivery of 5,000 bushels of wheat, and wheat futures prices are quoted in cents per bushel. Why do you think there are different wheat prices at these exchanges? Isn't wheat wheat?

WWW

For futures prices and price charts, visit these Web sites:
futures.tradingcharts.com
www.barchart.com

The reporting format for each futures contract is similar. For example, the first column of a price listing gives the contract delivery/maturity month. For each maturity month, the next six columns report futures prices observed during the previous day at the opening of trading ("Open"), the highest intraday price ("High"), an area to signal a life of contract high or low, the lowest intraday price ("Low"), the price at close of trading ("Settle"), and the change in the settle price from the previous day ("Chg"). The last column reports open interest for each contract maturity, which is the number of contracts outstanding at the end of that day's trading.

By now, we see that four of the contract terms for futures contracts are stated in the futures prices listing. These are:

1. The identity of the underlying commodity or financial instrument.
2. The futures contract size.
3. The futures maturity date.
4. The futures price.

Exact contract terms for the delivery process are available from the appropriate futures exchange on request.

EXAMPLE 14.2

Futures Prices

In Figure 14.1, locate the soybean contract with the greatest open interest. Explain the information provided.

The soybean (or just "bean") contract with the greatest open interest is specified by the contract maturity with the greatest number of contracts outstanding, so the March 2010 contract is the one we seek. One contract calls for delivery of 5,000 bushels of beans (a bushel, of course, is four pecks and weighs about 60 pounds). The closing price for delivery at maturity is quoted in cents per bushel. Because there are 5,000 bushels in a single contract, the total contract value is the quoted price per bushel of 1,044.50 cents times 5,000, or $52,225, for the March contract.

To get an idea of the magnitude of financial futures trading, take a look at the second entry under "Interest Rate Futures" in Figure 14.1, the CBT Treasury note contract. One contract calls for the delivery of $100,000 in par value notes. The total open interest in these contracts often exceeds a million contracts. Thus, the total face value represented by these contracts is over $100 billion.

Who does all this trading? The orders originate from money managers around the world and are sent to the various exchanges' trading floors and electronic systems for execution. On the floor, the orders are executed by professional traders who are quite aggressive at getting

GARISH JACKETS ADD TO CLAMOR OF CHICAGO PITS

For the inhabitants of Chicago's futures and options trading pits, dressing for success means throwing good taste to the wind.

Take James Oliff, a trader in the Chicago Mercantile Exchange's newly opened Mexican peso futures pit. Daily, he dons a multicolored jacket bedecked with cacti and sombreros, in keeping, he says, with the "theme" of the product he trades.

Twisting and turning to display his gaudy garb, the veteran currency options trader explains: "I wanted a jacket that would be easy to pick out in the crowd. Runners get orders to me more quickly, and clerks find me faster when I'm trying to do trades."

It's important to have what veterans of the mayhem describe as "pit presence" to make money in the crowded and noisy trading pits of the Merc and the Chicago Board of Trade. That elusive quality, they say, involves such stratagems as finding the best spot in the pit from which to communicate with clerks and other traders, maintaining good posture and using a loud, well-projected voice and forceful hand signals to attract attention.

Increasingly, in places such as the CBOT's bond pit, where hundreds of people cram into a space only slightly larger than a tennis court, garb is being used to grab attention. Hence the insatiable demand for magenta, lime-green, and silver-lamé jackets, featuring designs that run the gamut from the Mighty Morphin Power Rangers to bucolic farmhouses and sunflowers.

"I'd come in buck naked if I could," says Thomas Burke, a trader in the CBOT's overpopulated bond-futures pit. "As it is, the more obnoxious the jacket, the better. The louder it is, the more I can rest my voice and let my jacket draw the attention."

Chicago's exchanges quietly tolerate the proliferation of the garish trading jackets. Dress codes ban jeans and still require members to wear shirts with collars and don ties (although some of these may be little more than strings, having been worn daily for more than a decade). The rules also say that trading jackets must have sleeves that come below the elbow and contain pockets into which the traders stuff their trading cards and other documents. But during the past decade, traders say, exchange efforts to regulate the color and design of the jackets, or gently encourage their wearers to opt for something in quiet good taste, have been dropped as an exercise in futility.

Robert Pierce, who trades corn options at the CBOT, says the old brown jackets made him look like a UPS delivery man. "When someone gave me a UPS cap on the floor one day as a joke, I decided it was time for a change of style," he says. The switch, to a comparatively tasteful multicolored geometric pattern, has the added advantage of disguising pen and pencil marks, adds his wife, Cathy.

Dawn Guera, a former clerk at the CBOT, has spun the traders' need to stand out in the crowd into a four-year-old business designing and manufacturing custom trading jackets. Traders wander into her storefront operation next door to the CBOT to choose from dozens of fabrics with designs ranging from a subdued Harvard University crest on a crimson background to a slinky leopard skin pattern or turquoise frogs cavorting on a neon-pink background.

"Everyone has their own hobbies and interests and wants the jackets to reflect that," she explains, pointing to fabrics with designs of dice and cards aimed at traders willing to acknowledge their addiction to gambling in the markets. "It's like a vanity license plate."

And, at $50 a pop, traders are willing, even eager, to order multiple jackets, Ms. Guera says, especially since many believe that washing or dry cleaning a "lucky" jacket will launder out the luck in it. Some, like the CBOT's Gilbert Leistner, take a seasonal approach to jackets: in summer and fall he wears a brightly colored turquoise and aquamarine jacket decorated with tropical fish, but switches to a Southwestern theme come Thanksgiving.

"It's my version of going south for the winter," he says, adding he's contemplating donning something in gold lamé for New Year's celebrations.

Ms. Guera, a former sportswear designer in New York, says traders have a long way to go before they'll pull themselves off the worst-dressed lists. To be sure, some of the early emphasis on flashiness is easing a bit, she says, and demands for fluorescent geometric patterns are giving way to a new trend favoring subtler paisley-type patterns with lapels, cuffs, and pockets in a contrasting, solid color.

"I think it would be great if we could really push the fashion envelope here and remove the collar and cuffs from the jackets, or even persuade the exchanges to let traders wear vests instead," she says. "I'm looking for a way of making this whole trading process more artistic and creative."

---

the best prices. On the floor, futures traders can be recognized by their colorful jackets. As *The Wall Street Journal* article in the nearby *Investment Updates* box reports, these garish jackets add a touch of color to the clamor of the pits. Of course, garish jackets are not required for electronic trading. (Who knows what these traders are wearing!) In the next section, we will discuss how and why futures contracts are used for speculation and hedging.

CHECK THIS

14.1a	What is a forward contract?
14.1b	What is a futures contract, and why is it different from a forward contract?
14.1c	What is a futures price?

14.2 Why Futures?

The major economic purpose of futures contracts is to allow hedgers to transfer risk to speculators. Therefore, a viable futures market cannot exist without participation by both hedgers and speculators. We begin to help you understand the use of futures markets by describing how speculators use futures markets.

SPECULATING WITH FUTURES

To learn more about futures, visit www.usafutures.com

long position
A market position where the holder benefits from price increases and loses from price decreases.

short position
A market position where the holder benefits from price decreases and loses from price increases.

speculator
A person or firm that takes the risk of loss for the chance for profit.

Suppose you are thinking about speculating on commodity prices because you believe that you can accurately forecast future prices. The most convenient way to speculate is to use futures contracts. If you believe that gold prices will increase, then you can speculate on this belief by buying gold futures. Alternatively, if you think gold prices will decrease, you can speculate by selling gold futures.

Buying a futures contract is often referred to as "going long," or establishing a **long position**. Selling a futures contract is often called "going short," or establishing a **short position**. A **speculator** accepts price risk in an attempt to profit on the direction of prices. Speculators can go long or short futures contracts. A speculator who is long benefits from price increases and loses from price decreases. The opposite is true for a speculator who is short.

To illustrate the basics of speculating, suppose you believe the price of gold will go up. In particular, suppose the current price for delivery in three months is $1,000 per ounce (this $1,000 is called the "futures" price). You think that gold will be selling for much more than $1,000 three months from now, so you go long 100 gold contracts that expire in three months. When you do, you are obligated to take delivery of gold and pay the agreed-upon price, $1,000 per ounce. Each gold contract represents 100 troy ounces, so 100 contracts represents 10,000 troy ounces of gold with a total contract value of $10,000 \times \$1,000 = \$10,000,000$. In futures jargon, you have a $10 million long gold position.

Suppose your belief turns out to be correct, and three months later, the market price of gold is $1,020 per ounce. Your three-month futures contracts have just expired. So, to fulfill the terms of your long futures position, you accept delivery of 10,000 troy ounces of gold, pay $1,000 per ounce, and immediately sell the gold at the market price of $1,020 per ounce. Your profit is $20 per ounce, or $10,000 \times \$20 = \$200,000$. Of course, you will pay some brokerage commissions and taxes out of this profit.

Suppose your belief turns out to be incorrect and gold prices fall. You will lose money in this case because you are obligated to buy the 10,000 troy ounces at the agreed-upon price of $1,000 per ounce. If gold prices fell to, say, $975 per ounce, you would lose $25 per ounce, or $10,000 \times \$25 = \$250,000$. In addition, you will pay some brokerage commissions.

As this gold example shows, futures speculation can lead to substantial gains and losses. An important point is that your gains from futures speculation depend on accurate forecasts of the direction of future prices. You must ask yourself: Is it easy to forecast price changes?

Consider another example of commodity speculation. Suppose you analyze weather patterns and you are convinced that the coming winter months will be colder than usual. You believe that this will cause heating oil prices to rise. You can speculate on this belief by going long heating oil futures.

The standard contract size for heating oil is 42,000 gallons. Suppose you go long 10 contracts at a futures price of $1.90 per gallon. Your long position has a total contract value of $10 \times 42,000 \times \$1.90 = \$798,000$.

If the price of heating oil at contract maturity is, say, $1.50 per gallon, your loss before commissions would be 40 cents per gallon, or $10 \times 42{,}000 \times \$.40 = \$168{,}000$. Of course, if heating oil prices rose by 40 cents per gallon, you would gain $168,000 (less applicable commissions) instead.

Once again, futures speculation can lead to substantial gains and losses. The important point from this example is that your gains from futures speculation depend on you making more accurate weather forecasts than other traders. So ask yourself: How easy is it to out-forecast other traders?

EXAMPLE 14.3

What Would Juan Valdez Do?

After an extensive analysis of political currents in Central and South America, you conclude that future coffee prices will be lower than currently indicated by futures prices. Would you go long or short? Analyze the impact of a swing in coffee prices of 20 cents per pound in either direction if you have a 10-contract position, where each contract calls for delivery of 37,500 pounds of coffee.

You would go short because you expect prices to decline. Because you are short 10 contracts, you must deliver $10 \times 37{,}500 = 375{,}000$ pounds of coffee to fulfill your contract. If coffee prices fall to 20 cents below your originally contracted futures price, then you make 20 cents per pound, or $\$.20 \times 375{,}000 = \$75{,}000$. Of course, if you are wrong and the political situation destabilizes, the resulting $.20 increase in coffee prices would generate a $75,000 loss in your short futures position.

HEDGING WITH FUTURES

PRICE RISK   Many businesses face price risk when their activities require them to hold a working inventory. By a working inventory, we mean that firms purchase and store goods for later resale at market prices. Price risk is the risk that the firm will not be able to sell its goods at a price sufficiently higher than the acquisition cost.

For example, suppose you own a regional heating oil distributorship and must keep a large pre–heating season inventory of heating oil of, say, 2.1 million gallons. In futures market jargon, this heating oil inventory represents a long position in the underlying commodity. If heating oil prices go up, the value of the heating oil you have in inventory goes up in value, but if heating oil prices fall, the value of the heating oil you have to sell goes down. Your risk is not trivial, because even a 15-cent per gallon fluctuation in the price of heating oil will cause your inventory to change in value by $315,000. Because you are in the business of distributing heating oil, and not in the business of speculating on heating oil prices, you decide to remove this price risk from your business operations.

Investors face similar risks. For example, consider a U.S. investor who buys stock in Australia. The investor now has the risk of the investment itself and the risk of the currency exchange rate between Australia and the United States. For example, if the investment goes up in value but the Australian dollar depreciates sufficiently relative to the U.S. dollar, then the net result could be a loss for the investor. To shed the "price" (or currency) risk, the investor could use currency futures to "lock" in an Australian/U.S. dollar exchange rate. In this case, the investor would hedge by selling (i.e., take a short position) in Australian dollar futures contracts.

Whether the investor chooses to shift this risk depends on many factors. For example, when we discussed diversification, we saw that the lower the correlation the higher the diversification benefit from combining securities. So, to the extent that an investor desires diversification, the investor might choose to pass on hedging currency. Further, the investor might not know the planned holding period of the investment, making it difficult to place a precise hedge.

THE MECHANICS OF SHIFTING PRICE RISK   An important function of futures markets is that they allow firms that have price risk to shift it to others who want price risk. A person or company that wants to shift price risk to others is called a **hedger**. Hedgers transfer price risk by taking a futures market position that is the opposite of their existing position in the **underlying asset**. You can think about this using a portfolio approach. Hedgers look to add a futures market position to their position in the underlying asset that will provide cash to the hedgers when their position in the underlying asset declines in value. However, the cost of adding a futures position is that the futures position draws down cash when the position in the underlying asset generates value.

In the case of your heating oil enterprise, the heating oil you have in inventory represents a long position in the underlying asset. Therefore, the value of this heating oil inventory can be protected by taking a short position in heating oil futures contracts. Hedgers often say they are "selling" futures contracts when they are initiating a short position. Because you are using this short position for hedging purposes, you have created a **short hedge**.

With a short hedge in place, changes in the value of your long position in the underlying asset are offset by an approximately equal, but opposite, change in value of your short futures position.

AN EXAMPLE OF A SHORT HEDGE   One of the first questions a hedger has to answer is how many futures contracts are needed to shift risk. This question has many answers, and most can be found in a course devoted to futures contracts and other derivatives. However, a reasonable hedging strategy is known as a **full hedge**. When a hedger has an equal, but opposite, futures position to the position in the underlying asset, the hedger is said to have a full hedge.

Heating oil futures contracts are traded on the New York Mercantile Exchange (NYM), and the standard contract size for heating oil futures is 42,000 gallons per contract. Because you wish to full hedge 2.1 million gallons, you need to sell 2,100,000/42,000 = 50 heating oil contracts.

Suppose the average acquisition price of your 2.1 million gallons of heating oil is $1.30 per gallon and that today's futures price for delivery during your heating season is $1.90. In the past, market conditions in your distribution area were such that you could sell your heating oil to your customers at a price 20 cents higher than the prevailing futures price. To help finance your inventory purchases, you borrowed money. During the heating season, you have to make an interest payment of $500,000.

Given these numbers, you can forecast your pretax profit per gallon of heating oil. Revenues are 2,100,000 × $2.10 = $4,410,000. The cost of the heating oil is 2,100,000 × $1.30 = $2,730,000. Subtracting this cost and the debt payment of $500,000 from revenue results in a pretax profit of $1,180,000, or $1,180,000/2,100,000 = $.56 per gallon.

However, if heating oil prices decrease by $.40, your pretax profit per gallon of heating oil will only be $.16. You view this risk as unacceptable and decide to hedge by selling 50 heating oil futures contracts at a price of $1.90 per gallon. Table 14.1 summarizes three possible outcomes: heating oil prices remain steady, they increase by $.40, and they decrease by $.40.

As you can see in Table 14.1, your pretax profit will be $.56 in all three cases. To see this, suppose heating oil prices fall by $.40. In this case, revenues are 2,100,000 × $1.70 = $3,570,000. The cost of the heating oil is 2,100,000 × $1.30 = $2,730,000. Subtracting this cost and the debt payment of $500,000 from revenues results in an unhedged pretax profit of $340,000, or $340,000/2,100,000 = $.16 per gallon. However, if you had a short hedge in place, your pretax futures profit is $840,000 because ($1.90 − $1.50) × 42,000 × 50 = $840,000. Adding $840,000 to the unhedged pretax profit of $340,000 results in a hedged pretax profit of $1,180,000, which is $1,180,000/2,100,000 = $.56 per gallon.

In fact, your pretax profit will remain steady for a wide range of prices. We illustrate this result in Figure 14.2. In Figure 14.2, the blue line represents your pretax profit per gallon of heating oil for a wide range of possible heating oil selling prices. The red line represents your futures market gains or losses. Note that heating oil futures prices and futures contract gains (losses) appear across the top and on the right side of the graph. If futures prices remain unchanged at $1.90, you have no futures gain or loss. If futures prices fall to $1.50, your futures gain is $.40.

	Base Case: No Change in Heating Oil Price	Heating Oil Price Decrease	Heating Oil Price Increase
TABLE 14.1 — Hedging Heating Oil Inventory during the Heating Season			
Heating oil inventory (gal.)	2,100,000	2,100,000	2,100,000
Selling price, per gallon	$2.10	$1.70	$2.50
Average purchase price, per gallon	$1.30	$1.30	$1.30
Futures price	$1.90	$1.50	$2.30
Without a Hedge			
Revenue	$4,410,000	$3,570,000	$5,250,000
Cost of inventory sold	$2,730,000	$2,730,000	$2,730,000
Interest expense	$ 500,000	$ 500,000	$ 500,000
Pretax profit	$1,180,000	$ 340,000	$2,020,000
Pretax profit, per gallon	$ 0.56	$ 0.16	$ 0.96
With Short Hedge (short futures at $1.90)			
Revenue	$4,410,000	$3,570,000	$5,250,000
Cost of inventory sold	$2,730,000	$2,730,000	$2,730,000
Interest expense	$ 500,000	$ 500,000	$ 500,000
Futures gain (loss)	$ 0	$ 840,000	($ 840,000)
Pretax profit	$1,180,000	$1,180,000	$1,180,000
Hedge effect (constant pretax profit)	$ 0.56	$ 0.56	$ 0.56
Futures gain (loss), per gallon	$ 0.00	$ 0.40	($ 0.40)

FIGURE 14.2 — Heating Oil Selling Prices, Pretax Profits, and Futures Profits

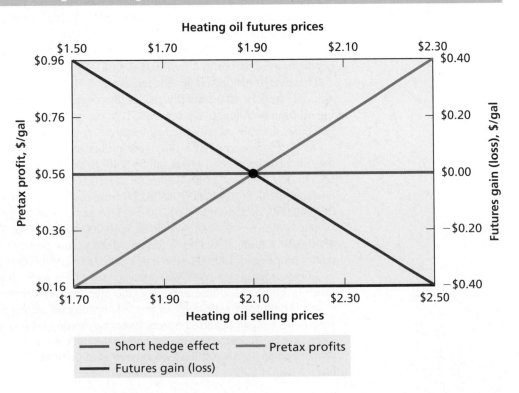

In Figure 14.2, the purple line remains steady at a value of $.56. This means that for a wide range of heating oil selling prices, your pretax profit remains unchanged if you employ the short hedge.

Your business activities may also include distributing other petroleum products like gasoline and natural gas. Futures contracts are also available for gasoline and natural gas, and therefore they may be used for hedging purposes. In fact, your business activities might dictate you use another common hedge, known as a **long hedge**.

long hedge

Adding a long futures position to a short position in the underlying asset.

Firms that use a long hedge do not currently own the underlying asset, but plan to acquire it in the future. In this case, it is as if the firm is "short" the underlying asset because if the price increases between now and the time at which the firm actually purchases the underlying asset, the firm will pay more than it thought. Note that the firm does not go into the market and establish a short position in the underlying asset. That would be speculating. Rather, its planned business activities create situations where the firm is exposed to price increases in the underlying asset. This exposure is what gives rise to the saying that the firm is effectively "short the underlying."

FINAL THOUGHTS ABOUT HEDGING In real hedging applications, many factors influence the exact profit recognized. But this example provides you with an overview of how hedging works. The important thing to remember is this: *If you want to shed risk, do not take risk.* That is, if you are long the underlying asset, do not buy futures too!

There is an easy way to remember which position to take in the futures market. In the heating oil example above, pretax profits per gallon change penny by penny with heating oil price changes. That is, the slope of the blue line in Figure 14.2 is one. To eliminate price risk, the hedger needs to add a futures position to the underlying position that results in a slope of zero. What number do we have to add to one to get zero? Obviously, the answer is negative one, which is the slope of the red line in Figure 14.2.

Figure 14.2 is sometimes called "the X" or "the cross" in that it shows how the risk of the futures position offsets the risk of the underlying position. If you can remember Figure 14.2, you will remember which futures position to take when you want to hedge.

Hedging greatly reduces and, in some cases, eliminates the possibility of a loss from a decline in the price of the underlying asset. However, by hedging with futures, the firm also eliminates the possibility of a gain from a price increase in the underlying asset. This is an important point. If the price of the underlying asset rises, you will incur a loss on your futures position.

However, forgone opportunities for increases in the value of the underlying asset represent the bulk of hedging costs. Failure to shift price risk through hedging means that the firm is actually holding price risk. Some people think that holding price risk that could be shifted is the same as taking price risk. The owners of the firm must decide whether they are price risk shifters or price risk holders.

EXAMPLE 14.4	Short Hedging

Suppose you have an inventory of 1.8 million pounds of soybean oil. Describe how you would hedge this position.

Because you are long in the underlying commodity, soybean oil, you need to go short in futures (i.e., sell). A single bean oil contract calls for delivery of 60,000 pounds of bean oil. To hedge your position, you need to sell 1.8 million/60,000 = 30 futures contracts.

EXAMPLE 14.5	More Hedging

You need to buy 360,000 pounds of orange juice concentrate in three months. How can you hedge the price risk associated with this planned purchase? One orange juice contract calls for delivery of 15,000 pounds of orange juice concentrate.

(continued)

In this example, if the price of concentrate increases between now and when you actually purchase the orange juice concentrate, you will pay more than you thought. So, effectively, you have a "short" position in the underlying asset because you do not currently own it (but you do plan to buy it later). To offset the risk of higher orange juice concentrate prices when you actually buy, you need to establish a long futures position today (this hedge is known as a long hedge). You should buy 360,000/15,000 = 24 contracts.

EXAMPLE 14.6

Even More Hedging

Suppose your company will receive payment of £15 million in three months, at which time your company will convert the British pounds to U.S. dollars. What is the standard futures contract size for British pounds? Describe how you could use futures contracts to lock in an exchange rate from British pounds to U.S. dollars for your planned receipt of £15 million, including how many contracts are required.

Your company will be receiving £15 million, so you are effectively long British pounds. So, if the British pound per U.S. dollar exchange rate falls, the British pounds you will receive will decline in terms of their value in U.S. dollars.

To hedge these British pounds, you can use a short hedge. That is, you short (or sell) British pound futures contracts today. As with any short position, your short position in British pound futures obligates you to deliver the underlying asset. In this case, when the futures contract expires, you are obligated to deliver British pounds and receive U.S. dollars at today's futures price for British pounds in terms of U.S. dollars. One British pound contract calls for delivery of £62,500. You will therefore sell £15 million/£62,500 = 240 contracts.

CHECK THIS

14.2a Explain what is meant by a long position in futures and what is meant by a short position in futures.

14.2b Suppose a hedger employs a futures hedge that is two-thirds the size of the underlying position. Why do you think this is called a "partial" hedge?

14.2c You have a short position in the underlying asset. How would you modify Figure 14.2 in this case?

14.2d Suppose a firm has a long position in the underlying asset. What happens if this firm buys futures contracts instead of selling futures contracts? Create an example like the one shown in Table 14.1 to help explain the consequences. (By the way, this activity is jokingly referred to as a "Texas hedge.")

14.3 Futures Trading Accounts

A futures exchange, like a stock exchange, allows only exchange members to trade on the exchange. Exchange members may be firms or individuals trading for their own accounts, or they may be brokerage firms handling trades for customers. Some firms conduct both trading and brokerage operations on the exchange. In this section, we discuss the mechanics of a futures trading account as it pertains to a customer with a trading account at a brokerage firm.

futures margin
Deposit of funds in a futures trading account dedicated to covering potential losses from an outstanding futures position.

initial margin
Amount required when a futures contract is first bought or sold. Initial margin varies with the type and size of a contract, but it is the same for long and short futures positions.

marking-to-market
In futures trading accounts, the process whereby gains and losses on outstanding futures positions are recognized on a daily basis.

maintenance margin
The minimum margin level required in a futures trading account at all times.

margin call
Notification to increase the margin level in a trading account.

reverse trade
A trade that closes out a previously established futures position by taking the opposite position.

The biggest customer trading accounts are those of corporations that use futures to manage their business risks and money managers who hedge or speculate with clients' funds. Many individual investors also have futures trading accounts of their own, although speculation by individual investors is not recommended without a full understanding of all risks involved. Whether a futures trading account is large or small, the mechanics of account trading are essentially the same.

There are several essential things to know about futures trading accounts. The first thing is that margin is required. In this way, futures accounts resemble the stock margin accounts we discussed in a previous chapter; however, the specifics are quite different. **Futures margin** is a deposit of funds in a futures trading account dedicated to covering potential losses from an outstanding futures position. An **initial margin** is required when a futures position is first established. The amount varies according to contract type and size, but margin requirements for futures contracts usually range between 5 percent and 15 percent of total contract value. Initial margin is the same for both long and short futures positions.

The second thing to know about a futures trading account is that contract values in outstanding futures positions are marked to market on a daily basis. **Marking-to-market** is a process whereby gains and losses on outstanding futures positions are recognized at the end of each trading day.

For example, suppose one morning you call your broker and instruct her to go long five U.S. Treasury bond contracts for your account. A few minutes later, she calls back to confirm order execution at a futures price of 110. Because the Treasury bond contract size is $100,000 par value, contract value is $110\% \times \$100,000 = \$110,000$ per contract. Thus, the total position value for your order is $550,000, for which your broker requires $35,000 initial margin. In addition, your broker requires that at least $27,500 in **maintenance margin** be present at all times. The necessary margin funds are immediately wired from a bank account to your futures account.

Now, at the end of trading that day Treasury bond futures close at a price of 108. Overnight, all accounts are marked to market. Your Treasury bond futures position is marked to $108,000 per contract, or $540,000 total position value, representing a loss of $10,000. This loss is deducted from your initial margin to leave only $25,000 of margin funds in your account.

Because the maintenance margin level on your account is $27,500, your broker will issue a **margin call** on your account. Essentially, your broker will notify you that you must immediately restore your margin level to the initial margin level of $35,000, or else she will close out your Treasury bond futures position at whatever trading price is available at the exchange.

This example illustrates what happens when a futures trading account is marked to market and the resulting margin funds fall below the maintenance margin level. The alternative, and more pleasant, experience occurs when a futures price moves in your favor, and the marking-to-market process adds funds to your account. In this case, marking-to-market gains can be withdrawn from your account so long as remaining margin funds are not less than the initial margin level.

The third thing to know about a futures trading account is that a futures position can be closed out at any time; you do not have to hold a contract until maturity. A futures position is closed out by simply instructing your broker to close out your position. To close out a position, your broker will enter a **reverse trade** for your account.

A reverse trade works like this: Suppose you are currently short five Treasury bond contracts, and you instruct your broker to close out the position. Your broker responds by going long five Treasury bond contracts for your account. In this case, going long five contracts is a reverse trade because it cancels exactly your previous five-contract short position. At the end of the day in which you make your reverse trade, your account will be marked to market at the futures price realized by the reverse trade. From then on, your position is closed out, and no more gains or losses will be realized.

This example illustrates that closing out a futures position is no more difficult than initially entering into a position. There are two basic reasons to close out a futures position before contract maturity. The first is to capture a current gain or loss, without realizing further price risk. The second is to avoid the delivery requirement that comes from holding a futures contract until it matures. In fact, over 98 percent of all futures contracts are closed out before contract maturity, which indicates that less than 2 percent of all futures contracts result in delivery of the underlying commodity or financial instrument.

Before closing this section, let's briefly list the three essential things to know about a futures trading account as discussed above:

1. Margin is required.

2. Futures accounts are marked to market daily.

3. A futures position can be closed out any time by a reverse trade.

Understanding the items in this list is important to anyone planning to use a futures trading account.

CHECK THIS

14.3a What are the three essential things you should know about a futures trading account?

14.3b What is meant by initial margin for a futures position? What is meant by maintenance margin for a futures position?

14.3c Explain the process of marking-to-market a futures trading account. What is a margin call, and when is one issued?

14.3d How is a futures position closed out by a reverse trade? What proportion of all futures positions are closed out by reverse trades rather than by delivery at contract maturity?

14.4 Cash Prices versus Futures Prices

We now turn to the relationship between today's price of some commodity or financial instrument and its futures price. We begin by examining current cash prices.

CASH PRICES

cash price
Price of a commodity or financial instrument quoted for current delivery. Also called the *spot price*.

cash market
Market in which commodities or financial instruments are traded for immediate delivery. Also called the *spot market*.

The **cash price** of a commodity or financial instrument is the price quoted for current delivery. The cash price is also called the *spot price*, as in "on the spot." In futures jargon, terms like "spot gold" or "cash wheat" are used to refer to commodities being sold for current delivery in what is called the **cash market** or the *spot market*.

Figure 14.3 reproduces the "Cash Prices" column of *The Wall Street Journal*, published the same day as the "Futures Prices" column seen in Figure 14.1. The column is divided into sections according to commodity categories. For example, the section "Grains and Feeds" lists spot price information for wheat, corn, soybeans, and similar crops. Other commodity sections include "Food," "Fats and Oils," "Energy," and "Metals." Each section gives commodity names along with cash market prices for the day of trading and one year earlier.

CASH-FUTURES ARBITRAGE

Intuitively, you might think that the cash price of a commodity is closely related to its futures price. If you do, then your intuition is quite correct. In fact, your intuition is backed up by strong economic argument and more than a century of experience observing the simultaneous operation of cash and futures markets.

As a routine matter, cash and futures prices are closely watched by market professionals. To understand why, suppose you notice that spot gold is trading for $1,030 per ounce while the two-month futures price is $1,080 per ounce. Do you see a profit opportunity?

You should, because buying spot gold today at $1,030 per ounce while simultaneously selling gold futures at $1,080 per ounce locks in a $50 per ounce profit. True, gold has storage costs

FIGURE 14.3 Commodity Cash Prices

Cash Prices

Wednesday, December 30, 2009

These prices reflect buying and selling of a variety of actual or "physical" commodities in the marketplace—separate from the futures price on an exchange, which reflects what the commodity might be worth in future months.

	Wednesday	Year ago
Energy		
European crude oil spot prices, 11 a.m. ET,		
Northwestern Europe		
Forties	77.98	33.03
Brent	77.83	34.68
Bonny light	79.28	37.43
Urals-Mediterranean	77.20	34.55
Domestic crude oil spot prices, 4 p.m. ET		
West Texas intmdt, Cushing	79.28	44.60
West Texas sour, Midlands	78.03	43.50
Louisiana sweet, St. James	81.68	48.30
Alaska North Slope, Pac delivery	80.68	39.00
Refined products		
Fuel oil, No. 2 NY	2.1080	1.4032
Diesel,500ppm low sulfur NY	2.1093	1.4057
Diesel,15ppm ultra-low sulf NY	2.1105	1.4457
Gasoline,conv prem NY	2.1106	1.1157
Gasoline,RBOB prem NY	2.1216	1.0982
Gasoline,conv reg NY	2.0293	1.0082
Gasoline,RBOB reg NY	2.0316	0.9744
Gasoline,CARBOB,reg LA-m	2.1650	1.2750
Propane,nontet,Mont Belvieu-g	1.3210	0.6150
Butane,normal,Mont Belvieu-g	1.5600	0.6900
Natural gas Henry Hub	5.830	5.620
Metals		
Gold, per troy oz		
Engelhard industrial	1090.00	863.11
Engelhard fabricated	1171.75	927.85
Handy & Harman base	1087.50	z
Handy & Harman fabricated	1174.50	E
London a.m. fixing	1092.50	865.00
London p.m. fixing	1087.50	z
Krugerrand,wholesale-e	1136.20	929.62
Maple Leaf-e	1136.20	929.62
American Eagle-e	1141.66	929.62
Mexican peso-e	1332.23	1065.40

	Wednesday	Year ago
Austria crown-e	1080.87	862.64
Austria phil-e	1136.20	929.62
Silver, troy oz.		
Engelhard industrial	16.8600	10.9000
Engelhard fabricated	20.2320	13.0800
Handy & Harman base	16.8900	z
Handy & Harman fabricated	20.2680	z
London fixing,spot price	£10.6717	£7.4082
(U.S.$ equivalent)	16.9200	10.7900
Coins,wholesale $1,000 face-a	12213	z
Other metals		
Platinum,free market	1461.0	z
Platinum,Engelhard industrial	1461.0	912.0
Platinum,Engelhard fabricated	1561.0	1012.0
Palladium,Engelhard industrial	395.0	185.0
Palladium,Engelhard fabricated	495.0	285.0
Aluminum, LME, $ per metric ton	2237.00	1455.0
Antimony-d	2.7850	2.0750
Copper,Comex spot	3.3255	1.3950
Lead,NA solder-d	143.424	64.340
Stainless steel scrap,US-d	1823	z
Tin,NA solder-d	1032.795	642.838
Zinc,NA-d	123.575	60.825
Fibers and Textiles		
Burlap,10-oz,40-inch NY yd-n,w	0.5950	0.4100
Cotton,1 1/16 std lw-mdMphs-u	0.7093	0.4602
Hides,hvy native steers fob-u	z	42.000
Wool,64s,staple,Terr del-u,w	2.48	z
Grains and Feeds		
Barley,top-quality Mnpls-u	3.50	5.15
Bran,wheat middlings, KC-u	98	132
Corn,No. 2 yellow,Cent IL bp,u	3.7400	3.7850
Corn gluten feed,Midwest-u,w	97.33	83.48
Cottonseed meal-u,w	290	240
Hominy feed,Cent IL-u,w	93	83
Meat-bonemeal,50% pro Mnpls-u,w	353	255
Oats,No.2 milling,Mnpls-u	2.7125	2.0750
Sorghum,(Milo) No.2 Gulf-u	7.8350	7.1350

	Wednesday	Year ago
SoybeanMeal,Cent IL,rail,ton48%-u	338.70	301.50
Soybeans,No.1 yllw IL-bp,u	10.1800	9.5800
Wheat,Spring14%-pro Mnpls-u	6.8625	7.6725
Wheat,No.2 soft red,St.Louis-bp,u	4.1050	4.8850
Wheat,hard,KC	5.1650	6.5700
Wheat,No.1soft white,Portld,OR-u	4.9500	5.7000
Food		
Beef,carcass equiv. index		
choice 1-3,600-900 lbs.-u	125.70	134.48
select 1-3,600-900 lbs.-u	119.35	125.81
Broilers,dressed 'A'-u	0.8250	0.8725
Broilers,12-city comp wghtd-u	0.7825	0.8203
Butter,AA Chicago	1.3275	1.1300
Cheddar cheese,bbl,Chicago	143.00	113.00
Cheddar cheese,blk,Chicago	145.00	113.25
Milk,Nonfat dry,Chicago	140	85
Cocoa,Ivory Coast	3722	z
Coffee,Brazilian,Comp	1.2771	1.0105
Correcting previous	1.2816	
Coffee,Colombian, NY	1.9246	1.3055
Correcting previous	1.9293	
Eggs,large white,Chicago-u	1.0450	1.1550
Flour,hard winter KC	z	z
Hams,17-20 lbs,Mid-US fob-u	0.60	z
Hogs,Iowa—So. Minnesota-u	60.78	52.16
Hogs,Sioux Falls,SD-u	42.75	34.50
Pork bellies,12—14 lb MidUS-u	z	0.7100
Pork loins,13—19 lb MidUS-u	1.0650	1.0000
Steers,Tex.-Okla. Choice-u	z	z
Steers,feeder,Okla. City-u	z	z
Sugar,cane,raw,world,fob	27.61	12.75
Fats and Oils		
Corn oil,crude wet/dry mill-u	40.5000	25.0000
Grease,choice white,Chicago-u	0.2650	0.2000
Lard,Chicago-u	0.2837	z
Soybean oil,crude;Centl IL-u	0.3633	0.3156
Tallow,bleach;Chicago-u	0.2900	0.2100
Tallow,edible,Chicago-u	0.3000	0.2100

KEY TO CODES: A=ask; B=bid; BP=country elevator bids to producers; C=corrected; D=Ryan's Notes; E=Manfra,Tordella & Brooks; G=ICE; M=midday; N=nominal; n.a.=not quoted or not available;U=USDA; W=weekly, Z=not quoted

Source: WSJ Market Data Group

(you have to put it somewhere), and a spot gold purchase ties up capital that could be earning interest. However, these costs are small relative to the $50 per ounce gross profit, which is $50 / $1,030 = 4.85% per two months, or about 33 percent per year (with compounding). Furthermore, this profit is risk-free! Alas, in reality, such easy profit opportunities are the stuff of dreams.

Earning risk-free profits from an unusual difference between cash and futures prices is called **cash-futures arbitrage**. In a competitive market, cash-futures arbitrage has very slim profit margins. In fact, the profit margins are almost imperceptible when they exist at all.

Comparing cash prices for commodities in Figure 14.3 with their corresponding futures prices reported in Figure 14.1, you will find that cash prices and futures prices are seldom equal. In futures jargon, the difference between a cash price and a futures price is called the **basis**.[1]

cash-futures arbitrage
Strategy for earning risk-free profits from an unusual difference between cash and futures prices.

basis
The difference between the cash price and the futures price for a commodity, i.e., Basis = Cash price − Futures price.

---

[1] The official Commodity Trading Manual of the Chicago Board of Trade defines basis as the difference between the cash and the futures price, i.e., Basis = Cash price − Futures price. We will be consistent with the CBOT definition. For nonagricultural futures, however, the basis is nearly always defined as the futures price minus the cash price.

For commodities with storage costs, the cash price is usually less than the futures price. This is referred to as a **carrying-charge market**, or *contango*. Sometimes, however, the cash price is greater than the futures price, and this is referred to as an **inverted market**, or *backwardation*. We can summarize this discussion of carrying-charge markets, inverted markets, and basis as follows:

Carrying-charge market: Basis = Cash price − Futures price < 0   (14.1)
Inverted market: Basis = Cash price − Futures price > 0

A variety of factors can lead to an economically justifiable difference between a commodity's cash price and its futures price, including availability of storage facilities, transportation costs, and seasonal price fluctuations. The primary determinants of the cash-futures basis, however, are storage costs and interest costs. Storage cost is the cost of holding the commodity in a storage facility, and interest cost refers to interest income forgone on funds used to buy and hold the commodity.

If a futures price rises far enough above a cash price to more than cover storage costs and interest expense, commodity traders will undertake cash-futures arbitrage by buying in the cash market and selling in the futures market. This drives down the futures price and drives up the cash price until the basis is restored to an economically justifiable level.

Similarly, if a futures price falls far enough relative to a cash price, traders will undertake cash-futures arbitrage by short selling in the cash market and buying in the futures market. This drives down the cash price and drives up the futures price until an economically justifiable basis is restored. In both cases, arbitrage ensures that the basis is kept at an economically appropriate level.

SPOT-FUTURES PARITY

We can be slightly more precise in illustrating the relationship between spot and futures prices for financial futures. Consider the example of futures contracts for shares of stock in a single company. One place such futures contracts are traded in the United States is OneChicago, a joint venture of the major Chicago exchanges. Single-stock futures contracts have a standard contract size of 100 shares of the underlying stock, but futures prices are quoted on a per-share basis.

Suppose we are examining a particular single-stock futures contract that calls for delivery of 100 shares of stock in one year. The current (i.e., cash or spot) stock price is $50 per share, and the stock does not pay dividends. Also, 12-month T-bills are yielding 6 percent. What should the futures price be? To answer, notice that you can buy 100 shares of stock for $50 per share, or $5,000 total. You can eliminate all of the risk associated with this purchase by selling one futures contract. The net effect of this transaction is that you have created a risk-free asset. Because the risk-free rate is 6 percent, your investment must have a future value of $5,000 × 1.06 = $5,300. In other words, the futures price should be $53 per share.

Suppose the futures price is, in fact, $52 per share. What would you do? To make money, you would short 100 shares of stock at $50 per share and invest the $5,000 proceeds at 6 percent.[2] Simultaneously, you would buy one futures contract.

At the end of the year, you would have $5,300. You would use $5,200 to buy the stock to fulfill your obligation on the futures contract and then return the stock to close out the short position. You pocket $100. This trading is just another example of cash-futures arbitrage.

More generally, if we let F be the futures price, S be the spot price, and r be the risk-free rate, then our example illustrates that:

$$F = S(1 + r)$$ (14.2)

In other words, the futures price is simply the future value of the spot price, calculated at the risk-free rate. This is the famous **spot-futures parity** condition. This condition must hold in the absence of cash-futures arbitrage opportunities.

---

[2] For the sake of simplicity, we ignore the fact that individual investors do not earn interest on the proceeds from a short sale, and we assume the stock does not pay dividends.

More generally, if r is the risk-free rate per period, and the futures contract matures in T periods, then the spot-futures parity condition is:

$$F_T = S(1 + r)^T \qquad (14.3)$$

Notice that T could be a fraction of one period. For example, if we have the risk-free rate per year, but the futures contract matures in six months, T would be 1/2.

EXAMPLE 14.7

Parity Check

A non-dividend-paying stock has a current price of $12 per share. The risk-free rate is 4 percent per year. If a futures contract on the stock matures in three months, what should the futures price be?

From our spot-futures parity condition, we have:

$$F_T = S(1 + r)^T$$
$$= \$12(1.04)^{1/4}$$
$$= \$12.12$$

The futures price should be $12.12. Notice that r and T are expressed in years for this example. Therefore, we set $r = .04$ and $T = 1/4$.

MORE ON SPOT-FUTURES PARITY

In our spot-futures parity example just above, we assumed that the underlying financial instrument (the stock) had no cash flows (no dividends). If there are dividends (for a stock future) or coupon payments (for a bond future), then we need to modify our spot-futures parity condition.

For a stock, we let D stand for the dividend, and we assume that the dividend is paid in one period, at or near the end of the futures contract's life. In this case, the spot-futures parity condition becomes:

$$F = S(1 + r) - D \qquad (14.4)$$

Notice that we have simply subtracted the amount of the dividend from the future value of the stock price. The reason is that if you buy the futures contract, you will not receive the dividend, but the dividend payment will reduce the stock price.

An alternative, and very useful, way of writing the dividend-adjusted spot-futures parity result in equation (14.4) is to define d as the dividend yield on the stock. Recall that the dividend yield is just the upcoming dividend divided by the current price. In our current notation, this is just $d = D/S$. With this in mind, we can write the dividend-adjusted parity result as:

$$F = S(1 + r) - D(S/S) \qquad (14.5)$$
$$= S(1 + r) - S(D/S)$$
$$= S(1 + r) - Sd$$
$$= S(1 + r - d)$$

Finally, as above, if there is something other than a single period involved, we would write:

$$F_T = S(1 + r - d)^T \qquad (14.6)$$

where T is the number of periods (or fraction of a period), and r is the interest rate per period.

For example, suppose there is a futures contract on a stock with a current price of $80. The futures contract matures in six months. The risk-free rate is 7 percent per year, and the stock has an annual dividend yield of 3 percent. What should the futures price be?

Plugging in the values to our dividend-adjusted parity equation, we have:

$$F_T = S(1 + r - d)^T$$
$$= \$80(1 + .07 - .03)^{1/2}$$
$$= \$81.58$$

Notice that we set T equal to 1/2 because the contract matures in six months.

14.4a   What is the spot price for a commodity?

14.4b   With regard to futures contracts, what is the basis?

14.4c   What is an inverted market?

14.4d   What is the spot-futures parity condition?

14.5   Stock Index Futures

There are a number of futures contracts on stock market indexes. Because these contracts are particularly important, we devote this entire section to them. We first describe the contracts and then discuss some trading and hedging strategies involving their use.

BASICS OF STOCK INDEX FUTURES

Locate the section labeled "Index Futures" in Figure 14.1. Here we see various stock index futures contracts. The third contract listed, on the S&P 500 Index, is the most important. With this contract, actual delivery would be very difficult or impossible because the seller of the contract would have to buy all 500 stocks in exactly the right proportions to deliver. Clearly, this is not practical, so this contract features cash settlement.

To understand how stock index futures work, suppose you bought one S&P 500 contract at a futures price of 1,240. The contract size is $250 times the level of the index. What this means is that, at maturity, the buyer of the contract will pay the seller $250 times the difference between the futures price of 1,240 and the level of the S&P 500 Index at contract maturity.

For example, suppose that at maturity the S&P had actually fallen to 1,210. In this case, the buyer of the contract must pay $250 \times (1,240 - 1,210) = \$7,500$ to the seller of the contract. In effect, the buyer of the contract has agreed to purchase 250 "units" of the index at a price of $1,240 per unit. If the index is below 1,240, the buyer will lose money. If the index is above that, then the seller will lose money.

WWW

For information on stock index futures visit the Web site at CME Group's www.cmegroup.com

---

EXAMPLE 14.8   **Index Futures**

Suppose you are convinced that the Dow stocks are going to skyrocket in value. Consequently, you buy 20 DJIA futures contracts maturing in six months at a price of 13,900. Suppose that the Dow Jones Index is at 14,320 when the contracts mature. How much will you make or lose?

The futures price is 13,900, and the contract size is $10 times the level of the index. At maturity, if the index is at 14,320, you make $10 \times (14,320 - 13,900) = \$4,200$ per contract. With 20 contracts, your total profit is $84,000.

INDEX ARBITRAGE

index arbitrage
Strategy of monitoring the futures price on a stock index and the level of the underlying index to exploit deviations from parity.

The spot-futures parity relation we developed above is the basis for a common trading strategy known as **index arbitrage**. Index arbitrage refers to monitoring the futures price on a stock index along with the level of the underlying index. The trader looks for violations of parity and trades as appropriate.

For example, suppose the S&P 500 futures price for delivery in one year is 1,540. The current level is 1,500. The dividend yield on the S&P is projected to be 3 percent per year, and the risk-free rate is 5 percent. Is there a trading opportunity here?

From our dividend-adjusted parity equation (14.6), the futures price should be:

$$F_T = S(1 + r - d)^T$$
$$= 1,500(1 + .05 - .03)^1$$
$$= 1,530$$

Thus, based on our parity calculation, the futures price is too high. We want to buy low, sell high, so we buy the index and simultaneously sell the futures contract.

Index arbitrage is often implemented as a **program trading** strategy. While this term covers a lot of ground, it generally refers to the monitoring of relative prices by computer to more quickly spot opportunities. In some cases it includes submitting the needed buy and sell orders using a computer to speed up the process.

Whether a computer is used in program trading is not really the issue; instead, a program trading strategy is any coordinated, systematic procedure for exploiting (or trying to exploit) violations of parity or other arbitrage opportunities. Such a procedure is a trading "program" in the sense that whenever certain conditions exist, certain trades are made. Thus, the process is sufficiently mechanical that it can be automated, at least in principle.

Technically, the NYSE defines program trading as the simultaneous purchase or sale of at least 15 different stocks with a total value of $1 million or more. Program trading can account for up to half the total trading volume on the NYSE, but not all program trading involves stock-index arbitrage.

Another phenomenon was often associated with index arbitrage and, more generally, futures and options trading. S&P 500 futures contracts have four expiration months per year, and they expire on the third Friday of those months. On these same four Fridays, options on the S&P Index and various individual stock options also expired. These Fridays were dubbed the "triple witching hour" because all three types of contracts expired, sometimes leading to unusual price behavior.

In particular, on triple witching hour Fridays, all positions must be liquidated, or "unwound." To the extent that large-scale index arbitrage and other program trading has taken place, enormous buying or selling sometimes occurs late in the day on such Fridays, as positions are closed out. Large price swings and, more generally, increased volatility are often seen. To curtail this problem, the exchanges have adopted rules regarding the size of a position that can be carried to expiration. In addition, options on the S&P 500 Index now expire on Friday morning.

HEDGING STOCK MARKET RISK WITH FUTURES

We earlier discussed hedging using futures contracts in the context of a business protecting the value of its inventory. We now discuss some hedging strategies available to portfolio managers based on financial futures. Essentially, an investment portfolio is an inventory of securities, and financial futures can be used to reduce the risk of holding a securities portfolio.

We consider the specific problem of an equity portfolio manager wishing to protect the value of a stock portfolio from the risk of an adverse movement of the overall stock market. Here, the portfolio manager wishes to establish a short hedge position to reduce risk and must determine the number of futures contracts required to properly hedge a portfolio.

In this hedging example, you are responsible for managing a broadly diversified stock portfolio with a current value of $185 million. Analysis of market conditions leads you to believe that the stock market is unusually susceptible to a price decline during the next few months. Of course, nothing is certain regarding stock market fluctuations, but you are still sufficiently concerned to believe that action is required.

A fundamental problem exists for you, however, in that no futures contract exactly matches your particular portfolio. As a result, you decide to protect your stock portfolio from a fall in value caused by a falling stock market using stock index futures. This is an example of a **cross-hedge**, where a futures contract on a related, but not identical, commodity or financial instrument is used to hedge a particular spot position.

Thus, to hedge your portfolio, you wish to establish a short hedge using stock index futures. To do this, you need to know how many index futures contracts are required to form an effective hedge. Four basic inputs are needed to calculate the number of stock index futures contracts required to hedge a stock portfolio:

1. The current value of your stock portfolio.
2. The beta of your stock portfolio.
3. The contract value of the index futures contract used for hedging.
4. The beta of the futures contract.

program trading

Computer-assisted monitoring of relative prices of financial assets; it sometimes includes computer submission of buy and sell orders to exploit perceived arbitrage opportunities.

For information on program trading, visit www.programtrading.com

For information on stock-index arbitrage, visit www.indexarb.com

cross-hedge

Hedging a particular spot position with futures contracts on a related, but not identical, commodity or financial instrument.

Based on previous chapters, you are familiar with the concept of beta as a measure of market risk for a stock portfolio. Essentially, beta measures portfolio risk relative to the overall stock market. We will assume that you have maintained a beta of 1.25 for your $185 million stock portfolio.

You believe that the market (and your portfolio) will fall in value over the next three months and you decide to eliminate market risk from your portfolio. Because you hold a stock portfolio, you know that you will need to establish a short hedge using futures contracts. You decide to use futures contracts on the S&P 500 Index, because this is the index you used to calculate the beta for your portfolio.

From *The Wall Street Journal,* you find that the S&P 500 futures price for contracts that mature in three months is currently 1,480. Because the contract size for the S&P 500 futures is 250 times the index level, the current value of a single S&P 500 Index futures contract is $250 × 1,480 = $370,000.

You now have all the information you need to calculate the number of S&P 500 Index futures contracts needed to hedge your $185 million stock portfolio. The number of stock index futures contracts needed to hedge the portfolio fully is:

$$\text{Number of contracts} = \frac{V_P}{V_F} \times \frac{\beta_P}{\beta_F} \qquad (14.7)$$

where: V_P = Value of the stock portfolio
V_F = Value of one stock index futures contract
β_P = Current beta of the stock portfolio
β_F = Current beta of the futures contract

For your particular hedging problem, β_P = 1.25, V_P = $185 million, and V_F = $370,000. We are not given the beta of the futures contract, but because we are using S&P 500 futures, the beta should be close to that of the S&P 500, which is 1. The only time β_F would be different from 1 is if the futures contract being used is different from the index being used to calculate the beta of the underlying portfolio. For example, if we calculate the beta of the underlying portfolio using the S&P 500 but we use Dow futures contracts to hedge, then we would also have to calculate the beta of these futures contracts using the S&P 500 Index.

Given the information in our example, the following calculation results:

$$\text{Number of contracts} = \frac{\$185,000,000}{\$370,000} \times \frac{1.25}{1} = 625$$

Thus, you can establish an effective short hedge by going short 625 S&P 500 index futures contracts. This short hedge will protect your stock portfolio against the risk of a general fall in the stock market during the remaining three-month life of the futures contract.

EXAMPLE 14.9	Hedging with Stock Index Futures

How many stock index futures contracts are required to completely hedge a $250 million stock portfolio, assuming a portfolio beta of .75 and an S&P 500 Index futures level of 1,500?

Using equation (14.7):

$$\text{Number of contracts} = \frac{250,000,000}{375,000} \times \frac{.75}{1} = 500$$

Therefore, you need to short 500 stock index futures contracts to hedge this $250 million portfolio. In this example, note that the value of one futures contract is given by $250 × 1,500 = $375,000.

HEDGING INTEREST RATE RISK WITH FUTURES

Having discussed hedging a stock portfolio, we now turn to hedging a bond portfolio. As we will see, the bond portfolio hedging problem is similar to the stock portfolio hedging problem.

Once again, we will be cross-hedging, but this time using futures contracts on U.S. Treasury notes. Here, our goal is to protect the bond portfolio against changing interest rates.

In this example, you are responsible for managing a bond portfolio with a current value of $100 million. Recently, rising interest rates have caused your portfolio to fall in value slightly, and you are concerned that interest rates may continue to trend upward for the next several months. You decide to establish a short hedge based on 10-year Treasury note futures.

The formula for the number of U.S. Treasury note futures contracts needed to hedge a bond portfolio is similar to equation (14.7):

$$\text{Number of contracts} = \frac{D_P \times V_P}{D_F \times V_F} \quad (14.8)$$

where: D_P = Duration of the bond portfolio
V_P = Value of the bond portfolio
D_F = Duration of the futures contract
V_F = Value of a single futures contract

We already know the value of the bond portfolio, which is $100 million. Also, suppose that the duration of the portfolio is given as eight years. Next, we must calculate the duration of the futures contract and the value of the futures contract.

As a useful rule of thumb, the duration of an interest rate futures contract is equal to the duration of the underlying instrument plus the time remaining until contract maturity:

$$D_F = D_U + M_F \quad (14.9)$$

where: D_F = Duration of the futures contract
D_U = Duration of the underlying instrument
M_F = Time remaining until contract maturity

For simplicity, let us suppose that the duration of the underlying U.S. Treasury note is 6 1/2 years and the futures contract has a maturity of 1/2 year, yielding a futures contract duration of 7 years.

The value of a single futures contract is the current futures price times the futures contract size. The standard contract size for U.S. Treasury note futures contracts is $100,000 par value. Now suppose that the futures price is 110, or 110 percent of par value. This yields a futures contract value of $100,000 \times 110 = \$110,000$.

You now have all inputs required to calculate the number of futures contracts needed to hedge your bond portfolio. The number of U.S. Treasury note futures contracts needed to hedge the bond portfolio is calculated as follows:

$$\text{Number of contracts} = \frac{8 \times \$100,000,000}{7 \times \$110,000} = 1{,}038.96$$

Thus, you can establish an effective short hedge by going short 1,039 futures contracts for 10-year U.S. Treasury notes. This short hedge will protect your bond portfolio against the risk of a general rise in interest rates during the life of the futures contracts.

EXAMPLE 14.10

Hedging with U.S. Treasury Note Futures

How many futures contracts are required to hedge a $250 million bond portfolio with a portfolio duration of 5 years using 10-year U.S. Treasury note futures with a duration of 7.5 years and a futures price of 105?

Using the formula for the number of contracts, we have:

$$\text{Number of contracts} = \frac{5 \times \$250,000,000}{7.5 \times \$105,000} = 1{,}587$$

You therefore need to sell 1,587 contracts to hedge this $250 million portfolio.

FUTURES CONTRACT DELIVERY OPTIONS

Many futures contracts have a delivery option, whereby the seller can choose among several different "grades" of the underlying commodity or instrument when fulfilling delivery requirements. Naturally, we expect the seller to deliver the cheapest among available options. In futures jargon, this is called the **cheapest-to-deliver option**. The cheapest-to-deliver option is an example of a broader feature of many futures contracts, known as a "quality" option. Of course, futures buyers know about the delivery option, and therefore the futures prices reflect the value of the cheapest-to-deliver instrument.

As a specific example of a cheapest-to-deliver option, the 10-year Treasury note contract allows delivery of *any* Treasury note with a maturity between 6 1/2 and 10 years. This complicates the bond portfolio hedging problem. For the portfolio manager trying to hedge a bond portfolio with U.S. Treasury note futures, the cheapest-to-deliver feature means that a note can be hedged only based on an assumption about which note will actually be delivered. Furthermore, through time the cheapest-to-deliver note may vary, and, consequently, the hedge will have to be monitored regularly to make sure that it correctly reflects the note issue that is most likely to be delivered. Fortunately, because this is a common problem, many commercial advisory services provide this information to portfolio managers and other investors.

cheapest-to-deliver option

Seller's option to deliver the cheapest instrument when a futures contract allows several instruments for delivery. For example, U.S. Treasury note futures allow delivery of any Treasury note with a maturity between 6 1/2 and 10 years.

CHECK THIS

14.5a What is a cross-hedge?

14.5b What are the basic inputs required to calculate the number of stock index futures contracts needed to hedge an equity portfolio?

14.5c What are the basic inputs required to calculate the number of U.S. Treasury note futures contracts needed to hedge a bond portfolio?

14.5d What is the cheapest-to-deliver option?

14.6 Summary and Conclusions

The topic of this chapter is futures markets. In this chapter, we surveyed the basics of futures markets and contracts—which we summarize by the chapter's important concepts.

1. **The basics of futures markets and how to obtain price quotes for futures contracts.**

   A. A futures contract is an agreement between a buyer and a seller for a future transaction at a price set today. Futures contracts are managed through organized futures exchanges. The existence of a futures exchange virtually eliminates default risk. Four major terms for standardized futures contracts are: (1) the identity of the underlying commodity or financial instrument; (2) the futures contract size; (3) the futures maturity date, and (4) the future price at which the contract will be fulfilled.

   B. Most commodity futures contracts call for delivery of a physical commodity. Financial futures require delivery of a financial instrument or, in many cases, cash. Futures contracts are a type of derivative security, because the value of the contract is derived from the value of an underlying instrument.

   C. Quotes for futures prices are available through the financial press. These days, however, delayed intradaily quotes for futures prices are available at the Web site of many futures exchanges.

2. **The risks involved in futures market speculation.**

   A. Speculators accept price risk in an attempt to profit on the direction of prices. Speculators can go long or short futures contracts. Speculators buy futures contracts if they think prices are going to go higher. Buying futures is often referred to as "going long," or establishing a long position. Speculators sell futures contracts if they think prices are going lower. Selling futures is often called "going short," or establishing a short position.

B. Futures speculation can lead to substantial gains and losses. An important point is that your gains from futures speculation depend on accurate forecasts of the direction of future prices.

 You must ask yourself: Is it easy to forecast price changes?

C. You can sustain losses in futures markets far in excess of your original margin deposit. As futures market prices move against your position, you could be asked to deposit more money into your futures trading account.

3. How cash prices and futures prices are linked.

A. The cash price of a commodity or financial instrument is the price quoted for current delivery. The cash price is also called the spot price.

B. The futures price is simply the future value of the spot price, calculated at the risk-free rate. This statement is the famous spot-futures parity condition. This condition must hold in the absence of cash-futures arbitrage opportunities.

4. How futures contracts can be used to transfer price risk.

A. Hedging is the major economic reason for the existence of futures markets. However, a viable futures market requires participation by both hedgers and speculators.

B. Hedgers transfer price risk to speculators, and speculators absorb price risk. Therefore, hedging and speculating are complementary activities.

C. Hedgers transfer price risk by taking a futures position opposite to their position in the spot market. For example, if the hedger has an inventory of some commodity, the hedger is said to be long in the spot market. Therefore, the hedger will offset price risk in the spot market by taking a short position in the futures market.

GET REAL

This chapter covered the essentials of what many consider to be a complex subject, futures contracts. We hope you realize that futures contracts per se are not complicated at all; in fact, they are, for the most part, quite simple. This doesn't mean that they're for everybody, of course. Because of the tremendous leverage possible, very large gains and losses can (and do) occur with great speed.

To experience some of the gains and losses from outright speculation, you should buy and sell a variety of contracts in a simulated brokerage account such as Stock-Trak. Be sure to go both long and short and pick a few of each major type of contract.

The Internet offers a rich source for more information on trading futures. Probably the best place to begin is by visiting the Web sites of the major futures exchanges: the CME Group (www.cmegroup.com), the IntercontinentalExchange (www.theice.com), and the Kansas City Board of Trade (www.kcbt.com). You might also visit the Web sites of some major international futures exchanges. The reference section of Numa's Web site (www.numa.com/ref/exchange) maintains an extensive list of the world's futures exchanges. Bear in mind that the list changes frequently due to mergers.

For information on futures markets regulation, the federal agency charged with regulating U.S. futures markets is the Commodities Futures Trading Commission (www.cftc.gov). The professional organization charged with self-regulation is the National Futures Association (www.nfa.futures.org). General information on futures markets and trading can be found at the Futures Industry Association (www.futuresindustry.org).

Useful Web sites on trading futures abound. For a large list of links to anything and everything related to futures, visit the commodities and futures section of Investor Links (www.investorlinks.com).

Key Terms

basis 483
carrying-charge market 484
cash-futures arbitrage 483
cash market 482
cash price 482
cheapest-to-deliver option 490
cross-hedge 487
forward contract 469
full hedge 477
futures contract 469
futures margin 481
futures price 469
hedger 477
index arbitrage 486

initial margin 481
inverted market 484
long hedge 479
long position 475
maintenance margin 481
margin call 481
marking-to-market 481
program trading 487
reverse trade 481
short hedge 477
short position 475
speculator 475
spot-futures parity 484
underlying asset 477

Chapter Review Problems and Self-Test

1. **Futures Gains and Losses (CFA2)**   Suppose you purchase 10 orange juice contracts today at the settle price of $1 per pound. How much do these 10 contracts cost you? If the settle price is lower tomorrow by 2 cents per pound, how much do you make or lose? The contract size is 15,000 pounds.

2. **Spot-Futures Parity (CFA1)**   There is a futures contract on a stock, which is currently selling at $200 per share. The contract matures in two months; the risk-free rate is 5 percent annually. The stock does not pay a dividend. What does the parity relationship imply the futures price should be?

Answers to Self-Test Problems

1. If you go long (purchase) 10 contracts, you pay nothing today (you will be required to post margin, but a futures contract is an agreement to exchange cash for goods later, not today). If the settle price drops by 2 cents per pound, you lose 15,000 pounds (the contract size) $\times$ $.02 = $300 per contract. With 10 contracts, you lose $3,000.

2. The spot-futures parity condition is:

$$F_T = S(1 + r - d)^T$$

where S is the spot price, r is the risk-free rate, d is the dividend yield, F is the futures price, and T is the time to expiration measured in years.

   Plugging in the numbers we have, with zero for the dividend yield and 1/6 for the number of years (2 months out of 12):

$$F_{1/6} = \$200(1 + .05)^{1/6} = \$201.63$$

Test Your Investment Quotient

1. **Futures versus Forward Contracts (LO1, CFA2)**   Which of the following statements is true regarding the distinction between futures contracts and forward contracts?

   a. Futures contracts are exchange-traded, whereas forward contracts are OTC-traded.
   b. All else equal, forward prices are higher than futures prices.
   c. Forward contracts are created from baskets of futures contracts.
   d. Futures contracts are cash-settled at maturity, whereas forward contracts result in delivery.

2. **Futures versus Forward Contracts (LO1, CFA2)** In which of the following ways do futures contracts differ from forward contracts?

   I. Futures contracts are standardized.
   II. For futures, performance of each party is guaranteed by a clearinghouse.
   III. Futures contracts require a daily settling of any gains or losses.
   a. I and II only
   b. I and III only
   c. II and III only
   d. I, II, and III

3. **Futures Contracts (LO1, CFA3)** The open interest on a futures contract at any given time is the total number of outstanding

   a. Contracts
   b. Unhedged positions
   c. Clearinghouse positions
   d. Long and short positions

4. **Futures Margin (LO2, CFA3)** Initial margin for a futures contract is usually

   a. Regulated by the Federal Reserve.
   b. Less than 2 percent of contract value.
   c. In the range between 2 percent and 5 percent of contract value.
   d. In the range between 5 percent and 15 percent of contract value.

5. **Futures Margin (LO2, CFA3)** In futures trading, the minimum level to which an equity position may fall before requiring additional margin is *most accurately* termed the

   a. Initial margin
   b. Variation margin
   c. Cash flow margin
   d. Maintenance margin

6. **Futures Margin (LO2, CFA3)** A silver futures contract requires the seller to deliver 5,000 troy ounces of silver. An investor sells one July silver futures contract at a price of $8 per ounce, posting a $2,025 initial margin. If the required maintenance margin is $1,500, the price per ounce at which the investor would first receive a maintenance margin call is closest to

   a. $5.92
   b. $7.89
   c. $8.11
   d. $10.80

7. **Futures Margin (LO2, CFA3)** Which of the following statements is false about futures account margin?

   a. Initial margin is higher than maintenance margin.
   b. A margin call results when account margin falls below maintenance margin.
   c. Marking-to-market of account margin occurs daily.
   d. A margin call results when account margin falls below initial margin.

8. **Futures Contracts (LO1, CFA2)** Which of the following contract terms changes daily during the life of a futures contract?

   a. Futures price
   b. Futures contract size
   c. Futures maturity date
   d. Underlying commodity

9. **Futures Delivery (LO1, CFA2)** On the maturity date, stock index futures contracts require delivery of

   a. Common stock
   b. Common stock plus accrued dividends
   c. Treasury bills
   d. Cash

10. **Spot-Futures Parity (LO3, CFA1)** A Treasury bond futures contract has a quoted price of 100. The underlying bond has a coupon rate of 7 percent, and the current market interest rate is 7 percent. Spot-futures parity then implies a cash bond price of

    a. 93
    b. 100

c. 107
   d. 114

11. **Spot-Futures Parity (LO3, CFA1)**   A stock index futures contract maturing in one year has a currently traded price of $1,000. The cash index has a dividend yield of 2 percent, and the interest rate is 5 percent. Spot-futures parity then implies a cash index level of

   a. $933.33
   b. $970.87
   c. $1,071
   d. $1,029

12. **Spot-Futures Parity (LO3, CFA1)**   A stock index futures contract matures in one year. The cash index currently has a level of $1,000 with a dividend yield of 2 percent. If the interest rate is 5 percent, then spot-futures parity implies a futures price of

   a. $943.40
   b. $970.87
   c. $1,060
   d. $1,030

13. **Futures Hedging (LO3, CFA2)**   You manage a $100 million stock portfolio with a beta of .8. Given a contract size of $100,000 for a stock index futures contract, how many contracts are needed to hedge your portfolio? Assume the beta of the futures contract is 1.

   a. 8
   b. 80
   c. 800
   d. 8,000

14. **Futures Hedging (LO4, CFA2)**   You manage a $100 million bond portfolio with a duration of 9 years. You wish to hedge this portfolio against interest rate risk using T-bond futures with a contract size of $100,000 and a duration of 12 years. How many contracts are required?

   a. 750
   b. 1,000
   c. 133
   d. 1,333

15. **Futures Hedging (LO4, CFA2)**   Which of the following is not an input needed to calculate the number of stock index futures contracts required to hedge a stock portfolio?

   a. The value of the stock portfolio.
   b. The beta of the stock portfolio.
   c. The contract value of the index futures contract.
   d. The initial margin required for each futures contract.

Concept Questions

1. **Understanding Futures Quotations (LO1, CFA2)**   Using Figure 14.1, answer the following questions:

   a. How many exchanges trade wheat futures contracts?
   b. If you have a position in 10 gold futures, what quantity of gold underlies your position?
   c. If you are short 20 oat futures contracts and you opt to make delivery, what quantity of oats must you supply?
   d. Which maturity of the gasoline contract has the largest open interest? Which one has the smallest open interest?

2. **Hedging with Futures (LO4, CFA2)**   Kellogg's uses large quantities of corn in its breakfast cereal operations. Suppose the near-term weather forecast for the corn-producing states is droughtlike conditions, so corn prices are expected to rise. To hedge its costs, Kellogg's decides to use the Chicago Board of Trade corn futures contracts. Should the company be a short hedger or a long hedger in corn futures?

3. **Hedging with Futures (LO4, CFA2)**   Suppose one of Fidelity's mutual funds closely mimics the S&P 500 Index. The fund has done very well during the year, and, in November, the fund manager wants to lock in the gains he has made using stock index futures. Should he take a long or short position in S&P 500 Index futures?

4. **Hedging with Futures (LO4, CFA2)** A mutual fund that predominantly holds long-term Treasury bonds plans on liquidating the portfolio in three months. However, the fund manager is concerned that interest rates may rise from current levels and wants to hedge the price risk of the portfolio. Should she buy or sell Treasury bond futures contracts?

5. **Hedging with Futures (LO4, CFA2)** An American electronics firm imports its completed circuit boards from Japan. The company signed a contract today to pay for the boards in Japanese yen upon delivery in four months; the price per board in yen was fixed in the contract. Should the importer buy or sell Japanese yen futures contracts?

6. **Hedging with Futures (LO4, CFA2)** Jed Clampett just dug another oil well, and, as usual, it's a gusher. Jed estimates that in two months, he'll have 2 million barrels of crude oil to bring to market. However, Jed would like to lock in the value of this oil at today's prices, since the oil market has been skyrocketing recently. Should Jed buy or sell crude oil futures contracts?

7. **Hedging with Futures (LO4, CFA2)** The town of South Park is planning a bond issue in six months and Kenny, the town treasurer, is worried that interest rates may rise, thereby reducing the value of the bond issue. Should Kenny buy or sell Treasury bond futures contracts to hedge the impending bond issue?

8. **Futures Markets (LO1, CFA3)** Is it true that a futures contract represents a zero-sum game, meaning that the only way for a buyer to win is for a seller to lose, and vice versa?

9. **Program Trading (LO1)** Program traders closely monitor relative futures and cash market prices, but program trades are not actually made on a fully mechanical basis. What are some of the complications that might make program trading using, for example, the S&P 500 contract more difficult than the spot-futures parity formula indicates?

10. **Short Selling (LO1, CFA3)** What are the similarities and differences in short selling a futures contract and short selling a stock? How do the cash flows differ?

Questions and Problems

1. **Understanding Futures Quotations (LO1, LO2, CFA2)** Using Figure 14.1, answer the following questions:

   a. What was the settle price for May 2010 coffee futures on this date? What is the total dollar value of this contract at the close of trading for the day?

   b. What was the settle price for February 2010 gasoline futures on this date? If you held 10 contracts, what is the total dollar value of your futures position?

   c. Suppose you held an open position of 25 March 2010 Dow Jones Industrial Average futures on this day. What is the change in the total dollar value of your position for this day's trading? If you held a long position, would this represent a profit or a loss to you?

   d. Suppose you are short 10 January 2010 soybean oil futures contracts. Would you have made a profit or a loss on this day?

2. **Futures Profits and Losses (LO2, CFA3)** You are long 20 March 2010 soybean futures contracts. Calculate your dollar profit or loss from this trading day using Figure 14.1.

3. **Futures Profits and Losses (LO2, CFA3)** You are short 15 December 2010 corn futures contracts. Calculate your dollar profit or loss from this trading day using Figure 14.1.

4. **Futures Profits and Losses (LO2, CFA3)** You are short 30 March 2010 five-year Treasury note futures contracts. Calculate your profit or loss from this trading day using Figure 14.1.

5. **Open Interest (LO1, CFA2)** Referring to Figure 14.1, what is the total open interest on the June 2010 Japanese yen contract? Does it represent long positions, short positions, or both? Based on the settle price on the contract, what is the dollar value of the open interest?

6. **Spot-Futures Parity (LO3, CFA1)** A non-dividend-paying stock is currently priced at $17.81. The risk-free rate is 5 percent, and a futures contract on the stock matures in six months. What price should the futures be?

7. **Spot-Futures Parity (LO3, CFA1)** A non-dividend-paying stock has a futures contract with a price of $94.90 and a maturity of two months. If the risk-free rate is 4.5 percent, what is the price of the stock?

8. **Spot-Futures Parity (LO3, CFA1)** A non-dividend-paying stock has a current share price of $58.13 and a futures price of $59.92. If the maturity of the futures contract is four months, what is the risk-free rate?

9. **Spot-Futures Parity (LO3, CFA1)** A stock has a current share price of $49.24 and a dividend yield of 1.5 percent. If the risk-free rate is 5.4 percent, what is the futures price if the maturity is four months?

10. **Spot-Futures Parity (LO3, CFA1)** A stock futures contract is priced at $27.18. The stock has a dividend yield of 1.25 percent, and the risk-free rate is 4.5 percent. If the futures contract matures in six months, what is the current stock price?

11. **Margin Call (LO2, CFA3)** Suppose the initial margin on heating oil futures is $8,400, the maintenance margin is $7,200 per contract, and you establish a long position of 10 contracts today, where each contract represents 42,000 gallons. Tomorrow, the contract settles down $.05 from the previous day's price. Are you subject to a margin call? What is the maximum price decline on the contract that you can sustain without getting a margin call?

12. **Marking-to-Market (LO2, CFA2)** You are long 10 gold futures contracts, established at an initial settle price of $975 per ounce, where each contract represents 100 troy ounces. Your initial margin to establish the position is $12,000 per contract, and the maintenance margin is $11,200 per contract. Over the subsequent four trading days, gold settles at $964, $960, $970, and $980, respectively. Compute the balance in your margin account at the end of each of the four trading days, and compute your total profit or loss at the end of the trading period. Assume that a margin call requires you to fund your account back to the initial margin requirement.

13. **Marking-to-Market (LO2, CFA2)** You are short 15 gasoline futures contracts, established at an initial settle price of $2.085 per gallon, where each contract represents 42,000 gallons. Your initial margin to establish the position is $7,425 per contract, and the maintenance margin is $6,500 per contract. Over the subsequent four trading days, gasoline settles at $2.071, $2.099, $2.118, and $2.146, respectively. Compute the balance in your margin account at the end of each of the four trading days, and compute your total profit or loss at the end of the trading period. Assume that a margin call requires you to fund your account back to the initial margin requirement.

14. **Futures Profits (LO2, CFA3)** You went long 20 December 2011 crude oil futures contracts at a price of $72.18. Looking back at Figure 14.1, if you closed your position at the settle price on this day, what was your profit?

15. **Futures Profits (LO2, CFA3)** You shorted 15 June 2010 British pound futures contracts at the high price for the day. Looking back at Figure 14.1, if you closed your position at the settle price on this day, what was your profit?

16. **Index Arbitrage (LO3, CFA1)** Suppose the CAC-40 Index (a widely followed index of French stock prices) is currently at 4,092, the expected dividend yield on the index is 2 percent per year, and the risk-free rate in France is 6 percent annually. If CAC-40 futures contracts that expire in six months are currently trading at 4,152, what program trading strategy would you recommend?

17. **Cross-Hedging (LO4, CFA2)** You have been assigned to implement a three-month hedge for a stock mutual fund portfolio that primarily invests in medium-sized companies. The mutual fund has a beta of 1.15 measured relative to the S&P Midcap 400, and the net asset value of the fund is $175 million. Should you be long or short in the Midcap 400 futures contracts? Assuming the Midcap 400 Index is at 658 and its futures contract size is 500 times the index, determine the appropriate number of contracts to use in designing your cross-hedge strategy.

18. **Spot-Futures Parity (LO3, CFA4)** Suppose the 180-day S&P 500 futures price is 1,281.55, while the cash price is 1,270.42. What is the *implied difference* between the risk-free interest rate and the dividend yield on the S&P 500?

19. **Spot-Futures Parity (LO3, CFA4)** Suppose the 180-day S&P 500 futures price is 1,395.62, while the cash price is 1,370.48. What is the *implied dividend yield* on the S&P 500 if the risk-free interest rate is 5 percent?

20. **Hedging Interest Rate Risk (LO4, CFA3)** Suppose you want to hedge a $300 million bond portfolio with a duration of 5.1 years using 10-year Treasury note futures with a duration of 6.7 years, a futures price of 102, and 3 months to expiration. The multiplier on Treasury note futures is $100,000. How many contracts do you buy or sell?

21. **Hedging Interest Rate Risk (LO4, CFA3)** Suppose you want to hedge a $400 million bond portfolio with a duration of 9.2 years using 10-year Treasury note futures with a duration of 6.2 years, a futures price of 102, and 94 days to expiration. The multiplier on Treasury note futures is $100,000. How many contracts do you buy or sell?

22. **Futures Arbitrage (LO3, CFA5)** A non-dividend-paying stock is currently priced at $62.12 per share. A futures contract maturing in five months has a price of $62.92 and the risk-free rate is 4 percent. Describe how you could make an arbitrage profit from this situation. How much could you make on a per-share basis?

23. **Futures Arbitrage (LO3, CFA5)** A stock is currently priced at $53.87 and the futures on the stock that expire in six months have a price of $55.94. The risk-free rate is 5 percent, and the stock is not expected to pay a dividend. Is there an arbitrage opportunity here? How would you exploit it? What is the arbitrage opportunity per share of stock?

CFA Exam Review by Schweser

[CFA2, CFA5, CFA6]

Jackson Inc. is a multinational company based in West Point, Mississippi, that makes freight cars. One third of Jackson's sales occur in the Netherlands. To manufacture the cars, the firm must import approximately half of the raw materials from Canada.

Two months from now, Jackson plans to sell freight cars to a Dutch firm for €15 million. To protect the company from any adverse moves in exchange rates, Jackson enters into a €15 million futures contract due in 60 days. Jackson also enters into a 60-day futures contract to lock in C$8.5 million, which will be used to purchase steel from a supplier.

The current euro to U.S. dollar exchange rate is €.79/$ while the Canadian dollar to U.S. dollar exchange rate is C$1.30/$. The 60-day euro to U.S. dollar rate is €.80/$, while the Canadian dollar to U.S. dollar rate is C$1.33/$. At the end of the two months, the actual euro to U.S. dollar exchange rate is €.90/$ and the actual Canadian dollar to U.S. dollar rate is C$1.20/$.

To help understand the relationships, Jackson's chief risk officer, Dr. Charles Miles, has put together the following table on hedging currency positions:

Currency Exposure	Position	Action
Receiving foreign currency	Long	Buy forward contracts
Paying foreign currency	Short	Sell forward contracts

1. When hedging its exchange rate risk on the freight car sale, Jackson used a futures contract to:
   a. Sell €15 million in exchange for $18.75 million.
   b. Buy €15 million in exchange for $18.75 million.
   c. Sell €15 million in exchange for $16.67 million.

2. To hedge the foreign exchange risk relative to the Canadian dollar, Jackson should:
   a. Buy a futures contract to exchange $7,083,333 for C$8.5 million.
   b. Buy a futures contract to exchange $6,390,977 for C$8.5 million.
   c. Sell a futures contract to exchange $6,390,977 for C$8.5 million.

3. In regard to the table that Dr. Miles constructed, which of the following is true?
   a. The receiving foreign currency position is correct; the action is incorrect.
   b. The receiving foreign currency position is incorrect; the action is also incorrect.
   c. The paying foreign currency position is correct; the action is also correct.

What's on the Web?

1. **One Chicago**   Go to www.onechicago.com. How many single-stock futures and narrow-based indexes are traded at One Chicago? What is the contract size of a single-stock future? What is the minimum tick size, contract month, and contract expiration? What is the margin requirement?

2. **Spot-Futures Parity**   Go to www.onechicago.com and find the futures quotes for eBay. Now go to finance.yahoo.com and find the current stock price for eBay. What is the implied risk-free rate using these prices? Does each different maturity give you the same interest rate? Why or why not?

3. **Contract Specifications**   You want to find the contract specifications for futures contracts. Go to the CME Group at www.cmegroup.com and find the contract specifications for corn, rough rice, butter, and lean hogs. What are the contract sizes for each of these contracts?

4. **The Juice**   Go to the IntercontinentalExchange Web site at www.theice.com. What contracts are traded on the IntercontinentalExchange? What does FCOJ stand for? What are the trading months for FCOJ futures contracts? What are the position limits for FCOJ futures contracts? What is the last trading day of the expiration month for FCOJ futures? What are the trading months and last trading day for FCOJ options contracts? What is the FCOJ Differential contract?

5. **Hedging with Futures**   You are working for a company that processes beef and will take delivery of 720,000 pounds of cattle in August. You would like to lock in your costs today because you are concerned about an increase in cattle prices. Go to the CME Group at www.cmegroup.com and find the contract size for live cattle. How many futures contracts will you need to hedge your exposure? Will you go long or short on these contracts? Now find the most recent price quote for live cattle futures on the CME Group Web site. What price are you effectively locking in if you traded at the last price? Suppose cattle prices increase 5 percent before the expiration. What is your profit or loss on the futures position? What if the price decreases by 5 percent? Explain how your futures position has eliminated your exposure to price risk in the live cattle market.

Stock-Trak Exercises

To access the Stock-Trak exercises for this chapter, please visit the book Web site at www.mhhe.com/jmd6e and choose the corresponding chapter.

CHAPTER 15

Stock Options

Learning Objectives

Give yourself some in-the-money academic and professional options by understanding:

1. The basics of option contracts and how to obtain price quotes.

2. The difference between option payoffs and option profits.

3. The workings of some basic option trading strategies.

4. The logic behind the put-call parity condition.

"I have no objection to the granting of options. Companies should use whatever form of compensation best motivates employees— whether this be cash bonuses, trips to Hawaii, restricted stock grants or stock options."

–Warren Buffett

Options have fascinated investors for centuries. The option concept is simple. Instead of buying stock shares today, you buy an option to buy the stock at a later date at a price specified in the option contract. You are not obligated to exercise the option, but if doing so benefits you, of course you will. Moreover, the most you can lose is the original price of the option, which is normally only a fraction of the stock price. Sounds good, doesn't it? ■

Options on common stocks have traded in financial markets for about as long as common stocks have been traded. However, it was not until 1973, when the Chicago Board Options Exchange (CBOE) was established, that options trading became a large and important part of the financial landscape. Since then, the success of options trading has been phenomenal.

Much of the success of options trading is attributable to the tremendous flexibility that options offer investors in designing investment strategies. For example, options can be used to reduce risk through hedging strategies or to increase risk through speculative strategies. As a result, when properly understood and applied, options are appealing both to conservative investors and to aggressive speculators.

CFA™ Exam Topics in This Chapter:

1 Derivative markets and instruments (L1, S17)

2 Option markets and contracts (L1, S17)

3 Risk management applications of option strategies (L1, S17)

4 Option markets and contracts (L2, S17)

5 Using credit derivatives to enhance return and manage risk (L2, S17)

6 Risk management applications of option strategies (L3, S15)

Go to www.mhhe.com/jmd6e for a guide that aligns your textbook with CFA readings.

In this chapter, we discuss options generally, but our primary focus is on options on individual common stocks. However, we also discuss options on stock market indexes, which are options on portfolios of common stocks. We begin by reviewing some of the ideas we touched on in an earlier chapter, where we very briefly discussed options.

15.1 Options on Common Stocks

OPTION BASICS

derivative security
Security whose value is derived from the value of another security. Options are a type of derivative security.

As we have discussed, options on common stock are a type of **derivative security** because the value of a stock option is "derived" from the value of the underlying common stock. For example, the value of an option to buy or sell IBM stock is derived from the value of IBM stock. However, the relationship between the value of a particular stock option and the value of the underlying stock depends on the specific type of option.

call option
Grants the holder the right, but not the obligation, to buy the underlying asset at a given strike price.

Recall that there are two basic option types: **call options** and **put options**. Call options are options to buy, and put options are options to sell. Thus, a call option on IBM stock is an option to buy IBM shares, and a put option on IBM stock is an option to sell IBM shares. More specifically, a call option on common stock grants the holder the right, but not the obligation, to buy the underlying stock at a given **strike price** before the option expiration date. Similarly, a put option on common stock grants the holder the right, but not the obligation, to sell the underlying stock at a given strike price before the option expiration date. The strike price, also called the *exercise price,* is the price at which stock shares are bought or sold to fulfill the obligations of the option contract.

put option
Grants the holder the right, but not the obligation, to sell the underlying asset at a given strike price.

strike price
Price specified in an option contract that the holder pays to buy shares (in the case of call options) or receives to sell shares (in the case of put options) if the option is exercised. Also called the *exercise price.*

Options are contracts, and, in practice, option contracts are standardized to facilitate convenience in trading and price reporting. Standardized stock options have a contract size of 100 shares of common stock per option contract. This means that a single call option contract involves an option to buy 100 shares of stock. Likewise, a single put option contract involves an option to sell 100 shares of stock.

Because options are contracts, an understanding of stock options requires that we know the specific contract terms. In general, options on common stock must stipulate at least the following six contract terms:

1. The identity of the underlying stock.
2. The strike price, also called the striking or exercise price.
3. The option contract size.
4. The option expiration date, also called the option maturity.
5. The option exercise style.
6. The delivery or settlement procedure.

First, a stock option contract requires that the specific stock issue be clearly identified. While this may seem to be stating the obvious, in financial transactions it is important that the "obvious" is in fact clearly and unambiguously understood by all concerned parties.

Second, the strike price, also called the exercise price, must be stipulated. The strike price is quite important, because the strike price is the price that an option holder will pay (in the case of a call option) or receive (in the case of a put option) if the option is exercised.

Third, the size of the contract must be specified. As stated earlier, the standard contract size for stock options is 100 stock shares per option.

The fourth contract term that must be stated is the option expiration date. An option cannot be exercised after its expiration date. If an option is unexercised and its expiration date has passed, the option becomes worthless.

American option
An option that can be exercised any time before expiration.

European option
An option that can be exercised only at expiration.

Fifth, the option's exercise style determines when the option can be exercised. There are two basic exercise styles: American and European. **American options** can be exercised any time before option expiration, but **European options** can be exercised only at expiration. Options on individual stocks are normally American style, and stock index options are usually European style.

Finally, in the event that a stock option is exercised, the settlement process must be stipulated. For stock options, standard settlement requires delivery of the underlying stock shares several business days after a notice of exercise is made by the option holder.

Like a stock exchange, or, for that matter, any securities exchange, an options exchange is a marketplace where buy and sell orders from customers are matched up with each other. Stock options are traded in financial markets in a manner similar to the way that common stocks are traded. For example, there are organized options exchanges, and there are over-the-counter (OTC) options markets. The largest volume of stock options trading in the United States takes place at the Chicago Board Options Exchange (CBOE). Stock options, however, are also actively traded at the Boston Stock Exchange (BSE), the International Securities Exchange (launched in late 2006), and the New York Stock Exchange Archipelago (NYSE).[1]

OPTION PRICE QUOTES

Closing prices for stock options traded at the major options exchanges are reported each day in the online version of *The Wall Street Journal,* www.wsj.com. Figure 15.1 reproduces a page from the "Listed Options" report available in the Markets Data Center section of the Web site.

For the Intel options listed in Figure 15.1, the first and second columns state expiration months and strike prices for the various options shown. By convention, standardized stock

_____
[1] The NYSE Archipelago acquired the parent company of the Pacific Stock Exchange (PSE) in 2005.

WWW

Visit these option exchanges:
www.cboe.com
www.nyse.com

FIGURE 15.1 Listed Options Quotations

Prices at close January 04, 2010

Intel (INTC) Underlying stock price*: 20.88

Expiration	Strike	Call			Put		
		Last	Volume	Open Interest	Last	Volume	Open Interest
Jan	15.00	5.85	99	47330	0.01	173	83864
Feb	15.00	6.00	15	402	0.11	46	7820
Jul	15.00	5.95	273	525	0.25	30	1000
Jan	16.00	4.95	130	16045	0.01	21	40123
Feb	16.00	4.90	13	22	0.04	28	271
Apr	16.00	5.00	25	1003	0.15	25	3168
Jul	16.00	5.15	31	113	0.37	3	5762
Feb	17.00	4.04	10	3	0.07	520	3649
Apr	17.00	4.00	64	1873	0.23	30	19074
Jul	17.00	4.25	15	283	0.53	313	10950
Jan	17.50	3.40	1033	89963	0.01	412	74721
Feb	18.00	3.05	186	163	0.14	299	3146
Apr	18.00	3.15	71	5143	0.36	93	12591
Jul	18.00	...	...	2667	0.75	532	9712
Jan	19.00	1.95	3381	43330	0.07	1492	72402
Feb	19.00	2.07	287	2543	0.26	3315	2489
Apr	19.00	2.32	274	16330	0.58	2136	15898
Jul	19.00	2.73	30	2953	1.04	385	9468
Jan	20.00	1.08	17234	250381	0.21	8457	93329
Feb	20.00	1.30	3695	10570	0.51	6178	11204
Apr	20.00	1.66	1668	36710	0.89	3362	19224
Jul	20.00	2.06	312	3967	1.40	537	4747
Jan	21.00	0.47	20902	97652	0.59	7750	24625
Feb	21.00	0.70	6776	6903	0.97	1971	9869
Apr	21.00	1.08	1234	22883	1.34	2481	9567
Jul	21.00	1.52	623	4354	1.91	28	433
Feb	22.00	0.33	8856	7595	1.59	1682	7223

Source: www.wsj.com. Reprinted with permission of *The Wall Street Journal,* January 4, 2010. © 2010 Dow Jones & Company, Inc. All Rights Reserved Worldwide.

options expire on the Saturday following the third Friday of their expiration month. Because of this convention, the exact date on which an option expires can be known exactly by referring to a calendar to identify the third Friday of its expiration month.

These first three contract terms—the identity of the underlying stock, the strike price, and the expiration month—will not change during the life of the option. However, because the price of a stock option depends in part on the price of the underlying stock, the price of an option changes as the stock price changes.

Option prices are reported in columns 3 and 6 of Figure 15.1. Column 3 gives call option prices, and column 6 gives put option prices. Option prices are stated on a per-share basis, but the actual price of an option contract is 100 times the per-share price. This is because each option contract represents an option on 100 shares of stock. Fractional contracts for, say, 50 shares, are not normally available.

In Figure 15.1, trading volume for each contract is reported in columns 4 and 7. Column 4 states the number of call option contracts traded for each available strike-maturity combination, while column 7 states the number of put option contracts traded for each strike-maturity combination. Columns 5 and 8 show open interest for each call and put option contract.

Useful online sources for option prices include the Chicago Board Options Exchange (quote.cboe.com) and Yahoo! Finance (finance.yahoo.com). The nearby *Work the Web* box contains an **option chain** for Starbucks Corp. (SBUX) stock options. The top box reports the time and price for the last trade in Starbucks stock, along with the change in price from the previous day and the trading volume so far for the current day. The bottom boxes contain the Starbucks option chain, one for call options and one for put options.

The second column of each section (labeled "Symbol") lists ticker symbols for specific options. Each of these new ticker symbols is 19 characters long. You can see that the first four values are the ticker symbol for Starbucks, SBUX. The next six values show you the expiration date of the option, in YYMMDD format. The expiration day is the Saturday following the last trading day. Following the expiration date, there is either a letter "C" or letter "P," which identifies the option as a call or a put, respectively. The last eight numbers are the strike price of the option. The first five numbers are the dollar value of the strike price and the last three numbers are the decimal part of the strike. For example, look at the entry for the first put option symbol, where you see the value "00021000." This value says that the strike price of the option is an integer (gleaned from the last three zeros) and the dollar value of the strike is 21. Of course, one can find the strike price by looking in the first column (labeled "Strike").

The third column ("Last") reports the option price for the last trade. The fourth column ("Chg") states the change in price from the previous day's last trade, where a zero indicates either no change in price or no trade that day. The next two columns ("Bid" and "Ask") contain representative bid and ask price quotes from dealers. Finally, the seventh column ("Vol") reports trading volume as the number of contracts traded that day, and the eighth column ("Open Int") states open interest as the total number of contracts outstanding.

option chain

A list of available option contracts and their prices for a particular security arrayed by strike price and maturity.

CHECK THIS

15.1a   What is a call option? What is a put option?

15.1b   What are the six basic contract terms that an options contract must specify?

15.1c   What is an option chain?

STOCK OPTION TICKER SYMBOLS

To trade stock options, it is useful to know something about option ticker symbols. The ticker symbol for a stock option identifies not only the underlying stock, but also the option type, the expiration date, and the strike price. Until recently, the format for option symbols had been the same for many years. In early 2010, however, the Options Clearing Corporation instituted a new, expanded approach for option symbols. This change was driven by the increasing size of the option market. Given the potential time lag associated with incorporating the new approach, we will address both the "former" and "current" approaches to decoding option symbols.

Here is a stock quote and an option chain for Starbucks Corp. (SBUX) from Yahoo! Finance (finance.yahoo.com).

Starbucks Corporation (NasdaqGS: SBUX)
Real Time: 26.17 ↓ 0.08 (0.30%) 12:09PM EDT

Last Trade:	**26.13**	Day's Range:	25.74 - 26.13
Trade Time:	**11:55AM EDT**	52wk Range:	18.69 - 28.50
Change:	↓ **0.12 (0.46%)**	Volume:	2,800,752
Prev Close:	**26.25**	Avg Vol (3m):	7,855,600
Open:	**26.08**	Market Cap:	19.34B
Bid:	**26.13 x 300**	P/E (ttm):	24.39
Ask:	**26.14 x 9600**	EPS (ttm):	1.07
1y Target Est:	**30.00**	Div & Yield:	0.52 (2.00%)

Add to Portfolio — Like 66

Starbucks Corporation — ■ SBUX — Oct 6, 11:54am EDT

(chart showing price 25.7 to 26.3, 10am to 4pm)

------ Previous Close

1d 5d 3m 6m 1y 2y 5y max

View By Expiration: Oct 10 | **Nov 10** | Jan 11 | Apr 11 | Jan 12 | Jan 13

Call Options — Expire At Close Friday, November 19, 2010

Strike	Symbol	Last	Chg	Bid	Ask	Vol	Open Int
22.00	SBUX101120C00022000	4.16	↑ 0.03	4.20	4.30	1	208
23.00	SBUX101120C00023000	3.20	0.00	3.30	3.40	3	291
24.00	SBUX101120C00024000	2.44	↓ 0.24	2.53	2.57	23	516
25.00	SBUX101120C00025000	1.56	↓ 0.26	1.77	1.79	86	745
26.00	SBUX101120C00026000	1.14	↓ 0.10	1.15	1.17	42	2,762
27.00	SBUX101120C00027000	0.60	↓ 0.17	0.68	0.69	10	1,162
28.00	SBUX101120C00028000	0.32	↓ 0.09	0.35	0.37	3	1,482
29.00	SBUX101120C00029000	0.15	↓ 0.05	0.16	0.18	100	395
30.00	SBUX101120C00030000	0.08	0.00	0.07	0.08	2	910

Put Options — Expire At Close Friday, November 19, 2010

Strike	Symbol	Last	Chg	Bid	Ask	Vol	Open Int
21.00	SBUX101120P00021000	0.13	↓ 0.04	0.12	0.15	3	10
22.00	SBUX101120P00022000	0.21	↓ 0.02	0.18	0.21	1	146
23.00	SBUX101120P00023000	0.34	↓ 0.07	0.29	0.31	4	165
24.00	SBUX101120P00024000	0.48	↑ 0.04	0.45	0.47	45	334
25.00	SBUX101120P00025000	0.85	↑ 0.20	0.70	0.72	40	491
26.00	SBUX101120P00026000	1.20	↑ 0.15	1.09	1.12	30	974
27.00	SBUX101120P00027000	1.79	↑ 0.24	1.62	1.65	30	1,070
28.00	SBUX101120P00028000	2.56	↑ 0.35	2.31	2.34	5	1,318
29.00	SBUX101120P00029000	2.98	0.00	3.10	3.20	51	308
30.00	SBUX101120P00030000	4.50	0.00	3.95	4.35	10	69

Highlighted options are in-the-money.

FORMER SYMBOLS A stock option ticker symbol has two parts. The first part contains a three-letter symbol for the underlying stock. The second part contains a two-letter symbol specifying the option type—put or call, the expiration month, and the strike price. For example, consider Coca-Cola call options with a $50 strike price with a March expiration. The ticker symbol is KO-CJ. The first part is KO, the ticker symbol for Coca-Cola stock. The second part is CJ, where C indicates a March call option and J indicates a $50 strike price. As another example, consider Disney put options with a $35 strike price and a September expiration. The ticker symbol is DIS-UG. The first part is DIS, the ticker symbol for Disney stock. The second part is UG, where U indicates a September put option and G indicates a $35 strike price.

Table 15.1 specifies the letters used to indicate option type, expiration month, and strike price. Notice that the 12 letters A–L denote the 12 expiration months January through December for call options. Similarly, the 12 letters M–X represent the 12 expiration months for put options. The 20 letters A–T represent strike prices from 5 through 100 in five-dollar increments. The six letters U–Z are reserved for the six strikes, 7.5, 12.5, 17.5, 22.5, 27.5, and 32.5, respectively. For strikes greater than 100, the letters repeat themselves. For example, the letter A represents strikes of 5, 105, 205, and so on.

Under the former system to create option tickers, options exchanges had to use special symbols for NASDAQ stocks, which have stock symbols of four or more letters. For example, the ticker symbol for Starbucks stock, SBUX, became SQX for Starbucks options. So, a Starbucks October call option with a $25 strike used to have the ticker symbol SQX-JF. Similarly, the stock ticker symbol for Sun Microsystems, SUNW, became SUQ for Sun

www

For information on option ticker symbols, see
www.cboe.com
www.schaeffersresearch.com
www.optionsxpress.com

INVESTMENT UPDATES

KEY DETAILS ABOUT CHANGES TO OPTIONS SYMBOLS

What Is Happening to Options Symbols?

The Options Clearing Corporation (OCC), an industry-wide body that oversees the clearance and settlement of exchange-listed options traded on all 7 options exchanges in the U.S., has instituted a change in the way options symbols are represented in data transmissions between financial services firms.

Options symbols have increased in length from 5 characters to 21 characters as part of a new industry standard format used in back-end operations, and now contain both numbers and letters.

Brokerage firms and data providers are allowed to create their own translation of the new industry standard format in their presentation of options symbols to the public.

Why Are Options Symbols Changing?

The OCC decided to undertake this change in response to changes in technology and the proliferation of new options products by the exchanges. The number and types of options products have grown substantially in recent years, straining the capacity of the original symbol format. The new, longer symbol format accommodates new products and supports future growth.

What Does the New Industry Standard Symbol Format Look Like?

The original options symbols contained up to 5 characters and consisted of 3 data elements. This format is known in the industry as the OPRA (Options Price Reporting Authority) code.

Original Symbol Format Example

Symbol		
	AAQED	
There are 3 data elements:		
1	**2**	**3**
Root symbol	Expiration date and call/put indicator	Strike price
AAQ	E	D
Meaning: A call on Apple that expires in May with a $20 strike price.		

In the example shown, AAQ is the root symbol that signifies the underlying security. E denotes both the expiration date and whether the symbol is for a call or a put. D conveys what the strike price is. So, AAQED designated a call option on Apple, Inc., that expired in May with a $20 strike price.

TABLE 15.1 Former Stock Option Ticker Symbol and Strike Price Codes

Expiration Month	Calls	Puts		Strike		Strike	
January	A	M		5	A	70	N
February	B	N		10	B	75	O
March	C	O		15	C	80	P
April	D	P		20	D	85	Q
May	E	Q		25	E	90	R
June	F	R		30	F	95	S
July	G	S		35	G	100	T
August	H	T		40	H	7.5	U
September	I	U		45	I	12.5	V
October	J	V		50	J	17.5	W
November	K	W		55	K	22.5	X
December	L	X		60	L	27.5	Y
				65	M	32.5	Z

The new industry standard symbol format (which is also known as the "OCC series key") has 21 characters and consists of 4 data elements.

Old:						
AAQED						
Becomes						
New:						
AAPL 100522C00020000						

The new symbol format has 4 data elements:

1				2	3	4
Underlying security (root symbol)	Expiration year	Expiration month	Expiration day	Call/Put indicator	Strike price (dollars)	Strike price (decimals)
AAPL	10	05	22	C	00020	000

Meaning: A call on Apple that expires May 22, 2010, with a $20 strike price.

Please note:

- The stock's underlying ticker symbol, which is the first data element, will always be used in the new symbol. In our example, "AAQ" becomes "AAPL," the actual stock ticker symbol for Apple.

- The data element for the underlying security has room for up to 6 characters. Spaces are officially considered part of this element, and are counted as part of the 21 characters. This means that a 4-character ticker like AAPL will be followed by 2 spaces; a 3-character ticker like IBM will be followed by 3 spaces, and so on. If a ticker took up all 6 character slots, then there would be no space between it and the next data element, which is the date.

- The second data element is the expiration date. In this case "100522" is 2010, 05, 22 or May 22, 2010.

- The third data element is the call/put indicator, denoted by a "C" or "P."

- The fourth data element is the strike price; 5 character spaces are assigned for the strike dollar price, with 3 spaces for any decimals. "00020000" means a strike price of $20.00.

Source: http://www.schwabcontent.com/symbology/us_eng/key_details.html#c.

stock options. A Sun November put option with a $5 strike used to have the ticker symbol SUQ-WA. Many brokers used to insulate their customers from this inconvenience and accepted option orders using the full NASDAQ stock ticker. So, for example, an order to buy SQX-JE options would have been accepted as SBUX-JE by most brokers. Also, options for many securities had even more complicated option ticker symbols. For these securities, option traders used to have to refer to an official list of ticker symbols maintained by option exchanges. The current system for option symbols is designed to reduce these ticker symbol inconveniences.

CURRENT SYMBOLS The former option symbol convention is particularly difficult to use for NASDAQ stocks and for other stocks with more complicated ticker symbols. Moreover, because of the number of options available on an individual security, even stocks with one-, two-, and three-letter tickers sometimes need additional option symbols. The new identification method for option symbols helps alleviate these issues. The trade-off, however, is that the symbol will increase from 5 letters to a combination of about 20 letters and numbers.

The new option symbols continue to provide the same information: underlying security, expiration date, option type, and strike price. But the expanded form allows investors to specify the actual symbol of the underlying security, as well as a broader range of strike prices. For more detail on the change take a look at the nearby *Investment Updates* box, which provides a summary of the change by a well-known brokerage house, Charles Schwab.

15.1d   Using Table 15.1, what are the option types, expiration months, and strike prices for the following Alcoa (AA) options: AA-FF, AA-RF, AA-HK, and AA-TL?

15.1e   What are the new option symbols for the Alcoa (AA) options listed in 15.1d? (Recall that options expire the day after the last trading day—which is the third Friday of the month.)

15.1f   What is the rationale for the change in option symbols?

15.2   The Options Clearing Corporation

WWW

Visit the OCC at
www.optionsclearing.com

Suppose that you order a new car through a local dealer and pay a $2,000 deposit. Further suppose that, two weeks later, you receive a letter informing you that your dealer had entered bankruptcy. No doubt, you would be quite upset at the prospect of losing your $2,000 deposit.

Now consider a similar situation where you pay $2,000 for several call options through a broker. On the day before expiration, you tell your broker to exercise the options, because they would produce, say, a $5,000 payoff. Then, a few days later, your broker tells you that the call writer entered bankruptcy proceedings and that your $2,000 call premium and $5,000 payoff were lost. No doubt, this default would upset you. However, this situation cannot occur if your option trade was made on a registered options exchange. In effect, the exchange eliminates counterparty risk.

Option traders who transact on option exchanges have an important ally. The **Options Clearing Corporation (OCC)**, founded in 1973, is the clearing agency for these options exchanges: the American Stock Exchange, the Chicago Board Options Exchange, the International Securities Exchange, NYSE Arca, Philadelphia Stock Exchange, and the Boston Stock Exchange.

Once an option trade is made on an options exchange, the Options Clearing Corporation steps in and becomes a party to both sides of the trade. In other words, the option buyer effectively purchases the option from the OCC, and the seller effectively sells the option to the OCC. In this way, each investor is free from the worry that the other party will default. Each option investor simply looks to the OCC.

Most options investors are unaware of the OCC because only member firms of an options exchange deal directly with it. However, in fact, all option contracts traded on U.S. options exchanges are originally issued, guaranteed, and cleared by the OCC. Brokerage firms merely act as intermediaries between investors and the OCC.

The OCC is an agency consisting of brokerage firms that are called "clearing members." The OCC's clearing members represent more than 100 of the largest U.S. broker-dealers, futures commission merchants, and non-U.S. securities firms. To guarantee the performance of all trades, the OCC has capital contributed by clearing members. If existing capital were to prove insufficient, the OCC could draw additional funds from its members. This structure ensures the integrity of the options markets.

The OCC began life as the clearinghouse for listed equity options. Today, however, the OCC clears many products. The OCC is regulated by both the Securities and Exchange Commission (SEC) and the Commodities Futures Trading Commission (CFTC). Under the watchful eye of the SEC, the OCC clears trades for put and call options on common stocks, stock indexes, foreign currencies, and single-stock futures. With CFTC oversight, the OCC clears and settles trades in futures contracts and options on futures contracts.

The OCC also sponsors the Options Industry Council (OIC). Founded in 1992, the OIC was created to educate investors about the benefits and risks of exchange-traded equity options. Today, each year the OIC conducts hundreds of seminars and webcasts, and it distributes thousands of interactive CDs and brochures. In addition, the OIC has an extensive Web site and there is even a "Help Desk" tab that focuses on options education.

Options Clearing Corporation (OCC)
Private agency that guarantees that the terms of an option contract will be fulfilled if the option is exercised; issues and clears all option contracts trading on U.S. exchanges.

WWW

Visit the OIC at
www.optionseducation.org

CHECK THIS

15.2a	Who makes up the OCC? Who regulates the OCC?	
15.2b	How does the OCC protect option traders?	
15.2c	What is the OIC and what does it do?	

15.3 Why Options?

As a stock market investor, a basic question you might ask is: "Why buy stock options instead of shares of stock directly?" Good question! To answer it properly, we need to compare the possible outcomes from two investment strategies. The first investment strategy entails simply buying stock. The second strategy involves buying a call option that allows the holder to buy stock any time before option expiration.

For example, suppose you buy 100 shares of IBM stock at a price of $90 per share, representing an investment of $9,000. Afterwards, three things could happen: the stock price could go up, go down, or remain the same. If the stock price goes up, you make money; if it goes down, you lose money. Of course, if the stock price remains the same, you break even.

To learn more about options, see
www.cboe.com/LearnCenter/

Now, consider the alternative strategy of buying a call option with a strike price of $90 expiring in three months at a per-share price of $5. This corresponds to a contract price of $500 since the standard option contract size is 100 shares. The first thing to notice about this strategy is that you have invested only $500, and therefore the most that you can lose is only $500.

To compare the two investment strategies just described, let's examine three possible cases for IBM's stock price at the close of trading on the third Friday of the option's expiration month. In case 1, the stock price goes up to $100. In case 2, the stock price goes down to $80. In case 3, the stock price remains the same at $90.

Case 1: If the stock price goes up to $100, and you originally bought 100 shares at $90 per share, then your profit is $100 \times (\$100 - \$90) = \$1,000$. As a percentage of your original investment amount of $9,000, this represents a return on investment of $\$1,000/\$9,000 = 11.11\%$.

Alternatively, if you originally bought the call option, you can exercise the option and buy 100 shares at the strike price of $90 and sell the stock at the $100 market price. After accounting for the original cost of the option contract, your profit is $100 \times (\$100 - \$90) - \$500 = \$500$. As a percentage of your original investment of $500, this represents a return on investment of $\$500/\$500 = 100\%$.

Case 2: If the stock price goes down to $80, and you originally bought 100 shares at $90 per share, then your loss is $100 \times (\$80 - \$90) = -\$1,000$. As a percentage of your original investment, this represents a return of $-\$1,000/\$9,000 = -11.11\%$.

If instead you originally bought the call option, exercising the option would not pay, and it would expire worthless. You would then realize a total loss of your $500 investment, and your return is −100 percent.

Case 3: If the stock price remains the same at $90, and you bought 100 shares, you break even, and your return is zero percent.

However, if you bought the call option, exercising the option would not pay, and it would expire worthless. Once again, you would lose your entire $500 investment.

As these three cases illustrate, the outcomes of the two investment strategies differ significantly, depending on subsequent stock price changes. Whether one strategy is preferred over another is a matter for each individual investor to decide. What is important is the fact that options offer an alternative means of formulating investment strategies.

Stock Returns

Suppose you bought 100 shares of stock at $50 per share. If the stock price goes up to $60 per share, what is the percentage return on your investment? If, instead, the stock price falls to $40 per share, what is the percentage return on your investment?

If the stock goes to $60 per share, you make $10/$50 = 20%. If it falls to $40, you lose $10/$50 = 20%.

Call Option Returns

In Example 15.1, suppose that you bought one call option contract for $200. The strike price is $50. If the stock price is $60 just before the option expires, should you exercise the option? If you exercise the option, what is the percentage return on your investment? If you don't exercise the option, what is the percentage return on your investment?

If the stock price is $60, you should definitely exercise. If you do, you will make $10 per share, or $1,000, from exercising. Once we deduct the $200 original cost of the option, your net profit is $800. Your percentage return is $800/$200 = 400%. If you don't exercise, you lose your entire $200 investment, so your loss is 100 percent.

More Call Option Returns

In Example 15.2, if the stock price is $40 just before the option expires, should you exercise the option? If you exercise the option, what is the percentage return on your investment? If you don't exercise the option, what is the percentage return on your investment?

If the stock price is $40, you shouldn't exercise since, by exercising, you will be paying $50 per share. If you did exercise, you would lose $10 per share, or $1,000, plus the $200 cost of the option, or $1,200 total. This would amount to a $1,200/$200 = 600% loss! If you don't exercise, you lose the $200 you invested, for a loss of 100 percent.

Of course, we can also calculate percentage gains and losses from a put option purchase. Here we make money if the stock price declines. So, suppose you buy a put option with a strike price of $20 for $.50. If you exercise your put when the stock price is $18, what is your percentage gain?

You make $2 per share since you are selling at $20 when the stock is worth $18. Your put contract cost $50, so your net profit is $200 − $50 = $150. As a percentage of your original $50 investment, you made $150/$50 = 300%.

CHECK THIS

15.3a If you buy 100 shares of stock at $10 and sell out at $12, what is your percentage return?

15.3b If you buy one call contract with a strike of $10 for $100 and exercise it when the stock is selling for $12, what is your percentage return?

15.4 Stock Index Options

Following the tremendous success of stock options trading on the Chicago Board Options Exchange, the exchange looked for other new financial products to offer to investors and portfolio managers. In 1982, the CBOE created stock index options, which, at the time, represented a new type of option contract.

INDEX OPTIONS: FEATURES AND SETTLEMENT

stock index option

An option on a stock market index. The most popular stock index options are options on the S&P 100 Index, S&P 500 Index, and Dow Jones Industrials Index.

A **stock index option** is an option on a stock market index. The first stock index options were contracts on the Standard & Poor's index of 100 large companies representative of American industry. This index is often simply called the "S&P 100." S&P 100 Index options trade under the ticker symbol OEX, and S&P 100 Index options are referred to as "OEX options." The second stock index options introduced by the CBOE were contracts on the Standard & Poor's index of 500 companies, the "S&P 500." S&P 500 Index options trade under the ticker symbol SPX and are referred to as "SPX options." In 1997, the CBOE introduced options on the Dow Jones Industrial Average (DJIA), which trade under the ticker symbol DJX.

Besides the different underlying indexes, the major difference between SPX, DJX, and OEX contracts is that OEX options are American style, whereas SPX and DJX options are European style. The CBOE also lists the "XEO option," which is based on the S&P 100 Index. The XEO option has European-style exercise. As we noted earlier, American-style options can be exercised any time before expiration, whereas European-style options can be exercised only on the last day before option expiration.

Learn more about trading index options at www.cboe.com

Before stock index options could be introduced, one very important detail that had to be worked out was what to do when an index option is exercised. Exchange officials saw that settlement by delivery was obviously impractical because of the number of stocks comprising an index. Instead, a cash settlement procedure was adopted for index options. For this reason, all stock index options are **cash-settled options**. With cash settlement, when a stock index option is exercised, the option writer pays a cash amount to the option buyer based on the difference between the exercise date index level and the option's strike price. For example, suppose you had purchased an SPX call option with a strike price of $1,520, and the S&P 500 Index was $1,540 on the day of exercise. The difference between the index level and the strike price is $1,540 − $1,520 = $20. Because the contract size for SPX options is 100 times the S&P 500 Index, the option writer must pay 100 × $20 = $2,000 to the option holder exercising the option.

cash-settled option

An option contract settled by a cash payment from the option writer to the option holder when the option is exercised.

In the example above, the contract size for SPX options was stated to be 100 times the S&P 500 Index. In fact, the contract size for almost all standardized stock index options is 100 times the underlying index. Thus, the actual price of a stock index option is 100 times the price stated on an index level basis. There are only a few exceptions to this rule. For example, the CBOE offers so-called Reduced Value index options with a contract size that is one-tenth the size of standard index options. Reduced Value index options are appealing to some individual investors, but they represent only a minuscule share of all index options trading.

INDEX OPTION PRICE QUOTES

Options now are available for a wide variety of stock market indexes. Each business day, the online version of *The Wall Street Journal* provides a summary of the previous day's activity in stock index options. Figure 15.2, "Index Options Trading," contains some information that can be found in the Markets Data Center at www.wsj.com.

Part One of Figure 15.2, "Ranges for Underlying Indexes," contains information on the major stock market indexes for which index options are now available. In the first column of this box, the name of each index and (in parentheses) its ticker symbol are listed. Columns 2, 3, 4, and 5 report the corresponding high, low, close, and net change values, respectively, for each stock market index from the previous day's trading. For each stock index, the columns labeled "From Dec. 31" and "% Change" report the index level value change and percentage value change, respectively, since the beginning of the current year.

The majority of trading in stock index options is conducted on the Chicago Board Options Exchange, which lists OEX and SPX options (among others). Part Two of Figure 15.2 is a partial listing of the options trading data for options on the S&P 500 Index (SPX). You might notice that the name of this option is "S&P 500-A.M." The name indicates that this option expires on the morning of the third Friday of the month (other options expire at the close of trading on the third Friday of the month).

Part Two of Figure 15.2 reports a portion of the options that expire in January 2010. The first column of data shows that these options all expire in January. The second column reports the strike and whether the option is a call or a put. The third column reports trading volume measured as the number of contracts traded during the previous day's trading. The fourth column, labeled "Last," reports the contract price for the last trade of the previous day, and the fifth column, labeled "Net Change," reports the price change from the last price on the previous day. Finally, the sixth column, labeled "Open Interest," lists the total number of contracts outstanding.

At the bottom of Part Two of Figure 15.2, you can see total volume and open interest for calls and puts. As noted, the unofficial trading volume is measured by the estimated number of contracts traded on a given day. Open interest is measured by the total number of contracts outstanding on the previous trading day.

FIGURE 15.2   Index Options Trading, Part One

Ranges for Underlying Indexes						
Prices at close Monday, January 4, 2010						
	High	Low	Close	Net Change	From Dec. 31	%Change
AM-Mexico (MXY)	227.37	220.72	227.36	6.64	6.64	3.01
Bank (BKX)	43.77	42.71	43.68	0.97	0.97	2.27
Biotechnology (BTK)	955.17	942.13	955.15	13.02	13.02	1.38
CB Tech (TXX)	752.41	739.30	751.06	11.76	11.76	1.59
DJ Industrials (DJX)	106.05	104.31	105.84	1.56	1.56	1.50
DJ Transportation (DTX)	414.97	410.19	413.08	3.12	3.12	0.76
DJ Utilities (DUX)	402.32	398.11	399.49	1.48	1.48	0.37
Eurotop 100 (EUR)	226.43	224.77	226.43	3.06	3.06	1.37
Gold/Silver (XAU)	175.56	169.55	174.02	5.77	5.77	3.43
HK Fltg (HKO)	388.34	388.34	388.34	-0.32	-0.32	-0.08
Institutional -A.M. (XII)	537.82	528.37	537.28	8.91	8.91	1.69
IW Internet (IIX)	237.56	233.86	236.92	3.06	3.06	1.31
Japan (JPN)			112.58	1.10	1.10	0.99
Leaps S&P 100 (OAX)	104.66	102.95	104.55	1.73	1.73	1.68
Leaps S&P 500 (LSY)	113.39	111.66	113.30	1.79	1.79	1.61
Major Market (XMI)	1169.73	1151.32	1167.77	16.45	16.45	1.43
MS Consumer (CMR)	678.13	670.32	676.71	6.39	6.39	0.95
MS Cyclical (CYC)	852.53	829.86	851.63	21.77	21.77	2.62
MS High Tech (MSH)	588.00	578.10	585.68	7.58	7.58	1.31
MS Internet (MOX)	23.46	22.97	23.46	0.49	0.49	2.13
MS Multi National (NFT)	633.98	622.71	633.05	10.32	10.32	1.66
Nasdaq 100 (NDX)	1890.02	1881.63	1886.70	26.39	26.39	1.42
Oil Services(OSX)	202.51	195.62	202.47	7.55	7.55	3.87
Pharmaceutical (DRG)	313.71	308.80	313.25	4.04	4.04	1.31
PSE Technology (PSE)	887.20	873.51	885.53	12.10	12.10	1.39
Russell 2000 (RUT)	640.10	628.11	640.10	14.71	14.71	2.35
S&P Midcap (MID)	739.57	726.65	738.15	11.48	11.48	1.58
S&P100 (OEX)	523.30	514.74	522.73	8.64	8.64	1.68
S&P500-A.M. (SPX)	1133.87	1116.56	1132.99	17.89	17.89	1.60
Semiconductor (SOX)	368.26	364.02	366.08	6.17	6.17	1.71
Utility (UTY)	421.58	417.05	418.33	0.33	0.33	0.08
Value Line (VLE)	2306.44	2269.94	2306.44	46.99	46.99	2.08
Volatility (VIX)	21.68	20.03	20.04	-1.64	-1.64	-7.56

FIGURE 15.2 Index Options Trading, Part Two

Prices at close January 04, 2010

S&P500-A.M. (SPX)   Chicago Exchange

Underlying Index	High	Low	Close	Net Change	From Dec.31	%Change
S&P500-A.M.	1133.87	1116.56	1132.99	17.89	17.89	1.60
		Strike	Volume	Last	Net Change	Open Interest
		⋮	⋮	⋮	⋮	⋮
Jan		1110.00 put	1,266	5.70	-7.90	9,468
Jan		1110.00 call	530	28.20	+8.95	14,635
Jan		1115.00 call	568	23.55	+7.41	18,970
Jan		1115.00 put	565	6.80	-9.16	10,058
Jan		1120.00 call	211	19.80	+6.36	26,151
Jan		1120.00 put	1,625	7.90	-10.10	7,757
Jan		1125.00 put	625	5.00	...	1,756
Jan		1125.00 call	341	12.20	...	12
Jan		1130.00 put	345	11.70	-11.30	2,331
Jan		1130.00 call	2,276	13.60	+4.90	15,435
Jan		1135.00 call	2,678	11.00	+4.50	14,539
Jan		1135.00 put	134	13.63	-12.47	86
Jan		1140.00 put	45	16.80	-6.20	184
Jan		1140.00 call	1,252	8.70	+3.70	16,675
Jan		1145.00 put	9	19.45	-8.15	8
Jan		1145.00 call	929	6.60	+2.87	8,181
Jan		1150.00 call	874	1.60	...	206
Jan		1150.00 put	6	18.90	...	...
		⋮	⋮	⋮	⋮	⋮
Call Vol.		261,553	Open Int.			3,943,095
Put Vol.		347,137	Open Int.			6,432,837

Volume figures are unofficial. Open interest reflects previous trading day.

EXAMPLE 15.4

Index Options

Suppose you bought 10 July 1290 SPX call contracts at a quoted price of $5. How much did you pay in total? At option expiration, suppose the S&P 500 is at 1300. What would you receive? What is your profit, if any?

The price per SPX contract is 100 times the quoted price. Because you bought 10 contracts, you paid a total of $5 × 100 × 10 = $5,000. If, at expiration, the S&P 500 is at 1300, you would receive $100 × (1300 − 1290) = $1,000 per contract, or $10,000 in all. This $10,000 would be paid to you in cash, because index options feature cash settlement. Your profit is $5,000.

CHECK THIS

15.4a   In addition to the underlying asset, what is the major difference between an ordinary stock option and a stock index option?

15.4b   In addition to the underlying index, what is the major difference between the OEX and SPX option contracts?

15.5 Option Intrinsic Value and "Moneyness"

To understand option payoffs and profits, we need to know some important concepts related to option value. The first important concept is called **intrinsic value**. The intrinsic value of an option is what the option would be worth if it were expiring immediately. Equivalently, the intrinsic value of an option is the payoff to an option holder if the underlying stock price does not change from its current value.

Computing the intrinsic value of an option is easy—all you need to know is whether the option is a call or a put, the strike price of the option, and the price of the underlying stock. The intrinsic value calculation, however, depends on whether the option is a call or a put.

You can calculate the intrinsic value of an option at any time, whether the option is dead or alive. For ease, we begin with examples where the option is just about to expire, and then show formulas that can be used at any time to calculate intrinsic value.

INTRINSIC VALUE FOR CALL OPTIONS

The first step to calculate the intrinsic value of a call option is to compare the underlying stock price to the strike price. Suppose a call option contract specifies a strike price of $50, and the underlying stock price is $45. Also, suppose this option was just minutes away from expiring. With the stock price at $45 and a strike price of $50, this call option would have no value. Why would you pay anything to buy the stock at $50, when you can buy it for $45? In this situation, the value of this call option is zero.

Alternatively, suppose the underlying stock price is $55. If the call option with a strike of $50 was just minutes from expiration, it would be worth just about $5. Why? This option grants the holder the right to buy the stock for $50, when everyone else would have to pay the going market price of $55.

Let's look at call options that are not just about to expire. If the underlying stock price is less than the strike price, the intrinsic value for a call option is set to zero. If, however, the underlying stock price, S, is greater than the strike price, K, the intrinsic value for a call option is the value $S - K$. Equation (15.1) shows how to calculate the intrinsic value of a call option.

$$\text{Call option intrinsic value} = \text{MAX}(S - K, 0) \qquad (15.1)$$

In equation (15.1), MAX stands for maximum and the comma stands for the word "or." You read equation (15.1) as follows: The **call option intrinsic value** is the maximum of the stock price minus the strike price *or* zero.

We assume that call option investors are rational and will prefer to exercise only call options that have a positive intrinsic value. For call options, rational exercise implies that the call option holder is able to purchase the stock for less than its current market price.

INTRINSIC VALUE FOR PUT OPTIONS

The first step to calculate the intrinsic value of a put option is also to compare the underlying stock price to the strike price. Suppose a put option contract specifies a strike price of $50, and the underlying stock price is $55. Also, suppose this option was just minutes away from expiring. With the stock price at $55 and a strike price of $50, this call option would have no value. Why would you pay anything to be able to sell the stock at $50, when you can sell shares for $55? In this situation, the value of this put option is zero.

Alternatively, suppose the underlying stock price is $45. If the put option with a strike price of $50 was just minutes from expiration, it would be worth just about $5. Why? This put option grants the holder the right to sell the stock for $50, when everyone else would have to sell at the going market price of $45.

Let's look at put options that are not just about to expire. If the underlying stock price is greater than the strike price, the intrinsic value for a put option is set to zero. If, however, the underlying stock price is less than the strike price, the intrinsic value for a put option is the value $K - S$. Equation (15.2) shows how to calculate the intrinsic value of a put option.

$$\text{Put option intrinsic value} = MAX(K - S, 0) \qquad (15.2)$$

In equation (15.2), MAX stands for maximum and the comma stands for the word "or." You read equation (15.2) as follows: The **put option intrinsic value** is the maximum of the strike price minus the stock price *or* zero.

We assume that put option investors are rational and will prefer to exercise only put options that have a positive intrinsic value. For put options, rational exercise implies that the put option holder is able to sell the stock for more than its current market price.

TIME VALUE

Now that you know how to calculate the intrinsic value of an option, you can think of intrinsic value as the amount of money an investor receives if exercising the option is rational. Note, however, that being rational and being smart are not the same thing. For example, in most cases the investor would be better off to sell the option rather than exercise it because the price of the option will be greater than intrinsic value.

The difference between the price of the option and the intrinsic value of the option is known as **option time value**. At expiration, the time value of an option is zero. Before expiration, the time value for options with American-style exercise is at least zero, but most always positive. Because options with American-style exercise can be exercised at any time, arbitrageurs will ensure that the price of these options remains at least as high as their intrinsic value. For options with European-style exercise, however, deep in-the-money put option prices that are less than intrinsic value are possible.

A full discussion of why investors exercise options is a topic generally covered in a derivatives course. Calculating option prices, including time value, is the topic of a whole chapter in this textbook.

THREE LESSONS ABOUT INTRINSIC VALUE

There are three important lessons about intrinsic value. First, investors can calculate intrinsic value whether the option is "dead" (at expiration) or "alive" (before expiration). Second, at expiration, the value of an option equals its intrinsic value because no time value is left at expiration. Third, before expiration, the value of an option equals its intrinsic value plus its time value.

SHOW ME THE MONEY

Option investors have developed shortcuts in the way they talk about the intrinsic value of options. Three important terms in this lingo are **in-the-money options**, **at-the-money options**, and **out-of-the-money options**.

Essentially, in-the-money options are those call options or put options with a positive intrinsic value. For an at-the-money call or put option, the strike price is exactly equal to the underlying stock price. For an out-of-the-money call option, the stock price is less than the strike price. For an out of-the-money put option, the strike price is less than the stock price. Exercising an out-of-the-money option does not result in a positive payoff.

Once you get the hang of all this "moneyness" and intrinsic value language, you will see that it is not difficult. Examples 15.5 through 15.10 give you some practice. Also, the chart immediately below summarizes the relationship between the stock price and the strike price for in-the-money, out-of-the-money, and at-the-money call and put options.

	In the Money	Out of the Money	At the Money
Call option	$S > K$	$S < K$	$S = K$
Put option	$S < K$	$S > K$	$S = K$

put option intrinsic value
The maximum of (*a*) the strike price minus the stock price or (*b*) zero.

option time value
The difference between the price of an option and its intrinsic value.

in-the-money option
Any option with a positive intrinsic value.

at-the-money option
Any option with a strike price exactly equal to the underlying price.

out-of-the-money option
An option that would not yield a positive payoff if the stock price remained unchanged until expiration.

EXAMPLE 15.5	In-the-Money Call Option

IBM stock is currently $55 per share. Let's look at a call option to buy IBM stock at $50 ($50 is the strike price). The stock price is greater than the strike price. If the call option were exercised immediately, there would be a positive payoff of $5 = $55 − $50. Because the option has a positive payoff if it is exercised immediately, this option is known as an in-the-money option.

EXAMPLE 15.6	Out-of-the-Money Call Option

IBM stock is currently $55 per share. Let's look at a call option to buy IBM stock at $60 ($60 is the strike price). Because the stock price is less than the strike price, immediate exercise would not benefit the option holder. Because option exercise would not yield a positive payoff, this option is called an out-of-the-money option.

EXAMPLE 15.7	Intrinsic Value for Calls

Suppose a call option exists with 20 days to expiration. It is selling for $1.65. The underlying stock price is $41.15. Calculate the intrinsic value and time value of: (1) a call with a strike price of 40, and (2) a call with a strike price of 45.

A call with a strike price of 40 has an intrinsic value of MAX($S − K$,0) = MAX($41.15 − $40,0) = $1.15. The time value of this call option equals the option price minus the intrinsic value, $1.65 − $1.15 = $.50.

A call with a strike price of 45 has an intrinsic value of MAX($S − K$,0) = MAX($41.15 − $45,0) = $0. The time value of this call option equals the option price minus the intrinsic value, $1.65 − $0 = $1.65.

EXAMPLE 15.8	In-the-Money Put Option

GE stock is selling at $33. Let's look at a put option to sell GE at a price of $40 per share ($40 is the strike price). Notice that the stock price is less than the strike price. If the put option were exercised immediately, it would yield a payoff of $7 = $40 − $33. Because the option has a positive payoff if exercised immediately, it is known as an in-the-money option.

EXAMPLE 15.9	Out-of-the-Money Put Option

GE stock is selling at $33. Let's look at a put option to sell GE at a price of $30 per share ($30 is the strike price). Because the stock price is greater than the strike price, immediate exercise would not benefit the option holder. Because option exercise would not yield a positive payoff, this option is called an out-of-the-money option.

EXAMPLE 15.10	Intrinsic Value for Puts

Suppose a put option exists with 15 days to expiration. It is selling for $5.70. The underlying asset price is $42.35. Calculate the intrinsic value and time value of: (1) a put with a strike price of 40, and (2) a put with a strike price of 45.

A put with a strike price of 40 has an intrinsic value of MAX($K − S$,0) = MAX($40 − $42.35,0) = $0. The time value of this put option equals the option price minus the intrinsic value, $5.70 − $0 = $5.70.

A put with a strike price of 45 has an intrinsic value of MAX($K − S$,0) = MAX($45 − $42.35,0) = $2.65. The time value of this put option equals the option price minus the intrinsic value, $5.70 − $2.65 = $3.05.

15.5a   All else equal, would an in-the-money option or an out-of-the-money option have a higher price? Why?

15.5b   Does an out-of-the-money option ever have value? Why?

15.5c   What is the intrinsic value of a call option? A put option?

15.5d   Suppose the stock price is $35. Is there a strike price for which a call option and a put option have the same intrinsic value?

15.6   Option Payoffs and Profits

Options are appealing because they offer investors a wide variety of investment strategies. In fact, there is essentially no limit to the number of different investment strategies available using options. However, fortunately for us, only a small number of basic strategies are available, and more complicated strategies are built from these. We discuss the payoffs from these basic strategies here and in the next section.

OPTION WRITING

Thus far, we have discussed options from the standpoint of the buyer only. However, options are contracts, and every contract must link at least two parties. The two parties to an option contract are the buyer and the seller. The seller of an option is called the "writer," and the act of selling an option is referred to as **option writing**.

By buying an option you buy the right, but not the obligation, to exercise the option before the option's expiration date. By selling or writing an option, you take the seller's side of the option contract. As a result, option writing involves receiving the option price and, in exchange, assuming the obligation to satisfy the buyer's exercise rights if the option is exercised.

For example, a **call writer** is obligated to sell stock at the option's strike price if the buyer decides to exercise the call option. Similarly, a **put writer** is obligated to buy stock at the option's strike price if the buyer decides to exercise the put option.

OPTION PAYOFFS

It is useful to think about option investment strategies in terms of their initial cash flows and terminal cash flows. The initial cash flow of an option is the price of the option, also called the option *premium*. To the option buyer, the option price (or premium) is a cash outflow. To the option writer, the option price (or premium) is a cash inflow. The terminal cash flow of an option is the option's payoff that could be realized from the exercise privilege. To the option buyer, a payoff entails a cash inflow. To the writer, a payoff entails a cash outflow.

For example, suppose the current price of IBM stock is $80 per share. You buy a call option on IBM with a strike price of $80. The premium is $4 per share. Thus, the initial cash flow is −$400 for you and +$400 for the option writer. What are the terminal cash flows for you and the option writer if IBM has a price of $90 when the option expires? What are the terminal cash flows if IBM has a price of $70 when the option expires?

If IBM is at $90, then you experience a cash inflow of $10 per share, whereas the writer experiences an outflow of $10 per share. If IBM is at $70, you both have a zero cash flow when the option expires because it is worthless. Notice that in both cases the buyer and the seller have the same cash flows, just with opposite signs. This shows that options are a "zero-sum game," meaning that any gains to the buyer must come at the expense of the seller and vice versa.

OPTION PAYOFF DIAGRAMS

When investors buy options, the price that they are willing to pay depends on their assessment of the likely payoffs (cash inflows) from the exercise privilege. Likewise, when investors write options, an acceptable selling price depends on their assessment of the likely payoffs (cash outflows) resulting from the buyers' exercise privilege. Given this,

option writing
Taking the seller's side of an option contract.

call writer
One who has the obligation to sell stock at the option's strike price if the option is exercised.

put writer
One who has the obligation to buy stock at the option's strike price if the option is exercised.

To learn more on options, see
www.numa.com
www.optionscentral.com
www.optionsxpress.com

FIGURE 15.3 Call Option Payoffs

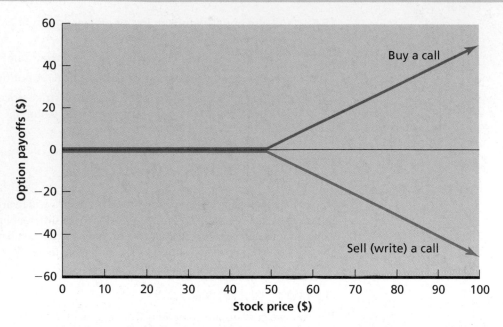

a general understanding of option payoffs is critical for understanding how option prices are determined.

A payoff diagram is a very useful graphical device for understanding option payoffs. The payoffs from buying a call option and the payoffs from selling (or writing) a call option are seen in the payoff diagram in Figure 15.3. The vertical axis of Figure 15.3 measures option payoffs, and the horizontal axis measures the possible stock prices on the option expiration date. These examples assume that the call option has a strike price of $50 and that the option will be exercised only on its expiration date.

In Figure 15.3, notice that the call option payoffs are zero for all stock prices below the $50 strike price. This is because the call option holder will not exercise the option to buy stock at the $50 strike price when the stock is available in the stock market at a lower price. In this case, the option expires worthless.

In contrast, if the stock price is higher than the $50 strike price, the call option payoff is equal to the difference between the market price of the stock and the strike price of the option. For example, if the stock price is $60, the call option payoff is equal to $10, which is the difference between the $60 stock price and the $50 strike price. This payoff is a cash inflow to the buyer, because the option buyer can buy the stock at the $50 strike price and sell the stock at the $60 market price. However, this payoff is a cash outflow to the writer, because the option writer must sell the stock at the $50 strike price when the stock's market price is $60.

Putting it all together, the distinctive "hockey-stick" shape of the call option payoffs shows that the payoff is zero if the stock price is below the strike price. Above the strike price, however, the buyer of the call option gains $1 for every $1 increase in the stock price. Of course, as shown, the call option writer loses $1 for every $1 increase in the stock price above the strike price.

Figure 15.4 is an example of a payoff diagram illustrating the payoffs from buying a put option and from selling (or writing) a put option. As with our call option payoffs, the vertical axis measures option payoffs, and the horizontal axis measures the possible stock prices on the option expiration date. Once again, these examples assume that the put has a strike price of $50, and that the option will be exercised only on its expiration date.

In Figure 15.4, the put option payoffs are zero for all stock prices above the $50 strike price. This is because a put option holder will not exercise the option to sell stock at the $50 strike price when the stock can be sold in the stock market at a higher price. In this case, the option expires worthless.

In contrast, if the stock price is lower than the $50 strike price, the put option payoff is equal to the difference between the market price of the stock and the strike price of the

FIGURE 15.4   Put Option Payoffs

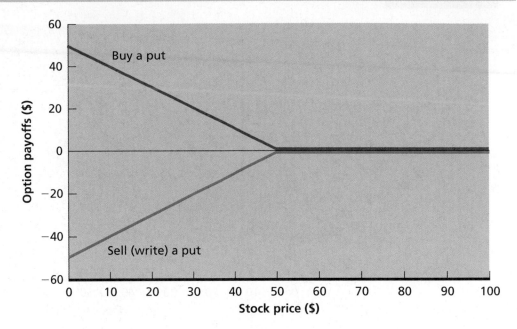

option. For example, if the stock price is $40, the put option payoff is equal to $10, which is the difference between the $40 stock price and the $50 strike price. This payoff is a cash inflow to the buyer, because the option buyer can buy the stock at the $40 market price and sell the stock at the $50 strike price. However, this payoff is a cash outflow to the writer, because the option writer must buy the stock at the $50 strike price when the stock's market price is $40.

Our payoff diagrams illustrate an important difference between the maximum possible gains and losses for puts and calls. Notice that if you buy a call option, there is no upper limit to your potential profit because there is no upper limit to the stock price. However, with a put option, the most you can make is the strike price. In other words, the best thing that can happen to you if you buy a put is for the stock price to go to zero. Of course, whether you buy a put or a call, your potential loss is limited to the option premium you pay.

Similarly, as shown in Figure 15.3, if you write a call, there is no limit to your possible loss, but your potential gain is limited to the option premium you receive. As shown in Figure 15.4, if you write a put, both your gain and loss are limited, although the potential loss could be substantial.

OPTION PROFIT DIAGRAMS

For even more on options, see
www.investorlinks.com

Between them, Figures 15.3 and 15.4 tell us essentially everything we need to know about the payoffs from the four basic strategies involving options, buying and writing puts and calls. However, these figures give the payoffs at expiration only and so do not consider the original cash inflow or outflow. Option profit diagrams are an extension of payoff diagrams that do take into account the initial cash flow.

As we have seen, the profit from an option strategy is the difference between the option's terminal cash flow (the option payoff) and the option's initial cash flow (the option price, or premium). An option profit diagram simply adjusts option payoffs for the original price of the option. This means that the option premium is subtracted from the payoffs from buying options and added to payoffs from writing options.

To illustrate, Figures 15.5 and 15.6 are profit diagrams corresponding to the four basic investment strategies for options. In each diagram, the vertical axis measures option profits, and the horizontal axis measures possible stock prices. Each profit diagram assumes that the option's strike price is $50 and that the put and call option prices are both $10. Notice that in each case the characteristic hockey-stick shape is maintained; the "stick" is just shifted up or down.

FIGURE 15.5 Call Option Profits

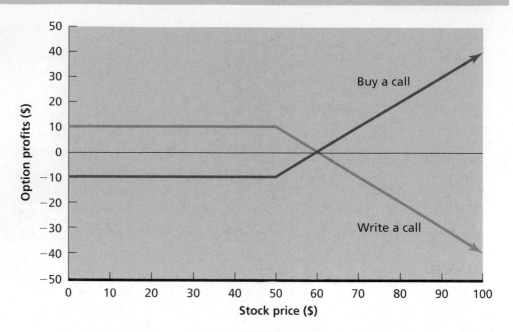

FIGURE 15.6 Put Option Profits

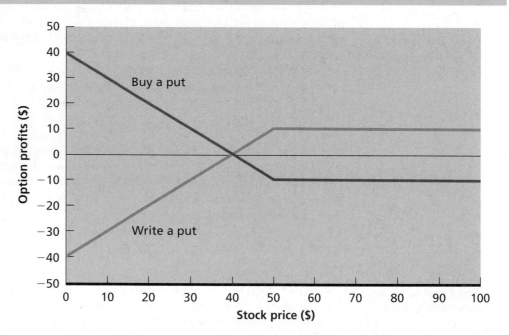

CHECK THIS

15.6a What is option writing?

15.6b What are the payoffs and profits from writing call options?

15.6c What are the payoffs and profits from writing put options?

15.6d Explain how a payoff diagram that shows option value at expiration can be thought of as a diagram that shows the intrinsic value of the option at expiration.

15.7 Using Options to Manage Risk

Thus far, we have considered the payoffs and profits from buying and writing individual calls and puts. In this section, we consider what happens when we start to combine puts, calls, and shares of stock. We could examine any of numerous combinations, but we will stick to just a few of the most basic and important strategies. Note that in the following discussion, the diagrams represent pretax outcomes.

THE PROTECTIVE PUT STRATEGY

Suppose you own a share of Emerson Electric Co. (EMR) stock, currently worth $45. Suppose you also purchase a put option with a strike price of $45 for $2. What is the net effect of this purchase?

To answer, we can compare what happens if Emerson stock stays at or above $45 to what happens if it drops below $45. If Emerson stock stays at or above $45, your put will expire worthless, because you would choose not to exercise it. You would lose the $2 you paid for the put option. However, if Emerson stock falls below $45, you would exercise your put, and the put writer would pay you $45 for your stock. No matter how far below $45 the price falls, you have guaranteed that you will receive $45 for your Emerson share of stock.

Thus, by purchasing a put option, you have protected yourself against a price decline. In the jargon of Wall Street, you have paid $2 to eliminate the "downside risk." For this reason, the strategy of buying a put option on a stock you already own is called a **protective put** strategy. Figure 15.7 shows the net effect of the protective put strategy. Notice that the net effect resembles the profit diagram of a long call. That is, when an investor, who owns stock, buys a put, the profit diagram of this new portfolio resembles the profit diagram of a long call.

The protective put strategy reduces the overall risk faced by an investor, so it is a conservative strategy. This fact is a good example of how options, or any derivative asset, can be used to decrease risk rather than increase it. Stated differently, options can be used to hedge as well as speculate, so they do not inherently increase risk.

protective put
Strategy of buying a put option on a stock already owned. This strategy protects against a decline in value.

CREDIT DEFAULT SWAPS

If you own a car, you surely have car insurance. Insurance is effectively a put option. You pay a premium to the insurance company. If you get into an accident (we hope not), then you have the right to "put" your car to the insurance company in exchange for a cash payout. This situation is not unique to cars or stocks—investors have the ability to buy "insurance" on many assets.

FIGURE 15.7 Protective Put on a Share of Emerson Stock

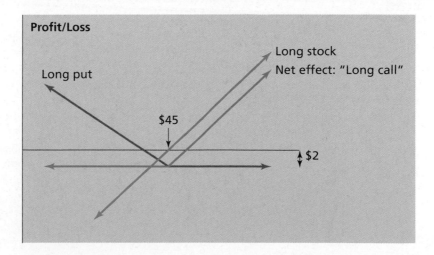

One type of put option that received quite a bit of attention during the 2008 financial crisis was credit default swaps (CDS). A CDS is essentially a put option on a fixed-income asset (i.e., a bond). For example, consider an investor that buys a bond of a distressed company. To hedge the risk of default, the investor might be able to purchase a CDS on the bond. If the bond issuer defaults, then the holder of a CDS is compensated according to the terms of the CDS contract.

While the example we provided is for a single bond, most CDS contracts are sold on baskets of fixed-income securities known as collateralized debt obligations, or CDOs. We discuss these in detail in a later chapter. But no matter how complex the underlying security, the CDS works pretty much the same: The CDS acts like a protective put option.

So, why were CDS contracts so important in the 2008 financial crisis? Well, two factors played key roles. First, at the height of the crisis, analysts estimated that about $55 *trillion* in securities were being hedged using credit default swaps. To put this dollar amount into perspective, at the same time the estimated net wealth of all U.S. citizens was $56 trillion. This comparison illustrates the importance of CDS contracts to the financial markets.

Second, historically most CDS contracts have not been traded on an exchange. Rather, these specialized contracts are bought and sold directly between buyers and sellers. This type of trading means that counterparty risk is prevalent. In fact, you might recall the fall of two investment banking stalwarts, Bear Stearns and Lehman Brothers, and the insurance giant AIG. These firms were active players in the CDS market, and each firm was undercapitalized relative to its position. As with any type of leverage, positions work well when asset prices move in the "right" direction. Disastrous ruin can occur, however, when prices move in the "wrong" direction. Such is the hard lesson about leverage learned time and again.

Because CDS contracts act like insurance contracts, the costs of the contracts can tell us something about the risk of default for the underlying firm. In fact, many investors pay great attention to CDS spreads, which are discussed in the nearby *Investment Updates* box.

THE PROTECTIVE PUT STRATEGY AND CORPORATE RISK MANAGEMENT

Suppose you own and operate a gold mine. Your revenue stream is risky because it will change as world gold prices change. However, your costs, which mostly consist of moving around tons of dirt and boulders, do not change as world gold prices change. Therefore, your profits change as world gold prices change.

This "underlying risk exposure" is the blue line in Figure 15.8. Suppose you decide to protect your operation from the possibility of low gold prices with the purchase of a put option. The put option profit is the red line in Figure 15.8. Your "net exposure" is the green line in Figure 15.8.

To construct your net exposure, you simply combine the blue line and the red line. Once you do, you see that to the left of the vertical axis, the result is that if gold prices fall, the

| FIGURE 15.8 | Using Puts to Manage Risk |

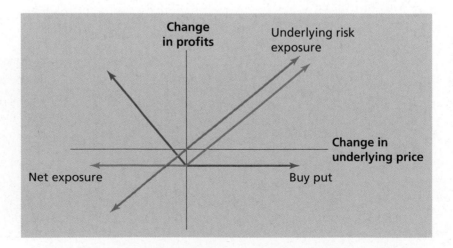

AIG: CDS MARKET STILL SHOWS SKEPTICISM

The market seems somewhat more skeptical about the health of AIG versus some of the other recipients of assistance from the Treasury Department under the TARP program. At least that's what this chart from today's TARP oversight report suggests.

The chart shows five-year CDS spreads for Citigroup, Bank of America, AIG and Morgan Stanley. CDS, or credit default swaps, are a type of derivative that insures against a company defaulting on its debt.

The spread—that is, the difference between the price of a CDS contract and the price of a Treasury with a similar maturity—can reflect market perception of a bank's health. The TARP panel explains the signaling mechanism succinctly: "If a bank's bondholders are worried about the bank defaulting on its debt, they can buy default protection through a credit default swap to hedge their bets. Therefore, the less healthy a bank is perceived to be, the more expensive a CDS contract against that bank will be."

As you can see from the chart, the prices on CDS for these institutions rocketed higher during the peak of the financial crisis in September 2008, a clear sign of the panic out in the market. Since then, Morgan Stanley, Bank of America and Citigroup have fallen back into a range roughly in line with where they were before the crisis struck. AIG, on the other hand, remains persistently elevated, signaling that the market remains skeptical on the outlook for the troubled, government-controlled insurance giant.

Interestingly, the TARP panel threw this tidbit into their analysis of exactly why the CDS spreads have contracted for the institutions that were bailed out by the government. "It is unclear the extent to which this decline in CDS spreads is due to confidence in major banks' stand-alone creditworthiness and to what degree this decline reflects CDS market confidence in implicit government guarantees of large banks."

The too-big-to-fail issue is alive and well. And it likely will be for a while. Even so, the government's deep involvement with AIG doesn't seem to be burnishing the insurance giant's reputation in the eyes of the market.

Source: Matt Phillips, *The Wall Street Journal*, December 9, 2009. Reprinted with permission of *The Wall Street Journal*. © 2009 Dow Jones & Company, Inc. All Rights Reserved Worldwide.

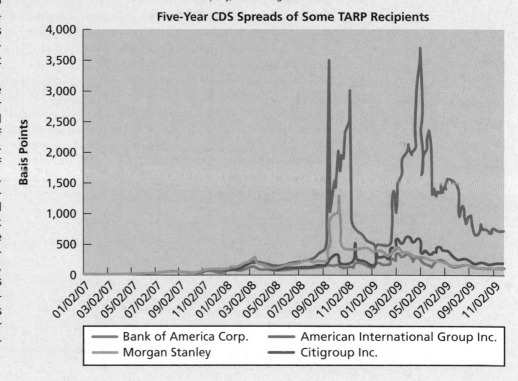

Five-Year CDS Spreads of Some TARP Recipients

Legend: Bank of America Corp. — American International Group Inc. — Morgan Stanley — Citigroup Inc.

decrease in profits reflects only the cost of purchasing the put option; decreases in the price of gold will not adversely affect your profits.

To the right of the vertical axis, if gold prices increase, your profits will increase too. However, they will be smaller than if you had not purchased the put option.

USING CALL OPTIONS IN CORPORATE RISK MANAGEMENT

Suppose you own and operate an airline that uses jet aircraft. Assume that you and your employees are skilled at competitively pricing seats on your flights. This skill results in a relatively stable revenue stream. Your operating costs, however, will vary with world prices for jet fuel because, after labor, jet fuel is the second largest operating expense for an airline.

FIGURE 15.9   Using Calls to Manage Risk

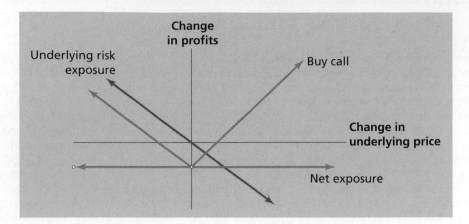

The competitive nature of the airline industry means that you cannot easily pass higher fuel prices on to passengers by raising fares. Changes in jet fuel prices thus could affect your profits. Fortunately, you can protect your profits using call options.

The red line in Figure 15.9 represents your underlying exposure to increases in jet fuel prices. Suppose you decide to protect your profits from the possibility of high jet fuel prices with the purchase of a call option. The call option profit is the blue line in Figure 15.9. Your net exposure is the green line in Figure 15.9.

To construct your net exposure, you simply combine the blue line and the red line. Once you do, you see that to the left of the vertical axis, the result is that if jet fuel prices fall, your profits will increase. However, because you purchased call options, your profits will decrease by the amount of the cost of purchasing the call options. Decreases in the price of jet fuel thus will increase your profits.

To the right of the vertical axis, if the price of jet fuel increases, the decrease in your profits reflects only the cost of purchasing the call option. That is, the increase in jet fuel prices will not adversely affect your profits.

CHECK THIS

15.7a	What is a protective put strategy, and how does it work?
15.7b	What is a credit default swap?
15.7c	Explain how a company can use options today to protect itself from higher future input prices.

15.8 Option Trading Strategies

For ideas on option trading strategies, see www.commodityworld.com

In this section, we present three types of option trading strategies. In the first type, traders add an option position to their stock position. Strategies in this category help traders modify their stock risk. The second type of option trading strategy is called a spread. A spread strategy involves taking a position on two or more options of the same type at the same time. By same type, we mean call options only or put options only. The third type of option trading strategy is called a combination. In a combination, the trader takes a position in a mixture of call and put options. Note that the effects of these strategies are pretax effects. Nonetheless, learning about these pretax effects is important for option traders.

THE COVERED CALL STRATEGY

Suppose you own a share of Emerson Electric Co. (EMR) stock, which is currently worth $45. Now, instead of buying a put, consider selling a call option for, say, $3, with an exercise price of $45. What is the net effect of this strategy?

FIGURE 15.10 Covered Call Option on Emerson Stock

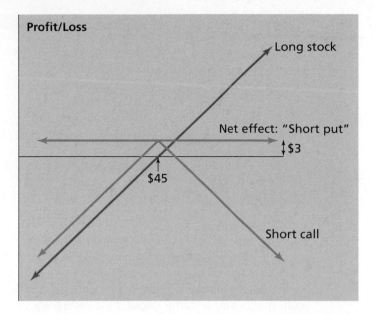

Profit/Loss

Long stock

Net effect: "Short put"

$3

$45

Short call

WWW

For more on covered calls, see
www.writecall.com

To answer, we can compare what happens if Emerson stock stays below $45 (the exercise price on the option you sold) to what happens if Emerson's stock price rises above $45. If Emerson stock stays below $45, the option will expire worthless, and you pocket the $3 premium you received from selling the call option. If Emerson stock rises above $45, the call option holder will exercise the call option against you, and you must deliver the Emerson stock in exchange for $45.

Thus, when you sell a call option on stock you already own, you keep the option premium no matter what. The worst thing that can happen to you is that you will have to sell your stock at the exercise price. Because you already own the stock, you are said to be "covered," and this is why the strategy is known as the **covered call** strategy.

Let's examine your covered call strategy further. Emerson stock is currently selling for $45. Because the strike price on the call option is $45, the net effect of this strategy is to give up the possibility of profits on the stock in exchange for the certain option premium of $3. Figure 15.10 shows the covered call option position on Emerson stock. Notice that the net effect resembles the profit diagram of a short put. That is, when an investor, who owns stock, sells a call, the profit diagram of this new portfolio resembles the profit diagram of a short put.

In the jargon of Wall Street, a covered call exchanges uncertain future "upside" potential for certain cash today, thereby reducing risk and potential reward. In contrast, a strategy of selling call options on stock you do not own is known as a "naked" call strategy and, as we saw earlier, has unlimited potential losses. Thus, selling call options is either highly risky or else acts to reduce risk, depending on whether you are covered or naked. This distinction is important to understand.

covered call
Strategy of selling a call option on stock already owned.

SPREADS

A **spread** strategy involves taking a position on two or more options of the same type. By same type, we mean call options only or put options only.

Three examples of spreads are:

spread
An option trading strategy involving two or more call options or two or more put options.

- *Bull call spreads.* This spread is formed by buying a call and also selling a call with a higher strike price. This spread is known as a "bull" spread because traders make a profit from this strategy if the underlying stock price increases in value.

- *Bear call spreads.* This spread is formed by buying a call and also selling a call with a lower strike price. This spread is known as a "bear" spread because traders make a profit from this strategy if the underlying stock price decreases in value.

FIGURE 15.11 Long Straddle Using a Long Call and a Long Put

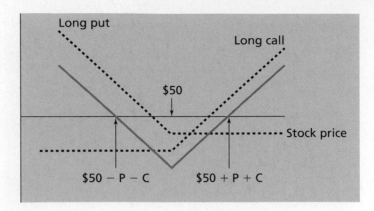

- *Butterfly spreads.* Using call options with equally spaced strikes, a "long" butterfly spread is formed by three option positions. To create a long butterfly spread, the trader buys one call option with the lowest strike price and buys one call option with the highest strike price while also selling two options with the middle strike. Traders profit from a long butterfly spread if the underlying stock price hovers around the strike price of the middle options.

There are many more examples of option spreads. For example, traders can form bull put spreads, bear put spreads, and short butterfly spreads. Traders can also form butterfly spreads using put options. These are just a few of the vast number of option spread strategies. You can learn more about these trading strategies in a derivatives course or online. For starters, see the terrific set of tutorials at www.cboe.com/LearnCenter.

COMBINATIONS

combination

An option trading strategy involving two or more call and put options.

For more information on trading options, see
www.optionetics.com
www.ino.com

In a **combination,** the trader takes a position in a mixture of call and put options. Perhaps the best known combination is called a *straddle.* Here is how a straddle works. Suppose a share of stock is currently selling at $50. You think the price is going to make a major move, but you are uncertain about the direction. What could you do? One answer is buy a call and buy a put, both with a $50 exercise price. That way, if the stock goes up sharply, your call will pay off; if it goes down sharply, your put will pay off. This combination is an example of a long straddle.

This strategy is called a straddle because you have, in effect, "straddled" the current $50 stock price. It is a long straddle because you bought both options. Figure 15.11 shows the profit from a long straddle. Note that the stock must make a major move for the trader to profit from this strategy. In fact, the stock price must either climb to a price equal to the option strike price plus the cost of both options, or it must fall to a price equal to the option strike price minus the cost of both options.

If you thought the stock price was not going to make a major move in either direction, you might sell a put and a call, thereby generating income today. This combination is an example of a short straddle. In this case, your income would be maximized if the stock price at option expiration equals the option strike price, $50 in this example. If the stock price is $50 at option expiration, both options would expire worthless.

There are many other combination strategies, with colorful names such as strips, straps, strangles, collars, and box "spreads" (which, for no known reason, are called spreads but are really combinations).

EXAMPLE 15.11 Another Option Strategy

You own a share of stock worth $80. Suppose you sell a call option with a strike price of $80 and also buy a put with a strike of $80. What is the net effect of these transactions on the risk of owning the stock?

(continued)

Notice that what you have done is combine a protective put and a covered call strategy. To see the effect of doing this, suppose that, at option expiration, the stock is selling for more than $80. In this case, the put is worthless. The call will be exercised against you, and you will receive $80 for your stock. If the stock is selling for less than $80, the call is worthless. You would exercise your put and sell the stock for $80. In other words, the net effect is that you have guaranteed that you will exchange the stock for $80 no matter what happens, so you have created a riskless asset.

Although option trading strategies are captivating, we really should move on. Up to now, we have mostly focused our attention on what options are worth when they expire. In our closing sections, we will put down the foundation we need to calculate option prices before expiration.

CHECK THIS

15.8a   What is the difference between option spreads and option combinations?

15.8b   What is a short straddle? When might it be appropriate?

15.9 Arbitrage and Option Pricing Bounds

The "hockey-stick" diagrams that show option payoffs can help you learn an extremely important concept, intrinsic value. The payoff diagrams, however, show what happens only at option expiration. Investors are also quite interested in option prices before expiration.

In our next chapter, we will calculate option prices before expiration. In this section and the next one, we will explore how arbitrage forces set some price limits on option prices before expiration. An arbitrage is a trading opportunity that (1) requires no net investment on your part, (2) has no possibility of loss, and (3) has at least the potential for a gain.

In general, option price limits depend on (1) whether the option in question is American or European and (2) whether a dividend is paid between today and the option expiration day. Dividends make discussing option price limits much more complicated. Therefore, in this section, we assume that the stock pays no dividends over the life of the option.

THE UPPER BOUND FOR CALL OPTION PRICES

What is the most a call option could sell for before expiration? Suppose we have a call option on a share of stock. The current stock price is $60 and the stock pays no dividends. Without more information, we cannot say a lot about the price of the call option, but we do know one thing: The price of the option must be less than $60. How do we know this?

If you think about it, the right to buy a share of stock cannot be worth more than the share itself. To illustrate, suppose the call option was actually selling for $65 when the stock was selling at $60. What would you do?

What you would do is get very rich, very fast. You would sell call options at $65 and buy stock at $60. You pocket the $5 difference. The worst thing that can happen to you is that the options are exercised, and you receive the exercise price. In this case, it is theoretically possible for you to make an unlimited amount of money at no risk. This trading strategy will work for options with either American- or European-style exercise.

This situation is an example of a true arbitrage opportunity. Unfortunately, such simple money machines don't exist very often (if at all) in the real world, so we know that a call option can't sell for more than the underlying stock.

THE UPPER BOUND FOR PUT OPTION PRICES

At expiration, we know that the value of a put option equals its intrinsic value. If the stock price is zero, then the intrinsic value is equal to the strike price of the put option. Therefore, at expiration, the most a put option can sell for is the strike price. What is the most that a put option can sell for before expiration? The answer is the present value of the strike price.

To begin to see this bound, suppose we have a put option with an exercise price of $50 and the put option price is $60. This situation is an arbitrage opportunity. What would you do? You would simply sell puts for $60 and deposit the proceeds in the bank. The worst thing that could happen to you at expiration is that you would have to buy the stock for $50 a share. However, you would also have $10 per share in cash (the difference between the $60 you received and the $50 you paid for the stock), and the interest on the proceeds.

Now suppose we have a put option with an exercise price of $50 and the put option price is also $50. This situation is also an arbitrage opportunity. You would sell puts for $50 and deposit the proceeds in the bank. Again, the worst thing that could happen to you at expiration is that you would have to buy the stock for $50 a share. However, you keep the interest on the proceeds from the sale of the put.

So, the upper bound on a European put's price is less than the strike price. How much less? The answer depends on the going interest rate on risk-free investments. We will have an arbitrage if the price of the put, plus the interest you could earn over the life of the option, is greater than the stock price. For example, suppose the risk-free rate is 3 percent per quarter. We have a put option selling for $49 with an exercise price of $50 and 90 days to maturity. Is there an arbitrage opportunity?

Yes, there is. You would sell the put and invest the $49 for 90 days at 3 percent to get $49 × 1.03 = $50.47. You will make at least $.47 guaranteed. At this point, you probably see where this is going. What is the maximum put value that does not result in an arbitrage opportunity? This value is:

$$\text{Maximum put price} \times (1.03) = \$50$$

$$\text{Maximum put price} = \$50/1.03 = \$48.54$$

Notice that our answer, $48.54, is the present value of the strike price computed at the risk-free rate. This result is the general answer: The maximum price for a European put option is the present value of the strike price computed at the risk-free rate.

The most put options with American-style exercise can sell for before expiration is the strike price. If an American put option had a price higher than the strike price, traders would sell these puts and invest the proceeds. The worst that could happen is that the stock price falls to zero and the holder of the American put exercises the put. The American put seller must buy the stock at the strike price—which is lower than the price of the put. The trader keeps the difference between the put price and the strike price, plus any interest earned before the put buyer exercised the put.

THE LOWER BOUNDS FOR CALL AND PUT OPTION PRICES

What is the lowest price possible for call and put options? Can an option have a negative value? A negative value means that holders would pay someone to take the option off their hands. However, option holders can simply let the option expire, so there would be no need to pay someone to haul away options. So, we conclude that options cannot have a negative value. This conclusion is true for European- and American-style options.

AMERICAN CALLS We can set a "higher" lower bound by answering this question: Is it possible for an American call option to sell for less than its intrinsic value? The answer is no. We know that sometimes the intrinsic value of an option is zero, and that the value of an option cannot be less than zero, but it can be zero. However, what about the cases in which the intrinsic value of an option is greater than zero? Why does the option have to sell for at least as much as its intrinsic value?

To see this result, suppose a current stock price is $S = \$60$, and a call option with a strike price of $K = \$50$ has a price of $C = \$5$. Clearly, this call option is in the money, and the $5 call price is less than the intrinsic value of $S - K = \$10$.

If you are presented with these actual stock and option prices, you have an arbitrage opportunity. That is, you have a way to obtain a riskless profit by following a simple three-step strategy.

First, buy the call option at its price of $C = \$5$. Second, immediately exercise the call option and buy the stock from the call writer at the strike price of $K = \$50$. At this point, you have acquired the stock for $55, which is the sum of the call price plus the strike price.

As a third and final step, simply sell the stock at the current market price of $S = \$60$. Because you acquired the stock for $55 and sold the stock for $60, you have earned an arbitrage profit of $5. Clearly, if such an opportunity continued to exist, you would repeat these three steps over and over until you became bored with making easy money. But realistically, such easy arbitrage opportunities do not exist, and it therefore follows that a American call option price is never less than its intrinsic value (even when dividends are paid). That is:

$$\text{American call option price} \geq \text{MAX}[S - K, 0] \qquad (15.3)$$

AMERICAN PUTS A similar arbitrage argument applies to American put options. For example, suppose a current stock price is $S = \$40$, and a put option with a strike price of $K = \$50$ has a price of $P = \$5$. This $5 put price is less than the option's intrinsic value of $K - S = \$10$. To exploit this profit opportunity, you first buy the put option at its price of $P = \$5$, and then buy the stock at its current price of $S = \$40$. At this point, you have acquired the stock for $45, which is the sum of the put price plus the stock price.

Now you immediately exercise the put option, thereby selling the stock to the option writer at the strike price of $S = \$50$. Because you acquired the stock for $45 and sold the stock for $50, you have earned an arbitrage profit of $5. Again, you would not realistically expect such an easy arbitrage opportunity to exist. Therefore, we conclude that the price of an American put option price is never less than its intrinsic value:

$$\text{American put option price} \geq \text{MAX}[K - S, 0] \qquad (15.4)$$

EUROPEAN CALLS Because European options cannot be exercised before expiration, we cannot use the arbitrage strategies that we used to set lower bounds for American options. We must use a different approach (which can be found in many textbooks that focus on options). It turns out that the lower bound for a European call option is greater than its intrinsic value.

$$\text{European call option price} \geq \text{MAX}[S - K/(1 + r)^T, 0] \qquad (15.5)$$

EUROPEAN PUTS The lower bound for a European put option price is less than its intrinsic value. In fact, in-the-money European puts will frequently sell for less than their intrinsic value. How much less? Using an arbitrage strategy that accounts for the fact that European put options cannot be exercised before expiration, the lower bound for a European put option is:

$$\text{European put option price} \geq \text{MAX}[K/(1 + r)^T - S, 0] \qquad (15.6)$$

To give you some intuition, let's look at an extreme case. Suppose the stock price falls to zero before expiration and there is absolutely no chance that the stock price will recover before expiration. American put holders would immediately exercise their puts because it is impossible for the puts to get further into the money. European put holders also would like to exercise their puts immediately for the same reason. However, they cannot. In this example, you can see that European put holders have a riskless asset that will be worth $K at expiration. Therefore, it is worth the present value of $K. Looking at equation (15.6), you can see that the lower bound increases as the option get closer to expiration.

A STRONGER BOUND When no dividends are paid, equation (15.5) also becomes the lower bound for American call option prices. Equation (15.5) is a "stronger" lower bound than equation (15.3). To illustrate why equation (15.5) is stronger, consider an example where $S = \$44$, $K = \$40$, $r = 10$ percent, and $T = 1$ year. Equation (15.5) says that for an American (or European) call option on a non-dividend-paying stock: $C \geq S - K/(1 + r)^T$, i.e., $C \geq \$44 - \$40/(1.1) = \$7.64$. Equation (15.3), however, says that, for American (not European) calls: $C \geq S - K$, or $C \geq \$44 - \$40 = \$4$. So, equation (15.5) is a stronger (i.e., higher) lower bound than equation (15.3). That is, stating that the American call price must exceed $7.64 is stronger than saying the American call price must exceed $4.

CHECK THIS

15.9a What is the most a European call option could be worth? How about an American call option?

15.9b What is the most a European put option could be worth? How about an American put option?

15.10 Put-Call Parity

Suppose an investor has a long stock position. Then, this investor decides to buy a protective put and sell a covered call at the same time. What happens in this case? That is, what kind of portfolio has this investor formed (assume both options have European-style exercise)? We will be creative and name the set of positions in these three risky assets "Portfolio A."

Table 15.2 presents the value of each position in Portfolio A when the options expire. For the put and the call, we calculate the intrinsic value of the option, and then determine whether the investor receives or pays the intrinsic value.

For example, if the expiration date stock price is less than the strike price, that is, if $S_T < K$, then the call option expires worthless and the put option has an intrinsic value of $K - S_T$. Because you bought the put option, you receive the intrinsic value.

If the stock price on option expiration day exactly equals the strike price, both the call and the put expire worthless. However, if the expiration day stock price is greater than the strike price, that is, $S_T > K$, the put option expires worthless and the call option intrinsic value is $S_T - K$. Because you sold the call, however, you must pay the call option holder the intrinsic value. So, to you, the value of the call option is $-(S_T - K)$.

In Table 15.2, notice that whether the expiration date stock price is less than, equal to, or greater than the strike price, the payoff to Portfolio A is always equal to the strike price, K. This means that this portfolio, which contains three risky assets, has a risk-free payoff at option expiration.

Because Portfolio A is risk-free, the cost of acquiring Portfolio A today should be equal to the cost of acquiring any other risk-free investment that will be worth K in one year. One such risk-free investment is a U.S. Treasury bill. The discounted amount, $K/(1 + r_f)^T$, is the cost of a U.S. Treasury bill paying K dollars at option expiration.[2]

We now use the fundamental principle of finance that states that two investments with the same risk and the same payoff on the same future date must have the same price today. If this fundamental principle were not true, then investors could create unlimited amounts of risk-free profits.

From Table 15.2, we see that Portfolio A and Portfolio B have the same payoff, K, at the option expiration date. The cost today of acquiring Portfolio A is $S + P - C$. The cost today of acquiring Portfolio B is $K/(1 + r_f)^T$. Setting these costs equal to one another yields this equation:

$$S + P - C = K/(1 + r_f)^T \qquad (15.7)$$

Equation (15.7) says something important about the relationship among the stock price, a put option, a call option, and a riskless asset. If we have any three prices, we can figure out

TABLE 15.2	Two Portfolios with the Same Value at Option Expiration				
			Value at Option Expiration in One Year If:		
Portfolio A	(cost today is)		$S_T < K$	$S_T = K$	$S_T > K$
Long stock	S		S_T	S_T	S_T
Long put	P		$K - S_T$	0	0
Short call	$-C$		0	0	$-(S_T - K)$
Total	$S + P - C$		K	K	K
Portfolio B	(cost today is)				
Long T-bill	$K/(1 + r_f)^T$		K	K	K

---

[2] In this discounted amount, r_f is the risk-free interest rate for one year, and T represents the time to maturity. In this case, the time to maturity is one year, so $T = 1$. If the time to maturity is, say, six months, then $T = \frac{1}{2}$. In other words, in the discounted amount, $K/(1 + r_f)^T$, the risk-free rate, r_f, is entered as an annual rate, and the time to maturity, T, is entered in years (or a fraction of a year).

EXAMPLE 15.12

Option Alchemy

Miss Molly, your eccentric (and very wealthy) aunt, wants you to explain something to her. Recently, at the Stable Club, she heard something fantastic. Her friend Rita said that there is a very interesting way to combine shares, puts, calls, and T-bills. Rita claims that having a share of stock and a put is the same as having a call and a T-bill. Miss Molly cannot believe it. Using the following information for Blue Northern Enterprises, show her that Rita is correct.

Stock price	$110
Put price	$5
Call price	$15
Strike price for both options	$105
Options expire in	1 year
One-year interest rate	5%

For $115, an investor can buy one share of stock and one put.[3] An investor can also take this $115, buy one call for $15, and invest $100. What happens in one year? We know the investment will grow to $105 in one year ($100 × 1.05 = $105). We know the options will be worth their intrinsic value in one year. However, we do not know what the stock price per share will be in one year. Therefore, we have listed some possible values below.

Gains and Losses from Investing $115 in Two Ways

First Way: Stock and Put

Stock Price in One Year	Value of Put Option ($K = \$105$)	Combined Value	Gain or Loss (from $115)
$125	$ 0	$125	$10
120	0	120	5
115	0	115	0
110	0	110	−5
105	0	105	−10
100	5	105	−10
95	10	105	−10
90	25	105	−10

Second Way: Call and T-Bill

Stock Price in One Year	Value of Call Option ($K = \$105$)	Value of T-bill	Combined Value	Gain or Loss (from $115)
$125	$20	$105	$125	$10
120	15	105	120	5
115	10	105	115	0
110	5	105	110	−5
105	0	105	105	−10
100	0	105	105	−10
95	0	105	105	−10
90	0	105	105	−10

(continued)

---

[3] This example uses prices per share. You know that exchange-traded option contracts are on 100 shares. An investor would have to buy 100 shares for $11,000 and one put for 100 × $5 = $500. This total outlay is $11,500 (or $115 per share).

What happens? We see that in both ways, you will have the same gain or loss for each stock price. That is, in one year, the combined value of a stock and a put is the same as the combined value of a call and a T-bill.

Therefore, the value today of a share of stock and a put is the same as today's value of a call and a T-bill (with a price equal to the strike price). It looks like Rita is correct.

put-call parity

The no-arbitrage relationship between put and call prices for European-style options with the same strike price and expiration date.

the price of the fourth. Also, note that we have three assets on one side of equation (15.7) and one on the other. By reading the signs of the terms in equation (15.7), we know what position to take in the three assets that have the same payoff as the fourth asset.

Rearranging equation (15.7) just a bit yields the **put-call parity** relationship, which is generally written as:

$$C - P = S - K/(1 + r_f)^T \qquad (15.8)$$

Put-call parity is the most basic relationship between two European option prices. Put-call parity states that the difference between a call option price and a put option price for options with the same strike price and expiration date is equal to the difference between the underlying stock price and the discounted strike price.

PUT-CALL PARITY WITH DIVIDENDS

The put-call parity argument stated above assumes that the underlying stock paid no dividends before option expiration. But what happens if the stock does pay a dividend before option expiration? To begin, we will rewrite the put-call parity relationship as:

$$S = C - P + K/(1 + r_f)^T \qquad (15.9)$$

Equation (15.9) says that holding a long stock position has the same payoff at option expiration as the portfolio consisting of long a call, short a put, and long a T-bill. However, will these payoffs be identical if the stock pays a dividend? The answer is no. The holder of the stock will receive a dividend at some time before option expiration. To get the same payoff, the holder of the portfolio needs an extra amount today. Because the dividend occurs at a later date, this extra amount is the *present value* of the dividend.

If the stock does pay a dividend before option expiration, then we adjust the put-call parity equation to:

$$C - P = S - \text{Div} - K/(1 + r_f)^T \qquad (15.10)$$

In equation (15.10), "Div" represents the present value of any dividend paid before option expiration.

EXAMPLE 15.13 | **Implied Put Option Prices**

A current stock price is $50, and a call option with a strike price of $55 maturing in two months has a price of $8. The stock will pay a $1 dividend in one month. If the interest rate is 6 percent, what is the price implied by put-call parity for a put option with a $50 strike price that matures in two months?

Rearranging the put-call parity equation yields the following price for a put option:

$$P = C - S + \text{Div} + K/(1 + r_f)^T$$
$$\$13.46 = \$8 - \$50 + \$1/(1.06)^{1/12} + \$55/(1.06)^{2/12}$$

WHAT CAN WE DO WITH PUT-CALL PARITY?

Put-call parity allows us to calculate the price of a call option before it expires. However, to calculate the call option price using put-call parity, you have to know the price of a put option with the same strike. No problem, you say. Put-call parity allows us to calculate the price of a put option. However, to calculate the put option price using put-call parity, you have to know the price of a call option with the same strike price. Uh-oh.

Do we abandon the notion of put-call parity? No. If you use an option pricing model to calculate a call option price, you can use put-call parity to calculate a put price. Option pricing models are the topic of the next chapter. As you can see in the following examples, put-call parity is also useful for arbitrageurs to align call and put option prices.

EXAMPLE 15.14

Identifying an Arbitrage Opportunity with Put-Call Parity

Suppose you observe the following market prices:

$$S = \$40$$
$$C = \$3$$
$$P = \$2$$

The strike price for the call and the put is $40. The riskless interest rate is 6 percent per year and the options expire in three months. The stock does not pay dividends. Is there an arbitrage opportunity?

To answer this question, use put-call parity (PCP) to calculate the "PCP-implied put price." Then compare this calculated price to the market price of puts. This difference, if any, is the potential arbitrage profit.

$$\text{PCP-implied put price} = C - S + K/(1 + r_f)^T$$
$$\$2.42 = \$3 - \$40 + \$40/(1.06)^{3/12}$$
$$\text{Potential arbitrage profit} = \text{PCP-implied put price} - \text{Market price of puts}$$
$$\$.42 = \$2.42 - \$2.00$$

EXAMPLE 15.15

Taking Advantage of an Arbitrage Opportunity

In Example 15.14, we calculated a $.42 potential arbitrage profit. How would an arbitrageur take advantage of this opportunity? How much profit will the arbitrageur make?

In Example 15.14, buying a call, selling stock, and investing the discounted strike has a value of $2.42. If an arbitrageur has these three positions, this portfolio is called a long "synthetic put." However, the arbitrageur can buy actual puts for $2.00. Arbitrageurs make money when they buy low and sell high. Therefore, the arbitrageur will buy a put for $2.00 and *sell* a synthetic put. That is, the investor will sell a call, buy stock, and borrow the difference. The arbitrageur can spend $2.00 to purchase an actual put and receive $2.42 for the sale of a synthetic put. This results in a potential profit of $.42. However, traders incur costs of trading. The realized pretax profit will be the potential profit minus trading costs.

CHECK THIS

15.10a Your friend Kristen claims that forming a portfolio today of long call, short put, and short stock has a value at option expiration equal to −K. Does it? (*Hint:* Create a table similar to Table 15.2.)

15.10b If a dividend payment occurs before option expiration, investors lower today's stock price to an "effective stock price." Why does this adjustment reduce call values and increase put values?

15.10c Exchange-traded options on individual stocks have American-style exercise. Therefore, put-call parity does not hold exactly for these options. Using option chain data from finance.yahoo.com or from the online version of *The Wall Street Journal*, compare the differences between selected call and put option prices with the differences between stock prices and discounted strike prices. You can find a short-term, riskless T-bill rate at www.reuters .com. How closely does put-call parity appear to hold for these equity options with American-style exercise?

15.11 Summary and Conclusions

In 1973, organized stock options trading began when the Chicago Board Options Exchange (CBOE) was established. Since then, options trading has grown enormously. In this chapter, we examined a number of concepts and issues surrounding stock options—which we have grouped by the chapter's important concepts.

1. **The basics of option contracts and how to obtain price quotes.**

   A. Options are contracts. Standardized stock options represent a contract size of 100 shares of common stock per option contract. We saw how standardized option prices are quoted online.

   B. Options on common stock are derivative securities because the value of a stock option is derived from the value of the underlying common stock. The two basic types of options are call options and put options. Holders of call options have the right, but not the obligation, to buy the underlying asset at the strike, or exercise, price. Holders of put options have the right, but not the obligation, to sell the underlying asset at the strike, or exercise, price.

   C. A stock index option is an option on a stock market index such as the S&P 500. All stock index options use a cash settlement procedure when they are exercised. With a cash settlement procedure, when a stock index option is exercised, the option writer pays a cash amount to the option buyer.

   D. The Options Clearing Corporation (OCC) is the clearing agency for all options exchanges in the United States. It guarantees that the terms of an option contract are fulfilled if the option is exercised.

2. **The difference between option payoffs and option profits.**

   A. The initial cash flow of an option is the price of the option, also called the option premium. To the option buyer, the option price (or premium) is a cash outflow. To the option writer, the option price (or premium) is a cash inflow. The terminal cash flow of an option is the option's payoff realized from the exercise privilege.

   B. At expiration, the value of the option is its intrinsic value. For call options, this value is the maximum of zero or the stock price minus the strike price. For put options, this value is the maximum of zero or the strike price minus the stock price.

   C. The profit from an option strategy is the difference between the option's terminal cash flow (the option payoff) and the option's initial cash flow (the option price, or premium). An option profit diagram simply adjusts option payoffs for the original price of the option. This means that the option premium is subtracted from the payoffs from buying options and added to payoffs from writing options. Note that these profits are pretax.

3. **The workings of some basic option trading strategies.**

   A. There are many option trading strategies. In one strategy type, traders add an option position to their stock position. Examples of this strategy include protective puts and covered calls.

   B. A spread is another type of option trading strategy. A spread strategy involves taking a position on two or more options of the same type at the same time. By same type, we mean call options only or put options only. A "butterfly" is a well-known example of a spread.

   C. A combination is the third type of option trading strategy. In a combination, the trader takes a position in a mixture of call and put options. A straddle is the best known combination.

   D. Option prices have boundaries enforced by arbitrage. A call option cannot sell for more than the underlying asset, and a put option cannot sell for more than the strike price on the option.

4. The logic behind the put-call parity condition.

A. Put-call parity is perhaps the most fundamental relationship between two option prices. Put-call parity states that the difference between a call price and a put price for European-style options with the same strike price and expiration date is equal to the difference between the stock price and the discounted strike price.

B. The logic behind put-call parity is based on the fundamental principle of finance stating that two securities with the same riskless payoff on the same future date must have the same price.

GET REAL

This chapter added to your understanding of put and call options by covering the rights, obligations, and potential gains and losses involved in trading options. How should you put this information to work? You need to buy and sell options to experience the gains and losses that options can provide. So, with a simulated brokerage account (such as Stock-Trak), you should first execute each of the basic option transactions: buy a call, sell a call, buy a put, and sell a put.

For help getting started, you can find an enormous amount of information about options on the Internet. A useful place to start is the Chicago Board Options Exchange (www.cboe.com). Excellent Web sites devoted to options education are the Options Industry Council (www.optionscentral.com) and the Options Clearing Corporation (www.optionsclearing.com). You might also look at the options section of Trading Markets (www.tradingmarkets.com) or Investor Links (www.investorlinks.com).

For information on option trading strategies, try entering the strategy name into an Internet search engine. For example, enter the search phrases "covered calls" or "protective puts" for online information about those strategies. For more general information, try the search phrase "options trading strategies" to find sites like Commodity World (www.commodityworld.com). For a sales pitch on writing covered calls, check out Write Call (www.writecall.com).

If you're having trouble understanding options ticker symbols, don't feel alone because almost everyone has trouble at first. For help on the net, try the search phrases "option symbols" or "options symbols" to find sites like www.optionscentral.com. Of course, the options exchanges listed above also provide complete information on the option ticker symbols they use.

Key Terms

American option 500
at-the-money option 513
call option 500
call option intrinsic value 512
call writer 515
cash-settled option 509
combination 524
covered call 523
derivative security 500
European option 500
in-the-money option 513
intrinsic value 512
option chain 502

Options Clearing Corporation (OCC) 506
option time value 513
option writing 515
out-of-the-money option 513
protective put 519
put-call parity 530
put option 500
put option intrinsic value 513
put writer 515
spread 523
stock index option 509
strike price 500

Chapter Review Problems and Self-Test

1. **Call Option Payoffs (CFA3)**   You purchase 25 call option contracts on Blue Ox stock. The strike price is $22, and the premium is $1. If the stock is selling for $24 per share at expiration, what are your call options worth? What is your net profit? What if the stock were selling for $23? $22?

2. **Stock versus Options (CFA2)**   Stock in Bunyan Brewery is currently priced at $20 per share. A call option with a $20 strike price and 60 days to maturity is quoted at $2. Compare the percentage gains and losses from a $2,000 investment in the stock versus the option in 60 days for stock prices of $26, $20, and $18.

3. **Put-Call Parity (CFA1)**   A call option sells for $8. It has a strike price of $80 and six months until expiration. If the underlying stock sells for $60 per share, what is the price of a put option with an $80 strike price and six months until expiration? The risk-free interest rate is 6 percent per year.

Answers to Self-Test Problems

1. Blue Ox stock is selling for $24. You own 25 contracts, each of which gives you the right to buy 100 shares at $22. Your options are thus worth $2 per share on 2,500 shares, or $5,000. The option premium was $1, so you paid $100 per contract, or $2,500 total. Your net profit is $2,500. If the stock is selling for $23, your options are worth $2,500, so your net profit is exactly zero. If the stock is selling for $22, your options are worthless, and you lose the entire $2,500 you paid.

2. Bunyan stock costs $20 per share, so if you invest $2,000, you'll get 100 shares. The option premium is $2, so an option contract costs $200. If you invest $2,000, you'll get $2,000/$200 = 10 contracts. If the stock is selling for $26 in 60 days, your profit on the stock is $6 per share, or $600 total. The percentage gain is $600/$2,000 = 30%.

    In this case, your options are worth $6 per share, or $600 per contract. You have 10 contracts, so your options are worth $6,000 in all. Since you paid $2,000 for the 10 contracts, your profit is $4,000. Your percentage gain is a whopping $4,000/$2,000 = 200%.

    If the stock is selling for $20, your profit is $0 on the stock, so your percentage return is 0 percent. Your options are worthless (why?), so the percentage loss is −100 percent. If the stock is selling for $18, verify that your percentage loss on the stock is −10 percent and your loss on the options is again −100 percent.

3. Using the put-call parity formula, we have:

$$C - P = S - K/(1 + r)^T$$

Rearranging to solve for P, the put price, and plugging in the other numbers gets us:

$$P = C - S + K/(1 + r)^T$$
$$= \$8 - \$60 + 80/(1.06)^{1/2}$$
$$= \$25.70$$

Test Your Investment Quotient

1. **Option Contracts (LO1, CFA2)**   Which of the following is *not* specified by a stock option contract?

    a. The underlying stock's price.
    b. The size of the contract.
    c. Exercise style—European or American.
    d. Contract settlement procedure—cash or delivery.

2. **Option Payoffs (LO2, CFA3)** All of the following statements about the value of a call option at expiration are true, except that the:

   a. Short position in the same call option can result in a loss if the stock price exceeds the exercise price.

   b. Value of the long position equals zero or the stock price minus the exercise price, whichever is higher.

   c. Value of the long position equals zero or the exercise price minus the stock price, whichever is higher.

   d. Short position in the same call option has a zero value for all stock prices equal to or less than the exercise price.

3. **Option Strategies (LO3, CFA2)** Which of the following stock option strategies has the greatest potential for large losses?

   a. Writing a covered call

   b. Writing a covered put

   c. Writing a naked call

   d. Writing a naked put

4. **Option Strategies (LO3, CFA6)** Which statement does not describe an at-the-money protective put position (comprised of owning the stock and the put)?

   a. Protects against loss at any stock price below the strike price of the put.

   b. Has limited profit potential when the stock price rises.

   c. Returns any increase in the stock's value, dollar for dollar, less the cost of the put.

   d. Provides a pattern of returns similar to a stop-loss order at the current stock price.

5. **Put-Call Parity (LO4, CFA1)** Which of the following is not included in the put-call parity condition?

   a. Price of the underlying stock.

   b. Strike price of the underlying call and put option contracts.

   c. Expiration dates of the underlying call and put option contracts.

   d. Volatility of the underlying stock.

6. **Put-Call Parity (LO4, CFA1)** According to the put-call parity condition, a risk-free portfolio can be created by buying 100 shares of stock and

   a. Writing one call option contract and buying one put option contract.

   b. Buying one call option contract and writing one put option contract.

   c. Buying one call option contract and buying one put option contract.

   d. Writing one call option contract and writing one put option contract.

7. **Option Strategies (LO3, CFA6)** Investor A uses options for defensive and income reasons. Investor B uses options as an aggressive investment strategy. What is an appropriate use of options for Investors A and B, respectively?

   a. Writing covered calls / buying puts on stock not owned.

   b. Buying out-of-the-money calls / buying puts on stock owned.

   c. Writing naked calls / buying in-the-money calls.

   d. Selling puts on stock owned / buying puts on stock not owned.

8. **Option Strategies (LO3, CFA2)** Which one of the following option combinations best describes a straddle? Buy both a call and a put on the same stock with

   a. Different exercise prices and the same expiration date.

   b. The same exercise price and different expiration dates.

   c. The same exercise price and the same expiration date.

   d. Different exercise prices and different expiration dates.

9. **Option Strategies (LO3, CFA2)** Which of the following strategies is the riskiest options transaction if the underlying stock price is expected to increase substantially?

   a. Writing a naked call option.

   b. Writing a naked put option.

   c. Buying a call option.

   d. Buying a put option.

10. **Option Gains and Losses (LO2, CFA3)**   You create a "strap" by buying two calls and one put on ABC stock, all with a strike price of $45. The calls cost $5 each, and the put costs $4. If you close your position when ABC stock is priced at $55, what is your per-share gain or loss?

   a. $4 loss
   b. $6 gain
   c. $10 gain
   d. $20 gain

11. **Option Gains and Losses (LO2, CFA3)**   A put on XYZ stock with a strike price of $40 is priced at $2.00 per share, while a call with a strike price of $40 is priced at $3.50. What is the maximum per-share loss to the writer of the uncovered put and the maximum per-share gain to the writer of the uncovered call?

	Maximum Loss to Put Writer	Maximum Gain to Call Writer
a.	$38.00	$ 3.50
b.	$38.00	$36.50
c.	$40.00	$ 3.50
d.	$40.00	$40.00

12. **Option Pricing (LO2, CFA4)**   If a stock is selling for $25, the exercise price of a put option on that stock is $20, and the time to expiration of the option is 90 days, what are the minimum and maximum prices for the put today?

   a. $0 and $5
   b. $0 and $20
   c. $5 and $20
   d. $5 and $25

13. **Option Strategies (LO3, CFA6)**   Which of the following strategies is most suitable for an investor wishing to eliminate "downside" risk from a long position in stock?

   a. A long straddle position.
   b. A short straddle position.
   c. Writing a covered call option.
   d. Buying a protective put option.

14. **Covered Calls (LO3, CFA2)**   The current price of an asset is $75. A three-month, at-the-money American call option on the asset has a current value of $5. At what value of the asset will a covered call writer break even at expiration?

   a. $70
   b. $75
   c. $80
   d. $85

15. **Option Strategies (LO3, CFA3)**   The current price of an asset is $100. An out-of-the-money American put option with an exercise price of $90 is purchased along with the asset. If the break-even point for this hedge is at an asset price of $114 at expiration, then the value of the American put at the time of purchase must have been

   a. $0
   b. $4
   c. $10
   d. $14

Concept Questions

1. **Basic Properties of Options (LO1, CFA2)**   What is a call option? A put option? Under what circumstances might you want to buy each? Which one has greater potential profit? Why?

2. **Calls versus Puts (LO1, CFA2)**   Complete the following sentence for each of these investors:

   a. A buyer of call options
   b. A buyer of put options

c. A seller (writer) of call options

d. A seller (writer) of put options

The (buyer/seller) of a (put/call) option (pays/receives) money for the (right/obligation) to (buy/sell) a specified asset at a fixed price for a fixed length of time.

3. **Option Break-even (LO2, CFA3)**   In general, if you buy a call option, what stock price is needed for you to break even on the transaction ignoring taxes and commissions? If you buy a put option?

4. **Protective Puts (LO3, CFA6)**   Buying a put option on a stock you own is sometimes called "stock price insurance." Why?

5. **Defining Intrinsic Value (LO2, CFA2)**   What is the intrinsic value of a call option? How do we interpret this value?

6. **Defining Intrinsic Value (LO2, CFA2)**   What is the intrinsic value of a put option? How do we interpret this value?

7. **Arbitrage and Options (LO2, CFA4)**   You notice that shares of stock in the Patel Corporation are going for $50 per share. Call options with an exercise price of $35 per share are selling for $10. What's wrong here? Describe how you could take advantage of this mispricing if the option expires today.

Use the following options quotations to answer questions 8 through 11:

Option & N. Y. Close	Strike Price	Expiration	Calls		Puts	
			Vol.	Last	Vol.	Last
Milson						
59	55	Mar	98	3.50	66	1.06
59	55	Apr	54	6.25	40	1.94
59	55	Jul	25	8.63	17	3.63
59	55	Oct	10	10.25	5	3.25

8. **Interpreting Options Quotes (LO1)**   How many options contracts on Milson stock were traded with an expiration date of July? How many underlying shares of stock do these options contracts represent?

9. **Interpreting Options Quotes (LO1, LO2, CFA2)**   Are the call options in the money? What is the intrinsic value of a Milson Corp. call option?

10. **Interpreting Options Quotes (LO1, LO2, CFA2)**   Are the put options in the money? What is the intrinsic value of a Milson Corp. put option?

11. **Interpreting Options Quotes (LO1, LO2, CFA4)**   Two of the options are clearly mispriced. Which ones? At a minimum, what should the mispriced options sell for? Explain how you could profit from the mispricing in each case.

12. **Option Strategies (LO3, CFA6)**   Recall the options strategies of a protective put and covered call discussed in the text. Suppose you have sold short some shares of stock. Discuss analogous option strategies and how you would implement them. (*Hint:* They're called protective calls and covered puts.)

13. **Put-Call Parity (LO4, CFA1)**   A put and a call option have the same maturity and strike price. If both are at the money, which is worth more? Prove your answer and then provide an intuitive explanation.

14. **Put-Call Parity (LO4, CFA1)**   A put and a call option have the same maturity and strike price. If they also have the same price, which one is in the money?

15. **Put-Call Parity (LO4, CFA2)**   One thing the put-call parity equation tells us is that given any three of a stock, a call, a put, and a T-bill, the fourth can be synthesized or replicated using the other three. For example, how can we replicate a share of stock using a put, a call, and a T-bill?

Questions and Problems

Core Questions

1. **Call Option Payoffs (LO2, CFA3)**   Suppose you purchase eight call contracts on Macron Technology stock. The strike price is $60, and the premium is $3. If, at expiration, the stock is selling for $64 per share, what are your call options worth? What is your net profit?

2. **Put Option Payoffs (LO2, CFA3)**   Suppose you purchase five put contracts on Testaburger Co. The strike price is $54, and the premium is $3. If, at expiration, the stock is selling for $47 per share, what are your put options worth? What is your net profit?

3. **Stock versus Options (LO2, CFA2)**   Stock in Cheezy-Poofs Manufacturing is currently priced at $65 per share. A call option with a $65 strike and 90 days to maturity is quoted at $2.75. Compare the percentage gains and losses from a $17,875 investment in the stock versus the option in 90 days for stock prices of $60, $65, and $70.

Use the following options quotations to answer questions 4 through 7:

Close	Strike Price	Expiration	Calls Vol.	Calls Last	Puts Vol.	Puts Last
Hendreeks						
103	100	Feb	72	5.20	50	2.40
103	100	Mar	41	8.40	29	4.90
103	100	Apr	16	10.68	10	6.60
103	100	Jul	8	14.30	2	10.10

4. **Option Quotes (LO1)**   Suppose you buy 50 April 100 call option contracts. How much will you pay, ignoring commissions?

5. **Calculating Option Payoffs (LO2, CFA3)**   In Problem 4, suppose that Hendreeks stock is selling for $105.70 per share on the expiration date. How much is your options investment worth? What if the stock price is $101.60 on the expiration date?

6. **Calculating Option Payoffs (LO2, CFA3)**   Suppose you buy 30 March 100 put option contracts. What is your maximum gain? On the expiration date, Hendreeks is selling for $84.60 per share. How much is your options investment worth? What is your net gain?

7. **Calculating Option Payoffs (LO2, CFA3)**   Suppose you write 30 of the July 100 put contracts. What is your net gain or loss if Hendreeks is selling for $90 at expiration? For $110? What is the break-even price, that is, the terminal stock price that results in a zero profit?

8. **Put-Call Parity (LO4, CFA1)**   A call option is currently selling for $5. It has a strike price of $65 and six months to maturity. What is the price of a put option with a $65 strike price and six months to maturity? The current stock price is $67, and the risk-free interest rate is 5 percent.

9. **Put-Call Parity (LO4, CFA1)**   A call option currently sells for $8. It has a strike price of $80 and five months to maturity. A put with the same strike and expiration date sells for $6. If the risk-free interest rate is 4 percent, what is the current stock price?

10. **Put-Call Parity (LO4, CFA1)**   A put option with a strike price of $40 sells for $4.80. The option expires in two months, and the current stock price is $42. If the risk-free interest rate is 5 percent, what is the price of a call option with the same strike price?

Intermediate Questions

11. **Put-Call Parity (LO4, CFA1)**   A call option is currently selling for $3.90. It has a strike price of $45 and five months to maturity. The current stock price is $47, and the risk-free rate is 5.3 percent. The stock will pay a dividend of $1.20 in two months. What is the price of a put option with the same exercise price?

12. **Put-Call Parity (LO4, CFA1)**   A call option is currently selling for $4.60. It has a strike price of $60 and four months to maturity. A put option with the same strike price sells for $8.30. The risk-free rate is 6 percent, and the stock will pay a dividend of $2.10 in three months. What is the current stock price?

13. **Put-Call Parity (LO4, CFA1)**   A put option is currently selling for $8.30. It has a strike price of $80 and seven months to maturity. The current stock price is $83. The risk-free rate is 5 percent, and the stock will pay a $1.40 dividend in two months. What is the price of a call option with the same strike price?

14. **Call Option Writing (LO2, CFA3)**   Suppose you write 20 call option contracts with a $50 strike. The premium is $3.45. Evaluate your potential gains and losses at option expiration for stock prices of $40, $50, and $60.

15. **Put Option Writing (LO2, CFA3)**   Suppose you write 25 put option contracts with a $45 strike. The premium is $3.80. Evaluate your potential gains and losses at option expiration for stock prices of $35, $45, and $55.

16. **Index Options (LO2, CFA2)**   Suppose you buy one SPX call option contract with a strike of 1200. At maturity, the S&P 500 Index is at 1218. What is your net gain or loss if the premium you paid was $14?

17. **Option Strategies (LO3, CFA6)**   You write a put with a strike price of $60 on stock that you have shorted at $60 (this is a "covered put"). What are the expiration date profits to this position for stock prices of $50, $55, $60, $65, and $70 if the put premium is $1.80?

18. **Option Strategies (LO3, CFA6)**   You buy a call with a strike price of $70 on stock that you have shorted at $70 (this is a "protective call"). What are the expiration date profits to this position for stock prices of $60, $65, $70, $75, and $80 if the call premium is $3.40?

19. **Option Strategies (LO3, CFA6)**   You simultaneously write a covered put and buy a protective call, both with strike prices of $80, on stock that you have shorted at $80. What are the expiration date payoffs to this position for stock prices of $70, $75, $80, $85, and $90?

20. **Option Strategies (LO3, CFA6)**   You simultaneously write a put and buy a call, both with strike prices of $80, naked, i.e., without any position in the underlying stock. What are the expiration date payoffs to this position for stock prices of $70, $75, $80, $85, and $90?

21. **Option Strategies (LO3, CFA6)**   You buy a straddle, which means you purchase a put and a call with the same strike price. The put price is $2.80 and the call price is $4.20. Assume the strike price is $75. What are the expiration date profits to this position for stock prices of $65, $70, $75, $80, and $85? What are the expiration date profits for these same stock prices? What are the break-even stock prices?

22. **Index Option Positions (LO3, CFA3)**   Suppose you buy one SPX call option with a strike of 1400 and write one SPX call option with a strike of 1425. What are the payoffs at maturity to this position for S&P 500 Index levels of 1350, 1400, 1450, 1500, and 1550?

23. **Index Option Positions (LO3, CFA3)**   Suppose you buy one SPX put option with a strike of 1400 and write one SPX put option with a strike of 1425. What are the payoffs at maturity to this position for S&P 500 Index levels of 1300, 1350, 1400, 1450, and 1500?

24. **Index Option Positions (LO3, CFA3)**   Suppose you buy one SPX call option with a strike of 1400 and write one SPX put option with a strike of 1400. What are the payoffs at maturity to this position for S&P 500 Index levels of 1300, 1350, 1400, 1450, and 1500?

25. **Index Option Positions (LO3, CFA3)**   Suppose you buy one each SPX call options with strikes of 1300 and 1500 and write two SPX call options with a strike of 1400. What are the payoffs at maturity to this position for S&P 500 Index levels of 1200, 1250, 1300, 1350, 1400, 1450, and 1500?

26. **Strangles (CFA6)**   A strangle is created by buying a put and buying a call on the same stock with a higher strike price and the same expiration. A put with a strike price of $100 sells for $6.75 and a call with a strike price of $110 sells for $8.60. Draw a graph showing the payoff and profit for a straddle using these options.

27. **Bull Spread with Calls (CFA6)**   You create a bull spread using calls by buying a call and simultaneously selling a call on the same stock with the same expiration at a higher strike price. A call option with a strike price of $20 sells for $4.55 and a call with a strike price of $25 sells for $1.24. Draw a graph showing the payoff and profit for a bull spread using these options.

28. **Bull Spread with Puts (CFA6)**   You can also create a bull spread using put options. To do so, you buy a put and simultaneously sell a put at a higher strike price on the same stock with the same expiration. A put with a strike price of $20 is available for $.45 and a put with a strike price of $25 is available for $1.64. Draw a graph showing the payoff and profit for a bull spread using these options.

29. **Butterfly Spread with Calls (CFA6)**   You create a butterfly spread using calls by buying a call at K_1, buying a call at K_3, and selling two calls at K_2. All of the calls are on the same stock and have the same expiration date. Additionally, butterfly spreads assume that $K_2 = \frac{1}{2}(K_1 + K_3)$. Calls on a stock with strike prices of $35, $40, and $45 are available for $7.00, $3.59, and $1.31, respectively. Draw a graph showing the payoff and profit for a butterfly spread using these options.

30. **Butterfly Spread with Puts (CFA6)**   You can also create a butterfly spread using puts by buying a put at K_1, buying a put at K_3, and selling two puts at K_2. All of the puts are on the same stock and have the same expiration date, and the assumption that $K_2 = \frac{1}{2}(K_1 + K_3)$ still holds. Puts on a stock with strike prices of $35, $40, and $45 are available for $.90, $2.35, and $5.10, respectively. Draw a graph showing the payoff and profit for a butterfly spread using these options.

CFA Exam Review by Schweser

[CFA1, CFA2]

Rachel Barlow is a recent finance graduate from Columbia University. She has accepted a position at a large investment bank but must first complete an intensive training program. Currently she is spending three months at her firm's Derivatives Trading Desk. To prepare for her assignment, Ms. Barlow decides to review her notes on option relationships, concentrating particularly on put-call parity. The data she will be using in her review are provided below. She also decides to assume continuous compounding.

	Option 1	Option 2
Stock price	$100	$110
Strike price	$100	$100
Interest rate	7%	7%
Dividend yield	0%	0%
Time to maturity (years)	0.5	0.5
Standard deviation of stock	20%	20%
Call option price	$7.38	$14.84

1. She would like to compute the value of the corresponding put option for Option 1. Which of the following is closest to Ms. Barlow's answer?

   a. $3.79
   b. $3.94
   c. $4.41

2. Ms. Barlow notices that the stock in the table above does not pay dividends. If the stock begins to pay a dividend, how will the price of the call option be affected?

   a. It will decrease.
   b. It will increase.
   c. It will not change.

3. She would like to compute the value of the corresponding put option for Option 2. Which of the following is closest to Ms. Barlow's answer?

   a. $0.98
   b. $1.41
   c. $4.84

What's on the Web?

1. **Option Prices**   You want to find the option prices for Intel (INTC). Go to finance.yahoo.com and find the option price quotes for Intel. What are the option premium and strike price for the highest and lowest strike price options that are nearest to expiring? What are the option premium and strike price for the highest and lowest strike price options expiring next month?

2. **Option Symbol Construction**   What is the option symbol for a call option on Cisco Systems (CSCO) with a strike price of $25 that expires in July? Go to www.cboe.com, and find the links for the option ticker symbol construction. Find the basic ticker symbol for Cisco Systems options, the codes for the expiration month, and strike price. Use these codes to construct the call option ticker symbol. Now construct the ticker symbol for a put option with the same strike price and expiration.

3. **Option Expiration**   Go to www.cboe.com, and find the expiration calendar for options traded on the CBOE. What day do equity options expire in the current month? What day do they expire next month?

4. **LEAPS**   Go to www.cboe.com and find the link for LEAPS. What are LEAPS? What are the two types of LEAPS? What are the benefits of equity LEAPS? What are the benefits of index LEAPS?

5. **FLEX Options**   Go to www.cboe.com and find the link for "FLEX Options." What is a FLEX option? When do FLEX options expire? What is the minimum size of a FLEX option?

Stock-Trak Exercises

To access the Stock-Trak Exercise for this chapter, please visit the book Web site at www.mhhe.com/jmd6e and choose the corresponding chapter.

CHAPTER 16

Option Valuation

Learning Objectives

Make sure the price is right by making sure that you have a good understanding of:

1. How to price options using the one-period and two-period binomial models.

2. How to price options using the Black-Scholes model.

3. How to hedge a stock portfolio using options.

4. The workings of employee stock options.

"I have compared the results of observation with those of theory . . . to show that the market, unwittingly, obeys a law which governs it, the law of probability."

–Louis Bachelier

Just what is an option worth? Actually, this is one of the more difficult questions in finance. Option valuation is an esoteric area of finance since it often involves complex mathematics. Fortunately, just like most options professionals, you can learn quite a bit about option valuation with only modest mathematical tools. But no matter how far you might wish to delve into this topic, you must begin with the Black-Scholes option pricing model. This model is the core from which all other option pricing models trace their ancestry. ■

The previous chapter introduced the basics of stock options. From an economic standpoint, perhaps the most important subject was the expiration date payoffs of stock options. Bear in mind that when investors buy options today, they are buying risky future payoffs. Likewise, when investors write options today, they become obligated to make risky future payments. In a competitive financial marketplace, option prices observed each day are collectively agreed on by buyers and writers assessing the likelihood of all possible future payoffs and payments. Option prices are set accordingly.

In this chapter, we spend a lot of time showing you how to calculate stock option prices. We begin with a simple way to calculate stock option prices and then discuss the binomial option pricing model. The discussion ends with the Black-Scholes option pricing model, which is widely regarded by finance professionals as the premier model of stock option valuation.

CFA™ Exam Topics in This Chapter:

1 Option markets and contracts I (L1, S17)
2 Option markets and contracts II (L2, S17)

3 Risk management applications of option strategies (L3, S15)

Go to www.mhhe.com/jmd6e for a guide that aligns your textbook with CFA readings.

16.1 A Simple Model to Value Options before Expiration

Calculating the value of an option before it expires can be complex. However, we can illustrate many of the key insights to this problem using a simple example. Suppose we are looking at a call option with one year to maturity and a $110 exercise price. The current stock price is $108, and the one-year risk-free rate, r, is 10 percent.

We know that an option is worth its intrinsic value at expiration. To calculate the intrinsic value, we need the strike price and the stock price at option expiration. We know the strike price today and at option expiration. We know the stock price today, but we do not know what the stock price will be in one year. A method frequently used to forge on and calculate option prices today is to assume that today we "know" the range of possible values for the underlying asset at option expiration.

We start with an uncomplicated example. Assume we know (somehow) that the stock price will be either $130 or $115 in one year. Keep in mind, though, that the stock price in one year is still uncertain. We do know that the stock price is going to be either $130 or $115 (but no other values). We do not know the odds associated with these two prices. In other words, we know the possible values of the stock, but not the probabilities associated with these two values.[1]

Because the strike price is $110, we know the call option value at expiration will be either $130 − $110 = $20 or $115 − $110 = $5. Once again, we do not know which one. We do know one very important thing: The call option is certain to finish in the money.

What about puts with a strike price of $110? In both cases, the put will finish out of the money. That is, the value of this put at expiration is zero regardless of the stock price. What is this put worth today? Think about it by answering this question: How much are you willing to pay today for a riskless asset that will have a zero value in one year? You are right, zero.

If you know the price of a put with the same strike, you can use put-call parity to price a call option before it expires. An expiration-day stock price of either $130 or $115 means that a put option with a $110 strike has a value of zero today and at expiration. Therefore, in this case, we can use put-call parity to calculate the value of a call with a strike of $110.

$$C - P = S_0 - K/(1 + r)^T$$
$$C - 0 = \$108 + \$110/(1.10)$$
$$C = \$108 - \$100 = \$8$$

Many other pairs of stock prices also result in a zero value for the put. Therefore, the fact that we selected these two particular stock prices is not what allows us to calculate the call option price. What allowed us to calculate the call option price were these two facts: (1) the chosen pair of stock prices guarantees that the call option will finish in the money; and (2) the chosen pair of stock prices also guarantees that a put option with the same strike will finish out of the money.[2]

We conclude that pricing a call option when we are certain that the call option will finish somewhere in the money is easy. We simply use a put option value of zero and the put-call parity equation to obtain the value of the call option before it expires.

---

[1] If we knew these probabilities, we could calculate the expected value of the stock price at expiration.

[2] You might be wondering what would happen if the stock price were less than the present value of the exercise price. In this event, the call price would be negative. But this cannot happen in this example because we are certain that the stock price will be at least K in one year because we know the call option will finish in the money. If the current price of the stock is less than $K/(1 + r)^T$, then the return on the stock is certain to be greater than the risk-free rate—which creates an arbitrage opportunity. For example, if the stock is currently selling for $80, then the minimum return will be $(115 − 80)/80 = 43.75\%$. Because we can borrow at 10 percent we can earn a certain minimum return of 33.75 percent per dollar borrowed. This, of course, is an arbitrage opportunity.

16.2 The One-Period Binomial Option Pricing Model

In the previous section, we made good use of the fact that the call option would always expire in the money. Suppose we want to allow the call option to expire in the money or out of the money.[3] How do we proceed in this case? Well, we need a different option pricing model. We will start our tour of option pricing models by looking at the one-period binomial option pricing model (BOPM).

THE ONE-PERIOD BINOMIAL OPTION PRICING MODEL—THE ASSUMPTIONS

Suppose the stock price today is S, and the stock pays no dividends. We will assume that the stock price in one period is either $S \times u$ or $S \times d$, where u (for "up" factor) is bigger than 1 and d (for "down" factor) is less than 1.[4] For example, suppose the stock price today is $100, and u and d are 1.10 and .95, respectively. With these numbers, the stock price in one period will either be $100 \times 1.10 = \$110$ or $100 \times .95 = \$95$.

THE ONE-PERIOD BINOMIAL OPTION PRICING MODEL—THE SETUP

Suppose we start with the values given in Table 16.1. To begin to calculate the call price today, suppose an investor

- Buys one share of stock, and
- Sells one call option.

TABLE 16.1	Inputs for the One-Period BOPM		
S	=	$100	Current stock price
u	=	1.10	Up factor
d	=	.95	Down factor
r	=	3%	Risk-free interest rate
K	=	$100	Strike price
T	=	1 period	Periods to option expiration

A key question to ask is: What is the value of this portfolio today and in one period when the option expires? To answer this question, we first write down all the prices that we know today and all the prices we know at expiration. We show these prices on two "trees" in Figure 16.1. In the world of option pricing models, a collection of stock or option prices is known as a tree.

As shown in Figure 16.1, we know the stock price today ($100) but we do not know the call price today (we are trying to calculate this). In one period when the option expires, we know that the stock price will either increase to $110 (which is $S \times u = \$100 \times 1.10$) or decrease to $95 (which is $S \times d = \$100 \times .95$).

At expiration, we know that the call option is worth its intrinsic value. If the stock price increases to $110, the intrinsic value of the call option, C_u, is MAX[110 − 100,0], or $10. Similarly, if the stock price decreases to $95, the call option intrinsic value, C_d, is MAX[95 − 100, 0], or $0.

What is the value of the portfolio of one share of stock and short one call option? If the stock price increases to $110, the call finishes in the money—with an intrinsic value equal to $10.

---

[3] We limit our discussion here to call options. Of course, we can make parallel statements for put options.
[4] Note that we are assuming that d is less than 1.0, but d does not necessarily have to be less than 1.0.

FIGURE 16.1   Stock Price Tree and Option Price Tree

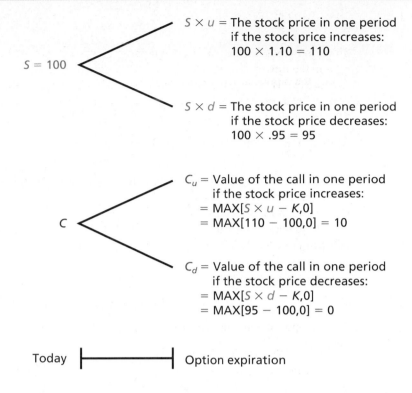

$S \times u$ = The stock price in one period
 if the stock price increases:
 $100 \times 1.10 = 110$

$S = 100$

$S \times d$ = The stock price in one period
 if the stock price decreases:
 $100 \times .95 = 95$

C_u = Value of the call in one period
 if the stock price increases:
 = MAX$[S \times u - K,0]$
 = MAX$[110 - 100,0] = 10$

C

C_d = Value of the call in one period
 if the stock price decreases:
 = MAX$[S \times d - K,0]$
 = MAX$[95 - 100,0] = 0$

Today ├───────────┤ Option expiration

Because the investor sold the call option, the investor owes the intrinsic value. Therefore, the portfolio value is $110 - \$10$, or $100. If the stock price decreases to $95, the call finishes out of the money, so it has an intrinsic value equal to $0. Therefore, the portfolio value is $95 + \$0 = \$95$.

THE ONE-PERIOD BINOMIAL OPTION PRICING MODEL—THE FORMULA

Is there a way to form a portfolio of stock and options that is worth the same amount regardless of the price of the stock in one period? It turns out that there is, and this way is a truly brilliant insight. Instead of buying one share, suppose the investor buys a "fractional" share of stock (which we will represent by the Greek letter delta, Δ). What happens in this case?

In Figure 16.2, we know all values at expiration except Δ. The key to the solution hinges on the fact that the investor can choose the size of the fractional share, Δ. That is, the investor can choose a value for Δ where the portfolio has the same value at expiration for both stock prices. In other words, the investor can choose Δ so that $\Delta S \times u - C_u = \Delta S \times d - C_d$.

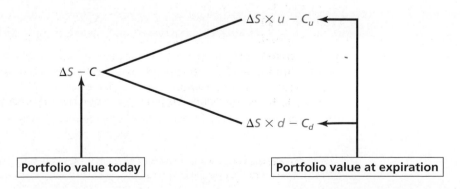

$\Delta S \times u - C_u$

$\Delta S - C$

$\Delta S \times d - C_d$

| Portfolio value today | Portfolio value at expiration |

For simplicity, we will drop the multiplication sign when we calculate Δ as follows:

$$\Delta Su - \Delta Sd = C_u - C_d$$
$$\Delta(Su - Sd) = C_u - C_d$$
$$\Delta = \frac{C_u - C_d}{Su - Sd}$$

Using the numbers in our example:

$$\Delta = \frac{C_u - C_d}{Su - Sd} = \frac{10 - 0}{110 - 95} = \frac{10}{15} = \frac{2}{3}$$

Have we succeeded in making the portfolio riskless? Yes:

$$(\Delta S \times u) - C_u = (\Delta S \times d) - C_d$$
$$(2/3)(100)(1.10) - 10 = (2/3)(100)(.95) - 0$$
$$73.33 - 10 = 63.33$$

We now have what we need to calculate the call price today, C. We choose Δ so that the portfolio has the same value for both possible stock prices. That is, the portfolio of long Δ shares and short one call option is riskless (for the right value of Δ). Therefore, a riskless portfolio today should be worth $(\Delta S - C)(1 + r)$ in one period. So,

$$(\Delta S - C)(1 + r) = \Delta S \times u - C_u \qquad (16.1)$$

The only unknown value in equation (16.1) is C. Rearranging the values in equation (16.1) results in:

$$C = \frac{\Delta S(1 + r - u) + C_u}{1 + r} \qquad (16.2)$$

We can calculate the call price today using equation (16.2):

$$C = \frac{\Delta S(1 + r - u) + C_u}{1 + r}$$
$$= \frac{(2/3)(100)(1 + .03 - 1.10) + 10}{1.03}$$
$$= \frac{(200/3)(-0.07) + 10}{1.03}$$
$$= \frac{5.33}{1.03} = \$5.18$$

Equation (16.2) is one way to write the formula for the one-period binomial option pricing model. Now that we know the price of the call, we can use put-call parity to calculate the price of a put with a strike of $100:

$$P + S = C + K/(1 + r_f)$$
$$P + 100 = 5.18 + 100/(1.03)$$
$$P = 5.18 + 100/(1.03) - 100$$
$$= \$2.27$$

EXAMPLE 16.1	**Using the One-Period Binomial Option Pricing Model**

A stock is currently selling for $25 per share. In one period, it will be worth either $20 or $30. The riskless interest rate is 5 percent per period. There are no dividends. What is today's price of a call option with a strike price of $27?

To answer this question, we can use the one-period binomial option pricing model:

$$C = \frac{\Delta S(1 + r - u) + C_u}{1 + r}$$

(continued)

To calculate Δ:

$$\Delta = \frac{C_u - C_d}{Su - Sd} = \frac{3 - 0}{30 - 20} = \frac{3}{10}$$

We also have to calculate u, which is \$30/\$25 = 1.20. We can now calculate the price of the call option:

$$C = \frac{\Delta S(1 + r - u) + C_u}{1 + r}$$

$$= \frac{(3/10)(\$25)(1 + .05 - 1.20) + \$3}{1.05}$$

$$= \frac{(\$75/10)(-.15) + \$3}{1.05}$$

$$= \frac{\$1.875}{1.05} = \$1.79$$

WHAT IS DELTA?

Delta, Δ, is an important proportion. We will use delta later in the chapter when we are talking about hedging the risk of adverse stock price movements using options.

An easy way to think about delta is to recall that delta is a proportion of shares to calls that is needed to form a risk-free portfolio. That is, a portfolio of shares and calls that does not change in value when the stock price changes. Remember, the investor can choose many values for delta. However, there is only one delta that helps the investor form a risk-free portfolio.

Therefore, a delta of 2/3 means that we need two shares and three calls to form a risk-free portfolio. The portfolio is risk-free because losses (gains) in the call options are offset by gains (losses) in the stock. So you can think of delta as the fractional share amount needed to offset, or hedge, changes in the price of one call.

In our detailed example, we calculated a delta of 2/3, or .67. This means that the number of shares to hedge one call is .67. Similarly, the number of calls to hedge one share is $1/\Delta$, or 3/2. That is, we need 3 call options to hedge 2 shares.

CHECK THIS

16.2a Suppose the stock price today is \$95, not \$100 as shown in Figure 16.1. Nothing else changes in the detailed example that follows Figure 16.1. Does delta still equal .67? What is the call price?

16.2b You calculate a delta of .8. How many shares and calls are needed to form a risk-free portfolio? What positions (i.e., long or short) does the investor have in shares and calls?

16.3 The Two-Period Binomial Option Pricing Model

In the previous section, we could price an option one period before it expires. Suppose there are two periods to expiration. What do we do in this case? It turns out that we repeat much of the process we used in the previous section.

In this section, we calculate the price of a European call option. However, we can use this method to calculate the price of a European put option, too. Using a slight modification to allow for early exercise, this technique can also be used to calculate prices for American calls and puts. In fact, this basic technique is so powerful that, with the right modifications, it can be used to price an exotic array of options.

TABLE 16.2	Inputs for the Two-Period BOPM	
S_0	=	$50	Stock price today
u	=	1.20	Up factor ($u > 1$) per period
d	=	.85	Down factor ($d < 1$) per period
r_f	=	8%	Risk-free interest rate per period
K	=	$55	Strike price
T	=	2 periods	Periods to option expiration

The best way to learn this technique is to work a detailed example. Suppose we have the set of inputs given in Table 16.2.

We need to point out one more important assumption. That is, in our detailed example, we assume that u, d, and r_f do not change in the two periods until option expiration. With this additional assumption and the inputs in Table 16.2, we will show that the call option is worth $6.29 today.

STEP 1: BUILD A PRICE TREE FOR STOCK PRICES THROUGH TIME

The upper part of Figure 16.3 shows the stock prices through time. Because there are more than two dates, we denote the stock price today as S_0. Starting at $S_0 = \$50$, S_1 (the stock price at time 1) is:

$$S_0 \times u = \$50 \times 1.20 = \$60 \quad \text{if the stock price increases}$$
$$S_0 \times d = \$50 \times 0.85 = \$42.50 \quad \text{if the stock price decreases}$$

Next, if the stock price in one period is $60, then the price in two periods will be either $60 × 1.20 = $72 or $60 × .85 = $51. Similarly, if the price in one period is $42.50, then the price in two periods will be either $42.50 × 1.20 = $51 or $42.50 × .85 = $36.13.

Thus, there are three stock prices in two periods, corresponding to a sequence of (1) two up moves, (2) two down moves, or (3) one up move and one down move. Notice that it doesn't matter if we go up, then down or down, then up. We end up at $51 either way. In symbols, the three possible S_2 stock prices are:

1. $S_2 = S_{uu} = S_0 \times u \times u = S_0 \times u^2$ (two up moves).
2. $S_2 = S_{dd} = S_0 \times d \times d = S_0 \times d^2$ (two down moves).
3. $S_2 = S_{ud} = S_0 \times u \times d = S_0 \times u \times d$ (one up move and one down move).

STEP 2: USE THE INTRINSIC VALUE FORMULA TO CALCULATE THE POSSIBLE OPTION PRICES AT EXPIRATION

As we calculated, the three possible stock prices at expiration are $72, $51, and $36.13. We plug each of these stock prices into the intrinsic value formula. Because the strike price is $K = \$55$, the possible values for the call option at expiration are:

$$\text{MAX}[S_T - K, 0] = \text{MAX}[\$72 - \$55, 0] = \$17$$
$$\text{MAX}[S_T - K, 0] = \text{MAX}[\$51 - \$55, 0] = \$0$$
$$\text{MAX}[S_T - K, 0] = \text{MAX}[\$36.13 - \$55, 0] = \$0$$

Notice that in two of the possible cases, the call has zero value at expiration.

Stock Price Tree

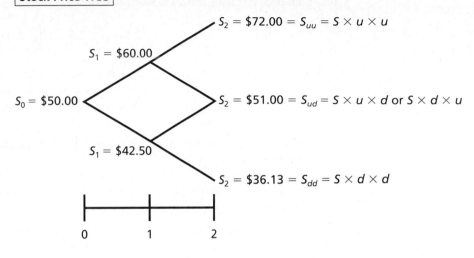

Call Price Tree

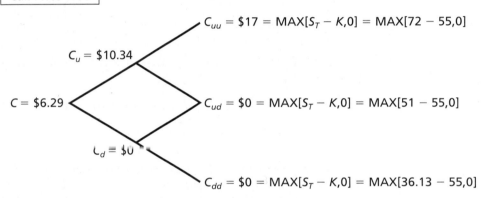

Delta Values

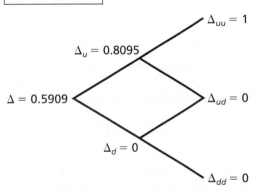

STEP 3: CALCULATE THE FRACTIONAL SHARE NEEDED TO FORM EACH RISK-FREE PORTFOLIO AT THE NEXT-TO-LAST DATE

To form the risk-free portfolios, we need to calculate the possible values for Δ in the next-to-last period. Recall that the portfolio is risk-free when the investor sells one call and buys a fraction, Δ, of one share.

Let us begin by looking at the point where the stock price is $60. You can see that the two possible stock prices from that point are $72 and $51. In addition, because the strike price is $55, two call option values, $17 and $0, are possible. You can see that it is as if we have an option with one period to expiration. Therefore, we can use the notation from the one-period binomial option pricing model to calculate Δ:

$$\Delta = \frac{C_u - C_d}{Su - Sd} = \frac{17 - 0}{72 - 51} = \frac{17}{21} = .8095$$

Likewise, from the point where the stock price is $42.50, the two possible stock prices are $51 and $36.13. Note, however, that because the strike price is $55, the option is worth $0 regardless of the stock price in one period. In this case, the Δ is:

$$\Delta = \frac{C_u - C_d}{Su - Sd} = \frac{0 - 0}{51 - 36.13} = \frac{0}{14.87} = 0$$

STEP 4: CALCULATE ALL POSSIBLE OPTION PRICES AT THE NEXT-TO-LAST DATE

We can now use these values for Δ to calculate the call prices when the stock price is $60 or when it is $42.50. When the stock price is $60, we use $\Delta = .8095$, $C_u = \$17$, $r = 8\%$, and $u = 1.20$ to calculate the call price:

$$C = \frac{\Delta S(1 + r - u) + C_u}{(1 + r)} = \frac{(.8095 \times 60)(1 + .08 - 1.20) + 17}{(1.08)} = \$10.34$$

When the stock price is $42.50, we use $\Delta = 0$, $C_u = \$0$, $r = 8\%$, and $u = 1.20$ to calculate the call price:

$$C = \frac{\Delta S(1 + r - u) + C_u}{(1 + r)} = \frac{(0 \times 42.50)(1 + .08 - 1.20) + 0}{(1.08)} = \$0$$

The intuition for a call with zero value is simple. Ask yourself: What price am I willing to pay today for a call option that will always have a value of zero in one period? Or think of it like this: This call option gives you the right to buy shares for $55 next period. However, the stock price will always be lower than $55 next period. How much are you willing to pay today for this call option? We are sure that you said zero (aren't we?).

STEP 5: REPEAT THIS PROCESS BY WORKING BACK TO TODAY

From the point where the stock price is $50, there are two possible stock prices, $60 and $42.50. If the stock price is $60, we know the call option is worth $10.34. When the stock price is $42.50, we know that the call option is worth $0. In this case, Δ is:

$$\Delta = \frac{C_u - C_d}{Su - Sd} = \frac{10.34 - 0}{60 - 42.50} = \frac{10.34}{17.50} = .5909$$

Using $\Delta = .5909$, $C_u = \$10.34$, $r = 8\%$, and $u = 1.20$, we calculate the call price as:

$$C = \frac{\Delta S(1 + r - u) + C_u}{(1 + r)} = \frac{(.5909 \times 50)(1 + .08 - 1.20) + 10.34}{(1.08)} = \$6.29$$

Using put-call parity, the price of the put with a $55 strike is:

$$P = C - S + \frac{K}{(1 + r)} = 6.29 - 50 + \frac{55}{1.08} = \$7.22$$

We summarize these calculations in Figure 16.3. Note that, over time, as S increases, so do Δ and C.

CHECK THIS

16.3a Look at Table 16.2. Suppose that $K = \$45$ and all other inputs remain the same. What is the price of a call option? What is the price of a put option?

16.3b Look at Table 16.2. Suppose that $u = 1.30$ and all other inputs remain the same. What is the price of a call option? What is the price of a put option?

16.4 The Binomial Option Pricing Model with Many Periods

When we have more than two periods, nothing really changes. We still work backwards one period at a time. Figure 16.4 shows a binomial tree with five periods to option expiration. Now there are six option values at expiration. To calculate today's option price, you would have to calculate 14 intermediate option prices, which would be fairly tedious and explains why computers come in handy to calculate option prices.

Looking at Figure 16.4, note the various paths that the stock can follow after the stock has increased or decreased in price. There are five ways that the stock could wind up at the black dot. For example, from the diamond marked U the stock could follow the blue or red path to the black dot at the end of the tree. The collection of possible stock price paths is also called the "lattice."

As another example, from the diamond marked D the stock could follow the orange or turquoise path to the yellow dot at the end of the tree. The stock price today can wind up at the yellow dot following 10 paths. In Figure 16.4, we show the number of ways that the stock can

---

FIGURE 16.4 A Five-Period Stock Price Tree

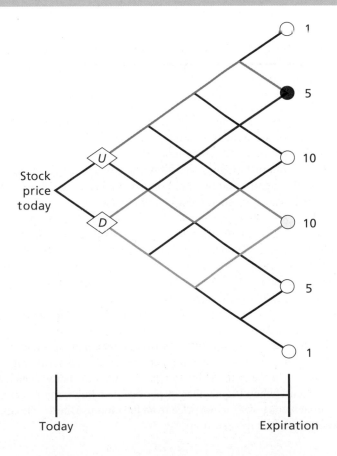

FIGURE 16.5   An 18-Period Stock Price Tree

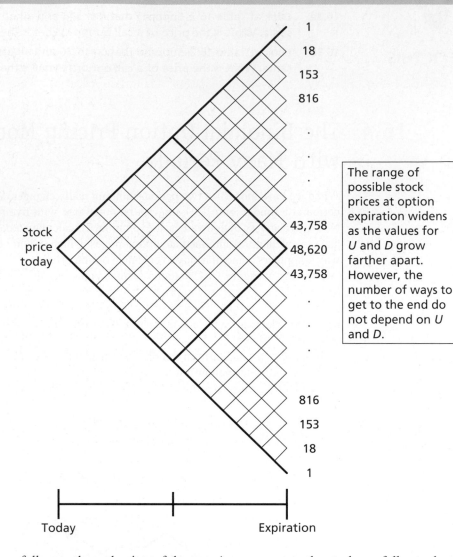

1
18
153
816
.
.
.

Stock price today

43,758
48,620
43,758
.
.
.

816
153
18
1

The range of possible stock prices at option expiration widens as the values for *U* and *D* grow farther apart. However, the number of ways to get to the end do not depend on *U* and *D*.

Today   Expiration

follow to the end points of the tree. As you can see, the stock can follow only one path to reach the highest and lowest possible prices. Also, you will notice that the way the numbers increase from 1 to 10 and then decrease back to 1 is symmetric.

Let's get crazy. Figure 16.5 shows a lattice with 18 periods to expiration. We have super-imposed a two-period binomial option pricing lattice over it. In this way, you can see that two periods can be subdivided into many periods.

There are many possible stock paths in Figure 16.5. In fact, there are 2^{18} (or 262,144) of them! Yikes! We have written down the possible ways that the stock price can wander to its ending prices at the option expiration date. As before, there is only one way to get to the highest possible stock price. However, there are 18 paths to the next highest stock price. You can see a symmetry to the way the paths increase in number from 1 to 48,620 and then decrease back to 1.

If you wanted to calculate today's option price, you don't have to worry about the number of paths. However, you do have to worry about the number of intersections at which the stock price can increase or decrease. With 18 periods to expiration, you would need to calculate 19 expiration-day stock prices and 170 intermediate option prices (that should seem like a lot to you).

What happens when the number of periods gets *really* big? The answer is that we could always use a computer to handle the calculations, but we can use a more elegant method. As it happens, when the number of periods gets huge, the price calculated using our binomial approach converges to the price from the famous Black-Scholes option pricing model, which we study in the next section.

16.4a Why is it that nothing really changes when there are more than two periods to expiration?

16.4b Why don't you have to worry about the number of paths the stock price can take before expiration? What do you have to worry about?

16.5 The Black-Scholes Option Pricing Model

Option pricing theory made a great leap forward in the early 1970s with the development of the Black-Scholes option pricing model by Fischer Black and Myron Scholes. Recognizing the important theoretical contributions by Robert Merton, many finance professionals knowledgeable in the history of option pricing theory refer to an extended version of the Black-Scholes model as the Black-Scholes-Merton option pricing model. In 1997, Myron Scholes and Robert Merton were awarded the Nobel Prize in Economics for their pioneering work in option pricing theory. Unfortunately, Fischer Black had died two years earlier and so did not share the Nobel Prize, which cannot be awarded posthumously. The nearby *Investment Updates* box presents *The Wall Street Journal* story of the Nobel Prize award.

Our focus is on the basic Black-Scholes model. The Black-Scholes option pricing model states the value of a European option on a non-dividend-paying stock as a function of these five input factors:

1. The current price of the underlying stock.

2. The strike price specified in the option contract.

3. The risk-free interest rate over the life of the option contract.

4. The time remaining until the option contract expires, sometimes called **expiry**.

5. The price volatility of the underlying stock (i.e., the distribution of possible stock prices at expiration).

expiry
A shortened way of saying "time to maturity."

In the model, the five inputs are defined as follows:

S = Current stock price

K = Option strike price

r = Risk-free interest rate

T = Time remaining until option expiration

σ = Sigma, representing stock price volatility

The CBOE has a free options calculator that will do most of the calculations in this chapter at www.cboe.com

In terms of these five inputs, the Black-Scholes formula for the price of a European call option on a single share of common stock is:

$$C = SN(d_1) - Ke^{-rT}N(d_2) \tag{16.3}$$

The Black-Scholes formula for the price of a European put option on a share of common stock is:

$$P = Ke^{-rT}N(-d_2) - SN(-d_1) \tag{16.4}$$

In these call and put option formulas, the numbers d_1 and d_2 are calculated as:

$$d_1 = \frac{\ln(S/K) + (r + \sigma^2/2)T}{\sigma\sqrt{T}} \quad \text{and} \quad d_2 = d_1 - \sigma\sqrt{T}$$

TWO U.S. ECONOMISTS WIN THE NOBEL PRIZE FOR WORK ON OPTIONS

Two economists with close ties to Wall Street, Robert C. Merton and Myron S. Scholes, won the Nobel Memorial Prize in Economic Science for path-breaking work that helped spawn the $148 billion stock-options industry.

The Nobel economics prize is given to innovators whose work breaks new ground and sires whole bodies of economic research. But this year, the prize committee chose laureates not only with distinguished academic records, but also with especially pragmatic bents, to split the $1 million award. Prof. Merton, 53 years old, teaches at Harvard Business School, while Prof. Scholes, 56, has emeritus status from the Stanford Graduate School of Business.

In the early 1970s, Prof. Scholes, with the late mathematician Fischer Black, invented an insightful method of pricing options and warrants at a time when most investors and traders still relied on educated guesses to determine the value of various stock-market products. Prof. Merton later demonstrated the broad applicability of the Black-Scholes options-pricing formula, paving the way for the incredible growth of markets in options and other derivatives.

"Thousands of traders and investors now use this formula every day to value stock options in markets throughout the world," the Royal Swedish Academy of Sciences said yesterday.

The Black-Scholes Formula

In their paper, Black and Scholes obtained exact formulas for pricing options.

$$C = SN(d) - Ke^{-rT} N(d - \sigma \sqrt{T})$$

According to the formula, the value of the call option C is given by the difference between the expected share value (the first term on the right-hand-side of the equation) and the expected cost (the second term) if the option is exercised at maturity.

The Black-Scholes option-pricing model "is really the classic example of an academic innovation that has been adopted widely in practice," said Gregg Jarrell, professor of economics at the University of Rochester's William E. Simon Business School and former chief economist at the Securities and Exchange Commission. "It is one of the most elegant and precise models that any of us has ever seen."

Options allow investors to trade the future rights to buy or sell assets—such as stocks—at a set price. An investor who holds 100 shares of International Business Machines Corp. stock today, for example, might buy an option that grants the right to sell 100 IBM shares at a fixed price in three months' time. The investor is therefore partially protected against a fall in the stock price during the life of the option.

Until the Black-Scholes model gained acceptance, the great minds of economics and finance were unable to develop a method of putting an accurate price on those options. The problem was how to evaluate the risk associated with options, when the underlying stock price changes from moment to moment. The risk of an option depends on the price of the stock underlying the option.

That breakthrough allowed the economists to create a pricing formula that included the stock price, the agreed sale or "strike" price of the option, the stock's volatility, the risk-free interest rate offered with a secure bond, and the time until the option's expiration. They published their work in 1973, the same year the Chicago Board Options Exchange turned the scattered world of options trading into a more formal market.

Prof. Merton himself forged a formal theoretical framework for the Black-Scholes formula, and extended the analysis to other derivative products—financial instruments in which the value of the security depends on the value of another indicator, such as mortgage, interest, or exchange rates. More broadly, his work allowed economists and financial professionals to view a wide variety of commonly traded financial instruments—such as corporate bonds—as derivatives and to price them using the ideas first expounded by Dr. Black and Prof. Scholes. "For the most part, the thing was conceived entirely in theory," said Prof. Merton.

The practical implications soon became apparent, however, as market participants flocked to the Black-Scholes-Merton approach to determine how much options are worth. "It's just a terrific yardstick for investors to help make that judgment," said Bill Kehoe, vice president and manager of the options marketing group at Merrill Lynch & Co., and an options trader since 1961.

Options markets have grown astronomically in the quarter century since the formula reached trading floors around the country. The value of U.S. exchange-traded options in 1995 was $118 billion. Last year, it surged to $148 billion, and in the first nine months of 1997, the figure hit $155 billion. More than 100,000 options series are now available. "Even now, we calculate the value of options world-wide using the Black-Scholes formula," said Yair Orgler, chairman of the Tel Aviv Stock Exchange.

Source: Michael M. Phillips, *The Wall Street Journal*, October 15, 1997. Reprinted with permission of *The Wall Street Journal*. © 1997 Dow Jones & Company, Inc. All Rights Reserved Worldwide.

For many links to option-related topics, see www.numa.com

In the formulas above, call and put option prices are algebraically represented by C and P, respectively. In addition to the five input factors S, K, r, T, and σ, the following three mathematical functions are used in the call and put option pricing formulas:

1. e^x, or $\exp(x)$, denoting the natural exponent of the value of x.
2. $\ln(x)$, denoting the natural logarithm of the value of x.
3. $N(x)$, denoting the standard normal probability of the value of x.

EXAMPLE 16.2

Computing Black-Scholes Option Prices

Calculate call and put option prices, given the following inputs to the Black-Scholes option pricing formula.

Stock price	$S = \$50$
Strike price	$K = \$45$
Time to maturity	$T = 3$ months
Stock volatility	$\sigma = 25\%$
Interest rate	$r = 6\%$

Referring to equations (16.3) and (16.4), first we compute values for d_1 and d_2:

$$d_1 = \frac{\ln(50/45) + (.06 + .25^2/2)\,.25}{.25\sqrt{.25}}$$

$$= \frac{.10536 + .09125 \times .25}{.125}$$

$$= 1.02538$$

$$d_2 = d_1 - .25\sqrt{.25}$$

$$= .90038$$

The following standard normal probabilities are provided:

$$N(d_1) = N(1.02538) = .84741 \qquad N(-d_1) = 1 - N(d_1) = .15259$$

$$N(d_2) = N(.90038) = .81604 \qquad N(-d_2) = 1 - N(d_2) = .18396$$

We can now calculate the price of the call option as:

$$C = \$50 \times .84741 - \$45 \times e^{-.06 \times .25} \times .81604$$

$$= \$50 \times .84741 - \$45 \times .98511 \times .81604$$

$$= \$6.195$$

and the price of the put option as:

$$P = \$45 \times e^{-.06 \times .25} \times .18396 - \$50 \times .15259$$

$$= \$45 \times .98511 \times .18396 - \$50 \times .15259$$

$$= \$.525$$

Exact standard normal probabilities provided in this example are obtained from Excel using the function NORMSDIST(x). A detailed example of how to use an Excel spreadsheet to calculate Black-Scholes option prices is shown in a *Spreadsheet Analysis* box later in this chapter.

EXAMPLE 16.3

Using a Web-Based Option Calculator

The purpose of Example 16.2 was to show you that the Black-Scholes formula is not hard to use—even if at first it looks imposing. If you are in a hurry to price an option or if you simply want to verify the price of an option that you have calculated, a number of option calculators are available on the Web. Let's check our previous answers by using the option calculator we found at www.numa.com.

(continued)

INPUT

Share Price: `50`   Strike Price: `45`   ⊙ dec ○ /8

Dividend Yld: `0`   Interest Rate: `6`   ☐ cc-int

Maturity: `3`   in ○ Days ⊙ Months ○ Years

CALCULATE:

⊙ theoretical option value =>enter- Volatility: `25`

or ○ implied volatility   =>enter- Option Price: [   ]

Option type: ⊙ Call ○ Put

OUTPUT

THEORETICAL VALUE CALCULATIONS		
Option Value: 6.195	Delta:	0.847

As you can see, our answers in Example 16.2 check out. You might be wondering what delta is. We discuss delta later in the chapter.

CHECK THIS

16.5a Consider the following inputs to the Black-Scholes option pricing model.

S = $65   r = 5%

K = $60   σ = 25%

T = .25 years

These input values yield a call option price of $6.78 and a put option price of $1.03.

Verify these prices from your own calculations.

16.6 Varying the Option Price Input Values

An important goal of this chapter is to provide an understanding of how option prices change as a result of varying each of the five input values. Table 16.3 summarizes the sign effects of the five inputs on call and put option prices. A plus sign indicates a positive effect, and a minus sign indicates a negative effect on the price of the option. For example, if the stock price increases, the call option price increases and the put option price decreases.

TABLE 16.3	Five Inputs Affecting Option Prices		
		Sign of Input Effect	
Input		**Call**	**Put**
Underlying stock price (S)		+	−
Strike price of the option contract (K)		−	+
Time remaining until option expiration (T)		+	+
Volatility of the underlying stock price (σ)		+	+
Risk-free interest rate (r)		+	−

FIGURE 16.6   Put and Call Option Prices

Input values:
$K = \$100$
$T = \frac{1}{4}$ year
$r = 5\%$
$\sigma = 25\%$

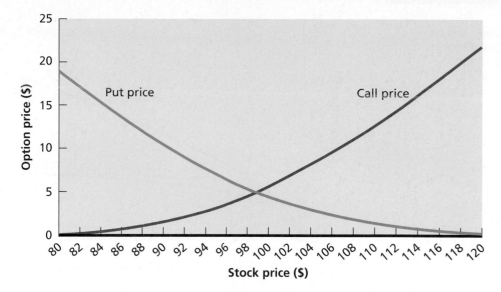

The two most important inputs determining stock option prices are the stock price and the strike price. However, the other input factors are also important determinants of option value. We next discuss each input factor separately.

VARYING THE UNDERLYING STOCK PRICE

Certainly, the price of the underlying stock is one of the most important determinants of the price of a stock option. As the stock price increases, the call option price increases and the put option price decreases. This is not surprising, because a call option grants the right to buy stock shares and a put option grants the right to sell stock shares at a fixed strike price. Consequently, a higher stock price at option expiration increases the payoff of a call option. Likewise, a lower stock price at option expiration increases the payoff of a put option.

For a given set of input values, the relationship between call and put option prices and an underlying stock price is illustrated in Figure 16.6. In Figure 16.6, stock prices are measured on the horizontal axis and option prices are measured on the vertical axis. Notice that the graph lines describing relationships between call and put option prices and the underlying stock price have a convex (bowed) shape. Convexity is a fundamental characteristic of the relationship between option prices and stock prices.

VARYING THE OPTION'S STRIKE PRICE

As the strike price increases, the call price decreases and the put price increases. This is reasonable, since a higher strike price means that we must pay a higher price when we exercise a call option to buy the underlying stock, thereby reducing the call option's value. Similarly, a higher strike price means that we will receive a higher price when we exercise a put option to sell the underlying stock, thereby increasing the put option's value. Of course, this logic works in reverse also; as the strike price decreases, the call price increases and the put price decreases.

VARYING THE TIME REMAINING UNTIL OPTION EXPIRATION

Time remaining until option expiration is an important determinant of option value. As time remaining until option expiration lengthens, both call and put option prices normally increase. This is expected, since a longer time remaining until option expiration allows more time for the stock price to move away from a strike price and increase the option's payoff, thereby making the option more valuable. The relationship between call and put option prices and time remaining until option expiration is illustrated in Figure 16.7, where time remaining until option expiration is measured on the horizontal axis and option prices are measured on the vertical axis.

FIGURE 16.7

Option Prices and Time to Expiration

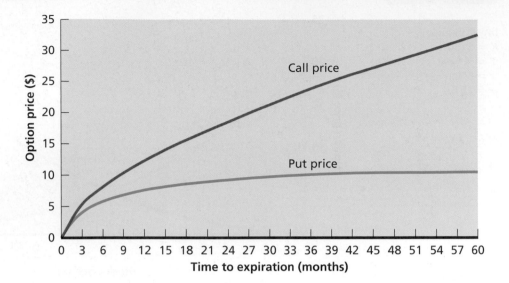

Input values:
$S = \$100$
$K = \$100$
$r = 5\%$
$\sigma = 25\%$

FIGURE 16.8

Option Prices and Sigma

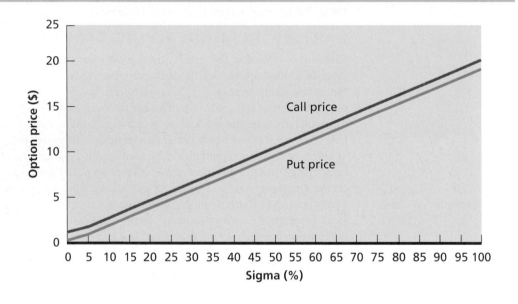

Input values:
$S = \$100$
$K = \$100$
$T = \frac{1}{4}$ year
$r = 5\%$

VARYING THE VOLATILITY OF THE STOCK PRICE

Stock price volatility (sigma, σ) plays an important role in determining option value. As stock price volatility increases, both call and put option prices increase. This is as expected, since the more volatile the stock price, the greater is the likelihood that the stock price will move farther away from a strike price and increase the option's payoff, thereby making the option more valuable. The relationship between call and put option prices and stock price volatility is graphed in Figure 16.8, where volatility is measured on the horizontal axis and option prices are measured on the vertical axis.

VARYING THE INTEREST RATE

Although seemingly not as important as the other inputs, the interest rate still noticeably affects option values. As the interest rate increases, the call price increases and the put price decreases. This is explained by the time value of money. A higher interest rate implies a greater discount, which lowers the present value of the strike price that we pay when we

FIGURE 16.9 · Option Prices and Interest Rates

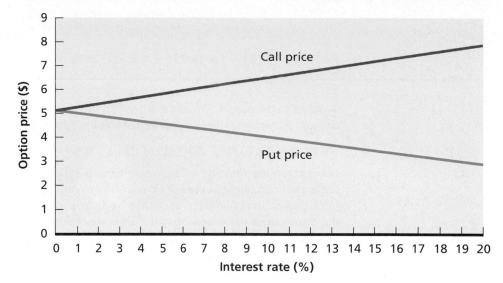

Input values:
$S = \$100$
$K = \$100$
$T = ¼$ year
$\sigma = 25\%$

exercise a call option or receive when we exercise a put option. Figure 16.9 graphs the relationship between call and put option prices and interest rates, where the interest rate is measured on the horizontal axis and option prices are measured on the vertical axis.

16.7 Measuring the Impact of Stock Price Changes on Option Prices

Investment professionals using options in their investment strategies have standard methods to state the impact of changes in input values on option prices. The two inputs that most affect stock option prices over a short period, say a few days, are the stock price and the stock price volatility. The approximate impact of a stock price change on an option price is stated by the option's **delta**.

delta

Measure of the dollar impact of a change in the underlying stock price on the value of a stock option. Delta is positive for a call option and negative for a put option.

You have seen delta earlier in this chapter. In the binomial model, we introduced the concept of delta, Δ. The difference between deltas in the binomial model and the Black-Scholes model is simple. Delta in the binomial model is calculated over discrete time periods, which can be very short. In the Black-Scholes model, time periods are infinitesimally short. In the Black-Scholes model, therefore, we measure delta as an instantaneous change in the option price when the stock price changes. In the Black-Scholes option pricing model, expressions for call and put option deltas are stated as follows, where the mathematical function and $N(x)$ were previously defined:

$$Call\ option\ delta = N(d_1) > 0$$
$$Put\ option\ delta = -N(-d_1) < 0$$

As shown above, a call option delta is always positive and a put option delta is always negative. This fact can be seen in Table 16.3, where the "+" indicates a positive change for a call option price and the "−" indicates a negative change for a put option price resulting from an increase in the underlying stock price.

EXAMPLE 16.4 · **Computing Call and Put Option Deltas**

Given the inputs to the Black-Scholes option pricing formula provided in Example 16.2, calculate call and put option deltas. The necessary values for d_1, $N(d_1)$, and $N(-d_1)$ were provided in Example 16.2.

$$N(d_1) = N(1.02538) = .84741 \quad N(-d_1) = 1 - N(d_1) = .15259$$

(continued)

Therefore:

$$\text{Call option delta} = N(d_1) = .84741$$

$$\text{Put option delta} = -N(-d_1) = -.15259$$

Notice that $N(d_1) - 1 = .84741 - 1 = -.15259 = -N(-d_1)$.

Refer to the nearby *Spreadsheet Analysis* box for examples of calculating Black-Scholes call and put option prices as well as deltas using a spreadsheet.

INTERPRETING OPTION DELTAS

Interpreting the meaning of an option delta is relatively straightforward. Delta measures the impact of a change in the stock price on an option price, where a $1 change in the stock price causes an option price to change by approximately delta dollars. For example, using the input values stated immediately below, we obtain a call option price (rounded) of $6.20 and a put option price (rounded) of $.52. These input values yield a call option delta of +.85 and a put option delta of −.15.

$$S = \$50 \qquad r = 6\%$$
$$K = \$45 \qquad \sigma = 25\%$$
$$T = .25$$

If we change the stock price from $50 to $51, we get a call option price of $7.06 and a put option price of $.39. Thus, a +$1 stock price change increased the call option price by $.86

SPREADSHEET ANALYSIS

	A	B	C	D	E	F	G
1							
2			Calculating Black-Scholes Option Prices				
3							
4	XYZ stock has a price of $50 and an annual return volatility of 25 percent. The riskless						
5	interest rate is 6 percent. Calculate call and put option prices with a strike price of $45						
6	and a 3-month time to expiration (0.25 years).						
7							
8	Stock =	50		d1 =	1.0254	N(d1) =	0.84741
9	Strike =	45				N(-d1) =	0.15259
10	Volatility =	0.25		d2 =	0.9004	N(d2) =	0.81604
11	Time =	0.25				N(-d2) =	0.18396
12	Rate =	0.06					
13						exp(-Rate x Time) =	0.98511
14							
15	Call Price =	Stock x N(d1) - Strike x exp(-Rate x Time) x N(d2) =					6.195
16	Put Price =	Strike x exp(-Rate x Time) x N(-d2) - Stock x N(-d1) =					0.525
17							
18							
19	Formula entered in E8 is =(LN(B8/B9)+(B12+0.5*B10^2)*B11)/(B10*SQRT(B11))						
20	Formula entered in E10 is =E8-B10*SQRT(B11)						
21	Formulas entered in G8 and G9 are =NORMSDIST(E8) and =NORMSDIST(-E8)						
22	Formulas entered in G10 and G11 are =NORMSDIST(E10) and =NORMSDIST(-E10)						
23							
24							
25			Calculating Black-Scholes Deltas				
26							
27	Call Delta =	N(d1) =					0.84741
28	Put Delta =	N(d1) - 1 = -N(-d1) =					-0.15259
29							
30							

and decreased the put option price by $.13. These price changes are close to, but not exactly equal to, the call option delta value of +.85 and put option delta value of −.15.

CHECK THIS

16.7a   Why do investors care about option deltas?

16.7b   Why do you think deltas for call options are positive but deltas for put options are negative?

16.8 Hedging Stock with Stock Options

Now that we know how to calculate option prices and option deltas, we turn our attention to an important way investors use options. Options provide investors with the opportunity to protect themselves against losses. Taking advantage of this opportunity is known as hedging.

Suppose you own 1,000 shares of XYZ stock, the stock we analyzed in the *Spreadsheet Analysis* earlier in the chapter. From the assumptions used in the *Spreadsheet Analysis,* we calculated prices and deltas for call and put options. If we had used all the same assumptions but used a stock price of $49 instead of $50, we would get a different set of prices and deltas for call and put options. Table 16.4 provides a convenient summary (notice we have rounded the option prices to two decimal places). In Table 16.4, all option prices use these inputs: a strike of $45, volatility of 25 percent, a risk-free rate of 6 percent, and three months to maturity.

Further, suppose that you want to protect yourself against declines in XYZ stock price. That is, you want to hedge: You want a portfolio that does not change in value if the stock price changes. To form this portfolio, you must add some options to your portfolio. How many options to add and whether you should be buying or selling options are two important questions that we answer. To begin, let us write down our goal:

$$\text{Change in value of stock portfolio} + \text{Change in value of options} = 0 \qquad (16.5)$$

The change in the value of the stock portfolio simply equals the change in the stock price times the number of shares. Similarly, the change in the value of options held is the change in the option price times the number of options. The one point to remember, however, is that the change in the option price depends on the change in the price of the stock.

From earlier in the chapter, we know that the delta of an option is a prediction of how the option price will change when the stock price changes by one dollar. If a call option has a delta of .58, the option price will change $.58 when the stock price changes by one dollar. If the stock prices increases by only $.50, then the option delta predicts that the call option price will increase by $.29. We generally assume that the stock price changes by one dollar when we are talking about hedging, but the stock price can change by other amounts. The lesson is that the change in the option price is equal to the option delta times the change in the stock price, which we denote as ΔS. So, if we multiply the change in the option price by the number of options held, we have the change in the value of options held. Knowing how to calculate these changes in value, we can write

$$\Delta S \times \text{Shares held} + \text{Option delta} \times \Delta S \times \text{Number of options} = 0 \qquad (16.6)$$

You can see that the change in the stock price, ΔS, can be eliminated from the equation. We know the number of shares we have and we can calculate an option delta using our favorite

TABLE 16.4	Using the Black-Scholes Option Model for Hedging				
XYZ Stock Price	**Call Price**	**Call Delta**	**Put Price**	**Put Delta**
$50	$6.195	0.8474	$0.525	−0.1526
$49	$5.368	0.8061	$0.698	−0.1939
Change in option price:	$−0.83		$0.17	

option pricing model. All we need to do is calculate the number of options that we need to add, which is:

$$\text{Number of options} = -\text{Shares held} \times (1/\text{Option delta})$$
$$= -\text{Shares held/Option delta} \qquad (16.7)$$

Equation (16.7) offers two important lessons. First, recall that an option delta tells us how many shares you need to hedge one call. The number of options that you need to hedge one share, therefore, is one divided by the option delta. Second, notice the minus sign out front. You can figure out whether to buy options depending on whether you get a positive number or a negative number in equation (16.7). We saw that deltas for call options are positive (but between zero and one), and deltas for put options are negative (but between minus one and zero). So, if we are hedging shares using call options, we need to sell call options. If we are hedging shares using put options, we need to purchase put options. A worked-out example will help you use these formulas.

HEDGING USING CALL OPTIONS—THE PREDICTION

As shown in Table 16.3, stock prices and call option prices are directly related. When the stock price increases, so do prices of call options on these shares. From Table 16.4, the call option delta is .8474 when XYZ stock price is $50. The call option delta is a prediction that the call option price will increase (decrease) by about $.85 if the stock price increases (decreases) by $1.00.

So, to hedge declines in XYZ share prices using call options, you need to write, or sell, call options to protect against a price decline. But notice that if the price of XYZ stock fell by $1.00 and you had 1,000 options, you would gain only $847.40. This would partially, but not fully, offset your loss of $1,000. You can do better by writing more options. Fortunately, you can use equation (16.7) to tell you how many call options to write:

$$\text{Number of options} = -\text{Shares} \times (1/\text{Option delta})$$
$$= -1,000/.8474 = -1,180.08$$

The minus sign confirms that you should write, or sell, call options. Because traded call options have 100 options per contract, you would need to write:

$$-1,180.08/100 \approx -12$$

call option contracts to create a hedge using call options with a strike of $45.

HEDGING USING CALL OPTIONS—THE RESULTS

Suppose you write 12 call option contracts at a price of $6.20 (rounded) per option, or $620 per contract. Further, just as you feared, XYZ stock fell in value by $1.00, so you suffered a $1,000 loss in the value of your shares. But what happened to the value of the call options you wrote? At the new XYZ stock price of $49, each call option is now worth $5.37 (rounded), a decrease of $.83 for each call, or $83 per contract. Because you wrote 12 call option contracts, your call option gain was $996.

Your gain in the call options nearly offsets your loss of $1,000 in XYZ shares. Why isn't it exact? You can see from Table 16.4 that delta also fell when the stock price fell. This means that you did not sell quite enough options. But because options contracts consist of 100 shares, you really did about as well as you could with this simple hedge.

HEDGING USING PUT OPTIONS—THE PREDICTION

As shown in Table 16.3, stock prices and put option prices are inversely related. When the stock price increases, put option prices on these shares decrease. From Table 16.4, the put option delta is −.1526 when the stock price is $50. The put option delta is a prediction that the put option price will decrease (increase) by about $.15 if the stock price increases (decreases) by $1.00.

Therefore, you want to purchase put options to profit from their price increase if the stock price decreases. But notice that if the price of XYZ stock fell by $1.00 and if you had 1,000 put options, you would gain only $152.60. This is insignificant when compared to your $1,000 loss in XYZ shares. You will have to purchase more put options if you are going to have a better hedge. Fortunately, equation (16.7) also tells you how many put options to purchase:

$$\text{Number of options} = -\text{Shares} \times (1/\text{Option delta})$$
$$= -1,000/-.1526 = 6,553.08$$

Because this number is positive, this confirms that you want to purchase put options. Because traded put options have 100 options per contract, you would need to purchase:

$$6,553.08/100 \approx 66$$

put option contracts to create a hedge using put options with a strike of $45.

HEDGING USING PUT OPTIONS—THE RESULTS

Suppose you purchase 66 put option contracts at a price of $.53 (rounded) per option, or $53 per contract. Again, as you feared, XYZ stock fell in value by $1.00, so you suffered a $1,000 loss in the value of your shares. But what happened to the value of the put options? At the new XYZ stock price of $49, each put option is now worth $.70, an increase of $.17 for each put option, or $17 per contract. Because you purchased 66 put option contracts, your put option gain was $1,122.

Your gain in the put options more than offsets your loss of $1,000 in XYZ shares. Why isn't it exact? You can see from Table 16.4 that the put delta also fell when the stock price fell (but it increased in absolute value). This means that you purchased too many put options. If you had purchased 59 put option contracts, you would have offset your share loss more closely. How would you have known that 59 put options make a better hedge than 66 options?

By constructing a table similar to Table 16.4 in advance, you would know that these put options increase in value by $.17 when the stock falls in value by $1. Therefore, each put option contract increases by about $17. Dividing $1,000 by $17 yields 58.82, telling us that 59 put contracts will provide a good hedge.

CHECK THIS

16.8a   What happens to call and put prices when the price of the underlying stock changes?

16.8b   What is the goal of a hedger who uses options?

16.9 Hedging a Stock Portfolio with Stock Index Options

Portfolio managers can hedge their entire equity portfolio by using stock index options. In this section, we examine how an equity portfolio manager might hedge a diversified stock portfolio using stock index options.

To begin, suppose that you manage a $10 million diversified portfolio of large-company stocks and that you maintain a portfolio beta of 1.00 for this portfolio. With a beta of 1.00, changes in the value of your portfolio closely follow changes in the Standard & Poor's 500 Index. Therefore, you decide to use options on the S&P 500 Index as a hedging vehicle. S&P 500 Index options trade on the Chicago Board Options Exchange (CBOE) under the ticker symbol SPX. SPX option prices are reported daily in the "Market Data Center" section at www.wsj.com. Each SPX option has a contract value of 100 times the current level of the S&P 500 Index.

SPX options are a convenient hedging vehicle for an equity portfolio manager because they are European style and because they settle in cash at expiration. For example, suppose you hold one SPX call option with a strike price of 1500 and at option expiration, the S&P 500 Index stands at 1507. In this case, your cash payoff is 100 times the difference between the index level and the strike price, or $100 \times (\$1507 - 1500) = \$700$. Of course, if the expiration date index level falls below the strike price, your SPX call option expires worthless.

Hedging a stock portfolio with index options requires first calculating the number of option contracts needed to form an effective hedge. While you can use either put options or call options to construct an effective hedge, we assume that you decide to use call options to hedge your $10 million equity portfolio. Using stock index call options to hedge an equity portfolio involves writing a certain number of option contracts. In general, the number of stock index option contracts needed to hedge an equity portfolio is stated by the equation:

$$\text{Number of option contracts} = -\frac{\text{Portfolio beta} \times \text{Portfolio value}}{\text{Option delta} \times \text{Option contract value}} \quad (16.8)$$

In your particular case, you have a portfolio beta of 1.00 and a portfolio value of $10 million. You now need to calculate an option delta and option contract value.

The option contract value for an SPX option is simply 100 times the current level of the S&P 500 Index. Checking the CBOE Web site, you see that the S&P 500 Index has a value of 1508, which means that each SPX option has a current contract value of $150,800.

To calculate an option delta, you must decide which particular contract to use. You decide to use options with an October expiration and a strike price of 1500, that is, the October 1500 SPX contract. From the Internet you find that the price for these options is 64.625 and their delta is .579.

You now have sufficient information to calculate the number of option contracts needed to construct an effective hedge for your equity portfolio. By using equation (16.8), we can calculate the number of October 1500 SPX options that you should write to form an effective hedge.

$$-\frac{1.00 \times \$10,000,000}{.579 \times \$150,800} \approx -115 \text{ contracts}$$

Furthermore, by writing 115 October 1500 call options, you receive $115 \times 100 \times 64.625 = \$743,187.50$.

To assess the effectiveness of this hedge, suppose the S&P 500 Index and your stock portfolio both immediately fall in value by 1 percent. This is a loss of $100,000 on your stock portfolio. After the S&P 500 Index falls by 1 percent, its level is 1492.92. Suppose the call option price is now $C = \$56.21$. If you were to buy back the 115 contracts, you would pay $115 \times 100 \times \$56.21 = \$646,415$. Because you originally received $743,187.50 for the options, this represents a gain of $\$743,187.50 - \$646,415 = \$96,772.50$, which cancels most of the $100,000 loss on your equity portfolio. In fact, your final net loss is only $3,227.50, which is a small fraction of the loss that would have been realized with an unhedged portfolio.

To maintain an effective hedge over time, you will need to rebalance your options hedge on, say, a weekly basis. Rebalancing simply requires calculating anew the number of option contracts needed to hedge your equity portfolio, and then buying or selling options in the amount necessary to maintain an effective hedge. The nearby *Investment Updates* box contains a brief *Wall Street Journal* report on hedging strategies using stock index options.

EXAMPLE 16.5

The Option Hedge Ratio for a Stock Portfolio

You are managing a $15 million stock portfolio with a beta of 1.1, which you decide to hedge by buying index put options with a contract value of $125,000 per contract and a delta of −.40. How many option contracts are required?

Plugging our information into equation (16.8) yields this calculation:

$$-\frac{1.1 \times \$15,000,000}{-.40 \times \$125,000} = 330 \text{ contracts}$$

Thus, you would need to buy 330 put option contracts.

MONEY MANAGERS USE OPTIONS TO HEDGE PORTFOLIOS

Traders and money managers began using options to hedge their portfolios yesterday after spending the past week ignoring defensive strategies to speculate on earnings and stock price movements.

The turning point came late in the morning when the Standard & Poor's 500 Index slid below 1,140. This wiped out many S&P 500 Index futures positions and market professionals responded by buying S&P 500 Index options to protect their portfolios from the market's volatility.

This hedging activity marked a change in the approach they have taken to the market. Many professionals recently stopped hedging their portfolios because the stock market has quickly corrected in the past. They spent money for hedges they ultimately didn't need.

"A lot of people were completely unhedged when the decline began," said Leon Gross, Salomon Smith Barney's options strategist. He noted that the S&P 500 Index's rise to 1,186 from 1,086 took six weeks, while it dropped 50 points in only four days.

The fear in the options market spiked higher as the S&P Index fell along with the Dow Jones Industrial Average.

The option market's fear gauge, the Chicago Board Options Exchange Volatility Index, rose 1.72, or 7.5%, to 24.66. "This is an indication that people are getting nervous and paying for puts," Mr. Gross said.

Options prices reflected this discomfort, which made hedging portfolios even more expensive than normal. For more aggressive traders, such as hedge funds, high options prices created opportunities to short sell puts and sectors.

The NASDAQ Index of the 100 largest nonfinancial stocks was a popular way to short the technology sector. Other traders sold put options because they think the fear is overdone and they'll be able to buy the contracts back for less money.

Source: Steven M. Sears, *The Wall Street Journal*, July 29, 1998. Reprinted with permission of *The Wall Street Journal*. © 1998 Dow Jones & Company, Inc. All Rights Reserved Worldwide.

CHECK THIS

16.9a   In the hedging example in the text, suppose that your equity portfolio had a beta of 1.50 instead of 1.00. What number of SPX call options would be required to form an effective hedge?

16.9b   Alternatively, suppose that your equity portfolio had a beta of .50. What number of SPX call options would then be required to form an effective hedge?

16.10 Implied Standard Deviations

implied standard deviation (ISD)

An estimate of stock price volatility obtained from an option price.

implied volatility (IVOL)

Another term for implied standard deviation.

WWW

For applications of implied volatility, see www.ivolatility.com

The Black-Scholes option pricing model is based on five inputs: a stock price, a strike price, an interest rate, the time remaining until option expiration, and the stock price volatility. Of these five factors, only the stock price volatility is not directly observable and must be estimated somehow. A popular method to estimate stock price volatility is to use an implied value from an option price. A stock price volatility estimated from an option price is called an **implied standard deviation** or **implied volatility**, often abbreviated as **ISD** or **IVOL**, respectively. Implied volatility and implied standard deviation are two terms for the same thing.

Calculating an implied volatility requires that all input factors have known values, except sigma, and that a call or put option price be known. For example, consider the following option price input values, absent a value for sigma.

$$S = \$50 \qquad T = .25$$
$$K = \$45 \qquad r = 6\%$$

Suppose we also have a call price of $C = \$6.195$. Based on this call price, what is the implied volatility? In other words, in combination with the input values stated above, what sigma value yields a call price of $C = \$6.195$? The answer comes from Example 16.2, which shows that a sigma value of .25, or 25 percent, yields a call option price of $6.195.

WORK THE WEB

Solving for an ISD using the other option price inputs (and the option price) can be tedious. Fortunately, many option calculators will do the work for you. Suppose you have a call option with a strike price of $45 that expires in three months. The stock currently sells for $50, the option sells for $7, and the interest rate is 6 percent per year. What is the ISD? To find out, we went to the options calculator at www.numa.com. After entering all this information, here is what we got:

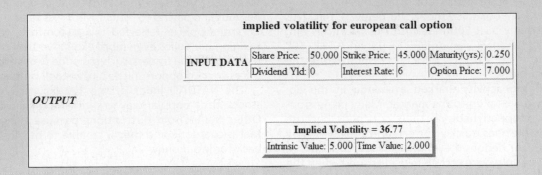

implied volatility for european call option					
INPUT DATA	Share Price: 50.000	Strike Price: 45.000	Maturity(yrs): 0.250
	Dividend Yld: 0	Interest Rate: 6	Option Price: 7.000

OUTPUT

Implied Volatility = 36.77
Intrinsic Value: 5.000 Time Value: 2.000

Notice the calculator changes the time to maturity to 0.250, because three months is one-fourth of a year. Based on the input data, the underlying stock has an ISD of 36.77 percent per year.

Now suppose we wish to know what volatility value is implied by a call price of $C = \$7$. To obtain this implied volatility value, we must find the value for sigma that yields this call price. By trial and error, you can try various sigma values until a call option price of $7 is obtained. This occurs with a sigma value of 36.77 percent, which is the implied standard deviation (ISD) corresponding to a call option price of $7. Our nearby *Work the Web* box shows how to get ISDs the easy way.

CBOE IMPLIED VOLATILITIES FOR STOCK INDEXES

VIX, VXO, VXN

Volatility indexes for the S&P 500, S&P 100, and NASDAQ 100 stock indexes, respectively, based on stock index options.

The Chicago Board Options Exchange (CBOE) publishes three implied volatility indexes: the S&P 500 Volatility Index (**VIX**), the S&P 100 Volatility Index (**VXO**), and the NASDAQ 100 Volatility Index (**VXN**). These indexes are three of the most popular measures of investor expectations of future stock market volatility. They are based on options traded on three major stock market indexes: the S&P 500, the S&P 100, and the NASDAQ 100. The ticker symbols for these three volatility indexes and the underlying stock indexes are summarized as follows:

Volatility Index Ticker	Stock Index	Stock Index Ticker
VIX	S&P 500	SPX
VXO	S&P 100	OEX
VXN	NASDAQ 100	NDX

Current levels for these volatility indexes are available at the CBOE Web site (www.cboe .com). You can also check them at Yahoo! Finance (finance.yahoo.com), along with the levels of their underlying stock indexes, using their ticker symbols. Note that the ticker symbols for these indexes do not correspond to traded securities and so must be preceded by a caret sign, that is, ^VIX, ^VXO, and ^VXN.

The VIX, VXO, and VXN implied volatility indexes are reported as annualized standard deviations. These volatility indexes provide investors with current estimates of expected market volatility in the month ahead. In fact, another name for the VIX is the "investor fear gauge." This name stems from the belief that the VIX reflects investors' collective prediction of near-term market volatility, or risk. Generally, the VIX increases during times of high financial stress and decreases during times of low financial stress.

Some investors use the VIX as a buy-sell indicator. This is because low levels of the VIX have, in many instances, preceded market selloffs. The market saying is: "When the VIX is high, it's time to buy; when the VIX is low, it's time to go!"

16.11 Employee Stock Options

In this section, we take a brief look at **employee stock options**, or **ESOs**. An ESO is, in essence, a call option that a firm gives to employees giving them the right to buy shares of stock in the company. The practice of granting options to employees has become widespread. It is almost universal for upper management, but some companies, like The Gap and Starbucks, have granted options to almost every employee. Thus, an understanding of ESOs is important. Why? Because you may very soon be an ESO holder!

ESO FEATURES

Because ESOs are basically call options, we have already covered most of the important aspects. However, ESOs have a few features that make them different from regular stock options. The details differ from company to company, but a typical ESO has a 10-year life, which is much longer than most ordinary options. Unlike traded options, ESOs cannot be sold. They also have what is known as a "vesting" period. Often, for up to three years or so, an ESO cannot be exercised and also must be forfeited if an employee leaves the company. After this period, the options "vest," which means they can be exercised. Sometimes employees who resign with vested options are given a limited time to exercise their options.

Why are ESOs granted? There are basically two reasons. First, the owners of a corporation (the shareholders) face the basic problem of aligning shareholder and management interests and also of providing incentives for employees to focus on corporate goals. ESOs are a powerful motivator because, as we have seen, the payoffs on options can be very large. High-level executives in particular stand to gain enormous wealth if they are successful in creating value for stockholders.

The second reason some companies rely heavily on ESOs is that an ESO has no immediate, upfront, out-of-pocket cost to the corporation. In smaller, possibly cash-strapped, companies, ESOs are simply a substitute for ordinary wages. Employees are willing to accept them instead of cash, hoping for big payoffs in the future. In fact, ESOs are a major recruiting tool, allowing businesses to attract talent that they otherwise could not afford.

ESO REPRICING

ESOs are almost always "at the money" when they are issued, meaning that the stock price is equal to the strike price. Notice that, in this case, the intrinsic value is zero, so there is no value from immediate exercise. Of course, even though the intrinsic value is zero, an ESO is still quite valuable because of, among other things, its very long life.

If the stock falls significantly after an ESO is granted, then the option is said to be "underwater." On occasion, a company will decide to lower the strike price on underwater options. Such options are said to be "restruck" or "repriced."

The practice of repricing ESOs is very controversial. Companies that do it argue that once an ESO becomes deeply out of the money, it loses its incentive value because employees recognize there is only a small chance that the option will finish in the money. In fact, employees may leave and join other companies where they receive a fresh options grant.

Critics of repricing point out that a lowered strike price is, in essence, a reward for failing. They also point out that if employees know that options will be repriced, then much of the incentive effect is lost. Today, many companies award options on a regular basis, perhaps annually or even quarterly. That way, an employee will always have at least some options that are near the money even if others are underwater. Also, regular grants ensure that employees always have unvested options, which gives them an added incentive to stay with their current employer rather than forfeit the potentially valuable options.

16.11a What are the key differences between a traded stock option and an ESO?

16.11b What is ESO repricing? Why is it controversial?

CHECK THIS

ESOs AT THE GAP, INC.

The Gap, Inc., is a large, well-known company whose stock trades under the ticker symbol GPS (GAP is the ticker symbol for Great Atlantic & Pacific Tea Co., which you probably know as A&P). The Gap grants employee stock options that are fairly standard. This description of The Gap's ESOs is taken from its annual report:

> Under our stock option plans, options to purchase common stock are granted to officers, directors, eligible employees and consultants at exercise prices equal to the fair market value of the stock at the date of grant. Stock options generally expire 10 years from the grant date, three months after termination, or one year after the date of retirement or death, if earlier. Stock options generally vest over a four-year period, with shares becoming exercisable in equal annual installments of 25 percent.

The GAP's ESOs are not European-style options because they vest in equal increments over a four-year period. By "vest," we mean the holders can exercise these options. If you were granted options on 500 shares of GPS stock, you could exercise options on 125 shares one year after the grant date, another 125 shares two years after the grant date, another 125 shares three years after the grant date, and the last 125 shares four years after the grant date. Of course, you wouldn't have to exercise your options this quickly. As long as you stay with the company you could wait 10 years to exercise your options just before they expire.

16.11c If you terminate your employment at The Gap, Inc., how long do you have to decide whether you will exercise your employee stock options?

CHECK THIS

VALUING EMPLOYEE STOCK OPTIONS

The Financial Accounting Standards Board issued FASB 123 to tell companies how to calculate the fair value of employee stock options. Basically, FASB 123 states that the fair value of ESOs should be determined using an option pricing model that takes into account the:

- Stock price at the grant date.
- Exercise price.
- Expected life of the option.
- Volatility of the underlying stock.
- Risk-free interest rate over the expected life of the option.
- Expected dividends.

As a practical matter, many companies calculate ESO prices using the Black-Scholes-Merton option pricing model. The Black-Scholes-Merton model is very similar to the Black-Scholes model. The difference between the two models is that expected dividends are an input for the Black-Scholes-Merton model.

INVESTMENT UPDATES

COKE PLAN FOR OPTION VALUING FIZZLES OUT AFTER FEW MONTHS: NEWS DASHES HOPES FOR ALTERNATIVE TO BLACK-SCHOLES EXPENSING MODELS

Coca-Cola Co.'s novel plan for valuing its employee stock-option compensation has fizzled out.

The world's biggest soft-drink company made a splash in July by announcing it would begin recognizing stock-option compensation as an expense on its financial statements. But it wasn't just Coke's decision to expense that piqued market interest. Even more noteworthy was the unique valuation method it planned to use, at Coke director Warren Buffett's urging. Instead of using Wall Street's much maligned, but widely used, Black-Scholes mathematical models, Coke said it would solicit quotations from two independent financial institutions to buy and sell Coke shares under the identical terms of the options to be expensed. Coke then would average the quotations to determine the value of the options.

So much for that plan.

Coke now concedes it won't work and that it will use Black-Scholes after all, notwithstanding the method's drawbacks. The disclosure almost certainly will disappoint investors who favor mandatory expensing of option-based compensation, but had been hoping for a feasible alternative to the subjective results often produced by Black-Scholes models.

It also signals that Black-Scholes, like it or not, may remain the norm even should the Financial Accounting Standards Board follow through with its plans to unveil a proposal this year mandating that public companies treat stock-option compensation as an expense.

Coke executives Thursday said they had no choice but to abandon the Buffett-backed plan. They said the company eventually concluded that current accounting standards wouldn't allow the new approach and instead require companies to perform their own value calculations.

In any event, the disclosure in Coke's proxy shows that dealer quotes wouldn't have yielded any different results than a Black-Scholes calculation. Coke says it determined the value of the options through Black-Scholes calculations—and only then obtained independent market quotes from two dealers "to ensure the best market-based assumptions were used." And, as it turned out, "our Black-Scholes value was not materially different from the independent quotes," Coke's proxy says. Coke declined to name the two financial institutions.

Because the dealer quotes were so similar, "you can assume they use Black-Scholes too," says Gary Fayard, Coke's chief financial officer. Asked if an alternative to Black-Scholes is needed, Mr. Fayard says, "I think it's something that business and the accounting profession need to work on and evaluate."

Given the lack of any meaningful difference, some accounting specialists say future efforts to seek market quotations for employee options likely will be pointless. "All they did was go to the expense of getting quotes from two independent parties who may have used the Black-Scholes model themselves," says Jack Ciesielski, publisher of the Analyst's Accounting Observer newsletter in Baltimore. "The whole affair winds up being an exercise in circularity."

While expensing options remains voluntary, all public companies are required to disclose what the effect on their earnings would be if they did expense options. Most such disclosures rely on variants of the model published in the 1970s by economists Fischer Black and Myron Scholes.

Like almost all valuation models, Black-Scholes hinges on lots of assumptions. For instance, option-pricing models typically require projections of the underlying security's future volatility, as well as the option's expected life. Those aren't easy to project with any precision. Even small changes in assumptions can make crucial differences in results and, consequently, a company's reported expenses. What's more, the Black-Scholes model wasn't designed to value options that, like the kind companies grant to employees, aren't freely transferable.

For example, SEC proxy rules required Coke to assume the options' time horizon would be the full life of the options' terms, or 15 years. That drove Coke to assume relatively lower volatility, given the lengthy time horizon. Using those assumptions, Coke calculated that the value of its options was $19.92 a share. However, accounting rules required Coke to use the options' "expected life" when calculating the time horizon. Coke assumed six years. That reduced the options' value, though the effect was partly offset by Coke's assumptions that volatility would be higher, given the shorter time span. The result: Under that Black-Scholes calculation, the value was $13.06 a share.

Source: Jonathan Weil and Betsy McKay, *The Wall Street Journal*, March 7, 2003. Reprinted with permission of *The Wall Street Journal*.

TABLE 16.5

Coca-Cola Employee Stock Options

Inputs	Input Value Assumptions	
Stock price	$44.55	$44.55
Exercise price	$44.655	$44.655
Time horizon	15 years	6 years
Volatility	25.53%	30.20%
Risk-free interest rate	5.65%	3.40%
Dividend yield	1.59%	1.70%
Black-Scholes-Merton option value	$19.92	$13.06

In terms of its six inputs, the Black-Scholes-Merton call option formula is:[5]

$$C = Se^{-yT}N(d_1) - Ke^{-rT}N(d_2)$$ (16.9)

One piece of equation (16.9) that is different from the Black-Scholes formula is that the stock price is discounted by the term e^{-yT}. In this discounting term, y represents the stock's dividend yield. In addition, the numbers d_1 and d_2 are calculated as

$$d_1 = \frac{\ln(S/K) + (r - y + \sigma^2/2)T}{\sigma\sqrt{T}} \quad \text{and} \quad d_2 = d_1 - \sigma\sqrt{T}$$

How do companies use the Black-Scholes-Merton formula to calculate ESO values? As an example, in December 2002, the Coca-Cola Company granted to several executives employee stock options representing more than half a million shares of Coke stock. The options had a stated term of 15 years, but, to allow for the fact that employee stock options are often exercised before maturity, Coca-Cola used two time horizon assumptions to value the options: the longest possible term of 15 years and an expected term of 6 years. The company then adjusted the interest rate, dividend yield, and volatility assumptions to each of these terms.

The different input values assumed and the resulting Black-Scholes option values are summarized in Table 16.5. Notice that Coca-Cola assumed a higher volatility and dividend yield, but a lower riskless interest rate for the six-year time horizon assumption. These assumptions seem reasonable because stock market volatility was relatively high and interest rates were relatively low in 2002. A *Wall Street Journal* article discussing the valuation of these Coke options is contained in the nearby *Investment Updates* box.

Visit the Coca-Cola Web site at
www.coca-cola.com
for more investor information

16.12 Summary and Conclusions

In this chapter, we examined stock option prices. Many important concepts and details of option pricing were covered. We summarize some of these aspects by the learning objectives of the chapter below. However, be warned. The following summary does not include important details of how to calculate option prices. You will need to study the body of the chapter to become proficient in these important details.

1. **How to price options using the one-period and two-period binomial models.**

   A. We show the details for a method to price European call options using the one-period and two-period binomial models. With a slight modification to allow for early exercise,

---

[5] Strictly speaking, the Black-Scholes-Merton formula is used for European options. ESOs are a hybrid between European options and American options. Before vesting, ESO holders cannot exercise these options, so ESOs are like European options in the vesting period. After vesting, ESO holders can exercise their ESOs before the ESO expires, so ESOs are like American options after the vesting period.

this technique can also be used to calculate prices for American calls and puts. In fact, this basic technique is so powerful that, with the right modifications, it can be used to price an exotic array of options.

B. The details of this method are:

- *Step 1:* Build a price tree for stock prices through time.
- *Step 2:* Use the intrinsic value formula to calculate the possible option prices at expiration.
- *Step 3:* Calculate the fractional share needed to form each risk-free portfolio at the next-to-last date.
- *Step 4:* Calculate all the possible option prices at the next-to-last date.
- *Step 5:* Repeat this process by working back to today.

2. How to price options using the Black-Scholes model.

A. The Black-Scholes option pricing formula states that the value of a stock option is a function of the current stock price, option strike price, risk-free interest rate, time remaining until option expiration, and the stock price volatility.

B. The two most important determinants of the price of a stock option are the price of the underlying stock and the strike price of the option. As the stock price increases, call prices increase and put prices decrease. Conversely, as the strike price increases, call prices decrease and put prices increase.

C. Time remaining until option expiration is an important determinant of option value. As time remaining until option expiration lengthens, both call and put option prices normally increase. Stock price volatility also plays an important role in determining option value. As stock price volatility increases, both call and put option prices increase.

D. Of the five input factors to the Black-Scholes option pricing model, only the stock price volatility is not directly observable and must be estimated somehow. A stock price volatility estimated from an option price is called an implied volatility or an implied standard deviation, which are two terms for the same thing.

E. The two input factors that most affect stock option prices over a short period, say, a few days, are the stock price and the stock price volatility. The impact of a stock price change on an option price is measured by the option's delta.

3. How to hedge a stock portfolio using options.

A. Call option deltas are always positive, and put option deltas are always negative. Delta measures the impact of a stock price change on an option price, where a one-dollar change in the stock price causes an option price to change by approximately delta dollars.

B. Options on the underlying stock can be used by investors to protect themselves from price declines in shares that they own. Option deltas can be used to calculate the number of options needed to hedge shares that are owned. Investors can write call options or purchase put options to provide protection from decreases in share prices.

C. Options on the S&P 500 Index are a convenient hedging vehicle for an equity portfolio because they are European style and because they settle for cash at option expiration. Hedging a stock portfolio with index options requires calculating the number of option contracts needed to form an effective hedge.

D. To maintain an effective hedge over time, hedgers should rebalance their hedge on a regular basis. Rebalancing requires (1) recalculating the number of option contracts needed to hedge an equity portfolio and then (2) buying or selling options in the amount necessary to maintain an effective hedge.

4. The workings of employee stock options.

A. An employee stock option (ESO) is, in essence, a call option that a firm gives to employees giving them the right to buy shares of stock in the company. The practice of granting options to employees has become widespread. ESOs provide an incentive for employees to work to increase the firm's stock price.

B. ESOs have a few features that make them different from regular stock options. The details differ from company to company, but a typical ESO has a 10-year life, which is much longer than most ordinary options. Unlike traded options, ESOs cannot be sold. They also have what is known as a "vesting" period. Often, for up to three years or so, an ESO cannot be exercised and also must be forfeited if an employee leaves the company. After this period, the options vest, which means they can be exercised.

C. The Financial Accounting Standards Board issued FASB 123 to tell companies how to calculate the fair value of employee stock options. As a practical matter, many companies calculate ESO prices using the Black-Scholes-Merton option pricing model. The Black-Scholes-Merton model is very similar to the Black-Scholes model. The difference between the two models is that expected dividends are an input for the Black-Scholes-Merton model.

GET REAL

This chapter began by introducing you to the Nobel-Prize-winning Black-Scholes option pricing formula. We saw that the formula and its associated concepts are fairly complex, but, despite that complexity, the formula is very widely used by traders and money managers. You can find out more about the Black-Scholes option pricing model on the Internet. Enter "Black-Scholes" into an Internet search engine for links to hundreds of Web sites.

To put into practice some real-world uses for the concepts we discussed, you should gather options trading information off the Web and then use the information to trade options through Stock-Trak. Some suggested Web sites are the Web Center for Futures and Options (www.ino.com), NUMA Derivatives (www.numa.com), and PM Publishing (www.pmpublishing.com). Of course, don't forget the most extensive Web site for options, the Chicago Board Options Exchange (www.cboe.com).

Another important use for option pricing theory is to gain some insight into stock market volatility. Recall that in Chapter 1 we discussed the probabilities associated with returns equal to the average plus or minus a particular number of standard deviations. Implied standard deviations (ISDs) provide a means of broadening this analysis to anything with traded options. You can learn a lot about implied volatilities and how they are used by options professionals on the Internet. Enter the search phrases "implied volatility" or "implied standard deviation" into your favorite Internet search engine for links to dozens of Web sites, like IVolatility (www.ivolatility.com).

Key Terms

delta 559
employee stock option (ESO) 567
expiry 553

implied standard deviation (ISD) 565
implied volatility (IVOL) 565
VIX, VXO, VXN 566

Chapter Review Problems and Self-Test

1. **Black-Scholes Formula (LO2, CFA2)** What is the value of a call option if the underlying stock price is $100, the strike price is $90, the underlying stock volatility is 40 percent, and the risk-free rate is 4 percent? Assume the option has 60 days to expiration.

2. **Black-Scholes Formula (LO2, CFA2)** What is the value of a put option using the assumptions from the previous problem?

1. We will use these input values to calculate the price of the call option:

S = current stock price = \$100
K = option strike price = \$90
r = risk-free interest rate = .04
σ = stock volatility = .40
T = time to expiration = 60 days

We first compute values for d_1 and d_2.

$$d_1 = \frac{\ln(100/90) + (.04 + .4^2/2) \times 60/365}{.4\sqrt{60/365}}$$

$$= \frac{.10536 + .12 \times .16438}{.16218}$$

$$= .77128$$

$$d_2 = d_1 - .16218$$

$$= .60910$$

The following standard normal probabilities are given:

$$N(d_1) = N(.77128) = .77973 \qquad N(d_2) = N(.60910) = .72877$$

We can now calculate the price of the call option as:

$$C = \$100 \times .77973 - \$90 \times e^{-.04 \times 60/365} \times .72877$$

$$= \$100 \times .77973 - \$90 \times .99345 \times .72877$$

$$= \$12.81$$

2. Since we already know the values for d_1 and d_2, we can solve for $N(-d_1)$ and $N(-d_2)$ as follows:

$$N(-d_1) = 1 - N(d_1) = 1 - .77973 = .22027$$

$$N(-d_2) = 1 - N(d_2) = 1 - .72877 = .27123$$

We can now calculate the price of the put option as:

$$P = \$90 \times e^{-.04 \times 60/365} \times .27123 - \$100 \times .22027$$

$$= \$90 \times .99345 \times .27123 - \$100 \times .22027$$

$$= \$2.22$$

Alternatively, using put-call parity (from the previous chapter):

$$P = C + Ke^{-rT} - S$$

$$= \$12.81 + \$90 \times e^{-.05 \times 90/365} - \$100$$

$$= \$12.81 + \$90 \times .99345 - \$100$$

$$= \$2.22$$

Test Your Investment Quotient

1. Black-Scholes Model (LO2, CFA2) The only variable in the Black-Scholes option pricing model that cannot be directly observed is the

   a. Stock price volatility.
   b. Time to expiration.
   c. Stock price.
   d. Risk-free rate.

2. Delta (LO2, CFA2) You purchase a call option with a delta of .34. If the stock price decreases by \$2.00, the price of the option will approximately

   a. Increase by \$.34.
   b. Decrease by \$.34.
   c. Increase by \$.68.
   d. Decrease by \$.68.

3. **Black-Scholes Model (LO2, CFA2)** In the Black-Scholes option pricing model, the value of an option contract is a function of five inputs. Which of the following is not one of these inputs?

   a. The price of the underlying stock.
   b. The strike price of the option contract.
   c. The expected return on the underlying stock.
   d. The time remaining until option expiration.

4. **Black-Scholes Formula (LO2, CFA2)** In the Black-Scholes option valuation formula, an increase in a stock's volatility

   a. Increases the associated call option value.
   b. Decreases the associated put option value.
   c. Increases or decreases the option value, depending on the level of interest rates.
   d. Does not change either the put or call option value because put-call parity holds.

5. **Option Prices (LO2, CFA2)** Which one of the following will increase the value of a call option?

   a. An increase in interest rates.
   b. A decrease in time to expiration of the call.
   c. A decrease in the volatility of the underlying stock.
   d. A decrease in the price of the underlying stock.

6. **Option Prices (LO2, CFA2)** Which one of the following would tend to result in a high value of a call option?

   a. Interest rates are low.
   b. The variability of the underlying stock is high.
   c. There is little time remaining until the option expires.
   d. The exercise price is high relative to the stock price.

7. **Option Price Factors (LO2, CFA2)** Which of the following incorrectly states the signs of the impact of an increase in the indicated input factor on call and put option prices?

	Call	Put
a. Strike price of the option contract.	+	−
b. Time remaining until option expiration.	+	+
c. Underlying stock price.	+	−
d. Volatility of the underlying stock price.	+	+

8. **Option Prices (LO2, CFA2)** Increasing the time to maturity of a call option will _____ the price of the option at a(n) _____ rate.

   a. Increase; increasing
   b. Decrease; decreasing
   c. Increase; decreasing
   d. Decrease; decreasing

9. **Option Prices (LO2, CFA2)** All else the same, an increase in which of the following will decrease the price of a call option?

   a. The strike price.
   b. The price of the underlying stock.
   c. The standard deviation of the underlying stock.
   d. The risk-free rate.

10. **Hedging with Options (LO3, CFA3)** All else the same, as the value of an option used to hedge an equity portfolio increases, the number of options needed to hedge the portfolio

    a. Increases.
    b. Decreases.
    c. Will not change.
    d. Increases only if the beta of the portfolio is less than 1.

11. **Hedging with Options (LO3, CFA3)** You wish to hedge a $5 million stock portfolio with a portfolio beta equal to 1. The hedging index call option has a delta equal to .5 and a contract value equal to $100,000. Which of the following hedging transactions is required to hedge the stock portfolio?

    a. Write 200 index call option contracts.
    b. Write 100 index call option contracts.

    c. Buy 200 index call option contracts.

    d. Buy 100 index call option contracts.

12. **Hedging with Options (LO3, CFA3)**   You wish to hedge a $10 million stock portfolio with a portfolio beta equal to 1. The hedging index put option has a delta equal to .5 and a contract value of $200,000. Which of the following hedging transactions is required to hedge the stock portfolio?

    a. Write 200 put option contracts.

    b. Write 100 put option contracts.

    c. Buy 200 put option contracts.

    d. Buy 100 put option contracts.

13. **Implied Volatility (LO4, CFA2)**   Which of the following provides the best economic interpretation of implied volatility for an underlying stock?

    a. Implied volatility predicts the stock's future volatility.

    b. Implied volatility states the stock's historical volatility.

    c. Implied volatility is unrelated to the underlying stock.

    d. Implied volatility is an accurate measure of interest rate risk.

14. **Implied Volatility (LO4, CFA2)**   Two call options on the same underlying stock with the same expiration dates have strike prices of $40 and $60 and yield implied volatilities of 45 percent and 35 percent, respectively. The stock price is $50. This means that

    a. The underlying stock has two different volatilities.

    b. Both options are incorrectly priced.

    c. The volatility skew has a negative slope.

    d. The underlying stock will soon pay a dividend.

15. **Implied Volatility (LO4, CFA2)**   The implied volatility for an at-the-money call option suddenly jumps from 25 percent to 50 percent. This most likely means that

    a. The underlying stock has just paid a dividend.

    b. The volatility jump is temporary.

    c. The option has a short time to expiration.

    d. An unforeseen event has increased the risk of the underlying stock.

Concept Questions

1. **Option Prices (LO2, CFA1)**   What are the six factors that determine an option's price?

2. **Options and Expiration Dates (LO2, CFA2)**   What is the impact of lengthening the time to expiration on an option's value? Explain.

3. **Options and Stock Price Volatility (LO2, CFA2)**   What is the impact of an increase in the volatility of the underlying stock on an option's value? Explain.

4. **Options and Dividend Yields (LO2, CFA2)**   What happens to the stock price when the stock pays a dividend? What impact does a dividend have on the prices of call and put options?

5. **Options and Interest Rates (LO2, CFA2)**   How do interest rates affect option prices? Explain.

6. **Time Value (LO2, CFA2)**   What is the time value of a call option? Of a put option? What happens to the time value of a call option as the maturity increases? What about a put option?

7. **Delta (LO2, CFA2)**   What does an option's delta tell us? Suppose a call option with a delta of .60 sells for $5.00. If the stock price rises by $1, what will happen to the call's value?

8. **Employee Stock Options (LO4)**   What is vesting in regard to employee stock options? Why would a company use a vesting schedule with employee stock options?

9. **Employee Stock Options (LO4)**   You own stock in a company that has just initiated employee stock options. How do the employee stock options benefit you as a shareholder?

10. **Employee Stock Options (LO4)**   In general, employee stock options cannot be sold to another party. How do you think this affects the value of an employee stock option compared to a market-traded option?

Questions and Problems

Core Questions

1. **Black-Scholes Model (LO2, CFA2)**   What is the value of a call option if the underlying stock price is $84, the strike price is $80, the underlying stock volatility is 42 percent, and the risk-free rate is 4 percent? Assume the option has 135 days to expiration.

2. **Black-Scholes Model (LO2, CFA2)**   What is the value of a call option if the underlying stock price is $86, the strike price is $90, the underlying stock volatility is 40 percent, and the risk-free rate is 3 percent? Assume the option has 60 days to expiration.

3. **Black-Scholes Model (LO2, CFA2)**   What is the value of a call option if the underlying stock price is $73, the strike price is $75, the underlying stock volatility is 37 percent, and the risk-free rate is 5 percent? Assume the option has 100 days to expiration.

4. **Black-Scholes-Merton Model (LO2, CFA2)**   A stock is currently priced at $63 and has an annual standard deviation of 43 percent. The dividend yield of the stock is 3 percent, and the risk-free rate is 6 percent. What is the value of a call option on the stock with a strike price of $60 and 45 days to expiration?

5. **Black-Scholes-Merton Model (LO2, CFA2)**   The stock of Nugents Nougats currently sells for $44 and has an annual standard deviation of 45 percent. The stock has a dividend yield of 2.5 percent, and the risk-free rate is 4.1 percent. What is the value of a call option on the stock with a strike price of $40 and 65 days to expiration?

6. **Black-Scholes Model (LO2, CFA2)**   The stock of Lead Zeppelin, a metal manufacturer, currently sells for $86 and has an annual standard deviation of 41 percent. The risk-free rate is 6 percent. What is the value of a put option with a strike price of $90 and 45 days to expiration?

7. **Black-Scholes Model (LO2, CFA2)**   What is the value of a put option if the underlying stock price is $42, the strike price is $35, the underlying stock volatility is 47 percent, and the risk-free rate is 5 percent? Assume the option has 140 days to expiration.

8. **Black-Scholes Model (LO2, CFA2)**   A stock with an annual standard deviation of 40 percent currently sells for $67. The risk-free rate is 6 percent. What is the value of a put option with a strike price of $80 and 60 days to expiration?

9. **Hedging with Options (LO3, CFA3)**   You are managing a pension fund with a value of $300 million and a beta of 1.07. You are concerned about a market decline and wish to hedge the portfolio. You have decided to use SPX calls. How many contracts do you need if the delta of the call option is .62 and the S&P Index is currently at 1230?

10. **Hedging with Options (LO3, CFA3)**   Suppose you have a stock market portfolio with a beta of .75 that is currently worth $300 million. You wish to hedge against a decline using index options. Describe how you might do so with puts and calls. Suppose you decide to use SPX calls. Calculate the number of contracts needed if the call option you pick has a delta of .50, and the S&P 500 Index is at 1160.

11. **One-Period Binomial Option Pricing (LO1, CFA2)**   A stock is currently selling for $45. In one period, the stock will move up by a factor of 1.15 or down by a factor of .87. A call option with a strike price of $50 is available. If the risk-free rate of interest is 2.5 percent for this period, what is the value of the call option?

12. **One-Period Binomial Option Pricing (LO1, CFA2)**   A stock is currently priced at $74 and will move up by a factor or 1.12 or down by a factor of .94 over the next period. The risk-free rate of interest is 4.2 percent. What is the value of a call option with a strike price of $75?

13. **One-Period Binomial Option Pricing (LO1, CFA2)**   A stock with a current price $58 has a put option available with a strike price of $55. The stock will move up by a factor of 1.13 or down by a factor of .88 over the next period and the risk-free rate is 3 percent. What is the price of the put option?

Intermediate Questions

14. **Black-Scholes Model (LO2, CFA2)**   A call option matures in six months. The underlying stock price is $85, and the stock's return has a standard deviation of 20 percent per year. The risk-free rate is 4 percent per year, compounded continuously. If the exercise price is $0, what is the price of the call option?

15. **Black-Scholes Model (LO2, CFA2)** A call option has an exercise price of $60 and matures in six months. The current stock price is $68, and the risk-free rate is 5 percent per year, compounded continuously. What is the price of the call if the standard deviation of the stock is 0 percent per year?

16. **Black-Scholes Model (LO2, CFA2)** A stock is currently priced at $55. A call option with an expiration of one year has an exercise price of $60. The risk-free rate is 12 percent per year, compounded continuously, and the standard deviation of the stock's return is infinitely large. What is the price of the call option?

17. **Employee Stock Options (LO4, CFA2)** In its 10-Q dated February 4, 2010, LLL, Inc., had outstanding employee stock options representing over 272 million shares of its stock. LLL accountants estimated the value of these options using the Black-Scholes-Merton formula and the following assumptions:

S = current stock price = $20.72
K = option strike price = $23.15
r = risk-free interest rate = .043
σ = stock volatility = .29
T = time to expiration = 3.5 years

What was the estimated value of these employee stock options per share of stock? (*Note:* LLL pays no dividends.)

18. **Hedging Employee Stock Options (LO4, CFA3)** Suppose you hold LLL employee stock options representing options to buy 10,000 shares of LLL stock. You wish to hedge your position by buying put options with three-month expirations and a $22.50 strike price. How many put option contracts are required? Use the same assumptions specified in the previous problem. (Note that such a trade may not be permitted by the covenants of many ESO plans. Even if the trade were permitted, it could be considered unethical.)

19. **Employee Stock Options (LO4, CFA3)** Immediately after establishing your put options hedge, volatility for LLL stock suddenly jumps to 45 percent. This changes the number of put options required to hedge your employee stock options. How many put option contracts are now required? (Except for the new volatility, use the same assumptions specified in the previous problem.)

20. **Two-Period Binomial Option Pricing (CFA2)** A stock is currently selling for $60. Over the next two periods, the stock will move up by a factor of 1.15 or down by a factor of .87 each period. A call option with a strike price of $60 is available. If the risk-free rate of interest is 3.2 percent per period, what is the value of the call option?

21. **Two-Period Binomial Option Pricing (CFA2)** A stock is currently priced at $35 and will move up by a factor or 1.18 or down by a factor of .85 each period over each of the next two periods. The risk-free rate of interest is 3 percent. What is the value of a put option with a strike price of $40?

22. **Two-Period Binomial Option Pricing (CFA2)** A stock with a current price $78 has a call option available with a strike price of $80. The stock will move up by a factor of .95 or down by a factor of .80 each period for the next two periods and the risk-free rate is 3.5 percent. What is the price of the call option today?

Spreadsheet Question

23. **Black-Scholes Model (LO2, CFA2)** A stock has a price of $26 and an annual return volatility of 45 percent. The risk-free rate is 2.9 percent. Using a computer spreadsheet program, calculate the call and put option prices with a strike price of $22.50 and a 90-day expiration. Also calculate the deltas of the call and put.

CFA Exam Review by Schweser

[CFA1, CFA2]
Ronald Franklin, CFA, is responsible for developing a new investment strategy for his firm. Given recent poor performance, the firm wants all of its equity portfolio managers to overlay options on all positions.

Mr. Franklin gained experience with basic option strategies at his previous job. As an exercise, he decides to review the fundamentals of option valuation using a simple example. Mr. Franklin recognizes that the behavior of an option's value is dependent on many variables and decides to spend some time closely analyzing this behavior, particularly in the context of the Black-Scholes option pricing model (and assuming continuous compounding). His analysis resulted in the information shown below:

Exhibit 1: Input for Option Pricing	
Stock price	$100
Strike price	$100
Interest rate	7%
Dividend yield	0%
Time to maturity (years)	1.0
Standard deviation of stock	0.20

Exhibit 2: Option Sensitivities		
	Call	Put
Delta	0.6736	−0.3264

1. Mr. Franklin wants to compute the value of the call option using the information in Exhibit 1. Which of the following is closest to his answer?

   a. $4.78
   b. $5.55
   c. $11.54

2. Mr. Franklin wants to compute the value of the put option that corresponds to the call value calculated in the previous question. Which of the following is the closest to his answer?

   a. $4.78
   b. $5.55
   c. $11.54

3. Mr. Franklin is interested in the sensitivity of the put option to changes in the volatility of the underlying equity's returns. If the volatility of the underlying equity's returns increases, the value of the put option:

   a. Decreases.
   b. Increases.
   c. Does not change.

4. Mr. Franklin wants to know how the put option in Exhibit 1 behaves when all the parameters are held constant except delta. Which of the following is the best estimate of the change in the put option's price when the underlying equity increases by $1?

   a. $.33
   b. −$.33
   c. −$3.61

What's on the Web?

1. **Black-Scholes Model** Go to www.numa.com and find the option pricing calculator. There is a call and a put option on a stock that expire in 30 days. The strike price is $55, and the current stock price is $58.70. The standard deviation of the stock is 45 percent per year, and the risk-free rate is 4.8 percent per year, compounded continuously. What is the price of the call and the put? What are the deltas for the call and the put?

2. **Black-Scholes Model** Go to www.cboe.com and find the option pricing calculator. A stock is currently priced at $98 per share and has a standard deviation of 58 percent per year. Options are available with an exercise price of $95, and the risk-free rate of interest is 5.2 percent per year, compounded continuously. What is the price of the call and the put that expire next month? What are the deltas of the call and the put? How do you interpret these numbers? How do your answers change for an exercise price of $100?

3. **Implied Standard Deviation** Go to www.numa.com and find the option pricing calculator. You purchased a call option for $11.50 that matures in 55 days. The strike price is $95, and the underlying stock has a price of $99.50. If the risk-free rate is 5.4 percent, compounded continuously, what is the implied standard deviation of the stock? Using this implied standard deviation, what is the price of a put option with the same characteristics?

4. **Black-Scholes-Merton Model** Recalculate the first two problems assuming a dividend yield of 2 percent per year. How does this change your answers?

CHAPTER 17

Projecting Cash Flow and Earnings

Learning Objectives

Help yourself grow as a stock analyst by knowing:

1. How to obtain financial information about companies.
2. How to read basic financial statements.
3. How to use performance and price ratios.
4. How to use the percentage of sales method in financial forecasting.

"Financial statements are like fine perfume; to be sniffed, but never swallowed."

–Abraham Briloff

Cash flow is a company's lifeblood, and, for a healthy company, the primary source of cash flow is earnings. Security analysts strive to make accurate predictions about future cash flow and earnings because an analyst who predicts these well has a head start in forecasting future stock performance. ■

Like any security analyst, we must examine financial statements to make cash flow and earnings projections. The quality of our financial statement analysis depends on accurate and timely financial statements. Generally, firms issue financial statements that provide a fair and accurate summary of the firm's financial health. You should know, however, that firms do have some discretion in reporting financial information. In rare cases, firms issue inaccurate, or even fraudulent, financial statements. Therefore, Abraham Briloff offers sound advice when he advocates a careful viewing of financial statements.

CFA™ Exam Topics in This Chapter:

1 Financial statement analysis: An introduction (L1, S7)
2 Financial reporting mechanics (L1, S7)
3 Financial reporting standards (L1, S7)
4 Understanding the income statement (L1, S8)
5 Understanding the balance sheet (L1, S8)
6 Understanding the cash flow statement (L1, S8)
7 Financial analysis techniques (L1, S10)
8 Financial reporting quality: Red flags and accounting warning signs (L1, S10)

9 Accounting shenanigans on the cash flow statement (L1, S10)
10 Financial statement analysis: Applications (L1, S10)
11 Financial statement analysis (L1, S11)
12 The lessons we learn (L2, S7)
13 Evaluating financial reporting quality (L2, S7)
14 Global equity strategy: The folly of forecasting (L3, S3)

Go to www.mhhe.com/jmd6e for a guide that aligns your textbook with CFA readings.

In a previous chapter, we examined some important concepts of stock analysis and valuation. Many of these concepts depend on either cash flow or earnings forecasts. In this chapter, we probe more deeply into the topic of stock valuation through an analysis of financial statements. In particular, we focus on cash flow and earnings forecasting. In this chapter, you will become acquainted with the financial accounting concepts necessary to understand basic financial statements and to make forecasts of cash flow and earnings. You may not become an expert analyst—this requires experience. But you will have a solid grasp of the fundamentals, which is a really good start.

Most investors have a difficult time reading the financial statements that are directly issued by firms. These investors rely on secondary sources of financial information. Bear in mind, however, that no one is paid well just for reading secondary sources of financial information.

By studying this chapter, you are taking an important step toward becoming "financial statement literate" (a good course in financial accounting is also very helpful). Ultimately, you learn how to read financial statements by reading financial statements! You know that your golf or tennis game improves with practice. Your financial statement reading skills also improve with practice. If you have an aptitude for it, financial statement analysis is a skill worth mastering. Good analysts are paid well because they provide good analyses. Who knows? Perhaps you, too, will become a financial analyst.

17.1 Sources of Financial Information

Good financial analysis begins with good financial information. An excellent primary source of financial information about any company is its annual report to stockholders. Most companies expend considerable resources preparing and distributing annual reports. In addition to their stockholders, companies also make annual reports available to anyone requesting a copy. A convenient way to request copies of annual reports from several companies simultaneously is to use the annual reports service provided by *The Wall Street Journal*. Just visit www.wsj.com and enter a stock symbol in the appropriate box. A company research page appears and you can click on "Annual Reports." *The Wall Street Journal* maintains an annual reports service where you can select documents for participating companies.

The Internet is a convenient source of financial information about many companies. For example, the NYSE Euronext Web site (www.nyse.com) provides a directory of Web sites for companies whose stock trades on the exchange. The content of company Web sites varies greatly, but many provide recent quarterly or annual financial reports—just surf to the investor relations section of their site.

In addition to company annual reports, a wealth of primary financial information is available to investors through the Securities and Exchange Commission. The SEC requires corporations with publicly traded securities to prepare and submit financial statements on a regular basis. When received, these documents are made available for immediate public access through the SEC's Electronic Data Gathering and Retrieval (EDGAR) archives. The **EDGAR** archives are accessible free of charge through the Internet (www.sec.gov) and are an excellent source of timely financial information.

The most important EDGAR document is the annual **10K** report, often simply called the "10K." Companies are required to submit an EDGAR-compatible 10K file to the SEC at the end of each fiscal year. They are also required to file quarterly updates, called 10Qs. The **10Q** is a mini-10K filed each quarter, except when the 10K is filed. Every 10K and 10Q report contains three important financial statements: a balance sheet, an income statement, and a cash flow statement. You must be familiar with these three financial statements to analyze company earnings and cash flow.

The Securities and Exchange Commission's **Regulation FD (Fair Disclosure)** stipulates that when a company discloses **material nonpublic information** to security analysts and stockholders who may trade on the basis of the information, it must also make a simultaneous disclosure of that information to the general public. Most companies satisfy

EDGAR
Electronic archive of company filings with the SEC.

10K
Annual company report filed with the SEC.

10Q
Quarterly updates of 10K reports filed with the SEC.

Regulation FD (Fair Disclosure)
Requires companies making a public disclosure of material nonpublic information to do so fairly without preferential recipients.

material nonpublic information
Any information that could reasonably be expected to affect the price of a security.

Review Regulation FD at
the SEC Web site
www.sec.gov

Regulation FD by distributing important announcements via e-mail alerts. To receive these e-mail alerts automatically, you can simply register for the service at the company's Web site. You can usually find the registration page in the investor relations section of the company's Web site.

17.2 Financial Statements

Financial statements reveal the hard facts about a company's operating and financial performance. This is why the SEC requires timely dissemination of financial statements to the public. It's also why security analysts spend considerable time poring over a firm's financial statements before making an investment recommendation. A firm's balance sheet, income statement, and cash flow statement are essential reading for security analysts. Each of these interrelated statements offers a distinct perspective. The **balance sheet** provides a snapshot view of a company's assets and liabilities on a particular date. The **income statement** measures operating performance over an accounting period, usually a quarter or a year, and summarizes company revenues and expenses. The **cash flow statement** reports how cash was generated and where it was used over the accounting period. Understanding the format and contents of these three financial statements is a prerequisite for understanding earnings and cash flow analysis.

We begin by considering the basic structure and general format of financial statements through a descriptive analysis of the balance sheet, income statement, and cash flow statement of a hypothetical intergalactic company—the Borg Corporation.

balance sheet
Accounting statement that provides a snapshot view of a company's assets and liabilities on a particular date.

income statement
Summary statement of a firm's revenues and expenses over a specific accounting period, usually a quarter or a year.

cash flow statement
Analysis of a firm's sources and uses of cash over the accounting period, summarizing operating, investing, and financing cash flows.

THE BALANCE SHEET

Table 17.1 presents year-end 2535 and 2536 balance sheets for Borg Corporation. The format of these balance sheets is typical of those contained in company annual reports distributed to stockholders and company 10K filings with the SEC. You will see quickly the accounting practice of specifying subtraction with parentheses and calculating subtotals with underlines. For example, Borg's 2536 fixed assets section is reproduced below, with the left numerical column following standard accounting notation and the right numerical column following standard arithmetic notation:

Look at the Portfolio/
Tools section at
www.thestreet.com

Fixed Assets	Accounting Style	Numeric Style
Plant facilities	$35,000	$35,000
Production equipment	20,000	+20,000
Administrative facilities	15,000	+15,000
Distribution facilities	10,000	+10,000
Accumulated depreciation	(20,000)	−20,000
Total fixed assets	$60,000	= $60,000

In the accounting style column, locate the row labeled "Total fixed assets." The single underline indicates this number will be used in another sum. Referring to Table 17.1, notice that total fixed assets is a subtotal used to calculate total assets, which is indicated by a double underline. With these conventions in mind, let us look over these sample balance sheets and try to become familiar with their format and contents.

The Borg Corporation balance sheet has four major **asset** categories: current assets, fixed assets, goodwill, and other assets. Current assets are cash or items that will be converted to cash or be used within a year. For example, inventory will be sold, accounts receivable will be collected, and materials and supplies will be used within a year. Cash is, of course, the quintessential current asset. Fixed assets have an expected life longer than one year and are used in normal business operations. Fixed assets may be tangible or intangible. Property, plant, and equipment are the most common tangible fixed assets. The Borg Corporation has no intangible fixed assets. However, rights, patents, and licenses are examples of intangible assets. Except for land, all fixed assets normally depreciate in value over time. Goodwill

asset
Anything a company owns that has value.

TABLE 17.1

Borg Corporation Balance Sheets, 2536 and 2535

	Year 2536	Year 2535
Current assets		
Cash	$ 2,000	$ 1,480
Accounts receivable	6,200	6,200
Prepaid expenses	1,500	1,500
Materials and supplies	1,300	1,300
Inventory	9,000	9,000
Total current assets	$20,000	$19,480
Fixed assets		
Plant facilities	$35,000	$35,000
Production equipment	20,000	20,000
Administrative facilities	15,000	15,000
Distribution facilities	10,000	
Accumulated depreciation	(20,000)	(17,000)
Total fixed assets	$60,000	$53,000
Goodwill	$ 5,000	
Other assets	3,000	3,000
Total assets	$88,000	$75,480
Current liabilities		
Short-term debt	$10,000	$10,000
Accounts payable	5,000	5,000
Total current liabilities	$15,000	$15,000
Long-term debt	$30,000	$20,000
Other liabilities	3,000	3,000
Total liabilities	$48,000	$38,000
Shareholder equity		
Paid-in capital	$10,000	$10,000
Retained earnings	30,000	27,480
Total shareholder equity	$40,000	$37,480
Total liabilities and equity	$88,000	$75,480
Shares outstanding	2,000	2,000
Year-end stock price	$40	$36

measures the premium paid over market value to acquire an asset. Other assets include miscellaneous items not readily fitting into any of the other asset categories.

liability
A firm's financial obligation.

The Borg balance sheet has three major **liability** categories: current liabilities, long-term debt, and other liabilities. Current liabilities normally require payment or other action within a one-year period. These include accounts payable and short-term debt. Long-term debt includes notes, bonds, or other loans with a maturity longer than one year. Other liabilities include miscellaneous items not belonging to any other liability category.

equity
An ownership interest in the company.

Shareholder **equity** is the difference between total assets and total liabilities. It includes paid-in capital, which is the amount received by the company from issuing common stock, and retained earnings, which represents accumulated income not paid out as dividends but instead used to finance company growth.

TABLE 17.2

Borg Corporation	Condensed 2536 Balance Sheet		
Cash	$ 2,000	Current liabilities	$15,000
Operating assets	18,000	Long-term debt	30,000
Fixed assets	60,000	Other liabilities	3,000
Goodwill and other assets	8,000	Shareholder equity	40,000
Total assets	$88,000	Total liabilities and equity	$88,000

The fundamental accounting equation for balance sheets states that assets are equal to liabilities plus equity:

$$\text{Assets} = \text{Liabilities} + \text{Equity} \qquad (17.1)$$

This equation says that the balance sheet must always "balance" because the left side must always equal the right side. If an imbalance occurs when a balance sheet is created, then an accounting error has been made and needs to be corrected.

Financial analysts often find it useful to condense a balance sheet down to its principal categories. This has the desirable effect of simplifying further analysis while still revealing the basic structure of the company's assets and liabilities. How much a balance sheet can be condensed and still be useful is a subjective judgment of the analyst. When making this decision, recall Albert Einstein's famous dictum: "Simplify as much as possible, but no more."

Table 17.2 is a condensed version of Borg's 2536 balance sheet that still preserves its basic structure. Notice that the current assets rows are reduced to two components, cash and operating assets. We separate cash from operating assets for a good reason.

Later, we show that the net cash increase from the cash flow statement is used to adjust cash on the balance sheet. This adjustment is more clearly illustrated by first separating current assets into cash and operating assets.

CHECK THIS

17.2a What are some examples of current assets?

17.2b What are some examples of fixed assets?

17.2c What are some examples of current liabilities?

17.2d Which accounts in Table 17.1 show changes between 2535 and 2536 balance sheets?

THE INCOME STATEMENT

Table 17.3 is a condensed income statement for Borg Corporation. This income statement reports revenues and expenses for the corporation over a one-year accounting period. Examine it carefully and be sure you are familiar with its top-down structure.

The income statement begins with net sales, from which cost of goods sold (COGS) is subtracted to yield gross profit. Cost of goods sold represents direct costs of production and sales, that is, costs that vary directly with the level of production and sales. Next, depreciation and operating expenses are subtracted from gross profit to yield operating **income**. Operating expenses are indirect costs of administration and marketing. That is, these costs do not vary directly with production and sales. Subtracting interest expense on debt from operating income yields pretax income. Finally, subtracting income taxes from pretax income yields net income. Net income is often referred to as the "bottom line" because it is normally the last line of the income statement. In this example, however, we have added dividends and retained earnings information (items that often appear in a separate financial statement). To avoid a separate statement, we show here that Borg Corporation paid dividends during the year. The sum of dividends and retained earnings is equal to net income:

income
The difference between a company's revenues and expenses, used to pay dividends to stockholders or kept as retained earnings within the company to finance future growth.

$$\text{Net income} = \text{Dividends} + \text{Retained earnings} \qquad (17.2)$$

TABLE 17.3

Borg Corporation Income Statement, Year 2536

	Year 2536
Net sales	$110,000
Cost of goods sold	(89,000)
Gross profit	$ 21,000
Depreciation	(3,000)
Other operating expenses	(10,000)
Operating income	$ 8,000
Interest expense	(2,000)
Pretax income	$ 6,000
Income taxes	(2,400)
Net income	$ 3,600
Dividends	(1,080)
Retained earnings	$ 2,520

In Table 17.3, note that we assume a 40 percent tax rate.

CHECK THIS

17.2e What is cost of goods sold (COGS)?

17.2f What is the difference between gross profit and operating income?

17.2g What is the difference between net income and pretax income?

17.2h What is meant by retained earnings?

THE CASH FLOW STATEMENT

The cash flow statement reports where a company generated cash and where cash was used over a specific accounting period. The cash flow statement assigns all cash flows to one of three categories: operating cash flows, investment cash flows, or financing cash flows.

Table 17.4 is a condensed cash flow statement for Borg Corporation. The cash flow statement begins with net income, which is the principal accounting measure of earnings for a corporation. However, net income and **cash flow** are not the same and often deviate greatly from each other. A primary reason why net income differs from cash flow is that net income contains **noncash items**. For example, depreciation is a noncash expense that must be added to net income when calculating cash flow. Adjusting net income for noncash items yields **operating cash flow**.

cash flow
Income realized in cash form.

noncash items
Income and expense items not realized in cash form.

operating cash flow
Cash generated by a firm's normal business operations.

TABLE 17.4

Borg Corporation Condensed 2536 Cash Flow Statement

	Year 2536
Net income	$ 3,600
Depreciation	3,000
Operating cash flow	$ 6,600
Investment cash flow[a]	(15,000)
Financing cash flow[b]	8,920
Net cash increase	$520

[a] December 31, 2536, purchase of distribution facilities from Klingon Enterprises for $15,000 (including $5,000 goodwill).

[b] Issue of $10,000 par value 5 percent coupon bonds, less a $1,080 dividend payout.

In your accounting classes, you learned that the difference between earnings and cash flow is generally the result of accrual accounting. Under this system, businesses recognize income and expenses as they are incurred, rather than when the cash flow is actually paid or received. As a result, earnings might not reflect cash flow accurately.

With this thought in mind, analysts generally agree that cash flow is a more reliable measure than earnings and agree that cash flow is better suited for cross-company comparisons. Moreover, analysts often refer to a company as having "high-" (or "low-") quality earnings. This distinction is simply a judgment of whether earnings accurately reflect the cash flow of the company. If they do, then the company is said to have high-quality earnings.

Operating cash flow is the first of three cash flow categories reported in the cash flow statement. The second and third categories are investment cash flow and financing cash flow. **Investment cash flow** (or "investing" cash flow) includes any purchases or sales of fixed assets and investments. For example, Borg's purchase of Klingon Enterprises's distribution facilities reported in footnote "a" is an investment cash flow. **Financing cash flow** includes any funds raised by issuing securities or expended by a repurchase of outstanding securities. In this example, Borg's $10,000 debt issue and $1,080 dividend payout reported in footnote "b" are examples of financing cash flows.

Standard accounting practice specifies that dividend payments to stockholders are financing cash flows, whereas interest payments to bondholders are operating cash flows. One reason is that dividend payments are discretionary, while interest payments are mandatory. Also, dividend payouts are not tax deductible, but interest payments are.

The sum of operating cash flow, investment cash flow, and financing cash flow yields the net change in the firm's cash. This change is the "bottom line" of the cash flow statement and reveals how much cash flowed into or out of the company's cash account during an accounting period. In this case, $520 of cash flowed into Borg Corporation (you can also see this change in cash by comparing the cash columns in Table 17.1).

investment cash flow

Cash flow resulting from purchases and sales of fixed assets and investments.

financing cash flow

Cash flow originating from the issuance or repurchase of securities and the payment of dividends.

CHECK THIS

17.2i What is the difference between net income and operating cash flow?

17.2j What are some noncash items used to calculate operating cash flow?

17.2k What is the difference between an investment cash flow and a financing cash flow?

17.2l What is meant by net increase in cash?

17.2m Can you explain why a cash item like interest expense does not appear on the cash flow statement?

PERFORMANCE RATIOS AND PRICE RATIOS

Annual reports and 10Ks normally contain various items of supplemental information about the company. For example, certain profitability ratios may be reported to assist interpretation of the company's operating efficiency. For Borg Corporation, some standard profitability ratios for 2536 are calculated immediately below:

Ratio	Formula	Calculation
Gross margin	$\dfrac{\text{Gross profit}}{\text{Net sales}}$	$\dfrac{\$21,000}{\$110,000} = 19.09\%$
Operating margin	$\dfrac{\text{Operating income}}{\text{Net sales}}$	$\dfrac{\$8,000}{\$110,000} = 7.27\%$
Return on assets (ROA)	$\dfrac{\text{Net income}}{\text{Total assets}}$	$\dfrac{\$3,600}{\$88,000} = 4.09\%$
Return on equity (ROE)	$\dfrac{\text{Net income}}{\text{Shareholder equity}}$	$\dfrac{\$3,600}{\$40,000} = 9.00\%$

WORK THE WEB

One of the more frequent uses of financial ratios is in stock screening. Stock screening is the process of selecting stocks based on specific criteria. A popular method used by the legendary investor Warren Buffett, among others, is searching for value stocks that have high growth potential. A value stock has relatively low price-earnings ratios. However, low price-earnings ratios can be an indication of low future growth potential, so we also want to determine if these stocks have future growth possibilities.

We went to www.cnbc.com, clicked on the "Investing" tab, and then the "Stock Screener" tab. You can see that there are some preset screens, like "Solid Stocks Solid Companies" and "Small Cap Value." By clicking on the "Create Custom Screen," we built our own screen looking for stocks that are large, growing, and cheap. That is, our screen looks for stocks with a market cap greater than $5 billion; P/E less than 20; estimated EPS growth greater than 20 percent; and P/S less than 1.3. Here is what we found:

Using stock screening as an investment tool is really not this simple. What we have done here is narrowed the universe of stocks to a few stocks that meet our criteria. It is now up to us to further examine the companies to determine if they are actually good investments. In other words, stock screening is not the end of the investment process—it simply narrows the field.

return on assets (ROA)
Net income stated as a percentage of total assets.

return on equity (ROE)
Net income stated as a percentage of shareholder equity.

Notice that **return on assets (ROA)** and **return on equity (ROE)** are calculated using current year-end values for total assets and shareholder equity. It could be argued that prior-year values should be used for these calculations. However, the use of current year-end values is more common.

Annual reports and 10Ks may also report per-share calculations of book value, earnings, and operating cash flow, respectively. Per-share calculations require the number of common stock shares outstanding. Borg's balance sheet reports 2,000 shares of common stock outstanding. Thus, for Borg Corporation, these per-share values are calculated as follows:

Check out the Investing section at www.moneyunder30.com

Ratio	Formula	Calculation
Book value per share (BVPS)	$\dfrac{\text{Shareholder equity}}{\text{Shares outstanding}}$	$\dfrac{\$40,000}{2,000} = \$20.00$
Earnings per share (EPS)	$\dfrac{\text{Net income}}{\text{Shares outstanding}}$	$\dfrac{\$3,600}{2,000} = \$1.80$
Cash flow per share (CFPS)	$\dfrac{\text{Operating cash flow}}{\text{Shares outstanding}}$	$\dfrac{\$6,600}{2,000} = \$3.30$

Notice that cash flow per share (CFPS) is calculated using operating cash flow—*not* the bottom line on the cash flow statement (see Table 17.4). Most of the time when you hear the term "cash flow," it refers to operating cash flow.

Recall that in a previous chapter, we made extensive use of price ratios to analyze stock values. Using per-share values calculated immediately above and Borg's year-end stock price of $40 per share, we get the following price ratios:

Ratio	Formula	Calculation
Price-book (P/B)	$\dfrac{\text{Stock price}}{\text{BVPS}}$	$\dfrac{\$40}{\$20} = 2.00$
Price-earnings (P/E)	$\dfrac{\text{Stock price}}{\text{EPS}}$	$\dfrac{\$40}{\$1.80} = 22.22$
Price-cash flow (P/CF)	$\dfrac{\text{Stock price}}{\text{CFPS}}$	$\dfrac{\$40}{\$3.30} = 12.12$

We use these price ratios later when assessing the potential impact of a sales campaign on Borg Corporation's future stock price. Our nearby *Work the Web* box shows another use for price ratios.

CHECK THIS

17.2n   What is the difference between gross margin and operating margin?

17.2o   What is the difference between return on assets and return on equity?

17.2p   What is the difference between earnings per share and cash flow per share?

17.2q   How is cash flow per share calculated?

17.3 Financial Statement Forecasting

In December 2536, Borg publicly announces the completion of an acquisition of some distribution outlets from Klingon Enterprises, LLC. The stated purpose of the acquisition was to expand sales. Complementing the acquisition, Borg also announces plans for a marketing campaign to increase next year's net sales to a targeted $137,500.

As a Borg analyst, you must examine the potential impact of these actions. You immediately contact Borg management to inquire about the details of the acquisition and the marketing campaign. Armed with this additional information, you decide to construct **pro forma financial statements** for Borg Corporation for the year 2537.

THE PERCENTAGE OF SALES APPROACH

A simple model to construct pro forma financial statements is one in which every item increases at the same rate as sales. This may be a reasonable assumption for some financial statement items. For others, such as long-term debt, it probably is not, because the amount of long-term debt is something set by company management. Therefore, long-term debt levels do not necessarily relate directly to the level of sales.

A more sophisticated model builds on the basic idea of separating the income statement and balance sheet items into two groups: those that do vary directly with sales and those that do not. Given a sales forecast, calculating how much financing the firm will need to support the predicted sales level is easy. This quick and practical model is known as the **percentage of sales approach**. You have decided to use this approach to generate pro forma financial statements for Borg Corporation for the year 2537.

THE PRO FORMA INCOME STATEMENT

The Borg Corporation announced projected sales for the year 2537 of $137,500—an increase of 25 percent over 2536. We use the 2536 Borg Corporation income statement and several assumptions to generate the pro forma income statement. From Table 17.3, we see that in the year 2536, the ratio of total costs to net sales was about 94.55 percent (actually 94.5454 percent). We assume the ratio of total costs to sales will be 94.55 percent in the year 2537 also.

Table 17.5 is our pro forma income statement for the Borg Corporation for 2537. To generate Table 17.5, we assume that the ratio of cost of goods sold to net sales will be the same in 2537 as it was in 2536 (80.91 percent).

We see in Table 17.4 that depreciation in the year 2536 was $3,000. Accountants grapple with various methods to produce depreciation schedules. Here, as a practical matter, we simply apply the percentage of sales approach. Depreciation expense as a percentage of sales in 2536 was $3,000/$110,000 \approx 2.7272$ percent. For the year 2537, we estimate depreciation

TABLE 17.5

Borg Corporation Pro Forma Income Statement, Year 2537

	Year 2536	Year 2537
Net sales	$110,000	$137,500
Cost of goods sold	(89,000)	(111,250)
Gross profit	$ 21,000	$ 26,250
Depreciation	(3,000)	(3,750)
Other operating expenses	(10,000)	(12,500)
Operating income	$ 8,000	$ 10,000
Interest expense	(2,000)	(2,500)
Pretax income	$ 6,000	$ 7,500
Income taxes	(2,400)	(3,000)
Net income	$ 3,600	$ 4,500
Dividends	(1,080)	(1,350)
Retained earnings	$ 2,520	$ 3,150
Profit margin	3.27%	3.27%
Total costs/Net sales	94.55%	94.55%

expense to be ($3,000/$110,000) × $137,500 = $3,750. (Note that we multiplied the actual ratio in 2536 to estimated sales in the year 2537.)

The Borg Corporation financed the purchase of the distribution outlets with 5 percent coupon bonds, which represent long-term debt. To estimate the 2537 interest expense, we assume that the Borg Corporation pays 4 percent simple interest on its short-term debt and 8 percent on its existing long-term debt. Given these assumptions, the 2536 interest expense of $2,000 was split $400 ($10,000 × .04) for short-term debt and $1,600 ($20,000 × .08) for long-term debt. Therefore, the additional $10,000 in long-term debt added at the end of 2536 will increase interest expense on long-term debt to $2,100 ($20,000 × .08 + $10,000 × .05). Adding an assumed $400 for interest on short-term debt, the total interest expense in the year 2537 will be $2,500.

Finally, recall that we assume that the ratio of total costs to net sales will be the same in 2537 as it was in 2536 (about 94.55 percent). To achieve this, we assume that the other operating expenses account is our "plug" and if we set this account to $12,500, we maintain the desired ratio of 94.55 percent.

The effect of assuming that total costs are a constant percentage of sales is to assume that the profit margin (net income/net sales) is constant. To check this, notice that in Table 17.5 Borg Corporation's profit margin was $3,600/$110,000 = 3.27 percent in 2536 and $4,500/$137,500 = 3.27 percent projected for 2537. In this calculation, a tax rate of 40 percent is assumed for both years.

Next, we need to project the dividend payment. The decision of how much of net income will be paid in dividends is a decision that rests with the management of the Borg Corporation. However, two dividend payment schemes are reasonable: one where the *dollar* payout is the same from year to year, and one where the *percentage* payout is the same from year to year.

We will assume that Borg management has a policy of paying a dividend that is a constant percentage of net income. For 2536, the dividend payout ratio was $1,080/$3,600 = 30 percent. We can also calculate the ratio of the addition to retained earnings to net income, which is $2,520/$3,600 = 70 percent for 2536. This ratio is called the *retention ratio* or *plowback ratio,* and it is equal to one minus the dividend payout ratio. The term "plowback ratio" is logical because if net income is not paid out to the shareholders, it must be retained by the company. Assuming the payout ratio is constant, the projected dividends are $4,500 × .30 = $1,350. Thus, the addition to retained earnings is $3,150.

THE PRO FORMA BALANCE SHEET

To generate a pro forma balance sheet, we start with the balance sheet for 2536 shown in Table 17.1. On this balance sheet, we assume that some of the items vary directly with sales and others do not. For the items that do vary with sales, we express each as a percentage of sales for the year just completed, year 2536. When an item does not vary directly with sales, we write "n/a" for "not applicable." For example, on the asset side, inventory is equal to about 8.2 percent of sales in 2536. We assume that this percentage also applies to 2537, so for each $1 increase in sales, inventory will increase by $.082.

capital intensity ratio
A firm's total assets divided by its sales, or the amount of assets needed to generate $1 in sales.

The ratio of total assets to sales for 2536 is $88,000/$110,000 = .80, or 80 percent. The ratio of total assets to sales is sometimes called the **capital intensity ratio**. This ratio tells us the amount of assets needed to generate $1 in sales. So the higher this ratio, the more capital intensive is the firm. For the Borg Corporation, $.80 in assets was needed to generate $1 in sales in 2536. If we assume that capital intensity ratio is constant, total assets of $110,000 will be needed to generate sales of $137,500 in 2537.

On the liability side of the balance sheet, we have assumed that only accounts payable vary with sales. The reason is that we expect Borg to place more orders with its suppliers as sales increase, so payables will change directly with sales. Short-term debt, on the other hand, represents bank borrowing. This account is not likely to vary directly with sales. Therefore, we write n/a in the "Percent of Sales" column for short-term debt in Table 17.6. Similarly, we write n/a for long-term debt because long-term debt will not vary directly with sales. The same is true for other liabilities and the paid-in capital account.

TABLE 17.6

Borg Corporation Partial Pro Forma Balance Sheet, Year 2537

	2536	Approximate Percent of Sales	2537	Change
Current assets				
Cash	$ 2,000	1.8%	$ 2,500	$ 500
Accounts receivable	6,200	5.6	7,750	1,550
Prepaid expenses	1,500	1.4	1,875	375
Materials and supplies	1,300	1.2	1,625	325
Inventory	9,000	8.2	11,250	2,250
Total current assets	$20,000	18.2	$ 25,000	$ 5,000
Total fixed assets	$60,000	54.5	$ 75,000	$15,000
Other assets	$ 8,000	7.3	$ 10,000	$ 2,000
Total assets	$88,000	80.0	$110,000	$22,000
Current liabilities				
Short-term debt	$10,000	n/a	$ 10,000	$ 0
Accounts payable	5,000	4.5	6,250	1,250
Total current liabilities	$15,000		$ 16,250	$ 1,250
Long-term debt	$30,000	n/a	$ 30,000	$ 0
Other liabilities	3,000	n/a	3,000	0
Total liabilities	$48,000		$ 49,250	$ 1,250
Shareholder equity				
Paid-in capital	$10,000	n/a	$ 10,000	$ 0
Retained earnings	30,000	n/a	33,150	3,150
Total shareholder equity	$40,000		$ 43,150	$ 3,150
Total liabilities and equity	$00,000		$ 92,400	$ 4,400
External financing needed:			$ 17,600	$17,600
Through short-term debt:				$ 2,500
Through long-term debt:				$15,100

Retained earnings, however, will change with an increase in sales, but the increase in retained earnings will not be a simple percentage of sales. Instead, we must calculate the change in retained earnings based on our projected net income and dividends, which come from our pro forma income statement.

We can now construct a partial pro forma balance sheet for the Borg Corporation, as shown in Table 17.6. We construct the column labeled 2537 by using the percentage of sales wherever possible to calculate projected amounts. For example, inventory in 2537 is projected to be ($9,000/$110,000) × $137,500 = $11,250. More generally, the ratio of total fixed assets to sales was about 54.5 percent in 2536. For 2537 total fixed assets is projected to be ($60,000/$110,000) × $137,500 = $75,000. This amount represents an increase of $15,000 from the total fixed assets in 2536.

For the items that do not vary directly with sales, note that we initially assume no change and simply write in the existing amounts. You can see the application of this method in the column labeled 2537 in Table 17.6. Notice that the change in retained earnings is projected to be $3,150—which is the amount shown in Table 17.5.

Inspecting the partial pro forma balance sheet for the Borg Corporation, we see that total assets are projected to increase by $22,000 in 2537. However, without additional financing, liabilities and equity will increase by only $4,400, leaving a shortfall, or imbalance, of $22,000 − $4,400 = $17,600. In Table 17.6, to be safe, we have calculated this $17,600 shortfall in two ways: as the difference between total assets ($110,000) and total liabilities and equity ($92,400) and as the difference between the change in total assets ($22,000) and the change in total assets and liabilities ($4,400). We have labeled the shortfall amount as *external financing needed (EFN)*.

SCENARIO ONE

The creation of a pro forma income statement and a pro forma balance sheet points out a potentially serious problem with Borg Corporation's projected sales increase of 25 percent—it isn't going to happen unless Borg Corporation can somehow raise $17,600 in new financing. For analysts working for the Borg Corporation, this is a good example of how the planning process can point out problems and potential conflicts. For example, if the Borg Corporation had a goal of not raising new financing, then an increase in sales of 25 percent is not possible.

If we take the need for $17,600 in new financing as given, we know that the Borg Corporation has three possible sources: short-term debt, long-term debt, and new equity. The choice of the exact combination of the three sources of financing is a decision that the management of the Borg Corporation must make. For illustration, however, we will choose one of the many possible combinations.

Suppose the Borg Corporation decides to borrow the needed funds, some via short-term debt and some via long-term debt. In Table 17.6, you can see that current assets increased by $5,000, but current liabilities increased only by $1,250 (the increase in accounts payable). If the Borg Corporation wanted to keep the ratio between current assets and current liabilities constant, it should borrow $2,500 in short-term debt. In 2536, the ratio between total current assets and total current liabilities was 4 to 3, or 1.3333 ($20,000/$15,000). In 2537, total current assets are $25,000, which means total current liabilities should be $18,750, or $2,500 more than the amount shown in Table 17.6.

If Borg borrows $2,500 in short-term debt, this leaves $15,100 to be raised by issuing additional long-term debt. These financing amounts are shown at the bottom of Table 17.6. Table 17.7 shows a completed pro forma balance sheet given this assumed financing decision.

We have used a combination of short-term debt and long-term debt to solve the financing problem for the Borg Corporation. It is extremely important for us to emphasize that this is only one possible strategy—and it might not even be the best strategy for the Borg Corporation. As analysts, we could (and should) investigate many other scenarios. For example, we would have to ask how the increased debt load would affect future earnings of the company.

SCENARIO TWO

The assumption that assets are a fixed percentage of sales is convenient, but it may not be suitable in many cases. In particular, we made a hidden assumption when we constructed pro forma financial statements for the Borg Corporation: We assumed that the Borg Corporation was using its fixed assets at 100 percent of capacity, because any increase in sales led to an increase in fixed assets. For most businesses, there would be some slack, or excess capacity, and production could be increased by, perhaps, running an extra shift or utilizing spare equipment.

If we assume that the Borg Corporation is running at 75 percent of capacity, then the need for external funds will be quite different. When we say "75 percent of capacity," we mean that the current sales level is 75 percent of the full-capacity sales level:

$$\text{Current sales} = \$110,000 = .75 \times \text{Full-capacity sales}$$
$$\text{Full-capacity sales} = \$110,000/.75 = \$146,667$$

This calculation tells us that sales could increase by one-third, from $110,000 to $146,667, before any new fixed assets would be needed.

TABLE 17.7

Borg Corporation Pro Forma Balance Sheet, Year 2537

	2536	Approximate Percent of Sales	2537	Change
Current assets				
Cash	$ 2,000	1.8%	$ 2,500	$ 500
Accounts receivable	6,200	5.6	7,750	1,550
Prepaid expenses	1,500	1.4	1,875	375
Materials and supplies	1,300	1.2	1,625	325
Inventory	9,000	8.2	11,250	2,250
Total current assets	$20,000	18.2	$ 25,000	$ 5,000
Total fixed assets	$60,000	54.5	$ 75,000	$15,000
Other assets	$ 8,000	7.3	$ 10,000	$ 2,000
Total assets	$88,000	80.0	$110,000	$22,000
Current liabilities				
Short-term debt	$10,000	n/a	$ 12,500	$ 2,500
Accounts payable	5,000	4.5	6,250	1,250
Total current liabilities	$15,000		$ 18,750	$ 3,750
Long-term debt	$30,000	n/a	$ 45,100	$15,100
Other liabilities	3,000	n/a	3,000	0
Total liabilities	$48,000	n/a	$ 66,850	$18,850
Shareholder equity				
Paid-in capital	$10,000	n/a	$ 10,000	$ 0
Retained earnings	30,000	n/a	33,150	3,150
Total shareholder equity	$40,000		$ 43,150	$ 3,150
Total liabilities and equity	$88,000		$110,000	$22,000
External financing needed (EFN):			$ 0	$ 0

In Scenario One, we assumed that adding $15,000 in net fixed assets would be necessary. In our current scenario, no spending on fixed assets is needed, because sales are projected to rise only to $137,500, which is substantially less than the $146,667 full-capacity sales level. As a result, our Scenario One estimate of $17,600 in external funds needed is too high. In fact, an argument could be made in Scenario Two that the level of external funds needed is $2,600.

To begin, you can see in Table 17.8 that we have now written n/a next to the total fixed assets account and we have written in a value of $60,000 (the same as for the year 2536). When no change is assumed for the total fixed assets account, the total assets account increases by $7,000. On the liability side of the balance sheet as shown in Table 17.5, a sales level of $137,500 generates an increase of $3,150 in retained earnings. In addition, this sales level means that the accounts payable account will increase by $1,250. The difference between the increase in total assets and the increase in total liabilities and equity would be $2,600 without any external financing ($7,000 − $3,150 − $1,250). In Table 17.8, a completed year 2537 pro forma balance sheet, we see that this is the amount that the short-term debt account has increased. That is, we have assumed that the Borg Corporation will use only short-term debt as its EFN source. You will note, however, that this assumption means that the ratio between total current assets and total current liabilities will decrease (slightly).

TABLE 17.8   Borg Corporation Pro Forma Balance Sheet, Year 2537

	2536	Approximate Percent of Sales	2537	Change
Current assets				
Cash	$ 2,000	1.8%	$ 2,500	$ 500
Accounts receivable	6,200	5.6	7,750	1,550
Prepaid expenses	1,500	1.4	1,875	375
Materials and supplies	1,300	1.2	1,625	325
Inventory	9,000	8.2	11,250	2,250
Total current assets	$20,000	18.2	$25,000	$5,000
Total fixed assets	$60,000	n/a	$60,000	$ 0
Other assets	$ 8,000	7.3	$10,000	$2,000
Total assets	$88,000		$95,000	$7,000
Current liabilities				
Short-term debt	$10,000	n/a	$12,600	$2,600
Accounts payable	5,000	4.5	6,250	1,250
Total current liabilities	$15,000		$18,850	$3,850
Long-term debt	$30,000	n/a	$30,000	$ 0
Other liabilities	3,000	n/a	3,000	0
Total liabilities	$48,000	n/a	$51,850	$3,850
Shareholder equity				
Paid-in capital	$10,000	n/a	$10,000	$ 0
Retained earnings	30,000	n/a	33,150	3,150
Total shareholder equity	$40,000		$43,150	$3,150
Total liabilities and equity	$88,000		$95,000	$7,000

EXAMPLE 17.1   EFN and Capacity Usage

Suppose the Borg Corporation was operating at 88 percent of capacity. What would sales be at full capacity? What is the EFN in this case? What is the capital intensity ratio at full capacity?

Full-capacity sales would be $110,000/.88 = $125,000. From Table 17.1, we know that fixed assets are $60,000. At full capacity, the ratio of fixed assets to sales is $60,000/$125,000 = .48. This tells us that the Borg Corporation needs $.48 in fixed assets for every $1 in sales once the Borg Corporation reaches full capacity. At the projected sales level of $137,500, the Borg Corporation needs $137,500 × .48 = $66,000 in fixed assets. This is $9,000 less than the year 2537 value of $75,000 shown in Table 17.6. Therefore, EFN is $17,600 − $9,000 = $8,600. Current assets and other assets would still be $25,000 and $10,000, respectively, so total assets would be $101,000. The capital intensity ratio would then be $101,000/$137,500 = .7345.

CHECK THIS

17.3a   What is the basic idea behind the percentage of sales approach?

17.3b   Unless it is modified, what does the percentage of sales approach assume about fixed asset capacity usage?

PROJECTED PROFITABILITY AND PRICE RATIOS

In addition to preparing pro forma financial statements, you also decide to calculate projected profitability ratios and per-share values under the new sales forecast. These are reported immediately below and compared with their original year-end values.

	Year 2536	Year 2537
Gross margin	19.09%	19.09%
Operating margin	7.27%	7.27%
Return on assets (ROA)	4.09%	4.09%/4.74%
Return on equity (ROE)	9.00%	10.43%
Book value per share (BVPS)	$20	$21.57
Earnings per share (EPS)	$ 1.80	$ 2.25
Cash flow per share (CFPS)	$ 3.30	$ 4.25

Note that two ROA numbers are provided for 2537. The first is from Scenario One, where we assume Borg is already running at 100 percent capacity. The second is from Scenario Two, where we assume Borg is running at 75 percent capacity.

One common method of analysis is to calculate projected stock prices under the new sales scenario using prior-period price ratios and projected per-share values from pro forma financial statements. For Borg Corporation, you decide to take your previously calculated year-end 2536 price ratios and multiply each ratio by its corresponding pro forma per-share value. The results of these projected stock price calculations (rounded) are shown immediately below.

$$\text{P/B} \times \text{BVPS} = 2 \times \$21.57 = \$43.14$$

$$\text{P/E} \times \text{EPS} = 22.22 \times \$2.25 = \$50.00$$

$$\text{P/CF} \times \text{CFPS} = 12.12 \times \$4.25 = \$51.51$$

Which projected stock price is correct? Well, it clearly depends on which sales level is realized and which price ratio the financial markets will actually use to value Borg Corporation's stock. This is where experience and breadth of knowledge count immensely. Of course, no one can make perfectly accurate predictions, but the analyst's job is to expertly assess the situation and make an investment recommendation supported by reasonable facts and investigation. But some analysts are better than others. Like professional baseball players, professional stock analysts with better batting averages can do very well financially.

17.4 Starbucks Corporation Case Study

After carefully reading the analysis of Borg Corporation, you should have a reasonably clear picture of how to do an earnings and cash flow analysis using pro forma financial statements. In this section, we present an analysis based on the 2009 financial statements for Starbucks Corporation. As you will see, using data for a real company is challenging.

This section begins with a review of the 2009 financial statements for Starbucks. We then proceed to analyze the effects on earnings and cash flow that might result from two sales projection scenarios. The analysis is similar to that for Borg Corporation, with a few important differences. Note that amounts shown are in thousands of dollars (except earnings per share).

Table 17.9 is the 2009 condensed balance sheet for Starbucks. This balance sheet shows that at fiscal year-end 2009 (September 27, 2009), Starbucks had $5,577 million of total assets and $3,046 million of shareholder equity. In Table 17.10, which is the 2009 condensed income statement for Starbucks, the bottom line reveals that Starbucks earned $390.8 million in net income from $9,775 million in net revenues.

From these values, we calculate Starbucks's return on assets (ROA) as 7.0 percent and return on equity (ROE) as 12.8 percent. As of its fiscal year-end date, Starbucks Corporation had 745.9 million shares outstanding. Therefore, earnings per share in 2009 were

TABLE 17.9

Starbucks Corporation Balance Sheets for 2009 and 2008 ($ in 000's)

	2009	2008
Current assets		
Cash and cash equivalents	$ 599,800	$ 269,800
Short-term investments	66,300	52,500
Accounts receivable	271,000	329,500
Inventory	664,900	692,800
Prepaid expenses	147,200	169,200
Deferred income taxes	286,600	234,200
Total current assets	$2,035,800	$1,748,000
Fixed assets		
Long-term investments	$ 423,500	$ 374,000
Property, plant and equipment, net	2,536,400	2,956,400
Other assets	253,800	261,100
Total fixed assets	$3,213,700	$3,591,500
Goodwill	$ 259,100	$ 266,500
Other intangible assets	68,200	66,600
Total assets	$5,576,800	$5,672,600
Current liabilities		
Accounts payable	$ 267,100	$ 324,900
Accrued expenses	1,313,700	1,151,100
Short-term debt	200	713,700
Total current liabilities	$1,581,000	$2,189,700
Long-term debt	$ 549,300	$ 549,600
Other long-term liabilities	400,800	442,400
Total liabilities	$2,531,100	$3,181,700
Shareholder equity		
Common stock	$ 700	$ 700
Paid-in capital	$ 186,400	$ 39,400
Retained earnings	$2,793,200	$2,402,400
Other stockholder equity	$ 65,400	$ 48,400
Total stockholder equity	$3,045,700	$2,490,900
Total liabilities and equity	$5,576,800	$5,672,600
Shares outstanding (000s)	745,900	741,700
(Fiscal) Year-end stock price	$19.83	$14.96

$.52, and book value per share was $4.08. Based on a fiscal year-end 2009 stock price of $19.83, the price-book ratio for Starbucks was 4.86, and the price-earnings ratio was 37.85.

Starbucks's stock price gradually increased in value before the company filed its annual financial information with the SEC on November 21, 2009. At the close of trading on December 18, 2009, Starbucks's stock price closed at $23.68. At this time, the price-book ratio for Starbucks was 5.80, and the price-earnings ratio was 45.20.

TABLE 17.10

Starbucks Corporation Income Statements for 2009 and 2008 ($ in 000's)

	2009	2008
Total net revenues	$9,774,600	$10,383,000
Cost of sales	4,324,900	4,645,300
Gross profit	$5,449,700	$ 5,737,700
Store operating expenses	$3,425,100	$ 3,745,100
Other operating expenses	264,400	330,100
Depreciation expense	534,700	549,300
General and administrative expenses	453,000	456,000
Restructuring charges	332,400	266,900
Total operating expenses	$5,009,600	$ 5,347,400
Income from equity investees	$ 121,900	$ 113,600
Operating income	$ 562,000	$ 503,900
Interest income and other income	$ 36,300	$ 9,000
Interest expense	(39,100)	(53,400)
Earnings before income taxes (EBT)	$ 559,200	$ 459,500
Income tax expense	168,400	144,000
Net income	$ 390,800	$ 315,500
Earnings per share	$0.52	$0.43
Shares outstanding (000s)	745,900	741,700
Operating margin	5.7%	4.9%
Income tax rate (EBT / Income tax expense)	30.1%	31.3%

PRO FORMA INCOME STATEMENT

To construct a 2010 pro forma income statement for Starbucks, we use forecasted sales and the percentage of sales approach, just as we did for the Borg Corporation. As shown in the nearby *Work the Web* box, we visited finance.yahoo.com and entered the ticker symbol for Starbucks, SBUX.

Clicking on the "Analyst Estimates" link, we saw that the highest estimate for Starbucks's 2010 revenue was $10.28 billion, or an increase of about 5.2 percent from Starbucks's 2009 revenue level of $9.77 billion. Finding ourselves in a frothy mood, however, we increased the highest revenue estimate to $10.90 billion. Our high revenue estimate is an increase of 11.5 percent from Starbucks's 2009 revenue level. The low estimate was $9.91 billion, so we rounded this low estimate to $9.90 billion. Note that our low revenue estimate is a revenue increase of about 1.3 percent over Starbucks's 2009 revenue. Analysts forecast earnings growth for Starbucks to be a whopping 25 percent. For our pro forma income statement for 2010, however, we will assume net income growth levels of 11.5 percent and 1.3 percent, respectively.

Table 17.11 is our pro forma income statement for Starbucks for 2010. We included 2009 for comparison. For both the high and low estimate for revenue, we assumed that gross margin, operating margin, interest income as a percentage of sales, and the income tax rate will be the same in 2010 as they were in 2009. This has the net effect of assuming that the profit margin will remain the same, about 4.0 percent.

Calculating company growth rates can involve detailed research. A major part of a stock analyst's job is to provide estimates of growth rates. One place to find earnings and sales growth rates is at finance.yahoo.com. We pulled up a quote for Starbucks (SBUX) and followed the "Analyst Estimates" link. Below, you will see an abbreviated look at the results.

Earnings Est	Current Qtr Dec-09	Next Qtr Mar-10	Current Year Sep-10	Next Year Sep-11
Avg. Estimate	0.27	0.22	1.00	1.15
No. of Analysts	18	17	20	15
Low Estimate	0.23	0.19	0.95	1.05
High Estimate	0.30	0.24	1.09	1.25
Year Ago EPS	0.15	0.16	0.80	1.00

Revenue Est	Current Qtr Dec-09	Next Qtr Mar-10	Current Year Sep-10	Next Year Sep-11
Avg. Estimate	2.58B	2.33B	10.03B	10.34B
No. of Analysts	14	14	15	12
Low Estimate	2.54B	2.30B	9.91B	10.08B
High Estimate	2.63B	2.38B	10.28B	10.64B
Year Ago Sales	2.62B	2.33B	9.77B	10.03B
Sales Growth (year/est)	-1.3%	-0.1%	2.6%	3.1%

You can see that analysts expect sales and earnings to increase at brisk rates.

Growth Est	SBUX	Industry	Sector	S&P 500
Current Qtr.	80.0%	1533.3%	56.6%	-32.0%
Next Qtr.	37.5%	631.6%	20.6%	15.8%
This Year	25.0%	-8.2%	3.4%	4.8%
Next Year	15.0%	93.3%	21.3%	27.1%
Past 5 Years (per annum)	4.803%	N/A	N/A	N/A
Next 5 Years (per annum)	16.38%	16.64%	12.2%	N/A
Price/Earnings (avg. for comparison categories)	23.68	35.37	18.73	18.09
PEG Ratio (avg. for comparison categories)	1.45	2.13	1.54	N/A

Analysts are also required to provide price targets for companies that they follow.

PRICE TARGET SUMMARY	
Mean Target:	22.60
Median Target:	24.00
High Target:	26.00
Low Target:	13.00
No. of Brokers:	15
Data provided by Thomson/First Call	

	2009	2010 (High Est.)	2010 (Low Est.)
Total net revenues	$ 9,774,600	$10,900,000	$ 9,900,000
Cost of sales	(4,324,900)	(4,822,848)	(4,380,385)
Gross profit	$ 5,449,700	$ 6,077,152	$ 5,519,615
Operating expenses	(5,009,600)	(5,586,381)	(5,073,869)
Operating income	$ 440,100	$ 490,771	$ 445,746
Net interest and other income	$ 119,100	$ 132,813	$ 120,628
Earnings before income taxes (EBT)	$ 559,200	$ 623,584	$ 566,374
Income tax expense (30.1%)	(168,400)	(187,789)	(170,560)
Net income	$ 390,800	$ 435,795	$ 395,814
Dividends	0	0	0
Retained earnings	$ 390,800	$ 435,795	$ 395,814
Gross margin	55.8%	55.8%	55.8%
Operating margin	4.5%	4.5%	4.5%
Interest and other income / Net sales	1.2%	1.2%	1.2%
Income tax rate	30.1%	30.1%	30.1%
Profit margin	4.0%	4.0%	4.0%
Earnings per share	$0.52	$0.58	$0.53
Shares outstanding (000s)	745,900	745,900	745,900

We assume that Starbucks will not declare any dividends in 2010 and assume that Starbucks will not issue or repurchase shares. Therefore, all net income will flow to retained earnings, and shares outstanding will remain at 745.9 million. Combined, these assumptions and the two sales forecasts result in a rounded earnings per share of $.58 given the high revenue estimate and $.53 per share with the low revenue estimate.

PRO FORMA BALANCE SHEET

Table 17.12 contains partial pro forma balance sheets for Starbucks for 2010 using the percentage of sales approach we discussed earlier in the chapter. Again, we included the actual 2009 balance sheet for comparison. Notice that we assumed that all asset accounts will increase with sales. However, short-term and long-term investment levels are certainly likely to reflect decisions made by senior management at Starbucks. Nevertheless, we will stick with our assumption that only two liability accounts will vary with sales—accounts payable and accrued expenses. In both cases, this assumption is reasonable.

Looking at the partial pro forma balance sheet using the high sales estimate, we see that the external financing needed is about $26.3 million. That is, we estimate that the amount of external financing needed to increase Starbucks's revenue by 11.5 percent is not a relatively large amount (keep in mind that Starbucks has $5.58 billion in assets, so $26.3 million represents only .5 percent of Starbucks's assets).

Looking at the partial pro forma balance sheet using the low sales estimate, we get a different scenario. Here, the external financing needed is a negative $343 million dollars. How does this happen, and what does it mean?

In this scenario, assets will grow by about $66 million and current liabilities will grow by about $13 million. The difference between the growth in current assets and the growth in current liabilities is $53 million. However, retained earnings increases by about $396 million, which is $343 million more than the difference between asset and liability growth. This

TABLE 17.12

Starbucks Corporation Partial Pro Forma Balance Sheet, 2010 ($ in 000's)

	2009	Percent of Sales*	2010 (High Est.)	Change	2010 (Low Est.)	Change
Current assets						
Cash and cash equivalents	$ 599,800	6.1%	$ 664,900	$ 65,100	$ 603,900	$ 4,100
Short-term investments	66,300	0.7	76,300	10,000	69,300	3,000
Accounts receivable	271,000	2.8	305,200	34,200	277,200	6,200
Inventory	664,900	6.8	741,200	76,300	673,200	8,300
Prepaid expenses	147,200	1.5	163,500	16,300	148,500	1,300
Deferred income taxes	286,600	2.9	316,100	29,500	287,100	500
Total current assets	$2,035,800		$2,267,200	$231,400	$2,059,200	$ 23,400
Fixed assets						
Long-term investments	$ 423,500	4.3%	$ 468,700	$ 45,200	$ 425,700	$ 2,200
Property, plant, and equipment, net	2,536,400	25.9	2,823,100	286,700	2,564,100	27,700
Other assets	253,800	2.6	283,400	29,600	257,400	3,600
Total fixed assets	$3,213,700		$3,575,200	$361,500	$3,247,200	$ 33,500
Goodwill	$ 259,100	2.7%	$ 294,300	$ 35,200	$ 267,300	$ 8,200
Other intangible assets	68,200	0.7	76,300	8,100	69,300	1,100
Total assets	$5,576,800		$6,213,000	$636,200	$5,643,000	$ 66,200
Current liabilities						
Accounts payable	$ 267,100	2.7%	$ 294,300	$ 27,200	$ 267,300	$ 200
Accrued expenses	1,313,700	13.4	1,460,600	146,900	1,326,600	12,900
Short-term debt	200	n/a	200	0	200	0
Total current liabilities	$1,581,000		$1,755,100	$174,100	$1,594,100	$ 13,100
Long-term debt	$ 549,300	n/a	$ 549,300	0	$ 549,300	0
Other long-term liabilities	400,800	n/a	400,800	0	400,800	0
Total liabilities	$2,531,100		$2,705,200	$174,100	$2,544,200	$ 13,100
Shareholder equity						
Paid-in capital & other equity	$ 252,500	n/a	$ 252,500	$ 0	$ 252,500	$ 0
Retained earnings	$2,793,200	n/a	$3,228,995	$435,795	$3,189,014	$ 395,814
Total stockholder equity	$3,045,700		$3,481,495	$435,795	$3,441,514	$ 395,814
Total liabilities and equity	$5,576,800		$6,186,695	$609,895	$5,985,714	$ 408,914
External financing needed:			$ 26,305	$ 26,305	($ 342,714)	($342,714)

*If you are a careful reader, you will discover that the numbers in this column are approximations of the actual percent of sales. For example, let's take a look at the "Cash and cash equivalents" line for the high estimate case for 2010. If we divide the 2009 level of this asset ($599,800) by the sales level in 2009 ($9,774,600), we get 6.1363 percent. Multiplying this percentage by the 2010 high estimated sales level of $10,900,000 provides an estimated cash and cash equivalents amount of $668,858. Like the growth in sales, this amount is 11.5 percent more than the 2009 level. We chose, however, to use a percent of sales approximation because we start with rounded numbers for 2009 and we wind up with rounded numbers for each 2010 estimate and its corresponding change. In addition, this method is simply intended to provide the analyst with an estimate of the amount of external financing required, if any.

means that under the low growth scenario (a sales increase of 1.3 percent), Starbucks becomes quite the "cash cow." That is, the existing profit margin Starbucks enjoys is such that considerable future growth can be financed out of sales. At a lower projected sales growth level, less cash is needed to finance this growth, so "excess" cash accumulates.

Under the low growth scenario, we estimate that Starbucks will generate about $343 million in additional, or excess, cash. Senior management at Starbucks could use this additional cash in many ways. In terms of investments, Starbucks could purchase other companies, look for new ways to expand the company, or buy back its own shares in the open market. Management at Starbucks could simply let this cash accumulate while looking for places to spend it. They could, if they chose to, declare a cash dividend and distribute some cash to shareholders.

At this point, we can generate a pro forma balance sheet that actually balances, depending on what sales forecast we use. Using the high sales forecast, we assume that management at Starbucks simply issues long-term debt for their external financing requirement. Using the low sales forecast, we assume that management puts the excess cash generated into the cash and cash equivalent accounts. Notice that the cash account balance would be $603,900 using the percentage of sales approach. The cash balance in Table 17.13 of $946,614 reflects the percentage of sales estimate in Table 17.12 ($603,900), plus $342,714. Table 17.13 presents these pro forma balance sheets.

CHECK THIS

17.4a Use the high sales estimate and data in Table 17.12 to determine the level of external financing needed if short-term and long-term investments were held at their 2009 levels.

17.4b Using the high sales estimate and data in Table 17.12, do you think it is more likely that Starbucks would use short-term or long-term debt if external financing needed was $3 billion? What financial data support your answer?

VALUING STARBUCKS USING RATIO ANALYSIS

We now turn our attention to valuing Starbucks using ratio analysis and the pro forma income statement and balance sheets that we generated. Immediately below, we report actual and projected profitability and per-share values for 2009 and 2010.

	2009	2010 (High Sales Forecast)	2010 (Low Sales Forecast)
Gross margin	55.8%	55.8%	55.8%
Operating margin	4.5%	4.5%	4.5%
Return on assets (ROA)	7.0%	7.0%	6.6%
Return on equity (ROE)	12.8%	12.5%	11.5%
Earnings per share (EPS)	$0.52	$0.58	$0.53
Book value per share (BVPS)	$4.08	$4.97	$4.61

For Starbucks, taking the 2009 price ratios and multiplying each ratio by its corresponding projected 2010 per-share value results in the following stock price calculations:

			2010 (High Sales Forecast)	2010 (Low Sales Forecast)
Using fiscal year-end stock price of $19.83				
P/E ratio	38.13	P/E × EPS	22.12	20.21
P/B ratio	4.86	P/B × BVPS	24.15	22.40
Using SEC reporting date stock price of $23.68				
P/E ratio	45.54	P/E × EPS	26.41	24.14
P/B ratio	5.80	P/B × BVPS	28.83	26.74

TABLE 17.13	Starbucks Corporation	Pro Forma Balance Sheet, 2010 ($ in 000's)				
	2009	Percent of Sales	2010 (High)	Change	2010 (Low)	Change
Current assets						
Cash and cash equivalents	$ 599,800	6.1%	$ 664,900	$ 65,100	$ 946,614	$346,814
Short-term investments	66,300	0.7	76,300	10,000	69,300	3,000
Accounts receivable	271,000	2.8	305,200	34,200	277,200	6,200
Inventory	664,900	6.8	741,200	76,300	673,200	8,300
Prepaid expenses	147,200	1.5	163,500	16,300	148,500	1,300
Deferred income taxes	286,600	2.9	316,100	29,500	287,100	500
Total current assets	$2,035,800		$2,267,200	$231,400	$2,401,914	$366,114
Fixed assets						
Long-term investments	$ 423,500	4.3%	$ 468,700	$ 45,200	$ 425,700	$ 2,200
Property, plant, and equipment, net	2,536,400	25.9	2,823,100	286,700	2,564,100	27,700
Other assets	253,800	2.6	283,400	29,600	257,400	3,600
Total fixed assets	$3,213,700	32.9%	$3,575,200	$361,500	$3,247,200	$ 33,500
Goodwill	$ 259,100	2.7%	$ 294,300	$ 35,200	$ 267,300	$ 8,200
Other intangible assets	68,200	0.7	76,300	8,100	69,300	1,100
Total assets	$5,576,800	57.1%	$6,213,000	$636,200	$5,985,714	$408,914
Current liabilities						
Accounts payable	$ 267,100	2.7%	$ 294,300	$ 27,200	$ 267,300	$ 200
Accrued expenses	1,313,700	13.4	1,460,600	146,900	1,326,600	12,900
Short-term debt	200	n/a	26,505	26,305	200	0
Total current liabilities	$1,581,000		$1,781,405	$200,405	$1,594,100	$ 13,100
Long-term debt	$ 549,300	n/a	$ 549,300	0	$ 549,300	0
Other long-term liabilities	400,800	n/a	400,800	0	400,800	0
Total liabilities	$2,531,100		$2,731,505	$200,405	$2,544,200	$ 13,100
Shareholder equity						
Paid-in capital & other equity	$ 252,500	n/a	$ 252,500	$ 0	$ 252,500	$ 0
Retained earnings	$2,793,200	n/a	$3,228,995	$435,795	$3,189,014	$395,814
Total stockholder equity	$3,045,700		$3,481,495	$435,795	$3,441,514	$395,814
Total liabilities and equity	$5,576,800		$6,213,000	$636,200	$5,985,714	$408,914
External financing needed:			$ 0	$ 0	$ 0	$ 0

Using ratio analysis, we generate Starbucks's prices that range from $20.21 to $28.83. Our estimated price range for Starbucks lies in the middle to high part of the price range ($13–$26) forecast by actual analysts (see the preceding *Work the Web* box).

Looking across sales forecasts, you can see that the prices we generate for Starbucks do not differ greatly. In fact, our projected Starbucks stock prices are more sensitive to the values picked for the price-earnings (P/E) ratio and price-book (P/B) ratio than they are to the value of the sales forecast picked.

VALUING STARBUCKS USING A TWO-STAGE RESIDUAL INCOME MODEL

In a previous chapter, we introduced the residual income model (RIM), which is an appropriate valuation model to use when you are trying to value the shares of a company, like Starbucks, that does not pay dividends. The version of RIM that we introduced earlier in the text incorporated the assumption that earnings would grow at a constant rate forever. However, for a fast-growing company like Starbucks, this is not really a reasonable assumption. Eventually, the growth rate in earnings for Starbucks must decrease.

Fortunately for us, the RIM can be modified to reflect the assumption that earnings grow at rate g_1 for T periods and then grow at rate g_2 forever thereafter. The RIM in this case is:

$$P_0 = BVPS_0 + \frac{EPS_0(1 + g_1) - BVPS_0 \times k}{k - g_1}\left[1 - \left(\frac{1 + g_1}{1 + k}\right)^T\right]$$
$$+ \frac{EPS_0(1 + g_1)^T(1 + g_2) - BVPS_0(1 + k)^T k}{(k - g_2)/(1 + k)^T} \tag{17.3}$$

In equation (17.3) we need values for earnings per share, EPS_0, and book value per share, $BVPS_0$, as of time 0 (2009 in this case). We can pluck these values, \$.52 and \$4.08, respectively, from data provided above. We need earnings growth rates for the two periods, however, and an appropriate discount rate.

From the preceding *Work the Web* box, we can see that analysts collectively think that Starbucks will be able to grow earnings at 16.4 percent for the next five years. After that, we will assume that Starbucks will be able to grow earnings *forever* at 5 percent. Even though this is a significant dropoff from 16.4 percent, it is still quite a bit higher than the long-term historical real growth rate of the U.S. economy, which is 3 percent. Therefore, in equation (17.3), $g_1 = .164$ and $g_2 = .05$.

We calculate an initial discount rate using the capital asset pricing model (CAPM). If we use a risk-free rate of 1.0 percent, a market risk premium of 7 percent, and a Starbucks beta of 1.15 (from *Value Line*), the discount rate, k, is $1.0 + 1.15 \times 7.0 = 9.05\%$.

Plugging these inputs into equation (17.3), we obtain this value for Starbucks:

$$P_0 = 4.08 + \frac{.52 \times 1.164 - 4.08 \times .0905}{.0905 \qquad .164}\left[1 - \left(\frac{1.164}{1.0905}\right)^5\right]$$
$$+ \frac{.52 \times (1.164)^5 \times 1.05 - 4.08 \times (1.0905)^5 \times .0905}{(.0905 - .05)/(1.0905)^5}$$
$$= 4.08 + 1.24 + 22.74 = \$28.06$$

This estimate of \$28.06 is about \$5 higher than the Starbucks stock price of \$23.68, which was observed at the time Starbucks filed its financial information with the SEC. Like any good analyst would, we now vary our inputs to see how sensitive the estimated price is to changes in these inputs. Even though we *could* change the growth rates, we will not. Instead, we will vary the discount rate and the length of time that Starbucks will exhibit an earnings growth rate of 16.4 percent.

We generate a set of additional discount rates by varying the beta for Starbucks. Beginning with the value of 1.15, we selected four other beta values, while keeping the risk-free rate and the market risk premium the same as before. We suspect that the length of time that Starbucks will grow earnings at the robust rate of 16.4 percent could be too long. But we cannot be sure, so we vary this length of time from three to five years. We then recalculate a Starbucks price for each of these combinations. The results appear immediately below.

Beta	Discount Rate	Number of Years Starbucks Grows Earnings at 16.4%		
		3	4	5
0.95	7.65	**27.17**	34.86	44.71
1.05	8.35	**21.11**	**27.09**	34.83
1.15	9.05	17.01	**21.80**	**28.06**
1.25	9.75	14.01	17.89	**23.02**
1.35	10.45	11.68	14.83	**19.03**

STARBUCKS SAYS DEMAND PERKING UP

Coffee Retailer Reports Surge in Earnings as Cost Cuts Pay Off, Raises Outlook for 2010

Starbucks Corp.'s profit soared in its fiscal fourth quarter, thanks mostly to cost-cutting efforts, but the retailer also saw improvement in demand for its coffee drinks.

Starbucks, which has been struggling in the recession as some consumers perceive its beverages as being too pricey, boosted its earnings outlook Thursday for the fiscal year that began a month ago and said it was cautiously optimistic about the coming holiday period.

The Seattle-based chain posted earnings of $150 million, or 20 cents a share, for the quarter ended Sept. 27, up from $5.4 million, or one cent a share, a year earlier. Revenue fell 3.7% to $2.42 billion.

Chief Executive Howard Schultz said in a conference call that a "more disciplined focus on operations" helped the company increase earnings and that it is seeing improvements in its surveys of customer satisfaction.

During the quarter, Starbucks cut prices on so-called easy-to-make coffees, while lifting prices by as much as 30 cents for larger and more complex drinks, such as a venti caramel macchiato.

Starbucks said sales at stores open at least a year, a key measure of retail health, declined 1%. That's an improvement from the fiscal third quarter, when same-store sales fell 5%, and marks the company's best same-store sales performance in about two years.

The company responded to the U.S. recession by closing stores, creating a multimillion-dollar marketing campaign and retooling business practices to make its cafes more efficient.

Starbucks said it reaped $580 million in cost savings in the latest fiscal year, topping its target of $550 million.

Mr. Schultz said the company is encouraged by the national rollout of its Via instant-coffee product. Via is "resonating with customers" and is having little negative impact on traditional coffee sales at Starbucks, he said.

Starbucks began making Via available in September in all its cafes in the U.S. and Canada, as well as in other locations such as hotels and bookstores. The company created Via, which costs $2.95 for a three pack, to try to reach consumers who aren't inclined to splurge on a regular coffee purchase.

For fiscal 2010, the company said it now expects earnings per share to increase 15% to 20%, up from its previous forecast of an increase of 13% to 18%.

Starbucks, which has about 11,000 U.S. outlets, reported $53.2 million in restructuring charges for its fourth quarter, almost all of which stemmed from store closings. The company said it had shuttered nearly all of the roughly 800 U.S. stores and 100 international stores in its previously announced store-closing plans.

Source: David Kesmodel, *The Wall Street Journal,* November 6, 2009. Reprinted with permission of *The Wall Street Journal.* © 2009 Dow Jones & Company, Inc. All Rights Reserved Worldwide.

From this sensitivity analysis, it appears that both the discount rate and the length of time that Starbucks grows its earnings by 16.4 percent are important in estimating a value for Starbucks. We highlighted seven values that are roughly in line with the Starbucks prices we generated with our ratio analysis. For an analyst, performing various "what-if" scenarios concerning input values that are used in valuation formulas is good practice.

VALUING STARBUCKS: WHAT DOES THE MARKET SAY?

As with many publicly traded companies, analysts frequently offer conflicting opinions concerning the future growth prospects of Starbucks and its current value. You can read an opinion about Starbucks in our nearby *Investment Updates* box. If you are a believer in the efficient markets hypothesis, the easiest way to value Starbucks is to look at what its shares are selling for in the open market. After all, the market price for Starbucks shares is the result of the collective assessment from thousands of analysts and investors. If, however, you believe that you are an above-average prognosticator for future sales and earnings growth for Starbucks, you can use the methods in this chapter to assist you in your personal investing decisions concerning Starbucks and other companies.

The methods presented in this chapter are intended to help you become a better financial analyst. Calibrating these methods to a publicly traded company is a useful way to get familiar with how inputs and assumptions affect the resulting valuation. These methods could be valuable to you if you are an internal analyst. For example, suppose you are asked to calculate whether the company you work for needs more financing to meet its expected sales growth levels. You can use the percentage of sales approach when you perform this task.

The methods in this chapter are especially useful if you are trying to value a nontraded company after you are given its financial data. Someday, you might find yourself working on calculating a per-share tender offer in a hostile takeover attempt. In any case, we are confident that this chapter will help you become more "financial-statement literate" and help you develop as a financial analyst.

17.5 Summary and Conclusions

In this chapter, we focus on earnings and cash flow analysis using financial statement information. Several important aspects of financial statements and their use were covered. We summarize these points by the important concepts of the chapter.

1. **How to obtain financial information about companies.**

   A. Good financial analysis begins with good financial information. A primary source of financial information is a company's annual report. In addition, the annual 10K report and the quarterly 10Q updates filed with the SEC are available from the EDGAR archives.

   B. The Internet is a convenient source of financial information about many companies. For example, the NYSE Euronext Web site (www.nyse.com) provides a directory of Web sites for companies whose stock trades on the exchange.

2. **How to read basic financial statements.**

   A. Three financial statements are essential reading for securities analysts: the balance sheet, the income statement, and the cash flow statement. The balance sheet has three sections: assets, liabilities, and equity. A fundamental accounting identity for balance sheets states that assets equal liabilities plus equity.

   B. The income statement reports revenues and expenses. Companies use their net income to pay dividends or to finance future growth. Net income is the "bottom line" for a company.

   C. The cash flow statement reports how cash was generated and where it was used. The cash flow statement assigns all cash flows to one of three categories: operating cash flow, investment cash flow, or financing cash flow.

3. **How to use performance and price ratios.**

   A. Profitability ratios based on financial statement information are often reported to help investors interpret a company's operating efficiency. Standard profitability ratios include gross margin, operating margin, return on assets (ROA), and return on equity (ROE).

   B. Annual reports, 10Ks, and 10Qs also report per-share calculations of book value, earnings, and operating cash flow, respectively. If we divide the stock price by these per-share values, we get three important ratios: the price to book ratio (P/B), the price-earnings ratio (P/E), and the cash flow per share (CFPS).

4. **How to use the percentage of sales method in financial forecasting.**

   A. Financial analysts often make projections about sales growth, future costs, and net income. These forecasts can be used to construct a forecasted, or pro forma, set of financial statements.

B. The percentage of sales approach is a method analysts can use to construct pro forma financial statements. This approach is based on the basic idea of separating the income statement and balance sheet items into two groups: those that do vary directly with sales and those that do not. Given a sales forecast, analysts can use the percentage of sales approach to calculate how much financing the firm will need to support the predicted sales level.

GET REAL

This chapter delves deeper into earnings and cash flow concepts, which are two of the most important tools of fundamental analysis. It focuses on using financial statement information to develop pro forma numbers to use in stock valuation. How should you, as an investor or investment manager, get started putting this information to work? The answer is that you need to get your fingers dirty! Dig into the financial statements of a few companies and develop your own pro forma financial statements.

Excellent sources for financial statement information are the SEC EDGAR database (www.sec.gov) and Free EDGAR (www.freeedgar.com). Other useful online sources are Annual Report Service (www.annualreportservice.com), Free Annual Reports (www.prars.com), and Corporate Information (www.corporateinformation.com).

A good place to start is to download the most recent financial reports for Starbucks from SEC EDGAR (www.sec.gov) or the Starbucks company Web site (www.starbucks.com). Then try your hand at developing pro forma financial statements for Starbucks similar to the ones developed in this chapter.

A next step is to pick a company you are interested in and examine its financial statements. As you read a company's financial statements, an important exercise is to try to understand what each number really represents. Why is it there? Is it a cash or market value? Or is it just an accounting number (like depreciation)? Once you are familiar with a company's current financial statements, try to develop pro forma statements for various sales scenarios as was done in this chapter. You really can learn a lot by doing this.

Key Terms

10K 581
10Q 581
asset 582
balance sheet 582
capital intensity ratio 590
cash flow 585
cash flow statement 582
EDGAR 581
equity 583
financing cash flow 586
income 584

income statement 582
investment cash flow 586
liability 583
material nonpublic information 581
noncash items 585
operating cash flow 585
percentage of sales approach 589
pro forma financial statements 589
Regulation FD (Fair Disclosure) 581
return on assets (ROA) 588
return on equity (ROE) 588

Chapter Review Problems and Self-Test

1. **Margin Calculations (CFA7)** Use the following income statement for Paul Bunyan Lumber Co. to calculate gross and operating margins.

Paul Bunyan Lumber 2011 Income Statement	
Net sales	$8,000
Cost of goods sold	(6,400)
Gross profit	$1,600
Operating expenses	(400)
Operating income	$1,200
Other income	80
Net interest expense	(120)
Pretax income	$1,160
Income tax	(464)
Net income	$ 696
Earnings per share	$ 3.48
Recent share price	$76.56

2. **Return Calculations (CFA7)** Use the following balance sheet for Paul Bunyan Lumber Co. along with the income statement in the previous question to calculate return on assets and return on equity.

Paul Bunyan Lumber 2011 Balance Sheet	
Cash and cash equivalents	$ 400
Operating assets	400
Property, plant, and equipment	3,160
Other assets	216
Total assets	$4,176
Current liabilities	$ 720
Long-term debt	612
Other liabilities	60
Total liabilities	$1,392
Paid-in capital	$ 600
Retained earnings	2,184
Total shareholder equity	$2,784
Total liabilities and equity	$4,176

3. **Pro Forma Income Statements (CFA2)** Prepare a pro forma income statement for Paul Bunyan Lumber Co. assuming a 5 percent increase in sales. Based only on the pro forma income statement, what is the projected stock price? (*Hint:* What is the price-earnings ratio?)

Answers to Self-Test Problems

1. Gross margin is $1,600/$8,000 = 20%
   Operating margin is $1,200/$8,000 = 15%

2. Return on assets is $696/$4,176 = 16.67%
   Return on equity is $696/$2,784 = 25%

3. With 5 percent sales growth, sales will rise to $8,400 from $8,000. The pro forma income statement follows. A constant gross margin is assumed, implying that cost of goods sold will also rise by 5 percent. A constant tax rate of 40 percent is used.

Paul Bunyan Lumber Pro Forma 2012 Income Statement	
Net sales	$8,400
Cost of goods sold	(6,720)
Gross profit	$1,680
Operating expenses	(400)
Operating income	$1,280
Other income	80
Net interest expense	(120)
Pretax income	$1,240
Income tax	(496)
Net income	$ 744
Earnings per share	$3.72

To get a projected stock price, notice that the 2011 price-earnings ratio was $76.56/$3.48 = 22. Using this ratio as a benchmark, the pro forma earnings of $3.72 imply a stock price of 22 × $3.72 = $81.84.

Test Your Investment Quotient

1. **Balance Sheet Assets (LO2, CFA11)**   White Company assets as of December 31, 2010:

Cash and cash equivalents	$ 150
Operating assets	$1,190
Property, plant, and equipment	$1,460
Total assets	$2,800

White Co. experienced the following events in 2011:

  Old equipment that cost $120 and that was fully depreciated was scrapped

  Depreciation expense was $125

  Cash payments for new equipment were $200

Based on the information above, what was White Co.'s net amount of property, plant, and equipment at the end of 2011?

  a. $1,415
  b. $1,535
  c. $1,655
  d. $1,660

2. **Cash Flow (LO2, CFA6)**   Cash flow per share is calculated as

  a. Net cash flow/Shares outstanding.
  b. Operating cash flow/Shares outstanding.
  c. Investing cash flow/Shares outstanding.
  d. Financing cash flow/Shares outstanding.

3. **Cash Flow (LO2, CFA6)**   Which of the following is *not* an adjustment to net income used to obtain operating cash flow?

  a. Changes in operating assets
  b. Changes in current liabilities

   c. Depreciation

   d. Dividends paid

4. **Cash Flow (LO2, CFA6)** The difference between net income and operating cash flow is at least partially accounted for by which of the following items?

   a. Retained earnings

   b. Cash and cash equivalents

   c. Depreciation

   d. Dividends paid

5. **Financial Ratios (LO3, CFA7)** Which of the following profitability ratios is incorrect?

   a. Gross margin = Gross profit/Cost of goods sold

   b. Operating margin = Operating income/Net sales

   c. Return on assets = Net income/Total assets

   d. Return on equity = Net income/Shareholder equity

6. **Financial Ratios (LO3, CFA7)** Which of the following per-share ratios is incorrect?

   a. Book value per share = Total assets/Shares outstanding

   b. Earnings per share = Net income/Shares outstanding

   c. Cash flow per share = Operating cash flow/Shares outstanding

   d. Dividends per share = Dividends paid/Shares outstanding

7. **Dividend Payment (LO2, CFA5)** A dividend payment has which of the following effects on the balance sheet?

   a. An increase in shares outstanding

   b. A decrease in shareholder equity

   c. A decrease in paid-in capital

   d. An increase in retained earnings

8. **Sales Growth (LO4, CFA10)** A particular firm is operating at less than full capacity. If sales are expected to grow at only a modest rate next year, which of the following is true?

   a. Assets will likely increase faster than sales in the short-term future.

   b. Dividends should be reduced to conserve cash.

   c. No further financial planning should be performed until the sales growth rate increases.

   d. External financing will likely not be needed next year.

9. **Capacity Usage (LO4, CFA11)** Which of the following is true regarding the full-capacity sales level of a firm?

   a. A firm that is operating at less than full capacity will never need external financing.

   b. For a firm that is operating at less than full capacity, fixed assets will typically increase at the same rate as sales.

   c. A firm with excess capacity has the room to expand without increasing its investment in fixed assets.

   d. Only firms operating at full capacity can grow rapidly.

Use the following raw data to answer the next four questions:

Net income:	$16
Depreciation/amortization:	$4
Repurchase of outstanding common stock:	$10
Issuance of new debt:	$18
Sale of property:	$12
Purchase of equipment:	$14
Dividend payments:	$4

10. **Cash Flow Analysis (LO2, CFA6)** Operating cash flow is

   a. $20

   b. $16

   c. $12

   d. $30

11. **Cash Flow Analysis (LO2, CFA6)** Investing cash flow is

   a. $2

   b. $(2)

    c. $12

    d. $(12)

12. **Cash Flow Analysis (LO2, CFA6)**   Financing cash flow is

    a. $8

    b. $(8)

    c. $4

    d. $(4)

13. **Cash Flow Analysis (LO2, CFA6)**   Net cash increase is

    a. $18

    b. $20

    c. $22

    d. $24

Use the following financial data to answer the next three questions:

Cash payments for interest:	$ (12)
Retirement of common stock:	$ (32)
Cash payments to merchandise suppliers:	$ (85)
Purchase of land:	$ (8)
Sale of equipment:	$30
Payments of dividends:	$ (37)
Cash payment for salaries:	$ (35)
Cash collection from customers:	$260
Purchase of equipment:	$(40)

14. **Cash Flow Analysis (LO2, CFA6)**   Cash flows from operating activities are

    a. $91

    b. $128

    c. $140

    d. $175

15. **Cash Flow Analysis (LO2, CFA6)**   Cash flows from investing activities are

    a. $(67)

    b. $(48)

    c. $(18)

    d. $(10)

16. **Cash Flow Analysis (LO2, CFA6)**   Cash flows from financing activities are

    a. $(81)

    b. $(69)

    c. $(49)

    d. $(37)

17. **Cash Flow Analysis (LO2, CFA6)**   A firm has net sales of $3,000, cash expenses (including taxes) of $1,400, and depreciation of $500. If accounts receivable increase over the period by $400, cash flow from operations equals

    a. $1,200

    b. $1,600

    c. $1,700

    d. $2,100

18. **Cash Flow Analysis (LO2, CFA6)**   A firm using straight-line depreciation reports gross investment in fixed assets of $80 million, accumulated depreciation of $45 million, and annual depreciation expense of $5 million. The approximate average age of fixed assets is

    a. 7 years

    b. 9 years

    c. 15 years

    d. 16 years

19. **Preferred Dividends (LO2)**   What proportion of preferred stock dividends received by a corporation is normally exempt from federal income taxation?

    a. 25–35 percent

    b. 50–60 percent

    c. 70–80 percent

    d. 90–100 percent

20. **Price Ratios (LO3, CFA7)**   All else the same, which of the following ratios is unaffected by an increase in depreciation?

    a. Price-earnings (P/E)

    b. Price-book (P/B)

    c. Price-cash flow (P/CF)

    d. Price-sales (P/S)

Concept Questions

1. **10K and 10Q (LO1, CFA1)**   What are the 10K and 10Q reports? Who are they filed by? What do they contain? Who are they filed with? What is the easiest way to retrieve one?

2. **Sales Forecast (LO4, CFA10)**   Why do you think most long-term financial planning begins with sales forecasts? Put differently, why are future sales the key input?

3. **Current Events (LO2, CFA5)**   What makes current assets and liabilities "current"? Are operating assets "current"?

4. **Income and EPS (LO2, CFA7)**   What is the relationship between net income and earnings per share (EPS)?

5. **Noncash Items (LO2, CFA6)**   Why do we say depreciation is a "noncash item"?

6. **Operating Cash Flow (LO2, CFA6)**   In the context of the standard cash flow statement, what is operating cash flow?

7. **Comparing ROE and ROA (LO3, CFA7)**   Both ROA and ROE measure profitability. Which one is more useful for comparing two companies? Why?

8. **Retained Earnings (LO2, CFA1)**   What is the difference between the "retained earnings" number on the income statement and the balance sheet?

9. **Gross! (LO3, CFA7)**   What is the difference between gross margin and operating margin? What do they tell us? Generally speaking, are larger or smaller values better?

10. **More Gross (LO3, CFA7)**   Which is larger, gross margin or operating margin? Can either be negative? Can both?

Questions and Problems

Core Questions

1. **Income Statements (LO2, CFA4)**   Given the following information for Smashville, Inc., construct an income statement for the year:

Cost of goods sold:	$164,000
Investment income:	$1,200
Net sales:	$318,000
Operating expense:	$71,000
Interest expense:	$7,400
Dividends:	$3,200
Tax rate:	35%

What are retained earnings for the year?

2. **Balance Sheets (LO2, CFA5)**   Given the following information for Smashville, Inc., construct a balance sheet:

Current liabilities:	$42,000
Cash:	$21,000
Long-term debt:	$102,000
Other assets:	$36,000
Fixed assets:	$150,000
Other liabilities:	$11,000
Investments:	$32,000
Operating assets:	$64,000

3. **Performance Ratios (LO3, CFA7)**   Given the information in the previous two problems, calculate the gross margin, the operating margin, return on assets, and return on equity for Smashville, Inc.

4. **Per-Share Ratios (LO3, CFA7)**   During the year, Smashville, Inc., had 15,000 shares of stock outstanding and depreciation expense of $15,000. Calculate the book value per share, earnings per share, and cash flow per share.

5. **Price Ratios (LO3, CFA7)**   At the end of the year, Smashville stock sold for $52 per share. Calculate the price-book ratio, price-earnings ratio, and the price-cash flow ratio.

6. **Calculating EFN (LO4, CFA10)**   The most recent financial statements for Bradley, Inc., are shown here (assuming no income taxes):

Income Statement		Balance Sheet			
Sales	$4,800	Assets	$14,200	Debt	$9,900
Costs	(3,180)			Equity	4,300
Net income	$1,620	Total	$14,200	Total	$14,200

Assets and costs are proportional to sales. Debt and equity are not. No dividends are paid. Next year's sales are projected to be $5,232. What is the external financing needed?

7. **Operating Cash Flow (LO3, CFA6)**   Weston Corporation had earnings per share of $1.64, depreciation expense of $310,000, and 190,000 shares outstanding. What was the operating cash flow per share? If the share price was $36, what was the price-cash flow ratio?

8. **Earnings per Share (LO3, CFA4)**   Alphonse Inc. has a return on equity of 15 percent, 36,000 shares of stock outstanding, and a net income of $98,000. What are earnings per share?

9. **Addition to Retained Earnings (LO2, CFA11)**   Lemon Co. has net income of $520,000 and 75,000 shares of stock. If the company pays a dividend of $1.42, what are the additions to retained earnings?

10. **Cash Flow Statement (LO2, CFA6)**   Given the following information for Hetrich, Inc., calculate the operating cash flow, investment cash flow, financing cash flow, and net cash flow:

Net income:	$175
Depreciation:	$52
Issuance of new stock:	$7
Repurchase of debt:	$18
Sale of property:	$10
Purchase of equipment:	$70
Dividend payments:	$9
Interest payments:	$32

11. **EFN (L04, CFA10)**   The most recent financial statements for Martin, Inc., are shown here:

Income Statement		Balance Sheet			
Sales	$27,500	Assets	$105,000	Debt	$43,000
Costs	(19,450)			Equity	62,000
Taxable income	$8,050	Total	$105,000	Total	$105,000
Taxes (34%)	(2,737)				
Net income	$ 5,313				

Assets and costs are proportional to sales. Debt and equity are not. A dividend of $1,050 was paid, and Martin wishes to maintain a constant payout ratio. Next year's sales are projected to be $33,000. What is the external financing needed?

Use the following financial statement information to answer the next five questions.
Amounts are in thousands of dollars (except number of shares and price per share):

Kiwi Fruit Company Balance Sheet

Cash and equivalents	$ 570
Operating assets	650
Property, plant, and equipment	2,700
Other assets	110
Total assets	$ 4,030
Current liabilities	$ 920
Long-term debt	1,280
Other liabilities	120
Total liabilities	$ 2,320
Paid in capital	$ 340
Retained earnings	1,370
Total equity	$ 1,710
Total liabilities and equity	$ 4,030

Kiwi Fruit Company Income Statement

Net sales	$ 7,800
Cost of goods sold	(5,900)
Gross profit	$ 1,900
Operating expense	(990)
Operating income	$ 910
Other income	105
Net interest expense	(200)
Pretax income	$ 815
Income tax	(285)
Net income	$ 530
Earnings per share	$ 2.00
Shares outstanding	265,000
Recent price	$34.50

Kiwi Fruit Company Cash Flow Statement

Net income	$ 530
Depreciation and amortization	175
Changes in operating assets	(90)
Changes in current liabilities	(120)
Operating cash flow	$ 495
Net additions to properties	$ 180
Changes in other assets	(80)
Investing cash flow	$ 100
Issuance/redemption of long-term debt	$ (190)
Dividends paid	(220)
Financing cash flow	$ (410)
Net cash increase	$ 95

12. **Calculating Margins (LO3, CFA7)**   Calculate the gross and operating margins for Kiwi Fruit.

13. **Calculating Profitability Measures (LO3, CFA7)**   Calculate ROA and ROE for Kiwi Fruit and interpret these ratios.

14. **Calculating Per-Share Measures (LO3, CFA7)**   Calculate the price-book, price-earnings, and price-cash flow ratios for Kiwi Fruit.

15. **Pro Forma Financial Statements (LO4, CFA10)**   Following the examples in the chapter, prepare a pro forma income statement, balance sheet, and cash flow statement for Kiwi Fruit assuming a 10 percent increase in sales.

16. **Projected Share Prices (LO4, CFA7)**   Based on the previous two questions, what is the projected stock price assuming a 10 percent increase in sales?

17. **Full-Capacity Sales (LO4, CFA11)**   Thorpe Mfg., Inc., is currently operating at only 75 percent of fixed asset capacity. Current sales are $480,000. How fast can sales grow before any new fixed assets are needed?

18. **Fixed Assets and Capacity Usage (LO4, CFA11)**   For the company in the previous problem, suppose fixed assets are $385,000 and sales are projected to grow to $645,000. How much in new fixed assets are required to support this growth in sales?

19. **Calculating EFN (LO4, CFA10)**   The most recent financial statements for Moose Tours, Inc., follow. Sales for 2011 are projected to grow by 15 percent. Interest expense will remain constant; the tax rate and the dividend payout rate will also remain constant. Costs, other expenses, current assets, and accounts payable increase spontaneously with sales. If the firm is operating at full capacity and no new debt or equity is issued, what is the external financing needed to support the 15 percent growth rate in sales?

MOOSE TOURS, INC. 2010 Income Statement	
Sales	$995,000
Costs	(782,000)
Other expenses	(15,000)
Earnings before interest and taxes	$198,000
Interest paid	(21,670)
Taxable income	$176,330
Taxes (35%)	(61,716)
Net income	$114,615
Dividends	$ 45,700
Addition to retained earnings	60,444

MOOSE TOURS, INC.
Balance Sheet as of December 31, 2010

Assets		Liabilities and Owners' Equity	
Current assets		Current liabilities	
Cash	$ 27,500	Accounts payable	$ 71,500
Accounts receivable	47,300	Notes payable	9,900
Inventory	83,600	Total	$ 81,400
Total	$158,400	Long-term debt	$171,600
Fixed assets		Owners' equity	
Net plant and		Common stock and paid-in surplus	$23,100
equipment	$400,400	Retained earnings	282,700
		Total	$305,800
Total assets	$558,800	Total liabilities and owners' equity	$558,800

20. **Capacity Usage and Growth (LO4, CFA11)**   In the previous problem, suppose the firm was operating at only 90 percent capacity in 2010. What is EFN now?

CFA Exam Review by Schweser

[CFA4, CFA6, CFA13, CFA14]

Laura Bond is a Senior VP of MediaInvests Partners (MIP), a late-stage venture capital firm. MIP is considering an investment in VirtualCon Corp. VirtualCon went public during the dot-com boom, and it currently trades at a small fraction of its IPO value; however, its recent financial statements have shown improvement.

Harry Darling, a former employee of MIP and current VirtualCon board member, thinks that VirtualCon is an excellent candidate to take private. He has presented the idea to MIP's board, pointing out the rising operating cash flows. Ms. Bond has the highest regard for Mr. Darling, but she remains dubious about his assessment of VirtualCon. She has come across several items in the footnotes to the financial statements that have raised concerns.

Ms. Bond noticed that six months ago VirtualCon created a special-purpose entity (SPE) to securitize its receivables. The firm sold off $12 million of its accounts receivable in those two quarters, which represented 80 percent of those outstanding and more than five months of revenue. She notes that a change in the default rate assumption and the discount rate at the time of sale caused the fair value of the receivables to exceed book value by $3.8 million, which VirtualCon booked as revenue.

Mr. Darling also points out, "VirtualCon has become more active in managing its accounts payable. It set up a financial arrangement with its principal bank so the bank makes payments to VirtualCon's suppliers on its behalf, and VirtualCon has 90 days to pay the bank. The suppliers are more willing to do business with VirtualCon because they have the assurance of being paid by the bank."

1. Ignoring interest, what is the effect on VirtualCon's total cash flow and cash flow from financing (CFF) from its financing arrangement for its accounts payable at the time of payment to the supplier?

	Total CF	CFF
a.	Unaffected	Increase
b.	Decrease	Unaffected
c.	Unaffected	Unaffected

2. Which of the following statements about VirtualCon's securitization of receivables is least accurate?

   a. Accelerates operating cash flow into the current period.
   b. Enables the firm to reclassify financing cash flow as operating cash flow.
   c. Could allow the firm to recognize a reduction in operating expenses.

3. If VirtualCon had decided to slow its payment of accounts payable by 90 days instead of entering into a financing arrangement with the bank, what would be the impact on its operating cash flow (CFO) and financing cash flow (CFF) during the 90 days relative to its cash flow under the financing arrangement, ignoring interest?

	CFO	CFF
a.	Higher	Lower
b.	Higher	Higher
c.	Lower	Higher

What's on the Web?

1. **Ratio Analysis**   Go to www.reuters.com/finance/stocks and enter the ticker symbol PFE for Pfizer. Click "View Full Quote" and look under the "Financials" link to find ratios for Pfizer, the industry, the sector, and the S&P 500. Discuss Pfizer's performance using the

following ratios: gross margin, operating margin, return on assets, return on equity, book value per share, earnings per share, cash flow per share, price-book, price-earnings, and price-cash flow.

2. **Ratio Calculation**   Under the Investor Center at Du Pont's Web site (www.dupont.com) you will find financial statements for the company. Using the most recent 10K form, calculate the following ratios for Du Pont over the three years reported: gross margin, operating margin, return on assets, return on equity, book value per share, earnings per share, cash flow per share, price-book, price-earnings, and price-cash flow. How have these ratios changed over this period?

3. **Cash Flow Statement**   You can find financial statements for 3M in the company's Annual Report located in the Investor Relations section of the company's Web site, www.3m.com. Locate the Statement of Cash Flows in the Annual Report. How have the items changed over the years? Explain 3M's most recent cash flow statement in words.

CHAPTER 18

Corporate Bonds

Learning Objectives

Conform to your fixed-income knowledge covenants by learning:

1. The basic types of corporate bonds.

2. How callable bonds function.

3. The different types of corporate bonds.

4. The basics of bond ratings.

"Creditors have better memories than debtors."

–Benjamin Franklin

A corporation issues bonds intending to meet all obligations of interest and repayment of principal. Investors buy bonds believing the corporation intends to fulfill its debt obligation in a timely manner. Although defaults can and do occur, the market for corporate bonds exists only because corporations are able to convince investors of their original intent to avoid default. Reaching this state of trust is not easy—it normally requires elaborate contractual arrangements. ■

Almost all corporations issue notes and bonds to raise money to finance investment projects. Indeed, for many corporations, the value of notes and bonds outstanding can exceed the value of common stock shares outstanding. Nevertheless, most investors do not think of corporate bonds when they think about investing. This is because corporate bonds represent specialized investment instruments that are usually bought by financial institutions like insurance companies and pension funds. For professional money managers at these institutions, a knowledge of corporate bonds is absolutely essential. This chapter introduces you to the specialized knowledge that these money managers possess.

CFA™ Exam Topics in This Chapter:

1 Features of debt securities (L1, S15)
2 Risks associated with investing in bonds (L1, S15)
3 Overview of bond sectors and instruments (L1, S15)
4 Understanding yield spreads (L1, S15)
5 General principles of credit analysis (L2, S14)
6 Valuing bonds with embedded options (L2, S14)

Go to www.mhhe.com/jmd6e for a guide that aligns your textbook with CFA readings.

18.1 Corporate Bond Basics

Corporate bonds represent the debt of a corporation owed to its bondholders. More specifically, a corporate bond is a security issued by a corporation that represents a promise to pay to its bondholders a fixed sum of money at a future maturity date, along with periodic payments of interest. The fixed sum paid at maturity is the bond's *principal,* also called its par or face value. The periodic interest payments are called *coupons.*

From an investor's point of view, corporate bonds represent an investment distinct from common stock. The three most fundamental differences are these:

1. Common stock represents an ownership claim on the corporation, whereas bonds represent a creditor's claim on the corporation.

2. Promised cash flows—that is, coupons and principal—to be paid to bondholders are stated in advance when the bond is issued. By contrast, the amount and timing of dividends paid to common stockholders may change at any time.

3. Most corporate bonds are issued as callable bonds, which means that the bond issuer has the right to buy back outstanding bonds before the maturity date of the bond issue. When a bond issue is called, coupon payments stop and the bondholders are forced to surrender their bonds to the issuer in exchange for the cash payment of a specified call price. By contrast, common stock is almost never callable.

WWW

For more information on corporate bonds visit www.investinginbonds.com

The corporate bond market is large, with several trillion dollars of corporate bonds outstanding in the United States. The sheer size of the corporate bond market prompts an important inquiry: Who owns corporate bonds and why? The answer is that most corporate bond investors belong to only a few distinct categories. The single largest group of corporate bond investors is life insurance companies, which hold about a third of all outstanding corporate bonds. Remaining ownership shares are roughly equally balanced among individual investors, pension funds, banks, and foreign investors.

The pattern of corporate bond ownership is largely explained by the fact that corporate bonds provide a source of predictable cash flows. While individual bonds occasionally default on their promised cash payments, large institutional investors can diversify away most default risk by including a large number of different bond issues in their portfolios. For this reason, life insurance companies and pension funds find that corporate bonds are a natural investment vehicle to provide for future payments of retirement and death benefits, because both the timing and amount of these benefit payments can be matched with bond cash flows. These institutions can eliminate much of their financial risk by matching the timing of cash flows received from a bond portfolio to the timing of cash flows needed to make benefit payments—a strategy called cash flow matching. For this reason, life insurance companies and pension funds together own more than half of all outstanding corporate bonds. For similar reasons, individual investors might own corporate bonds as a source of steady cash income. However, since individual investors cannot easily diversify default risk, they should normally invest only in bonds with higher credit quality.

Every corporate bond issue has a specific set of issue terms associated with it. The issue terms associated with any particular bond can range from a relatively simple arrangement, where the bond is little more than an IOU of the corporation, to a complex contract specifying in great detail what the issuer can and cannot do with respect to its obligations to bondholders. Bonds issued with a standard, relatively simple set of features are popularly called **plain vanilla bonds** or "bullet" bonds.

plain vanilla bonds

Bonds issued with a relatively standard set of features. Also known as *bullet bonds.*

As an illustration of a plain vanilla corporate debt issue, Table 18.1 summarizes the issue terms for a note issue by Jack Russell Corp. Referring to Table 18.1, we see that the Jack Russell Corp. notes were issued in December 2010 and mature five years later in December 2015. Each individual note has a face value denomination of $1,000. Because the total issue amount is $20 million, the entire issue contains 20,000 notes. Each note pays a $100 annual coupon, which is equal to 10 percent of its face value. The annual coupon is split between two semiannual $50 payments made each June and December. Based on the original offer

TABLE 18.1

Jack Russell Corp. Five-Year Note Issue

Issue amount	$20 million	Note issue total face value is $20 million
Issue date	12/15/2010	Notes offered to the public in December 2010
Maturity date	12/31/2015	Remaining principal due December 31, 2015
Face value	$1,000	Face value denomination is $1,000 per note
Coupon interest	$100 per annum	Annual coupons are $100 per note
Coupon dates	6/30, 12/31	Coupons are paid semiannually
Offering price	100	Offer price is 100 percent of face value
Yield to maturity	10%	Based on stated offer price
Call provision	Not callable	Notes may not be paid off before maturity
Security	None	Notes are unsecured
Rating	Not rated	Privately placed note issue

unsecured debt

Bonds, notes, or other debt issued with no specific collateral pledged as security for the bond issue.

price of 100, which means 100 percent of the $1,000 face value, the notes have a yield to maturity of 10 percent. The notes are not callable, which means that the debt may not be paid off before maturity.

The Jack Russell Corp. notes are **unsecured debt**, which means that no specific collateral has been pledged as security for the notes. In the event that the issuer defaults on its promised payments, the noteholders may take legal action to acquire sufficient assets of the company to settle their claims as creditors.

When issued, the Jack Russell Corp. notes were not reviewed by a rating agency like Moody's or Standard & Poor's. Thus, the notes are unrated. If the notes were to be assigned a credit rating, they would probably be rated as "junk grade." The term "junk," commonly used for high-risk debt issues, is unduly pejorative. After all, the company must repay the debt. If the company is in a high-risk industry, however, the probability is high that the company might have difficulty paying off the debt in a timely manner.

Reflecting their below-average credit quality, the Jack Russell Corp. notes were not issued to the general public. Instead, the notes were privately placed with two insurance companies. Such private placements are common among relatively small debt issues. Private placements will be discussed in greater detail later in this chapter.

18.2 Types of Corporate Bonds

debentures

Unsecured bonds issued by a corporation.

Debentures are the most frequently issued type of corporate bond. Debenture bonds represent an unsecured debt of a corporation. Debenture bondholders have a legal claim as general creditors of the corporation. In the event of a default by the issuing corporation, the bondholders' claim extends to all corporate assets. However, they may have to share this claim with other creditors who have an equal legal claim or yield to creditors with a higher legal claim.

In addition to debentures, there are three other basic types of corporate bonds: mortgage bonds, collateral trust bonds, and equipment trust certificates. **Mortgage bonds** represent debt issued with a lien on specific property, usually real estate, pledged as security for the bonds. A mortgage lien gives bondholders the legal right to foreclose on property pledged by the issuer to satisfy an unpaid debt obligation. However, in actual practice, foreclosure and sale of mortgaged property following a default may not be the most desirable strategy for bondholders. Instead, it is common for a corporation in financial distress to reorganize itself and negotiate a new debt contract with bondholders. In these negotiations, a mortgage lien can be an important bargaining tool for the trustee representing the bondholders.

mortgage bond

Debt secured with a property lien.

collateral trust bond

Debt secured with financial collateral.

Collateral trust bonds are characterized by a pledge of financial assets as security for the bond issue. Collateral trust bonds are commonly issued by holding companies, which may pledge the stocks, bonds, or other securities issued by their subsidiaries as collateral for their own bond issue. The legal arrangement for pledging collateral securities is similar to that for a mortgage lien. In the event of an issuer's default on contractual obligations to bondholders, the bondholders have a legal right to foreclose on collateralized securities in the amount necessary to settle an outstanding debt obligation.

equipment trust certificate
Shares in a trust with income from a lease contract.

Equipment trust certificates represent debt issued by a trustee to purchase heavy industrial equipment that is leased and used by railroads, airlines, and other companies with a demand for heavy equipment. Under this financial arrangement, investors purchase equipment trust certificates, and the proceeds from this sale are used to purchase equipment. Formal ownership of the equipment remains with a trustee appointed to represent the certificate holders.

The trustee then leases the equipment to a company. In return, the company promises to make a series of scheduled lease payments over a specified leasing period. The trustee collects the lease payments and distributes all revenues, less expenses, as dividends to the certificate holders. These distributions are conventionally called dividends because they are generated as income from a trust. The lease arrangement usually ends after a specified number of years when the leasing company makes a final lease payment and may take possession of the used equipment.

From the certificate holders' point of view, this financial arrangement is superior to a mortgage lien since they actually own the equipment during the leasing period. Thus, if the leasing corporation defaults, the equipment can be sold without the effort and expense of a formal foreclosure process. Because the underlying equipment for this type of financing is typically built according to an industry standard, the equipment can usually be quickly sold or leased to another company in the same line of business.

Figure 18.1 is a *Wall Street Journal* bond announcement for an aircraft equipment trust for Northwest Airlines (recently acquired by Delta). Notice that the $243 million issue is split into two parts: $177 million of senior notes paying 8.26 percent interest and $66 million of subordinated notes paying 9.36 percent interest. The senior notes have a first claim on the aircraft in the event of a default by the airline, while the subordinated notes have a secondary claim. In the event of a default, investment losses for the trust will primarily be absorbed by the subordinated noteholders. For this reason, the subordinated notes are riskier and, therefore, pay a higher interest rate. Of course, if no default actually occurs, the subordinated notes would turn out to be a better investment. For risky bonds, however, there is no way of knowing in advance that the company will not default.

CHECK THIS

18.2a Given that a bond issue is one of the four basic types discussed in this section, how would the specific bond type affect the credit quality of the bond?

18.2b Why might some bond types be more or less risky with respect to the risk of default?

18.2c Given that a default has occurred, why might the trustee's job of representing the financial interests of the bondholders be easier for some bond types than for others?

18.3 Bond Indentures

indenture summary
Description of the contractual terms of a new bond issue included in a bond's prospectus.

prospectus
Document prepared as part of a security offering detailing information about a company's financial position, its operations, and investment plans.

A bond indenture is a formal written agreement between the corporation and the bondholders. It is an important legal document that spells out in detail the mutual rights and obligations of the corporation and the bondholders with respect to the bond issue. Indenture contracts are often quite long, sometimes several hundred pages, and make for very tedious reading. In fact, very few bond investors ever read the original indenture, but instead might refer to an **indenture summary** provided in the **prospectus** that was circulated when the bond issue was originally sold to the public. Alternatively, a summary of the most important features of an indenture is published by debt rating agencies.

The Trust Indenture Act of 1939 requires that any bond issue subject to regulation by the Securities and Exchange Commission (SEC), which includes most corporate bond and note issues sold to the general public, must have a trustee appointed to represent the interests of

| FIGURE 18.1 | Equipment Trust Notes Issue |

$243,000,000

NWA Trust No. 1

$177,000,000 8.26% Class A Senior Aircraft Notes

$66,000,000 9.36% Class B Subordinated Aircraft Notes

The 8.26% Class A Senior Aircraft Notes and the 9.36% Class B Subordinated Aircraft Notes are secured by, among other things, a security interest in certain aircraft sold by Northwest Airlines, Inc. ("Northwest") to an owner trust for a purchase price of $443 million and the lease relating to such Aircraft, including the right to receive amounts payable by Northwest under such lease. The Noteholders also have the benefit of a liquidity facility, initially provided by General Electric Capital Corporation, to support certain payments of interest on the Notes.

Lehman Brothers   BT Securities Corporation

Source: Reprinted with permission of *The Wall Street Journal*, via Copyright Clearance Center, Inc. © 1994 Dow Jones & Company, Inc. All Rights Reserved Worldwide.

the bondholders. Also, all responsibilities of a duly appointed trustee must be specified in detail in the indenture. Some corporations maintain a blanket or open-ended indenture that applies to all currently outstanding bonds and any new bonds that are issued, while other corporations write a new indenture contract for each new bond issue sold to the public.

Descriptions of the most important provisions frequently specified in a bond indenture agreement are presented next.

BOND SENIORITY PROVISIONS

The Trust Indenture Act of 1939 is available at the SEC Web site
www.sec.gov

A corporation may have several different bond issues outstanding; these issues normally can be differentiated according to the seniority of their claims on the firm's assets. Seniority usually is specified in the indenture contract.

Consider a corporation with two outstanding bond issues: (1) a mortgage bond issue with certain real estate assets pledged as security and (2) a debenture bond issue with no specific assets pledged as security. In this case, the mortgage bond issue has a senior claim on the pledged assets but no specific claim on other corporate assets. The debenture bond has a claim on all corporate assets not specifically pledged as security for the mortgage bond, but it would have only a residual claim on assets pledged as security for the mortgage bond issue. This residual claim would apply only after all obligations to the mortgage bondholders have been satisfied.

As another example, suppose a corporation has two outstanding debenture issues. In this case, seniority is normally assigned to the bonds first issued by the corporation. The bonds issued earliest have a senior claim on the pledged assets and are called **senior debentures**. The bonds issued later have a junior or subordinate claim and are called **subordinated debentures**.

The seniority of an existing debt issue is usually protected by a **negative pledge clause** in the bond indenture. A negative pledge clause prohibits a new issue of debt with seniority over a currently outstanding issue. However, it may allow a new debt issue to share equally in the seniority of an existing issue. A negative pledge clause is part of the indenture agreement of most senior debenture bonds.

CALL PROVISIONS

Most corporate bond issues have a call provision allowing the issuer to buy back all or part of its outstanding bonds at a specified call price sometime before the bonds mature. The most frequent motive for a corporation to call outstanding bonds is to take advantage of a general fall in market interest rates. Lower interest rates allow the corporation to replace currently outstanding high-coupon bonds with a new issue of bonds paying lower coupons. Replacing existing bonds with new bonds is called **bond refunding**.

TRADITIONAL FIXED-PRICE CALL PROVISIONS   There are two major types of call provisions, *traditional fixed-price* and *make-whole*. From an investor's point of view, a fixed-price call provision has a distinct disadvantage. For example, suppose an investor is currently holding bonds paying 10 percent coupons. Further suppose that, after a fall in market interest rates, the corporation is able to issue new bonds that only pay 8 percent coupons. By calling existing 10 percent coupon bonds, the issuer forces bondholders to surrender their bonds in exchange for the fixed call price. But this happens at a time when the bondholders can reinvest funds only at lower interest rates. If instead the bonds were noncallable, the bondholders would continue to receive the original 10 percent coupons.

For this reason, callable bonds are less attractive to investors than noncallable bonds. Consequently, a callable bond will sell at a lower price (or, equivalently, a higher yield) than a comparable noncallable bond. Despite their lower prices, corporations generally prefer to issue fixed-price callable bonds. However, to reduce the price gap between callable and noncallable bonds, issuers typically allow the indenture contract to specify certain restrictions on their ability to call an outstanding bond issue. Three features are commonly used to restrict an issuer's call privilege:

1. Callable bonds usually have a *deferred call provision* which provides a *call protection period* during which a bond issue cannot be called. For example, a bond may be call-protected for a period of five years after its issue date.

2. A call price often includes a *call premium* over par value. A standard arrangement stipulates a call premium equal to one year's coupon payments for a call occurring at the earliest possible call date. Over time, the call premium is gradually reduced until it is eliminated entirely. After some future date, the bonds become callable at par value.

3. Some indentures specifically prohibit an issuer from calling outstanding bonds for the purpose of refunding at a lower coupon rate but still allow a call for other reasons. This *refunding provision* prevents the corporation from calling an outstanding bond

---

senior debentures
Bonds that have a higher claim on the firm's assets than other bonds.

subordinated debentures
Bonds that have a claim on the firm's assets after those with a higher claim have been satisfied.

negative pledge clause
Bond indenture provision that prohibits new debt from being issued with seniority over an existing issue.

bond refunding
Process of calling an outstanding bond issue and refinancing it with a new bond issue.

FIGURE 18.2 Noncallable Bonds and Fixed-Price Callable Bonds

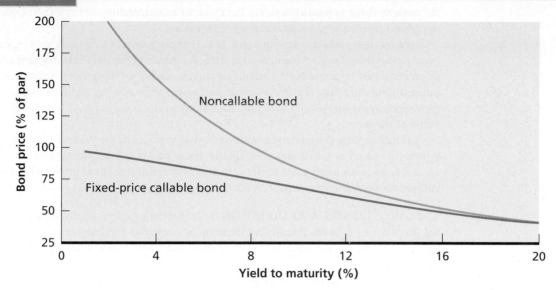

issue solely as a response to falling market interest rates. However, the corporation can still pay off its bond debt ahead of schedule by using funds acquired from, say, earnings, or funds obtained from the sale of newly issued common stock.

After a bond's call protection period has elapsed, a rational investor would be unwilling to pay much more than the call price for the bond since the issuer might call the bond at any time and pay only the call price for the bond. Consequently, a bond's call price serves as an effective ceiling on its market price. It is important for bond investors to understand how the existence of a price ceiling for callable bonds alters the standard price-yield relationship for bonds.

The relationship between interest rates and prices for comparable callable and noncallable bonds is illustrated in Figure 18.2. In this example, the vertical axis measures bond prices, and the horizontal axis measures bond yields. In this two-bond example, both bonds pay an 8 percent coupon and are alike in all respects except that one of the bonds is callable any time at par value.

As shown in Figure 18.2, the noncallable bond has the standard *convex price-yield relationship,* where the price-yield curve is bowed toward the origin. When the price-yield curve is bowed to the origin this is called *positive convexity.* In contrast, the fixed-price callable bond has a convex or bowed price-yield relationship in the region of high yields, but is bowed away from the origin in the region of low yields. This is called *negative convexity.* The important lesson here is that no matter how low market interest rates might fall, the maximum price of an unprotected fixed-price callable bond is generally bounded above by its call price.

CHECK THIS

18.3a After a call protection period has elapsed, why is the call price an effective ceiling on the market price of a callable bond with a fixed-price call provision?

MAKE-WHOLE CALL PROVISION   In just the last few years, a new type of call provision, a "make-whole" call, has become common in the corporate bond market. If a callable bond has a make-whole call provision, bondholders receive approximately what the bond is worth if the bond is called. This call provision gets its name because the bondholder does not suffer a loss in the event of a call; that is, the bondholder is "made whole" when the bond is called.

Like a fixed-price call provision, a make-whole call provision allows the borrower to pay off the remaining debt early. Unlike a fixed-price call provision, however, a make-whole call provision requires the borrower to make a lump-sum payment representing the present value of all payments that will not be made because of the call. The discount rate used to calculate the present value is usually equal to the yield on a comparable maturity U.S. Treasury security plus a fixed, prespecified *make-whole premium.*

Because the yield of a comparable U.S. Treasury security changes over time, the call price paid to bondholders changes over time. As interest rates decrease, the make-whole call price increases because the discount rate used to calculate the present value decreases. As interest rates increase, the make-whole call price decreases. In addition, make-whole call provisions typically specify that the minimum amount received by a bondholder is the par value of the bond.

As interest rates decline, even in the region of low yields, the price of bonds with a make-whole call provision will increase. That is, these bonds exhibit the standard *convex price-yield relationship* in all yield regions. In contrast, recall that bond prices with a fixed-price call provision exhibit *negative convexity* in the region of low yields.

CALLABLE BONDS AND DURATION In an earlier chapter, we discussed the concept of the duration of a bond. Recall that duration is a weighted average measure of when cash flows are received. We use duration to estimate how sensitive bond prices are to changes in interest rates.

To determine the duration of plain vanilla bonds, either the Macaulay or the modified duration measure we discussed earlier is appropriate. For bonds with embedded options, such as callable bonds, these standard duration measures will not correctly estimate the price and interest rate relationship. For callable bonds we must calculate the *effective* duration of the bond. We can also use effective duration to estimate how sensitive bond prices are to changes in interest rates. When we calculate effective duration, however, we use option pricing methods to account for the embedded option to call the bond.

EXAMPLE 18.1

Calculating the Make-Whole Call Premium

Assume that LKD Energy Inc. sold a total of $1.25 billion worth of notes and bonds, and the first tranche issue of $300 million in notes has the following terms:

Settlement date:	7/16/2010
First payment:	2/1/2011
Maturity:	8/1/2015
Coupon:	5.90%
Price:	99.864
Yield:	5.931%
Spread:	90 basis points above U.S. Treasury notes
Make-whole call:	15 basis points above U.S. Treasury notes
Ratings:	Baa2 (Moody's); BBB (S&P)

If these notes were called immediately, what price would LKD Energy have to pay to these note holders? To calculate the make-whole call premium of these notes, we need to add 15 basis points to the yield of comparable-maturity U.S. Treasury notes.

We find the yield of comparable-maturity U.S. Treasury notes by subtracting the 90 basis point spread from the yield of the LKD notes, 5.931% − .90% = 5.031%. Then we add the 15 basis point make-whole premium: 5.031% + .15% = 5.181%. Discounting the remaining cash flows of the note at 5.181 percent, we get a make-whole call price of about $103.13—which is about $3.27 more than the current price of the notes ($99.864). You must remember to use the standard bond pricing formula to discount these cash flows.

You can verify this price using Excel. Using the information above, enter =PRICE("7/16/2010","8/1/2015",0.059,0.05181,100,2) into an Excel cell and you will get a price of $103.15.

CHECK THIS

18.3b Suppose you hold a bond with a make-whole call provision. The coupon rate on this bond is 5.90 percent. At what yield to maturity will this bond sell for par?

PUT PROVISIONS

put bonds
Bonds that can be sold back to the issuer at a prespecified price on any of a sequence of prespecified dates. Also called *extendible bonds.*

A bond issue with a put provision grants bondholders the right to sell their bonds back to the issuer at a special *put price,* normally set at par value. These so-called **put bonds** are "putable" on each of a series of designated *put dates.* These are often scheduled to occur annually but sometimes occur at more frequent intervals. At each put date, the bondholder decides whether to sell the bond back to the issuer or continue to hold the bond until the next put date. For this reason, put bonds are often called *extendible bonds* because the bondholder has the option of extending the maturity of the bond at each put date.

Notice that by granting bondholders an option to sell their bonds back to the corporation at par value, the put feature provides an effective floor on the market price of the bond. Thus, the put feature offers protection to bondholders from rising interest rates and the associated fall in bond prices.

A put feature also helps protect bondholders from acts of the corporation that might cause a deterioration of the bond's credit quality. However, this protection is not granted without a cost to bond investors, because a putable bond will command a higher market price than a comparable nonputable bond.

CHECK THIS

18.3c Using Figure 18.2 as a guide, what would the price-yield relationship look like for a noncallable bond putable at par value?

18.3d Under what conditions would a put feature not yield an effective floor for the market price of a put bond? (*Hint:* Think about default risk.)

BOND-TO-STOCK CONVERSION PROVISIONS

convertible bonds
Bonds that holders can exchange for common stock according to a prespecified conversion ratio.

Some bonds have a valuable bond-to-stock conversion feature. These bonds are called convertible bonds. **Convertible bonds** grant bondholders the right to exchange each bond for a designated number of common stock shares of the issuing firm. To avoid confusion in a discussion of convertible bonds, it is important to understand some basic terminology.

1. The number of common stock shares acquired in exchange for each converted bond is called the *conversion ratio*:

   Conversion ratio = Number of stock shares acquired by conversion

2. The par value of a convertible bond divided by its conversion ratio is called the bond's *conversion price*:

$$\text{Conversion price} = \frac{\text{Bond par value}}{\text{Conversion ratio}}$$

3. The market price per share of common stock acquired by conversion times the bond's conversion ratio is called the bond's *conversion value*:

   Conversion value = Price per share of stock × Conversion ratio

For example, suppose a convertible bond with a par value of $1,000 can be converted into 20 shares of the issuing firm's common stock. In this case, the conversion price is

There is a convertible
bond calculator at:
www.numa.com

$1,000/20 = \$50$. Continuing this example, suppose the firm's common stock has a market price of \$40 per share; then the conversion value of a single bond is $20 \times \$40 = \$800$.

Figure 18.3 is *The Wall Street Journal* announcement of an issue of convertible subordinated notes by Advanced Micro Devices (AMD). The notes pay a 6 percent coupon rate and mature in 2005. The conversion price for this note issue is \$37 per share, which

FIGURE 18.3	Convertible Notes Issue

This announcement is neither an offer to sell, nor a solicitation of an offer to buy, any of these securities.
The offer is made only by the Prospectus and related Prospectus Supplement.

$517,500,000

AMD

Advanced Micro Devices, Inc.

6% Convertible Subordinated Notes due 2005

The 6% Convertible Subordinated Notes due 2005 (the "Notes") will be convertible at the option of the holder into shares of common stock, par value \$.01 per share (the "Common Stock"), of Advanced Micro Devices, Inc. (the "Company") at any time at or prior to maturity, unless previously redeemed or repurchased, at a conversion price of \$37.00 per share (equivalent to a conversion rate of 27.027 shares per \$1,000 principal amount of Notes), subject to adjustment in certain events.

Price 100%

Copies of the Prospectus and related Prospectus Supplement may be obtained in any State from such of the undersigned as may legally offer these securities in compliance with the securities laws of such State.

Donaldson, Lufkin & Jenrette
Securities Corporation

Salomon Smith Barney

Source: Reprinted with permission of *The Wall Street Journal*. © 1998 Dow Jones & Company, Inc. All Rights Reserved Worldwide.

implies a conversion ratio of 27.027 shares of common stock for each $1,000 face value note.

From an investor's perspective, the conversion privilege of convertible bonds has the distinct advantage that bondholders can receive a share of any increase in common stock value. However, the conversion option has a price. A corporation can sell convertible bonds at par value with a coupon rate substantially less than the coupon rate of comparable nonconvertible bonds. This forgone coupon interest represents the price of the bond's conversion option.

When convertible bonds are originally issued, their conversion ratio is customarily set to yield a conversion value of 10 percent to 20 percent less than par value. For example, suppose the common stock of a company has a price of $30 per share and the company issues convertible bonds with a par value of $1,000 per bond. To set the original conversion value at $900 per bond, the company would set a conversion ratio of 30 stock shares per bond. Thereafter, the conversion ratio is fixed, but each bond's conversion value becomes linked to the firm's stock price, which may rise or fall in value. The price of a convertible bond reflects the conversion value of the bond. In general, the higher the conversion value the higher the bond price, and vice versa.

Investing in convertible bonds is more complicated than owning nonconvertible bonds, because the conversion privilege presents convertible bondholders with an important timing decision. When is the best time to exercise a bond's conversion option and exchange the bond for shares of common stock? The answer is that investors should normally postpone conversion as long as possible, because while they hold the bonds they continue to receive coupon payments. After converting to common stock, they lose all subsequent coupons. In general, unless the total dividend payments on stock acquired by conversion are somewhat greater than the forgone bond coupon payments, investors should hold on to their convertible bonds to continue to receive coupon payments.

The rational decision of convertible bondholders to postpone conversion as long as possible is limited, however, since convertible bonds are almost always callable. Firms customarily call outstanding convertible bonds when their conversion value has risen by 10 percent to 15 percent above bond par value, although there are many exceptions to this rule. When a convertible bond issue is called by the issuer, bondholders are forced to make an immediate decision whether to convert to common stock shares or accept a cash payment of the call price. Fortunately, the decision is simple—convertible bondholders should choose whichever is more valuable, the call price or the conversion value.

18.3e Describe the conversion decision that convertible bondholders must make when the bonds mature.

GRAPHICAL ANALYSIS OF CONVERTIBLE BOND PRICES

The price of a convertible bond is closely linked to the value of the underlying common stock shares that can be acquired by conversion. A higher stock price implies a higher bond price, and, conversely, a lower stock price yields a lower bond price.

The relationship between the price of a convertible bond and the price of the firm's common stock is depicted in Figure 18.4. In this example, the convertible bond's price is measured on the vertical axis, and the stock price is measured along the horizontal axis. The straight, upward-sloping line is the bond's conversion value; the slope of the line is the conversion ratio. The horizontal line represents the price of a comparable nonconvertible bond with the same coupon rate, maturity, and credit quality.

A convertible bond is said to be an **in-the-money bond** when its conversion value is greater than its call price. If an in-the-money convertible bond is called, rational bondholders will convert their bonds into common stock. When the conversion value is less

in-the-money bond
A convertible bond whose conversion value is greater than its call price.

FIGURE 18.4 Convertible Bond Prices

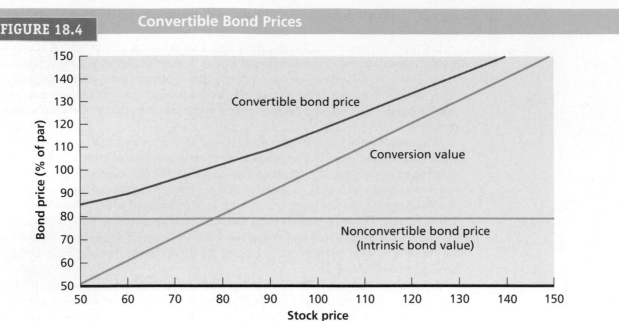

than the call price, a convertible bond is said to be *out of the money*. If an out-of-the-money bond is called, rational bondholders will accept the call price and forgo the conversion option. In practice, however, convertible bonds are seldom called when they are out of the money.

The curved line in Figure 18.4 shows the relationship between a convertible bond's price and the underlying stock price. As shown, there are two lower bounds on the value of a convertible bond. First, a convertible bond's price can never fall below its **intrinsic bond value**, also commonly called its *investment value* or *straight bond value*. This value is what the bond would be worth if it were not convertible, but otherwise identical in terms of coupon, maturity, and credit quality. Second, a convertible bond can never sell for less than its *conversion value* because, if it did, investors could simply buy the bond and convert, thereby realizing an immediate, riskless profit.

intrinsic bond value
The price below which a convertible bond cannot fall, equal to the value of a comparable nonconvertible bond. Also called *investment value.*

Thus, the *floor value* of a convertible bond is its intrinsic bond value or its conversion value, whichever is larger. As shown in Figure 18.4, however, a convertible bond will generally sell for more than this floor value. This extra is the amount that investors are willing to pay for the right, but not the obligation, to convert the bond at a future date at a potentially much higher stock price.

An interesting variation of a bond-to-stock conversion feature occurs when the company issuing the bonds is different from the company whose stock is acquired by the conversion. In this case, the bonds are called **exchangeable bonds**. Figure 18.5 presents a *Wall Street Journal* announcement of an issue of exchangeable subordinated debentures by the McKesson Corporation. These debentures are exchangeable for common stock shares of Armor All Products Corporation. McKesson is a retail distributor, and Armor All markets consumer chemical products. Exchangeable bonds, while not unusual, are less common than convertible bonds.

exchangeable bonds
Bonds that can be converted into common stock shares of a company other than the issuer's.

CHECK THIS

18.3f For nonconvertible bonds, the call price is a ceiling on the market price of the bond. Why might the call price not be an effective ceiling on the price of a convertible bond?

FIGURE 18.5   Exchangeable Debentures Issue

This announcement is neither an offer to sell nor a solicitation of an offer to buy any of these Securities.
The offer is made only by the Prospectus.

$180,000,000

McKesson Corporation

4¹/₂% Exchangeable Subordinated Debentures
Due 2004

Exchangeable for Shares of Common Stock of
Armor All Products Corporation

Interest Payable March 1 and September 1

Price 100% and Accrued Interest, if any

Copies of the Prospectus may be obtained in any State from only such
of the undersigned as may legally offer these Securities in
compliance with the securities laws of such State.

MORGAN STANLEY & CO.
Incorporated

MONTGOMERY SECURITIES

MONNESS, CRESPI, HARDT & CO. INC.   **WHEAT FIRST BUTCHER & SINGER**
                                                       Capital Markets

BOND MATURITY AND PRINCIPAL PAYMENT PROVISIONS

term bonds
Bonds issued with a single maturity date.

Term bonds represent the most common corporate bond maturity structure. A term bond issue has a single maturity date. On this date, all outstanding bond principal must be paid off. The indenture contract for a term bond issue normally stipulates the creation of a *sinking fund*. As we discuss elsewhere, a sinking fund is an account established to repay bondholders through a series of fractional redemptions before the bond reaches maturity. Thus, at maturity, only a fraction of the original bond issue will still be outstanding.

An alternative maturity structure is provided by **serial bonds**, where a fraction of an entire bond issue is scheduled to mature in each year over a specified period. Essentially, a serial bond issue represents a collection of subissues with sequential maturities. As an example, a serial bond issue may stipulate that one-tenth of an entire bond issue must be redeemed in each year over a 10-year period, with the last fraction redeemed at maturity. Serial bonds generally do not have a call provision, whereas term bonds usually do have a call provision.

When originally issued, most corporate bonds have maturities of 30 years or less. However, in recent years some companies have issued bonds with 40- and 50-year maturities. In 1993, Walt Disney Company made headlines in the financial press when it sold 100-year maturity bonds. This bond issue became popularly known as the "Sleeping Beauty" bonds, after the classic Disney movie. However, the prince might arrive early for these bonds since they are callable after 30 years. Nevertheless, this was the first time since 1954 that 100-year bonds were sold by any borrower in the United States. Only days later, however, Coca-Cola issued $150 million of 100-year maturity bonds. Both the Disney and Coke bond issues locked in the unusually low interest rates prevailing in 1993.

SINKING FUND PROVISIONS

sinking fund

An account used to provide for scheduled redemptions of outstanding bonds.

The indentures of most term bonds include a **sinking fund** provision that requires the corporation to make periodic payments into a trustee-managed account. Account reserves are then used to provide for scheduled redemptions of outstanding bonds. The existence of a sinking fund is an important consideration for bond investors mainly for two reasons:

1. A sinking fund provides a degree of security to bondholders, since payments into the sinking fund can be used only to pay outstanding obligations to bondholders.

2. A sinking fund provision requires fractional bond issue redemptions according to a preset schedule. Therefore, some bondholders will be repaid their invested principal before the stated maturity for their bonds whether they want repayment or not.

As part of a *scheduled sinking fund redemption,* some bondholders may be forced to surrender their bonds in exchange for cash payment of a special *sinking fund call price.* For this reason, not all bondholders may be able to hold their bonds until maturity, even though the entire bond issue has not been called according to a general call provision. For example, the indenture for a 25-year maturity bond issue may require that one-twentieth of the bond issue be retired annually, beginning immediately after an initial 5-year call protection period.

Typically, when a redemption is due, the sinking fund trustee will select bonds by lottery. Selected bonds are then called, and the affected bondholders receive the call price, which for sinking fund redemptions is usually par value. However, the issuer normally has a valuable option to buy back the required number of bonds in the open market and deliver them to the sinking fund trustee instead of delivering the cash required for a par value redemption. Issuers naturally prefer to exercise this option when bonds can be repurchased in the open market at less than par value.

18.3g For bond investors, what are some of the advantages and disadvantages of a sinking fund provision?

CHECK THIS

COUPON PAYMENT PROVISIONS

Coupon rates are stated on an annual basis. For example, an 8 percent coupon rate indicates that the issuer promises to pay 8 percent of a bond's face value to the bondholder each year. However, splitting an annual coupon into two semiannual payments is an almost universal practice in the United States. An exact schedule of coupon payment dates is specified in the bond indenture when the bonds are originally issued.

KATRINA CLAIMS COULD LEAVE HOLDERS OF A "CAT BOND" WITH MAJOR LOSSES

As Hurricane Katrina approached the Gulf Coast, those anxiously following the storm included big investors around the globe. They are owners of $5.3 billion of "catastrophe bonds" that insurers issued in recent years to help pay claims from natural disasters.

Now, it appears holders of one such "cat bond" may be out of pocket by almost $200 million, while most of the other investors have avoided such losses.

The bond in question: a special-purpose vehicle called Kamp Re. Under the terms of the $190 million bond, issued in August, investors lose their money if Zurich Financial Services, the big Swiss insurance company, pays insurance claims of more than $1 billion on any hurricane or earthquake in the United States within five years. Zurich's total losses from Katrina, which hit New Orleans and the Gulf Coast on Aug. 29, are estimated at almost $2 billion, according to the company.

Several people in the market said the Kamp Re bonds are being quoted at zero value in anticipation that investors have been wiped out. The bonds were sold in a private placement to institutional investors, like most cat bonds. If the Kamp Re bondholders lose all of their investment, it would be the first cat-bond issue to totally call in investors' funds, though some have cost investors modest chunks of their principal in past years. The event could lead investors to demand more protection, such as higher trigger points and interest payments, some market participants said.

Catastrophe bonds, or "cat bonds" for short, were launched in the 1990s by financial wizards on Wall Street and elsewhere to provide insurance companies an alternative to steeply priced reinsurance. In short, reinsurance is coverage insurers buy to spread the risk of losses from policies they sell to individuals and companies.

Here is how cat bonds generally work: Insurance companies sell bonds to investors and agree to pay them an annual interest rate, typically three to five percentage points above the benchmark London interbank offered rate, or LIBOR. At current rates, the cost would be about 7% to 9%. The money raised is placed in a trust fund.

If a natural catastrophe strikes of sufficient magnitude—measured by wind speed, earthquake force, or, as in the Kamp Re instance, insured losses—the issuer gets to keep the cash to help pay its policyholders' claims. The bonds typically have a three-year maturity but often are rolled over.

Buyers of cat bonds are mostly sophisticated investors like hedge funds, pension funds, and banks, which see them as an opportunity to diversify their investment portfolios. Since they first appeared, the global insurance industry has issued $13.41 billion of natural-catastrophe bonds. The largest single issuer is Swiss Re, also based in Zurich, which has more than $1 billion in catastrophe bonds outstanding.

Katrina, to be sure, was a big deal: U.S. risk-management firm ISO estimated Tuesday that total private-sector insurance claims would amount to $34.4 billion, making it the costliest natural disaster in history.

If a company suspends payment of coupon interest, it is said to be in default. Default is a serious matter. In general, bondholders have an unconditional right to the timely payment of interest and principal. They also have a right to bring legal action to enforce such payments. Upon suspension of coupon payments, the bondholders could, for example, demand an acceleration of principal repayment along with all past-due interest. However, a corporation in financial distress has a right to seek protection in bankruptcy court from inflexible demands by bondholders. As a practical matter, it is often in the best interests of both the bondholders and the corporation to negotiate a new debt contract. Indeed, bankruptcy courts normally encourage a settlement that minimizes any intervention on their part.

18.4 Protective Covenants

protective covenants

Restrictions in a bond indenture designed to protect bondholders.

In addition to the provisions already discussed, a bond indenture is likely to contain a number of **protective covenants**. These agreements are designed to protect bondholders by restricting the actions of a corporation that might cause a deterioration in the credit quality of a bond issue. Protective covenants can be classified into two types: negative covenants and positive, or affirmative, covenants.

A *negative covenant* is a "thou shalt not" for the corporation. Here are some examples of negative covenants that might be found in an indenture agreement:

1. The firm cannot pay dividends to stockholders in excess of what is allowed by a formula based on the firm's earnings.

2. The firm cannot issue new bonds that are senior to currently outstanding bonds. Also, the amount of a new bond issue cannot exceed an amount specified by a formula based on the firm's net worth.

3. The firm cannot refund an existing bond issue with new bonds paying a lower coupon rate than the currently outstanding bond issue it would replace.

4. The firm cannot buy bonds issued by other companies, nor can it guarantee the debt of any other company.

A *positive covenant* is a "thou shalt." It specifies things that a corporation must do, or conditions that it must abide by. Here are some common examples of positive covenants:

1. Proceeds from the sale of assets must be used either to acquire other assets of equal value or to redeem outstanding bonds.

2. In the event of a merger, acquisition, or spinoff, the firm must give bondholders the right to redeem their bonds at par value.

3. The firm must maintain the good condition of all assets pledged as security for an outstanding bond issue.

4. The firm must periodically supply audited financial information to bondholders.

CHECK THIS

18.4a Why would a corporation voluntarily include protective covenants in its bond indenture contract?

18.5 Event Risk

event risk
The possibility that the issuing corporation will experience a significant change in its bond credit quality.

Protective covenants in a bond indenture help shield bondholders from event risk. **Event risk** is broadly defined as the possibility that some structural or financial change to the corporation will cause a significant deterioration in the credit quality of a bond issue, thereby causing the affected bonds to lose substantial market value.

A classic example of event risk, and what could happen to bondholders without adequate covenant protection, is provided by an incident involving Marriott Corporation, best known for its chain of hotels and resorts. In October 1992, Marriott announced its intention to spin off part of the company. The spinoff, called Host Marriott, would acquire most of the parent company's debt and its poorly performing real estate holdings. The parent, Marriott International, would be left relatively debt-free with possession of most of the better performing properties, including its hotel management division.

On the announcement date, the affected Marriott bonds fell in value by about 30 percent, reflecting severe concern about the impact of the spinoff on the credit quality of the bonds. On the same day, Marriott stock rose in value by about 30 percent, reflecting a large wealth transfer from bondholders to stockholders. A subsequent bondholder legal challenge was unsuccessful. Standard & Poor's later announced that it was formally revising its credit

MARRIOTT TO SPLIT, MAKING 2 FIRMS

Marriott Corp. shareholders approved a plan to split the company into a real-estate concern, with most of Marriott's debt, and a high-growth hotel-management company.

The split, approved by 85% of the shares voted, was the main issue at Marriott's annual meeting Friday. Under the plan, which is expected to take effect in September, stockholders will receive a share of Marriott International, Inc., the hotel-management operation, for each Marriott share they own. Then Marriott Corp. will be renamed Host Marriott Corp., an entity that will operate the real-estate side of the business.

The plan stunned bondholders when it was announced in October. They argued that the financial support of their debt was being undermined, and a suit by some of the bondholders is still pending.

Marriott shares have risen 60% since the plan's announcement. In New York Stock Exchange trading Friday, Marriott closed at $27.785, up 12.5 cents. The stock has traded as low as $15.50 in the past year.

The Marriott family controls more than 25% of the 100.8 million shares outstanding as of Jan. 1.

Marriott's directors set a distribution date for the split dividend of Sept. 10 for shares of record Sept. 1.

J. W. Marriott, 61 years old and currently chairman and president of the company, will be chairman, president, and chief executive officer of Marriott International, while his brother, Richard E. Marriott, 54, will be chairman of Host Marriott. Richard Marriott is currently vice chairman and executive vice president of the company.

In addition to the bondholders' lawsuit seeking to block the reorganization, Marriott had faced a suit by holders of preferred stock. Marriott said that the holders have agreed to dismiss their case and convert their preferred shares into common stock.

The suit by the group of bondholders, representing about a dozen institutional investors, is still pending, however. Under the reorganization plan, holders of about $1.5 billion in Marriott bonds would have the option to swap their notes for new notes of a unit of the new real-estate entity. The company will retain $2.1 billion of Marriott's $3 billion long-term debt and will own 139 hotels and other real-estate assets.

Larry Kill, attorney for the bondholders, said the suit would proceed despite the shareholder vote. "This was a very unfair transaction," he said.

As a separate company, Host Marriott would have had about $1.2 billion in sales in 1992, according to the company's estimates. Marriott International, Inc., the new hotel concern, will operate more than 760 hotels through Marriott's four hotel-management units and related management services. Marriott International would have had $7.8 billion in sales last year, the company estimates.

In 1992, Marriott had net income of $85 million, or 64 cents a share, on sales of $8.72 billion. It had about $3 billion in long-term debt as of Jan. 1.

Moody's Investors Service, Inc., downgraded its ratings on the senior unsecured debt of Marriott Corp., affecting about $2.3 billion in debt, to Ba-2 from single-B-2. Moody's said the bond-exchange plan will leave a Host Marriott unit highly leveraged "with modest debt protection." Moody's said it expects only gradual improvement in operating earnings, given the sluggish economy and glut of hotel rooms. Moody's said, however, that the Host Marriott unit will be well-positioned for increased earnings when the recovery hits full speed.

WWW

Visit Marriott and Host Marriott Web sites at
www.marriott.com
and
www.hostmarriott.com

ratings on Marriott bonds to recognize the impact of the spinoff. (Credit ratings are discussed in detail in a later section.) Debt remaining with Marriott International would have an investment-grade rating, while bonds assigned to Host Marriott would have junk bond status. *The Wall Street Journal* report covering the story is reproduced in the nearby *Investment Updates* box.

✓

CHECK THIS

18.5a What are some possible protective covenants that would have protected Marriott bondholders from the adverse impact of the spinoff described here?

18.6 Bonds without Indentures

private placement
A new bond issue sold to one or more parties in private transactions not available to the public.

The Trust Indenture Act of 1939 does not require an indenture when a bond issue is not sold to the general public. For example, the bonds may be sold only to one or more financial institutions in what is called a **private placement**. Private placements are exempt from registration requirements with the SEC. Nevertheless, even privately placed debt issues often have a formal indenture contract.

When a corporation issues debt without an indenture, it makes an unconditional promise to pay interest and principal according to a simple debt contract. Debt issued without an indenture is basically a simple IOU of the corporation. Bond analysts sometimes reserve the designation "bonds" to mean corporate debt subject to an indenture and refer to corporate debt not subject to an indenture as "notes." However, bonds and notes are more commonly distinguished on the basis of maturity, where bonds designate relatively long maturities, say, 10 years or longer, and notes designate maturities less than 10 years. Both definitions overlap since most long-term debt is issued subject to an indenture, and most privately placed short-term debt is issued as a simple IOU. In between, however, privately placed intermediate-maturity debt may or may not be issued subject to an indenture and therefore might be referred to as either a bond or a note regardless of the existence of an indenture. As in any profession, the jargon of investments is sometimes ambiguous.

18.7 Preferred Stock

preferred stock
A security with a claim to dividend payments that is senior to common stock.

Preferred stock has some of the features of both bonds and common stock. Preferred stockholders have a claim to dividend payments that is senior to the claim of common stockholders—hence the term "preferred stock." However, their claim is subordinate to the claims of bondholders and other creditors. A typical preferred stock issue has the following basic characteristics:

1. Preferred stockholders do not normally participate with common stockholders in the election of a board of directors. However, a few preferred stock issues do grant voting rights to their holders.
2. Preferred stockholders are promised a stream of fixed dividend payments. Thus, preferred dividends resemble bond coupons.
3. Preferred stock normally has no specified maturity, but it is often callable by the issuer.
4. Management can suspend payment of preferred dividends without setting off a bankruptcy process, but only after suspending payment of all common stock dividends.
5. If preferred dividends have been suspended, all unpaid preferred dividends normally become a cumulative debt that must be paid in full before the corporation can resume any payment of common stock dividends. Preferred stock with this feature is termed *cumulative preferred*.
6. Some preferred stock issues have a conversion feature similar to convertible bonds. These are called *convertible preferred stock*.

All else equal, preferred stock normally pays a lower interest rate to investors than do corporate bonds. This is because, when most investors buy preferred stock, the dividends received are taxed at the same rate as bond interest payments. However, if a business corporation buys preferred stock, it can usually exclude at least 70 percent of the preferred dividends from income taxation. As a result, most preferred stock is owned by corporations that can take advantage of the preferential tax treatment of preferred dividends. However, companies that issue ordinary preferred stock must treat preferred dividends the same as common stock dividends for tax purposes and, therefore, cannot deduct preferred dividends from their taxable income.

18.7a From the perspective of common stockholders and management, what are some of the advantages of issuing preferred stock instead of bonds or new shares of common stock?

18.8 Adjustable-Rate Bonds

adjustable-rate bonds
Securities that pay coupons that change according to a prespecified rule. Also called *floating-rate bonds* or simply *floaters*.

Many bond, note, and preferred stock issues allow the issuer to adjust the annual coupon according to a rule or formula based on current market interest rates. These securities are called **adjustable-rate bonds**; they are also sometimes called *floating-rate bonds* or *floaters*.

For example, a typical adjustment rule might specify that the coupon rate be reset annually to be equal to the current rate on 180-day maturity U.S. Treasury bills plus 2 percent. Alternatively, a more flexible rule might specify that the coupon rate on a bond issue cannot be set below 105 percent of the yield to maturity of newly issued five-year Treasury notes. Thus, if five-year Treasury notes have recently been sold to yield 6 percent, the minimum allowable coupon rate is $1.05 \times 6\% = 6.3\%$.

Adjustable-rate bonds and notes are often putable at par value. For this reason, an issuer may set a coupon rate above an allowable minimum to discourage bondholders from selling their bonds back to the corporation.

Most adjustable-rate bonds have coupon rates that rise and fall with market interest rates. The coupon rates of some adjustable-rate bonds, however, move opposite to market interest rates. These bonds are called *inverse floaters*. A fall in the benchmark interest rate results in an increase in the coupon rate of an inverse floater.

This relationship magnifies bond price fluctuations. For example, if interest rates fall, bond prices rise. Further, the higher coupon rate that results will cause the inverse floater bond price to rise even more. The opposite is true if rates rise. Thus, prices of inverse floaters can be extremely volatile.

18.8a How does an adjustable coupon rate feature affect the interest rate risk of a bond?

18.8b How might bondholders respond if the coupon rate on an adjustable-rate putable bond was set below market interest rates?

18.9 Corporate Bond Credit Ratings

credit rating
An assessment of the credit quality of a bond issue based on the issuer's financial condition.

WWW
Visit these rating agency Web sites: Duff & Phelps at **www.duffandphelps.com** Fitch at **www.fitchratings.com** Moody's at **www.moodys.com** S&P at **www.standardandpoors.com**

When a corporation sells a new bond issue to investors, it usually subscribes to several bond rating agencies for a credit evaluation of the bond issue. Each contracted rating agency then provides a **credit rating**—an assessment of the credit quality of the bond issue based on the issuer's financial condition. Rating agencies charge a fee for this service. As part of the contractual arrangement between the bond issuer and the rating agency, the issuer agrees to allow a continuing review of its credit rating even if the rating deteriorates. Without a credit rating a new bond issue would be very difficult to sell to the public, which is why almost all bond issues originally sold to the general public have a credit rating assigned at the time of issuance. Also, most public bond issues have ratings assigned by several rating agencies.

Established rating agencies in the United States include Duff & Phelps, Inc. (D&P); Fitch Investors Service (Fitch); Moody's Investors Service (Moody's); and Standard & Poor's Corporation (S&P). Of these, the two best known rating agencies are Moody's and Standard & Poor's. These companies publish regularly updated credit ratings for thousands of domestic and international bond issues.

TABLE 18.2

Corporate Bond Credit Rating Symbols

Moody's	Rating Agency Duff & Phelps	Standard & Poor's	Credit Rating Description
Investment-Grade Bond Ratings			
Aaa	1	AAA	Highest credit rating, maximum safety
Aa1	2	AA+	
Aa2	3	AA	High credit quality, investment-grade bonds
Aa3	4	AA−	
A1	5	A+	
A2	6	A	Upper-medium quality, investment-grade bonds
A3	7	A−	
Baa1	8	BBB+	
Baa2	9	BBB	Lower-medium quality, investment-grade bonds
Baa3	10	BBB−	
Speculative-Grade Bond Ratings			
Ba1	11	BB+	Low credit quality, speculative-grade bonds
Ba2	12	BB	
Ba3	13	BB−	
B1	14	B+	Very low credit quality, speculative-grade bonds
B2	15	B	
B3	16	B−	
Extremely Speculative-Grade Bond Ratings			
Caa	17	CCC+	Extremely low credit standing, high-risk bonds
		CCC	
		CCC−	
Ca		CC	Extremely speculative
C		C	
		D	Bonds in default

It is important to realize that corporate bond ratings are assigned to particular bond issues and not to the issuer of those bonds. For example, a senior bond issue is likely to have a higher credit rating than a subordinated issue even if both are issued by the same corporation. Similarly, a corporation with two bond issues outstanding may have a higher credit rating assigned to one issue because that issue has stronger covenant protection specified in the bond's indenture contract.

Seniority and covenant protection are not the only things affecting bond ratings. Bond rating agencies consider a number of factors before assigning a credit rating, including an appraisal of the financial strength of the issuer, the caliber of the issuer's management, the issuer's position in an industry, and the industry's position in the economy.

Table 18.2 summarizes corporate bond rating symbols and definitions used by Moody's (first column), Duff & Phelps (second column), and Standard & Poor's (third column). As shown, bond credit ratings fall into three broad categories: investment-grade, speculative-grade, and extremely speculative-grade.

In general, a bond rating is intended to be a comparative indicator of overall credit quality for a particular bond issue. The rating in itself, however, is not a recommendation to buy or sell a bond. In fact, few investors realize that the ratings themselves are not guaranteed by the rating agencies. Moreover, the ratings are subject to an upgrade or a downgrade at any time. The rating agencies design their rating systems to provide an independent review of the bond. Bond ratings, like any analyst recommendation, are subject to error.

The system to rate bonds attracted considerable attention during the crash of 2008. Many real estate loans had been packaged together and sold as a type of fixed-income investment, known as mortgage-backed securities (MBS). We discuss MBS in detail in our online chapter. The rating agencies provided ratings on many of these investments, and most were rated as "triple A," the highest investment grade possible. After the underlying mortgages began to default, however, many of these securities lost significant value. The rating agencies subsequently received considerable criticism for being inaccurate in their assessment and rating of these securities.

WHY BOND RATINGS ARE IMPORTANT

Even with the errors discussed above, bond credit ratings assigned by independent rating agencies remain quite important to bond market participants. Only a few institutional investors have the resources and expertise necessary to properly evaluate a bond's credit quality on their own. Bond ratings provide investors with reliable, professional evaluations of bond issues at a reasonable cost. This information is indispensable for assessing the economic value of a bond.

prudent investment guidelines
Restrictions on investment portfolios stipulating that securities purchased must meet a certain level of safety.

Furthermore, many financial institutions have **prudent investment guidelines** stipulating that only securities with a certain level of investment safety may be included in their portfolios. For example, bond investments for many pension funds are limited to investment-grade bonds rated at least Baa by Moody's or at least BBB by Standard & Poor's. Bond ratings provide a convenient measure to monitor implementation of these guidelines.

Individual investors investing in bonds also find published bond ratings useful. Individual investors generally do not have the ability to diversify as extensively as do large institutions. With limited diversification opportunities, an individual should invest only in bonds with higher credit ratings.

AN ALTERNATIVE TO BOND RATINGS

Bond ratings are not the only way to evaluate the credit quality of a bond. One particularly important measure is a bond's credit spread. The credit spread is simply an estimate of the difference in yield between the bond and a comparable maturity Treasury security. The higher the credit spread, the higher the level of perceived default risk.

Credit spreads and credit ratings should show a strong correlation. High-grade bonds should have a lower spread than low-grade bonds. The potential benefit of using credit spreads instead of bond ratings, however, is that credit spreads are updated nearly continuously through the trading activities of many bond market participants. By way of contrast, credit ratings tend to be more stable and therefore could be a lagging indicator of the bond's quality.

For more insight on this issue, check out the nearby *Investment Updates* box on yield spreads. From the graph provided in the article, note that average credit spreads are not constant through time. These spreads clearly widen during recessions, such as the one associated with the recent crash of 2008.

CHECK THIS

18.9a   Does a low credit rating necessarily imply that a bond is a bad investment?

18.9b   What factors besides the credit rating might be important in deciding whether a particular bond is a worthwhile investment?

18.10 Junk Bonds

high-yield bonds
Bonds with a speculative credit rating that is offset by a yield premium offered to compensate for higher credit risk. Also called *junk bonds*.

Bonds with a speculative or low grade rating—that is, those rated Ba or lower by Moody's or BB or lower by Standard & Poor's—are commonly called **high-yield bonds**, or, more colorfully, *junk bonds*. The designation "junk" is somewhat misleading and often unduly pejorative, since junk bonds *have* economic value. Junk bonds simply represent debt with a higher than average credit risk. To put the term in perspective, one should realize that most

CORPORATE BONDS STILL HAVE A GOOD PULSE

After a blistering 2009, corporate bond markets are set for a more sedate 2010. No longer obviously cheap, the market faces a number of hurdles. But that doesn't mean investors should write off corporate bonds as last year's fad. Technical and fundamental forces suggest corporate bonds could keep running a while longer.

For a start, corporate-bond investors may have less to fear than their government-bond counterparts from central bankers reducing the extraordinary support that fueled 2009's sharp rally in risk assets. While government bond supply is set to rise as central banks ease back on quantitative and credit easing measures, pushing yields higher, cash-rich corporations are expected to reduce their borrowing in 2010. Net nonfinancial supply could fall by 30% in the U.S. and 25% in Europe, according to Barclays Capital.

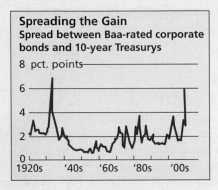

Spreading the Gain
Spread between Baa-rated corporate bonds and 10-year Treasurys

Source: Moody's Investors Service.

Meanwhile, corporate bonds are set to throw off record amounts of cash in absolute terms. The investment-grade euro-denominated bond market generates an average of 50 billion euros ($71.9 billion) a quarter in interest and principal payments for the next two years, according to Deutsche Bank, meaning 400 billion euros will be available for reinvestment. The picture is similarly rosy in dollars and sterling.

Meanwhile, the importance of corporate bonds as a funding mechanism has gained wider appreciation as a result of the crisis. The continued need for banks to reduce the size of their balance sheets means policy makers are likely to seek to support the corporate bond market as a key alternative source of funding, particularly in Europe. Meanwhile, executives are likely to remain protective of their credit ratings, meaning bond investors may still have the upper hand over their equity counterparts. Default rates are expected to drop sharply in 2010.

Of course, investors will have to adjust their return expectations. In 2009, U.S. investment-grade corporate bonds returned 19.4%, according to Bank of America-Merrill Lynch, while Europe turned in 15.1%. Junk-bond returns were even more startling: 57% for U.S. high-yield and 74.5% for euro high-yield.

That performance can't be repeated. Rising government bond yields have already started to take their toll. A sharp rise in Treasury yields in December means U.S. investment grade bonds have returned −1.27% in a month, even as spreads continued to tighten.

The best trade might be to focus on the relative performance of corporate bonds versus government bonds rather than on total returns. After all, among the biggest risks for corporate bonds is higher government debt yields. One option is to hedge overall interest-rate risk in 2010 and bet that the credit spread between free-spending sovereigns and thriftier corporations continues to narrow.

consumer debt and small business debt represents higher than average credit risk. Yet it is generally considered desirable from an economic and social perspective that credit be available to consumers and small businesses.

Junk bonds that were originally issued with an investment-grade credit rating that subsequently fell to speculative grade because of unforeseen economic events are called *fallen angels*. Another type, *original-issue junk*, is defined as bonds originally issued with a speculative-grade rating.

Junk bonds are attractive investments for many institutional investors with well-diversified portfolios. The logic of junk bond investing revolves around the possibility that the *yield premium* for junk bonds might be high enough to justify accepting the higher default rates of junk bonds. As an example of this logic, consider the following back-of-the-envelope calculations.

The yield, or credit, spread is the extra return, in the form of an increased yield to maturity, that investors receive for buying a bond with a lower credit rating. Because of the credit risk, investors demand a risk premium for investing in lower rated bonds. You can create a yield curve for bonds with different credit ratings. We went to finance.yahoo.com and looked up the composite bond yields for U.S. Treasuries and corporate bonds. Here is what we found:

US TREASURY BONDS

MATURITY	YIELD	YESTERDAY	LAST WEEK	LAST MONTH
3 MONTH	0.03	0.03	0.03	0.04
6 MONTH	0.12	0.12	0.13	0.15
2 YEAR	0.89	0.87	0.92	0.90
3 YEAR	1.47	1.44	1.49	1.47
5 YEAR	2.44	2.41	2.49	2.46
10 YEAR	3.67	3.65	3.74	3.75
30 YEAR	4.55	4.54	4.63	4.61

CORPORATE BONDS

MATURITY	YIELD	YESTERDAY	LAST WEEK	LAST MONTH
2YR AA	1.41	1.39	1.41	1.47
2YR A	1.57	1.54	1.54	1.82
5YR AAA	2.93	2.91	2.99	2.96
5YR AA	3.28	3.26	3.26	3.37
5YR A	3.31	3.29	3.31	3.41
10YR AAA	3.38	3.38	3.38	3.57
10YR AA	4.92	4.93	4.97	4.58
10YR A	4.53	4.53	4.52	4.72
20YR AAA	5.42	5.35	5.18	5.48
20YR AA	5.39	5.41	5.48	5.45
20YR A	6.36	6.29	6.12	6.43

If you calculate the yield spread for a five year AAA credit–rated corporate bond, you should find it is 49 basis points (2.93% – 2.44%). Similarly, the yield spread for a five-year A credit–rated corporate bond is 87 basis points (3.31% – 2.44%). Although these yield spreads look small, remember they are for highly rated corporate bonds. A yield spread on junk bonds exceeding 10 percent is not uncommon.

Suppose that the average yield on junk bonds is 10 percent when U.S. Treasury bonds yield 7 percent. In this case, the yield premium of junk bonds over default-free Treasury bonds is 3 percent. Further suppose that an investor expects about 4 percent of all outstanding junk bonds to default each year, and experience suggests that when junk bonds default bondholders on average receive 50 cents for each dollar of bond face value. Based on these rough assumptions, diversified junk bond investors expect to lose 2 percent (.04 × .50) of their portfolio value each year through defaults. But with a junk bond yield premium of 3 percent, the junk bond portfolio is expected to outperform U.S. Treasury bonds by 1 percent per year.

It is true that a junk bond portfolio is much more expensive to manage than a Treasury bond portfolio. For a $1 billion bond portfolio, however, a junk bond yield premium of 1 percent represents $10 million of additional interest income per year.

Of course, actual default rates could turn out to be much different than expected. History suggests that the major determinant of aggregate bond default rates is the state of economic activity. During an expansionary economic period, bond default rates are usually low. But in a recession, default rates can rise dramatically. For this reason, the investment performance of corporate bond portfolios, including junk bond portfolios, largely depends on the health of the economy. Therefore, as you can see in the nearby *Work the Web* box, yield spreads also exist for higher-rated corporate bonds.

YIELD JUNKIES RETURN TO BOND MARKET

Risk Takes a Backseat as Demand for High-Yield Credit Sets a Record; Forgetting 2008 Happened

In the high-yield credit markets, it is time to party like it's 2006. Companies left for dead a year ago are now finding that investors are clamoring for their high-yield debt. Private equity–backed businesses are paying their owners dividends out of new bond issues. In all, companies raised $11.7 billion last week in the high-yield bond market, the biggest in history, according to Thomson Reuters.

The previous record: $11.4 billion, set at the apex of the mid-decade credit boom in November 2006.

The latest demand seems all the more remarkable coming just over a year after the greatest financial panic in generations. The panic and a bleak economy helped push 11% of high-yield issuers into default in 2009, according to Standard & Poors.

Such sobering figures appear to be overlooked by investors. "It looks like risk is on the backburner again as investors are reaching for yield," said Adam Cohen, co-founder of Covenant Review, an independent credit research firm. "And issuers are all too happy to oblige in meeting the insatiable demand."

For most issuers, the new debt isn't going toward building new factories or funding big acquisitions. Instead, these new deals are improving the companies' balance sheets by repaying existing debt and pushing back maturities. These overleveraged companies hope they can get more time to improve operations and benefit from an economic recovery.

The average gap between yields on high-yield bonds and U.S. Treasury bonds stands at about 6 percentage points, after starting the year at 6.4 percentage points. At the height of the credit bubble in early 2007, the spread had narrowed to under three percentage points. By December 2008, at the peak of the financial crisis, that so-called risk premium stood at about 22 percentage points, creating big returns for distressed investors.

After such a rally, return expectations in the high-yield market for 2010 are more modest.

"The period of picking up dollars for 50 cents is behind us," said Dean Kehler, co-portfolio manager of New York–based Trian Credit Fund.

Oaktree Chairman Howard Marks said that, unlike the last several months, investing in the high-yield bond market now requires a discerning eye.

"A year ago everyone thought the world was ending, few people would invest at any price, and that brought the bargains of a lifetime," he said. "Today the market isn't overpriced or underpriced, so success lies in buying the right credits."

Source: Peter Lattman and Mike Spector, *The Wall Street Journal*, January 19, 2010. Reprinted with permission of *The Wall Street Journal*.
© 2010 Dow Jones & Company, Inc. All Rights Reserved Worldwide.

FIGURE 18.6 **High Yield Bond Trading**

Most Active High Yield Bonds

Issuer Name	Symbol	Coupon	Maturity	Rating Moody's/S&P/Fitch	High	Low	Last	Change	Yield %
FORD MOTOR CREDIT CO	F.GSL	9.750%	Sep 2010	B3/B-/B+	104.360	103.250	104.260	0.415	2.958
WILLIAMS PARTNERS LP	WPZ.GE	7.250%	Feb 2017	Ba2/BBB-/BB	112.750	111.750	111.750	-0.750	5.228
NEWPAGE CORP	NPGP.GD	10.000%	May 2012	Caa2/CCC-/--	78.000	69.500	69.500	-8.500	29.290
FORD MOTOR CREDIT	F.IT	7.250%	Oct 2011	B3/B-/B+	103.750	98.680	101.875	0.125	6.096
KINDER MORGAN	KMI.GP	5.150%	Mar 2015	Ba1/BB/BB+	99.250	98.125	98.562	0.108	5.476
CRICKET COMM	LEAP.GC	9.375%	Nov 2014	B3/B-/--	101.700	100.000	101.563	0.552	8.717
SPRINT CAPITAL	S.IU	7.625%	Jan 2011	Ba3/BB/BB	103.678	101.210	103.250	0.500	4.313
CIT GP	CIT.GCF	7.000%	May 2017	--/--/--	89.000	77.000	88.250	3.740	9.260
ACCELLENT	ACCE.GB	10.500%	Dec 2013	Caa2/CCC+/--	99.750	98.750	99.250	0.000	10.734
CIT GP	CIT.GCE	7.000%	May 2016	--/--/--	91.541	78.000	88.000	3.240	9.568

Source: www.wsj.com, January 21, 2010.

Prices and yields of selected junk bonds are published online at www.wsj.com in its "Most Active High Yield Bonds" report. A sample report is displayed in Figure 18.6. For an interesting discussion on investing in junk bonds, see the nearby *Investment Updates* box.

18.11 Bond Market Trading

Consistent with the need to hold bonds for predictable cash flows, many corporate bond investors buy and hold bonds until they mature. However, many investors need to liquidate some bonds before they mature, and others wish to purchase outstanding bonds originally issued by a particular corporation several years earlier. For these and many other reasons, the existence of an active secondary market for corporate bonds is important for most bond investors. Fortunately, an active secondary market with a substantial volume of bond trading does exist to satisfy most of the liquidity needs of investors.

Almost as many different bond issues are listed on the New York Stock Exchange (NYSE) as there are different common stock issues. These NYSE-traded bond issues represent the most actively traded bonds of large corporations. However, there are many more thousands of different corporate debt issues outstanding. Most of these debt issues trade in the over-the-counter (OTC) market. In fact, it is estimated that less than 1 percent of all corporate bond trading actually takes place on the New York Stock Exchange. While some bond trading activity occurs on the American Stock Exchange and other regional exchanges, corporate bond trading is characteristically an OTC activity.

Learn more about TRACE and see TRACE data at www.finra.org

Before mid-2002, the OTC corporate bond market had limited transparency, meaning that, unlike stocks, relatively little information was available on trading. This lack of transparency made it difficult for bond investors to get accurate, up-to-date prices. At the request of the Securities and Exchange Commission (SEC), however, recently adopted rules require reporting of corporate bond trades through what is known as the Trade Reporting and Compliance Engine (TRACE). Transparency has dramatically improved. As this is written, transaction prices are now reported on more than 5,550 bonds, which represent more than 75 percent of investment-grade market volume.

18.12 Summary and Conclusions

In this chapter, we cover the important topic of corporate bonds. Bonds are a major source of capital used by corporations. This chapter covers many aspects of this market, including the following items—grouped by the chapter's important concepts.

1. **The basic types of corporate bonds.**

   A. A corporate bond represents a corporation's promise to pay bondholders a fixed sum of money at maturity, along with periodic payments of interest. The sum paid at maturity is the bond's principal, and the periodic interest payments are coupons. Most bonds pay fixed coupons, but some pay floating coupon rates adjusted regularly according to prevailing market interest rates.

B. The largest category of corporate bond investors is life insurance companies, which own about a third of all outstanding corporate bonds. Remaining ownership shares are roughly equally distributed among individual investors, pension funds, banks, and foreign investors.

C. The existence of an active secondary market for corporate bonds is important to most bond investors. The greatest total volume of bond trading occurs in the OTC market.

2. How callable bonds function.

A. Corporate bonds are usually callable, which means that the issuer has the right to buy back outstanding bonds before maturity. When a bond issue is called, bondholders surrender their bonds in exchange for a prespecified call price.

B. Make-whole call provisions have become common in the corporate bond market. If a callable bond is called and has a make-whole call provision, bondholders receive the approximate value of what the bond is worth. This call provision gets its name because the bondholder does not suffer a loss if the bond is called.

3. The different types of corporate bonds.

A. Debentures are the most common type of corporate bond. Debenture bonds represent the unsecured debt of a corporation. Mortgage bonds represent debt issued with a lien on specific property pledged as security for the bonds. Collateral trust bonds are characterized by a pledge of financial assets as security for a bond issue. Equipment trust certificates are issued according to a lease form of financing, where investors purchase equipment trust certificates and the proceeds from this sale are used to purchase equipment that is leased to a corporation.

B. A bond indenture is a formal agreement between the corporation and bondholders that spells out the legal rights and obligations of both parties with respect to a bond issue. An indenture typically specifies the seniority of a bond issue, along with any call provisions, put provisions, bond-to-stock conversion provisions, and sinking fund provisions.

4. The basics of bond ratings.

A. When a corporation sells a new bond issue to the public, it usually has a credit rating assigned by several independent bond rating agencies. Without a credit rating, a new bond issue would be difficult to sell, which is why almost all bond issues sold to the public have credit ratings assigned.

B. Bonds with a speculative or lower grade rating, commonly called high-yield bonds, or junk bonds, represent corporate debt with higher than average credit risk. Credit ratings for junk bonds are frequently revised to reflect changing financial conditions.

GET REAL

This chapter explored the world of corporate bonds, an important category of investments for institutions such as pension funds and life insurance companies, and also for individuals. This category also includes convertible bonds and preferred stock. How should you put this information to work?

Now that you understand the most important features of corporate bonds, you need to buy several different issues to experience the real-world gains and losses that come with managing a bond portfolio. So, with a simulated brokerage account (such as Stock-Trak), try putting roughly equal dollar amounts into three or four different corporate bond issues. Be sure to include some junk bonds in your selections. Check the credit ratings of the bond issues you have selected at a site such as Bonds Online (www.bondsonline.com).

You can find out more information about corporate bonds at the many Web sites now specializing in bonds, including Investing In Bonds (www.investinginbonds.com). The Web sites of bond rating agencies such as Moody's (www.moodys.com), Standard & Poor's (www.standardandpoors.com), Duff & Phelps (www.duffandphelps.com), and Fitch (www.fitchratings.com) are also quite informative.

As you monitor the prices of your bonds, notice how interest rates influence their prices. You may also notice that for bonds with lower credit ratings, the stock price of the issuing company is an important influence. Why do you think this is so?

Of course, with the convertible issues the bond price will definitely be influenced by the underlying stock value, but the impact depends on the specific conversion features of the bond, including whether the bond is in the money or not.

Key Terms

adjustable-rate bonds 635
bond refunding 622
collateral trust bond 619
convertible bonds 625
credit rating 635
debentures 619
equipment trust certificate 620
event risk 632
exchangeable bonds 628
high-yield bonds 637
indenture summary 620
in-the-money bond 627
intrinsic bond value 628
mortgage bond 619

negative pledge clause 622
plain vanilla bonds 618
preferred stock 634
private placement 634
prospectus 620
protective covenants 631
prudent investment guidelines 637
put bonds 625
senior debentures 622
serial bonds 630
sinking fund 630
subordinated debentures 622
term bonds 629
unsecured debt 619

Chapter Review Problems and Self-Test

1. **Callable Bonds (CFA2)**   A particular bond matures in 30 years. It is callable in 10 years at 110. The call price is then cut by 1 percent of par each year until the call price reaches par. If the bond is called in 12 years, how much will you receive? Assume a $1,000 face value.

2. **Convertible Bonds (CFA6)**   A convertible bond features a conversion ratio of 50. What is the conversion price? If the stock sells for $30 per share, what is the conversion value?

3. **Convertible Bonds (CFA6)**   A convertible bond has an 8 percent coupon, paid semiannually, and will mature in 15 years. If the bond were not convertible, it would be priced to yield 9 percent. The conversion ratio on the bond is 40, and the stock is currently selling for $24 per share. What is the minimum value of this bond?

Answers to Self-Test Problems

1. The call price will be 110% − 2 × 1% = 108% of face value, or $1,080.

2. The conversion price is face value divided by the conversion ratio, $1,000/50 = $20. The conversion value is what the bond is worth on a converted basis, 50 × $30 = $1,500.

3. The minimum value is the larger of the conversion value and the intrinsic bond value. The conversion value is 40 × $24 = $960. To calculate the intrinsic bond value, note that we have a face value of $1,000 (by assumption), a semiannual coupon of $40, an annual yield of 9 percent (4.5 percent per half-year), and 15 years to maturity (30 half-years). Using the standard bond pricing formula from an earlier chapter, the bond's price (be sure to verify this) if it were not convertible is $918.56. This convertible bond thus will sell for more than $960.

Test Your Investment Quotient

1. **Trust Certificates (LO1, CFA1)**   An airline elects to finance the purchase of some new airplanes using equipment trust certificates. Under the legal arrangement associated with such certificates, the airplanes are pledged as collateral, but which other factor applies?

   a. The airline still has legal title to the planes.
   b. Legal title to the planes resides with the manufacturer.
   c. The airline does not get legal title to the planes until the manufacturer is paid off.
   d. Legal title to the planes resides with a third party who then leases the planes to the airline.

2. **Callable Bonds (LO2, CFA2)**   What does the call feature of a bond mean?

   a. Investor can call for payment on demand.
   b. Investor can only call if the firm defaults on an interest payment.
   c. Issuer can call the bond issue prior to the maturity date.
   d. Issuer can call the issue during the first three years.

3. **Callable Bonds (LO2, CFA2)**   Who primarily benefits from a call provision on a corporate bond?

   a. The issuer
   b. The bondholders
   c. The trustee
   d. The government regulators

4. **Callable Bonds (LO2, CFA2)**   Which of the following describes a bond with a call feature?

   a. It is attractive, because the immediate receipt of principal plus premium produces a high return.
   b. It is more likely to be called when interest rates are high, because the interest savings will be greater.
   c. It would usually have a higher yield than a similar noncallable bond.
   d. It generally has a higher credit rating than a similar noncallable bond.

5. **Callable Bonds (LO2, CFA2)**   Two bonds are identical, except one is callable and the other is noncallable. Compared to the noncallable bond, the callable bond has

   a. Negative convexity and a lower price.
   b. Negative convexity and a higher price.
   c. Positive convexity and a lower price.
   d. Positive convexity and a higher price.

6. **Convexity (LO1, CFA2)**   What does positive convexity on a bond imply?

   a. The direction of change in yield is directly related to the change in price.
   b. Prices increase at a faster rate as yields drop than they decrease as yields rise.
   c. Price changes are the same for both increases and decreases in yields.
   d. Prices increase and decrease at a faster rate than the change in yield.

7. **Convexity (LO1, CFA2)** A bond with negative convexity is best described as having a price-yield relationship displaying

 a. Positive convexity at high yields and negative convexity at low yields.
 b. Negative convexity at high yields and positive convexity at low yields.
 c. Negative convexity at low and high yields and positive at medium yields.
 d. Positive convexity at low and high yields and negative at medium yields.

8. **Duration (LO1, CFA2)** Which of the following *most accurately* measures interest rate sensitivity for bonds with embedded options?

 a. Convexity
 b. Effective duration
 c. Modified duration
 d. Macaulay duration

9. **Refundings (LO1, CFA2)** The refunding provision of an indenture allows bonds to be retired unless

 a. They are replaced with a new issue having a lower interest cost.
 b. The remaining time to maturity is less than five years.
 c. The stated time period in the indenture has not passed.
 d. The stated time period in the indenture has passed.

10. **Debentures (LO1, CFA1)** Holders of unsecured debentures with a negative pledge clause can claim which of the following assurances?

 a. No additional secured debt will be issued in the future.
 b. If any secured debt is issued in the future, the unsecured debentures must be redeemed at par.
 c. The debentures will be secured, but to a lesser degree than any secured debt issued in the future.
 d. The debentures will be secured at least equally with any secured debt issued in the future.

11. **Credit Risk (LO1, CFA5)** An "original issue junk" bond is *best* described as a bond issued

 a. Below investment grade.
 b. At an original issue discount.
 c. As investment grade, but declined to speculative grade.
 d. As below investment grade, but upgraded to speculative grade.

12. **Credit Risk (LO1, CFA5)** A "fallen angel" bond is *best* described as a bond issued

 a. Below investment grade.
 b. At an original issue discount.
 c. As investment grade, but declined to speculative grade.
 d. As a secured bond, but the collateral value declined below par value.

13. **Preferred Stock** Nonconvertible preferred stock has which of the following in comparison to common stock?

 a. Preferential claim on a company's earnings.
 b. A predetermined dividend rate.
 c. Preferential voting rights.
 d. All of the above.

14. **Preferred Stock** A preferred stock that is entitled to dividends in arrears is known as

 a. Convertible
 b. Cumulative
 c. Extendible
 d. Participating

15. **Convertible Bonds (LO3, CFA2)** Which one of the following statements about convertible bonds is true?

 a. The longer the call protection on a convertible, the less the security is worth.
 b. The more volatile the underlying stock, the greater the value of the conversion feature.
 c. The smaller the spread between the dividend yield on the stock and the yield to maturity on the bond, the more the convertible is worth.
 d. The collateral that is used to secure a convertible bond is one reason convertibles are more attractive than the underlying common stocks.

16. **Convertible Bonds (LO3, CFA6)** Which one of the following statements about convertible bonds is false?

   a. The yield on the convertible will typically be higher than the yield on the underlying common stock.

   b. The convertible bond will likely participate in a major upward movement in the price of the underlying common stock.

   c. Convertible bonds are typically secured by specific assets of the issuing company.

   d. A convertible bond can be valued as a straight bond with an attached option.

17. **Convertible Bonds (LO3, CFA6)** A convertible bond sells at $1,000 par with a conversion ratio of 40 and an accompanying stock price of $20 per share. The conversion price and conversion value are, respectively,

   a. $20 and $1,000

   b. $20 and $800

   c. $25 and $1,000

   d. $25 and $800

18. **Convertible Bonds (LO3, CFA6)** A convertible bond sells at $1,000 par with a conversion ratio of 25 and conversion value of $800. What is the price of the underlying stock?

   a. $12

   b. $48

   c. $40

   d. $32

19. **Convertible Bonds (LO3, CFA6)** A convertible bond has a par value of $1,000 and a conversion ratio of 20. The price of the underlying stock is $40. What is the conversion value?

   a. $20

   b. $800

   c. $1,000

   d. $25

20. **International Bonds (LO1, CFA3)** A U.S. investor who buys Japanese bonds will most likely maximize his return if interest rates

   a. Fall and the dollar weakens relative to the yen.

   b. Fall and the dollar strengthens relative to the yen.

   c. Rise and the dollar weakens relative to the yen.

   d. Rise and the dollar strengthens relative to the yen.

Concept Questions

1. **Bond Types (LO1, CFA1)** What are the four main types of corporate bonds?

2. **Bond Features (LO2, CFA2)** What is a bond refunding? Is it the same thing as a call?

3. **Callable Bonds (LO2, CFA2)** With regard to the call feature, what are call protection and the call premium? What typically happens to the call premium through time?

4. **Put Bonds (LO1, CFA6)** What is a put bond? Is the put feature desirable from the investor's perspective? The issuer's?

5. **Bond Yields (LO1, CFA4)** What is the impact on a bond's coupon rate from

   a. A call feature?

   b. A put feature?

6. **Exchangeable Bonds (LO3, CFA2)** What is the difference between an exchangeable bond and a convertible bond?

7. **Event Risk (LO1, CFA4)** What is event risk? In addition to protective covenants, which bond feature do you think best reduces or eliminates such risk?

8. **Floaters (LO1, CFA4)** From the bondholder's perspective, what are the potential advantages and disadvantages of floating coupons?

9. **Effective Duration (LO2, CFA3)** Why is effective duration a more accurate measure of interest rate risk for bonds with embedded options?

10. **Embedded Options (LO2, CFA2)** What are some examples of embedded options in bonds? How do they affect the price of a bond?

11. **Junk Bonds (LO1, CFA2)** Explain the difference between an original issue junk bond and a fallen angel bond.

12. **Put Bonds (LO1, CFA6)** What is the difference between put bonds and extendible bonds?

13. **Callable Bonds (LO2, CFA2)** All else the same, callable bonds have less interest rate sensitivity than noncallable bonds. Why? Is this a good thing?

14. **Callable Bonds (LO2, CFA2)** Two callable bonds are essentially identical, except that one has a refunding provision while the other has no refunding provision. Which bond is more likely to be called by the issuer? Why?

15. **Inverse Floaters (LO1, CFA1)** What is the impact of an inverse floating coupon on a bond's price volatility?

Questions and Problems

Core Questions

1. **Conversion Price (LO3, CFA6)** A convertible bond has a $1,000 face value and a conversion ratio of 50. What is the conversion price?

2. **Conversion Price (LO3, CFA6)** A convertible bond has a conversion ratio of 22 and a par value of $1,000. What is the conversion price?

3. **Conversion Ratio (LO3, CFA6)** A company just sold a convertible bond at a par value of $1,000. If the conversion price is $64, what is the conversion ratio?

4. **Conversion Value (LO3, CFA6)** A convertible bond has a $1,000 face value and a conversion ratio of 36. If the stock price is $42, what is the conversion value?

5. **Conversion Value (LO3, CFA6)** A convertible bond has a conversion ratio of 17 and a par value of $1,000. If the stock is currently priced at $38, what is the conversion value?

6. **Conversion Ratio (LO3, CFA6)** You find a convertible bond outstanding with a conversion value of $1,120. The stock is currently priced at $33. What is the conversion ratio of the bond?

7. **Callable Bonds (LO2, CFA2)** A bond matures in 25 years, but is callable in 10 years at 120. The call premium decreases by 2 percent of par per year. If the bond is called in 14 years, how much will you receive?

8. **Call Premium (LO2, CFA2)** You own a bond with a 6 percent coupon rate and a yield to call of 6.90 percent. The bond currently sells for $1,070. If the bond is callable in five years, what is the call premium of the bond?

9. **Convertible Bonds (LO3, CFA6)** A convertible bond has a 6 percent coupon, paid semiannually, and will mature in 10 years. If the bond were not convertible, it would be priced to yield 5 percent. The conversion ratio on the bond is 20 and the stock is currently selling for $49 per share. What is the minimum value of this bond?

10. **Convertible Bonds (LO3, CFA6)** You own a convertible bond with a conversion ratio of 20. The stock is currently selling for $72 per share. The issuer of the bond has announced a call; the call price is 108. What are your options here? What should you do?

Intermediate Questions

11. **Callable Bonds (LO3, CFA2)** There is a 30-year bond with a 7 percent coupon and a 5 percent yield to maturity. The bond is callable in 10 years at par value. What is the Macaulay duration of the bond assuming it is not called? What is the Macaulay duration if the bond is called? Which number is more relevant?

12. **Convertible Bonds (LO3, CFA6)** Steven Long, a bond analyst, is analyzing a convertible bond. The characteristics of the bond are given below.

Convertible Bond Characteristics	
Par value	$1,000
Annual coupon rate (annual pay)	7.2%
Conversion ratio	25
Market price	105% of par
Straight value	99% of par
Underlying Stock Characteristics	
Current market price	$32 per share

Compute the bond's conversion value and market conversion price.

13. **Convertible Bonds (LO3, CFA6)** Determine whether the value of a callable convertible bond will increase, decrease, or remain unchanged if there is an increase in stock price volatility. What if there is an increase in interest rate volatility? Justify each of your responses.

Use the following information to answer the next two questions: Stephanie Podendorf is evaluating her investment alternatives in Sands Incorporated by analyzing a Sands convertible bond and Sands common equity. Characteristics of the two securities are as follows:

Characteristic	Convertible Bond	Common Equity
Par value	$1,000	
Coupon (annual payment)	6%	
Current market price	$960	$42 per share
Straight bond value	$940	
Conversion ratio	25	
Conversion option	At any time	
Dividend		$0
Expected market price in one year	$1,080	$54 per share

14. **Convertible Bonds (LO3, CFA6)** Calculate the following:
    a. The current market conversion price for the Sands convertible bond.
    b. The expected one-year rate of return for the Sands convertible bond.
    c. The expected one-year rate of return for the Sands common equity.

15. **Convertible Bonds (LO3, CFA6)** One year has passed and Sands's common equity price has increased to $58 per share. Name the two components of the convertible bond's value. Indicate whether the value of each component should increase, stay the same, or decrease in response to the increase on Sands's common equity.

CFA Exam Review by Schweser

[CFA2, CFA6]

Patrick Wall is a new associate at a large international financial institution. Mr. Wall recently completed his finance degree and is currently a CFA Level 1 candidate. Mr. Wall's new position is as the assistant to the firm's fixed-income portfolio manager. His boss, Charles Johnson, is responsible for familiarizing Mr. Wall with the basics of fixed-income investing. Mr. Johnson asks Mr. Wall to evaluate the bonds shown below. The bonds are otherwise identical except for the call feature present in one of the bonds. The callable bond is callable at par and exercisable on the coupon dates only.

	Noncallable	Callable
Price	$100.83	$98.79
Time to maturity (years)	5	5
Time to first call date	—	0
Annual coupon	$6.25	$6.25
Interest payment	Semiannual	Semiannual
Yield to maturity	6.0547%	6.5366%
Price value per basis point	428.0360	—

1. Mr. Johnson asks Mr. Wall to compute the value of the call option. Using the given information, what is the value of the embedded call option?
   a. $0.00
   b. $1.21
   c. $2.04

2. Mr. Wall is a little confused over the relationship between the embedded option and the callable bond. How does the value of the embedded call option change when interest rate volatility increases?

   a. It increases.
   b. It may increase or decrease.
   c. It decreases.

3. Mr. Wall believes he understands the relationship between interest rates and straight bonds but is unclear how callable bonds change as interest rates increase. How do prices of callable bonds react to an increase in interest rates? The price:

   a. Increases.
   b. May increase or decrease.
   c. Decreases.

What's on the Web?

1. **Bond Quotes**   Go to cxa.marketwatch.com/finra/MarketData and find the corporate bond search. Enter "Ford Motor" for Ford Motor Company in the Issue box and search for Ford bonds. How many bonds are listed for sale? What are the different credit ratings for these bonds? What is the yield to maturity for the longest maturity bond? What is its price?

2. **Credit Spreads**   What are the current credit spreads? Go to finance.yahoo.com and find the U.S. Treasury yields and the corporate bond yields. Calculate the yield spreads for AAA, AA, and A credit–rated bonds for 2-, 5-, and 10-year bonds. Are the yield spreads linear? In other words, does the yield spread increase by the same number of basis points for each decline in credit rating? Why or why not? Why are the yield spreads higher for longer term bonds?

3. **Historical Credit Spreads**   The Federal Reserve Bank of St. Louis has files with historical interest rates on its Web site at www.stlouisfed.org. Go to the site and find the monthly Moody's Seasoned Aaa Corporate Bond Yield and the monthly Moody's Seasoned Baa Corporate Bond Yield. You can calculate a credit spread as the difference between these two returns. When was the largest credit spread? The smallest? What factors do you think led to the large credit spreads and the small credit spreads?

4. **Bond Terminology**   Go to www.investinginbonds.com and find the definitions for the following terms: bond resolution, cap, collar, defeasance, extraordinary redemption, overcollateralization, and refunding.

Stock-Trak Exercises

To access the Stock-Trak Exercise for this chapter, please visit the book Web site at www.mhhe.com/jmd6e and choose the corresponding chapter.

CHAPTER 19

Government Bonds

Learning Objectives

Before you loan money to Uncle Sam (and his relatives), you should know:

1. The basics of U.S. Treasury securities and how they are sold.

2. The workings of the STRIPS program and pricing Treasury bonds.

3. How federal agencies borrow money.

4. How municipalities borrow money.

"I am for a government rigorously frugal and simple, applying all the possible savings of the public revenue to the discharge of the national debt."

–Thomas Jefferson

U.S. Treasury bonds are among the safest investments available because they are secured by the considerable resources of the federal government. Many bonds issued by federal government agencies, and by state and local municipal governments, are also nearly free of default risk. Consequently, government bonds are generally excellent vehicles for conservative investment strategies seeking predictable investment results. ■

The largest and most important debt market is that for debt issued by the U.S. government. This market is truly global in character because a large share of federal debt is sold to foreign investors, and it thereby sets the tone for debt markets around the world. In contrast, the market for debt issued by states and municipalities is almost exclusively a domestic market. This is because almost all U.S. municipal securities are owned by U.S. investors. These two broad categories make up the government bond market. In this chapter, we examine securities issued by federal, state, and local governments. These securities represent a combined value of many trillions of dollars.

CFA™ Exam Topics in This Chapter:

1 Features of debt securities (L1, S15)

2 Risks associated with investing in bonds (L1, S15)

3 Overview of bond sectors and instruments (L1, S15)

4 Fixed-income portfolio management (L3, S9)

Go to www.mhhe.com/jmd6e for a guide that aligns your textbook with CFA readings.

19.1 Government Bond Basics

The U.S. federal government is the largest single borrower in the world. As of September 2010, the public debt of the U.S. government exceeded $13 trillion. Responsibility for managing outstanding government debt belongs to the U.S. Treasury, which acts as the financial agent of the federal government.

The U.S. Treasury finances government debt by issuing marketable securities and non-marketable securities. Most of the gross public debt is financed by the sale of marketable securities at regularly scheduled Treasury auctions. Marketable securities include Treasury bills, Treasury notes, and Treasury bonds, often simply called T-bills, T-notes, and T-bonds, respectively. Outstanding marketable securities trade among investors in a large, active financial market called the Treasury market. Nonmarketable securities include U.S. Savings Bonds, Government Account Series, and State and Local Government Series. Many individuals are familiar with U.S. Savings Bonds since they are sold only to individual investors. Government Account Series are issued to federal government agencies and trust funds, in particular, the Social Security Administration trust fund. State and Local Government Series are purchased by municipal governments.

Treasury security ownership is registered with the U.S. Treasury. When an investor sells a U.S. Treasury security to another investor, registered ownership is officially transferred by notifying the U.S. Treasury of the transaction. However, only marketable securities allow registered ownership to be transferred. Nonmarketable securities do not allow a change of registered ownership and therefore cannot be traded among investors. For example, a U.S. Savings Bond is a nonmarketable security. If an investor wishes to sell a U.S. Savings Bond, it must be redeemed by the U.S. Treasury. This is normally a simple procedure. For example, most banks handle the purchase and sale of U.S. Savings Bonds for their customers.

Another large market for government debt is the market for municipal government debt. There are more than 85,000 state and local governments in the United States, most of which have issued outstanding debt obligations. In a typical year, well over 10,000 new municipal debt issues are brought to market. Total municipal debt outstanding in the United States is estimated to be over $2 trillion. Of this total, individual investors hold about half, either through direct purchase or indirectly through mutual funds. The remainder is split about equally between holdings of property and casualty insurance companies and commercial banks.

The value of the outstanding U.S. federal government debt can be found at www.treasurydirect.gov

Visit www.investinginbonds.com for more information on U.S. Treasury securities

19.2 U.S. Treasury Bills, Notes, Bonds, and STRIPS

face value
The value of a bill, note, or bond at its maturity when a payment of principal is made. Also called *redemption value.*

discount basis
Method of selling a Treasury bill at a discount from face value.

imputed interest
The interest paid on a Treasury bill determined by the size of its discount from face value.

Treasury bills are short-term obligations that mature in six months or less. They are originally issued with maturities of 4, 13, or 26 weeks. A T-bill entitles its owner to receive a single payment at the bill's maturity, called the bill's **face value** or *redemption value.* The smallest denomination T-bill has a face value of $1,000. T-bills are sold on a **discount basis**, where a price is set at a discount from face value. For example, if a $10,000 bill is sold for $9,500, then it is sold at a discount of $500, or 5 percent. The discount represents the **imputed interest** on the bill.

Treasury notes are medium-term obligations with original maturities of 10 years or less, but more than 1 year. They are normally issued with original maturities of 2, 5, or 10 years, and they have face value denominations as small as $1,000. Besides a payment of face value at maturity, T-notes also pay semiannual coupons.

Treasury bonds are long-term obligations with much longer original-issue maturities. Since 1985, the Treasury has only issued T-bonds with a maturity of 30 years in its regular bond offerings. Like T-notes, T-bonds pay their face value at maturity, pay semiannual coupons, and have face value denominations as small as $1,000.

The coupon rate for T-notes and T-bonds is set according to interest rates prevailing at the time of issuance. For example, if the prevailing interest rate for a Treasury note of a certain maturity is 5 percent, then the coupon rate—that is, the annual coupon as a percentage of par value—for a new issue with that maturity is set at or near 5 percent. Thus, a $10,000 par value T-note paying a 5 percent coupon would pay two $250 coupons each year. Coupon payments normally begin six months after issuance and continue to be paid every six months until the last coupon is paid along with the face value at maturity. Once set, the coupon rate remains constant throughout the life of a U.S. Treasury note or bond.

Treasury STRIPS are derived from Treasury notes originally issued with maturities of 10 years and from Treasury bonds issued with 30-year maturities. Since 1985, the U.S. Treasury has sponsored the **STRIPS** program, an acronym for *Separate Trading of Registered Interest and Principal of Securities*. This program allows brokers to divide Treasury bonds and notes into *coupon strips* and *principal strips*, thereby allowing investors to buy and sell the strips of their choice. Principal strips represent face-value payments, and coupon strips represent coupon payments. For example, a 30-year maturity T-bond can be separated into 61 strips, representing 60 semiannual coupon payments and a single face value payment. Under the Treasury STRIPS program, each of these strips can be separately registered to different owners.

The terms "STRIPS" and "strips" can sometimes cause confusion. The acronym STRIPS is used when speaking specifically about the Treasury STRIPS program. The term *strips*, however, now popularly refers to any note or bond issue broken down into its component parts. In this generic form, the term strips is acceptable.

Since each strip created under the STRIPS program represents a single future payment, STRIPS securities effectively become **zero coupon bonds** and are commonly called *zeroes*. The unique characteristics of Treasury zeroes make them an interesting investment choice.

The yield to maturity of a zero coupon bond is the interest rate that an investor will receive if the bond is held until it matures. Table 19.1 lists bond prices for zero coupon bonds with a face value of $10,000, maturities of 5, 10, 20, and 30 years, and yields from 3 percent to 15 percent. As shown, a $10,000 face-value zero coupon bond with a term to maturity of 20 years and an 8 percent yield has a price of $2,082.89.

STRIPS
Treasury program allowing investors to buy individual coupon and principal payments from a whole Treasury note or bond. Acronym for *Separate Trading of Registered Interest and Principal of Securities.*

zero coupon bond
A note or bond paying a single cash flow at maturity. Also called *zeroes.*

Visit the U.S. Treasury at www.ustreas.gov

EXAMPLE 19.1   Calculating a STRIPS Price

What is the price of a STRIPS maturing in 20 years with a face value of $10,000 and a yield to maturity of 7.5 percent?

The STRIPS price is calculated as the present value of a single cash flow as follows:

$$\text{STRIPS price} = \frac{\$10,000}{(1 + .075/2)^{40}}$$

$$= \$2,293.38$$

You can also calculate a STRIPS price using a built-in spreadsheet function. For example, the nearby *Spreadsheet Analysis* box contains this STRIPS price calculation using an Excel spreadsheet.

EXAMPLE 19.2   Calculating a STRIPS Yield

What is the yield to maturity of a STRIPS maturing in 10 years with a face value of $10,000 and a price of $5,200?

The STRIPS yield is calculated as a yield to maturity of a single cash flow as follows:

$$\text{STRIPS yield} = 2 \times \left[\left(\frac{\$10,000}{\$5,200} \right)^{1/20} - 1 \right]$$

$$= 6.65\%$$

The nearby *Spreadsheet Analysis box* contains an example of this STRIPS yield calculation using an Excel spreadsheet.

Figure 19.1 graphs prices of zero coupon bonds with a face value of $10,000. The vertical axis measures bond prices, and the horizontal axis measures bond maturities. Bond prices for yields of 4, 8, and 12 percent are illustrated.

652   Part 6 ■ **Topics in Investments**

TABLE 19.1 — Zero Coupon Bond Prices, $10,000 Face Value

Yield to Maturity	Bond Maturity			
	5 Years	10 Years	20 Years	30 Years
3.0%	$8,616.67	$7,424.70	$5,512.62	$4,092.96
3.5	8,407.29	7,068.25	4,996.01	3,531.30
4.0	8,203.48	6,729.71	4,528.90	3,047.82
4.5	8,005.10	6,408.16	4,106.46	2,631.49
5.0	7,811.98	6,102.71	3,724.31	2,272.84
5.5	7,623.98	5,812.51	3,378.52	1,963.77
6.0	7,440.94	5,536.76	3,065.57	1,697.33
6.5	7,262.72	5,274.71	2,782.26	1,467.56
7.0	7,089.19	5,025.66	2,525.72	1,269.34
7.5	6,920.20	4,788.92	2,293.38	1,098.28
8.0	6,755.64	4,563.87	2,082.89	950.60
8.5	6,595.37	4,349.89	1,892.16	823.07
9.0	6,439.28	4,146.43	1,719.29	712.89
9.5	6,287.23	3,952.93	1,562.57	617.67
10.0	6,139.13	3,768.89	1,420.46	535.36
10.5	5,994.86	3,593.83	1,291.56	464.17
11.0	5,854.31	3,427.29	1,174.63	402.58
11.5	5,717.37	3,268.83	1,068.53	349.28
12.0	5,583.95	3,118.05	972.22	303.14
12.5	5,453.94	2,974.55	884.79	263.19
13.0	5,327.26	2,837.97	805.41	228.57
13.5	5,203.81	2,707.96	733.31	198.58
14.0	5,083.49	2,504.19	667.80	172.57
14.5	4,966.23	2,466.35	608.29	150.02
15.0	4,851.94	2,354.13	554.19	130.46

FIGURE 19.1 — Zero Coupon Bond Prices ($10,000 Face Value)

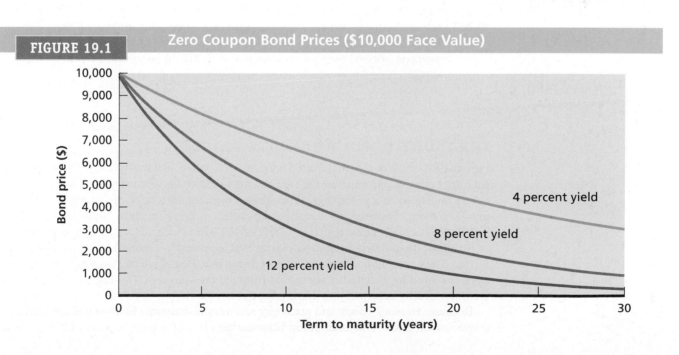

	A	B	C	D	E	F	G
1							
2			Calculating the Price of a Zero-Coupon STRIPS				
3							
4	A STRIPS traded on June 30, 2010, matures in 20 years on June 30, 2030.						
5	Assuming a 7.5 percent yield to maturity, what is the STRIPS price?						
6	Hint: Use the Excel function PRICE with the coupon rate set to zero.						
7							
8		$22.9338	=PRICE("6/30/2010","6/30/2030",0,0.075,100,2)				
9							
10	For a bond with a $10,000 face value, multiply the price by 100 to get $2,293.38.						
11							
12			Calculating the Yield to Maturity of a STRIPS				
13							
14	A STRIPS traded on June 30, 2010, matures in 10 years on June 30, 2020.						
15	The STRIPS price is $52. What is its yield to maturity?						
16	Hint: Use the Excel function YIELD with the coupon rate set to zero.						
17							
18		6.65%	=YIELD("6/30/2010","6/30/2020",0,52,100,2)				
19							
20							

CHECK THIS

19.2a What are some possible reasons why individual investors might prefer to buy Treasury STRIPS rather than common stocks?

19.2b What are some possible reasons why individual investors might prefer to buy individual Treasury STRIPS rather than whole T-notes or T-bonds?

19.2c For zero coupon bonds with the same face value and yield to maturity, is the price of a zero with a 15-year maturity larger or smaller than the average price of two zeroes with maturities of 10 years and 20 years? Why?

TREASURY BOND AND NOTE PRICES

Figure 19.2 displays a partial *Wall Street Journal* online (www.wsj.com) listing of prices and other relevant information for Treasury notes and bonds. Treasury bond and note price quotes are stated on a percentage of par basis. For example, a price of 101 equals par value plus 1 percent. Fractions of a percent are stated in thirty-seconds. Thus, a price stated as 101:12 is actually equal to 101 + 12/32, or 101.375.

To illustrate, the first column in Figure 19.2 is maturity, reported in a year-month-day format. The next column states the annual coupon rate. Dealer bid and ask price quotes come next, followed by changes in ask quotes from the previous day. The last column gives the yield to maturity implied by an asked price quote.

Because Treasury bonds and notes pay semiannual coupons, bond yields are stated on a semiannual basis. The relationship between the price of a note or bond and its yield to

FIGURE 19.2   U.S. Treasury Quotes

U.S. Treasury Quotes

TREASURY NOTES & BONDS

GO TO: Bills

Wednesday, January 20, 2010   Find Historical Data [ ] | WHAT'S THIS?

Treasury note and bond data are representative over-the-counter quotations as of 3pm Eastern time. Figures after colons in bid and ask quotes represent 32nds; 101:26 means 101 26/32, or 101.8125% of face value; 99:01 means 99 1/32, or 99.03125% of face value. For notes and bonds callable prior to maturity, yields are computed to the earliest call date for issues quoted above par and to the maturity date for issues below par.

Maturity	Coupon	Bid	Ask	Chg	Asked yield
2010 Jan 31	2.125	100:02	100:02	unch.	-0.1732
2010 Feb 15	3.500	100:07	100:08	-1	0.0707
2010 Feb 15	4.750	100:10	100:11	unch.	0.1037
2010 Feb 15	6.500	100:14	100:14	unch.	0.1911
2010 Feb 28	2.000	100:06	100:07	-1	-0.0090
2010 Mar 15	4.000	100:18	100:19	-1	0.0709
2010 Mar 31	1.750	100:10	100:11	unch.	0.0435
2010 Apr 15	4.000	100:29	100:29	unch.	0.0838
2010 Apr 30	2.125	100:18	100:18	unch.	0.0599
2010 May 15	3.875	101:06	101:07	unch.	0.0862
2010 May 15	4.500	101:12	101:13	-1	0.0960
2010 May 31	2.625	100:20	100:23	unch.	0.0947
2010 Jun 15	3.625	101:12	101:13	-1	0.1168
2010 Jun 30	2.875	101:07	101:07	unch.	0.1155
2010 Jul 15	3.875	101:26	101:26	unch.	0.1364
2010 Jul 22	0.000	00:04	00:04	unch.	0.1268
2010 Jul 31	2.750	101:12	101:12	unch.	0.1458
2010 Aug 15	4.125	102:08	102:08	unch.	0.1715

Source: www.wsj.com. Reprinted with permission of *The Wall Street Journal*, January 20, 2010. © 2010 Dow Jones & Company, Inc. All Rights Reserved Worldwide.

maturity was discussed in an earlier chapter. For convenience, the bond price formula from that chapter is restated here:

$$\text{Bond price} = \frac{\text{Annual coupon}}{YTM} \times \left[1 - \frac{1}{(1 + YTM/2)^{2M}} \right] + \frac{\text{Face value}}{(1 + YTM/2)^{2M}}$$

Figure 19.3 illustrates the relationship between the price of a bond and its yield to maturity for 2-year, 7-year, and 30-year terms to maturity. Notice that each bond has a price of 100 when its yield is 8 percent. This price indicates that each bond has an 8 percent coupon rate, because when a bond's coupon rate is equal to its yield to maturity, its price is equal to its par value.

bid-ask spread
The difference between a dealer's ask price and bid price.

The difference between a dealer's ask and bid prices is called the **bid-ask spread**. The bid-ask spread measures the dealer's gross profit from a single round-trip transaction of buying a security at the bid price and then selling it at the ask price.

FIGURE 19.3   Bond Prices ($100 Face Value)

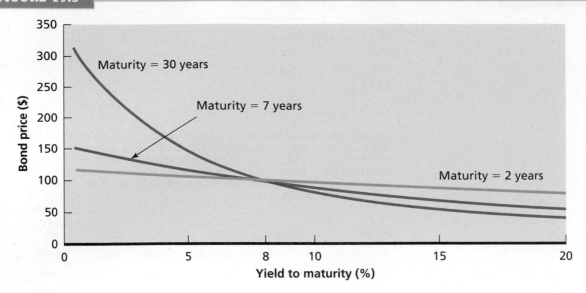

CHECK THIS

19.2d   What would Figure 19.3 look like if the three bonds all had coupon rates of 6 percent? What about 10 percent?

19.2e   In Figure 19.2, which Treasury issues have the narrowest spreads? Why do you think this is so?

19.2f   Examine the spreads between bid and ask prices for Treasury notes and bonds listed online at www.wsj.com.

TREASURY INFLATION-PROTECTED SECURITIES

In recent years, the U.S. Treasury has issued securities that guarantee a fixed rate of return in excess of realized inflation rates. These inflation-indexed Treasury securities, commonly called TIPS, pay a fixed coupon rate on their current principal and adjust their principal semiannually according to the most recent inflation rate.

For example, suppose an inflation-indexed note is issued with a coupon rate of 3.5 percent and an initial principal of $1,000. Six months later, the note will pay a coupon of $1,000 × 3.5%/2 = $17.50. Assuming 2 percent inflation over the six months since issuance, the note's principal is then increased to $1,000 × 102% = $1,020. Six months later, the note pays $1,020 × 3.5%/2 = $17.85, and its principal is again adjusted to compensate for recent inflation.

Price and yield information for inflation-indexed Treasury securities is reported online at www.wsj.com, as shown in Figure 19.4. In Figure 19.4, we see that the first and second columns report the maturity and fixed coupon rate, respectively. The third, fourth, and fifth columns report current bid/ask prices and the price change from the previous trading day. Prices for inflation-indexed securities are reported as a percentage of current accrued principal. The sixth and seventh columns list an inflation-adjusted yield to maturity and current accrued principal reflecting all cumulative inflation adjustments.

For investors wanting long-term protection against inflation along with the safety of U.S. Treasury bonds, inflation-indexed Treasury securities are perhaps the perfect investment. The nearby *Investment Updates* box further discusses the attractive features of inflation-indexed Treasury securities.

Treasury Inflation-Protected Securities

Wednesday, January 20, 2010   Find Historical Data [ ] | WHAT'S THIS?

Treasury Inflation-Protected Securities, or TIPS, are securities whose principal is tied to the Consumer Price Index (CPI). The principal increases with inflation and decreases with deflation. When the security matures, the U.S. Treasury pays the original or adjusted principal, whichever is greater. TIPS pay interest every six months. Figures after periods in bid and ask quotes represent 32nds; 101.26 means 101 26/32, or 101.8125% of 100% face value; 99.01 means 99 1/32, or 99.03125% of face value.

Maturity	Coupon	Bid	Ask	Chg	Yield*	Accrued principal
2010 Apr 15	0.875	100.13	100.13	- 1	-0.896	1141
2011 Jan 15	3.500	104.08	104.08	unch.	-0.804	1242
2011 Apr 15	2.375	103.25	103.26	unch.	-0.691	1089
2012 Jan 15	3.375	107.22	107.23	+ 1	-0.485	1218
2012 Apr 15	2.000	105.10	105.11	+ 2	-0.376	1065
2012 Jul 15	3.000	108.15	108.16	+ 1	-0.396	1202
2013 Apr 15	0.625	102.19	102.20	+ 1	-0.185	1023
2013 Jul 15	1.875	106.16	106.17	+ 3	0.004	1177
2014 Jan 15	2.000	106.26	106.27	+ 1	0.275	1170
2014 Apr 15	1.250	104.10	104.11	+ 2	0.222	1021
2014 Jul 15	2.000	107.06	107.07	+ 3	0.378	1147
2015 Jan 15	1.625	105.05	105.06	+ 2	0.568	1132
2015 Jul 15	1.875	106.20	106.21	+ 2	0.638	1111
2016 Jan 15	2.000	107.00	107.01	+ ?	0.791	1009
2016 Jul 15	2.500	110.12	110.13	+ 5	0.847	1070
2017 Jan 15	2.375	109.14	109.15	+ 5	0.969	1072
2017 Jul 15	2.625	111.16	111.17	+ 6	1.023	1043
2018 Jan 15	1.625	103.28	103.29	+ 7	1.114	1032
2018 Jul 15	1.375	101.25	101.26	+ 8	1.150	1002
2019 Jan 15	2.125	107.22	107.23	+ 10	1.215	1007
2019 Jul 15	1.875	105.15	105.16	+ 11	1.260	1012
2020 Jan 15	1.375	100.20	100.21	+ 11	1.306	1000
2025 Jan 15	2.375	106.14	106.15	+ 12	1.878	1147

*Yield to maturity on accrued principal.

Source: www.wsj.com. Reprinted with permission of *The Wall Street Journal,* January 20, 2010.

19.3   U.S. Treasury Auctions

The Federal Reserve Bank conducts regularly scheduled auctions for Treasury securities. At each Treasury auction, the Federal Reserve accepts sealed bids of two types: competitive bids and noncompetitive bids. Competitive bids for T-bills specify a bid price and a bid quantity. The bid price is what the bidder is willing to pay, and the bid quantity is the face value amount that the bidder will purchase if the bid is accepted. Noncompetitive

"INFLATION-LINKED TREASURYS HOLD SURPRISING APPEAL"

Inflation-indexed treasury bonds don't quite rival the Swiss Army Knife. But it's amazing what you can do with them. Need income? Worried about stocks? Want a place to park some cash? Inflation bonds can come in handy. Here's how:

RISING INCOME: Each year, the value of inflation bonds is stepped up along with consumer prices. Investors also collect interest based on this ever-rising principal value. Those twin attributes make the bonds an intriguing investment for retirees.

Suppose you invested $1,000 in inflation bonds at the current yield of 3.8%. If consumer prices rose 2.5% over the next year, your principal would climb to $1,025 and you would earn interest equal to 3.8% of this growing sum. Thus, if you spent the interest but didn't cash in any bonds, you would enjoy a rising stream of income, while keeping your principal's spending power intact.

Retirees should still keep some money in stocks, so they have a shot at even higher returns. After all, many folks won't have a big enough portfolio to live off inflation bonds' 3.8% yield. Still, inflation bonds are a good choice for at least part of your portfolio. "The long-run total return may not be as high as it is from stocks," says Ken Volpert, co-manager of Vanguard Inflation Protected Securities Fund, a no-load fund with $120 million in assets. "But you have greater certainty that the rise in your income and your principal will be in line with inflation."

INFLATION INSURANCE: Need protection against rising consumer prices? Inflation bonds may be just the ticket. Suppose you are going to retire next year, and you plan to buy an annuity at that point. If you buy inflation bonds now, you have protected yourself against a short-term spike in inflation.

Alternatively, suppose you sold your house and won't buy another for a few years. Maybe you are taking a job overseas or planning to rent while you look for the perfect spot to retire. If you plunked your home equity into inflation bonds and earned 3.8 percentage points a year more than inflation, you should have a good shot at keeping pace with real-estate prices.

PORTFOLIO PROTECTION: If inflation takes off or the economy tumbles into recession, stocks will get whacked. Want to cushion that blow? Traditionally, stock investors have added a dollop of regular bonds to their portfolios. That works well in a recession, when interest rates tend to fall, driving up the price of regular bonds, whose fixed-interest payouts now seem more attractive. But when inflation takes off, interest rates climb. Result: Both stocks and regular bonds get crushed.

That is where inflation bonds come in. They won't do as well as regular bonds in a recession. But during periods of rising consumer prices, inflation bonds will sparkle, thus helping to offset your stock-market losses.

PARKING PLACE: Because inflation bonds don't perform as erratically as regular bonds, they can be a good place to stash your emergency money. You never know when you will need this emergency money. Maybe you will have to call on your reserve next month—or maybe the money will sit untouched for the next decade. Because your time horizon is uncertain, you want the money to be readily available, but you also want it to earn healthy returns. Inflation bonds look good on both counts. Mr. Volpert figures your chances of losing money in any given year are slim. "You might even have better downside protection than you would with a short-term bond fund," he says.

WWW

For recent information on Treasury auctions visit www.treasurydirect.gov

stop-out bid
The lowest competitive bid in a U.S. Treasury auction that is accepted.

bids specify only a bid quantity since the price charged to noncompetitive bidders will be determined by the results of the competitive auction process. Individual investors can submit noncompetitive bids, but only Treasury securities dealers can submit competitive bids.

At the close of bidding, all sealed bids are forwarded to the U.S. Treasury for processing. As a first step, all noncompetitive bids are accepted automatically and are subtracted from the total issue amount. Then a **stop-out bid** is determined; this is the price at which all competitive bids are sufficient to finance the remaining issue amount. Competitive bids at or above the stop-out bid are accepted, and bids below the stop-out bid are rejected.

Since 1998, all U.S. Treasury auctions have been single-price auctions in which all accepted competitive bids pay the stop-out bid. The stop-out bid is also the price paid by noncompetitive bidders. For example, suppose an auction for T-bills with $20 billion of face value receives $28 billion of competitive bids and $4 billion of noncompetitive bids. Noncompetitive bids are automatically accepted, leaving $16 billion for competitive bidders. Now suppose the stop-out bid for this $16 billion amount is $9,700 for a $10,000 face-value T-bill. Accepted competitive bidders and all noncompetitive bidders pay this price of $9,700.

The process is similar for T-bond and T-note issues, except that bids are made on a yield basis, where competitive bids state yields instead of prices. A coupon rate for the entire issue is then set according to the average competitive-bid yield.

CHECK THIS

19.3a The Federal Reserve announces an offering of Treasury bills with a face value amount of $25 billion. The response is $5 billion of noncompetitive bids, along with the following competitive bids:

Bidder	Price Bid	Quantity Bid
A	$9,500	$5 billion
B	9,550	5 billion
C	9,600	5 billion
D	9,650	5 billion
E	9,700	5 billion

In a single-price auction, which bids are accepted and what prices are paid by each bidder? How much money is raised by the entire offering?

19.4 U.S. Savings Bonds

The U.S. Treasury offers an interesting investment opportunity for individual (U.S.) investors in the form of savings bonds. Two types of savings bonds are currently available, Series EE and Series I. (Other types exist, but they are no longer available or can be obtained only by converting from one type to another.)

SERIES EE SAVINGS BONDS

For the latest on savings bonds visit
www.savingsbonds.com
or the savings bond section of
www.treasurydirect.gov

Series EE bonds are available in face value denominations ranging from $25 to $10,000, but the original issue price of a Series EE bond is always set at exactly half its face value. Thus, Series EE bonds are sold to resemble zero coupon securities. However, individuals purchasing Series EE bonds receive monthly interest accruals. This interest is paid as an accrual to the redemption value of the bond, where the current redemption value is the original price of the bond plus all prior accrued interest.

Savings bonds purchased after May 1, 2005, pay a fixed rate of interest. Rates for new issues are set each May 1 and November 1, with each new rate effective for all bonds issued during the following six months. Interest accrues monthly and is compounded semiannually. Savings bonds must be held at least one year, and a three-month interest penalty is applied to bonds held less than five years. However, the bond's value is guaranteed to double if it is held until its original 20-year maturity. For example, suppose a $10,000 face value savings bond pays 3 percent interest. Compounding semiannually for 20 years yields a value of $9,070, which is less than a doubling of its original issue price of $5,000. If you hold the bond until maturity, you are guaranteed to receive its face value of $10,000. This works out to an effective interest rate of about 3.496 percent.

SERIES I SAVINGS BONDS

Series I bonds are designed for investors seeking to earn a guaranteed real rate of return. Series I bonds are an accrual-type security with interest added to the bond monthly and paid when the bond is redeemed. Series I bonds are available in face value denominations ranging from $50 to $10,000 and are sold at face value (i.e., investors pay $100 for a $100 Series I bond).

Series I bonds earn interest for up to 30 years. The interest rate on these bonds comes from two rates: a fixed rate of return (which is constant for the life of the bond) and a variable semiannual inflation rate. Interest on Series I bonds accrues monthly and is compounded semiannually.

Fixed rates for new Series I bonds are announced each May and November. The fixed rate of return announced in May of a given year is the fixed rate of return over the entire life of the I bond purchased between May 1 and October 31 of that year. Likewise, the fixed rate of return announced in November of a given year applies to the entire life of an I bond purchased between November 1 and April 30 of the following year.

The semiannual inflation rate is also announced each May and November. The semiannual inflation rate is based on changes in the Consumer Price Index for all Urban consumers (CPI-U). The inflation rate reflects a three-month lag. That is, the semiannual inflation rate announced in May is a measure of inflation over the preceding October through March; the inflation rate announced in November is a measure of inflation over the preceding April through September.

Investors can redeem Series I bonds after 12 months. At redemption, investors receive their original investment plus interest earned. However, an investor who redeems a Series I bond within the first five years of purchase incurs a three-month earnings penalty. For example, if you redeem a Series I bond after 24 months, you will get 21 months of earnings.

CHECK THIS

19.4a What are the differences between Series EE savings bonds and Series I savings bonds?

19.4b Compare the methods by which interest is paid for Series EE savings bonds and Series I bonds. Which method would be preferred if inflation decreased? Which would be preferred if inflation increased?

19.4c Compare the methods by which interest is paid for Series EE savings bonds and Series I inflation-indexed Treasury securities.

19.5 Federal Government Agency Securities

Visit
www.investinginbonds.com
for more information on agency
securities

Most U.S. government agencies consolidate their borrowing through the Federal Financing Bank, which obtains funds directly from the U.S. Treasury. However, several federal agencies are authorized to issue securities directly to the public. For example, the Resolution Trust Funding Corporation, the World Bank, and the Tennessee Valley Authority issue notes and bonds directly to investors.

Bonds issued by U.S. government agencies share an almost equal credit quality with U.S. Treasury issues. Most agency debt does not carry an explicit guarantee of the U.S. government. A federal agency on the verge of default, however, would probably receive government support to ensure timely payment of interest and principal on outstanding debt. This perception is supported by historical experience and the political reality that Congress would likely feel compelled to rescue an agency that it created if it became financially distressed.

This conjecture was confirmed in September 2008. The Federal Housing Finance Agency (FHFA) placed two government-sponsored enterprises (GSE), Fannie Mae and Freddie Mac, into conservatorship. This decision was supported by the U.S. Treasury and the Federal Reserve Bank. The U.S. Treasury pledged taxpayer money to keep these GSEs solvent.

Government agency notes and bonds are attractive to many investors because they offer higher yields than comparable U.S. Treasury securities. For example, Figure 19.5 presents dealer price quotes for agency issues as reported online at www.wsj.com. The listing format is similar to Treasury notes and bonds described previously, except that callable bonds are indicated by an asterisk with only the maturity date shown. Note that Figure 19.5 presents quotes only for Fannie Mae (Federal National Mortgage Association). At www.wsj.com, however, you can also find Freddie Mac (the Federal Home Loan Mortgage Corporation) bond

FIGURE 19.5 Agency Securities

Government Agencies & Similar Issues

Wednesday, January 20, 2010

Over-the-Counter mid-afternoon quotations based on large transactions, usually $1 million or more. Colons in bid and ask quotes represent 32nds; 101:01 means 101 1/32. All yields are calculated to maturity, and based on the ask quote. *Callable issue, maturity date shown. For issues callable prior to maturity, yields are computed to the earliest call date for issues quoted above par, or 100, and to the maturity date for issues below par.

Fannie Mae Issues

Rate	Maturity	Bid	Ask	Yield
3.88	2-10	100:08	100:09	...
7.13	6-10	102:25	102:26	0.11
6.63	11-10	105:04	105:05	0.29
6.25	2-11	104:19	104:20	1.69
5.50	3-11	105:21	105:22	0.53
6.00	5-11	106:30	106:31	0.68
5.38	11-11	107:30	107:31	0.94
6.13	3-12	110:16	110:17	1.15
4.88	5-12	108:05	108:06	1.29
5.25	8-12	107:31	108:00	1.98
4.38	9-12	107:10	107:10	1.54
4.63	5-13	105:09	105:10	2.91
4.63	10-13	109:07	109:09	2.04
5.13	1-14	106:05	106:06	3.44
4.13	4-14	106:30	106:31	2.38
6.25	5-29	116:27	116:29	4.89
7.13	1-30	128:08	128:10	4.89
7.25	5-30	130:00	130:02	4.90
6.63	11-30	122:09	122:11	4.90

Source: www.wsj.com. Reprinted with permission of *The Wall Street Journal,* January 20, 2010. © 2010 Dow Jones & Company, Inc. All Rights Reserved Worldwide.

quotes. In addition, quotes are available for bonds issued by the Federal Farm Credit Bank, the Federal Home Loan Bank, GNMA mortgage issues, and the Tennessee Valley Authority.

If you compare bid and ask dealer price quotes for agency bonds listed in Figure 19.5 with similar Treasury bonds listed in Figure 19.2, you will find that agency bonds have a higher bid-ask spread than Treasury bonds. The reason for the higher bid-ask spread is that agency bond trading volume is much lower than Treasury bond trading volume. To compensate for the lower volume, dealers charge higher spreads. Thus, trading agency bonds is costlier than trading Treasury bonds. Consequently, agency bonds are usually purchased by institutional investors planning to hold the bonds until they mature. Another reason for the higher yields on agency bonds compared to Treasury bonds is that interest income from agency bonds is subject to federal, state, and local taxation, whereas Treasury interest payments are subject only to federal taxation.

19.5a If you saw a quote with an asterisk in Figure 19.5, what would the asterisk indicate?

19.5b Examine spreads between bid and ask prices for government agency notes and bonds listed online at www.wsj.com. What is the typical bid-ask spread?

19.6 Municipal Bonds

WWW

Visit
www.investinginbonds.com
for more about municipal bonds

Municipal notes and bonds are intermediate- to long-term interest-bearing obligations of state and local governments or agencies of those governments. The defining characteristic of municipal notes and bonds, often called "munis," is that coupon interest is usually exempt from federal income tax. Consequently, the market for municipal debt is commonly called the *tax-exempt market*. Most of the 50 states also have an income tax, but their tax treatment of municipal debt interest varies. Only a few states exempt coupon interest on out-of-state municipal bonds from in-state income tax, but most states do allow in-state municipal debt interest to be an exemption from in-state income tax. In any case, state income tax rates are normally much lower than federal income tax rates, and state taxes can be used as an itemized deduction from federal taxable income. Consequently, state taxes are usually a secondary consideration for municipal bond investors.

The federal income tax exemption makes municipal bonds attractive to investors in the highest income tax brackets. This includes many individual investors, commercial banks, and property and casualty insurance companies—precisely those investors who actually hold almost all municipal debt. However, yields on municipal debt are less than on corporate debt with similar features and credit quality. This eliminates much, but not all, of the advantage of the tax exemption. Therefore, tax-exempt investors, including pension funds and retirement accounts of individuals, nonprofit institutions, and some life insurance companies, normally do not invest in municipal bonds. Instead, they prefer to invest in higher-yielding corporate bonds. For some more interesting details on the tax status of various municipal bonds, see the nearby *Investment Updates* box.

default risk

The risk that a bond issuer will cease making scheduled payments of coupons or principal or both.

Municipal bonds are typically less complicated investments than corporate bonds. However, while municipal debt often carries a high credit rating, **default risk** does exist. Thus, investing in municipal debt requires more care than investing in U.S. Treasury securities.

To illustrate some standard features of a municipal bond issue, Table 19.2 summarizes the issue terms for a hypothetical bond issued by the city of Bedford Falls. We see that the bonds were issued in December 1999 and mature 30 years later in December 2029. Each bond has a face value denomination of $5,000 and pays an annual coupon equal to 6 percent of face value. The annual coupon is split between two semiannual payments each June and December. Based on the original offer price of 100, or 100 percent of par value, the bonds have a yield to maturity of 6 percent. The Bedford Falls bonds are call-protected for 10 years, until January 2010. Thereafter, the bonds are callable any time at par value.

general obligation bonds (GOs)

Bonds issued by a municipality that are secured by the full faith and credit of the issuer.

The Bedford Falls bonds are **general obligation bonds (GOs)**, which means that the bonds are secured by the full faith and credit of the city of Bedford Falls. "Full faith and credit" means the power of the municipality to collect taxes. The trustee for the bond issue is the Potters Bank of Bedford Falls. A trustee is appointed to represent the financial interests of bondholders and administer the sinking fund for the bond issue. A sinking fund requires a bond issuer to redeem for cash a fraction of an outstanding bond issue on a periodic basis. The sinking fund in this example requires that, beginning 10 years after issuance, the city must redeem at par value $2.5 million of the bond issue each year. At each annual redemption, a fraction of the bond issue is called and the affected bondholders receive the par value call price.

NOT ALL TAX-FREE MUNI BONDS ARE REALLY EXEMPT FROM TAX

For safety-conscious investors looking for tax-free income, this is a good time to consider municipal bonds. Just be careful: Not all tax-free bonds are really tax-free. Even tax experts agree the $1.7 trillion market for state and local government bonds can be surprisingly tricky. Municipal bonds come in many different shades and flavors. The Bond Market Association, a trade group that represents securities firms and banks that buy, sell, and trade bonds, estimates there are more than 50,000 state and local entities that issue "munis," and there are more than two million separate bond issues outstanding. So never purchase a muni without carefully investigating the bond's tax status with your broker or financial advisor. This subject can get so tricky that I recommend you ask the same question of more than one expert. I speak from experience here: I covered the credit markets for *The Wall Street Journal* for nearly a decade and found many myths and misconceptions about this area. Here are just a few tax considerations to keep in mind when you're shopping for munis:

State and Local Taxes. Muni-bond income isn't always exempt from state and local taxes. The general rule of thumb is that bonds issued by the state you live in, or municipalities of that state, pay tax-free interest. But if you live in a state with an income tax and you buy out-of-state bonds, the interest typically would be taxable in your home state.

For example, I live in New York City. If I buy a New York City or New York State bond, I typically wouldn't owe any federal, state, or local taxes on the interest. Those bonds are, as bond peddlers like to call them, "triple tax-free." But if I buy an out-of-state bond, such as one issued by California, the interest income would be fully taxable in New York. That's why many investors in high-tax areas such as New York City favor bonds issued within their home state. Or they may buy shares of mutual funds that specialize in bonds only from a single state. Just don't be a slave to this strategy. Sometimes, investors can do better by buying out-of-state bonds, even though it means having to pay their home state's tax.

Unfortunately, you also can't assume that all in-state bonds will be free from your state tax. That can depend on what state you call home, says Alexandra Lebenthal, president of Lebenthal & Co., a New York–based firm specializing in municipal bonds. Check this not only with your broker but also with your state tax department. The Federation of Tax Administrators in Washington, D.C., has a Web site that includes links to state tax departments.

Intangible Property. Naturally, you don't have to worry about such state income-tax considerations if you're from a state with no income tax, such as Florida or Texas. But Floridians have another taxing issue to consider: The state has an "intangible personal property" tax, an annual tax based on the market value of stock holdings and other "intangible" personal property. Some types of investments, such as bonds issued by the state of Florida, aren't subject to this tax. To find out what other investments are exempt from this tax, see the Web site of the Florida Department of Revenue.

Alternative Minimum Tax. Lawmakers created the AMT decades ago to prevent high-income people from escaping all federal income taxes through a combination of tax credits, deductions, and other items. But since the tax wasn't adjusted for inflation, it's now hitting rapidly growing numbers of Americans. Unfortunately, some types of bonds pay interest that is considered income when you're calculating the AMT.

Investinginbonds.com, another Web site run by the Bond Market Association, offers a helpful primer on muni-bond income and the AMT. (Click on "Taxation of Municipals" in the left-hand navigation bar and then scroll way down to the "Alternative Minimum Tax" section.) If you're subject to this tax and you're on the phone with an eager bond salesman, be sure to ask if a bond you're considering is an "AMT bond."

Social Security. One of the biggest surprises for many elderly investors is that buying munis can affect how much, if any, of their Social Security benefits are taxable. The law says that you have to include tax-exempt bond income when you're doing the number-crunching. The Investinginbonds.com Web site also has more information on this subject—in fact, you'll find it right below the section mentioned above on the AMT. So if you're receiving Social Security income, be sure to have a tax professional evaluate your situation before purchasing muni bonds.

Taxable Munis. A taxable muni is just what it sounds like: It's a muni bond where the interest "is not excluded from the gross income of its owners for federal income tax purposes," says Lynnette K. Hotchkiss, senior vice president and associate general counsel of the Bond Market Association. She says some munis are taxable because they were issued "for purposes that the federal government deems not to provide a significant benefit to the public at large," such as certain types of economic-development projects that solely benefit a corporation.

Capital Gains and Losses. There also may be capital-gains tax considerations. If you sell a muni bond—or a muni-bond fund—for more than you paid for it, capital gains taxes may have to be considered.

While this isn't a comprehensive list, it's a reminder that buying munis can be much trickier than it may seem at first glance.

Source: Tom Herman, *The Wall Street Journal*, May 21, 2002. Reprinted with permission of *The Wall Street Journal*. © 2002 Dow Jones & Company, Inc. All Rights Reserved Worldwide.

TABLE 19.2 | **City of Bedford Falls General Obligation Bonds**

Issue amount	$50 million	Bond issue represents a total face value amount of $50 million
Issue date	12/15/99	Bonds were offered to the public on December 15, 1999
Maturity date	12/31/29	All remaining principal must be paid at maturity on December 31, 2029
Par value	$5,000	Each bond has a face value of $5,000
Coupon rate	6%	Annual coupons of $300 per bond
Coupon dates	12/31, 6/30	Semiannual coupons of $150
Offering price	100	Offer price is 100% of par value
Yield to maturity	6%	Based on stated offer price
Call provision	Callable after 12/31/09	Bonds are call-protected for 10 years
Call price	100	Bonds are callable at par value
Trustee	Potters Bank of Bedford Falls	The trustee is appointed to represent the bondholders and administer the sinking fund
Sinking fund	$2.5 million annual par redemptions after 12/31/09	City must redeem at par value $2.5 million of the bond issue each year beginning in 2010

MUNICIPAL BOND FEATURES

Municipal bonds are typically callable, pay semiannual coupons, and often have a par value denomination of $5,000. Municipal bond prices are stated as a percentage of par value. Thus, a price of 102 indicates that a bond with a par value of $5,000 has a price of $5,100. By convention, however, municipal bond dealers commonly use yield quotes rather than price quotes in their trading procedures. For example, a dealer might quote a bid-yield of 6.25 percent for a 5 percent coupon bond with seven years to maturity, indicating a willingness to buy at a price determined by that yield. The actual dollar bid price in this example is $4,649.99, as shown in the following bond price calculation:

$$\frac{\$250}{.0625} \times \left[1 - \frac{1}{(1.03125)^{14}}\right] + \frac{\$5,000}{(1.03125)^{14}} = \$4,649.99$$

Because many thousands of different municipal bond issues are outstanding, only a few large issues trade with sufficient frequency to justify having their prices reported in the financial press. A partial *Wall Street Journal* online listing of some actively traded municipal bonds is seen in Figure 19.6. The listing reports the name of the issuer, the coupon rate, the maturity of the issue, the most recent bid price quote, the change from an earlier price quote, and a yield to maturity based on a dealer's bid yield.

A **call provision** is a standard feature of most municipal bond issues. A call provision allows an issuer to retire outstanding bonds before they mature, usually to refund with new bonds after a fall in market interest rates. When the bond is called, each bondholder receives the bond's call price in exchange for the bond. However, two bond features often limit an issuer's call privilege. First, callable municipal bonds usually offer a period of call protection following their original issue date. Since a bond issue is not callable during this period, the earliest possible call date is the end of the call protection period. Second, a call price is often specified with a call premium. A call premium is the difference between a bond's call price and its par value. A common arrangement is to specify a call premium equal to one year's coupons for a call occurring at the earliest possible call date. This is then followed by a schedule of call premium reductions, until about 5 to 10 years before maturity, when the call premium is eliminated entirely. Thereafter, the bond issue is callable any time at par value.

WWW

Check out municipal bonds at
www.municipalbonds.com

call provision

Feature of a municipal bond issue that specifies when the bonds may be called by the issuer and the call price that must be paid.

FIGURE 19.6

Municipal Securities

Tax Exempt Bonds

Wednesday, January 20, 2010

Issue	Coupon	Maturity	Price	Change	Bid Yield
CA Hlth Facs Fin Auth bd	5.000	08-15-39	93.701	.278	5.43
CA Hlth Facs Fin Auth bd	5.000	11-15-36	97.825	-.142	5.15
CA Palomar Pmrd Hlth Care Dt cert	6.750	11-01-39	102.444	.145	6.41
CA Palomar Pmrd Hlth Care Dt cert	6.625	11-01-29	103.515	.148	6.15
CA St Pub Wks lease rev Ser 0	6.125	11-01-29	102.765	.075	5.75
CA St Pub Wks lease rev Ser 0	6.000	11-01-34	103.199	.227	5.58
CA state var purp gen obl	6.000	04-01-38	102.546	.144	5.64
Chrltte NC wtr&swr sys rev Ser 09 B	5.000	07-01-38	108.202	.529	4.04
Colorado Hlth Facs Auth rev bds Ser 09A	5.000	07-01-39	100.221	.224	4.97
Illinois Fin Auth rev bds Ser 09 B	5.500	04-01-39	98.845	.284	5.58
Indiana Fin Auth hlth sys rev Ser 09 A	5.250	11-01-39	102.140	.232	4.97
Maryland Hlth & Hgr Educ Facs rev Ser 10	5.125	07-01-39	100.183	.149	5.10
Maryland Hlth & Hgr Educ Facs rev Ser 10	5.000	07-01-34	99.857	.279	5.01
Massachusetts HEFA rev bds Ser 10 J-1	5.000	07-01-34	100.746	.225	4.90
Massachusetts HEFA rev bds Ser 10 J-1	5.000	07-01-39	100.596	.225	4.92
Michigan St Hosp Fin Auth rev ref Ser 09	5.750	11-15-39	98.587	.277	5.85
Missouri Hlth & Educ Facs Auth hlth facs	5.625	05-15-39	101.111	.145	5.47
Montgomery Cnty OH rev bds Ser 09 A	5.000	05-01-39	100.213	.221	4.97
NC Med Care Comm hlthcare	5.000	06-01-42	100.738	.224	4.90
NC Med Care Comm hlthcare	5.000	06-01-39	101.338	.225	4.82
New Jersey Tpke Auth tpke rev bds Ser 09	5.000	01-01-35	103.001	-.161	4.62
New Orleans Aviation Bd LA gulf oppt zon	6.500	01-01-40	103.980	.210	5.93
North Texas Tollway Auth system first ti	5.250	01-01-44	99.058	.465	5.31
NYC Trt for Cultural Res rev bds Ser 0	5.000	12-01-39	102.420	.237	4.69
NYS Dorm Auth rev bds Ser 09 A	5.000	07-01-39	103.500	.155	4.54
NYS Dormitory Auth rev bds Ser 09 B	5.000	07-01-39	103.500	.155	4.54
OH State hosp rev bds Ser	5.500	01-01-39	103.788	.219	4.98
Penn Turnpke Comm Rv	5.125	12-01-40	101.191	-.312	4.97
Penn Turnpke Comm Rv	5.300	12-01-41	102.542	-.315	4.97
Puerto Rico Pub Tax Fin	6.000	08-01-42	104.346	.074	5.42
Puerto Rico Pub Tax Fin	5.750	08-01-37	104.319	.075	5.18

Source: Reprinted with permission of *The Wall Street Journal*, January 20, 2010. © 2010 Dow Jones & Company, Inc. All Rights Reserved Worldwide.

serial bonds
Bonds issued with maturity dates scheduled at intervals, so that a fraction of the bond issue matures in each year of a multiple-year period.

Municipal bonds are commonly issued with a serial maturity structure, hence the term **serial bonds**. In a serial bond issue, a fraction of the total issue amount is scheduled to mature in each year over a multiple-year period. As an example, a serial bond issue may contain bonds that mature in each year over a 5-year period, with the first group maturing 11 years after the original issue date and the last group maturing 15 years after issuance. The purpose of a serial maturity structure is to spread out the principal repayment, thereby avoiding a lump-sum repayment at a single maturity date.

term bonds
Bonds from an issue with a single maturity date.

When an entire bond issue matures on a single date, the bonds are called **term bonds**. Term bonds normally have a sinking fund provision. A sinking fund is a trustee-managed account to which the issuer makes regular payments. Account reserves are dedicated to redeeming a fraction of the bond issue on each of a series of scheduled redemption dates. Each redemption usually proceeds by lottery, where randomly selected bonds are called and the affected bondholders receive the sinking fund call price. Alternatively, scheduled redemptions can be implemented by purchasing bonds from investors at current market prices. This latter option is usually selected by the issuer when the bonds are selling at a discount from par value. The motive for a sinking fund provision is similar to that for a serial maturity structure; it provides a means for the issuer to avoid a lump-sum principal repayment at a single maturity date.

put bonds
Bonds that can be sold back to the issuer.

Some municipal bonds are putable, and these are called **put bonds**. The holder of a put bond, also called a *tender offer bond,* has the option of selling the bond back to the issuer, normally at par value. Some put bonds can be tendered any time, whereas others can be tendered only on regularly scheduled dates. Weekly, monthly, quarterly, semiannual, and annual put date schedules are all used. Notice that with a put bond, maturity is effectively the choice of the bondholder. This feature protects bondholders from rising interest rates and the associated fall in bond prices. However, a putable bond will have a higher price than a comparable nonputable bond. The price differential simply reflects the value of the put option to sell back the bonds.

variable-rate notes
Securities that pay an interest rate
that changes according to market
conditions. Also called *floaters*.

While most municipal bonds maintain a constant coupon rate (hence the term fixed-rate bonds), interest rate risk has induced many municipalities to issue **variable-rate notes,** often called *floaters.* For these debt issues, the coupon rate is adjusted periodically according to an index-based rule. For example, at each adjustment the coupon rate may be set at 60 percent of the prevailing rate on 91-day maturity U.S. Treasury bills. A variable-rate note may also be putable, in which case it is called a *variable-rate demand obligation,* often abbreviated to VRDO. A stipulation attached to most VRDOs allows the issuer to convert an entire variable-rate issue to a fixed-rate issue following a specified conversion procedure. Essentially, the issuer notifies each VRDO holder of the intent to convert the outstanding VRDO issue to a fixed-rate issue on a specific future date. In response, VRDO holders have the option of tendering their VRDOs for cash, or they can accept conversion of their VRDOs into fixed-rate bonds.

TYPES OF MUNICIPAL BONDS

There are two basic types of municipal bonds: revenue bonds and general obligation bonds, often referred to as GOs. General obligation bonds are issued by all levels of municipal governments, including states, counties, cities, towns, school districts, and water districts. They are secured by the general taxing powers of the municipalities issuing the bonds. For state governments and large city governments, tax revenue is collected from a diverse base of income taxes on corporations and individuals, sales taxes, and property taxes. In contrast, tax revenues for smaller municipalities are largely derived from property taxes, although sales taxes have become increasingly important. Because of their large, diverse tax bases, general obligation bonds issued by states and large cities are often called *unlimited tax bonds* or *full faith and credit bonds.*

However, some general obligation bonds are called *limited tax bonds.* The distinction between limited and unlimited tax bonds arises when a constitutional limit or other statutory limit is placed on the power of a municipality to assess taxes. For example, an amendment to the California state constitution, popularly known as Proposition 13 when it was enacted, placed rigid limits on the ability of California municipalities to assess taxes on real estate.

revenue bonds
Municipal bonds secured by
revenues collected from a specific
project or projects.

Revenue bonds constitute the bulk of all outstanding municipal bonds. **Revenue bonds** are bonds secured by proceeds collected from the projects they finance. Thus, the credit quality of a revenue bond issue is largely determined by the ability of a project to generate revenue. A few examples of the many different kinds of projects financed by revenue bonds are listed below.

Airport and seaport bonds: Used to finance development of airport and seaport facilities. Secured by user fees and lease revenues.

College dormitory bonds: Used to finance construction and renovation of dormitory facilities. Secured by rental fees.

Industrial development bonds: Used to finance development of projects ranging from factories to shopping centers. Secured by rental and leasing fees.

Multifamily housing bonds: Used to finance construction of housing projects for senior citizens or low-income families. Secured by rental fees.

Highway and road gas tax bonds: Used to finance highway construction. May be secured by specific toll revenues or general gas tax revenues.

Student loan bonds: Used to purchase higher education guaranteed student loans. Secured by loan repayments and federal guarantees.

hybrid bonds
Municipal bonds secured by
project revenues with some
form of general obligation credit
guarantees.

Many municipal bonds possess aspects of both general obligation and revenue bonds; these are called **hybrid bonds.** Typically, a hybrid is a revenue bond secured by project-specific cash flows, but with additional credit guarantees. A common form of hybrid is the *moral obligation bond.* This is a state-issued revenue bond with provisions for obtaining general revenues when project-specific resources are inadequate. Usually, extra funds can be obtained only with approval of a state legislature, which is said to be "morally obligated" to assist a financially distressed state-sponsored project. However, a moral obligation is not a guarantee, and the likelihood of state assistance varies. Municipal bond credit analysts consider each state's history of assistance, as well as current state financial conditions, when evaluating the credit-quality enhancement of the moral obligation. In general, experienced municipal bond investors agree that a state will first service its own general obligation debt before providing service assistance to moral obligation debt. This is typically evidenced by the higher yields on moral obligation debt compared to general obligation debt.

Since 1983, all newly issued municipal bonds have had to be registered—that is, with the identity of all bondholders registered with the issuer. With registered bonds, the issuer sends coupon interest and principal payments only to the registered owner of a bond. Additionally, it is now standard practice for registered bonds to be issued in book entry form; bondholders are not issued printed bond certificates, but instead receive notification that their ownership is officially registered. The actual registration record is maintained by the issuer in computer files. This contrasts with the now defunct practice (in the United States) of issuing bearer bonds, where coupon interest and principal were paid to anyone presenting the bond certificates.

MUNICIPAL BOND CREDIT RATINGS

WWW

Check out these rating agency Web sites: Moody's at www.moodys.com Fitch at www.fitchratings.com S&P at www.standardandpoors.com

Municipal bond credit rating agencies provide investors with an assessment of the credit quality of individual bond issues. As part of the issuance and credit rating process, the rating agency is paid a fee to assign a credit rating to a new bond issue, to periodically reevaluate the issue, and to make these ratings available to the public. The three largest municipal bond credit rating agencies are Moody's Investors Service, Standard & Poor's Corporation, and Fitch Investors Service. Among them, they rate thousands of new issues each year. Table 19.3 compares and briefly describes the credit rating codes assigned by these three agencies.

The highest credit rating that can be awarded is "triple-A," which indicates that interest and principal are exceptionally secure because of the financial strength of the issuer. Notice that "triple-A" and "double-A" ratings are denoted as AAA and AA, respectively,

TABLE 19.3 Municipal Bond Credit Ratings

Rating Agency			
Standard & Poor's	Moody's	Fitch	Credit Rating Description
Investment-Grade Bond Ratings			
AAA	Aaa	AAA	Highest credit quality
AA	Aa	AA	High credit quality
A	A	A	Good credit quality
BBB	Baa	BBB	Satisfactory credit quality
Speculative-Grade Bond Ratings			
BB	Ba	BB	Speculative credit quality
B	B	B	Highly speculative quality
CCC	Caa	CCC	Poor credit quality
CC	Ca	CC	Probable default
Extremely Speculative-Grade Bond Ratings			
C	C	C	Imminent default
D		DDD	In default
		DD, D	

MUNIS HAVE WEATHERED STORMS BEFORE

Financial markets have been resilient in the wake of Hurricane Katrina, but a question mark hangs over one market that has traditionally been considered among the safest: municipal bonds.

Though states and municipalities in the Gulf face potential financial hardships, the risk for muni investors flows largely from what Katrina's aftermath could do to the companies whose business it is to stand behind municipal-bond issuers. Four big bond-insurance companies—MBIA Inc.'s MBIA Insurance Corp., Ambac Financial Group Inc.'s Ambac Assurance Corp., FGIC Corp.'s Financial Guaranty Insurance Co., and Financial Security Assurance Inc.—guarantee payments on about 80% of the $2 trillion in muni bonds outstanding. (Financial Security is a unit of French-Belgian financial services firm Dexia.)

Bonds issued by governments in Louisiana, Mississippi, and Alabama comprise less than 1% of the entire muni market, but if hurricane-related claims put pressure on the bond insurers' triple-A credit ratings, they could in turn affect the ratings and potentially the prices of tens of thousands of insured bonds across the country—bonds owned mostly by individual investors, either directly or through mutual funds.

"The more global issue is the effect on the bond insurers," says Judy Wesalo Temel, director of credit research at Samson Capital Advisors, an investment-management firm that focuses on muni bonds. "The triple-A rating is key."

It is still early to guess how bad the financial damage will be, and states, cities, and other entities that sell tax-free muni bonds almost never renege on their debts, even after major natural disasters. Most bond-market professionals think the insurers will be fine, and might actually benefit from the opportunity to demonstrate the value of their service by stepping in to meet missed payments. "If we get through this OK, it will justify the bond-insurance industry," says Gary Pollack,

head of fixed income at Deutsche Bank Private Wealth Management.

Katrina, however, has wrought more damage than any of its predecessors, wiping out or damaging many of the parks, housing projects, and other public works built with muni-bond money as well as the ports and other businesses that generate money to make payments on the bonds. Ratings firms Moody's and Standard & Poor's have put about $9.5 billion in affected bonds on watch for a potential downgrade. S&P issued a report saying that "more severe downgrades" or "actual long-term default by multiple issuers" could threaten bond insurers' triple-A ratings.

"The history has been that we have not seen material, if any, defaults," says Richard Smith, credit analyst at S&P. "Unfortunately, this hurricane is different than what we've experienced before. So I'm not sure that I would count on that history." Fitch Ratings has said it doesn't expect hurricane-related losses to affect its ratings of the bond insurers.

So far, the insurers say they have paid out more than $2 million to cover missed bond payments in the affected areas.

Most bond-market professionals tend to agree that the area's credit will ultimately rebound as federal money pours in and New Orleans rebuilds. "In the long run New Orleans is not a city that's just going to go away," says Peter Coffin, president of Breckinridge Capital, an asset-management firm that specializes in municipal bonds. "At this point the view is that they'll rebuild, and that through that rebuilding and with some assistance they'll manage."

by Standard & Poor's and Fitch, but as Aaa and Aa, respectively, by Moody's. Also notice that "triple-B" and "double-B" ratings—that is, BBB and BB, respectively—by Standard & Poor's and Fitch correspond to "B-double-a" and "B-single-a" ratings—Baa and Ba, respectively—by Moody's. The same pattern holds for C ratings.

The highest four credit ratings, BBB or Baa and above, designate investment-grade bonds. As a matter of policy, many financial institutions will invest only in investment-grade bonds. Lower rankings indicate successively diminishing levels of credit quality. Ratings of BB or Ba and below designate speculative-grade bonds. Individual investors should probably avoid speculative-grade bonds. A rating of C or below indicates that actual or probable default makes the bond issue unsuitable for most investors.

It is not unusual for the ratings assigned to a particular bond issue to differ slightly across credit rating agencies. For example, a bond issue may be rated AA by Standard & Poor's, Aa by Moody's, but only A by Fitch. When this occurs, it usually reflects a difference in credit rating methods rather than a disagreement regarding basic facts. For example, Moody's may focus on the budgetary status of the issuer when assigning a credit rating, while Standard & Poor's may emphasize the economic environment of the issuer. Remember that Standard & Poor's, Moody's, and Fitch are competitors in the bond rating business, and, like competitors in any industry, they try to differentiate their products.

MUNICIPAL BOND INSURANCE

insured municipal bonds
Bonds secured by an insurance policy that guarantees bond interest and principal payments should the issuer default.

In the last two decades, it has become increasingly common for municipalities to obtain bond insurance for new bond issues. **Insured municipal bonds**, besides being secured by the issuer's resources, are also backed by an insurance policy written by a commercial insurance company. The policy provides for prompt payment of coupon interest and principal to municipal bondholders in the event of a default by the issuer. The cost of the insurance policy is paid by the issuer at the time of issuance. The policy cannot be canceled while any bonds are outstanding. With bond insurance, the credit quality of the bond issue is determined by the financial strength of the insurance company, not the municipality alone. Credit rating agencies are certainly aware of this fact. Consequently, a bond issue with insurance can obtain a higher credit rating than would be possible without insurance, and therefore sell at a higher price.

Visit Web sites of these municipal bond insurers:
www.mbia.com
www.ambac.com

Municipal bond insurance companies manage default risk in three ways. First, they insure bond issues only from municipalities that have a good credit rating on their own. Second, municipal bond insurers diversify default risk by writing insurance policies for municipalities spread across a wide geographic area. Third, and perhaps most important, to compete in the municipal bond insurance business, insurers must maintain substantial investment portfolios as a source of financial reserves. Without sizable reserves, a company's insurance policies are not credible and municipalities will avoid purchasing insurance from them. The ability of municipal bond insurance companies to maintain triple-A credit ratings for the municipal bonds they insure was severely tested during the 2005 hurricane season (see *The Wall Street Journal* article in the nearby *Investment Updates* box).

19.7 Equivalent Taxable Yield

Consider an individual investor who must decide whether to invest in a corporate bond paying annual coupon interest of 8 percent or a municipal bond paying annual coupon interest of 5 percent. Both bonds are new issues with a triple-A credit rating, both bonds sell at par value, and the investor plans to hold the bonds until they mature. Since both bonds are purchased at par value, their coupon rates are equal to their originally stated yields to maturity. For the municipal bond this is a tax-exempt yield, and for the corporate bond this is a taxable yield.

Clearly, if the investment was for a tax-exempt retirement account, corporate debt is preferred since the coupon interest is higher and tax effects are not a consideration. But if the investment is not tax-exempt, the decision should be made on an aftertax basis. Essentially, the investor must decide which investment provides the highest return after accounting for income tax on corporate debt interest. This is done by comparing the tax-exempt yield of 5 percent on municipal bonds with an equivalent taxable yield. An equivalent taxable yield depends on the investor's marginal tax rate and is computed as follows:

$$\text{Equivalent taxable yield} = \frac{\text{Tax-exempt yield}}{1 - \text{Marginal tax rate}}$$

For example, suppose the investor is in a 35 percent marginal tax bracket. Then a tax-exempt yield of 5 percent is shown to correspond to an equivalent taxable yield of 7.69 percent as follows:

$$\text{Equivalent taxable yield} = \frac{5\%}{1 - .35} = 7.69\%$$

In this case, the investor would prefer the taxable yield of 8 percent on the corporate bond to the equivalent taxable yield of 7.69 percent on the municipal bond.

Alternatively, the investor could compare the aftertax yield on the corporate bond with the tax-exempt yield on the municipal bond. An aftertax yield is computed as follows:

$$\text{Aftertax yield} = \text{Taxable yield} \times (1 - \text{Marginal tax rate})$$

To change the example, suppose that the investor is in a 40 percent marginal tax bracket. This results in an aftertax yield of 4.8 percent, as shown below.

$$\text{Aftertax yield} = 8\% \times (1 - .40) = 4.8\%$$

In this case, the tax-exempt yield of 5 percent on the municipal bond is preferred to the aftertax yield of 4.8 percent on the corporate bond.

Another approach is to compute the critical marginal tax rate that would leave an investor indifferent between a given tax-exempt yield on a municipal bond and a given taxable yield on a corporate bond. A critical marginal tax rate is found as follows:

$$\text{Critical marginal tax rate} = 1 - \frac{\text{Tax-exempt yield}}{\text{Taxable yield}}$$

For the example considered here, the critical marginal tax rate is 37.5 percent, determined as follows:

$$\text{Critical marginal tax rate} = 1 - \frac{5\%}{8\%} = 37.5\%$$

Investors with a marginal tax rate higher than the critical marginal rate would prefer the municipal bond, whereas investors in a lower tax bracket would prefer the corporate bond.

CHECK THIS

19.7a An investor with a marginal tax rate of 30 percent is interested in a tax-exempt bond with a yield of 6 percent. What is the equivalent taxable yield of this bond?

19.7b A taxable bond has a yield of 10 percent, and a tax-exempt bond has a yield of 7 percent. What is the critical marginal tax rate for these two bonds?

19.8 Taxable Municipal Bonds

private activity bonds
Taxable municipal bonds used to finance facilities used by private businesses.

The Tax Reform Act of 1986 imposed notable restrictions on the types of municipal bonds that qualify for federal tax exemption of interest payments. In particular, the 1986 act expanded the definition of **private activity bonds**. Private activity bonds include any municipal security where 10 percent or more of the issue finances facilities used by private entities and is secured by payments from private entities.

Interest on private activity bonds is tax-exempt only if the bond issue falls into a so-called qualified category. Qualified private activity bonds that still enjoy a tax-exempt interest privilege include public airport bonds, multifamily housing bonds, nonvehicular mass commuting bonds, and various other project bonds. The major types of private activity bonds that do not qualify for tax-exempt interest are those used to finance sports stadiums, convention facilities, parking facilities, and industrial parks. However, these taxable private activity bonds may still enjoy exemption from state and local income tax. In any case, as a result of the 1986 act and the continuing need to finance private activity projects, new issues of taxable municipal revenue bonds are frequently sold with yields similar to corporate bond yields.

19.9 Summary and Conclusions

The topic of this chapter is government bonds. The government bonds covered in this chapter include U.S. Treasury bonds, notes, and bills, as well as state, city, county, and local municipal bonds. In this chapter, we cover many aspects of these investments—which we summarize by the chapter's important concepts.

1. **The basics of U.S. Treasury securities and how they are sold.**

   A. The U.S. federal government is the largest single borrower in the world, with about $13 trillion of publicly held debt. Responsibility for managing this debt belongs to the U.S. Treasury, which issues Treasury bills, notes, and bonds at regular auctions to finance government debt.

   B. Treasury bills are short-term obligations that are sold on a discount basis. Treasury notes are medium-term obligations that pay fixed semiannual coupons as well as payment of face value at maturity. Treasury bonds are long-term obligations that pay their face value at maturity and pay fixed semiannual coupons.

2. **The workings of the STRIPS program and pricing Treasury bonds.**

   A. The U.S. Treasury sponsors the STRIPS program, where Treasury bonds and notes are broken down into principal strips, which represent face-value payments, and coupon strips, which represent individual coupon payments. Because each strip created under the STRIPS program represents a single future payment, strips effectively become zero coupon bonds.

   B. Treasury bond and note price quotes are stated on a percentage of par basis: a price of 102 equals par value plus 2 percent. Fractions of a percent are stated in thirty-seconds. Thus, a price stated as 102:28 is actually equal to 102 + 28/32, or 102.875. Because Treasury bonds and notes pay semiannual coupons, bond yields are stated on a semiannual basis.

   C. The U.S. Treasury also issues securities that guarantee a fixed rate of return in excess of realized inflation rates. These inflation-indexed Treasury securities are commonly called TIPS. TIPS pay a fixed coupon rate on their current principal and adjust their principal semiannually according to the most recent inflation rate.

3. **How federal agencies borrow money.**

   A. Several federal agencies are authorized to issue securities directly to the public. Bonds issued by U.S. government agencies have a credit quality almost identical to U.S. Treasury issues, but agency notes and bonds are attractive to many investors because they offer higher yields than comparable U.S. Treasury securities. However, the market for agency debt is less active than the market for U.S. Treasury debt and investors are potentially subject to state income taxes on agency debt interest, while U.S. Treasury debt interest is not subject to state taxes.

   B. Another large market for government debt is the market for municipal government debt. Total municipal debt outstanding currently exceeds $2 trillion, divided among most of the more than 85,000 state and local governments in the United States. Individual investors hold about half this debt, while the remainder is roughly split equally between holdings of property and casualty insurance companies and commercial banks.

4. **How municipalities borrow money.**

   A. Municipal notes and bonds are intermediate- to long-term interest-bearing obligations of state and local governments or agencies of those governments. Municipal debt is commonly called the tax-exempt market because the coupon interest is usually exempt from federal income tax, which makes municipal bonds attractive to investors in the highest income tax brackets. However, yields on municipal debt are less than yields on corporate debt with similar features and credit quality, thus eliminating much of the advantage of the tax exemption.

B. Most municipal bonds pay a constant coupon rate, but some municipal notes pay variable coupon rates that change according to prevailing market interest rates. Also, a call provision is a standard feature of most municipal bond issues. A call provision allows an issuer to retire outstanding bonds before they mature.

C. There are two basic types of municipal bonds: revenue bonds and general obligation bonds. Revenue bonds, which constitute the bulk of all outstanding municipal bonds, are secured by proceeds collected from the projects they finance. General obligation bonds, which are issued by all levels of municipal governments, are secured by the general taxing powers of the municipalities issuing the bonds.

D. As part of the process for issuing municipal bonds to the public, a rating agency is paid a fee to assign a credit rating to a new bond issue. In the last two decades, municipalities have increasingly been obtaining bond insurance for new bond issues through an insurance policy written by a commercial insurance company. With bond insurance, the credit quality of the bond issue is determined by the financial strength of the insurance company, not the municipality alone.

GET REAL

This chapter covered government bonds, a large and important securities market. How should you put your knowledge to work? Begin by purchasing (in a simulated brokerage account like Stock-Trak) the various types of government securities that are available for trading out there. Observe how their prices and yields change over time.

You should also learn more about buying Treasury securities. A great place to start is www.treasurydirect.gov. There you can examine and download the forms needed to bid in the regular auctions. You can also obtain current Treasury auction information, including forthcoming auctions and the results of previous auctions. You can also read about the *Treasury Direct* program, which is probably the best way of purchasing Treasury issues for individual investors. But if you prefer U.S. Savings Bonds, you can check out the section of the Web site that tells you all you need to know about them.

You will probably find that you cannot trade municipal bonds through a simulated brokerage account. The reason is that the market for municipals is so thin that getting timely price information for a particular issue isn't possible. In practice, municipal bonds are best suited for buy-and-hold investors who buy the bonds when originally issued and hold them until maturity. You can now buy municipal bonds online through a number of brokers. Try, for example, FMS Bonds (www.fmsbonds.com) or Lebenthal Investments (www.lebenthal.com).

Key Terms

bid-ask spread 655
call provision 664
default risk 662
discount basis 651
face value 651
general obligation bonds (GOs) 662
hybrid bonds 666
imputed interest 651
insured municipal bonds 669

private activity bonds 670
put bonds 665
revenue bonds 666
serial bonds 665
stop-out bid 658
STRIPS 652
term bonds 665
variable-rate notes 666
zero coupon bond 652

Chapter Review Problems and Self-Test

1. **Treasury Yields (CFA3)** A Treasury bond's price is 140:25. It has a coupon rate of 10 percent, makes semiannual payments, and matures in 16 years. What yield would be reported in the financial press?

2. **Equivalent Yields (CFA3)** A particular investor faces a 40 percent tax rate. If a AA-rated municipal bond yields 4 percent, what must a similar taxable issue yield for the investor to be impartial to them?

Answers to Self-Test Problems

1. We have a bond with a price of 140.78125 (after converting from thirty-seconds), a coupon of 10 percent paid semiannually, and a maturity of 16 years (or 32 periods). Verify, using the standard bond formula from an earlier chapter, that the semiannual yield is 3 percent, so the reported yield would be 6 percent.

2. The equivalent taxable yield is the municipal yield "grossed up" by one minus the tax rate:

$$\frac{4\%}{1 - .40} = 6.67\%$$

Test Your Investment Quotient

1. **Zero Coupon Bonds (LO2)** What is the yield to maturity (YTM) on a zero coupon bond?
   a. The interest rate realized if the bond is held to maturity.
   b. The interest rate realized when the bond is sold.
   c. The coupon yield for an equivalent coupon bond.
   d. A fixed rate when the bond is issued.

2. **Treasury Notes (LO1, CFA3)** The coupon rate for a Treasury note is set
   a. The same for all Treasury note issues.
   b. By a formula based on the size of the Treasury note issue.
   c. According to prevailing interest rates at time of issuance.
   d. According to the supply and demand for money.

3. **Treasury Notes and Bonds (LO1, CFA3)** U.S. Treasury notes and bonds have face value denominations as small as
   a. $1,000
   b. $5,000
   c. $10,000
   d. $25,000

4. **Treasury Bonds (LO1, CFA3)** What is the dollar value of a U.S. Treasury bond quoted at 92:24?
   a. $922.75
   b. $922.40
   c. $927.50
   d. Indeterminable

5. **Treasury Bonds (LO1, CFA3)** The following are quotes for a U.S. Treasury bond:

Bid	Ask
102:02	102:05

   If the face value of the bond is $1,000, the price an investor should pay for the bond is *closest* to
   a. $1,020.63
   b. $1,021.56
   c. $1,025.00
   d. $1,026.25

6. **Treasury Bonds (LO1, CFA3)** A trader purchases $5 million face value of Treasury bonds at 95:16 and then later sells the bonds at 95:24. What is the round-trip gain on these transactions?

   a. $1,250
   b. $12,500
   c. $4,000
   d. $40,000

7. **Treasury STRIPS (LO2, CFA3)** When originally issued, a 10-year maturity Treasury note can be stripped into how many separate components?

   a. 10
   b. 11
   c. 20
   d. 21

8. **Treasury Bills (LO1)** Treasury bills are sold on a discount basis, meaning that the difference between their issue price and their redemption value is

   a. The same for all T-bill issues.
   b. The imputed interest on the T-bill.
   c. Never less than the issue price.
   d. The bond equivalent yield for the T-bill.

9. **Treasury Auctions (LO1, CFA3)** Which of the following statements about single-price Treasury auctions is true?

   a. Competitive bidders pay their bid prices.
   b. Noncompetitive bidders pay the stop-out bid plus a 10% premium.
   c. Noncompetitive bidders pay the stop-out bid.
   d. All of the above are true.

10. **Treasury Dealers (LO1, CFA3)** When trading U.S. Treasury securities, Treasury dealers

    a. Buy at the bid price and sell at the ask price.
    b. Sell at the bid price and buy at the ask price.
    c. Buy at the stop-out bid price and sell at the market price.
    d. Sell at the stop-out bid price and buy at the market price.

11. **Savings Bonds (LO1, CFA3)** A Series EE Savings Bond with a face value of $1,000 is originally sold for

    a. $1,000.
    b. $500.
    c. A price based on the recent inflation rate.
    d. 90 percent of the price of a recently issued five-year T-note.

12. **Savings Bonds (LO1, CFA3)** Series EE savings bonds are guaranteed to double in price if they are held for

    a. 10 years
    b. 5 years
    c. 15 years
    d. 20 years

13. **Savings Bonds (LO1, CFA3)** A Series I savings bond with a face value of $1,000 is originally sold at a price of

    a. $1,000.
    b. $500.
    c. A price based on the recent inflation rate.
    d. 90 percent of the price of a recently issued five-year T-note.

14. **Savings Bonds (LO1, CFA3)** The interest rate on Series I savings bonds is reset every six months as

    a. 90 percent of the rate on newly issued five-year T-notes.
    b. 90 percent of the rate on newly issued five-year T-notes plus the recent inflation rate.
    c. A fixed rate plus the recent inflation rate.
    d. An adjustable rate plus the recent inflation rate.

15. **Agency Bonds (LO3, CFA3)**   Which statement applies to a bond issued by an agency of the U.S. government?

    a. It is exempt from the federal income tax on interest.
    b. It becomes a direct obligation of the U.S. Treasury in case of default.
    c. It is secured by assets held by the agency.
    d. None of the above.

16. **Agency Bonds (LO3, CFA3)**   Which is true for bonds issued by all agencies of the U.S. government?

    a. They become direct obligations of the U.S. Treasury.
    b. They are secured bonds backed by government holdings.
    c. They are exempt from federal income tax.
    d. None of the above.

17. **Agency Bonds (LO3, CFA3)**   Which of the following investors is most likely to invest in agency bonds?

    a. High-income individual with a need for liquidity.
    b. High-income individual living in a triple income tax municipality.
    c. Commercial bank.
    d. Life insurance company.

18. **Municipal Bonds (LO4, CFA3)**   Which of the following constitutes the bulk of all outstanding municipal bonds?

    a. Revenue bonds
    b. General obligation bonds
    c. Moral obligation bonds
    d. Private activity bonds

19. **Municipal Bonds (LO4, CFA3)**   Which of the following investors is most likely to invest in locally issued municipal bonds?

    a. High-income individual with a need for liquidity.
    b. High-income individual living in a triple income tax municipality.
    c. Commercial bank.
    d. Life insurance company.

20. **Revenue Bonds (LO4, CFA3)**   A revenue bond is distinguished from a general obligation bond in that revenue bonds have which of the following characteristics?

    a. They are issued by counties, special districts, cities, towns, and state-controlled authorities, whereas general obligation bonds are issued only by the states themselves.
    b. They are typically secured by limited taxing power, whereas general obligation bonds are secured by unlimited taxing power.
    c. They are issued to finance specific projects and are secured by the revenues of the project being financed.
    d. They have first claim to any revenue increase of the issuing tax authority.

21. **Insured Municipal Bonds (LO4, CFA3)**   Which of the following is not a method used by municipal bond insurers to manage default risk?

    a. Only insure bonds from municipalities with a good credit rating.
    b. Diversify default risk by writing insurance policies for municipalities spread across a wide geographic area.
    c. Maintain substantial investment portfolios as a source of financial reserves.
    d. All of the above are used to manage default risk.

22. **Insured Municipal Bonds (LO4, CFA3)**   Which one of the following generally is not true of an insured municipal bond?

    a. The price on an insured bond is higher than that on an otherwise identical uninsured bond.
    b. The insurance can be canceled in the event the issuer fails to maintain predetermined quality standards.
    c. The insurance premium is a one-time payment made at the time of issuance.
    d. The insurance company is obligated to make all defaulted principal and/or interest payments in a prompt and timely fashion.

23. **Taxable Equivalent Yield (LO4, CFA3)**   A municipal bond carries a coupon of 6 3/4 percent and is trading at par. To a taxpayer in the 34 percent tax bracket, what would the taxable equivalent yield of this bond be?

   a. 4.5 percent
   b. 10.2 percent
   c. 13.4 percent
   d. 19.9 percent

24. **Taxable Equivalent Yield (LO4, CFA3)**   A 20-year municipal bond is currently priced at par to yield 5.53 percent. For a taxpayer in the 33 percent tax bracket, what equivalent taxable yield would this bond offer?

   a. 8.25 percent
   b. 10.75 percent
   c. 11.40 percent
   d. None of the above

25. **Taxable Equivalent Yield (LO4, CFA3)**   The coupon rate on a tax-exempt bond is 5.6 percent, and the coupon rate on a taxable bond is 8 percent. Both bonds sell at par. At what tax bracket (marginal tax rate) would an investor show no preference between the two bonds?

   a. 30.0 percent
   b. 39.6 percent
   c. 41.7 percent
   d. 42.9 percent

Concept Questions

1. **Bills versus Bonds (LO1, CFA3)**   What are the key differences between T-bills and T-bonds?

2. **Notes versus Bonds (LO1, CFA3)**   What are the key differences between T-notes and T-bonds?

3. **Zeroes (LO1, CFA3)**   What two Treasury securities are zeroes?

4. **Spreads (LO1, CFA3)**   What are typical spreads for T-notes and T-bonds? Why do you think they differ from issue to issue?

5. **Agencies versus Treasuries (LO3, CFA3)**   From an investor's standpoint, what are the key differences between Treasury and agency issues?

6. **Municipals versus Treasuries (LO4, CFA3)**   From an investor's standpoint, what are the main differences between Treasury and municipal issues?

7. **Serial Bonds (LO4, CFA3)**   What are serial bonds? What purpose does this structure serve?

8. **VRNs (LO4, CFA3)**   In the context of the muni market, what are variable-rate notes? What is likely true about their risks compared to those of ordinary issues?

9. **Revenues versus General Obligation Munis (LO4, CFA3)**   What is the difference between a revenue bond and a general obligation bond?

10. **Private Activity Munis (LO4, CFA3)**   What is a private activity muni? What type of investor would be interested in it?

11. **Treasury versus Municipal Bonds (LO4, CFA3)**   Treasury and municipal yields are often compared to calculate critical tax rates. What concerns might you have about such a comparison? What do you think is true about the calculated tax rate?

12. **Callable Treasury Bonds (LO1, CFA3)**   For a callable Treasury bond selling above par, is it necessarily true that the yield to call will be less than the yield to maturity? Why or why not?

13. **Callable Agency Issues (LO3, CFA3)**   For a callable agency bond selling above par, is it necessarily true that the yield to call will be less than the yield to maturity? Why or why not?

14. **Treasury versus Municipal Bonds (LO4, CFA3)**   Why might the yield to maturity on, say, a BBB-rated municipal bond with moderate default risk actually be less than that of a U.S. Treasury bond with no default risk?

15. **Treasury versus Municipal Bonds (LO4, CFA3)**   In a recent issue of *The Wall Street Journal*, compare the yields on U.S. Treasury bonds with the yields on municipal bonds. Why might these yield spreads depend on the state of the economy?

Questions and Problems

1. **STRIPS Price (LO2, CFA3)** What is the price of a STRIPS with a maturity of 14 years, a face value of $10,000, and a yield to maturity of 5.2 percent?

2. **STRIPS YTM (LO2, CFA3)** A STRIPS with 9 years until maturity and a face value of $10,000 is trading for $7,241. What is the yield to maturity?

3. **Treasury Auctions (LO1, CFA3)** The Federal Reserve announces an offering of Treasury bills with a face value of $60 billion. Noncompetitive bids are made for $11 billion, along with the following competitive bids:

Bidder	Price Bid	Quantity Bid
A	$9,400	$15 billion
B	9,405	14 billion
C	9,410	11 billion
D	9,415	8 billion
E	9,425	10 billion
F	9,430	9 billion

   In a single-price auction, which bids are accepted and what prices are paid by each bidder? How much money is raised by the entire offering?

4. **Municipal Bonds (LO4, CFA3)** A municipal bond with a coupon rate of 2.7 percent has a yield to maturity of 3.9 percent. If the bond has 10 years to maturity, what is the price of the bond?

5. **Yield to Maturity (LO4, CFA1)** A municipal bond with a coupon rate of 4.1 percent sells for $4,920 and has seven years until maturity. What is the yield to maturity of the bond?

6. **Yield to Maturity (LO4, CFA1)** A municipal bond has 18 years until maturity and sells for $5,640. If the coupon rate on the bond is 5.70 percent, what is the yield to maturity?

7. **Yield to Call (LO4, CFA2)** Assume the bond in the previous problem can be called in 10 years. What is the yield to call if the call price is 110 percent of par?

8. **Aftertax Yield (LO4, CFA3)** A municipal bond has a yield to maturity of 3.8 percent. What corporate bond yield would make an investor in the 29 percent tax bracket indifferent between the two bonds, all else the same?

9. **Tax Equivalent Yields (LO4, CFA 3)** A taxable corporate issue yields 6.5 percent. For an investor in a 35 percent tax bracket, what is the equivalent aftertax yield?

10. **Tax Rates (LO4, CFA3)** A taxable issue yields 6.4 percent, and a similar municipal issue yields 4.7 percent. What is the critical marginal tax rate?

11. **Treasury Prices (LO1, CFA3)** A Treasury bill has a bid yield of 2.75 and an ask yield of 2.73. The bill matures in 140 days. What is the least you could pay to acquire a bill? (*Note:* You may need to review material from an earlier chapter for the relevant formula.)

12. **Treasury Prices (LO1, CFA3)** At what price could you sell the Treasury bill referred to in the previous question? What is the dollar spread for this bill? (*Note:* You may need to review material from an earlier chapter for the relevant formula.)

13. **Treasury Prices (LO1, CFA3)** A Treasury issue is quoted at 102:09 bid and 102:12 ask. What is the least you could pay to acquire a bond?

14. **Treasury Prices (LO1, CFA3)** A noncallable Treasury bond has a quoted yield of 4.28 percent. It has a 5.25 percent coupon and 11 years to maturity. What is its dollar price assuming a $1,000 par value? What is its quoted price?

15. **Treasury Yields (LO1, CFA3)** A Treasury bond with the longest maturity (30 years) has an ask price quoted at 99:14. The coupon rate is 4.6 percent, paid semiannually. What is the yield to maturity of this bond?

16. **STRIPS Price (LO2, CFA3)** A STRIPS traded on May 1, 2010, matures in 18 years on May 1, 2028. Assuming a 4.1 percent yield to maturity, what is the STRIPS price?

17. **STRIPS YTM (LO2, CFA3)** A STRIPS traded on November 1, 2010, matures in 12 years on November 1, 2022. The quoted STRIPS price is 52.75. What is its yield to maturity?

[CFA3, CFA4]

Fixed Income Asset Management, Inc. (FIAM), has traditionally managed fixed-income portfolios for pension and endowment funds employing immunization and cash-matching strategies. Recently, FIAM accepted the responsibility for managing funds for which indexed and enhanced indexed strategies are appropriate. Ms. Debra Truxell, CFA, is a senior manager at FIAM and has been asked to lead the company in this new direction. She begins by conducting a series of in-house seminars.

Cara Moore, an expert in bond indexing, presented the first seminar. She opened the session with a discussion of the risk characteristics that distinguish bond management styles. She stated the key risk factor that distinguishes indexing from active management is that indexing takes no position on duration but may differ in terms of sector, yield expectations, and quality differences. The differences depend upon how far the portfolio falls along the indexing versus active management continuum.

Ms. Moore's associate, James Higgins, noted that "lower costs, diversification, and stable performance are all advantages of indexing a portfolio to a large, well-diversified bond index." He also said, "Simple replication of a bond index such as the Lehman Aggregate Bond Index is known as pure bond indexing. I recommend pure bond indexing for most passively managed portfolios because it is the most efficient means of reducing tracking error and is the easiest indexing strategy to implement in most circumstances." Ms. Truxell supported his statement by saying, "The greatest cost benefit of indexing lies in pure bond indexing."

1. Regarding bond indexing:

   a. Ms. Moore is correct regarding the primary factor that distinguishes indexing from active management; Ms. Truxell is incorrect regarding the cost savings from pure bond indexing.

   b. Ms. Moore is correct regarding the primary factor that distinguishes indexing from active management; Ms. Truxell is correct regarding the cost savings from pure bond indexing.

   c. Ms. Moore is incorrect regarding the primary factor that distinguishes indexing from active management; Ms. Truxell is incorrect regarding the cost savings from pure bond indexing.

2. The statement made by Mr. Higgins about bond indexing is:

   a. Correct with respect to the advantages of indexing but incorrect in his conclusions regarding pure bond indexing.

   b. Correct both with respect to the advantages of indexing and in his conclusions regarding pure bond indexing.

   c. Incorrect both with respect to the advantages of indexing and in his conclusions regarding pure bond indexing.

3. Frederick Jackson, a recent college graduate and CFA candidate, asked Ms. Truxell if she felt that return enhancements could be realized through sector exposure. Truxell accurately replied, "Yes, it is possible to increase the yield of the portfolio without a proportionate increase in risk by:

   a. Overweighting one- to five-year Treasuries and underweighting one- to five-year corporates."

   b. Underweighting long-term Treasuries and overweighting long-term corporates."

   c. Underweighting one- to five-year Treasuries and overweighting one- to five-year corporates."

What's on the Web?

1. **Treasury Auctions** Go to www.treasurydirect.gov and find the next Treasury auctions scheduled. When are the auctions scheduled? What instruments will be offered at these auctions?

2. **Treasury Auctions** Go to www.treasurydirect.gov and find the recently completed Treasury auctions for bills and notes. When did the auctions occur? What were the yields for each bill and note sold at these auctions?

3. **Municipal Bond Spreads** Go to www.municipalbonds.com. What was the highest bid-side spread for the most recent quarter? What was the highest offer-side spread over this same period? What were the dollar amounts of these spreads?

4. **Municipal Bond Prices**   Go to www.municipalbonds.com and find the municipal bonds traded yesterday for your state. What was the most active bond in terms of the number of trades? Which bond traded the highest dollar amount? How many bonds had a spread of more than one point in trading yesterday?

5. **Savings Bonds**   In this chapter, we discussed U.S. Series EE and Series I savings bonds. There are also Series HH savings bonds, which the Treasury stopped issuing in 2004. These three bonds are different in several respects. Go to www.treasurydirect.gov and find out how the Series HH bonds work. What are the differences in these three types of savings bonds?

Stock-Trak Exercises

To access the Stock-Trak Exercise for this chapter, please visit the book Web site at www.mhhe.com/jmd6e and choose the corresponding chapter.

Appendix A

Answers to Test Your Investment Quotient Questions

Chapter 1

1-1	b
1-2	b
1-3	c
1-4	b
1-5	b
1-6	c
1-7	d
1-8	a
1-9	a
1-10	d
1-11	d
1-12	d
1-13	d
1-14	a
1-15	b

Chapter 2

2-1	a
2-2	c
2-3	c
2-4	c
2-5	b
2-6	b
2-7	b
2-8	a
2-9	c
2-10	b
2-11	a
2-12	a
2-13	c
2-14	c
2-15	d

Chapter 3

3-1	d
3-2	a
3-3	c
3-4	a
3-5	c
3-6	b
3-7	c
3-8	c
3-9	c
3-10	c

Chapter 4

4-1	c
4-2	b
4-3	d
4-4	d
4-5	d
4-6	d
4-7	b
4-8	a
4-9	a
4-10	a
4-11	b
4-12	d
4-13	a
4-14	a
4-15	d

Chapter 5

5-1	b
5-2	a
5-3	b
5-4	c
5-5	a
5-6	b
5-7	c
5-8	a
5-9	a
5-10	b
5-11	c
5-12	b
5-13	a
5-14	c
5-15	c

Chapter 6

6-1	c
6-2	a
6-3	a
6-4	b
6-5	b
6-6	c
6-7	d
6-8	c
6-9	c
6-10	a

6-11	a
6-12	d
6-13	d
6-14	c
6-15	c
6-16	c
6-17	c
6-18	a
6-19	a
6-20	b

Chapter 7

7-1	d
7-2	c
7-3	d
7-4	d
7-5	c
7-6	a
7-7	a
7-8	d
7-9	c
7-10	d
7-11	c
7-12	d
7-13	b
7-14	d
7-15	d

Chapter 8

8-1	d
8-2	c
8-3	d
8-4	b
8-5	a
8-6	b
8-7	c
8-8	b
8-9	a
8-10	d
8-11	c
8-12	b
8-13	c
8-14	b
8-15	d

Chapter 9

9-1	b
9-2	a
9-3	a
9-4	d
9-5	d
9-6	b
9-7	a
9-8	c
9-9	c
9-10	b
9-11	a
9-12	a
9-13	d
9-14	a
9-15	b
9-16	a
9-17	b
9-18	c
9-19	d
9-20	d

Chapter 10

10-1	b
10-2	c
10-3	d
10-4	a
10-5	a
10-6	b
10-7	a
10-8	a
10-9	b
10-10	c
10-11	a
10-12	a
10-13	c
10-14	c
10-15	c
10-16	a
10-17	a
10-18	b
10-19	a
10-20	d
10-21	b
10-22	a
10-23	c
10-24	c
10-25	c

Chapter 11

11-1	d
11-2	c
11-3	c
11-4	b
11-5	c
11-6	a
11-7	a
11-8	b
11-9	b
11-10	a
11-11	d
11-12	b
11-13	d
11-14	c
11-15	a

Chapter 12

12-1	d
12-2	a
12-3	a
12-4	d
12-5	b
12-6	b
12-7	b
12-8	c
12-9	d
12-10	d
12-11	d
12-12	a
12-13	b
12-14	a
12-15	b

Chapter 13

13-1   b
13-2   a
13-3   b
13-4   c
13-5   a
13-6   b
13-7   b
13-8   d
13-9   c
13-10   c
13-11   d
13-12   a
13-13   d
13-14   b
13-15   c

Chapter 14

14-1   a
14-2   d
14-3   a
14-4   d
14-5   d
14-6   c
14-7   d
14-8   a
14-9   d
14-10   b
14-11   b
14-12   d
14-13   c
14-14   a
14-15   d

Chapter 15

15-1   a
15-2   c
15-3   c
15-4   b
15-5   d
15-6   a
15-7   a
15-8   c
15-9   a
15-10   b
15-11   a
15-12   b
15-13   d
15-14   a
15-15   d

Chapter 16

16-1   a
16-2   d
16-3   c
16-4   a
16-5   a
16-6   b
16-7   a
16-8   c
16-9   a
16-10   b
16-11   b

16-12   d
16-13   a
16-14   c
16-15   d

Chapter 17

17-1   b
17-2   b
17-3   d
17-4   c
17-5   a
17-6   a
17-7   b
17-8   d
17-9   c
17-10   a
17-11   b
17-12   c
17-13   c
17-14   b
17-15   c
17-16   b
17-17   a
17-18   b
17-19   c
17-20   d

Chapter 18

18-1   d
18-2   c
18-3   a
18-4   c
18-5   a
18-6   b
18-7   a
18-8   b
18-9   a
18-10   d
18-11   a
18-12   c
18-13   b
18-14   b
18-15   b
18-16   c
18-17   d
18-18   d
18-19   b
18-20   a

Chapter 19

19-1   a
19-2   c
19-3   a
19-4   c
19-5   b
19-6   b
19-7   d
19-8   b
19-9   c
19-10   a
19-11   b
19-12   d
19-13   a
19-14   c

19-15	d		20-4	c
19-16	d		20-5	a
19-17	d		20-6	c
19-18	a		20-7	b
19-19	b		20-8	c
19-20	c		20-9	b
19-21	d		20-10	a
19-22	b		20-11	a
19-23	b		20-12	c
19-24	a		20-13	a
19-25	a		20-14	b
			20-15	d

Chapter 20 (Web site only)

20-1	d
20-2	a
20-3	c

Appendix B

Answers to Selected Questions and Problems.

Chapter 1

1-1 $428
1-5 Cherry average return = 8.60%
Straw average return = 10.20%
1-9 Arithmetic average = 8.17%
Geometric average = 7.30%
1-15 12.56%
1-17 Small company stocks = 11.93%
Large company stocks = 9.70%
Long-term government bonds = 5.28%
Treasury bills = 3.77%
Inflation = 3.01%

Chapter 2

2-1 3,039.22 shares
2-5 $40,000
2-9 Critical stock price = $41.33
Account equity = $14,470
2-13 $45.71
2-17 $2,057.66
2-21 20.47%
2-25 Effective annual return = 15.19%

Chapter 3

3-1 Closing price = $57.69
Round lots = 186,491
3-5 Next payment = $108,000
Payment at maturity = $3,108,000
3-9 Current yield = 7.347%
3-13 −$7,593.75
3-20 104.08%

Chapter 4

4-1 $20.73
4-5 $52.29
4-9 $21.81; −11.74%
4-13 −1.25%
4-17 8.19%; 5.59%
4-21 $42,800

Chapter 5

5-1 2.03106
5-5 10.75%
5-9 4.15528
5-13 0.13266118

Chapter 6

6-1 $34.93
6-4 12.1%
6-9 $1.98; $2.13
6-13 $30.24
6-17 $5.95
6-22 $42.44
6-25 23.20 times
6-29 −$26.05

Chapter 7

None

Chapter 8

8-2 .967, .760, 1.343, .730, 1.029
8-6 .5207, .5620, .6116, .5868, .6446
8-15 1.149, 1.1234, 1.1069, 1.0965

Chapter 9

9-1 70.68%
9-5 6.8%
9-9 $988,115.56
9-13 BEY = 5.802%
Discount yield = 5.642%
9-17 5-year STRIP = 75.550
$f_{1,5} = 5.768\%$
2-year STRIP = 90.516
$f_{2,3} = 5.109\%$
9-21 $f_{1,1} = 5.50\%$
$f_{1,2} = 6.26\%$
$f_{1,3} = 7.11\%$

Chapter 10

10-1 $848.55
10-5 7.23%
10-9 5.56%
10-13 8.28%
10-19 9.07 years
10-21 YTM = 4.97%
Realized yield = −1.34%
10-25 $0.445
10-29 Macaulay duration = 10.498
Modified duration = 10.143

Chapter 11

11-1 9.70%
11-5 Roll = 18.62%
 Ross = 6.37%
11-9 *a.* 2.73%
 b. 0.02800; 16.73%
11-17 Standard deviation = 23.71%
 Expected return = 14.10%
11-20 Standard deviation = 32.34%
 Expected return = 13.30%

Chapter 12

12-1 1.29
12-5 1.175
12-9 $38.86
12-13 1.22%
12-17 1.53

Chapter 13

13-1 22.05%
13-4 0.0439
13-9 −13.59%
13-16 −11.64%
13-19 Sharpe = .2034
 Treynor = .0350

Chapter 14

14-1 *a.* $51,918.75
 b. $863,772
 c. $750
 d. $36,000
14-5 $50,210,212.50
14-9 $49.87
14-13 Day 1: $120,195
 Day 2: $102,555
 Day 3: $111,375
 Day 4: $111,375
 Profit = −$38,430
14-17 611.70
14-21 5,587.03

Chapter 15

15-1 $800
15-5 $28,500; $8,000

15-9 $80.70
15-13 $12.16
15-16 $400

Chapter 16

16-1 $11.11
16-5 $5.62
16-9 Write 4,209 contracts
16-13 $1.54
16-17 $4.76
16-20 $5.92

Chapter 17

17-1 $46,720
17-5 P/B = 5.27 times
 P/E = 15.63 times
 P/CF = 12.01 times
17-9 $413,500
17-13 ROA = 13.15%
 ROE = 30.99%
17-17 Maximum sales growth = 33.33%

Chapter 18

18-1 $20.00
18-5 $646
18-8 $150.94
18-12 Conversion value = $800
 Conversion price = $42.00

Chapter 19

19-1 $4,873.87
19-5 4.37%
19-9 4.23%
19-13 $1,023.75

Chapter 20 (Web site only)

20-1 $1,671.79
20-5 0.6029%
20-9 $93,710.71
20-13 $145.09
20-17 50 PSA: 0.1682%
 200 PSA: 0.6924%
 400 PSA: 1.4424%

Appendix C

Key Equations

Chapter 1

1. Dividend yield = D_{t+1}/P_t (1.1)
2. Capital gains yield = $(P_{t+1} - P_t)/P_t$ (1.2)
3. Total return = $(D_{t+1} + P_{t+1} - P_t)/P_t$ (1.3)
4. $1 + EAR = (1 + \text{Holding period percentage return})^m$ (1.4)
5. $\text{Var}(R) = [(R_1 - \bar{R})^2 + (R_2 - \bar{R})^2 + \cdots + (R_N - \bar{R})^2]/(N - 1)$
6. Geometric average return $= [(1 + R_1) \times (1 + R_2) \times \cdots \times (1 + R_N)]^{1/N} - 1$ (1.5)
7. Blume's formula:
$$R(T) = \frac{T-1}{N-1} \times \text{Geometric average} + \frac{N-T}{N-1} \times \text{Arithmetic average}$$

Chapter 2

1. $\text{Margin} = \dfrac{\text{Account equity}}{\text{Value of stock}}$

Buying on margin:

2. Maintenance margin
$$= \frac{\text{Number of shares} \times P^* - \text{Amount borrowed}}{\text{Number of shares} \times P^*}$$

In equation 2:

3. $P^* = \dfrac{\text{Amount borrowed/Number of shares}}{1 - \text{Maintenance margin}}$ (2.1)

Short selling:

4. Maintenance margin
$$= \frac{\text{Initial margin deposit} + \text{Short proceeds} - \text{Number of shares} \times P^*}{\text{Number of shares} \times P^*}$$

In equation 4:

5. $P^* = \dfrac{(\text{Initial margin deposit} + \text{Short proceeds})/\text{Number of shares}}{1 + \text{Maintenance margin}}$

Chapter 3

1. $EAR = [1 + (APR/m)]^m - 1$

Chapter 4

1. $\text{Net asset value} = \dfrac{\text{Asset value}}{\text{Number of shares outstanding}}$

Chapter 5

1. $\text{Price-weighted index level} = \dfrac{\text{Sum of stock prices}}{\text{Divisor}}$

Chapter 6

1. $P_0 = \dfrac{D_1}{(1+k)} + \dfrac{D_2}{(1+k)^2} + \dfrac{D_3}{(1+k)^3} + \cdots + \dfrac{D_T}{(1+k)^T}$ (6.1)

2. $P_0 = \dfrac{D_0(1+g)}{k-g}$ $(g < k)$ (6.2)

3. $P_0 = \dfrac{D_1}{k-g}$ $(g < k)$ (6.3)

4. $g = \left[\dfrac{D_N}{D_0}\right]^{1/N} - 1$ (6.7)

5. Payout ratio $= D/EPS$

6. Sustainable growth rate = ROE $\times$ Retention ratio
= ROE $\times$ (1 − Payout ratio) (6.8)

7. Return on equity (ROE) = Net income/Equity (6.9)

8. $\text{ROE} = \dfrac{\text{Net income}}{\text{Sales}} \times \dfrac{\text{Sales}}{\text{Assets}} \times \dfrac{\text{Assets}}{\text{Equity}}$ (6.10)

9. The two-stage dividend growth model:
$$P_0 = \frac{D_0(1 + g_1)}{k - g_1} \times \left[1 - \left(\frac{1 + g_1}{1 + k}\right)^T\right] + \left(\frac{1 + g_1}{1 + k}\right)^T$$
$$\times \frac{D_0(1 + g_2)}{k - g_2}$$ (6.11)

10. Discount rate = U.S. T-bill rate + (Stock beta
$\times$ Stock market risk premium) (6.17)
In this equation:
U.S. T-bill rate = Return on 90-day U.S. T-bills
Stock beta = Risk relative to an average stock
Stock market risk premium = Risk premium for an
average stock

11. $P_0 = B_0 + \dfrac{EPS_1 - B_0 \times k}{(1+k)^1} + \dfrac{EPS_2 - B_1 \times k}{(1+k)^2}$
$+ \dfrac{EPS_3 - B_2 \times k}{(1+k)^3} + \cdots$ (6.18)

12. $P_0 = B_0 + \dfrac{EPS_0(1+g) - B_0 \times k}{k - g}$ (6.19)

13. $P_0 = \dfrac{EPS_1 - B_0 \times g}{k - g}$ (6.20)

14. $D_1 = EPS_1 + B_0 - B_1 = EPS_1 + B_0 - B_0(1+g)$
$= EPS_1 - B_0 \times g$ (6.21)

15. $\beta_{\text{Equity}} = \beta_{\text{Asset}} \times \left[1 + \dfrac{\text{Debt}}{\text{Equity}}(1 - t)\right]$ (6.23)

16. Expected price = Historical P/E ratio $\times$ Projected EPS
= Historical P/E ratio $\times$ Current EPS
$\times$ (1 + Projected EPS growth rate)

17. Expected price = Historical P/CF ratio $\times$ Projected CFPS
= Historical P/CF ratio $\times$ Current CFPS
$\times$ (1 + Projected CFPS growth rate)

18. Expected price = Historical P/S ratio $\times$ Projected SPS
= Historical P/S ratio $\times$ Current SPS
$\times$ (1 + Projected SPS growth rate)

Chapter 7

1. Abnormal return = Observed return − Expected return   (7.1)

Chapter 8

1. Market Sentiment Index (MSI)

$$= \frac{\text{Number of bearish investors}}{\text{Number of bullish investors} + \text{Number of bearish investors}}$$

2. $\text{Arms} = \dfrac{\text{Declining volume/Declining issues}}{\text{Advancing volume/Advancing issues}}$ (8.1)

Chapter 9

1. Future value = Present value $\times (1 + r)^N$ (9.1)

2. Present value $= \dfrac{\text{Future value}}{(1 + r)^N}$ (9.3)

3. Present value = Future value $\times (1 + r)^{-N}$ (9.4)

4. Current price

$$= \text{Face value} \times \left(1 - \frac{\text{Days to maturity}}{360} \times \text{Discount yield}\right) \quad (9.5)$$

5. Bond equivalent yield

$$= \frac{365 \times \text{Discount yield}}{360 - \text{Days to maturity} \times \text{Discount yield}} \quad (9.6)$$

6. Bill price

$$= \frac{\text{Face value}}{1 + \text{Bond equivalent yield} \times \text{Days to maturity}/365} \quad (9.7)$$

7. $1 + EAR = \left(1 + \dfrac{APR}{m}\right)^m$ (9.8)

8. STRIPS price $= \dfrac{\text{Face value}}{(1 + YTM/2)^{2M}}$ (9.9)

9. $YTM = 2 \times \left[\left(\dfrac{\text{Face value}}{\text{STRIPS price}}\right)^{\frac{1}{2M}} - 1\right]$ (9.10)

10. Real interest rate = Nominal interest rate − Inflation rate   (9.11)

11. $\int_{1,1} \dfrac{(1 + r_1)^2}{1 + r_1}$

12. NI = RI + IP + RP + LP + DP   (9.13)

In this equation:

NI = Nominal interest rate

RI = Real interest rate

IP = Inflation premium

RP = Interest rate risk premium

LP = Liquidity premium

DP = Default premium

Chapter 10

1. Coupon rate $= \dfrac{\text{Annual coupon}}{\text{Par value}}$ (10.1)

2. Current yield $= \dfrac{\text{Annual coupon}}{\text{Bond price}}$ (10.2)

3. Bond price

$$= \frac{C}{YTM}\left[1 - \frac{1}{(1 + YTM/2)^{2M}}\right] + \frac{FV}{(1 + YTM/2)^{2M}} \quad (10.3)$$

In this formula:

C = Annual coupon, the sum of two semiannual coupons

FV = Face value

M = Maturity in years

YTM = Yield to maturity

4. Premium bonds:

Coupon rate > Current yield > Yield to maturity

5. Discount bonds:

Coupon rate < Current yield < Yield to maturity

6. Par value bonds:

Coupon rate = Current yield = Yield to maturity

7. Callable bond price

$$= \frac{C}{YTC}\left[1 - \frac{1}{(1 + YTC/2)^{2T}}\right] + \frac{CP}{(1 + YTC/2)^{2T}} \quad (10.4)$$

In this formula:

C = Constant annual coupon

CP = Call price of the bond

T = Time in years until earliest possible call date

YTC = Yield to call assuming semiannual coupons

8. Percentage change in bond price $\approx$

$$-\text{Duration} \times \frac{\text{Change in } YTM}{(1 + YTM/2)} \quad (10.5)$$

9. Modified duration $= \dfrac{\text{Macaulay duration}}{(1 + YTM/2)}$ (10.6)

10. Percentage change in bond price $\approx$

$-$Modified duration $\times$ Change in YTM (10.7)

11. Par value bond duration

$$= \frac{(1 + YTM/2)}{YTM}\left[1 - \frac{1}{(1 + YTM/2)^{2M}}\right] \quad (10.8)$$

In this formula:

M = Bond maturity in years

YTM = Yield to maturity assuming semiannual coupons

12. Duration

$$= \frac{1 + YTM/2}{YTM} - \frac{(1 + YTM/2) + M(CPR - YTM)}{YTM + CPR[(1 + YTM/2)^{2M} - 1]} \quad (10.9)$$

In this formula:

CPR = Constant annual coupon rate

M = Bond maturity in years

YTM = Yield to maturity assuming semiannual coupons

13. Dollar value of an 01 $\approx$ Modified duration

$\times$ Bond price $\times$ 0.0001   (10.10)

14. Yield value of a 32nd $\approx \dfrac{1}{32 \times \text{Dollar value of an 01}}$ (10.11)

Chapter 11

1. Risk premium = Expected return − Risk-free rate   (11.1)

Risk premium $= E(R_j) - R_f$

2. Portfolio return for N-asset portfolio:

$$E(R_P) = x_1 \times E(R_1) + x_2 \times E(R_2) + \cdots + x_n \times E(R_n) \quad (11.2)$$

3. Portfolio variance for two-asset portfolio:

$$\sigma_P^2 = x_A^2\sigma_A^2 + x_B^2\sigma_B^2 + 2x_Ax_B\sigma_A\sigma_B\text{Corr}(R_A, R_B) \quad (11.3)$$

4. Portfolio variance for three-asset portfolio:

$$\sigma_P^2 = x_A^2\sigma_A^2 + x_B^2\sigma_R^2 + x_C^2\sigma_C^2 + 2x_Ax_B\sigma_A\sigma_B\text{Corr}(R_A, R_B)$$
$$+ 2x_Ax_C\sigma_A\sigma_C\text{Corr}(R_A, R_C) + 2x_Bx_C\sigma_B\sigma_C\text{Corr}(R_B, R_C) \quad (11.4)$$

5. The weight in asset A in the minimum variance portfolio:

$$x_A^* = \frac{\sigma_B^2 - \sigma_A\sigma_B\text{Corr}(R_A, R_B)}{\sigma_A^2 + \sigma_B^2 - 2\sigma_A\sigma_B\text{Corr}(R_A, R_B)} \quad (11.5)$$

6. Portfolio return for three-asset portfolio:

$$R_P = x_FR_F + x_SR_S + x_BR_B \quad (11.6)$$

7. Portfolio variance for three-asset portfolio when all correlations are zero:

$$\sigma_P^2 = x_F^2\sigma_F^2 + x_S^2\sigma_S^2 + x_B^2\sigma_B^2 \quad (11.7)$$

Chapter 12

1. Total return − Expected return = Unexpected return   (12.1)

$\quad\quad R \quad\quad - \quad\quad E(R) \quad\quad = \quad\quad U$

2. Announcement = Expected part + Surprise (12.2)

3. $R - E(R)$ = Systematic portion + Unsystematic portion (12.3)

4. $R - E(R) = U = m + \epsilon$ (12.4)

5. Total risk = Systematic risk + Unsystematic risk (12.5)

6. $\dfrac{E(R_A) - R_f}{\beta_A} = \dfrac{E(R_B) - R_f}{\beta_B}$ (12.6)

7. SML slope $= \dfrac{E(R_M) - R_f}{\beta_M} = \dfrac{E(R_M) - R_f}{1} = E(R_M) - R_f$

8. $E(R_i) = R_f + [E(R_M) - R_f] \times \beta_i$ (12.7)

9. $R - E(R) = m + \epsilon$ (12.8)

10. $m = [R_M - E(R_M)] \times \beta$ (12.9)

11. $R - E(R) = m + \epsilon = [R_M - E(R_M)] \times \beta + \epsilon$ (12.10)

12. $\beta_i = \text{Corr}(R_i, R_M) \times \sigma_i / \sigma_M$ (12.11)

Chapter 13

1. Sharpe ratio $= \dfrac{R_P - R_f}{\sigma_P}$ (13.1)

2. Treynor ratio $= \dfrac{R_P - R_f}{\beta_P}$ (13.2)

3. $E(R_P) = R_f + [E(R_M) - R_f] \times \beta_P$ (13.3)

4. Jensen's alpha $= \alpha_P = R_P - E(R_P)$
$= R_P - \{R_f + [E(R_M) - R_f] \times \beta_P\}$ (13.4)

5. $\dfrac{E(R_P) - R_f}{\sigma_P} = \dfrac{x_S E(R_S) + x_B E(R_B) - R_f}{\sqrt{x_S^2 \sigma_S^2 + x_B^2 \sigma_B^2 + 2x_S x_B \sigma_S \sigma_B \text{Corr}(R_S, R_B)}}$ (13.7)

6. $E(R_{P,T}) = E(R_P) \times T$ (13.8)

7. $\sigma_{P,T} = \sigma_P \times \sqrt{T}$ (13.9)

8. Value-at-Risk:

$\text{Prob}[R_{P,T} \leq E(R_P) \times T - 2.326 \times \sigma_P \sqrt{T}] = 1\%$

$\text{Prob}[R_{P,T} \leq E(R_P) \times T - 1.96 \times \sigma_P \sqrt{T}] = 2.5\%$ (13.10)

$\text{Prob}[R_{P,T} \leq E(R_P) \times T - 1.645 \times \sigma_P \sqrt{T}] = 5\%$

Chapter 14

1. Basis = Cash price − Futures price (14.1)

2. Spot-futures parity: $F_T = S(1 + r)^T$ (14.3)

3. Spot-futures parity (with dividend yield):
$F_T = S(1 + r - d)^T$ (14.6)

4. Number of index futures contracts, N, needed to hedge fully:

$N = \dfrac{V_P}{V_F} \times \dfrac{\beta_P}{\beta_F}$ (14.7)

5. Number of U.S. Treasury note futures contracts, N,
needed to hedge a bond portfolio:

$N = \dfrac{D_P \times V_P}{D_F \times V_F}$ (14.8)

6. Duration of an interest rate futures contract
(rule of thumb):

$D_F = D_U + M_F$ (14.9)

Chapter 15

1. Call option intrinsic value = MAX$(S - K, 0)$ (15.1)

2. Put option intrinsic value = MAX$(K - S, 0)$ (15.2)

3. The put-call parity relationship:
$C - P = S - K/(1 + r_f)^T$ (15.8)

4. The put-call parity relationship (with dividends):
$C - P = S - \text{Div} - K/(1 + r_f)^T$ (15.10)

Chapter 16

1. Delta, one-period binomial model:

$\Delta = \dfrac{C_u - C_d}{Su - Sd}$

2. Call value, one-period binomial model: (16.2)

$C = \dfrac{\Delta S(1 + r - u) + C_u}{1 + r}$

3. Black-Scholes call option pricing model:
$C = SN(d_1) - Ke^{-rT}N(d_2)$ (16.3)

4. Black-Scholes put option pricing model:
$P = Ke^{-rT}N(-d_2) - SN(-d_1)$ (16.4)

Where, in the Black-Scholes formula, d_1 and d_2 are:

5. $d_1 = \dfrac{\ln(S/K) + (r + \sigma^2/2)T}{\sigma\sqrt{T}}$

6. $d_2 = d_1 - \sigma\sqrt{T}$

7. Call option delta = $N(d_1) > 0$

8. Put option delta = $-N(-d_1) < 0$

9. A useful option hedging equation:
Change in value of stock portfolio + Change in value
of options = 0 (16.5)

10. Number of stock options needed to hedge shares held:

Number of options $= \dfrac{-\text{Shares held}}{\text{Option delta}}$ (16.7)

11. Number of option contracts needed to hedge an equity portfolio:

$= \dfrac{\text{Portfolio beta} \times \text{Portfolio value}}{\text{Option delta} \times \text{Option contract value}}$ (16.8)

12. Black-Scholes-Merton call option formula:
$C = Se^{-yT}N(d_1) - Ke^{-rT}N(d_2)$ (16.9)

Where, in the Black-Scholes-Merton call option formula,
d_1 and d_2 are:

13. $d_1 = \dfrac{\ln(S/K) + (r - y + \sigma^2/2)T}{\sigma\sqrt{T}}$

14. $d_2 = d_1 - \sigma\sqrt{T}$

Chapter 17

Profitability ratios:

1. Gross margin $= \dfrac{\text{Gross profit}}{\text{Net sales}}$

2. Operating margin $= \dfrac{\text{Operating income}}{\text{Net sales}}$

3. Return on assets (ROA) $= \dfrac{\text{Net income}}{\text{Total assets}}$

4. Return on equity (ROE) $= \dfrac{\text{Net income}}{\text{Shareholder equity}}$

Per-share calculations:

5. Book value per share (BVPS) $= \dfrac{\text{Shareholder equity}}{\text{Shares outstanding}}$

6. Earnings per share (EPS) $= \dfrac{\text{Net income}}{\text{Shares outstanding}}$

7. Cash flow per share (CFPS) $= \dfrac{\text{Operating cash flow}}{\text{Shares outstanding}}$

Price ratios:

8. Price-book (P/B) $= \dfrac{\text{Stock price}}{\text{BVPS}}$

9. Price-earnings (P/E) $= \dfrac{\text{Stock price}}{\text{EPS}}$

10. Price-cash flow (P/CF) $= \dfrac{\text{Stock price}}{\text{CFPS}}$

Two-stage residual income model (RIM):

11. $P_0 = BVPS_0 + \dfrac{EPS_0(1 + g_1) - BVPS_0 \times k}{k - g_1}\left[1 - \left(\dfrac{1 + g_1}{1 + k}\right)^T\right]$

$\qquad + \dfrac{EPS_0(1 + g_1)^T(1 + g_2) - BVPS_0(1 + k)^T k}{(k - g_2)/(1 + k)^T}$ (17.3)

Chapter 18

Convertible bond-to-stock conversion formulas:

1. Conversion ratio = Number of stock shares acquired by conversion

2. Conversion price = $\dfrac{\text{Bond par value}}{\text{Conversion ratio}}$

3. Conversion value = Price per share of stock $\times$ Conversion ratio

Chapter 19

1. STRIPS price = $\dfrac{\text{Face value}}{(1 + (YTM/2))^{2N}}$

2. STRIPS yield = $2\left[\left(\dfrac{\text{Face value}}{\text{Price}}\right)^{\frac{1}{2N}} - 1\right]$

3. Bond price = $\dfrac{\text{Annual coupon}}{YTM} \times \left[1 - \dfrac{1}{(1 + YTM/2)^{2M}}\right]$

$\qquad + \dfrac{\text{Face value}}{(1 + YTM/2)^{2M}}$

4. Equivalent taxable yield = Tax-exempt yield / (1 − Marginal tax rate)

5. After-tax yield = Taxable yield $\times$ (1 − Marginal tax rate)

6. Critical marginal tax rate = 1 − (Tax-exempt yield/Taxable yield)

Name Index

Page numbers followed by n indicate notes.

McGee, Suzanne, 474n
McKay, Betsy, 569n
McMurray, Jamie, 289
Merton, Robert, 553, 554
Milligan, Spike, 1
Milstead, Larry, 314
Morgan, J. P., 441, 457

N

Newman, Ryan, 289
Norstad, J., 384n

O

O'Brien, William, 163
Odean, Terrance, 265
Oliff, James, 474
O'Neal, Shaquille, 225
Opdyke, Jeff D., 46n
Orgler, Yair, 554

P

Patrick, Danica, 157
Patton, George S., 105
Perfumo, Diego, 163
Phillips, Matt, 67n, 521n
Phillips, Michael M., 554n
Picard, Irving, 53
Pierce, Cathy, 474
Pierce, Robert, 474

Pollack, Gary, 668
Pulliam, Susan, 234n

R

Richardson, Karen, 234n
Roeser, Donald "Buck
        Dharma," 243n
Rogers, Will, 42, 441
Rom, Brian, 44
Rossa, Jennifer, 149n
Russo, J. E., 266n
Russolillo, Steven, 430n

S

Santayana, George, 2
Scannell, Kara, 66n
Scholes, Myron, 553, 554, 569
Schonberger, Jennifer, 134n
Schowmaker, P. J. H., 266n
Schultz, Howard, 604
Scott, David, 382
Sears, Steven M., 565n
Sharpe, William F., 443, 455
Shiller, Robert, 21
Siegel, Jeremy J., 9n, 301n
Silverblatt, Rob, 120n
Smith, Adam, 146
Smith, Richard, 668
Sokol, David, 234
Sortino, Frank, 455

Spector, Mike, 640n
Statman, Meir, 381n
Staunton, Michael, 16, 17
Stewart, Martha, 232

T

Temel, Judy Wesalo, 668
Thottam, Jyoti, 633n
Train, Mark, 468
Treynor, Jack L., 416n, 443
Tversky, Amos, 267, 270
Twain, Mark, 2, 25n, 181

V

Volpert, Ken, 658

W

Waskal, Sam, 232
Weil, Jonathan, 569n
Welch, Ivo, 16
Whitehouses, Mark, 668n
Wiener, Daniel, 27
Wong, Sally, 455

Z

Zweig, Jason, 89n

Equation Index

Page numbers followed by n indicate notes.

Subject Index

Page numbers followed by n indicate notes; by f, figures; by t, tables.

Frequency distribution, 18–19
Front-end load, 111
Full faith and credit bonds, 666
Full hedge, 477
Full price of a bond, 345
Full-service brokers, 50
Fundamental analysis, 182, 226
Funds of funds, 137
Futures contracts
    cash prices versus futures prices, 482–486
    commodity, 90–91, 469, 470, 473, 475–479
    definition and introduction, 90–93, 469,
        470–471
    delivery options, 93, 469, 490
    features of, 470–471
    gains and losses on, 93
    hedging with, 476–480, 487–489
    history, 469–470
    option contracts compared with, 94
    price quotes, 91–93, 471–474
    purpose of, 475–480
    reverse trades, 481–482
    single-stock, 484–485
    speculating with, 475–476
    standardization of, 469
    stock index, 469, 486–490
    trading accounts, 480–482
Futures margin, 481
Futures price, 469
Future value, 302, 318–320, 359

G

GAAP (Generally Accepted Accounting
        Principles), 164
Gambler's fallacy, 270
Games of chance, 44, 261, 267–269, 270
The Gap, 567–568
Gender and trading frequency, 265
General cash offer, 150
General Electric Capital Corporation, 305
General Electric Company, 514
General equity mutual funds (GEFs), 236–238
General funds, 121
Generally Accepted Accounting Principles
        (GAAP), 164
General Motors (GM), 105, 171, 203,
        265–266, 385
General obligation bonds (GOs), 317,
        662–664, 666–667
Geometric average dividend growth rate,
        185–187
Geometric average return, 27–30, 133
Ginnie Mae; *see* Government National
        Mortgage Association
GlaxoSmithKline, 430
Global funds, 118
Global Investment Performance Standards
        (GIPS), 451
Global stock markets, 15–18
GMO LLC, 21
GNMA; *see* Government National Mortgage
        Association
Gold, 9, 90–91, 470, 473
Golden mean, 287
Goldman Sachs, 134, 150

Goldman Sachs Group Inc., 163
Goldman Sachs Private Equity, 289
Google, 151, 162, 272, 428
GOs (general obligation bonds), 317,
        662–664, 666–667
Government bonds; *see* U.S. government bonds
Government National Mortgage Association
        (GNMA)
    agency bond quotes, 661
    interest rate reports for, 317
    mortgage mutual funds, 121
Government-sponsored enterprises (GSEs), 660
Great Depression, 89
Gross margin, 586
Growth and income funds, 117
Growth funds, 117, 118
Growth stocks, 25–26, 122, 202–203
GSEs (government-sponsored enterprises), 660
Guaranty Bancorp, 149
Gymboree, 408

H

Harley-Davidson, 2–3, 412, 413t
Harrah's Entertainment, 150
Harvard Business School, 554
Head and shoulders patterns, 282
Hedge funds, 135–137, 147–148, 455
Hedgers, 477
Hedging
    cross-hedging, 487
    with futures, 476–480, 487–489
    with index options, 563–565
    interest rate risk, 488–489
    price risk, 476–477
    stock market risk, 487–488
    with stock options, 561–563
"Hemline" indicator, 287
Herding, 271
Herzfeld Caribbean Basin Fund, 120
Heuristics, 271
Hewlett-Packard, 274
HIBOR (Hong Kong Interbank Offered Rate),
        306
High-yield bond funds, 121
High-yield bonds, 317, 619, 637–641
Hippo markets, 382
Historical growth rates, 185–187
Historical perspective
    diversification and, 380–381
    futures contracts, 469–470
    inflation rates, 12f, 322
    interest rates, 301–303, 321
    S&P 500 index, 234
    T-bill rates, 322
Historical returns; *see also* Large-company
        stocks; Risk and return history; Small-
        company stocks
    average returns, 15
    corporate bonds, 7–14, 17t, 23f, 28t
    government bonds, 7–14, 15, 17t, 22, 23f,
        28t, 33
    growth stocks, 25–26
    S&P 500 Index, 12–14, 20–21, 89
    stock markets, 1, 7–14, 20–21, 24–25, 34, 89
    Treasury bills, 7–14, 15, 28t, 33, 34

Treasury bonds, 89
Historical variance, 19–22
H-model, 195
Holding period, 6
Honda, 273
Hong Kong Interbank Offered Rate (HIBOR),
        306
Hong Kong Investment Funds Association, 455
Horizon as investor constraint, 43–46, 69
Host Marriott, 632–633
"Hot-hand" fallacy, 267–270
House money, 263–264
Hurricane Katrina, 631, 668
Hybrid bonds, 666–667
Hybrid market, 157
Hybrid securities, 81, 86
Hypothecation, 58

I

Ibbotson Associates, 20
IBM, 85, 105, 157, 412, 413t, 500, 505, 507,
        514, 515, 554
ICE (IntercontinentalExchange), 470
Illusion of knowledge, 265–266
Imclone, 232
IMM (International Monetary Market), 469
Immunization, 361–363
Implementation costs, 274
Implied standard deviation (ISD), 565–567
Implied volatility (IVOL), 565
Imputed interest, 651
Income, 584
Income funds, 122
Income statement, 582, 584–585, 589–590,
        595, 597t
Indenture, 620–621, 634, *see also* Bond
        indenture provisions
Indenture summary, 620
Independent deviations from rationality,
        224–225, 260
Index arbitrage, 486–487
Index divisors, 170–171
Indexes, stock market, 166–170, 566–567
Index funds, 118–119, 130–131, 132,
        236–238, 445
Index futures, 469, 486–490
Index options, 508–511, 563–565
Index staleness, 172
Individual retirement accounts (IRAs), 59–60
Indymac, 149
Inefficient portfolios, 390
Inflation
    Fed monetary policy and, 302–303, 305, 321
    historical rates of, 12f, 322
    real interest rates and, 321–323, 327–328
    term structure theories and, 325, 327
Inflation-indexed Treasury securities, 322–323,
        656–657, 658
Inflation premium, 327–328
Information effect on price
    news and announcements, 228–230, 243,
        407–409, 410
    nonpublic, 231, 581–582
    past returns as predictor of future, 227–228
    performance incentive, 227

M

Macaulay duration, 353–356
MACD (moving average convergence divergence), 285
Macro funds, 137
Macron Technology, 96–97
Mad Money (TV show), 271
Maintenance margin, 55–56, 481
Make-whole call price, 347
Make-whole call provisions, 622, 623–624
Make-whole premium, 624
Malkiel's theorems, 350–351
Management fees, 112
Management of investments, 48
Margin, 54
Margin accounts
  account balance sheet, 54, 62–63
  account equity, 54
  annualizing returns, 58
  call money rate, 54, 305
  definition, 54
  effects of, 56–58
  as financial leverage, 56
  for futures trading, 480–482
  hypothecation, 58
  initial margin, 55, 481
  maintenance margin, 55–56, 481
  margin calls, 55–56, 57, 481
  short sales, 61–67
  spread, 54
  street name registration, 58–59
Margin call, 55–56, 57, 481
Margin purchase, 54
Market anomalies, 239–243
Market-book ratio, 203–204
Market capitalization, 7, 118, 122–123, 429
Market efficiency
  anomalies, 239–243
  "beating the market," 224
  bubbles and crashes, 243–250
  driving forces, 226–227
  efficient markets hypothesis, 224
  expected and unexpected returns, 409
  forms of, 225–226
  foundations of, 224–225, 260
  implications, 227–231, 235
  informed traders, 231
  insider trading, 231–232
  introduction, 223–224
  money manager performance and, 236–238
  testing, 233–235
Market makers, 156, 158–159, 162
Market neutral funds, 136
Marketocracy Masters 100 Fund, 120
Market orders, 159
Market portfolios, 420, 430, 445
Market risk, 409, 411, 422t, 456, 487–488
Market risk premium, 420
Market segmentation theory, 326
Market sentiment index (MSI), 276–277
Market timing, 48, 69, 235
Market timing funds, 137
Marking-to-market, 481
Markowitz efficient frontier, 392–395, 451–452
Marriott Corporation, 632–633

Marriott International, 632–633
Martha Stewart Living Omnimedia, Inc., 232, 428
Massachusetts Institute of Technology, 272, 273, 455
Material nonpublic information, 231, 581–582
Mathematical models, 382
Maturity; *see also* Duration; Yield to maturity
  of bond funds, 119
  bond principal payments at, 618, 629–630
  effective, 354
  expiry, 553
  interest rate risk and, 349–350, 357–358
  100-year bonds, 630
Maturity preference theory, 325
Maturity premium, 325
MBIA Inc., 668
MBIA Insurance Corp., 668
MBSs; *see* Mortgage-backed securities
McDonald's, 105, 120
McGraw-Hill Company analysis, 205–210
McKesson Corporation, 628, 629
Medifast, 373
Mental accounting, 263–264
Merrill Lynch, 50, 109, 156, 315, 316f, 554, 638
Mezzanine-level financing, 148
Microcaps, 164
Microsoft, 5, 105, 162, 165, 231, 267, 272, 284–286, 408, 413t
MidAmerica Commodity Exchange, 469
MidAmerican Energy, 234
Midcap funds, 118, 122–123
Middle market, 148–149
Minimum variance portfolio, 389–390
Minneapolis Grain Exchange (MPLS), 469, 473
MMDAs (money market deposit accounts), 116
MMMFs (money market mutual funds), 114–116
Modern portfolio theory (MPT), 382, 450
Modified duration, 353–354
Molson Coors, 120
Monetta Young Investor Fund, 120
Money flow, 285–286
Money illusion, 264
Money managers, 48, 106, 114, 233–238, 442, 565
Money market deposit accounts (MMDAs), 116
Money market instruments
  banker's acceptances, 306
  CDs, 305–306, 311
  commercial paper, 305
  definition and introduction, 81–82, 301
  Eurodollars, 306
  pure discount securities, 307, 317–318
Money market interest rates
  bank discount basis, 307–308
  bellwether rate, 303
  call money rate, 305
  on CDs, 305–306, 311
  discount basis, 82
  discount rate, 305
  Federal funds rate, 304–305
  LIBOR, 306
  money market prices and, 307–313
  mortgage market effect on, 306
  prime rate, 303
  on Treasury bills, 306, 308–310, 322

Money market mutual funds (MMMFs), 114–116
Money market prices and yields
  bank discount yield versus bond equivalent yield, 310–311
  bond equivalent yields, 310–313
  Treasury bills, 308–310
Moody's Investors Service, Inc., 619, 633, 635–637, 667–669, 668
Moral obligation bonds, 666–667
Morgan Stanley, 134, 521
Morningstar Inc., 89, 115, 124, 125n
Mortgage-backed securities (MBSs)
  credit ratings, 637
  issuers, 317
  subprime mortgages, 249
Mortgage bonds, 619, 622
Mortgage debt, 352
Mortgage funds, 121
Mortgage market, 306, 317
Mortgages; *see* Mortgage-backed securities
Moving average convergence divergence (MACD), 285
Moving averages, 282–284, 285
MPLS (Minneapolis Grain Exchange), 469, 473
MPT (modern portfolio theory), 382, 450
MSI (market sentiment index), 276–277
Municipal bond funds, 119–121
Municipal bonds
  credit ratings, 662, 667–669
  default risk, 662
  equivalent taxable yield, 669–670
  features of, 664–666
  GOs, 317, 662–664, 666–667
  hybrid, 666–667
  insurance, 668, 669
  overview, 651, 662
  revenue, 666–667
  taxable, 663
  tax treatment of, 116, 317, 328–329, 662, 663
Mutual funds
  advantages and drawbacks, 106–107
  behavioral finance and, 269–270
  bond funds, 119–121, 388–390
  as brokerage account alternative, 60
  closed, 108
  closed-end, 107–108, 128–130
  costs and fees, 110–114, 135–136
  definition and overview, 105–106
  diversification with, 106, 388–390, 392–395
  exchange-traded funds, 130–135
  expenses, 112–114
  general equity, 236–238
  hedge funds, 135–137, 455
  index, 118–119, 130–131, 132, 236–238
  as investment companies, 107–109
  long-term, 117–123
  money managers, 106, 114, 233–238, 442, 565
  money market, 114–116
  net asset value, 108–109
  objectives, 117, 122–123
  open-end, 107–108
  operations, 109–110
  organization and creation, 109–110
  past returns as predictor of future, 269–270
  performance, 125–128

Stock price behavior
anomalies, 239–243
bubbles and crashes, 243–250
event studies, 228–230
news announcements, 228–230, 243,
407–409, 410
past returns as predictor of future, 227–228
random walk, 227–228
volatility, 558, 566–567
Stocks
blue chip, 125n
growth, 25–26, 122, 202–203
hedging with stock options, 561–563
listed, 157–158
option investments compared with, 96–97,
507–508
preferred, 85–86, 634–635
price trees, 545, 548–549, 551–552
spot-futures parity, 484–485
ticker symbols, 5
value, 122, 202–203
Stock screening, 587
Stock splits, 170–171
Stop-buy orders, 159
Stop-limit orders, 160
Stop-loss orders, 159–160
Stop orders, 159
Stop-out bid, 657–659
Stop-sell orders, 159
Straddles, 524
Straight bonds, 339, 340–341, 628
Straight bond value, 628
Strategic allocation, 70
Street name, 58–59
Strike (exercise) price, 94, 500
Strips, generic, 652
STRIPS (Separate Trading of Registered
Interest and Principal of Securities),
318–320, 652
Strong-form efficient markets, 225–226
Subordinated debentures, 622, 636
Subordinated notes, 620
Subprime mortgages, 249
Sunk cost fallacy, 264
Sun Microsystems, 282, 503, 505
Super Bowl indicator, 287–288
Super Display Book system (SDBK), 156–157
SuperDOT system, 156
Supernormal growth, 194–195
Supplemental liquidity providers (SLPs), 156
Support levels, 278
Surprise announcements, 408
Sustainable growth rate, 187–188
Swiss Re, 631
Syndicates, 151–153
Synthetic puts, 531
Systematic risk
beta and, 412–415, 423–424
definition, 409, 422t
diversification and, 411
expected returns and, 412, 419
measuring, 412–414
principle of, 412
return and, 410
security market line and, 420–421
Treynor ratio and, 443–444
Systematic risk principle, 412, 422t

T

Tactical asset allocation, 70
Target, 120
Target date, 358–363
Target-date funds, 115, 122
Taxable municipal bonds, 663
Taxes
bond funds, 119–121
Buffett on, 47
equivalent taxable yield, 669–670
as investor constraint, 46–47, 69, 107
money market funds, 116
municipal securities, 116, 317,
662, 663
mutual funds, 107, 110
preferred stock dividends, 634
state and local, 662, 663
Tax-exempt bonds, 317, 328–329
Tax-exempt market, 662
Tax-managed funds, 119
Tax Reform Act of 1986, 670
T-bills; see U.S. Treasury bills
Technical analysis
advance/decline line, 278–280
block trades, 280
charting, 281–286
Closing Arms, 280
Daytona 500 indicator, 289
definition, 276
Dow theory, 277
Elliott wave theory, 277–278
Fibonacci numbers, 287
hemline indicator, 287
indicators, 278–280
market sentiment index, 276–277
odd-lot indicator, 287
popularity of, 276–277
relative strength, 281
Super Bowl indicator, 287–288
support and resistance levels, 278
volume indicators, 280
weak-form efficient market and, 226
Tel Aviv Stock Exchange, 554
Templeton Global Income Fund, 128–130
10-K, 581, 588
10-Q, 581
Tender offer bond, 665
Tennessee Valley Authority (TVA), 317,
660, 661
Term bonds, 629–630, 665
Terminal dividend, 183
Term structure of interest rates
definition, 317
expectations theory, 324–325
liquidity and default risk, 327–329
market segmentation theory, 326
maturity preference theory, 325
modern theories, 326–329
nominal versus real interest rates, 321–323,
327–328
traditional theories, 324–326
Treasury STRIPS, 318–320
Tetra Technologies, 430
Third market, 163
Thomson Reuters, 640
3Com/Palm, 274–275

3M Company, 54, 83, 157
Three-asset portfolios, 378–379, 387,
392–393
TIAA-CREF, 44
Ticker symbols, 5, 89, 502–506
Ticker tape, 88, 89
Time diversification fallacy, 383–385
Time value of an option, 513
Time value of money, 32, 196, 302,
318–320, 421
Time Warner Cable, 84
Timothy Plan Aggressive Growth Fund, 120
Tippers and tippees, 231
TIPS (Treasury inflation-protected securities),
322–323, 656–657, 658
Tombstones, 153, 154f
Total dollar return, 3
Total market capitalization, 7
Total percent return, 4
Total return, 410, 422t, 423
Total risk, 411, 414, 422t, 443
TPC Group, 289
TPG Capital, 149, 150
TRACE (Trade Reporting and Compliance
Engine), 83–84, 641
Tracking error, 447–448
Trading accounts, 50
Trading costs, 112
Trading frequency, 47, 264–265
Trading volume indicators, 280
Traditional fixed-price call provisions,
622–623
Travelers Cos., 171
Treasury bills; see U.S. Treasury bills
Treasury bonds; see U.S. Treasury bonds
Treasury inflation-protected securities (TIPS),
322–323, 656–657, 658
Treasury notes; see U.S. Treasury notes
Treasury securities; see U.S. Treasury securities
Treasury STRIPS, 318–320, 652
Treasury yield curve, 314–315
Treynor ratio, 416n, 443–444, 449, 450
Trian Credit Fund, 640
TR(ading) IN(dex) (TRIN), 280
Triple witching hour, 487
Trust Indenture Act of 1939, 620–621, 634
Turn-of-the-month effect, 242
Turn-of-the-year effect, 242
Turnover, 112
TVA (Tennessee Valley Authority), 317,
660, 661
12b-1 fees, 111–112
Two-asset portfolios, 385–390, 395,
452–453
Two-period binomial option pricing model,
547–551
Two-stage dividend growth model
advantages and disadvantages, 196
definition and introduction, 190–193
discount rates for DDMs, 195–196
H-model, 195
nonconstant growth in first stage, 193–195
Two-stage residual income model, 603–604
Two states of the economy, 374
2008 stock market crash; see Financial
crisis of 2008
TXU Corp., 149, 150